JURISDICTION AND ENFORCEMENT OF JUDGMENTS IN CIVIL AND COMMERCIAL MATTERS

ECJ JUDGMENTS

VOLUME I

JURISDICTION AND ENFORCEMENT OF JUDGMENTS IN CIVIL AND COMMERCIAL MATTERS

ECJ JUDGMENTS

VOLUME I

Edited by
Paolo Galizzi

BIICL
British Institute of
International and
Comparative Law

Published and Distributed by
The British Institute of International and Comparative Law
Charles Clore House, 17 Russell Square, London WC1B 5JP

British Library Cataloguing in Publication Data
A Catalogue record of this book is available from the British Library

ISBN 0–903067–85–4

The texts of the cases have been reproduced from the 'Reports of Cases before the Court of Justice' and from the website of the European Court of Justice.

Printed in Great Britain by Biddles Ltd.,
Guildford and King's Lynn

Contents

* Numbering under the 1968 Brussels Convention in bold.
New numbering under Regulation 44/2001 in square brackets and italics

TITLE III *[Chapter III]*

RECOGNITION AND ENFORCEMENT
[Recognition and Enforcement]

Foreword

This is a very welcome collection of the case law of the European Court on the Brussels Convention. It comes at the end of the practical life of the Brussels Convention, which (like the parallel Lugano Convention) has for most practical purposes been replaced by Council Regulation (EC) 44/2001 on jurisdiction and the recognition and enforcement of judgments in civil and commercial matters. In the last 26 years the European Court has given judgment in more than 100 references on the Brussels Convention. What is remarkable is that, although the Court does not have, and does not pretend to have, specialist expertise in this area, very few of its decisions on the Convention are thought to have taken a wrong direction, or have required correction by amendments to the Convention or by new provisions in the Council Regulation. That is probably a tribute to the excellence of the Advocates General and their staff.

The Council Regulation is in force from March 1, 2002, and that Regulation will be the source of ECJ judgments in this area once the 13 references which are still pending on the Brussels Convention as of 1 August 2002 have been decided. Some of them are of considerable importance, especially the reference in Case C-281/02 *Owusu v. Jackson*, in which the English Court of Appeal has made a reference which raises the question left undecided in *Re Harrods (Buenos Aires) Ltd (No. 2)* [1992] Ch 72 on the relationship between proceedings in Convention countries and those in non Contracting States. This collection will be of great practical and continuing utility under the new regime.

Lawrence Collins
Royal Courts of Justice
London
November 2002

Preface and Acknowledgements

The *Brussels Convention on Jurisdiction and the Enforcement of Judgments in Civil and Commercial Matters* was concluded on 27 September 1968 among the original six Member States of the then EEC. The Convention, as modified by the various Accession Conventions, applied to all the fifteen Members of the European Union.

On 1 March 2002 the Convention has been replaced by *EC Regulation No 44/2001 of 22 December 2000 on Jurisdiction and the Recognition and Enforcement of Judgments in Civil and Commercial Matters*. The new regulation applies to all Member States of the European Union with the exclusion of Denmark (the Convention will therefore continue to apply between Denmark and the Member States bound by the new Regulation). Regulation 44/2001 has modified several provisions of the Convention and left many unaltered. Some of the modifications have been introduced to take into account decisions of the ECJ.

These two volumes contain the decisions of the European Court of Justice on the interpretation of the Brussels Convention from 1976 to 2000.[1] Since 1976, when the Court gave its first judgment on the interpretation of the Convention, there have been over 100 cases. This book is an essential tool for all those that want to better understand the provisions of the Convention. The Convention could not properly be understood and applied without reference to the case law of the ECJ, whose invaluable contribution is recognised in this book.

The case law of the ECJ on the 1968 Brussels Convention will continue to be of fundamental importance for an understanding of the provisions of the new Regulation. This importance is specifically recognised in the Preamble to the Regulation: "…continuity between the Brussels Convention and this Regulation should be ensured, and transitional provisions should be laid down to that end. The same need for continuity applies as regards the interpretation of the Brussels Convention by the Court of Justice of the European Communities….".

The cases have been reproduced and grouped following the structure

[1] **Note:** *The authoritative version of these texts is that published in the "Reports of Cases before the Court of Justice" which alone are authentic.*

of the Convention (and of Regulation 44/2001). The cases have been grouped into three main sections: Title I, including cases dealing with the scope of the Convention (Chapter I of the Regulation), Title II, including all cases interpreting specific jurisdictional rules (Chapter II of the Regulation) and Title III, containing all cases deal with provisions on recognition and enforcement (Chapter III of the Regulation). Cases under Title II, Jurisdiction, have been divided into sub-categories: cases on the general rule on jurisdiction; on jurisdiction in matters related to contracts; jurisdiction in matters relating to maintenance; jurisdiction in matters related to tort, delict or quasi-delict; jurisdiction in matters arising out of the operations of a branch, agency or other establishment; jurisdiction in case of plurality of defendants; jurisdiction in matters relating to insurance; jurisdiction over consumer contracts; exclusive jurisdiction; prorogation of jurisdiction by consent; prorogation of jurisdiction by appearance; examination as to jurisdiction and admissibility; lis pendens; provisional measures. Cases under Title III have also been divided into three sub-headings: definition of judgment; recognition and enforcement. Cases which did not fit neatly into any of the above groups have been included as miscellaneous cases.

Many of the judgments reproduced in these volumes deal with several provisions of the Convention. Such judgments are only reproduced under one section, with cross-references to the other relevant sections. For example, the first case appearing in these two volumes, *LTU v Eurocontrol,* in which the Court interprets the concept of civil and commercial matters, is reproduced under Title I, Scope of the Convention. However, the decision also incidentally deals with the enforcement of judgments and therefore a cross-reference is also found under that heading. In a few cases, it was rather more difficult to make a choice on where a judgment should be reproduced. For example, the case of *Zelger v Salinitri I,* dealing with Articles 5(1) and 17, could have been reproduced under the section on jurisdiction in matters relating to contracts or under the section on prorogation of jurisdiction by consent. In such cases, a decision had to be made to avoid duplication.

This book, as already mentioned, includes all the decisions of the ECJ on the Convention, including those which have been superseded by modifications of the Convention (for example, *Roesler v Rottwinkel*). This book includes also the Advocate Generals' opinions for each case. This was thought useful for a better understanding of the judgmetns and reasoning of the Court.

Notwithstanding the several judgments on the Convention, questions and uncertainties on its interpretation persist and are testified by the numerous cases decided by the ECJ after completion of the work for this book. 7 cases have in fact been decided between 2001 and 1 August 2002.

13 more cases are currently pending before the Court. It is predictable that Regulation 44/2001 will also soon be the object of requests for clarification.

These two volumes, containing all the judgments of the Court on the "old" Brussels Convention, will hopefully provide a useful tool to all those interested in the "new" Regulation, in the spirit of continuity between the "old" and "new" European rules on jurisdiction and the enforcement of judgments in civil and commercial matters.

My interest in private international law and more specifically on the 1968 Brussels Convention on Jurisdiction and Enforcement of Judgments in Civil and Commercial Matters dates back to my years at the University of Milan. During my final year at the Faculty of Law, I started writing my undergraduate dissertation under the supervision of Professors Tullio Treves and Nerina Boschiero on the interpretation of the 1968 Brussels Convention by the European Court of Justice. Once I finished my dissertation, I moved to London and I started working at the British Institute of International and Comparative Law on this project: a comprehensive and systematic collection of the cases of the ECJ on the Brussels Convention.

The then Director of the Institute, Piers Gardner, and the then Fellow in Private International Law, Richard Fentiman asked me to work on this project and I enthusiastically accepted. I would like to express my gratitude to both and in particular to Richard Fentiman, whose invaluable guidance and ideas were of great assistance in the initial stages. My thanks also to Joe McDonald Hill, former Assistant Editor of the ICLQ, with whom I discussed developments and whose advice and guidance I much appreciated.

The final publication of these volumes owes much to the new Director of the Institute, Mads Andenas, who has given new impetus to this project. This publication is largely due to his commitment and encouragement. My gratitude also extends to Michael Anderson, Director of Projects at the Institute, who has always been very encouraging and supportive.

Many people have assisted me in researching and editing this book. I would like to thank all of them for their invaluable help. I would like to mention in particular those who helped me in the final stages of this work: Louise Doble, Angela Blomfield and Pieter Vervoort, my LLM students at the University of Nottingham. A particular mention to Caroline Boyle and Edem Kuenyehia for proof reading the text of the cases. Special thanks are due to Professor James Fawcett, University of Nottingham, and Professor Nerina Boschiero, University of Verona, for their invaluable comments and advice.

I would also like to thank Mirella Mauri, formerly Publications

Assistant at the Institute, and Margaret Wilkerson, formerly Assistant Editor, ICLQ. Last but not least, my appreciation to the hard work of Olivia Skinner, Assistant Editor at the Institute, without whom this book would have never been published.

Needless to say, errors or omissions, which may remain in these two volumes, are solely my responsibility.

Paolo Galizzi

London, 1 August 2002

Tables

Numerical Index of cases

49/84	*Debaecker and Plouvier v Bouwman* [1985] ECR 1779	1388
119/84	*Capelloni and Aquilini v Pelkmans* [1985] ECR 3147	1533
148/84	*Deutsche Genossenschaftsbank v Brasserie du Pêcheur* [1985] ECR 1981	1523
220/84	*AS-Autoteile Service v Malhé* [1985] ECR 2267	816
221/84	*Berghoefer v ASA* [1985] ECR 2699	955
22/85	*Anterist v Crédit Lyonnais* [1986] ECR 1951	964
198/85	*Carron v Germany* [1986] ECR 2437	1548
266/85	*Shenavai v Kreischer* [1987] ECR 239	252
313/85	*Iveco Fiat v Van Hool* [1986] ECR 3337	975
144/86	*Gubisch Maschinenfabrik v Palumbo* [1987] ECR 4861	1142
145/86	*Hoffmann v Krieg* [1988] ECR 645	1409
218/86	*SAR Schotte GmbH v Parfums Rothschild* [1987] ECR 4905	609
9/87	*Arcado v Haviland* [1988] ECR 1539	263
158/87	*Scherrens v Maenhout* [1988] ECR 3791	826

189/87	*Kalfelis v Schröder* [1988] ECR 5565	635
32/88	*Six Constructions v Humbert* [1989] ECR 341	271
C-115/88	*Reichert v Dresdner Bank I* [1990] ECR I-27	834
C-220/88	*Dumez France v Hessische Landesbank* [1990] ECR I-49	473
C-305/88	*Lancray v Peters und Sickert* [1990] ECR I-2725	1426
C-365/88	*Kongress Agentur Hagen v Zeehaghe* [1990] ECR I-1845	646
C-190/89	*Rich v Società Italiana Impianti* [1991] ECR I-3855	78
C-214/89	*Powell Duffryn v Petereit* [1992] ECR I-1745	988
C-351/89	*Overseas Union Insurance v New Hampshire Insurance* [1991] ECR I-3317	1152
C-183/90	*Van Dalfsen v van Loon* [1991] ECR I-4743	1556
C-261/90	*Reichert v Dresdner II* [1992] ECR I-2149	488
C-280/90	*Hacker v Euro-Relais* [1992] ECR I-1111	843
C-26/91	*Soc. Jakob Handte v TMCS* [1992] ECR I-3967	287
C-89/91	*Shearson Lehman Hutton v TVB* [1993] ECR I-139	689

Alphabetical Index of cases

Cases decided up to 1 August 2002 (not included in these volumes)[1]

1. *C-518/99 – Order of 5 April 2001*
Richard Gaillard v Alaya Chekili

Article 16(1) - Exclusive jurisdiction in proceedings which have as their object rights *in rem* in immovable property - Scope - Action for rescission of a contract of sale of immovable property and for damages.

Operative Part of the Court's Order

"The Court (Sixth Chamber), in answer to the question referred to it by the Cour d'appel de Bruxelles by judgment of 22 December 1999, hereby rules:

> **An action for rescission of a contract for the sale of land and consequential damages is not within the scope of the rules on exclusive jurisdiction in proceedings which have as their object rights *in rem* in immovable property under Article 16(1) of the Convention of 27 September 1968 between the Member States of the European Economic Community on jurisdiction and the enforcement of judgments in civil and commercial matters, as amended by the Convention of 9 October 1978 on the accession of the Kingdom of Denmark, Ireland and the United Kingdom of Great Britain and Northern Ireland and by the Convention of 25 October 1982 on the accession of the Hellenic Republic."**

2. *C-256/00 – Judgment of 19 February 2002*
Besix SA v WABAG and Plafog

Article 5(1) - Jurisdiction in matters relating to a contract - Place of performance of the obligation in question - Obligation not to do something, applicable without geographical limit - Undertakings given by two companies not to bind themselves to other partners when tendering for a public contract - Application of Article 2.

[1] The full text of these cases can be found on the website of the European Court of Justice at www.curia.eu.int under "Recent case-law of the Court of Justice". The text of these cases can also be found on Eur-lex (The Portal to European Union Law) at http://europa.eu.int/eur-lex/en/index.html

Operative Part of the Court's Judgment

"The Court, in answer to the question referred to it by the Cour d'appel of Brussels by judgment of 19 February 2000, hereby rules:

> **The special jurisdictional rule in matters relating to a contract, laid down in Article 5(1) of the Convention of 27 September 1968 on Jurisdiction and the Enforcement of Judgments in Civil and Commercial Matters, as amended by the Convention of 9 October 1978 on the Accession of the Kingdom of Denmark, Ireland and the United Kingdom of Great Britain and Northern Ireland, is not applicable where, as in the present case, the place of performance of the obligation in question cannot be determined because it consists in an undertaking not to do something which is not subject to any geographical limit and is therefore characterised by a multiplicity of places for its performance. In such a case, jurisdiction can be determined only by application of the general criterion laid down in the first paragraph of Article 2 of that Convention."**

3. Case C-37/00 – Judgment of 27 February 2002
Herbert Weber v Universal Ogden Services Ltd.

Article 5(1) - Courts for the place of performance of the contractual obligation - Contract of employment - Place where the employee habitually carries out his work - Definition - Work performed partly at an installation positioned over the continental shelf adjacent to a Contracting State and partly in the territory of another Contracting State

Operative Part of the Court's Judgment

"THE COURT (Sixth Chamber), in answer to the questions referred to it by the Hoge Raad der Nederlanden by judgment of 4 February 2000, hereby rules:

> **1. Work carried out by an employee on fixed or floating installations positioned on or above the part of the continental shelf adjacent to a Contracting State, in the context of the prospecting and/or exploitation of its natural resources, is to be regarded as work carried out in the territory of that State for the purposes of applying Article 5(1) of the Convention of 27 September 1968 on Jurisdiction and the Enforcement of Judgments in Civil and Commercial Matters, as amended by**

the Convention of 9 October 1978 on the Accession of the Kingdom of Denmark, Ireland and the United Kingdom of Great Britain and Northern Ireland, the Convention of 25 October 1982 on the Accession of the Hellenic Republic and the Convention of 26 May 1989 on the Accession of the Kingdom of Spain and the Portuguese Republic.

2. Article 5(1) of that convention must be interpreted as meaning that where an employee performs the obligations arising under his contract of employment in several Contracting States the place where he habitually works, within the meaning of that provision, is the place where, or from which, taking account of all the circumstances of the case, he in fact performs the essential part of his duties *vis-à-vis* his employer.

In the case of a contract of employment under which an employee performs for his employer the same activities in more than one Contracting State, it is necessary, in principle, to take account of the whole of the duration of the employment relationship in order to identify the place where the employee habitually works, within the meaning of Article 5(1).

Failing other criteria, that will be the place where the employee has worked the longest.

It will only be otherwise if, in light of the facts of the case at hand, the subject-matter of the dispute is more closely connected with a different place of work, which would, in that case, be the relevant place for the purposes of Article 5(1) of the convention.

In the event that the criteria laid down by the Court of Justice do not enable the national court to identify the habitual place of work, as referred to in Article 5(1) of the convention, the employee will have the choice of suing his employer either in the courts for the place where the business which engaged him is situated, or in the courts of the Contracting State in whose territory the employer is domiciled.

3. National law applicable to the main dispute has no bearing on the interpretation of the concept of the place where an employee habitually works, within the meaning of Article 5(1) of the convention, to which the second question relates."

4. *C-24/02 – Order of 22 March 2002*
Marseille Fret SA v Seatrano Shipping Company Ltd

Protocol on the interpretation of the Convention by the European Court of Justice – Regulation 44/2001 – National jurisdiction with competence to refer questions for preliminary rulings – ECJ manifestly lacked jurisdiction to decide questions submitted.

5. *C-69/02 – Order of 22 March 2002*
Tilly Reichling v Leon Wampach

Protocol on the interpretation of the Convention by the European Court of Justice – National courts authorised to refer questions of interpretation to the European Court of Justice – ECJ manifestly lacked jurisdiction to decide questions submitted.

6. *C-80/00 – Judgment of 6 June 2002*
Italian Leather SpA v Weco Polstermöbel GmbH & Co.

Article 27(3) – Irreconcilable judgments – Different national requirements for provisional measures – Enforceable judgment – Restraining order – Enforceability under law of State of foreign judgment.

Operative part of the Court's Judgment

"THE COURT (Fifth Chamber), in answer to the questions referred to it by the Bundesgerichtshof by order of 10 February 2000, hereby rules:

> **1. On a proper construction of Article 27(3) of the Convention of 27 September 1968 on Jurisdiction and the Enforcement of Judgments in Civil and Commercial Matters, as amended by the Convention of 9 October 1978 on the Accession of the Kingdom of Denmark, Ireland and the United Kingdom of Great Britain and Northern Ireland, by the Convention of 25 October 1982 on the Accession of the Hellenic Republic and by the Convention of 26 May 1989 on the Accession of the Kingdom of Spain and the Portuguese Republic, a foreign decision on interim measures ordering an obligor not to carry out certain acts is irreconcilable with a decision on interim measures refusing to grant such an order in a dispute between the same parties in the State where recognition is sought.**
> **2. Where a court of the State in which recognition is sought finds that a judgment of a court of another Contracting State**

is irreconcilable with a judgment given by a court of the former State in a dispute between the same parties, it is required to refuse to recognise the foreign judgment."

7. *Case C-96/00 - Judgment of 11 July 2002*
Rudolf Gabriel v Schlank & Schick gmbH

Consumer contracts – Prize notifications – Applicability of Article 13, first paragraph, point 3 - Articles 5(1) and 5(3) – Entitlement of a consumer to whom misleading advertising has been sent to seek payment, in judicial proceedings, of the prize which he has apparently won – Classification – Action of a contractual nature covered by Article 13, first paragraph, point 3 – Conditions.

Operative part of the Court's Judgment

"THE COURT (Sixth Chamber), in answer to the question referred to it by the Oberster Gerichtshof by order of 15 February 2000, hereby rules:

The jurisdiction rules set out in the Convention of 27 September 1968 on Jurisdiction and the Enforcement of Judgments in Civil and Commercial Matters, as amended by the Convention of 9 October 1978 on the Accession of the Kingdom of Denmark, Ireland and the United Kingdom of Great Britain and Northern Ireland, by the Convention of 25 October 1982 on the Accession of the Hellenic Republic, by the Convention of 26 May 1989 on the Accession of the Kingdom of Spain and the Portuguese Republic, and by the Convention of 29 November 1996 on the Accession of the Republic of Austria, the Republic of Finland and the Kingdom of Sweden, are to be construed as meaning that judicial proceedings by which a consumer seeks an order, in the Contracting State in which he is domiciled and pursuant to that State's legislation, requiring a mail-order company established in another Contracting State to pay him a financial benefit in circumstances where that company had sent to that consumer in person a letter likely to create the impression that a prize would be awarded to him on condition that he ordered goods to a specified amount, and where that consumer actually placed such an order in the State of his domicile without, however, obtaining payment of that financial benefit, are contractual in nature in the sense contemplated in Article 13, first paragraph, point 3, of that Convention.

List of Pending Cases (up to 1 August 2002)[2]

1. *C-167/00* *Verein für Konsumenteninformation v Karl Heinz Henkel*
(Opinion of the Advocate General delivered on 14 March 2002)

Reference for a preliminary ruling from the Oberster Gerichtshof (Supreme Court), Austria - Action by a consumers' association to obtain an injunction prohibiting the use of unlawful general contractual terms and conditions – Whether a matter relating to tort, delict or quasi-delict within the meaning of Article 5(3).

2. *C-271/00* *Gemeente Steenbergen v Luc Baten*
(Opinion of the Advocate General delivered on 18 April 2002)

Reference by the Hof van Beroep Antwerp (Belgium) – Interpretation of article 1, first sentence and 2, third sentence – Civil matters and social security – Field of application.

3. *C-334/00* *Fonderie Officine Meccaniche Tacconi SpA v HWS Heinrich Wagner Sinto Maschinenfabrik GmbH*
(Opinion of the Advocate General delivered on 31 January 2002)

Reference by the Corte di Cassazione (Italy) – Jurisdiction – Pre-contractual liability – Whether matter falling within Article 5(3) (delict or Quasi-delict) or Article 5(1) (contract) – Whether criterion of defendant's domicile applies.

4. *C-437/00* *Giulia Pugliese v Finmeccanica SpA Alenia Aerospazio Division*

Reference by the Landesarbeitsgericht München (Higher Labour Court)

---

[2] An up to date list of pending cases can be found in *Interntional Litigation Procedure* (*I.L.Pr.*) or on the website of the ECJ.

Munich – Article 5(1) – Place of habitual performance of empoyee's obligations – Place of work other than that stated in contract.

5. C-111/01 Gantner Electronic GmbH v. Basch Exploitatie Maatschappij BV

Reference by the Oberster Gerichtshof (Austria) – Interpreation of Article 21 – Action with same object and same cause – Effect of judicial or extrajudicial compensation – Effects of a implicit decision on preliminary questions.

6. C-266/01 Préservatrice Foncière Tiard SA v The Netherlands

Reference by Hoge Raad der Nederlanden (Netherlands) – Interpretation of Article 1 – Civil and commercial matters – Custom matters.

7. C- 280-01 Brian Watson v. First Choice Holidays and Flights Ltd and Apartada Hotels Caledonia SA

Reference by the Court of Appeal (Civil Division) (United Kingdom) – Interpreation of Article 6(1) – Plurality of defendants – Jurisdiction of the court where one of the co-defendants is domiciled – Conditions – Risk of irreconcilable judgments.

8. C-433/01 Freistaat Bayern v Jan Blijdenstein

Reference by the Bundesgerichtshof (Germany) – Interpretation of Article 5(2) – Special jurisdictions – Action by public authority for recovery of maintenance payment.

9. C-464/01 Johann Gruber v Bay Wa AG

Reference by the Oberster Gerichtshof (Austria) – Interpretation of Article 13 – Jurisdiction in contracts concluded by consumer – Criteria for identification of consumer – Contract between parties resident in different States.

10. *C-18/02* *Danmarks Rederiforening v LO Landsorganisationen i Sverige*

Reference by the Arbejdsretten (Denmark) – Interpretation of Article 5(3) – Whether definition includes collective industrial actions – Court having jurisdiction to hear claims in such cases.

11. *C-27/02* *Petra Engler v Janus Versand GmbH*

Reference by the Oberlandesgericht Innsbruck (Austria) – Interpretation of Article 13(3) – Article 5(1) and (3) – Claim of prizes by consumers – Court having jurisdiction.

12. *C-39/02* *Mærsk Olie & Gas A/S v Firma M. de Haan en W. de Boer*

Reference by the Hojesteret (Denmark) – Interpretation of Articles 21, 25 and 27(2) of the Convention – Definition of proceedings under the Convention – Notion of Judgment – Recognition.

13. *C-116/02* *Erich Gasser GmbH v Misat Srl*

Reference by the Oberlandesgericht Innsbruck (Austria) – Interpretation of Article 21 of the Convention.

ECJ JUDGMENTS

TITLE I *[Chapter 1]*

SCOPE *[Scope]*

Scope – Article 1 *[Article 1]*

See also

Case C-29/76 - 14 October 1976

LTU Luftransportunternehmen GmbH & Co. KG
v
Eurocontrol

Article 1 - Area of application of Convention - Civil and commercial matters - Interpretation - Action between a public authority and a person governed by private law - Exercise of powers of public authority - Judgment - Exclusion.

Summary

1. In the interpretation of the concept 'civil and commercial matters' for the purposes of the application of the Convention of 27 September 1968 on jurisdiction and the enforcement of Judgments in Civil and Commercial Matters, in particular Title III thereof, reference must be made not to the law of one of the States concerned but, first, to the objectives and scheme of the Convention and, secondly, to the general principles which stem from the corpus of the national legal systems.

2. Although certain judgments given in actions between a public authority and a person governed by private law may fall within the area of application of the Convention, this is not so where the public authority acts in the exercise of its powers. Such is the case in a dispute which concerns the recovery of charges payable by a person governed by private law to a national or international body governed by public law for the use of equipment and services provided by such body, in particular where such use is obligatory and exclusive. This applies in particular where the rate of charges, the methods of calculation and the procedures for collection are fixed unilaterally in relation to the users.

JUDGMENT OF THE COURT

Kutscher, President, Donner and Pescatore, Presidents of Chambers, Mertens de Wilmars, Sorensen, Lord Mackenzie Stuart and O'Keeffe, Judges

1. By order dated 16 February 1976 received at the Court Registry on the following 18 March, the Oberlandesgericht Düsseldorf referred to the Court of Justice pursuant to the Protocol of 3 June 1971 on the interpretation of the Convention of 27 September 1968 on jurisdiction and the enforcement of Judgments in Civil and Commercial Matters (hereinafter referred to as 'the Convention') the question whether, for the purposes of interpreting the concept 'civil and commercial matters' within the meaning of the first paragraph of Article 1 of the Convention, the law to be applied is the law of the State in which judgment was given or the law of the State in which proceedings for an order for enforcement were issued.

2. The file shows that the question arose within the context of proceedings under Title III, Section 2, of the Convention in which Eurocontrol asked the competent German courts to authorize the enforcement of an order by the Belgian courts that LTU pay to it certain sums by way of charges imposed by Eurocontrol for the use of its equipment and services.

3. Under Article 1, the Convention 'shall apply in civil and commercial matters whatever the nature of the court or tribunal'. The second paragraph of Article 1 states that it shall not apply to: '(1) the status or legal capacity of natural persons, rights in property arising out of a matrimonial relationship, wills and succession; (2) bankruptcy, proceedings relating to the winding-up of insolvent companies or other legal persons, judicial arrangements, compositions and analogous proceedings; (3) social security; (4) arbitration'.

Apart from providing that the Convention shall apply whatever the nature of the court or tribunal to which the matter is referred and excluding certain matters from its area of application, Article 1 gives no further details as to the meaning of the concept in question.

As Article 1 serves to indicate the area of application of the Convention it is necessary, in order to ensure, as far as possible, that the rights and obligations which derive from it for the Contracting States and the persons to whom it applies are equal and uniform, that the terms of that provision should not be interpreted as a mere reference to the internal law of one or other of the States concerned.

By providing that the Convention shall apply 'whatever the nature of the court or tribunal' Article 1 shows that the concept 'civil and commercial matters' cannot be interpreted solely in the light of the division of jurisdiction between the various types of courts existing in certain States.

The concept in question must therefore be regarded as independent and must be interpreted by reference, first, to the objectives and scheme of the Convention and, secondly, to the general principles which stem from the corpus of the national legal systems.

4. If the interpretation of the concept is approached in this way, in particular for the purpose of applying the provisions of Title III of the Convention, certain types of judicial decision must be regarded as excluded from the area of application of the Convention, either by reason of the legal relationships between the parties to the action or of the subject-matter of the action.

Although certain judgments given in actions between a public authority and a person governed by private law may fall within the area of application of the Convention, this is not so where the public authority acts in the exercise of its powers.

Such is the case in a dispute which, like that between the parties to the main action, concerns the recovery of charges payable by a person governed by private law to a national or international body governed by public law for the use of equipment and services provided by such body, in particular where such use is obligatory and exclusive.

This applies in particular where the rate of charges, the methods of calculation and the procedures for collection are fixed unilaterally in relation to the users, as is the position in the present case where the body in question unilaterally fixed the place of performance of the obligation at its registered office and selected the national courts with jurisdiction to adjudicate upon the performance of the obligation.

5. The answer to be given to the question referred must therefore be that in the interpretation of the concept 'civil and commercial matters' for the purposes of the application of the Convention and in particular of Title III thereof, reference must not be made to the law of one of the States concerned but, first, to the objectives and scheme of the Convention and, secondly, to the general principles which stem from the corpus of the national legal systems.

On the basis of these criteria, a judgment given in an action between a public authority and a person governed by private law, in which a public authority has acted in the exercise of its powers, is excluded from the area of application of the Convention.

On those grounds, the court, in answer to the question referred to it by the Oberlandesgericht Düsseldorf, by order dated 16 February 1976, hereby rules:

1. In the interpretation of the concept 'civil and commercial matters' for the purposes of the application of the Convention of 27 September 1968 on jurisdiction and the enforcement of Judgments in Civil and Commercial Matters, in particular Title III thereof, reference must not be made to the law of one of the States concerned but, first, to the objectives and scheme of the Convention and, secondly, to the general principles which stem from the corpus of the national legal systems;

2. A judgment given in an action between a public authority and a person governed by private law, in which the public authority has acted in the exercise of its powers, is excluded from the area of application of the Convention.

OPINION OF MR ADVOCATE GENERAL REISCHL

The question referred for a preliminary ruling, on which I am giving opinion today, relates to the expression 'civil and commercial matters', which appears in Article 1 of the Convention on jurisdiction and the enforcement of Judgments in Civil and Commercial matters in short the Convention on Jurisdiction - and which defines the Convention's field of application. In this connection the Oberlandsgericht, Düsseldorf, pursuant to the Protocol on the interpretation of the said Convention, has raised the question whether the interpretation of the said expression is governed by the law of the State in which the judgment on the claim was given (in this case Belgium) or the law of the State in which the order for its enforcement has to be issued (in this case the Federal Republic of Germany).

I must first of all make some preliminary observations on the facts underlying this question. On 13 November 1960 an international agreement for cooperation in connection with the safety of air navigation was concluded by several States, *inter alia* the Member States of the Community except for Denmark and Italy. It set up the European Organization for the Safety of Air Navigation - Eurocontrol - an international organization having a legal personality and its seat in Brussels. So called route charges are levied on aircraft owners who wish to make use of the air safety services provided by Eurocontrol.

The levying of these charges is authorised not only by the clauses of the agreement but also by bilateral and multilateral agreements, in the Case of the Federal Republic of Germany by a regulation of the Federal Minister for Transport of 27 October 1971. Paragraph 3 of this regulation prescribes that the charges are payable in Brussels; as far as the rates of the charges, the detailed rules for their application and the procedure for their collection are concerned reference must be made to an order made on 16 June 1971 by the executive organ of Eurocontrol, the agency providing the air safety service. Relying on these provisions Eurocontrol issued bills for the charges payable for the period from December 1971 to October 1972 to the German air transport undertaking LTU, the appellant in the main action. In these bills there is a clause conferring jurisdiction on the Belgiancourts, in the same way moreover as the conditions which regulate payment of the charges for using the services and which constitute Appendix 2 of the Annex to the above-mentioned order of 16 June 1971 issued by the Eurocontrol agency mention that the Belgian courts have jurisdiction. As LTU disputed the validity of the account of charges, Eurocontrol sued in the Tribunal de commerce, Brussels, for part of the amount claimed. This court ordered LTU to pay the charges. In these proceedings it is important to note that the court refused to uphold the plea that the claim for payment of the charges was a matter governed by public law. On the contrary it specifically held that the charges are not to be regarded as taxes and that the determinative factor must be that the payment of the charges is ascribable to operations which must be described as commercial. It is Eurocontrol's intention to enforce this judgment, which was declared to be provisionally enforceable and in the meantime has become final, in the Federal Republic of Germany, because both the appeal to the Cour d'Appel in Brussels and the appeal on a point of law to the Belgian Cour de Cassation were dismissed. For this purpose it sought on the basis of Article 31 of the Convention on Jurisdiction leave to enforce the judgment and the issue of an order for its enforcement. Eurocontrol produced as proof of service of the judgment in accordance with Article 47 of the Convention on Jurisdiction a certificate of Service issued by the Registrar of the Amtsgericht Düsseldorf. By an order of 13 August 1974 leave to enforce the judgment was granted and an order for its enforcement was issued. However, on appeal by LTU to the Oberlandes-gericht, Düsseldorf, the 19th Civil Senate of that court by an order of 24 March 1975 set aside the order of 13 August 1974 and dismissed the application for leave to enforce the judgment. The decisive factor for the Oberlandesgericht was that it did not feel able to find that there had been proper service of the judgment of the Tribunal de commerce, Brussels. In the meantime, another Civil Senate of the Oberlandesgericht, Düsseldorf, had made an order for the annulment of the certificate of service of the Registrar of the Amtsgericht, Düsseldorf, on the ground that its content - in fact the certificate refers to the service of a statement of claim - was incorrect. On appeal by Eurocontrol on a point of law to the Bundesgerichtshof that court rejected the view of the Oberlandes-gericht, Düsseldorf, on proof of service and pointed out that the effectiveness of the service, for which proof was available, is not invalidated by the setting aside of the certificate of service. The Bundesgerichtshof also declared that the negative order of the Oberlandeagericht, Düsseldorf, could not be upheld on other grounds. The Belgian court, to the jurisdiction of which LTU has submitted, regarded the issue as a commercial matter. This was binding on the Court of the State in which enforcement was sought, since the question whether a judgment is to be regarded as having been given in a civil or a commercial matter must be answered in accordance with the law of the State in which the judgment was given. As, however, further findings on the final nature of the Belgian judgment were necessary - its finality had not then been established and, being a question of fact, could not be ascertained by the Bundesgerichtshof itself - the matter was referred back to the Oberlandesgericht, Düsseldorf. The Oberlandesgericht, Düsseldorf, when it reconsidered the matter, took the view that it could not confine itself to an examination of the only question which in the view of the Bundesgerichishof was still outstanding but had in addition - apparently because it did not share the view of the Bundesgerichtshof on this point - to go into the question of the proper construction of the expression 'civil and commercial matters.'Consequently by an order of 16 February 1976 it stayed the proceedings and referred the question which I mentioned at the outset to the Court of Justice for a preliminary ruling.

It is perhaps also of interest to note that LTU for its part has brought the matter of Eurocontrol's bills for outstanding charges before the appropriate German administrative court (Verwaltungsgericht). This court, however, dismissed the application as being inadmissible, because the German courts did not have jurisdiction. The Oberverwaltungsgericht for the Land of North Rhine-Westphalia in its judgment of 7 July 1975 on the appeal against the judgment of the Verwaltungsgericht held that the action for annulment was inadmissible, because the bills for the charges payable to Eurocontrol were not administrative measures capable of being challenged under German law. No decision has apparently yet been made as to the alternative application for a declaration that the charges are not due and owing, and similarly the decision on the appeal on a point of law to the Bundesverwaltungsgericht against the judgment of the Oberverwaltungsgericht is still awaited.

1. Let me preface my opinion on this case with two preliminary observations.

(a) The first relates to the application in time of the Convention on Jurisdiction and can be dealt with quite briefly. The distinguishing feature of this case is that the action was brought in Brussels *before* the entry into force of the Convention and that the Court made its decision *afterwards*. Under the second paragraph of Article 54 this is of no importance 'if jurisdiction founded upon rules which accorded with those provided for either in Table II of this Convention or in a convention concluded between the State in which judgment was given and the State in which recognition or enforcement is sought and which was in force when proceedings were instituted'. In my view the Commission has convincingly shown that these conditions have been fulfilled in this Case. As far as the territorial jurisdiction of the Brussels court is concerned reference can in fact be made not only to the German-Belgian Convention of 30 June 1971 but also to the provisions in the Eurocontrol order of 16 June 1971, which has already been mentioned, and in the Regulation of 27 October 1971 of the Federal Minister for Transport, which provides that air safety charges are payable in Brussels.

(b) The second preliminary observation relates to Eurocontrol's objection that the reference is inadmissible. Eurocontrol submits that the court applying for a preliminary ruling has already given its ruling in the appeal proceedings and the matter was then brought before the Bundesgerichshof. The latter court only referred the matter back to the Oberlandesgericht, because in its view there were still findings to be made on the question whether the judgment to be enforced was final. However, a reference to the Court for an interpretation of the Convention on Jurisdiction is unnecessary for such a finding of fact. Furthermore it is significant that the Bundesgerichtshof, without considering a reference to be necessary, has already ruled on the problem which has arisen in this case. The Oberlandesgericht is under national law bound by this ruling.

This objection is clearly unfounded. That can be said straight away, although there is no doubt that in the context of the Protocol on Interpretation the Court has on occasion to consider national law, and this is so whenever the question arises whether a reference from a court or tribunal *acting as a court of appeal* is admissible. However, it is something entirely different to examine national law from the point of view of relevance to the decision, that is to say, to look into the question of the extent of the powers of an appeal court after a superior court has referred a matter back to it and into the question whether therefore the interpretation requested is necessary to enable the subsequent judgment to be given. The Court has never carried out such an examination of national law and with good reason.

On the other hand, so far as the right of courts other than those of last resort to refer questions to the Court when they have to make a decision in cases referred back to them is concerned, the case-law is clear. Thus the Court in Case 166/73 (*Rheinmühlen-Düsseldorf* v *Einfuhrund Vorratstelle für Getreide und Futtermittel*, Judgment of 16 January 1974, [1974] ECR 37 *et seq.*) found and in Case 146/73 (*Rheinmühlen-Düsseldorf* v *Einfuhrund Vorratsstelle für Getreide und Futtermittel*, Judgment of 12 February 1974, [1974] ECR 147 *et seq.*) confirmed that the national court has an unfettered right to refer questions to the Court of Justice. It went out of its way to emphasize that a Court which is not one of last instance 'must be free, if it considers that the ruling on law made by the superior court could lead it to give a judgment contrary to Community law, to refer to the Court questions which concern it'. It is true that these rulings were given in proceedings under Article 177. However I have no doubt that because of the similarity of the procedure under the Protocol on interpretation for referring questions to the Court these rulings must also apply to that procedure. In particular, so far as this point is concerned, no importance can be attached to the fact that in connexion with the *duty* of supreme courts to request preliminary rulings the words 'if that court or tribunal consider that a decision on the question is necessary to enable it to give judgment' are found in the Protocol on interpretation, and only in that Protocol, as it has been obvious for a long time that a corresponding rule also applies without any express mention to the third paragraph of Article 177.

2. The question referred by the Oberlandesgericht, Düsseldorf, which I will now deal with, relates - as I have already said - to the field of application of the Convention on Jurisdiction. In this connexion problems arise because its scope - if the matters to which it does not apply, which are specifically mentioned in the second paragraph of Article 1 of the Convention are disregarded is simply defined by use of the expression 'civil and commercial matters', without there being any indication of the way in which this expression is to be interpreted.

It is therefore not surprising that this particular problem, soon after the Convention had been drawn up, became the subject of academic scrutiny and that it has already played a part in national case-law. In this connexion a large number of proposals for solutions were worked out - the Commission has, in fact, described them in detail - proposals which, moreover, are in no way exhausted by the alternative which appears in the question as formulated. Some people take the view, which I will now outline briefly, that the law of the State in which enforcement is sought is applicable, an argument upon which LTU too, mainly relies. Others on the contrary advocate the law of the State in which judgment was given. Sometimes this is done without any reservation, sometimes importance is attached to the question whether there is any express designation in the judgment which it is sought to enforce. If not, then designation under the law of the State in which enforcement is sought is also regarded as permissible. There are other views which, where designation by the State in which judgment was given is recognized in principle, make different reservations. Thus, there is the view that in proceedings brought before the entry into force of the Convention it cannot be accepted that the court before which enforcement is sought is bound by the designation made in the State in which judgment was given, because the first court was not bound by the Convention when it gave judgment. Others deny that the designation made in the State in which judgment was given is binding in matters clearly governed by public law; at the very least it is wondered whether recourse may be had to the exception of public policy as mentioned in Article 27 of the Convention. There is an entirely different view advocated by those who argue that the expression 'civil and commercial matters' is not to be defined by reference to national law but that on the contrary it must be assumed to be an independent concept just as Community law concepts are independent. The Italian Government and the Government of the Federal Republic of Germany have expressed their support for this view. In considering this question the Italian Government, relying on bilateral agreements and provisions of the EEC Treaty (Article 84) comes to the conclusion that sea and air transport do not fall within the field of application of the Convention. The Government of the Federal Republic of Germany qualified its view by an alternative suggestion that the crucial question for the second court might be whether the definition of the expression in question by the first court and that only if there are grave doubts in this respect should consideration be given to refusing the matter to the Court or clarification of the delimitation question.

In dealing with this problem, and considering the arguments put forward in support of the various solutions, I was at first strongly attracted to the view that the expression 'civil and commercial matters' must be assumed to have a meaning determined by *Community law*. Unquestionably its great advantage - the Commission says that it is an ideal solution - is that it secures a uniform application of the Convention and binds the Member States equally. One of the chief advantages would be to prevent any risk of the expression, which is of importance both in the section on jurisdiction as well as that on enforcement, being interpreted in different ways. To proceed in this way would moreover mean that, in the absence of an accurate definition, the same methods would be used as those adopted in cases where there are gaps in Community law; the basic concepts common to the Member States would have to be ascertained, perhaps taking into account the bilateral and multilateral conventions of the Member States which were earlier in force. In any case it would certainly not be practicable to proceed in the way which LTU's representative - I will comment on this basic attitude later - considers to be correct and only to regard those matters as civil and commercial, which in the opinion of the Member State accepting the widest definition of the field of public law merits such a designation; for this would mean taking as one's basis the legal system of one Member State, but not common concepts. It is also clear that the view of the Italian Government that matters relating to sea and air transport were not included in the Convention cannot be accepted. This view cannot be inferred from Article 84 of the EEC Treaty - its functions under the Treaty are quite different - and further a comparison with other Treaties is not conclusive for the very good reason that under the Convention on Jurisdiction air and sea transport are not mentioned as one of the specific fields to which the Convention does not apply. On the other hand it is interesting to note that in the latest draft of an agreement for the accession of the new Member States sea and air transport are in no way excluded that, on the contrary, bearing in mind that in their case too a field of civil law is concerned, the assumption is that the definition of the field in question is arrived at by following criteria which are generally accepted as being valid.

The deciding factor would therefore have to be whether the relationship of superordination and subordination, which is the distinguishing feature of public law relations, existed when Eurocontrol - those functions of air safety which are plainly governed by police law are not at issue in this connection - prosecuted its *claim for charges*. That it is possible by taking this view of the problem to hold that the Convention on Jurisdiction does apply to the facts in the main action results in my opinion from two considerations. First, as is made clear by the report sent to the Governments with the draft Convention, the Convention was intended by its authors to be given a *wide* interpretation. Secondly, it is important to note that according to the provisions which I mentioned at the beginning of my opinion Eurocontrol's charges are to be regarded as consideration for services tendered and that the Belgian civil courts were given jurisdiction to enforce their collection.

Nevertheless, however regrettable this may be, serious objections can be raised against the view that the expression 'civil and commercial matters' is governed by Community law.

In view of the divergent interpretations in the various Member States it must be conceded straight away that the definition of a Community law concept of civil and commercial matters would be anything but easy; this would apply to an even greater degree after Great Britain acceded to the Convention, because in the English legal world the difference between civil and public law is far less marked than on the continent. For this reason the experts who drafted the Convention have not dared to attempt a definition and that is why there are only certain negative attempts at definitions in the draft of an Accession Agreement with reference to tax, customs and administrative matters.

The working out of a Community law concept, and this is the experience of the courts in the Member States which acknowledge such a distinction, would therefore undoubtedly be time-consuming and consequently entail a longer period of uncertainty. This would mean that frequently - and whenever an element of public law emerges - references would be made to the Court for a preliminary ruling and this would happen even if the alternative argument of the Government of the Federal Republic of Germany is accepted, i.e. whenever attention is drawn to the fact that serious doubts exist. The enforcement proceedings would thereby be delayed and could not be prosecuted as expeditiously as the authors of the Convention undoubtedly imagined. The main purpose and the paramount objectives of the Convention do not therefore favour an interpretation which would involve such serious disadvantages as continuing uncertainty and delayed proceedings. In this connection I need only recall the preamble to the Convention which stresses the need to expedite the enforcement procedure. I also refer to the Joint Declaration annexed to the Convention which states that the Convention is to be applied as effectively and uniformly as possible. Finally, I refer to the above-mentioned report on the Convention which speaks of encouraging to the maximum possible extent the mobility of judgments given in the Member States.

If, however, the argument in favour of an independent Community law concept of 'civil and commercial matters' has to be dropped, if only for pragmatic reasons - the above-mentioned report goes out of its way to emphasize that the Convention must be applied as pragmatically as possible - the only course which in fact remains open is to have recourse to national law. In principle, therefore, only the designation by the first court or by the court making the enforcement order can be decisive, that is to say, essentially a choice has to be made between the alternatives mentioned in the order making the reference, although naturally this does not mean - contrary to what was thought by one of the parties to the proceedings - that when the Court deals with the reference for a preliminary ruling it is in principle confined to the choices of interpretation which the court making the reference may have mentioned.

As far as the two possible solutions which have been mentioned are concerned, it further becomes very quickly apparent that the arguments advanced in favour of a designation in principle under the law of the State in which enforcement is sought are hardly convincing.

In this connection LTU submitted that international treaties are in cases of doubt to be given a narrow interpretation and construed in such a way that they affect the sovereign powers of the contracting States to the least possible extent. With reference to the Convention on jurisdiction it stated that it cannot be assumed that the State in which enforcement is sought subjects itself, as it were, to foreign law without any express direction to that effect in the Convention and that, in particular, it is prepared to enforce judgments in matters which it regards as being governed by public law and in respect of which enforcement abroad is not in principle permitted. In my opinion this reasoning starts off on the wrong foot. It overlooks the fact that the Convention fulfils an important function within the framework of the Economic Community. It is intended to ensure that the facilitation of trade and commerce between States should be accompanied and complemented by the simplification of legal proceedings. For this reason and also by virtue of the fact that there is a not *a world of difference* between the legal situation in the Member States, but more importantly because the legal and procedural guarantees are approximately the same, it is certainly more inappropriate to accept as valid for the Convention principles of interpretation however justified they may be in the case of conventions of a public international law nature.

On the other hand, there are good reasons for accepting in principle as the deciding factor designation by the court of the State in which judgment was given.

Thus it is to be inferred from the above-mentioned report that one of the main purposes of the Convention is to strengthen the State in which judgment was given. In the first place this is expressed - and the report refers to this, too - in the very wide rules for the recognition of judgments, which result in extending recognition on the widest possible basis. In fact, the grounds for refusing to recognize a judgment are exhaustively enumerated in Articles 27 and 28 and that is why in legal articles the writers go so far as to talk about a presumption of recognition. On the other hand, it is also expressed in the field of enforcement by Article 34 which provides that enforcement may only be refused for one of the reasons specified in Articles 27 and 28. Also there is in principle no review of jurisdiction, because according to the third paragraph of Article 28 the test of public policy may not be applied to the rules relating to jurisdiction. In particular the legality of judgments which have been given may not be reviewed.

The view that the designation by the State in which the judgment was given is in principle the deciding factor as far as the expression 'civil and commercial matters' is concerned is unquestionably the one which least corresponds to this basic trend which favours, in principle making the decision in the State in which judgment was given the deciding factor. This is also the best way of adhering to the manifest aim of the Convention to ensure the greatest possible mobility of judgments as well as to the principle of ensuring that they are applied as effectively and as widely as possible. On the other hand, a corresponding review by the State in which enforcement is sought would perhaps imperil the attainment of this objective and lead to differing enforcement procedures. I am, therefore, convinced that the question referred can only be answered in the way in which I have just described.

Furthermore, it is my impression that for the purposes of the judgment in the main action this basic view is quite sufficient. Contrary to the view advocated by LTU there is in fact no reason to doubt that the Belgian courts have expressly designated the dispute as a civil matter. In this respect it is enough that a request was made for legal assistance on the ground that the matter in question is a civil matter and the Tribunal de commerce has dealt with the objection relating thereto raised by LTU. In addition the appeal court in its judgment dismissing the appeal expressly based itself on the Hague Convention on Civil Procedure of 1 March 1954 as far as the question of service is concerned. On the other hand, it may also be well to recall what I said earlier in connection with the designation of Eurocontrol's claim for payment of its charges in the light of common legal principles and which, moreover, appears to prove that there is relatively little danger of an incorrect classification of such matters.

Viewed in this way there is therefore no reason for examining those other aspects of the problems dealt with which have been partially revealed during the proceedings. In particular there is now no need to consider how to proceed if in the State in which judgment was given no express designation was made - whether in such circumstances this question is determined by the State in which enforcement is sought and whether that State's own legal principles are applicable or whether, and this would unquestionably be time-consuming and onerous, it would be necessary to have recourse to the law of the State in which judgment was given.

Similarly, there is nothing in the present case to warrant an examination of the question whether in certain circumstances the designation might not have to be reviewed, perhaps having regard to the exception of public policy under Article 27 of the Convention, in extreme cases by the court in which enforcement is sought, in particular, for example, when endeavours are made to enforce what are clearly decisions given in matters of tax law and criminal law. In my view the further development of the law in this field should be awaited. When an appropriate occasion arises the necessary examination of these undoubtedly difficult questions can be carried out.

3. In view of the foregoing I suggested that the question referred be the Oberlandsgericht, Düsseldorf, be answered as follows: the first paragraph of Article 1 of the Convention on jurisdiction and the enforcement of Judgments in Civil and Commercial matters is to be interpreted as meaning that the courts of the State in which enforcement is sought are bound by the classification adopted by the courts of the State in which the judgment was given at least in those cases in which the latter courts have expressly designated the legal dispute in question as a civil or commercial matter.

Case 133/78 - 22 February 1979

Henri Gourdain
v
Franz Nadler

Interpretation - Article 1 - Concepts serving to indicate the scope of the Convention - Independent interpretation - Scope - Matters to which the Convention does not apply - Bankruptcy proceedings relating to the winding-up of insolvent companies or other legal persons, judicial arrangements, compositions and analogous proceedings - Exclusion from the scope of the Convention - Conditions.

Summary

1. The concepts used in Article 1 of the Convention which serve to indicate its scope must be regarded as independent concepts which must be interpreted by reference, first, to the objectives and scheme of the Convention and, secondly, to the general principles which stem from the corpus of the national legal systems.

2. Bankruptcy, proceedings relating to the winding-up of insolvent companies or other legal persons, judicial arrangements, compositions and analogous proceedings are proceedings founded, according to the various laws of the Contracting Parties relating to debtors who have declared themselves unable to meet their liabilities, insolvency or the collapse of the debtor's credit- worthiness, which involve the intervention of the courts culminating in the compulsory 'liquidation des biens' in the interest of the general body of creditors of the person, firm or company or at least in supervision by the courts. If decisions relating to bankruptcy and winding-up are to be excluded from the scope of the Convention they must derive directly from bankruptcy or winding-up and be closely

connected with proceedings for the 'liquidation des biens' or the 'règlement judiciaire'.

JUDGMENT OF THE COURT

Kutscher, President, Mertens de Wilmars and Lord Mackenzie Stuart, Presidents of Chambers, Donner, Pescatore, Sorensen, O'Keeffe, Bosco and Touffain, Judges

1. By an order of 22 May 1978 which was received at the Court Registry on 12 June 1978 the Bundesgerichtshof [Federal Court of Justice], pursuant to the Protocol of 3 June 1971 on the interpretation of the Convention of 27 September 1968 on jurisdiction and the enforcement of judgments in civil and commercial matters (hereinafter referred to as 'the Convention'), referred to the Court of Justice for a preliminary ruling a question on the interpretation of subparagraph 2 of the second paragraph of Article 1 which provides that the Convention shall not apply to 'bankruptcy, proceedings relating to the winding-up of insolvent companies or other legal persons, judicial arrangements, compositions and analogous proceedings'.

2. This question has been referred to the Court following an order by the Cour d'Appel, Paris, dated 15 March 1976, which ordered the *de facto* manager of a French company, in respect of which there had been a previous declaration that the conditions existed for a 'liquidation des biens', to bear a part of the company's debts pursuant to Article 99 of the French Law No 67-563 of 13 July 1967 on the 'règlement judiciare', the 'liquidation des biens', the 'faillite personnelle' and 'banqueroutes'. The 'syndic' of the said company has applied for leave to enforce the order in the Federal Republic of Germany submitting that it relates to a special case concerning civil liability which falls within the field of application of the first paragraph of Article 1 of the Convention.

The Oberlandesgericht [Higher Regional Court] Frankfurt, before the matter was brought before the Bundesgerichtshof, refused an application for leave by way of exequatur to enforce the order on the grounds that the order *in personam* under Article 99 of the French Law, which is not known in the German legal system, did not come within the scope of decisions in civil and commercial matters covered by the Convention but was part of the proceedings for the 'liquidation des biens'.

It is in these circumstances that the Bundesgerichtshof has referred to the Court the following question:

'Is a judgment given by French civil courts on the basis of Article 99 of the French Law No 67-563 of 13 July 1967 against the *de facto* manager of a legal person for payment into the assets of a company in liquidation to be regarded as having been given in bankruptcy proceedings, proceedings relating to the winding-up of insolvent companies or other legal persons and analogous proceedings (subparagraph 2 of the second paragraph of Article 1 of the Convention) or is such a judgment a decision given in a civil and commercial matter (first paragraph of Article 1 of the Convention)?'

3. The Convention, the particular aim of which is to secure the simplification of formalities governing the reciprocal recognition and enforcement of judgments of courts and tribunals and to strengthen in the Community the legal protection of persons who are established there has laid down as a matter of principle that its scope includes 'civil and commercial matters' without, however, defining this expression.

However, because of the special nature of certain matters and of the profound differences between the laws of the Contracting States the Convention does not apply to certain fields including 'bankruptcy, proceedings relating to the winding-up of insolvent companies or other legal persons, judicial arrangements, compositions and analogous proceedings' without the meaning of these concepts being defined either.

As Article 1 serves to indicate the scope of the Convention it is necessary, in order to ensure, as far as possible, that the rights and obligations which derive from it for the Contracting States and the persons to whom it applies are equal and uniform, that the terms of that provision should not be interpreted as a mere reference to the internal law of one or other of the States concerned.

By providing that the Convention shall apply 'whatever the nature of the court or tribunal' the first paragraph of Article 1 shows that the concept of 'civil and commercial matters' cannot be interpreted solely in the light of the division of jurisdiction between the various types of courts existing in certain States.

The concepts used in Article 1 must be regarded as independent concepts which must be interpreted by reference, first, to the objectives and scheme of the Convention and, secondly, to the general principles which stem from the corpus of the national legal systems.

4. As far as concerns bankruptcy, proceedings relating to the winding-up of insolvent companies or other legal persons, judicial arrangements, compositions and analogous proceedings, according to the various law's of the Contracting Parties relating to debtors who have declared

themselves unable to meet their liabilities, insolvency or the collapse of the debtor's creditworthiness, which involve the intervention of the courts culminating in the compulsory 'liquidation des biens' in the interest of the general body of creditors of the person, firm or company, or at least in supervision by the courts, it is necessary, if decisions relating to bankruptcy and winding-up are to be excluded from the scope of the Convention, that they must derive directly from the bankruptcy or winding-up and be closely connected with the proceedings for the 'liquidation des biens' or the 'règlement judiciaire'.

In order to answer the question referred to the Court by the national court it is therefore necessary to ascertain whether the legal foundation of an application such as that provided for in Article 99 of the French Law is based on the law relating to bankruptcy and winding-up as interpreted for the purposes of the Convention.

5. The application under Article 99, called an application to make good a deficiency in the assets, for which special provision is made in a law on bankruptcy and winding-up is made only to the court which made the order for the 'règlement judiciaire' or the 'liquidation des biens'.
It is only the 'syndic' - apart from the court which can make the order of its own motion - who can make this application on behalf of and in the interest of the general body of creditors with a view to the partial reimbursement of the creditors by respecting the principle that they rank equally and by taking account of any preferential rights lawfully acquired.

In this application, which derogates from the general rules of the law of liability, the *de jure* or *de facto* managers of the company are presumed to be liable and they can only discharge this burden by proving that they managed the affairs of the company with all the requisite energy and diligence.

The period of limitation of three years for the application runs from the date when the final list of claims is drawn up and is suspended for the duration of any scheme of arrangement which may have been entered into and begins to run again if such a scheme is terminated or declared void.

If the application directed against the manager of the company succeeds it is the general body of creditors which benefits, some assets being added to the funds to which they are entitled, as happens where the 'syndic' establishes a claim which benefits the general body of creditors.

Furthermore, the court may order the 'règlement judiciaire' or the 'liquidation des biens' of those managers who have been made responsible for part or all of the liabilities of a legal person and who do not discharge the said liabilities, without having to verify whether the said managers are businessmen and whether they are unable to meet their liabilities.

6. It is quite apparent from all these findings that the legal foundation of Article 99, the object of which, in the event of the winding-up of a commercial company, is to go beyond the legal person and proceed against its managers and their property is based solely on the provisions of the law of bankruptcy and winding-up as interpreted for the purpose of the Convention.

A decision such as that of a French civil court based on Article 99 of the French Law No 67-563 of 15 July 1967 ordering the *de facto* manager of a legal person to pay a certain sum into the assets of a company must be considered as given in the context of bankruptcy, proceedings relating to the winding-up of insolvent companies or other legal persons or analogous proceedings within the meaning of subparagraph 2 of the second paragraph of Article 1 of the Convention.

On those grounds, the court, in answer to the question referred to it by the Bundesgerichtshof by an order of 22 May 1978, hereby rules:

> **A decision such as that of a French civil court based on Article 99 of the French Law No 67-563 of 15 July 1967, ordering the *de facto* manager of a legal person to pay a certain sum into the assets of a company must be considered as given in the context of bankruptcy, proceedings relating to the winding-up of insolvent companies or other legal persons or analogous proceedings within the meaning of subparagraph 2 of the second paragraph of Article 1 of the Convention.**

OPINION OF MR ADVOCATE GENERAL REISCHL

In March 1974 proceedings were begun for the winding-up of the French limited liability company 'Fromme France Manutention', Paris, after the German parent company had become insolvent. The applicant and appellant on a point of law in the main proceedings, in which the present request for a preliminary ruling originated, was appointed 'syndic [liquidator or trustee for the creditors]'. Since the assets of the French company were not sufficient to pay its debts, in June 1974, on application by the 'syndic', the defendant and respondent on a point of law in the main action, who had been managing director of the German parent company and apparently since 1971 - also managing director of the French company, was as *de facto* manager of the French company made a party to the proceedings for the winding-up of that company. This was done pursuant to French Law No 67-753 of 13 July 1967 on the 'réglement judicaire [administration of the affairs of an insolvent person, firm or company expected to continue in business under the supervision of the court]', the 'liquidation des biens [the winding-up of an insolvent person, firm or company not expected to continue in business]', the 'faillite personnelle [mandatory or optional deprivation or prohibition by the Council of the exercise of rights required to carry on business when the debtor or manager has been imprudent or dishonest]' and 'banqueroutes [ordinary and criminal bankruptcies]', Article 99 whereof reads:

'Lorsque le règlement judiciaire ou la liquidation des biens d'une personne morale fait apparaître une insuffisance d'actif, le tribunal peut décider, à la requête du syndic, ou même d'office, que les dettes sociales seront supportées, en tout ou en partie, avec ou sans solidarité, par tous les dirigeants sociaux, de droit ou de fait, apparents ou occultes, rémunérés ou non, ou par certains d'entre eux.

L'action se prescrit par trois ans à compter de l'arrêté définitif des créances. En cas de résolution ou d'annulation du concordat, Ia prescription, suspendue pendant le temps qu'a duré le concordat, recommence à courir. Toutefois, le syndic dispose a nouveau, pour exercer l'action, d'un délai qui ne peut en aucun cas être inférieur a un an. Pour dégager leur responsabilité, les dirigeants impliqués doivent faire la preuve qu'ils ont apporté à la gestion des affaires sociales toute l'activité et la diligence nécessaires'.

'[If the 'règlement judiciaire' or the 'liquidation des biens' of a legal person discloses that the assets are insufficient, the court may, on the application of the 'syndic' or even of its own motion, order that the debts of the company shall be borne in whole or in part, with or without joint and several liability, by some or all of the *de jure* or *de facto* managers, apparent or concealed, paid or unpaid, of the company.

The right to make such an application is barred on the expiration of the period of three years from the date when the final list of claims is drawn up. If the scheme of arrangement is terminated or declared void the period of limitation suspended for the duration of any scheme of arrangement begins to run again. Nevertheless, the 'syndic' is allowed a further period, which may under no circumstances be less than one year, within which to make his application.

In order to discharge their liability the managers involved must prove that they managed the company's business with the requisite energy and diligence.]'

The Commercial Court, Paris, granted the application. The order was partially varied in March 1976 by the Court of Appeal, Paris. Pursuant to the latter's decision the defendant has to pay FF 743 563.15 of the liabilities of the French company amounting to FF 859 575.39 which are not covered by the assets, and also to bear the costs of the appeal, - less a lawyer's charges. The Court of Appeal also confirmed the order of the Commercial Court insofar as it declared, pursuant to Article 108 of the before-mentioned Law No 67-563, that the defendant had lost the right to direct, manage, conduct or supervise a commercial undertaking.

In order to be able to enforce this order, against which an appeal to have it set aside has been lodged, in the Federal Republic of Germany at any rate insofar as the order for payment against the defendant is concerned the 'syndic' pursuant to Article 31 of the Convention on jurisdiction and the enforcement of judgments in civil and commercial matters (often referred to as the 'Convention on jurisdiction and enforcement') applied for leave to have that order enforced there. The judge of the competent court, the President of the First Zivilkammer [Civil Chamber] of the Landgericht [Regional Court] Limburg/Lahn granted this application in April 1977 but ordered that the enforcement might not go further than protective measures, until the creditor produced a certificate that execution could proceed without any restriction and that, so long as the execution might not go further than protective measures, the debtor could effect a stay of execution by giving security in the sum of FF 743 563.15.

However, on appeal by the defendant this order was set aside by an order of the Oberlandesgericht [Higher Regional Court] Frankfurt of 7 September 1977 and the application for the issue of a writ of execution refused on the ground that the order against the *de facto* manager of an insolvent company in accordance with the before-mentioned French Law is founded on the insolvency of the company and is part and parcel of the winding-up proceedings. Consequently, such a matter forms part of bankruptcy or winding-up and does not fall within the scope of the Convention on jurisdiction and enforcement which in Article 1 thereof is defined as follows: 'This Convention shall apply in civil and commercial matters whatever the nature of the court or tribunal. The Convention shall not apply to: 1...; 2. bankruptcy, proceedings relating to the winding-up of insolvent companies or other legal persons, judicial arrangements, compositions and analogous proceedings;'.

The applicant in the main action considers that this classification is wrong. In his view it is important to note that Article 99 of the French law provides for a special form of liability *under civil* law and the 'syndic' must bring a *civil action* against the person or persons liable. He therefore appealed to the Bundesgerichtshof [Federal Court of Justice].

Since the Bundesgerichtshof finds that the interpretation of Article 1 of the Convention on jurisdiction and enforcement which I have quoted is not entirely free from doubt, it has, pursuant to Article 3 of the Protocol annexed to this Convention upon which the High Contracting Parties have agreed in connection with its interpretation, stayed proceedings and referred the following question to the Court for a preliminary ruling: 'Is a judgment given by French civil courts on the basis of Article 99 of the French Law No 67-563 of 13 July 1967 against the *de facto* manager of a legal person for payment into the assets of a company in liquidation to be regarded as having been given in bankruptcy proceedings, proceedings relating to the winding-up of insolvent companies or other legal persons and analogous proceedings (subparagraph 2 of the second paragraph of Article 1 of the Convention) or is such a judgment a decision given in a civil and commercial matter (first paragraph of Article 1 of the Convention)?'

My view on this question is as follows:

1. The respondent has expressed misgivings as to the wording of the question. They are that the Court is wrongly asked to classify the proceedings taken under Article 99 of the French Law No 67-653, that is to say, to bring them within the concepts of the Convention on jurisdiction and enforcement. This is nothing but an invitation to the Court to apply the law which it is not empowered to do in a reference for an interpretation and, moreover, such application also concerns the interpretation of national law, namely the French Law which has been mentioned.

That view must be endorsed and it must be confirmed that the Court's only task - and the question has to be construed in this way - is to give an abstract interpretation of Community law and to this end, if necessary, to extract the essential criteria according to subparagraph 2 of the second paragraph of Article 1 of the Convention on jurisdiction and enforcement. On the other hand, it also goes without saying, however, that this must only be done with reference to the issues in the main action and that here the special features of the national rules under consideration, insofar as they are not disputed, can definitely be taken into consideration.

2. A preliminary observation can be made without any difficulty. Although subparagraph 2 of the second paragraph of Article 1 of the Convention on jurisdiction and enforcement reads that the Convention shall not apply to bankruptcy, proceedings relating to the winding-up of insolvent companies or other legal persons, judicial arrangements, compositions and analogous proceedings, this certainly is not to be taken as indicating that the law to be applied is, for example, the national law either of the State in which the judgment was given or of the State where enforcement is sought. On the contrary we are concerned with a concept of Community law which has to be interpreted independently, to be precise, taking into account the objective and system of the Convention and also the general legal principles which can be found in this field in the Member States. In my view, which is also shared by all the parties to these proceedings, this point was settled by the findings relating to the concept 'civil and commercial matters', which is also found in Article 1 of the Convention, in the Court's judgment of 14 October 1976 in Case 29/76 *LTU Lufttransportunternehmen GmbH & Co. KG* v *Eurocontrol* [1976] 2 ECR 1541. If this applies to the basic concept which demarcates the scope of the Convention then logically it can only be assumed that the same applies to the concepts which specify the exceptions to the scope of the Convention. In the interest of a uniform application of the Convention they must naturally be given a uniform definition as well. Any other view would be contrary to the recognizable common intention of the parties to the Convention on jurisdiction and enforcement when they drew it up, their intention being that the scope of this Convention should be the complement to that of the Convention on Bankruptcy which was in preparation at the time (cf. Schlosser, Konkurs und konkursähnliche Verfahren im geltenden Europarecht [Bankruptcy and winding-up and analogous proceedings in current European law], in Festschrift für Friedrich Weber [commemorative publication for Friedrich Weber], 1975, p. 396).

3. Before I turn my attention to the interpretation of the concept 'bankruptcy, proceedings relating to the winding-up of insolvent companies or other legal persons, judicial arrangements, compositions and analogous proceedings' allow me now, first of all, to summarize what has been stated in these proceedings about the development and the distinctive features of the statutory liability in Article 99 of the French Law No 67-563 of managers of legal persons, which apparently is not found in a similar form in the legal systems of other Member States.

As far as I can see, originally provision was simply made for the liability of managers of legal persons in France and presumably also in the legal systems of all the Member States - in the Companies Acts. According to those Acts members of the Board of Directors of an Aktiengesellschaft [incorporated public company] - the same applied to Gesellschaften mit beschränkter Haftung [limited liability companies] - were liable under general principles of law for mistakes and negligence in the management of the company, their liability being the same as that of a paid agent under the Code Civil [Civil Code]. Then, in 1940, there was a change in the law relating to incorporated public companies, which from 1953 also applied to limited liability companies, to the effect that a legal person's liabilities which have been ascertained in winding-up proceedings, could, if the assets were insufficient, be imposed on to the managers of the legal person. Even this modification - so we were told - was, in fact, based on liability for mistakes and negligence. The change consisted in essence of a reversal of the burden of proof, this liability being avoidable only if the manager concerned could prove that he had shown the diligence and energy expected of a paid agent. Furthermore, the liability was not linked to a findings of damage and according to the case-law it also attached to *de facto* managers of the legal person; the court was able to decide in the matter whether the managers of a legal person and which of them had to bear the liabilities.

The French Law No 67-563 went a step further. As is stated in the legal opinion produced by the respondent this Law further reinforced those elements of the law on the winding-up of the affairs of companies which relate to the liability of the managers of legal persons. According to that opinion there is no reference to the general legal principles of the law of obligations - and this applies equally to *de jure* and *de facto* managers; reference is no longer made to the energy and diligence of a paid agent. Accordingly, it is no longer sufficient and it is, therefore, better to talk about a presumption of liability than about a presumption of negligence to prove that there was no mismanagement; on the contrary the manager of a legal person has to show that he made every effort to look after its interests. It must, in addition, be borne in mind - this emerges clearly from the wording of Article 99 of the French Law which I have just quoted - that the manager of a legal person can be proceeded against not only on the application of the 'syndic' for the 'faillite' or 'règlement judiciaire' but also by the court having jurisdiction in the winding-up of its own motion. Furthermore, a notable feature is that the application is barred on the expiration of the period of three years from the date when the final list of claims is drawn up, that the court in the event of non-compliance 'prononce le règlement judiciaire ou la liquidation des biens de ceux des dirigeants à la charge desquels a été mis tout ou partie du passif d'une personne morale [shall order the 'règlement judiciaire' on the 'liquidation des biens' of those managers who have been made responsible for all or part of the assets of a legal person]' (Article 100) and that the court 'peut prononcer la faillite personnelle ou l'interdiction de diriger, gérer, administrer ou contrôler, soit toute entreprise commerciale, soit seulement une personne morale, contre le débiteur ou, s'il s'agit d'une personne morale commerciale, contre les dirigeants de droit ou de fait, apparents ou occultes, rémunérés ou non' [may order the 'faillite personnelle' of the debtor or, if the debtor is a legal person engaged in business of the *de jure* or *de facto* managers, apparent or concealed, paid or unpaid, or prohibit the said debtor or managers from directing, managing, conducting or supervising either any commercial undertaking or a legal person alone]' (Article 108).

4. I would also like to make some preliminary observations on the method of interpretation.

(a) As is known the Commission with reference to the Jenard Report on the Convention on jurisdiction and enforcement has stressed the need to give a broad interpretation to the provisions defining its scope, because it is a general agreement, and conversely to give the exceptions specified a narrow construction in order to ensure its efficacy.

In this connection, it is to be noted, without this assertion having to be restricted in principle, that it is at least doubtful whether it also applies to a field such as bankruptcy and winding-up which is also covered by a convention, or to be more precise by a convention in respect of which, even if the original intention to bring it into force at the same time as the Convention on jurisdiction and enforcement could not be achieved, it can be assumed that preparation will be completed in the foreseeable future. In this field - if I correctly understand the position the finding in the Jenard Report was made in another connection - account has to be taken of the fact that there will, in the not too distant future, be a legally effective set of uniform Community rules similar to the Convention on jurisdiction and enforcement. On the other hand, it must not be forgotten that a broad interpretation of the Convention on jurisdiction and enforcement carries within it the danger of encroaching on the field within which Convention on bankruptcy is to be concluded.

However, in any case, it must be said in connection with the claim that the Convention on jurisdiction and enforcement is to be given a broad interpretation, that to circumscribe its scope to this extent cannot be justified if, according to the nature of the matter, that is to say according to the subject-matter of the field to be demarcated, it appears to be unwarranted.

(b) Furthermore, the Commission's reasoning conveyed the impression that the main point of its argument is unequivocally based on the Preliminary Draft of a Convention on bankruptcy and winding-up which has been produced to the Court.

I also consider that to be questionable and take the contrary view that the determinative starting point for interpretation is to be sought in the Convention which is already in force. Even if it may, in fact, be assumed that many of the provisions of the Preliminary Draft will probably be reproduced in the final version of the future Convention there can however be no certainty that they will be. This is shown by Article 12 of the Preliminary Draft which was quoted in the proceedings. It read originally as follows: 'The courts of the Contracting State in which a firm, company or legal person has been declared bankrupt shall have exclusive jurisdiction to entertain actions concerning the liability incurred by the persons specified in Article 2 of Annex I by reason of their management. Actions may be brought only by the liquidator of the firm, company or legal person'.

After discussions which took place in November 1978 because some delegations had made reservations we now, on the other hand, have to proceed on the basis of the following wording of which there is for the time being only the version in French: 'Les juridictions de l'Etat contractant où a été prononcée la faillite d'une société ou personne morale sont exclusivement compétentes pour connaître des actions relatives (a) à la responsabilité encourue en raison de sa gestion par tout dirigeant de cette société ou de cette personne morale pour réparer le dommage subi par elle,...[The courts of the Contracting State in which a firm, company or legal person has been declared insolvent shall have exclusive jurisdiction to entertain actions concerning (a) the liability incurred by reason of his management by any manager of this firm, company or legal person for the purpose of making good the damage which it has suffered,...]'.

Calling in aid the Preliminary Draft of a Convention on bankruptcy and winding-up can, therefore, only be effected with the utmost caution and be limited at best to confirming that it results in the validation and substantiation of an interpretation of the Convention on jurisdiction and enforcement which has been arrived at essentially by a different route.

The same applies, of course, to the view recorded in the minutes of discussions on 15, 16 and 17 November 1978, which, moreover, is shared by only a *majority* of the delegations that, if an order against a manager of a company in an action for a declaration of liability does not lead to 'liquidation collective' [a creditor's winding-up] it does not fall within subparagraph 2 of the second paragraph of Article 1 of the Convention on jurisdiction and enforcement, but is to be classified as a civil and commercial matter. It is all the more necessary to accept this since it is not entirely clear from the extract from the minutes whether in this connection a distinction was drawn between general actions for a declaration of liability and those brought in the field of bankruptcy and winding-up.

(c) Finally, it may also be noted in this connection that some other facts, which have come to light during the proceedings, are undoubtedly not conclusive for the purpose of interpreting the Convention on jurisdiction and enforcement.

For instance, the fact that the French provision, which is relevant in this case, was included in a law on bankruptcy and winding-up is certainly not in itself of importance.

This applies also to the determination of jurisdiction under national law since 'the nature of the court or tribunal' in accordance with Article of the Convention is not in question.

Finally, this also applies to the fact that in the case of the application in question the wording used in civil actions was chosen and that the application was so to speak put forward in the guise of a civil action. On this point the representative of the Federal Government referred with justification to the liability of the heirs for the debts owing by the deceased, which, since the administration of estates has not been included in the Convention on jurisdiction and enforcement, is not covered by the Convention, notwithstanding the civil law wording chosen. In this connection reference was also made to the concept 'place of performance' used in the judgment of 14 October 1976 in Case 29/76 *LTU Lufttransportunternehmen GmbH & Co. KG* v *Eurocontrol* [1976] 2 ECR 1541, which did not exclude the presumption of a dispute governed by public law.

5. If we now consider how the concepts 'bankruptcy, proceedings relating to the winding-up of insolvent companies or other legal persons, judicial arrangements, compositions and analogous proceedings' in Article 1 of the Convention on jurisdiction and enforcement are to be understood the starting point chosen by the respondent is, in my view, the correct one. According to him the first thing to do is to determine the essential nature of the bankruptcy, winding-up or analogous proceedings with reference to the principles applicable in the legal systems of the Member States. In this way one comes to the conclusion that the purpose of such bankruptcy and winding-up proceedings is to get in and realize under the supervision of an officially appointed liquidator or trustee in bankruptcy the assets of the insolvent company or property of the person unable to meet his debts in order to pay off the creditors on a *pro rata* basis. The essential concern of such a proceeding is to get in the entire assets or property of the insolvent company or debtor by adopting a procedure specially designed for this purpose.

The finding in the Jenard Report that individual proceedings connected with bankruptcy or winding-up are to be regarded as bankruptcy or winding-up proceedings if they arise directly out of the bankruptcy or winding-up is useful. Moreover Article 22(4) of the relevant Benelux Treaty, which has not yet entered into force, uses such wording. In the corresponding bilateral treaties such as the Franco-Belgian Treaty of 8 July 1899 or the Belgo-Netherlands Treaty of 28 February 1925 the determinative question is whether the claim put forward is founded in bankruptcy or winding-up, whether the legal consequence of the claim put forward is provided for by the law of bankruptcy or winding-up (cf. Schlosser *loc. cit.*, p. 406). So with individual actions the question is whether there is a very close material connection with bankruptcy or winding-up proceedings so that those rules and special features as it were determine the nature of the proceedings.

The latter undoubtedly applies to rights such as those arising out of the invalidation of certain assignments and payments prior to bankruptcy or winding-up which are peculiar to bankruptcy and winding-up and which are therefore granted under the law of bankruptcy and winding-up and are not merely general rights modified for the purpose of bankruptcy and winding-up. I draw the Court's attention to the Report on the Preliminary Draft of a

Convention on bankruptcy and winding-up by Noël-Lemontey, which in this connexion contains the conclusion that the rights to invalidate certain assignments and payments prior to bankruptcy or winding-up have their origin in bankruptcy and winding-up. I also refer to comparative law research by Schlosser in his treatise (page 407), to which I again refer, and which shows that such an opportunity of invalidating pre-bankruptcy assignments and payments is known in the law of bankruptcy and winding-up of all six original Member States of the Community.

However, the same must also be assumed to apply to rights, which, although they arise under the general law, are modified by the law of bankruptcy and winding-up to such a substantial extent as to suggest the conclusion that viewed as a whole their nature is entirely determined by the law of bankruptcy and winding-up. In my view this represents an intelligible formula enabling decisions to be given which is definitely supported by the conclusions of the Jenard Report. This formula also includes the liability created in Article 99 of the relevant French Law in this case. That liability presupposes the winding-up of a company; the court which made the winding-up order also has jurisdiction to consider it. The 'syndic' may ask for a declaration of liability or the court may make the declaration of its own motion and the purpose of the declaration is to make the manager answerable for the company's debts and consequently not give compensation for specific damage. We also come across an unusual reversal of the burden of proof, which, moreover, is not limited to negligence and, what is more, is only discharged if it is proved that the person whom it is sought to make liable, has applied himself to the management of the business with the requisite energy and diligence. Last but not least, it must also be borne in mind that if the company's debts are not paid the manager whom it is sought to make liable may himself be adjudicated bankrupt and penalties may be imposed upon him for specific bankruptcy offences.

Viewed in this way the interpretation given by the applicant in the main action that the application is simply a special application for a declaration of liability based on a particular rule concerning liability of civil and commercial law according to which liability arises if particular conditions are fulfilled can certainly not be regarded as convincing. A comparison between Article 244 and Article 248 of the French 'Code des Sociétés [Companies Act]' surely refutes this interpretation. According to the first mentioned article the 'administrateurs [directors]' of a public company are liable for breaches of the provisions governing public companies, and of the Memorandum and Articles and for mistakes made in the management of the company and according to the commentaries they give rise to payment of compensation if 'faute [negligence]' is proved. On the other hand Article 248 provides: 'En cas de règlement judiciaire ou de liquidation des biens de la société, les personnes visées par la legislation sur le réglement judiciaire, la liquidation des biens, la faillite personelle et les banque-routes, peuvent être rendues responsables du passif social dans les conditions prévues par ladite législation. [In the event of a 'règlement judiciaire'or a 'liquidation des biens' of a company the persons specified by the laws relating to the 'règlement judiciaire', the 'liquidation des biens', the 'faillite personnelle' and 'banqueroutes' may be declared liable for the company's liabilities in accordance with the conditions laid down by the said laws]'.

On the contrary, more convincing is the respondent's interpretation which stresses that the real purpose of the proceedings in question is to get in all the outstanding assets of a company, so that there is a sort of restitution in kind in that the situation which would exist had it not been for the mistakes in the management of the company has to be reestablished. If, however, the proceedings are for compensation for running down the assets it is, in fact, natural, having regard to the function of the proceedings under Article 99 of Law No 67-563, to say that they are clearly part and parcel of the winding-up proceedings. In support of the view that the issue is whether a claim arises out of bankruptcy or winding-up the representative of the Federal Government has referred lastly, with justification, to Article 27 of the Convention on jurisdiction and enforcement. This article provides in connection with the recognition of judgments for the court of the Member State in which recognition is sought to consider certain preliminary questions, for example, status. Although, however, this only applies to the matters mentioned in subparagraph 1 of the second paragraph of Article 1 to which the Convention does not apply and does not relate to the law on bankruptcy and winding-up, there is surely every reason to define with caution the scope of the Convention as far as concerns rights which are conditional upon an adjudication or winding-up order.

6. However, I do not intend to end my examination of the case yet in that way without considering the Preliminary Draft of a Convention on bankruptcy and winding-up which has been mentioned and upon which the Commission's main argument had rested, in order to see whether it could upset the result which has so far been arrived at.

In the first place, the Commission attaches importance to the fact that the Convention on bankruptcy and winding-up does not provide any general definition of the proceedings specified in subparagraph 2 of the second paragraph of Article 1 of the Convention on jurisdiction and enforcement to which the latter Convention does not apply. These proceedings on the contrary are listed in detail in a Protocol annexed to the Convention on bankruptcy and winding-up and the scope of that Convention is defined in this way. Since however - the Commission reasons - the proceeding under Article 99 of the French Law on bankruptcy and winding-up is not included in the list set out it cannot be assumed that it is intended to fall within the scope of a Convention on bankruptcy and winding-up. Although on the other hand Article 12 of the latter Convention mentions proceedings such as those instituted under Article 99 of the French Law that is done merely for the purpose of establishing a particular jurisdiction but not to give expression thereby to the fact that they fall in general within the scope of the Convention on bankruptcy and winding-up. In any case it is significant that according to Article 61 of the Preliminary Draft of this Convention the recognition and enforcement of judgments in actions concerning liability referred to in Article 12 are to be governed by the Convention on jurisdiction and enforcement but this must be understood as being only *declaratory* having regard to the other conclusions already mentioned which are to be drawn concerning the Convention on bankruptcy and winding-up.

This argument seems to me - quite apart from the objections in principle to invoking the Preliminary Draft of a Convention on bankruptcy and winding-up as being determinative - to be unconvincing.

As far as I am concerned, the conclusion that only those proceedings expressly mentioned in the Protocol annexed to the Convention on bankruptcy and winding-up can be regarded as forming part of bankruptcy and winding-up is not convincing. It is clear that only the so-called basic proceedings are for the most part mentioned there. Consequently, the question whether any particular proceedings fall within the Convention on bankruptcy and winding-up must also be deducible from other provisions, otherwise such proceedings which arise directly out of bankruptcy and winding-up and to which according to the beforementioned Jenard Report the Convention on jurisdiction and enforcement is simply not intended to apply would be governed by that Convention.

On the other hand, as far as concerns the value and significance of the reference in Article 61 of the Preliminary Draft of a Convention on bankruptcy and winding-up it cannot only be pointed out in connection with the view that the provision is only declaratory that it can scarcely be assumed that the legislature is providing for the incorporation in the Convention of a superfluous and, consequently, rather confusing provision. In particular it must not be overlooked that Article 61 also refers to the proceedings set out in Article 17 of the Convention on bankruptcy and winding-up. However, it is quite certain judging by a number of them - I call attention again on this point to the beforementioned treatise by Schlosser - that they are typical proceedings in bankruptcy and winding-up. Thus, it is reasonable not only to find in Articles 12 and 17 of the Convention on bankruptcy and winding-up rules for determining jurisdiction but also to assume that they are intended to give expression to the inclusion of these matters in that Convention, and furthermore Article 59(4) of the Convention on bankruptcy and winding-up supports this view. This suggests that the reference in Article 61 of the Convention on bankruptcy and winding-up be regarded as substantive.

Moreover, this interpretation of the Convention on bankruptcy and winding-up seems also to be in every way appropriate. It leads to the conclusions that only when the general recognition of bankruptcy and winding-up has been secured by a specific convention can there also be recognition of judgments concerning rights, which are conditional on a valid bankruptcy or winding-up and which rank as rights arising out of the very essence of bankruptcy and winding-up.

7. I, therefore, suggest that the following answer be given to the question referred to the Court by the Bundesgerichtshof for a preliminary ruling.

In addition to the basic proceedings those proceedings connected with bankruptcy and winding-up proceedings which must be presumed to stem from bankruptcy or winding-up and arise directly thereout fall within the exception contained in subparagraph 2 of the second paragraph of Article 1 of the Convention on jurisdiction and enforcement. This applies to proceedings concerning rights which arise only under the law of bankruptcy and winding-up as well as to rights which exist under the general civil law but which in the law relating to bankruptcy and winding-up undergo such a decisive modification that, having regard to their specific object they are to be regarded as falling within the law of bankruptcy and winding-up.

Case 143/78 - 27 March 1979

Jacques de Cavel
v
Luise de Cavel I

Article 1 - Sphere of application - Matters excluded - 'Rights in property arising out of a matrimonial relationship' - Concept - Provisional measures ordered in the course of proceedings for divorce - Exclusion - Conditions - Article 24 - Distinction between provisional and definitive measures - None.

Summary

1. The term 'rights in property arising out of a matrimonial relationship' within the meaning of the second paragraph of Article 1 of the Convention, includes not only property arrangements specifically and exclusively envisaged by certain national legal systems in the case of marriage but also any proprietary relationships resulting directly from the matrimonial relationship or the dissolution thereof.

2. Judicial decisions authorizing provisional protective measures - such as the placing under seal or the freezing of the assets of the spouses - in the course of proceedings for divorce do not fall within the scope of the Convention as defined in Article 1 thereof if those measures concern or are closely connected with either questions of the status of the persons involved in the divorce proceedings or proprietary legal relations resulting directly from the matrimonial relationship or the dissolution thereof.

3. In relation to the matters covered by the Convention, no legal basis is to be found therein for drawing a distinction between provisional and definitive measures.

JUDGMENT OF THE COURT

Kutscher, President, Mertens de Wilmars and Lord Mackenzie Stuart, Presidents of Chambers, Donner, Pescatore, Sorensen, O'Keeffe, Bosco and Touffait, Judges

1. By an order of 22 May 1978, which was received at the Court on 19 June 1978, the Bundesgerichtshof referred to the Court of Justice for a preliminary ruling pursuant to the Protocol of 3 June 1971 on the Interpretation by the Court of Justice of the Convention of 27 September 1968 on Jurisdiction and the Enforcement of Judgments in Civil and Commercial (hereinafter referred to as 'the Convention') a question relating to the interpretation of subparagraph (1) of the second paragraph of Article 1 of the Convention which excludes from the scope of the Convention the status or legal capacity of natural persons, rights in property arising out of a matrimonial relationship, wills and succession.

2. The question was raised in the context of a dispute concerning the enforcement in the Federal Republic of Germany of an order made on 19 January 1977 by the judge of family matters at the Tribunal de Grande Instance, Paris, authorizing, as a protective measure in divorce proceedings pending between the parties, the putting under seal of furniture, effects and other objects in the flat at Frankfurt-am-Main belonging to the parties and the freezing of the assets and accounts of the respondent at two banking establishments in that city.

In reliance on Article 31 of the Convention the husband, who had commenced proceedings for the divorce, and in whose favour the authorization to freeze the assets was made, applied to the President of the Landgericht Frankfurt-am-Main for an order for the enforcement of the decision of the French court, but that application was dismissed on the ground that the applicant had not produced the documents referred to in Article 47 of the Convention.

On appeal, the Oberlandesgericht Frankfurt-am-Main also rejected the application, on the ground that the protective measures enforcement of which was sought formed part of divorce proceedings and were therefore excluded from the scope of the Convention by subparagraph (1) of the second paragraph of Article 1.

3. The case was then brought before the Bundesgerichtshof which referred to the Court of Justice the following question: 'Is the Convention of the European Community of 27 September 1968 on Jurisdiction and

the Enforcement of Judgments in Civil and Commercial Matters inapplicable to an order made by a French judge of family matters simultaneously with proceedings for the dissolution of marriage pending before a French court for putting under seal and freezing assets, since it relates to proceedings incidental to an action concerning personal status or right in property arising out of a matrimonial relationship (subparagraph (1) of the second paragraph of Article 1 of the Convention)?'

4. The Commission and the appellant argue that the answer should be given that the proceedings referred to fall within the scope of the Convention, while the Governments of the United Kingdom and of the Federal Republic of Germany and the respondent contend that the answer should be that the Convention is inapplicable.

5. It appears from the file on the case that the matters in dispute before the German courts concern, on the one hand, the connection between the measures ordered by the French judge of family matters and the divorce proceedings and, on the other, the question whether the Convention is applicable in view of the proprietary nature of the protective measures in question.

6. In the words of Article 1, the Convention is to apply in 'civil and commercial matters'.
Nevertheless, because of the specific nature of certain matters, including 'the status or legal capacity of natural persons, rights in property arising out of a matrimonial relationship, wills and succession', disputes relating to such matters are excluded from its scope.

7. The enforced settlement on a provisional basis of proprietary legal relationships between spouses in the course of proceedings for divorce is closely linked to the grounds for the divorce and the personal situation of the spouses or any children of the marriage and is, for that reason, inseparable from questions relating to the status of persons raised by the dissolution of the matrimonial relationship and from the settlement of rights in property arising out of the matrimonial relationship.

Consequently, the term *'rights in property arising out of a matrimonial relationship' includes* not only property arrangements specifically and exclusively envisaged by certain national legal systems in the case of marriage but also any proprietary relationships resulting directly from the matrimonial relationship or the dissolution thereof.

Disputes relating to the assets of spouses in the course of

proceedings for divorce may therefore, depending on the circumstances, concern or be closely connected with:

(1) questions relating to the status of persons; or

(2) proprietary legal relationships between spouses resulting directly from the matrimonial relationship or the dissolution thereof; or

(3) proprietary legal relations existing between them which have no connection with the marriage.

Whereas disputes of the latter category fall within the scope of the Convention, those relating to the first two categories must be excluded therefrom.

8. The foregoing considerations are applicable to measures relating to the property of spouses whether they are provisional or definitive in nature.

As provisional protective measures relating to property - such as the affixing of seals or the freezing of assets - can serve to safeguard a variety of rights, their inclusion in the scope of the Convention is determined not by their own nature but by the nature of the rights which they serve to protect.

9. Furthermore, in relation to the matters covered by the Convention, no legal basis is to be found therein for drawing a distinction between provisional and definitive measures.

That conclusion is not affected by Article 24 of the Convention whereby:

'Application may be made to the courts of a Contracting State for such provisional, including protective, measures as may be available under the law of that State, even if, under this Convention, the courts of another Contracting State have jurisdiction as to the substance of the matter'.

In fact, that provision expressly envisages the case of provisional measures in a Contracting State where 'under this Convention' the courts of another Contracting State have jurisdiction as to the substance of the matter and it cannot, therefore, be relied on to bring within the scope of the Convention provisional or protective measures relating to matters which are excluded therefrom.

10. It may, therefore, be concluded that judicial decisions authorizing provisional protective measures - such as the placing under seal or the freezing of the assets of the spouses - in the course of proceedings for divorce do not fall within the scope of the Convention as defined in Article 1 thereof if those measures concern or are closely connected with either questions of the status of the persons involved in the divorce

proceedings or proprietary legal relations resulting directly from the matrimonial relationship or the dissolution thereof.

On those grounds, the court, in answer to the question referred to it by the Bundesgerichtshof by order of 22 May 1978, hereby rules:

> **Judicial decisions authorizing provisional protective measures - such as the placing under seal or the freezing of the assets of the spouses - in the course of proceedings for divorce do not fall within the scope of the Convention of 27 September 1968 on Jurisdiction and the Enforcement of Judgments in Civil and Commercial Matters as defined in Article 1 thereof if those measures concern or are closely connected with either questions of the status of the persons involved in the divorce proceedings or proprietary legal relations resulting directly from the matrimonial relationship or the dissolution thereof.**

OPINION OF MR ADVOCATE GENERAL WARNER

This case comes to the Court by way of a reference for a preliminary ruling ordered by the Bundesgerichtshof under the Protocol of 3 June 1971 on the interpretation by the Court of the Convention of 27 September 1968 on Jurisdiction and Enforcement of Judgments in Civil and Commercial Matters.

The question raised by the reference concerns the field of application of the Convention and, more particularly, the scope of the exceptions from that field made by subparagraph 1 of the second paragraph of Article 1 for matters relating to 'the status ... of natural persons' and 'rights in property arising out of a matrimonial relationship'.

As Your Lordships know, the Convention is at present in force only in the original Member States and the only authentic texts of it are the German, French, Italian and Dutch texts. It has been my practice, in opinions dealing with pre-1973 Community instruments of which there has been no authentic English text, to refer to the French text. Your Lordships also know, however, that a Convention on the Accession of the new Member States to the 1968 Convention and to the Protocol on its interpretation by the Court was signed at Luxembourg on 9 October 1978 ('the Accession Convention'). Versions of the original Convention and Protocol in Danish, English and Irish are annexed to the Accession Convention and Article 37 of the Convention provides that those versions 'shall be authentic under the same conditions as the original texts of the 1968 Convention and the 1971 Protocol'. That being so I propose to cite from what is to become, when ratification of the Accession Convention is complete, the authentic English text. There is this advantage in my doing so that that text shows to some extent what the authors of the Accession Convention (at least) thought that the original Convention meant.

I turn to the facts of the present case. On 12 January 1977 M. Jacques de Cavel ('the husband') instituted, in the Tribunal de Grande Instance of Paris, proceedings against his wife, Mme. Luise de Cavel ('the wife') for divorce. The husband is a French citizen, working in Frankfurt-am-Main. The wife is of German origin. They had a flat in Frankfurt and another in Cannes. It seems that in November 1976 the wife caused to be removed from the flat in Cannes, and to be sold for her benefit, some valuable carpets which the husband claims were his. He also alleges that, when he returned to Frankfurt from holiday at the beginning of January 1977, he found that a number of objects had similarly been removed from the flat there and from his office. On the strength of those allegations, he coupled with his divorce petition an application to the Tribunal de Grande Instance of Paris for protective measures ('mesures conservatoires').

On 19 January 1977 the Judge in Matrimonial Matters ('Juge aux Affaires Matrimoniales') of the Tribunal ordered, first, the placing of seals ('l'apposition des scellés') on the furniture and effects in the flat in Frankfurt and on a safe deposit box hired in the wife's name at a bank in Frankfurt and, secondly, the freezing ('saisie arret') of two accounts in the wife's name with banks in Frankfurt. It is, I think, common ground that that order was made ex parte and that it was made under Article 257 of the French Civil Code, which empowers a Judge to order emergency measures ('des mesures urgentes') as soon as a divorce petition has been filed. Reference was made, in the course of argument, to Article 220 of the Code, which enables such measures to be ordered independently of divorce proceedings, but an order under that Article can be made only by the President of the Tribunal, and the order here in question was not made by him.

The husband applied to the Landgericht of Frankfurt for enforcement under Article 31 of the 1968 Convention of the order of 12 January 1977. On 3 May 1977 his application was rejected by that Court on the ground that documents had not been produced, as required by Article 47 of the Convention, to show that 'according to the law of the State in which it has been given, the Judgment is enforceable and has been served'.

The husband appealed to the Oberlandesgericht of Frankfurt which, in its turn, refused to enforce the order, on the different ground that interim measures adopted in the course of divorce proceedings form part of those proceedings and must, therefore, be regarded as measures relating to the status of natural persons which, under the second paragraph of Article 1 of the Convention, fall outside its field of application. In the view of the Oberlandesgericht it made no difference that the object of the measures was to protect interests of a proprietary nature, since the same paragraph refers explicitly to 'rights in property arising out of a matrimonial relationship'.

The husband now appeals to the Bundesgerichtshof, which has referred to this Court the question whether, to put it shortly, the 1968 Convention is inapplicable to an order such as that made by the French Judge in this case, on the grounds that that order was made in proceedings relating to personal status or rights in property arising out of a matrimonial relationship.

For the purposes of their arguments the Commission, the German

Government and the United Kingdom Government broke that question down into two:

(1) Can the 1968 Convention apply to an ancillary order made in proceedings in which the substantive claim is outside the scope of the Convention; more particularly can the Convention apply to an order for interim measures made in divorce proceedings?

(2) If the answer to the first question is 'yes', do measures of the kind ordered by the French Judge in the present case relate to 'the status of natural persons' or to 'rights in property arising out of a matrimonial relationship' within the meaning of those phrases in the second paragraph of Article 1 of the Convention?

The United Kingdom Government submitted that the first question should be answered in the negative. In support of that submission it put forward four main arguments:

(i) There are wide differences both in the bases on which courts of Member States assume jurisdiction over divorce and in the grounds (if any) on which they will allow a marriage to be dissolved. That is the primary reason for the exclusion of matters relating to the status of natural persons from the scope of the Convention. Because divorce laws are rooted in deeply held social, moral and religious attitudes, the courts of one country may find it difficult to assist the courts of another country in exercising that jurisdiction. It would be illogical and contrary to the spirit of the Convention if it, nevertheless, required ancillary orders made in the exercise of the same jurisdiction to be enforced by the courts of another country.

(ii) Since divorce proceedings are outside the Convention, a court entertaining such proceedings does not have to comply with the rules of the Convention concerning jurisdiction over persons domiciled elsewhere in the Community. It follows that an ancillary order might be made in divorce proceedings by a court lacking jurisdiction under the Convention to make the order. There would be no means of checking on this, because Article 28 of the Convention prevents re-examination of the basis of jurisdiction.

(iii) Jurisdiction to make ancillary orders falling within the scope of the Convention would have to be based on the rules of the Convention itself. A court exercising divorce jurisdiction on a ground not generally authorized by the Convention would be deprived of its power to make ancillary orders of that kind in the proceedings.

(iv) Article 5(2) of the Convention gives jurisdiction 'in matters relating to maintenance' to 'the courts for the place where the maintenance creditor is domiciled or habitually resident'. It is amended by the Accession Convention which adds the following: 'or if the matter is ancillary to proceedings concerning the status of a person, in the court which, according to its own law, has jurisdiction to entertain these proceedings, unless that jurisdiction is based solely on the nationality of one of the parties'.

That amendment would have been unnecessary, the United Kingdom Government submits, if maintenance proceedings ancillary to status proceedings already fell within the scope of the Convention.

Those are powerful arguments, particularly to my mind the second and the third. I have, however, come to the conclusion that, on balance, they are outweighed by considerations urged upon us by the Commission and by the German Government.

The first paragraph of Article 1 of the Convention expressly provides that the answer to the question whether or not the Convention applies in a particular case does not depend on 'the nature of the court or tribunal' concerned. The subsequent provisions of the Convention seem to me to make it clear that the answer to that question does not in general depend on the nature of the proceedings either. In general the determining factor is the subject-matter of the case. To that general principle there are express exceptions, such as those for bankruptcy and analogous proceedings, and for arbitration, in subparagraphs 2 and 4 of the second paragraph of Article 1.

That is as one would expect. It would be odd if the applicability of the Convention depended on the particular forum or type of procedure chosen by the plaintiff, petitioner or other claimant; if, for instance, in the present case, the situation would have been different if the husband had applied to the President of the Tribunal under Article 220 of the Civil Code independently of divorce proceedings or if the enforceability of an order of the High Court in England, designed to preserve property owned by a husband and wife in common, were to depend on whether it was made by the Chancery Division in the exercise of its equitable jurisdiction (as in *Wailer* v *Waller* [1967] 1 WLR 451) or by the Family Division in the course of divorce proceedings.

In my opinion the United Kingdom Government's interpretation of Article 5(2) of the Convention and of the effect of the amendment thereof to be made by the Accession Convention are mistaken. Article 5(2) as it stands at present makes an exception to the general rule in Article 2 that a person is to be sued in the courts of the State where he is 'domiciled'. That exception is to the effect that a 'maintenance creditor' may also sue in the courts of a State where he or she is domiciled or habitually resident. Article 5(2) is silent on the question whether the Convention applies to a maintenance order made in divorce proceedings. Professor Schlosser's Report on the draft of the Accession Convention (paragraph 32) identifies the reason for that as being that when the 1968 Convention was drawn up the principle still applied in the original Member States that maintenance proceedings could not be combined with proceedings relating to status. Since 1968, however, widespread reforms of family law in those States have led to an increasing number of combined proceedings there. The result may be seen in the Judgment of 4 June 1976 of the Oberlandesgericht of Karlsruhe in *B.K.* v *P.K.* (2 W 7/76 - Synopsis of Case Law on the 1968 Convention, Part 2, No 54). The Oberlandesgericht had no difficulty in holding that a maintenance order made by the Tribunal de Grande Instance of Paris in divorce proceedings was enforceable under the Convention. Indeed the Oberlandesgericht thought the point too clear to warrant a reference to this Court. On that view the effect of the amendment to Article 5(2) must be that a court of a Member State which is neither that of the domicile of the 'maintenance debtor' nor that of the domicile or habitual residence of the 'maintenance creditor' will have power to make an order in the latter's favour provided that the order is made as an ancillary matter in proceedings concerning the status of a person that that court has jurisdiction to entertain according to its own law and provided that that jurisdiction is not based solely on the nationality of one of the parties.

The Commission and the German Government found support for their interpretation of Article 1 (with which I agree) in other provisions of the Convention, notably Article 42, Article 5(4) and Article 24.

The first paragraph of Article 42 provides: 'Where a foreign judgment has been given in respect of several matters and enforcement cannot be authorized for all of them, the Court shall authorize enforcement for one or more of them'.

That appears to mean that, where a judgment covers matters that are and matters that are not within the Convention, enforcement is to be ordered in respect of those that are. It would seem to be inconsistent with the approach there evinced to hold that an ancillary order relating to a matter within the Convention cannot be enforced if made in proceedings relating also to matters outside the Convention.

Article 5(4) gives a court seized of criminal proceedings jurisdiction to hear civil claims for damages or restitution based on the act giving rise to those proceedings. That is a case where the Convention expressly applies to an ancillary proceeding, although the main proceedings clearly fall outside its scope.

Article 24 I shall have to advert to, later, in a different context. On the present point it seems to me neutral.

I turn to the second question. As to that it seems to me abundantly clear that an order of the kind made by the French Judge in the present case does not relate to the status of any natural person. It relates only to property. So the real question is whether it relates to 'rights in property arising out of a matrimonial relationship'. In approaching that question is confronted with two main difficulties. The first is that, as the Commission pointed out to us, the phrases corresponding to 'rights in property arising out of a matrimonial relationship' in the texts of the Convention in the several official languages do not all have the same meaning. It seems that the phrase in the German text 'ehelicher Güterstand'is especially narrow.

Secondly there is a great disparity, even among the legal systems of the original Member States, in the rules governing proprietary relationships between spouses. In all of those States, it seems, such relationships are governed by 'regimes' each consisting of a more or less comprehensive set of rules, e.g. 'community of property', 'separation of property' or 'community limited to after-acquired property', for which couples are required to opt at the time of their marriage. In some countries (e.g. Germany) the regime applicable to a particular couple can be changed subsequently. In others it cannot. In some countries (e.g. France) there are rules, referred to as the 'regime matrimonial primaire', that apply irrespective of the particular regime opted for. In others there are not. Moreover, the rules applicable under each regime differ from country to country. In the result it is never possible to determine without detailed enquiry what a spouse's rights over particular property are, nor the extent to which those rights are derived from the general law or from the relevant matrimonial regime. With the accession to the Convention of Ireland and the United Kingdom, where such regimes are unknown but where a spouse's rights may also be derived wholly or partly either from the general law of property or from his or her position as a spouse (and in the latter case wholly or partly either from a marriage settlement or from general law applicable as between spouses) the disparities will be increased.

One thing is certain. It is that the very purpose of the Convention must be defeated if, in each case in which enforcement is sought in one Member State of a judgment of a court of another Member State, the court before which enforcement is sought has to enquire to what extent the property rights to which the judgment gives effect, or purports to give effect, are derived from a matrimonial regime, from a marriage settlement, from general matrimonial law, from the general law of property, or (perhaps) from other branches of the general law. In order for the Convention to work as it is intended to, the Court before which enforcement is sought must be able to tell, virtually at a glance, whether the judgment is or is not one to which the Convention applies. Moreover, in the case of an order for protective measures such as is here in question, an enquiry of that kind would be futile, since such an order is designed not to give effect to proprietary rights but merely to preserve the property to which it relates so that the respective rights of the spouses over that property may be effectively adjudicated upon later.

In the argument before us three solutions of the problem were canvassed.

One, which was the solution in favour of which the Commission came down, was to give to the phrase 'rights in property arising from a matrimonial relationship' a very narrow interpretation, confining it to matters relating to the adoption, existence or dissolution of a matrimonial regime, and to exclude any question as to rights arising from the existence or dissolution of such a regime. That solution might, I suppose, be workable in the period before the entry into force of the Accession Convention and it may be consistent with the four now authentic texts of the 1968 Convention. But it would not be workable after the entry into force of the Accession Convention and would be irreconcilable with what will then be the English text of Article 1. In other words it would defeat the expressed intention of the authors of the Accession Convention, unless one were to hold that the entry into force of the Accession Convention will alter the meaning of Article 1.

The second possible solution was to interpret the phrase 'rights in property arising from a matrimonial relationship' quite literally as excluding any rights subsisting between spouses that would have existed as between them even had they not been married. No-one, as I understood the arguments, actually supported that solution. Its adoption would be incompatible with the purpose of the Convention as a whole for the reason, which I alluded to a moment ago, that it would require in each case an enquiry by the enforcing court into the sources of the rights to which the judgment was intended to give effect.

There remains only the solution contended for by the German Government (if I understood it rightly), by the United Kingdom Government (albeit briefly) and on behalf of the wife. This is to give to the phrase a broad meaning, on the footing that, in practice, in few disputes between spouses about property is it likely that the 'matrimonial relationship' between them will play no part. A case in which that relationship plays no part can no doubt occur, but then that fact can be made clear in the judgment, and will no doubt be made clear in it if it is widely enough known among the legal profession and among Judges in the Member States that that is a precondition to the judgment's enforceability under the Convention in other Member States.

The upshot is that, in my opinion, a judgment or order relating to a property dispute between spouses should be presumed to be outside the scope of the Convention unless it is apparent on the face of the particular judgment or order in question that it is not.

I do not overlook the argument of the Commission that that interpretation must necessarily restrict the field of application of the Convention. That does not, however, mean that it is not the right interpretation, as is borne out by the Judgment that Your Lordships have just delivered in Case 133/78 *Gourdain* v *Nadler*, where a like argument was put forward by the Commission.

It was also argued on the Commission that such an interpretation would be inconsistent with the fact that the Convention applies to maintenance orders. I do not think so. Maintenance orders are, in general, orders for the payment of money. They operate *in personam* and do not affect property rights, except where secured maintenance is ordered, but then the affection of property is of a limited and special kind.

The Commission further submitted that that interpretation would be inconsistent with the deliberate departure by the authors of the 1968 Convention from the text of The Hague Convention on the Recognition and Enforcement of Foreign Judgments in Civil and Commercial Matters which refers, in the provision corresponding to subparagraph 1 of the second paragraph Article 1 of the 1968 Convention, to 'the status or capacity of persons or questions of family law, including personal or financial rights and obligations between parents and children or between spouses'. One has only, however, to turn to M. Jenard's Report on the draft of the 1968 Convention (Chapter III, para. IV (A)) to see why its authors made that departure. Their reasons had nothing to do with the present issue, except insofar as they wished to make the Convention apply to maintenance orders.

Virtually the whole of the argument submitted to us on behalf of the husband rested on Article 24 of the Convention, which reads as follows: 'Application may be made to the courts of a Contracting State for such provisional, including protective, measures as may be available under the law of that State, even if, under this Convention, the courts of another Contracting State have jurisdiction as to the substance of the matter'.

In my opinion that Article is not in point, because it applies only where under the Convention jurisdiction as to the substance of a particular matter is allocated to the courts of a particular 'Contracting State'. In other words Article 24 does not apply where 'the substance of the matter' is outside the field of application of the Convention. It would be astonishing if it were otherwise, because it would mean that, in cases outside the scope of the Convention, the courts of the Member States were, nonetheless, bound to enforce each other's provisional orders.

In the result I am of the opinion that, in answer to the question referred to the Court by the Bundesgerichtshof, Your Lordships, should rule that an order for protective measures made by a court of a Member State in proceedings for divorce is not, on the mere ground that it is made in such proceedings, outside the scope of the Convention of 27 September 1968, but that, where the order relates to property that is the subject-matter of a dispute between the parties of those proceedings, that order must be taken to be outside the scope of the Convention unless it appears on the face of the order that the rights in dispute arise independently of the matrimonial relationship between the parties.

Case 120/79 - 6 March 1980

Luise de Cavel
v
Jacques de Cavel II

Article 1 - Scope - Subject of maintenance obligations - Inclusion - Scope - Claim ancillary to proceedings which are excluded by virtue of their subject-matter - Inclusion - Articles 1 and 24 - Scope - Distinction between interim and final measures - None - Interlocutory measure ordering the payment of a maintenance allowance during divorce proceedings - Interim compensation payment awarded by a divorce judgment - Inclusion.

Summary

1. The subject of maintenance obligations falls of itself within the concept of 'civil ... matters' within the meaning of the first paragraph of Article 1 of the Convention and accordingly comes within the scope of the Convention since it has not been excepted by the second paragraph of that article.

2. A claim falls within the scope of the Convention where its own subject-matter is one of the matters covered by the Convention even if it is ancillary to proceedings which, because of their subject-matter, do not come within the Convention's sphere of application.

3. The interim or final nature of a judgment is not relevant to whether the judgment comes within the scope of the Convention.

4. The Convention is applicable, on the one hand, to the enforcement of an interlocutory order made by a French court in divorce proceedings whereby one of the parties to the proceedings is awarded a monthly maintenance allowance and, on the other hand, to an interim

compensation payment, payable monthly, awarded to one of the parties by a French divorce judgment pursuant to Article 270 *et seq.* of the French Civil Code.

JUDGMENT OF THE COURT

Kutscher, President, Mertens de Wilmars, Lord Mackenzie Stuart, Judges

1. By order of 27 June 1979 which was received at the Court on 30 July 1979 the Bundesgerichtshof submitted to the Court of Justice, under the Protocol of 3 June 1971 on the Interpretation of the Convention of 27 September 1968 on Jurisdiction and the Enforcement of Judgments in Civil and Commercial Matters (hereinafter referred to as 'the Convention'), two questions on the interpretation of subparagraph (1) of the second paragraph of Article 1 and subparagraph (2) of Article 5 of the Convention.

2. The first question is directed towards ascertaining whether the Convention, and in particular Article 31 thereof which relates to the enforcement of judgments given in another Contracting State, apply to 'the enforcement of an interlocutory order made by a French judge in divorce proceedings, whereby one of the parties to the proceedings is awarded maintenance payable monthly' or whether, on the contrary, such a judgment must be considered as not being a 'civil matter' within the meaning of subparagraph (1) of the second paragraph of Article 1 of the Convention. This question is raised in the context of proceedings relating to the enforcement in the Federal Republic of Germany of an order made on 18 May 1977 by the judge in matrimonial matters at the Tribunal de Grande Instance, Paris, awarding the wife, pursuant to Article 253 *et seq.* of the French Civil Code, an interim maintenance allowance pending divorce.

3. The second question asks, likewise, whether the Convention - in particular its provisions relating to the enforcement of judgments - is applicable 'to the payment of interim compensation, on a monthly basis, granted to one of the parties in a French judgment dissolving a marriage pursuant to Article 270 *et seq.* of the Code Civil'. In terms of the said Article 270, the payment in question is intended to compensate, so far as possible, for the disparity which the breakdown of the marriage creates in the parties' respective living standards. Article 271 provides further that the compensatory payment is to be fixed according to the needs of the spouse to whom it is paid and the means of the other, having regard to the

position at the time of divorce and its development in the foreseeable future.

4. According to the first paragraph of Article 1 of the Convention its scope extends to 'civil and commercial matters'. However, certain matters, although falling within that concept, have been removed from that field, by way of exception, by the second paragraph of the same provision. Such is the case in regard to, *inter alia,* the status or legal capacity of natural persons, rights in property arising out of a matrimonial relationship, wills and succession.

5. It is well settled that the subject of maintenance obligations itself falls within the concept of a 'civil matter' and that since it is not taken out by the exceptions provided for in the second paragraph of Article 1 of the Convention it therefore falls within the scope of the Convention. Article 5(2) of the Convention provides confirmation, should such be necessary, that is so falls. On the other hand, the 'compensatory payments' provided for in Article 270 *et seq.* of the French Civil Code and referred to in the second question are concerned with any financial obligations between former spouses after divorce which are fixed on the basis of their respective needs and resources and are equally in the nature of maintenance. They are therefore civil matters within the meaning of the first paragraph of Article 1 of the Convention and accordingly come within the scope of the Convention since they have not been excepted by the second paragraph of that article.

6. Accordingly, all that has to be considered is whether the fact that the maintenance judgment is given in the context of divorce proceedings - which unquestionably concern the status of persons and are consequently outside the field of application of the Convention - has the consequence that the maintenance proceedings must, as being ancillary to the divorce proceedings, also be excepted from that field of application, with the result that they may not benefit from, *inter alia,* the simplified procedures for recognition and enforcement provided by Articles 26 to 30 and Articles 31 to 45 respectively.

7. Insofar as its field of application is concerned, no provision of the Convention links the treatment of ancillary claims to the treatment of principal claims. On the contrary, various provisions confirm that the Convention does not link the treatment of claims classified as 'ancillary' to the treatment of the principal claim. In particular, such is the case with Article 42 which provides that, where a foreign judgment has been given

in respect of several matters and enforcement cannot be authorised for all of them, the Court shall authorise enforcement for one or more of them, and with Article 24, which provides that application for such provisional, including protective, measures - which are, by definition, ancillary measures - as may be available under the law of a Contracting State may be made to the courts of that State ‘even if, under this Convention, the courts of another Contracting State have jurisdiction as to the substance of the matter’.

8. These provisions demonstrate unequivocally that the general scheme of the Convention does not necessarily link the treatment of an ancillary claim to that of a principal claim. In accordance with that principle, and in regard precisely to the Convention’s scope, a criminal court, the judgments of which, when given in its proper area of activity, are clearly excluded from the scope of the Convention, has jurisdiction conferred upon it by Article 5(4) of the Convention to entertain an ancillary civil claim, with the result that a judgment given on that claim will benefit from the Convention as regards its recognition and enforcement. That provision thus expressly provides that a claim ancillary to criminal proceedings, which are obviously excluded from the scope of the Convention, comes within it.

9. Ancillary claims accordingly come within the scope of the Convention according to the subject-matter with which they are concerned and not according to the subject-matter involved in the principal claim. It was by way of applying that rule that the Court held in its judgment of 27 March 1979 in Case 143/78 *de Cavel* [1979] ECR 1055, involving the same parties, that an application in the course of divorce proceedings for placing assets under seal did not come within the scope of the Convention, not on account of its ancillary nature, but because it appeared that, having regard to its true function, it concerned, in that case, rights in property arising out of the spouses’ matrimonial relationship.

10. On the other hand, the Court has already recognised in that same judgment that the interim or final nature of a judgment is not relevant to whether the judgment comes within the scope of the Convention. Accordingly, the argument to the effect that the maintenance obligation is only an interim one pending divorce must be rejected.

11. It follows from the foregoing considerations that the scope of the Convention extends also, and for the same reasons, to maintenance

obligations which legislation or the Court places on spouses for the period after divorce.

12. The answer to the questions put by the Bundesgerichtshof should therefore be that the Convention is applicable, on the one hand, to the enforcement of an interlocutory order made by a French court in divorce proceedings whereby one of the parties to the proceedings is awarded a monthly maintenance allowance and, on the other hand, to an interim compensation payment, payable monthly, awarded to one of the parties by a French divorce judgment pursuant to Article 270 *et seq.* of the French Civil Code.

On those grounds, the court (Third Chamber), in answer to the questions submitted to it by the Bundesgerichtshof by order of 27 June 1979 received at the Court on 30 July 1979, hereby rules:

> **The Convention of 27 September 1968 on Jurisdiction and the Enforcement of Judgments in Civil and Commercial Matters (English version, Official Journal 1978 L 304, p. 36) is applicable, on the one hand, to the enforcement of an interlocutory order made by a French court in divorce proceedings whereby one of the parties to the proceedings is awarded a monthly maintenance allowance and, on the other hand, to an interim compensation payment, payable monthly, awarded to one of the parties by a French divorce judgment pursuant to Article 270 *et seq.* of the French Civil Code.**

OPINION OF MR ADVOCATE GENERAL WARNER

I hope that I shall not be thought lacking in regard for the arguments of Counsel if I say that I do not in this case need time to consider my opinion. There cannot be the slightest doubt that the Convention of 1968 applies to maintenance orders. That is plain from Article 5(2) of the Convention itself. Counsel for Monsieur *de Cavel* sought to escape from that conclusion by invoking the judgment of the Court in Case 143/78, the first de Cavel case. But that case was not about a maintenance order. It was about an order affecting property of the spouses. As I ventured to point out in my opinion in that case a maintenance order and an order relating to property are different things. The relevant passage was read to us by Counsel for Madame de Cavel this afternoon. (The reference to it is [1979] ECR at p. 1075). The Court could not and did not hold in Case 143/78 that maintenance orders were outside the scope of the Convention.

That being so, the only substantial question is whether the Convention can apply to an ancillary order made in proceedings in which the main claim is outside the scope of the Convention; more particularly it is whether the Convention can apply to a maintenance order made in divorce proceedings? I considered that question very fully in my opinion in Case 143/78 and came to the conclusion that the answer was 'Yes' (see [1979] ECR at pp. 1070-1073). I need not, I think, repeat what I there said, nor has anything put forward in argument in the present case persuaded me that it was wrong.

In the result I am of the opinion that Your Lordships should, in answer to the Bundesgerichtshof, rule that the Convention applies as regards the enforcement in one Contracting State of a maintenance order, whether interlocutory or otherwise, made by a court of another Contracting State, even though that order was made in divorce proceedings. If Your Lordships adopt that formula, the problem of the admissibility of the Bundesgerichtshof's second question will disappear. That problem exists because the proceedings at present pending before the Bundesgerichtshof are only about the enforcement in Germany of the order for maintenance pending suit made by the Tribunal de Grande Instance of Paris in Madame de Cavel's favour on 18 May 1977. Those proceedings are not concerned with the order for interim periodical payments incorporated by the Tribunal in its decree of divorce dated 27 June 1978. One can understand, of course that the Bundesgerichtshof should wish, in an endeavour to save time and costs, to have the Court's ruling in relation to that order too, in anticipation of the question of its enforceability coming up for decision. Nonetheless, for the reasons that I gave recently in my opinion in Case 104/79 *Foglia* v *Novello*, I do not think that, strictly speaking, the Court has jurisdiction to answer the question.

Nor does it appear to me from the order for reference that the Court is thereby invited to define the concept of 'maintenance' for the purposes of the Convention. Much less is it for this Court to rule on the effect or on the validity of any judgment of the Tribunal de Grande Instance of Paris.

Case 814/79 - 16 December 1980

Netherlands State
v
Reinhold Rüffer

Article 1 - Ambit - Civil and commercial matters - Concept - Independent interpretation - Criteria - Ambit of the Convention - Determination - Factors to be taken into consideration - Civil and commercial matters - Actions brought by a public authority against a private person on the basis of its public authority powers - Recovery of the costs of removing a wreck - Exclusion - Claim for redress before civil courts - Not available.

Summary

1. The concept 'civil and commercial matters' used in Article 1 of the Convention must be regarded as an independent concept which must be construed with reference, first, to the objectives and scheme of the Convention and, secondly, to the general principles which stem from the corpus of the national legal systems.

2. As the Convention must be applied in such a way as to ensure, as far as possible, that the rights and obligations which derive from it for the Contracting States and the persons to whom it applies are equal and uniform it must be interpreted solely in the light of the division of jurisdiction between the various types of courts existing in certain States; its ambit must therefore be essentially determined by reason of the legal relationships existing between the parties to the action or of the subject matter of the action.

3. The concept of 'civil and commercial matters' within the meaning of the first paragraph Article 1 of the Convention does not include actions brought by the agent responsible for administering public waterways

against the person having liability in law in order to recover the costs incurred in the removal of a wreck carried out by or at the instigation of the administering agent in the exercise of its public authority. The fact that the agent responsible for administering public waterways is seeking to recover those costs by means of a claim for redress before the civil courts and not by administrative process cannot be sufficient to bring the matter in dispute within the ambit of the Convention.

JUDGMENT OF THE COURT

Mertens de Wilmars, President, Pescatore and Koopmans, Presidents of Chambers, Lord Mackenzie Stuart, O'Keeffe, Bosco and Touffait, Judges

1. By judgment of 14 December 1979 which was received at the Court on 17 December 1979 the Hoge Raad [Supreme Court] applied to the Court in proceedings based on Article 1 of the Protocol on the interpretation by the Court of Justice of the Convention of 27 September 1968 on Jurisdiction and the Enforcement of Judgments in Civil and Commercial Matters.

2. That application was ordered in the course of a dispute concerning a claim for redress brought by the Netherlands State against a waterman, the owner of a German river motor vessel, the *Otrate* which on 26 October 1971 collided with the Dutch motor vessel *Vechtborg* in the Bight of Watum and as a result of that collision sank on the spot.

3. The Bight of Watum is a public waterway in the mouth of the Ems located in an area over which both the Kingdom of the Netherlands and the Federal Republic of Germany claim sovereign rights. Co-operation in that waterway between the two bordering States is governed by the Ems-Dollard Treaty of 8 April 1960 Article 19(1) (a) of that Treaty provides that the Kingdom of the Netherlands shall be responsible, in the Bight of Watum and other places for river-police functions which, under Article 20(2) (d), include 'removal of wrecks'. Article 21 of the same Treaty stipulates further that 'in carrying out river-police functions, each Contracting Party Commission shall be notified'.

4. In accordance with that Treaty and on the basis of the provisions of the Netherlands Law on Wrecks of 19 June 1934 (hereinafter referred to as the 'Wrakkenwet') the Kingdom of the Netherlands had the wreck of the German boat which had sunk in the Bight of Watum removed by a Netherlands firm. The remains of the boat recovered in that way together

with its cargo were sold pursuant to Article 6 of the 'Wrakkenwet' by public auction in order that the Netherlands State might recover the costs involved in the removal of the wreck. After the proceeds of that sale were deducted from those costs a debit balance remained which the Netherlands State sought to recover from the waterman and owner of the boat in question by the claim for redress referred to above.

5. The District Court of the Hague before which the matter was brought at first instance declared that it had no jurisdiction to entertain the application. Its ground was the finding that owing to the German flag of the boat which sunk the place where the harmful event occurred, namely the wreck of the *Otrate*, must be regarded as the Federal Republic of Germany in this case so that jurisdiction to entertain the application lay with German courts by virtue of Article 5(3) of the Brussels Convention of 27 September 1968 on Jurisdiction and the Enforcement of Judgments in Civil and Commercial Matters (hereinafter referred to as 'the Brussels Convention'). The decision by that court was upheld by the Gerechtshof [Regional Court of Appeal] of The Hague and the Netherlands State appealed in cassation to the Hoge Raad of the Netherlands. Before ruling on the substance of the matter that court decided to submit several questions to the Court of Justice on the interpretation of the Brussels Convention.

The first question

6. In its first question the Hoge Raad asks the Court to state first of all whether the concept 'civil and commercial matters' in Article 1 of the Convention must be construed as including a claim for redress such as that brought in the instant case by the Netherlands State.

7. It is apparent from the case-law of the Court (judgment of 14 October 1976 in Case 29/76 LTU [1976] ECR 1541; judgment of 14 July 1977 in Cases 9 and 10/77 *Bavaria-Germanair* [1977] ECR 1517; judgment of 22 February 1979 in Case 133/78 *Gourdain* [1978] ECR 733) that the concept 'civil and commercial matters' used in Article 1 of the Brussels Convention must be regarded as an independent concept which must be construed with reference first to the objectives and scheme of the Convention and secondly to the general principles which stem from the corpus of the national legal systems.

8. In the light of those considerations the Court has specifically held in that same case-law that whilst certain judgments given in an action

between a public authority and a person governed by private law may come within the area of application of the Convention that is not the case if the public authority is acting in the exercise of its public authority powers.

9. Such a case is an action for the recovery of the costs involved in the removal of a wreck in a public waterway, administered by the State responsible in performance of an international obligation and on the basis of provisions of national law which, in the administration of that waterway, confer on it the status of public authority in regard to private persons.

10. It is common ground that in this case the Netherlands State had the wreck of the Otrate removed in performance of an obligation which was assumed under Article 19(1) (a) and 20(2) (d) of the Ems-Dollard Treaty within the framework of the river-police functions conferred on it in that waterway by the said Treaty and that consequently it acted in this case as the body invested with public authority.

11. The granting of such status to the agent responsible for policing public waterways, for the purpose of removing wrecks located in those waterways, is, furthermore, in keeping with the general principles which stem from the corpus of the national legal systems of the Member States whose provisions on the administration of public waterways precisely show that the agent administering those waterways does so, when removing wrecks, in the exercise of public authority.

12. In view of those factors the action brought by the Netherlands State before the national court must be regarded as being outside the ambit of the Brussels Convention, as defined by the concept of 'civil and commercial matters' within the meaning of the first paragraph of Article 1 of that Convention, since it is established that the Netherlands State acted in the instant case in the exercise of public authority.

13. The fact that in this case the action pending before the national court does not concern the actual removal of the wreck but the costs involved in that removal and that the Netherlands State is seeking to recover those costs by means of a claim for redress and not by administrative process as provided for by the national law of other Member States cannot be sufficient to bring the matter in dispute within the ambit of the Brussels Convention.

14. As the Court has stated in the authorities cited above the Brussels Convention must be applied in such a way as to ensure, as far as possible, that the rights and obligations which derive from it for the Contracting States and the persons to whom it applies are equal and uniform. By that same case-law such a requirement rules out the possibility of the Convention's being interpreted solely in the light of the division of jurisdiction between the various types of courts existing in certain States: on the contrary it implies that the area of application of the Convention is essentially determined either by reason of the legal relationships between the parties to the action or of the subject-matter of the action.

15. The fact that in recovering those costs the administering agent acts pursuant to a debt which arises from an act of public authority is sufficient for its action, whatever the nature of the proceedings afforded by national law for that purpose, to be treated as being outside the ambit of the Brussels Convention.

16. For those reasons the answer to the first question must be that the concept of 'civil and commercial matters' within the meaning of the first paragraph of Article 1 of the Convention of 27 September 1968 on Jurisdiction and the Enforcement of Judgments in Civil and Commercial Matters does not include actions such as that referred to by the national court brought by the agent responsible for administering public waterways against a person having liability in law in order to recover the costs incurred in the removal of a wreck carried out by or at the instigation of the administering agent in the exercise of its public authority.

The other questions

17. The other questions were submitted by the national court in case the answer to the first question were in the affirmative. As the answer to that question is in the negative there is no further point in considering them.

On those grounds, the court, in answer to the questions referred to it by the Hoge Raad by judgment of 14 December 1979, hereby rules:

> **The concept of 'civil and commercial matters' within the meaning of the first paragraph of Article 1 of the Convention of 27 September 1968 on Jurisdiction and the Enforcement of Judgments in Civil and Commercial Matters does not include actions such as that referred to by the national court brought**

by the agent responsible for administering public waterways against the person having liability in law in order to recover the costs incurred in the removal of a wreck carried out by or at the instigation of the administering agent in the exercise of its public authority.

OPINION OF MR ADVOCATE GENERAL WARNER

Introductory

This case comes to the Court by way of a reference for a preliminary ruling ordered by the Hoge Raad of the Netherlands under the Protocol of 3 June 1971 on the interpretation by the Court of the Convention of 27 September 1968 on Jurisdiction and the Enforcement of Judgments in Civil and Commercial Matters. As Your Lordships know, that Convention is at present in force only as between the original Member States, and the only authentic texts of it are the German, French, Italian and Dutch texts. Your Lordships also know, however, that a Convention on the Accession of the new Member States to the 1968 Convention and to the 1971 Protocol was signed on 9 October 1978 and is at present in the process of being ratified. I shall call this 'the Accession Convention'. Annexed to it are versions of the 1968 Convention and 1971 Protocol in Danish, English and Irish, and it provides (by Article 37) that those versions are to be authentic under the same conditions as the original texts of the 1968 Convention and 1971 Protocol. That being so, I propose to cite, as and where appropriate, from what are to become, when the process of ratification has been completed, the authentic Danish, English and Irish texts.

The appellant in the proceedings before the Hoge Raad is the State of the Netherlands, which I shall call for short 'the State'. The respondent is described in the order for reference as 'Reinhold Rüffer', but it has been indicated to us on his behalf that his surname is actually 'Rüffer'. He is a German citizen, 'domiciled' (within the meaning of that term in the 1968 Convention) in the Federal Republic of Germany. He was the owner and skipper of a German barge, the *Otrate*, which, on the night of 26 October 1971, as the result of a collision with a Dutch ship called the *Vechtbor* sank in the Bight of Watum in the Ems Estuary, and became a wreck. The State alleges that the collision was due, wholly or in part, to the negligent navigation of the *Otrate*, albeit that the person at her helm at the time was a local pilot.

The root of the problems to which the case gives rise lies in the surprising fact that the frontier between the Netherlands and the Federal Republic of Germany in the Ems Estuary is disputed. The Bight of Watum is within an area over which both States claim sovereignty. Since this Court is not called upon to resolve that dispute, I need not trouble Your Lordships with the origins and details of it, interesting though they be.

By a treaty between the Netherlands and the Federal Republic signed at the Hague on 8 April 1960 (the 'Ems-Dollard Treaty'), which was supplemented by later instruments the provisions of which are not material for present purposes, arrangements were made between the two States for co-operation in the Ems Estuary without prejudice to their respective territorial claims. The relevant provisions of the Ems-Dollard Treaty may be summarised as follows: Article 16 provides that 'each Contracting Party shall bear the costs of those works and measures which it is entitled or required to carry out or to take under the terms of this Treaty'. Article 19 defines the areas in which each Contracting Party is to be responsible for what the Treaty calls 'river-police functions'. The Netherlands are to be responsible for them in the Bight of Watum. Article 20 defines 'river-police functions' as including among other things 'measures for the location, marking and removal of wrecks'. Article 21 provides that 'in carrying out river-police functions, each Contracting Party shall apply its own laws and regulations'.

Article 32 prescribes rules to be applied 'where the applicability of any legal provision depends upon the question within which territory a vessel is situated or through which territory its course lies'. In such a case, 'save as otherwise provided in ... international treaties to which both Contracting Parties are parties ... German vessels shall be deemed to be within the territory of the Federal Republic, and Netherlands vessels shall be deemed to be within the territory of the Kingdom of the Netherlands'. The situation of a vessel of a third country is to be ascertained by reference to the situation of its port of destination or of departure within the Estuary. Article 33 provides that 'Article 32 shall apply *mutatis mutandis* with respect to the jurisdiction of the police authorities, the, prosecuting authorities and the courts'.

Article 46(1) states: 'The provisions of this Treaty shall not affect the question of the course of the international frontier in the Ems Estuary. Each Contracting Party reserves its legal position in this respect'. Article 46(2) enables either Contracting Party to refer that question to the International Court of Justice or to arbitration, but it does not appear that either of them has done so.

Thus, under Articles 19 to 21 of the Treaty, it fell to the competent Dutch authority, i.e. the State in the shape of the 'Ministerie Van Verkeer en Waterstaat' (Ministry of Transport and Water Management), to deal with the wreck of the *Otrate* in accordance with the relevant Dutch legislation, which was the 'Wrakkenwet' (Statute on Wrecks) of 19 June 1934. Under powers conferred by that Statute, in particular Article 6, the Ministry caused the remains of the vessel and its cargo to be raised and taken to the Port of Delfzijl, where they were sold by the Burgemeester. The cost of their removal amounted to 113994.55 guilders and the net proceeds of their sale to 6 530.37 guilders. The balance of 107 564.18 guilders was claimed by the State from Mr Rüffer under Article 10 of the 'Wrakkenwet', which provides: 'Costs incurred pursuant to this statute shall, insofar as they have not been repaid by the persons concerned, or cannot be covered by the proceeds of the articles sold pursuant to Article 6, be borne by the authority, subject always to its power, pursuant to this article, to recover costs incurred by it from persons who, pursuant to the law, are liable therefore'.

From what is stated by the Hoge Raad in the order for reference and further explained by the State in its observations to this Court, it appears that the liability referred to in the last part of Article 10 is liability under the general law, in this instance, according to the State's claim, liability under the combined effect of Article 780 of the 'Wetboek van Koophandel' (the Dutch Commercial Code), which imposes on the owner of a ship vicarious liability for damage caused by the wrongful acts of those employed on the ship, whether permanently or temporarily, in the course of their employment, and Articles 1401 and 1403 of the 'Burgerlijk Wetboek' (the Dutch Civil Code) which relate to torts. At all events the Hoge Raad expressly states that the State's claim against Mr Rüffer is to be classified in Dutch law as a claim in tort ('als verbintenis uit onrechtmatige daad').

Mr Rüffer having denied liability, the State brought an action against him the Arrondissementsrechtbank of The Hague to enforce its claim. By interlocutory application, objection was taken on behalf of Mr Rüffer to the jurisdiction of that Court. By a judgment dated 20 February 1976 the Arrondissementsrechtsbank declared that it had no jurisdiction to hear the action. The State appealed to the Gerechtshof of The Hague, which by judgment of the Arron-dissementsrechtbank. I need not, I think, trouble Your Lordships with the details of the contentions put forward on behalf of the parties before those courts or with the reasons given by the latter for deciding as they did.

The State now appeals to the Hoge Raad. Before that Court it rests its case entirely on Article 5(3) of the 1968 Convention. That provision is as follows: 'A person domiciled in a Contracting State may, in another Contracting State, be sued: ... (3) in matters relating to tort, delict or quasi-delict, in the courts for the place where the harmful event occurred.

Before the Hoge Raad the State put its case in four ways. First it contended that, since in the view of the Dutch Government the Bight of Watum forms part of Dutch territory, a Dutch court ought to hold that the place where the *Otrate* sank and from which its wreck was removed, if that was to be regarded as 'the place where the harmful event occurred' within the meaning of Article 5(3), was a place within Dutch territory. Alternatively it contended that, in a case such as this where the State of the Netherlands, pursuant to Articles 19 to 21 of the Ems-Dollard Treaty and to the Dutch Wrakkenwet, has removed a wreck from a part of the Ems Estuary in respect of which the Netherlands are, under the Ems-Dollard Treaty, responsible for river-police functions, a reasonable and proper ('redelijke en doelmatige') interpretation of Article 5(3) requires that, for the purposes of that provision, the place from which the wreck was removed should be regarded as being within Dutch territory. In the further alternative the State contended that the collision between the *Otrate* and the *Vechtborg* was part of the 'harmful event' within the meaning of Article 5(3) and that, whilst the *Otrate*, being a German vessel, might be deemed by virtue of Article 32 of the Ems-Dollard Treaty to be within German territory, the Vechtborg a Dutch vessel, was by the same token deemed to be within Dutch territory, so that the 'harmful event' occurred also in Dutch territory. Lastly the State contended that 'the place where the harmful event occurred' within the meaning of Article 5(3) was not the place where the *Otrate* sank, but the place where the State suffered damage, consisting in the cost of removing the wreck insofar as that could not be recovered from the proceeds of sale of the wreck and of its cargo; and that that place was either The Hague, where the State had its seat government, or Delfzijl, where it transpired that the proceeds of the sale would be insufficient to cover the cost of removing the wreck.

The essence of Mr Rüffer's case is that Article 5(3) does not apply and that he can be sued only before a German court. He relies primarily (so far as relevant for present purposes) on Articles 32 and 33 of the Ems-Dollard Treaty and on Article 57 of the 1968 Convention, which provides: 'This Convention shall not affect any conventions to which the Contracting States are or will be parties and which, in relation to particular matters, govern jurisdiction and the recognition and enforcement of judgments'.

Mr Rüffer contends that the EmsDollard Treaty, and in particular Articles 33 and 22 thereof, is a convention which governs jurisdiction 'in relation to particular matters', so that, by virtue of Article 57, the application of the 1968 Convention is excluded. He contends, as I understand it, in the alternative, that, by virtue of Article 32, the 'harmful event', the sinking of the *Otrate*, is deemed to have occurred in Germany, so that Article 5(3) cannot confer jurisdiction on the Dutch courts.

Such are the circumstances in which the Hoge Raad has referred to this Court five questions, which are lettered (a) to (e).

Question (a)

Question (a) is:

'Does the concept 'civil and commercial matters' referred to in Article 1 of the Convention include a claim such as that brought by the State against Rüffer?'

All those on whose behalf observations were submitted to the Court (namely, the State, Mr Rüffer, the United Kingdom government, and the Commission) agreed that that question should be answered in the affirmative. In the written observations lodged on behalf of Mr Rüffer it was said that, in the circumstances, this Court need not answer the question, but at the hearing Counsel for Mr Rüffer, whilst maintaining that it was irrelevant because of Article 57, expressed his agreement with the view that the matter was a 'civil' one. The United Kingdom government, whilst concurring in that view, said that it wished to submit observations only on question (b); it did not develop any argument on question (a). Thus only the State and the Commission put forward arguments on question (a).

The argument of the State was, in a nutshell, that the administration of a waterway need not be vested in a public authority. There were formerly in the Netherlands canals that were owned and managed by private companies. Moreover, the claim in question was a claim in tort, typically a 'civil' matter. In putting it forward the State was not therefore acting as a public authority exercising its powers as such, so as to bring the case within the principle laid down by this Court in Case 28/76 *LTU* v *Eurocontrol* [1976] 2 ECR 1541.

The argument of the Commission was slightly different in that the Commission accepted that, in removing a wreck from a public waterway, a public authority was exercising public powers in the sense meant by the Court in *LTU* v *Eurocontrol*. It did not, however, follow, the Commission submitted, that an action based on Article 10 of the 'Wrakkenwet' was an action brought in the exercise of public powers. It was an action in tort, brought to recover from those responsible for the wreck being there the amount of a financial loss occasioned by their wrongdoing. It was analogous to any action brought by the victim of a collision at sea against the person responsible for that collision.

I do not think, for my part, that the answer is as simple as that. One must, in my opinion, bear in mind that the expressions used in Article 1, which defines the scope of the Convention, connote concepts that are 'independent' of the law of any particular Member State and which 'must be interpreted by reference, first, to the objectives and scheme of the Convention and, secondly, to the general principles which stem from the corpus of the national legal systems' - see *LTU* v *Eurocontrol* Cases 9 and 10/77 *Bavaria Fluggesellschaft and Germanair* v *Eurocontrol* [1977] 2 ECR 1517 and Case 133/78 Gourdain v Nadler [1979] ECR 733. As the Court explained in each of those cases that approach 'is necessary in order to ensure, as far as possible, that the rights and obligations which derive from [the Convention] for the Contracting States and the persons to whom it applies are equal and uniform'. In *LTU* v *Eurocontrol* the Court went on to say that 'if the interpretation of the concept ['civil and commercial matters'] is approached in this way ... certain types of judicial decision must be regarded as excluded from the area of application of the Convention, either by reason of the legal relationships between the parties to the action or of the subject-matter of the action'. It was on that footing that the Court there held that 'although certain judgments given in actions between a public authority and a person governed by private law may fall within the area of application of the Convention, this is not so where the public authority acts in the exercise of its powers as such'. (The English translation of the judgment in the ECR does not have the words 'as such', but I think they must be added to render the full meaning of the original, which has 'hoheitliche Befugnisse').

Thus, in order to decide whether an action of the kind brought by the State against Mr Rüffer is within the scope of the Convention, it is not enough to look at its classification in Dutch law. It is necessary to consider the legal systems of all the Member States to see whether there can be regarded as stemming from them a general principle according to which such an action is to be regarded as a 'civil' or 'commercial' matter.

An examination of the laws of the original Member States evinces that, among them, Dutch law is unique in affording to a harbour or waterway authority an action of that kind in tort. In Belgium the matter is governed by Articles 49, 102 and 109(4) of an 'Arrêté Royal' dated 15 October 1935 laying down a 'Règlement général des voies navigables di Royaume', read with Articles 220, 221 and 224 of the 'Code des droits d'enregistrement, d'hypothèque et de greffe'. Shortly stated the effect of those provisions is to empower the 'Office de la Navigation', where a wreck has not been removed by its owner, to remove it and to claim the cost of doing so from the owner. If he fails to pay, the amount is recovered from him by the 'Administration de l'Enregistrement et des Domaines' through the issue of a 'contrainte' the execution of which the owner can only stop by himself taking proceedings before the appropriate court. The procedure is thus typically administrative. There is, it appears, no right for any public authority, if the use of that procedure fails to produce full reimbursement, to sue the owner or anyone else in tort.

In Germany there are two relevant instruments, one of 18 May 1874, the 'Strandungsordnung' (Wrecks Order) and one of 2 April 1968, the 'Bundeswasserstrassengesetz' (Statute on Federal Waterways). Particularly in point are paragraphs 25 *et seq.* of the former (as amended) and paragraphs 24(1), 25, 28 and 30 of the latter. Between them they envisage two possibilities:

(i) The competent authority may, by an administrative act, which is susceptible of challenge in the administrative courts ('Verwaltungsgerichte'), enjoin upon the owner of the wreck, or upon any other person whom it considers responsible for its presence, to remove it at his own expense. If he fails to do so within the time prescribed, the authority may itself remove the wreck and charge him with the cost of doing so, again by an administrative act susceptible of challenge in the administrative courts.

(ii) In a case of urgency, the authority may itself remove the wreck without notice to the owner or to anyone else. It then acquires a charge over the wreck for the cost of removal. That charge is enforceable by an administrative process for the recovery of debt known as 'Verwaltungszwangsverfahren'. If the cost exceeds the value of the wreck, the excess is irrecoverable (see the Judgment of the Bundesverwaltungsgericht dated 22 August 1975 cited in 'Die öffentliche Verwaltung', 1976, p. 100).

There again, therefore, the whole matter is administrative, though it was not always so. Until the enactment of the Statute of 1968, there were circumstances in which an action similar to that in question here could be brought under the provisions of the 'Burgeliches Gesetzbuch' (the German Civil Code) relating to 'Geschäftsführung ohne Auftrag' (*negotiorum gestio*), not tort.

In France the law as respects maritime wrecks is to be found in a Statute of 24 November 1961 relating to 'la police des épaves maritimes' and in two instruments implementing it, a 'Décret' of 26 December 1961 and an 'Arrêté' of 4 February 1965. As respects wrecks in inland waterways it is to be found in the 'Règlement général de police de la navigation intérieure', promulgated by a 'Décret' of 21 September 1973. The gist of it is that, failing removal of a wreck by the owner, the competent authority may itself cause it to be removed and issue a 'titre exécutoire' entitling the authority to recover from the owner any excess of the cost over the proceeds of the wreck. It is up to the owner to challenge that 'titre exécutoire', if he wishes to, in the administrative courts. There is, it appears, no possibility for the competent authority to sue the owner or anyone else in the ordinary courts.

In Italy the 'Codice della Navigazione' (Maritime Code) enacted by a 'Decreto Reale' (Royal Decree) No 327 of 30 March 1942 empowers a competent authority, failing removal of a wreck by its owner or in a case of urgency, to remove the wreck. In such a case the property in the wreck passes to the authority. If the cost of removal exceeds the proceeds of sale of the wreck and the wrecked vessel was of more than 300 tonnes, the authority is entitled, under Articles 73 and 84 of the Codice, to issue an 'ingiunzione' (an order) requiring the owner (but no-one else) to pay the difference. That 'ingiunzione' becomes executory upon receiving by 'decreto' the fiat of the Pretore. There appears to have been some controversy among Italian lawyers as to whether the need for the Pretore's fiat converts what starts as an administrative act into a judicial one, but the better view appears to be that it does not, in particular because once the 'ingiunzione' has become executory, it is left to the owner to challenge it, if he thinks fit, before the appropriate court, which need not be the Pretore's. There is no possibility, it appears, for the competent authority to take ordinary civil proceedings against anyone, in tort or otherwise, even where the vessel was of less than 300 tonnes or where the owner has insufficient means to pay for the cost of its removal.

In Luxembourg the problem can arise only, of course, as regards the Moselle. The only legislation about it is the 'Règlement de police pour a navigation de la Moselle' promulgated by an 'Arrêté Grand-Ducal' of 18 June 1971. That imposes on the skipper of a wrecked vessel the obligation to remove the wreck, but empowers the competent authority to remove it where its removal is urgent. The cost to the authority of so doing is recoverable from the owner of the wreck or, where the wreck is the result of a collision, from the owner of the vessel considered by the authority to have been responsible for the collision. The authority has, however, no power to sell the wreck or to issue a 'titre exécutoire'. Should it need to enforce its rights it must take proceedings in the appropriate court. It seems that in practice that need does not arise because all vessels navigating the Moselle are insured. So the law is little developed.

The question is whether, if that be a correct summary of the laws of the original Member States, there can be attributed to the authors of the 1968 Convention an intention that the phrase 'civil and commercial matters' in Article 1 of that Convention should comprise an action of the present kind. I find it impossible to answer that question in the affirmative. This is an action by a public authority against a private person arising out of what is considered, in the laws of all the original Member States except possibly the Netherlands, to have been an exercise by that authority of its powers as such. It is, moreover, an action of a kind virtually unknown in the laws of any of the original Member States other than the Netherlands. That being so, the only real ground on which one could hold it to be a 'civil' or 'commercial' matter would be that it was considered to be such in Dutch law. But that would be incompatible, so it seems to me, with the principles laid down by the Court in *LTU* v *Eurocontrol* and incompatible also with the concept of reciprocity which is enshrined in the preamble to the Convention.

I doubt if, on such a question, the laws of the new Member States or the provisions of the Accession Convention can be relevant, but I will, for the sake of completeness, advert to them briefly. Danish law appears to be in line with the laws of the majority of the original Member States. The laws of Ireland and of the United Kingdom, on the other hand are broadly in line with Dutch law; they enable a harbour or waterway authority, independently of statutory powers, to sue in tort, for the cost of removing a wreck, a person whose negligent navigation - or the negligent navigation of anyone for whose acts he is vicariously liable - is responsible for the wreck having got there (see as regards Irish law *The Edith* (1883) 11 L.R.Ir. 270, as regards English law *The Ella* [1915] p. 111 and *Dee Conservancy Board* v *McConnell* [1928] 2 K.B. 159 and as regards Scots law per Lord Murray in *Clyde Navigation Trustees* v *Kelvin Shipping Co* [1927] S.C. at p. 626).

The Accession Convention 'adjusts' Article 1 of the 1968 Convention by adding to the first paragraph a sentence providing that the Convention 'shall not extend, in particular, to revenue, customs or administrative matters'. In his report on the draft of that Convention, Professor Dr Peter Schlosser, the rapporteur of the working party responsible for preparing the draft, has this to say about the actual background against which that adjustment was proposed (Official Journal C 59 of 5 March 1979 at p.82): 'The distinction between civil and commercial matters on the one hand and matters of public law on the other is well recognised in the legal systems of the original Member States and is, in spite of some important differences, on the whole arrived at on the basis of similar criteria. Thus the term 'civil law' also includes certain important special subjects which are not public law, especially, for example, parts of labour law. For this reason the draughtsmen of the original text of the 1968 Convention, and the Jenard Report, did not include a definition of civil and commercial matters and merely stated that the 1968 Convention also applies to decisions of criminal and administrative courts, provided they are given in a civil or commercial matter, which occasionally happens. In this last respect, the accession of the three new Member States presents no additional problems. But as regards the main distinction referred to earlier considerable difficulties arise. In the United Kingdom and Ireland the distinction commonly made in the original EEC States between private law and public law is hardly known. This meant that the problems of adjustment could not be solved simply by a reference to these classifications. In view of the Judgment of the Court of Justice of the European Communities of 14 October 1976 [i.e. the judgment in *LTU* v *Eurocontrol*], which was delivered during the final stages of the discussions and which decided in favour of an interpretation which made no reference to the 'applicable' national law, the Working Party restricted itself to declaring, in Article 1, paragraph 1, that revenue, customs or administrative matters are not civil or commercial matters within the meaning of the Convention'.

I see nothing in all that to disturb the conclusion that I reached from a consideration of the 'unadjusted' terms of the 1968 Convention and of the laws of the original Member States.

In the result I would, in answer to Question (a), say that a claim of the kind referred to in that question is not within the concept of 'civil and commercial matters' referred to in Article 1 of the 1968 Convention.

If that is right the Hoge Raad's subsequent questions do not call for any answer. Lest, however, Your Lordships should differ from me on Question (a), I must deal with them.

Question (b)

Question (b), which the Hoge Raad asks only in case Question (a) should be answered in the affirmative, is whether a claim of the present kind is within the concept of 'matters relating to tort, delict or quasi-delict' referred to in Article 5(3) of the Convention.

The arguments of the State and of Mr Rüffer on that question were scant. The State confined itself to saying, if I understood it rightly, that the answer must be in the affirmative because it was so in Dutch law. On Mr Rüffer's behalf it was submitted, first, that the question was irrelevant because the *Otrate* had in fact complied with the relevant rules of navigation so that he was not liable for any tort, secondly that the question was irrelevant because of Article 57 and of the provisions of the Ems-Dollard Treaty, but thirdly that, if and insofar as the question was relevant, the answer to it must clearly be that the claim was in tort.

The United Kingdom government, founding on the judgment of the Court in Case 12/76 *Tessili* v *Dunlop* [1976] 2 ECR 1473, submitted that one must first consider whether the phrase 'matters relating to tort, delict or quasi-delict' in Article 5(3) should (in the words of paragraph 10 of that judgment) be interpreted as having its 'own independent meaning and as being thus common to all the Member States or as referring to substantive rules of the law applicable in each case under the rules of conflict of laws of the court before which the matter is first brought'; and the United Kingdom government submitted that the latter was the correct interpretation. Indeed, in flat contradiction of what the Court said in Case 33/78 *Somafer* v *Saar-Ferngas* [1978] ECR 2183 (paragraphs 5 to 8 of the judgment), the United Kingdom government went so far as to submit that 'such a determination in accordance with the *lex fori* should be adopted for the interpretation of all the special jurisdictions set out in Article 5 of the Convention unless there are special reasons to the contrary'.

I need not, I think, take up Your Lordships' time rehearsing the detailed arguments put forward by the United Kingdom in support of its submission. Your Lordships have read them and they were summarised in the Report for the Hearing. In my opinion some of them are weighty, others less so. For instance, the fact that, unless in interpreting concepts that are found in the Convention a national court applies its own law, inconsistencies will result between the meaning attributed to a term in the Convention and in national law seems to me far less important a consideration than the need, stressed by the Court in the cases that I cited earlier, to ensure as far as possible that the rights and obligations that derive from the Convention for the Member States and the persons to whom it applies are equal and uniform. The authors of the Convention clearly accepted that terms used in it might have there a connotation different from their connotation in national law. For example the English text of the Convention uses the word 'domiciled' in a sense manifestly different from its sense in the law of Ireland or of the United Kingdom.

In my opinion, however, there are two clear reasons why the submission of the United Kingdom government should be rejected.

The first is that it is inconsistent with the principles on which this Court has decided cases since *Tessili* v *Dunlop*. It is true that, in *Tessili* v *Dunlop*, which was the first case on the Convention ever to be decided by the Court, the Court held that 'the place of performance of the obligation in question' in Article 5(1) of the Convention was to be ascertained by reference to the law governing that obligation according to the rules of conflict of laws of the court before which the matter was brought. It did so because 'having regard to the differences obtaining between national laws of contract and to the absence, at this stage of legal development, of any unification in the substantive law applicable, it does not appear possible to give any more substantial guide to the interpretation of that phrase' (paragraph 14 of the judgment). The Court added that that was 'all the more true since the determination of the place of performance of obligations depends on the contractual context to which these obligations belong'. The decision in *Tessili* v *Dunlop* stands, however, alone and is probably to be explained on the ground of the peculiar complexities that exist in the field of contract. In every subsequent case where the question has arisen whether an expression used in the Convention had an 'independent' meaning or was to be interpreted as a reference to national concepts, the Court has either proceeded on the tacit assumption that the former view was correct - as in Case 14/76 *De Bloos* v *Bouyer* [1976] 2 ECR 1497 and Case 21/76 *Bier* v *Mines de Potasse d'Alsace*, ibid. p. 1735, in each of which, however, the question was discussed by the Advocate General - or has expressly decided in favour of that view - as in *LTU* v *Eurocontrol* (already cited), Case 43/77 *Industrial Diamond Supplies* v *Riva* [1977] 2 ECR 2175, Case 140/77 Bertrand v Ott [1978] ECR 1431, *Somafer* v *Saar-Ferngas* (already cited) and *Gourdain* v *Nadler* (already cited). In the later cases the Court has stressed that the dominant consideration is the need for the equal and uniform application of the Convention in all the Member States and also, in relation to Article 5, the need to avoid a proliferation of special jurisdictions which would defeat one of the main purposes of the Convention. In some of the cases (*Industrial Diamond Supplies* v *Riva and Bertrand* v *Ott*) divergencies between national legal concepts have been given as a reason for holding that a term in the Convention must be given an independent meaning. I conclude that such a term is to be interpreted as a reference to national concepts only where to give it an independent meaning is for some reason impossible. Weighty though some of the considerations put forward by the United Kingdom government are, they do not in my opinion go that far.

The second reason why I would reject the United Kingdom government's submission - and this is in my opinion decisive - is that to treat the phrase 'matters relating to tort, delict or quasi- delict' as a reference to national legal concepts would only be possible if the corresponding phrase in the authentic text of the Convention in the official language or languages of each Member State connoted a concept known to the law of that State. In fact that is not so.

The authentic texts in the languages of the original Member States use the following phrases: German: 'wenn eine unerlaubte Handlung oder eine Handlung, die einer unerlaubten Handlung gleichgestellt ist, oder wenn Ansprüche aus einer solchen Handlung den Gegenstand des Verfahrens bilden';

French: 'en matière dèlictuelle ou quasi-dèlictuelle';

Italian: 'in materia di delitti o quasi delitti';

Dutch: 'ten aanzien van verbintenissen it onrechtmatige daad'.

No difficulty arises over the French or the Dutch. 'En matière dèlictuelle ou quasi-dèlictuelle' is an appropriate phrase to connote the concept of French law corresponding to tort, and also, in French, the corresponding concepts of Belgian and Luxembourg law. Similarly 'ten aanzien van verbintenissen uit onrechtmatige daad' is appropriate to connote the corresponding concepts of Dutch law and, in Dutch, of Belgian law. In the German text, however, whilst the phrase 'eine unerlaubte Handlung' connotes the German concept of tort, the circumlocution 'eine Handlung, die einer unerlaubten Handlung gleichgestellt ist' does not, I understand, refer to any concept known to German law. For its part the Italian phrase 'in materia di delitti o quasi-delitti', whilst it is intelligible to an Italian lawyer familiar with Justinian, the Napoleonic Codes and the erstwhile Italian Civil Code, is not appropriate to modern Italian law, in which the term of art is 'fatti illeciti'.

Here again I do not think that the laws of the new Member States are relevant, but I will deal with them briefly for the sake of completeness. In the English text 'tort' is of course appropriate to English law and to Irish law, whilst 'delict or quasi-delict' appears to be appropriate to Scots law. The Irish text has 'in abhair a bhaineann le tort, mighniomh no samhail mhighnimh' which is, I understand, a direct rendering of the English. The last four words, corresponding to 'delict or quasi-delict' do not connote any concept known to Irish law. Lastly the Danish text has 'i sager om erstatning uden for kontrakt', which literally means 'in matters concerning compensation unconnected with contract'. As I understand it that phrase, or phrases like it, are used in Denmark only in certain procedural statutes where they are taken to connote a wide and somewhat undefined range of claims arising otherwise than out of contract.

I am thus of the opinion that it is impossible to interpret the phrase 'tort, delict or quasi-delict' in Article 5(3) as referring to national legal concepts and that it must be taken to have an independent meaning.

The Commission, which also takes that view, attempted a definition of that independent concept. As, however, emerges from Professor André Tunc's Introduction to Volume XI of the *International Encyclopedia of Comparative Law*, the volume on 'Torts', no-one has ever succeeded, even in the context of any national legal system, in formulating an accurate definition of tort that did not beg one or more questions. Like the proverbial elephant, tort is easier to recognise than to define.

I do not think it necessary in this case to attempt a definition of the concept of tort for the purposes of the Convention.

I am content to observe that in the three Member States where the subject-matter of an action of the present kind is not considered to belong exclusively to the sphere of public or administrative law (the Netherlands, Ireland and the United Kingdom) it is considered to belong to the province of tort.

For those reasons I would hold that, if such an action is within the scope of the Convention at all, it is within the scope of Article 5(3).

I turn to the Hoge Raad's Question (c) with which I can deal much more shortly.

Question (c)

That question is: 'What is the effect of Article 5(3) in a situation where the harmful event occurred in territory that is, according to the Ems-Dollard Treaty, regarded by the Kingdom of the Netherlands as belonging to the Netherlands and by the Federal Republic of Germany as belonging to the Federal Republic of Germany? Does Article 5(3) mean that for the Dutch courts that place must be regarded as (also) being situated in the Netherlands? Having regard to the nature of the present claim is it in this respect relevant that the place lies in territory in which, pursuant to the Ems-Dollard Treaty, the Kingdom of the Netherlands is responsible for river-police functions and is therefore obliged to remove a wreck lying in the said territory?'

The question is asked, of course, on the footing that the subject-matter of the present action is within the scope of the Convention and within the scope of Article 5(3). It is prompted by the first two contentions advanced by the State before the Hoge Raad, to which I have referred.

Underlying the question, however, so it seems to me, is the false assumption that, if in a particular case 'the place where the harmful event occurred', within the meaning of Article 5(3), lies in territory over which sovereignty is claimed by two Member States, the issue whether that place should for the purposes of that case be taken to lie in the territory of one or the other of those States can be resolved as a matter of interpretation of Article 5(3). In my opinion the 1968 Convention is in no way concerned with resolving issues of that kind. Its provisions are, as the Commission put it, 'neutral' with regard to them. The Convention is framed on the basis that the situation of a particular place in the territory of this or that Member State has been or will be determined *aliunde*. That in my opinion is all that can be said in answer to Question (c), if as a result of Your Lordships' answers to Questions (a) and (b) an answer to Question (c) is called for at all.

Question (d)

Question (d), which is also put on the footing that Questions (a) and (b) are both to be answered in the affirmative, is as follows: 'Can 'the place where harmful event occurred' be the place where the damage as alleged by the State occurred, namely either The Hague, where the State has its seat of government, or Delfzijl (in the Arrondissement of Groningen) where the goods salvaged from the wreck were sold by the State revealing to what extent the costs incurred by the State in removing the wreck were not covered?'

That question, manifestly, reflects the fourth contention put forward by the State before the Hoge Raad. That contention is in my opinion ill-founded. The State relied in support of it on the decision of the Court in *Bier* v *Mines de Potasse d'Alsace* (already cited). But that authority does not in my opinion justify the contention. It was there held that the expression 'the place where the harmful event occurred' in Article 5(3) was apt to cover both 'the place where the damage occurred' and 'the place of the event giving rise to it'. But the relevant damage in that case was the harm to the plaintiff company's seed beds in the Netherlands caused by the pollution of the Rhine. The place of the event giving rise to it was Alsace, where the defendant discharged saline waste into the Rhine. It was never suggested there, much less held by the Court, that the place where the harmful event occurred could be the place where the plaintiff company had its seat or the place where the amount of the damage to its business was quantified. As was pointed out to us in argument both on behalf of Mr Rüffer and on behalf of the Commission, to hold here that the place where the State has its seat could be regarded as being 'the place where the harmful event occurred' would be tantamount to holding that, under the Convention, a plaintiff in tort had the option of suing in the courts of his own domicile, which would be quite inconsistent with the scheme of Article 2 et seq. of the Convention. As for the suggestion that the 'harmful event' in this case might be regarded as having occurred in Delfzijl, I think it enough to point out that the sale of the wreck by the Burgemeester was not a harmful event but a means of mitigating *pro tanto* the damage that the State had suffered.

I would therefore answer Question (d), if it be relevant, in the negative.

I turn lastly to Question (e).

Question (e)

That is in these terms:

'If the Ems-Dollard Treaty is to be understood as giving the Dutch Courts jurisdiction over a claim such as the present one (which question is not referred to the Court of Justice for a preliminary ruling) does Article 57 of the Brussels Convention leave scope for the application of the opening words and paragraph 3 of Article 5 regarding jurisdiction?'

I confess that I am unsure as to what lies behind that question. I doubt if it can be any contention of Mr Rüffer's, since his case is that the Ems-Dollard Treaty confers jurisdiction on the German courts. Possibly it is the State's third contention, to the effect that the Vechtborg's involvement in the collision meant that, under the Ems-Dollard Treaty, the harmful event must be taken to have occurred in Dutch territory as well as in German territory.

At all events, it was contended on behalf of Mr Rüffer that the Ems-Dollard Treaty was a *lex specialis* governing the respective jurisdictions of the Dutch and German courts in a matter such as this, so that, by virtue of Article 57, any application of the 1968 Convention was precluded. On behalf of the State and of the Commission, on the other hand, it was submitted that that consequence would follow only if the provisions of the Ems-Dollard Treaty as to jurisdiction were intended to be exclusive of the application of any other possible rules on the subject.

I have come to the conclusion that, on that point, the State and the Commission are right. Article 57 forms part of Title VII in the Convention, which is headed 'Relationship to other Conventions'. That title opens with Article 55, which list *nominatim* the conventions concluded between two or more Member States that the 1968 Convention is to 'supersede'. Then follows Article 56, which provides that, nonetheless those conventions are to 'continue to have effect in relation to matters to which this Convention does not apply' and also (putting it briefly) in relation to judgments and instruments dated before the entry into force of the Convention. Then Articles 57 and 58 provide that the Convention 'shall not affect' certain other conventions. (The corresponding terms in the other texts are: German 'läßt...unberührt' in Article 57, 'berührt nicht' in Article 58, French 'ne déroge pas aux' in Article 57, 'ne porte pas préjudice aux' in Article 58, Italian 'non deroga alle' in Article 57, 'non pregiudicano i' in Article 58, Dutch 'laat onverlet' in Article 57, 'maken geen inbreuk' in Article 58. The Danish and Irish texts, like the English, use the same expression in both Articles: 'bererer ikke' and 'Ni dheanfaidh seo difear' respectively.) If a convention relating to 'particular matters', within the meaning of Article 57, such as the Ems-Dollard Treaty, prescribes rules as to jurisdiction that are intended to apply to the exclusion of any other rules, its operation will obviously be affected if the rules in the 1968 Convention are held to be applicable in the alternative at the option of the plaintiff. That will not be so, however, if the particular convention envisages that rules other than those that it contains may apply.

I would therefore answer Question (e), if Your Lordships consider it relevant, by saying that the existence of a convention governing jurisdiction in relation to particular matters does not preclude the application, as an alternative, of the rules as to jurisdiction contained in the 1968 Convention, unless the first-mentioned convention is to be interpreted as prescribing rules that are intended to apply to the exclusion of any other possible rules.

Case 25/81 - 31 March 1982

C. H. W.
v
G. J. H.

Article 1 - Scope of the Convention - Application for interim measures relating to a dispute concerning the proprietary relationships between spouses - Exclusion - Conditions - Article 24 - Provisional or protective measures relating to excluded matters - Inclusion - None - Article 18 - Prorogation of Jurisdiction - Appearance of defendant before the court seised - Appearance not only to contest the jurisdiction but also to make submissions on the substance - Appearance not conferring jurisdiction.

Summary

1. An application for provisional measures to secure the delivery up of a document in order to prevent it from being used as evidence in an action concerning a husband's management of his wife's property does not fall within the scope of the Convention of 27 September 1968 on Jurisdiction and the Enforcement of Judgments in Civil and Commercial Matters if such management is closely connected with the relationship resulting directly from the marriage bond.

2. Article 24 of the Convention of 27 September 1968 may not be relied on to bring within the scope of the Convention provisional or protective measures relating to matters which are excluded from it.

3. Article 18 of the Convention of 27 September 1968 must be interpreted as meaning that it allows the defendant not only to contest the jurisdiction but to submit at the same time in the alternative a defence on the substance of the action without, however, losing the right to raise an objection of lack of jurisdiction.

JUDGMENT OF THE COURT

Mertens de Wilmars, President, Bosco, Touffait, Due, Presidents of Chambers, Pescatore, Lord Mackenzie Stuart, O'Keeffe, Koopmans, Everling, Chloros and Grévisse, Judges

1. By judgment dated 6 February 1981 which was received at the Court on 17 March 1981 the Hoge Raad der Nederlanden [Supreme Court of the Netherlands] referred to the Court for a preliminary ruling under the Protocol of 3 June 1971 on the interpretation by the Court of Justice of the Convention of 27 September 1968 on Jurisdiction and the Enforcement of Judgements in Civil and Commercial Matters (hereinafter referred to as 'the Conventions') four questions as to the interpretation of Articles 1, 18 and 24 of that Convention.

2. Those questions were raised in the context of proceedings between a married couple of Netherlands nationality domiciled in Belgium concerning the husband's management of his wife's separate property. Because the wife wished to produce in evidence a document drawn up by the husband marked 'codicil' the terms of which were intended to exempt the wife's separate property from the liabilities resulting from his management of that property, the husband made an application to the President of the Arrondissementsrechtbank [District Court], Rotterdam, for an order requiring the document to be returned to him and an injunction against its being used as evidence.

3. The jurisdiction of the President of the Arrondissementsrechtbank to order delivery up of the document was challenged and the case was brought before the Gerechtshof [Regional Court of Appeal], The Hague, and then before the Hoge Raad which decided that an interpretation of the Convention was needed to resolve the dispute and referred the following questions to the Court:

'1. Does the exclusion of 'wills and succession' from the application of the Convention, provided for by the opening words of the second paragraph of Article 1 and subparagraph (1) thereof, apply to applications by the person making a codicil held by another person for the delivery up of that codicil, the destruction of photocopies, transcripts and reproductions thereof, and an injunction against holding or using (or causing to be held or used) any photocopy, transcript or reproduction of that document for the purpose of preventing the declarations contained in the codicil from being used against the person making the codicil as evidence in a legal dispute which does not relate to a will or succession?

2. Does the exclusion of 'rights in property arising out of a matrimonial relationship' from the application of the Convention, provided for by the opening words of the Convention, provided for by the opening words of the second paragraph of Article 1 and subparagraph (1) thereof, apply to applications as described in 1. above if they are made in order to prevent the declarations contained in the codicil from being used against the person making the codicil in a legal dispute about alleged unauthorized or improper management by that person of his wife's separate property, where that management must be regarded as being closely connected with proprietary relationships flowing directly from the marriage bond?

3. Does the concept of 'provisional, including protective, measures' referred to in Article 24 cover the possibility, provided for in the Eighteenth Section of Part 13 of the First Book of the Netherlands Code of Civil Procedure [Wetboek van Burgerlijke Rechtsvordering], of applying for interim relief in interlocutory proceedings? Does the fact that the relief is sought in connection with other proceedings pending in the Netherlands affect the answer?

4. Must the entering of appearance by the defendant solely in order to contest the jurisdiction of the court, referred to in the second sentence of Article 18, be taken to cover a case where the defendant contests the court's jurisdiction and at the same time challenges in the alternative the substance of the application in case the court decides that it has jurisdiction?'

The first and second questions

4. The issue raised by the first and second questions is whether an application for a provisional measure for the return of a document marked 'codicil' which is likely to be used as evidence in an action relating to a husband's management of his wife's separate property should be excluded from the scope of the Convention in accordance with the second paragraph of Article 1 thereof because it is related to either 'wills and succession' or 'rights in property arising out of a matrimonial relationship'.

5. The second question, relating to 'rights in property arising out of a matrimonial relationship' within the meaning of Article 1 of the Convention, should be examined first.

6. As the Court held in its judgment of 27 March 1979 in Case 143/78 *de Cavel* [1979] ECR 1055 that term includes not only property

arrangements specifically and exclusively envisaged by certain national legal systems in the case of marriage but also any proprietary relationships resulting directly from the matrimonial relationship or the dissolution thereof.

7. By its very wording the second question has in view a case in which the management of the wife's property in question must be considered as being closely connected with the proprietary relationship between the spouses flowing directly from their marriage bond.

8. Therefore, an application for provisional measures to secure the delivery up of a document in order to prevent the statements which it contains from being used as evidence in an action concerning the management of the wife's property must also be considered to be connected with rights in property arising out of a matrimonial relationship within the meaning of the Convention because of its ancillary nature.

9. Therefore, the answer to the second question must be that an application for provisional measures to secure the delivery up of a document in order to prevent it from being used as evidence in an action concerning a husband's management of his wife's property does not fall within the scope of the Convention if such management is closely connected with the proprietary relationship resulting directly from the marriage bond.

10. In view of that answer there is no need to reply to the first question.

The third question

11. The foregoing conclusion is not affected by Article 24 of the Convention which states that: 'Application may be made to the courts of a Contracting State for such provisional, including protective, measures as may be available under the law of that State, even if, under this Convention, the courts of another Contracting State have jurisdiction as to the substance of the matter'.

12. That provision, in fact, has in view cases in which provisional measures are ordered in a Contracting State where 'under this Convention' a court of another Contracting State has jurisdiction as to the substance of the matter. Therefore, it may not be relied on to bring within the scope of the Convention provisional or protective measures relating

to matters which are excluded from it. That is how the third question must be answered.

The fourth question

13. As to the fourth question, it suffices to recall that in its judgments of 24 June 1981 in Case 150/80 *Elefanten Schuh GmbH* [1981] ECR 1671 and of 22 October 1981 in Case 27/81 *Rohr* [1981] ECR 2431 the Court held that Article 18 of the Convention must be interpreted as meaning that it allows the defendant not only to contest the jurisdiction but to submit at the same time in the alternative a defence on the substance of the action without, however, losing his right to raise an objection of lack of jurisdiction.

On those grounds, the Court, in answer to the question submitted to it by the Hoge Raad der Nederlanden by judgment of 6 February 1981, hereby rules:

> **1. An application for provisional measures to secure the delivery up of a document in order to prevent it from being used as evidence in an action concerning a husband's management of his wife's property does not fall within the scope of the Convention of 27 September 1968 on Jurisdiction and the Enforcement of Judgments in Civil and Commercial Matters if such management is closely connected with the proprietary relationship resulting directly from the marriage bond.**
>
> **2. Article 24 of the Convention on Jurisdiction and the Enforcement of Judgments in Civil and Commercial Matters may not be relied on to bring within the scope of the Convention provisional or protective measures relating to matters which are excluded from it.**
>
> **3. Article 18 of the Convention of 27 September 1968 on Jurisdiction and the Enforcement of Judgments in Civil and Commercial Matters must be interpreted as meaning that it allows the defendant not only to contest the jurisdiction but to submit at the same time in the alternative a defence on the substance of the action without, however, losing the right to raise an objection of lack of jurisdiction.**

OPINION OF MRS ADVOCATE GENERAL ROZES

The Hoge Raad [Supreme Court] of the Netherlands has applied to the Court for a preliminary ruling in the case W. v H. These are the facts.

I - Proceedings are pending in the Netherlands between Mr H., a Netherlands national residing in Belgium, and his wife (W.), who is also a Netherlands national residing in Belgium, concerning the management by the husband of his wife's separate property. In the proceedings the wife wishes to use as evidence the terms of a 'codicil' drawn up by her husband which is now in the possession of her advocate in Rotterdam. The couple are also suing for divorce in the Netherlands.

The husband applied to the President of the Arrondissementsrechtbank [District Court], Rotterdam, seeking as a matter of urgent interlocutory relief an order requiring the delivery up of that 'codicil' and an injunction restraining his wife from using its content against him in legal proceedings or otherwise.

The wife appeared at the interlocutory hearing and challenged the jurisdiction of the President and, in the alternative, contested the substance of the application for protective relief.

The President of the Rotterdam court held that he had jurisdiction but found against the husband on the substance.

The husband then appealed from that judgment to the Gerechtshof [Regional Court of Appeal], The Hague, and the wife cross-appealed on the ground that the President of the Rotterdam court had erred in finding that he had jurisdiction.

The Court of Appeal rejected the cross-appeal and in its decision on the main appeal overturned the interlocutory judgment. It ordered the 'codicil' to be delivered up to the husband's advocate and granted an injunction restraining the wife from using the document upon penalty of a fine.

Both the husband and the wife appealed in cassation against that judgment, the wife lodging the main appeal, the husband a cross-appeal.

The main appeal once again raises the question of the jurisdiction of the President of the Rotterdam court to entertain the application for provisional relief to restrain use being made of the 'codicil'. These, then, are the circumstances in which the Hoge Raad of the Netherlands submits to the Court under Articles 1 and 2 of the Protocol on the interpretation of the Brussels Convention of 27 September 1968 on Jurisdiction and the Enforcement of Judgments in Civil and Commercial Matters the following questions:

'1. Does the exclusion of 'wills and succession' from the application of the Convention, provided for by the opening words of the second paragraph of Article 1 and subparagraph (1) thereof, apply to applications by the person making a codicil held by another person for the delivery up of that codicil, the destruction of photocopies, transcripts and reproductions thereof, and an injunction against holding or using (or causing to be held or used) any photocopy, transcript or reproduction of that document for the purpose of preventing the declarations contained in the codicil from being used against the person making the codicil as evidence in a legal dispute which does not relate to a will or succession?

2. Does the exclusion of 'rights in property arising out of a matrimonial relationship' from the application of the Convention, provided for by the opening words of the second paragraph of Article 1 and subparagraph (1) thereof, apply to applications as described in (a) above if they are made in order to prevent the declarations contained in the codicil from being used against the person making the codicil in a legal dispute about alleged unauthorized or improper management by that person of his wife's separate property, where that management must be regarded as being closely connected with proprietary relationships flowing directly from the marriage bond?

3. Does the concept of provisional, including protective, measures referred to in Article 24 cover the possibility, provided for in the Eighteenth Section of Part 13 of the First Book of the Netherlands Code of Civil Procedure [Wetboek van Burgerlijke Rechtsvordering], of applying for interim relief in interlocutory proceedings? Does the fact that relief is sought in connection with other proceedings pending in the Netherlands affect the answer?

4. Must the entering of appearance by the defendant solely in order to contest the jurisdiction of the court referred to in the second sentence of Article 18, be taken to cover a case where the defendant contests the court's jurisdiction and at the same time challenges in the alternative the substance of the application in case the court decides that it has jurisdiction?'

II - In civil and commercial matters within the meaning of Article 1 of the Convention, the ordinary rule laid down in the first paragraph of Article 2 thereof confers jurisdiction on the courts of the State in which the defendant is domiciled. In the present case the wife is domiciled in Belgium.

However, rights in property arising out of a matrimonial relationship, wills and succession are among the matters *excluded* from the application of the Convention (Article 1(1)). According to the appeal judgment, that rule means that the courts of the Netherlands have jurisdiction because, although the spouses are domiciled in Belgium they are both Netherlands nationals and when the husband dies his property will probably devolve in accordance with the laws of the Netherlands.

But there are two exceptions to that exclusion.

First, under Article 18: 'Apart from jurisdiction derived from other provisions of this Convention, a court of a Contracting State before whom a defendant enters an appearance shall have jurisdiction. This rule shall not apply where appearance was entered solely to contest the jurisdiction, or where another court has exclusive jurisdiction by virtue of Article 16'.

Secondly, under Article 24: 'Application may be made to the courts of a Contracting State for such provisional, including protective, measures as may be available under the laws of that State, even if, under this Convention, the courts of another contracting State have jurisdiction as to the substance of the matter'.

The Supreme Court of the Netherlands wonders whether, if either of those provisions is applicable, the President of the Rotterdam Court had jurisdiction to rule upon the husband's interlocutory application.

I think it would be useful to examine the last two questions first.

1. Proceedings relating to rights in property arising out of a matrimonial relationship, wills and succession are expressly excluded from the application of the Convention. Article 24 does not have the effect of conferring jurisdiction on the courts of a Contracting State to order a provisional or protective measure unless the *substance of the action*, whilst falling within the jurisdiction of a court of another Contracting State, concerns matters covered by the Convention. Therefore on no account may that article be used to circumvent the provision of public policy constituted by Article 1 of the Convention.

The Court decided in the *de Cavel* judgment of 27 March 1979 ([1979] ECR 1056) that, in relation to the matters covered by the Convention, no legal basis is to be found therein for drawing a distinction between provisional and definitive measures. Article 24 does not affect that conclusion at all because it expressly envisages cases in which provisional measures are ordered in a Contracting State when, "*under the Convention*", the courts of another Contracting State have jurisdiction as to the substance of the matter. That article cannot, therefore, be relied on to bring within the scope of the Convention the adoption of provisional or protective measures relating to matters which are excluded from it.

2. Even supposing that the jurisdiction of Netherlands courts were excluded under Article 1, the Hoge Raad, nevertheless, wonders whether they would not still have jurisdiction owing to the fact that the wife has entered an appearance to contest not only the jurisdiction of the President of the Rotterdam court but also, in the alternative, the substance of the application (Article 18).

The question calls for two answers.

First, and by analogy with the observations which I made with regard to Article 24, it appears that, even if the defendant enters an appearance and does so not just to contest the jurisdiction, the conferment of jurisdiction which Article 18 provides for in such a case may not result in bringing within the scope of the Convention a matter which is basically excluded from it by Article 1. Moreover, the second sentence of Article 18 states that 'this rule shall not apply ... where another court has exclusive jurisdiction by virtue of Article 16'; however, the exclusive jurisdiction itself, dealt with by that article, relates only to actions in civil and commercial matters.

Secondly, the second sentence of Article 18 excludes the conferment of jurisdiction on a court of a contracting State other than that in which the defendant is domiciled, before which the defendant appears when he contests not only the jurisdiction of the court but also the substance of the application. In fact the Court has held in Case 150/80 *Elefanten Schuh* [1981] ECR 1671 that the rule on jurisdiction which the first sentence of Article 18 lays down does not operate even if the challenge to jurisdiction is not the primary submission or is not preliminary to any defence as to the substance; it need only precede what under the national law of the court seised is considered to be 'the first defence addressed to it'. Sir Gordon Slynn was more explicit in his opinion on the case when he stated that 'a defendant's act in advancing arguments on the substance of the action does not necessarily indicate that he has submitted to the jurisdiction, if these arguments are *alternative* to his primary submission that the court has no jurisdiction'.

In the *Rohr* judgment of 22 October 1981 the Court stated that Article 18 'allows the defendant not only to contest the jurisdiction but to submit at the same time in the alternative a defence on the substance of the action *without, however, losing his right to raise an objection of lack of jurisdiction*'.

3. Therefore, the issue confronting the national court is confined to the question whether the substance of the action between the spouses is a matter pertaining to rights in property arising out of a matrimonial relationship or succession in the broad sense, or on the contrary to a 'civil and commercial matter'.

The first two questions have been put to the Court in a very direct form and it is not for the Court when ruling pursuant to the Protocol on the *interpretation* of the Brussels Convention to determine the nature of the husband's application.

To assist the court which has made the reference I would only wish to stress the following point which was brought out by the Court's decision in de Cavel cited above: It is because of the specific nature of certain matters, in particular 'the status or legal capacity of natural persons, rights in property arising out of a matrimonial relationship, wills and succession' that disputes relating to such matters are excluded from the scope of the Convention.

The enforced settlement on a provisional basis of 'proprietary ... relationships between spouses in the course of proceedings for divorce ... is ... inseparable from questions relating to the status of persons raised by the dissolution of the matrimonial relationship and from the settlement of rights in property arising out of the matrimonial relationship'.

Consequently, the term 'rights in property arising out of a matrimonial relationship' includes 'not only property arrangements specifically and exclusively envisaged by certain national legal systems in the case of marriage but also any proprietary relationships resulting directly from the matrimonial relationship or the dissolution thereof' (paragraph 7, p. 1066).

Disputes relating to the property of spouses suing for divorce may, therefore, depending on the circumstances, be loosely connected with either: questions relating to the status of either persons; or proprietary legal relationships resulting directly from the matrimonial relationship or the dissolution thereof; or proprietary legal relations existing between the spouses which has no connection with the marriage.

The convention applies only in the last case.

For my part I would point out that, according to the wording of the second question, the management conducted by the husband must be regarded 'as being closely connected with proprietary relationships flowing directly from the marriage bond'.

4. As to the succession or testamentary aspect of the dispute between the parties, I would merely observe that the rights, in support of which the wife intends to adduce in evidence the 'codicil' drawn up by her husband, are only contingent in nature because they are based on future succession In such circumstances it seems difficult to accept that a court to which an interlocutory application is made can order even a provisional or protective measure: a plaintiff in other proceedings pending may rely on an existent or contingent debt

as against the defendant only on the basis of an already existing legal situation: by definition, however, the husband has not yet given rise to any succession.

In answer to the questions raised I submit that the Court should rule:

1. Judgments ordering provisional or protective measures under Article 24 of the Brussels Convention fall within the scope of the Convention as defined in Article 1 thereof provided that the action in connection with which such a measure is sought relates to proprietary relationships independent of the matrimonial relationship of the parties or the dissolution thereof.

2. The rule on jurisdiction laid down in Article 18 of the Convention does not apply where, in a matter falling within the scope of the Convention, the defendant enters an appearance to challenge the jurisdiction and at the same time submits in the alternative a defence as to the substance.

Case C-190/89 - 25 July 1991

Marc Rich and Co. AG
v
Società Italiana Impianti PA

Scope of the Convention - Matters excluded - Article 1(4) - Arbitration - Meaning - Application to a court for the appointment of an arbitrator - Included - Need to settle a preliminary question concerning the existence or validity of the arbitration clause - No effect.

Summary

By excluding arbitration from the scope of the Convention of 27 September 1968 on Jurisdiction and the Enforcement of Judgment in Civil and Commercial Matters, by virtue of Article 1(4) thereof, on the ground that it was already covered by international conventions, the Contracting Parties intended to exclude arbitration in its entirety, including proceedings brought before national courts.

Consequently, the abovementioned provision must be interpreted as meaning that the exclusion provided for therein extends to litigation pending before a national court concerning the appointment of an arbitrator, even if the existence or validity of an arbitration agreement is a preliminary issue in that litigation.

JUDGMENT OF THE COURT

Due, President, Mancini, O' Higgins, Rodriguez Iglesias, Presidents of Chambers, Sir Gordon Slynn, Joliet, Schockweiler, Grèvisse and Zuleeg, Judges

1. By order of 26 January 1989, which was received at the Court Registry on 31 May 1989, the Court of Appeal of England and Wales referred to the Court for a preliminary ruling under the Protocol of 3 June 1971 on the interpretation by the Court of Justice of the Convention of 27 September 1968 on Jurisdiction and the Enforcement of Judgments in Civil and Commercial Matters (hereinafter referred to as 'the Convention') three questions on the interpretation of certain provisions of the Convention.

2. The questions were raised in proceedings pending before that court between Marc Rich and Co. AC (hereinafter referred to as 'Marc Rich'), whose registered office is in Zug, Switzerland, and Società Italiana Impianti PA (hereinafter referred to as 'Impianti'), whose registered office is in Genoa, Italy.

3. It appears from the documents forwarded to the Court that, by telex message of 23 January 1987, Marc Rich made an offer to purchase a quantity of Iranian crude oil on fob terms from Impianti. On 25 January 1987, Impianti accepted the offer subject to certain further conditions. On 26 January, Marc Rich confirmed acceptance of those further conditions and on 28 January sent a further telex message setting out the terms of the contract and including the following clause: 'Law and arbitration. Construction, validity and performance of this contract shall be construed in accordance with English law. Should any dispute arise between buyer and seller the matter in dispute shall be referred to three persons in London. One to be appointed by each of the parties hereto and the third by the two so-chosen, their decision or that of any two of them shall be final and binding on both parties.'

4. The vessel which Marc Rich then nominated completed loading by 6 February. On the same day Marc Rich complained that the cargo was seriously contaminated, causing it to incur a loss in excess of USD 7 000 000.

5. On 18 February 1988, Impianti summoned Marc Rich to appear before the Tribunale (Regional Court), Genoa, Italy, in an action for a declaration that it was not liable to Marc Rich. The summons was served on Marc Rich on 29 February 1988, and on 4 October 1988 the latter, relying on the existence of the arbitration clause, lodged submissions to the effect that the Italian court had no jurisdiction.

6. Also on 29 February 1988, Marc Rich commenced arbitration

proceedings in London, in which Impianti refused to take part. On 20 May 1988, Marc Rich commenced proceedings before the High Court of Justice, London, for the appointment of an arbitrator pursuant to section 10(3) of the Arbitration Act 1950. By decision of 19 May 1988, the High Court had granted leave to serve an originating summons on Impianti in Italy.

7. On 8 July 1988, Impianti requested that the order granting leave be set aside, contending that the real dispute between the parties was linked to the question whether or not the contract in question contained an arbitration clause. It considered that such a dispute fell within the scope of the Convention and should therefore be adjudicated on in Italy. Marc Rich on the other hand, took the view that the dispute fell outside the scope of the Convention by virtue of Article I thereof.

8. On 5 November 1988, the High Court held that the Convention did not apply, that the putative proper law of the contract between the parties was English and that it was a proper case to give leave to serve out of the jurisdiction.

9. On appeal, the Court of Appeal decided to stay the proceedings and refer the following questions to the Court of Justice for a preliminary ruling:

'1. Does the exception in Article 1(4) of the Convention extend:

(a) to any litigation or judgments and, if so, (b) to litigation or judgments where the initial existence of an arbitration agreement is in issue?

2. If the present dispute falls within the Convention and not within the exception to the Convention, whether the buyers can nevertheless establish jurisdiction in England pursuant to:

(a) Article 5(1) of the Convention, and/or (b) Article 17 of the Convention.

3. If the buyers are otherwise able to establish jurisdiction in England than under paragraph 2 above, whether:

(a) the Court must decline jurisdiction or should stay its proceedings under Article 21 of the Convention or, alternatively, (b) whether the Court should stay its proceedings under Article 22 of the Convention, on the grounds that the Italian court was first seised.'

10. Reference is made to the Report for the Hearing for a fuller account of the facts of the case, the course of the procedure and the written observations submitted to the Court, which are mentioned or discussed hereinafter only in so far as is necessary for the reasoning of the Court.

The first question

11. The first question submitted by the national court seeks, in substance, to determine whether Article 1(4) of the Convention must be interpreted in such a manner that the exclusion provided for therein extends to proceedings pending before a national court concerning the appointment of an arbitrator and, if so, whether that exclusion also applies where in those proceedings a preliminary issue is raised as to whether an arbitration agreement exists or is valid. These two points will be considered successively.

12. The first paragraph of Article 1 of the Convention provides that it is to apply in civil and commercial matters whatever the nature of the court or tribunal. According to the second paragraph of that article, the Convention shall not apply to: '1. ...; 4. arbitration'.

Exclusion of proceedings for the appointment of an arbitrator from the scope of the Convention

13. Impianti considers that the exclusion in Article 1(4) of the Convention does not apply to proceedings before national courts or to decisions given by them. It contends that 'arbitration' in the strict sense concerns proceedings before private individuals on whom the parties have conferred the authority to settle the dispute between them. Impianti bases that view essentially on the purpose of Article 220 of the Treaty which, it argues, is to establish a complete system for the free movement of decisions determining a dispute. Consequently, it is legitimate to interpret Article 1(4) of the Convention in such a way as to avoid lacunae in the legal system for ensuring the free movement of decisions terminating a dispute.

14. Marc Rich and the governments which have submitted observations support a wide interpretation of the concept of arbitration, which would exclude completely from the scope of the Convention any disputes relating to the appointment of an arbitrator.

15. The purpose of the Convention, according to the preamble thereto, is to implement the provisions of Article 220 of the EEC Treaty concerning the reciprocal recognition and enforcement of judgments of courts or tribunals. Pursuant to the fourth paragraph of Article 220, the Member States shall, so far as is necessary, enter into negotiations with each other with a view to securing for the benefit of their nationals the simplification

of formalities governing the reciprocal recognition and enforcement of judgments of courts or tribunals and of arbitration awards.

16. In referring to decisions of courts and tribunals and to arbitration awards, Article 220 of the Treaty thus relates both to proceedings brought before national courts and tribunals which culminate in a judicial decision and to those commenced before private arbitrators which culminate in arbitral awards. However, it does not follow that the Convention, whose purpose is in particular the reciprocal recognition and enforcement of judicial decisions, must necessarily have attributed to it a wide field of application. In so far as the Member States are called upon, by virtue of Article 220, to enter into negotiations 'so far as necessary', it is incumbent on them to determine the scope of any agreement concluded between them.

17. With respect to the exclusion of arbitration from the scope of the Convention, the report by the group of experts set up in connection with the drafting of the Convention (Official Journal 1979 C 59, p. 1) explains that 'There are already many international agreements on arbitration. Arbitration is, of course, referred to in Article 220 of the Treaty of Rome. Moreover, the Council of Europe has prepared a European Convention providing a uniform law on arbitration, and this will probably be accompanied by a Protocol which will facilitate the recognition and enforcement of arbitral awards to an even greater extent than the New York Convention. This is why it seemed preferable to exclude arbitration'.

18. The international agreements, and in particular the above-mentioned New York Convention on the recognition and enforcement of foreign arbitral awards (New York, 10 June 1958, *United Nations Treaty Series*, Vol. 330, p. 3), lay down rules which must be respected not by the arbitrators themselves but by the courts of the Contracting States. Those rules relate, for example, to agreements whereby parties refer a dispute to arbitration and the recognition and enforcement of arbitral awards. It follows that, by excluding arbitration from the scope of the Convention on the ground that it was already covered by international conventions, the Contracting Parties intended to exclude arbitration in its entirety, including proceedings brought before national courts.

19. More particularly, it must be pointed out that the appointment of an arbitrator by a national court is a measure adopted by the State as part of the process of setting arbitration proceedings in motion. Such a measure

therefore comes within the sphere of arbitration and is thus covered by the exclusion contained in Article 1(4) of the Convention.

20. That interpretation is not affected by the fact that the international agreements in question have not been signed by all the Member States and do not cover all aspects of arbitration, in particular the procedure for the appointment of arbitrators.

21. That conclusion is also corroborated by the opinion expressed by the experts in the report drawn up by them at the time of the accession of Denmark, Ireland and the United Kingdom to the Convention, according to which the Convention does not apply to court proceedings which are ancillary to arbitration proceedings, for example the appointment or dismissal of arbitrators (Official Journal 1979 C 59, p. 93). Similarly, in the report drawn up at the time of the accession of the Hellenic Republic to the Convention, the experts considered that cases where a court is instrumental in setting up the arbitration body are not covered by the Convention (Official Journal 1986 C 298, p. 1).

Whether a preliminary issue concerning the existence or validity of an arbitration agreement affects the application of the Convention to the dispute in question

22. Impianti contends that the exclusion in Article 1(4) of the Convention does not extend to disputes or judicial decisions concerning the existence or validity of an arbitration agreement. In its view, that exclusion likewise does not apply where arbitration is not the principal issue in the proceedings but is merely a subsidiary or incidental issue.

23. Impianti argues that, if that were not so, a party could avoid the application of the Convention merely by alleging the existence of an arbitration agreement.

24. Impianti contends that, in any event, the exception in Article 1(4) of the Convention does not apply where the existence or validity of an arbitration agreement is being disputed before different courts to which the Convention applies, regardless of whether that issue has been raised as a main issue or as a preliminary issue.

25. The Commission shares Impianti's opinion in so far as the question of the existence or validity of an arbitration agreement is raised as a preliminary issue.

26. Those interpretations cannot be accepted. In order to determine whether a dispute falls within the scope of the Convention, reference must be made solely to the subject-matter of the dispute. If, by virtue of its subject-matter, such as the appointment of an arbitrator, a dispute falls outside the scope of the Convention, the existence of a preliminary issue which the court must resolve in order to determine the dispute cannot, whatever that issue may be, justify application of the Convention.

27. It would also be contrary to the principle of legal certainty, which is one of the objectives pursued by the Convention (see judgment in Case 38/81 *Effer* v *Kantner* [1982] ECR 825, paragraph 6) for the applicability of the exclusion laid down in Article 1(4) of the Convention to vary according to the existence or otherwise of a preliminary issue, which might be raised at any time by the parties.

28. It follows that, in the case before the Court, the fact that a preliminary issue relates to the existence or validity of the arbitration agreement does not affect the exclusion from the scope of the Convention of a dispute concerning the appointment of an arbitrator.

29. Consequently, the reply must be that Article 1(4) of the Convention must be interpreted as meaning that the exclusion provided for therein extends to litigation pending before a national court concerning the appointment of an arbitrator, even - if the existence or validity of an arbitration agreement is a preliminary issue in that litigation.

The second and third questions

30. In view of the answer given to the first question, the second and third questions do not call for a reply.

On those grounds, the Court, in reply to the questions submitted to it by the Court of Appeal, London, by order of 26 January 1989, hereby rules:

> **Article 1(4) of the Convention must be interpreted as meaning that the exclusion provided for therein extends to litigation pending before a national court concerning the appointment of an arbitrator even if the existence or validity of an arbitration agreement is a preliminary issue in that litigation.**

OPINION OF MR ADVOCATE GENERAL DARMON

1. The interpretation of the Brussels Convention (hereinafter referred to as 'the Convention') raises numerous difficulties since, as well as being inherently complex, it uses concepts which the various national laws define precisely but in a manner which often differs from one Member State to another, with the result that the Court has often felt it necessary to educe from it an independent meaning. For that purpose, the objectives of the Convention, which pursue the 'free movement of judgments', are reliable points of reference which may be used in order to reject solutions which might lead to a multiplicity of actions before different courts and the associated risk of irreconcilable decisions.

2. However, these constant and justified concerns which are evident in the decisions of the Court are subject to an obvious limitation: the scope of the Convention itself. The present preliminary-ruling proceedings, which are concerned with the scope of Article 1(4) of the Convention, according to which the Convention is not to apply to arbitration, must serve as a reminder that, however constructive and specific it may be, the Court's interpretation of the Convention must not lead to a result which strays beyond the limits of its wording, its scheme and the coherence of its provisions.

3. Those preliminary remarks are prompted by some of the analyses made in the present case, which refer in a somewhat ritualistic manner to the objectives of the Convention and leave aside all other considerations, even those which stem from the logic of that instrument and the specific features of the problem before the Court: international arbitration. The issues raised in this case cannot be tackled without reference first being made to the fundamental importance of arbitration today within the 'international business community', to use the expression adopted by academic writers. Contributing to the expansion of world trade, international arbitration has universally become the 'most frequently used method of resolving disputes in international trade'. That pronounced trend may be illustrated by the following quotation from the Final Act of the Helsinki Conference (ECSC) of 1 August 1975: 'The participating States, considering that the prompt and equitable settlement of any disputes which may arise from commercial transactions relating to goods and services and contracts for industrial co-operation would contribute to expanding and facilitating trade and co-operation; considering that arbitration is an appropriate means of settling such disputes, recommend, where appropriate, to organizations, enterprises and firms in their countries to include arbitration clauses in commercial contracts and industrial co-operation contracts or in special agreements; recommend that the provisions on arbitration should provide for arbitration under a mutually acceptable set of arbitration rules, and permit arbitration in a third country, taking into account existing intergovernmental and other agreements in this field.'

4. The author of a major work on the New York Convention of 1958 - the main multilateral arbitration instrument - perfectly describes the deeply felt needs which are satisfied by international arbitration, which distinguish it very clearly from domestic arbitration: 'The foreign court can be an alien

environment for a businessman because of his unfamiliarity with the procedure which may be followed, the laws to be applied, and even the mentality of the foreign judges. In contrast, with international commercial arbitration parties coming from different legal systems can provide for a procedure which is mutually acceptable. They can anticipate which law shall be applied: a particular law or even a *lex mercatoria* of a trade. They can also appoint a person of their choice having expert knowledge in the field.'
The author goes on to say: 'These and other advantages are only potential until the necessary legal framework can be internationally secured. This legal framework should at least provide that the commitment to arbitrate is enforceable and that the arbitral decision can be executed in many countries, precluding the possibility that a national court review the merits of the decision.'

5. The decision which the Court is called on to make in the present case is not without impact on the juridical stability which international arbitration enjoys within the territory of the Community. Indeed, certain of the views put to the Court might, if the Court were amenable to accepting them, be liable to call in question well-established principles, disturbing expectations in this area for an indefinite period. Moreover, as the Court cannot be unaware, the territory of the European Community includes major international arbitration centres, whose development has recently been favoured by intense activity in the areas of legal literature, legislation and case-law. As a result, the difficulty raised by the question submitted by the Court of Appeal for a preliminary ruling must be examined in detail.

6. Article 220 of the Treaty of Rome - the scope of Community law is certainly not such that it bears no relation whatsoever to arbitration - provides: 'Member States shall, so far as is necessary, enter into negotiations with each other with a view to securing for the benefit of their nationals: .. the simplification of formalities governing the reciprocal recognition and enforcement of judgments of courts or tribunals and of arbitration awards'.

7. Despite the wording of that provision, Article 1 of the Brussels Conventions - the text of which has not been changed in that respect by the accession conventions - provides: 'This Convention shall apply in civil and commercial matters whatever the nature of the court or tribunal.
The Convention shall not apply to:

1. The status or legal capacity of natural persons, rights in property arising out of a matrimonial relationship, wills and successions;
2. Bankruptcy, proceedings relating to the winding up of insolvent companies or other legal persons, judicial arrangements, compositions and analogous proceedings;
3. Social security;
4. *Arbitration.*'

8. Without at this stage considering the scope to be attributed to that provision, I shall refer here to the statements made by the committee of experts which prepared the draft Convention: 'There are already many international agreements on arbitration. Arbitration is, of course, referred to in Article 220 of the Treaty of Rome. Moreover, the Council of Europe has prepared a European

Convention providing a uniform law on arbitration, and this will probably be accompanied by a protocol which will facilitate the recognition and enforcement of arbitral awards to an even greater extent than the New York Convention'.

9. Brief historical details of the drafting of the international conventions on international arbitration are called for here. Until the end of the First World War, the law applicable to arbitration was almost exclusively governed by national laws which, like the court, were often hostile towards arbitration. The development of international arbitration following the First World War was to result in substantial international legislative activity under the auspices of the League of Nations. The adoption of the Geneva Protocol of 1923 - upholding the validity of arbitration clauses which at that time were prohibited by many national laws, and imposing an obligation on national courts to refer to arbitration disputes in respect of which an arbitration agreement had been concluded - and then, in 1927, the Geneva Convention on the enforcement of foreign judgments, brought about an improvement in the legal circumstances of international arbitration.

10. However, certain restrictive aspects of those conventions still limited the extent to which they promoted the satisfactory functioning of international arbitration. In particular, the manner in which Article 1 of the Geneva Convention of 1927 was interpreted, whereby the award to be recognized or enforced was required to have become final in the country in which it was made, frequently made it necessary to obtain 'a double order for enforcement', the first by the courts of the place of arbitration and the second by the courts of the State of enforcement. Thus, further efforts at achieving an international solution were made following the Second World War. The proceedings of the Economic and Social Committee of the United Nations included preparation of the draft New York Convention of 10 June 1958. That instrument, which makes numerous significant amendments to the Geneva Conventions, deals with two essential features of international commercial arbitration: the effectiveness of arbitration agreements and the enforcement of arbitration awards. It must be noted in particular that the requirement of the 'double order for enforcement' was removed. More than 80 States, including 11 EEC Member States, acceded to that Convention, which is now the principal basis for international arbitration.

'The modern tendency is for a coming together of the different systems of law which govern the procedural aspects of international commercial arbitration and the recognition and enforcement of international awards. This is partly because of the unifying effect of conventions on arbitration, most importantly the New York Convention'.

'The New York Convention (...) is easily the most important international treaty relating to international commercial arbitration. The general level of success of the Convention may be seen as one of the factors responsible for the rapid development over recent decades of arbitration as a means of resolving international trade disputes'.

11. Whilst the New York Convention thus constitutes a major instrument of international arbitration, mention must also be made of the potential impact of the recent Model Law (Uncitral) of 1985 on international commercial

arbitration, the provisions of which provide a pattern for national legislation concerning the arbitration agreement, the composition of the arbitration tribunal, the arbitration procedure, the making of awards, appeals against awards and recognition and enforcement thereof. Reflecting the development of national laws, the Model Law adopts the principle of the competence/competence' of arbitrators, according to which an arbitrator may himself, subject to subsequent judicial review, appraise his own jurisdiction.

'In adopting the concept of "competence/competence", the Model Law has recognized the general trend of modern national legal systems, and of international conventions, which allow an arbitral tribunal to determine its own jurisdiction. However, the Model Law does not give an arbitral tribunal the final word; there is provision for concurrent control by the court specified by Article 6'.

12. Alongside those instruments, there are numerous regional conventions on international arbitration. Within the confines of Europe, two treaties must be mentioned: the European Convention on International Commercial Arbitration of 21 April 1961 and the European Convention providing a uniform law on arbitration of 20 January 1966 (the Strasbourg Convention). The first of those instruments, supplementing the New York Convention, limits the grounds on which recognition and enforcement of arbitral awards may be refused. More precisely, annulment of an award by the courts of the State in which it was delivered can serve as a basis for withholding an order for enforcement only if made for certain specified reasons. Moreover, the 1961 European Convention establishes in particular the principle of arbitrators' 'competence/competence' and provides for cases of *lis pendens* as between arbitration proceedings and proceedings subsequently instituted before national courts. The Convention is binding on twenty Member States, seven being Member States of the Community. On the other hand, the Strasbourg Convention has not achieved the success initially expected of it, since only one State, Belgium, has so far ratified it.

13. At the same time, national laws have increasingly recognized the needs of international commercial arbitration by accepting the ramifications of the independence accorded to the wishes of parties in international arbitration. This trend is particularly pronounced in Europe and is apparent both in legislation and in the attitudes of national courts which show no hostility to international arbitration.

14. 'It used occasionally to be suggested that the English courts were hostile to the process of arbitration. Whether this was ever true, in the distant past, is a matter of opinion. What must be clear, to anyone reading the judgments delivered during the past 60 years, is that this is now a complete misconception'.

Although it refers to the United Kingdom courts, that opinion could no doubt be extended to most other national courts.

15. The foregoing general outline, which should be supplemented by a description of the essential role of the permanent arbitration institutions or the emergence of a new *lex mercatoria*, gives a general picture of international arbitration which, having progressively fewer links with national legal systems, is tending, according to some commentators, to become 'denationalized' or indeed 'delocalized'.

16. The present case, which marks the first occasion on which a United Kingdom court has made a reference to this Court on the Brussels Convention and also the first time that this Court is called on to give a decision on the scope of the exclusion of arbitration from the Convention, is of considerable importance in both respects. It derives from circumstances which must be described if the issues involved are to be properly understood.

17. By a telex message of 23 January 1987, Marc Rich and Co. AG (hereinafter referred to as 'Marc Rich') made an offer to purchase Iranian crude oil from Società Italiana Impianti PA (hereinafter referred to as 'SII'). On the 25th of the same month, the latter accepted the offer, subject to certain further conditions which appear to have been accepted by Marc Rich on 26 January, on which date SII considers that a contract was thus concluded. On 28 January, Marc Rich sent a further telex message setting out the terms of the contract and including the following clause: 'Law and arbitration. Construction, validity and performance of this contract shall be construed in accordance with English law. Should any dispute arise between buyer and seller the matter in dispute shall be referred to three persons in London. One to be appointed by each of the parties hereto and the third by the two so chosen, their decision or that of any two of them should be final and binding on both parties.'

There was no reply to that telex message.

18. Some days later, the cargo of oil was loaded aboard the vessel *Atlantic Emperor* the operation being completed on 6 February. It seems that, on the same day, Marc Rich complained that the cargo was seriously contaminated, giving rise to damage in excess of USD 7 000 000.

19. On 18 February 1988, the Italian company commenced legal proceedings in Italy for a declaration that it was not liable to Marc Rich. The writ was served on that company on 29 February 1988 and, on the same day, Marc Rich commenced arbitration proceedings in London, appointing its arbitrator, and on 4 October 1988 claimed that the Italian court had no jurisdiction as a result of the arbitration agreement. Moreover, Marc Rich subsequently commenced proceedings directly before the Italian Corte di Cassazione for a declaration that the Italian courts lacked jurisdiction, in view of the existence of the arbitration agreement. Since SII had not appointed an arbitrator, on 20 May 1988 Marc Rich commenced proceedings for an arbitrator to be appointed by the High Court under the Arbitration Act 1950. The English court gave leave for a notice of writ to be served on SII in Italy. On 8 July 1988 the Italian company applied for that leave to be withdrawn, contending that the real dispute between the parties turned on the question whether or not the contract at issue contained an arbitration clause. It claimed that a dispute of that kind fell within the scope of the Brussels Convention and should therefore be heard before the courts in Italy. According to Marc Rich, the dispute fell outside the scope of the Convention as a result of Article 1 thereof which excludes arbitration.

20. Hirst J. held that the Convention did not apply to the dispute, also taking the view that the contract was subject to English law and granting leave for service out of the jurisdiction. An appeal was lodged against that decision. Although it appears that both parties of the main proceedings showed some

reticence concerning a reference for a preliminary ruling and asked the Court of Appeal itself to decide on the interpretation of the Convention in this case, that court referred three questions to the Court of Justice: 'Does the exception in Article 1(4) of the Convention extend:

(a) to any litigation or judgments and, if so, (b) to litigation or judgments where the initial existence of an arbitration agreement is in issue?

If the present dispute falls within the Convention and not within the exception to the Convention, whether the buyers can nevertheless establish jurisdiction in England pursuant to:

(a) Article 5(1) of the Convention, and/or (b) Article 17 of the Convention.

If the buyers are otherwise able to establish jurisdiction in England than under paragraph 2 above, whether:

(a) the Court must decline jurisdiction or should stay its proceedings under Article 21 of the Convention or, alternatively, (b) whether the Court should stay its proceedings under Article 22 of the Convention on the grounds that the Italian court was first seised.'

21. Two preliminary remarks are called for.

22. The first is prompted by the opinions of Messrs Jenard and Schlosser produced to the Court by SII. It is well known that they also prepared the reports of the Committees of Experts which drafted the initial Convention and the convention concerning the accession thereto of Denmark, Ireland and the United Kingdom. Accordingly, the Court has taken those reports into account. It should also be remembered that the Civil Jurisdiction and Judgments Act 1982 expressly refers to those reports for the purpose of interpretation of the Convention by the United Kingdom courts. On the other hand, it is beyond doubt that the opinions submitted to the Court in these proceedings merely have the status of a statement of views to which, of course, there must be accorded only the weight which their intrinsic merits deserve. This clarification is particularly necessary since Mr Schlosser, for his part, puts forward a view which in every respect contradicts the official report signed by him concerning application of the Convention to disputes relating to arbitration before national courts.

23. The second remark relates to the scope of the answer to be given by the Court to the first question, which is formulated in very general terms by the Court of Appeal. Strictly on its wording, the Court might be prompted to consider a very wide range of hypotheses concerning the extent of the exclusion of arbitration from the scope of the Brussels Convention. I am thinking in particular of a delicate question which arose during the negotiations prior to the accession of the United Kingdom. The United Kingdom delegation had, it seems, contended that the Convention did not apply to recognition and enforcement of a judgment on the subject-matter of a dispute delivered by a national court because it overlooked an arbitration agreement or considered it wholly invalid. Although that view does not appear to have been accepted by the original Member States, that difference of opinion did not lead to any change to the wording of the Convention. According to the Schlosser Report, 'the new Member States can deal with this problem of interpretation in their implementing legislation'. Whatever the analysis which one may be inclined to adopt in that

respect, it must be stated that that difficulty bears no relation to the dispute pending before the English court which made the reference. Consequently, contrary to the suggestion made by the French Government on that point, I suggest that this matter should not be dealt with in the Court's reply to the Court of Appeal. I share the view of the German Government that the Court's answer should be limited to the clarifications necessary for a decision to be given in the main proceedings.

24. Marc Rich's application is concerned with *the appointment of an arbitrator*, that is to say the constitution of the arbitral tribunal. Counsel for SII raises the initial question *whether an arbitration agreement exists at all*. These are undeniably the essential features of the dispute *before the* national court and provide the basis on which I propose that the Court give an interpretation of Article 1(4) of the Convention.

25. It also seems that some confusion has arisen in that connection owing to the fact that SII denies that the proceedings pending before the national court are concerned with the appointment of an arbitrator. The 'principal or real dispute between the parties', it contends, relates to the existence of an arbitration agreement. Without doubt, that question appears at the present stage of the proceedings to be the most important. From the procedural point of view, it is merely an incidental issue or, more precisely, a preliminary issue. SII itself stated at the hearing that the question of the existence of an arbitration agreement must be settled before the appointment of an arbitrator can be proceeded with. And its written observations clearly state: 'The buyers' application in the English court is for the appointment of an arbitrator. But, as held by Hirst, J and not challenged by the buyers, the buyers are not in a position to obtain this relief unless or until they have established the existence of a valid arbitration agreement'. No better description could be given of a preliminary issue.

26. I would also point out that that distinction between a preliminary issue and the main issue, which is familiar to continental lawyers, has already been made in this very area by Common Lawyers. In fact, in a decision of the High Court - concerning the powers of arbitrators whose jurisdiction is challenged - the question of jurisdiction, prior to an assessment of the substance of the dispute, was specifically described as a '*preliminary matter*' in the following terms: 'They are entitled to inquire into the merits of the issue whether they have jurisdiction or not, not for the purpose of reaching any conclusion which will be binding upon the parties - because that they cannot do - but for the purpose of satisfying themselves as a preliminary matter whether they ought to go on with the arbitration or not'.

27. Although that statement was made concerning the question of an arbitrator's jurisdiction raised before that arbitrator, the analysis - which is, moreover, logical and obvious - that the question is a preliminary matter does not differ in that respect where the proceedings are before a national court which has been asked to appoint an arbitrator.

28. According to the view put forward by SII, which is based largely on the views expressed by Messrs Jenard and Schlosser, the Convention applies to the proceedings instituted before the national court which referred the question.

At first sight, that conclusion contradicts the solution which would be arrived at from the hitherto accepted principles regarding application of the exclusions provided for in the Convention, which I shall first describe. That solution was perfectly set out in the German Government's observations. It is clear and precise. The starting point of the analysis is the undeniable principle that 'matters falling outside the scope of the Convention do so only if they constitute the principal subject-matter of the proceedings'.

29. As we have seen, in this case the principal subject-matter of the proceedings is the appointment of an arbitrator. Mr Schlosser's report is wholly unambiguous in that respect: 'The 1968 Convention does not cover court procedures which are ancillary to arbitration proceedings, for example the appointment or dismissal of arbitrators'.

Similarly, all authors who have dealt with this point agree in excluding that particular type of proceedings from the scope of the Convention.

30. Short of adopting the radical view contained in Mr Schlosser's updated opinion, according to which the Convention applies to all disputes concerning arbitration brought before the courts, a view which I shall consider in due course, there is no room for any hesitation: the Convention does not apply to the principal subject-matter of the proceedings pending before the national court. But the national court has before it the preliminary issue of whether or not an arbitration agreement exists.

31. At this point I must lay great emphasis on the fact that, under the scheme of the Convention, where a court is seised of a principal issue not falling within the scope of the Convention its jurisdiction to deal with a preliminary issue is in no case governed by the Convention but is a matter for the *lex fori*, and that is so even if the preliminary matter falls within the scope of the Convention.

32. Messrs Gothot and Holleaux expressed that view very clearly: The Convention does not operate with respect to principal questions excluded from its scope even if they incidentally raise an issue covered by the Convention. The jurisdiction of the court concerning the principal subject-matter (social security, for example...), which is excluded from the scope of the Convention, *and the incidental issue* (concerning a contract for employment, for example), which falls within the scope of the Convention; depends on the national lex fori of that court and not on the Convention (the judgment delivered obviously cannot benefit from the conditions laid down in the Convention concerning recognition and enforcement)'.

33. Two conclusions must be drawn from this. The first is that it is the lex fori alone, that is to say English law in this case, which must determine whether the court has jurisdiction to deal with the preliminary matter. The second is that the dispute, of which the principal subject-matter falls outside the scope of the Convention, clearly cannot be brought within the scope of the Convention by the effect of a preliminary matter, even if the latter falls within one of the subject areas covered by the Convention. In this connection, it is unnecessary, in my opinion, for the Court to express a view in this case as to whether or not the question of the existence of an arbitration agreement raised as a main issue

before a court falls within the scope of the Convention. In my view, it would be sufficient to find that, where such a question is in the nature of a preliminary matter in a dispute whose principal subject-matter falls outside the Convention, the Convention does not apply and, consequently, the decision whether the court seised may dispose of the preliminary issue is a matter for the lex fori. That conclusion seems to me to follow naturally from the principles to which I have referred.

34. But if the Court declines to take that course, considering, regardless of any procedural analysis, that the main issue in this case relates to whether an arbitration agreement exists between the parties, the Court will not as a result decide that the dispute brought before the national court falls within the scope of the Convention. In my opinion, a dispute as to the existence of an arbitration agreement falls outside the scope of the Convention.

35. It is appropriate here to quote from the Schlosser Report: 'A judgment determining whether an arbitration agreement is valid or not, or, because it is invalid, ordering the parties not to continue the arbitration proceedings, is not covered by the 1968 Convention'.

That opinion is also expressed by an academic writer: 'Furthermore, it is considered, perhaps controversially, that legal proceedings concerning purely the contractual validity of the arbitration agreement should also be regarded as being excluded from the Convention as involving arbitration under Article 1, paragraph 2(4), through being more closely related to the arbitration process itself than, for example, are contractual questions in respect of matrimonial property rights - likewise excluded under Article 1, paragraph 2(1) - related thereto'.

The United Kingdom correctly emphasized in that connection that there is no good reason for distinguishing between a non-existent arbitration agreement and an invalid agreement. The 1961 European Convention in fact draws no distinction between a challenge as to the existence of an arbitration agreement and a challenge as to its validity. In both cases, it is the jurisdiction of the arbitrator which is referred to. Moreover, I do not see any reason for drawing a distinction, as Mr Jenard does in the opinion produced to this Court, between a challenge as to the existence or the validity of the arbitration agreement before the arbitration proceedings commence, which would fall within the scope of the Convention, and a challenge as to the arbitrator's jurisdiction brought before the Court in the course of the arbitration proceedings, which, for its part, would fall outside the scope of the Convention.

36. In certain legal systems, review by the courts of an arbitrator's jurisdiction is essentially exercised *ex post facto*. That is the position under French law, for example, which, except in the case of a manifestly void arbitration agreement, requires courts to refer matters to arbitration, and the arbitrator's assessments concerning his own jurisdiction are subsequently reviewed by the Court if an action for annulment of the award is brought. The Jenard and Schlosser reports state that the Convention is not applicable to judgments setting aside an arbitration award. However, the ground of annulment may reside precisely in the fact that the arbitrator has no jurisdiction. It seems

therefore that, according to Mr Jenard, the Convention does not apply to review of that kind whereas, on the other hand, it does govern initial challenges to the arbitrator's jurisdiction in systems of law which allow a review of that jurisdiction *ab initio*.

37. Such a solution would result in an arbitrary dividing line between proceedings which all lead to a ruling on the question of the arbitrator's jurisdiction: some would be subject to the Convention and others would be excluded from its scope.

38. Finally the following argument put forward by SII must be considered: 'Arbitration depends on consent. Absent consent, there is no "arbitration". The Sellers therefore submit that on its natural meaning "arbitration" does not extend to a dispute in which the initial existence of an agreement to arbitrate is in issue'. In other words, the subject-matter of a dispute does not concern arbitration if the very existence of an agreement to arbitrate is contested.

39. In the light of the previous decisions of this Court, that analysis is unconvincing. In the Court's judgment in *Effer* a claim for the payment of fees was countered by a defence argument that no contractual relations had been established between the parties. The question put to the Court was whether the challenge as to the very existence of a contract prevented the application of Article 5(1) of the Convention, within whose scope the claim for payment undoubtedly fell. The Court held that the plaintiff was entitled to invoke the jurisdiction of the courts of the place of performance of the contract 'even where the existence of the contract on which the claim is based is in dispute between the parties'. In other words, the Court considered that an allegation as to the non-existence of a contract whose performance was sought was not sufficient to take the matter out of the field of contract law. Applied to the present case, that reasoning must lead to the conclusion that the allegation that no arbitration agreement exists likewise cannot lead to the conclusion that the dispute brought before the national court - seeking the appointment of an arbitrator, in other words implementation of the said arbitration agreement - does not fall within the subject area of arbitration.

40. Consequently, whatever analysis is made of the question whether the existence of an arbitration agreement is a preliminary or principal issue, it seems that the principal subject-matter of the dispute before the national court relates to arbitration. I should also be noted that in his opinion Mr Jenard himself conceded that arbitration is the 'main issue' in the dispute before the English court, but he draws a conclusion - which I shall consider in due course - that the Convention applies to this dispute.

41. That is not the result which would be arrived at by application of the traditional principles in this area, a result challenged by SII and by the Commission.

42. Before I consider the Italian company's argument, which relies principally on a radical interpretation according to which the Convention applies to all disputes concerning arbitration which are brought before the courts, I must first set out the Commission's view, which advocates application of the Convention in this case on the basis of an analysis which seems to me totally to disregard the principles to which I have just referred.

43. In the Commission's view, the key to the difficulty is provided by the following passage from the Evrigenis and Kerameus report: 'However, the verification, as an incidental question, of validity of an arbitration agreement which is cited by a litigant in order to contest the jurisdiction of the court before which he is being sued pursuant to the Convention, must be considered as falling within its scope'.

44. Let me say at the outset that I would have very serious doubts as to the correctness of that statement if it meant that it is the Convention which confers on a court seised of a main action within the scope of the Convention jurisdiction to deal with an incidental issue falling outside the Convention. That is a matter for the *lex fori* of the court seised and not a matter to be determined by the Convention. As Messrs Gothot and Holleaux state: 'In fact, the Convention does not operate in that respect: it is a matter for the general law of the court seised concerning jurisdiction and procedure to decide whether an incidental issue of that kind must be treated merely as a preliminary or pre-trial issue'.

45. It therefore seems to me preferable to take the view that the authors of the report in fact intended to refer to the application of the Convention to recognition and enforcement of a judgment which disposes of a dispute within the scope of the Convention after giving a decision on the validity of an arbitration agreement. As we have seen, that question was raised during the negotiations prior to the accession of the United Kingdom. In my view, the question remains open and in any event is not pertinent to the dispute before the national court.

46. But even if it is assumed that the authors of the report considered that the Convention determined the jurisdiction of a court seised under the Convention to deal, as a preliminary issue, with the validity of an arbitration agreement, the passage quoted does not in any case lead to the conclusion drawn by the Commission.

47. In fact, the situation expressly referred to is that of a court seised *pursuant to the Convention* which is called on to review the incidental issue of the arbitration agreement. In other words, it is of decisive importance to determine whether the principal issue before the national court falls within the scope of the Convention. That is the first essential stage in the process of reasoning, which the Commission seems to me to have dispensed with.

48. One can only guess as to the grounds for its view that arbitration is 'only an incidental matter' in this case. Does the Commission mean by that that, *before the English Court*, the appointment of an arbitrator is an incidental issue and the existence of an arbitration agreement the principal issue? If that is its analysis, it represents a spectacular challenge of fundamental procedural concepts. But even such a view can lead to application of the Convention to the dispute before the English court only if it is proved that the question as to the existence of an arbitration agreement falls within the Convention. I have found no answer to those questions in the observations submitted to the Court.

49. The particularly detailed arguments put forward by SII will require much longer consideration by the Court.

50. The view that the Convention is applicable to the present case is

essentially based on two alternative propositions: primarily - and this is a radical analysis in which the Italian company relies in particular on the observations of Mr Schlosser - the Convention *applies to all proceedings* before courts concerning arbitration; consequently, the Court is asked to make a ruling of considerable importance regarding the scope of Article 1(4); in the alternative - and SII's view is based in particular on Mr Jenard's opinion here - the application of the Convention to the present case is justified by the true objectives of the Convention.

51. I shall consider those two arguments successively.

52. The view that the Brussels Convention applies to all court proceedings concerning arbitration has the apparent merit of simplicity. However, it is contradicted by the scheme of the Convention and involves serious difficulties which are not offset by any significant advantage whatsoever.

53. According to Mr Schlosser's opinion, Article 1(4) of the Convention is purely declaratory. In other words, the purpose of that provision is solely to make clear that the Convention does not apply to the recognition and enforcement of arbitration awards. On the other hand, both the jurisdiction of national courts to deal with disputes concerning arbitration and the recognition and enforcement of decisions made on conclusion of such proceedings are said to fall within the scope of the Convention.

54. Contrary to the various reports of the Committees of Experts, that analysis is vitiated in the first place by defective logic if the provision in question is examined. Let me quote an authoritative commentator: 'The Brussels Convention expressly excludes this subject area, by contrast with the Hague Convention on the enforcement of judgments. It is true that conventions which are concerned with the recognition and enforcement of decisions given by national courts and tribunals do not apply, ex hypothesi, to the enforcement of arbitration awards. However, a doubt which did not worry the negotiators in The Hague persisted in the minds of those in Brussels and the latter sought, by means of a formal provision, to eliminate any attempt to provide for the recognition or enforcement of judicial decisions dealing with proceedings concerning arbitration, such as an action for annulment for example. *Moreover, since the Brussels Convention relates to international jurisdiction, it is expressly stated that it does not purport to determine the jurisdiction of courts and tribunals for proceedings concerning arbitration'*.

55. It should also be observed that the very wording of the text supports that analysis. In fact, if Article I of the Convention enumerates in indents 1 (status of persons ...), 2 (bankruptcy ...), 3 (social security...) matters which, although subject to the jurisdiction of the courts, are excluded from the Convention, it is logical that the fourth and final indent of the same provision should have the same effect on matters brought before national courts. If the exclusion of arbitration was merely declaratory, as contended by SII and Mr Schlosser - in other words if its purpose were merely to recall what was self-evident, namely that the Convention on jurisdiction and recognition and enforcement of judgments does not apply to arbitration proceedings or to the recognition and enforcement of arbitration awards - then the scheme of the text would lack coherence.

56. SII's argument is clearly undermined by the various reports of the Committees of Experts. The Jenard Report in the first place: 'The Brussels Convention does not apply to the recognition and enforcement of arbitral awards... ; it does not apply for the purpose of determining the jurisdiction of courts and tribunals in respect of litigation relating to arbitration - for example, proceedings to set aside an arbitral award, and, finally, it does not apply to the recognition of judgments given in such proceedings'.

57. Then the Schlosser Report, more clearly still: '... the 1968 Convention does not cover court proceedings which are ancillary to arbitration proceedings, for example, the appointment or dismissal of arbitrators, the fixing of the place of arbitration, the extension of the time-limit for making awards or the obtaining of a preliminary ruling on questions of substance as provided under English law in the procedure known as 'statement of special case' (Section 21 of he Arbitration Act 1950). In the same way a judgment determining whether an arbitration agreement is valid or not, or because it is invalid, ordering the parties not to continue the arbitration proceedings, is not covered by the 1968 Convention. Nor does the 1968 Convention cover proceedings and decisions concerning applications for the revocation, amendment, recognition and enforcement of arbitration awards'.

58. It should also be noted that, according to the latter report, it was clear to all the States that were parties to the Convention that the exclusion relates at least to 'proceedings before national courts... if they refer to arbitration proceedings, whether concluded, in progress or to be started'. That indeed was the entirely unambiguous position of the original States, although it was regarded as more restrictive than the United Kingdom's position concerning the difficulty to which I have referred.

59. Finally, the Evrigenis and Kerameus Report: 'Proceedings which are directly concerned with arbitration as the principal issue, for example cases where the court is instrumental in setting up the arbitration body, judicial annulment or recognition of the validity or the defectiveness of an arbitration award, are not covered by the Convention'.

60. Legal writers agree that the Convention does not apply to disputes relating to arbitration. The only disputed point concerns the difficulty with which I have already dealt, concerning the recognition and enforcement under the Brussels Convention of a judgment which disposes of the substance of a dispute despite the existence of an arbitration agreement. But even in the view of those authors who favour application of the Convention in such cases, all disputes concerning arbitration fall outside the scope of the Convention.

61. Since the wording of the Convention is supported by a complete Convergence of views in the reports of the Committees of Experts - giving rise, it must be emphasized, to legitimate expectations in the circles affected - there would, it seems to me, have to be solid substantive reasons for the radical solution now advocated by Mr Schlosser to be seriously considered. However, when reviewed, the reasons put forward to justify that view are highly debatable.

62. The thesis put to the Court invokes in particular the lack of continuity that would exist between the Brussels Convention and international conventions

if the Brussels Convention were not applicable to disputes concerning arbitration brought before courts and tribunals.

63. In the first place, let me observe that, in the opinion of Professor Schlosser himself, 'Very often in practice arbitral awards have been enforced extra-territorially despite the fact that some other court (namely the court of the place where the arbitration was conducted) had previously interfered in the arbitration proceedings by, for example, appointing an arbitrator. The courts in the country of enforcement often find it quite normal and self-evident that the courts at the place of arbitration have jurisdiction over the arbitration proceedings if the judicial measures at issue are familiar to other legal regimes. Problems of the integrity of such kind of judicial proceedings, such as the fair hearing to both parties involved in arbitration, apparently have never arisen. Therefore very often no attention has been paid to the issue whether judgments relating to arbitration must really be recognized in another country under the respective bilateral treaty'.

64. However, Professor Schlosser does not seem satisfied by the apparently efficient pragmatic approach adopted by the various national courts. He goes on to say: 'A closer scrutiny of these treaties, however, reveals that this approach is superficial. A judgment relating to arbitration is a judgment like any other. It can be recognized in another country only if a legal basis exists for doing so. Such a legal basis may be found in the respective bilateral treaty'. The author goes on to draw attention to the deficiencies which, in that respect, he perceives in those bilateral treaties,

65. I am far from convinced by that analysis.

66. Whereas the national courts, when recognizing arbitral awards, apparently see no disadvantage in the intervention of national courts at the place where the arbitration takes place, it is nevertheless proposed that the Court adopt a 'revised' reading of the Brussels Convention because close legal examination should prompt the courts to raise difficulties. It does not seem to me to be satisfactory to draw attention to a purely theoretical problem, since it is conceded that in practice the system operates normally, and then to claim that that problem militates in favour of a new interpretation of the Convention. The view expressed by Mr Schlosser and SII would be worthy of note if it constituted a response to indisputable practical preoccupations. However, it is clear that the needs referred to here do not add up to a convincing case.

67. On the one hand, Mr Schlosser refers to the recognition and enforcement of awards merged into judgments - a situation that, according to the author, arises frequently in the United Kingdom - which in his view makes it necessary for the Convention to apply to proceedings concerning arbitration, having regard to the United Kingdom's importance as an arbitration centre. The situation to which Mr Schlosser refers arises where the court or tribunal at the place of arbitration grants an order for enforcement in a special form: judgment is given in terms of the award'.

68. That argument could be dismissed merely by pointing out that the recognition and enforcement of judgments into which an award has 'merged' have in fact not raised any difficulties in the circumstances referred to by Mr

Schlosser. In any event, that is what appears from the judgments mentioned by him in which a decision had to be given on enforcement in such circumstances.

69. But to that practical finding must be added a more fundamental legal observation. Under the New York Convention, there is no doubt that, where an award is merged into a judgment, the award can as such be recognized. Indeed, 'The fact that the leave for enforcement has the effect of absorbing the award in the country of origin is a technical aspect for the purposes of enforcement within that country. The award can therefore be deemed to remain a cause of action for enforcement in other countries'. Accordingly, the 'merger' of the award must be regarded as limited to the territory of the court which delivered the judgment and only the award must be taken into account for the purpose of recognition and enforcement in other States. In any event,it is clear that the solution of limiting recognition only to the judgment in which the award is 'merged' must be rejected.

70. However, the prevailing trend in legal literature and case-law is to grant the beneficiary of a 'merged' arbitral award an option between the possibility of enforcing the award itself under the New York Convention or of enforcing the judgment under bilateral conventions or domestic law. In those circumstances, the successful party always retains the possibility of securing recognition and enforcement of the arbitral award, under the New York Convention, even if the award has been 'merged'. The difficulty referred to by Mr Schlosser does not in fact arise unless only the judgment can be recognized. That is not the solution adopted by the courts. The advantages claimed in that respect by Mr Schlosser are not therefore persuasive.

71. Furthermore, Mr Schlosser refers to the interest in applying the Convention to recognition of judgments which annul an arbitral award. There again, the need referred to - somewhat laconically - by Mr Schlosser appears far from pressing. Article V(e) of the New York Convention specifically provides for the possibility of refusal of recognition and enforcement of the arbitral award where it 'has been set ... by a competent authority of the country in which, or under the law of which, that award was made', and Article IX of the 1961 European Convention, for its part, states that an order for enforcement of an arbitral award may be withheld on a limited number of specific grounds of annulment. Recognition of a judgment annulling an arbitral award appears therefore to be governed by those provisions.

72. I confess that I do not see therefore for what reason it would be 'desirable' to apply the Brussels Convention to judgments annulling arbitral awards. Perhaps Mr Schlosser has in mind those cases where an award has been annulled by the courts of a State other than that in whose territory the award was made? It remains to be shown that it is desirable for such judgments to enjoy 'transnational' recognition. It would be inappropriate not to mention here the analysis according to which the courts of the 'country of origin' have exclusive jurisdiction to annul the award. Against that background, there can be no question therefore of invoking the need to recognize judgments annulling awards made in other States.

73. But reference must be made above all to the clear trend obtaining at the present time, which inspires certain national legislation, to challenge the very need systematically to recognize judgments annulling arbitration awards. A feature of that trend is to recognise only review by the courts in whose territory enforcement is to be pursued, in order to ensure the maximum effectiveness of arbitral awards. It is obvious that the automatic transnational recognition of judgments annulling arbitral awards, referred to by Mr Schlosser, goes directly against those objectives. '...those who consider that the international arbitrator makes awards in accordance with a specific legal order, the *lex mercatoria* cannot think of making recognition and enforcement of the award in the territory of a State conditional on the view expressed by another State legal order: such a solution could only be accounted for by intrinsic inferiority of the *lex mercatoria* by comparison with national laws'. The positive law of certain European States is based on such views, for example where it excludes actions for the annulment of an international arbitral award delivered within national territory (Article 1717 of the Belgian Judicial Code) or, again, by not providing that annulment of an arbitral award in its State 'of origin' is a ground for refusal of an order for enforcement (Article 1502 of the new French Code of Civil Procedure). The latter solution shows how the view put forward by Mr Schlosser runs counter to such approaches. It is sufficient to bear in mind that the Brussels Convention would require the courts of every Member State to recognize judgments annulling an international arbitral award.

74. Finally, according to SII, Article 11(3) - of the New York Convention 'says nothing at all about the recognition and enforcement' of a decision that there is no arbitration agreement. The provision at issue provides: 'The Court of a Contracting State, when seized of an action in a matter in respect of which the parties have made an agreement within the meaning of this article, shall, at the request of one of the parties, refer the parties to arbitration, unless it finds that the said agreement is null and void, inoperative or incapable of being performed'. In that respect, SII concedes that clearly there is no difficulty if the court considers that an arbitration agreement exists. In such a case, the parties will be referred to arbitration.

75. On the other hand, if the Court concludes that no arbitration agreement exists, is there a need to recognize such a judgment which is so imperative as to justify application of the Brussels Convention to disputes concerning arbitration? In the first place, in the event of a national court's deciding, as an incidental issue, that an arbitration agreement exists or is invalid, thereupon concluding that it has jurisdiction and then adjudicating on a dispute falling within the scope of the Brussels Convention, the application of the latter to the recognition and enforcement of such a judgment again raises the question which was considered at the time of the United Kingdom's accession. But, even if it were assumed that it was appropriate to decide that such a judgment was covered by the Brussels Convention, that solution certainly does not make it necessary for the Convention to apply to all disputes concerning arbitration brought before the courts. As we have seen, the original States, which favoured such a solution, also clearly considered that the exclusion extended to proceedings before

national courts relating to arbitration procedures which had been concluded, were pending or were yet to be started.

76. Finally, let us consider - although SII has not cited a case where this problem has arisen - the question of recognition or otherwise of a judgment dealing, as a principal issue, with the existence and validity of an arbitration agreement. The difficulty might be as follows. Before commencing any litigation, a party applies to a court in State A to give a decision on the validity of an arbitration agreement and obtains a judgment finding that it is invalid. A difference having arisen between the parties, that judgment is produced in State B where the arbitration proceedings are commenced. Is it desirable to apply to such a judgment the rules regarding recognition under the Convention? That judgment may have been delivered elsewhere than at the place of arbitration. The possibility that several national courts might give a decision on an arbitrator's jurisdiction has been dealt with by academic writers, whose conclusions on this point, it seems to me, very clearly favour assessments made by the courts of the place of arbitration by reason of their neutrality.

'A. International recognition of the first judgment given by a national court ... Judgments given in response to an objection of lack of jurisdiction raised in order to resist a substantive claim likewise hardly qualify for international recognition, since their direct purpose of the dispute. But that in itself ensures the all-important neutrality. In any event there is no alternative if the aim is to endeavour to centralize control in order to harmonize decisions at international level'. It must be stated that that solution will not be promoted by application of the Brussels Convention, which would allow recognition of any judgment given by any court in a contracting State without any special attention being paid to the courts of the place of arbitration. Harmonization of the solutions adopted by national courts does not constitute an aim in itself, at the expense of the specific features of the area concerned.

77. If the Brussels Convention is applied to disputes concerning arbitration, there is a great risk that solutions will be arrived at which, although doubtless in harmony with each other, would be wholly inappropriate to the specific needs of international arbitration. The unsuitability of the Brussels Convention in that respect casts doubt on the advantages attributed to it by SII. Moreover, that unsuitability is illustrated by a major disadvantage. By virtue of a well-established practice, courts at the place of arbitration give their support and assistance to the arbitration process: appointment of an arbitrator, protective measures, interim measures and measures for the obtaining of evidence. 'For example, the assistance of a national court may be needed for the appointment, replacement or challenge of an arbitrator. It is a generally accepted principle of the international division of judicial competence that the court of the country under the arbitration law of which the arbitration is to take, is taking, or took place, is the competent authority in relation to arbitration'. Such collaboration between national courts at the place where the arbitration is taking place could be severely undermined if the Brussels Convention were to be applied to arbitration. Indeed, it would then be necessary to determine what provision of the Convention conferred jurisdiction on the court at the place of arbitration, This

difficulty has been perfectly described by one author: 'it is right and proper that judicial proceedings connected with the prosecution of an arbitration agreement, such as are mentioned above, should be held to be excluded from the Convention's scope under Article 1, paragraph 2(4), and accordingly be subject to national jurisdiction rules: for, just as the law of the place of arbitration will normally govern the latter proceedings in the absence of a different choice, so too it is believed should courts of the same country be regarded as being particularly appropriate and well- placed to control arbitration activities within its territory at national law; thus, if Convention grounds were to apply to any such court proceedings, the English courts might find themselves unable to adjudicate in respect of English arbitration proceedings where the defendant was domiciled in a foreign contracting state (unless, perhaps, Article 5(1) were able to be construed as affording local jurisdiction)'.

78. Although it denies that the purpose of the exclusion under Article 1(4) is to recognize the jurisdiction of courts at the place of arbitration, SII itself acknowledges that looking for a head of jurisdiction in the Convention is a 'legitimate concern' and in Mr Schlosser's opinion efforts are made to 'construct' jurisdiction for the benefit of the courts at the seat of arbitration on the basis of Articles 5(1) or 17 of the Convention.

79. With respect, first, to Article 5(1), Mr Schlosser states that the parties to an arbitration agreement are required to cooperate to ensure the proper conduct of the arbitration proceedings. The penalty for failure to fulfil those obligations, envisaged by certain authors, implies that there is a place of enforcement for those obligations. According to the opinion, that place must be regarded as being the place of arbitration as a result of the agreement of the parties as to the place of arbitration. Consequently, Article 5(1) confers jurisdiction on the courts at the seat of the arbitration.

80. Strong objections must be made to that proposition, In the first place, an arbitration agreement is an agreement of a procedural nature whose purpose differs fundamentally from that of substantive contracts creating obligations for the parties. 'It is, however, of a different nature from the other provisions of the contract: not merely because the rights which it creates are procedural rather than substantive'. Moreover, many actions commenced before the courts at the seat of arbitration can hardly be regarded as seeking enforcement of an obligation deriving from the arbitration agreement: for example, applications for protective measures and applications for more time to be allowed for the arbitrator to complete his task.

81. Finally, and most importantly, Mr Schlosser himself concedes that the jurisdiction of the court at the seat of arbitration under Article 5(1) cannot be exclusive. Accordingly, he envisages that the courts of a contracting State other than that at the seat of the arbitration may 'give support to arbitration conducted or to be conducted pursuant to the rules of a foreign legal order'. Such an eventuality is not realistic. Could it be imagined, for example, that an English court would agree to take action to support arbitration being conducted in Paris? Mr Schlosser also concedes in that respect that the national courts have almost invariably refused to intervene in arbitration proceedings which are not governed by their own law.

82. As regards the efforts to found jurisdiction on Article 17, they likewise appear open to criticism. It would indeed be dangerous to suggest that an arbitration agreement must be seen as implying a submission to the jurisdiction of the courts at the seat of the arbitration. That solution, advocated by Mr Schlosser, would result in a requirement that arbitration agreements should satisfy the conditions laid down in Article 17 in order to found the jurisdiction of the courts at the seat of the arbitration. It is easy to see what insoluble problems might arise, if Mr Schlosser's thesis were adopted, when measures were sought from courts at the seat of the arbitration. In particular, considerable reservations might be expressed concerning the author's suggestion that Article II(2) of the New York Convention, regarding the *form of the arbitration agreement*, contains the form customarily accepted in international trade, referred to in Article 17 of the Brussels Convention for *agreements conferring jurisdiction*.

83. The complexities which would be associated with the 'discovery in the arbitration agreement of an implied clause conferring jurisdiction on the courts at the place of arbitration render unacceptable that solution, which is put forward in an attempt to palliate the disadvantages of the 'revised' reading of the Convention suggested to the Court.

84. If Articles 5(1) and 17 of the Convention must be interpreted as boldly as Mr Schlosser suggests, it is precisely because the Convention made no provision for any jurisdiction for the courts at the place of arbitration, and the absence thereof is accounted for precisely by the exclusion of arbitration from the scope of the Convention. 'Had it been decided expressly to include such legal proceedings within the Convention's scope, it may have required an additional exclusive jurisdiction ground of courts of place of arbitration in Section 5 of Title II'.

85. The negotiations preceding the United Kingdom's accession to the Brussels Convention clearly showed that for all the contracting States court proceedings relating to arbitration were excluded from the scope of the Convention. The Report on the Accession Convention of 1978 is unequivocal on this point. In the absence of any convincing justification, SII's thesis must, in view of its inherent disadvantages, be firmly rejected.

86. In his opinion, Mr Jenard proposes an apparently less radical solution than Mr Schlosser's since he does not expressly challenge the principle whereby disputes relating to arbitration are excluded from the scope of the Convention. He nevertheless reaches the conclusion that the Convention governs the proceedings before the national court in this case. According to Mr Jenard, the Convention applies to a case where a court with jurisdiction under the Convention has to dispose of the incidental issue of the existence or the validity of an arbitration agreement. He also refers to the judgment of the Court in *Effer*. In the latter case, as we have seen, the Court held that Article 5(1) of the Convention did not cease to apply to proceedings in which a main claim covered by the Convention - for the payment of fees - was contested on the ground that the contract whose performance was sought did not exist. It is unclear how this prompted Mr Jenard to form the view that the proceedings before the national court in this case are nevertheless governed by the Convention. He concedes, in

fact, that the arbitration is 'a main issue' before the English courts. However, the existence of the proceedings pending before the Italian court, in his opinion, renders the Convention applicable to the proceedings brought before the English court. That result, he says, follows from the objectives and the spirit of that instrument.

87. That view gives rise to very strong objections.

88. The question whether or not an action comes within the scope of the Convention is determined by its subject-matter. That is an objective criterion. In order to decide that the Convention is applicable, it is necessary to establish that, *ratione materiae*, a dispute is, by virtue of its particular features, covered by the provisions of the Convention. But in no circumstances can the existence of another action pending before another court entail the result that application of the Convention is extended to the dispute concerned if it was not already covered by the Convention by virtue of its subject-matter. Nevertheless, that is the view advanced by Mr Jenard. That view might in fact lead to the conclusion that the same dispute would come within the scope of the Convention if another action were pending before a court in another contracting State, but on the other hand would not be governed by the Convention if the other proceedings did not exist. The applicability of the Convention to a particular dispute cannot be made subject to variable geometry in that way.

89. According to Mr Jenard's opinion, the scope of the Convention may be shaped to suit different situations in a purely opportunistic manner. For that purpose, it is only necessary to refer to its objectives in order to render it applicable to any dispute, whether or not the latter falls within its purview.

90. Without doubt, the objectives of the Brussels Convention are of decisive importance for the interpretation of those provisions. But a mere reference to those objectives cannot justify neglect of the requirements of legal consistency or total disregard for the consequences which necessarily follow from the logic of the instrument but which are regarded as inconvenient.

91. By saying purely and simply that if two actions, one being concerned principally with arbitration and the other being merely incidental thereto, are pending before the courts of two contracting States, the Convention applies to the first, Mr Jenard seeks, in his Opinion, to evade the conclusion which inevitably follows from the exclusion of arbitration, which, moreover, he does not challenge as a matter of principle.

92. To arrive at the conclusion that the Convention is applicable, it must, as already stated, be established that proceedings fall within its purview. The reliance placed solely on the objectives of the Convention in order to circumvent the impossibility of establishing that fact shows the legal weakness of a position which cannot accept the obvious, namely that the proceedings before the referring court fall outside the scope of the Convention.

93. In view of the answer which I think must be given to the first question, I shall not consider in detail the second and third questions from the Court of Appeal but will merely make a number of brief observations.

94. My analysis of Mr Schlosser's opinion has enabled me to show how the creation of a jurisdiction based on Articles 5(1) or 17 for courts at the seat of

the arbitration appears artificial and inappropriate. In my opinion therefore, if the Court were to uphold the thesis that all disputes relating to arbitration fell within the scope of the Convention, it would ineluctably be compelled to create such a jurisdiction in a praetorian manner.

95. Finally, the Court will not have to answer the question concerning Articles 21 and 22 of the Convention unless it should consider that the Convention governs the proceedings before the referring court and the latter has jurisdiction on the basis of Article 5(1) or Article 17.

96. I would point out in the first place that a situation where an action is pending for the appointment of an arbitrator and another is pending concerning the actual substance of the dispute cannot be described as one of *lis pendens*. The Commission itself, although favouring the Italian company's view, also admits that there is no lis pendens in the present case.

97. With respect to Article 22, I shall not go into the question whether the various conditions imposed by it are satisfied in this case. I shall merely say that, even if that is the case, that provision 'imposes no obligation on the court before which one of the related actions is brought in the second place'. That court is merely *entitled* to stay the proceedings or, if the requirements laid down in the second paragraph of Article 22 are fulfilled, to decline jurisdiction. In other words, in no case can the interpretation of the Convention suggested by SII have the result of *compelling* the referring court to stay the proceedings. To put it another way, the exercise of that entitlement by that court is liable to be influenced by its conviction concerning the correctness of the solution rendering the Convention applicable to the proceedings before it.

98. In other words, a solution which is clearly illogical and contrary to legal certainty, adopted in the name of the objectives of the Convention, would not necessarily lead to the result pursued by those objectives: a decision only by the Italian court as to the existence or otherwise of an arbitration agreement. It would be necessary to find indisputable reasons militating in favour of application of the Convention to the proceedings before the national court. As far as I am concerned, the attempts to do so have been totally unsuccessful.

99. I shall now conclude with a number of general observations. In the first place, there is nothing exceptional about the proceedings before the English court. It often happens that there is a dispute as to whether or not an arbitration agreement exists, a situation which is accounted for particularly by the fact that the enforcement of arbitral awards is today a well-established procedure in the international community.

100. It is recognized that dilatory tactics by a recalcitrant party to arbitration seriously jeopardize the effectiveness of international arbitration. Of course, this is a general observation and I certainly do not intend it to indicate that the attitude of either of the parties to the main proceedings in this case is inspired by such motives. But it must be stated that the application of the Convention to such proceedings would in certain circumstances make available an additional means of 'forum shopping', in breach of the agreement to refer the matter to arbitration.

101. In that connection, a clarification is called for. By deciding that the Brussels Convention does not apply to proceedings concerning arbitration, the

Court will not thereby decide that arbitrators should be left to decide as to their own jurisdiction. It seems that in the present case it may well be the English courts which themselves decide that question. But it must not be forgotten that national laws and the international conventions generally tend to grant arbitrators the right to rule as to their own jurisdiction, although their assessment is always subject to judicial review. That is a trend which the Brussels Convention of course cannot go against. However, application of the Convention to proceedings concerning arbitration might favour certain dilatory manoeuvres where the reluctant party commences proceedings before the court of a contracting State in order to avoid the application of laws of other contracting States which are more favourable to the arbitration process. The place of arbitration is fortuitous. It would be paradoxical if the choice of a seat of arbitration within the Community, where one of the parties is domiciled within the territory of the Community, could slow down the arbitration procedure by operation of the Brussels Convention - which, on the other hand, would not be applicable in any event if the arbitration were to be conducted outside the Community.

102. Finally, SII emphasized the risks of irreconcilability if the application were not applied to the proceedings before the English court. For my part, I am fully convinced that as far as possible it is necessary to arrive at solutions which prevent such risks, but at the same time it is necessary to describe correctly and precisely the context in which this difficulty arises. In the first place, let me say again, the machinery provided by Articles 21 and 22 can be put into operation only within the scope of the Convention. Insofar as the Convention does not apply to certain matters, the risk inevitably arises that there may be irreconcilable decisions in some cases. That inevitably follows from the fact that the authors of the Convention excluded certain matters from its scope. The fact that two courts, one dealing with a case covered by the Convention and the other with a case not so covered, may arrive at a different decision on the same preliminary matter may, in the abstract, appear regrettable. Situations of that type are the result of the exclusions contained in the Convention. The Court has already had occasion to consider cases of irreconcilability between a judgment covered by the Convention and a judgment falling outside its scope. Clearly, in this case, if the Italian court and the English court take differing views as to the existence of an arbitration agreement, the possibility cannot be excluded that in due course, for example, an arbitral award may be made which is irreconcilable with the judgment on the substance of the case delivered in Italy. That possibility must be accepted by the Court.

103. Moreover, irreconcilability between an arbitral award and a national judgment, although obviously not desirable, is susceptible of remedy. The ways of remedying the problem have been set out in a paper dealing with conflicts between judgments and arbitral awards. And its author considered in particular the situation where a judgment protected by the Brussels Convention and an arbitral award conflict and the solutions which would be applicable in such circumstances. In any event, it is clear from that paper that the applicable principles make it possible to say, according to the conflicting situations, whether the judgment or the award should prevail.

104. Finally, let me say that I was not at all concerned by the Commission's observation at the hearing that the solution advocated by it is of a 'Community' character by contrast with the views of the three intervening Member States, according to which the Convention does not apply to the proceedings before the English court. For my part, I see no advantage for the Community in ignoring the specific legal requirements of international arbitration, a universal method of resolving disputes in international trade. Those needs, as I hope I have shown, are not necessarily identifiable with those set out in the Brussels Convention, an instrument which is designed to ensure the proper administration of justice by the State within the Community.

105. Consequently, I propose that the Court give a clear reminder of the scope of the Convention and rule as follows: 'The question of the existence of an arbitration agreement raised before a court called upon to appoint an arbitrator is covered by the exclusion laid down in Article 1(4) of the Convention of 27 September 1968 concerning jurisdiction and the enforcement of judgments in civil and commercial matters'.

Case C-172/91 - 21 April 1993

Volker Sonntag
v
Hans Waidmann and Others

Scope - Civil and commercial matters - Concept of 'civil matters' - Claim brought before a criminal court for compensation for loss caused to an individual by a person committing a criminal offence - Claim brought against a State-school teacher who has failed to fulfil his duty of supervision vis-à-vis his pupils - Included

Enforcement - Remedies - Appeal in cassation and 'Rechtsbeschwerde' -Remedy available to interested third parties under domestic law - Excluded

Recognition and enforcement - Grounds for refusal - Document which instituted the proceedings not served in due form and in sufficient time on defendant in default - Concept of 'default' - Defendant to a civil claim made in the context of criminal proceedings - Appearance to the civil claim precluding default.

Summary

1. A claim for compensation for loss to an individual resulting from a criminal offence, even though made in the context of criminal proceedings, is civil in nature unless the person against whom it is made is to be regarded as a public authority which acted in the exercise of its powers. That is not the case where the activity called in question is the supervision by a State-school teacher of his pupils during a school trip. It follows that 'civil matters' within the meaning of the first sentence of the first paragraph of Article 1 of the Convention of 27 September 1968 on jurisdiction and the enforcement of judgments in civil and commercial

matters covers a claim for damages brought before a criminal court against a State-school teacher who, during a school trip, occasioned loss to a pupil as a result of a culpable and unlawful breach of his duties of supervision, even where there is coverage by a scheme of social insurance under public law.

2. The second paragraph of Article 37 of the Convention must be interpreted as precluding any appeal by interested third parties against the judgment given on an appeal against authorisation to enforce a judgment given in another Contracting State, even where the domestic law of the State in which enforcement is sought confers on such third parties a right of appeal.

3. Since non-recognition of a judgment given in another Contracting State for the reasons set out in Article 27(2) of the Convention is possible only where the defendant was in default of appearance in the original proceedings, that provision may not be relied upon where the defendant appeared. A defendant is deemed to have appeared for the purposes of Article 27(2) of the Convention where, in connection with a claim for damages made in the context of the criminal proceedings pending before the criminal court, the defendant, through defence counsel of his own choice, answered the criminal charges at the trial but did not express a view on the civil claim, on which oral argument was also submitted in the presence of his counsel.

JUDGMENT OF THE COURT

Due, President, Kakouris, Rodrígues Iglesias, Zuleeg, Murray, Presidents of Chambers, Mancini, Joliet, Schockweiler, Moitinho de Almeida, Grévisse, Diez de Velasco, Kapteyn and Edward, Judges

1. By order of 28 May 1991 received at the Court on 1 July 1991, the Bundesgerichtshof (Federal Court of Justice) referred to the Court for a preliminary ruling pursuant to the Protocol of 3 June 1971 on the interpretation by the Court of Justice of the Convention of 27 September 1968 on Jurisdiction and the Enforcement of Judgments in Civil and Commercial Matters (*Journal Officiel* 1972 L 299, p.32), as amended by the Convnetion of 9 October 1978 on the accession of the Kingdom of Denmark, Ireland and the United Kingdom of Great Britain and Northern Ireland (OJ 1978 L 304, p.1, hereinafter 'the Convention') a number of questions on the interpretation of the first paragraph in Articles 1, 27(2) and 37(2) of the Convention.

2. Those questions arose in proceedings between Mr V. Sonntag, supported by the Land Baden-Württemberg, and Mr and Mrs H. Waidmann and their son Stefan Waidmann (hereinafter 'the parties seeking enforcement'), concerning the enforcement in the Federal Republic of Germany of the civil-law provisions of a judgment given by an Italian criminal court.

3. It appears from the documents before the Court that the parties seeking enforcement are the parents and brother of Thomas Waidmann, a pupil in a school administered by the Land Baden-Württemberg who, on 8 June 1984, during a school trip to Italy, suffered a fatal accident in the mountains. Criminal proceedings were brought against the accompanying teacher, Mr Volker Sonntag, in the Bolzano Criminal Court for causing death by negligence.

4. On 22 September 1986 the parties seeking enforcement joined those criminal proceedings as civil parties seeking an order against the accused teacher for compensation for the loss caused by the accident. The court document drawn up for that purpose was served on Mr Sonntag on 16 February 1987.

5. The trial took place before the Bolzano Criminal Court on 25 January 1988. During the hearing Mr Sonntag was represented by counsel. In the judgment given on the same day Mr Sonntag was found guilty of causing death by negligence and ordered to make a provisionally enforceable payment on account of LIT 20 million to the Waidmann family together with costs. The judgment was served on Mr Sonntag and became final.

6. On application by the parties seeking enforcement, the Landgericht (Regional Court) Ellwangen granted them, on 29 September 1989, an order for enforcement of the civil-law part of the judgment of the Bolzano court.

7. Mr Sonntag appealed to the Oberlandesgericht (Higher Regional Court) against that decision and in the course of those proceedings he served notice of the dispute on the Land Baden-Württemberg, contending in that document that if the decision in the proceedings were unfavourable to him, he was entitled under the law governing the civil service to be relieved by the Land Baden-Württemberg of his obligation to pay damages. The Land Baden-Württemberg intervened in the proceedings in support of the form of order sought by Mr Sonntag.

8. The Oberlandesgericht dismissed the appeal on 20 July 1990 on the ground, *inter alia*, that the criminal judgment of the Bolzano court related to a civil matter within the meaning of the first sentence of the first paragraph of Article 1 of the Convention and that the civil claim had been served on Mr Sonntag in sufficient time.

9. Mr Sonntag and the Land Baden-Württemberg appealed to the Bundesgerichtshof against that decision. Both maintained, *inter alia*, that the criminal judgment of the Bolzano court related to a claim under public law, since the supervision of pupils by Mr Sonntag in his capacity as a civil servant was a matter that fell within the province of administrative law. They also considered that the document of 22 September 1986 giving notice of the civil parties' claims was too vague to be regarded as a 'document which instituted the proceedings' within the meaning of Article 27(2) of the Convention.

10. Taking the view that the dispute raised questions regarding the interpretation of the Convention, the Bundesgerichtshof decided to stay proceedings and to refer the following questions to the Court for a preliminary ruling:

'1. Does the second paragraph of Article 37 of the Convention preclude any appeal by interested third parties against the decision given on the appeal under Article 36 of the Convention, even where the domestic law of the State in which enforcement is sought allows such parties to appeal?

2. (a) Where the holder of a public office who has caused injury to another person by reason of an unlawful breach of his official duties is personally sued by that person for damages, does such an action constitute a civil matter within the meaning of the first sentence of the first paragraph of Article 1 of the Convention?

(b) If the question under (a) is answered in the affirmative: is this also the case where the accident is covered under a social insurance scheme governed by public law?

3. If the defendant is given notice by a procedural document that in criminal proceedings a claim will also be made against him for compensation for material and non-material damage, although the document in question gives no additional details of the civil claim which is to be made, is such a document capable of being treated as a 'document which instituted the proceedings' within the meaning of Article 27(2) of the Convention?

4. Has a defendant appeared for the purposes of Article 27(2) of the Convention where a case concerns a civil claim for damages in

connection with charges brought before a criminal court (Article 5(4) of the Convention) and the person against whom enforcement is sought, through counsel of his own choice, answered to the criminal charges but did not express a view on the civil claim, on which oral argument was also submitted in the presence of his counsel?

11. Reference is made to the Report for the Hearing for a fuller account of the facts of the case before the national court, the procedure and the written observations submitted to the Court, which are mentioned or discussed hereinafter only insofar as is necessary for the reasoning of the Court.

12. Insofar as the questions referred by the national court concern the interpretation of a number of provisions of the Convention, the first point for consideration is whether the action for damages which has given rise to the dispute in this case, as described in the order for reference, falls within the scope of the Convention. Accordingly, the second question must be answered first.

The second question

13. The wording of the question submitted and the grounds of the order for reference show that the national court is essentially seeking to ascertain whether 'civil matters' within the meaning of the first sentence of the first paragraph of Article 1 of the Convention cover a claim for damages made before a criminal court against a teacher in a State school who, during a school trip, caused injury to a pupil through a culpable and unlawful breach of his duties of supervision, and whether this is so even where cover is provided under a social scheme governed by public law.

14. In order to answer that question, it is necessary first to determine whether a claim for damages made before a criminal court may fall within the scope of the Convention.

15. In the words of the first paragraph of Article 1, the Convention 'shall apply in civil and commercial matters whatever the nature of the court or tribunal'.

16. It follows from the wording of that provision that the Convention also applies to decisions given in civil matters by a criminal court.

17. It must next be determined whether an action for damages against a

teacher in a State school who caused injury to a pupil during a school trip as a result of a breach of his official duties constitutes a 'civil matter' within the meaning of the first sentence of the first paragraph of Article 1 of the Convention.

18. As the Court has consistently held (see, in particular, Case 29/76 *LTU* v *Eurocontrol* [1976] ECR 1541, paragraphs 3 and 4; Case 133/78 *Gourdain* v *Nadler* [1979] ECR 733, paragraph 3; and Case 814/79 *Netherlands* v *Rüffer* [1980] 3807, paragraphs 7 and 8), the concept of 'civil matters' in Article 1 of the Convention must be regarded as an independent concept to be interpreted by reference, first, to the objectives and scheme of the Convention and, secondly, to the general principles which stem from the corpus of the national legal systems.

19. Even though it is joined to criminal proceedings, a civil action for compensation for injury to an individual resulting from a criminal offence is civil in nature. In the legal systems of the Contracting States the right to obtain compensation for injury suffered as a result of conduct regarded as culpable in criminal law is generally recognised as being a civil-law right. That, moreover, is the conception underlying Article 5(4) of the Convention.

20. It follows from the judgments in the *LTU* and *Rüffer* cases, cited above, that such an action falls outside the scope of the Convention only where the author of the damage against whom it is brought must be regarded as a public authority which acted in the exercise of public powers.

21. The first point to be noted in that respect is that the fact that a teacher has the status of civil servant and acts in that capacity is not conclusive. Even though he acts on behalf of the State, a civil servant does not always exercise public powers.

22. Secondly, in the majority of the legal systems of the Member States the conduct of a teacher in a State school, in his function as a person in charge of pupils during a school trip, does not constitute an exercise of public powers, since such conduct does not entail the exercise of any powers going beyond those existing under the rules applicable to relations between private individuals.

23. Thirdly, a teacher in a State school assumes the same functions *vis-à-vis* his pupils, in a case such as that in point in the main proceedings, as those assumed by a teacher in a private school.

24. Fourthly, the Court has already held, although in a different factual and legal context, in Case 66/85 *Lawrie-Blum* v *Land Baden-Württemberg* [1986] ECR 2121, paragraph 28 in conjunction with paragraph 24, that a teacher does not exercise public powers even when he awards marks to pupils and participates in the decisions on whether they should move to a higher class. That must be so a *fortiori* in relation to the duty of a teacher, as a person in charge of pupils, to supervise them during a school trip.

25. Finally, it should be added that even if the activity of supervising pupils is characterised in the Contracting State of origin of the teacher concerned as an exercise of public powers, that fact does not affect the characterisation of the dispute in the main proceedings in the light of Article 1 of the Convention.

26. It follows from all the foregoing considerations that the action for damages brought in the main proceedings against the State-school teacher by the parties seeking enforcement is covered by the term 'civil matters' within the meaning of the first sentence of the first paragraph of Article 1 of the Convention.

27. It still remains to be considered whether that interpretation may be invalidated by the fact that the accident giving rise to the action is covered by a social insurance scheme governed by public law.

28. In that respect, it need only be stated that the availability of insurance cover is irrelevant since the basis of the civil claim, that is to say liability in tort or delict, is not affected by the existence of that public insurance.

29. The answer to the second question referred by the national court must therefore be that 'civil matters' within the meaning of the first sentence of the first paragraph of Article 1 of the Convention covers an action for damages brought before a criminal court against a teacher in a State school who, during a school trip, caused injury to a pupil through a culpable and unlawful breach of his duties of supervision and that this is so even where cover is provided under a social insurance scheme governed by public law.

The first question

30. By this question the national court seeks essentially to ascertain whether the second paragraph of Article 37 of the Convention must be

interpreted as meaning that it precludes any appeal by interested third parties against a judgment given on an appeal brought under Article 36 of the Convention, even where the domestic law of the State in which enforcement is sought confers on such parties a right of appeal.

31. In order to answer that question, it should first be pointed out that according to the first paragraph of Article 36 of the Convention it is the party against whom enforcement is sought who may appeal against the decision authorising enforcement. According to the second paragraph of Article 37(2) of the Convention, in the Federal Republic of Germany the judgment given on the appeal may be contested only by a *Rechtsbeschwerde* (appeal on a point of law).

32. Secondly, the Court has found in favour of a narrow interpretation of the concept 'judgment given on appeal' in Article 37(2) of the Convention and has ruled that under the general scheme of the Convention, and in the light of one of its principal objectives, which is to simplify procedures in the State in which enforcement is sought, that provision cannot be extended so as to enable an appeal in cassation to be lodged against a judgment other than that given on the appeal (Case 258/83 *Brennero* v *Wendel* [1984] ECR 3971, paragraph 15, and Case C-183/90 *Van Dalfsen* v *van Loon* [1991] ECR I-4743, paragraph 19).

33. Finally, the Court made it clear in its judgment in Case 148/84 *Deutsche Genossenschaftsbank* v *Brasserie du Pêcheur* [1985] ECR 1981, paragraph 17), that the Convention has established an enforcement procedure which constitutes an autonomous and complete system, including the matter of appeals, and that it follows that Article 36 of the Convention excludes procedures whereby interested third parties may challenge an enforcement order under domestic law.

34. That principle must also be applied to a subsequent appeal brought under Article 37(2) of the Convention. To preclude an interested party from bringing an appeal under Article 36, whilst allowing that party to intervene at a later stage in the proceedings by means of an appeal under Article 37, would be contrary to the above-mentioned system and also to one of the principal objectives of the Convention which is to simplify the procedure in the State in which enforcement is sought.

35. The answer to the second question referred by the national court must therefore be that the second paragraph of Article 37(2) of the Convention must be interpreted as meaning that it precludes any appeal by interested

third parties against a judgment given on an appeal brought under Article 36 of the Convention, even where the domestic law of the State in which enforcement is sought confers on such third parties a right of appeal.

The third and fourth questions

36. By these last two questions, which must be examined together and which concern the interpretation of Article 27(2) of the Convention, the national court seeks to ascertain, first, whether there is a 'document which instituted the proceedings' within the meaning of that article where the defendant is given notice by a procedural document that he will be called upon, in the context of criminal proceedings, to make reparation for both material and non-material damage, even though that document does not mention the amount of the claim under civil law that will be made against him. Secondly, the national court seeks to ascertain whether a defendant has appeared for the purposes of Article 27(2) of the Convention where, in the context of a claim for compensation joined to criminal proceedings, the defendant, through counsel of his choice, answered at the trial to the criminal charges but did not express a view on the civil claim, on which oral argument was also submitted in the presence of his counsel.

37. Article 27 lists the conditions to which recognition in a Contracting State of judgments given in another Contracting State is subject. Under point 2 of that article it is provided that recognition must be refused 'if the defendant was not duly served with the document which instituted the proceedings or with an equivalent document in sufficient time to enable him to arrange for his defence'.

38. As the Court has consistently held, Article 27(2) is intended to ensure that a judgment is not recognised or enforced under the Convention if the defendant has not had an opportunity of defending himself before the court first seised (Case 166/80 *Klomps* v *Michel* [1981] ECR 1593, paragraph 9, and Case C-123/91 *Minalmet* v *Brandeis* [1992] ECR I-5661, paragraph 18).

39. It follows that non-recognition of a judgment for the reasons set out in Article 27(2) of the Convention is possible only where the defendant was in default of appearance in the original proceedings. Consequently, that provision may not be relied upon where the defendant appeared, at least if he was notified of the elements of the claim and had the opportunity to arrange for his defence.

40. In view of the facts in the main proceedings, it should be recalled that, according to the first paragraph of Article II of the Protocol annexed to the Convention, '[w]ithout prejudice to any more favourable provisions of national laws, persons domiciled in a Contracting State who are being prosecuted in the criminal courts of another Contracting State of which they are not nationals for an offence which was not intentionally committed may be defended by persons qualified to do so, even if they do not appear in person'.

41. Where a defendant, through his counsel, answers at the trial to the charges against him and is aware of the civil-law claim made against him in the context of the criminal prosecution, he must in principle be regarded as having appeared in the proceedings taken as a whole, without there being any need to distinguish between the criminal prosecution and the civil-law claim. This, however, does not preclude the possibility for the defendant to decline to appear in the civil action; but if he does not do so his reply to the criminal charges is to be taken as constituting, at the same time, an appearance for the purposes of the civil-law claim.

42. It is apparent from the order for reference that the counsel chosen by the defendant in the main proceedings raised no objections to the civil claim, even during oral argument on that claim.

43. It follows that in this case the defendant cannot be regarded as being in default of appearance and that Article 27(2) of the Convention must therefore be declared inapplicable. Consequently, it is unnecessary to consider whether there was a document instituting the proceedings within the meaning of that provision.

44. The answer to be given to the national court must therefore be that non-recognition of a judgment for the reasons set out in Article 27(2) of the Convention is possible only where the defendant was in default of appearance in the original proceedings. Consequently, that provision may not be relied upon where the defendant appeared. A defendant is deemed to have appeared for the purposes of Article 27(2) of the Convention where, in connection with a claim for compensation joined to criminal proceedings, he answered at the trial, through counsel of his own choice, to the criminal charges but did not express a view on the civil claim, on which oral argument was also submitted in the presence of his counsel.

On those grounds, the Court, in answer to the questions referred to it by the Bundesgerichtshof, by order of 28 May 1991, hereby rules:

1. Civil Matters' within the meaning of the first sentence of Article 1 of the Convention cover an action for compensation for damage brought before a criminal court against a teacher in a State school who, during a school trip, caused injury to a pupil through a culpable and unlawful breach of his duties of supervision; this is so even where cover is provided under a social insurance scheme governed by public law.

2. Article 37(2) of the Convention must be interpreted as precluding any appeal by interested third parties against a judgment given on an appeal under Article 36 of the Convention, even where the domestic law of the State in which enforcement is sought confers on such third parties a right of appeal.

3. Non-recognition of a judgment for the reasons set out in Article 27(2) of the Convention is possible only where the defendant was in default of appearance in the original proceedings. Consequently, that provision may not be relied upon where the defendant appeared. A defendant is deemed to have appeared for the purposes of Article 27(2) of the Convention where, in connection with a claim for compensation joined to criminal proceedings, he answered at the trial, through counsel of his own choice, to the criminal charges but did not express a view on the civil claim, on which oral argument was also submitted in the presence of his counsel.

OPINION OF MR ADVOCATE GENERAL DARMON

1. By means of the questions it has referred to the Court, the Bundesgerichtshof (Federal Court of Justice) asks the Court to rule on the interpretation of the first sentence of Article 1, Article 27(2) and the second paragraph of Article 37 of the Brussels Convention of 27 September 1968 on Jurisdiction and the Enforcement of Judgments in Civil and Commercial Matters, as amended by the 1978 accession Convention, hereinafter the 'Convention'.

2. The facts which give rise to the main proceedings are as follows.

3. Thomas Waidmann, a pupil in a school administered by the Land Baden-Württemberg, suffered a fatal fall on 8 June 1984 during a school visit to Italy. The accompanying teacher, Mr Volker Sonntag, a German civil servant, was prosecuted by the Italian authorities before the Bolzano criminal court, for causing death by negligence.

4. On 22 September 1986 the victim's parents and brother joined the criminal proceedings as civil parties by a court document served on Mr Sonntag on 16 February 1987, in order to obtain, before the Bolzano court, compensation for both pain and suffering and material damage.

5. On 25 January 1988, at the criminal trial, when Mr Sonntag was legally represented, the civil parties lodged claims in order to obtain a provisionally enforceable payment on account of LIT 20 million together with costs.

6. According to a judgment given on the same day, Mr Sonntag was found guilty of causing death by negligence and ordered to make the provisionally enforceable payment claimed.

7. The judgment was served on Mr Sonntag and, in the absence of an appeal, became final.

8. On 29 September 1989, upon application by the parties seeking enforcement, the Landgericht (Regional Court) Ellwangen made an order for the enforcement of the civil provisions of that judgment.

9. Mr Sonntag appealed against the enforcement under Article 36 of the Convention. In those proceedings he served notice of the dispute on the Land Baden-Württemberg, contending that it must relieve him of his obligations to pay damages, since, in his view, under the law governing the civil service that obligation fell on the *Land* employing him.

10. The Oberlandesgericht (Higher Regional Court) dismissed the appeal, taking the view that the judgment of the Bolzano court concerned a civil matter within the meaning of the first sentence of Article 1 of the Convention.

11. Mr Sonntag and the Land Baden-Württemberg appealed to the Bundesgerichtshof on a point of law on the basis of the second paragraph of Article 37 of the Convention; that court has submitted four questions for a preliminary ruling, which are set out in the Report for the Hearing and which essentially ask the Court to state:

- whether the right of appeal provided for in the second paragraph of Article 37 of the Convention may be exercised by an interested third party where the domestic law of the State in which enforcement is sought allows such a party to contest the judgment in question;
- whether the expression 'civil matters' in the first sentence of Article 1 of the Convention includes an action for damages against a public official who, in breach of the duties with which he was entrusted, has caused injury to another person, and whether this is so even where cover is provided under a social insurance scheme governed by public law;
- whether a procedural document which informs the defendant of the existence of a claim for damages but without specifying the amount claimed is to be regarded as a 'document which instituted the proceedings' within the meaning of Article 27(2) of the Convention.
- whether a defendant against whom a civil action is brought and joined to criminal proceedings - a situation provided for in Article 5(4) of the Convention - must be regarded as having duly appeared within the meaning of Article 27(2) where, at the trial on the substance of the case, and through his

counsel, he answered to the criminal charges but did not express a view on the civil claim, on which oral argument was submitted in the presence of his counsel.

12. It is necessary as a matter of priority to determine the nature of the action brought by the victim's family before the criminal court against an agent of the State. Whether or not the Convention may apply to the facts in issue depends on the answer to that question. I shall therefore begin with the second question.

13. By virtue of Article 1, the Convention is to apply in civil matters 'whatever the nature of the court or tribunal'. It follows that the nature of the court or tribunal cannot serve as a criterion and that the scope of the Convention includes the civil provisions of a judgment delivered by a criminal court.

14. Even though it is joined to criminal proceedings, a civil action for compensation for damage caused by a criminal offence loses none of its civil character. Consequently, a judgment given by a criminal court can be recognised and enforced in the territory of the other Contracting States as regards its civil provisions.

15. The report by Mr Jenard confirms that the authors of the Convention expressly intended to bring this type of proceeding within its scope.

'The Convention covers civil proceedings brought before criminal courts, both as regards decisions relating to jurisdiction, and also as regards the recognition and enforcement of judgments given by criminal courts in such proceedings.'

16. That is also apparent from Article 5(4) of the Convention, which provides that: 'A person domiciled in a Contracting State may, in another Contracting State, be sued: ... as regards a civil claim for damages or restitution which is based on an act giving rise to criminal proceedings, in the court seised of those proceedings, to the extent that that court has jurisdiction under its own law to entertain civil proceedings.'

17. But are the rules on jurisdiction the same where the person responsible for the damage is, like Mr Sonntag, the 'holder of a public office'? Do the proceedings still relate to 'civil matters'? Or do they concern 'administrative matters', which are precluded by Article 1 of the Convention?

18. That article sets out a positive and negative definition of the substantive scope of the Convention: 'This Convention shall apply in civil and commercial matters whatever the nature of the court or tribunal. It shall not extend, in particular, to revenue, customs or administrative matters ...'.

19. However, Article 1 does not define what is meant by 'civil matters'. The Brussels Convention is not alone in that respect:

it is an approach shared by many multilateral and bilateral treaties.

20. Whilst it is rare in a bilateral context to draw up an exhaustive list of matters coming under civil or commercial law, such an approach is even less conceivable in the wider context formed by the corpus of the signatory States, owing to the diversity of their legal systems.

21. The special nature of the Convention, however, is the result of its link with the EEC Treaty, which must also make it possible to establish 'closer relations between the States belonging to [the Community]'.

22. In order to achieve a uniform application of the rules on jurisdiction in the Contracting States and, in doing so, to maintain cohesion in the interpretation of the law, it is therefore necessary to develop an independent definition of the matters falling within the sphere of private law. In that respect, the case-law of the Court has certainly been extremely innovative.

23. It was in that sense that the Court stated in its judgment in *LTU* v *Eurocontrol* that: 'The concept in question must therefore be regarded as independent and must be interpreted by reference, first, to the objectives and scheme of the Convention and, secondly, to the general principles which stem from the corpus of the national legal systems'.

In the same decision the Court went on to state that:

'If the interpretation of the concept is approached in this way ..., certain types of judicial decision must be regarded as excluded from the area of application of the Convention, either by reason of the legal relationships between the parties to the action or of the subject-matter of the action'.

Having laid down this principle of interpretation, the Court went on to apply it in these terms: 'Although certain judgments given in actions between a public authority and a person governed by private law may fall within the area of application of the Convention, this is not so where the public authority acts in the exercise of its powers'.

24. This approach to the interpretation of the concept of civil matters within the meaning of the Convention was restated and explained in the *Netherlands* v *Rüffer* judgment, the facts of which merit a brief description.

25. The Netherlands State had brought proceedings against Mr Rüffer, a German waterman, to recover the costs incurred in that State in removing a wreck owned by him. The Hoge Raad der Nederlanden had referred a question to the Court for a preliminary ruling on the nature of the proceedings.

26. In order to determine whether the State had acted within the framework of its public powers, the Court analysed not only the objective of the action and the nature of the links between the parties but also the general principles stemming from the corpus of the national legal systems of the Contracting States.

27. Therefore, unlike the German Government, I do not believe that it is sufficient to consider the classification of the dispute only from the viewpoint of domestic law. On the contrary, it is essential to derive from the legal systems of all the signatory States a general principle for determining whether such proceedings constitute a 'civil matter'.

28. It should be observed at once that the law of the common law countries rarely allows the victim to take part in proceedings before the criminal courts. In those courts the victim does not take part in the proceedings as the 'civil party' even when a compensation order is sought. In order to obtain compensation for the damage suffered he must bring proceedings before the civil courts and the author of the damage will be judged in accordance with the rules of civil law. The concept of administrative law does not, moreover, apply in those countries.

29. With regard to the Continental legal systems, the fact that criminal proceedings are brought against the holder of a public office may, it is true, affect the conditions for bringing a civil action, and even call in question the expedience of bringing such an action against the official, but in general has no effect on the characterisation of the proceedings on the substance of the case.

30. Accordingly, in Denmark a civil claim in criminal proceedings can be pursued only against the person who actually caused the injury. The claim for damages will be pursued against the public employer in the civil courts and the proceedings retain their civil character.

31. In Spain a person who has committed a criminal offence may be sued in the civil or criminal courts. Where the person concerned is an official the same rules apply, but the vicarious liability of the State may be invoked before the same courts.

32. In Belgium, a civil claim against an official and against the State is governed exclusively by civil law and is heard by the ordinary courts.

33. The same applies in Italy, where the liability of the State may be incurred if the official has committed the offence in the performance of his duties. The action brought by the victim retains its civil-law character whether claim for damages is made against the official or the State.

34. In Portugal the State is jointly and severally liable, and although acts to which public law applies come within the jurisdiction of the administrative courts, acts of the State in connection with private administration must be sought before the ordinary courts. However, even in the case of acts of public administration the victim may, where there has been a criminal offence, seek reparation from the official alone by making a civil claim which will fall to be examined by the criminal courts.

35. In the Netherlands the victim may obtain reparation exclusively from the State in certain cases and/or against the official; the liability of the authorities and/or the official is determined in accordance with the rules of civil law.

36. In France a special system applies to offences committed by members of the public education system, in which State liability is substituted for that of the official. In the event of personal fault on the part of the official or a fault committed in the course of his duties, the victim can bring proceedings in the ordinary courts, which apply the rules of the Civil Code; the criminal courts are not excluded, and where appropriate the civil claim against the State is joined to the criminal proceedings against the official.

37. In Luxembourg the Constitution does not allow proceedings having civil rights as their subject-matter to be removed from the civil courts. Proceedings are rarely brought against a teacher because the loss is covered by compulsory accident insurance, and the victim can take action only in the event of intentional fault by the person responsible. Notwithstanding that insurance, liability is predominantly civil in nature.

38. In Germany, before the introduction of Article 34 of the Basic Law, the victim has to make a claim (Paragraph 839 of the BGB) against the official in the civil courts, which applied the rules of civil liability. Since that liability was considered particularly onerous, the State itself now assumes sole responsibility

for reparation for damage such as that referred to by the national court, but may, in the event of serious fault, bring recourse proceedings against its official. Academic writing is divided as regards how such an action is to be characterised: some writers consider that it is of a civil nature, while others take the view that it is of a public nature. By a Law of 26 June 1981, the State intended to repeal Paragraph 839 and introduce liability in public law. However, that law was declared unconstitutional by the Bundesverfassungsgericht (Federal Constitutional Court). Although the nature of the victim's claim against the State is uncertain, the ordinary courts nonetheless have sole jurisdiction and apply the rules of civil law.

39. In Greek law, on the other hand, an action of this type must be brought against the official and the State and liability is a matter of public law.

40. Examination of the various national laws therefore shows that the liability of the State and/or of the official is, in almost all of those laws, either of a purely civil nature or of a predominantly private-law nature. There are, however, some special features regarding the circumstances giving rise to and the form of the liability, which may be either excluded or exclusive, or vicarious or joint and several, none of this, however, entailing any change in the nature of the action.

41. Those, then, are the general principles emerging from the legal systems of the various Contracting States. An action of the type in point in this case must therefore be regarded as a civil matter within the meaning of Article 1 of the Convention.

42. Let us now turn to the nature of this action where the accident, like the one to which the national court refers, is covered by a social insurance scheme governed by public law. Can the existence of such a scheme have the effect of altering the original classification of the action?

43. It follows from the judgments in *LTU* v *Eurocontrol* and *Netherlands* v *Rüffer*, cited above, that proceedings do not fall within the scope of the Convention:

- if their subject-matter is an act of a public authority acting in the exercise of public powers;
- if the right on which the proceedings are founded has its source in such an act.

44. In line with that reasoning, it must be considered that where the right on which the action is based originates not in an act of the public authority acting in the exercise of public powers, but in a breach by a public servant of his official duties, the consequences of his liability being borne by an insurance scheme governed by public law, the existence of such insurance, which is not among the criteria established by this Court, cannot exclude from the scope of the Convention an act which, by its nature, falls within it.

45. No derogation from the free movement of judgments can be accepted on the sole ground that a signatory State is involved in a dispute: the concept of administrative matters referred to in Article 1 must be construed narrowly.

46. The Convention does, moreover, refer to such disputes: it covers proceedings concerned with designs, trade marks and patents which may be

brought by a public authority owning intellectual property against a private person (Article 16).

47. Furthermore, the fact that the administrative courts have jurisdiction is not sufficient to preclude proceedings before them from the scope of the Convention. The French and Belgian Conseils d'Etat and the Bundesverwaltungsgericht, among other courts, are empowered under Article 2 of the Protocol on the interpretation of the Convention by the Court of Justice to request the Court to give preliminary rulings on questions of interpretation.

48. That concept of administrative matters must cover only the sphere in which the State is clearly acting in the full exercise of its powers. Here I am adopting the concept of sovereignty referred to in the Schlosser Report: 'In the legal systems of the original Member States, the State itself and corporation exercising public functions such as local authorities may become involved in legal transactions in two ways. Having regard to their special functions and the fact that they are formally part of public law they may act outside private law in a "sovereign" capacity ... The State and public corporations can also incur tortious liability in the same way as private individuals, for example as a result of a traffic accident in which an official car is involved'.

49. I am therefore unable to subscribe to the German Government's assertion that damages claimed from the State arising from 'breach of a public-service obligation' necessarily come under the heading of administrative matters.

50. That concept of 'public service' is undoubtedly recognised in a number of national legal systems, but, in the interest of maintaining uniformity in the law emanating from the Convention, cannot prevail for the purposes of an *independent classification* of administrative matters.

51. As the case-law of the Court makes clear, disputes between a private person and a public person not acting in the exercise of public powers fall within the scope of the Convention, no matter what classification is given to such disputes in national law.

52. A claim against a servant of a signatory State must therefore come within the scope of the Convention when the acts in question do not entail the exercise of public powers.

53. Since the dispute comes within the scope of the Convention, it is necessary to answer the other questions submitted by the Bundesgerichtshof.

54. Let me begin by considering the first of them.

55. May an interested third party contest, under the second paragraph of Article 37, the judgment given on the appeal provided for in Article 36 even though he was merely an intervener in that appeal, where domestic law provides for such an appeal?

56. Such a possibility cannot be accepted, since, in the context of Article 36, the fact that an appeal may be brought by an interested third party under domestic law has never been taken into consideration in the case-law of the Court.

57. It follows from the judgment in the *Deutsche Genossenschaftsbank* case that the principal objective of the Convention is to simplify enforcement procedures:

'In order to attain that objective the Convention established an enforcement procedure which constitutes an autonomous and complete system, including the matter of appeals'.

58. It would therefore be wrong to analyse Article 37 in isolation when the link between that Article and Article 37 is clear.

59. Article 36 determines the persons entitled to appeal against a decision authorising enforcement and the period within which that right must be exercised. Article 37 designates the courts with jurisdiction to determine such appeals (paragraph (1)) and the remedies available against the judgments given by those courts (paragraph (2)).

60. On the other hand, Article 37 does not specify the parties entitled to contest the decision authorising enforcement. It is therefore necessary to refer to the concept of 'party' in Article 36.

61. That narrow construction of Article 37 is consistent with the Court's judgment in the *Brennero* case.

'Under the general scheme of the Convention, and in the light of one of its principal objectives which is to simplify procedures in the State in which enforcement is sought, that provision cannot be extended so as to enable an appeal in cassation to be lodged against a judgment other than that given on the appeal'.

62. The Court also expressly stated in the judgment in *Van Dalfsen* v *van Loon* that the second paragraph of Article 37 must be narrowly construed.

63. As may be seen from the Court's interpretation of Article 36, that provision

'excludes procedures whereby interested third parties may challenge an enforcement order under domestic law'.

Similarly, a third party cannot be allowed to appeal under the second paragraph of Article 37.

64. It is to that effect that I propose that the Court answer the first question.

65. That, in my view, is consistent with the objective of the Convention, which is to facilitate the freedom of movement of judgments within the Community, without however compromising the protection of the rights of third parties.

66. That protection will be fully guaranteed by the national law of each State, not at the stage of the decision authorising enforcement but at the stage of actual enforcement, which does not come within the Convention.

67. As we know, the Convention applies only to proceedings whereby a decision (or an authentic instrument) issued in a Contracting State can be made enforceable in another Contracting State; on the other hand, it leaves the detailed rules regarding execution of the enforcement order to the jurisdiction of the domestic legal orders of the signatory States.

68. The last two questions concern the rules relating to the principle of respect for the rights of defence in Article 27(2) and give the Court its first opportunity to consider the relevance and, possibly, the scope of that provision in a situation where the defendant is not in default of appearance.

69. Allow me briefly to mention the logic of the system underlying the Brussels Convention.

70. The Convention is based on the principle of the recognition of judgments delivered by the national courts with a view to ensuring and facilitating the movement of judgments within the European Community. Thus the free movement of judgments takes its place alongside the four fundamental freedoms set out in the Treaty and bears witness to the Member States' desire to strengthen their links through the Convention.

71. The principle of the recognition of judgments is based on the Member States' mutual trust in their respective legal systems and judicial institutions.

72. This trust allows the Member States to waive their internal rules on the recognition and enforcement of foreign judgments. This prerequisite must remain unassailable, which explains why, for proceedings within the scope of the Convention, review of the legality of the foreign decision is confined to:

- public policy: Article 27(1);
- the rights of the defence: Article 27(2); and
- whether the judgment is irreconcilable with another judgment: Article 27(3).

73. The principle of respect for the rights of the defence is also enshrined in Article 20, which provides that a court is to declare of its own motion that it has no jurisdiction if the defendant fails to enter an appearance unless its jurisdiction is derived from the provisions of the Convention; it also provides that a court is to stay proceedings so long as it is not shown that the defendant in default of appearance was able to receive the document instituting the proceedings in sufficient time to enable him to arrange for his defence.

74. It is also appropriate to refer to Article 46, under which a party seeking recognition or applying for enforcement of a judgment is to produce the original or a certified copy of the document which establishes that the party in default was served with the document instituting the proceedings.

75. Article 27(2) provides that 'a judgment shall not be recognised ... if the defendant was not duly served with the document which instituted the proceedings or with an equivalent document in sufficient time to enable him to arrange for his defence'.

76. Therefore the series of provisions designed to protect the rights of the defence is fundamentally concerned solely with defendants *in default of appearance.*

77. Furthermore, the Jenard Report, it should be noted, refers to such protection only in relation to this category of defendants.

78. However, in order usefully to answer the third question submitted by the Bundesgerichtshof, can there be said to be an infringement of the rights of defence where the document which instituted the proceedings is vague as regards the quantum of the claim, even though the defendant is not in default of appearance?

79. Although, as I have observed, questions have been referred to the Court for a preliminary ruling on Article 27(2), that provision has never been relied upon in favour of a defendant who is not in default of appearance.

80. It certainly seems to follow from the judgment of the Court in *Klomps v Michel* that only the capacity of 'defendant in default of appearance' can justify

the applicability of Article 27(2). The Court stated that that provision 'is intended to ensure that a judgment is not recognised or enforced under the Convention *if the defendant has not had an opportunity of defending himself before the court first seised'*.

81. That objective of protecting a defendant in default of appearance was repeated in the *Minalmet* judgment, according to which 'Article 27, point 2, of the Brussels Convention is intended to protect the rights of the defence and to ensure that a judgment is not recognised or enforced under the Convention if the defendant has not had an opportunity of defending himself before the court first seised'.

82. In order to be applicable, Article 27(2) necessarily implies, in my view, that the defendant is in default of appearance, and must have been found to be so by the court of the State where the proceedings were first brought; I shall attempt to define 'in default' below, in relation to the final question referred by the Bundesgerichtshof.

83. If a defendant who has appeared were able to rely on that provision, then the court of the State in which enforcement is sought would be empowered to review the finding, already made, after an *inter partes* hearing by the court of the State in which the judgment was given, that the proceedings before it were in no way defective.

84. It cannot in such circumstances be permissible to review the questions whether the notice to appear was in order or served in sufficient time for the party concerned to arrange for his defence. The defendant, or his counsel, had the opportunity before that court to object that the document instituting the proceedings was defective and to submit defence arguments going both to admissibility and the merits. He was also in a position to make use of the legal remedies available to him if the decision appeared unfavourable to him.

85. That, moreover, is the position adopted by Messrs Gothot and Holleaux, among others, who express themselves as follows: 'The question whether the proceedings before the court first seised were defective may be reviewed only in the case of the recognition and enforcement of judgments given in default ... It is therefore only when the court before which enforcement is sought is faced with a judgment given following proceedings of an *inter partes* nature before the court first seised, but in which the defendant was in default of appearance, that it is necessary to verify whether the document which instituted the proceedings or an equivalent document was served or notified in proper form and in sufficient time to enable the defendant to arrange for his defence'.

86. Similarly, Mr Droz considers that: 'The judgment must have been given in default. ... Article 27(2) refers only to cases where the defendant is in default of appearance. In the Convention the view seems to be taken that if the defendant has appeared, even belatedly, he will have been able to assert his rights and, in particular, request and obtain the necessary time to prepare his defence ...'

87. Under those circumstances, Article 27(2) must be declared inapplicable where the defendant is not in default of appearance.

88. However, is that necessarily so in the case of a defendant who, intentionally or inadvertently, did not express a view on the civil claim?

89. That is the subject-matter of the fourth and final question.

90. Article 27, point 2, does not define what is meant by 'default of appearance'.

91. Must that term be defined independently or with reference to the domestic law of the State in which the judgment was given?

92. It would appear that, since that concept depends on the assessment made by the court first seised under its domestic law, it must be interpreted by reference to that law.

93. I would refer, here again, to the judgment in *Klomps* v *Michel.* The Court had to decide whether a judgment given in default had to be regarded as such even though the party against whom enforcement was sought had lodged an objection against that decision and that objection had been adjudged inadmissible by the court of the State in which the judgment was given.

94. The Court held that: 'In the case with which the question is concerned the defendant did not submit a defence as to the substance of the case before the court first seised. The dismissal of the objection to the enforcement order as inadmissible means that the decision given in default remains intact. For that reason the objective of Article 27, point 2, requires that in the case with which this question is concerned the court in the State in which enforcement is sought should carry out the examination prescribed by that provision.

The reply ... should therefore be that Article 27, point 2, remains applicable where the defendant has lodged an objection against the decision given in default and *a court of the State in which the judgment* was given has held the objection to be inadmissible on the ground that the time for lodging an objection has expired'.

95. The Court therefore considered that it was the defendant's default, as determined by the court of the State in which the judgment was given, that enabled the court in which enforcement was sought to apply Article 27(2).

96. Likewise, it follows from the judgment in *Lancray* v *Peters* that '[t]he Brussels Convention does not determine which law is to be applied to that question [whether the document instituting the proceedings was properly served]. Since the rules governing the service of the document instituting the proceedings *form part of the procedure before the court of the State in which judgment was given,* the question whether service was duly effected can only be answered by reference to *the law to be applied by that court,* including any relevant international conventions'.

97. It is therefore by application of the law of the State in which judgment was given that it must be determined whether or not a defendant was in default of appearance.

98. Provided that the defendant appeared according to the law of the State in which the judgment was given, the decision cannot be regarded as being given in default of appearance; in that connection there is no need to take into consideration the fact that the defendant, whether intentionally or inadvertently, failed to respond to the claims of the civil parties.

99. I therefore propose that the Court rules as follows:

(1) The concept of 'civil and commercial matters' within the meaning of

the first paragraph of Article 1 of the Convention of 27 September 1968 on jurisdiction and the enforcement of judgments in civil and commercial matters includes proceedings in which an individual seeks compensation for loss caused by the breach by a public servant of the duties entrusted to him, notwithstanding the fact that the consequences are covered by insurance governed by public law.

(2) Article 37(2) of the Convention precludes any appeal by interested third parties against a judgment given in pursuance of Article 36 of the Convention even though such a remedy is available to those third parties under the law of the State in which enforcement is sought.

(3) Article 27(2) of the Convention is not applicable where the defendant was not in default of appearance in the proceedings before the court first seised; the concept of default of appearance is to be assessed according to the law of the State in which the judgment was given.

Case C-220/95 - 27 February 1997

Antonius van den Boogaard
v
Paula Laumen

Article 1, second paragraph - Scope - Civil and commercial matters - Matters relating to maintenance - Decisions rendered in divorce proceedings ordering payment of a lump sum and transfer of ownership in certain property - Included - Conditions.

Summary

1. If the reasoning of a decision rendered in divorce proceedings shows that the provision which it awards is designed to enable one spouse to provide for himself or herself of if the needs and resources of each of the spouses are taken into consideration in the determination of its amount, the decision will be concerned with maintenance and will therefore fall within the scope of the Convention of 27 September 1968 on Jurisdiction and the Enforcement of Judgments in Civil and Commercial matters, as amended by the Convention of 9 October 1978 on the Accession of the Kingdom of Denmark, Ireland and the United Kingdom of Great Britain and Northern Ireland and by the Convention of 25 October 1982 on the Accession of the Hellenic Republic. On the other hand, where the provision awarded is solely concerned with dividing property between the spouses, the decision will be concerned with rights in property arising out of a matrimonial relationship and will not therefore be enforceable under the Brussels Convention. A decision which does both these things may, in accordance with Article 42 of the Brussels Convention, be enforced in part if it clearly shows the aims to which the different parts of the judicial provision correspond.

2. It follows that a decision rendered in divorce proceedings ordering payment of a lump sum and transfer of ownership in certain property by one party to his or her former spouse must be regarded as relating to maintenance and therefore as falling within the scope of the Convention if its purpose is to ensure the former spouse's maintenance. The fact that in its decision the court of origin disregarded a marriage contract is of no account in this regard.

JUDGMENT OF THE COURT

Moitinho de Almeida, President of the Fifth Chamber, Gulmann, Edward, Puissochet and Jann, Judges

1. By a judgment of 14 June 1995, received at the court on 21 June 1995, the Arrondissementsrechtbank te Amsterdam referred to the Court from a preliminary ruling under the Protocol of 3 June 1971 on the interpretation by the Court of Justice of the Convention of 27 September 1968 on Jurisdiction and the Enforcement of Judgments in Civil and Commercial Matters, as amended by the Convention of 9 October 1978 on the accession of the Kingdom of Denmark, Ireland and the United Kingdom of Great Britain and Norther Ireland (OJ 1978 L 304, p.77) and by the Convention of 25 October 1982 on the Accession of the Hellenic Republic (OJ 1982 L 388, p. 1, hereinafter 'the Brussels Convention'), a question on the interpretation of Article 1 of that Convention.

2. The question has been raised in proceedings between Antonius van den Boogaard and Paula Laumen concerning an application for enforcement, in the Netherlands, of a judgment given on 25 July 1990 by the High Court of Justice of England and Wales.

3. According to the order of reference, Mr Van den Boogaard and Miss Laumen were married in the Netherlands in 1957 under the regime of community of property. In 1980, they entered into a marriage contract, again in the Netherlands, which altered their matrimonial regime into one of separation of goods. In 1982, they moved to London. By judgment of 25 July 1990, the High Court dissolved the marriage and also dealt with an application made by Miss Laumen for full ancillary relief. Since the wife sought a 'clean break' between herself and her husband, the English court awarded her a capital sum so that periodic payments of maintenance would be unnecessary. It also held that the Netherlands separation of goods agreement was of no relevance for the purposes of its decision in the case.

4. In its decision the High Court set the total amount which Miss Laumen should be awarded in order to provide for herself at £875000. Part of that amount, £535000, was covered by her own funds, by the sale of moveable property, by the transfer of painting and, finally, by the transfer of immovable property. For the rest, the English court ordered Mr Van den Boogaard to pay Miss Laumen a lump sum of £340000, to which was added £15000 to meet the costs of earlier proceedings.

5. By application lodged on 14 April 1992 at the Arrondissementsrechtbank te Amsterdam, Miss Laumen sought enforcement of the English judgment, relying on the Hague Convention of 2 October 1973 on the Recognition and Enforcement of Decisions relating to Maintenance Obligations (hereinafter 'the Hague Convention').

6. On 21 May 1992 the President of the Arrondissementsrechtbank granted that application.

7. On 19 July 1993 Mr Van den Boogaard appealed against the grant of leave to enforce.

8. The Arrondissementsrechtbank te Amsterdam, which had jurisdiction to hear and determine that appeal, was uncertain whether the High Court's judgment of 25 July 1990 was to be classified as a 'judgment given in matters relating to maintenance', in which case leave to enforce would be properly granted, or whether it was to be classified as a 'judgments given in a matter relating to right in property arising out of a matrimonial relationship', in which case the Hague Convention could provide no basis for enforcement.

9. The Amsterdam Court considered that the High Court's judgment had such consequences for the parties' relations as regards as property rights that it could not be regarded as a 'decision in respect of maintenance obligations' within the meaning of Article 1 of the Hague Convention. It therefore considered that enforcement was not to be granted on the basis of that Convention. It then went on to consider whether the Brussels Convention could provide a basis for granting leave for enforcement.

10. Article 1 of the Brussels Convention provides: 'This Convention shall apply in civil and commercial matters whatever the nature of the court or tribunal. It shall not extend, in particular, to revenue, customs or administrative matters. The Convention shall not apply to:

1. the status or legal capacity of natural persons, rights in property arising out of a matrimonial relationship, wills and successions; ...'.

11. Article 5 of the Convention provides: 'A person domiciled in a Contracting State may, in another Contracting State, be sued:

1. ... ; 2. in matters relating to maintenance, in the courts for the place where the maintenance creditor is domiciled or habitually resident or, if the matter is ancillary to proceedings concerning the status of a person, in the court which, according to its own law, has jurisdiction to entertain those proceedings, unless that jurisdiction is based solely on the nationality of one of the parties; ...'.

12. The first paragraph of Article 57 of the Brussels Convention provides: 'This Convention shall not affect any conventions to which the Contracting States are or will be parties and which, in relation to particular matters, govern jurisdiction or the recognition or enforcement of judgments'.

13. Article 23 of the Hague Convention is worded as follows: 'This Convention shall not restrict the application of an international instrument in force between the State of origin and the State addressed or other law of the State addressed for the purpose of obtaining recognition or enforcement of a decision or settlement'.

14. Unsure about the interpretation to be given to the Brussels Convention, the Arrondissementsrechtbank te Amsterdam referred the following question to the Court for a preliminary ruling: 'Must the decision of the English judge, which in any case relates in part to a maintenance obligation, be regarded as a decision which relates (in part) to rights in property arising out of a matrimonial relationship within the meaning of indent 1 of the second paragraph of Article 1 of the Brussels Convention even though: (a) the income requirement is capitalized; (b) an order was made to transfer the house and the De Heem painting which, according to the decision, belong to the husband; (c) in his decision, the English judge himself expressly stated that he did not regard the marriage settlement as binding; (d) it cannot be made out from that decision to what extent the factor mentioned in (c) influenced the English judge's decision?'

15. By this question the national court is asking in substance whether a decision rendered in divorce proceedings ordering payment of a lump sum and transfer of ownership in certain property by one party to his or

her former spouse is excluded from the scope of the Brussels Convention by virtue of point 1 of the second paragraph of Article 1 thereof on the ground that it relates to rights in property arising out of a matrimonial relationship, or whether it may be covered by that Convention on the ground that it relates to maintenance. It also inquires whether the fact that the court of origin disregarded a marriage contract in arriving at his decision is relevant.

16. As a preliminary point, it must be observed that at the hearing it was asserted that Mr Van den Boogaard had lodged an appeal after the two-month period laid down in Article 36 of the Brussels Convention for appealing against decisions authorizing enforcement had expired. That fact does not affect in any way the Court's jurisdiction to give a preliminary ruling since, according to settled case-law, it is solely for national courts before which disputes are brought and which must assume responsibility for the subsequent judicial decision, to determine in the light of the particular circumstances of each case both the need for a preliminary ruling in order to enable them to deliver judgment and the relevance of the questions which they submit to the Court (see the judgment in Case C-127/92 *Enderby* [1993] ECR I-5535, paragraph 10).

17. It must also be observed that, for the reasons explained by the Advocate General in paragraphs 24 to 29 of his Opinion, the Hague Convention, by virtue of Article 23 thereof, does not preclude application of the Brussels Convention, notwithstanding Article 57 of the latter Convention.

18. It is common ground that the Brussels Convention does not define 'rights in property arising out of a matrimonial relationship' or 'maintenance'. These two terms must be distinguished, however, since only maintenance is covered by the Brussels Convention.

19. As is stated in the Schlosser Report, in no legal system of a Member State 'do maintenance claims between spouses derive from rules governing "matrimonial regimes" (Report on the Convention on the accession of the Kingdom of Denmark, Ireland and the United Kingdom of Great Britain and Northern Ireland to the Convention on Jurisdiction and the Enforcement of Judgments in Civil and Commercial Matters and to the Protocol on its interpretation by the Court of Justice, OJ 1979 C 59, p. 71, paragraph 49).

20. As the Advocate General points out in paragraphs 54 to 62 of his Opinion, on divorce courts in England and Wales have a wide discretion to make financial provisions. They may, in particular, order periodical payments or lump sum payments to be made and ownership in property belonging to one spouse to be transferred to the former spouse. Thus, they have the task of regulating, in a single decision, the matrimonial relationship and maintenance obligations arising from the dissolution of a marriage.

21. Owing precisely to the fact that on divorce an English court may, by the same decision, regulate both the matrimonial relationships of the parties and matters of maintenance, the court from which leave to enforce is sought must distinguish between those aspects of the decision which relate to rights in property arising out of a matrimonial relationship and those which relate to maintenance, having regard in each particular case to the specific aim of the decision rendered.

22. It should be possible to deduce the aim from the reasoning of the decision in question. If this shows that a provision awarded is designed to enable one spouse to provide for himself or herself or if the needs and resources of each of the spouses are taken into consideration in the determination of its amount, the decision will be concerned with maintenance. On the other hand, where the provision awarded is solely concerned with dividing property between the spouses, the decision will be concerned with rights in property arising out of a matrimonial relationship and will not therefore be enforceable under the Brussels Convention. A decision which does both these things may, in accordance with Article 42 of the Brussels Convention, be enforced in part if it clearly shows the aims to which the different parts of the judicial provision correspond.

23. It makes no difference in this regard that payment of maintenance is provided for in the form of a lump sum. This form of payment may also be in the nature of maintenance where the capital sum set is designed to ensure a predetermined level of income.

24. In the present case, as the Advocate General points out in paragraph 59 of his Opinion, the court of origin was under an obligation to consider whether it had to impose a clean break between the spouses and to order payment of a lump sum instead of periodical payments. It is clear that the choice of the method of payment made by the court of origin cannot alter the nature of the aim pursued by the decision.

25. Likewise, the fact that the decision of which enforcement is sought also orders ownership in certain property to be transferred between the former spouses cannot call in question the nature of that decision as an order for the provision of maintenance. The aim is still to make provision, by means of a capital sum, for the maintenance of one of the former spouses.

26. Finally, for the reasons explained by the Advocate General in paragraphs 69 to 72 of his Opinion, the English court's statement that it did not consider itself bound by the separation of goods agreement should be read in its context and in any event is not relevant for the purposes of defining the nature of the decision in question.

27. Consequently, the answer to be given must be that a decision rendered in divorce proceedings ordering payment of a lump sum and transfer of ownership in certain property by one party to his or her former spouse must be regarded as relating to maintenance and therefore as falling within the scope of the Brussels Convention if its purpose is to ensure the former spouse's maintenance. The fact that in its decision the court of origin disregarded a marriage contract is of no account in this regard.

On those grounds, the Court (Fifth Chamber), in answer to the question referred to it by the Arrondissementsrechbank te Amsterdam by judgment of 14 June 1995, hereby rules:

> **A decision rendered in divorce proceedings ordering payment of a lump sum and transfer of ownership in certain property by one party to his or her former spouse must be regarded as relating to maintenance and therefore as falling within the scope of the Convention of 27 September 1968 on Jurisdiction and the Enforcement of Judgments in Civil and Commercial Matters, as amended by the Convention of 9 October 1978 on the accession of the Kingdom of Denmark, Ireland and the United Kingdom of Great Britain and Northern Ireland and by the Convention of 25 October 1982 on the Accession of the Hellenic Republic, if its purpose is to ensure the former spouse's maintenance. The fact that in its decision the court of origin disregarded a marriage contract is of no account in this regard.**

OPINION OF MR ADVOCATE GENERAL JACOBS

1. The essential issue before the Court in this case, which has come by way of reference for a preliminary ruling from the Arrondissementsrechtbank te Amsterdam (District Court, Amsterdam), is how an order for the payment of a lump sum made by the High Court of Justice of England and Wales in the context of divorce proceedings is to be classified for the purposes of the Brussels Convention on jurisdiction and the enforcement of judgments in civil and commercial matters. More particularly, does such an order relate to 'rights in property arising out of a matrimonial relationship' within the meaning of Article 1 of the Convention, in which case it may not be enforced pursuant to the Convention, or does it relate to maintenance, in which case it is enforceable thereunder?

Relevant provisions of the Brussels Convention

2. The second paragraph of Article 1 of the Brussels Convention provides that that Convention is not to apply to '(1) the status or legal capacity of natural persons, rights in property arising out of a matrimonial relationship

3. Article 5 of the Brussels Convention provides: 'A person domiciled in a Contracting State may, in another Contracting State, be sued:

1. .... 2. in matters relating to maintenance, in the courts for the place where the maintenance creditor is domiciled or habitually resident or, if the matter is ancillary to proceedings concerning the status of a person, in the court which, according to its own law, has jurisdiction to entertain those proceedings, unless that jurisdiction is based solely on the nationality of one of the parties; ...'.

4. It is clear therefore that the Brussels Convention applies to matters relating to maintenance, including those arising in the context of the dissolution of a marriage. Indeed the reason for including such matters among the exceptions enumerated in Article 5 to the general rule that proceedings must be brought in the State of the defendant's domicile was precisely to enable a married but separated woman to sue her husband for maintenance in courts local to her. In order to effect this, a further exception to the general scheme of the Convention was necessary: Article 5(2) is the only provision in the Convention which offers habitual residence as an alternative criterion to domicile for establishing jurisdiction. Since in most jurisdictions there is substantial overlap between the two concepts, it may be wondered why Article 5(2) so derogates from the general rule. The reason is that in some Contracting States a woman acquires on marriage the domicile of her husband; accordingly conferring jurisdiction solely on the courts of the place where a married but separated woman was domiciled would not always have achieved its objective of enabling the woman to sue in her, rather than her estranged husband's, local courts.

Background to the order sought to be enforced

5. Mr Van den Boogaard and Miss Laumen, who both have Netherlands

nationality, were married in 1957 in the Netherlands under the regime of community of property. In 1980, as permitted by Netherlands law, they entered into a separation of goods agreement, thereby dividing their assets in approximately equal shares.

6. In early 1982, the parties settled in the United Kingdom. The marriage was dissolved by the High Court of Justice, London, in 1988; the English court presumably assumed jurisdiction on the basis that one or both of the parties had been habitually resident in England for one year before commencement of the divorce proceedings. The former wife subsequently applied to the High Court for full ancillary relief, namely for financial provision and property adjustment orders in accordance with sections 23 and 24 of the Matrimonial Causes Act 1973. On 25 July 1990 Cazalet J made an order of which the essential elements are that the husband (i) transfer to the wife the matrimonial home and a De Heem painting; (ii) pay the wife a lump sum of £355,000 and (iii) make periodical payments (initially £35,000 per annum pursuant to an order made earlier in the proceedings, subsequently £30,000 per annum) to the wife without interruption until payment of the lump sum and transfer of the home and painting.

7. The order for reference sets out a number of extracts from Cazalet J's judgment, including the following: 'The formal application before me is an application by a wife against her husband for full ancillary relief, including periodical payments for herself and the two youngest children of the family. I have been told that she does not at this stage wish to pursue her claim for periodical payments in regard to the two children; she reserves her right to come back and pursue that claim at a later stage.

She has further told me through counsel that she would wish, if it could be achieved, that there should be a clean break between herself and her former husband. It would then follow that, if and when any appropriate capital sums were to be paid to her, her periodical payments claim could be dismissed. That would then ensure that she was no longer reliant on her husband by way of support. ... So for the compelling reasons that I have given, I do not consider that the 1980 Dutch separation agreement has any bearing or significance on the decision that I am to make in these proceedings. ... If one then deducts from the sum total of those figures, that is, the £10,000 she has and the £35,000 which she can find from her chattel sales, £430,000 from 39 Connaught Square and the £60,000 for the De Heem which I order to be transferred to her so that she can sell for that net sum of money, she should be able to raise or have available to her £535,000 towards the total which I consider she requires of £875,000 in terms of cash to provide for herself. A deduction of £535,000 from £875,000 leaves £340,000. From the evidence before me, I am satisfied that the husband has the means to meet this order. Furthermore I am satisfied that he will still thereafter be left with ample funds to provide suitably for his own needs and those of the two youngest children. I also consider that this is preeminently a case in which it is appropriate for there to be a 'clean break' with the parties' financial obligations to each other terminated.

As to how the order is to be drawn I shall hear further argument, but I envisage her having her full capital sum within three months, again subject to argument that I hear, with the interim payments continuing meanwhile. Also there is to be a further sum of £15,000 added on to the lump sums paid to her to meet the costs of the Swiss proceedings. So that will bring £340,000 up to £355,000.

That is the lump sum order that I propose to make.'

8. The 'compelling reasons' for disregarding the Dutch separation of goods agreement mentioned by Cazalet J were mainly that the wife had entered into the agreement fearing that her husband was facing imminent bankruptcy and that the husband had entered into it in the undisclosed knowledge of an imminent and substantial commission payment. As explained further below, under English law an agreement between spouses as to the ownership of their property will not bind the court with power to make financial and property arrangements on their divorce.

9. There are in addition a couple of further matters in the judgment which may be relevant to the issue before the Court and which have not been mentioned by the referring court.

10. First, it is clear from the judgment that Cazalet J's starting figure of £875,000 in the above calculation, being the total which he considered that the former wife required to provide for herself, represents the total of (i) £375,000 to acquire and move into appropriate accommodation and (ii) £500,000 being the capitalized sum, calculated in accordance with English case-law, required to provide annual income of £30,000, considered by Cazalet J to be the appropriate figure for her.

11. Secondly, Cazalet J made the point that the former wife could not properly be regarded as having any earning capacity, being 55 and still being occupied with looking after the three younger of the six children of the marriage.

The enforcement proceedings

12. On 21 May 1992 on application by Miss Laumen, the former wife, the President of the Arrondissementsrechtbank te Amsterdam granted leave to enforce the earlier order and the final order pursuant to the Hague Convention of 2 October 1973 on the recognition and enforcement of decisions relating to maintenance obligations, considered further below. There is some confusion in the terminology employed by both parties: it appears from the national court's file that what was sought to be enforced was not in fact the earlier periodical payments order - which had expired in July 1991 - but the periodical payments part of the final order, which replaced it, and that the reference to the final order means the lump sum element of that order.

13. On 19 July 1993 Mr Van den Boogaard, the former husband, appealed to the Arrondissementsrechtbank te Amsterdam against the grant of leave to enforce in so far as it referred to the final order, apparently on the basis that that order was not a decision relating to maintenance obligations and hence was not enforceable pursuant to the Hague Convention. Before the national court he appears to accept that the earlier annual payment of £35,000 is maintenance and states his readiness to comply. He submits however that the final order (by

implication apart from the periodical payments aspect), in so far as it concerns divorce, concerns the status of persons, and in so far as it concerns the division of assets, concerns rights in property arising out of a matrimonial relationship. It is accordingly enforceable neither under the Hague Convention nor under the Brussels Convention.

14. It will be observed that Mr Van den Boogaard's appeal was lodged outside the two-month time-limit for appeals against decisions authorizing enforcement laid down by Article 36 of the Brussels Convention. It is of course in the first instance solely for the national court to determine in the light of the particular circumstances of the case the need for a preliminary ruling in order to enable it to deliver judgment; it may however be noted that, if the national court had considered that the Brussels Convention applied, it would have had (and may still have) to apply Article 36 of its own motion.

15. The Arrondissementsrechtbank tends towards the view that the final order 'relates (partly) to "rights in property arising out of a matrimonial relationship" within the meaning of ... Article 1 of the Brussels Convention', in which case the order for enforcement could not have been given on the basis of either the Brussels Convention or the Hague Convention. In reaching that view it stated: 'having regard to the obligations imposed on Van den Boogaard which amount to a transfer of assets - in particular the transfer of the house belonging to Van den Boogaard and of his painting - and, in addition, to the reasoning of the English judge - who expressly stated that he did not consider that the marriage settlement was binding -, the decision has such consequences for the relations as regards property rights between the parties that it cannot be regarded as a "decision in respect of maintenance obligations"'.

16. However, partly because the English legal system diverges from the continental systems and the term 'rights in property arising out of a matrimonial relationship' ('huwelijksgoederenrecht') is unknown to the common law, the court referred the following questions for a preliminary ruling: 'Must the decision of the English judge, which in any case relates in part to a maintenance obligation, be regarded as a decision which relates (in part) to rights in property arising out of a matrimonial relationship within the meaning of indent 1 of the second paragraph of Article 1 of the Brussels Convention even though:

(a) the income requirement is capitalized;

(b) an order was made to transfer the house and the De Heem painting which, according to the decision, belong to the husband;

(c) in his decision, the English judge himself expressly stated that he did not regard the marriage settlement as binding;

(d) it cannot be made out from that decision to what extent the factor mentioned in (c) influenced the English judge's decision?'

17. It is not clear from the order for reference precisely what is meant by 'the decision of the English judge', which encompassed the orders for the transfer of the house and the painting, the order for the lump sum payment and the order for periodical payments. As indicated above, it appears from the national court's file that what was at issue before it was the enforceability of the lump sum order, and I am assuming that it is that aspect of Cazalet J's order with

which the national court is concerned. It also however seeks guidance as to the relevance in determining whether the lump sum order is enforceable of the factors listed in (a) to (d) in the question, including the parallel property transfer orders.

18. Written observations were submitted only by the Austrian Government and the Commission; the parties and the Commission were represented at the hearing.

19. The national court's question is highly specific, referring as it does to the enforcement of the actual order made by Cazalet J. As I shall explain, however, in my view it would be more appropriate for the Court to lay down some general guidelines which could be applied both by the referring court in this case and by other courts faced in future with a similar problem. Before attempting to formulate some guidelines, I propose to review in some detail the history and scope of the relevant provisions of the Convention: this will I hope both illustrate the differences separating the civil law and common law approaches to the issues raised in this case and assist in reconciling them. First however I will consider another issue which has arisen, namely the interrelationship between the two conventions invoked by the parties to the main proceedings.

Relationship between the Brussels Convention and the Hague Convention

20. Although Miss Laumen relied on the Hague Convention in her application for enforcement, the referring court has interpreted the application 'as signifying that Laumen also sought to rely in the alternative on the Brussels Convention in so far as it would afford her a more favourable outcome than relying on the ... Hague Convention'.

21. The Hague Convention, which has been in force between the United Kingdom and the Netherlands since 1981, establishes a system for the reciprocal recognition and enforcement of decisions relating to maintenance obligations in respect of adults. Article 1 provides that that convention: 'shall apply to a decision rendered by a judicial or administrative authority in a Contracting State in respect of a maintenance obligation arising from a family relationship, parentage, marriage ... between - 1. a maintenance creditor and a maintenance debtor;...'.

22. The relevant provisions of Articles 1 and 5(2) of the Brussels Convention are set out above (paragraphs 2 and 3).

23. There is accordingly an overlap between the Hague Convention and the Brussels Convention with regard to the enforcement of decisions relating to maintenance, whereas decisions relating to rights in property arising out of a matrimonial relationship are enforceable under neither convention.

24. The first paragraph of Article 57 of the applicable version of the Brussels Convention provides that the Brussels Convention is not to affect any conventions to which the Contracting States are or will be parties and which in relation to particular matters govern jurisdiction or the recognition or enforcement of judgments. Thus the operation of the Hague Convention remains

intact notwithstanding the fact that maintenance obligations are within the scope of the Brussels Convention.

25. Article 25(2) of the 1978 Accession Convention provides as follows: 'With a view to its uniform interpretation, paragraph 1 of Article 57 shall be applied in the following manner: ... (b) ... Where a convention on a particular matter to which both the State of origin and the State addressed are parties lays down conditions for the recognition or enforcement of judgments, those conditions shall apply. In any event, the provisions of the 1968 Convention as amended which concern the procedures for recognition and enforcement of judgments may be applied.'

26. Article 23 of the Hague Convention, however, provides: 'This Convention shall not restrict the application of an international instrument in force between the State of origin and the State addressed ... for the purposes of obtaining recognition or enforcement of a decision or settlement.'

27. The combined effect of those provisions appears to be that, where the same ground is covered by the Brussels Convention and a particular convention, either convention may be relied on for recognition and enforcement, but the procedural framework put in place by the Brussels Convention - simpler and swifter - is in any event available.

28. That interpretation is borne out by the *travaux préparatoires* of the Hague Convention. It appears from the Report " of the Special Commission entrusted by the Hague Conference on private international law to prepare the work of the Twelfth Session on maintenance obligations, the genesis of the Hague Convention of 1973, that Article 23 was designed to enable a maintenance creditor to invoke provisions concerning recognition and enforcement which would be more advantageous to him. The Report states that, as a result in particular of 'the impending entry into force of [the Brussels Convention], this rule is of capital importance ... One may assume that Article [23] will be often invoked, especially in private relationships between nationals of Common Market countries.'

29. The Report then sets out the view of the Special Commission that every maintenance creditor retains the right, notwithstanding Article 57 of the Brussels Convention, to opt for the application of the Brussels Convention rather than the Hague Convention, by virtue of Article 23 of the latter Convention.

The background to Article 1 - 'rights in property arising out of a matrimonial relationship'

30. The original six States party to the Brussels Convention each had (and have) a distinct legislative framework governing the ownership of matrimonial property (in the broadest sense, including goods and finances). The spouses may opt on marriage for a specific pattern of ownership, ranging from joint ownership of all property to separate ownership of all property with various permutations in between. If no express option is made, the law imposes a statutory regime; in some States moreover there are overriding statutory provisions which apply notwithstanding the specific choice of regime made by

the spouses. In some States the initial regime may subsequently be changed: thus for example the former spouses in this case, having been married under the Netherlands regime of common property, subsequently changed the regime to that of universal separation of property.

31. It appears from the Jenard Report that Article 1 of the Convention was intended to exclude from the Convention this mosaic of national rules governing proprietary relationships between spouses. There were two separate but overlapping reasons for excluding such regimes from the Brussels Convention.

32. First, both the substantive laws, including the overriding and default rules and the specific regimes, and the conflict rules, which, in the case of a marriage with an international element, determined which State's matrimonial regime applied, varied significantly between the original Contracting States. It seems to have been regarded as 'politically impossible' and 'Utopian' to seek to ensure quasi-automatic mutual enforcement of decisions in these matters without a preliminary harmonization of, in particular, the conflict rules. According to the Jenard Report, the extent of the disparity between the various systems of law, in particular regarding the conflict rules, meant that 'it would have been difficult not to re-examine the rules of jurisdiction at the enforcement stage [which] would have meant changing the nature of the Convention and making it much less effective'.

33. Secondly, there were public policy considerations. These are of course particularly strong in the often associated context of divorce, where 'laws are rooted in different moral and religious attitudes which make it difficult for one country to accept the decisions of another country in these matters'; that was even more so when the Convention was drafted 30 years ago. Including such sensitive matters within the scope of the Convention would surely have encouraged national courts to abuse the notion of public policy by refusing recognition on the basis of the exception on that ground in Article 27(1), intended 'to operate only in exceptional cases'. It would obviously have undermined the Convention's aim of automatic recognition and enforcement if, again to borrow the words of Droz, 'les situations, jugées choquantes aux yeux du juge requis, [avaient été] purement et simplement éliminées par le moyen de l'ordre public'. By way of illustration of how this could arise in the context of matrimonial regimes, Droz gives as an example a Netherlands judgment based on community of property under Netherlands law concerning a Dutch/Italian couple married after a divorce regarded as non-existent in Italy.

34. The committee of experts which drafted the Brussels Convention was of the opinion that there might possibly be grounds for resuming discussion of the problems which led to the exclusions in the first indent in the second paragraph of Article 1 after the Convention had entered into force. In 1994 a working group on the extension of the Brussels Convention was created through the Council. It is currently engaged in negotiating a new convention, popularly known as 'Brussels II'. It appears however that the new convention will be restricted to jurisdiction in the matters of divorce, legal separation, validity of marriage and possibly custody of children and will not attempt to regulate matrimonial property issues.

35. The terminology used in Article 1 of the Brussels Convention posed a particular problem on the accession of the United Kingdom and Ireland. In those jurisdictions, there is nothing equivalent either to the concept of overriding or default legislation regulating property rights between spouses during the currency of the marriage or to the concept of a specific matrimonial regime which may be chosen by the spouses. Although both ante-nuptial and post-nuptial settlements are made, agreements between spouses regulating their property rights are subject to the general law, being treated no differently from agreements with third parties.

36. As a result of the conflict between the approach of the common-law acceding States and that of the original six civil-law States, the concept of rights in property arising out of a matrimonial relationship is considered in some detail in the Schlosser Report. Schlosser analyses in greater depth than Jenard the position in the original six Contracting States, pointing out that the concept does not cover the same legal relations in all the systems concerned. The report states: 'For the purpose of governing the relations between spouses in respect of property, these legal systems do not, or at least not predominantly, employ the legal concepts and institutions otherwise used in their civil law. Instead, they have developed exclusive legal institutions the application of which is limited to relations between spouses, and whose most important feature is a comprehensive set of rules governing property. However, there is not merely one such set of rules in each legal system. Instead, spouses have a choice between several, ranging from general a "community of property" to strict "separation of property". Even the latter, when chosen by the spouses, is a special form of "property regime", although special features arising from marriage can then hardly be said to exist any longer. ... If the spouses do not make a choice, one of the sets of rules governing property rights applies to them by law (known as the "statutory matrimonial regime").

... Some provisions apply to all marriages, irrespective of the particular "matrimonial regime" under which spouses live ... It is within the spirit of Article 1, second paragraph, point 1 of the 1968 Convention to exclude those provisions concerning property rights affecting all marriages from its scope of application, in so far as they are not covered by the term "maintenance claims" ...

These findings raise problems similar to those with which the Working Party was faced in connection with the concept 'civil and commercial matters'. It was, however, possible to define the concept of 'matrimonial regimes' not only in a negative manner ... but also positively, albeit rather broadly. This should enable implementing legislation in the United Kingdom and Ireland, in reliance on these statements, to indicate to the courts which legal relations form part of 'matrimonial regimes' ... Consequently, no formal adjustment of the 1968 Convention became necessary.

As a negative definition, it can be said with certainty that in no legal system do maintenance claims between spouses derive from rules governing 'matrimonial regimes'; nor are maintenance claims confined to claims for periodic payments ... The Convention does not apply ... if the subject matter of the proceedings concerns issues which have arisen between spouses ... during or after dissolution of their marriage, and which affect rights in property arising out of the matrimonial relationship. The expression 'rights in property' includes all rights of administration and disposal - whether by marriage contract or by statute - of property belonging to the spouses.'

37. Unfortunately the United Kingdom implementing legislation did not take up the invitation to indicate which legal relations form part of 'matrimonial regimes', merely setting out the text of the Convention. As explained below, however, English law subsequently developed in a way which did not make it feasible to draw a clear legislative distinction.

The background to Article 5(2) - 'maintenance'

38. There is no definition of 'maintenance' in the Brussels Convention. Schlosser states that there is no significant difference regarding the concept of maintenance as used in that convention and in the 1973 Hague Convention. That convention similarly contains no definition: the Report of the Special Commission which drafted it explains: 'The Experts recalled that their colleagues meeting in 1956 under the auspices either of the Hague Conference or of the United Nations Organization when confronted with the difficulty of drafting such definitions, had attempted in vain to arrive at a satisfactory text'.

39. The most that can be derived from the *travaux préparatoires* for the Hague Convention of 24 October 1956 on the law applicable to maintenance obligations towards children and the Hague Convention of 15 April 1958 concerning the recognition and enforcement of decisions relating to maintenance obligations towards children, referred to in the above quotation, is that it was intended that the term should be interpreted broadly.

40. In considering the concept of maintenance under Article 5(2) of the Brussels Convention, one can derive several useful points from the Schlosser Report.

41. First (and as already mentioned), it is not necessary in order for a claim to be for maintenance that it should be for periodic payments. As Schlosser points out: 'The mere fact that the courts in the United Kingdom have power to order not only periodic payments by one spouse to the other after a divorce, but also the payment of a single lump sum of money, does not therefore prevent the proceedings or a judgment from being treated as a maintenance matter. Even the creation of charges on property and the transfer of property as provided on the Continent, for example in Article 8 of the Italian divorce law, can be in the nature of maintenance.'

42. Secondly, it is difficult to distinguish between claims for maintenance on the one hand and claims for damages and the division of property on the other. As Schlosser explains: 'In Continental Europe a motivating factor in assessing the amount of maintenance due to a divorced spouse by his former partner is to compensate an innocent spouse for his loss of matrimonial status. ... However, English law, which is characterized by judicial discretionary powers and which does not favour inflexible systematic rules, does not make a distinction as to whether the payments ordered by the court are intended as damages or as maintenance.'

The notion of compensating the innocent party must, however, be now regarded as considerably less relevant given the marked trend in European divorce laws away from a fault-centred concept in favour of divorce by mutual consent, which in one form or another was introduced between 1970 and 1978 in Austria, Belgium, France, Germany, Italy, Luxembourg, the Netherlands, Portugal and the United Kingdom.

43. Finally, in the case of a lump sum payment between spouses, a division of property or damages may well be the underlying factor; more particularly, where both spouses are earning well, payment of a lump sum can only serve the purpose of a division of property or compensation for non-material damage, in which case the obligation to pay is not in the nature of maintenance. Schlosser reiterates that the Convention is not applicable at all where the payments claimed or ordered are governed by matrimonial property law and that whether or not Article 5(2) applies depends, in the case of a lump sum payment, solely on whether the payment is in the nature of maintenance.

The case-law

44. The case-law on the interpretation of the relevant provisions of Articles 1 and 5(2) of the Brussels Convention is unfortunately sparse and relatively unhelpful.

45. In *de Cavel* v *de Cavel ('de Cavel I')* the Court considered the scope of the exclusion of 'rights in property arising out of a matrimonial relationship' in Article 1. That case concerned the enforcement in Germany of a French order 'authorizing, as a protective measure in divorce proceedings pending between the parties, the putting under seal of furniture, effects and other objects in the flat [in Germany] belonging to the parties and the freezing of the assets and accounts of the respondent at two banking establishments [in Germany]'.

46. The Court stated: 'The enforced settlement on a provisional basis of proprietary legal relationships between spouses in the course of proceedings for divorce is closely linked to the grounds for the divorce and the personal situation of the spouses or any children of the marriage and is, for that reason, inseparable from questions relating to the status of persons raised by the dissolution of the matrimonial relationship and from the settlement of rights in property arising out of the matrimonial relationship.

Consequently, the term 'rights in property arising out of a matrimonial relationship' includes not only property arrangements specifically and exclusively envisaged by certain national legal systems in the case of marriage but also any proprietary relationships resulting directly from the matrimonial relationship or the dissolution thereof.

Disputes relating to the assets of spouses in the course of proceedings for divorce may therefore, depending on the circumstances, concern or be closely connected with:

(1) questions relating to the status of persons; or

(2) proprietary legal relationships between spouses resulting directly from the matrimonial relationship or the dissolution thereof., or

(3) proprietary legal relations existing between them which have no connection with the marriage.
Whereas disputes of the latter category fall within the scope of the Convention, those relating to the first two categories must be excluded therefrom.'

47. That statement echoed the view of Advocate General Warner, who had proposed: 'to give to the phrase a broad meaning, on the footing that, in practice, in few disputes between spouses about property is it likely that the 'matrimonial relationship' between them will play no part. ... The upshot is that, in my opinion, a judgment or order relating to a property dispute between spouses should be presumed to be outside the scope of the Convention unless it is apparent on the face of the particular judgment or order in question that it is not.'

48. The Advocate General went on briefly to consider maintenance orders, stating that they 'are, in general, orders for the payment of money. They operate *in personam* and do not affect property rights, except where secured maintenance is ordered, but then the affection of property is of a limited and special kind.'

49. The Court's reasoning in *de Cavel I* is somewhat opaque. Scrutiny of the ruling suggests that the Court regarded as crucial that the protective measures at issue were of their nature ancillary: since such measures 'can serve to safeguard a variety of rights, their inclusion in the scope of the Convention is determined not by their own nature but by the nature of the rights which they serve to protect'. It appears therefore that the *ratio decidendi* was that since the measures were ancillary to proceedings which were clearly outside the scope of the Convention (divorce and the consequential dissolution of the matrimonial regime governing the French marriage in question), they were thereby also outside its scope.

50. The subsequent case between the same parties *de Cavel* v *de Cavel ('de Cavel II')* concerned *inter alia* the enforceability of a French court's order for monthly compensatory payments in the context of divorce proceedings. The relevant provisions (Art. 270 et seq.) of the French Civil Code provided that such payments were intended to compensate, so far as possible, for the disparity which the breakdown of the marriage created in the parties' respective living standards and that the amount was to be fixed according to the needs of the spouse to whom it was paid and the means of the other. The specific issue before the Court was whether maintenance orders made in the context of divorce proceedings were within the scope of the Convention. The case was brought before Article 5(2) was amended on the accession of the United Kingdom, Ireland and Denmark so as to make it clear that such orders ancillary to divorce proceedings were included. Unsurprisingly the Court found that the payments were in the nature of maintenance, and concluded that the scope of the Convention extended 'to maintenance obligations which legislation or the court places on spouses for the period after divorce'.

51. In its ruling in *de Cavel II* the Court additionally sought to reformulate the reasoning underlying the earlier judgment. However in the third case on the exclusion of 'rights in property arising out of a matrimonial relationship', *W.* v *H.* (which needs no further mention since it offers no further guidance on the meaning of the phrase), the Court restated the principle laid down in *de Cavel I*

unaffected by the comments of the Court in the intervening case; the first case accordingly remains applicable.

52. Against the broad interpretation of 'rights in property arising out of a matrimonial relationship' endorsed by the Court it may be objected that, as an exception to the 'civil and commercial matters' governed by the Convention, the phrase should rather be narrowly construed. It is indicated in the Jenard Report that the expression 'civil and commercial matters' is very wide and that the formula of specific exclusion rather than an exhaustive positive definition of the scope of the Convention was adopted with a view to preserving that breadth: 'in this respect the Convention should be interpreted as widely as possible'.

53. It should perhaps also be borne in mind that the Court in *de Cavel I* was not focusing on the frontier between 'rights in property arising out of a matrimonial relationship' and maintenance. Where the dividing line between those two concepts is at issue, a broad interpretation of the former will inevitably be at the expense of the scope of the latter. I can see no reason for thus disturbing the equilibrium of two provisions of equal standing.

Financial relief on divorce in England and Wales

54. At issue in this case is whether an order made by an English court in the context of a divorce is excluded from the Brussels Convention by virtue of Article 1. It is obvious that the rules on matrimonial property in the United Kingdom do not dovetail with those in the continental Contracting States: the issue is to what extent they therefore fall outside the exclusion. Before turning to this question, it may first be useful to describe briefly the legislative framework within which an English court will grant financial relief on divorce.

55. Since the enactment of the Married Women's Property Act 1882, which provided that a married woman was capable of acquiring, holding, and disposing of property as if she were a feme sole (unmarried woman), English law has started from a presumption of separate ownership of property in marriage; that presumption may of course be rebutted by actual or inferred intention that specific property is jointly owned.

56. The powers of English courts to order lump sum payments and transfers of property on divorce are relatively recent. The power to order a lump sum payment was first introduced in 1963 (although the power to grant such a sum as secured maintenance may be traced further back via the Matrimonial Causes Act 1950 and the Judicature Act 1925 into the nineteenth century). The power to make transfer of property orders dates from the Matrimonial Proceedings and Property Act 1970: until then, the courts had no power on divorce to transfer the ownership of property between spouses; their powers to make property orders were restricted to reflecting existing patterns of ownership. Most of the 1970 Act survives in the current legislation, the Matrimonial Causes Act 1973. The provisions of particular relevance for the present case are sections 21, 23, 24, 25 and 25A of the 1973 Act; their effect is as follows.

57. On divorce (or nullity or judicial separation), the English courts have a wide discretion to order financial provision, including periodical and lump sum

payments between spouses, and property adjustment orders, including transfer of property between spouses. The discretionary power to adjust property rights between spouses is in marked contrast to certain civil-law systems, where a court on divorce has no power to order transfers of property, being bound by existing patterns of ownership which will in turn normally derive from a prior agreement or from overriding legal provisions.

58. In exercising its discretion, the English court is required to have regard to all the circumstances of the case, first consideration being given to the welfare of any minor child of the family. In exercising its powers to make a lump sum order or a property adjustment order in relation to the other spouse (as opposed to a child of the family), the court is required to have regard to each spouse's income, earning capacity, property and other financial resources; their respective financial needs, obligations and responsibilities; the standard of living enjoyed by the family before the breakdown of the marriage; the age of each spouse and the duration of the marriage; any physical or mental disability of either spouse; each spouse's contributions to the welfare of the family, including any contribution by looking after the home or caring for the family; their respective conduct, if it is such that it would in the opinion of the court be inequitable to disregard it; and the value to each spouse of any benefit, for example a pension, which that spouse will lose the chance of acquiring.

59. Beyond these specific guidelines, the Act does not impose an overall objective to be sought by the court in framing its order. Before amendment in 1984, the Act required the court so to exercise its statutory powers 'as to place the parties, so far as it is practicable and, having regard to their conduct, just to do so, in the financial position in which they would have been if the marriage had not broken down and each had properly discharged his or her financial obligations and responsibilities towards the other'. That provision was dropped when section 25 was recast in 1984. At the same time, the Act was amended so as to require the court in all cases where it makes an order in favour of a party to the marriage on or after a decree of divorce or nullity to consider whether it would be appropriate so to exercise its powers 'that the financial obligations of each party towards the other will be terminated as soon after the grant of the decree as the court considers just and reasonable'. In other words, the court is now under a duty to consider whether to impose a 'clean break'.

60. The court's powers under the Matrimonial Causes Act 1973 cannot be ousted by private agreement between the parties. A previous agreement between spouses as to the ownership of their property will therefore not be binding on the court making an order on their divorce, although it will be a circumstance to which the court must have regard. This is again in stark contrast to the position in certain civil-law systems, where the court on a dispute between spouses as to the ownership of their property must give effect to any agreement between them or to the pattern of ownership imposed by the law in default of an agreement.

61. One of the changes wrought by the 1970 Act, the precursor of the 1973 Act, was the abolition of the previous terminology, which had distinguished between alimony, maintenance and periodical payments. All are now described as financial provision and may take the form of periodical payments or a lump

sum payment. The term 'maintenance' was rejected as suggesting some inferiority on the part of the recipient. Although a lump sum may be for maintenance - indeed on a 'clean break', which the court is now directed to impose if it considers it appropriate, it will be the only means of ordering a maintenance payment between spouses - the 'more important use of the power ... is to adjust the parties' capital assets. If, for example, the husband owns shares, the court may wish the benefit of a proportion of these to be given to the wife. ... it may do this directly by ordering them to be transferred to her in specie; it will be much more common, however, to order him to make a lump sum payment to her.'

62. Considered as a whole, the provisions summarized above suggest that it may be arbitrary to try to draw a clear distinction with regard to a given order between an equitable division of assets and maintenance. That in turn suggests that, in keeping with the Court's readiness to develop an autonomous interpretation of terms and concepts used in the Convention with a view to its uniform application, it may in some cases be necessary to look for the essential object of the order. I shall return shortly to this crucial point.

Guidelines for the national court

63. In the light of the above, I will now propose some indications to assist the national court to judge whether a lump sum order made by an English court in the context of divorce proceedings relates to 'rights in property arising out of a matrimonial relationship' within the meaning of Article 1 of the Convention or whether it relates to maintenance. In the course of formulating these guidelines I will also consider the relevance, for categorizing an order, of the specific matters raised by the national court, namely the capitalization of an income requirement, the parallel transfer of property order and the disregard by the English court of the civil-law matrimonial property agreement.

The status of English orders on divorce in the scheme of the Convention: some general points

64. I would make the preliminary point that the mere fact that there is no separate framework of matrimonial property regimes in English law does not mean that orders on divorce made by an English court will therefore always fall outside the exclusion in Article 1 and hence, by virtue of being a civil matter not expressly excluded, be enforceable under the Convention.

65. First, it appears beyond doubt that it was intended that on the accession of the United Kingdom and Ireland the definition would have some application in those States: see the comments in the Schlosser Report set out in paragraph 36 above, including the invitation to the legislature of those States to frame a definition. That was moreover the understanding of Advocate General Warner, who in *de Cavel I* stated his view that the accession to the Convention of the United Kingdom and Ireland would increase the disparities in the rules governing proprietary relationships between spouses which were intended to be excluded by Article 1.

66. There is in any event no compelling conceptual reason for treating a legal system characterized by a common-law assumption of separate ownership of property in marriage, subject to a discretionary power on the part of the courts to make adjustments to that ownership on dissolution of the marriage, any differently from a legal system which achieves the same pattern of ownership of property on marriage by the imposition of a legislative rule. That approach also finds support in the Schlosser Report, where it is stated that even strict separation of property, when chosen by the spouses (as it is in England by default) 'is a special form of a "property regime"'.

67. It may also be added that the reasons for excluding 'rights in property arising out of a matrimonial relationship' from the framework set in place by the Brussels Convention - namely public policy and the disparity in substantive law and conflict rules - apply equally to the English system. The public policy issue is clearly of equal force, and the differences separating both the substantive law and the conflict rules from their civil law counterparts are, at least as regards the substantive law, greater than the differences between the various civil law regimes. With regard in particular to the conflict rules, it should not be thought that those applying to matrimonial property rights in the common law jurisdictions are any less complex or multifarious than those applying to civil law regimes: see the response of the United Kingdom to the questionnaire on the conflict of laws in matrimonial property matters prepared by the Hague Conference on private international law.

68. Finally, the alternative view, namely that the English rules do not fall within the definition because they are part of the general law rather than imposed by specific matrimonial property legislation, is difficult to reconcile with the broad interpretation of the term 'rights in property arising out of a matrimonial relationship' given by the Court in *de Cavel I* and in particular with its statement that the term 'includes not only property arrangements specifically and exclusively envisaged by certain national legal systems in the case of marriage but also any proprietary relationships resulting directly from the matrimonial relationship or the dissolution thereof.'

The relevance of the prior civil-law matrimonial agreement

69. The referring court has raised the question of the significance of the Netherlands marriage settlement (meaning the regime of universal separation of goods adopted by the spouses while their marriage, originally under the regime of common property, was still current) to the categorization and hence enforceability of the English order. More specifically, the referring court asks whether it is relevant that the English judge stated that he did not regard the marriage settlement as binding on him and that it cannot be made out from the judgment to what extent that view influenced his decision.

70. On an application under the Brussels Convention to enforce this or any analogous order, the sole question is whether - or to what extent - the order is in the nature of maintenance, in which case it falls within the scope of the Convention and is enforceable.

71. I do not see how the English judge's statement that he did not regard the separation of goods agreement as binding on him is relevant to the categorization of the final order. As a matter of English law it was not binding on him, although it is a circumstance to which he was required to have regard. It is clear from his judgment that he considered the agreement and its implications for the issues before him in some depth. He appears in fact to have regarded it as applicable in so far as he assumed that the various matrimonial assets were owned separately by the former husband and wife in accordance with the agreement. He was not however prepared to find that the wife had abrogated any right to further capital provision by virtue of the agreement. The reasons which the judge gave for disregarding it to that extent appear to be solely to do with the fairness of the agreement in the circumstances in which it was entered into.

72. In this case, therefore, I do not consider that the English judge's disregard of that aspect of the agreement is relevant to the issue before the Court, namely the question whether the lump sum order finally made is enforceable as relating to maintenance.

The lump sum as maintenance

73. Turning to the criteria for the categorization of particular lump sum orders, it is clear that, at one end of the spectrum, where the recipient has no earning power and the lump sum is awarded in the context of a 'clean break' in lieu of periodical payments for the recipient spouse, at least part of that sum must be in the nature of maintenance. This is expressly recognized by Schlosser; indeed he goes further, and states that the transfer of property on divorce may in certain circumstances be in the nature of maintenance. The Commission makes the same point, noting that a transfer of property is not automatically excluded as such from the scope of the Convention, but only to the extent that it is not in the nature of maintenance. The Commission refers to the view it expressed in its written observations in *de Cavel II* to the effect that if 'a payment fixed in the course of divorce proceedings is intended to ensure the support of the spouse who is in need, this is a matter of a maintenance obligation within the meaning of the 1968 Convention'. The Commission rightly concludes that a lump sum payment or a transfer of property will, if it has that objective, be in the nature of maintenance notwithstanding its form; the Austrian Government similarly considers that a lump sum will be in the nature of maintenance to the extent that the spouses' respective needs and resources have been taken into account in determining the amount. What must be looked at, therefore, are the objectives sought to be achieved by the particular order, and it is to be hoped that national courts when drawing up orders will bear in mind the need for those objectives to be readily ascertainable from the reasoning given by the court.

74. The national court asks whether the fact that the income requirement is capitalized is relevant. That question in fact encompasses two separate issues.

75. First is the question whether a lump sum may in any event be maintenance:

I have already indicated my view that that is so.

76. Second is the question of the significance to that categorization of the fact that a lump sum was quantified so as to be capable of generating a predetermined level of income. In my view, and as the Commission points out, that fact is likely to be strong evidence that the lump sum is intended to generate income rather than redistribute capital; that in turn will suggest that it is in the nature of maintenance notwithstanding its expression as a lump sum: it demonstrates that the court is seeking to provide income without having recourse to periodical payments. In this case, for example, in the context of the sum of £500,000, part of the total awarded, the judge made it clear that the reason for capitalizing the income requirement was to ensure that the former wife was 'no longer reliant on her [former] husband by way of support'.

77. Once it is accepted that a lump sum may properly be regarded as relating to maintenance notwithstanding its capital nature, it is obvious that the mere fact that in determining the appropriate amount the court took account of the former spouses' respective ownership of the matrimonial property and, in the same order as that in which it ordered payment of the lump sum, ordered certain adjustments of that property as between the former spouses cannot invalidate that conclusion: the calculation of the appropriate lump sum following dissolution of a marriage will, in order to be both accurate and equitable, require the court to take account of those factors, and there may be circumstances where it is more appropriate to order the direct transfer of property rather than - or as well as - a lump sum payment.

78. It should also be borne in mind that a parallel transfer of property order may - indeed frequently will - lead to a lower lump sum than would otherwise have been the case, since it will enable the recipient to realize part of the total capital sum which the court considers appropriate. That factor is well illustrated by the present case: although Cazalet J started from a total of £875,000 which he considered that the former wife 'requires ... in terms of cash to provide for herself', the amount awarded by way of lump sum order was £340,000 since most of the balance was granted to the former wife by means of orders that property directly or indirectly owned by the former husband be transferred to her with a view to their sale to raise cash.

79. Accordingly, since it appears from the judgment of Cazalet J that the £875,000 awarded in total was the amount which he considered the former wife required to provide for herself and since the lump sum of £340,000 whose enforcement is at issue represents part of that total, it would be proper for the referring court to regard that lump sum as in the nature of maintenance and hence enforceable pursuant to both the Brussels and the Hague Convention.

The lump sum as a division of property

80. At the other end of the spectrum, where both parties are earning well an order awarding a lump sum will frequently be intended as a division of assets rather than maintenance in any sense: at that extreme, in my view, it will concern 'rights in property arising out of a matrimonial relationship' and hence be unenforceable under the Convention.

Combined orders

81. There will however inevitably be lump sum orders which fall somewhere in the continuum between the extremes of manifest maintenance and manifest property division. Some such orders may well partake of the attributes of both types, with a proportion destined to ensure maintenance and the remainder intended to effect a division of the matrimonial property. Provided that the order is clearly and fully reasoned, the court before which enforcement is sought should be in a position itself to ascertain the intended proportions. In addition to clear reasoning, it is imperative that an order intended to combine maintenance and a division of property be mathematically transparent, so that the court before which enforcement is sought is able to sever the enforceable from the unenforceable. Even where it is not apparent from the face of a lump sum order that it was intended to reflect both the need for maintenance and a division of property, it would in my view be reasonable for the enforcing court to conclude that, in circumstances where a level of maintenance regarded as appropriate has already been assured (for example by a specified level of income to be generated by a capital sum representing part of the total lump sum ordered) the balance of the total sum relates to rights in property arising out of a matrimonial relationship.

82. If a national court in a particular case were to decide that an English lump sum order related in part to rights in property and in part to maintenance, it may, by virtue of the second paragraph of Article 42 of the Brussels Convention, order enforcement to the extent that the order related to maintenance notwithstanding that the order would be unenforceable to the extent that it related to rights in property.

83. Article 42 provides: 'Where a foreign judgment has been given in respect of several matters and enforcement cannot be authorized for all of them, the court shall authorize enforcement for one or more of them. An applicant may request partial enforcement of a judgment.'

84. The second paragraph is intended to cater for situations where, for example, the judgment whose enforcement is sought orders the payment of a sum of money part of which has been paid since the judgment was given, in contrast to the first paragraph which is intended to cater for situations where a judgment deals with separate and independent heads of claim, the decision on some of which is unenforceable. In my view, there is no reason why partial enforcement under the second paragraph should not also be available, by analogy with the first paragraph, where part of the sum of money in question relates to a matter enforceable under the Convention and the balance to a matter unenforceable thereunder. The question whether the court before which enforcement is sought may order partial enforcement of its own motion, or grant leave to amend the application, will depend on its domestic procedural rules.

85. To conclude, where the judgment, taken as a whole, can be regarded as having maintenance as its essential object, it should be recognized and enforced as a whole. Where it is clearly severable, those parts which can be so regarded should be recognized and enforced in application of the above provision.

Conclusion

Accordingly the question referred by the Arrondissementsrechtbank te Amsterdam should in my opinion be answered as follows: 'An order made by a court in the context of divorce proceedings will fall within the scope of the Brussels Convention if it can be regarded as having maintenance as its essential object, notwithstanding its form. Accordingly, an order for a lump sum payment will be enforceable if maintenance is its essential object. The fact that an order for a lump sum payment is accompanied by an order for the transfer of property between spouses does not of itself prevent its being in the nature of maintenance'.

TITLE II *[Chapter II]*

JURISDICTION *[Jurisdiction]*

General Rule on Jurisdiction – Article 2 *[Article 2]*

See also

Case C-412/98 - 13 July 2000

Société Group Josi Reinsurance Company SA
v
Compagnie d'Assurances Universal General Insuance Company (UGIC)

Personal scope - Plaintiff domiciled in a non-Contracting State - Material scope - Rules of jurisdiction in matters relating to insurance - Dispute concerning a reinsurance contract.

Summary

1. Title II of the Convention is in principle applicable where the defendant has his domicile or seat in a Contracting State, even if the plaintiff is domiciled in a non-member country. It will otherwise only in exceptional cases where an express provision of the Convention provides that the application of the rule of jurisdiction which it sets out is dependent on the plaintiff's domicile being in a Contracting State.

2. The rules of special jurisdiction in matters relating to insurance set out in Articles 7 to 12a of the Convention do not cover disputes between a reinsurer and a reinsured in connection with a reinsurance contract.

JUDGMENT OF THE COURT

Presiding, Lecourt, Moitinho de Almeida, President of Chambers, Schintgen, Rapporteur, Puissochet, Hirsch and Macken, Judges

1. By judgment of 5 November 1998, received at the Court on 19 November 1998, the Cour d'Appel (Court of Appeal), Versailles, referred to the Court for a preliminary ruling under the Protocol of 3 June 1971 on

the interpretation by the Court of Justice of the Convention of 27 September 1968 on Jurisdiction and the Enforcement of Judgments in Civil and Commercial Matters two questions on the interpretation of the provisions of Title II of that convention (OJ 1972 L 299, p. 32), as amended by the Convention of 9 October 1978 on the Accession of the Kingdom of Denmark, Ireland and the United Kingdom of Great Britain and Northern Ireland (OJ 1978 L 304, p. 1; amended version of the Convention at p. 77), by the Convention of 25 October 1982 on the Accession of the Hellenic Republic (OJ 1982 L 388, p. 1) and by the Convention of 26 May 1989 on the Accession of the Kingdom of Spain and the Portuguese Republic (OJ 1989 L 285, p. 1) (hereinafter 'the Convention').

2. Those questions were raised in proceedings between Universal General Insurance Company ('UGIC'), in liquidation, an insurance company incorporated under Canadian law, having its registered office in Vancouver, Canada, and Group Josi Reinsurance Company SA ('Group Josi'), a reinsurance company incorporated under Belgian law, having its registered office in Brussels, concerning a sum of money claimed by UGIC from Group Josi in its capacity as party to a reinsurance contract.
The Convention

3. The rules of jurisdiction laid down by the Convention are to be found in Title II thereof, which contains Articles 2 to 24.

4. Article 2 of the Convention, which forms part of Section 1, entitled 'General provisions', of Title II, states: 'Subject to the provisions of this convention, persons domiciled in a Contracting State shall, whatever their nationality, be sued in the courts of that State.

Persons who are not nationals of the State in which they are domiciled shall be governed by the rules of jurisdiction applicable to nationals of that State'.

5. The first paragraph of Article 3 of the Convention, which is part of the same section, provides: 'Persons domiciled in a Contracting State may be sued in the courts of another Contracting State only by virtue of the rules set out in Sections 2 to 6 of this title'.

6. The second paragraph of Article 3 of the Convention prohibits a plaintiff from relying on special rules of jurisdiction in force in the Contracting States which are based, in particular, on the nationality of the parties and on the plaintiff's domicile or residence.

7. Article 4, which also forms part of Section 1 of Title II of the Convention, states: 'If the defendant is not domiciled in a Contracting State, the jurisdiction of the courts of each Contracting State shall, subject to the provisions of Article 16, be determined by the law of that State'.

As against such a defendant, any person domiciled in a Contracting State may, whatever his nationality, avail himself in that State of the rules of jurisdiction there in force, and in particular those specified in the second paragraph of Article 3, in the same way as the nationals of that State.

8. In Sections 2 to 6 of Title II, the Convention lays down rules of special or exclusive jurisdiction.

9. Thus, under Article 5, which is part of Section 2, entitled 'Special jurisdiction, of Title II of the Convention: 'A person domiciled in a Contracting State may, in another Contracting State, be sued:

1. in matters relating to a contract, in the courts for the place of performance of the obligation in question; ...

2. in matters relating to maintenance, in the courts for the place where the maintenance creditor is domiciled or habitually resident ...

...'.

10. Articles 7 to 12a constitute Section 3, entitled 'Jurisdiction in matters relating to insurance', of Title II of the Convention.

11. Article 7 of the Convention states: 'In matters relating to insurance, jurisdiction shall be determined by this section ...'.

12. Article 8 of the Convention provides: 'An insurer domiciled in a Contracting State may be sued:

1. in the courts of the State where he is domiciled, or

2. in another Contracting State, in the courts for the place where the policy-holder is domiciled, or

3. if he is a co-insurer, in the courts of a Contracting State in which proceedings are brought against the leading insurer.

An insurer who is not domiciled in a Contracting State but has a branch, agency or other establishment in one of the Contracting States shall, in disputes arising out of the operations of the branch, agency or establishment, be deemed to be domiciled in that State'.

13. Section 4 of Title II of the Convention contains rules of jurisdiction over consumer contracts.

14. The first paragraph of Article 14, which is part of that section, states: 'A consumer may bring proceedings against the other party to a contract either in the courts of the Contracting State in which that party is domiciled or in the courts of the Contracting State in which he is himself domiciled'.

15. Article 16, which constitutes Section 5 of Title II of the Convention, lays down certain rules of exclusive jurisdiction and states that they are to apply 'regardless of domicile'.

16. Under the first paragraph of Article 17, which is part of Section 6, entitled 'Prorogation of jurisdiction, of Title II of the Convention: 'If the parties, one or more of whom is domiciled in a Contracting State, have agreed that a court or the courts of a Contracting State are to have jurisdiction to settle any disputes which have arisen or which may arise in connection with a particular legal relationship, that court or those courts shall have exclusive jurisdiction. ...'.

17. Article 18, which also forms part of Section 6, states: 'Apart from jurisdiction derived from other provisions of this convention, a court of a Contracting State before whom a defendant enters an appearance shall have jurisdiction. This rule shall not apply where appearance was entered solely to contest the jurisdiction, or where another court has exclusive jurisdiction by virtue of Article 16'.

The main proceedings

18. It is apparent from the documents in the case in the main proceedings that UGIC instructed its broker, Euromepa, a company incorporated under French law, having its registered office in France, to procure a reinsurance contract with effect from 1 April 1990 in relation to a portfolio of comprehensive home-occupiers' insurance polices based in Canada.

19. By fax dated 27 March 1990, Euromepa offered Group Josi a share in that reinsurance contract, stating that 'the main reinsurers are Union Ruck with 24% and Agrippina Ruck with 20%'.

20. By fax of 6 April 1990, Group Josi agreed to acquire a 7.5% share.

21. On 28 March 1990, Union Ruck had told Euromepa that it did not intend to retain its share after 31 May 1990 and, by letter of 30 March

1990, Agrippina Ruck had informed the same broker that it would reduce its share to 10% with effect from 1 June 1990, the reason for those withdrawals being changes in economic policy imposed by the American-based parent companies of those insurance undertakings.

22. On 25 February 1991, Euromepa sent Group Josi first a statement of account showing a debit balance and then a final calculation showing that Group Josi owed CAD 54 679.34 in respect of its share in the reinsurance transaction.

23. By letter of 5 March 1991, Group Josi refused to pay that amount, essentially on the ground that it had been induced to enter into the reinsurance contract by the provision of information which subsequently turned out to be false.

24. In those circumstances, on 6 July 1994, UGIC brought proceedings against Group Josi before the Tribunal de Commerce (Commercial Court), Nanterre, France.

25. Group Josi argued that that court lacked jurisdiction since the Tribunal de Commerce, Brussels, within whose territorial jurisdiction it has its registered office, had jurisdiction, and it relied, first, on the Convention and, second, in the event of the general law being found to apply, on Article 1247 of the French Code Civil (Civil Code).

26. By judgment of 27 July 1995, the Tribunal de Commerce, Nanterre, held that it had jurisdiction on the ground that UGIC is a company incorporated under Canadian law without a place of business in the Community and that the objection of lack of jurisdiction raised on the basis of the Convention cannot be applied to it. On the substance, the court ordered Group Josi to pay the sum claimed by UGIC, plus statutory interest as from 6 July 1994.

27. Group Josi subsequently appealed against that judgment before the Cour d'Appel, Versailles.

28. In support of its appeal, Group Josi submitted that the Convention applies to any dispute in which a connecting factor with the Convention is apparent. In the present case, the Convention should apply. The main connecting factor is that specified in the first paragraph of Article 2 of the Convention, namely the defendant's domicile. Since Group Josi has its registered office in Brussels and no subsidiary place of business in

France, it can, in accordance with that provision, be sued only in a Belgian court. In addition, Group Josi relied on Article 5(1) of the Convention, arguing in this respectthat the obligation in question, being payment of a contractual debt, was, in the absence of any stipulation to the contrary in the reinsurance contract, to be performed in the debtor's place of domicile, namely Brussels.

29. UGIC, on the other hand, contended that the rules of jurisdiction established by the Convention can apply only if the plaintiff is also domiciled in a Contracting State. Since UGIC is a company incorporated under Canadian law with no subsidiary place of business in a Contracting State, the Convention is not applicable in the present case.

30. The Cour d'Appel observed, first, that, although a dispute may be regarded as sufficiently integrated into the European Community to justify jurisdiction being vested in the courts of a Contracting State where, as in the present case, the defendant is domiciled in a Contracting State, it is a different question whether the specific rules of that convention can be used against a plaintiff domiciled in a non-Contracting State, which would necessarily entail extending Community law to non-member countries.

31. Second, the Cour d'Appel noted that Article 7 of the Convention simply refers to matters relating to 'insurance without specifying further, so that the question arises whether reinsurance falls within the scope of the autonomous system of jurisdiction established by Articles 7 to 12a of the Convention. In this respect, it might be considered that the purpose of those articles is to protect the insured as the weak party to the insurance contract and that there is no such characteristic in matters of reinsurance, but, on the other hand, the text of the Convention does not contain any exclusion on that point.

The questions referred for preliminary ruling

32. Taking the view that, in those circumstances, the resolution of the dispute required an interpretation of the Convention, the Cour d'Appel, Versailles, decided to stay proceedings and to refer the following two questions to the Court for a preliminary ruling: '1. Does the Brussels Convention of 27 September 1968 on Jurisdiction and the Enforcement of Judgments in Civil and Commercial Matters apply not only to intra-Community disputes but also to disputes which are integrated into the Community? More particularly, can a defendant established in a

Contracting State rely on the specific rules on jurisdiction set out in that convention against a plaintiff domiciled in Canada? 2. Do the rules on jurisdiction specific to matters relating to insurance set out in Article 7 *et seq*. of the Brussels Convention apply to matters relating to reinsurance?'

The first question

33. By its first question, the national court essentially seeks to ascertain whether the rules of jurisdiction laid down by the Convention apply where the defendant has its domicile or seat in a Contracting State, even if the plaintiff is domiciled in a non-member country.

34. In order to answer that question, it is important to state at the outset that the system of common rules on conferment of jurisdiction established in Title II of the Convention is based on the general rule, set out in the first paragraph of Article 2, that persons domiciled in a Contracting State are to be sued in the courts of that State, irrespective of the nationality of the parties.

35. That jurisdictional rule is a general principle, which expresses the maxim *actor sequitur forum rei*, because it makes it easier, in principle, for a defendant to defend himself (see, to that effect, Case C-26/91 *Handte* v *Traitements Mécano-chimiques des Surfaces* [1992] ECR I-3967, paragraph 14; see also the Jenard Report on the Brussels Convention (OJ 1979 C 59, p. 1, 18)).

36. It is only by way of derogation from that fundamental principle, that the courts of the Contracting State in which the defendant has its domicile or seat are to have jurisdiction, that the Convention provides, under the first paragraph of Article 3 thereof, for the cases, exhaustively listed in Sections 2 to 6 of Title II, in which a defendant domiciled or established in a Contracting State may, where the situation is covered by a rule of special jurisdiction, or must, where it is covered by a rule of exclusive jurisdiction or a prorogation of jurisdiction, be excluded from the jurisdiction of the courts of the State in which it is domiciled and sued in a court of another Contracting State.

37. In that context, Sections 2 to 6 of Title II of the Convention include certain specific provisions which, for the purpose of determining which court has jurisdiction, depart from the general criterion of the domicile of the defendant by according, exceptionally, a certain influence to the domicile of the plaintiff.

38. Thus, first, in order to facilitate the proceedings brought by a maintenance creditor, Article 5(2) of the Convention gives that person the option to sue the defendant, in a Contracting State other than that of the defendant's domicile, in the courts for the place where the plaintiff is domiciled or habitually resident.

39. Similarly, also with the aim of protecting the party deemed to be weaker than the other party to the contract, point 2 of the first paragraph of Article 8 and the first paragraph of Article 14 of the Convention provide, respectively, that a holder of an insurance policy and a consumer have the right to bring proceedings against the other party to their contract in the courts of the Contracting State in which they are domiciled.

40. Although those rules of special jurisdiction give importance, exceptionally, to the plaintiff's domicile being in a Contracting State, they none the less constitute only an additional option for the plaintiff, alongside the forum of the courts of the ContractingState where the defendant is domiciled, which constitutes the general rule underlying the Convention.

41. Second, Article 17 of the Convention provides for the exclusive jurisdiction of a court or the courts of a Contracting State chosen by the parties, so long as one of the parties is domiciled in a Contracting State.

42. That condition does not necessarily refer to the defendant's domicile, so that the place of the plaintiff's domicile may, where appropriate, be decisive. However, it also follows from that provision that the rule of jurisdiction set out therein is applicable if the defendant is domiciled in a Contracting State, even if the plaintiff is domiciled in a non-member country (see, to that effect, the Jenard Report, cited above, p. 38).

43. On the other hand, the other provisions in Sections 2 to 6 of Title II of the Convention do not attach any importance to the plaintiff's domicile.

44. Admittedly, under Article 18 of the Convention, the voluntary appearance of the defendant establishes the jurisdiction of a court of a Contracting State before which the plaintiff has brought proceedings, without the place of the defendant's domicile being relevant.

45. However, although the court seised must be that of a Contracting State, that provision does not further require that the plaintiff be domiciled in such a State.

46. The same conclusion can be drawn from Article 16 of the Convention, which states that the rules of exclusive jurisdiction which it lays down are to apply without the domicile of the parties being taken into consideration. The fundamental reason for those rules of exclusive jurisdiction is the existence of a particularly close connection between the dispute and a Contracting State, irrespective of the domicile both of the defendant and of the plaintiff (as regards, more specifically, in proceedings having as their object tenancies of immovable property, the exclusive jurisdiction of the courts of the Contracting State in which the property is situated, see, in particular, Case C-8/98 *Dansommer* v *Götz* [2000] ECR I-0000, paragraph 27).

47. In the light of the foregoing, the Court finds that it is only in quite exceptional cases that Title II of the Convention accords decisive importance, for the purpose of conferring jurisdiction, to the plaintiff's domicile being in a Contracting State. That is the case only if the plaintiff exercises the option open to him under Article 5(2), point 2 of the first paragraph of Article 8 and the first paragraph of Article 14 of the Convention, and also in matters relating to prorogation of jurisdiction under Article 17 of the Convention, solely where the defendant's domicile is not situated in a Contracting State.

48. None of those specific cases is applicable in the case in the main proceedings.

49. Furthermore, it is settled case-law that the rules of jurisdiction which derogate from the general principle, set out in the first paragraph of Article 2 of the Convention, that the courts of the Contracting State in which the defendant is domiciled or established are to have jurisdiction, cannot give rise to an interpretation going beyond the cases expressly envisaged by the Convention (see, in particular, *Handte*, paragraph 14; Case C-89/91 *Shearson Lehman Hutton* v *TVB* [1993] ECR I-139, paragraphs 15 and 16; Case C-269/95 *Benincasa* v *Dentalkit* [1997] ECR I-3767, paragraph 13; and Case C-51/97 *Réunion Européenne and Others* [1998] ECR I-6511, paragraph 16).

50. In addition, as is already clear from the second paragraph of Article 3 of the Convention, which prohibits a plaintiff from invoking against a defendant domiciled in a Contracting State national rules of jurisdiction based, in particular, on the plaintiff's domicile or residence, the Convention appears clearly hostile towards the attribution of jurisdiction to the courts of the plaintiff's domicile (see Case C-220/88 *Dumez*

France and Tracoba [1990] ECR I-49, paragraph 16; and *Shearson Lehman Hutton*, paragraph 17). It follows that the Convention must not be interpreted as meaning that, otherwise than in the cases expressly provided for, it recognises the jurisdiction of the courts of the plaintiff's domicile and therefore enables a plaintiff to determine the court with jurisdiction by his choice of domicile (see, to that effect, *Dumez France and Tracoba*, paragraph 19).

51. Article 4 of the Convention provides, admittedly, for a derogation from the rule laid down in the second paragraph of Article 3. Article 4 states that, if the defendant is not domiciled in a Contracting State, jurisdiction is to be determined by the law in force in each Contracting State, subject only to Article 16, which applies regardless of domicile, and that, as against such a defendant, a plaintiff domiciled in a Contracting State has the right to avail himself in that State of the special rules of jurisdiction there in force of which an illustrative list appears in the second paragraph of Article 3 of the Convention.

52. However, in so far as Article 4 of the Convention provides that the rules of jurisdiction laid down by the Convention are not applicable where the defendant is not domiciled in a Contracting State, it constitutes a confirmation of the fundamental principle set out in the first paragraph of Article 2 of the Convention.

53. In the light of all the foregoing, it must be concluded that the system of rules on conferment of jurisdiction established by the Convention is not usually based on the criterion of the plaintiff's domicile or seat.

54. Moreover, as is clear from the wording of the second paragraph of Article 2 and the second paragraph of Article 4 of the Convention, nor is that system based on the criterion of the nationality of the parties.

55. The Convention enshrines, on the other hand, the fundamental principle that the courts of the Contracting State in which the defendant is domiciled or established are to have jurisdiction.

56. As is clear from paragraph 47 above, it is only by way of exception to that general rule that the Convention includes certain specific provisions which, in clearly defined cases, accord an influence to the plaintiff's domicile.

57. It follows that, as a general rule, the place where the plaintiff is domiciled is not relevant for the purpose of applying the rules of

jurisdiction laid down by the Convention, since that application is, in principle, dependent solely on the criterion of the defendant's domicile being in a Contracting State.

58. It would be otherwise only in exceptional cases where the Convention makes that application of the rules of jurisdiction expressly dependent on the plaintiff being domiciled in a Contracting State.

59. Consequently, the Convention does not, in principle, preclude the rules of jurisdiction which it sets out from applying to a dispute between a defendant domiciled in a Contracting State and a plaintiff domiciled in a non-member country.

60. As the Advocate General observed in paragraph 21 of his Opinion, it is thus fully in accordance with that finding that the Court has interpreted the rules of jurisdiction laid down by the Convention in cases where the plaintiff had his domicile or seat in a non-member country, although the provisions of the Convention in question did not establish any exception to the general principle that the courts of the Contracting State in which the defendant is domiciled are to have jurisdiction (see Case C-190/89 *Rich* [1991] ECR I-3855; and Case C-406/92 *The Tatry* [1994] ECR I-5439).

61. In those circumstances, the answer to the first question must be that Title II of the Convention is in principle applicable where the defendant has its domicile or seat in a Contracting State, even if the plaintiff is domiciled in a non-member country. It would be otherwise only in exceptional cases where an express provision of the Convention provides that the application of the rule of jurisdiction which it sets out is dependent on the plaintiff's domicile being in a Contracting State.

The second question

62. In this respect, it must be observed, first, that the rules of jurisdiction in matters relating to insurance, laid down in Section 3 of Title II of the Convention, apply expressly to certain specific types of insurance contracts, such as compulsory insurance, liability insurance, insurance of immovable property and marine and aviation insurance. Furthermore, point 3 of the first paragraph of Article 8 of the Convention expressly refers to co-insurance.

63. On the other hand, reinsurance is not mentioned in any of the provisions of that section.

64. First, according to settled case-law, it is apparent from a consideration of the provisions of Section 3 of Title II of the Convention in the light of the documents leading to their enactment that, in affording the insured a wider range of jurisdiction than that available to the insurer and in excluding any possibility of a clause conferring jurisdiction for the benefit of the insurer, they reflect an underlying concern to protect the insured, who in most cases is faced with a predetermined contract the clauses of which are no longer negotiable and is the weaker party economically (Case 201/82 *Gerling and Others* v *Amministrazione del Tesoro dello Stato* [1983] ECR 2503, paragraph 17).

65. The role of protecting the party deemed to be economically weaker and less experienced in legal matters than the other party to the contract which is fulfilled by those provisions implies, however, that the application of the rules of special jurisdiction laid down to that end by the Convention should not be extended to persons for whom that protection is not justified (see, by analogy, in respect of Article 13 *et seq.* of the Convention in relation to jurisdiction over consumer contracts, *Shearson Lehmann Hutton*, paragraph 19).

66. No particular protection is justified as regards the relationship between a reinsured and his reinsurer. Both parties to the reinsurance contract are professionals in the insurance sector, neither of whom can be presumed to be in a weak position compared with the other party to the contract.

67. It is thus in accordance with both the letter and the spirit and purpose of the provisions in question to conclude that they do not apply to the relationship between a reinsured and his reinsurer in connection with a reinsurance contract.

68. That interpretation is confirmed by the system of rules of jurisdiction established by the Convention.

69. Thus Section 3 of Title II of the Convention includes rules which confer jurisdiction on courts other than those of the Contracting State in which the defendant is domiciled. In particular, point 2 of the first paragraph of Article 8 of the Convention provides that the courts for the place where the policy-holder is domiciled are to have jurisdiction.

70. As has already been noted in paragraph 49 above, it is settled case-law that the rules of jurisdiction which derogate from the general principle, laid down in the first paragraph of Article 2 of the Convention,

that the courts of the Contracting State in which the defendant is domiciled are to have jurisdiction, cannot give rise to an interpretation going beyond the cases envisaged by the Convention.

71. That interpretation is all the more valid in the case of a rule of jurisdiction such as that laid down in point 2 of the first paragraph of Article 8 of the Convention, which enables the policy-holder to sue the defendant in the courts of the Contracting State in which the plaintiff is domiciled.

72. For the reasons more fully set out in paragraph 50 above, the framers of the Convention demonstrated their hostility towards the attribution of jurisdiction to the courts of the plaintiff's domicile otherwise than in the cases for which it expressly provides.

73. It follows that Section 3 of Title II of the Convention may not be regarded as applying to the relationship between a reinsured and his reinsurer in connection with a reinsurance contract.

74. That interpretation is also supported by the Schlosser Report on the Convention of Accession of the Kingdom of Denmark, Ireland and the United Kingdom of Great Britain and Northern Ireland to the Brussels Convention (OJ 1979 C 59, p. 71, 117), according to which '[r]einsurance contracts cannot be equated with insurance contracts. Accordingly, Articles 7 to 12 do not apply to reinsurance contracts'.

75. However, as the Commission rightly pointed out, although the rules of special jurisdiction in matters relating to insurance do not refer to disputes between a reinsured and his reinsurer in connection with a reinsurance contract, such as that at issue in the main proceedings, they are, on the other hand, fully applicable where, under the law of a Contracting State, the policy-holder, the insured or the beneficiary of an insurance contract has the option to approach directly any reinsurer of the insurer in order to assert his rights under that contract as against that reinsurer, for example in the case of the bankruptcy or liquidation of the insurer. In such a situation, the plaintiff is in a weak position compared with the professional reinsurer, so that the objective of special protection inherent in Article 7 *et seq*. of the Convention justifies the application of the special rules which it lays down.

76. In the light of all the foregoing, the answer to the second question must be that the rules of special jurisdiction in matters relating to

insurance set out in Articles 7 to 12a of the Convention do not cover disputes between a reinsurer and a reinsured in connection with a reinsurance contract.

On those grounds, the Court (Sixth Chamber), in answer to the questions referred to it by the Cour d'Appel, Versailles, by judgment of 5 November 1998, hereby rules:

> **1. Title II of the Convention of 27 September 1968 on Jurisdiction and the Enforcement of Judgments in Civil and Commercial Matters, as amended by the Convention of 9 October 1978 on the Accession of the Kingdom of Denmark, Ireland and the United Kingdom of Great Britain and Northern Ireland, by the Convention of 25 October 1982 on the Accession of the Hellenic Republic and by the Convention of 26 May 1989 on the Accession of the Kingdom of Spain and the Portuguese Republic, is in principle applicable where the defendant has its domicile or seat in a Contracting State, even if the plaintiff is domiciled in a non-member country. It would be otherwise only in exceptional cases where an express provision of that convention provides that the application of the rule of jurisdiction which it sets out is dependent on the plaintiff's domicile being in a Contracting State.**
>
> **2. The rules of special jurisdiction in matters relating to insurance set out in Articles 7 to 12a of that convention do not cover disputes between a reinsurer and a reinsured in connection with a reinsurance contract.**

OPINION OF ADVOCATE GENERAL FENNELLY

1. This Brussels Convention reference raises two questions: the first is whether the Convention applies where the plaintiff is domiciled in a third country; the second is whether the special rules concerning 'jurisdiction in matters relating to insurance' apply to disputes concerning reinsurance.

I - The legal and factual background

A - The relevant provisions of the Brussels Convention

2. Section 1 of Title II of the Convention contains Article 2 which sets out the general rule of jurisdiction, whereby 'persons domiciled in a Contracting

State shall, whatever their nationality, be sued in the courts of that State'. This general domiciliary rule of jurisdiction is subject to the rules of 'special jurisdiction' set out in section 2 of Title II. They include Article 5 which, *inter alia*, provides that: 'A person domiciled in a Contracting State may, in another Contracting State, be sued: 1.in matters relating to a contract, in the courts for the place of performance of the obligation in question; ...' .

3. Section 2 is also subject to the rules of section 3, comprising Articles 7 to 12a, concerning 'jurisdiction in matters relating to insurance. Article 8 provides that: 'An insurer domiciled in a Contracting State may be sued:

1. in the courts of the State where he is domiciled, or
2. in another Contracting State, in the courts for the place where the policy-holder is domiciled, or
3. if he is a co-insurer, in the courts of a Contracting State in which proceedings are brought against the leading insurer.

An insurer who is not domiciled in a Contracting State but has a branch, agency or other establishment in one of the Contracting States shall, in disputes arising out of the operations of the branch, agency or establishment, be deemed to be domiciled in that State'.

B - The main proceedings and reference

4. Universal General Insurance Company ('UGIC'), now in liquidation, is domiciled in British Columbia, Canada. It had instructed its broker, Euromepa, a French-domiciled company, to enter into a reinsurance contract with effect from 1 April 1990 in relation to a portfolio of Canadian home-occupiers' insurance policies. Acting on these instructions, Euromepa contacted Group Josi Reinsurance Company (hereinafter 'Group Josi'), a Belgian-domiciled company, by a fax dated 27 March 1990 and offered a share in the reinsurance contract, stating that 'the main reinsurers are Union Ruck with 24% and Agrippina Ruck with 20% ...'. By a faxed reply of 6 April 1990, Group Josi agreed to acquire a 7.5% share.

5. In the meantime, on 28 March 1990, Union Ruck told Euromepa that it did not intend to retain its share after 31 May 1990, and, by letter of 30 March 1990, Agrippina Ruck said it would reduce its share from 20% to 10% as of 1 June 1990. It is common case that Euromepa did not inform Group Josi of these communications.

6. On 25 February 1991, Euromepa sent Group Josi a statement of account showing that CAD 54 679.34 was owing in respect of the latter's share of the risk. Group Josi refused to pay, claiming that it had been induced to enter into the reinsurance contract on foot of information which 'subsequently transpired to be false'.

7. On 6 July 1994, UGIC brought proceedings against Group Josi before the Tribunal de Commerce (Commercial Court), Nanterre. Group Josi submitted that the French courts lacked jurisdiction because the Tribunal de Commerce, Brussels, within whose territorial jurisdiction it had its registered office, had jurisdiction. Group Josi relied both on the Brussels Convention and on Article 1247 of the French Code Civil (Civil Code).

8. On 27 July 1995, the Tribunal de Commerce, Nanterre, held that it had jurisdiction under French law on the basis that the Brussels Convention did not apply in respect of a Canadian company. It found against Group Josi and ordered it to pay to UGIC the sum of CAD 54 679.34 plus interest.

9. Group Josi appealed against that decision to the French Cour d'Appel (Court of Appeal), Versailles (hereinafter 'the referring court'). It contended that the Brussels Convention applied since it, as the defendant, was domiciled in a Contracting State. UGIC contended that the jurisdictional rules established by the Convention could only apply if both the plaintiff and the defendant were domiciled in a Contracting State. Since it was a company incorporated under Canadian law with no subsidiary establishment within the European Community, it concluded that the Convention could not apply and the dispute as to jurisdiction fell to be resolved according to national rules of private international law, pursuant to which the French courts had jurisdiction.

10. Having consulted the Ministère Public (Advocate General), the referring court decided to refer the following questions to the Court under the Protocol of 3 June 1971 on the Interpretation by the Court of Justice of the Brussels Convention:

'1. Does the Convention of 27 September 1968 on jurisdiction and the enforcement of judgments in civil and commercial matters apply not only to "intra-Community" disputes but also to disputes which are "integrated into the Community"? More particularly, can a defendant established in a Member State rely on the specific rules on jurisdiction set out in that Convention against a plaintiff domiciled in Canada?

2. Do the rules on jurisdiction specific to matters relating to insurance set out in Article 7 *et seq.* of the Convention apply to matters relating to reinsurance"?

II - Analysis

11. Written observations have been submitted by UGIC, Group Josi, the French Republic, the United Kingdom of Great Britain and Northern Ireland and the Commission. Only France and the Commission submitted oral observations.

A - The applicability of the Brussels Convention

12. All of the observations submitted to the Court, with the exception of those from UGIC, contend that the Brussels Convention is applicable in circumstances such as those involved in the main proceedings.

13. The Commission, the United Kingdom and France submit that, once the subject-matter of a dispute falls within the material scope of the Brussels Convention and, in particular, where the defendant is domiciled in a Contracting State, the domicile of the plaintiff is irrelevant.

14. There is nothing in the Jenard Report on the Brussels Convention which would indicate that any general restriction on the application of the basic rule is predicated upon the plaintiff's domicile being within the territory of a

Contracting State. Moreover, only exceptionally is the place of domicile of the plaintiff significant under the Convention. The explicit references made in those exceptional cases to that place indicate that in all other cases it is irrelevant.

15. Group Josi agrees but adds that disputes which are connected with the Community fall within its scope. A dispute will be 'integrated' ('intégré) into the Community if it is covered by one of the Convention's jurisdictional rules. France contends that, as UGIC may be regarded as being domiciled in France through the medium of its French agent, the first question does not arise. Moreover, the application of Article 2, notwithstanding a plaintiff's place of domicile, would increase legal certainty for non-Contracting-State domiciliaries, who would then not have to face the uncertainty of the vagaries of application of national rules of private international law.

16. I agree with the United Kingdom and France that it would be inappropriate, for the purposes of determining the personal scope of a Brussels Convention that was designed to promote legal certainty, to resort to such an indefinite concept as that of whether disputes are integrated into the Community. 'Legal certainty, as the Jenard Report noted, 'is most effectively secured by conventions based on direct jurisdiction' - i.e. where the jurisdictional rules established are applicable in the State of the original legal proceedings rather than merely in the courts of the place where it is sought to have a judgment recognised and enforced - 'since, under them, judgments are given by courts deriving their jurisdiction from the conventions themselves'. This is precisely what the Brussels Convention does; it establishes 'common rules of jurisdiction ... to achieve ... in the field which it was required to cover, a genuine legal systematisation which will ensure the greatest possible degree of legal certainty'. In a Convention whose central jurisdictional tenet is that a defendant must normally be sued in the courts for the place where he is domiciled, it would be odd if the place of domicile of the plaintiff were relevant.

17. It is sufficient to recall the scheme of the Brussels Convention to conclude that the domicile of the plaintiff is irrelevant. The scope of the Convention is defined in Article 1 so as to 'apply in civil and commercial matters whatever the nature of the court or tribunal'. The Court has confirmed that the Convention contains rules of jurisdiction which enumerate *exhaustively* the cases in which a person may be *sued* outside the State in which he is domiciled. Article 26 on the recognition of judgments and Article 31 on their enforcement, the key provisions in Title III of the Convention on 'Recognition and Enforcement' of judgments, are drafted in similarly general terms. In short, the language of all the principal provisions presumes that the material scope of the Convention is defined by reference to the actions which are brought before the courts of the Contracting States regardless of the parties.

18. The Brussels Convention takes the domicile of *the defendant* consistently as its primary point of reference for the exercise of jurisdiction. The basic rule in Article 2 and the special rules in, *inter alia*, Articles 5 and 6 invariably refer to where a 'person domiciled in a Contracting State' may be sued. Neither in those provisions nor in any of the special provisions such as Article 13 (consumer contracts) or Article 16 (exclusive jurisdiction) is any

reference made to the domicile of the plaintiff. Indeed, such indications as appear from the text suggest that the Convention is presumed to apply to litigation involving domiciliaries of non-Contracting States. The second paragraph of Article 13 provides that where 'a consumer enters a contract with a party who is not domiciled in a Contracting State, the latter is 'deemed to be domiciled' in a Contracting State when it has a branch or agency there and the dispute arises out of its operations. The latter provision is merely designed to identify the Contracting State' which may, in proceedings brought by a consumer, exercise jurisdiction. Article 17 confers exclusive jurisdiction on the courts of a Contracting State nominated for that purpose in a contract between parties 'one or more of whom is domiciled in a Member State'.

19. The jurisdictional provisions of the Brussels Convention comprise two distinct sets of provisions which establish the framework for the operation of Title III. Firstly, Article 2 confers jurisdiction based on the defendant's domicile, subject to a number of special provisions such as Articles 5, 6, 7 to 12a, 13 to 15, 16 and 17. Article 4 provides for the cases where 'the defendant is not domiciled in a Contracting State', in which case the jurisdiction of each Contracting State is to be determined 'by the law of that State', viz. by the private international law of the respective Contracting States. Thus, the Convention establishes a comprehensive scheme covering all defendants whether or not they are domiciled in a Contracting State.

20. The exclusion of the *plaintiffs* domiciled in non-Contracting States from Article 2, as argued by UGIC, would create a major and illogical gap in the scheme of the Brussels Convention. Firstly, it would make no sense to exclude cases where plaintiffs are domiciled in non-Contracting States from the scope of the Convention when cases involving *defendants* from such States are included. In particular, actions covered by Article 4 would be regulated, where necessary, by the provisions of Articles 21 and 22 regarding *lis alibi pendens* and related actions, whereas actions by non-domiciled plaintiffs even against persons domiciled within a Contracting State would not necessarily be so regulated. While the latter provisions do not confer jurisdiction, their language presumes, like that of Articles 26 and 31, that the Convention applies comprehensively to all cases brought before the courts of the various Contracting States.

21. Furthermore, no support for non-application of the Brussels Convention may be derived from the fact that it does not apply to proceedings concerning the recognition and enforcement of judgments given in non-Contracting States. The proceedings at the origin of such application, unlike an action brought against a defendant domiciled in one Contracting State before the courts of another, have manifestly no connection with the Community. Moreover, as the Commission observes, some support for dismissing the relevance of the plaintiff's domicile may be derived from certain case-law which has concerned actions brought by non-Contracting-State-domiciled plaintiffs but in which that domicile was not viewed as being pertinent. Thus, in *Rich*, the Court did not comment on the fact that the main proceedings involved a Swiss plaintiff who had brought an application before the English courts for the appointment of an arbitrator against an Italian domiciliary. While, in *The Tatry*,

although one of the various series of actions involved in that case comprised proceedings brought in the Netherlands by Polish shipowners for a declaration that they were not liable for the alleged contamination of certain cargo carried on board one of their ships from Brazil to Rotterdam, it was not suggested that the courts in the subsequently commenced English actions could ignore the *lis alibi pendens* requirements of Article 21 of the Convention on the basis that the Convention was inapplicable in respect of the first-in-time Netherlands action.

22. Accordingly, I recommend that the Court confirm that the non-Contracting-State domicile of the plaintiff is irrelevant for the purposes of the application of the Brussels Convention. In my opinion, it may only have a bearing in those cases where it is stated explicitly, whether directly or indirectly, by the Convention to constitute a relevant factor.

B - The Brussels Convention and reinsurance

23. Only UGIC favours treating reinsurance as falling within the scope of section 3 of Title II of the Brussels Convention. It refers particularly to the potentially very weak position of the insurer in certain 'fronting' situations, and submits that reinsurance should be subject to the special insurance rules.

24. Group Josi, supported on this point by France and the United Kingdom, submits that the special rules regarding insurance (especially Article 8(2) of the Brussels Convention, which allows the policy-holder to sue in the courts for the place where it is domiciled) do not apply. They are designed to protect insured persons as the presumptively weaker contracting parties. This is not the case with reinsurance. Group Josi, along with France and the United Kingdom, draws support from the Schlosser Report on the 1978 Accession Convention, which states that '[r]einsurance contracts cannot be equated with insurance contracts. Accordingly, Articles 7 to 12 do not apply to reinsurance contracts'. France notes that, although reinsurance has arisen in the context of certain Article 21 cases, the Court did not consider that the special rules concerning insurance applied. It also contends that, even if reinsurance were covered, Article 8(2) of the Convention could only apply where the insured is the weaker party and where it is domiciled in a Contracting State, neither of which conditions is satisfied by UGIC.

25. The Commission observes that the relationship between the reinsured and the reinsurer does not affect that between the insurer and the original insured person and that the relevant provisions of the Convention are ambiguous. However, it has decided to reconsider the view it expressed in its observations in *Overseas Union Insurance and Others.* Accordingly, it now submits that the insurance rules are designed to protect the 'weaker' party, which would tend to exclude reinsurance contracts. The rules on insurance should be viewed as being inspired by the same philosophy as that underlying the rules concerning consumer contracts in section 4 of Title II (Articles 13 to 15) of the Brussels Convention.

26. There are two possible bases upon which reinsurance may be regarded as falling within the scope of the special insurance rules. The first is that there is

no fundamental difference between insurance and reinsurance that would justify excluding the latter from the scope of section 3 of Title II of the Brussels Convention. The second is the textual argument that, while certain large risks are expressly excluded by Article 12a, which was inserted by the 1978 Accession Convention, reinsurance is not among them. Some indirect support for this view could be drawn, as suggested by UGIC, from the French legislature's decision, so as to exclude reinsurance from the scope of the French Code des Assurances (Insurance Code), to insert an express provision (Article L.111-1) into the Code to that effect.

27. However, I do not find these arguments convincing. In the first place, insurance and reinsurance, though related, 'are conceptually distinct'. Thus, while there is no generally accepted broad definition of reinsurance, it may, in substance, be distinguished from ordinary insurance contracts, because '[i]t is neither an assignment nor transfer of the original insurance business from one insurer to another, nor is it a relationship of partnership or agency between insurers', but, rather, it constitutes 'an independent contract of insurance whereby the reinsurer engages to indemnify the reinsured wholly or partially against losses for which the latter is liable to the insured under the primary contract of insurance'.

28. The decisive consideration, however, is to be found in the policy behind the special rules on jurisdiction in respect of insurance. It is clear from the Jenard Report that 'social considerations for the protection of certain categories of person, such as insured persons ...' necessitated certain exceptions from the general domiciliary jurisdiction rule, 'aimed in particular at preventing abuses which could result from the terms of contracts in standard form'. The notion of protecting the insured, jurisdictionally, against the (usually) economically more powerful insurer would seem to have inspired even the original text of section 3 of Title II of the Brussels Convention. Indeed, the Court had taken the view in *Bertrand* v *Ott*, several months before even the signature of the 1978 Accession Convention, that protection of the weaker private (final-consumer) party formed the basis for the rules of the original section 4 of Title II, notwithstanding that its provisions made no reference to 'consumers'. This view was expressly confirmed in 1983, as regards section 3 of Title II of the original Brussels Convention, in *Gerling* v *Amministrazione del Tesoro dello Stato*, where the Court held that it was 'apparent from a consideration of the provisions of that section in the light of the documents leading to their enactment that, in affording the insured a wider range of jurisdiction than that available to the insurer and in excluding any possibility of a clause conferring jurisdiction for the benefit of the insurer, their purpose was to protect the insured who is most frequently faced with a predetermined contract the clauses of which are no longer negotiable and who is in a weaker economic position'.

29. It is in this context that the unequivocal view regarding reinsurance expressed in paragraph 151 of the Schlosser Report must be considered. Since it categorically rejects the equation of reinsurance contracts with insurance contracts and since Article 9 of the 1978 Accession Convention inserted a new Article 12a into the Brussels Convention so as explicitly to exclude certain (but

not all) business-risk insurance contracts, the authors of the 1978 Accession Convention must be regarded as having accepted the Schlosser Report's view that there was no need to remove any types of reinsurance contracts because reinsurance had never been covered in the first place.

30. Moreover, the Court has consistently held that all exceptions to the general rule that a defendant be sued in the courts for the place of his domicile are to be narrowly construed. Since it is, at the very least, doubtful that it was originally intended to include reinsurance within the scope of section 3 of Title II of the Brussels Convention or, even if it were so originally included, to maintain that inclusion following the adoption of the 1978 Accession Convention, the Court should now confirm that the general jurisdictional rules of the Brussels Convention apply. Indeed, the whole thrust of section 3 of Title II is to prescribe a series of alternative rules of jurisdiction intended to benefit those suing 'an insurer domiciled in a Contracting State' (see Article 8). Only Article 11 addresses the right of an insurer to 'bring proceedings'. Yet it provides, apart from counterclaims which may always be made in the court in which the original claim is pending, that insurer-initiated proceedings must be brought 'in the courts of the Contracting State in which the defendant is domiciled'. In effect, therefore, as France points out, in so far as the right of action of insurers is concerned section 3 of Title II merely confirms the general rule of Article 2. If those provisions also extended to reinsurance, it might, not unreasonably, be contended that the reassured could only sue the 'reinsurer' at the latter's place of domicile because, after all, it would remain an 'insurer', while the reinsurer, since it would fall to be equated with an 'insurer', could also only sue the reinsured 'insurer' at the reassured's place of domicile. It seems to me highly unlikely that the authors of the Brussels Convention intended to deprive either insurers or reinsurers of the right, in disputes between themselves, to bring proceedings in particular pursuant to Article 5.

31. I would draw additional support for this conclusion from both the academic and judicial reaction to the provisions of section 3 of Title II of the Brussels Convention, as amended by the 1978 Accession Convention. In 1990, one commentator, '[i]n anticipation of a request being made for ... a ruling from the Court at some future date, ... submitted that reinsurance should most certainly be excluded from section 3'. It is noteworthy that the English courts - which, since much of the international reinsurance business is placed on the London market, have a particular familiarity with reinsurance - have taken a consistent position against the inclusion of reinsurance within the special rules.

32. Consequently, I am satisfied that reinsurance contracts, i.e. those which create relationships between a reinsured and his reinsurer, do not fall to be considered as 'matters relating to insurance' for the purpose of the Brussels Convention. This conclusion is unaffected by the Commission's submission that reinsurance should be so considered where the original policy-holder(s) is placed, whether as a result of national legislation or otherwise, in a direct relationship with the reinsurer. In those circumstances, the reinsurer would effectively act as an insurer and would, therefore, be subject to the special jurisdictional rules of section 3 of Title II. In other words, it would, vis-à-vis such

a policy-holder, fall to be considered as subrogated to the position of the insurer for the purpose of section 3.

III - Conclusion

33. In the light of the foregoing, I recommend that the Court answer the questions referred by the Cour d'Appel, Versailles as follows:

(1) The Convention of 27 September 1968 on jurisdiction and the enforcement of judgments in civil and commercial matters, as amended, applies to any civil or commercial action brought in a Contracting State to that Convention, against a defendant who is domiciled in that or another Contracting State to the Convention, regardless of the place of domicile of the plaintiff;

(2) The rules on jurisdiction specific to matters relating to insurance set out in section 3 of Title II, as amended, of the Brussels Convention do not apply in matters relating to reinsurance.

TITLE II *[Chapter II]*

JURISDICTION *[Jurisdiction]*

Jurisdiction in matters relating to contracts – Article 5(1) *[Article 5(1) – Also Articles 18 - 21]*

See also

Case 12/76 - 6 October 1976

Industrie Tessili Italiana Como
v
Dunlop AG

Principles of interpretation - Special jurisdiction - Article 5(1) - Matter relating to a contract - Place of performance of the obligation.

Summary

1. The new Member States are entitled to submit observations in the context of proceedings relating to the interpretation of one of the Conventions, for which provision is made in Article 220 of the Treaty, to which they are required by Article 3(2) of the Act of Accession to become parties.

2. The Convention of 27 September 1968 must be interpreted having regard both to its principles and objectives and to its relationship with the Treaty. As regards the question, whether the words and concepts used in the Convention must be regarded as having their own independent meaning and as being thus common to all the Member States or as referring to substantive rules of the law applicable in each case under the rules of conflict of laws of the court before which the matter is first brought, the appropriate choice can only be made in respect of each of the provisions of the Convention to ensure that it is fully effective having regard to the objectives of Article 220 of the Treaty.

3. The 'place of performance of the obligation in question' within the meaning of Article 5(1) of the Convention of 27 September 1968 is to be determined in accordance with the law which governs the obligation in

question according to the rules of conflict of laws of the court before which the matter is brought.

JUDGMENT OF THE COURT

Presiding, Lecourt, President, Kutscher and O'Keeffe, Presidents of Chambers, Donner, Mertens de Wilmars, Pescatore, Sorensen, Lord Mackenzie Stuart and Capotorti, Judges; Mayras, Advocate General

1. By order dated 14 January 1976, received at the Court Registry on 13 February 1976, the Oberlandesgericht Frankfurt am Main referred to the Court for a preliminary ruling under the Protocol of 3 June 1971 on the Interpretation of the Convention of 27 September 1968 on Jurisdiction and Enforcement of Judgments in Civil and Commercial Matters (hereinafter referred to as 'the Convention') a question on the interpretation of Article 5(1) of the Convention.

2. It appears from the order of reference that at this stage the case, which has been brought as an appeal to the Oberlandesgericht, relates to the jurisdiction of the court of first instance at Hanau to hear a case brought by an Italian undertaking with its registered office at Como in connection with the performance of a contract relating to the delivery by the Italian undertaking in accordance with instructions given by the German undertaking and delivered to a carrier in Como appointed by the German undertaking.

3. The German undertaking after taking delivery of the goods and selling some of them considers as a result of complaints from its customers that the suits delivered by the manufacturer are defective and do not correspond to the specifications agreed between the parties. For this reason it brought an action in its local court against the Italian manufacturer.

4. The Court by interlocutory judgment dated 10 May 1974 declared itself to have jurisdiction to hear the case whereupon the Italian undertaking brought an appeal before the Oberlandesgericht Frankfurt am Main. In the view of this latter court the question of jurisdiction raised must be settled in accordance with the provisions of the Convention. In its view there is no valid agreement between the parties conferring jurisdiction within the meaning of Article 17 of the Convention. On the other hand the Oberlandesgericht does not rule out the possibility that the court of first instance may have jurisdiction under Article 5(1) of the

Convention as being the place 'of performance of the obligation in question'. To settle this question it asks the Court of Justice to rule on the interpretation of that provision.

Procedure

5. The Republic of Ireland and the United Kingdom submitted observations during the written procedure and the Court therefore requested the parties in the main action, the Member States and the Commission to give their views on the question whether the new Member States which are not yet parties to the Convention are entitled to participate in proceedings relating to its interpretation.

6. Article 3(2) of the Act of Accession provides that 'The new Member States undertake to accede to the Conventions provided for in Article 220 of the EEC Treaty, and to the Protocols on the interpretation of those Conventions by the Court of Justice, signed by the original Member States, and to this end they undertake to enter into negotiations with the original Member States in order to make the necessary adjustments thereto'. The first paragraph of Article 63 of the Convention provides that 'The Contracting States recognize that any State which becomes a member of the European Economic Community shall be required to accept this Convention as a basis for the negotiations between the Contracting States and that State necessary to ensure the implementation of the last paragraph of Article 220 of the Treaty establishing the European Economic Community'. The new Member States thus have an interest in expressing their views when the Court is called upon to interpret the Convention to which they are required to become parties.

7. It should further be observed that Article 5(1) of the Protocol of 3 June 1971 stipulates that, except as otherwise provided, 'the provisions of the Treaty establishing the European Economic Community and those of the Protocol on the Statute of the Court of Justice annexed thereto, which are applicable when the Court is requested to give a preliminary ruling, shall also apply to any proceedings for the interpretation of the Convention'.

8. As a result the new Member States to which Article 177 of the EEC Treaty and Article 20 of the Protocol on the Statute of the Court of Justice apply are entitled to submit observations in accordance with the said articles in proceedings for the interpretation of the Convention. No valid objection to this conclusion is constituted by Article 4(4) of the Protocol

of 3 June 1971 on a special procedure which is not relevant for the present purposes. Further in the context of that Protocol, which originated before the enlargement of the European Communities, the words 'Contracting States' refer to all the Member States.

The interpretation of the Convention in general

9. Article 220 of the EEC Treaty provides that Member States shall, so far as necessary, enter into negotiations with each other with a view to securing for the benefit of their nationals the establishment of rules intended to facilitate the achievement of the common market in the various spheres listed in that provision. The Convention was established to implement Article 220 and was intended according to the express terms of its preamble to implement the provisions of that article on the simplification of formalities governing the reciprocal recognition and enforcement of judgments of courts or tribunals and to strengthen in the Community the legal protection of persons therein established. In order to eliminate obstacles to legal relations and to settle disputes within the sphere of intra-Community relations in civil and commercial matters the Convention contains, *inter alia*, rules enabling the jurisdiction in these matters of courts of Member States to be determined and facilitating the recognition and execution of courts' judgments. Accordingly the Convention must be interpreted having regard both to its principles and objectives and to its relationship with the Treaty.

10. The Convention frequently uses words and legal concepts drawn from civil, commercial and procedural law and capable of a different meaning from one Member State to another. The question therefore arises whether these words and concepts must be regarded as having their own independent meaning and as being thus common to all the Member States or as referring to substantive rules of the law applicable in each case under the rules of conflict of laws of the court before which the matter is first brought.

11. Neither of these two options rules out the other since the appropriate choice can only be made in respect of each of the provisions of the Convention to ensure that it is fully effective having regard to the objectives of Article 220 of the Treaty. In any event it should be stressed that the interpretation of the said words and concepts for the purpose of the Convention does not prejudge the question of the substantive rule applicable to the particular case.

The question raised by the national court

12. Article 5 of the Convention provides: 'A person domiciled in a Contracting State may, in another Contracting State, be sued: (1) in matters relating to a contract, in the courts for the place of performance of the obligation in question'. This provision must be interpreted within the framework of the system of conferment of jurisdiction under Title II of the Convention. In accordance with Article 2 the basis of this system is the general conferment of jurisdiction on the court of the defendant's domicile. Article 5, however, provides for a number of cases of special jurisdiction at the Option of the plaintiff.

13. This freedom of choice was introduced in view of the existence in certain well-defined cases of a particularly close relationship between a dispute and the court which may be most conveniently called upon to take cognizance of the matter. Thus in the case of an action relating to contractual obligations Article 5(1) allows a plaintiff to bring the matter before the Court for the place 'of performance' of the obligation in question. It is for the Court before which the matter is brought to establish under the Convention whether the place of performance is situate within its territorial jurisdiction. For this purpose it must determine in accordance with its own rules of conflict of laws what is the law applicable to the legal relationship in question and define in accordance with that law the place of performance of the contractual obligation in question.

14. Having regard to the differences obtaining between national laws of contract and to the absence at this stage of legal development of any unification in the substantive law applicable, it does not appear possible to give any more substantial guide to the interpretation of the reference made by Article 5(1) to the 'place of performance' of contractual obligations. This is all the more true since the determination of the place of performance of obligations depends on the contractual context to which these obligations belong.

15. In these circumstances the reference in the Convention to the place of performance of contractual obligations cannot be understood otherwise than by reference to the substantive law applicable under the rules of conflict of laws of the court before which the matter is brought.

On those grounds, the Court in answer to the question referred to it by the

Oberlandesgericht Frankfurt am Main by order dated 14 January 1976, hereby rules:

The 'place of performance of the obligation in question' within the meaning of Article 5(1) of the Convention of 27 September 1968 on Jurisdiction and the Enforcement of Judgments in Civil and Commercial Matters is to be determined in accordance with the law which governs the obligations in question according to the rules of conflict of laws of the court before which the matter is brought.

OPINION OF MR ADVOCATE GENERAL MAYRAS

I. This is the first case to be referred to you under the Protocol of 3 June 1971 on the interpretation of the Convention on Jurisdiction of 27 September 1968, a text which has been in force in the relations between the six original Member States of the European Economic Community since September 1975.

The facts which have given rise to this action may be summarized as follows: on 29 April 1971 the German company Dunlop AG of Hanau ordered on the basis of samples a certain number of women's ski-suits from the Italian company Industrie Tessili of Como. The Italian company made up the articles in question and despatched them on 31 July 1971 by a carrier designated by the German company. They were received by that company on 18 August 1971. At the same time as it sent the goods the Italian company made out an invoice which was received by the German Company on 3 August 1971.

When a dispute arose between the parties to the transaction over the conformity of the goods with the specifications in the order, the German company brought an action against its supplier before the Landgericht Hanau. We do not know exactly what the company is seeking: t is either the termination of the transaction or the payment of damages. Be that as it may, its cause of action lies in the defective performance by the Italian company of its contractual obligation. That company has appeared before the German court, but only in order to contest its jurisdiction. That court found that the parties had during their negotiations validly chosen it to be the tribunal with jurisdiction to entertain any disputes which might arise out of their transaction and in a judgment on a preliminary issue. It dismissed the objection of lack of jurisdiction.

The Italian company then appealed from this decision to the Oberlandesgericht Frankfurt. That court is inclined to take the view that the parties have concluded no valid agreement on a choice of forum in the sense of Article 17 of the Convention. As the respondent has not sued the appellant in a court of the State in which the appellant is domiciled (according to the general provision contained in Article 2 of the Convention) and as no exclusive jurisdiction *ratione materiae* vests in an Italian court rather than in a court of the Federal Republic of Germany, the Oberlandesgericht Frankfurt considers that the

Landgericht Hanau may only have jurisdiction if it is 'the court for the place where the obligations has been or is to be performed' within the meaning that you will give to this phrase. It is quite unnecessary to emphasize the importance of the reply that you are called upon to give, since it may be assumed that actions arising out of contractual obligations will form a large proportion of the disputes to which the Convention will apply.

II. The problem of the conflict of jurisdiction is not new in the six original Member States of the EEC. The Convention was concluded between these six States precisely in order to try to determine 'the international jurisdiction of their courts'. The preamble sets out the guiding principle of its authors, that is, the desire 'to strengthen in the Community the legal protection of persons therein established'.

In contractual matters the competent court - and the law applicable to the contract - may be determined according to rigid rules or according to more flexible provisions. To limit ourselves to the private law of the six original Member States, conflicts of jurisdiction in this field are resolved in various ways: certain legislations refer both to the place where the contract or obligation was concluded or came into being and the place for their performance (Belgium, Italy); other legislations give jurisdiction in actions concerning sales of a commercial character either to the court for the place where the promise was made and the goods delivered by the seller or to the court for the place where payment was to be made by the buyer (France, Luxembourg); others accept in all cases only the jurisdiction of the court for the place of performance (Federal Republic of Germany); finally, others pay no attention to any criterion of connection with the conclusion or performance of a contract (The Netherlands). The law laid down by conventions also provides many different solutions to this problem and it is for this reason that Article 55 of the Convention stipulates that 'for the States which are parties to it' shall 'supersede' a whole series of bilateral agreements which it lists.

Whatever the arguments which motivated their choice - a desire to avoid 'splitting' the jurisdiction between the court for the place where the contract was concluded (in actions concerning its formation and effects) and the court for the place of performance (in actions concerning performance), or the advisability of granting jurisdiction to the court of the State in which it will be necessary to seek to enforce a judgment concerning delivery and in which the goods to be delivered are situated - the preparatory work, commentaries by legal writers and text of the Convention show clearly that its authors have opted in all cases for the criterion of the 'place where the obligation has been or is to be performed' ('lieu où l'obligation a été ou doit être exécutée'). They considered performance to be the ingredient which best distinguished the transaction as a whole and that it was therefore necessary to retain the criterion attaching it to a particular locality. Article 5(1) therefore refers to the 'place where the obligation has been or is to be performed'. Similarly, in matters relating to quasi-delict, the criterion adopted is the 'place where the harmful event occurred', a fact which is giving rise to certain problems with which you will soon be required to deal.

III. Although the substantive nature of the provision contained in Article

5(1) is of particular importance, as is emphasized by the use of the singular noun ('the obligation'), the apparent simplicity and unity of this criterion must not be allowed to create an illusion. First of all, this criterion must be adopted in the light of the possible multiplicity of the places of performance; it often happens that a single contract must be performed in several countries. In particular, however, this criterion varies according to the particular type of obligation in question. It is thus appropriate, first, to define the legal relationship or the contract out of which the main action has arisen. In this respect - without in any way prejudicing the power of the national court to classify the facts submitted to it - I consider that this dispute has arisen out of an 'international sale of goods' within the meaning of the Uniform Law on this matter annexed to The Hague Convention of 1 July 1964, that is, out of a 'forward sale' or of a 'contract for the supply of goods to be manufactured or produced', since the seller has to provide all the materials necessary for such manufacture or production or, at least, since the buyer is not required to provide an essential part of the materials which are necessary. These classifications are those of the Hague Convention of 15 June 1955 on the law relating to the international sale of goods and The Hague Convention of 1 July 1964 on the same subject. When the events which gave rise to this case occurred the latter text was not in force between Italy and the Federal Republic of Germany but it has been in force subsequently. Secondly, in the case of a bilateral contract, a distinction must be made according to whether the facts are considered from the point of view of one contracting party or the other, for example, as regards a sale - a description which seems to me to cover the transaction involved in this instance - according to whether we consider the facts from the point of view of the seller or the buyer. The authors of the Convention themselves made this distinction in matters relating to instalment sales and loans (Articles 14 and 15). Furthermore, this distinction between the obligations of the seller and the obligations of the buyer is taken up again in the Uniform Law on the International Sales of Goods which the authors of the Convention certainly had in their minds.

In a transaction of this type the seller undertakes:

1 - to effect delivery,

2 - to hand over any documents relating thereto,

3 - to transfer the property in the goods.

For his part, the buyer undertakes:

1 - to pay the price for the goods,

2 - to take delivery of the goods.

The aims of the parties are, on the one hand, to sell and to deliver the product and, on the other, to pay the price and to take delivery of the goods. The place where the obligation is to be performed is the place in which the service which *characterises* the transaction must be provided. Of these three obligations on the seller, the one whose performance characterises or typifies the contract of sale from the point of view of the buyer is the taking of delivery or handing over of the goods and thus if the buyer brings an action the competent court will be determined by reference to the place of delivery.

IV. Is it, however, necessary to 'divide' or 'split' still further the place of performance of the obligation and to look for the place in which a debt resulting from the termination of a contract of sale by reason of the wrongful conduct of the seller *is to be paid* and the place where the article sold must be returned, if such is the subject of the action before the court dealing with the substance of the case. This is the real question before the Oberlandesgericht Frankfurt. As the contractual obligation has been performed and as the dispute concerns the defective nature of that performance, the court asks whether the phrase 'the obligation *is to be* performed' may refer to the substitute obligation into which the breach of the main obligation may be resolved.

According to one argument, although it is correct that a failure to perform or, on the other hand, the proper performance, of the obligation which is, from the point of view of the seller, the essential feature of the contract of sale, will be established in the place of delivery, acceptance of delivery and approval of the goods, it may be that hidden defects in the article sold only appear later in a different place from the original place of delivery. It is in the former that the terms, conditions for performance (arrangements for examining the goods) or consequences of the breach (termination on grounds of breach, the raising of the issue of the seller's liability, etc.) must be brought before the courts. Therefore, any obligation on the seller which is brought before the courts for this reason by using one of the many means of redress available under national law (termination of the contract, damages, duty to provide a guarantee, etc.) may and must be performed in a place different from that in which the original, essential obligation (delivery in the case of a sale) was performed. This may be either the place where the goods are to be found, or the place where the sum owed by the buyer is to be recovered, according to whether it must be collected (as is the case in France, Belgium and the Federal Republic of Germany) or is payable at the address of the payee (as is the case in Italy and the Netherlands). Thus, the problem which arises in the present case is to discover whether the obligation referred to in Article 5(1) is the original obligation or its substitute, represented according to customs or national laws, by an action for specific performance, in whole or in part, of the contract or for its termination or by an action for the payment of damages for failure to perform or insufficient performance. If taken to its logical conclusion, this argument amounts to maintaining that if a contract contains several obligations to be performed by the defendant the plaintiff could choose the competent court from among all those which are, to a greater or lesser degree, concerned with any one of the obligations under the contract, even if that obligation were not itself in dispute. This explains why Article 5(1) refers to the place where the obligation has been or is to be performed.

I do not consider that it is possible to go so far. The Italian version of Article 5(1) assumes that the obligation in question must at least be in dispute, since it refers to it as '*dedotta in giudizio*'. More particularly, such an argument would not be compatible with the intentions of the authors of the Convention. Of course, the rules established by that text are intended essentially to resolve conflicts of jurisdiction; they are not principally rules of substantive law. However, I consider one of the assumptions of the system set up by the Convention to be that although distinctions may be made according to the type of contract and the parties to it, taken as a whole a contract constitutes a legal and economic entity and all questions connected with the performance of the essential obligation of the contract must fall within the jurisdiction of the court for the place of performance of that obligation. Any disputes which have arisen or which may arise in connection with the 'particular legal relationship' (Article 17) constituted by the obligation to deliver must be brought before the court for the place where delivery must take place. Any contract draws its dominant feature from one of the obligations which result from it, even if such obligations may differ according to the circumstances. The expectations of the parties are turned towards the performance of that particular obligation and it is in the place of performance that the failure to perform will normally be found and the consequences of such failure drawn. The contrary argument would amount to perfectionism and would bring us back to the criterion of the place in which the goods are to be found (*lex rei sitae*) or to that of the *forum conveniens*. An approach which would without further qualification adopt the court of the place which has the closest links with the performance of the obligation, or which appears to be the most appropriate for such performance - 'the court with the closest connection' (by analogy with Article 4 of the draft of the Convention on the law applying to contractual and non-contractual obligations) - would be too vague and general and would make it impossible to advance the basic values in the matter of contract, namely legal certainty and the possibility of foreseeing the law which will be applied.

It has been stated by authoritative commentators (Droz, Compétence Judiciaire et Effets des Jugements dans le Marché Commun, 1972, p. 128), that 'the Convention rejects the theory of the *forum conveniens*; serious difficulties of a practical nature may arise in determining the connection between the case and the designated court'. The same author states further (pp. 45-46) that 'These rules of jurisdiction (in Articles 5 and 6) form a whole and are self subsistent...'. It must be accepted in principle that the silence of the Treaty as to a ground of jurisdiction means that such a ground must be excluded: this will apply for example, not only to the *forum* of the place where the contract was made, but also to the forum ascertained by reference to connection with the contract, a principle which the Treaty has not accepted, as a ground for direct jurisdiction.

As Mr Bourel observes (Les Conflits de Lois en Matière d'Obligations Extracontractuelles, 1961, p. 145), 'if the obligations which result from the contract are determined by the will of the parties, those which result from a breach of the contract are created by law and are thus covered by the territorial rule, in the same way as obligations arising in matters of tort'. The result of this is that, by reason of the disparity in the territorial rules, the obligations which result from a breach of contract may vary considerably according to whether the rules are optional, subject to the law chosen independently by the parties, or constitute mandatory provisions, covered by the law governing performance of the contract. Such a result would jeopardize, the aim of grouping and concentrating the disputes in the court hearing the *original* application which was in the minds of the authors of the Convention when they drafted Article 6 (third-party proceedings, counterclaim).

In fact, unlike the authors of the Benelux Treaty on jurisdiction of 1961, which has not yet come into force, the authors of the Convention adopted the criterion of the place of performance of the obligation rather than the place where it came into being. Article 4 of the Treaty provides that: 'Any dispute which arises in matters concerning personal rights and obligations and rights and obligations relating to recoverable property and in civil or commercial matters, may be brought by the plaintiff before the court of the place in which the obligation came into being, or in which it has been or *is to be performed*'. Article 1(2) of the Protocol states: 'The Grand duchy of Luxembourg shall not be obliged to recognize judgments given in matters of contract by a Belgian or a Netherlands court or to declare them enforceable where the jurisdiction of such court was based on the place where the obligation came into being or where it was performed, if, when the action was brought, the defendant was domiciled in Luxembourg or, if he was not domiciled in one of the three countries, had his residence there'.

If the authors of the Convention had not simply referred to the 'place of performance of the contract', this is because the Convention applies both to commercial and civil matters. In employing the phrase 'the place where the obligation is to be performed' they are referring to the original and principal obligation which forms the essential feature of the contract.

It would only be useful to resort - and then only on a subsidiary basis - to the criterion that jurisdiction shall vest in the court of the place which has the *closest link* with the performance of the obligation if the act which forms the essence of the transaction cannot be defined. This is, however, not the case as regards the sale of goods.

V. I consider that the view that these are actions which concern the obligation which constitutes the essential feature of the contract in question and disputes engendered by that obligation which have arisen or which may arise in connection with a particular legal relationship (Article 17(1)) is confirmed by the Convention relating to a uniform law on the international sale of goods to which I have already referred. According to this Convention, having regard to legal remedies open to the buyer, the obligations on the seller may be divided into two types. First, there are obligations as regards the date and place of delivery. The buyer's remedies for the seller's failure to perform the obligations arising out of that relationship are (Article 24):

- either to require performance of the contract, or
- to declare the contract avoided.

In either case he may also claim damages, the amount of which varies according to which whether or not the contract is avoided. Secondly, there are obligations as regards the conformity of the goods. Where the seller has handed over goods which do not conform to the terms of the contract and where performance of the contract has nevertheless begun to take place, the seller *is regarded as having failed to fulfil his obligation to deliver the goods* (Article 33). The buyer's remedies for the seller's failure to perform the obligations arising out of that relationship are (Article 41):

- to require performance of the contract by the seller, or
- to declare the contract avoided, or
- to reduce the price.

The buyer may also obtain damages, the amount of which varies according to whether or not the contract is avoided. Therefore, whether the seller is at fault as regards the terms and conditions of delivery of the goods or as regards their conformity, he is regarded as having failed to perform his obligation to deliver the goods.

I do not regard it as relevant whether the obligation to deliver has been *performed* (in which case the buyer claims a reduction in price or the avoidance of the contract, plus damages for lack of conformity) or *is to be performed* (in which case the buyer seeks the performance of the contract, plus damages): in either case the place referred to in Article 5(1) of the Convention is the place where delivery is taken.

VI. The reservation set out in Article I of the Protocol annexed to the Convention provides further confirmation for the interpretation which I am putting forward. The first paragraph of Article I of the Protocol provides that the rule concerning jurisdiction contained in Article 5(1) shall not apply to persons domiciled in Luxembourg. In the Grand Duchy of Luxembourg economic relationships are characterized by the fact that many contracts concluded by persons domiciled there are international in nature. In this type of contract it is normally the buyer who is resident in the Grand Duchy; the seller has his place of business abroad - in particular in Belgium - and generally stipulates that a fob clause be put in the contract. According to the specialists (Jenard, Rapport sur la Convention, Supplement to the Bulletin of the EC, November 1972, English version, p. 109), this reservation 'is justified by the particular nature of the economic relationships between Belgium and Luxembourg, in consequence of which the *greater part* of the contractual obligations between persons residing in the two countries are performed or are to be performed in Belgium'. Therefore *in most* cases a buyer-plaintiff domiciled in Luxembourg could not bring before the Luxembourg courts actions which concern a seller-defendant domiciled in Belgium (under Article 2(1)) but may, on the other hand, be sued in the Belgian courts. As Alphonse Huss has said (Le Contrat Economique International 1975, p. 226) this could give rise to the fear that 'the domestic tribunals would be largely divested of jurisdiction whilst, too often, plaintiffs would be obliged to take proceedings abroad'. For this reason, not only has the criterion of the place where the contract is concluded, which confers a marked advantage on the more powerful of the contracting parties, been set aside by virtue of the basic option contained in the Convention (Article 2(1)), but even the criterion of the place of performance only applies if it has been expressly and specifically accepted (Article 17 of the Convention and second paragraph of Article I of the Protocol). This same specialist has also stated that 'the direct usefulness of this exceptional provision is weakened by the third paragraph of Article 28 of the Convention, which rules out any review of jurisdiction by the court recognizing and enforcing the judgment and does not allow the recourse to the plea founded on public policy. Thus, where the foreign court fails to observe the safeguard clauses in the

Protocol, the party concerned may find himself obliged to defend his rights before a court which has no jurisdiction'.

Whatever the practical use of this reservation and its justification from the point of view of the freedom of establishment of lawyers may be, these comments constitute an authentic interpretation of the Convention by its authors themselves and are of great value in replying to the question before us.

The phrase 'the place where the obligation has been or is to be performed' must be given a wide interpretation: as regards the sale of goods it covers 'the greater part' of the seller's contractual obligations, in particular, those connected with the delivery of the goods.

VII. As regards the actual ascertainment of the place where the seller's obligations with regard to delivery have been or are to be performed and, therefore, the ascertainment of the place of delivery, the reply will vary according to the terms of the contract or, in the absence of such terms, according to the particular circumstances of the case. In this respect the clauses of the contract concerning delivery will be decisive: it may be the place where the seller's principal place of business (fob sale) or on the other hand a place in the State in which the buyer is domiciled (cif sale). It is for the court trying the substance of the case to determine such place and, by interpreting the contract or by classifying the facts in the light of its own law (such a reference to the internal law and private international law of each Contracting State is provided for, for example, as regards the recognition of judgments (Article 27(4)) or the determination of domicile and seats of companies (Articles 52 and 55) to rule whether performance has taken place or was to take place within its area of jurisdiction. It is not impossible for this place to be found in the buyer's State and not, as the seller maintains, at its own registered office. Conversely, if the place where the goods have been or were to be handed over to the buyer or to the person responsible for receiving them on his behalf were situated in the seller's State, jurisdiction would vest in a court in that State. It is thus possible that if the plaintiff had addressed itself directly to a court of the State in which the seller is domiciled (Article 2) that court would have decided that delivery took place in the buyer's State and that it was incompetent to entertain the action. There will not necessarily be any correlation between the law applicable and the court before which the action is brought, that is, between the legislative power and the judicial power. In short, this provision of the Convention may well be of no help to a buyer who would like to sue a seller-defendant outside his State. But it is only suppletive in nature: it is in no way intended to allow the plaintiff to avoid the rule in Article 2 *in all cases* and to institute proceedings against the defendant outside the jurisdiction of the court of his domicile (Article 6(2)). The plaintiff *may* avail himself of this provision only if the place of performance of the obligation is to be found in the Contracting State in which he himself is domiciled. In fact, assuming that the legal relationship is international in nature and at the place of performance of the obligation may be regarded as situated in a State other than that in which the defendant is domiciled, the aim of Article 5(1) is to determine the court which, *in that State*, has jurisdiction. Its aim is not to depart in all cases from the rule laid down in Article 2(1).

At the present stage of European development, it is difficult to go any further as long as no uniform rules governing the conflict *of laws* have been adopted as regards contractual obligations. The intention of the authors of the Convention was not to adopt uniform legislation but 'to ensure that these provisions are applied as effectively and as uniformly as possible' (Joint Declaration of 3 June 1971 attached to the Protocol on the interpretation of the Convention) and 'to prevent differences of interpretation of the Convention from impairing its unifying effect' (Joint Declaration of 27 September 1961 attached to the Convention). As Georges Droz has said (Clunet 1973, p. 23), 'It will no longer be a case of truth on this side of the Pyrenees, error beyond; in future, in France or the Netherlands, it will be a case of two truths'. However, to arrive at a uniform interpretation of the concept of the place of performance would be an important step, even if reference were still made on a subsidiary level to the national law of the court seised of the matter. If the Convention did not exist it would first be necessary to decide on the criterion which determines jurisdiction. As we have already seen, one might hesitate before making this decision, at least between the place where the contractual obligation came into being and the place of its performance. Had the Convention retained these two grounds of jurisdiction, the court before which an action was brought would still have had to resort to its national law in order to attach each ground to a particular area. Thus, in relation to the situation existing earlier the Convention represents clear progress and constitutes a middle course between the principle that, as far as possible, all questions concerning a contract must be submitted to a single court (and to a single ideal law) and the opposing principle that a contract must be divided into various separate parts.

I am therefore of the opinion that you should rule that: in the relationships between the High Contracting Parties to the Convention of 27 September 1968 and subject to the provisions of the first paragraph of Article 2 and to Article 17 of the Convention and to Article 1 of the Protocol annexed to the Convention, any disputes relating to the performance of the obligation which constitutes the essential feature of the contract in question may, under Article 5(1), be brought before the court for the place where that obligation has been or was to be performed. In the case of sales and as regards the seller, this obligation concerns the delivery of the goods. It is for the court before which the action was first brought to determine where the place of performance of this obligation is situated.

Case 14/76 - 6 October 1976

Ets. A. De Bloos, S.P.R.L.
v
Société en commandite par actions Bouyer

Matters relating to a contract - Article 5(1) - Concept of obligation - Exclusive concession - Action brought by grantee against grantor - Compensation by way of damages - Action for payments - Powers of the national court - Article 5(5) -Control of branch, agency or other establishment - Criteria for distinction.

Summary

1. For the purpose of determining the place of performance within the meaning of Article 5 of the Convention of 27 September 1968 the obligation to be taken into account is that which corresponds to the contractual right on which the plaintiff's action is based. In a case where the plaintiff asserts the right to be paid damages or seeks the dissolution of the contract by reason of the wrongful conduct of the other party, the obligation referred to in Article 5(1) is still that which arises under the contract and the non-performance of which is relied upon to support such claims.

2. In disputes in which the grantee of an exclusive sales concession charges the grantor with having infringed the exclusive concession, the word 'obligation' contained in Article 5(1) of the Convention of 27 September 1968 on jurisdiction and the enforcement of Judgments in Civil and Commercial Matters refers to the obligation forming the basis of the legal proceedings, namely the contractual obligation of the grantor which corresponds to the contractual right relied upon by the grantee in support of the application. In disputes concerning the consequences of the infringement by the grantor of a contract conferring an exclusive concession, such as the payment of damages or the dissolution of the

contract, the obligation to which reference must be made for the purposes of applying Article 5(1) of the Convention is that which the contract imposes on the grantor and the non-performance of which is relied upon by the grantee in support of the application for damages or for the dissolution of the contract.

In the case of actions for the payment of compensation by way of damages, it is for the national court to ascertain whether, under the law applicable to the contract, an independent contractual obligation or an obligation replacing the unperformed contractual obligation is involved.

3. When the grantee of an exclusive sales concession is not subject either to the control or to the direction of the grantor, he cannot be regarded as being at the head of a branch, agency or other establishment of the grantor within the meaning of Article 5(5) of the Convention of 27 September 1968.

JUDGMENT OF THE COURT

Lecourt, President, Kutscher, O'Keeffe, Presidents of Chambers, Donner, Mertens de Wilmars, Pescatore, Sørensen, Lord Mackenzie Stuart, Capotorti, Judges

1. By order of 9 December 1975, received at the Court Registry on 13 February 1976, the Court d'Appel, Mons, has referred to the Court under the Protocol of 3 June 1971 concerning the interpretation of the Convention of 27 September 1968 on jurisdiction and the enforcement of Judgments in Civil and Commercial Matters (hereinafter referred to as 'the Convention') questions concerning the interpretation of Article 5(1) and (5) of the said Convention.

2. From the order making the reference it appears that the case is at this stage concerned with the question whether the Belgian court has jurisdiction to hear an action which the grantee of an exclusive distributorship contract, whose registered office is in Belgium, has brought against the grantor, who is established in France.

3. Complaining of a unilateral breach, without notice, of the said contract, the grantee brought proceedings against the grantor before the Belgian court seeking, in accordance with Belgian law, the dissolution of the contract by the court, on the ground of the grantor's wrongful conduct, and the payment of damages.

4. When the Belgian court of first instance decided that it had no jurisdiction to hear the case, the grantee appealed before the Cour d'Appel, Mons.

5. In the first question, the Court is asked whether, in an action brought by the grantee of an exclusive sales concession against the grantor in which he claims that the latter has infringed the exclusive concession, the term 'obligation' in Article 5(1) of the Convention is to be interpreted as applying without distinction to any obligation arising out of the outline contract granting an exclusive sales concession or even arising out of the successive sales concluded in performance of the said contract, or as referring exclusively to the obligation forming the basis of the legal proceedings.

6. If the last-mentioned possibility is the correct one, the Court is further asked to rule whether the word 'obligation' in the aforementioned Article 5(1) refers to the original obligation, the obligation to provide the equivalent of the original obligation or to obligation to pay damages where the effect of the dissolution or termination of the contract is to render void the original obligation, or, finally, to the obligation to pay 'fair compensation' or even 'additional compensation' within the meaning of the Belgian Law of 27 July 1961.

7. Under Article 5(1) of the Convention, a person domiciled in a Contracting State may, in another Contracting State, be sued: 'in matters relating to a contract, in the courts for the place of performance of the obligation in question.'

8. As stated in its preamble, the Convention is intended to determine the international jurisdiction of the courts of the Contracting States, to facilitate the recognition and to introduce an expeditious procedure for securing the enforcement of judgments.

9. These objectives imply the need to avoid, so far as possible, creating a situation in which a number of courts have jurisdiction in respect of one and the same contract.

10. Because of this, Article 5(1) of the Convention cannot be interpreted as referring to any obligation whatsoever arising under the contract in question.

11. On the contrary, the word 'obligation' in the article refers to the contractual obligation forming the basis of the legal proceedings.

12. This interpretation is, moreover, clearly confirmed by the Italian and German versions of the article.

13. It follows that for the purposes of determining the place of performance within the meaning of Article 5, quoted above, the obligation to be taken into account is that which corresponds to the contractual right on which the plaintiff's action is based.

14. In a case where the plaintiff asserts the right to be paid damages or seeks a dissolution of the contract on the ground of the wrongful conduct of the other party, the obligation referred to in Article 5(1) is still that which arises under the contract and the non-performance of which is relied upon to support such claims.

15. For these reasons, the answer to the first question must be that, in disputes in which the grantee of an exclusive sales concession charges the grantor with having infringed the exclusive concession, the word 'obligation' contained in Article 5(1) of the Convention of 27 September 1968 on jurisdiction and the enforcement of Judgments in Civil and Commercial Matters refers to the obligation forming the basis of the legal proceedings, namely the contractual obligation of the grantor which corresponds to the contractual right relied upon by the grantee in support of the application.

16. In disputes concerning the consequences of the infringement by the grantor of a contract conferring an exclusive concession, such as the payment of damages or the dissolution of the contract, the obligation to which reference must be made for the purposes of applying Article 5(1) of the Convention is that which the contract imposes on the grantor and the non-performance of which is relied upon by the grantee in support of the application for damages or for the dissolution of the contract.

17. In the case of actions for the payment of compensation by way of damages, it is for the national court to ascertain whether, under the law applicable to the contract, an independent contractual obligation or an obligation replacing the unperformed contractual obligation is involved.

18. In the second question, the Court is asked to rule whether, in circumstances where, on the one hand, the grantee of an exclusive sales concession is not empowered either to negotiate in the name of the grantor or to bind him and, on the other hand, is not subject either to the control or direction of the grantor, he should be regarded as being at the

head of a branch, agency or other establishment of the grantor within the meaning of Article 5(5) of the Brussels Convention.

19. Under Article 5(5) of the Convention, a person domiciled in a Contracting State may, in another Contracting State, be sued: 'as regards a dispute arising out of the operations of a branch, agency or other establishment, in the courts for the place in which the branch, agency or other establishment is situated.'

20. One of the essential characteristics of the concepts of branch or agency is the fact of being subject to the direction and control of the parent body.

21. It is clear from both the object and the wording of this provision that the spirit of the Convention requires that the concept of 'establishment appearing in the said article shall be based on the same essential characteristics as a branch or agency.

22. It is, in consequence, impossible to extend the concepts of branch, agency or other establishment to the grantee of an exclusive concession whose operations are of the kind indicated by the national court.

23. For the foregoing reasons, the answer to the second question must be that, when the grantee of an exclusive sales concession is subject neither to the control nor to the direction of the grantor, he cannot be regarded as being at the head of a branch, agency or other establishment of the grantor within the meaning of Article 5(5) of the Convention of 27 September 1968.

On those grounds the Court in answer to the question referred to it by the Cour d'Appel, Mons, by order 9 December 1975, hereby rules:

1. In disputes in which the grantee of an exclusive sales concession is charging the grantor with having infringed the exclusive concession, the word 'obligation' contained in Article 5(1) of the Convention of 27 September 1968 on jurisdiction and the enforcement of Judgments in Civil and Commercial Matters refers to the contractual obligation forming the basis of the legal proceedings namely the obligation of the grantor which corresponds to the contractual right relied upon by the grantee in support of the application.

In disputes concerning the consequences of the infringement by the grantor of a contract conferring an exclusive concession such as the payment of damages or the dissolution of the contract the obligation to which reference must be made for the purposes of applying Article 5(1) of the Convention is that which the contract imposes on the grantor and the non-performance of which is relied upon by the grantee in support of the application for damages or for the dissolution of the contract.

In the case of actions for payment of compensation by way of damages, it is for the national court to ascertain whether, under the law applicable to the contract, an independent contractual obligation or an obligation replacing the unperformed contractual obligation is involved.

2. When the grantee of an exclusive sales concession is not subject either to the control or to the direction of the grantor, he cannot be regarded as being at the head of a branch, agency or other establishment of the grantor within the meaning of Article 5(5) of the Convention of 27 September 1968.

OPINION OF MR ADVOCATE GENERAL REISCHL

In order to understand the reference for a preliminary ruling made to the Court by the Cour d'Appel, Mons, by order of 9 December 1975 the following preliminary remarks must be made: on 24 October 1959 the French company Bouyer, the registered office of which is in Tomblaine, Meurthe et Moselle, concluded a contract with the Belgian company De Bloos, the registered office of which is in Leuze, whereby the exclusive distribution rights of the products produced by Bouyer for Belgium, Luxembourg and the former Belgian Congo were granted to the above-mentioned Belgian company. The contract was initially for three years but subsequently, as neither party had given notice to terminate it, it was impliedly extended. In accordance with Regulation No.17 it was notified to the Commission; however no individual exemption was necessary as, by virtue of communication from the Commission in 1969, it fell within the scope of the regulation providing for exemption of categories of agreements (Regulation No 67/67, OJ English Special Edition 1967, p. 10). In the autumn of 1972 difficulties evidently arose between the parties to the contract. They were caused by the fact that Bouyer had entered into negotiations in Belgium with another undertaking concerning the distribution of its products. De Bloos regards this as a breach of contract having certain legal consequences. In this respect it relies on a Belgian Law of 27 July 1961 as amended by the Law of 13 April 1971. Thereby contracts such as the one at issue are deemed to have been concluded for an indefinite period if they are extended on two occasions. In addition the law provides that the injured party in the case of unilateral revocation without compliance with a reasonable period of notice has a right to fair compensation, and that, if notice is given by the grantor on grounds other than the wrongful act of the grantee then reasonable additional compensation is payable. In reliance on these provisions De Bloos appealed to the commercial court in Tournai. It sought a ruling that the exclusive dealing agreement had been dissolved on 1 October 1972 through breach of contract by Bouyer and an order that the French company should pay damages.

The defendant company challenges the jurisdiction of the court in which the action was brought. The above mentioned Belgian law provides that actions by the grantee under a contract conferring an exclusive concession against his supplier for breach of contract can be brought in the court which has jurisdiction at the place of residence of the trader if the exclusive dealing contract produces effects in Belgium. However, the commercial court did not take account of this provision as, clearly correctly, it regarded it as being superseded by the Convention of 27 September 1968 on jurisdiction and the enforcement of Judgments in Civil and Commercial Matters which entered into force on 1 March 1973. It relied rather on the Convention in particular Article 5 thereof which provides that: 'A person domiciled in a Contracting State may, in another contracting State, be sued:

(1) in matters relating to a contract, in the courts for the place of performance of the obligation in question...'. The commercial court implied from clauses in business letters and invoices from the defendant which specified that the courts of Nancy were to have jurisdiction, that the bills were payable in Nancy and that the goods were to be delivered to the business premises of the defendant, that the defendant company had to perform its obligations not in Belgium but in France. Therefore it decided that the jurisdiction of Belgian courts to deal with the case was excluded.

De Bloos appealed against this judgment to the Cour d'Appel in Mons. In its assessment of the facts the Cour d'Appel at first reached another conclusion in that it found no agreement that the place of performance be in France and thus no agreement conferring jurisdiction within the meaning of Article 17 of the above-mentioned Convention in respect of the disputed obligation. It decided that the above-mentioned clauses only applied to individual business transactions but not for the outline contract which was the sole object of the court proceedings. In addition the court thought it conceivable that the Belgian courts might have jurisdiction either on the basis of above-mentioned Article 5(1) of the Convention on jurisdiction or under Article 5(5) thereof which runs as follows: 'as regards a dispute arising out of the operations of a branch, agency or other establishment, in the courts for the place in which the branch, agency or other establishment is situated'. The Cour d'Appel is not without its doubts in this respect for the following reasons: In applying Belgian law - it is Belgian law that is to be applied to the particular situation by the court on the basis of a provision for conflict of laws contained in the Belgian law of 1961 as the exclusive dealing agreement produces effects in Belgium - the court reached the conclusion, with regard to Article 5(1) of the Convention, that is with regard to the courts for the place of performance, that the claim made could be classified in various ways. One view was that it may be decisive that the duty to pay compensation replaces the obligation to comply with a reasonable period of notice; in the principal obligation of the grantee, may be found the basis for the claim to compensation which may therefore be regarded as a contractual right. Another view was that the grantor has a choice between complying with a reasonable period of notice or paying damages, the duty to pay damages being a legal consequence of the dissolution of the contract, that is to say, a new, independent obligation. Accordingly the place of performance is regarded as being either in Belgium, that is the area where the principal obligations of the grantee are to be performed where the debtor resides, then the place of performance is that at which the defendant French debtor resides. The Cour d'Appel finds difficulties in the application of Article 5(5) of the Convention on jurisdiction in that according to the facts as stated in the proceedings the exclusive dealer was not entitled to deal *in the name* of the supplier and that he was not subject to the control and direction of the supplier. Therefore it has doubts whether the Belgian exclusive dealer can be regarded as a branch etc. Within the meaning of Article 5(5) of the Convention. For these reasons the court stayed proceedings in order to obtain a preliminary ruling on the interpretation of the Convention on jurisdiction and the enforcement of Judgments.

The following questions were formulated in its order for reference of 9 December 1975:

I - In an action brought by the grantee of an exclusive sales concession against the grantor in which he claims that the latter has infringed the exclusive concession, may the term '*obligation*' in Article 5(1) of the Convention of 27 September 1968 on jurisdiction and the enforcement of Judgments in Civil and Commercial Matters be applied without distinction to each of the obligations set out below or must its application to any of them be excluded:

1. Any obligation arising out of the outline contract granting an exclusive sales concession or even arising out of the successive sales concluded in performance of this outline contract;

2. The obligation in dispute or forming the basis of the legal proceedings and, if so, (a) the original obligation (such as the obligation not to sell to others in the territories agreed upon or the obligation to give reasonable notice in the event of unilateral breach);(b) or the obligation to provide the equivalent of the original obligation (to pay compensation or damages); (c) or the obligation to pay damages where the effect of novation arising from the dissolution or termination of the contract is to render void the original obligation, (d) or, finally, the obligation to pay 'fair compensation' or even 'additional compensation' provided for in Articles 2 and 3 of the Belgian Law of 27 July 1961 concerning the unilateral termination of exclusive sales concessions of indefinite duration, as amended by the Law of 13 April 1971;

II - Where, on the one hand, the grantee of an exclusive sales concession is not empowered either to negotiate in the name of the grantor or to bind him and, on the other hand, he is not subject either to the control or direction of the grantor, is such a person at the head of a branch, agency or other establishment of the grantor within the meaning of Article 5(5) of the Brussels Convention?

I - Before I can examine these questions I must first state my opinion concerning a problem of procedural law. This results from the fact that the Government of the United Kingdom also submitted observations concerning the reference for a preliminary ruling which, in accordance with the usual practice, was communicated to all Member States of the Community although the Convention on jurisdiction and the enforcement of Judgments and the Protocol on its interpretation for the time being only apply in relation to the original Member States of the Community. As became evident in the course of the procedure there is no unanimity on the question whether such observations are admissible from the three new Member States. In support of their admissibility, reference is particularly made to Article 5 of the Protocol on interpretation which refers to the EEC Protocol on the Statute of the Court of Justice in respect of references for a preliminary ruling. The view is taken that since Article 20 of the above-mentioned Protocol certainly refers to all Member States the same must also apply in relation to proceedings under Article 3 of the Protocol on interpretation. In addition reference is made to Article 37 of the EEC Protocol on the Statute of the Court of Justice whereby all Member States have the right to 'intervene in cases before the Court'. Against this the French Government, which was the only party to raise objections, stated that exclusion of the new Member States from the proceedings is supported by the fact that only courts of the original Member States and their 'competent authorities' within the meaning of Article 4 of the Protocol on interpretation are able to refer questions to the Court of Justice. Moreover only the *Contracting States*, that is those States which concluded the Convention, are in a position to define its contents. In our examination of this problem doubts may certainly be felt whether reference to Article 5 of the Protocol on interpretation is sufficient to justify the participation of the new Member States in the reference for a preliminary ruling concerning the Convention on jurisdiction. It must not be overlooked that Article 5 begins with the words 'except where this Protocol otherwise provides'.This may be understood in the sense that the point at issue is the purpose and system of the Protocol and that the determining factor is for which Member States is the Protocol already binding. In addition reference may be made to Article 4 of the Protocol in which - apart from the Commission and the Council - reference is only made to notice being given to the Contracting States. This may be regarded as a general clarification of the right of participation but it is difficult to see why, in relation to proceedings under Article 4 of the Protocol on interpretation which also concerns only questions of interpretation, there should be a different sphere of application in respect of Member States from that relating to proceedings under Article 3. On the other hand it must be acknowledged that the references made in the course of the proceedings to Article 3(2) of the Act concerning the Conditions of Accession and the Adjustments to the Treaties and Article 63 of the Convention on jurisdiction have considerable force. Article 3(2) of the Act concerning the Conditions of Accession provides that the new Member States undertake, 'to accede to the conventions provided for in Article 220 of the EEC

Treaty, and to those protocols on the interpretation of those conventions by the Court of Justice, signed by the original Member States and to this end they undertake to enter into negotiations with the original Member States in order to make the necessary adjustments thereto'. As we know these negotiations have already reached the first stage. Article 63 of the Convention on jurisdiction provides that: 'The Contracting States recognize that any State which becomes a member of the European Economic Community shall be required to accept this Convention as a basis for the negotiations between the Contracting States and that State necessary to ensure the implementation of the last paragraph of Article 220 of the Treaty establishing the European Economic Community. The necessary adjustments may be the subject of a special Convention between the Contracting States of the one part and the new Member State of the other part.'

According to the Report on the Convention on jurisdiction and the enforcement of Judicial Decisions in Civil and Commercial Matters - which for the sake of brevity I shall call 'the Report' - this means that the basic principles of the Convention may not be departed from and therefore that the fundamental principles of the Convention will also apply in respect of the new Member States. Consequently future Contracting States have a genuine interest which should be protected in taking part in proceedings concerning its interpretation; the corresponding legal decisions will - at least in respect of the basic principles of the Convention - form part of the body of law which must be adopted by the new Member States. However, since it is certainly not easy to define what is fundamental to the Convention and what allows of adjustment, I believe there should be no hesitation in allowing new Member States in general to submit observations in respect of requests for a preliminary ruling concerning the Convention on jurisdiction and the enforcement of Judgments. This conclusion is further supported by the fact that we are here concerned with objective proceedings intended to ascertain the purport of the Convention in which in principle nothing is left open to the parties thereto. In addition, if occasion arises, the intentions which the Contracting States had at the time of concluding the Convention may be taken into account as regards statements by the original Member States.

I do not think it is necessary to examine in detail Article 37 of the EEC Protocol on the Statute of the Court of Justice as its application to proceedings of the present nature appears to me to be extremely doubtful and I therefore suggest that it be ruled that there is no objection to collaboration by the new Member States in any proceedings concerning the interpretation of the Convention on jurisdiction and the enforcement of Judgments.

II - 1. The *first question* to which I must turn relates to the interpretation of Article 5(1) of the Convention, that is the provision which provides for the jurisdiction of the place of performance for the enforcement of contractual rights.

A problem arises here in so far as, where a national court, examining its jurisdiction on the basis of this provision and in view of the fact that substantive law including international private law in the Community has - still - not been harmonised, has to determine, according to its own private international law, the law which is applicable to the legal situation concerned and then has to ascertain, on the basis of this law, where the obligations in question are to be performed. If this produces several places of performance then under the Convention the question arises whether they are all equally important or whether the above-mentioned provision is to be so interpreted as to leave some places of performance out of account.

After all the observations submitted in this respect in the course of the proceedings I have no doubt that the Commission is correct in stating that the 'performance of the obligation' arising out of a contract, mentioned in Article 5, has to a certain extent an independent meaning, a Community law meaning as it were, and that national law alone is not decisive in this respect.

In principle it may be assumed that terms used in such agreements which are of significance for the life of the Community - the Convention on jurisdiction and enforcement of Judgments concerns the facilitation of legal proceedings - have a meaning for the purposes of Community law at least in so far as there exists no clear and unambiguous reference to national law as, for example, in Article 52 in respect of the concept of domicile.

It is particularly important for the Convention on jurisdiction and the enforcement of Judgments that a *uniform* system of jurisdiction is created. Its provisions must be observed by national courts and, with a few exceptions, once jurisdiction has been accepted there is in principle no occasion for reopening the matter. This is evident from the above-mentioned Report. However, it may be said that fundamental autonomous concepts are a necessary precondition for the definition of common rules of jurisdiction.

It is further relevant that the Convention is based on the attempt not to have duplication of jurisdiction except where this is necessary. In this respect it is *inter alia* characteristic that the place where the contract was concluded is not taken into consideration. However, as the court seised of the matter rules as to the law applicable and as, apart from a few exceptions, the matter is subsequently no longer open to dispute, the danger of duplication of jurisdiction cannot be entirely ruled out where the national law alone is decisive, as is illustrated by the present case.

Even if it is going too far to say the place of performance results from the Convention itself there is no support for such an extensive incursion into national law and moreover in the absence of further details this would entail the danger of considerable legal uncertainty - nevertheless in view of the above-mentioned factors there remains the consideration that places of performance which may be determined in relation to a particular legal situation on the basis of national law are not necessarily decisive for the application of the Convention.

If, on the basis of the principles that we have deduced, we examine the different aspects of the question before us as formulated with regard to the factual situation in the main action, then a further consideration may be deduced without any particular difficulties. Article 5(1) of the Convention is certainly not to be understood as meaning that *one* place of performance applies in respect of a whole contractual relationship, in particular for such a complex relationship as that of an exclusive dealing agreement in the context of which are included numerous individual contracts of sale. Its view of the customary method of determining jurisdiction of the place of performance in legal systems which already used the concept, the contrary assumption must appear quite unacceptable. It is also clear that Article 5(1) refers to the obligation which is the object of the dispute. This is expressed in the above-mentioned Report, which was submitted together with the draft Convention to the Governments, in which reliance is placed on the obligation *on which the claim is based (klagebegründende Verplifchtung)*. This view is supported by numerous authors such as Martha Weser in 'Convention Communautaire sur la compétence judiciaire et l'exécution des décisions' (page 248). She draws clear support from the German and Italian texts of the Convention. Furthermore an appropriate amendment of the French and Dutch texts is provided for in the context of the work in respect of the accession of the new Member States of the Convention. This is evident, having regard to the intentions of the authors of the Convention from a report of the working party of the Council of 20 November 1975 which was submitted by the Commission. In the case of synallagmatic contracts Article 5(1) of the Convention provides, according to the obligation at issue, a different jurisdiction as the place of performance differs. Therefore, in exclusive dealing agreements it is natural that the obligations of the grantor and those of the grantee must be kept apart and that for the enforcement of claims for breach of contract by the grantor, the individual contracts of sale which were undertaken within the context of the agreement must be left out of consideration because of their legal independence.

It is not quite so simple to resolve what may be regarded as the central problem of the main action, that is the question whether rights against the grantor for breach of an exclusive dealing agreement must also be regarded separately in so far as they are not regarded as contractual obligations under national law or whether, irrespective of the fact that they are provided for by law, the place of performance of the principal obligation is decisive as this is the basis of the claim and as the action fundamentally concerns the improper performance of them.

In this respect it is possible to opt for a strict interpretation of the text of Article 5(1) and to take the view that since reference is made to rights arising out of a *contract,* it does not apply to legal obligations which have arisen in the case of failure to perform contractual obligations. Finally, however, it must be admitted that there are stronger arguments in support of the view of the Commission which advocates a broader interpretation. Therefore, the principle of concentration of jurisdiction applies in relation to the Convention the intention being to avoid as far as possible conflicting decisions in the various Contracting States. This interpretation is clearly evidenced by the above-mentioned Report. In this respect reference may also be made to Article 21 by virtue of which, in cases where proceedings involving the same cause of action and between the same parties are brought in the courts of different Contracting States, any court other than the court first seised shall of its own motion decline jurisdiction in favour of the first court. This is also supported by Article 22 which provides, in cases where related action are brought in the courts of different Contracting States, that a court other than the court first seised may, while the actions are pending at first instance, stay its proceedings. For the purposes of that article actions are deemed to be related where they are so closely connected 'that it is expedient to hear and determine them together to avoid the risk of irreconcilable judgments resulting from separate proceedings'.

Any other interpretation which might lead to division of jurisdiction would fail to take account of the principle of good administration of justice and would therefore appear rather strange in the context of an agreement the purpose of which is to ensure effective pursuit of legal actions. The main action in the present case shows that such an interpretation would give rise to considerable problems; the jurisdiction of the Belgian courts would have to be recognized for the application for judicial dissolution of the contractual relations as this is clearly dependent on the principal obligation of the grantor and thus leads to a place of performance in Belgium. However, if in respect of the claim for damages, which depends on the decision as to the dissolution of the contractual relations, any other qualification were made, the place of performance would have to be taken to be in France and the French courts would therefore have jurisdiction.

Finally, it is also relevant - we need not here decide whether it is decisive - that if the solution advocated by the Commission is adopted the result is that the competent court of the place of performance is in the territory of the State the law of which is applicable to the disputed situation - a result which was expressly declared to be desirable in the above-mentioned Report. This is not only evident from Belgian private international law but it is also apparent from the appropriate rules as to conflict of laws of most of the Member States whereby matters depend on the sphere of operations of the grantee. In addition this is also contained in the proposed Convention on the law applicable to contractual and non-contractual obligations; Article 4 of a draft text already prepared provides that - except where the parties have agreed otherwise - the contract is to be governed by the law of the country with which it is most closely connected.

Thus, in answer to the first question referred for a preliminary ruling it should be stated that the application of Article 5(1) of the Convention on jurisdiction is dependent on the contractual obligation which is the basis of the dispute and that in the case of disputes concerning the consequences of the breach of an exclusive dealing agreement by the grantee, the main obligation of the grantee forms the subject of the proceedings even if the consequences of the breach of this obligation are prescribed by law.

2. As we have seen interpretation of Article 5(5) of the Convention on jurisdiction and the enforcement of judgments is also required by the court making the reference. The *second question* of the order for reference makes it necessary to determine what is to be understood by 'branch', 'agency' and 'other establishment' and how the phrase 'a dispute arising out of the operations of branch' etc. is to be interpreted. A lengthy explanation is not necessary. I feel that the statements submitted by the Commission which were also supported by the representative of the British Government are convincing. Thus it may be said that characteristics of a branch are, on the one hand, a certain autonomy and, on the other, being subordinate to the parent company and subject to the control of

that company. Particular characteristics are the absence of its own legal personality and the authority to act on behalf of the parent company. An agency is similar but its autonomy is certainly less marked. This was supported by reference to the legal systems of the Member States, to earlier bilateral or multilateral conventions and to provisions of the EEC Treaty which certainly have some value as a means of interpretation for a convention which was concluded within the context of the EEC Treaty. It may be deduced from Article 52 of the EEC Treaty contrasting agencies and branches on the one hand and subsidiaries on the other, that the former possess no legal personality. Accordingly and after what has become evident in the course of the main action it is certain that in the present case the jurisdiction of the Belgian courts cannot be deduced from Article 5(5) of the Convention at least in so far as it concerns the terms branch and agency.

With regard to the term 'other establishment' the Commission showed that this does not entail any greater independence and therefore that the subordination to another undertaking is characteristic. As legal personality is not the decisive legal factor in economic matters it is conceivable that these terms might also include bodies with legal personality such as a wholly controlled subsidiary company which operates as though it were a department of the undertaking. It appears feasible for those having an exclusive dealing right to be regarded as such establishments as in one part of the modern doctrine on the subject, economic dependence, the grantor's ability to determine the conditions of disposal stands to the fore. Even if it is presumed that the Belgian undertaking - although this does not appear to be the case according to the facts as they appear - is included in the term 'other establishments' understood in this way, then no jurisdiction for the claims against the grantor could be assumed by virtue of Article 5(5) of the Convention. As the Commission rightly emphasized it is important in this respect that as Article 5(5) provides for an exception it must in principle be strictly construed. In addition it is important that, in drawing up the Convention, jurisdictions linked to the nationality or residence of the plaintiff were not taken into account. On this basis it cannot be presumed that Article 5(5) permits a legally independent establishment to bring an application before the court competent for the area in which that establishment is situated insofar as such application concerns a controlling undertaking, the parent company. Clearly Article 5(5) rather has the sole purpose of facilitating legal proceedings for *third parties* who are involved with a subsidiary establishment in that they are not obliged to lodge their application where the parent company is situated. Thus it was solely for their benefit that jurisdiction was established in a place nearer to that in which the case of action arose.

Thus in answer to the second question it should be ruled that Article 5(5) of the Convention can in no way allow of an interpretation giving jurisdiction to the Belgian courts for the main action in this case.

3. In conclusion I therefore suggest that the questions referred, for a preliminary ruling by the Cour d'Appel, Mons, should be answered as follows:

(a) For the application of Article 5(1) of the Convention on jurisdiction and the enforcement of Judgments, in disputes concerning an exclusive dealing agreement regard must not be had to *any* obligation arising from the contractual relationship but exclusively to *that* obligation which is the basis of the dispute. In particular, in disputes concerning compliance with exclusive dealing agreements, those agreements which result from contracts of sale concluded in the context of the exclusive dealing agreement must not be taken into consideration. In disputes concerning the consequences of breach of an exclusive dealing agreement by the grantor the subject of the proceedings is the basic obligation of the grantor irrespective of the question whether the consequences of a breach are laid down by law and irrespective of how the obligation to pay compensation is regarded in national law.

(b) Article 5(5) of the Convention only applies in respect of establishments which are subordinate to another undertaking and in respect of which the parent establishment possesses powers of control and direction. Insofar as legally independent undertakings may be regarded as establishments because of their economic dependence, Article 5(5) does not apply to disputes with the controlling undertaking.

Case 56/79 - 17 January 1980

Siegfried Zelger
v
Sebastiano Salinitri

Relationship between Article 5(1) and Article 17 - Jurisdiction of the court for the place of performance - Jurisdiction of the court designated by the parties - Nature and foundation of both - Designation of place of performance by a clause valid according to the law applicable - Observance of formal conditions provided for under Article 17 not required.

Summary

1. The provisions of Article 5(1) of the Convention, to the effect that in matters relating to a contract a defendant domiciled in a Contracting State may be sued in the courts for the place of performance of the obligation in question, introduce a criterion for jurisdiction, the selection of which is at the option of the plaintiff and which is justified by the existence of a direct link between the dispute and the court called upon to take cognizance of it. By contrast, Article 17 of the Convention, which provides for the exclusive jurisdiction of the court designated by the parties in accordance with the prescribed form, puts aside both the rule of general jurisdiction - provided for in Article 2 - and the rules of special jurisdiction - provided for in Article 5 - and dispenses with any objective connexion between the legal relationship in dispute and the court designated. It thus appears that the jurisdiction of the court for the place of performance and that of the selected court are two distinct concepts and only agreements selecting a court are subject to the requirements of form prescribed by Article 17 of the Convention.

2. If the place of performance of a contractual obligation has been specified by the parties in a clause which is valid according to the national law applicable to the contract, the court for that place has jurisdiction to take cognizance of disputes relating to that obligation under Article 5(1) of the Convention, irrespective of whether the formal conditions provided for under Article 17 have been observed.

JUDGMENT OF THE COURT

Kutscher, President, O'Keeffe and Touffait, Presidents of Chambers, Mertens de Wilmars, Pescatore, Lord Mackenzie Stuart, Koopmans and Due, Judges

1. By order of 15 March 1979, received at the Court Registry on 11 April 1979, the Bundesgerichtshof [Federal Court of Justice] referred to the Court, under Article 3 of the Protocol of 3 June 1971 on the Interpretation of the Convention of Brussels of 27 September 1968 (hereinafter referred to as 'the Convention'), a question concerning the interpretation of Article 5(1) and 17 of the said Convention.

This question has been raised in the course of litigation between two merchants, one domiciled in Munich, in the Federal Republic of Germany, and the other in Mascari, in Italy, relating to the repayment by the defendant in the main action of a loan said to have been made to him by the plaintiff in the main action. The latter, relying upon an oral agreement under which Munich is said to have been fixed as the place of repayment, instituted proceedings before the Landgericht München [Munich Regional Court] which held that it had no jurisdiction on the grounds that, on the one hand, a mere oral agreement on the place of performance was not sufficient to establish international jurisdiction and, on the other hand, that that agreement could only have the effect of conferring jurisdiction if the form prescribed by Article 17 of the Convention had been observed. That decision was upheld by the Oberlandesgericht München [Munich Higher Regional Court] and the plaintiff in the main action appealed on a point of law to the Bundesgerichtshof which posed the following question:

'Does an informal agreement which is effective under national - in this case German - law between full-scale merchants (Vollkaufleute) concerning the place of performance of the obligation which is at issue in the proceedings suffice to found jurisdiction in that place under Article 5(1) of the Convention, or is the capacity of such an agreement to found jurisdiction dependent upon observance of the form laid down in Article 17 of the Convention?'

2. It follows from the wording of this question that the national court is asking whether an agreement such as that described, in order to found jurisdiction under Article 5(1) of the Convention, is dependent upon observance of the form prescribed by Article 17 of the Convention, according to which provision the court of the Contracting State specified by the parties - of whom at least one must have his domicile in the territory of a Contracting State - as having jurisdiction to settle any disputes which have arisen or may arise in connexion with a particular legal relationship shall have exclusive jurisdiction, provided that it has been specified by an agreement in writing or an oral agreement evidenced in writing.

3. It is appropriate to point out that Article 5(1), which occurs in Section 2 of Title II of the Convention entitled 'special jurisdiction', creates a ground of jurisdiction which is an exception to the general rule of jurisdiction provided for in Article 2 of the Convention; the provisions of Article 5, which provide that in matters relating to a contract a defendant domiciled in a Contracting State may be sued in the courts for the place of performance of the obligation in question, introduce a criterion for jurisdiction, the selection of which is at the option of the plaintiff and which is justified by the existence of a direct link between the dispute and the court called upon to take cognizance of it.

4. By contrast, Article 17, which occurs in Section 6 of the Convention entitled 'Prorogation of jurisdiction' and which provides for the exclusive jurisdiction of the court designated by the parties in accordance with the prescribed form, puts aside both the rule of general jurisdiction - provided for in Article 2 - and the rules of special jurisdiction - provided for in Article 5 - and dispenses with any objective connexion between the legal relationship in dispute and the court designated. It thus appears that the jurisdiction of the court for the place of performance (provided for in Article 5(1)) and that of the selected court (provided for in Article 17) are two distinct concepts and only agreements selecting a court are subject to the requirements of form prescribed by Article 17 of the Convention.

5. Consequently, if the parties to the contract are permitted by the law applicable to the contract, subject to any conditions imposed by that law, to specify the place of performance of an obligation without satisfying any special condition of form, an agreement on the place of performance of the obligation is sufficient to found jurisdiction in that place within the meaning of Article 5(1) of the Convention.

6. The answer to the question put by the Bundesgerichtshof must therefore be that if the place of performance of a contractual obligation has been specified by the parties in a clause which is valid according to the national law applicable to the contract, the court for that place has jurisdiction to take cognizance of disputes relating to that obligation under Article 5(1) of the Convention of Brussels of 27 September 1968, irrespective of whether the formal conditions provided for under Article 17 have been observed.

On those grounds, the court, in answer to the question referred to it by the Bundesgerichtshof by order of 15 March 1979, hereby rules:

> **If the place of performance of a contractual obligation has been specified by the parties in a clause which is valid according to the national law applicable to the contract, the court for that place has jurisdiction to take cognizance of disputes relating to that obligation under Article 5(1) of the Convention of Brussels of 27 September 1968, irrespective of whether the formal conditions provided for under Article 17 have been observed.**

OPINION OF MR ADVOCATE GENERAL CAPOTORTI

1. The Convention of Brussels of 27 September 1968 on Jurisdiction and the Enforcement of Judgments in Civil and Commercial Matters provides, as the Court is aware, that in the field contracts the 'courts for the place of performance of the obligation in question' may also have jurisdiction (Article 5(1)). That place is not always defined by rules of law alone; the contracting parties may agree to fix it, thereby producing the *indirect* result of invoking a 'special jurisdiction' in terms of the Brussels Convention.

On the other hand, the exclusive jurisdiction of a court or of the courts of a Contracting State may be *directly* conferred by the parties, by means of an appropriate agreement conferring jurisdiction, which is required by Article 17 to meet certain conditions of form and substance. The issue raised by the request for a preliminary ruling on a question of interpretation which has been referred to the Court by the German Bundesgerichtshof [Federal Court of Justice], and which is the basis of this case, is that of comparing contractual clauses determining the place of performance and agreements conferring jurisdiction, in order to see whether the restrictive conditions applicable to the latter ought to be considered applicable to clauses of the former kind.

In this case a German national, resident in Munich, Bavaria, (Zelger), claiming to have lent a sum of money to an Italian national, resident in Sicily (Salinitri), and to be still owed a part of that sum, sued the alleged debtor in the Landgericht München [Munich Regional Court]. According to the plaintiff, that court had jurisdiction because, at the time, the parties had agreed orally that the repayment of the loan would be made in Munich. The defendant disputed the existence of both the obligation and any agreement concerning the place of performance.

The Landgericht, by judgment of 18 April 1977, declared that it did not have international jurisdiction since it was unable to hold that an oral agreement on the place of performance could have any bearing on jurisdiction, within the meaning of Article 5(1) of the Convention, and thus circumvent the provisions of Article 17 which permit the prorogation of jurisdiction only by means of an agreement in writing or an oral agreement evidenced in writing. In holding that it lacked jurisdiction, the German court proceeded upon the rule of German law which provides that, unless otherwise agreed, the place of performance of a contractual obligation is the residence of the debtor (Article 269 of the Bürgerliches Gesetzbuch) [German Civil Code].

The decision at first instance was upheld on appeal by the Oberlandesgericht München [Munich Higher Regional Court] by judgment dated 9 November 1977. That court held that the rule laid down in Article 17 of the Convention of Brussels, in the absence of express provision to the contrary, applied to all agreements conferring jurisdiction; and that agreements specifying the place of performance could therefore have no effect upon jurisdiction unless they fulfilled the formal requirements set out in Article 17.

The Bundesgerichtshof, to which the matter was taken on a point of law, by order of 15 March 1979 referred to the Court of Justice of the European Communities the following preliminary question: 'Does an informal agreement which is effective under national - in this case German - law between full-scale merchants (Vollkaufleute) concerning the place of performance of the obligation which is at issue in the proceedings suffice to found jurisdiction in that place under Article 5(1) of the Convention, or is the capacity of such an agreement to found jurisdiction dependent upon observance of the form by the objective link which exists laid down in Article 17 of the Convention?'

2. I make the observation first of all that the issue has to be considered upon the hypothesis that two parties to a contract have concluded an oral agreement concerning the place of performance of the obligation which later forms the subject of dispute; it is not necessary to know whether, in this case, the hypothesis matches the true facts. For what it is worth, the plaintiff in the main proceedings maintained that there was also agreed, at the time, an oral agreement conferring jurisdiction, but that remains outside our purview.

In the view of the German courts of first and second instance, clauses conferring jurisdiction and those relating to the place of performance must be subjected to the same rules of form before the latter clauses may have a bearing on the issue of jurisdiction. But, in truth, the Issue concerns two wholly different types of agreement: the one has a purely procedural purpose, the other a substantive purpose accompanied by a procedural result arising, independently of any specific intention of the parties, from the provisions of Article 5(1). Further, agreements conferring jurisdiction give exclusive jurisdiction to the court or courts specified, with the consequence that they suspend the operation of both the general rule on jurisdiction (Article 2) and the rules relating to special jurisdiction (Article 5); whereas the place of performance, however determined, is the basis of a special jurisdiction which is concurrent with the general jurisdiction and any other equally special jurisdictions. Finally, jurisdiction settled upon pursuant to Article 17 leaves out of account any objective factor connecting the legal relationship in dispute and the chosen tribunal whereas jurisdiction based on Article 5(1) is really warranted by the objective link which exists between an important aspect of the contract and the court recognised as having jurisdiction.

On a purely exegetical level, it has to be said that Article 17, in referring to agreements whereby the parties have 'agreed that a court or the courts of a Contracting State are to have jurisdiction to settle any disputes which have arisen or which may arise in connexion with a particular legal relationship', precisely describes their particular content, clearly distinguishing them from agreements which settle the place at which performance must take place.

In turn, Article 5(1) contains nothing which would lead one to hold that it has in contemplation only the place of performance of the contractual obligation fixed *ex lege* and excludes a place agreed upon for that purpose by the parties in the exercise of the freedom of contract recognised by law.

In regard to the manner in which the criterion for jurisdiction laid down in Article 5(1) is to be interpreted, reference has properly been made in the course of the present proceedings to the Judgment of the Court of 6 October 1976 in Case 12/76 *Tessili* v *Dunlop* [1976] ECR 1474. That judgment laid down that it was for the national court to determine, in accordance with its own rules of conflict of laws, the law governing the legal relationship in question and accordingly to determine, on the basis of that law, the place of performance of the contractual obligation in question. If, therefore, the law which is applicable gives to the contracting parties power to determine the place in which the obligation to be concluded is to be performed, without imposing any special requirements of form, the choice freely arrived at by the parties will be binding both for the purposes of the law governing the substantive elements of the contract and for the purposes of Article 5(1) of the Convention of Brussels. To separate the one consequence from the other would mean holding that, although the contract was to be performed in the place fixed by the parties, the jurisdiction of the courts of that place could nevertheless not be recognized; but that would strike against both the letter and the spirit of the provision which has been cited and which, as I have already mentioned, reflects the idea that the location of the contract during the phase of its performance is sufficient to found jurisdiction in that same place.

A further support for the view which I have just set forth is provided by the argument which the Commission properly drew from Article 1 of the Protocol annexed to the Convention of Brussels. In the first paragraph of that article it is provided that any person domiciled in Luxembourg who is sued in a court of another Contracting State pursuant to Article 5(1) may refuse to submit to the jurisdiction of that court; if the defendant does not enter an appearance, the court shall declare of its own motion that it has no jurisdiction. In the second paragraph, a rule, also making an exception in favour of persons domiciled in Luxembourg, is drawn up in regard to Article 17, it being there laid down that agreements conferring jurisdiction shall be valid with respect to such persons only if they are expressly and specifically agreed. The manner in which the aforesaid two provisions are formulated and set out evidently implies that the system applying to the court of the place of performance and that applying to the selected court are two quite distinct things.

3. The answer to the question which has been referred to the Court therefore seems so clear that one may wonder how the courts of first and second instance were ever able to decide it differently. It is likely that they were influenced to a certain degree by the direction recently taken in the law of civil procedure in the Federal Republic, which has restricted both cases of prorogation of jurisdiction (by amending Article 38 of the Zivilprozebordnung [Code of Civil Procedure]) and the possibility of founding jurisdiction on the place of performance of the contract where that is determined by means of agreement between the parties (Article 29(2) of that Code has also been amended). There are naturally good reasons for this approach: the intention was to avoid the formal barriers against agreements conferring jurisdiction being circumvented by the specifying of the place of performance in agreements free of all formality so as to achieve, in the end, the same result that of specifying a different court from the one generally having jurisdiction by different and simpler means.

In my opinion the risk of that happening may be neither excluded nor ignored. The conditions prescribed by Article 17 are generally known to have been conceived with the intention of protecting the weaker party to the contract and, for the same reasons, a solution such as that recently adopted by German law in regard to the procedural result of agreements on the place of performance would be very welcome. Even though, during the oral procedure, the Commission declared itself satisfied with Article 5 as it stands, I consider that *de lege ferenda* the problem deserves to be examined again and I personally regret that the negotiation of the Convention of 9 October 1978 relating to the accession of the other three States to the Convention of Brussels of 1968 did not give rise to such a re-examination. Nor does it appear to me that the nature of the problem has been changed merely because, as the British Government observed in this case, the recent Convention diminished the formal requirements of Article 17; in truth, that diminution consisted in the recognition, as regards international trading relationships, of the forms which accord with practice and of which the parties are presumed to have been aware but the rule has retained the criterion of subjecting the validity of an agreement conferring jurisdiction to certain conditions of form and substance.

The Commission concluded by saying that, if the selection of the place of performance is effective, then jurisdiction is well founded, leaving it to be seen what will be required to establish the true or fictional nature of the agreement to determine the place of performance. It will, however, be for the applicable national law to establish whether, and in what circumstances, a national court may possibly hold the selection to be fictitious and therefore of no effect or else declare that the parties have abused the power given to them in order to circumvent the formalities necessary for agreements conferring jurisdiction. Nonetheless, it remains settled that, under the scheme of the Convention, jurisdiction is effected by the place selected for performance of the contract, in whatever way that place may be determined (whether *ex lege* or by agreement between the parties and without any additional formality being required for the latter). Accordingly, in my opinion, the answer which ought to be given to the request for an preliminary ruling made by the Bundesgerichtshof by order of 15 March 1979 is as follows: 'If the place of performance of a contractual obligation has been determined by the parties in an agreement which is valid under the national law applicable to the contract, the courts for that place have jurisdiction to take cognizance of disputes relating to that obligation by virtue of Article 5(1) of the Convention of Brussels of 27 September 1968, irrespective of whether the formal conditions laid down by Article 17 have been observed'.

Case 38/81 - 4 March 1982

Effer SpA
v
Hans-Joachim Kantner

Article 5(1) - Jurisdiction in matters relating to a contract - Scope - Dispute between the parties as to the existence of the contract - Jurisdiction extends to that question.

Summary

In the cases provided for in Article 5(1) of the Convention of 27 September 1968, the national court's jurisdiction to determine questions relating to a contract includes the power to consider the existence of the constituent parts of the contract itself, since that is indispensable in order to enable the national court in which proceedings are brought to examine whether it has jurisdiction under the Convention. Therefore, the plaintiff may invoke the jurisdiction of the courts of the place of performance in accordance with Article 5(1) of the Convention, even when the existence of the contract on which the claim is based is in dispute between the parties.

JUDGMENT OF THE COURT

Bosco, President of the First Chamber, O'Keeffe, Koopmans, Judges

1. By an order dated 29 January 1981 which was received at the Court Registry on 19 February 1981, the Bundesgerichtshof [Federal Court of Justice] referred to the Court for a preliminary ruling under the Protocol of 3 June 1971 on the Interpretation by the Court of Justice of the

Convention of 27 September 1968 on Jurisdiction and the Enforcement of Judgments in Civil and Commercial Matters a question on the interpretation of Article 5(1) of that Convention, pursuant to which: 'A person domiciled in a Contracting State may, in another Contracting State, be sued: (1) in matters relating to a contract, in the courts of the place of performance of the obligation in question'.

2. The question was raised in the context of a dispute between Effer SpA of Castel Maggiore (Bologna, Italy) and Mr Kantner, a patent agent practising in Darmstadt (Federal Republic of Germany).

3. Effer SpA, the appellant on a point of law in the main proceedings, is an undertaking which manufactures cranes. They were distributed in the Federal Republic of Germany through the Hydraulikkran undertaking (hereinafter referred to as 'Hykra'). Effer developed a new machine and it was necessary to establish whether the sale of that machine was contrary to existing patent rights. After a discussion with Effer, Hykra commissioned Mr Kantner, patent agent, in December 1971 to carry out investigations in Germany for that purpose. The dispute between the parties to the main action concerns the question whether Hykra, which has since become insolvent, commissioned Mr Kantner in the name of Effer or in its own name. In order to obtain payment of his fees - the amount of which is not in dispute - Mr Kantner brought an action before a German court in December 1974. Effer denied the existence of a contractual relationship between it and the patent agent. Owing to the alleged absence of a contract, Effer argued that the German courts had no jurisdiction. The German courts found in favour of Mr Kantner, at first instance and on appeal. Effer then appealed on a point of law to the Bundesgerichtshof, which decided to stay the proceedings and refer the following question to the Court for a preliminary ruling: 'May the plaintiff invoke the jurisdiction of the courts of the place of performance in accordance with Article 5(1) of the Convention even when the existence of the contract on which the claim is based is in dispute between the parties?'

4. Mr Kantner, the respondent in the appeal on a point of law, and the Commission of the European Communities take the view that this question must be answered in the affirmative. The United Kingdom, although it does not wholly accept that argument, nevertheless, considers that a dispute as to the existence of the contract does not prevent Article 5(1) of the Convention from being applied, provided that the obligation is *prima facie* of a contractual nature and the action is *bona fide* brought

by the plaintiff. Only Effer is of the opinion that the plaintiff may not invoke the jurisdiction of the courts for the place of performance of the contract when the existence of the contract on which the claim is based is in dispute.

5. It is established that the wording of Article 5(1) of the Convention does not resolve this question unequivocally. Whilst the German version of that provision contains the words 'Vertrag oder Ansprüche aus einem Vertrag', the French and Italian versions contain the expressions 'en matière contractuelle' and 'in materia contrattuale' respectively. Under these circumstances, in view of the lack of uniformity between the different language versions of the provision in question, it is advisable, in order to arrive at the interpretation requested by the national court, to have regard both to the context of Article 5(1) and to the purpose of the Convention.

6. It is clear from the provisions of the Convention, and in particular from the preamble thereto, that its essential aim is to strengthen in the Community the legal protection of persons therein established. For that purpose, the Convention provides a collection of rules which are designed *inter alia* to avoid the occurrence, in civil and commercial matters, of concurrent litigation in two or more Member States and which, in the interests of legal certainty and for the benefit of the parties, confer jurisdiction upon the national court territorially best qualified to determine a dispute.

7. It follows from the provisions of the Convention, and in particular from those in Section 7 of Title II, that, in the cases provided for in Article 5(1) of the Convention, the national court's jurisdiction to determine questions relating to a contract includes the power to consider the existence of the constituent parts of the contract itself, since that is indispensable in order to enable the national court in which proceedings are brought to examine whether it has jurisdiction under the Convention. If that were not the case, Article 5(1) of the Convention would be in danger of being deprived of its legal effect, since it would be accepted that, in order to defeat the rule contained in that provision it is sufficient for one of the parties to claim that the contract does not exist. On the contrary, respect for the aims and spirit of the Convention demands that that provision should be construed as meaning that the court called upon to decide a dispute arising out of a contract may examine, of its own motion even, the essential preconditions for its jurisdiction, having regard to conclusive and relevant evidence adduced by the party concerned,

establishing the existence or the inexistence of the contract. This interpretation is, moreover, in accordance with that given in the judgment of 14 December 1977 in Case 73/77 (*Sanders* v *Van der Putte* [1977] ECR 2383) concerning the jurisdiction of the courts of the State where the immovable property is situated in matters relating to tenancies of immovable property (Article 16(1) of the Convention). In that case the Court held that such jurisdiction applies even if there is a dispute as to the 'existence' of a lease.

8. It is therefore necessary to reply to the question put by the Bundesgerichtshof that the plaintiff may invoke the jurisdiction of the courts of the place of performance in accordance with Article 5(1) of the Convention of 27 September 1968 on Jurisdiction and the Enforcement of Judgments in Civil and Commercial Matters even when the existence of the contract on which the claim is based is in dispute between the parties.

The Court (First Chamber), in answer to the question submitted to it by the Bundesgerichtshof by an order dated 29 January 1981, hereby rules:

> **The plaintiff may invoke the jurisdiction of the courts of the place of performance in accordance with Article 5(1) of the Convention of 27 September 1968 on Jurisdiction and the Enforcement of Judgments in Civil and Commercial Matters even when the existence of the contract on which the claim is based is in dispute between the parties.**

OPINION OF MR ADVOCATE GENERAL REISCHL

The question on which I am giving my opinion today relates to Article 5(1) of the Convention on Jurisdiction and the Enforcement of Judgments in Civil and Commercial Matters [hereinafter referred to as 'the Convention'], which provides: 'A person domiciled in a Contracting State may, in another Contracting State, be sued: 1. in matters relating to a contract, in the courts for the place of performance of the obligation in question'.

In this regard the Bundesgerichtshof [Federal Court of Justice] wishes to know whether a plaintiff may invoke this jurisdiction even when the existence of the contract on which the claim is based is in dispute between the parties.

The appellant in the main proceedings is an undertaking based in Italy which manufactures cranes. They were distributed in the Federal Republic of Germany through the undertaking Hydraulikkran of Böblingen, which has apparently since - in October 1974 - gone into liquidation. In order to ascertain whether the sale of equipment developed by the appellant was contrary to patent rights, a patent agent was to carry out investigations in Germany. As far as I can understand from the order for reference, it seems that, following a conversation with the appellant, Hydraulikkran commissioned the respondent in the main proceedings, a patent agent practising in the Federal Republic of Germany, for that purpose.

The patent agent subsequently claimed from Effer payment of a fee and brought an action for that purpose before a German court in December 1974. Effer, in fact, denies that there were contractual relations between it and the patent agent. It admits that it commissioned Hydraulikkran but claims that the latter was not authorized to employ the respondent *on behalf of* the appellant; furthermore, another patent agent was engaged by Hydraulikkran to carry out the desired investigation. In this dispute the respondent at first succeeded before the Landgericht [District Court] Frankfurt. However - proceeding on the basis that the German courts had jurisdiction under Article 5(1) of the Convention - the Sixth Civil Senate of the Oberlandesgericht [Higher Regional Court] Frankfurt set aside the judgment of the Landgericht on the ground that it had no local jurisdiction and, because in reality it was not a patent dispute, referred the case to the Landgericht Darmstadt. However, that court also ordered Effer to pay the fee, and the appeal against that decision was unsuccessful, among other reasons because the Thirteenth Civil Senate of the Oberlandesgericht Frankfurt took the view that the German courts had jurisdiction under the above-mentioned provision of the Convention, in view of the fact that, for the application of that rule, it did not matter that there was a dispute over the *existence* of the contract on which the claim was based.

Thereafter, the matter reached the Bundesgerichtshof in an appeal on a point of law. The action having been brought in the court of the place of performance, the Bundesgerichtshof held that the place of performance was to be determined in accordance with German law because the main emphasis of the contract indicated German law. Accordingly, it was assumed that there is a single place of performance in relation to a contract with a patent agent, at the place where the services are to be provided, that is to say, where the patent agent has his office. According to the Bundesgerichtshof, however, it was not clear, in view of the appellant's submissions, whether a German court in fact had jurisdiction under Article 5(1) of the Convention or whether - because the conditions laid down in Article 5(1) were not met - the action should instead be brought at the place where Effer had its registered office. It therefore stayed the proceedings by an order dated 29 January 1981 and referred the above-mentioned question to the Court for a preliminary ruling.

Only the appellant has argued in favour of a negative answer to the question, whilst all the other parties to the proceedings, the respondent, the Commission and the United Kingdom Government, favour an answer in the affirmative.

I share the latter point of view. It is, incidentally, supported in academic writings (Bülow-Böckstiegel, *'Internationaler Rechtsverkehr in Zivil- und Handelssachen, Kommentar zum Vollstreckungsübereinkommen'*, p. 57; Piltz, 'Der Gerichtsstand des Erfüllungsortes nach dem Europäischen

Gerichtsstandsund Vollstreckungs-fibereinkommen', Neue Juristische Wochenschrift 1981, p. 1876; Spellenberg, 'Die Vereinbarung des Erfüllungsortes und Artikel 5 Nummer 1 des Europäischen Gerichtsstands- und Vollstreckungsübereinkommens', Praxis des internationalen Privat- und Verfahrensrechts 1981, p.75); there are also judgments of certain national courts to that effect (Oberlandesgericht Bamberg, Neue Juristische Wochenschrift 1977, p. 505; Oberlandesgericht Hamm, Recht der Internationalen Wirtschaft, 1980, p. 663).

I give the following grounds for my view.

1. First, with regard to the *wording* of Article 5(1), the German version, which I quoted earlier, certainly supports the assumption that a dispute over the existence of a contract does not a *priori* exclude the jurisdiction of the courts of the place of performance. Versions in other languages are not as clear, especially the French and Italian, on which the appellant focused particular attention and which may not, of course, be disregarded. However, I do not see how the phrases used there ('en matière contractuelle', 'in materia contrattuale') should necessarily give rise to the conclusion that the formation of a contract must not be in dispute and that jurisdiction under Article 5(1) is ruled out where there is a dispute as to the existence of a contract.

2. Persuasive authority in favour of an affirmative answer is undoubtedly to be found in the judgment of 14 December 1977 in Case 73/77 *Sanders* v *Van der Putte* ([1977] ECR 2383 at p.2388 *et seq.*). That case concerned the interpretation of Article 16(1) of the Convention, which provides: 'The following courts shall have exclusive jurisdiction, regardless of domicile: 1. in proceedings which have as their object rights *in rem* in, or tenancies of, immovable property, the courts of the Contracting State in which the property is situated'.

It seems that in that case there was a similar dispute over the question whether a tenancy agreement had ever existed. Nevertheless, the application of the above-mentioned provision was not ruled out. That is clear from paragraphs 12 to 15 of the decision, in which the following sentence appears: 'The foregoing considerations explain the assignment of exclusive jurisdiction to the courts of the State in which the immovable property is situated in the case of disputes relating to tenancies of immovable property so-called, that is to say, in particular, *disputes* between lessors and tenants *as to the existence* or interpretation of leases or to compensation for damage caused by the tenant and to giving up possession of the premises'.

3. If it were to be accepted that the presence of a dispute over the existence of a contractual relationship *ipso facto* excludes an action under Article 5(1) of the Convention, then it would be possible by a simple denial on the part of the defendant to render that provision largely ineffective, as well as that contained in Article 5(3) - jurisdiction in matters relating to tort - where indeed the defendant's defence as a rule consists of denying the existence of a tort. That cannot be practical or what was intended. Although it must be conceded that Article 5(1) constitutes an exception to the general rule contained in Article 2 - jurisdiction of the courts of the defendant's domicile - and consequently it cannot

be presumed that the former provision is to be interpreted broadly, yet such considerations may certainly not lead to an interpretation which would make it possible to render an exceptional provision practically ineffective.

4. On the other hand, a plaintiff who invokes jurisdiction under Article 5(1) of the Convention can hardly be required to give more than a coherent statement of his claim. That was indeed the opinion of the representative of the United Kingdom in stating that the plaintiff must *bona fide* claim that there is a contractual relationship and, indeed, on the basis of facts which *prima facie* indicate the existence of a contract.

In this regard the Commission correctly pointed out that recourse to the Convention's jurisdiction rules is not in principle tied to formal conditions or compliance with minimum standards of evidence and that the requirement of writing laid down in Article 17 of the Convention for jurisdiction agreements must rather be regarded as a definite exception. Thus, it was held in the judgment of 17 January 1980 in Case 56/79 *Zelger* v *Salinitri* ([1980] ECR 89 at p. 97), that an informal agreement as to the place of performance is sufficient for Article 5(1).

5. Further support for the proposition that a dispute over the existence of a contract does not deprive the courts of the place of performance of jurisdiction may be derived from the fact that a court whose jurisdiction is invoked in reliance on the Convention must - as a result of Article 20 of the Convention - *examine*, of its own motion, the question of its jurisdiction under the provisions of the Convention (see the Jenard Report on Article 19 of the Convention and Bülow- Böckstiegel, *op. cit*, Point III on Article 20 of the Convention). That can only mean that all the conditions necessary for the alleged jurisdiction are to be established and also a legal appraisal is to be undertaken. It follows that the same must also be true with regard to the question whether a contract, and with it a contractual place of performance, is to be taken to exist.

In this connection the better view must be that no relevance is to be attached to the fact that the examination of the question of jurisdiction wholly or partly overlaps with the examination of the substance of the claim. The possibility that the examination of the facts founding jurisdiction may also affect the determination of the substantive claim is not to be ruled out in other cases either. One needs only to look at the example given by the Commission, of a jurisdiction agreement in a firm's general trading conditions, where the examination of the question whether the agreement was validly concluded may also prejudge questions relating to the claim, since in many cases other matters are determined in the trading conditions. Otherwise a distinction would be drawn according to whether there was a separate agreement on the place of performance or not, which scarcely seems justified. The view that jurisdiction under the Convention could not be recognized if the examination of the question of jurisdiction wholly or partly overlapped with the examination of the facts founding the claim would not be compatible with the principle, clearly expressed in the Jenard Report, that the Convention should be given a wide application.

It is clear, however, that the judicial practice described by the Commission of requiring no evidence of the facts founding jurisdiction if they are at the same time ingredients of the substantive claim would also be incompatible with the rules of the Convention, precisely because those rules require an examination as to jurisdiction by the court *of its own motion* and with it, if necessary, the hearing of evidence limited to the determination of jurisdiction.

6. Finally, it should not be forgotten that the interpretation which I have set out does not lay an unreasonable burden on defendants who may find themselves obliged to defend themselves before foreign courts. Thus the second paragraph of Article 20 of the Convention which provides that the court shall stay the proceedings so long as it is not shown that the defendant has been able to receive the document instituting the proceedings in sufficient time to enable him to arrange for his defence, ensures that the defendant has an opportunity to submit his point of view. Moreover, if he is sued before the courts of a Contracting State in which he is not domiciled, he is not obliged to attend and enter an appearance. In such a case the first paragraph of Article 20 of the Convention requires the court to examine the question of jurisdiction of its own motion. In this respect an alleged fact cannot be regarded as admitted on account of the defendant's failure to enter an appearance; on the contrary, full proof of the facts founding jurisdiction is to be required of the plaintiff (see Bülow-Böckstiegel, *op. cit*).

7. Without going into the problem raised by the United Kingdom, as to whether, in fact, jurisdiction which has been correctly invoked under Article 5(1) of the Convention still exists even if the claim that there is no contract is later shown to be justified, I propose that the question submitted by the Bundesgerichtshof should be answered as follows: 'A plaintiff may invoke the jurisdiction of the courts of the place of performance in accordance with Article 5(1) of the Convention even when the existence of the contract on which the claim is based is in dispute between the parties'.

Case 133/81 - 26 May 1982

Roger Ivenel
v
Helmut Schwab

Special jurisdiction - Article 5(1) - Court for the place of performance of a contractual obligation - Claims based on different obligations resulting from a contract of employment - Obligation to be taken into account for the purpose of jurisdiction - Obligation characterizing the contract in question.

Summary

The obligation to be taken into account for the purposes of the application of Article 5(1) of the Convention of 27 September 1968 in the case of claims based on different obligations arising under a contract of employment as a representative binding a worker to an undertaking is the obligation which characterizes the contract.

JUDGMENT OF THE COURT

Mertens de Wilmars, President, Bosco, Touffait, Due, Lord Mackenzie Stuart, O'Keeffe, Koopmans, Chloros and Grévisse, Judges

1. By judgment of 2 April 1981, received at the Court on 3 June 1981, the French Cour de Cassation referred to the Court of Justice for a preliminary ruling pursuant to the Protocol of 3 June 1971 on the interpretation by the Court of Justice of the Convention of 27 September 1978 on Jurisdiction and the Enforcement of Judgments in Civil and Commercial Matters, a question on the interpretation of Article 5(1) of the Convention.

2. That question was raised in proceedings between Mr Ivenel, who resides in Strasbourg, and the undertaking Schwab Maschinenbau, whose place of establishment is at Oettingen in Bavaria, relating to an alleged breach of a contract for representation which gave rise to a claim for payment of commission, compensation for goodwill, in lieu of notice and in respect of paid holidays.

3. The Conseil de Prud'hommes, Strasbourg, before which the claim was brought, dismissed the two objections founded on lack of jurisdiction which were raised by Mr Schwab. It based its jurisdiction *ratione materiae* on the fact that in its opinion the contract between the parties was to be considered as a contract of employment. As regards its jurisdiction *ratione loci* it considered that, according to Article 5(1) of the Convention, in matters of contract an action might be brought against a defendant ordinarily resident in the territory of another Member State before the court for the place where the obligation was, or was to be, performed and that in the case in point the obligation to be taken into account was that of the work carried out by the representative who had his office in Strasbourg where he collated orders and attended to their execution.

4. When an appeal by Schwab was brought before the Cour d'Appel, Colmar, that court, whilst confirming the judgment of the Conseil de Prod'hommes insofar as it found that there was a contract of employment, set aside that judgment for lack of jurisdiction *ratione loci.* The Cour d'Appel considered that the obligation to be taken into account for the purpose of applying Article 5(1) of the Convention was that which constituted the basis of the court action. In the case in point that obligation was the payment of the commission and other amounts claimed from Schwab, which were payable at the address of the debtor and not the creditor.

5. Mr Ivenel appealed in cassation against that judgment and maintained that the Cour d'Appel had infringed Article 5(1) of the Convention.

6. The Cour de Cassation took cognizance of the grounds relied on by the Cour d'Appel in deciding that the French courts had no jurisdiction in the case but, nevertheless, considered that since the action related to the performance of a contract for representation involving mutual obligations some of which, at least, were performed in France the question which was the place of performance of the obligation within the meaning of

Article 5(1) raised an issue of interpretation. It, therefore, stayed the proceedings and asked the Court for a ruling on the interpretation to be given to that provision.

7. It must be observed that, as the Court of Justice has already stated, in particular in its judgment of 6 October 1976 in Case 12/76 *Tessili* [1976] ECR 1473, the 'place of performance' within the meaning of Article 5(1) of the Convention is to be determined in accordance with the law which governs the obligation in question according to the conflict rules of the court before which the matter is brought.

8. The question raised by the national court concerns the obligation to be taken into account for the purposes of that definition when the claim before the court is based on different obligations under a single contract for representation which has been classified by the courts concerned with the substance of the case as a contract of employment.

9. In its judgment of 6 October 1976 in Case 14/76 *de Bloos* [1976] ECR 1497 the Court has already stated that the obligation to be taken into account for the purposes of Article 5(1) of the Convention in the case of a claim based on a contract granting an exclusive sales concession between two commercial undertakings is that which forms the basis of the legal proceedings. The problem raised by this case is whether the same criterion must be applied to cases of the kind described by the national court.

10. It is appropriate to examine that problem in the light of the objectives of the Convention and the general scheme of its provisions.

11. Adoption of the special rules of jurisdiction as contained in Articles 5 and 6 of the Convention is justified *inter alia* by the fact that there must be a close connecting factor between the dispute and the court with jurisdiction to resolve it. The report drawn up by the committee of experts (Official Journal 1979, C 59, p. 1) which drafted the text of the Convention stresses that connection by stating *inter alia* that the court for the place of performance of the obligation will be useful in proceedings for the recovery of fees since the creditor will have a choice between the courts of the State where the defendant is ordinarily resident by virtue of the general provisions contained in Article 2 of the Convention and the courts of another State within whose jurisdiction the services were provided, particularly where, according to the appropriate law, the obligation to pay must be performed where the services were provided.

12. The above-mentioned report also refers to the reasons why those drafting the Convention did not consider it appropriate to insert into the Convention a provision giving exclusive jurisdiction in contracts of employment. According to the report it is desirable as far as possible for disputes to be brought before the courts of the State whose law governs the contract whereas at the time the Convention was being drafted work was in progress to harmonise the application of the rules of employment law in the Member States of the Community. The report concludes that at present the existing provisions of the Convention, such as Article 2 stipulating the forum for the place where the defendant is ordinarily resident and Article 5(1) the forum for the place of performance of the obligation, are likely to satisfy the relevant interests.

13. It should be noted that on 19 June 1980 a Convention on the law applicable to contractual obligations was opened for signature by the Member States (Official Journal 1980, L 266, p. 1). Article 6 thereof provides that a contract of employment is to be governed, in the absence of choice of the applicable law, by the law of the country in which the employee habitually carries out his work in performance of the contract unless it appears from the circumstances as a whole that the contract is more closely connected with another country.

14. The experts' report on the Convention on the law applicable to contractual obligations (Official Journal 1980, C 282, p. 1) explains in that respect that the adopting of a special conflict rule in relation to contracts of employment was intended to provide an appropriate arrangement for matters in which the interests of one of the contracting parties were not the same as those of the other and to secure thereby adequate protection for the party who from the socio-economic point of view was to be regarded as the weaker in the contractual relationship.

15. It follows from the foregoing account that in the matter of contracts Article 5(1) of the Convention is particularly concerned to attribute jurisdiction to the court of the country which has a close connection with the case; that in the case of a contract of employment the connection lies particularly in the law applicable to the contract; and that according to the trend in the conflict rules in regard to this matter that law is determined by the obligation characterising the contract in question and is normally the obligation to carry out work.

16. It emerges from an examination of the provisions of the Convention that in establishing special or even exclusive jurisdiction for insurance,

instalment sales and tenancies of immovable property those provisions recognise that the rules on jurisdiction, too, are inspired by concern to afford proper protection to the party to the contract who is the weaker from the social point of view.

17. Those factors must be taken into account in answering the question which has been put to the Court.

18. In a case such as the one in point, where the national court has before it claims relating to obligations under a contract for representation, some of which concern remuneration due to the employee from an undertaking established in one State and others concern compensation based on the manner in which the work has been done in another State, it is necessary to interpret the provisions of the Convention in such a way that the national court is not compelled to find that it has jurisdiction to adjudicate upon certain claims but not on others.

19. Such a result would be even less compatible with the objectives and general structure of the Convention in the case of a contract of employment for which, as a general rule, the law applicable contains provisions protecting the worker and is normally that of the place where the work characterising the contract is carried out.

20. It follows from the foregoing considerations, taken as a whole, that the obligation to be taken into account for the purposes of the application of Article 5(1) of the Convention in the case of claims based on different obligations arising under a contract of employment as a representative binding a worker to an undertaking is the obligation which characterises the contract.

On those grounds, the Court, in answer to the question submitted to it by the French Cour de Cassation by judgment of 2 April 1981, hereby rules:

> **The obligation to be taken into account for the purposes of the application of Article 5(1) of the Convention of 27 September 1968 on Jurisdiction and the Enforcement of Judgments in Civil and Commercial Matters in the case of claims based on different obligations arising under contract of employment as a representative binding a worker to an undertaking is the obligation which characterises the contract.**

OPINION OF MR ADVOCATE GENERAL REISCHL

A contract was made in September 1971 between Mr Ivenel, the plaintiff in the main action, resident in Strasbourg, and Mr Schwab, the defendant in the main action who runs an engineering works in the Federal Republic of Germany. According to the contract the plaintiff was to sell machinery in France on behalf of the defendant and receive therefor commission at the rate of 15% of the amount of the relevant orders. Since August 1975 the defendant allegedly ceased to pay commission which led to the plaintiff's having to give up his work for the defendant in July 1976.

The plaintiff sees that as discharge of the contract for which the defendant is responsible. In January 1977 the plaintiff, therefore, brought the matter before the Conseil de Prud'Hommes Commerciaux in Strasbourg claiming that the defendant be ordered to pay, various sums (commission, compensation for goodwill, payment in lieu of notice and holiday payments and the balance of a so-called internal account).

Since the defendant objected to the territorial and substantive jurisdiction of the court before which the matter was brought, that court gave judgment on 17 April 1978 on the question of jurisdiction. On the one hand, it confirmed that it had jurisdiction *ratione materiae* because the claims made derived from a *contract of employment.* Further, it held that it had jurisdiction *ratione loci* on the basis of Article 5(1) of the Convention on Jurisdiction and the Enforcement of Judgments in Civil and Commercial Matters which provides: 'A person domiciled in a Contracting State may, in another Contracting State, be sued: (1) In matters relating to a contract, in the courts for the place of performance of the obligation in question'.

In that regard the court took the view that the various obligations in a mutual contract did not have to be separated but that the essential issue was what was the *characteristic* obligation. In a contract for representation that was the obligation of the representative; since, however, that was to be performed in the place in which the representative had his office, the French courts had jurisdiction in the present case, and in particular because there was no agreement on jurisdiction.

The defendant appealed against the judgment, which adjourned the hearing of the claims to a later date, to the Cour d'Appel in Colmar where he was partly successful. The Social Affairs Division of the Cour'd'Appel in its judgment of 10 October 1978 confirmed the view of the court of first instance that there was a *contract of employment* and in consequence the relevant courts had jurisdiction *ratione materiae.* On the other hand, it held that under Article 5(1) of the Convention on Jurisdiction the French courts had no jurisdiction *ratione loci.* The criterion for that purpose was the obligations on which the action was based. Since, however, both under French and German law claims for the payment of commission and other amounts were payable at the address of the debtor and not the creditor the place of performance could in that respect be only in the Federal Republic of Germany.

Upon the plaintiff's appeal in cassation on 22 December 1978 the Social

Affairs Division of the French Cour de Cassation came to the view in considering the case that in a contract for representation giving rise to mutual obligations some of which were to be performed in France the question of the *determination* of a place of performance for the purposes of the Convention on Jurisdiction was fraught with difficulties. It, therefore, decided to stay the proceedings and by judgment of 2 April 1981 requested an interpretation of Article 5(1) of the Convention on Jurisdiction with reference to the particular features of the facts before it.

My opinion on that question is as follows.

1. Where the issue is one of determining the court for the place of performance within the meaning of Article 5(1) of the Convention on Jurisdiction, that is to say, of ascertaining the place in which certain contractual obligations are to be performed, the court before which the matter comes must first of all solve a problem of conflict of laws. It has to determine, in accordance with the private international law by which it is bound, the law applicable to the contractual relationship and then ascertain, on the basis of the rules of that law, the place of performance. That was the tenor of the decision in Case 12/76, in view of the fact that the Convention on Jurisdiction contains no definition of the concept 'place of performance', and that no doubt must remain the situation, since the present case and the observations made with regard thereto in any event give no cause to contemplate other possible solutions.

This preliminary analysis, of course, raises the issue of a determination of the contractual relationship in question. In the present case, as is known, the courts of first and second instance took the view that it was an *employment relationship.*

On that assumption the conclusion is obviously that French law applies, namely Article L 751 - 1 et seq. of the Code du Travail. That seems to be the opinion of French legal writers; the plaintiff cited *Battifol*, Traité de Droit International Privé 1976, No 576. It is, however, also in conformity with what is provided for in the Convention on the Law Applicable to Contractual Obligations (Official Journal L 266, 9 October 1980, p. 1), which has not yet entered into force. Article 6 provides that in the absence of a choice of law the contract of employment is to be governed by the law of the country in which the employee habitually carries out his work in performance of the contract and it even provides that a choice of law is not to have the result of depriving the employee of the protection afforded to him by the mandatory rules of the law to which reference has just been made as in general governing the matter.

The plaintiff in the main action and the Commission have argued exclusively on that legal basis. My view, however, is that this leads to an unacceptable restriction of the area for consideration.

The defendant in the main action, in fact, puts forward a number of reasons, which I will not now mention since we do not have to resolve the problem of definition, against the finding that there is a contract of employment and he vigorously propounds the view that the plaintiff is to be regarded as an *independent commercial representative.* It may be that we cannot even be certain that the question of definition has already been finally decided. That is because, on the one hand, since in any event the jurisdiction *ratione loci* of the French courts was denied by the Cour d'Appel in Colmar, the defendant has so far had no cause to challenge the finding that the labour courts have jurisdiction, and on the other, because the Cour de cassation which has not been asked to decide the question of jurisdiction *ratione materiae*, may come to another conclusion as regards the question of definition when it applies Article 5(1) of the Convention on Jurisdiction.

It is more reasonable, therefore, to undertake the interpretation of Article 5(1) of the Convention on Jurisdiction, as we have been requested, not only from the point of view that a contract of employment is at issue in the main proceedings but rather more comprehensively.

2. The court making the reference which has to determine, in the manner which I have described, the place (or places) of performance of the contract at issue must in addition be referred to the judgment in Case 14/76 *[de Bloos]* for the correct application of Article 5(1) of the Convention on Jurisdiction.

(a) In that judgment it was held, following my Opinion in which I had set out the conclusive arguments therefor, that Article 5(1) was not based on the notion of a *single* place of performance which had to apply to the contract as a whole and was to be determined according to the obligation *characterizing* the contract. On the contrary the term 'obligation' within the meaning of Article 5(1) was that contractual obligation which formed the basis of the legal proceedings; the relevant obligation was, therefore, that which corresponded to the contractual right on which the action was based.

That must be stressed in view of certain references in the very brief judgment making the reference which give the impression that in the view of the Cour de Cassation it may suffice for the purposes of the application of Article 5(1) that *some* of the obligations mutually entered into in the contract at issue have to be performed in France even though they themselves are not at issue.

Moreover, there is nothing in the present proceedings to provide a basis for a general derogation from the said principle. I shall later discuss the question whether a certain modification may be appropriate for normal contracts of employment.

(b) Two other statements in the *de Bloos* judgment must, however, also be recalled.

On one hand, it was held that, in the case of claims after dissolution of a contract conferring an exclusive concession for compensation for goodwill built up by the representative, the national court had to ascertain whether under the law applicable to the contract *independent* contractual obligations or obligations *replacing* the unperformed contractual obligations were involved. That was apparently done because in that respect there were serious problems in Belgian law and the case was concerned with the application of that law (cf. *Vander Elst* in Journal des Tribunaux 1976, p. 733 *et seq.*). If I understand the position correctly there can, however, be no question of that in the present case according to the relevant laws. Under French law it seems to be clear (the observations of the defendant warrant this inference) that the claims which arise under the Code du Travail after dissolution of a contract for representation are not to be regarded as independent but replace the original claims corresponding to the main obligations of the employer. There is, therefore, probably no reason at present to dwell any longer on that part of the judgment in Case 14/76, which, as the Commission has pointed out, has led to divergent commentaries and, for example, to inquire into the question whether considerations, to which I shall come in a moment, might make it appear appropriate to depart therefrom and to regard *all* claims in such a case as similar *contractual* claims even if they are not directed to performance of the contract but to actions in substitution therefor in the widest sense. In my opinion there are good reasons for such a view.

Further, it was made clear in the said judgment that in an action concerning the consequences of a breach by the supplier of a contract conferring an exclusive concession, which has as its object the payment of compensation or discharge of the contract, the decisive factor is the contractual obligation of the supplier, the non-performance *of which* is alleged, so that *that* determines the ascertainment of the court for the place of performance. This conveys the notion that a *multiplicity* of courts having jurisdiction is to be avoided, a notion clearly formulated in another part of the judgment, and with the express reference to the need 'to avoid, so far as it is possible, creating a situation in which a number of courts have jurisdiction in respect of one and the same contract' (paragraph 9 of the decision). I also spoke in favour of this in support of the Commission's view in my Opinion and expressly proposed that Article 5(1) should be interpreted in accordance with the underlying intention of the Convention that in the event of a multiplicity of obligations arising for a party out of a contract regard should be had to the *main obligation* of that party. What could be done, and in my opinion should be done, in the present case to clarify and perhaps build upon the decision in Case 14/76 is to emphasize with the necessary clarity that principle of the determinant nature of the main obligation on the part of the defendant.

3. Those guidelines could lead to the result, and obviously we do not have to decide that now, that in the case at issue in the main proceedings a place of performance in France and thus jurisdiction of the French courts is to be assumed as regards the claims which have been brought.

As we know, the plaintiff is essentially claiming that the defendant be ordered to pay commission, compensation for failure to give notice and for goodwill, conceived as compensation for the unjustified termination of the contract. What is at issue, therefore, is partly performance of the contract (payment of commission, settlement of an 'internal account' through which sums collected and claims of the plaintiff were to be taken into account) and partly claims for non-performance (holiday allowance, compensation for failure to give notice and for unwarranted unilateral termination of the contract).

As regards the first-mentioned matters it is possible to gain the impression, in view of what has been submitted, that they are to be complied with in France, at least if it is assumed that the contract is one of *employment*. In that respect I would refer to the plaintiff's observations, which he supported with references to the case-law, to the effect that according to French law payments of salary are to be made at the place in which the work is done, that, furthermore, emoluments to travellers are to be paid at their residence and that in such cases where there is an obligation to pay by cheque or bank transfer that likewise generally means performance at the place of residence of the employee.

The same should apply to the claims for non-performance (damages for termination of the contract and compensation for failure to give notice) since they are based on the defendant's obligation not to disturb the plaintiff in the performance of his work and thus obviously only one place of performance can be contemplated, namely in the area in which the plaintiff should do his work. In that respect reference may be made to the above-mentioned article by *Vander Elst* and the case-law of Belgian courts (Cour d'Appel, Mons, judgment of 3 May 1974, Cour de Cassation, judgment of 6 April 1978, Cour d'Appel, Liège, judgment of 12 May 1977, printed in the Digest of Case-law Relating to the European Communities, Series D, Article 5 of the Convention of 27 September 1968).

If that is so, and the national court has in the end to decide that, as well as to adjudicate upon the defendant's objections to the effect that the plaintiff insisted on the application of the terms of payment applied to German representatives and the payment of his remuneration in German marks, it would, in fact, to some extent be consistent with the judgment, cited by the Commission, of the Cour d'Appel, Angers, of 29 January 1980 in a similar case. That can be said to be so at least insofar as the judgment proceeds on the basis that the relevant obligations in regard to payment replace the obligations in the contract which have not been performed and that as regards the claims for compensation for failure to give notice and for goodwill acquired, these are claims for the breach of the obligation to continue to perform the contract. On the other hand, the view, which is also to be found in the judgment, to the effect that the claims for commission and holiday allowance are based on the non-performance of obligations which are to be treated as *consideration* for work done and that, therefore, in the case of those obligations the place of performance is that where the work is carried out, must be queried in view of the previous case-law of this Court.

The result which I have indicated would further be in conformity with the desire expressed in the Jenard Report to recognize the venue of the place of performance as being in the country whose law governs the contract at issue.

4. In conclusion, however, I would like to return, as I previously mentioned, to the question whether at least for *contracts of employment* a very clear modification of the law as laid down in the judgment in Case 14/76 does not appear to be appropriate.

The Commission has evolved a line of thought which points in that direction. It obviously has in mind to ascertain in the case of legal relationships of this kind *one* focal point (namely the area in which the work has to be done and whose mandatory legal provisions require application) which alone would determine the place of performance for the purposes of Article 5(1), that is to say, there would be one place of performance only for the whole contract. In that way the argument that the determinant factor is the obligation *characterizing* a contract and that the venue of the place of performance is to be ascertained accordingly would be recognized at least as far as the law of employment is concerned.

That, however, seems to me a difficult case to argue in the present state of the law.

It must be admitted that in the Jenard Report which is unquestionably of importance in interpreting the Convention on Jurisdiction it is stated that in drafting the Convention the *special problems* of contracts of employment were seen and that it emphasizes that 'it is desirable that disputes over contracts of employment should as far as possible be brought before the courts of the State whose law governs the contract'. I cannot, however, disregard the fact that the provision contained in the preliminary draft of the Convention to the effect that in matters relating to contracts of employment the courts of the Contracting State in which the undertaking concerned was situated or in which the work was to have been performed was not included in the Convention. It is expressly stated in the Report that it was decided not to insert in the Convention any special provisions on jurisdiction in the matter of the law on employment, obviously having regard to the work undertaken by the EEC Commission in harmonizing the provisions on employment law in the Member States; further it is expressly stated that the general rules of the Convention will apply to contracts of employment and, as has been shown in Case 14/76, with regard to Article 5 (1), the theory that the determinant factor is the obligation *characterizing* a contract is not compatible with those rules. Finally, there can also be no question of departing from this because in the meantime the Convention, which has not yet entered into force, on the law applicable to contractual obligations has come into existence, for it is stated quite clearly in the Jenard Report (Official Journal C 59, 5 March 1979, p. 24): 'Once the work of the Commission in this field has been completed, it will always be possible to *amend* the provisions of the Convention, either by means of an additional protocol, or by the drafting of a convention governing the whole range of problems relating to contracts of employment ... '.

5. I can, therefore, propose only that the question put by the French Cour de Cassation should be answered as follows: 'Article 5(1) of the Convention on Jurisdiction must be interpreted to the effect that in the case of contracts imposing mutual obligations there can be no question of determining one place of performance according to the criterion of the obligation which characterises the contract but rather account must be taken of that obligation which provides the basis on which the claim is brought. In the case of claims for breach of contractual obligations the obligation whose non-performance is alleged is to be taken as the criterion. If several claims are brought in relation to one contract then it is necessary to ascertain according to the law applicable to the contract what is to be considered as the corresponding *main obligation* of the defendant; its place of performance then determines the venue of legal proceedings with regard thereto.

Case 34/82 - 22 March 1983

Martin Peters Bauunternehmung GmbH
v
Zuid Nederlandse Aannemers Vereniging

Article 5(1) - Special jurisdiction - Jurisdiction in matters relating to a contract - Independent concept - Concept of matters relating to a contract - Obligations to pay money having their basis in the relationship between an association and its members by virtue of membership - Inclusion.

Summary

1. The concept of matters relating to a contract in Article 5(1) of the Convention of 27 September 1968 on Jurisdiction and the Enforcement of Judgments in Civil and Commercial Matters should not be interpreted simply as referring to the national law of one or other of the Member States concerned, but should be regarded as an independent concept which, for the purposes of the application of the Convention, must be interpreted by reference chiefly to the system and objectives of the Convention, in order to ensure that it is fully effective.

2. Obligations in regard to the payment of a sum of money which have their basis in the relationship existing between an association and its members by virtue of membership are 'matters relating to a contract' within the meaning of Article 5(1) of the Convention, whether the obligations in question arise simply from the act of becoming a member or from that act in conjunction with one or more decisions made by organs of the association.

JUDGMENT OF THE COURT

Mertens de Wilmars, President, O'Keeffe, Everling, Presidents of Chambers, Bosco, Koopmans, Bahlmann and Galmot, Judges

1. By a judgment dated 15 January 1982 which was received at the Court on 21 January 1982, the Hoge Raad der Nederlanden [Supreme Court of the Netherlands] referred to the Court of Justice for a preliminary ruling under the Protocol of 3 June 1971 on the Interpretation by the Court of Justice of the Convention of 27 September 1968 on Jurisdiction and the Enforcement of Judgments in Civil and Commercial Matters (hereinafter referred to as 'the Convention') two questions on the interpretation of Article 5(1) of the Convention.

2. Those questions arose in the course of a dispute between Zuid Nederlandse Aannemers Vereniging (South Netherlands Contractors' Association), hereinafter referred to as 'the Association', an association under Netherlands law, having its registered office in Maastricht and its administrative office at Heeze (North Brabant) and one of its members, Martin Peters Bauunternehmung GmbH (hereinafter referred to as 'Peters'), a company incorporated under German law having its registered office in Aachen, in the Federal Republic of Germany, concerning the recovery of sums payable by the latter by virtue of an internal rule adopted by the organs of the Association and binding on its members.

3. The Association brought a claim before the Arrondissementsrechtbank [District Court], 's-Hertogenbosch, which dismissed the objection of lack of jurisdiction raised by Peters. It ruled that it had jurisdiction on the ground that in its view the dispute arose out of a contract and that it, therefore, had jurisdiction under Article 5(1) of the Convention, which provides that a person, in this case Peters, domiciled in a Contracting State may, in another Contracting State, be sued in matters relating to a contract in the courts for the place of performance of the obligation in question.

4. Peters appealed against that decision to the Gerechtshof [Regional Court of Appeal], s'-Hertogenbosch, which confirmed the judgment at first instance on the ground that the obligation to pay the amounts claimed by the Association from Peters should be regarded as a contractual obligation for the purposes of Article 5(1) of the Convention.

5. Peters brought an appeal on a point of law against that decision before the Hoge Raad der Nederlanden challenging the analysis made by the Gerechtshof, s'-Hertogenbosch, in relation to the nature of the relationship between it and the Association.

6. The Hoge Raad decided, before giving a decision, to refer to the Court of Justice the following two questions on the interpretation of the Brussels Convention: '1. Does Article 5(1) of the Convention apply to claims which are made by an association constituted under private law possessing legal personality against one of its members in a matter relating to obligations in to the payment of a sum of money and which have their basis in the relationship between the parties by virtue of membership, such relationship arising from the defendant party's joining the association as a member by virtue of a legal transaction entered into for that purpose. 2. Does it make any difference whether the obligations in question arise simply from the act of becoming a member, or from that act in conjunction with one or more decisions made by organs of the association?'

1. First question

7. Article 5 of the Convention makes provision in a number of cases for a special jurisdiction which the plaintiff may choose, in derogation from the general jurisdiction provided for in Article 2(1) of the Convention.

8. According to Article 5(1) of the Convention: 'A person domiciled in a Contracting State may, in another Contracting State, be sued: (1) in matters relating to a contract, in the courts for the place of performance of the obligation in question'.

9. Thus, the concept of matters relating to a contract serves as a criterion to define the scope of one of the rules of special jurisdiction available to the plaintiff. Having regard to the objectives and the general scheme of the Convention, that it is important that, in order to ensure as far as possible the equality and uniformity of the rights and obligations arising out of the Convention for the Contracting States and the persons concerned, that concept should not be interpreted simply as referring to the national law of one or other of the States concerned.

10. Therefore, and as the Court ruled on similar grounds in relation to the words 'the operation of a branch, agency or other establishment'

referred to in Article 5(5) of the Convention (judgment of 22. 11. 1978 in Case 33/78 *Somafer* v *Saar-Ferngas* AG [1978] ECR 2183), the concept of matters relating to a contract should be regarded as an independent concept which, for the purpose of the application of the Convention, must be interpreted by reference chiefly to the system and objectives of the Convention, in order to ensure that it is fully effective.

11. In this regard it should be pointed out that although Article 5 makes provision in a number of cases for a special jurisdiction which the plaintiff may choose, this is because of the existence, in certain clearly-defined situations, of a particularly close connecting factor between a dispute and the court which may be called upon to hear it, with a view to the efficacious conduct of the proceedings.

12. In that context, the designation by Article 5(1) of the Convention of the courts for the place of performance of the obligation in question expresses the concern that, because of the close links created by a contract between the parties thereto, it should be possible for all the difficulties which may arise on the occasion of the performance of a contractual obligation to be brought before the same court: that for the place of performance of the obligation.

13. In that regard it appears that membership of an association creates between the members close links of the same kind as those which are created between the parties to a contract and that consequently the obligations to which the national court refers may be regarded as contractual for the purpose of the application of Article 5(1) of the Convention.

14. Since under national legal systems it is usually stipulated that the place in which the association is established is to be the place of performance obligations arising out of the act of becoming a member, the application of Article 5(1) of the Convention also has practical advantages: the court for the place in which the association has its seat is, in fact, usually the best fitted to understand the documents of constitution, rules and decisions of the association, and also the circumstances out of which the dispute arose.

15. Under those circumstances the answer to the first question should be that the obligations in regard to the payment of a sum of money which have their basis in the relationship between an association and its members by virtue of membership must be regarded as 'matters relating to a contract' within the meaning of Article 5(1) of the Convention.

2. Second question

16. The national court asks the Court of Justice to state whether, in order to determine whether or not an obligation of a member towards an association falls within 'matters relating to a contract', a distinction should be drawn according to whether the obligation in question arises simply from the act of becoming a member or results from that act in conjunction with a decision made by an organ of the association.

17. It should be noted that multiplication of the bases of jurisdiction in one and the same type of case is not likely to encourage legal certainty and effective legal protection throughout the territory of the Community. The provisions of the Convention should therefore be interpreted in such a way that the court seised is not required to declare that it has jurisdiction to adjudicate upon certain applications but has no jurisdiction to hear certain other applications, even though they are closely related. Moreover, respect for the purposes and spirit of the Convention requires an interpretation of Article 5 which enables the national court to rule on its own jurisdiction without being compelled to consider the substance of the case.

18. On those grounds, the answer should be that the fact that the obligation in question arises simply from the act of becoming a member or results from that act in conjunction with a decision of an organ of the association has no effect on the application of the provisions of Article 5(1) of the Convention to a dispute concerning that obligation.

On those grounds, the Court, in answer to the questions submitted to it by the Hoge Raad der Nederlanden by judgment of 15 January 1982, hereby rules:

1. Obligations in regard to the payment of a sum of money which have their basis in the relationship existing between an association and its members by virtue of membership are 'matters relating to a contract' within the meaning of Article 5(1) of the Convention of 27 September 1968 on Jurisdiction and the Enforcement of Judgments in Civil and Commercial Matters.

2. It makes no difference in that regard whether the obligations in question arise simply from the act of becoming a member or from that act in conjunction with one or more decisions made by organs of the association.

OPINION OF MR ADVOCATE GENERAL MANCINI

1. This reference for a preliminary ruling concerns the interpretation of certain aspects of the expression 'matters relating to a contract' which appears in Article 5(1) of the Brussels Convention of 27 September 1968 on Jurisdiction and Enforcement of Judgments in Civil and Commercial Matters. According to that provision, 'a person domiciled in a Contracting State may, in another Contracting State, be sued: (1) in matters relating to a contract, in the courts for the place of performance of the obligation in question'.

It must first be ascertained whether the above expression is to be interpreted independently or with reference to the lex causae. It must then be established whether the obligations incurred by a member of an association are of a contractual nature or not. This Court has already given rulings on other aspects of the same provision. I refer to the judgment of 6 October 1976 in Case 14/76 *De Bloos* v *Bouyer* [1976] ECR 1497). In that case the Court defined the effect of the expression 'obligation' and held that it referred to the contractual obligation forming the basis of the proceedings. I would also recall the judgment of the same date in Case 12/76 *Tessili* v *Dunlop* ([1976] ECR 1473) which interpreted the words 'the place of performance of the obligation in question' by reference to the law which is applicable under the rules of the conflict of laws of the court before which the matter is brought. There are, however, no previous decisions which concern specifically the concept of 'matters relating to a contract' on which the Court is now asked to give a ruling.

2. For the purposes of a proper understanding of the matters at issue in the dispute it is appropriate to note from the outset a number of details relating to the structure and function of the organisation which is the appellant in the main proceedings. Its name is the Zuid Nederlandse Aannemers Vereniging [South Netherlands Contractors' Association] (hereinafter referred to as 'the Association') and its registered office is in the Netherlands. It is a legal association of the construction undertakings which operate in the southern provinces of the Netherlands, in Limburg, North Brabant, Zeeland and in part of the province of Gelderland. As is stated in paragraph 1 of the judgment making the reference, the object of the Association 'is to promote the economic, financial, legal and other interests of its members and of undertakings in the building industry in general insofar as those interests relate to ... price regulation in the context of invitations to tender for contracts and the consequences thereof for undertakings'. So as to enable it to carry out those functions, the Association's documents of constitution specifically empower it both to adopt internal rules of a general character, which are binding upon the members, and to take decisions. Such decisions are also binding and are based on both the documents of constitution and the above-mentioned general rules. They concern solely the position of individual contractors.

Amongst the decisions of the first type, the 'Guidelines on private tenders for public works and utilities' are of particular relevance for the purposes of the dispute in this case they were adopted on 28 November 1972 and entered into force on 1 January 1973. They require that certain rules be complied with by those members who submit tenders for work within the Association's area of activity: in particular the members must inform the Association of their intention to tender (Article 3 of the Guidelines); and, if other contractors who are members of the Association propose to submit competing tenders for the same work, they must participate, directly or through a representative, in a special meeting of all contractors concerned organized by the central office of the Association (Article 4). The meeting is presided over by a representative of the Association and its purpose is to fix certain compensatory sums to be paid by the member to whom the contract is awarded. Such sums are contributions: (a) amounting to 6% or less of the value of the work, designed to cover 'expenses and work of members connected with the tender for the work' (Article 11); (b) intended to reimburse the Association for its expenses (Article 12(1)); (c) intended for one or more contractors' organisations (Article 12(2)).

The decisions which determine the amount of the contributions come under the second category of binding decisions which I have mentioned earlier: those which govern individual situations concerning the relations between members.

Therefore, as a result of those provisions, the contractor who finally carries out the work is automatically required to pay the Association the compensatory sums fixed in the course of the preliminary meeting. Payment must, moreover, be made within the period and in the manner prescribed by the Guidelines, that is to say in principle as soon as the member has started to carry out the work and, so far as the place of payment is concerned, at the Association's head office (Articles 18 and 19 of the Guidelines).

3. Having thus explained the context of the litigation in the main proceedings, I will now give a brief summary of the facts in the case.

The undertaking Martin Peters Bauunternehmung GmbH (hereinafter referred to as 'Peters') has its registered office in Aachen, in the Federal Republic of Germany. After it had become a member of the Association Peters was awarded a contract to works which involved the construction of an office and industrial buildings for Medtronic in Kerkrade. It failed, however, to inform the Association of this and did not participate in the preliminary meeting which was organized by the Association and held in the prescribed manner at Heerlen on 3 May 1977. In the course of that meeting the contributions to be paid by the undertaking which had obtained the contract were determined. Subsequently, when it was established that Peters had started the work, it was asked by the Association to pay the contributions in relation thereto which had already been fixed. Peters refused to pay the contributions and by writ of 12 May 1978 the Association summoned it to appear before the Arrondissementsrecht-bank [District Court], 's-Hertogenbosch, and sought an order against it for the payment of the sum of HFL 112 725, together with statutory interest and costs, in respect of the contributions which it was required to pay as the successful tenderer. The German company contended that the above-mentioned court before which the proceedings are instituted did not have jurisdiction in view of the fact that the company's registered office was situated in the Federal Republic of Germany. It maintained that by virtue of Article 2 of the Brussels Convention this factor prevented the Association from being able to sue it in a Netherlands court.

By judgment of 2 March 1979 the Arrondissementsrechtbank, 's-Hertogenbosch, dismissed the objection and held that the obligation which was the subject of the proceedings was contractual in nature and was to be performed at the Association's head office in the Netherlands. The Court, therefore, had jurisdiction under Article 5(1) of the above-mentioned Convention which, as we know, provides that for contractual obligations the court which has jurisdiction is that for the place 'of performance' of the obligation. Peters then appealed to the Gerechtshof [Regional Court of Appeal], 's-Hertogenbosch, which confirmed the judgment of the court of first instance. The undertaking then brought an appeal on a point of law in which it contested the contractual nature of the relationship which bound it to the Association. By judgment of 15 January 1982, the Hoge Raad [Supreme Court of the Netherlands] stayed the proceedings and referred to the Court of Justice the following question for a preliminary ruling: 'Does Article 5(1) of the Convention apply to claims which are made by an association constituted under private law and possessing legal personality against one of its members in a matter relating to obligations in regard to the payment of a sum of money and which have their basis in the relationship between the parties by virtue of membership, such relationship arising from the defendant party's joining the association as a member by virtue of a legal transaction entered into for that purpose? Does it make any difference whether the obligations in question arise simply from the act of becoming a member, or from that act in conjunction with one or more decisions made by organs of the association?'

4. The first matter which has to be clarified concerns the scope of the expression 'matters relating to a contract'. It is well known that the expressions and legal concepts drawn from civil, commercial and procedural law which appear in the Brussels Convention may be interpreted in two ways. They may be given an independent meaning which is therefore common to all the Member States or they may be held to refer to the law applicable under the rules of conflict of laws of the court before which the matter was first brought. On that subject this Court has stated that 'neither of these two options rule out the other since the appropriate choice can only be made in respect of each of the provisions of the Convention to ensure that it is fully effective having regard to the objectives of Article 220 of the Treaty'. (judgment of 6.10.1976 in Case 12/76 *Tessili* v *Dunlop* [1976] ECR 1473, at p. 1485, paragraph 11 of the decision).

It should, however, be added that the Court has adopted the second approach only in the above-mentioned judgment (which concerned, as we know, the definition of the 'place of performance' of contractual obligations) and it did so in view of the 'differences obtaining between national laws of contract and [having regard to] the absence at this stage of legal development of any unification in the substantive law applicable', (*ibid.* paragraph 14 of the decision). In all the other judgments hitherto given in proceedings for preliminary rulings relating to the Brussels Convention, the first interpretation has been adopted. It is, thus, acknowledged in those judgments that the legal terms of art used in the Convention have a significance of their own which is, therefore, the same for the various Member States. Amongst the judgments to that effect I would recall the following: the judgments of 14 October 1976 in Case 29/76 *LTU* v *Eurocontrol* ([1976] ECR 1541) and of 16 December 1980 in Case 814/79 *Netherlands* v *Rüffer* ([1980] E.C.R. 3807) relating to the expression civil and commercial matters in Article 1; the judgment of 30 November 1976 in Case 21/76 *Bier* v *Mines de Potasse d'Alsace* ([1976] ECR 1735), on the concept of 'the place where the harmful event occurred' which appears in Article 5(3)); the judgment of 21 June 1976 in Case 150/77 *Bertrand* v *Ott* ([1976] ECR 1431), on the concept of 'sale of goods on instalment credit terms' within the meaning of Article 13; the judgments of 22 November 1978 in Case 33/78 *Somafer* v *Saar-Ferngas* ([1978] ECR 2183) and 18 March 1981 in Case 13/80 *Blanckaert & Willems* v *Trost* ([1981] ECR 819), on the interpretation of the expression 'operations of a branch, agency or other establishment' in Article 5(5).

I consider that the expression 'matters relating to a contract' to which the questions of the Netherlands court refer should be interpreted independently. I arrive at this conclusion by referring, on the one hand, to the general principles which on this matter may be derived from the national legal systems taken as a whole and, on the other, to the objectives and scheme of the Convention itself. In the latter respect, it is especially important to note that the aim of the Convention is to ensure, as far as possible, the equality and uniformity of the rights and obligations deriving from it, for the Contracting States and the persons to whom it applies. The importance of those interpretative criteria has been repeatedly emphasised by this Court; I refer, amongst others, to the judgments of 22 February 1979 in Case 133/78 *Gourdain* v *Nadler* ([1979] ECR 733), and of 16 December 1980 in Case 814/79 *Netherlands* v *Rüffer*, cited above (in particular, paragraphs 8 and 14 of the decision).

5. In almost all the legal systems of the Member States the relationships between an association and its members are recognized as being contractual in nature. Under Belgian, French, Italian, Danish and English law and under the law of Scotland contractual status attaches either to the act of becoming a member of the organization or to the rights and obligations resulting from membership. For example, according to French legal literature the creation of an association depends on the intention of the parties and in French case-law the relationships between an association and its members are considered to be 'contractual'. The Italian system follows the same line. Article 1420 of the Civil Code provides that the participation of more than two persons in an agreement (as in the case of an association's documents of constitution) is a genuine contract, even if 'the contributions of each [member] are directed towards the achievement of a common aim'. As regards the obligations laid upon the members as the result of their belonging to an association, the Italian Corte di Cassazione [Court of Cassation] has held that the act which creates the bond between a member and an association brings about the same situation as that which normally exists under bilateral contracts; the association may, therefore, apply to the courts under Article 1453 of the Civil Code (on the dissolution of commutative contracts on grounds of non-performance) for the expulsion of

those members who fail to fulfil their obligations (Court of Cassation, 2 March 1973, No 579). English law adopts the same position with reference both to an association's documents of constitution and to the obligations laid upon the members as the result of their belonging to that association. I would mention in this respect the case of *Lee* v *Showmen's Guild of Great Britain* [1952] 2 QB, 329, 341 in which Lord Denning emphasised the contractual nature of the relationship between a member and an association in order to show that the jurisdiction of the court was not restricted to the protection of proprietary rights.

As regards the German system, the courts and academic writers agree that the act by which a person becomes a member of an association is to be regarded as contractual. However, their views differ as to the relations which exist after membership has been acquired. The case-law seems to suggest that such relations are covered by the 'institutional law' of the organization, whilst in legal literature the opinion of writers is divided, in the sense that some writers accept the contractual theory and others support the institutional theory. Finally, in the Netherlands under the new Civil Code the act by which an association is formed is regarded as a multilateral legal transaction *sui generis* and the relations which derive from membership of the association are similarly *sui generis* (or based on the institutional concept).

It follows from the above-mentioned factors, in brief, that with the exception of the Netherlands system, all the national legal systems consider the act by which an association is created to be a contract in the strict sense. A similar approach seems to be taken as regards the relationships which arise between the organization and its members as the result of membership. Apart from the so-called institutional theory for which the new Netherlands Civil Code and the case-law of the Federal Republic of Germany have opted (although I would recall that in German legal literature opinion is divided on the subject), under all the other systems these relationships are considered to be of a contractual nature. The Commission's representative drew attention to that situation in his written observations of 26 March 1982 (in particular, paragraph 6, p. 21). From this it is but a short step to saying that the prevailing tendency of the legal systems of Community States is to consider that both the act by which an association is created and the relationships between the members and the association are governed by the law of contract. In the present case that step is important for the purposes of my conclusion namely that the obligations which directly or indirectly bind the members of an association are included in the concept of 'matters relating to a contract' within the meaning of Article 5(1) of the Brussels Convention. The correctness of that interpretation is, moreover, fully confirmed by reference to the objectives and the scheme of the Convention.

6. Articles 5 and 6 of the Convention list the situations in which a defendant may be sued in a Contracting State other than that in which he is ordinarily resident. As is noted in the Jenard Report (OJ C 59, 1979, p. 1 *et seq.*, in particular p. 22), 'the forums provided for in these articles supplement those which apply under Article 2', that is to say the courts of the Contracting State in whose territory the defendant is ordinarily resident. The introduction of alternative forums directly ascertainable by reference to the Convention (that is

to say without its being necessary to refer to the rules of territorial jurisdiction in force under the *lex fori*) is essentially designed to meet a requirement of foreseeability or, if the term is preferred, of legal certainty. In that way, the report states (p. 22), it is intended 'to facilitate implementation of the Convention' because 'by ratifying the Convention, the Contracting States will avoid having to take any other measures to adapt their internal legislation to the criteria laid down in Articles 5 and 6'. Indeed, it is clear that the most appropriate means of meeting the need for certainty to which I have alluded is the independent interpretation of the expression 'matters relating to a contract' which results in a uniform concept applicable in the same manner in all the Member States.

However, as the report continues, there is another particularly important consideration which justifies 'the adoption of special rules of jurisdiction', namely that there must be 'a close connecting factor between the dispute and the court with jurisdiction to resolve it' (*ibid.* p. 22). In drafting Article 5(1) (and the other provisions of that article and of the article which follows it) the authors of the Convention started from the premise that the court of the place 'of performance of the obligation in question' has by virtue of its physical proximity to the relationship at issue the best chances of determining the nature of that relationship in the fullest possible knowledge of the facts of the case. That argument may be thought to be particularly persuasive when the question concerns, as in this case, the obligations to be fulfilled within an organisation. It seems clear that, in cases of that kind, the court for the place in which the obligation is to be performed is in a better position than any other to obtain the appropriate information on the functioning of the creditor organisation and, therefore, in a better position to rule on the issues which may be inherent in such obligations.

Such considerations support the so-called contractual theory. On the other hand, no arguments come to mind, and the parties have not suggested any, which might justify excluding the obligations arising from the bond between an association and its members from the sphere of application of Article 5(1). On the contrary, the reasons for stipulating, for contractual obligations in general, the special forum of the place of performance are equally valid for obligations arising from that bond. In both cases an alternative forum is established founded on the jurisdiction of the court closest to the disputed relationship.

Following the same line of thought, a further consideration may be noted. I have already stated that according to this Court, the Convention is intended to guarantee as far as possible the equality and uniformity of the legal situations arising from it for Member States and for the persons to whom it applies. That objective is attained with greater efficacy if the independent nature of the expression 'matters relating to a contract' is recognised. It is obvious that if that expression is interpreted with reference to the *lex causae* which is applicable in each particular case, the functioning of the special forum provided for by Article 5(1) will be as diverse as the different concepts of contractual obligation which prevail in the different systems whereas if, as I propose, the expression is given an independent interpretation it would represent a common criterion for all the Member States.

7. In the written procedure and at the hearing, attention was drawn to the connection between the Brussels Convention and the Convention on the Law Applicable to Contractual Obligations, opened for signature in Rome on 19 June 1980 (OJ L 266, 1980, p. 1). Article 1(e) of the latter Convention (which, however, is not yet in force) excludes from its field of application 'questions governing the law of companies and other bodies corporate or incorporate and the personal liability of officers and members as such for the obligations of the company or body'. Peters' representative argues on the basis of the above-mentioned rule that the obligations laid upon the members of an association as a result of their joining it do not have a contractual basis and that confirmation of their non-contractual nature is to be found precisely in the fact that they are excluded from the scope of the Convention which determines the laws applicable to contractual obligations. On the other hand, the Commission and the Federal Republic of Germany infer from the same conclusion that the obligations in question are contractual in character. They observe that to have foreseen the necessity of providing for that exclusion suggests a fear that in the absence of an express provision such obligations would by virtue of their contractual nature fall within the sphere of application of the Convention.

I do not think that arguments of that kind are in themselves decisive for the purpose of resolving, in one way or the other, the problem before the Court. However, in view of the considerations which I have put forward earlier concerning the aim of the Convention of 1968 and in particular of Article 5(1), it seems to me that the argument *a contrario* which may be derived from the Rome Convention may at least amount to a confirmation of the view which I am advocating.

8. In addition to asking whether the claims which the association bases on the obligations arising from membership come within the scope of application of Article 5(1), the Hoge Raad also asks whether it makes 'any difference whether the obligations in question arise simply from the act of becoming a member, or from that act in conjunction with one or more decisions made by organs of the association'. I consider that this second question should be answered in the negative. The obligations arising from a decision of such a body are founded on the agreement by which a bond of association is created. By means of such an agreement the contracting parties manifest their intention to accept the internal rules of the association and, therefore, agree *inter alia* to be bound by the decisions taken by the organs of the association. In other words, it may be said that ultimately the binding effect of such decisions is, like that of the act of becoming a member, based on the contractual intention of the parties.

That being the case, it seems to me that from the theoretical point of view there is no difficulty in restoring the decisions of associations to the contractual sphere. Moreover, it has already been seen that such a conclusion exactly reflects the prevailing tendency in the legal systems of the Member States.

9. In the light of all the considerations set out above I propose that the Court give the following answer to the question referred to it for a preliminary ruling by the Hoge Raad der Nederlanden by judgment of 15 January 1952 in the action which the Zuid Nederlandse Aannemers Vereniging brought, by writ dated 12 May 1978, against Martin Peters Bauunternehmung GmbH:

'1. The expression 'matters relating to a contract' which appears in Article 5(1) of the Brussels Convention of 27 September 1968 on Jurisdiction and the Enforcement of Judgments in Civil and Commercial Matters should be interpreted as applying to the relationships between an association endowed with legal personality and its members where such relationships result from the act of becoming a member of the organization and involve the obligation to pay a sum of money to the organization or to perform a different service for its benefit.

2. It makes no difference, for the purposes of the above paragraph, whether the obligations derive directly from the act of becoming a member of the association or from that act in conjunction with subsequent decisions of the organs of the association'.

Case 266/85 - 15 January 1987

Hassan Shenavai
v
Klaus Kreischer

Article 5(1) - Special jurisdiction - Court of the place of performance of a contractual obligation - Relevant obligation for purposes of determining jurisdiction - Action for recovery of architect's fees.

Summary

Whereas in the case of an action based on an obligation under a contract of employment or another contract with the same particularities for work other than on a self-employed basis the relevant obligation for the purpose of determining the place of performance within the meaning of Article 5(1) of the Convention of 27 September 1968 the obligation which characterises that contract, the position is different where no such particularities exist, as in the case of most contracts, where the general rule applies that the relevant obligation is that on which the plaintiff's action is based. In a dispute concerning proceedings for the recovery of fees commenced by an architect commissioned to draw up plans for the building of houses, therefore, the obligation to be taken into consideration is the contractual obligation which forms the actual basis of the legal proceedings.

JUDGMENT OF THE COURT

Lord Mackenzie Stuart, President, Kakouris, O'Higgins, Schockweiler, Presidents of Chambers, Bosco, Koopmans, Bahlmann, Joliet and Rodríguez Iglesias, Judges

1. By an order of 5 March 1985, which was received at the Court on 30 August 1985, the Landgericht [Regional Court] Kaiserslautern referred to the Court for a preliminary ruling under the Protocol of 3 June 1971 on the interpretation by the Court of Justice of the Convention of 27 September 1968 on Jurisdiction and the Enforcement of Judgments in Civil and Commercial Matters a question concerning the interpretation of Article 5(1) of the Convention.

2. The question arose in the course of proceedings between Mr Shenavai, an architect of Rockenhausen, Federal Republic of Germany, and Mr Kreischer, residing at Geleen, Netherlands, concerning the recovery of architect's fees for the preparation of plans for the construction of three holiday homes near Rockenhausen.

3. The Amtsgericht [Local Court] Rockenhausen, before which the action was brought, allowed Mr Kreischer's objection that it lacked jurisdiction on the ground that the place of performance of the obligation to pay architect's fees was the domicile of the person who commissioned the work; Mr Kreischer was domiciled in the Netherlands, so that the requisite conditions for him to be sued in a German court were not satisfied.

4. Mr Shenavai appealed to the Landgericht Kaiserslautern which took the view that under German law the place of performance of the architect's contract was the place where his office was situated and where the planned buildings were to be erected. Thus the place of performance of all the obligations arising under the contract was to be found at the 'focal point' of the contractual relationship seen as a whole.

5. The Landgericht went on to state that it was not certain that the same interpretation had to be followed as regards Article 5(1) of the Convention, since some judgments of the Court made international territorial jurisdiction dependent on the place of performance of the contractual obligation on which the judicial proceedings were based - in this case, the obligation to pay the fees. In those circumstances the Landgericht deemed it necessary to refer the following question to the Court for a preliminary ruling: 'For the purposes of Article 5(1) of the Convention of 27 September 1968 on Jurisdiction and the Enforcement of Judgments in Civil and Commercial Matters, is the place of performance, in the specific case of a claim for fees by an architect engaged solely in planning work, to be determined by reference to the contractual obligation which forms the actual basis of the legal

proceedings (in this case a debt payable under German law at the place where the defendant is domiciled), or by reference to the obligation typical of the contract and characterising the contractual relationship as a whole (that is to say, the place where the architect has his practice and/or the site of the planned building)?'

6. It should be recalled that Article 2 of the Convention lays down the general rule that jurisdiction is to be based on the defendant's domicile, but that Article 5(1) thereof further provides that, in matters relating to a contract, the defendant may also be sued 'in the courts for the place of performance of the obligation in question'. As The Court observed in its judgment of 6 October 1976 (Case 12/76 *Tessili* v *Dunlop* [1976] ECR 1473), that freedom of choice was introduced in view of the existence in certain cases of a particularly close relationship between a dispute and the court which may be most conveniently called upon to take cognizance of the matter.

7. In the same judgment, the Court ruled that the question of the location of the 'place of performance' of an obligation was to be determined pursuant to the law governing the obligation at issue and in accordance with the rules on the conflict of laws of the court before which the matter was brought.

8. In another judgment of 6 October 1976 (Case 14/76 *De Bloos* v *Bouyer* [1976] ECR 1497) the Court observed that the Convention was intended to determine the international jurisdiction of the courts of the Contracting States, to facilitate the recognition of judgments and to introduce an expeditious procedure for securing the enforcement of judgments; it held that those objectives implied the need to avoid, so far as possible, creating a situation in which a number of courts had jurisdiction in respect of one and the same contract, and that Article 5(1) of the Convention could therefore not be interpreted as referring to any obligation whatsoever arising under the contract in question.

9. The Court concluded that, for the purposes of determining the place of performance within the meaning of Article 5, the obligation to be taken into account was that which corresponded to the contractual right on which the plaintiff's action was based. It ruled that, in a case where the plaintiff asserted the right to be paid damages or sought dissolution of the contract on the ground of the wrongful conduct of the other party, that obligation was still that which arose under the contract and the non-performance of which was relied upon to support such claims.

10. The general rule thereby defined admits, however, of certain exceptions on the ground that 'matters relating to a contract' cover relationships of widely differing kinds, both from the viewpoint of their social importance and from that of the obligations entered into. The Convention takes account of that diversity by laying down certain special rules which apply to specific contractual relationships. For example, Article 16 of the Convention provides for exclusive jurisdiction in cases concerning tenancies of immovable property.

11. Guided by similar considerations, the Court, in its judgment of 26 May 1982 (Case 133/81 *Ivenel* v *Schwab* [1982] ECR 1891), held that in the case of a claim based on different obligations arising under a single contract for commercial representation which had been described by the national court as a contract of employment, the obligation to be taken into consideration for the purposes of Article 5(1) of the Convention was the obligation which characterised the contract and was normally the obligation to carry out work.

12. In those circumstances, the question submitted by the Landgericht must be regarded as seeking to establish in particular whether, in proceedings for the recovery of architect's fees, the general rule set out in the aforesaid *De Bloos* judgment must apply, under which the obligation to be taken into consideration is the one on which the plaintiff's action is based, or conversely whether the case displays special features analogous to those which were in evidence in the *Ivenel* case.

13. The argument presented to the Court dealt not only with the problem whether regard should be had to the nature of the disputed contract in determining the obligation to be taken into account, but also with the problem raised by the presence, within one and the same dispute, of a number of obligations forming the basis of the judicial proceedings.

14. On the first point the United Kingdom advocates a generalised application of the criterion adopted by the Court in the above mentioned Ivenel judgment with reference to a contract of employment, arguing that the application of that criterion to all contracts for professional services would offer certain advantages. To interpret Article 5(1) accordingly would in particular have the effect of avoiding a situation in which courts in different Contracting States had jurisdiction over different claims based on one and the same contract, and would locate the forum in the Contracting State whose law was normally applicable to the contract. In a case such as the present one it would have the further advantage of

affording a genuine alternative to the forum of the defendant's domicile - the usual forum under the Convention.

15. The German and Italian Governments and the Commission do not subscribe to that point of view. The German Government admits that some arguments militate in favour of a single contractual forum but emphasises, first, that some contracts do not embody a characteristic obligation, for example, when the obligations of the two parties are of an equivalent nature (as in the case of a contract of barter), and, secondly, that it was the intention of the authors of the Convention, as reflected in certain language versions of Article 5(1) thereof, to establish the forum of the place of performance by reference to the contractual obligation on which the judicial proceedings were actually based.

16. In that connection it should first be observed that contracts of employment, like other contracts for work other than on a self-employed basis, differ from other contracts - even those for the provision of services - by virtue of certain particularities: they create a lasting bond which brings the worker to some extent within the organisational framework of the business of the undertaking or employer, and they are linked to the place where the activities are pursued, which determines the application of mandatory rules and collective agreements. It is on account of those particularities that the court of the place in which the characteristic obligation of such contracts is to be performed is considered best suited to resolving the disputes to which one or more obligations under such contracts may give rise.

17. When no such particularities exist, it is neither necessary nor appropriate to identify the obligation which characterises the contract and to centralise at the place of performance thereof jurisdiction, based on place of performance, over disputes concerning all the obligations under the contract. The variety and multiplicity of contracts as a whole are such that the above criterion might in those other cases create uncertainty as to jurisdiction, whereas it is precisely such uncertainty which the Convention is designed to reduce.

18. On the other hand, no such uncertainty exists for most contracts if regard is had solely to the contractual obligation whose performance is sought in the judicial proceedings. The place in which that obligation is to be performed usually constitutes the closest connecting factor between the dispute and the court having jurisdiction over it, and it is this connecting factor which explains why, in contractual matters, it is

the court of the place of performance of the obligation which has jurisdiction.

19. Admittedly, the above rule does not afford a solution in the particular case of a dispute concerned with a number of obligations arising under the same contract and forming the basis of the proceedings commenced by the plaintiff. However, in such a case the court before which the matter is brought will, when determining whether it has jurisdiction, be guided by the maxim *accessoriam sequitur principale*; in other words, where various obligations are at issue, it will be the principal obligation which will determine its jurisdiction. That complication does not, however, arise in the case referred to in the question raised by the Landgericht Kaiserslautern.

20. The answer to be given to the question referred to the Court should therefore be that, for the purposes of determining the place of performance within the meaning of Article 5(1) of the Convention, the obligation to be taken into consideration in a dispute concerning proceedings for the recovery of fees commenced by an architect commissioned to draw up plans for the building of houses is the contractual obligation which forms the actual basis of legal proceedings.

On those grounds, the Court, in answer to the question referred to it by the Landgericht Kaiserslautern by order of 5 March 1985, hereby rules:

> **For the purposes of determining the place of performance within the meaning of Article 5(1) of the Convention of 27 September 1968 on Jurisdiction and the Enforcement of Judgments in Civil and Commercial Matters, the obligation to be taken into consideration in a dispute concerning proceedings for the recovery of fees commenced by an architect commissioned to draw up plans for the building of houses is the contractual obligation which forms the actual basis of legal proceedings.**

OPINION OF MR ADVOCATE GENERAL MANCINI

1. Article 2 of the Convention of 27 September 1968 on Jurisdiction and the Enforcement of Judgments in Civil and Commercial Matters refers to the domicile of the defendant as the general criterion in determining which court shall have jurisdiction. In addition to that rule - and not in derogation from it - Article 5 enables a plaintiff to bring proceedings before a different court, to be

determined according to special criteria. The Court has held: 'This freedom of choice was introduced in view of the existence in certain ... cases of a particularly close relationship between a dispute and the court which may be most conveniently called upon to take cognizance of the matter' (judgment of 6 October 1976, Case 12/76 *Tessili* v *Dunlop* [1976] ECR 1473, at paragraph 13 of the Decision). Thus, in resolving disputes in matters relating to a contract, a creditor may sue a debtor domiciled in another Contracting State 'in the courts for the place of performance of the obligation in question' (Article 5(1)).

However, contracts usually give rise to a relationship involving a number of obligations. It is therefore understandable that, when the Convention came to be interpreted, doubts arose as to which of those obligations the provision refers to the obligation whose non-performance is the subject of the plaintiff's action, the obligation which characterises the relationship, or one of the many other obligations flowing from the contract. When called upon to resolve the question, the Court of Justice had no hesitation in holding that Article 5(1) 'refers to the contractual obligation forming the basis of the legal proceedings' (judgment of 6 October 1976, Case 14/76 *De Bloos* v *Bouyer* [1976] ECR 1497, at paragraph 11 of the Decision).

The principle thereby established aroused some doubt in academic circles, but, being expressed in unequivocal terms which leave no room for uncertainty, it was received favourably by almost all the courts of the Contracting States (see the Digest of Case-Law Relating to the European Communities, D Series, under 1-5.1.1.-B). The fact that, a decade after that judgment, the Court should have received a request for a preliminary ruling to clarify yet again the meaning of 'obligation' under Article 5(1) might therefore seem surprising. As will be seen, however, the request from the national court is explained by the particular rules of its domestic law and by a judgment of the Court subsequent to *De Bloos* which seems to introduce problems into the clearly defined framework mentioned above.

2. Mr Shenavai, a German architect residing at Rockenhausen in the Federal Republic of Germany, brought proceedings before the Amtsgericht [Local Court] Rockenhausen against Mr Kreischer, a German national residing in the Netherlands, claiming payment on the fees due to him for the preparation of plans for the construction of three houses in the district of Rockenhausen. The Amtsgericht held that the place in which payment ought to be made was the client's domicile, and declared the application to be outside its territorial jurisdiction. On appeal, however, the Landgericht [Regional Court] Kaiserslautern deemed it necessary to stay the proceedings and to refer the following question to the Court: 'For the purposes of Article 5(1)..., is the place of performance, in the specific case of a claim for fees by an architect...to be determined by reference to the contractual obligation which forms the actual basis of the legal proceedings (in this case a debt payable under German law at the place where the defendant is domiciled), or by reference to the obligation typical of the contract and characterising the contractual relationship as a whole (that is to say the place where the architect has his practice and/or the site of the planned building)?'

As it stands, the question confuses two issues which, according to Article 5(1), ought to be kept apart, namely on the one hand, the identification of the obligation, and on the other, the determination of the place in which it is to be performed. However, the Court has already given replies to both parts of the question: the first was resolved, as was seen above, by the *De Bloos* judgment, and the second by the *Tessili* judgment. At paragraph 13 of the Decision in the latter case, the Court held: 'It is for the court before which the matter is brought to establish ... whether the place of performance is situated within its territorial jurisdiction. For this purpose it must determine in accordance with its own rules of conflict of laws what is the law applicable to the legal relationship in question and define in accordance with that law the place of performance of the contractual obligation in question.'

In the light of those explanations, it seems to me that the problem raised by the Landgericht Kaiserslautern vanishes altogether. The order requesting the preliminary ruling cannot be said to contain elements of fact or law such as would justify the Court revising its previous approach. On the other hand, the impression one forms of the order of the national court is that the real difficulty in this case is one of domestic law. The Landgericht Kaiserslautern informs the Court that, under German law, the place of payment of an architect's fees is not clearly established. And it is well known that the simplest way to supply lacunae of this sort - that is, of resolving by indirect means the vexed question of domestic territorial jurisdiction - is to resort to an international forum, whose conclusions obviously take priority. In the present case, for example, it would be sufficient to read Article 5(1) as if it referred, not to the obligation in dispute before the court (namely the payment of the fees), but to the obligation which characterises the relationship, namely the architect's services, in order to infer furthermore that performance of that obligation will necessarily take place in the architect's office; and it is precisely with that result in view that the German court wishes to know whether, in the dispute brought before it, it may refer to the criterion of the 'characteristic obligation' for the purposes of the application of that article.

When viewed in that perspective, therefore, the question referred to the Court by the Landgericht Kaiserslautern is not without purpose; that does not, however, alter the answer to be given to it. There can be no doubt that, for procedural purposes, the term 'obligation' in Article 5(1) is autonomous and cannot vary according to the different contractual relationships in dispute before a court. It is equally certain, moreover, that the doubts in German law as to the place in which the fees are to be paid do not, in themselves, warrant a derogation from the general rule enshrined in the *De Bloos* judgment. In Conclusion I can only repeat that, if the problem on which the Court is requested to give a ruling is appraised by reference to the facts of the case alone, a comprehensive solution is to be found in the *De Bloos* judgment and the *Tessili* judgment.

3. The same problem assumes quite different dimensions, on the other hand, if the circumstances of the case are disregarded and account is taken - although the national court did not do so - of another, more recent judgment of the Court of 26 May 1982 (Case 133/81 *Ivenel* v *Schwab* [1982] ECR 1891). The

plaintiff had put forward several claims based on the various obligations arising under a contract of employment, and the Court held that in such a case the provisions of the Convention must be interpreted 'in such a way that the national court is not compelled to find that it has jurisdiction to adjudicate upon certain claims but not on others' and that therefore 'the obligation to be taken into account for the purposes of the application of Article 5(1) ... is the obligation which characterises the contract' (paragraphs 18 and 20 of the Decision).

In the present case, however, there is no doubt that what is at issue is a contract (other than a contract of employment) for services of an intellectual nature, and that the plaintiff's claim is founded on a single obligation. If, therefore, the solution formulated in the *Ivenel* case were to be applied, that solution would need to be treated not as an exceptional expedient dictated by the particularities of the case, but as the expression of a new and general Criterion overturning that in *De Bloos*. The question is, however, whether it is possible and, above all, desirable to adopt that approach. On that point the United Kingdom, the German and Italian Governments and the Commission of the European Communities have expressed opinions which should now be considered.

4. The United Kingdom maintains that, if the criterion of 'characteristic obligation' became the general rule, the application of Article 5(1) would become more rational; it would serve to avoid the 'fragmentation' of jurisdiction (that is, the possibility that several courts in different States might have jurisdiction over different claims arising from the same contractual relationship), and to prevent the plaintiff from determining the jurisdiction at will, according to the type of application which he decides to submit. The United Kingdom points out that that solution would, furthermore, (a) allow the forum under Article 5(1) to be used as a genuine alternative to the general forum under Article 2, and (b) enable the rules of the Convention of 27 September 1968 to be harmonised with the aims and provisions of the Convention on the Law Applicable to Contractual Obligations, which was opened for signature in Rome on 19 June 1980.

In the view of the German Government, too, the Criterion established by *De Bloos* might bring about the fragmentation of jurisdiction and hence the delivery of divergent judgments in relation to one and the same contract. In practice, however, that danger is reduced by the option open to the defendant of lodging a counterclaim against the plaintiff (Article 6(3) of the Convention), and by the fact that, where related actions are brought in the courts of different Contracting States, 'any court other than the court first seised may ... stay its proceedings ... [or] ... decline jurisdiction' (first and second paragraphs of Article 22; but see also the obligations imposed on that court by the first paragraph of Article 21). In any event, since the forum under Article 5(1) does not exclude the forum under Article 2, raising the criterion in *Ivenel* to the status of a general rule would not eliminate the risk of divergent judgments and, in that case, it is as well to take the same approach as in the past.

Lastly, the Italian Government and the Commission contend that, far from being in conflict, the principles set out in the De Bloos and Ivenel judgments are complementary. The first is the general rule whilst the second applies only in circumstances analogous to those which caused it to be adopted in the first place, namely an employment relationship (or more generally, according to the Commission, any relationship where there is disparity of bargaining power between the parties) and a number of claims which a plaintiff bases on various obligations arising under the same contract.

5. Of the standpoints summarised above I prefer the last. The United Kingdom's argument cannot withstand the objections raised by the Federal Republic of Germany and, as far as the reference to the Rome Convention of 19 June 1980 is concerned, is open to three simple counter-arguments:

(a) far from reducing the risk of 'fragmentation of jurisdiction', that Convention enables the parties to arrange for the obligations arising under the contract to be governed by different legal systems (Article 3(1));

(b) in its general scheme, reference to the performance which is 'characteristic of the contract' is merely subsidiary and is not in any event a reliable Criterion for determing the forum;

(c) with regard to contracts of employment, the Rome Convention safeguards the employee not by designating the *lex loci laboris* (law of the place where the work is performed) as the legal system governing the obligation characterising the contract but by providing that the 'mandatory rules of law', even those of a foreign country, are to override the *lex contractus* (Article 6(1)).

Having said that, I must observe that, although it correctly defines the relationship between *De Bloos* and *Ivenel* in terms of rule and exception, the Commission's line of argument attributes too wide a scope to the principle laid down by the second judgment; I do not think that the principle may be applied outside the context of an employment relationship; in particular, it does not apply to dealings which are characterised merely by the economic inferiority of one party. It seems to me that this is demonstrated by the case of insurance contracts, for which the 1968 Convention determines jurisdiction by means of rules (Articles 7 to 11) which, according to the Jenard Report, 'are dictated by social considerations which are aimed in particular at preventing abuses which could result from the terms of contracts in standard form' (Official Journal C 59 of 5 March 1979, p.29). Article 8 provides a number of forums for legal proceedings brought by the insured, and it adopts as the determining criterion not the place in which the 'characteristic obligation' is to be performed (that is, the business operations of the insurer), but the place in which the harmful event occurs or the parties' domiciles. The question arises whether insurance may be considered for present purposes, of course, to be representative of the whole range of contracts concluded between parties having disparate bargaining power, including contracts for professional and other services. In my opinion it may, and the conclusion to be drawn is that where such contracts are concerned, the 1968 Convention does not provide for a single forum for all conceivable disputes which may arise from the contractual relationship, but leaves the 'weaker' party with an option. That conclusion is, moreover, consistent with the rationale of Article 5 which, as the *Tessili* judgment establishes, is to enable a creditor to commence proceedings before the court of the place which, from the point of view of court proceedings, is most closely connected with the subject-matter of his claim.

It follows from the foregoing that the requirement in Article 5(1) that 'the obligation to be taken into account' be 'that which corresponds to the contractual right on which the plaintiff's action is based' (*De Bloos* judgment, cited above, at paragraph 13 of the Decision) also applies to disputes concerning contracts of the kind at issue in the present case.

6. In view of all the foregoing considerations I propose that the Court should give the following answer to the question referred to it by the Landgericht Kaiserslautern in its Order of 5 March 1985 in the proceedings brought by Mr Shenavai against Mr Kreischer: 'In a dispute concerning the payment of an architect's fees, the term 'obligation' under Article 5(1) of the Convention of 27 September 1968 refers to the contractual obligation forming the basis of the legal proceedings, which in the present instance means the obligation to pay the fees. The place in which that obligation has been, or should be, performed is determined in accordance with the law which governs the obligation in question according to the rules of conflict of laws of the court before which the matter is brought.'

Case 9/87 - 8 March 1988

SPRL Arcado
v
SA Haviland

Article 5(1) - Special Jurisdiction - Jurisdiction 'in matters relating to a contract' - Concept - Independent interpretation - Independent commercial agency agreement - Claims for the payment of commission and compensation for wrongful repudiation of a contract - Inclusion.

Summary

The concept of 'matters relating to a contract' in Article 5(1) of the Convention of 27 September 1968 on Jurisdiction and the Enforcement of Judgments in Civil and Commercial Matters is to be regarded as an independent concept which, for the purpose of the application of the Convention, must be interpreted by reference principally to the system and objectives of the Convention in order to ensure that it is fully effective.

Proceedings relating to the wrongful repudiation of an independent commercial agency agreement and the payment of commission due under such an agreement are proceedings in matters relating to a contract within the meaning of Article 5(1) of the Convention.

JUDGMENT OF THE COURT

Due, President of the Chamber, Koopmans, Bahlmann, Kakouris and O'Higgins, Judges

1. By judgment of 11 September 1986, which was received at the Court on 16 January 1987, the Cour d'appel, Brussels, referred to the Court for

a preliminary ruling, under the Protocol of 3 June 1971 on the Interpretation by the Court of Justice of the Convention of 27 September 1968 on Jurisdiction and the Enforcement of Judgments in Civil and Commercial Matters (hereinafter referred to as 'the Convention'), a question concerning the interpretation of Article 5(1) of the Convention.

2. That question was raised in the context of proceedings concerning the performance of an independent commercial agency agreement by which SA Haviland, whose registered office is in Limoges (France) appointed SA Agecobel, whose registered office is in Belgium, as its agent for the sale of porcelain products in Belgium and Luxembourg.

3. Following the termination of that agreement by Haviland, Agecobel instituted proceedings against Haviland on 13 November 1978 before the Tribunal de commerce (Commercial Court), Brussels, seeking the payment of compensation for wrongful termination of the agreement and the balance of outstanding commission. Haviland objected that the court had no jurisdiction *ratione loci* on the ground that the action for compensation was based on a quasi-delict committed at the place from which termination of the agreement was notified to the other party, namely its registered office.

4. By judgment of 26 May 1982 the Tribunal de commerce rejected the objection that it lacked jurisdiction because it considered that the dispute was contractual in origin and that it therefore had jurisdiction under Article 5(1) of the Convention. By judgment of 22 June 1983 the Tribunal de commerce ordered Haviland to pay compensation for its sudden and premature repudiation of the agreement and to pay arrears of commission. In addition, it granted Haviland's counterclaim and therefore ordered Agecobel to pay outstanding balances on invoices and compensation.

5. Agecobel lodged an appeal before the Cour d'appel, Brussels seeking an increase in the compensation awarded and an order that Haviland pay statutory interest. In a cross-appeal Haviland relied on Article 5(3) of the Convention and contested the jurisdiction of the Belgian courts. By a document lodged at the registry of the Cour d'Appel, Brussels on 5 June 1985, SPRL Arcado, whose registered office is in Belgium and which had succeeded to the rights of Agecobel, took over the proceedings instituted by the latter.

6. The Cour d'appel took the view that whilst the dispute concerning the payment of commission clearly suggested that the matters at issue were contractual in nature it was, nevertheless, necessary to determine whether the claim for compensation for the sudden and premature repudiation of the contract falls within the concept of matters relating to a contract within the meaning of Article 5(1) of the Convention according to the independent interpretation of that concept.

7. The Cour d'appel also decided to stay the proceedings and to refer the following question to the Court of Justice for a preliminary ruling: 'Are proceedings relating to the wrongful repudiation of an (independent) commercial agency agreement and the payment of commission due under such an agreement proceedings in matters relating to a contract within the meaning of Article 5(1) of the Brussels Convention of 27 September 1968?'

8. Reference is made to the Report for the Hearing for a fuller account of the facts, the course of the procedure and the written observations submitted to the Court by the parties to the main proceedings, the Commission, the Government of the Italian Republic and the United Kingdom, which are mentioned or discussed hereinafter only insofar as is necessary for the reasoning of the Court.

9. By way of derogation from the general rule governing jurisdiction set out in the first paragraph of Article 2 of the Convention, Article 5(1) of the Convention provides as follows: 'A person domiciled in a contracting State may, in another contracting State, be sued: (1) in matters relating to a contract, in the courts of the place of performance of the obligation in question ... '.

10. As the Court held in its judgment of 22 March 1983 in Case 34/82 (*Martin Peters Bauunternehmung GmbH* v *Zuid Nederlandse Aannemers Vereniging* [1983] ECR 987) the concept of 'matters relating to a contract' serves as a criterion to define the scope of one of the rules of special jurisdiction available to the plaintiff. Having regard to the objective and the general scheme of the Convention, it is important that, in order to ensure as far as possible the equality and uniformity of the rights and obligations arising out of the Convention for the Contracting States and the persons concerned, that concept should not be interpreted simply as referring to the national law of one or other of the States concerned.

11. Consequently, the concept of 'matters relating to a contract is to be regarded as an independent concept which, for the purpose of the application of the Convention, must be interpreted by reference principally to the system and objectives of the Convention in order to ensure that it is fully effective.

12. There is no doubt that a claim for the payment of commission due under an independent commercial agency agreement finds its very basis in that agreement and consequently constitutes a matter relating to a contract within the meaning of Article 5(1) of the Convention.

13. The same view must be taken of a claim for compensation for the wrongful repudiation of such an agreement as the basis for such compensation is the failure to comply with a contractual obligation.

14. As regards, more particularly, the right of a self-employed commercial agent to notice, its contractual nature and therefore the contractual nature of the compensation in lieu of notice were recognised in Articles 15 and 17 of Council Directive 86/653 of 18 December 1986 on the co-ordination of the laws of the Member States relating to self-employed commercial agents (Official Journal 1986, L 382, p. 17).

15. In addition, Article 10 of the Convention on the Law applicable to Contractual Obligations of 19 June 1980 (Official Journal 1980, L 266, p. 1) confirms the contractual nature of judicial proceedings such as those in point in as much as it provides that the law applicable to a contract governs the consequences of a total or partial failure to comply with obligations arising under it and consequently the contractual liability of the party responsible for such breach.

16. The reply to the question raised by the Cour d'appel, Brussels, must therefore be that proceedings relating to the wrongful repudiation of an independent commercial agency agreement and the payment of commission due under such an agreement are proceedings in matters relating to a contract within the meaning of Article 5(1) of the Convention of 27 September 1968.

On those grounds, the Court (Sixth Chamber), in answer to the question referred to it by the Cour d'appel, Brussels, by a judgment of 11 September 1986, hereby rules:

Proceedings relating to the wrongful repudiation of an independent commercial agency agreement and the payment of commission due under such an agreement are proceedings in matters relating to a contract within the meaning of Article 5(1) of the Brussels Convention of 27 September 1968.

OPINION OF ADVOCATE GENERAL SIR GORDON SLYNN

SA Haviland, which is incorporated and has its registered office in France, appointed (it seems in 1967) SA Agecobel as its agent for the sale of Haviland's products in Belgium and Luxembourg. By 1975 Haviland had, it alleges, received many complaints about Agecobel and accordingly it terminated the agency agreement with effect from the end of October 1975. Agecobel brought proceedings against Haviland in the Tribunal de commerce in Brussels for outstanding commission and for compensation for the unlawful termination of the agreement. Haviland objected that the court had no jurisdiction to hear the claim and counterclaimed for monies due on unpaid invoices.

The Tribunal de commerce accepted that it had jurisdiction by virtue of Article 5(1) of the Convention of 27 September 1965 on Jurisdiction and the Enforcement of Judgments in Civil and Commercial Matters ('the Convention') and ordered Haviland to pay compensation and monies due on unpaid invoices.

SPRL Arcado, apparently incorporated in and having its registered offices in Belgium, has, in a way which is not explained, succeeded to the rights and obligations of Agecobel. As such successor it became party to an appeal from the judgment of the Tribunal de commerce to the Court of Appeal in Brussels in which the amount of commission and of the compensation awarded at first instance are in issue. Haviland objected in reply that the claim being made for compensation for unlawful termination was a matter 'relating to tort, delict or quasi-delict' within the meaning of Article 5(3) of the Convention and that the Brussels courts had no jurisdiction.

The Court of Appeal took the view that whereas the claim for payment of commission clearly suggested that the proceedings were contractual in nature there was room for doubt as to whether a claim for compensation for unlawful repudiation was within Article 5(1) of the Convention if that Article was to be given an independent meaning. If it was to be construed in accordance with Belgian or French law it seemed that the claim would properly be categorised as relating to a contract.

Accordingly, the Court of Appeal asked for a preliminary ruling on the question: 'Are proceedings relating to the unlawful repudiation of an (independent) commercial agency agreement and the payment of omission due under such an agreement proceedings in matters relating to a contract within the meaning of Article 5(1) of the Brussels Convention of 27 September 1968?'

Article 5 of the Convention, by way of derogation from the basic rule linking jurisdiction with domicile set out in Article 2, provides that: 'A person domiciled in a contracting State may, in another contracting State, be sued: (1)

in matters relating to a contract, in the courts for the place of performance of the obligation in question; ... (3) in matters relating to tort, delict or quasi-delict, in the courts for the place where the harmful event occurred'.

Whether phrases in the Convention are to be construed as such so that they apply uniformly in all Member States or whether they are to be taken as requiring courts before which disputes come to apply their own conflict of laws rules has already been much debated. On the one hand, it is said that to apply an 'independent' interpretation ensures a uniform and equal body of rules applicable throughout the Member States party to the Convention. On the other hand, an interpretation which leaves it to the conflict of laws rules of Member States to decide issues like the present does not by any means necessarily conflict with the overriding aims of the Convention to facilitate the automatic recognition and enforcement of judgments given in circumstances which are wholly acceptable as bases for jurisdiction.

The Court has recognised in Case 12/76 (*Tessili* v *Dunlop* [1976] ECR 1473) that, 'Neither of these two options rules out the other since the appropriate choice can only be made in respect of each of the provisions of the Convention to ensure that it is fully effective having regard to the objectives of Article 220 of the Treaty' and taking national law including its conflicts rules may be necessary in view of the 'differences obtaining between national laws of contract and ... the absence at this stage of legal development of any unification in the substantive law applicable'.

Whether words or concepts which may have a different meaning in different Member States should be given an independent meaning, or decided by reference to the substantive law accepted as applicable by the conflict of laws rules of the court seised of the matter, must be decided according to which of them is likely to be most effective in enabling the Convention to achieve the objectives it pursues. This is so not least since the derogations in Article 5 are created 'because of the existence, in certain clearly defined situations, of a particularly close connecting factor between a dispute and the court which may be called upon to hear it, with a view to the efficacious conduct of the proceedings' (Case 33/78 *Somafer* v *Saar-Ferngas* [1978] ECR 2183, at p. 2191, paragraph 7).

If the matter were free from authority, it seems to me that where claims are made in respect of alleged contracts there is much to be said for adopting a rule that the court in which the proceedings are brought should decide what is the proper law governing the circumstances in dispute and then decide under that law whether the matter relates to a contract and where is the place of performance of the obligation in question. This might well produce different results in different courts as to whether the matter did or did not relate to a contract. On the other hand, it would avoid the conflict which can arise if an independent interpretation decides that the matter is one relating to a contract whereas under the proper law governing the circumstances, or the law of the place of performance of the obligation, there is no contract at all.

The matter, however, is not free from authority. The term 'civil and commercial matters' in Article 1 of the Convention was held to be an independent concept which must be construed with reference first, to the objectives and scheme of the Convention and, secondly, to the general principles which stem from the corpus of the national legal systems (Case 814/79 *Netherlands* v *Rüffer* [1980] ECR 3807, at p. 3819, paragraph 7) following Case 29/76 (*Lufttransportunternehmen* (LTU) v *Eurocontrol* [1976] ECR 1541, at p. 1551, paragraph 3). Similarly, in Case 33/71 *Somafer* the Court held that the need to ensure legal certainty and equality of rights and obligations for the parties as regards the power to derogate from the general jurisdiction of Article 2 required an independent interpretation, common to all the Member States, of the concepts contained in Article 5(5) (*Somafer*, p. 2191, paragraph 8). In particular, the Court has already held in Case 34/82 (*Martin Peters* v *ZNAV* [1983] ECR 987) that the phrase 'matters relating to a contract' in Article 5(1) should be regarded as a Community concept and interpreted in the light of the Convention and its aims (at p. 1002, paragraphs 9 and 10).

The approach of the Court has therefore been that concepts contained in the Convention relating to the scope of the Convention and the scope of the derogations, under Article 5, from the general role contained in Article 2(1) should be defined independently in accordance with the objectives and system of the Convention, rather than be defined by reference to individual national laws. By contrast, the place of performance of the obligation to be taken into account is to be determined in accordance with the law which governs the obligation in question according to the conflict rules of the court before which the matter is brought (Case 133/81 *Ivenel* v *Schwab* [1982] ECR 1891, at p. 1899 (paragraph 7), following Case 12/76 *Tessili* v *Dunlop* [1976] ECR 1473). That approach is also confirmed by Case 266/85 (*Shenavai* v *Kreischer* ECR 239), judgment of 15 January 1987. The identification of the scope of the derogation and the determination of the place in which it is to be performed have thus been treated as separate issues and the Court has adopted different approaches.

In the light of these decisions it seems to me that the question posed has to be answered by reference to the Convention rather than by reference to a specific national law.

As already indicated the Convention itself must be interpreted with reference first, to the objectives and scheme of the Convention and, secondly, to the general principles which stem from the corpus of national legal systems (Case 814/79 *Netherlands* v *Rüffer*, supra). In many cases it may be necessary, as it was in Peters, to refer in detail to the legal systems of Member States to see whether the claim made is to be treated as relating to a contract. That examination in detail may not always be necessary in clear cases. Thus in Case 14/76 (*De Bloos* v *Bouyer* [1976] ECR 1497) the Court accepted, without a detailed comparison, a claim by the grantee of an exclusive sales concession against the grantor, claiming unilateral breach, dissolution of the contract by the court and payment of damages, as being matters relating to a contract.

It seems to me that if proceedings are brought which as an essential element of the claim allege the existence of what it is agreed would be a contract if it was made (even if the existence of the contract is in dispute (Case 31/81 *Effer SpA* v *Kantner* [1912] ECR 825)) then they are to be regarded as covering 'matters relating to a contract' for the purposes of Article 5(1) of the Convention.

That test is clearly satisfied in the present case. The claim for commission due under the commercial agency agreement is now agreed by the parties to be, and plainly is, a matter relating to a contract. So in my view is the claim for compensation for what is said to be a premature and sudden termination of the agreement. The essence of that claim is that the contract itself required reasonable notice of the termination; that term of the contract was broken; compensation is claimed for the breach.

Accordingly, in my opinion the question referred falls to be answered on the following lines: 'Proceedings relating to the wrongful repudiation of an (independent) commercial agency agreement and the payment of commission due under such an agreement are proceedings in matters relating to a contract within the meaning of Article 5(1) of the Brussels Convention.'

Case 32/88 - 15 February 1989

Six Constructions Ltd
v
Paul Humbert

Special jurisdictions - Article 5(1) - Court for the place in which the contractual obligation is to be performed - Contract of employment - Obligation to be taken into consideration - Obligation to carry out the agreed work - Performance outside the territory of the Contracting States - Article 5(1) of the Convention not applicable - Application of Article 2 of the Convention.

Summary

Article 5(1) of the Convention of 27 September 1968 on Jurisdiction and the Enforcement of Judgments in Civil and Commercial Matters must be interpreted as meaning that, as regards contracts of employment, the obligation to be taken into consideration is that which characterizes such contracts, in particular the obligation to carry out the agreed work. Where the obligation of the employee to carry out the agreed work was performed and had to be performed outside the territory of the Contracting States, Article 5(1) of the Convention is not applicable; in such a case jurisdiction is to be determined on the basis of the place of the defendant's domicile in accordance with Article 2 of the Convention.

JUDGMENT OF THE COURT

Koopmans, President of the Chamber, O'Higgins, Mancini, Schockweiler and Diez de Velasco, Judges

1. By judgment dated 14 January 1988, which was received at the

Court on 28 January 1988, the French Cour de cassation referred to the Court for a preliminary ruling pursuant to the Protocol of 3 June 1971 on the interpretation by the Court of Justice of the Convention of 27 September 1968 on Jurisdiction and the Enforcement of Judgments in Civil and Commercial Matters, two questions on the interpretation of Article 5(1) of that Convention.

2. Those questions arose in proceedings between Paul Humbert, residing in Labrède, France, and Six Constructions Ltd, established in Brussels, concerning a breach of a contract of employment which gave rise to an application for the payment of several amounts by way of payment in lieu of notice, damages, gratuities and various amounts by way of compensation and arrears of salary.

3. It is apparent from the documents before the Court that Six Constructions Ltd is a company incorporated under the law of Sharjah, one of the United Arab Emirates, which has a branch in Brussels. During the main proceedings, it asserted that its registered office was in Brussels. That assertion was accepted by the French courts because it was not contested at the proper time.

4. Two problems of jurisdiction arose before the conseil de prud'hommes (Labour Conciliation Tribunal), Bordeaux, before which the application was brought, and before the cour d'appel (Court of Appeal). On the one hand, Six Constructions Ltd invoked a term of the contract of employment according to which disputes concerning the performance of the contract were subject to the jurisdiction of the Brussels courts. However, the written instrument containing the terms of the contract had never been signed by Mr Humbert. On the other hand, Six Constructions Ltd contested the jurisdiction of the French courts on the ground that the contract of employment was performed not in France but in several countries outside the territory of the Community, since between March 1979, when he was taken on as a deputy project manager and December 1979, when he was dismissed, Mr Humbert had been sent to Libya, Zaïre and Abu Dhabi, one of the United Arab Emirates.

5. The Cour de cassation considered the two submissions mentioned above. It decided in regard to the first that the term attributing jurisdiction did not fulfil the conditions for validity under Article 17 of the Convention. With regard to the second, the Cour de cassation pointed out that, under Article 5(1) of the Convention, in matters relating to a contract, a person may be sued in the courts of the place of performance

of the obligation in question and it is clear from the previous decisions of the Court of Justice that the obligation to be taken into account in the case of a contract of employment is the obligation which characterizes the contract, in particular the obligation to carry out the agreed work. However, the Cour de cassation considered that the question of which obligation was to be taken into account where the work was performed outside the territory of the Community raised a problem of interpretation.

6. In those circumstances, the Cour de cassation stayed proceedings and referred the following questions to the Court of Justice for a preliminary ruling:

'(1) What is the obligation to be taken into account for the purposes of the application of Article 5(1) of the Brussels Convention of 27 September 1968 where the court is hearing an action based on obligations arising under a contract of employment binding an employee residing in France to a company having its registered office in Belgium which posted him to several countries outside Community territory?

(2) Must the characteristic obligation be considered as being performed in the establishment which engaged him, or must jurisdiction be determined pursuant to Article 2 of the Brussels Convention?'

7. Reference is made to the Report for the Hearing for a fuller account of the facts of the main proceedings, the course of the procedure and the written observations submitted to the Court which are mentioned or discussed hereinafter only insofar as is necessary for the reasoning of the Court.

8. It should be observed at the outset that the main proceedings were brought before 1 November 1986, the date on which the version of the Convention amended as a result of the accession of new Member States came into effect. The provisions to be interpreted are therefore those of the Convention in the form in which it existed in 1971.

First question

9. The first question covers the case in which, as in the main proceedings, proceedings have been brought before a court on the basis of several obligations arising under a single contract of employment. For the purposes of applying Article 5(1) of the Convention, it must be determined, in that situation, where the 'place of performance of the obligation in question' is situated.

10. According to the Court's case-law, as the national court rightly pointed out, the obligation to be taken into consideration for the purposes of applying Article 5(1) of the Convention to contracts of employment is the obligation which characterizes such a contract, in particular, the obligation to carry out the agreed work (judgments of 26 May 1982 in Case 133/81 *Ivenel* v *Schwab* [1982] ECR 1891, and of 15 January 1987 in Case 266/85 *Shenavai* v *Kreischer* [1987] ECR 239). In that regard, the Court based its decision on the finding that contracts of employment, and more generally contracts for the performance of work other than work on a self-employed basis differ from other contracts by virtue of certain particularities inasmuch as they create a lasting bond which brings the worker to some extent within the organisational framework of the business of the undertaking or employer and they are linked to the place where the activities are pursued, which determines the application of mandatory rules and collective agreements.

11. On the basis that in this case the employee carried out work not in Brussels where, according to the documents before the Court, he regularly returned to make reports, but only in African and Arab countries to which he was posted to take part there in certain construction work, the national court asked how it should apply the criterion of the place where the work is carried out in order to determine which courts have jurisdiction.

12. In that regard, the French Government, the German Government and the United Kingdom argued that if an employed person does not normally perform his work in a single country, it must be the courts for the place in which the business which engaged the employee is situated that have jurisdiction under Article 5(1) of the Convention for disputes arising under the contract of employment. That interpretation is in accordance with the solution envisaged in such situations by the Rome Convention on the Law Applicable to Contractual Obligations (Official Journal 1980, L 266, p. 1) and with the wording chosen in the draft Convention on Jurisdiction and the Enforcement of Judgments in Civil and Commercial Matters to be concluded by the Member States of the Community and the Member States of the European Free Trade Association (the 'parallel' convention to the Brussels Convention). After the observations had been submitted in this case, that Convention was concluded in Lugano on 16 September 1988 (Official Journal L 319, p. 9). Article 5(1) thereof provides that in matters relating to a contract of employment, the place of performance of the obligation is the place 'where the employee habitually carries out his work, or if the employee does not habitually carry out his

work in any one country, this place shall be the place of business through which he was engaged'.

13. That argument was contested by the Italian Government and the Commission. According to the latter, the interpretation put forward by those three governments has the twofold weakness of departing significantly from the actual terms of Article 5(1) of the Convention and of not taking account of the need to ensure adequate protection to the socially weaker contracting party, namely the employee. In that regard, the Commission argues that the effect of the criterion of the place of business through which the employee was engaged is to give jurisdiction to the courts for the place where the employer's registered office is located, even if the employer is the plaintiff, and to establish thereby a forum actoris, whereas the underlying idea of the Convention, as is clearly stated in Articles 2 and 3, is precisely to limit the number of cases in which a person may be sued in the courts of the plaintiff's domicile.

14. The Commission's arguments on that point must be accepted. As the Court held in its judgments of 26 March 1982 and 15 January 1987, cited above, on account of the particularities of contracts of employment, it is the courts of the place in which the work is to be carried out which are best suited to resolving disputes to which one or more obligations under such contracts may give rise. Those particularities of contracts of employment do not justify an interpretation of Article 5(1) of the Convention which would permit account to be taken of the place of business through which the employee was engaged if it is difficult or impossible to determine in which State the work was performed.

15. The reply to the first question should therefore be that Article 5(1) of the Convention must be interpreted as meaning that, as regards contracts of employment, the obligation to be taken into consideration is that which characterizes such contracts, in particular the obligation to carry out the agreed work.

Second question

16. The second question concerns how to apply, in regard to contracts of employment, the criterion of the characteristic obligation when the employee carries out all his work outside the territory of the Community. It asks in particular whether, in such a case, jurisdiction is determined by reference to the place of business in which the employee was engaged or whether it must be determined pursuant to Article 2 of the Convention.

17. The possible choice of the criterion of the place of business in which the employee was engaged has already been considered in regard to the first question.

18. It should be added in that regard that, as the Court pointed out in its judgment of 27 September 1988 in Case 189/87 *Kalfelis* v *HEMA* [1988] ECR 5565, the provisions on 'special jurisdiction' in Articles 5 and 6 of the Convention constitute derogations from the principle that jurisdiction is vested in the courts of the State of the defendant's domicile, laid down in the general provisions of Articles 2 and 3 and, therefore, those provisions on special jurisdiction must be interpreted restrictively.

19. In those circumstances when a court finds that claims made before it are based on obligations arising from a contract of employment and that the employee's obligation to carry out the agreed work was and must be fulfilled outside the territory of the Contracting States, it has no choice but to conclude that the place provided for in Article 5(1) of the Convention cannot serve as a basis for attributing jurisdiction to a court within that territory and that Article 5(1) cannot therefore be applicable.

20. Although there are indeed some disadvantages in the alternative jurisdiction envisaged by the Convention in contract matters being precluded by the manner in which the parties to the contract have agreed that it is to be performed, it should be observed that the plaintiff is always entitled to bring his action before the courts of the place of the defendant's domicile in accordance with Article 2 of the Convention, which thereby provides a certain and reliable criterion.

21. It should also be noted that interpretation corresponds to the system laid down by the laws of the Contracting States in regard to jurisdiction in disputes arising out of contracts of employment. A comparative study of those laws shows that the criteria most often applied are those of the defendant's domicile and the place where the work is performed. In most cases, those laws give the plaintiff the choice between those two places.

22. The reply to the second question should therefore be that where, in the case of a contract of employment, the obligation of the employee to carry out the agreed work was performed and has to be performed outside the territory of the Contracting States, Article 5(1) of the Convention is not applicable and that in such a case jurisdiction is determined on the basis of the place of the defendant's domicile in accordance with Article 2 of the Convention.

On those grounds, the Court (Sixth Chamber), in answer to the questions referred to it by the Cour de cassation, by judgment of 14 January 1988, hereby rules:

(1) Article 5(1) of the Convention of 27 September 1968 on Jurisdiction and the Enforcement of Judgments in Civil and Commercial Matters must be interpreted as meaning that, as regards contracts of employment, the obligation to be taken into consideration is that which characterizes such contracts, in particular the obligation to carry out the agreed work.

(2) Where, in the case of a contract of employment, the obligation of the employee to carry out the agreed work was performed and has to be performed outside the territory of the Contracting States, Article 5(1) of the Convention is not applicable; in such a case jurisdiction is to be determined on the basis of the place of the defendant's domicile in accordance with Article 2 of the Convention.

OPINION OF MR ADVOCATE GENERAL TESAURO

1. By judgment of 14 January 1988 the French Cour de cassation (Court of Cassation) has sought a ruling from the Court of Justice on the interpretation of Article 5(1) of the Brussels Convention on Jurisdiction and the Enforcement of Judgments in Civil and Commercial Matters.

The facts of the case and the arguments of the parties which have submitted observations to the Court during the procedure are set out in detail in the Report for the Hearing. It therefore suffices for me, before examining the questions referred to the Court, to mention the essential points of those arguments.

The plaintiff, Mr Humbert, a French national resident in France, brought proceedings before a French tribunal against the company for which he had worked for a period of nine months seeking the payment of compensation under various heads. There are reasons for doubting whether the defendant is established in a Member State although that question is of decisive importance for the purposes of the application of the Brussels Convention. It appears from documents before the Court that Six Constructions Ltd, a company whose registered office is alleged to be in Brussels, is a company incorporated under the law of the United Arab Emirate of Sharjah and that it has a 'branch' in Brussels.

Since, however, in proceedings for a preliminary ruling, the Court must rely, as regards the facts of the proceedings before the national court, on the conclusions arrived at by that court in those proceedings, it is necessary to proceed in this case on the assumption that the defendant's registered office is in Belgium.

The French court which was called upon to consider the defendant's objection of lack of jurisdiction was unable, on procedural grounds, to consider that question in greater detail since it was not raised in the proper manner in the course of the procedure.

I therefore put that question aside nolens volens and return to the characteristics of the case referred to the Court by the Cour de cassation.

A significant factor in this case is the fact that the plaintiff did not perform his work for the defendant in any Member State of the Community. It is apparent from the order for reference and from the documents before the Court that Mr Humbert worked for the defendant exclusively in non-member countries. It is for that reason that the Cour de cassation has referred two questions to the Court, to ascertain first what obligation is to be taken into account for the purposes of the application of Article 5(1) and secondly whether the characteristic obligation must be considered as being performed at the registered office of the company which engaged him or whether, on the other hand, the general rule that the defendant is to be sued in the courts of the place where it is domiciled, in accordance with Article 2 of the Convention, is to be applied.

2. The Court's case-law concerning the interpretation of Article 5(1) of the Brussels Convention is not very extensive. It has, however, given some judgments first on the more general question of determining the obligation to be taken into account for the purposes of Article 5(1) and secondly on the more specific problem arising in that connection with regard to contracts of employment.

There is no concealing the fact that considerable divergences between those judgments have led to questions - often of a somewhat critical nature - being raised by legal writers. The ruling which the Court is asked to give in the present case is therefore of particular importance for the purpose of clarifying the Court's case-law. It is no coincidence that the observations submitted in the course of the written procedure and at the hearing, whilst citing the Court's case-law, reach divergent conclusions.

3. Let us begin by a systematic examination of the principles which have been laid down by the Court in the past and may come into play in the present case.

(a) I would refer in the first place to the principle laid down in Case 14/76 *De Bloos* v *Bouyer* [1976] ECR 1497 according to which the obligation to be taken into account for the purpose of determining the place of enforcement is that which corresponds to the right on which the plaintiff's action is based, that is to say the obligation *in respect of which the proceedings were brought.*

(b) Secondly, in its judgment in Case 12/76 *Tessili* v *Dunlop* [1976] ECR 1473, the Court laid down the principle that the place where the obligation in question was performed, or was to be performed, is to be determined by means of two steps. First the court before which the matter is brought must determine 'in accordance with its own rules of conflict of laws what is the law applicable to the legal relationship in question'; then it must define, in accordance with that law, the place of performance of the contractual obligation in question.

(c) Thirdly, and in relation to contracts of employment, the Court, in its judgment in Case 133/81 *Ivenel* v *Schwab* [1982] ECR 1891, laid down the principle that in the case of a contract of employment the connection which must subsist between the court hearing the matter and the dispute before it is determined by the obligation *characterizing* the contract in question and is normally the obligation to carry out work.

(d) Finally, in Case 266/85 *Shenavai* v *Kreischer* [1987] ECR 239, the Court reiterated that contracts of employment have certain particularities in the light of which the court of the place in which the characteristic obligation of such contracts is to be performed is considered best suited to resolving disputes which may arise, and stated that 'where no such particularities exist' regard is to be had solely to the contractual obligation whose performance is sought in the judicial proceedings.

4. On applying the principles derived from the aforementioned cases to the questions referred to the Court by the Cour de cassation, it becomes clear that the solution will differ depending on which line of decisions is relied upon.

An application of the principles laid down in the *De Bloos* and *Shenavai* cases leads to the conclusion that the obligation to be taken into account is the obligation which corresponds to the right on which the plaintiff's action is based. In this case the Cour de cassation states in its order that in his action Mr Humbert is seeking the payment of compensation under various heads deriving from his contract of employment. The obligations upon which his action is based could be regarded as the obligation on the part of the employer to pay the compensation.

Consequently, it is not precluded, in theory, that the place of performance of the obligation could be the place where the worker is resident if that is what is provided by the rules of substantive law to be applied according to the rules of conflict of laws of the court before which the matter is brought, according to the judgment in the *Tessili* case. Unsurprisingly, that is the view to which Mr Humbert subscribes in his observations to the Court, although on the basis of reasoning which fails to take account of the judgment in the *De Bloos* case.

On the basis, however, of the principle laid down in the *Ivenel* case that the obligation which characterizes the contract, normally the obligation to carry out work, is to be taken into account, it must be the courts of the State in which the work is carried out that have jurisdiction. Needless to say such a conclusion inevitably makes it impossible in this instance, the characteristic of which is, as has already been seen, that the work is not carried out in any Member State of the Community, to apply Article 5(1) unless, as Mr Humbert argued, other features of the employment relationship are regarded as characterizing the contract for the purpose of locating the relationship in a specific State.

In order to overcome that difficulty the parties which sought to rely on the *Ivenel* judgment have had to show considerable ingenuity in their observations to the Court.

5. On the one hand, some governments have suggested the adoption in a case such as the present of a criterion according to which the court of the place where the employer has its registered office would have jurisdiction. That criterion was also envisaged by the Cour de cassation in its second question.

On the other hand, the Commission, which considered that criterion and rejected it, proposes that in such a case it is completely impossible to apply

Article 5(1) and that recourse must be had to the general rule of jurisdiction set out in Article 2, namely the place of the defendant's domicile.

6. Before I consider which of the two alternatives is to be preferred or whether to propose a further solution, may I be permitted to make some observations on the argument put forward in the second question by the Cour de cassation and developed by some of the governments which submitted observations to the Court, namely that the Court should lay down the principle of the jurisdiction of the courts of the place where the employer has its registered office as such (or, in this case, as the place of recruitment).

7. I must say that such an innovative solution, although presented in an authoritative manner, leaves me so seriously perplexed, in the light of the aforementioned judgments of the Court, that it does not seem justified to recommend its adoption.

In order to explain my perplexity I do not believe it necessary to examine the various arguments which the governments put forward in support of this proposition, based in particular on the provisions of two international conventions, the Rome Convention on the Law Applicable to Contractual Obligations and the Lugano Convention on the Recognition and Enforcement of Judgments (the so-called 'parallel convention'), for one very simple reason: even if such an examination would provide support for that proposition, I am convinced that its merits must be assessed by reference to the Brussels Convention, that is to say the only one which the Court has jurisdiction to interpret.

8. In other words, it is not excluded that provisions of other conventions or criteria for the interpretation of other conventions could provide logical arguments in favour of a given interpretation of the Brussels Convention.

What is excluded, however, insofar as it is contrary to the most basic principles of interpretation, is that a connective criterion adopted under one convention could be used, in its own right, that is to say not as a result of a process of interpretation, in the application of Article 5(1) of the Brussels Convention.

9. Reference to the criterion of the place of the company's registered office is inconsistent with the following:

(a) the wording of the provision which the Court is called upon to interpret;

(b) the intention of the drafters of the 1968 Convention confirmed in 1978;

(c) the *ratio decidendi* of the judgment in the *Ivenel* case;

(d) a systematic reading of the Convention;

(e) the legal position in almost all the Member States.

(a) The Brussels Convention certainly does not lay down any specific rules on jurisdiction, neither special nor exclusive, for disputes in employment matters. Consequently jurisdiction is governed either by the general provision contained in Article 2 or by the *special* alternative provision for contracts contained in Article 5(1), which the Court is to interpret in this case and which is, without doubt, a provision which must be interpreted strictly.

It is also beyond doubt that neither of those other provisions refers as such to the place where a company has its registered office as a connective criterion. On the contrary, Article 2 refers to the courts of the place of the defendant's domicile and Article 5(1) provides the plaintiff with the alternative of the courts for the place of performance of the obligation in respect of which the legal proceedings were brought.

(b) The Jenard Report clearly explains the reasons why the final version of the Brussels Convention, the preliminary draft of which included a provision on exclusive jurisdiction for cases relating to employment matters (and also particularly provided, it may be emphasized, the criterion of the place of the company's registered office), did not lay down a special jurisdiction for such cases. It is, moreover, significant that the Jenard Report concludes its discussion of contracts of employment by referring to the possibility of amending the scope of the Brussels Convention, in particular by means of an additional protocol. However, no such change has been made even as a result of the amendment of the Convention to take account of the accession of three new States. That clearly shows that the Member States' intention is still not to provide for a special jurisdiction in employment cases.

Moreover, not only did the Convention of Accession of 1978 not introduce a special jurisdiction for contracts of employment, in contrast to other situations, but it laid down the authentic interpretation of Article 5(1) by expressly bringing the French and Dutch texts into line with the Italian text so as to refer to the courts for 'the place of performance of the obligation in question. In addition, the Schlosser Report expressly referred in that connection to the judgment in the *De Bloos* case.

(c) As regards the judgment in the *Ivenel* case, the reasons why the Court had recourse to the concept of the characteristic obligation as the criterion for determining the place of performance in cases concerning employment relationships are, on the one hand, to provide an alternative which is potentially closer to the interests of the employee, who is regarded as the weaker party, and, on the other, to avoid the risk, feared by many persons, of a multiplication of courts having jurisdiction.

The proposition in question would lead to the paradox that by establishing the place where the company has its registered office as such as the criterion for determining jurisdiction, the same criterion would also be applicable in cases in which the plaintiff was the employer.

In other words, to maintain that the place of performance must be defined as the place where the company has its registered office, in cases where the characteristic obligation, represented by the work carried out, is performed outside the territory of the Member States, would have the result of enabling the employer to bring the employee, the weaker party, before its own *forum actoris*.

In my view, the paradox seems so glaring as to make it fundamentally impossible to endorse that proposition.

(d) This is all the more clear if it is considered that in the cases where the Convention has explicitly laid down special rules on jurisdiction - alternatives to the general rule contained in Article 2 - in order to protect the weaker party (as for matters relating to insurance and to consumer contracts), the Convention has also expressly provided (in Articles 11 and 14, as amended in 1978) that proceedings may be brought only in the courts of the State in which the weaker party is domiciled. That means in practice that an insurer may never bring an insured person before its own courts. The same principle applies to consumer contracts. In the case, however, of contracts of employment the employer would be able to bring the employee before the employer's own courts. That result is at the very least debatable.

Undoubtedly, it is the employee who is the plaintiff in the majority of cases concerning employment. In the scheme of the Convention the general provision regarding jurisdiction contained in Article 2, namely that the courts of the place where the defendant is domiciled have jurisdiction, is available to the plaintiff. Accordingly, if it is desired to give substance to the need for protection for the weaker party, and therefore to offer the plaintiff a genuine alternative, which is plainly the object of the Convention, the proper course, in my opinion, is not to create something which in many cases will be none other than a duplicate of the general rule. In view of the need to provide effective protection for the weaker party so as to enable him to defend his interests without being burdened by legal costs (not to mention other costs) which may be a disincentive, forcing him to bring proceedings in the courts of the place where the employer has its registered office, I feel that another avenue should be explored seeking to establish an alternative forum to that afforded by Article 2 within the limits of a teleological interpretation.

This is borne out by the fact that, as was emphasized in the Jenard Report, the Brussels Convention, which is based on the principle of direct jurisdiction, provides a higher degree of legal certainty because the decision whether to recognize or enforce a judgment in the State requested to do so emanates from a court whose jurisdiction is derived from the same Convention itself.

(e) An examination of the national rules of jurisdiction applicable in Member States with regard to employment relationships leads to the following conclusions:

(i) the vast majority of national laws lay down the rule that actions are to be brought in the courts of the defendant's domicile;

(ii) in many cases, and mostly concomitantly with the courts of the defendant's domicile, it is possible to bring proceedings before the courts of the place where the work was performed or was to be performed;

(iii) it is rare for jurisdiction to be attributed to the courts of the place of the employer's domicile or registered office as such.

It is therefore possible to discern a general trend in the national legal systems to affording the worker a forum close to his place of work. In addition, some States seek to facilitate the legal protection of *workers alone* by allowing them a greater choice in comparison with an employer.

The Italian rules (Article 413 of the codice di procedurale civile (Code of Civil Procedure)) which envisage in the alternative the jurisdiction of the place where a company has its registered office, are only at first sight contrary to the foregoing. That provision makes it clear that the reason for the choice is the need to confer jurisdiction on the courts of the place where, on the basis of the principle of *id quod plerumque accidit*, the work is carried out because that is where the company is established. That is confirmed by the alternative provision for the jurisdiction of the courts of the place of a subsidiary establishment of the company where the work is carried out. In addition, it must not be overlooked that it is one thing to provide for the courts of the place where the company is situated to have jurisdiction for the purposes of determining jurisdiction in the national territory and quite another for it to be laid down for the purposes of determining international jurisdiction.

Whilst it is possible to justify the national legislature's choice of the courts of the place where the company has its registered office insofar as it is based on the reasonable assumption that in general the place where the company has its registered office is also the place where the work is carried out, it would be unacceptable for such a choice to be adopted by court ruling, as proposed by the Cour de cassation and certain governments, inasmuch as in the present case the fact that the worker has not worked in the country where the company has its registered office is in fact the premise on which the argument is based. Nor is this an exceptional case; it is a recurring situation where problems of international jurisdiction are at issue.

10. In conclusion, I believe that the argument that jurisdiction be conferred on the courts of the place where the company has its registered office as such, that is to say in absolute terms and *ex hypothesi* without reference to any link either with the place of performance or with the place of the other obligations inherent in an employment relationship, must be firmly rejected. To propose such a solution, which could, moreover, quite conceivably be extended from the case in point to all cases in general, would be to ask the Court not just to interpret Article 5(1) of the Convention but rather to establish a new connective criterion. Whilst the solution of the characteristic obligation (*Ivenel* case) could still be ascribed to the efforts to interpret Article 5(1) and in particular to the determination of the obligation to be taken into account, the hypothesis of the jurisdiction of the courts of the place where the company has its registered office as such would constitute the culmination not of a process of interpretation but rather one of real innovation: a new criterion would be established, one which was moreover deliberately excluded by the Contracting States. It hardly needs to be pointed out that it is for those States and not for the Court to make amendments to the Convention.

Since therefore the solution of the jurisdiction of the courts of the place where the company has its registered office as such or as the 'place of recruitment', which is a different way of saying the same thing, has been rejected, it is necessary to consider other ways of giving a satisfactory reply to the Cour de cassation.

11. In essence, the dispute may be reduced to two alternatives: the national court may consider either that the payment of the compensation which the plaintiff is seeking represents the performance of the contractual obligation to which the proceedings relate or that payment of the compensation does not relate to a *sole obligation* but to 'various obligations' resulting from the contract of employment.

In the first case, that is to say, if there is a single obligation, the solution seems relatively simple. The wording of Article 5(1) of the Convention, in itself and as interpreted by the Court (in the *De Bloos*, *Shenavai* and *Tessili* cases), leads the court before which the proceedings are brought to consider whether, in accordance with the rules of substantive law which are to be applied under its rules of conflict of laws, that court or some other court has jurisdiction in the matter. In addition, the court before which the matter is brought is not prevented from otherwise determining its jurisdiction (or lack of jurisdiction) by reference to the place of performance of the obligation which forms the basis of the action: for example, where that appears to be the precise intention of the parties, perhaps confirmed by the method of performance adopted by the parties in the course of the employment relationship in question, and in any event in the case of a mere factual connective criterion.

12. In the second case, that is to say of a multiplicity of obligations, the position would be that underlying the *Ivenel* case and it would be difficult to apply the principles laid down in that judgment to this case in which the obligation which 'characterizes' the labour relationship is located outside the Community.

An examination of this argument is considerably simplified if account is taken of the reasons upon which the judgment in the *Ivenel* case was based. It is significant that the Court's reasoning hinged on two elements: the protection of the weaker party and the advisability of correlation between the courts having jurisdiction and the law applicable to the contract which 'contains provisions protecting the worker'. The Court states in paragraph 19 of its judgment that, 'the law applicable ... is normally that of the place where the work characterizing the contract is carried out'.

In my view the logic of the Court's reasoning leads to the conclusion that in a case where the rules of substantive law protecting the worker are unable to perform that function of providing a connection between the law applicable and the courts having jurisdiction simply because the place where the work is carried out is outside the territory of the Member States of the EEC, that interpretation cannot be developed further, at least if the focus is on the obligation to carry out the work.

13. In such a case it is possible either to disregard for the purposes of this hypothesis the 'obligation which characterizes the contract' and to go back to the general scheme of Article 5(1) according to the wording of the provision itself (*De Bloos* and *Shenavai* cases) or to hold Article 5(1) to be wholly inapplicable and to have recourse, as is proposed by the Commission, to the normal rule of jurisdiction contained in Article 2, that is to say the place where the defendant is domiciled.

14. Without wishing to cast doubt on the Court's approach in its judgment in the *Ivenel* case, I do consider that the Court should verify whether recourse to the concept of the characteristic obligation, insofar as that is taken to be the work carried out, constitutes the hoped-for panacea in all cases where a multiplicity of obligations is at issue, particularly in cases where, for factual reasons - work performed outside the Member States - the connection between the place where

the work is carried out and the court having jurisdiction is impracticable; otherwise further uncertainty will be created rather than removed (work carried out in more than one State).

In examining that question certain elements which have been emphasized by academic writers on the subject must, in my view, be taken into account. I refer, in particular, to the criticism provoked by the connection between the law applicable and the court with jurisdiction, which emerges from the judgment in the *Ivenel* case. In that connection I would point out that Article 6 of the Rome Convention, which relates to employment contracts, certainly does not constitute a specific application of the principle of the characteristic obligation which is referred to in Article 4 but provides for a derogation from the application of that principle. In the absence of Article 6, or in a case where it is not applicable, the effect of Article 4 would be the application of the law of the country of habitual *residence* of the worker, as the party performing the obligation which is characteristic of the contract.

More generally then, without there being any need to invoke fundamental principles, there is no doubt that the problem of determining the law applicable is different from that of determining the court with jurisdiction, above all in the area with which this case is concerned where many aspects of the employment relationship are subject to mandatory rules (either rules of public law or rules which must necessarily be applied) of the State in which the work is carried out, with the consequence that the actual choice of the law applicable is often merely residual. The determination of the court with jurisdiction, on the other hand, involves other conditions and implications which are centred, in most legal systems, on the interests of the worker.

In addition, as has already been emphasized, in comparison with the legislative choice regarding jurisdiction within the national territory, that is to say in relation to employment relationships where there is generally no foreign element, the choice of the court with jurisdiction in the international context is much more delicate. In that connection the most common situation is of an employment relationship containing subjective and objective elements located in two or more countries so that it is all the more necessary that the worker who is bringing the proceedings has a real alternative to the courts of the place where the defendant company has its registered office. Whilst it may be true that the protection of the worker's interests is foreign to the 'philosophy' contained in the Brussels Convention, that is not a reason for denying him a genuine alternative, as may be said to be offered to a plaintiff, in accordance with a judicial tradition which has been consistently enshrined in all legal systems and also, undeniably, in the Brussels Convention.

15. On the basis of those considerations, I take the view that the existence of a factual element, namely that the work is carried out in one or more non-member countries, should not be capable of exercising such a significant influence as to exclude the normal operation of Article 5(1) . In other words, it is difficult to understand why the mere fact that:

(a) the plaintiff founds his action on, for example, *two* obligations rather than a *single* obligation,

(b) the place where the work is carried out is partially or totally in the territory of a non-member country, should always and inevitably deprive the plaintiff of the alternative forum afforded by Article 5(1), as interpreted by the Court in its judgments in the *De Bloos* and *Shenavai* cases.

Rather, I believe that it is more consistent with the general structure of the rules of the Convention, which seek to afford the plaintiff - clearly, where the relevant conditions are met - a genuine alternative forum by means of special rules of jurisdiction, to propose to the Court a solution which enables the provisions of Article 5(1) to be applied in an appropriate case.

In my opinion therefore, at least in a situation such as that in the present case, but also where there are held to exist a multiplicity of obligations, the court before which the matter is brought must have regard to the obligations actually at issue before it and ignore the characteristic obligation which may obviously not in fact be the subject of the proceedings and may lead to a forum outside the Community or in any event to a substantial separation between the place of performance and the employment relationship considered as a whole.

I do not consider that the risk of a 'multiplication' of proceedings which has sometimes been feared constitutes a decisive hindrance to the acceptance of that proposition. The national courts do not lack the means to avoid that risk. The Brussels Convention itself offers solutions based on well-known judicial concepts, such as related actions and collateral actions. Furthermore, it does not follow that the determination of the 'principal' obligation amongst those which are the subject of legal proceedings is incapable of satisfying all the relevant requirements: the need for certainty, the need to adhere to the wording of the Convention and the intention of the Contracting States and also those requirements which I can but endorse, formed the basis of the Court's judgment in the *Ivenel* case.

In conclusion I propose that the following reply be given to the Cour de cassation: 'In a dispute arising out of employment in which the work is carried out outside the territory of the Contracting States, the court before which the matter is brought must take into account, for the purposes of deciding whether it has jurisdiction in accordance with Article 5(1) of the Brussels Convention, the contractual obligations in respect of which the legal proceedings were brought'.

Case C-26/91 - 17 June 1992

Jakob Handte & Co. GmbH
v
Traitements Mécano-chimiques des Surfaces SA (TMCS)

Special jurisdiction - Jurisdiction 'in matters relating to a contract' - Concept - Independent interpretation - Chain of contracts - Action to establish liability brought by a sub-buyer against the manufacturer - Excluded.

Summary

The phrase 'matters relating to a contract' in Article 5(1) of the Convention of 27 September 1968 on Jurisdiction and the Enforcement of Judgments in Civil and Commercial Matters, which must be interpreted independently, is not to be understood as covering a situation in which there is no obligation freely assumed by one party towards another. Strengthening legal protection of persons established in the Community, which is one of the objectives of the Convention, also requires that the jurisdictional rules which derogate from the general principle set out in Article 2 of the Convention should be interpreted in such a way as to enable a normally well informed defendant reasonably to predict before which courts, other than those of the State in which he is domiciled, he may be sued. It follows that Article 5(1) of the Convention is to be understood as meaning that it does not apply to an action between a sub-buyer of goods and the manufacturer, who is not the seller, relating to defects in those goods or to their unsuitability for their intended purpose.

JUDGMENT OF THE COURT

Due, President, Schockweiler, President of Chamber, Mancini, Kakouris, Moitinho de Almeida, Diez de Velasco and Zuleeg, Judges

1. By judgment of 8 January 1991, received at the Court on 25 January 1991, the French Cour de Cassation (Court of Cassation) referred to the Court for a preliminary ruling under the Protocol of 3 June 1971 on the Interpretation by the Court of Justice of the Convention of 27 September 1968 on Jurisdiction and the Enforcement of Judgments in Civil and Commercial Matters (OJ 1978 L 304, p. 36), as amended by the Convention of 9 October 1978 on the Accession of the Kingdom of Denmark, Ireland and the United Kingdom of Great Britain and Northern Ireland (OJ 1978 L 304, p. 1) (hereinafter 'the Convention'), a question concerning the interpretation of Article 5(1) of the Convention.

2. The question has arisen in proceedings between Jakob Handte & Co. GmbH, whose registered office is at Tuttlingen (Federal Republic of Germany) (hereinafter 'Handte Germany'), and Traitements Mécano-chimiques des Surfaces, a limited liability company whose registered office is at Bonneville (France) (hereinafter 'TMCS').

3. It appears from the documents submitted to the Court that in 1984 and 1985 TMCS purchased from Bula et Fils (hereinafter 'Bula'), which is a limited liability company governed by Swiss law, two metal-polishing machines to which TMCS had a suction system fitted that was manufactured by Handte Germany but sold and installed by Société Handte France S.à.r.l. (hereinafter 'Handte France'), whose registered office is at Strasbourg (France).

4. In 1987 TMCS instituted proceedings against Bula, Handte Germany and Handte France in the Tribunal de Grande Instance (Regional Court), Bonneville (France), seeking compensation for damage incurred by reason of the fact that the equipment manufactured and sold did not comply with rules on hygiene and safety at work and was unsuitable for its intended purpose.

5. By judgment of 4 May 1988, that court ruled that it had no jurisdiction *ratione loci* to entertain the action against Bula but that it did have jurisdiction under Article 5(1) of the Convention to rule on the claim against Handte Germany and Handte France.

6. By judgment of 20 March 1989, the Cour d'Appel (Court of Appeal), Chambéry (France), dismissed Handte Germany's appeal on the ground that the action brought by TMCS against that company was an action to establish the manufacturer's liability for defects in the goods sold, that such a direct action by a sub-buyer against the manufacturer related to a contractual matter under both French law and the Convention and that the lower court was accordingly right in finding that it had jurisdiction under Article 5(1) of the Convention as the court for the place of performance of the obligation.

7. Handte Germany considered that Article 5(1) of the Convention was not applicable where there was a chain of contracts and appealed on a point of law against the judgment of the Cour d'Appel, Chambéry.

8. The French Cour de Cassation found that the dispute raised a problem concerning interpretation of the Convention and accordingly decided to stay proceedings until the Court of Justice has given a preliminary ruling on the following question: 'Does Article 5(1) of the Convention, which provides for special jurisdiction in matters relating to a contract, apply to an action between a sub-buyer of goods and the manufacturer, who is not the seller, relating to defects in those goods or to their unsuitability for their intended purpose?'

9. Reference is made to the Report for the Hearing for a fuller account of the facts of the main proceedings, the course of the procedure and the written observations submitted to the Court, which are mentioned or discussed below only in so far as is necessary for the reasoning of the Court.

10. In replying to the question from the national court, it should first be observed that the Court has consistently held that the phrase 'matters relating to a contract' in Article 5(1) of the Convention is to be interpreted independently, having regard primarily to the objectives and general scheme of the Convention, in order to ensure that it is applied uniformly in all the Contracting States (see the judgment in Case 34/82 *Martin Peters Bauuntenehmung* v *Zuid Nederlandse Aannemers Vereniging* [1983] ECR 987, paragraphs 9 and 10, and the judgment in Case 9/87 *Arcado* v *Haviland* [1988] ECR 1539, paragraphs 10 and 11). The phrase should not therefore be taken as referring to how the legal relationship in question before the national court is classified by the relevant national law.

11. Secondly, it should be noted that, according to the preamble to the Convention, one of its objectives is to 'strengthen in the Community the legal protection of persons therein established'.

12. In that connection, the expert report prepared at the time when the Convention was drawn up (OJ 1979 C 59, p. 1) states that: '...the purpose of the Convention is ..., by establishing common rules of jurisdiction, to achieve, ... in the field which it was required to cover, a genuine legal systematization which will ensure the greatest possible degree of legal certainty. To this end, the rules of jurisdiction codified in Title II determine which State's courts are most appropriate to assume jurisdiction, taking into account all relevant matters ...'.

13. The Convention achieves that objective by laying down a number of jurisdictional rules which determine the cases, exhaustively listed in Sections 2 to 6 of Title II of the Convention, in which a defendant domiciled or established in a Contracting State may, under a rule of special jurisdiction, or must, under a rule of exclusive jurisdiction or prorogation of jurisdiction, be sued before a court of another Contracting State.

14. The rules on special and exclusive jurisdiction and those relating to prorogation of jurisdiction thus derogate from the general principle, set out in the first paragraph of Article 2 of the Convention, that the courts of the Contracting State in which the defendant is domiciled are to have jurisdiction. That jurisdictional rule is a general principle because it makes it easier, in principle, for a defendant to defend himself. Consequently, the jurisdictional rules which derogate from that general principle must not lead to an interpretation going beyond the situations envisaged by the Convention.

15. It follows that the phrase 'matters relating to a contract', as used in Article 5(1) of the Convention, is not to be understood as covering a situation in which there is no obligation freely assumed by one party towards another.

16. Where a sub-buyer of goods purchased from an intermediate seller brings an action against the manufacturer for damages on the ground that the goods are not in conformity, it must be observed that there is no contractual relationship between the sub-buyer and the manufacturer because the latter has not undertaken any contractual obligation towards the former.

17. Furthermore, particularly where there is a chain of international contracts, the parties contractual obligations may vary from contract to contract, so that the contractual rights which the sub-buyer can enforce against his immediate seller will not necessarily be the same as those which the manufacturer will have accepted in his relationship with the first buyer.

18. The objective of strengthening legal protection of persons established in the Community, which is one of the objectives which the Convention is designed to achieve, also requires that the jurisdictional rules which derogate from the general principle of the Convention should be interpreted in such a way as to enable a normally well-informed defendant reasonably to predict before which courts, other than those of the State in which he is domiciled, he may be sued.

19. However, in a situation such as that with which the main proceedings are concerned, the application of the special jurisdictional rule laid down by Article 5(1) of the Convention to an action brought by a sub-buyer of goods against the manufacturer is not foreseeable by the latter and is therefore incompatible with the principle of legal certainty.

20. Apart from the fact that the manufacturer has no contractual relationship with the sub-buyer and undertakes no contractual obligation towards that buyer, whose identity and domicile may, quite reasonably, be unknown to him, it appears that in the great majority of Contracting States the liability of a manufacturer towards a sub-buyer for defects in the goods sold is not regarded as being of a contractual nature.

21. It follows that the answer to the question submitted by the national court must be that Article 5(1) of the Convention is to be understood as meaning that it does not apply to an action between a sub-buyer of goods and the manufacturer, who is not the seller, relating to defects in those goods or to their unsuitability for their intended purpose.

On those grounds, the Court, in answer to the question referred to it by the French Cour de Cassation by judgment of 8 January 1991, hereby rules:

> **Article 5(1) of the Convention of 27 September 1968 on Jurisdiction and the Enforcement of Judgments in Civil and Commercial Matters is to be understood as meaning that it does not apply to an action between a sub-buyer of goods and**

the manufacturer, who is not the seller, relating to defects in those goods or to their unsuitability for their intended purpose.

OPINION OF MR ADVOCATE GENERAL JACOBS

1. The French Cour de Cassation has asked for a preliminary ruling on the interpretation of Article 5(1) of the Convention of 27 September 1968 on Jurisdiction and the Enforcement of Judgments in Civil and Commercial Matters (hereafter 'the Convention'), as amended by the Convention of 9 October 1978 on the Accession of Denmark, Ireland and the United Kingdom. The question referred is in substance whether proceedings brought by a purchaser of a product against the manufacturer of the product are to be classified as contractual and so as falling under Article 5(1) of the Convention where there is no direct contractual link between the parties. The question arises because in French law the purchaser of a product may bring proceedings based in contract directly against the manufacturer, notwithstanding the absence of a contract between them.

The background

2. The first respondent in the main proceedings is Traitements Mécano-chimiques des Surfaces ('TMCS'), whose registered office is at Bonneville, Haute-Savoie (France). The appellant in the main proceedings is Jakob Handte GmbH ('Handte Germany'), whose registered office is at Tuttlingen, Württemberg (Germany). In 1984 and 1985 TMCS purchased two metal-polishing machines from a Swiss company, Bula et Fils, which is the second respondent. It fitted to those machines a suction system manufactured by Handte Germany, but sold and installed by Société Handte France ('Handte France'). It is not clear what the relationship is between Handte France and Handte Germany.

3. On 8 and 9 April 1987 TMCS commenced proceedings against Bula et Fils, Handte France and Handte Germany in the Tribunal de Grande Instance, Bonneville, claiming damages on the ground that the equipment did not comply with the rules on hygiene and safety at work and was unfit for its purpose. That court declined jurisdiction over the Swiss defendant, but held that it had jurisdiction over Handte Germany on the ground that TMCS's action against that company was of a contractual nature under French law, with the result that the court had jurisdiction under Article 5(1) of the Convention. By way of derogation from the general jurisdiction rule set out in the first paragraph of Article 2 of the Convention, Article 5(1) confers jurisdiction, in matters relating to a contract, on the courts for the place of performance of the obligation in question.

4. Handte Germany's appeal to the Cour d'Appel, Chambéry, was dismissed by judgment of 20 March 1989. It then took the matter to the Cour de Cassation, which has requested a preliminary ruling on the question: 'Whether

Article 5(1) of the Convention, which provides for special jurisdiction in matters relating to a contract, applies to a dispute between a subsequent purchaser and the manufacturer, who is not the seller, of an object, in connection with defects in that object or its unsuitability for the purpose for which it was intended.'

5. It should be noted at the outset that it is not clear whether an answer to the question posed in these terms will necessarily determine the issue of jurisdiction in the circumstances of the present case. In the first place, it cannot be assumed, for reasons which I will give later, that, if Article 5(1) applies, the court in Bonneville may exercise jurisdiction over TMCS's claim against Handte Germany as the court for the place of performance of the obligation in question. If on the other hand Article 5(1) is not applicable, it cannot be assumed that Handte Germany must be sued in the courts for the place at which it has its seat, in accordance with Article 2 of the Convention. Indeed, there are several other provisions on which the jurisdiction of the French courts (though not necessarily those in Bonneville) might possibly be founded. Those provisions are as follows:

(a) Article 5(3), which confers jurisdiction in matters relating to tort, delict or quasi-delict on the courts for the place where the harmful event occurred.

This Court has construed that provision as conferring on the plaintiff a choice of jurisdiction; he may sue either at the place where the damage occurred or at the place of the event giving rise to it: Case 21/76 *Bier* v *Mines de Potasse d'Alsace* [1976] ECR 1735.

(b) Article 5(5), which provides that, as regards a dispute arising out of the operations of a branch, agency or other establishment, proceedings may be brought in the courts for the place in which the branch, agency or other establishment is situated: see in particular, in relation to this head of jurisdiction, Case 33/78 *Somafer* v *Saar-Ferngas* [1978] ECR2183 and Case 218/86 *SAR Schotte* v *Parfums Rothschild* [1987] ECR 4905.

In the absence of any information about the legal relationship between Handte Germany and Handte France, it is impossible to say whether the latter might constitute a 'branch, agency or other establishment' of the former.

(c) Article 6(1), under which a person domiciled in a Contracting State may be sued, where he is one of a number of defendants, in the courts for the place where any one of them is domiciled.

It may be noted that Handte Germany could be sued in Bonneville under Article 6(1) only if the jurisdiction of the Bonneville court over Handte France were based on Article 2 of the Convention (i.e. if Handte France has its seat there). If, on the other hand, jurisdiction over Handte France were based solely on Article 5(1) or (3), it would not be possible to sue Handte Germany in Bonneville under Article 6(1), since none of the defendants would be domiciled there. Although the Order for Reference does not state where Handte France is domiciled, it may be noted that there is appended to Handte Germany's observations the judgment of the Cour d'Appel, Chambéry, of 20 March 1989, from which it is clear that Handte Germany argued that Article 6(1) was not applicable on the ground that Handte France was domiciled in Strasbourg.

(d) Article 6(2), (under which a person domiciled in a Contracting State may be sued as a third party in an action on a warranty or guarantee or any other third party proceedings in the court seised of the original proceedings, unless these were instituted solely with the object of removing him from the jurisdiction of the court which would be competent in his case.

TMCS attempted to invoke Article 6(2) in the proceedings before the Cour d'Appel, which did not, however, make any ruling on the point.

6. In my view, the essential issue on which the Cour de Cassation seeks guidance is whether an action of this kind should be treated, for the purposes of the Convention, as contractual, with the consequence that Article 5(1) of the Convention will apply, or as founded in tort, delict or quasi-delict (for convenience, I shall refer to "delict" alone), with the consequence that Article 5(3) will apply. That also appears to be the way in which the issue has been understood by those who have submitted observations to this Court, namely Handte Germany, the German Government and the Commission.

7. Handte Germany criticises the French courts for having classified TMCS's claim under the *lex fori*, with the result that it is treated as contractual. Instead, the claim should receive an independent classification based on the system and aims of the Convention. The main obstacle to classifying the claim as contractual is the absence of any contractual link between the manufacturer and the sub-buyer. Moreover, the French classification of the claim as contractual is not adopted by all the other legal systems in the Contracting States, notably by English law.

8. The German Government also points out that the question whether a claim is contractual must be determined independently, rather than by reference to the *lex fori*. The French classification of the claim is not followed in German law, which treats the manufacturer's liability towards the sub-buyer as delictual. The German Government considers that the delictual nature of such liability is borne out by Council Directive 85/374/EEC on the approximation of the laws, regulations and administrative provisions of the Member States concerning liability for defective products (OJ 1985 L 210, p. 29), which imposes liability without fault and prohibits the limitation of liability by contract. Moreover, liability in contract pre-supposes that the manufacturer has, by some independent act on his part, bound himself vis-à-vis the plaintiff; there is no such act as between the manufacturer and the enduser of a product.

9. The Commission gives a brief comparative survey of the law of several Member States. German, English and Dutch law are said to treat the sub-buyer's claim against the manufacturer as delictual, while French, Belgian and Italian law treat it as contractual. In fact, the information about Italian law appears to be incorrect (see paragraph 18 below).

10. The Commission considers that it is necessary to avoid interpreting Article 5(1) in such a way that different results ensue, as regards jurisdiction, depending on whether the plaintiff sues the manufacturer alone, the seller alone (with the possibility of third party proceedings against the manufacturer), or the manufacturer and the seller together.

11. The Commission cites the judgment in Case 189/87 *Kalfelis* v

Bankhaus Schröder [1988] ECR 5565, in which the Court held that: '... the term 'matters relating to tort, delict or quasi-delict' within the meaning of Article 5(3) of the Convention must be regarded as an independent concept covering all actions which seek to establish the liability of a defendant and which are not related to a 'contract' within the meaning of Article 5(1).'
Delictual liability is therefore a residual category encompassing liability that is not contractual. Hence, if a contractual link can be identified in the relationship between the manufacturer and the sub-buyer, the action falls to be classified as contractual. Such a link exists in the form of the chain of contracts connecting the two parties. That is particularly so when the manufacturer could foresee that his product would be resold.

12. The disadvantage of classifying the action as contractual, according to the Commission, is that it may result in conferring jurisdiction on the courts at the place where the plaintiff is domiciled. Article 3 of the Convention and the Court's decision in Case C-220/88 *Dumez France and Tracoba* [1990] ECR I-49 do not look favourably on such a result. However, if TMCS had sued Handte France alone in Bonneville, Handte France could have brought Handte Germany in as a third-party under Article 6(2) of the Convention. Hence, in order to avoid the abusive conferring of jurisdiction on the courts of the plaintiff's place of domicile, the Commission considers it necessary to make the contractual classification of the sub-buyer's direct action against the manufacturer subject to the condition that such classification results in jurisdiction being conferred on the same court before which the manufacturer could be sued as a third-party under Article 6(2) of the Convention.

13. Before examining the principal issues raised by this case I will make two brief comments on the observations submitted to the Court. First, I do not think that Council Directive 85/374 ("the Product Liability Directive"), which was referred to by the German Government, is directly relevant in this case. The Product Liability Directive is concerned only with damage to persons or to property other than the defective product itself. If the suction system bought by TMCS were so defective that it injured a worker at TMCS's factory, there might be a case of product liability. But no such injury is alleged to have occurred and TMCS is claiming damages for purely economic loss, namely the loss caused by the supply of goods that are not fit for their purpose. That type of claim has nothing to do with product liability, in the sense in which the term is generally understood and in the sense in which it is used in Directive 85/374. None the less, that directive does, as I shall explain, have some indirect bearing on the issue raised in this case.

14. Secondly, I will say at the outset that I cannot agree with the analysis put forward by the Commission. That analysis is, in my view, founded on dubious policy considerations. In particular, I disagree with the Commission's view that it is necessary to avoid interpreting Article 5(1) in such a way that different results ensue depending on whether the plaintiff is able to sue the manufacturer alone, the seller alone or both of them together. Certainly, I do not think that the Court should attempt to avoid that consequence by distorting the meaning of terms such as 'contract' and 'tort, delict or quasi-delict' in Article 5

of the Convention. In particular, I fail to see how the construction of the expression 'matters relating to a contract' in Article 5(1) can depend on national rules relating to third-party proceedings. If the sub-buyer's action against the manufacturer should properly be classified as contractual, it cannot cease to be contractual simply because that classification confers jurisdiction on a court that would not have jurisdiction over the manufacturer by way of a third-party claim brought under Article 6(2).

15. One other point should be noted at this stage. As I have already observed, we have no information about the precise relationship between Handte Germany and Handte France. The sharing of a name may suggest a relationship of parent and subsidiary or principal and agent. I have already alluded to the possibility that, if that is indeed the relationship between the parties, the courts in Strasbourg may acquire jurisdiction under Article 5(5) of the Convention as 'the courts for the place in which the branch, agency or other establishment is situated'. Furthermore, if Handte France acted as agent for Handte Germany when it contracted with TMCS, there might be a direct contractual relationship between TMCS and Handte Germany, in which case the issue now before the Court would not arise. However, in the absence of any information to the contrary, I shall assume in the remaining discussion that Handte Germany and Handte France are independent of each other. That indeed appears to be the premise underlying the national court's question.

The distinction between contract and delict

16. The distinction between contractual and delictual liability is an old one and doubtless exists in all developed legal systems. Contractual liability may be defined as civil liability for a failure to perform an obligation that one person owes to another by virtue of an agreement entered into by the parties. Delictual liability may be defined as civil liability for a failure to perform an obligation which the law imposes independently of any agreement between the parties, e.g. an obligation to exercise reasonable care when driving a motor vehicle.

17. Most legal systems have a rule to the effect that a contract cannot confer rights or impose obligations on persons who are not parties to the contract, except in limited circumstances. In English law that principle is known as the doctrine of privity of contract. In French law it is known as the "théorie de l'effet relatif des contrats". At first sight that rule would seem to preclude a contractual classification of the sub-buyer's claim against the manufacturer, in the absence of any contract between the two parties. That does indeed appear to be the case in all the legal systems of the Contracting States, with the exceptions of France, Belgium and Luxembourg. Certainly in English law the sub-buyer could not sustain a contractual action against the manufacturer, unless he could show the existence of a collateral warranty, i.e. a promise by the manufacturer which led him to buy the goods from the intermediate supplier (see Chitty on Contracts, 26th edition, 1989, vol.1, paragraphs 1321 *et seq.*). Similar rules exist in German law (H. Messer, in Produzenthaftung, by H. J. Kullmann and B. Pfister (eds.), vol.1, 1350 *et seq*; Graf von Westphalen,

Produkthaftungshandbuch, vol.1, p. 99 *et seq.*) The doctrine of privity also exists in Irish law and, in a modified form, in Scots law.

18. The sub-buyer cannot bring a contractual action against the manufacturer, in the absence of a contractual relationship, in Italian law (judgment of the Corte di Cassazione of 28 July 1986, No 4833, with a note by M. Moretti, in Nuova Gurisprudenza Civile Commentata 1987, p. 246), Spanish law (judgment of the Tribunal Supremo (Sala Civil) of 25 November 1967, Aranzadi, Repertorio Cronologico de Jurisprudencia, 1967, No. 4769), Portuguese law (J. Calvao da Silva, Responsabilidade Civil do Produtor, 1990, p. 278), Greek law and, probably, Danish law (H. Nielsen, Produktansvar, 1987, p. 24).

19. As regards Dutch law, there is some caselaw establishing that the sub-buyer may in certain circumstances bring a delictual action against the manufacturer if the goods are not fit for their purpose (see, for example, judgment of the Hoge Raad of 25 March 1966, Nederlandse Jurisprudentie 1966, No. 279, judgment of the Gerechtshof 's-Hertogenbosch of 21 December 1967, Nederlandse Jurisprudentie 1968, No. 402). A contractual action is excluded in the absence of a contract between the two parties. Although there was a proposal to introduce a direct contractual action for the benefit of consumers (which was referred to by the Commission in its observations), the proposal was apparently not adopted.

20. In the three legal systems which grant the sub-buyer a contractual claim against the manufacturer (France, Belgium and Luxembourg) the theoretical justification offered for such a solution is that the intermediate supplier transmits to the sub-buyer his contractual rights against the manufacturer (or against a previous intermediary) as an accessory of the goods. The theory was explained by a Luxembourg court, the Tribunal d'arrondissement, Diekirch, in a judgment of 24 March 1904 (Pasicrisie Luxembourgeoise, vol. VI, p. 503) in the following terms: 'L'obligation de délivrer la chose vendue comprend tous ses accessoires, donc également tous les droits compétents de ce chef au vendeur, lequel partant estcensé transmettre la chose 'cum omni sua causa', subrogeant son successeur également dans toutes les actions découlant de la convention, lequel peut dès lors à son choix rechercher en garantie son propre vendeur, conformément à l'article 1641 du même Code [civil], ou bien, s'il le préfère pour éviter des frais et des lenteurs, s'en prendre au premier vendeur'.

It should be noted that the subject is not free from controversy in French law and that the case-law is not entirely consistent. In particular, the judgment of the plenary session of the Cour de Cassation of 12 July 1991 in the Besse case (Recueil Dalloz Sirey 1991, jurisprudence, p. 549) appears to mark a move away from contractual liability in favour of a delictual classification. In that case the Cour de Cassation held that an action against a sub-contractor in respect of badly executed building work was delictual in accordance with the basic proposition in Article 1165 of the Code Civil that 'les conventions n'ont d'effet qu'entre les parties contractantes'. It is not clear to what extent that judgment affects the traditional view of the French courts that the sub-buyer's action against the manufacturer is necessarily contractual. Some authors conclude that such an action continues to be contractual, where the alleged damage is due to a failure to supply goods of the appropriate quality (see J. Ghestin, Recueil Dalloz Sirey 1991, jurisprudence, p. 549; C. Jamin, Recueil Dalloz Sirey, 1991, Chronique, p. 257).

21. It would, however, be an over-simplification to conclude from the above survey of national law that a claim by the sub-buyer against the manufacturer is classified as contractual in only three legal systems among the Contracting States and as delictual in all the remainder. So far as the type of claim in issue in these proceedings is concerned, which is a claim for economic loss alone (namely the loss caused by the supply of goods that are not fit for their purpose), where there is a chain of contracts but in the absence of any direct contractual link between the sub-buyer and the manufacturer, the fact is that most of the legal systems do not recognize such a claim at all, while those legal systems which do recognize it tend to treat it as contractual. If however the claim in issue were in respect of the harm caused to the plaintiff by the product, for example, physical damage to his person or property caused by the defective nature of the goods, rather than in respect of economic loss alone, then it would be right to say that such a claim would be classified by most of the Contracting States' laws as delictual.

The choice between an autonomous or national interpretation

22. According to the case-law of the Court, the term 'matters relating to a contract in Article 5(1) must not be interpreted by reference to the national law of one or other of the States concerned. Instead it must be regarded as an independent concept to be interpreted by reference principally to the system and objectives of the Convention in order to ensure that the Convention is fully effective: see in particular Case 9/87 *Arcado* v *Haviland* [1988] ECR 1539, paragraphs 10 and 11.

23. It is true that in his Opinion in that case Advocate General Slynn said that, if the matter were free from authority, he thought there was much to be said for determining whether the case was contractual under the *lex causae*. That would avoid the conflict that might arise if an independent interpretation decided that the matter was contractual, whereas under the *lex causae* it was classified otherwise. However he considered that he was bound by the judgment in Case 34/82 *Martin Peters* v *Zuid Nederlandse Aannemers Vereniging* [1983] ECR 987. It might seem paradoxical if, for example, the Court were to hold that the sub-buyer's action against the manufacturer were delictual and the French courts were to take jurisdiction under Article 5(3) of the Convention, but then apply the law of contract to the substance of the action. But I do not think that that entails serious consequences; see the Opinion of Advocate General Darmon in Case 189/87 *Kalfelis* v *Schröder* [1988] ECR 5565, paragraph 19. Such paradoxes are a frequent phenomenon of private international law. In fact, for more elaborate scenarios can be imagined. The French courts might, for example, take jurisdiction under Article 5(3) on the basis that the action is delictual, then

classify it as contractual, then decide that the *lex causae* is German law and then discover that under the *lex causae* the action is delictual.

24. It is above all important to stress that the jurisdiction rules of the Convention deal solely with the issue of jurisdiction. They do not affect the classification of the action for such purposes as determining the applicable principles of liability or deciding what limitation period applies. A court that acquires jurisdiction under Article 5(1) is not prevented by the Convention from proceeding with the action on the basis that it is delictual and a court that acquires jurisdiction under Article 5(3) is not prevented by the Convention from proceeding with the action on the basis that it is contractual.

The choice between a contractual or delictual classification of the sub-buyer's action

25. It follows from the Court's existing case-law that it must determine, by reference to the system and objectives of the Convention, whether the sub-buyer's action against the manufacturer is contractual or delictual. The distinction between contractual and delictual liability was touched on in Kalfelis. There the Court regarded delictual liability as a residual category, stating (at paragraph 17) that: '... the concept of 'matters relating to tort, delict and quasi-delict' covers all actions which seek to establish the liability of a defendant and which are not related to a 'contract' within the meaning of Article 5(1)'; see also Case C-261/90 *Reichert* v *Dresdner Bank AG*, judgment of 26 March 1992, ECR 2149, paragraph 16. However, I do not think that the residual nature of delictual liability makes Article 5(1) a dominant jurisdiction rule in relation to Article 5(3). Nor do I think that it may be inferred from the *Kalfelis* judgment that an indirect relationship between the parties, through a chain of contracts, necessarily makes Article 5(1) applicable at the expense of Article 5(3).

26. In deciding whether the sub-buyer's claim against the manufacturer is contractual or delictual for the purposes of the Convention, I do not think that too much weight can be attached to the classification adopted in the laws of the Contracting States. In the first place, the results of the comparative survey set out above are inconclusive. Secondly, and more importantly, the policy considerations on which classification is based in national law may be very different from those that are relevant in interpreting the Convention. As I have remarked already, it is by reference to the system and objectives of the Convention that the issue now before the Court must be resolved.

27. The purpose of the special jurisdiction rules laid down in Article 5 is to ensure that certain actions which are closely connected with a particular locality are dealt with by the courts at the place in question. Stated negatively, that proposition means that Article 5 should not operate so as to confer jurisdiction on the courts for a place that has no real connection with the substance of the action. In particular, it should not be allowed to derogate from the general jurisdiction rule laid down in Article 2, unless there is a sound reason for removing the defendant from his natural forum. It is therefore necessary to

examine what practical consequences would flow from the classification of the sub-buyer's action as contractual or delictual.

28. If TMCS's claim against Handte Germany is classified as contractual, the courts for the place of performance of the obligation in question will have jurisdiction under Article 5(1). The obligation in question is the one forming the basis of the legal proceedings (Case 14/76 *De Bloos* v *Bouyer* [1976] ECR 1497). In the present case the obligation in question was presumably Handte Germany's obligation to supply equipment of the appropriate quality to Handte France. The place of performance of that obligation is to be determined in accordance with the law that is applicable to the contract under the conflict rules of the court seised (Case 12/76 *Industrie Tessili* v *Dunlop* [1976] ECR 1473). Whichever law is applicable, it seems unlikely that the place of performance could be at TMCS's factory in Bonneville, unless of course Handte Germany was required by its contract with Handte France to deliver the equipment directly to TMCS in Bonneville. If, on the other hand, Handte Germany was required to deliver the equipment to Handte France's premises in Strasbourg, the courts for that city may have jurisdiction under Article 5(1). In this respect there is an important difference between the general jurisdiction rule laid down in Article 2 and the special jurisdiction rules laid down in Article 5. Article 2 confers jurisdiction on the courts of the Contracting State in which the defendant is domiciled, leaving to domestic law the task of determining in which part of that State the defendant may be sued. The provisions of Article 5 (with the exception of Article 5(6)) confer jurisdiction not on the courts in general of a Contracting State but on the courts of a particular place within a Contracting State (see the Jenard Report, OJ 1979 C 59, at p. 22).

29. It is only if the contractual classification is applied in the way indicated above that the outcome will be consistent with the principle that Article 5 should not operate so as to confer jurisdiction on a forum which has no real connection with the substance of the action. If, for example, a manufacturer in Dublin sells a product to a dealer in London who then resells it to someone in Marseille, and the product turns out not to be as sound as the French sub-buyer was entitled to expect in the light of his contract with the dealer in London, it would in my view be strange if the Dublin manufacturer, who may have had no intention of doing business in France, could be sued in Marseille. It might of course be different if the manufacturer had known that the dealer intended to resell the goods to an end user in France and it would certainly be different if the manufacturer agreed to deliver the goods directly to the sub-buyer. In the latter case the place of performance of the obligation in question would probably be Marseille.

30. If the action were classified as delictual, the courts for the 'place where the harmful event occurred' would have jurisdiction under Article 5(3) of the Convention. That expression means either the place where the damage occurred or the place of the event giving rise to it: Case 21/76 *Bier* v *Mines de Potasse d'Alsace*, cited above in paragraph 5. In the present case the harmful event giving rise to the damage was the supply of allegedly defective equipment by Handte Germany to Handte France. That event occurred at the place of performance of Handte Germany's obligation to supply goods of sound quality

to Handte France (i.e. presumably either at Handte Germany's premises in Tuttlingen or at Handte France's premises in Strasbourg). The place where the damage occurred was arguably TMCS's place of business in Bonneville. Does that mean that the court in Bonneville would have jurisdiction under Article 5(3)?

31. If the test laid down in *Bier* v *Mines de Potasse d'Alsace* were applied literally, the answer to that question would be affirmative. However, it is clear from the Court's judgment in Case C-220/88 *Dumez France and Tracoba* [1990] ECR 1-49 that the scope of the rule laid down in *Mines de Potasse d'Alsace* is much more limited. In *Dumez France* French plaintiffs sought compensation in France for damage which they claimed to have suffered as a result of the insolvency of their German subsidiaries; the insolvency was allegedly caused by the wrongful cancellation of loans by the defendant banks. The Court held (at paragraph 20) that the concept of the place where the damage occurred, used in the Mines de Potasse d'Alsace judgment, 'can be understood only as indicating the place where the event giving rise to the damage, and entailing tortious, delictual or quasidelictual liability, directly produced its harmful effects upon the person who is the immediate victim of that event'. In the present case, if we assume that Handte Germany did not deliver the goods directly to TMCS's factory at Bonneville and did not know that the goods were intended for TMCS, the immediate victim of the harmful event was Handte France and the place where the damage was directly produced upon that company was the place where Handte Germany supplied the goods to Handte France. (i. e. presumably either Tuttlingen or Strasbourg, but not Bonneville).

32. Applied in this way, a delictual classification is again consistent with the principle that Article 5 should not operate so as to confer jurisdiction on a forum that has no real connection with the substance of the action. As in the case of Article 5(1), a different result might be produced if Handte Germany knew that the goods were intended for TMCS or actually undertook to deliver them directly to TMCS's factory in Bonneville. Certainly, in the case of direct delivery the harmful event itself would occur at the sub-buyer's premises; and if the manufacturer knows that the goods are specifically intended for a particular sub-buyer it might be possible to regard the sub-buyer as the immediate victim of the harmful event. But in the ordinary case of a manufacturer (or other supplier) who sells goods to a dealer, not knowing where or by whom the goods will ultimately be used, there seems little justification for allowing the manufacturer to be sued, under Article 5(3), at the place where the sub-buyer suffers the damage, if the damage complained of is purely financial loss due to the diminished value of the goods. Different considerations would of course apply if the goods, instead of simply being of inferior quality, were dangerous and caused physical damage to the sub-buyer's person or property. In such a case the sub-buyer would be the immediate victim.

33. The strongest argument in favour of a contractual classification is that the sub-buyer's right of action does not arise independently of contract. A right to claim damages for the supply of defective goods, where the alleged loss consists solely in the diminished value of the goods supplied, does not, it would

seem, arise in the absence of a contractual link. The type of damage is essentially of a contractual nature and can only be measured by reference to a failure to fulfil obligations imposed by contract. The laws of the Contracting States do not appear to recognise any general obligation, owed by the manufacturer to the world at large, to ensure that goods placed in circulation are of a particular quality (other than an obligation to ensure that goods are safe). As I have observed already, the matter would be very different if the goods were dangerous and caused physical damage to the sub-buyer's person or property. One solution would be to distinguish between the two types of damage. An action in respect of damage consisting solely in the failure of the product to conform to the contractual stipulations as to quality would be treated as contractual, while an action in respect of physical damage to the sub-buyer's person or property would be treated as delictual. Tempting though that solution is, I think that it must be rejected because it would hardly be satisfactory in practice to treat differently two claims which in practice will often arise together.

34. The main argument in favour of a delictual classification of the sub-buyer's action against the manufacturer for failure to supply goods of the appropriate quality is simply that there is no contract between the two parties. The 'contractual' link between the parties consists of two or more separate contracts which may of course contain very different terms, including conflicting jurisdiction clauses, and may be governed by different *lex causae*. This appears to pose a major obstacle to a contractual classification of the sub-buyer's direct action, because it seems difficult to determine precisely what contractual obligations were owed by the manufacturer to the sub-buyer. The national court may, as a result, have considerable difficulty in determining the place of performance of the obligation. The question that will inevitably arise, in many such cases, is 'which obligation?' Is it the manufacturer's obligation to his purchaser, or the obligation of that purchaser - or of a subsequent purchaser - to the sub-buyer? In many internal situations, this may not matter; but in a case arising under the Convention, there are likely to be different answers available.

35. I have already suggested a solution to some of these problems (see paragraph 28). However, it cannot be pretended that that solution would be easy to apply in practice. Even in the case of much simpler transactions, the practical application of Article 5(1) has given rise to unexpected difficulties, as is proved by the Court's case-law. It seems to me that, if the sub-buyer's action against the manufacturer were classified as contractual, there is a danger, owing to the complexity of the jurisdiction rule contained in Article 5(1), that the defendant would unfairly be brought before a forum with which he has no real connexion. That is demonstrated by the willingness of the French courts in the present case to hold that Bonneville was the place of performance of the obligation in question, without apparently identifying the precise obligation owed by Handte Germany to TMCS and determining by what law that obligation was governed.

36. If, on the other hand, the action were classified as delictual, the practical application of the relevant jurisdiction rule would be relatively simple. The test laid down in *Bier* v *Mines de Potasse d'Alsace*, subject to the qualification introduced in *Dumez France*, should not give rise to major

problems and should produce a logical and equitable result (see paragraphs 31 and 32 above).

37. There are other reasons which militate in favour of a delictual classification. As already mentioned, classification for the purposes of the Convention should not depend on the type of harm in respect of which the claim arises. There seems little justification for treating certain forms of direct action as contractual, and therefore adopting different jurisdictional rules, simply because the loss claimed is purely economic. But where the loss is not purely economic, a part of the rationale for the contractual classification disappears: the sub-buyer can in any event sue the manufacturer of the product in delict. From the point of view of the Convention, it then seems logical that such an action should be treated as delictual, that is, treated in the same way as an action against the manufacturer by any other person, excluding only a person who has a contractual relationship with the manufacturer.

38. It may be noted, finally, that another part of the rationale for a contractual classification also disappears in such cases. Liability in contract is traditionally strict, while delictual liability historically required proof of fault. But in consequence of the developments in the law of product liability, and in particular in consequence of the Product Liability Directive, the same principles of liability are likely to govern both types of action in such cases. That consideration is not directly relevant under the Convention, since issues of liability are independent of questions of jurisdiction. It is however not irrelevant that the Product Liability Directive in effect requires the laws of the Member States to treat actions falling within its scope as in substance delictual, notably by precluding any contractual derogation: see Article 12 of the Directive. That may be regarded as providing confirmation of the view which seems to me in any event correct on the grounds previously stated, that the action should be regarded as delictual.

Conclusion

39. I am therefore of the opinion that the question referred to the Court by the Cour de Cassation should be answered as follows: 'Where an action is brought against the manufacturer of a product by a subsequent purchaser in the absence of any direct contractual relationship between the parties, in connection with defects in that product or its suitability for the purpose for which it was intended, such an action is to be classified as an action relating to tort, delict or quasi-delict with the consequence that the courts for the place where the harmful event occurred have jurisdiction in accordance with Article 5(3) of the Convention of 27 September 1968 on Jurisdiction and the Enforcement of Judgments in Civil and Commercial Matters. That place is to be understood as the place where the event giving rise to the damage occurred or where it directly produced its harmful effects upon the person who was the immediate victim of that event'.

Case C-125/92 - 13 July 1993

Mulox IBC Ltd.
v
Hendrick Geels

Rules of jurisdiction - Autonomous interpretation - Article 5(1) - Special jurisdiction - Court of the place of performance of the contractual obligation - Contract of employment - Place of performance of the obligation characterising the contract - Autonomous concept - Place of performance by the employee of the work stipulated - Work performed in more than one Contracting State - Place where or from which the employee principally discharges his obligations.

Summary

1. The terms used in the Convention of 27 September 1968 on Jurisdiction and the Enforcement of Judgments in Civil and Commercial Matters must be interpreted autonomously. Only such an interpretation is capable of ensuring uniform application of the Convention, the objectives of which include unification of the rules on jurisdiction of the Contracting States, so as to avoid as far as possible the multiplication of the bases of jurisdiction in relation to one and the same legal relationship and to reinforce the legal protection available to persons established in the Community by, at the same time, allowing the plaintiff easily to identify the court before which he may bring an action and the defendant reasonably to foresee the court before which he may be sued.

2. In view of the specific nature of contracts of employment, the place of performance of the obligation in question, for the purposes of applying Article 5(1) of the Convention of 27 September 1968 on Jurisdiction and the Enforcement of Judgments in Civil and Commercial Matters, must, in the case of such contracts, be determined by reference not to the

applicable national law in accordance with the conflict rules of the court seised but, rather, to uniform criteria laid down by the Court of Justice on the basis of the scheme and the objectives of the Convention. The place of performance is the place where the employee actually carries out the work covered by the contract with his employer.

Where the employee performs his work in more than one Contracting State, the place of performance of the contractual obligation, within the meaning of that provision, must be defined as the place where or from which the employee discharges principally his obligations towards his employer.

JUDGMENT OF THE COURT

Due, President, Zuleeg and Murray, Presidents of Chambers, Mancini, Schockweiler, Moitinho de Almeida, Grévissa, Diez de Velasco and Kapteyn, Judges

1. By judgment of 17 March 1992, received at the Court on 17 April 1992, the Cour d'Appel, Chambéry, referred to the Court for a preliminary ruling under the Protocol of 3 June 1971 on the interpretation by the Court of Justice of the Convention of 27 September 1968 on Jurisdiction and the Enforcement of Judgments in Civil and Commercial Matters (OJ 1978 L 304, p.97), as amended by the Convention of 9 October 1978 on the Accession of the Kingdom of Denmark, Ireland and the United Kingdom of Great Britain and Northern Ireland (OJ 1978 L 304, p.1, hereinafter 'the Convention'), a question on the interpretation of Article 5(1) of the Convention.

2. That question was raised in the course of proceedings between Mulox IBC Ltd., a company incorporated under English law whose registered office is in London (hereinafter 'Mulox'), and one of its former employees, Hendrick Geels, a Netherlands national residing in Aix-les-Bains, France, following termination of his contract of employment by his employer.

3. It is apparent from the documents before the Court that Mr Geels, who had been employed by Mulox as international marketing director since 1 November 1988, established his office in Aix-les-Bains and sold Mulox products initially in Germany, Belgium, the Netherlands and the Scandinavian countries, to which he travelled frequently. As from January 1990, Mr Geels worked in France.

4. Following termination of his contract of employment, Mr Geels sued his former employer before the Conseil de Prud'Hommes, Aix-les-Bains, for compensation in lieu of notice and for damages.

5. By judgment of 4 December 1990, that court declared that it had jurisdiction under Article 5(1) of the Convention and, applying French law, ordered Mulox to pay Mr Geels various sums by way of compensation.

6. Mulox then appealed to the Cour d'Appel, Chambéry, claiming that the French courts lacked jurisdiction to hear the case on the grounds that the place of performance of the contract at issue was not confined to France and that Mulox was established in the United Kingdom.

7. The Cour d'Appel, Chambéry, entertained doubts as to whether the French courts had jurisdiction to hear the case, whereupon it stayed the proceedings and referred the following question to the Court of Justice for a preliminary ruling: 'Does the application of the jurisdiction rule under Article 5(1) of the Brussels Convention of 27 September 1968 require the obligation characterising the employment contract to have been performed wholly and solely in the territory of the State of the court seised of the dispute, or is it sufficient for its operation that part of the obligation - possibly the principal part - has been performed in the territory of that State?'

8. Reference is made to the Report of the Judge-Rapporteur for a fuller account of the facts of the case, the procedure and the written observations submitted to the Court, which are mentioned or discussed hereinafter only insofar as is necessary for the reasoning of the Court.

9. In answering the question from the national court, it must be borne in mind first of all that, by way of derogation from the general principle laid down in the first paragraph of Article 2 of the Convention, namely that the courts of the State where the defendant is domiciled are to have jurisdiction, Article 5(1) of the Covnention provides: 'A person domiciled in a Contracting State may, in another Contracting State, be sued: 1. in matters relating to a contract, in the courts for the place of performance of the obligation in question'.

10. It is settled case-law that, as far as possible, the Court of Justice will interpret the terms of the Convention autonomously so as to ensure that

it is fully effective having regard to the objectives of Article 220 of the EEC Treaty, for the implementation of which it was adopted.

11. That autonomous interpretation alone is capable of ensuring uniform application of the Convention, the objectives of which include unification of the rules on jurisdiction of the Contracting States, so as to avoid as far as possible the multiplication of the bases of jurisdiction in relation to one and the same legal relationship and to reinforce the legal protection available to persons established in the Community by, at the same time, allowing the plaintiff easily to identify the court before which he may bring an action and the defendant reasonably to foresee the court before which he may be sued.

12. It is true that, with regard to the rule in Article 5(1) of the Convention on special jurisdiction, the Court has already held (Case 12/76 *Tessili* v *Dunlop* [1976] ECR 1473) that, for contracts in general, 'the place of performance of contractual obligations', within the meaning of that provision, cannot be understood otherwise than by reference to the law which governs the obligations in question under the conflict rules of the court before which the matter is brought.

13. In reaching that conclusion, the Court stated that the various Contracting States have very different views as to the meaning of the place of performance of the relevant obligation under a contract such as the sales transaction at issue in that case.

14. However, no such problem arises in relation to contracts of employment. The Court has consistently held that, in view of the specific nature of contracts of that kind (Case 133/81 *Ivenel* v *Schwab* [1982] ECR 1891, paragraph 20, Case 266/85 *Shenavai* v *Kreischer* [1987] ECR 239, paragraph 11, and Case 32/88 *Six Constructions* v *Humbert* [1989] ECR 341, paragraph 10), the obligation to be taken into consideration for the purposes of the application of Article 5(1) of the Convention to contracts of employment is always the obligation which characterises such contracts, namely the employee's obligation to carry out the work stipulated.

15. The Court found in *Ivenel, Shenavai* and *Six Constructions,* cited above, that such contracts display certain particular features compared with other contracts in that they create a lasting bond which brings the worker to some extent within the organisational framework of the employer's business and they are linked to the place where the activities

are pursued, which determines the application of mandatory rules and collective agreements protecting the employee.

16. It follows that, in the case of a contract of employment, it is appropriate to determine the place of performance of the relevant obligation, for the purposes of applying Article 5(1) of the Convention by reference not to the applicable national law in accordance with the conflict rules of the court seised but, rather, to uniform criteria which it is for the Court to lay down on the basis of the scheme and the objectives of the Convention.

17. In order specifically to define the place of performance, it must first be noted that, in *Ivenel* and *Shenavai*, the Court held that the rule on special jurisdiction in Article 5(1) of the Convention was justified by the existence of a particularly close relationship between a dispute and the court which may most conveniently be called on to take cognizance of the matter. In its judgments in *Shenavai* and *Six Constructions*, the Court added that, in view of the particular features of contracts of employment, it is the courts of the place in which the work is to be carried out which are best suited to resolving the disputes to which one or more obligations under such contracts may give rise.

18. Furthermore, in *Ivenel* and *Six Constructions*, the Court took the view that, in interpreting that provision of the Convention, account must be taken of the concern to afford proper protection to the party to the contract who is the weaker from the social point of view, in this case the employee.

19. Proper protection of that kind is best assured if disputes relating to a contract of employment fall within the jurisdiction of the courts of the place where the employee discharges his obligations towards his employer. that is the place where it is least expensive for the employee to commence, or defend himself against, court proceedings.

20. It follows that in relation to contracts of employment, the place of performance of the relevant obligation must be interpreted as meaning, for the purposes of Article 5(1) of the Convention, the place where the employee actually performs the work covered by the contract with his employer.

21. Where, as in this case, the work is performed in more than one Contracting State, it is important to interpret the Convention so as to

avoid any multiplication of courts having jurisdiction, thereby precluding the risk of irreconcilable decisions and facilitating the recognition and enforcement of judgments in States other than those in which they were delivered (Case 220/88 *Dumez France* and *Tracoba* [1990] ECR I-49, paragraph 18).

22. In that connection, the Court has held that, where the various obligations derive from the same contract and form the basis of the plaintiff's action, it is the principal obligation which must be relied on in order to determine jurisdiction (*Shenavai*, paragraph 19).

23. It follows that Article 5(1) of the Convention cannot be interpreted as conferring concurrent jurisdiction on the courts of each Contracting State in whose territory the employee performs part of his work.

24. Where the work entrusted to the employee is performed in the territory of more than one Contracting State, it is important to define the place of performance of the contractual obligation, within the meaning of Article 5(1) of the Convention, as being the place where or from which the employee principally discharges his obligations towards his employer.

25. In order to determine the place of performance, which is a matter for the national court, it is necessary to take account of the fact that, in this case, the work entrusted to the employee was carried out from an office in a Contracting State, where the employee had established his residence from which he performed his work and to which he returned after each business trip. Furthermore, it is open to the national court to take account of the fact that, when the dispute before it arose, the employee was carrying out his work solely in the territory of that Contracting State. In the absence of other determining factors, that place must be deemed, for the purposes of Article 5(1) of the Convention, to be the place of performance of the obligation on which a claim relating to a contract of employment is based.

26. It follows from all the foregoing considerations that Article 5(1) of the Convention must be interpreted as meaning that, in the case of a contract of employment in pursuance of which the employee performs his work in more than one Contracting State, the place of performance of the obligation characterising the contract, within the meaning of that provision, is the place where or from which the employee principally discharges his obligations towards his employer.

On those grounds, the Court, in answer to the question referred to it by the Cour d'Appel, Chambéry, by judgment of 17 March 1992, hereby rules:

Article 5(1) of the Convention of 27 September 1968 on Jurisdiction and the Enforcement of Judgments in Civil and Commercial Matters must be interpreted as meaning that, in the case of a contract of employment in pursuance of which the employee performs his work in more than one Contracting State, the place of performance of the obligation characterising the contract, within the meaning of that provision, is the place where or from which the employee principally discharges his obligations towards his employer.

OPINION OF MR ADVOCATE GENERAL JACOBS

1. The Cour d'Appel, Chambéry, has asked for a preliminary ruling on the interpretation of Article 5(1) of the Convention of 27 September 1968 on Jurisdiction and the Enforcement of Judgments in Civil and Commercial Matters (hereafter 'the Brussels Convention'), as amended by the Convention of 9 October 1978 on the accession of Denmark, Ireland and the United Kingdom (OJ 1978 L 304, p.79).

2. Mr H. Geels, a Netherlands national, was appointed by Mulox IBC Limited (hereafter 'Mulox'), a company incorporated under English law with its registered office in London, as international marketing manager, with effect from 1 November 1988. During his employment with Mulox, Mr Geels resided at Aix-les-Bains (France) and appears to have used his home as an office and base of operations. Initially he performed his task of canvassing customers and establishing a distribution system for Mulox products in Germany, Belgium, the Netherlands and Scandinavia, which countries he visited frequently. It appears from a report of the year's business which he sent to his employer in December 1989 that after visiting Germany, Belgium and spain he pursued his marketing activities during 1989 in Germany and then in Scandinavia, Belgium and the Netherlands - French territory being excluded from his area of responsibility until September 1989. According to a memorandum which Mr Geels prepared for his employer, dated 19 April 1990, it was not until January 1990 that he worked with Mulox agents in France and serviced his employer's French customers. Dissatisfied with the results of Mr Geels' work, Mulox decided to dispense with his services and the employment relationship seems to have ended on 7 May 1990, when he wrote to Mulox acknowledging the termination of his contract and demanding compensation in lieu of notice equal to 12 months' salary, plus damages.

3. Mr Geels took the matter to the Conseil des Prud-hommes, Aix-les-Bains, which, having held that it had jurisdiction under Article 5(1) of the Brussels Convention and that the dispute was governed by French law, gave a

judgment largely favourable to Mr Geels. Mulox appealed against that judgment to the Cour d'Appel, Chambéry, arguing principally that the French courts had no jurisdiction because the place of performance of the employment contract covered the whole of Europe and the defendant's place of establishment was in London. It argued in the alternative that the contract was governed by English law, which was chosen by the parties and indicated by the Rome Convention of 19 June 1980 on the Law Applicable to Contractual Obligations (OJ 1980 L 266, p.1) as the Law of the employer's place of establishment, and that Mr Geels was not entitled under English law to compensation in lieu of notice, compensation for dismissal or damages. It argued in the further alternative that Mr Geels' claims were unfounded under French law.

4. The Cour d'Appel, Chambéry, noted that, according to the Court of Justice's judgment in Case 133/81 *Ivenel* v *Schwab* [1982] ECR 1891, the obligation to be taken into account for the purposes of the application of Article 5(1) of the Brussels Convention in the case of claims based on different obligations arising under a contract of employment was the obligation which characterised the contract. The French court observed that in that judgment the Court of Justice indicated that it was desirable for disputes arising from contracts of employment to be brought before the coruts of the State whose law governed the contract and that, according to the trend in conflict rules, as reflected in Article 6 of the Rome Convention, the law applicable to a contract of employment was determined by reference to the obligation characterising the contract, which was normally the obligation to carry out work. The French court took the view that in the present case, under the aforesaid Article 6, the contract was probably governed by English law. Doubting therefore whether Article 5(1) of the Brussels Convention should be interpreted so as to confer jurisdiction on the French courts in the circumstances of the present case, the Cour d'Appel referred the following question to the Court of Justice for a preliminary ruling:

'Does the application of the jurisdiction rule under Article 5(1) of the Brussels Convention of 27 September 1968 require the obligation characterising the employment contract to have been performed wholly and solely in the territory of the State of the court seised of the dispute, or is it sufficient for its operation that part of the obligation - possibly the main part - has been peformed in the territory of that State?'

The relevant Convention provisions and case-law

5. Article 2 of the Brussels Convention lays down the general rule that persons domiciled in a Contracting State are to be sued in the courts of that State. The only exceptions to that rule, according to Article 3, are those provided for in Sections 2 to 6 of Title II of the Convention. They are justified by the fact that, as stated in the Jenard Report (OJ 1979 C 59, p.1, and p.22), 'there must be a close connecting factor between the dispute and the court with jurisdiction to resolve it'. The exceptions are subject to strict interpretation: Case 189/87 *Kalfelis* v *Schröder* [1988] ECR 5565, at paragraph 8, and Case 32/88 *Six Constructions* v *Humbert* [1989] ECR 341, at paragraph 18. One such exception

is contained in Article 5(1), which provides that: 'A person domiciled in a Contracting State may, in another Contracting State, be sued: 1. in matters relating to a contract, in the courts for the place of performance of the obligation in question'.

6. In order to apply that jurisdiction rule it is necessary to determine (a) the relevant obligation and (b) the place of performance of that obligation. As regards the first point, the general rule is that the obligation be taken into account for the purposes of applying Article 5(1) is the obligation which corresponds to the contractual right on which the plaintiff's action is based: Case 14/76 *de Bloos* v *Bouyer* [1976] ECR 1497, at paragraph 11. However, in the case of employment contracts the relevant obligation is the obligation which characterises the contract, usually the obligation to carry out work: *Ivenel* v *Schwab* (cited above, in paragraph 4), confirmed in Case 266/85 *Shenavai* v *Kreischer* [1987] ECR 239. In *Ivenel* v *Schwab* the Court justified that exception to the general rule for employment contracts on a number of grounds, including the view that jurisdiction should be conferred on the courts of the place closely connected with the dispute, the need to provide adequate protection for employees, the desirability of conferring jurisdiction on the courts of the State whose law governs the contract and the necessity of interpreting the Convention in such a way that a court is not compelled to find that it has jurisdiction to adjudicate on certain claims and not on others. In *Shenavai* v *Kreischer* the Court further justified its decision that in the case of employment contracts the relevant obligation is the obligation to perform work on the ground that employment contracts differ from other contracts inasmuch as 'they create a lasting bond which brings the worker to some extent within the organisational framework of the business of the undertaking or employer, and they are linked to the place where the activities are pursued, which determines the application of mandatory rules and collective agreements' (paragraph 16 of the judgment).

7. As regards the determination of the place of performance of the relevant obligation, the general rule is that that determination must be made in accordance with the law which governs the obligation in accordance with the conflict rules of the court seised: Case 12/76 *Tessili* v *Dunlop* [1976] ECR 1473. The unusual feature of that judgment is that the Court ruled that a term used in the Convention should be interpreted by reference to the national law of a specific country. More frequently the Court has held that the terms used in the Convention should be given an autonomous meaning to be determined in the light of the objectives of the Convention. One of the issues that will have to be decided in the present case is whether the rule laid down in *Tessili* v *Dunlop*, to the effect that the place of performance of the obligation in question should in general be determined by reference to the applicable national law, also applies to contracts of employment or whether in the employment field the place of performance must be determined in accordance with independent criteria to be formulated by the Court.

8. In most cases the determination of the place of performance of the characteristic obligation under a contract of employment is not subject to doubt, since the typical employee performs his work at a single location. The only case

in which the Court has had to rule in relation to a situation in which an employee worked in a number of different countries is *Six Constructions* (cited above, in paragraph 5). In that case the employee performed his obligations in a number of non-contracting States. The Court held that in such circumstances Article 5(1) of the Brussels Convention could not be relied upon to confer jurisdiction upon a territory within the scope of the Convention. More interestingly, however, the Court rejected the view that, where it was difficult or impossible to determine in which State the work was performed, the courts of the place of business through which the employee was engaged should have jurisdiction. The Court rejected that view, accepting the argument that it might operate unfairly to the detriment of the employee, since it would enable the employer to sue him at the employer's place of business, thus creating a *forum actoris* which would be contrary to the basic principle of the Brussels Convention.

9. It should be noted that Article 5(1) of the Brussels Convention has now been amended by Article 4 of the San Sebastian Convention of 26 May 1989, which provides for the accession of Spain and Portugal to the Brussels Convention (OJ 1989 L 285, p.1). A further sentence has been added to Article 5(1), which now reads: 'A person domiciled in a Contracting State may, in another Contracting State, be sued:

1. in matters relating to a contract, in the courts for the place of performance of the obligation in question; in matters relating to individual contracts of employment, this place is that where the employee habitually carries out his work, or if the employee does not habitually carry out his work in any one country, the employer may be sued in the courts for the place where the business which engaged the employee was or is now situated'.

10. However, as the Commission pointed out in its written observations, the San Sebastian Convention entered into force, as regard France, the Netherlands and Spain, on 1 February 1991, in accordance with Article 32 thereof. The amendments made by the San Sebastian Convention apply only to legal proceedings instituted after its entry into force in the State of origin (Article 29(1)). Since it is clear from the order for reference that Mr Geels instituted proceedings against Mulox before 1 February 1991, the version of the Brussels Convention which is applicable in the present case is the 1978 version established by the Convention on the accession of Denmark, Ireland and the United Kingdom.

11. For the sake of completeness I will mention to other Conventions which may cast some light on the issues before the Court. The Lugano Convention of 16 September 1988 (OJ 1988 L 319, p.9) extended the principles of the Brussels Convention to the countries of the European Free Trade Association. Article 5(1) of the Lugano Convention, which is not applicable to the present case, provides that: 'A person domiciled in a Contracting State may, in another Contracting State, be sued:

1. in matters relating to a contract, in the courts for the place of performance of the obligation in question; in matters relating to individual contracts of employment, this place is that where the employee habitually carries out his work, or if the employee does not habitually carry out his work in any

one country, this place shall be the place of business through which he was engaged'.

12. The amendments made to Article 5(1) of the Brussels Convention by the San Sebastian Convention were modelled on the Lugano Convention but account was also taken of the comments made by the Court in the *Six Constructions* judgment, which was delivered after the adoption of the Lugano Convention: see the Report on the San Sebastian Convention by M. de Almeida Cruz, M. Desantes Real and P. Jenard (OJ 1990 C 189, p. 35, at pp. 44 and 45). As a result, under the San Sebastian Convention, the jurisdiction based on the place of the business which engaged the employee is available only to the employee. Under the Lugano Convention it is available to both parties. An unusual feature of Article 5(1) of the Lugano Convention is that it is based party on a legal fiction: where the work is not habitually performed in a single country, the place of performance is deemed to be the place of the business ('*établissement*' in the French version) which engaged the employee, even though neither the employer nor the employee may have been required to perform any obligations under the contract at that place. Although the San Sebastian Convention lays down a similar jurisdiction rule, it does so without recourse to legal fictions: it simply provides that the employer may be sued at a particular place without pretending that that is the place of performance of any obligation under the contract.

13. The Rome Convention of 19 June 1980 on the Law Applicable to Contractual Obligations, which came into force on 1 April 1991, lays down choice-of-law rules for application in contractual disputes. The basic rule, laid down in Article 3, is that a contract is governed by the law chosen by the parties. Article 6(2) provides that: '... a contract of employment shall, in the absence of choice in accordance with Article 3, be governed:

(a) by the law of the country in which the employee habitually carries out his work in performance of the contract, even if he is temporarily employed in another country; or

(b) if the employee does not habitually carry out his work in any one country, by the law of the country in which the place of business through which he was engaged is situated;

unless it appears from the circumstances as a whole that the contract is more closely connected with another country, in which case the contract shall be governed by the law of that country'.

14. The Rome Convention applies in each Contracting State to contracts made after the date on which the Convention entered into force with respect to that State (Article 17). The Court does not yet have jurisdiction to interpret the Rome Convention and it is in any event not the Court's task to give the courts of the Contracting States any guidance on the determination of the *lex causae*. In *Ivenel* v *Schwab* the Court did, however, refer to the Rome Convention and indicated that it was desirable to interpret Article 5(1) of the Brussels Convention in such a way as to confer jurisdiction on the courts of the country whose substantive law governed the contract of employment. I shall say more on that subject later.

The observations submitted to the Court

15. Written observations have been submitted by the French and German Governments and by the Commission. The French Government considers that Article 5(1) of the Brussels Convention may now be interpreted in the light of the San Sebastian Convention; therefore, since the employee did not habitually carry out his work in a single country, jurisdiction should be conferred upon the courts of the State in which the business which engaged him is or was situated. That would, according to the French Government, ensure that the choice of forum coincides with the choice of law, since the contract is in its view governed by English law pursuant to Article 6(2) of the Rome Convention.

16. The German Government takes the view that it is sufficient for part of the characteristic obligation to have been performed within the territorial jurisdiction of the court seised for jurisdiction to be conferred upon that court pursuant to Article 5(1) and favours conferring jurisdiction, in circumstances in which the obligation was performed in a number of different States, on the courts of the place which coincides with the employee's domicile, in this instance the French courts. Paradoxically, the German Government, like the French Government, considers that its proposed solution has the advantage that the choice of forum and the choice of law coincide, since it believes that, under Article 6(2) of the Rome Convention, the law governing the contract is French law on the ground that the contract bears close links with France.

17. The Commission points out that, according to the judgment in *Tessili* v *Dunlop* (cited above, in paragraph 7), the place of performance of the obligation in question is to be determined by the law which governs the obligation according to the conflict rules of the court before which the proceedings are brought. However, the Commission questions whether it is appropriate to apply that solution to contracts of employment and suggests that it would be preferable to give an autonomous definition of the concept of place of performance in relation to such contracts. According to the Commission, the considerations which led the Court to treat contracts of employment as a special category for the purposes of the identification of the relevant obligation also justify treating those contracts differently with regard to the determination of the place of performance of that obligation. The Commission notes that that approach is confirmed by the San Sebastian Convention, which gives an autonomous definition of the place of performance of employment contracts, but considers that a similar result can be reached on the basis of the 1978 version of the Convention.

18. As regards the content of the autonomous definition of the place of performance, the Commission considers that, where the work is undertaken in several Contracting States, jurisdiction should be conferred upon the courts of the place in which the work is habitually carried out. The Commission suggests that in the present type of case that place will normally be the place where the employee has his office and where he centralises orders from clients. Where it is impossible, on the facts, to establish a principal place of performance of the obligation, the Commission concludes that Article 5(1) should not apply and that

jurisdiction should be determined according to the general principle laid down in Article 2 of the Convention.

The choice between a national and an autonomous interpretation of the term 'place of performance'

19. The simplest solution - and one which would, moreover, be entirely consistent with the existing case-law - would be (a) to confirm the ruling in *Ivenel* v *Schwab* to the effect that the relevant obligation for the purpose of applying Article 5(1), in disputes arising out of a contract of employment, is the obligation which characterises the contract (normally the obligation to perform work) and (b) to confirm the ruling in *Tessili* v *Dunlop* to the effect that the place of performance of the relevant obligation is to be determined by reference to the law which governs the obligation according to the conflict rules of the court before which the proceedings are brought. If such an approach were taken, there would be no need for the Court to give further consideration to the criteria to be used in determining the place of performance of an employment contract under which the employee works in a number of Contracting States. That would be an issue for the national court to resolve in accordance with the law applicable to the contract under its own conflict rules.

20. Like the Commission, I do not think that that would be an appropriate solution. I say so, notwithstanding that in *Ivenel* v *Schwab* the Court cited *Tessili* v *Dunlop* (at paragraph 7) and repeated the general rule that the place of performance is to be determined in accordance with the applicable national law (see also the comments of Advocate General Reischl at p.1904). That was, however, very much an *obiter dictum*, since there does not seem to have been any doubt in that case that the employee was required to work in a single Contracting State and so the interpretation of the term 'place of performance' was never in issue; the case was concerned with the issue which obligation should be taken into account for the application of Article 5(1).

21. An autonomous interpretation of the terms used in the Convention is preferable in principle because it helps to secure the uniform application of the Convention and thus contributes to the realisation of its underlying purpose, which is to unify the jurisdiction rules of the Contracting States. Such unification is inevitably impeded if the meaning of the terms used in the Convention varies according to the applicable law. That doubtless explains why the Court has always regarded autonomous interpretation as the norm and has resorted to interpretation by reference to national law only in exceptional cases where special considerations applied. But the grounds given by the Court in *Tessili* v *Dunlop* for determining the place of performance by reference to national law do not seem nearly so compelling in relation to a contract of employment, especially if the relevant obligation is the obligation to perform work (see paragraphs 22 and 23, below). Moreover, the grounds given in *Ivenel* v *Schwab* and *Shenavai* v *Kreischer* for treating contracts of employment differently from other contracts as regards the determination of the relevant obligation seem to apply with equal force to the

determination of the place of performance of that obligation (see paragraph 24, below).

22. In *Tessili* v *Dunlop* the Court justified recourse to national law for the purpose of determining the place of performance on the ground that it was impossible for the Court to give substantial guidance on the interpretation of that concept 'having regard to the differences obtaining between national laws of contract and to the absence at this stage of legal development of any unification in the substantive law applicable'. In that case a German buyer claimed damages from an Italian seller as a result of the latter's alleged breach of an obligation to deliver goods of sound quality; the seller, whose seat was in Como, had delivered the goods to a carrier in Como appointed by the buyer. All legal systems contain rules for determining the place of performance of that type of obligation; those rules are often of a highly technical nature, they vary according to the type of contract (cif, fob, ex works etc.), they take into account legal presumptions about the intention of the parties and they are anything but uniform. It would have been manifestly inappropriate for the Court to attempt to devise a uniform rule and impose it on the courts of the Contracting States. Similar considerations apply to pecuniary obligations, whose place of performance is often determined by arbitrary rules stating that a debt is payable at the residence of the creditor or of the debtor. Once again it would be inappropriate for the Court to impose a uniform rule even for the purpose of determining jurisdiction.

23. Those difficulties do not arise in relation to contracts of employment, once it is accepted that the relevant obligation is the employee's obligation to perform work. There is little scope for the application of technical rules of law in order to determine where someone does his job; it is largely a question of fact. It may not be an easy question of fact, if the person works in more than one place. but no major difficulty would ensue if the Court laid down a uniform test for determining jurisdiction in such cases.

24. It is clear from the judgments in *Ivenel* v *Schwab* and in *Shenavai* v *Kreischer* that the overriding reason for treating employment contracts as a special case is the existence of a close and enduring connection with a particular legal system within which the employment relationship unfolds and under which the employee enjoys the protection of mandatory legislation (see in particular paragraphs 15 and 19 of *Ivenel* v *Schwab* and paragraph 16 of *Shenavai* v *Kreischer*). If then the aim, when applying Article 5(1) to employment contracts, must be to identify the country with which that close and enduring link exists, that leaves little scope for the application of any rule of national law which might locate the place of performance in some other country and which might, like Article 5(1) of the Lugano Convention, be based on a legal fiction. It follows that the place of performance should be determined, not by reference to the applicable national law, but on the basis of uniform criteria to be established by the Court. In other words the term 'place of performance' must be interpreted autonomously.

25. Confirmation of that view is provided - as the Commission has pointed out - by the San Sebastian Convention, which gives an autonomous definition of the place of performance in relation to individual contracts of employment. For

the reasons given above, I share the Commission's view that, even though the San Sebastian Convention does not apply to the present proceedings, it is possible to conclude on the basis of the earlier version of Article 5(1) that the term 'place of performance' must be interpreted autonomously.

The interpretation of the term 'place of performance'

26. The judgment in *Ivenel* v *Schwab* appears to suggest that one of the principal criteria governing the interpretation of Article 5(1) is the desirability of conferring jurisdiction on a court which will be able to apply its own law, rather than a foreign law. Thus in paragraph 15 the Court stated: 'It follows from the foregoing account that in the matter of contracts Article 5(1) of the Convention is particularly concerned to attribute jurisdiction to the court of the country which has a close connection with the case; that in the case of a contract of employment the connection lies particularly in the law applicable to the contract; and that according to the trend in the conflict rules in regard to this matter that law is determined by the obligation characterising the contract in question and is normally the obligation to carry out work'.

A variant of that idea appears in *Shenavai* v *Kreischer*, where the Court suggests (at paragraph 16) that Article 5(1) must be interpreted in such a way as to ensure the application of the 'mandatory rules and collective agreements' in force at the place where the work is done. The link between jurisdiction and the applicable law has also been stressed by the Cour d'Appel, Chambéry, in the order for reference and by the French and German Governments in their observations.

27. Desirable though it may be to confer jurisdiction over employment disputes on the courts of the country whose law is applicable, that will not always be possible in practice, even after the harmonisation of the choice-of-law rules effected by the Rome Convention. It is clear from Articles 3 and 6(1) of the Rome Convention that the parties are in principle free to choose the law applicable to a contract of employment; the chosen law might not necessarily be the law of the competent court, unless of course the parties include in their contract a jurisdiction clause specifying the courts of the country whose law is chosen as the *lex causae*. But even without those complications, there cannot be any certainty that the *lex causae* will always coincide with the *lex fori*, especially while the Court of Justice does not have jurisdiction to interpret the Rome Convention as well as the Brussels Convention. The present case is proof of that. The French court, which appears to read *Ivenel* v *Schwab* as establishing a necessary link between the applicable law and jurisdiction, considers that under Article 6 of the Rome Convention the contract between Mulox and Mr Geels is governed by English law. It could be argued that on a proper interpretation of Article 6 the contract is governed by French law. Certainly an English court might arrive at that conclusion, either on the basis of Article 6 of the Rome Convention or on the basis of its own rules of private international law. The paradoxical result is that if, after the Court's preliminary ruling, the dispute is finally litigated in France English law will be applied, whereas if the litigation

were to take place in England French law might be applied. (Article 15 of the Rome Convention excludes *renvoi.*) It must also be remembered that jurisdiction under Article 5(1) is not exclusive and that the plaintiff could in any event choose to sue at the defendant's domicile under Article 2 of the Brussels Convention, regardless of the place of performance. There must be many cases in which a contract of employment is governed by a law other than the law of the country in which the defendant is domiciled.

28. I conclude from the above that it would be a mistake to exaggerate the importance of the link between jurisdiction and *lex causae* in employment disputes. As regards the reference to mandatory rules in *Shenavai* v *Kreischer*, it is of course important to prevent an employer from evading the application of legislation which has been enacted for the protection of employees and which cannot be excluded by contract. But that merely begs the question which country's mandatory legislation should be applied. Matters such as working hours, annual leave, maternity leave and unfair dismissal should presumably be governed by the mandatory provisions of the *lex causae*. As regards matters such as safety and hygiene (e.g., rules on fire exits or the use of asbestos as an insulator), it would seem appropriate to apply the mandatory legislation in force at each of the several places of employment. Articles 6 and 7 of the Rome Convention contain provisions which appear to be capable of achieving the desired results, regardless of the country in which litigation takes place.

29. In my view, the true basis for the Court's ruling that the relevant obligation, for the purpose of applying Article 5(1) of the Brussels Convention in employment disputes, is the characteristic obligation under the contract of employment lies not so much in the desirability of establishing jurisdiction in the country whose law governs the contract, but rather in the simple proposition that the worker should be entitled to sue his employer (and vice versa, of course) at the place where he works. That is the natural forum for such disputes and it will in most cases be the most convenient forum for the employee. He should not be deprived of the convenience of suing there simply because his employer is domiciled in another Contracting State. That derogation from the general rule laid down in Article 2 of the Convention is justified by the particularly close connection between the dispute and the courts at the place where the work is done.

30. Having thus established the basis for the rule that jurisdiction is determined by the characteristic obligation in employment disputes, I turn to the relatively straightforward task of determining the place of performance of that obligation in a case such as the present, where the work was done in more than one Contracting State.

31. In view of the wording of the question formulated by the Cour d'Appel, two preliminary points need to be made. First, I do not think that the work must have been performed 'wholly and solely' in a single Contracting State in order for Article 5(1) to apply; where the worker is normally employed in one country, its courts should not lose jurisdiction simply because he makes an isolated excursion into another country in the performance of his duties. Secondly, where small portions of the work are performed in a number of

different countries, I do not think that Article 5(1) can be interpreted as conferring concurrent jurisdiction on the courts of all those countries, at the election of the plaintiff; if, for example, Mr Geels made a single business trip to Denmark, that should not mean that he could sue or be sued in Denmark. The connection with Denmark would be insufficiently strong to justify establishing jurisdiction there. Moreover, although the Court has occasionally interpreted the special jurisdiction rules of the Convention as granting the plaintiff a choice of jurisdictions (as in Case 21/76 *Bier* v *Mines de Potasse d'Alsace* [1976] ECR 1735, which was concerned with jurisdiction in tort where different considerations apply), the general rule is that Article 5(1) should be interpreted in such a way as to 'avoid, so far as possible, creating a situation in which a number of courts have jurisdiction in respect of one and the same contract': Case 14/76 *de Bloos* v *Bouyer* (cited above, in paragraph 6), at paragraph 9. It must also be borne in mind, as the Commission and the German Government point out, that if the plaintiff were given a choice of jurisdictions that choice would apply to actions brought by the employer as well as the worker. It would hardly be fair to allow the employer to remove the worker from his natural forum simply by requiring him to perform a small part of his duties in some other Contracting State.

32. It follows from those preliminary remarks that, where the work is performed in more than one Contracting State, Article 5(1) of the Brussels Convention should be construed as establishing jurisdiction at the principal place of employment. That term will in most situations be largely synonymous with the concept of the 'habitual' place of employment used in Article 6 of the Rome Convention and in the Lugano and San Sebastian Conventions. However, the expression 'principal place of employment' seems preferable, since it more effectively conveys the idea that one of the worker's several places of employment must in normal circumstances be more important than the others. The unhelpful nature of the term 'habitual' is demonstrated by the facts of the present case: a person who is employed in several States may not have a habitual place of employment in any of them, but may yet have a principal place of employment in one of them. The question which place is the principal place of employment is largely a question of fact and must ultimately be left to the national court, though the Court of Justice may offer some guidance in the light of the established facts of the case. Bearing in mind the need for caution, since our knowledge of the facts is necessarily limited, I will confine myself to the following remarks.

33. Where a person employed as a commercial representative has an office in one Contracting State, which he uses as a base for his operations, and from time to time travels from that base to other Contracting States for the purpose of visiting his clients, there must be a strong presumption that his principal place of employment is located at the place where he has his office, especially if, as in the present case, he also resides at that place. It is there that he receives instructions from his employer; it is from there that he communicates with his clients by post, telephone, telefax, etc., from there that he plans his business trips to other Contracting States and to that place that he returns after each trip. Even if he

spends more than half of the year travelling in other countries and does not in fact visit a single client in the country in which he has his office, it seems to me very difficult to rebut the presumption that his principal place of employment is located at the place where he has his centre of operations.

34. I will briefly make three final points. First, the German Government argued that in preference to jurisdiction at the principal place of employment, which might be difficult to determine, it would be more practical to use the worker's domicile as the connecting factor; he could thus sue at the place where he lives, provided - I assume - that part of his work is performed there. In the present case that approach produces a satisfactory result because Mr Geels' office was situated in his residence. There is, however, no guarantee that it would always produce a satisfactory result. If, for example, Mr Geels lived in Italy and had his office and centre of operations just across the border in France and if he occasionally visited clients in Italy, the German Government's approach would mean that he could sue in the Italian courts under Article 5(1), even though an insignificant part of his work was done in Italy. I do not see how the worker's domicile can be a decisive connecting factor for the purposes of Article 5(1).

35. Secondly, it is conceivable that unusual cases will occur in which two or more work-places are equally important. If, for example, Mr Geels managed Mulox's French office in Aix-les-Bains and its Italian office in Turin and spent roughly half his time at each of those places, it might be difficult to classify one of them as principal and the other as subsidiary. The Commission implies that in such a case Article 5(1) of the Brussels Convention should cease to apply and that Mr Geels would have to sue Mulox under Article 2 at its domicile in England, even though he had never worked there at all. Such a result would, in my view, be regrettable and unfair. It would be as illogical as saying that Mr Smith and Mr Jones are both equally deserving of promotion and that, in order to avoid making a difficult choice between them, the promotion should be given to Mr Brown, whose merits are considerably less. Even in difficult cases it should be possible to find relevant criteria for giving priority to one place of employment rather than another (e.g., the place where social security contributions and income tax are paid or the place where the employee's salary is paid). In the rare cases in which it is not possible to identify a principal place of employment, it would be reasonable, notwithstanding what I said earlier about the need to avoid a multiplicity of forums, to allow the plaintiff to sue at any of the places which have an equal claim to be the principal place of employment.

36. Thirdly, although Mulox could be sued in England, where it has its registered office, under Article 2 of the Brussels Convention, I disagree with the French Government's view that the English courts could acquire jurisdiction under Article 5(1) of the Convention. As the French Government recognises, such a result could only be achieved under the new version of Article 5(1) introduced by the San Sebastian Convention. The old version relied on a single connecting factor: namely, the place of performance of the obligation in question, which the Court has held to mean, in employment disputes, the place where the work is performed. The San Sebastian Convention has introduced a

substitute connecting factor (namely, the place where the business which engaged the employee was or is situated) which applies only for the benefit of the employee and only where he is not habitually employed in a single country. That substitute connecting factor is entirely different from the one used in the old version of Article 5(1) and it may have the result of conferring jurisdiction on the courts of a country in which no obligation under the contract was to be performed. Clearly such a result could not be justified under the old version of Article 5(1) and there can be no case for applying the new version in proceedings instituted before its entry into force. Consequently, if in the present case it is impossible to identify the principal place of employment, recourse must be had, not to the new rule introduced by the San Sebastian Convention, but to the general jurisdiction rule contained in Article 2 of the Brussels Convention.

37. That is not to say, however, that the amendments made by the San Sebastian Convention should be disregarded entirely. The substitute connecting factor introduced by that Convention is capable of producing somewhat anomalous results: if, for example, Mr Geels had been engaged in Luxembourg by an entity which had since transferred itself to Italy, that might be sufficient to confer jurisdiction on the courts of Luxembourg or Italy, even though he had never worked in either country. That highlights the importance of making a determined effort to identify a principal (or habitual) place of employment. It will thus be possible to ensure that jurisdiction is conferred on the courts of a country which has a genuine connection with the dispute - a result that will not always be possible if recourse is had to the substitute connecting factor introduced by the San Sebastian Convention. For that reason I consider that, if the San Sebastian Convention were applicable in a case such as the present one, the term ‘habitually’ should not be construed too literally but should be read as indicating the principal place of employment.

Conclusion

38. Accordingly, I am of the opinion that the question submitted to the Court by the Cour d’Appel, Chambéry, should be answered as follows:

Article 5(1) of the Convention of 27 September 1968 on Jurisdiction and the Enforcement of Judgments in Civil and Commercial Matters must be interpreted as meaning that in disputes arising from a contract of employment under which work is performed in more than one Contracting State jurisdiction is conferred on the courts for the principal place of employment. It is for the national court to determine that place in the light of all the relevant facts. In the case of an international marketing manager who has an office in one Contracting State which serves as his centre of operations and address for correspondence and from which he travels from time to time to other Contracting States and non-contracting States for the purpose of visiting clients, that office will normally constitute the principal place of employment, unless there is some factor of such a kind as to establish a closer connection with another Contracting State.

Case C-288/92 - 29 June 1994

Custom Made Commercial Ltd
v
Stawa Metallbau GmbH

Special jurisdiction - Article 5(1) - Court of the place of performance of a contractual obligation - Determination of the place of performance according to the substantive law, including, if appropriate, the uniform law on international sales, applicable according to the conflicts rules of the court seised.

Summary

The place of performance of the obligation in question was chosen as the criterion of jurisdiction in Article 5(1) of the Convention on Jurisdiction and the Enforcement of Judgments in Civil and Commercial Matters because, being precise and clear, it fits into the general aim of the Convention, which is to establish rules guaranteeing certainty as to the allocation of jurisdiction among the various national courts before which proceedings in matters relating to a contract may be brought. That criterion makes it possible for a defendant to be sued in the courts for the place of performance of the obligation in question, even where the court thus designated is not that which has the closest connection with the dispute.

The court before which the matter is brought must determine in accordance with its own rules of conflicts of laws, including, if appropriate, a uniform law, what is the law applicable to the legal relationship in question and define, in accordance with that law, the place of performance of the contractual obligation in question. Article 5(1) of the Convention, as amended by the Convention on the Accession of the Kingdom of Denmark, Ireland and the United Kingdom of Great Britain and Northern Ireland, must be interpreted as meaning that, in the case of a demand for payment made by a supplier to his customer under a contract of manufacture and supply, the place of performance of the obligation to pay the price is to be determined pursuant to the substantive law governing the obligation in dispute under the conflicts rules of the court seised, even where those rules refer to the application to the contract of provisions such as those of the Uniform Law on the International Sale of Goods, annexed to the Hague Convention of 1 July 1964.

JUDGMENT OF THE COURT

Due, President, Moitinho de Almeida and Diez de Velasco, Presidents of Chambers, Kakouris, Schockweiler, Grévisse, Zuleeg, Kapteyn and Murray, Judges

1. By order of 26 March 1992, received at the Court on 30 June 1992, the Bundesgerichtshof referred to the Court for a preliminary ruling under the Protocol of 3 June 1971 on the interpretation by the Court of Justice of the Convention of 27 September 1968 on Jurisdiction and the Enforcement of Judgments in Civil and Commercial Matters (OJ 1978 L 304, p. 36) ('the Convention'), as amended by the Convention of 9 October 1978 on the Accession of the Kingdom of Denmark, Ireland and the United Kingdom of Great Britain and Northern Ireland (OJ 1978 L 304, p. 1 and - amended version - p. 77), a number of questions on the interpretation of Article 5(1) and the first paragraph of Article 17 of the Convention.

2. Those questions arose in proceedings between Stawa Metallbau GmbH ('Stawa'), which has its seat in Bielefeld (Germany), and Custom Made Commercial Ltd ('Custom Made'), which has its seat in London, concerning the payment by the latter of merely part of the price agreed under a contract for the supply of windows and doors to be manufactured by Stawa.

3. According to the order for reference, Stawa gave a verbal undertaking in London on 6 May 1988, following negotiations conducted in English, to supply the goods to Custom Made. The goods were to be used for a building complex in London. The contract, the first to be concluded between the parties, stipulated that payment was to be in sterling.

4. Stawa confirmed the conclusion of the contract by a letter of 9 May 1988 written in English, to which it attached for the first time its general business conditions written in German. Paragraph 8 of those general conditions stated that in the event of a dispute between the parties the place of performance and jurisdiction was to be Bielefeld. Custom Made did not raise any objection to those general conditions.

5. When Custom Made paid only part of the stipulated price, Stawa brought proceedings for recovery of the balance before the Landgericht (Regional Court) Bielefeld. On 13 December 1989 that court delivered a default judgment in which it ordered Custom Made to pay to Stawa the sum of £144,742.08 plus interest.

6. In its application to have that judgment set aside, Custom Made submitted, *inter alia*, that the German courts lacked international jurisdiction. On 9 May 1990 the Landgericht Bielefeld delivered an interlocutory judgment declaring Stawa's claim to be admissible.

7. Custom Made appealed against that decision to the Oberlandesgericht (Higher Regional Court) Hamm, once again claiming that the German courts lacked international jurisdiction.

8. The Oberlandesgericht dismissed that appeal by judgment of 8 March 1991, in which it based the international jurisdiction of the German courts on Article 5(1) of the Convention, in conjunction with the first part of Article 59(1) of the Uniform Law on the International Sale of Goods annexed to the Hague Convention of 1 July 1964 *(United Nations Treaty Series*, 1972, Vol. 834, p. 107 *et seq.*), which provides that the buyer must pay the price to the seller at the seller's place of business or, if he does not have a place of business, at his habitual residence.

9. Custom Made brought an appeal on a point of law before the Bundesgerichtshof against the judgment of the Oberlandesgericht.

10. The Bundesgerichtshof took the view that the dispute gave rise to problems of interpretation of the Convention and for that reason decided to stay the proceedings until the Court had delivered a preliminary ruling on the following questions:

'1. (a) Is the place of performance under Article 5(1) of the Brussels Convention on Jurisdiction and the Enforcement of Judgments in Civil and Commercial Matters to be determined pursuant to the substantive law applicable to the obligation in issue under the conflicts rules of the court hearing the case where the case concerns a claim for payment of the price brought by the supplier against the customer under a contract for manufacture and supply, according to the conflicts rules of the court hearing the case that contract is governed by uniform sales law and under that law the place of performance of the obligation to pay the price is the place of establishment of the plaintiff supplier?

(b) In the event that the Court of Justice replies in the negative to Question 1(a): How is the place of performance under Article 5(1) of the Convention to be determined in such a case?

2. In the event that according to the answers to Questions 1(a) and (b) the German courts cannot derive jurisdiction from Article 5(1) of the Convention:

(a) Can a jurisdiction agreement validly be made under the third hypothesis in the second sentence of Article 17, first paragraph, of the Convention (in the 1978 version) where after the oral conclusion of a contract the supplier confirms the conclusion of the contract in writing and that written confirmation is accompanied for the first time by general business conditions containing a jurisdiction clause, the customer does not dispute the jurisdiction clause, there is no trade practice at the place where the customer is established to the effect that the absence of response to such a document is to be regarded as assent to the jurisdiction clause, the customer is not aware of any such trade practice and it is the first time that the parties have done business with each other?

(b) In the event that the Court of Justice replies in the affirmative to Question 2(a): Is that also true where the general business conditions containing the jurisdiction clause are in a language which the customer does not understand and is not that in which the contract was negotiated and concluded and where the written confirmation of the contract, written in the language in which the contract was negotiated and concluded, refers generally to the attached general business conditions but not specifically to the jurisdiction clause?

3. In the event that the Court of Justice replies in the affirmative to Questions 2(a) and (b): In relation to a jurisdiction clause contained in general business conditions which meets the requirements laid down in Article 17 of the Convention for a valid jurisdiction agreement, does Article 17 preclude further examination, under the national substantive law which is applicable in accordance with the conflicts rules of the court hearing the case, of the question whether the jurisdiction clause is validly incorporated in the contract?'

Question 1(a)

11. In this question, as elucidated by the grounds of the order for reference, the national court asks whether Article 5(1) of the Convention is to be understood as meaning that, in the case of a claim for payment by a supplier against his customer under a contract for manufacture and supply, the place of performance of the obligation to pay must be determined pursuant to the substantive law applicable to the obligation in issue under the conflicts rules of the court seised, even if those rules refer to the application to the contract of provisions such as those of the Uniform Law on the International Sale of Goods, annexed to the Hague Convention of 1 July 1964.

12. Article 2 of the Convention sets out the general rule that the jurisdiction of a court is based on the place of the defendant's domicile, although Article 5 also confers jurisdiction on other courts, the choice of which is a matter for the applicant. This freedom of choice was introduced in view of the existence in certain well-defined cases of a particularly close relationship between a dispute and the court which may most conveniently be called upon to take cognizance of the matter (see Case 12/76 *Tessili* v *Dunlop* [1976] ECR 1473, paragraph 13). However, Article 5 does not establish that connecting factor itself as the criterion for the choice of the competent forum. It is not possible for an applicant to sue a defendant before any court having a connection with the dispute since Article 5 lists exhaustively the criteria for linking a dispute to a specific court.

13. Article 5(1) provides in particular that a defendant may, in matters relating to a contract, be sued in the courts 'for the place of performance of the obligation in question'. That place usually constitutes the closest connecting factor between the dispute and the court having jurisdiction over it and explains why that court has jurisdiction in contractual matters (see Case 266/85 *Shenavai* v *Kreischer* [1987] ECR 239, paragraph 18).

14. Although the connecting factor is the reason which led to the adoption of Article 5(1) of the Convention, the criterion employed in that provision is not the connection with the court seised but, rather, only the place of performance of the obligation which forms the basis of the legal proceedings.

15. The place of performance of the obligation was chosen as the criterion of jurisdiction because, being precise and clear, it fits into the general aim of

the Convention, which is to establish rules guaranteeing certainty as to the allocation of jurisdiction among the various national courts before which proceedings in matters relating to a contract may be brought.

16. It has been submitted, certainly, that the criterion of the place of performance of the obligation which specifically forms the basis of the applicant's action, a criterion expressly laid down in Article 5(1) of the Convention, may in certain cases have the effect of conferring jurisdiction on a court which has no connection with the dispute, and that, in such a case, the criterion explicitly laid down should be departed from on the ground that the result it yields would be contrary to the aim of Article 5(1) of the Convention.

17. That last argument cannot be accepted, however.

18. The use of criteria other than that of the place of performance, where that confers jurisdiction on a court which has no connection with the case, might jeopardize the possibility of foreseeing which court will have jurisdiction and for that reason be incompatible with the aim of the Convention.

19. The effect of accepting as the sole criterion of jurisdiction the existence of a connecting factor between the facts at issue in a dispute and a particular court would be to oblige the court before which the dispute is brought to consider other factors, in particular the pleas relied on by the defendant, in order to determine whether such a connection exists and would thus render Article 5(1) nugatory.

20. Such an examination would also be contrary to the purposes and spirit of the Convention, which requires an interpretation of Article 5 enabling the national court to rule on its own jurisdiction without being compelled to consider the substance of the case (see Case 34/82 *Peters* v *ZNAV* [1983] ECR 987, paragraph 17).

21. It follows that under Article 5(1), in matters relating to a contract, a defendant may be sued in the courts for the place of performance of the obligation in question, even where the court thus designated is not that which has the closest connection with the dispute.

22. It is accordingly necessary to identify the 'obligation' referred to in Article 5(1) of the Convention and to determine its 'place of performance'.

23. The Court has ruled that the obligation cannot be interpreted as referring to any obligation whatsoever arising under the contract in question, but is rather that which corresponds to the contractual right on which the plaintiff's action is based (see Case 14/76 *De Bloos* v *Bouyer* [1976] ECR 1497, paragraphs 10 and 13).

24. Having allowed an exception in the case of contracts of employment presenting certain special features (see, in particular, Case 133/81 *Ivenel* v *Schwab* [1982] ECR 1891), in paragraph 20 of its judgment in Shenavai, cited above, the Court confirmed that the obligation referred to in Article 5(1) is the contractual obligation which forms the actual basis of the legal proceedings.

25. That interpretation was endorsed on the conclusion of the Convention of 26 May 1989 on the Accession of the Kingdom of Spain and the Portuguese Republic to the Convention on Jurisdiction and the Enforcement of Judgments in Civil and Commercial Matters (OJ 1989 L 285, p. 1). On that occasion the rule in Article 5(1) of the Convention was maintained in the same terms and was supplemented by a single exception relating to contracts of employment which had already been recognized by way of interpretation in the Court's case-law cited above.

26. With regard to the 'place of performance', the Court has ruled that it is for the court before which the matter is brought to establish under the Convention whether the place of performance is situated within its territorial jurisdiction and that it must for that purpose determine in accordance with its own rules of conflict of laws what is the law applicable to the legal relationship in question and define, in accordance with that law, the place of performance of the contractual obligation in question (see *Tessili*, cited above, paragraph 13, as referred to in paragraph 7 of *Shenavai*, cited above).

27. That interpretation must also be accepted in the case where the conflicts rules of the court seised refer to the application to contractual relations of a 'uniform law' such as that in issue in the main proceedings.

28. That interpretation is not called in question by a provision such as Article 59(1) of the Uniform Law, under which the place of performance of the obligation on the buyer to pay the price to the seller is the seller' place of business or, if he does not have a place of business, his habitual residence, subject only to the proviso that the parties to the contract have

not stipulated a different place for the performance of that obligation under Article 3 of that Law.

29. It follows that Article 5(1) of the Convention must be interpreted as meaning that, in the case of a demand for payment made by a supplier to his customer under a contract of manufacture and supply, the place of performance of the obligation to pay the price is to be determined pursuant to the substantive law governing the obligation in dispute under the conflicts rules of the court seised, even where those rules refer to the application to the contract of provisions such as those of the Uniform Law on the International Sale of Goods, annexed to the Hague Convention of 1 July 1964.

30. In view of the reply to Question 1(a), it is not necessary to reply to the other questions asked by the national court.

On those grounds, the Court, in answer to a question referred to it by the Bundesgerichtshof, by order of 26 March 1992, hereby rules:

Article 5(1) of the Convention of 27 September 1968 on Jurisdiction and the Enforcement of Judgments in Civil and Commercial Matters, as amended by the Convention of 9 October 1978 on the Accession of the Kingdom of Denmark, Ireland and the United Kingdom of Great Britain and Northern Ireland, must be interpreted as meaning that, in the case of a demand for payment made by a supplier to his customer under a contract of manufacture and supply, the place of performance of the obligation to pay the price is to be determined pursuant to the substantive law governing the obligation in dispute under the conflicts rules of the court seised, even where those rules refer to the application to the contract of provisions such as those of the Uniform Law on the International Sale of Goods, annexed to the Hague Convention of 1 July 1964.

OPINION OF MR ADVOCATE GENERAL LENZ

A - Introduction

1. In its request for a preliminary ruling, the Bundesgerichtshof (Federal Court of Justice) raises questions concerning the interpretation of two important provisions of the Brussels Convention, namely Article 5(1) on jurisdiction in respect of the place of performance and (possibly) Article 17 on jurisdiction

agreements. According to the particulars given by the national court, those two provisions are applicable either in the 1978 version or in the (identical) 1982 version.

2. The questions arose in proceedings in which Stawa Metallbau GmbH seeks in the court for the place at which its registered office is located, Bielefeld, from a party to a contract with it, Custom Made Commercial Ltd, (part) payment for doors and windows of its manufacture.

3. Those articles were intended for a building complex in London. The price agreed was denominated in sterling. The contract on which the claim is based was the first one concluded between the parties. It was concluded orally in London on 6 May 1988 after negotiations conducted in English.

4. The plaintiff confirmed the conclusion of the contract by a letter of 9 May 1988 written in English. That letter contains the following passage: 'We refer to our meeting on May 6th and confirm your order for the manufacturing of windows and doors for the Project "Cranbrook Estate", subject to our terms of sale and supply. ...'.

5. That letter was accompanied for the first time by the plaintiff's general business conditions written in German, Paragraph 8 of which reads as follows:
'Paragraph 8: Jurisdiction
Where the purchaser is a registered trader, a legal person governed by public law or a special entity governed by public law, the place of performance and jurisdiction for all disputes between the parties which may arise out of the contractual relationship shall be Bielefeld.'

6. The defendant did not dispute those business conditions.

7. The Bundesgerichtshof held that the contract in question was governed by the Uniform Law on the International Sale of Goods (the 'Uniform Law') forming the annex to the Hague Convention of 1 July 1964. According to the first part of Article 59(l) of the Uniform Law, which is applicable in this case, the place of performance of the obligation to pay the purchase price is the seller's place of business or, if he does not have a place of business, his habitual residence.

8. As regards the procedure before the national courts, it should be observed that the plaintiff first obtained default judgment before the Landgericht (Regional Court) Bielefeld under which the defendant was ordered to pay it the sum at issue. The defendant applied to set aside that judgment, upon which the Landgericht, by interlocutory judgment, held the claim to be admissible. The Oberlandesgericht (Higher Regional Court) Hamm dismissed the defendant's appeal against that judgment. It based the jurisdiction of the German courts on Article 5(1) of the Brussels Convention, since it held that, under Article 59 of the Uniform Law, the plaintiff's head office was the place of performance within the meaning of that provision.

9. In an appeal on a point of law against the judgment of the Oberlandesgericht Hamm, the Bundesgerichtshof requested the Court of Justice for a preliminary ruling on the following questions:

'1. (a) Is the place of performance under Article 5(1) of the Brussels Convention on jurisdiction and the enforcement of judgments in civil and commercial matters to be determined pursuant to the substantive law applicable to the obligation in issue under the conflicts rules of the court hearing the case where the case concerns a claim for payment of the price brought by the supplier against the customer under a contract for manufacture and supply, according to the conflicts rules of the court hearing the case that contract is governed by uniform sales law and under that law the place of performance of the obligation to pay the price is the place of establishment of the plaintiff supplier?

(b) In the event that the Court of Justice replies in the negative to question 1(a):

How is the place of performance under Article 5(1) of the Convention to be determined in such a case?

2. In the event that according to the answers to questions 1(a) and (b) the German courts cannot derive jurisdiction from Article 5(1) of the Convention:

(a) Can a jurisdiction agreement validly be made under the third hypothesis in the second sentence of Article 17, first paragraph, of the Convention (in the 1978 version) where after the oral conclusion of a contract the supplier confirms the conclusion of the contract in writing and that written confirmation is accompanied for the first time by general business conditions containing a jurisdiction clause, the customer does not dispute the jurisdiction clause, there is no trade practice at the place where the customer is established to the effect that the absence of response to such a document is to be regarded as assent to the jurisdiction clause, the customer is not aware of any such trade practice and it is the first time that the parties have done business with each other?

(b) In the event that the Court of Justice replies in the affirmative to question 2(a):

Is it also true where the general business conditions containing the jurisdiction clause are in a language which the customer does not understand and is not that in which the contract was negotiated and concluded and where the written confirmation of the contract, written in the language in which the contract was negotiated and concluded, refers generally to the attached general business conditions but not specifically to the jurisdiction clause?

3. In the event that the Court of Justice replies in the affirmative to questions 2(a) and (b):

In relation to a jurisdiction clause contained in general business conditions which meets the requirements laid down in Article 17 of the Convention for a valid jurisdiction agreement, does Article 17 preclude further examination, under the national substantive law which is applicable in accordance with the conflicts rules of the court hearing the case, of the question whether the jurisdiction clause is validly incorporated in the contract?'

B - Appraisal

The national court's first question

10. I - Article 5(1) of the Brussels Convention, which has to be considered

as a result of the national court's first question, reads as follows: 'A person domiciled in a Contracting State may, in another Contracting State, be sued: 1. in matters relating to a contract, in the courts for the place of performance of the obligation in question ...'.

11. As can clearly be seen from the national court's order, it wishes to clarify the concept contained in that provision of 'the place of performance of the obligation in question'. More precisely, it seeks to establish whether the meaning of that concept - 'the place of performance' - should be determined, in cases such as this, 'pursuant to the substantive law applicable to the obligation in issue under the conflicts rules of the court hearing the case'. If that question is answered in the negative, the national court wishes to know in what (other) way the place of performance should be determined.

12. II - In my view, in order to resolve those problems it is important to take a more detailed look at their context, namely Article 5(1) of the Convention - the source of the concept at issue - and its place in the Brussels Convention and the relevant case-law of the Court.

13. (1) As far as the aim of Article 5(1) is concerned, it appears from the Jenard Report that the adoption of special rules of jurisdiction in the Convention was justified 'by the fact that there must be a close connecting factor between the dispute and the court with jurisdiction to resolve it'.

14. With regard specifically to Article 5(1), the Jenard Report lists a number of examples showing the interest in defining the jurisdiction of the court for the place of performance in this way: 'The court for the place of performance of the obligation will be useful in proceedings for the recovery of fees: the creditor will have a choice between the courts of the State where the defendant is domiciled and the courts of another State within whose jurisdiction the services were provided, particularly where, according to the appropriate law, the obligation to pay must be performed where the services were provided. This forum can also be used where expert evidence or inquiries are required.'

15. That interpretation of the aim of Article 5(1) has been expressly adopted by the Court. In the judgment in *Tessili* v *Dunlop*, it is stated as follows with regard to the freedom of choice between courts having special jurisdiction under Article 5: 'This freedom of choice was introduced in view of the existence in certain well-defined cases of a particularly close relationship between a dispute and the court which may be most conveniently called upon to take cognizance of the matter.

16. In other words, that is to say, those of Advocate General Mancini the court of the place of performance of the obligation in question 'has by virtue of its physical proximity to the relationship at issue the best chances of determining the nature of that relationship in the fullest possible knowledge of the facts of the case'.

17. But in some instances the aim of Article 5(1) is interpreted differently.

18. Thus, for different reasons, the court of the place of performance is regarded as part of a system in which the advantages and risks with regard to jurisdiction are allocated fairly between the plaintiff and the defendant. Proponents of this view seek in this way - with very different results - to turn Article 5(1) into a counterweight to the rule set out in Article 2.

19. In this regard, I take the view that such a fair allocation of advantages and risks is a completely legitimate aim. Evidently, the authors of the Convention also took that sort of consideration into account. As the passages which I have just quoted from the Jenard Report show, however, the authors of the Convention started out from the premiss that Article 5(1) did in fact satisfy the principle of 'fair allocation', since it is justified on objective grounds connected with each individual 'dispute'.

20. It may be doubted whether such an idea stands up to critical examination in the context of the whole of the scope of Article 5(1). However, what is involved is a fundamental legal-policy choice which the Court is bound to respect. As a result, the Court should not try to define the aim of Article 5(1) systematically on the basis of its own conception of what is 'fair'. Moreover, in this regard the Court takes a particularly cautious approach. It is only in the field of employment law, which is characterized by the particular social importance of employment contracts, that the Court has allowed considerations relating to the protection of the weaker party to be taken into account, and solely as a complementary consideration to its considerations as to the court which is the most appropriate to try the case by virtue of its physical proximity.

21. Neither do I share the view that the justification for Article 5(1) is that the debtor should be answerable in the court for the place where he had to perform his obligation under the rules of the substantive law. That view seems to be based on the idea that that potential defendant undertook, by contract, to perform an obligation at a particular place and should therefore also accept that he should be sued there. Against that argument I would point out that, in so far as it is prescribed by statute, the place of performance under the substantive law does not warrant that conclusion. Such a conclusion is, moreover, all the more questionable in cases such as the one now before the Court. The place of performance of obligations to make payment under the substantive law generally determines merely the allocation of the risks and burdens connected with the transfer of money, the availability of which does not depend on the place of performance of the obligation in question. I cannot understand what that purely economic allocation of risks has to do with the question whether the debtor has to accept the creditor's suing him at a particular place.

22. (2) I would now turn to the concept of the place of performance, which, for the authors of the Convention, should, where Article 5(1) applies, yield a court physically proximate to the relationship at issue.

23. The concept of the *place of performance* originates in the *substantive* law.

24. In this sphere, *performance* constitutes an act by which the obligation due is fulfilled *vis-à-vis* the creditor, thus extinguishing his claim, If that claim is based on a contract - and it is only then that it can be covered by Article 5(1) - the word 'performance' also means that one of the contractual objectives defined by the parties has been achieved, at any event in the case of a claim relating to one of the two principal obligations (exchanged).

25. It might therefore be inferred from this that the place of performance, which is the spatial dimension of performance, is the place where the creditor's

claim is extinguished by the debtor's having performed the obligation required of him and, as regards the principal obligations, the place where the aim of the contract is wholly or partly achieved.

26. However, a two-fold reservation must be entered with regard to that conclusion. First, it does not accurately mirror the aim of the substantive provisions relating to the place of performance. Not only do those provisions have, in the absence of agreement, to crystallize the parties' obligations, they must also demarcate the areas for which each of the parties are responsible, in case irregularities should arise in carrying out the contract. Depending on the contractual obligation concerned, the accent falls sometimes on the one objective, sometimes on the other. As regards the obligation to pay the contract price, determination of the place of performance serves, as I have already explained, principally to allocate risks. This is also true of the rule applicable in this case, set out in Article 59(1) of the Uniform Law, which provides that the purchaser's obligation to make payment is to be performed at the creditor's place of business. That rule is based on the view that the person from whom a sum of money is due has to bear the risk attaching to the payment operation.

27. Secondly, it should be pointed out that, in demarcating the parties' responsibilities in this way, the place of the act of performance and the place at which performance *achieves its outcome* may differ. Article 19(2) of the Uniform Law will serve as an example. According to that provision, where the contract involves carriage of the goods and no other place for delivery has been agreed upon, delivery is to be effected by handing over the goods to the carrier for transmission to the buyer. The aim of the contract, which is to give the purchaser possession of the goods, is not achieved until he takes delivery of them. In contrast, the seller's responsibility comes to an end once he has duly handed the goods over to the carrier (see also Articles 97(1) and 96 of the Uniform Law).

28. It should be added that, under the *substantive* law, each contractual obligation may have its own place of performance. It is therefore not precluded that, even if they are closely related economically, two obligations arising under a single contract may have different places of performance.

29. (3) The conclusion to be reached from what has been considered so far is that a forum based on a concept derived from the substantive law is justified on *procedural grounds*, namely a ground such as physical proximity to the relationship at issue.

30. In this case, that tension is particularly striking. It is sufficient to observe that Article 59(1) of the Uniform Law serves primarily to allocate the risk, in any event in the present circumstances relating to payment.

31. Before going into the case-law of the Court of Justice, I would profit by that observation in order to avoid a misunderstanding which might arise from a superficial reading of the national court's order.

32. More specifically, I consider that the combination of Article 5(1) of the Convention and Article 59(1) of the Uniform Law should not be regarded as giving rise to difficulty merely because it causes jurisdiction to be based on the plaintiff's place of business or residence. Such a reservation could be justified only if a species of general 'antipathy' to conferring jurisdiction on the plaintiff's

courts were to be read into the Convention and became a criterion for correcting, where necessary, the outcome of an interpretation. Admittedly, it must be allowed that Article 2 of the Convention adopted the general rule that the courts of the defendant's domicile should have jurisdiction, whilst Article 3 ruled out the application of various national provisions conferring jurisdiction on the plaintiff's courts. Neither can it be contested that, in view of the aforementioned articles, 'apart from the cases expressly provided for, the Convention appears clearly hostile towards the attribution of jurisdiction to the courts of the plaintiff's domicile'. Yet such 'exceptions' to the conditions laid down by Article 5 et seq. are by no means rare. Articles 13 and 14 on jurisdiction over consumer contracts show this clearly. The court having jurisdiction under Article 5(3) (place where the harmful event occurred) may turn out, in the event, to be the court of the plaintiff's domicile. There is therefore no justification for inferring conclusions favouring a particular interpretation from the Convention's more or less marked 'antipathy' to the plaintiff's court.

33. The only cogent conclusion resulting from the system laid down by Articles 2, 3 and 5 et seq. seems to me to be that which the Court used as its starting point in the judgments in *Shearson Lehman Hutton* and *Dumez France*, namely that where an interpretation of Article 5 et seq. has the result that the court having jurisdiction is that of the plaintiff's domicile, particular care should be taken to see whether that interpretation accords with the aim of the provision in question. Consequently, the Bundesgerichtshof is at the heart of the matter in so far as it bases its doubts on the fact that the combination of Article 5(1) of the Convention and Article 59(1) of the Uniform Law means that 'as a general rule the courts for the place where ... the plaintiff ... is established have jurisdiction'.

34. (4) How has the Court reacted in decided cases to the structure of Article 5(1) as I have defined it?

35. (a) Already in its first two judgments on the Convention, which it delivered on 6 October 1976, the Court had to lay down the rules for determining the place of performance, on the one hand, as regards the choice of the obligation(s) to be taken into account and, on the other, as regards the choice of applicable provisions or principles from which the place of performance for that obligation (those obligations) arises.

36. As far as those two aspects are concerned, the Court came down in favour of an substantive interpretation of Article 5(1).

37. In accordance with the considerations which I have set out above, that is to say that, under the substantive law, obligations arising under a contract are not all bound to be performed at the same place, the Court held in *De Bloos* v *Bouyer*, which was concerned with claims of the grantee of an exclusive distribution contract towards its suppliers, that: '... for the purposes of determining the place of performance within the meaning of Article 5 ... the obligation to be taken into account is that which corresponds to the contractual right on which the plaintiff's action is based'.

38. According to the wording used by the Court of Justice, that solution strives to avoid, as far as possible, a situation in which a number of courts have jurisdiction in respect of one and the same contract: for that reason, the Court

refused to interpret Article 5(1) as 'referring to any obligation whatsoever arising under the contract in question'. In addition, it is based on the German and Italian wording of that article, which was applicable at the material time in the 1968 version.

39. However, the Court has attenuated that principle where the obligations at issue have taken the place of contractual obligations which have not been performed. In such case, the obligation for the purposes of Article 5(1) continues to be the contractual obligation whose non-performance is relied upon in order to support such claims. As a comparison of the judgment and the Opinion in that case shows, that principle also aims at avoiding a number of courts having jurisdiction and, more specifically, at encouraging related questions to be dealt with by the same court.

40. It was also on the basis of an approach guided by the substantive law that, in the judgment in *Tessili* v *Dunlop*, the Court laid down the criterion for choosing the principles and provisions for determining the actual place of performance.

41. According to that judgment, 'the place of performance of the obligation in question within the meaning of Article 5(1) of the Convention 'is to be determined in accordance with the law which governs the obligations in question according to the rules of conflict of laws of the court before which the matter is brought'.

42. Three points from the grounds of that judgment should be stressed.

43. The first relates to the criterion according to which it has to be assessed whether a concept in the Convention is to be interpreted independently - and hence in a manner common to all the Member States - or as a reference to the substantive rules which are applicable in accordance with the conflicts rules of the first court seised. In that connection, the Court of Justice held as follows: 'Neither of these two options rules out the other since the appropriate choice can only be made in respect of each of the provisions of the Convention to ensure that it is fully effective having regard to the objectives of Article 220 of the Treaty.'

44. The Court added a reservation concerning the restricted scope of the Convention: 'In any event, it should be stressed that the interpretation of the said words and concepts for the purpose of the Convention does not prejudge the question of the substantive rule applicable to the particular case.'

45. With regard to the choice between an independent interpretation and a reference to the conflicts rules of the forum, the Court initially opted for a pragmatic criterion: the aim should be an 'appropriate choice'. Account should be taken to that end of the fact that the Convention as such pursues very different aims: strengthening the legal protection of persons established in the Community with a view to the elimination of obstacles to legal relations and the resolution of disputes; equality of rights and obligations for the Contracting States and the persons concerned; the need to avoid a number of courts having jurisdiction; predictability as regards the application of the jurisdiction rules. In addition, each provision and indeed each concept appearing in the Convention has its own function, which may be more or less closely connected with the aforementioned

aims. Accordingly, even though in its more recent decisions it has shown a general preference for an independent interpretation, the Court has held that it was appropriate in the final analysis to reserve the possibility in each case of choosing an appropriate interpretation.

46. The second important point in the grounds of the judgment in *Tessili* v *Dunlop* is, as I have already pointed out, the reference made to the aims of the special jurisdictions provided for in the Convention. The Court apparently did not consider it questionable to satisfy the aims of the Convention by referring to the *lex causae.* That is not surprising, since none of parties which submitted observations in that case questioned that solution. Admittedly, the desirability of an independent interpretation was discussed, but from quite different points of view. The discussion essentially came down to weighing the advantages of such an interpretation from the point of view of the uniform application of the Convention against certain disadvantages, namely the ensuing difficulties in the field of comparative law and the (undesired) effects on the substantive law of the Member States.

47. For his part, Advocate General Mayras concentrated on which contractual obligations ought to be taken into account for the purposes of Article 5(1) where the subject-matter of the proceedings is not the seller's principal obligation to deliver the goods, but a claim by the purchaser based on defective performance. After stating that in such case it was appropriate to take account of the said principal obligation, he discussed the application of the *lex causae* relatively briefly. As in the case of the observations submitted to the Court, he discussed only the question of the harmonization (or lack of harmonization) of the conflict rules and of the substantive law.

48. We are now touching on the third relevant point of the grounds of the judgment in *Tessili* v *Dunlop* for present purposes. In that point, the Court discussed whether in the interests of harmonization of the concept of the place of performance it might go further than merely referring to the *lex causae.* According to the Court, that was impossible 'at this stage of legal development' regard being had to 'the differences obtaining between national laws of contract and to the absence ... of any unification in the substantive law applicable ..., [especially since] the determination of the place of performance of obligations depends on the contractual context to which these obligations belong'.

49. If a balance-sheet is drawn up, on the basis of all these considerations, of the judgments in *De Bloos* v *Bouyer* and *Tessili* v *Dunlop* it will be seen that in neither of those judgments did the Court take physical proximity as a reason for examining whether it was necessary to deviate from the substantive law (of the contract) in interpreting Article 5(1). The Court's considerations on the basis of which it examined such a step were of another kind: in so far as in the judgment in *De Bloos* v *Bouyer* it decided that the same court that had jurisdiction in respect of the principal obligations should have jurisdiction in respect of obligations derived from principal obligations, it sought to avoid more than one court having jurisdiction over related issues. The question considered in the judgment in *Tessili* v *Dunlop* as to whether it was necessary to go beyond

a reference to the *lex causae* was raised in view of the possible aim of unifying the concept of the place of performance.

50. (b) In its subsequent case-law, the Court gradually introduced special rules for disputes relating to employment law, but, in general, remained consistent with that which I have just described. I shall now consider those matters in detail.

51. In *Ivenel* v *Schwab*, cited above, which was delivered in response to a request for a preliminary ruling from the French Cour de Cassation (Court of Cassation), what was at issue was various claims of a commercial traveller following the alleged termination of his contract, which the national appeal court described as a contract of employment. The national court asked what was the obligation to be taken into account for the purposes of the criterion defined in *Tessili* v *Dunlop*. Consequently, the Court had to consider whether it should in that case adhere to the principles set out in *De Bloos* v *Bouyer* or diverge from them. It decided to do the latter, declaring that: 'The obligation to be taken into account for the purposes of the application of Article 5(1) of the Convention ... in the case of claims based on different obligations arising under a contract of employment as a representative binding a worker to an undertaking is the obligation which characterizes the contract'.

52. The Court gave three different reasons for that decision. *First*, it took account of the aim of Article 5(1) of conferring jurisdiction on a court which has *a close connection with the case*. In the case of a contract of employment, the Court saw that connection as lying 'particularly in the law applicable to the contract', which 'as a general rule, ... contains provisions protecting the worker'. According to the trend in the conflict rules in regard to that matter, that law is determined by the obligation characterizing the contract in question, which is normally the obligation to carry out work. It will usually be the law of the place where the work is carried out.

53. *Secondly*, the Court took account of the idea of protecting the party who is the weaker from the social point of view.

54. Lastly, basing itself on the considerations set out in the judgment in *De Bloos* v *Bouyer*, the Court came down in favour of interpreting the Convention in such a way that 'the national court is not compelled to find that it has jurisdiction to adjudicate upon certain claims but not on others'.

55. In the judgment in *Shenavai* v *Kreischer*, the Court felt itself constrained - albeit the question raised did not arise in the sphere of employment law, but related to an action brought by an architect with a view to recovering his fees - to supplement the arguments set out in *Ivenel* v *Schwab* relating to physical proximity to the effect that, in employment disputes, proceedings should, where possible, be brought before a court for the place where the work in question was performed, since it is, generally speaking, the substantive provisions of that place which will be applicable. In the Court's view, the fact that employment contracts and other similar contracts 'create a lasting bond which brings the worker to some extent within the organizational framework of the business of the undertaking or employer' also militates in favour of the solution adopted in *Ivenel* v *Schwab*.

56. After the Court confirmed the *Ivenel* v *Schwab* case-law, as refined by the judgment in *Six Constructions*, it had to consider the case of *Mulox*, which was also concerned with a dispute relating to a contract of employment. However, unlike the cases with which it had hitherto had to deal, *Mulox* was not concerned with the choice of the obligation to be taken into account, but with determining the place of performance of the obligation in question.

57. The Court came to the conclusion that in the field of employment law the place of performance should not be determined in accordance with the *lex causae*, but - independently - on the basis of uniform criteria which, in its view, should be defined on the basis of the system and aims of the Convention. The difficulties arising from the different views as to *the place of performance* of the *obligation in question* which the Court had used in *Tessili* v *Dunlop* as justification for deciding that the place of performance should be determined in accordance with the lex causae did not exist in the sphere of employment law. In that sphere, the employee's obligation to carry out the agreed work as the characteristic obligation of the contract of employment is the obligation in question within the meaning of Article 5(1). The Court referred in this connection to the particularities of contracts of employment which it had already described in its earlier case-law: they create a lasting bond bringing the worker within the framework of the employer's business and are linked to the place where the activities are pursued, which determines the application of mandatory rules and collective agreements.

58. As to where it was appropriate in this case actually to localize the place of performance (which was to be determined independently), the Court held that it was the place where the employee actually carried out the activity agreed with his employer. The Court referred in this regard to the criteria which it had evolved in its previous case-law, namely a close connection with the dispute and protection of the weaker party.

59. If you would bear with me, I would now take stock of the case-law from *Ivenel* v *Schwab* to *Mulox*.

60. It is clear at first glance that the criteria set out in *Mulox* with a view to determining the place of performance were already determined in advance by the choice which the Court had made since *Ivenel* v *Schwab* as regards the obligation in question. In order to justify that solution, the Court based itself in Mulox solely on arguments on which it had already relied in *Ivenel* v *Schwab* (as refined in subsequent judgments). The decision in favour of an independent interpretation of the place of performance had therefore been taken ever since the judgment in *Ivenel* v *Schwab*.

61. Having regard to the grounds of the judgment in *Ivenel* v *Schwab*, it can be seen that, as early as this, the Court already took the view that to determine the place of performance on the basis of the substantive law of the contract did not square with the aim of Article 5(1) - at any event, not in the sphere of contracts of employment.

62. Accordingly, a twofold conclusion can be reached.

63. First, the case-law discussed above shows that although the Court intended that the place of performance should continue to be determined as a

general rule on the basis of the substantive law of the contract, it will depart from that principle where its application, *in a given case, manifestly does not square with the aim of Article 5(1)*. To my mind, this correctly constitutes a *via media* between two extremes (which should be rejected): (a) a rigid application of Article 5(1) which sticks strictly to its wording, but departs from its aim and (b) an interpretation which takes account solely of the court's proximity to the dispute, but which might undermine the concept of place of performance and turn Article 5(1) into a vague *forum conveniens* rule. On closer inspection, the Court had already left the door open in *Tessili* v *Dunlop* to making such an exceptional distinction between the substantive and procedural places of performance (cf. section 44, *supra*).

64. Secondly, it turns out that the problem of the choice of the obligation to take into consideration and that of the test to be used in order to determine the place of performance are closely linked. Any interpretation which, by diverging from the substantive law of the contract (and also from the wording of some language versions of Article 5(1), takes account of an obligation other than the obligation at issue constitutes a step towards an independent interpretation (in relation to the substantive law governing the contract). Such an interpretation affects, intentionally or unintentionally, the relationship between the aim of Article 5(1) and the outcome of applying it. Conversely, such a correction may - as one conceivable means - be deliberately employed in order to take account of the aim of Article 5(1) when it is applied. Such a manner of proceeding may, as the case-law discussed above shows, constitute a better potential solution than determining the place of performance by using comparative law, especially since the use of comparative law does not necessarily guarantee that criteria unsuited to determine a court physically proximate to the relationship at issue will be replaced by more appropriate criteria. Determining the place of performance by means of comparative law may instead reinforce the harmonizing effect of Article 5(1): the criterion of the lex causae is a uniform one. However, in view of its very nature, it is relatively remote from the actual determination of the place of performance.

65. In this context, I would further point out that the concept of 'independent interpretation' should not lead one to suppose that there are only two possibilities available in any given case: that is to say, to determine the place of performance *absolutely consistently* with the substantive law or *completely independently* of it. On the contrary - and still in the interest of having an interpretation consistent with the aims of the provision in question - many intermediate solutions are conceivable. I would mention in this context as an example only the judgment in *De Bloos* v *Bouyer*, which I have already discussed. In that judgment, the Court held, as regards claims for damages or claims seeking the dissolution of the contract in question, that the contractual obligation to be taken into account was the obligation the non-performance of which was relied upon in support of such claims. That step towards an independent interpretation of Article 5(1) was again accompanied, however, by a reference to the *lex causae*: 'In the case of actions for the payment of compensation by way of damages, it is for the national court to ascertain

whether, *under the law applicable to the contract*, an independent contractual obligation or an obligation replacing the unperformed contractual obligation is involved.

66. Let us now turn to the case-law not dealing with contracts of employment.

67. In *Shenavai* v *Kreischer*, the Court held that, in proceedings relating to an action for the recovery of fees brought by an architect for the preparation of building plans, the obligation to be taken into account was the contractual obligation on which the legal action was actually based. In order to justify that solution, as against the different one which it reached in *Ivenel* v *Schwab*, the Court first rehearsed the arguments to the effect that an employee was brought within the framework of the employer's business and that the contracts were localized at the place where the activities were pursued, which determined the application of mandatory rules and collective agreements. The Court added that: 'When no such particularities exist, it is neither necessary nor appropriate to identify the obligation which characterizes the contract and to centralize at the place of performance thereof jurisdiction, based on place of performance, over disputes concerning all the obligations under the contract. The variety and multiplicity of contracts as a whole are such that the above criterion might in those cases create uncertainty as to jurisdiction, whereas it is precisely such uncertainty which the Convention is designed to reduce.

On the other hand, no such uncertainty exists for most contracts if regard is had solely to the contractual obligation whose performance is sought in the judicial proceedings. The place in which that obligation is to be performed usually constitutes the closest connecting factor between the dispute and the court having jurisdiction over it, and it is this connecting factor which explains why, in contractual matters, it is the court of the place of performance of the obligation which has jurisdiction.'

68. Those considerations show, in the first place, that the Court clearly recognized the imperfect nature of Article 5(1), since it allows that the place of performance of the obligation at issue (only) 'usually' constitutes the closest connecting factor between the dispute and the court having jurisdiction over it. Secondly, the Court's considerations only cover a limited number of the problems arising. On the one hand, the question as to whether the rules relating to the place of performance of the obligation to make payment are such as to confer jurisdiction on a court physically proximate to the relationship at issue was not discussed. Although the German Government drew attention to the fact that taking account of the characteristic obligation of the contract corresponded more nearly to the aim of Article 5(1) than taking account of the obligation to make payment (which was at issue in *Shenavai* v *Kreischer*), neither it or any of the other parties concerned, nor the Court raised the idea that Article 5(1) had manifestly not achieved its objective. On the other hand, as clearly emerges from paragraph 17 of the judgment, the only alternative to the chosen situation which was discussed was that of '*centralizing*' at the place of performance of the '*obligation which characterizes the contract* ... jurisdiction ... over disputes concerning all the obligations under the contract'. The Court rejected that

approach on account of the 'uncertainty' which it would, in its view, create. Consequently, it can be considered that the question as to *whether* it is possible to effect limited corrections having predictable effects still remains open.

69. Outside the sphere of contracts of employment, mention should also be made of the judgment in *Zelger* v *Salinitri* in addition to *Shenavais* v *Kreischer*. That judgment was concerned with a clause relating to the place of performance with regard to the repayment of a loan. In it, the Court confirmed the *Tessili* v *Dunlop* case-law, since it held that the place of performance within the meaning of Article 5(1) was the place which had been 'specified by the parties in a clause which is valid according to the national law applicable to the contract'. The question as to whether that solution was warranted in practice by the 'existence of a direct link between the dispute and the court called upon to take cognizance of it' was not raised. The main theme of the judgment was the relationship between Article 5(1) and Article 17.

70. III - The reply to be given to the national court's first question should take account of all those considerations.

71. (1) The question raised by question 1(a), namely whether it is appropriate to diverge from the application of the lex causae has to be assessed in the light of the test formulated from the case-law: it must be ascertained whether its application in the instant case is manifestly inconsistent with the aim of Article 5(1).

72. In this connection, it should be observed that, in disputes relating to the payment of the purchase price - where the actual conclusion of the contract is not in issue -, it is a question in most cases as to whether the performance provided by the seller was duly effected. Of the courts which are geographically close to the events in connection with the performance of the contract, the one which is to be taken into consideration for the purposes of the aim contemplated by Article 5(1) is that which is in the best position to assess the due nature of that performance.

73. The first part of Article 59(1) of the Uniform Law results in contrast in the courts for the creditor's domicile systematically having jurisdiction, since the creditor should be placed at an advantage as far as the allocation of risks of international payment transactions is concerned. In my view, this in itself supports an independent definition of the place of performance. In that connection, account should be taken of the fact that, for the first part of Article 59(1) of the Uniform Law, the place of performance of the obligation to pay the purchase price is, by definition, independent of the place of performance of the obligation in kind (consideration), the alleged defective performance of which is generally the cause of the dispute about the payment of the purchase price. It is only in the case mentioned in the second part of the provision that the places of performance coincide.

74. It is therefore clear that the criterion set out in the first part of Article 59(1) is manifestly not able to confer jurisdiction on a court which is physically proximate to the relationship at issue. Consequently, question 1(a) should be answered in the negative.

75. (2) In order to answer question 1(b), that is to say, *how* the place of

performance is to be determined if question 1(a) is answered in the negative, a direct link can be made with that which I have already stated.

76. To my mind, it is not appropriate here to take into consideration the obligation to make payment, but the seller's obligation to provide the consideration. As is clear from the discussions above, in the case of contractual relations between the parties, it is a question of the 'place of performance' which most readily enables a court to be determined which is physically proximate to the relationship at issue. This is particularly true in this case, since, according to the judgment given on appeal by the Oberlandesgericht Hamm, to which the Bundesgerichtshof expressly refers, the windows delivered had to be to British technical and quality standards.

77. Before setting out this solution in somewhat more detail, I would describe very briefly its relationship with the judgments in *De Bloos* v *Bouyer* and *Tessili* v *Dunlop*, from which it in fact diverges only very slightly. As far as the judgment in *De Bloos* v *Bouyer* is concerned, it should be observed that the proposed solution does not refer to just 'any' contractual obligation, but to the one which is far more likely to result in the determination of a court physically proximate to the relationship than the obligation at issue. In addition, that solution is consistent with the principle set out in *De Bloos* v *Bouyer* and confirmed in *Shenavai* v *Kreischer*, to which some writers refer as the 'isolation principle', that as a general rule a place of performance is to be determined separately for each obligation. Only the method of determining the place of performance differs from that laid down in *De Bloos* v *Bouyer*.

78. As far as the judgment in *Tessili* v *Dunlop* is concerned, it should be observed that the *lex causae* continues to apply, albeit not for the purposes of determining the place of performance of the obligation at issue, but the place of performance of the counter-obligation of the other party.

79. However, that statement should be qualified somewhat with a view to the more detailed specification of the solution proposed. In this connection, I should like to set out the following considerations before setting forth my proposal.

80. The rules of the *lex causae* relating to the place of performance of the seller's obligation to supply the goods may, like the rules on the place of performance with regard to the payment of the purchase price, embody elements which serve solely to apportion the risk - more specifically in this case the carriage risk - and do not provide reliable indications about the economic objective of the seller's obligations. As I used such elements when I examined the rules on the place of performance of the obligation to make payment as a reason for diverging from the substantive law of the contract on the ground that those rules could not serve to determine a court which was physically proximate to the relationship at issue, it would seem illogical to use another method when considering the rules on the place of performance of the seller's obligation to deliver the goods. It should be held in that regard that, in the case of disputes about the payment of the price arising on account of the alleged defective performance of the counter-obligation - which I considered was the typical case - the court for the place at which the goods were intended to be supplied is, as a

general rule, nearer to the facts than the courts for the place from which they were sent. This is true irrespective as to which of those two places is the 'place of performance' under the substantive law and hence irrespective as to which of the contracting parties is to bear the carriage risk.

81. It therefore seems that the Bundesgerichtshof's question should be qualified in this way. It follows from the judgment given on appeal by the Oberlandesgericht Hamm that that court interpreted the clause delivery 'free site in London' simply as an agreement on the circumstances in which delivery was to be made. It seems that it therefore did not consider that London was the place of performance of the (plaintiff's) obligation in kind and this is precisely why it was *not* the *second part* of Article 59(1) of the Uniform Law but the first part which was applied.

82. IV - For all those reasons, I propose that the reply to questions 1(a) and (b) of the Bundesgerichtshof should be as follows: Where a supplier makes a claim against a customer for the payment of the price due under a contract for manufacture and supply to which the Uniform Law is applicable and the first part of Article 59(1) of the Uniform Law is applicable to that payment under the substantive law, the place of performance within the meaning of Article 5(1) of the Brussels Convention is the place agreed in the contract at which the goods are intended to be supplied, irrespective as to which of the parties have to bear the risk of conveying the goods to that place.

The national court's second question

General observations

83. The Bundesgerichtshof's second question is to be answered in the event that in view of the answer to the first question 'the German courts cannot derive jurisdiction from Article 5(1) of the Convention'. Since the place of performance within the meaning of that article, as I have just interpreted it, cannot be in Germany in this case, it is necessary to answer the second question.

84. In that question, the Bundesgerichtshof seeks to establish whether, in the circumstances described in the question, 'a jurisdiction agreement [can] validly be made' within the meaning of Article 17 of the Convention. As the Bundesgerichtshof considers that such agreement was not made 'in writing' (second sentence of the first paragraph of Article 17; the first hypothesis mentioned in that article) and was not 'evidenced in writing' (*loc. cit.*; second hypothesis), it opts for the *third hypothesis* mentioned in Article 17. That provision, which was added on the accession of new Member States in 1978, enables a jurisdiction agreement to be concluded, 'in international trade or commerce, in a form which accords with practices in that trade or commerce of which the parties are or ought to have been aware'.

85. It appears from the Schlosser Report that, in the case of the other two hypotheses contemplated by Article 17, the Court's interpretation 'does not cater adequately for the customs and requirements of international trade'. The authors of the addition to Article 17 sought in particular to attenuate the consequences of

the judgment in *Segoura*. In that case, faced with an orally concluded contract of sale embodying no oral jurisdiction agreement within the meaning of Article 17, the Court refused to give any effect to a letter of confirmation from the seller to which the latter had appended its general conditions of sale which did embody a jurisdiction clause. The Court held that such a clause did not form part of the contract unless the purchaser agreed to it in writing. The fact that the purchaser did not raise any objections against a confirmation issued unilaterally by the other party did not amount to acceptance on his part of the clause conferring jurisdiction unless the oral agreement came within the framework of a continuing trading relationship between the parties which was based on the general conditions of one of them, and those conditions contained a clause conferring jurisdiction. The Schlosser Report states in this regard that 'the requirement that the other party to a contract with anyone employing general conditions of trade has to give written confirmation of their inclusion in the contract before any jurisdiction clause in those conditions can be effective is unacceptable in international trade'.

86. In the following appraisal of the questions raised by the Bundesgerichtshof I shall consider the meaning of the provision in question in more detail.

Question 2(a)

87. I - In this part of the question, the Bundesgerichtshof starts by describing the *conduct of the parties* which might possibly form the basis of a valid jurisdiction clause (under the third hypothesis):

- after the oral conclusion of a contract, the supplier confirms the conclusion of the contract in writing;
- the written confirmation is accompanied for the first time by general business conditions containing a jurisdiction clause; and
- the customer does not dispute the jurisdiction clause.

88. The Bundesgerichtshof goes on to set out certain accompanying *factual and legal circumstances* which might be relevant:

- there is 'no trade practice' at the place where the customer is established to the effect that the absence of response to such a document is to be regarded as assent to the jurisdiction clause;
- the customer is not aware of any such trade practice; and
- it is the first time that the parties have done business with each other.

89. Since the Court has not yet had to consider the third hypothesis provided for in Article 17 (in its 1978 version), the Bundesgerichtshof has not related its question to the various conditions for the application of that provision, but to the provision as a whole. According to the Bundesgerichtshof, the question arises whether Article 17, despite its narrow wording, concerns not merely the form but also the substantive preconditions for a jurisdiction agreement. The question further arises, in its view, as to how the concepts of international trade or commerce and international trade practices, which must be defined more specifically, and the subjective factors which give rise to the application of that provision are to be interpreted.

90. It seems appropriate in these circumstances to discuss the conditions imposed by the provision at issue individually while taking account of the circumstances mentioned by the Bundesgerichtshof.

91. II - (1) First, it should be ascertained whether this case is concerned with '*international trade or commerce*' within the meaning of Article 17. That question, which has not been specifically argued before the Court, should, in my view, be answered in the affirmative. There is no doubt that the transaction covered by the jurisdiction clause, as a contract of sale relating to the supply of goods from one Contracting State to another the parties to which are established as commercial companies in those States, is *international* in character. Admittedly, that condition could be construed as limiting the application of the provision in question to specific commercial sectors capable of being clearly defined. It was this situation that the Select Committee on the European Communities of the House of Lords seems to have had in mind when it proposed adding a third case to Article 17. However, jurisdiction clauses in contracts going unnoticed - does not support such an interpretation. Without limiting the scope of the article in question *from the outset* in this way, it seems appropriate to take into consideration, when interpreting the concept of a commercial or trade practice and the subjective conditions for the application of the third hypothesis, any differences between institutionalized trade and commerce (in the commodities sector, for example) and other international transactions.

92. Since the parties to the contract at issue are commercial companies and both were acting in their own sector of business, there is no doubt to my mind that the transactions at issue relate to (international) *commerce or trade.*

93. (2) It should next be considered what guidance can be provided to the Bundesgerichtshof for the purposes of interpretation having regard to the obligation for a jurisdiction clause to be concluded in a '*form which accords with practices in that trade or commerce*'.

94. (a) As has been seen, the third hypothesis contemplated by Article 17 was introduced so as to authorize modes of concluding valid jurisdiction clauses other than clauses in writing or evidenced in writing. In view of the structure of Article 17, it is clear that jurisdiction agreements according with the, relevant 'practices in the trade or commerce' should be authorized as valid types of jurisdiction agreement.

95. In contrast, the scope of that criterion is not absolutely clear. As the Bundesgerichtshof has correctly observed, according to the wording of Article 17, it refers solely to the 'form' of the jurisdiction agreement at issue, and it may be asked whether it is not also supposed to relate to the agreement itself - namely to *consensus*.

96. In my view, the latter view is correct. Admittedly, the Commission rightly points out that the Schlosser Report regards the third hypothesis in Article 17 'merely' as a 'relaxation of the formal provisions' and raises the question as to whether 'questions of consensus other than the matter of form should be decided according to the national laws applicable or to unified EEC principles'. However, the aim of the 1978 amendment would not be achieved if merely a formal provision were involved. In the judgment in Segoura, the Court held that

there was no valid jurisdiction clause, precisely because there was no proof of actual consensus between the parties as required by Article 17: the fact that the purchaser does not respond to written confirmation does not 'amount to acceptance'. If the new version referred only to the form, the need for actual consensus would still have be examined *in accordance with that case-law*, without any relaxation being achieved having regard to the needs of international commerce or trade. More generally, it should be observed that, in accordance with a consistent line of cases of the Court, including *Segoura*, the formal requirements set out in Article 17 do not have an aim in themselves but perform the function of '[ensuring] that the consensus between the parties is in fact established'.

97. The Court of Justice confirmed this approach again very recently in the judgment in *Powell Duffryn*, which was concerned with a clause conferring jurisdiction contained in a company's statutes. After observing that in the legal systems of the Contracting States the statutes of a company are in writing and constitute the basic instrument governing the relations between a shareholder and the company, the Court held that '*irrespective of how shares are acquired*, every person who becomes a shareholder of a company *knows, or ought to know*, that he is bound by the company's statutes ...'.

98. As far as the instant case is concerned, it should be added that commercial practices concerning *purely formal* requirements in the field in question can arise only with great difficulty, if at all. Such requirements come under *procedural law*, the mandatory rules of which can be formulated differently and amended at any time by the Member States. As the Schlosser Report shows, it may, in contrast, very well be that, for the purposes of determining the court having jurisdiction, there exist commercial practices relating to the way in which *consensus is formed*, since that question is a matter of *substantive* law. Such practices, like that relating to absence of response to a commercial letter of confirmation, may be a mixture of elements relating to form and elements relating to substantive consensus. In other words, they may relate to a certain *form*, in the sense of the *manner* in which consensus is formed. The third hypothesis contemplated by Article 17 therefore refers to a situation in which the conformity of the parties' conduct with commercial practices, combined with certain subjective conditions, guarantees that which, outside its sphere of application, is guaranteed only by writing or 'evidence in writing': jurisdiction clauses must not pass unnoticed in a contract.

99. (b) It is no accident that the Bundesgerichtshof provides details of the parties' conduct and of the legal situation in the United Kingdom with a view to the interpretation of Article 17. The relevance of those factors is to be assessed depending on how the concept of 'commercial or trade practices' is understood, in particular where there is no response to a commercial letter of confirmation. This point is disputed in academic writing, where the following three different approaches are to be found:

- With regard to a particular method of reaching consensus, a commercial or trade practice means a *de facto* usage which is generally and continuously followed and regularly observed by the circles concerned in commercial transactions corresponding, objectively and from the point of view of their localization, to the commercial transaction at issue, and which warrants the conclusion that the conduct concerned embodies an agreement (or consent on the part of the party concerned). Article 17 confers legal effect on such a usage. From that point of view, the existence of a relevant commercial practices has to be *proved*.

- Under Article 17, in international trade the absence of a response to a commercial letter of confirmation may, by virtue of a commercial or trade practice, signify agreement to a jurisdiction clause added by that confirmation (in any event, where the parties are or ought to be aware of that practice). Such a practice does not have to be specifically proved.
- There is a commercial or trade practice with regard to a manner of reaching consensus where it is recognized by (a) legal system(s) to be determined that the parties conduct constitutes agreement (or consent) by virtue of a commercial or trade practice. The criterion for determining that legal system or those legal systems has to be established by interpreting Article 17.

100. I would propose that the Court should adopt the *first* approach set out above, for the following reasons.

101. The conclusion following from the second approach set out above, namely that the Convention itself recognizes the practice of the commercial letter of confirmation as a commercial practice is certainly not justified. It can, admittedly, be inferred from the Schlosser Report that the judgment in *Segoura*, cited above, which related to that practice, was the *reason* for the revamping of Article 17. However, it is not possible to determine the exact content of the commercial practice allegedly recognized. It is sufficient to observe in that regard that, in the States signatory to the Convention, there are completely different conceptions of the legal significance of the practice in question and that it cannot be ruled out that there are differences depending on the commercial sector in question.

102. The third approach which I described, which confers on Article 17 the character of a conflicts rule, or of a reference to a national conflicts rule, is linked directly to that consideration. As far as that approach is concerned, it must be objected that it may be difficult to determine in practice commercial practices in the field of international trade (except in those fields which are intrinsically international). However, that fact does not give rise to any argument according to which Article 17 can be interpreted in the sense sought by that view.

103. In the first place, it appears from the system of the provision in question, in particular the English and French versions, that the relevant commercial practices must relate to 'international trade'. The German version refers, albeit in a somewhat ambiguous manner, to 'internationale Handelsgebräuche' (international commercial usages). The introduction into Article 17, through the intermediary of conflicts rules, of local usages which are not proven to be imposed in the sphere of the relevant international trade would have the result of facilitating the incorporation of jurisdiction clauses to an extent exceeding that required by the reform. In that regard, attention should be drawn to the wording of the Lugano and San Sebastian Conventions, which, in addition

to the conditions laid down in the 1978 version, require that the usage should 'in such trade or commerce [be] widely known to, and regularly observed by, parties to contracts of the type involved in the particular trade or commerce concerned'. According to the Jenard/Müller Report on the Lugano Convention, 'having regard to the words "internationale Handelsbräuche" and "usages" which are used in the French and German versions of Article 17 of the Brussels Convention, it seems that there are at least no major differences in substance between the provisions concerned in the two Conventions'. To my mind, that commentary is hard to square with the new version if Article 17 of the 1978 version was a mere conflicts rule or a reference to national conflict rules.

104. Secondly, as I have already mentioned, the Court has viewed the formal requirements laid down in the first two hypotheses in Article 17 as guaranteeing actual consensus and has accordingly laid down certain *independent requirements with regard to consensus itself* in that regard, it has avoided bringing into that provision complex, very controversial problems relating to conflicts of laws. Moreover, regret has been expressed since the outset that Article 17 was not coupled with an express conflict rule on account of certain preconditions for consensus (namely legal capacity and agency). In my view, the interpretation of the third hypothesis in Article 17 should remain consistent with this and therefore, as in the case of the other two hypotheses, should give rise to an independent interpretation.

105. (c) The application of that solution to the present case calls for the following observations.

106. (aa) It should first be observed that the legal situation in the United Kingdom, as described by the Bundesgerichtshof, is not decisive in itself, no more than the legal situation in Germany: Article 17 is not a conflicts rule. I shall be returning shortly to the question of the - limited - importance of national law for the purposes of proving the existence of a commercial practice and as regards the subjective conditions for the application of Article 17.

107. (bb) I would next explain the importance, from two points of view, of the criterion which I have just put forward with a view to giving a useful answer to the questions raised by the Bundesgerichtshof. The first relates to the need for the practice in question to be sufficiently widespread, having regard to the characteristics of the transaction at issue. In order to achieve the aim of Article 17 when applying that criterion, only trade or commercial practices which are geographically and objectively related to transactions of the type at issue may be taken into account. The protection against jurisdiction clauses being incorporated unnoticed which Article 17 aims to afford would, for instance, not be achieved if in a case such as this reliance could be placed on practices in force in the automobile sector or in Franco-German trade.

108. The second point of view relates to the authority which the trade or commercial practice must have acquired in the sector concerned. For the purposes of Article 17, it must be established that the practice is regularly observed in circles involved in the particular trade or commerce. It is only on that condition, which is also prescribed by the Lugano and San Sebastian Conventions following the example of Article 9(2) of the Vienna Convention on

contracts for the international sale of goods, that the practice acquires the practical effectiveness which will enable it also to be legally recognized through Article 17. As regards the practice of the subsequent incorporation of general business conditions into a contract by means of a commercial letter of confirmation, the conditions for the third hypothesis to apply are fulfilled only where participants in the trade or commerce concerned regard conditions incorporated in this way as binding.

109. I would observe in passing that it is my impression that those conditions are not met by all transactions falling within the scope of the Convention. In fields characterized by frequent repetition of identical transactions in an essentially closed circle of traders, such practices find more fertile soil than elsewhere.

110. (cc) However that may be, it is for the tribunal of fact to carry out the necessary investigations into the circumstances which are relevant in regard to that criterion with the assistance of the International Chamber of Commerce or of a bilateral chamber of commerce.

111. When assessing the circumstances pleading for or against the existence of a commercial or trade practice, it is possible, in an individual case, also to take into account with all the requisite circumspection - the national legal systems concerned. The *emergence* and *continuance* of usages in international trade or commerce depend, *inter alia*, on the extent to which judicial notice is taken of such practices by the courts in the Member States. Thus, in trade between two Member States whose courts attach no importance to the practice of the commercial letter of confirmation in signifying possible consensus, a usage to that effect can scarcely ever come about. The contrary will apply where the courts in the two Member States are prepared to take judicial notice of such a usage. At the present stage of the proceedings, those indications - which are, of necessity, very general - should suffice.

112. (dd) This brings me to the last issue to be discussed in this context. As has been seen, according to the 1968 version of the Convention, jurisdiction clauses could be incorporated only in the ways covered by the first and second hypotheses set out in Article 17. Consequently, within the scope of that article, differing practices relating to the inclusion of clauses into contracts could not extend to jurisdiction clauses, even if such practices existed under other rules relating to incorporation. The old version of Article 17 necessarily precluded this. On that ground, when the trade or commercial practices are examined, it is necessary to ignore the effects of the old version of Article 17 on the incorporation of jurisdiction clauses. If the 1978 reform is to have practical effect, practices relating to other contractual provisions must decide the matter. In other words, It is necessary to interpret the third hypothesis in Article 17 as conferring on general practices the legal effects in the sphere of jurisdiction clauses which they were denied by the old version of Article 17.

113. (3) I would now turn to the subjective conditions of Article 17, where it provides that '*the parties are or ought to have been aware*' of the practices in trade or commerce.

114. Those conditions are intended to prevent jurisdiction clauses -

whatever the practices in a given trade or commerce - from having effects *vis-à-vis* persons who were unaware or should not have been aware of those practices and therefore were unaware or should not have been aware of the manners of incorporating clauses into a contract to which those usages relate.

115. If the criterion of 'practices in trade or commerce' is essentially a matter of fact, the same must also be true of the above-mentioned subjective conditions. Accordingly, account can be taken of all relevant circumstances.

116. As far as the present case is concerned, it appears from the order for reference that the customer was unaware of the commercial practice relied on, to the effect that absence of response to a letter of confirmation of the type described by the Bundesgerichtshof has to be regarded as assent to a jurisdiction clause. That fact is relevant in any event where the party concerned was not aware in a general way - irrespective of the question of jurisdiction clauses - of the commercial usage alleged by the other party.

117. In answering the question as to whether that party *ought to have been aware* of that practice, it is possible to take account of two of the circumstances which the Bundesgerichtshof has brought to the Court's notice: the fact that the alleged practice does not apply at the place where the customer has its head office and that this was the first time that the parties had done business. As far as the first point is concerned, the academic writings cited by the Bundesgerichtshof suggest that in English law generally - that is to say, not only in the sphere of jurisdiction clauses - absence of response to a commercial letter of confirmation to which general business conditions are appended for the first time is not regarded as signifying assent to the content of those conditions. In such a case, the practice in question cannot be regarded as being known to the customer, unless other circumstances (for instance, commercial contracts with other economic operators in the trade or commerce) sufficiently supporting the opposite view are relied upon and proved. This is also a matter for the tribunal of fact.

118. III - For all the above reasons, I consider that the reply to question 2(a) should be as follows: In the circumstances adverted to by the Bundesgerichtshof, a jurisdiction agreement can be validly made under the third hypothesis in the second sentence of Article 17, first paragraph, of the Convention only where a practice exists which is followed generally, continuously and regularly by the circles concerned in transactions which correspond, both objectively and in point of their localization, to the transaction at issue and warrants the conclusion that the parties' conduct implies assent to the content of the letter of confirmation and the general business conditions appended thereto.

If, in view of the fact that one of the parties was unaware of such a practice - if any -, the resolution of the dispute turns on whether that party ought to have been aware of that usage, the question should be answered in the negative if no such practice existed at the place at which that party has its head office and it was the first time that that party did business with a party adopting such a usage. Matters will be different where other circumstances are relied on and proved which bear out to a sufficient degree the fact that the party concerned ought to have been aware of the commercial practice in question.

Question 2(b)

119. The Bundesgerichtshof raised this part of the question in case a jurisdiction clause may be validly concluded in the circumstances set out in question 2(a). If, as regards the subjective conditions set out in Article 17, there should be no circumstances other than those set out in the order for reference, question 2(a) should be answered in the negative and there would be no need to answer question 2(b). I consider that if the Court should follow my view it should merely answer question 2(a).

120. Be that as it may, the question of the 'language risk' raised in the part of the question which I am now to consider does not seem to me to be particularly complex.

121. Reference should be made *in limine* to the judgment in *Elefanten Schuh*, according to which legislation of a Contracting State requiring a particular language to be used in private relations does not have to be taken into consideration in the field of application of Article 17. This should also hold good, however, of rules relating to the 'language risk' developed by case-law in a Member State, since such rules, like the legislation referred to in *Elefanten Schuh*, have an effect on the requirements relating to the manner in which the agreement is reached (form and substantive conditions).

122. In those circumstances, the Bundesgerichtshof asks whether a jurisdiction clause can be validly concluded regard being had to the following facts:

- the general business conditions appended to the letter of confirmation were in a language other than the language in which the contract was drawn up and the negotiations were conducted;
- the customer did not know that language; and
- the letter of confirmation written in the language in which the contract was negotiated and concluded, referred generally to the general business conditions but not specifically to the jurisdiction clause.

123. It is further known that this was the first time that the parties did business with each other.

124. In those circumstances - and in particular in the absence of any specific reference to the jurisdiction clause in the language in which the contract was drawn up and the negotiations were conducted it cannot be claimed as a general rule that the party concerned was given adequate notice of the jurisdiction clause. Consequently, a basic precondition for actual consensus would be absent. In such a case, if the third hypothesis in Article 17 is applied, a jurisdiction agreement could be concluded only if the practice in force itself authorized a language to be used other than the language in which the contract was drawn up and the negotiations were conducted. Question 2(b) should be answered to this effect.

The national court's third question

125. For completeness' sake, I would briefly rehearse the issues raised by

this question, that is to say, whether, in the event that a validly concluded jurisdiction clause under Article 17 is involved, there should be a 'further examination, under the national substantive law which is applicable in accordance with the conflicts rules of the court hearing the case, of the question whether the jurisdiction clause is validly incorporated in the contract'.

126. In the context in which this question is raised, it should be answered in the negative. Article 17 is intended to create, within its field of application, independent and, hence, uniform law. Article 17 provides an exhaustive definition of the requirements with regard to substantive consensus and the necessary forms for guaranteeing those requirements. Accordingly, there is no room for provisions of domestic law carrying out the same function in addition thereto. The third question should be answered to this effect.

C - Conclusion

127. For the reasons set out above, I propose that the Court should answer the questions raised by the Bundesgerichtshof as follows:

Question 1(a) and (b):

1. Where a supplier makes a claim against a customer for the payment of the price due under a contract for manufacture and supply to which the Uniform Law on the International Sale of Goods is applicable and the first part of Article 59(1) of the Uniform Law is applicable to that payment under the substantive law, the place of performance within the meaning of Article 5(1) of the Brussels Convention is the place agreed in the contract at which the goods are intended to be supplied, irrespective as to which of the parties has to bear the risk of conveying the goods to that place.

The reply to the following questions, in so far as they need to be answered, should be as follows:

2. (a) In the circumstances adverted to by the Bundesgerichtshof, a jurisdiction agreement can be validly made under the third hypothesis in the second sentence of Article 17, first paragraph, of the Convention only where a practice exists which is followed generally, continuously and regularly by the circles concerned in transactions which correspond, both objectively and in point of their localization, to the transaction at issue and warrants the conclusion that the parties' conduct implies assent to the content of the letter of confirmation and the general business conditions appended thereto.

If, in view of the fact that one of the parties was unaware of such a practice - if any - the resolution of the dispute turns on whether that party ought to have been aware of that usage, the question should be answered in the negative if no such practice existed at the place at which that party has its head office and it was the first time that that party did business with a party adopting such a usage. Matters will be different where other circumstances are relied on and proved which bear out to a sufficient degree the fact that the party concerned ought to have been aware of the commercial practice in question.

(b) Agreement on a jurisdiction clause cannot be validly concluded for the purposes of Article 17 by silence following receipt of a commercial letter of confirmation where the general business conditions attached to the letter of confirmation and containing the jurisdiction clause are in a language other than that in which the contract was concluded and the negotiations were conducted, the addressee of the letter does not know the language in question, no specific reference to that clause was made in the language in which the negotiations were conducted and the contract was concluded, and it is the first time that the parties did business with each other. The situation would be different only if the commercial practice in force itself authorized a language to be used other than the language in which the contract was concluded and the negotiations were conducted.

3. Rules of national law relating to the effective incorporation of contractual provisions and, in particular, of provisions set out in general business conditions and covering effective consensus and the form to be taken by such consensus are not applicable alongside Article 17 of the Brussels Convention. Accordingly, such rules of the national substantive law which is applicable in accordance with the conflicts rules of the court hearing the case cannot be used in order to determine whether a jurisdiction clause satisfying the conditions laid down by Article 17 has been validly incorporated into a contract.

Case C-383/95 - 9 January 1997

Petrus Wilhelmus Rutten
v
Cross Medical Ltd.

Article 5(1) - Courts for the place of performance of the contractual obligation - Contract of employment - Place where the employee habitually carries out his work - Work performed in more than one country.

Summary

Article 5(1) of the Convention of 27 September 1968 on Jurisdiction and the Enforcement of Judgments in Civil and Commercial Matters, as amended by the Convention of 26 May 1989 on the Accession of the Kingdom of Spain and the Portuguese Republic, must be interpreted as meaning that where, in the performance of a contract of employment, an employee carries out his work in several Contracting States, the place whee he habitually carries out his work, within the meaning of that provision, is the place where he has established the effective centre of his working activities. When identifying that place, it is necessary to take into account the fact that the employee spends most of his working time in one of the Contracting States in which he has an office where he organizes his activities for his employer and to which he returns after each business trip abroad.

JUDGMENT OF THE COURT

Mancini, President, Murray, Kakouris, Ragnemalm and Schintgen (Rapporteur), Judges

1. By judgment of 1 December 1995, received at the Court on 7 December 1995, the Hoge Raad der Nederlanden (Netherlands Supreme Court) referred to the Court for a preliminary ruling under the Protocol of 3 June 1971 on the interpretation by the Court of Justice of the Convention of 27 September 1968 on Jurisdiction and the Enforcement of Judgments in Civil and Commercial Matters (OJ 1972 L 299, p. 32), as amended by the Convention of 9 October 1978 on the Accession of the Kingdom of Denmark, Ireland and the United Kingdom of Great Britain and Northern Ireland (OJ 1978 L 304, p. 1, and - amended text - p. 77), by the Convention of 25 October 1982 on the Accession of the Hellenic Republic (OJ 1982 L 388, p. 1) and by the Convention of 26 May 1989 on the Accession of the Kingdom of Spain and the Portuguese Republic (OJ 1989 L 285, p. 1), hereinafter 'the Convention', three questions on the interpretation of Article 5(1) of the Convention.

2. The questions were raised in proceedings between Mr Rutten, a Netherlands national residing in Hengelo, Netherlands, and Cross Medical Ltd, a company incorporated under English law whose registered office is in London, following termination of his contract of employment by his employer.

3. It appears from the documents in the main proceedings that Mr Rutten was engaged on 1 August 1989 by Cross Medical BV, a company incorporated under Netherlands law whose registered office is in the Netherlands and which is a subsidiary of Cross Medical Ltd.

4. On 31 May 1990 the contract of employment between the parties was terminated on account of the poor financial situation of Cross Medical BV and, with effect from 1 June 1990, Mr Rutten was employed by Cross Medical Ltd.

5. It is common ground that Mr Rutten carried out his duties on behalf of his two successive employers not only in the Netherlands, but also - for approximately one third of his working hours - in the United Kingdom, Belgium, Germany and the United States of America. He carried out his work from an office established in his home at Hengelo to which he returned after each business trip. Cross Medical Ltd paid his salary to him in pounds sterling.

6. Following his dismissal by Cross Medical Ltd on 1 October 1991, Mr Rutten brought an action against that company on 19 June 1992

before the Kantonrechter (Cantonal Court) Amsterdam claiming payment of arrears of salary and interest.

7. That court declared that it had jurisdiction to try the case, whereupon Cross Medical Ltd appealed against that judgment to the Rechtbank (District Court), Amsterdam, which set aside the judgment of the Kantonrechter.

8. Mr Rutten then appealed in cessation to the Hoge Raad der Nederlanden.

9. Since it was uncertain as to the interpretation of Article 5(1) of the Convention, the Hoge Raad submitted the following three questions to the Court of Justice for a preliminary ruling:

'1. Where, in the performance of an employment contract, an employee carries out his work in more than one country, what are the criteria according to which he should be regarded as *habitually* carrying out his work in one of those countries, within the meaning of Article 5(1) of the Brussels Convention?

2. Is the fact that he spends most of his working time in one of those countries, or the fact that he spends more of his working time in another country or countries, decisive or significant in that regard?

3. Is the fact that the employee resides in one of those countries and maintains there an office where he prepares or administers his work outside that country, and to which he returns after every trip which he makes in connection with his work, significant in that regard?'

10. The three questions, which should be considered together, essentially seek a ruling on the interpretation of 'place ... where the employee habitually carries out his work'within the meaning of Article 5(1), second sentence, of the Convention, where a contract of employment is performed in more than one Contracting State.

11. In order to answer those questions, it should first be observed that, as an exception to the general rule laid down in the first paragraph of Article 2 of the Convention, namely that the courts of the Contracting State in which the defendant has his domicile have jurisdiction, Article 5(1) of the Convention provides that: 'A person domiciled in a Contracting State may, in another Contracting State, be sued:

1. in matters relating to a contract, in the courts for the place of performance of the obligation in question; in matters relating to individual contracts of employment, this place is that where the employee

habitually carries out his work, or if the employee does not habitually carry out his work in any one country, the employer may also be sued in the courts for the place where the business which engaged the employee was or is now situated.'

12. It is settled law (see, in particular, Case C-125/92 *Mulox IBC* v *Hendtick Geels* [19931 ECR I-4075, paragraph 10) that, in principle, the Court of Justice will interpret the terms of the Brussels Convention autonomously so as to ensure that it is fully effective, having regard to the objectives of Article 220 of the EEC Treaty, for the implementation of which it was adopted.

13. That autonomous interpretation alone is capable of ensuring uniform application of the Convention, the objectives of which include unification of the rules on jurisdiction of the Contracting States, so as to avoid as far as possible the multiplication of the bases of jurisdiction in relation to one and the same legal relationship and to reinforce the legal protection available to persons established in the Community by, at the same time, allowing the plaintiff easily to identify the court before which he may bring an action and the defendant reasonably to foresee the Court before which he may be sued (*Mulox IBC*, paragraph 11).

14. Moreover, in *Mulox IBC* the Court has already interpreted Article 5(1) of the Brussels Convention, in the version prior to its amendment by the Convention of 26 May 1989, cited above (hereinafter 'the San Sebastian Convention').

15. In *Mulox IBC* the Court held that Article 5(1) had to be interpreted as meaning that in relation to contracts of employment the place of performance of the relevant obligation, for the purposes of that provision, refers to the place where the employee actually performs the work covered by the contract with his employer and that where the employee performs his work in more than one Contracting State, that place refers to the place where or from which the employee principally discharges his obligations towards his employer (paragraphs 20 and 26).

16. As justification for that interpretation, the Court stated, first (paragraph 17), that the rule on special jurisdiction in Article 5(1) of the Brussels Convention was justified by the existence of a particularly close relationship between a dispute and the court which could most conveniently be called on to take cognizance of the matter (Case 133/81 *Ivenel* v *Schwab* [1982] ECR 1891 and Case C-266/85 *Shenavai* v

Kreischer [1987] ECR 239), and that the courts for the place in which the employee is to carry out the agreed work were best suited to resolving the disputes to which the contract of employment could give rise (*Shenavai* and Case 32/88 *Six Constructions* v *Humbert* [1989] ECR 341).

17. It considered, secondly (*Mulox IBC*, paragraphs 18 and 19), that, in regard to contracts of employment, interpretation of Article 5(1) of the Brussels Convention had to take account of the concern to afford proper protection to the employee as the party to the contract who was the weaker from the social point of view (Ivenel and Six Constructions) and that such protection was best assured if disputes relating to a contract of employment fell within the jurisdiction of the courts of the place where the employee discharged his obligations towards his employer, since that was the place where it was least expensive for the employee to commence, or defend himself in, court proceedings.

18. The Court stated, thirdly (*Mulox IBC*, paragraphs 21 and 23), that where the work was performed in more than one Contracting State, it was important to avoid any multiplication of courts having jurisdiction in order to preclude the risk of irreconcilable decisions and to facilitate the recognition and enforcement of judgments in States other than those in which they were delivered (see also, to that effect, the judgment in Case C-220/88 *Dumez France and Tracoba* [1990] ECR I-49, paragraph 18) and that consequently, Article 5(1) of the Brussels Convention could not be interpreted as conferring concurrent jurisdiction on the courts of each Contracting State in whose territory the employee performed part of his work.

19. That case-law is also relevant for the purposes of interpreting Article 5(1) of the Convention as amended by the San Sebastian Convention, which is the version applicable in the main proceedings.

20. As the Court observed in Case C-288/92 *Custom Made Commercial* v *Stava Metallbau* [1994] ECR I-2913, paragraph 25, it had already interpreted the Convention as establishing the rule of special jurisdiction relating to contracts of employment, which the San Sebastian Convention inserted in Article 5(1) of the Brussels Convention. In that regard, it is clear from the report by Almeida Cruz, Desantes Real and Jenard on the San Sebastian Convention (OJ 1990 C 189, pp. 35, 44 and 45) that the new version of Article 5(1) of the Convention takes into account not only the wording of Article 5(1) of the Convention on Jurisdiction and the Enforcement of Judgments in Civil and Commercial Matters signed at

Lugano on 16 September 1988 (OJ 1988 L 319, p. 9), which was itself based on the interpretation which the Court adopted in *Ivenel and Shenavai*, but also of the need to afford proper protection to the employee, as stated by the Court in *Six Constructions*.

21. Consequently, not only did the amendment by the San Sebastian Convention to the wording of Article 5(1) of the Brussels Convention leave the rationale and purpose of that provision unaffected, but, moreover, the new wording of that provision following the entry into force of the San Sebastian Convention was intended in fact to support the interpretation given by the Court to that article in regard to contracts of employment.

22. It follows that in order to determine the meaning of the words 'place ... where the employee habitually carries out his work'for the purposes of Article 5(1) of the Convention, as amended by the San Sebastian Convention, in a case where, as in the main proceedings, the employee carries out his work in more than one Contracting State, the Court's previous case-law must be taken into account when determining the place with which the dispute has the most significant link, while taking due account of the concern to afford proper protection to the employee as the weaker party to the contract.

23. Having regard to the requirements set out in the previous paragraph, where a contract of employment is performed in several Contracting States, Article 5(1) of the Convention, as amended by the San Sebastian Convention, must be understood to refer to the place where the employee has established the effective centre of his working activities and where, or from which, he in fact performs the essential part of his duties *vis-à-vis* his employer.

24. That is the place where it is least expensive for the employee to commence proceedings against his employer or to defend himself in such proceedings. The courts for that place are also best placed and, therefore, the most appropriate to resolve the dispute relating to the contract of employment.

25. When identifying that place in the particular case, which is a matter for the national court in the light of the facts before it, the fact that the employee carried out almost two-thirds of his work in one Contracting State - the remainder of his work being performed in several other States - and that he has an office in that Contracting State where he organized

his work for his employer and to which he returned after each business trip abroad, as was the case in the main proceedings, is relevant.

26. In a situation such as that at issue in the main proceedings, that is the place where the employee established the effective centre of his activities under the contract of employment concluded with his employer. That place must, therefore, be deemed, for the purposes of the application of Article 5(1) of the Convention, as amended by the San Sebastian Convention, to be the place where the employee habitually carries out his work.

27. Accordingly, Article 5(1) of the Convention, as amended by the San Sebastian Convention, must be interpreted as meaning that where, in the performance of a contract of employment an employee carries out his work in several Contracting States, the place where he habitually carries out his work, within the meaning of that provision, is the place where he has established the effective centre of his working activities. When identifying that place, it is necessary to take into account the fact that the employee spends most of his working time in one of the Contracting States in which he has an office where he organizes his work for his employer and to which he returns after each business trip abroad.

On those grounds, the Court in answer to the questions referred to it by the Hoge Raad der Nederlanden by judgment of 1 December 1995, hereby rules:

> **Article 5(1) of the Convention of 27 September 1968 on Jurisdiction and the Enforcement of Judgments in Civil and Commercial matters, as amended by the Convention of 26 May 1989 on the Accession of the Kingdom of Spain and the Portuguese Republic, must be interpreted as meaning that where, in the performance of a contract of employment, an employee carries out his work in several Contracting States, the place where he habitually carries out his work, within the meaning of that provision, is the place where he has established the effective centre of his working activities. When identifying that place, it is necessary to take into account the fact that the employee spends most of his working time in one of the Contracting States in which he has an office where he organizes his activities for his employer and to which he returns after each business trip abroad.**

OPINION OF MR ADVOCATE GENERAL JACOBS

1. The Netherlands Hoge Raad (Supreme Court) has asked for a preliminary ruling on the interpretation of Article 5(1) of the Convention of 27 September 1968 on jurisdiction and the enforcement of judgments in civil and commercial matters (hereafter 'the Brussels Convention'), as amended by the Convention of 9 October 1978 on the accession of Denmark, Ireland and the United Kingdom, by the Convention of 25 October 1982 on the accession of the Hellenic Republic and by the Convention of 26 May 1989 on the accession of the Kingdom of Spain and the Portuguese Republic ('the San Sebastian Convention').

2. Article 5(1) of the Brussels Convention, in so far as relevant to this case, essentially confers jurisdiction in disputes arising out of employment contracts on, *inter alia*, the courts of the place where the employee *habitually* carries out his work.

Background

3. Mr Rutten, a Netherlands national resident in the Netherlands, was employed from 1 August 1989 by Cross Medical BV, a Netherlands subsidiary of Cross Medical Ltd, a company incorporated in Great Britain and established in London. His contract of employment contained clauses conferring jurisdiction in the event of employment disputes on the Amsterdam Kantonrechter (Cantonal Court) and stipulating that the contract was to be governed by Netherlands law. On 31 May 1990 Mr Rutten's employment with Cross Medical BV was terminated because of that company's financial difficulties and he entered into a new contract of employment with Cross Medical Ltd. That contract surprisingly contained neither a choice of law clause nor a submission to jurisdiction clause.

4. Mr Rutten continued to live in the Netherlands. Both before and after his change of employer, he carried out some two-thirds of his work in the Netherlands; the remaining third appears to have been spent in several other countries (there is slight divergence between the documents on the file, but England, Scotland, Ireland, the United States, Germany and Belgium are variously mentioned). He carried out the preparation and planning for his trips in his Netherlands office (which appears to have been in his house), where he kept all relevant documentation and where he returned after every trip.

5. Mr Rutten's employment was terminated by Cross Medical Ltd with effect from 1 October 1991. He sought payment of arrears of salary and interest before the Amsterdam Kantonrechter. Cross Medical Ltd contests the jurisdiction of the Netherlands courts, arguing that Rutten *habitually* carried out his work in the United Kingdom. The Kantonrechter declared that it had jurisdiction to hear and determine the claim; on appeal on the issue of jurisdiction, the Rechtbank (District Court), Amsterdam, set aside the judgment of the Kantonrechter. Mr Rutten appealed in cessation to the Netherlands Hoge Raad, which referred the following questions to the Court:

'(a) Where, in the performance of an employment contract, an employee carries out his work in more than one country, what are the criteria according to which he should be regarded as *habitually* carrying out his work in one of those countries, within the meaning of Article 5(1) of the Brussels Convention?

(b) Is the fact that he spends most of his working time in one of those countries, or the fact that he spends more of his working time in another country or countries, decisive or significant in that regard?

(c) Is the fact that the employee resides or maintains in one of those countries an office from which he prepares or administers his work outside that country, and to which he returns after every trip which he makes in connection with his work, of significance in that regard?'

Article 5(1) of the Brussels Convention

6. Article 5(1) represents one of the exceptions to the general rule set out in Article 2, namely that persons domiciled in a Contracting State are to be sued in the courts of that State. Those exceptions are justified by the fact that, as stated in the Jenard Report on the Convention, 'there must be a close connecting factor between the dispute and the court with jurisdiction to resolve it'.

7. Until 1989, Article 5(1) read as follows: 'A person domiciled in a Contracting State may, in another Contracting State, be sued: 1. in matters relating to a contract, in the courts for the place of performance of the obligation in question; ...

8. The San Sebastian Convention amended Article 5(1) so that it reads as follows: 'A person domiciled in a Contracting State may, in another Contracting State, be sued: 1. in matters relating to a contract, in the courts for the place of performance of the obligation in question; in matters relating to individual contracts of employment, this place is that where the employee *habitually* carries out his work, or if the employee does not *habitually* carry out his work in any one country, the employer may also be sued in the courts for the place where the business which engaged the employee was or is now situated; ...'

9. What is at issue in this case is the meaning of the words '[the place] where the employee *habitually* carries out his work'. The identification of that place in a specific case is a question of fact to be determined by the national court, and the Court has been asked in particular to give guidance as to the factors which may be relevant to that determination in circumstances where the employee works in more than one country.

10. The Court has not yet had occasion to rule on the meaning of the above terms. In the absence of any judicial guidance, I will briefly review the history of the provision. A fuller discussion of the background may be found in my Opinion in *Mulox IBC* v *Geels*.

11. The amendment made to Article 5(1) by the San Sebastian Convention is discussed in the Report on that convention by Almeida Cruz, Desantes Real and Jenard. It is stated that the solution adopted 'attempts to improve on that adopted by the Lugano Convention without departing from it too greatly, while following the guidelines laid down by the Court of Justice on the protection of

the weaker party in the contractual relationship'. The Report refers in particular to the decision of the Court of Justice in *Six Constructions* v *Humbert*, delivered after signature of the Lugano Convention but before finalisation of the San Sebastian Convention.

12. The relevant provision in the Lugano Convention, also Article 5(1), reads as follows: 'A person domiciled in a Contracting State may, in another Contracting State, be sued: 1. in matters relating to a contract, in the courts for the place of performance of the obligation in question; in matters relating to individual contracts of employment, this place is that where the employee *habitually* carries out his work, or if the employee does not *habitually* carry out his work in any one country, this place shall be the place of business through which he was engaged; ...'

13. The only difference between the wording of Article 5(1) of the Lugano Convention and Article 5(1) of the Brussels Convention as amended by the San Sebastian Convention is that it is made clear in the latter that the option (where the employee does not *habitually* carry out his work in any one country) of suing in the place of business of engagement is available only to the employee. That is the improvement referred to in the Report on the San Sebastian Convention, intended to reflect the concern to protect the socially weaker party to the contract. It was prompted by *Six Constructions*, in which the Court pointed out that the wording of the Lugano Convention could work against the interests of the socially weaker party to the employment contract by conferring jurisdiction on the courts for the place where the employer is located even where the employer is the plaintiff.

14. Article 5(1) of the Lugano Convention was apparently intended to reflect the decisions of the Court of Justice in *Ivenel* v *Schwab* and *Shenavai* v *Kreischer* (see the Report on the San Sebastian Convention, paragraph 23(a)) and also to be consistent with the Rome Convention on the law applicable to contractual obligations (see the Jenard-Möller Report on the Lugano Convention, paragraphs 37 to 40).

15. In the absence of any specific provision for contracts of employment in the pre-1989 versions of the Brussels Convention, the Court had ruled in *Ivenel* v *Schwab* that the obligation to be taken into account for the purposes of Article 5(1) in the case of claims based on different obligations arising under a contract of employment was the obligation which characterised the contract, which was normally the obligation to carry out work. In *Shenavai* v *Kreischer* the Court had stated *obiter* that, in the case of a dispute concerned with a number of obligations arising under the same contract and forming the basis of the proceedings in question, the court before which the matter was brought should, when determining whether it had jurisdiction, be guided by the maxim *accessorium sequitur principale*: in other words, where various obligations are at issue, it will be the principal obligation which will determine its jurisdiction. Those two propositions, together with Article 6(2) of the Rome Convention, are the source of the reference in Article 5(1) of the Lugano Convention (and hence also of that in Article 5(1) of the Brussels Convention) to the place 'where the employee *habitually* carries out his work'.

16. Article 6(2) of the Rome Convention provides that, in the absence of choice of law, a contract of employment is to be governed:

'(a) by the law of the country in which the employee *habitually* carries out his work in performance of the contract, even if he is temporarily employed in another country; or

(b) if the employee does not *habitually* carry out his work in any one country, by the law of the country in which the place of business through which he was engaged is situated;

unless it appears from the circumstances as a whole that the contract is more closely connected with another country, in which case the contract shall be governed by the law of that country'.

17. It is clear from the Giuliano-Lagarde Report on the Rome Convention that the wording of Article 6 took account of the fact that the interests of the parties to an employment contract differ and sought to secure 'more adequate protection for the party who from the socioeconomic point of view is regarded as the weaker in the contractual relationship'.

18. That the concern to afford proper protection to the party to the contract who is the weaker from the social point of view is a factor to be taken into account in interpreting Article 5(1) of the Brussels Convention was confirmed by the Court of Justice in *Ivenel* v *Schwab*, in relation to the pre-1989 version of the article. The Court in that case additionally stated, after reviewing the legislative history of the provision, that in the matter of contracts Article 5(1) was particularly concerned to attribute jurisdiction to the court of the country which had a close connection with the case, and that in the case of a contract of employment the connection lay particularly in the law applicable to the contract. I will revert to these points later.

The *Mulox* case

19. The pre-1989 version of Article 5(1) came before the Court again in *Mulox IBC* v *Geels*, a case where the employee performed his work in more than one Contracting State. In my view, the Court's ruling, although concerned with the earlier wording, is none the less helpful in interpreting the present wording. This is because the Court interpreted the pre-1989 version in the light of its decisions in *Ivenel* v *Schwab* and *Shenavai* v *Kreischer*; as has been seen, it was those decisions which largely shaped the 1989 amendment currently before the Court.

20. The Court ruled that, in the case of a contract of employment, it was appropriate to determine the place of performance of the relevant obligation, for the purposes of applying Article 5(1) of the Convention, by reference not to the applicable national law in accordance with the conflict rules of the court seised but, rather, to uniform criteria which it was for the Court to lay down on the basis of the scheme and the objectives of the Convention.

21. The Court moreover referred to its statement in *Ivenel* v *Schwab* that account must be taken of the concern to afford proper protection to the party to the contract who is the weaker from the social point of view, namely in these

cases the employee. Proper protection of that kind is best assured if disputes relating to a contract of employment fall within the jurisdiction of the courts of the place where the employee discharges his obligations towards his employer. That is the place where it is least expensive for the employee to commence, or defend himself against, court proceedings.

22. That proposition echoes the view I expressed in my Opinion in that case that the worker should be entitled to sue his employer at the place where he works: that is the natural forum for such disputes and it will in most cases be the most convenient forum for the employee, who should not be deprived of the convenience of suing there simply because his employer is domiciled in another Contracting State.

23. The Court in *Mulox* referred to earlier case-law (set out above) holding that, where various obligations derive from the same contract and form the basis of the plaintiff's action, it is the principal obligation which must be relied on in order to determine jurisdiction. The Court then stated that, where the work was performed in more than one Contracting State, the place of performance of the contractual obligation within the meaning of Article 5(1) was the place where or from which the employee principally discharged his obligations towards his employer. In order to determine the place of performance, which was a matter for the national court, it was necessary to take account of the fact that, in that case, the work entrusted to the employee was carried out from an office in a Contracting State, where the employee had established his residence, from which he performed his work and to which he returned after each business trip.

Application to the present case

24. The issue before the Court in this case is essentially whether the wording of Article 5(1) of the Brussels Convention as amended by the San Sebastian Convention, and in particular the words '[the place] where the employee *habitually* carries out his work', differs to any significant extent from the Court's interpretation of the unamended provision in *Mulox*, and in particular the concept 'the place where or from which the employee principally discharges his obligations towards his employer'; and if so whether that difference warrants departing from the guidelines laid down by the Court in *Mulox* for determining where that place is in a specific case.

25. I remain of the view which I expressed in my Opinion in *Mulox*, to the effect that the pre-1989 version of Article 5(l): 'should be construed as establishing jurisdiction at the principal place of employment. That term will in most situations be largely synonymous with the concept of the "habitual" place of employment used in Article 6 of the Rome Convention and in the Lugano and San Sebastian Conventions. However, the expression 'principal place of employment'seems preferable, since it more effectively conveys the idea that one of the worker's several places of employment must in normal circumstances be more important than the others. ... if the San Sebastian Convention were applicable in a case such as the present one, the term 'habitually'should not be

construed too literally but should be read as indicating the principal place of employment.'

26. That interpretation accords with a number of factors.

27. First, it affords protection to the party to the contract who is weaker from a social point of view, namely in employment contracts the employee: as has been seen, the concern to ensure such protection has been recognised by the Court and coloured the 1989 amendment to Article 5(1).

28. Secondly, it reflects the requirement of a close connecting factor between the dispute and the court with jurisdiction to resolve it.

29. Thirdly, it should mean that the courts with jurisdiction will almost invariably be at the place where it is least expensive for the employee to commence, or defend himself against, court proceedings.

30. Against that interpretation it might be argued that it will not necessarily confer jurisdiction on courts of the country whose law is applicable. As stated above, the desirability of conferring jurisdiction on a court which will be able to apply its own law, rather than a foreign law, was mentioned by the Court in *Ivenel* v *Schwab* as one of the principal criteria governing the interpretation of Article 5(1).

31. I do not however think that that objection is sufficient to override the advantages of the interpretation I propose. As I stated in my Opinion in *Mulox*, desirable though it may be to confer jurisdiction over employment disputes on the courts of the country whose law is applicable, that will not always be possible in practice, even after the harmonisation of the choice-of-law rules effected by the Rome Convention. In that Opinion I discussed in some depth the difficulties inherent in any attempt to ensure coincidence of *lex causae and lex fori,* and concluded that it would be a mistake to exaggerate the importance of the link between jurisdiction and *lex causae* in employment disputes. I remain of that view.

32. Where, therefore, in the performance of an employment contract, an employee carries out his work in more than one country, the criteria according to which he should be regarded as *habitually* carrying out his work in one of those countries within the meaning of Article 5(1) of the Brussels Convention are essentially the same as the criteria according to which he would formerly have been regarded as principally discharging his obligations towards his employer. The Court in *Mulox* has already suggested some of those criteria: in particular the location of the employee's office in a Contracting State, where he had established his residence, from which he performed his work and to which he returned after each business trip.

33. The Commission, although it endorses the view I expressed in my Opinion in *Mulox* that the term 'habitually'should not be interpreted too literally, sees difficulties in simply equating the meaning of 'habitually'and 'principally'. It submits that the first concept refers rather to the temporal organisation of the employee's work whereas the second refers to the central point of the work. However, it then states that the term 'principally'implies, as shown by the judgment in *Mulox*, that in relation to the previous version of Article 5(1) various criteria should be taken into account, including the time spent in each of the

countries concerned. The new wording, and in particular the use of the word 'habitually', confirms that latter criterion. The Commission concludes that the national court must therefore first establish the periods during which the employee worked in the various different countries. If a clear majority of days were spent in one Contracting State, it is the courts of that State which in principle have jurisdiction to hear disputes arising out of the contract of employment.

34. Although that reasoning will in all probability lead to the correct result in the majority of cases, I am not convinced of the wisdom of such a wide formulation. I remain of the view which I expressed in my Opinion in *Mulox* that the location and use made of the employee's office cannot be overlooked. In that case, I stated that, even if the employee spent more than half of the year travelling in other countries and did not in fact visit a single client in the country in which he had his office, it seemed to me very difficult to rebut the presumption that his principal place of employment was located at the place where he had his centre of operations. I do not consider that that proposition has been made less cogent by the new wording of Article 5(1). If an employee who travels to several different countries prepares and plans his work from his office and returns there after every trip, it is artificial to regard him as 'habitually'or 'principally'carrying out his work in any country other than that where he has his office, the hub of his working activities.

35. The Commission adds that other factors, such as location of office and residence, are also significant. It draws a distinction as to the weight to be attached to those factors depending on whether the criterion of time points to the same or a different place as the other factors. This seems to me to be unnecessarily complex in the context of this case, where it is clear that there is no such difficulty. It also shows the dangers of attaching too much weight to the criterion of time and too little to the location of the employee's centre of operations.

36. As to the criterion of residence, I would merely comment that, although it may be a relevant factor in the circumstances of a particular case, for the reasons given in my Opinion in *Mulox* I do not consider that it should be decisive.

37. I would stress the importance in any case involving an employee who works in several different countries of making a determined effort to identify a principal place of employment, in order to ensure that jurisdiction is conferred on the courts of a country which has a genuine connection with the dispute. That result will not necessarily be achieved if recourse is had to the substitute connecting factor introduced by the San Sebastian Convention, namely the place where the business which engaged the employee was or is situated. Other than to draw attention to the risk, however, I do not consider that it is necessary for the purposes of this case to analyse the scope of that substitute connecting factor.

38. To conclude, therefore, I consider that the additional factors mentioned in the national court's questions are all relevant criteria for determining where the employee *habitually* carries out his work.

39. It may finally be noted that the main proceedings in this case provide

a good illustration of the advantages of the interpretation of Article 5(1) which I advocate. Mr Rutten is resident in the Netherlands. He has an office in the Netherlands from which he plans and prepares his work and to which he returns after each trip, and he spends some two-thirds of his working time in the Netherlands, the remaining third being divided between several other countries. Clearly the employment dispute at issue has numerous close connecting factors with the Netherlands. For Mr Rutten to be compelled to bring his action before a court in the United Kingdom would be consistent neither with the general concern to protect the socially weaker party nor with the specific application of that concern in such cases, namely the aim of ensuring that the employee may bring proceedings in the forum most convenient to him.

Conclusion

40. Accordingly, I am of the opinion that the Court should give the following reply to the questions put by the Hoge Raad: For the purposes of Article 5(1) of the Convention of 27 September 1968 on jurisdiction and the enforcement of judgments in civil and commercial matters, as most recently amended by the Convention of 26 May 1989 on the accession of the Kingdom of Spain and the Republic of Portugal, the place where an employee *habitually* carries out his work means, in the case of a contract of employment in pursuance of which the employee performs his work in more than one State, the place where or from which the employee principally discharges his obligations towards his employer. It is for the national court to determine that place in the light of all the relevant facts, which include in particular the fact that the employee spends most of his working time in one of those States where he resides and maintains an office from which he prepares or administers his work outside that State and to which he returns after every trip which he makes in connection with his work.

Case C-440/97 - 28 September 1999

GIE Groupe Concorde and Others v The Master of the Vessel Suhadiwarno Panjan and Others

Contract of carriage of goods - Article 5(1) - Place of performance of obligation - Law governing the obligation in question - Conflict of law rules of the court seised.

Summary

The "place of the performance of the obligation in question" within the meaning of Article 5(1) of the Court of 27 September 1968 is to be determined in accordance with the law governing the obligation in question according to the conflict rules of the court seised.

JUDGMENT OF THE COURT

Iglesias, President, Kapteyn, Puissochet, Hirsch and Jann, Presidents of Chambers, Moitinho de Almeida, Gulmann, Murray, Ragnemalm, Sevón, Wathelet and Schintgen, Judges

1. By judgment of 9 December 1997, received at the Court on 29 December 1997, the French Cour de Cassation (Court of Cassation) referred to the Court for a preliminary ruling under the Protocol of 3 June 1971 on the interpretation by the Court of Justice of the Convention of 27 September 1968 on Jurisdiction and the Enforcement of Judgments in Civil and Commercial Matters a question on the interpretation of Article 5(1) of that Convention (OJ 1978 L 304, p. 36), as amended by the Convention of 9 October 1978 on the Accession of the Kingdom of

Denmark, Ireland and the United Kingdom of Great Britain and Northern Ireland (OJ 1978 L 304, p. 1 and - amended version - p. 77), by the Convention of 25 October 1982 on the Accession of the Hellenic Republic (OJ 1982 L 388, p. 1) and by the Convention of 26 May 1989 on the Accession of the Kingdom of Spain and the Portuguese Republic (OJ 1989 L 285, p. 1) (hereinafter 'the Brussels Convention').

2. That question has arisen in a dispute between seven insurance companies and GIE Groupe Concorde, their lead insurer, which has its registered office in Paris (hereinafter 'the insurers'), on the one hand, and, on the other, the Master of the vessel *Suhadiwarno Panjan*, Pro Line Ltd (hereinafter 'Pro Line'), which has its registered office in Hamburg (Germany), and four other defendants, after a cargo of bottles of wine in cartons was found on delivery to be damaged.

The Brussels Convention

3. Article 5(1) of the Brussels Convention provides that: 'A person domiciled in a Contracting State may, in another Contracting State, be sued:

1. in matters relating to a contract, in the courts for the place of performance of the obligation in question; in matters relating to individual contracts of employment, this place is that where the employee habitually carries out his work ...'

The main proceedings

4. Cartons containing bottles of wine were loaded in containers on board the vessel *Suhadiwarno Panjan* in the port of Le Havre (France). They were to be carried by sea to the port of Santos (Brazil) by Pro Line. Upon arrival at their destination, the goods were found to be damaged and short-delivered.

5. The insurers paid compensation to the consignee. Having been subrogated to the latter's rights, the insurers commenced proceedings, by application of 22 September 1991, against, inter alios, the Master of the vessel and Pro Line before the Tribunal de Commerce (Commercial Court), Le Havre, which, by a decision of 3 January 1995, declined jurisdiction.

6. On appeal by the insurers, the Cour d'Appel (Court of Appeal), Rouen, by judgment of 24 May 1995, confirmed that the first court lacked jurisdiction on the ground, in particular, that Le Havre was not the place where the contract of carriage was to be performed.

7. The insurers appealed to the Cour de Cassation on a point of law against that judgment on two grounds. Their first ground of appeal was dismissed by the Cour de Cassation. By their second ground of appeal, the insurers claim that the Cour d'Appel, Rouen, was wrong to rule that the place of performance of the obligation at issue was not Le Havre without first investigating which law governed the contract of carriage.

8. The Cour de Cassation found that, in its judgment in Case 12/76 *Tessili* v *Dunlop* [1976] ECR 1473, the Court of Justice had held that the place of performance of the obligation within the meaning of Article 5(1) of the Brussels Convention is to be determined in accordance with the law which governs the obligation in question according to the conflict rules of the court before which the matter is brought, which may include the provisions of an international convention laying down uniform law (Case C-288/92 *Custom Made Commercial* v *Stawa Metallbau* [1994] ECR I-2913), unless the parties themselves specify that place by means of a clause which is valid under the law applicable to the contract (Case 56/79 *Zelger* v *Salinitri* [1980] ECR 89). However, the Cour de Cassation considered it appropriate to ask the Court of Justice whether an independent Community solution could be found.

9. It therefore decided to stay proceedings and refer the following question to the Court: 'With a view to the application of Article 5(1) of the Brussels Convention ..., must the place of performance of the obligation, within the meaning of that provision, be determined in accordance with the law which, pursuant to the rules on conflicts of laws of the court seised, governs the obligation at issue, or should national courts determine the place of performance of the obligation by seeking to establish, having regard to the nature of the relationship creating the obligation and the circumstances of the case, the place where performance actually took place or should have taken place, without having to refer to the law which, under the rules on conflict of laws, governs the obligation at issue?'

The question submitted for preliminary ruling

10. By its question, the national court is essentially asking whether the expression 'place of performance of the obligation in question' used in Article 5(1) of the Brussels Convention to establish special jurisdiction in contractual matters is to be construed as referring to the substantive law applicable under the conflict rules of the court seised or whether it must be given an independent interpretation.

11. As far as possible, the Court of Justice gives the terms used in the Brussels Convention an autonomous interpretation, rather than by reference to national law, so as to ensure that the Convention is fully effective, having regard to the objectives of Article 220 of the EC Treaty (now Article 293 EC), in the implementation of which the Convention was adopted (Case C-125/92 *Mulox IBC* v *Geels* [1993] ECR I-4075, paragraph 10).

12. The Court has, however, made it clear that neither option excludes the other, since the appropriate choice can be made only in relation to each of the provisions of the Brussels Convention (*Tessili*, paragraph 11, and Case 144/86 *Gubisch Maschinenfabrik* v *Palumbo* [1987] ECR 4861, paragraph 7).

13. As regards the expression 'place of performance of the obligation in question', the Court has repeatedly ruled that this expression is to be interpreted as referring to the law which governs the obligation in question according to the conflict rules of the court seised (*Tessili*, paragraph 13, and *Custom Made Commercial*, paragraph 26).

14. It is true that, in the case of contracts of employment, the Court has ruled that the place of performance of the relevant obligation should be determined by reference, not to the applicable national law in accordance with the conflict rules of the court seised, but to uniform criteria which it is for the Court to lay down on the basis of the scheme and the objectives of the Brussels Convention (*Mulox IBC*, paragraph 16). These criteria lead to the choice of the place where the employee actually performs the work covered by the contract with his employer (*Mulox IBC*, paragraph 20).

15. The German and United Kingdom Governments and the Commission advocate that the approach adopted in *Mulox IBC* should be extended to cover all types of contract. They submit that the objectives of the Brussels Convention, which are to enable potential litigants to foresee which courts will have jurisdiction and to provide legal certainty and equal treatment, favour the establishment of uniform criteria so that, for each type of contractual obligation, or at least for each type of contract, the place of performance for the purposes of Article 5(1) of the Brussels Convention could be determined independently.

16. The French and Italian Governments, however, argue that the Court's present case-law should not be changed. They accept that

recourse to conflict rules to determine the place of performance may cause difficulties of implementation and lead to unsatisfactory results. But they point out that an autonomous interpretation of place of performance could work only in the case of a few simple contracts and that this solution would be incompatible with the constant evolution of contractual practice in international trade. Given the diversity of the alternative proposals, it is for the Contracting States, should they consider it expedient, to make a choice in the context of the review of the Brussels Convention.

17. It should be noted that in paragraph 14 of *Tessili* the Court, in explaining its reasons for determining the place of performance of contractual obligations by reference to the law applicable to the contract, pointed out that determination of the place of performance depends on the contractual context of the obligations in question and that the contract laws of the Contracting States had very divergent views of the place of performance.

18. In the case of contracts of employment, however, abandonment of the criterion of reference to the law applicable to the contract for the purpose of determining the place of performance and preferring the place where the acts constituting performance of the relevant obligation were localised could be justified by the particular characteristics of this type of contract (see *Mulox IBC*, paragraph 15). These had already led the Court to hold that, in the case of such contracts, the obligation to be taken into consideration for the purpose of applying Article 5(1) of the Brussels Convention is always the obligation which characterises the contract, namely the employee's obligation to carry out the work stipulated (see, in particular, Case 133/81 *Ivenel* v *Schwab* [1982] ECR 1891, paragraph 20, and *Mulox IBC*, paragraph 14).

19. The Court has confirmed that, where no such particular features exist, it is neither necessary nor appropriate to identify the obligation which characterises the contract and to centralise at its place of performance a jurisdiction, based on place of performance, over disputes concerning all the obligations under the contract (Case 266/85 *Shenavai* v *Kreischer* [1987] ECR 239, paragraph 17).

20. That interpretation, as regards both maintenance of the general rule applicable to all contracts and the special rule laid down for contracts of employment, was corroborated by the Convention of 26 May 1989 on the Accession of the Kingdom of Spain and the Portuguese Republic to the

Brussels Convention, which gave to Article 5(1) of the Brussels Convention the version at present in force.

21. Moreover, a review of the Brussels Convention is at present being carried out, in which the difficulties associated with the application of Article 5(1), in its present version as hitherto interpreted by the Court, have been raised. Several proposals for reforming this provision have been submitted and examined.

22. Argument before the Court in the present case has also highlighted, not only the contradictory positions of, on the one hand, two governments which submitted observations in favour of keeping the present case-law and, on the other, two other governments and the Commission, which advocate a new approach, but also substantial differences between the alternative proposals put forward.

23. In these circumstances, it must be stressed that the principle of legal certainty is one of the objectives of the Brussels Convention (see, in particular, Case C-129/92 *Owens Bank* v *Fulvio Bracco and Bracco Industria Chimica* [1994] ECR I-117, paragraph 32).

24. This principle requires, in particular, that the jurisdictional rules which derogate from the basic principle of the Brussels Convention, such as Article 5(1), should be interpreted in such a way as to enable a normally well-informed defendant reasonably to foresee before which courts, other than those of the State in which he is domiciled, he may be sued (Case C-26/91 *Handte* v *Traitements Mécano-chimiques des Surfaces* [1992] ECR I-3967, paragraph 18).

25. Determination of the place of performance by reference to the nature of the relationship of obligation and the circumstances of the case, as suggested by the national court, would, as Article 5(1) of the Brussels Convention stands at present, be insufficient to resolve all questions linked to application of that provision.

26. Some of the questions which might arise in this context, such as identification of the contractual obligation forming the basis of proceedings, as well as the principal obligation where there are several obligations, could hardly be resolved without reference to the applicable law.

27. It follows that adoption of the criteria proposed by the national court would not make it entirely unnecessary for the court seised to determine

the law governing the obligation in dispute, in order to rule on its jurisdiction under Article 5(1) of the Brussels Convention.

28. Moreover, bearing in mind the important position generally accorded by national contract law to the intention of the parties, the Court has held that, if the parties to the contract are permitted by the applicable law, subject to the conditions it lays down, to specify the place of performance of an obligation without satisfying any special condition of form, that agreement on the place of performance of the obligation is sufficient to found jurisdiction in that place within the meaning of Article 5(1) of the Brussels Convention (*Zelger*, paragraph 5), on condition that this place has a real connection with the true substance of the contract (Case C-106/95 *MSG* v *Gravières Rhénanes* [1997] ECR I-911, paragraphs 30 and 31).

29. In these circumstances, it does not appear justified to substitute the criteria proposed by the national court for the interpretation previously given by the Court, to the effect that the place of performance must be determined in accordance with the law which governs the obligation at issue. That solution also has the advantage that the competent court is the court of the place where the obligation in question is to be performed in accordance with the law applicable to it. Indeed, it was because the place of performance usually constitutes the closest connecting factor between the dispute and the court of competent jurisdiction that, with a view to efficient organisation of procedure, the rule of special jurisdiction provided for by Article 5(1) of the Brussels Convention in contractual matters was adopted (*Shenavai*, paragraph 18, and *Custom Made Commercial*, paragraphs 12 and 13).

30. It should be added that there is no risk that the law applicable to the determination of the place of performance will vary depending on the court seised, since the conflict rules enabling the law applicable to the contract to be determined have been standardised in the Contracting States by the Convention of 19 June 1980 on the Law applicable to Contractual Obligations (OJ 1980 L 266, p. 1), as amended by the Convention of 10 April 1984 on the Accession of the Hellenic Republic (OJ 1984 L 146, p. 1), by the Convention of 18 May 1992 on the Accession of the Kingdom of Spain and the Portuguese Republic (OJ 1992 L 333, p. 1), and by the Convention of 29 November 1996 on the Accession of the Republic of Austria, the Republic of Finland and the Kingdom of Sweden (OJ 1997 C 15, p. 10).

31. It is for the national legislature, which has exclusive competence in

this field, to define a place of performance which takes fairly into account both the interests of the sound administration of justice and the interests of adequate protection for individuals. It may well be that, in so far as national law allows, the national court will have to determine the place of performance by reference to the criteria suggested by the referring court - i.e. by identifying, by reference to the nature of the obligations undertaken and the circumstances of the case, the place where the thing or service contracted for was, or should have been, provided.

32. It follows from all of the foregoing considerations that, on a proper construction of Article 5(1) of the Brussels Convention, the place of performance of the obligation, within the meaning of that provision, is to be determined in accordance with the law governing the obligation in question according to the conflict rules of the court seised.

On those grounds, the court, in answer to the question referred to it by the Cour de Cassation by judgment of 9 December 1997, hereby rules:

> **On a proper construction of Article 5(1) of the Convention of 27 September 1968 on Jurisdiction and the Enforcement of Judgments in Civil and Commercial Matters, as amended by the Convention of 9 October 1978 on the Accession of the Kingdom of Denmark, Ireland and the United Kingdom of Great Britain and Northern Ireland, by the Convention of 25 October 1982 on the Accession of the Hellenic Republic, and by the Convention of 26 May 1989 on the Accession of the Kingdom of Spain and the Portuguese Republic, the place of performance of the obligation, within the meaning of that provision, is to be determined in accordance with the law governing the obligation in question according to the conflict rules of the court seised.**

OPINION OF MR ADVOCATE GENERAL RUIZ-JARABO COLOMER

"'Child," said Don Quixote then in a loud voice, "follow the thread of your story' and do not meander or go off on sidetracks"'.

I - Introduction

1. This case raises the question whether the Court should abandon its traditional case-law and adopt an autonomous interpretation of the phrase 'place of performance of the obligation in question' in Article 5, point (1), of the

Convention of 27 September 1968 on Jurisdiction and the Enforcement of Judgments in Civil and Commercial Matters ('the Brussels Convention' or simply 'the Convention').

2. The Court's case-law, laid down more than 20 years ago in the *Tessili* judgment and followed in the *Custom Made Commercial* judgment, requires a court dealing with a matter relating to a contract to ascertain first of all the law applicable to the legal transaction in question and then to determine the place of performance according to that law. The method used in the *Tessili* judgment, the conflictualist logic of which is contrary to the spirit of the Convention and even to the rest of the Court's case-law on the subject, is not satisfactory. It has been severely criticised by many commentators and has been applied unequally and often incorrectly by the national courts. For all these reasons, at meetings taking place within the Council with a view to revising the Brussels Convention, the possibility of amending Article 5, point (1), or removing it altogether is being discussed.

3. The draftsmen of the Brussels Convention tried above all to facilitate what is customarily called the 'free movement of judgments'. With regard to jurisdictional competence, the aim was to lay down simple, uniform criteria for the whole of European territory, so that the process of unification can also be reflected in the field of the administration of justice. Therefore, it seems to me paradoxical that a matter which fundamentally requires simple, practical answers enabling European courts preferably at first instance to establish quickly whether they have international jurisdiction or not has been characterised, in both case-law and legal theory, by a high degree of theoretical thinking which has lost sight of the problems which have to be faced by the regular practitioners of judicial business.

4. I do not think that, so far as international jurisdiction is concerned any more than in domestic jurisdiction there are any particular reasons for this theoretical approach: priority should not be given to finding the interpretative solution which is the most perfect in theory, but to providing courts and litigants with working criteria.

II - The facts of the main proceedings

5. The facts given in the order for reference and the documents in the file accompanying it may be summarised as follows.

6. Two containers with almost 1 000 cases of bottles of wine were loaded in Le Havre, France, on board the vessel *Suhadiwamo Panjan*, flying the Indonesian flag, for shipment under a bill of lading to the port of Santos, in Brazil. The carrier was the German firm Pro Line Limited and Co., having its registered office in Hamburg. As it was found on arrival at the port of destination that some of the goods were missing and others were damaged, nine cargo insurers ('the insurers'), of which GIE Groupe Concorde was the leading insurer, indemnified the consignee for a total of FRF 666 279. The insurers were subrogated to the consignee's rights and on 22 September 1991 they brought an action for compensation before the Tribunal de Commerce de Terre et de Mer,

Le Havre, against the master and the owner of the vessel, the carrier Pro Line and the Swedish company which insured the vessel for civil liability.

7. Pro Line and the Swedish insurer pleaded clauses conferring exclusive jurisdiction on the courts of Hamburg and Goteborg respectively. The Tribunal de Commerce accepted those pleas and declined jurisdiction by judgment of 3 January 1995. The insurers then appealed on the question of jurisdiction. The judgment was upheld, although on different grounds, by the Cour d'Appel, Rouen, by judgment of 24 May 1995. The Cour d'Appel found that, although the jurisdiction clauses were not valid as they did not fulfil the requirements of Article 17 of the Convention, it was still correct to decline the international jurisdiction of the French courts pursuant to Article 5, point (1), of the Convention because that provision provides that in matters relating to a contract, in addition to the general forum of the defendant's domicile, the court for the place of performance of the contract, which, according to the French court, was none other than the Brazilian port of Santos, has jurisdiction.

8. The insurers appealed on a point of law against that judgment, relying in particular on a breach of Article 5, point (1), of the Brussels Convention, as interpreted by the Court of Justice since the *Tessili* judgment of 6 October 1976, cited above.

9. The Commercial, Financial and Economic Chamber of the Cour de Cassation (France) confirmed that the French courts had no jurisdiction to entertain the action in so far as it had been brought against the master of the vessel. However, the Cour de Cassation considered that jurisdiction to entertain the action in so far as it had been brought against the carrier raised a serious difficulty of interpretation of the Brussels Convention. Consequently, pursuant to Article 1 of the Protocol of 3 June 1971 on the Interpretation by the Court of Justice of the European Communities of the Brussels Convention, judgment was stayed and the following question was referred to the Court of Justice: 'With a view to the application of [Article 5, point (1), of the Brussels Convention], must the place of performance of the obligation in question, within the meaning of that provision, be determined in accordance with the law which, in accordance with the rules on conflict of laws of the court seised, governs the obligation at issue, or should national courts determine the place of performance of the obligation by seeking to establish, having regard to the nature of the relationship creating the obligation and the circumstances of the case, the place where performance actually took place or should have taken place, without having to refer to the law which, under the rules on conflict of laws, governs the obligation at issue?'

III -The applicable provisions of the Brussels Convention

10. The first paragraph of Article 2 of the Brussels Convention lays down the following general rule of jurisdiction: 'Subject to the provisions of this Convention, persons domiciled in a Contracting State shall, whatever their nationality, be sued in the courts of that State.'

11. The special jurisdictions include that of Article 5, point (1), the relevant part of which is worded as follows: 'A person domiciled in a

Contracting State may, in another Contracting State, be sued: (1) in matters relating to a contract, in the courts for the place of performance of the obligation in question ....'

Consequently, point (1) of Article 5 creates an exceptional jurisdiction by virtue of which the plaintiff may, provided the conditions prescribed in the provision are fulfilled, choose between two forums: that of the defendant's domicile or that of the place of performance of the contractual obligation, which thereby becomes a concurrent or optional jurisdiction.

IV - Brief summary of the case-law

12. Just as a reminder, I shall review briefly the Court's case-law on Article 5, point (1), of the Convention in so far as it is relevant to the present case.

13. The *Tessili* case produced the first judgment on the subject. On that occasion, the Court found that the place of performance of the seller's obligation to guarantee against hidden defects in goods was to be determined in accordance with the law applicable to the contract of sale according to the rules of conflict of laws of the court before which the matter was brought.

In another judgment, delivered on the same day in the *De Bloos* case, the Court made it clear, with regard to the former wording of Article 5, that the contractual obligation to be taken into account was that on which the action was based.

14. The Court allowed only one exception to the general rule laid down in the *Tessili* judgment. I refer to the obligations arising from a contract of employment. In *Ivenel* the Court held that, among all the obligations arising under a contract of employment, the only obligation to be taken into account for the purposes of the application of Article 5, point (1), of the Convention, was the obligation which 'characterised' the contract. This obligation was to be deemed to have been performed in practice at the place where the worker supplied his services. The Court refused to extend this interpretation to other situations.

15. In *Custom Made*, cited above, in spite of the Opinion of Advocate General Lenz, who proposed that the court of the place having the closest connection with the dispute should have jurisdiction, the Court preferred to abide by its traditional method: the place of performance was to be determined pursuant to the substantive law governing the obligation in dispute, even where that law incorporated the 1964 Uniform Law on the International Sale of Goods.

V - The observations submitted to the Court

(a) The observations of the parties to the main proceedings

16. Counsel for GIE Group Concorde and the other plaintiffs contend that, by referring the present question to the Court of Justice, the Cour de Cassation is in essence asking the Court to abandon its settled case-law and to give an autonomous interpretation to the phrase 'place of performance of the obligation'.

As no circumstances have arisen which would support this new development of case-law, the plaintiffs in the main proceedings consider that the place of performance of contractual obligations must continue to be determined in accordance with the substantive law applicable under the rules of conflict of the court before which the matter is brought.

17. In their observations, the defendants Pro Line and the company insuring the vessel reach the same conclusion after stressing the considerable differences still existing in the various European legal systems with regard to the determination of the place of performance of a contractual obligation and the consequences which this has on ability to foresee the competent court in matters relating to a contract, desirable as that is.

(b) The observations of the intervening governments

18. The German Government supports an autonomous interpretation of 'the place of performance of the obligation'. As there are many different types of contract, the place of performance should be determined by reference to each type. Furthermore, according to the German Government, to maintain the necessary equilibrium between the parties, the place of performance of a contract should be determined in each case according to the particular obligation in question.

Thus, in the case of contracts for the sale or use of property in return for consideration, where the characteristic obligation is the basis of the action, the place of performance could be determined to be the place where the immovable property is situated or where the movable property is located, depending on the stipulations of the contract.

In contracts for services other than contracts of employment, the place of performance could be deemed to be the place where the service in question is to be mainly carried out, where it forms the basis of the action.

On the other hand, where the action relates to the pecuniary consideration, the place of performance could be deemed to be the defendant's forum at the time when the contract was concluded.

19. The United Kingdom Government also advocates an independent definition of 'place of performance'. According to this Government, an independent definition would not only promote legal certainty and ensure the equality and uniformity of the rights and obligations arising under the Convention, but would also reduce, in accordance with the aims of the Convention, the potential for forum shopping.

The United Kingdom adds that the practical application of an independent definition must be effected case by case. So far as the present case is concerned, as the action arises from the delivery of damaged goods on the basis of a contract of carriage, the place of performance of the obligation is the place at which it was agreed that those goods were to be delivered.

20. The French Government accepts, firstly, that it has been found that certain national courts have had difficulty in applying the principles of the *Tessili* judgment and that they have given rise to a certain lack of foreseeability with

regard to the competent court in matters relating to a contract. However, as relationships creating obligations are not always governed by uniform legal rules, to permit the national court to designate the place of performance according to the *de facto* circumstances of each of those relationships would give rise to unforeseeability and, therefore, legal uncertainty. Consequently, the French Government considers that it is not desirable to accept the solution indirectly proposed by the Cour de Cassation, which would consist in giving 'place of performance' an independent definition.

21. The Italian Government agrees that Article 5, point (1), of the Convention has given rise to differing interpretations, and that is why the question whether it would be advisable to amend it, by the addition of a uniform point of connection, is now being studied. Therefore, it does not appear to be the right time to abandon the *Tessili* case-law. For the present, it would suffice to add the proviso that where, under Article 5, point (1), the defendant's forum has jurisdiction, it must be the same as the forum for the place of performance of the obligation, understood uniformly as an autonomous concept by the court before which the matter is brought.

(c) The Commission's observations

22. According to the Commission, the Court's approach in *Tessili* was from the beginning an interim solution in so far as, at that time, it was not possible to arrive at a Community interpretation which would ensure the uniform application of Article 5, point (1), of the Brussels Convention. The Commission adds that this approach gives rise to certain practical and theoretical difficulties. The court before which the matter is brought must first establish, by reference to its own rules of conflict, the law applying to the obligation in question and must then determine the competent forum according to that law. However, this method departs from the general rule in private international law that the determination of the competent court is independent of the determination of the applicable law.

The Commission therefore proposes that the Court should interpret the term 'place of performance' independently. This is appropriate particularly in the case of contracts for carriage by sea, the specific characteristics of which make it difficult to apply the principles of the *Tessili* judgment effectively. After examining the existing possibilities of interpretation for determining the place for performance of the obligation to deliver goods without damage under a contract for the international carriage of goods by sea, the Commission favours 'the place where the goods have been or are to be delivered'.

VI - Discussion of the solution adopted in *Tessili*

23. The question on which the Cour de Cassation seeks a preliminary ruling does not appear in principle to require the attention of the full Court of Justice. The question relates to the interpretation of Article 5, point (1), of the Brussels Convention, namely the meaning of 'place of performance of the obligation in question' for the purposes of this European code of procedure.

However, the Court has been giving rulings on this question since 1976, when it gave what was to become the first judgment delivered on the subject of the Brussels Convention. To ascertain whether it has jurisdiction, the court before which the matter is brought 'must determine in accordance with its own rules of conflict of laws what is the law applicable to the legal relationship in question and define in accordance with that law the place of performance of the contractual obligation in question'. This case-law was followed recently, in the same terms, in *Custom Made* on a reference for a preliminary ruling from the Bundesgerichtshof. The Court has been giving virtually the same answer for more than 20 years.

24. It is true that, in relation to *Tessili*, the *Custom Made* case had a new element in so far as the law applicable to the legal relationship arose, not from the rules of conflict, but from a uniform law originating from a convention relating to international transactions, namely the Uniform Law on the International Sale of Goods, annexed to the Hague Convention of 1 July 1964. However, this reference is not valid in the present case. The Cour de Cassation does not indicate any particular feature of the present case which might justify a reply other than that already given by the Court in relation to the *Tessili* and *Custom Made* cases. Nor can it be said - at least, in my opinion - that the circumstances underlying the *Custom Made* judgment have changed appreciably. By referring once again the question of the interpretation of Article 5, point (1), of the Convention, the Cour de Cassation has exercised the right of the national courts, which has been recognised by the Court of Justice in relation to questions referred under Article 177 of the EC Treaty, to refer settled questions of interpretation to the Court again, if they consider it desirable to do so.

25. The Brussels Convention lays down a general rule *(actor sequitur forum rei)*, known in almost all legal systems, that the courts of the defendant's domicile have jurisdiction. However, in addition to this true general forum, the Convention creates other bases of jurisdiction, some of which are special or optional while others are exclusive. The former include that which interests us here: the plaintiff may sue the defendant in the courts for 'the place of performance of the obligation in question'. Later on I shall set out the reason for this special forum. For the present it is sufficient to say that a plaintiff who wishes to assert in court a right arising from a contractual obligation has the option of bringing an action, at his convenience, before at least two courts: that of the defendant's domicile and that for the place of performance of the obligation.

26. The phrase 'place of performance of the obligation', seemingly so simple, soon gives rises to many questions. What is meant by 'matters relating to a contract'? What obligation is referred to? The obligation to deliver the goods or to carry out the service, for example, or the obligation to pay the price? How is the place of performance to be determined? In accordance with which law? The law of the court before which the matter is brought, or some other law?

27. Since its judgment in *Tessili*, the Court has given replies to all these questions. First, the word 'obligation' and the phrase 'in matters relating to a contract' must be construed independently, that is to say, independently of the

terms used by the national legal systems. Secondly, the national court must assess the obligation on which the claim is based and establish the law applying to that obligation in order, finally, to determine the place of performance designated by virtue of that law. If it is the same as the place designated by the court's own law, the court will have jurisdiction, otherwise it will not.

28. In theory, the *Tessili* principles appear technically flawless. In an ideal world, where legal rules are unambiguous and courts omniscient, the *Tessili* principles permit foreseeable, uniform answers which comply with the letter - and perhaps even the spirit - of the Convention. In practice, however, there is more than one disagreeable surprise in store. *Tessili* requires a court to carry out three rather painstaking tasks from the legal viewpoint. First, it must, taking account of the information in its possession, classify or characterise the contractual obligation in question. For this purpose, the court will establish whether the legal relationship is contractual and will classify the relationship creating an obligation in the generally accepted categories (contracts of sale or carriage, leases and loan agreements, etc.). Although this first task is perhaps the simplest, it is not always straightforward. For example, what is the nature of the relationship between an association and its members? Or again, what are the limits of a right to damages in contract as compared with a claim in tort? In any case, the court will have to examine initially in more detail the conditions of the claim.

29. Secondly, the court will have to ascertain whether the legal relationship in question is subject to uniform international rules, a task which the constant proliferation of international agreements sometimes makes more difficult, rather than easier. If there are no uniform international rules, the court must apply its own rules of private international law to discover which law is applicable or, as the case may be, the Rome Convention of 19 June 1980 on the Law Applicable to Contractual Obligations, since the date when it came into force. This work may necessitate even more detailed study of aspects going to the substance of the case. Every legal practitioner knows the difficulties involved in referring to the rules of conflict of a given legal system, the magnitude of the difficulties being equalled only by the fascination with which they are studied by university professors.

30. Thirdly, once the applicable law has been identified, the court must determine, by reference to that law, the place of performance of the obligation in question. If no uniform rules in this connection are found, the court will have to seek them in its own law or in a foreign system. The difficulties arising in the latter case, which depend on the venue and on the applicable law in question, may be practically insurmountable. In any case, determining the place of performance of a particular type of obligation comes up against the general antipathy of most legal systems to theoretical definitions. With the possible exception of obligations for the payment of a sum of money, national legal systems are usually content with a general reference to the will, express or implied, of the parties. This situation will compel the court to study the substance of the case in even greater depth.

31. At best, all this effort will have served to confirm the jurisdiction of the

court before which the matter has been brought or, at worst, to rule out the application of Article 5 or to confer jurisdiction upon the courts of another Member State which, if a new case is brought before them, will nevertheless have to go through the same procedure to verify their jurisdiction.

32. I now propose to apply to the present case the steps which I have just described.

VII - Application of the *Tessili* judgment to the present case

33. The plaintiffs in the main proceedings are insurance companies. They insured the carriage by sea of certain goods between the ports of Le Havre in France and Santos in Brazil. On arrival at the port of destination, it was found that some of the goods were damaged or missing and the insurance companies therefore indemnified the consignee. Having been subrogated to the latter's remedies and rights, the insurers had recourse to those responsible for carrying the goods (the master of the vessel, the shipping company which owns it, the carrier and the insurance company covering the civil liability of the vessel) by bringing before a court of first instance in Le Havre the action which has led to this reference to the Court of Justice.

34. Confronted with the question of its own jurisdiction, the court of Le Havre ought, according to the *Tessili* judgment, to have established, by means of autonomous interpretation, whether the matter before it related to a contract. It would appear that this question need not have detained the court for long. The action undoubtedly originates, at least indirectly, from a contract for the carriage of goods. In actual fact, this is true only with regard to the action against the carrier. So far as the other defendants are concerned, the basis of the action for indemnity probably lies in tort. In the latter case, and in accordance with the case-law of the Court of Justice, the court of Le Havre ought to have refrained from applying Article 5, point (1), of the Convention in relation to the other defendants as the obligations in question were not a 'matter relating to a contract'.

35. After establishing that the action is contractual, the court of Le Havre should have ascertained the specific obligation on which the action was based, at least in relation to one of the defendants. As, according to the Court, 'in a case where the plaintiff asserts the right to be paid damages ... the obligation referred to in Article 5, point (1), is still that which arises under the contract and the non-performance of which is relied upon to support such claims', it is clear that the obligation which the national court ought to have considered decisive is the obligation to transport the goods delivered to the port of destination without damage.

36. Next, the court ought to have determined the law applicable. For this purpose, still according to the *Tessili* judgment, the court ought to have used its own rules of conflict. There are many different points of connection in the rules of conflict with regard to contracts. Let us imagine, for the sake of argument, that the possibilities which could have been considered were, in sequence, the law chosen by the parties, the national law common to the parties, the law of the

place where the contract was concluded and, finally, the law of the place of performance. As there is no indication of the law chosen by the parties, who in any case do not appear to have the same nationality, and as there may be serious doubt as to the place where the contract was concluded in so far as it is between a carrier and a consignee of goods to whom the bill of lading was to be delivered - the court will probably have to determine the law applicable to the contract by reference to ... the place of its performance!

37. Now let us imagine that the court before which the matter is brought reaches the conclusion, by reference to the express or implied will of the parties or by applying an imperative or dispositive rule in the course of its conflictualist examination, that the law applicable is that of Brazil. The court will then have to determine the place designated by Brazilian law as the place of performance of the obligation of carriage by sea. As it is unlikely that a French court of first instance will have sufficient knowledge of Brazilian law or adequate means of understanding it, the court will probably abandon such a complicated method and will apply a different solution which would take account, if possible, of the particular circumstances of the case.

38. If, perhaps, the French court has sufficient knowledge of Brazilian law, it will probably find that the law of that country, like every other legal system, prefers to refrain from theoretical definitions in matters of contract, leaving it to the parties to define the terms of the contract. If the information available to the court leads it to conclude that the parties' intention was to agree that the place of performance was to be the destination port of the goods, the court must find that the port of Santos was designated.

39. As a place situated in Brazil is designated as the place of performance of the contractual obligation, the French court has no choice but to decline jurisdiction and to refrain from taking further cognisance of the action as regards the application of Article 5, point (1), of the Convention. The difficulty arises from the fact that the first paragraph of Article S provides, in so far as we are concerned, that 'a person domiciled *in a Contracting State may, in another Contracting State*, be sued ...'. When a court finds that an action before it is based on an obligation which has been or must be fulfilled 'outside the territory of the Contracting States, it has no choice but to conclude that the place provided for in Article 5, point (1), of the Convention cannot serve as a basis for attributing jurisdiction to a court within that territory and that Article 5, point (1), cannot therefore be applicable'.

40. Just for the sake of illustration, if the case had been brought in Spain, the court would have applied the law to which the parties to the legal transaction had expressly submitted, provided that it had a connection with the transaction in question; failing an express choice, the national law common to the parties; failing that, the law of the common habitual residence and, finally, the law of the place where the contract was concluded. The particulars in the order for reference do not show which law would have been applied but, in all probability, to determine the law in question it would have been necessary to define terms such as 'habitual residence' in relation to companies and their establishments, or 'place of conclusion of the contract' in relation to 'contracts concluded at a distance'.

41. However, from the information available I think I may conclude that the French court ought to have referred to the Rome Convention of 19 June 1980 on the Law Applicable to Contractual Obligations in order to determine the lex causae. So far as the French Republic is concerned, the Convention came into force on 1 April 1991, while the action was brought before the court of Le Havre on 22 September 1991 (see paragraph 6 above). Therefore the solution would have been somewhat simpler and, of course, uniform throughout the Contracting States. However, it could not in itself have eliminated the risk of diverging interpretations. The reason is that Article 4(1) of the Convention provides that, where the applicable law has not been chosen by the parties, the contract is to be governed by the law of the country with which it is most closely connected. With regard to the present case, Article 4(4) provides that 'if the country in which, at the time the contract is concluded, the carrier has his principal place of business is also the country in which the place of loading or the place of discharge or the principal place of business of the consignor is situated, it shall be presumed that the contract is most closely connected with that country'. This does not appear to be the case, so that the only criterion for choosing the applicable law is simply 'most closely connected' of Article 4(1).

42. If the contract was concluded in France and the damage was attributable to a mistake in loading or stowing, it could be argued that the contractual obligation was most closely connected with France and therefore French law is applicable. If, on the other hand, we consider that, from the viewpoint of the obligation in question, the actual work of unloading or the State where the goods were located is of greater importance, Brazil will be the designated country and Brazilian law will apply. With regard to characteristic obligations, reference to the lex causae merely displaces the moment of uncertainty, and with it the subsequent risk of fragmenting jurisdiction, to a later stage of reasoning, without eliminating uncertainty altogether.

43. However, once the proper law of the contract has been identified, the difficulties of determining the place of performance according to that law remain, and also the problems arising from the unsuitability of reference to the lex causae for resolving questions of jurisdiction. I shall revert to this point later.

VIII - The criticism of the *Tessili* judgment

44. The criticism of the case-law laid down in *Tessili* and *Custom Made* has concentrated essentially on two aspects: the practical difficulty of applying that case-law and the undesirable consequences of seeking the applicable substantive law in order to determine a question of jurisdiction. The fact that the courts of the plaintiff's domicile are more and more often imposed as a general forum for matters relating to contracts must be mentioned as one of these undesirable effects.

(a) The difficulties of applying the Tessili case-law

45. As I have said, the *Tessili* case-law imposes a three-fold task on the court before which the matter is brought: independently classifying the

obligation on which the claim is based; determining the law applicable to that obligation in accordance with the court's own rules of conflict; and ascertaining the place of performance of the obligation in accordance with that law.

46. I think I have shown sufficiently, using the present case as an example, that the *Tessili* method is extremely laborious, particularly when considered in relation to its only purpose, which is to determine whether the court before which the matter is brought has jurisdiction. This complexity has not only led to much criticism from commentators but also–and this is more serious–caused considerable disaffection on the part of the national courts. In a word, *Tessili* is not followed. And in cases where it is actually followed, this is often because the law applicable to the obligation in question is the law of the place in which the case is heard, namely, the law which the court knows best or, as the case may, uniform international law.

47. I should add that, in my view, the correct application of the *Tessili* judgment requires the court not only to go through the stages of reasoning described above in its internal legal system, but also to explain them and state grounds. A court which, in its decision, merely indicates a place of performance of the obligation in question for the purpose of Article 5, point (1), which is the same as that to which correct application of the *Tessili* judgment would have led has not applied that case-law.

48. Where a court does not apply the conflictualist method, it usually proceeds on the basis of the circumstances of the particular case to determine the place of performance. Finally, there have been cases of open 'rebellion' against the *Tessili* judgment, among which must be mentioned, because of its special features, that of the Cour de Cassation, the court which has referred the present question.

49. However, perhaps the most discouraging aspect of the painstaking exercise required of the national court is that, in practice, the result it will obtain will be either the defendant's domicile, in which case it would have been sufficient to apply the general forum provided for by Article 2 of the Convention, or the plaintiff's domicile, which contradicts not only most European procedural traditions, but also the system of the Brussels Convention itself, *while there is still no guarantee that either of those places is most closely connected with the case* -- the criterion which is the specific justification for Article 5, point (1), as we shall see. This occurs particularly in relation to obligations to pay a price.

(b) Reference to the lex causae to resolve questions of jurisdiction is inappropriate

50. The second main criticism of the Court's method of interpreting Article 5(1) deplores the fact that criteria which have their *raison d'etre* in substantive law are transposed into the field of jurisdictional competence, in that elements specific to rules of conduct are transferred to the field of conceptual rules or rules which create rights, such as rules of competence. Such transposition also destroys the theoretical purity which was supposed to be found in the *Tessili* method.

51. Specifically, the criticism is in essence directed at the introduction of a general jurisdiction in contractual matters which coincides with the domicile of the plaintiff, or rather the seller.

52. There can be no doubt that the most frequent type of contract in international commercial relations is the contract of sale. Furthermore, most disputes relate to the payment of the agreed price. As regards the place where payment is to be made, traditionally there have been two trends in Europe: the place of the debtor's domicile (Germany, Belgium, Spain, France) and that of the creditor's domicile (Denmark, Greece, Ireland, Italy, Netherlands, United Kingdom). The first option has been continuously eroded in favour of the second. Thus, Article 59(1), first sentence, of the 1964 Uniform Law on the International Sale of Goods provided that the place of performance of the obligation to pay the selling price is the place where the seller is established or, in the absence of an establishment, the place of his customary residence. Article 57 of the United Nations Convention on Contracts for the International Sale of Goods, which came into force on 1 January 1988, is, if possible, in even more general terms with regard to the obligation to make payment at the seller's domicile.

53. In the order for reference which gave rise to the *Custom Made* case, the Bundesgerichtshof rightly questioned whether the place of performance should be determined according to the lex causae 'even in a matter governed by the Uniform Law on Sales, which would lead to generalising the *forum actoris* in actions for payment of the price of the goods'.

54. When replying in the affirmative, the Court of Justice facilitated the research work of the national court which could, for that purpose, refer to a uniform international law. At the same time, this increased the likelihood of a uniform reply. Unfortunately, it also aggravated the pernicious tendency to use substantive-law criteria for resolving procedural problems, such as those relating to jurisdiction.

55. Nevertheless, it must be said that, in principle, there is nothing pernicious in the fact - which, on the contrary, is perfectly logical - that, so far as contractual obligations are concerned, the place of performance should be the same as the domicile of one of the parties, even if it is that of the seller. In most contracts it is customary for the respective obligations to be performed at the domicile of one of the parties. What is not legitimate is to distort the function of substantive law itself, which in this case consists in sharing out the contractual risks between the different parties, in order to establish competent courts conforming with those same criteria for sharing risks. This occurs where the increasingly general acceptance, in the international field, of the seller's domicile as the place of performance of the payment obligation opens the door, by virtue of the *Tessili* and *De Bloos* case-law, to a vast *forum actoris* in relation to pecuniary obligations, having no connection whatever with the place where the characteristic consideration of the contract was to be given. The defendant, who will generally claim that what he has received does not conform with what was agreed, will be obliged to put his case before a court perhaps a very long way from his domicile. For its part, the court before which the case is brought

must find that it has jurisdiction even if it has to use long and costly letters rogatory to obtain essential evidence, that is to say, to verify the defendant's allegations of contractual non-conformity.

56. In his Opinion in the *Custom Made* case, Advocate General Lenz devoted the greater part of his criticism of the Court's case-law to this problem. After observing that, according to the intention of the draftsmen of the Convention, the concept of 'place of performance' was to enable a court closely connected with the facts to be designated, Mr Lenz observed that 'the rules of the *lex causae* relating to the place of performance may ... embody elements which serve solely to apportion the risk ... and do not provide reliable indications about the economic *objective* of the seller's obligations'. It follows that this rule is not appropriate for designating a court closely connected with the facts of the case.

Consequently, for Mr Lenz, the main defect of the method consisting in determining the *forum contractus* by reference to the substantive law applicable by virtue of the rules of conflict is not so much an alleged general 'antipathy' to the jurisdiction of the defendant's domicile - which he does not find to exist as the fact that this method is useless for attaining the specific objective of Article 5, point (1), namely the creation of a special forum in contractual matters with physical proximity to the facts.

57. Although the criticism which I have just set out is entirely justified, it must be recognised that it arises from the *De Bloos* judgment and the isolation of bilateral obligations which it establishes, rather than from the *Tessili* method. As I indicated above, the controversy concerning the correct classification of the obligation for the purpose of Article 5(1) is outside the scope of these proceedings. Even though in the present case the plaintiffs in the main proceedings claim a sum of money, there is no doubt that they are acting by virtue of subrogation to the consignee of the goods and therefore they have brought an action based on the characteristic obligation of the contract, namely the obligation to carry the goods and to deliver them in good condition to the consignee.

58. I should like to add, however, that determining the place of performance by reference to the *lex causae* contributes greatly to complicating the practical application of the *Tessili* principles. As I said previously, the main concern of substantive law in the matter of contractual obligations - is in general to share out the responsibilities or, in other words, the risk, between the contracting parties. It follows that civil or commercial legislation rarely lays down what is meant by the place of performance of an obligation, in the absence of express agreement between the parties. The law usually defines the moment at which the risk passes from one contracting party to the other. Normally that is the only indication offered by substantive law to the court to enable it to define what could be meant by 'place of performance'. I doubt seriously whether it is legitimate to define the place of performance of an obligation by reference to the rules on sharing out contractual responsibilities. What happens if it is agreed that the goods are to be carried at the consignee's risk? Does this mean that, by shifting to the port of loading the moment of the passing of the risk, the place

where the obligation is to be performed is also moved? Or, where the law provides that, in certain circumstances, the carrier is not liable for damage arising from the fact that the vessel is not seaworthy, does this mean that, for the purpose of an action for breach of contract, a carrier who pleads the statutory defence may claim that the place where he put goods on board the defective ship should be regarded as the place of performance of his obligation, on the ground that that is where his responsibility ceased in the case in question?

The rules on the sharing of commercial risks are of no use at all for designating the competent court.

IX - The objectives of Article 5, point (1), of the Convention

59. Any attempt to interpret Article 5, point (1), of the Brussels Convention must begin by determining the purpose of what is called the forum contractus. What is the purpose of Article 5, point (1), in the framework of the Brussels Convention? Why is it capable of creating a special jurisdiction at the place of performance of a contractual obligation and not, for example, at the place where the contract was concluded?

(a) The general objectives of the Brussels Convention

60. Article 5, point (1), forms part of the Convention which was adopted by the Member States on the basis of Article 220 of the EC Treaty, which provides that 'the Member States shall, so far as is necessary, enter into negotiations with each other with a view to securing for the benefit of their nationals ... the simplification of formalities governing the reciprocal recognition and enforcement of judgments of courts or tribunals and of arbitration awards'. The scope of the Brussels Convention is clearly much wider than the specific objective laid down by Article 220. However, I wish to emphasise the aim of 'simplification' which it mentions.

The preamble to the Convention states that the 'simplification of formalities' referred to by Article 220 and the 'legal protection' of persons established in the European Community are among the objectives of the Convention.

61. The corollary of the second objective of 'legal certainty' which imbues the whole of the Convention is to provide parties to actions with foreseeable decisions.

62. In the *Mulox* judgment, the Court described the objectives of uniform application of the Convention, which include 'unification of the rules on jurisdiction of the courts of the Contracting States, so as to avoid ... the multiplication of the bases of jurisdiction in relation to one and the same legal relationship and to reinforce the legal protection available to persons established in the Community, by, at the same time, allowing the plaintiff easily to identify the court before which he may bring an action and the defendant reasonably to foresee the court before which he may be sued'.

(b) The specific objectives of Article 5, point (1), of the Convention

63. The main aims of the Brussels Convention as a whole are reflected most clearly in what is conventionally called its general forum, that is to say, the defendant's domicile. That forum meets, appropriately and at one and the same time, the aims of uniformity, foreseeability, avoiding a multiplicity of jurisdictions, ease of designation and legal protection. However, the Convention provides for a limited number of special jurisdictions, the justification for which varies from case to case. Thus, in proceedings concerning immovable property, Article 16 provides that the courts of the State in which the property is situated are to have exclusive jurisdiction by reason of the advantages for the administration of justice arising from the proximity of those courts to the subject-matter of the dispute. Similarly, with regard to insurance, the insured may choose to bring an action before the court of his domicile in order to have greater legal protection. Consequently, there is no doubt that the adoption of a special, optional forum in contractual matters must also have an equally specific justification.

64. Article 5, point (1), is generally said to have two main objectives: the proximity of the court with jurisdiction to the subject-matter of the dispute and procedural balance between the parties.

65. The justification of proximity to the subject-matter has been recognised since the Jenard Report. In principle, there is no doubt that the fact that the court is close to the place where the obligation in question was to be performed appears likely, in most cases, to facilitate the administration of evidence. That is usually the place where the goods are located or where the obligation is to be fulfilled. It is also the place where witnesses can most easily be reached and where expert reports can be obtained at less cost, by avoiding slow and costly letters rogatory. In fact, however, this is true only with regard to the place where the characteristic obligation of the contract is to be fulfilled. That is why I said previously that I am in favour of rectifying the *De Bloos* case-law so that a merely pecuniary obligation, that is to say, one not characteristic of the contract, would no longer be taken into account for the purpose of Article 5, point (1). Even if the plaintiff claims that the agreed price has not been paid, the place of performance of the obligation *in kind* serves best to designate a court with proximity to the dispute because, firstly, the defendant generally pleads in his defence that the plaintiff has not fulfilled or has only partly fulfilled his obligation and, secondly, proof of payment is normally in documentary form: that is why it is to a greater extent independent of a specific place in proximity to which a basis of jurisdiction should be established. In any case, I repeat that these considerations, although important, have no direct bearing on the outcome of the main proceedings, which concern, as we know, the performance of the characteristic obligation of the contract.

66. The Court has accepted this justification in its case-law on more than one occasion.

67. Personally, I think it is more correct to speak of 'connection with the contract' rather than 'proximity to the subject-matter', in so far as the links

between the competent court and the contract may be based on mere declarations of intention rather than facts proper. This usually applies in the case of total non-performance of the obligation due. In that case, the place where the obligation was to be performed can be determined only on the basis of hypothetical factors.

From this viewpoint, the criterion of connection derives further legitimacy, apart from considerations of the proper administration of justice, from the general principle of the autonomy of the contracting parties' intention.

68. Certain commentators add that the creation of the *forum solutionis* enables the advantages and risks connected with determining the competent court to be shared fairly between the plaintiff and the defendant. In this way, Article 5, point (1), is said to act as a counterweight to the general rule of the forum of the defendant's domicile.

69. Some of these writers use this supposed purpose of the above mentioned provision to support a broad interpretation of it. They contend that Article 5 of the Convention, read in conjunction with Article 2, is based on the idea that, in certain particular cases, the plaintiff's interest must take precedence over the protection of the defendant and therefore that he should be given an option with regard to jurisdiction. To be effective, this right of option must not be construed restrictively, otherwise Article 5, point (1), and Article 2 could be fused into one and the same provision, the former being left with no effect at all.

70. Personally, I think that this last argument, although original, has insufficient support in the legal traditions of the Member States to be regarded as authentic. Furthermore, I do not think this justification is necessary or useful. It is true that in practice Article 5, point (1), by conferring jurisdiction in many cases on the courts of the plaintiffs domicile, may to some extent counterbalance the general forum. However, this is due more to the simple fact that, generally, obligations have to be performed where at least one of the parties resides, rather than to a supposed intention to achieve a balance between the parties to a contract so far as jurisdiction is concerned.

(c) First provisional conclusion

71. At this stage of the discussion, I think it useful to set out a first provisional conclusion regarding the general and particular objectives which, in my opinion, are pursued by the establishment of the *forum contractus* in the framework of the Brussels Convention.

It follows from what has been said that the proper interpretation of Article 5, point (1), must lead to designating as the competent court that which is situated at a place having a close connection with the contractual obligation in question, a place which is determined by reference to the general requirements of foreseeability, of avoiding a multiplicity of jurisdictions, of uniform criteria and of ease of designation.

X - The possible methods of interpretation

72. As I have already said, the first judgment given by the Court under the Protocol of 3 June 1971 related precisely to Article 5, point (1), of the Brussels Convention. The issue then was to determine the place of performance of the seller's obligation to deliver goods in conformity with the contract. The defendant company in the main proceedings, Dunlop AG, even then set out in its written observations the two main possibilities open to the Court: on the one hand, a uniform interpretation based on elements of comparative law and, on the other, a conflictualist interpretation dependent on the substantive law applicable in each case. With regard to the latter possibility, counsel for Dunlop even then pointed out the danger in treating the place of performance of the obligation as that of the seller's domicile and finally proposed as the place of performance the place where the obligation was actually to be carried out, namely the place indicated by the circumstances of the case, by reference to the relationship creating the obligation in question.

73. More than 20 years have elapsed and, although Article 5, point (1), has been the subject of more judicial controversy and has been given more attention by commentators than any other provision of the Brussels Convention, the possible solutions are in substance still the same, namely:

(a) uniform interpretation in the framework of the Convention, which is in itself independent of the interpretations prevailing in the Member States, even if it is based on them, and which is now commonly called 'autonomous interpretation';

(b) the conflictualist method, generally used by the Court, which consists in determining the place of performance of the obligation by reference to the substantive law applicable to the particular case according to the rules of conflict of the court before which the matter is brought;

(c) the designation of the place of performance by reference to the particular circumstances of the case and the nature of the relationship creating the obligation in question; this is the solution which the Cour de Cassation appears to suggest.

74. These three categories, as described above, must be understood as means of analysis rather than true, completely defined scientific options. The third variant is really only a sub-category of the first. This makes it necessary first of all to choose between, on the one hand, recourse to the *lex causae* and, on the other, autonomous interpretation. When this choice has been made, it is necessary to find the criterion of interpretation which best satisfies the general and particular requirements of the *forum executionis*, which I have listed above. In other words, I think it prudent to distinguish between methods and criteria of interpretation and to examine them one after the other.

(a) Autonomous interpretation

75. 'An autonomous interpretation of the terms used in the Convention is preferable in principle because it helps to secure the uniform application of the

Convention and thus contributes to the realisation of its underlying purpose, which is to unify the jurisdiction rules of the Contracting States. Such unification is inevitably impeded if the meaning of the terms used in the Convention varies according to the applicable law.' I fully concur with the views of Advocate General Jacobs expressed in the *Mulox* case.

76. Autonomous interpretation fulfils one of the fundamental purposes of the Brussels Convention: to attain a high degree of uniformity within Europe with regard to the treatment of questions of international jurisdiction.

77. Autonomous interpretation also facilitates to a large extent the application of the Convention by avoiding constant recourse to the law applicable to the legal relationship in question. As I have already stressed with regard to the *locus solutionis*, the need to construe the terms used in the Convention by recourse to the *lex causae* means that the mere designation of the competent court raises difficulties associated with the substance of the case, which are aggravated by the special features of the technique of conflict of laws (classification, preliminary question, public policy and other concepts).

78. It is not surprising that the Court has preferred autonomous interpretation in almost all cases. Thus, it has interpreted independently not only the phrase 'matters relating to a contract', but also, among others, 'civil and commercial matters', so 'matters relating to tort, delict or quasi-delict' and 'maintenance creditor'. It seems to have abandoned this method only in very rare cases, namely those in which the Convention itself calls for recourse to national law (for example, in relation to the term 'domicile') and, precisely, Article 5, point (1), but even with regard to the latter, only in relation to the definition of 'place of performance'.

79. Autonomous interpretation therefore meets the aims of uniform criteria and ease of designation. In the following paragraphs I wish to make the point that, in relation to the other aims of the Convention, the technique of the *Tessili* judgment offers no advantages.

(b) The conflictualist method

80. The supporters of the conflictualist method stress mainly the limitations inherent in the autonomous interpretation of the terms of an international convention. They also maintain that there is nothing to indicate that the jurisdiction of the court of the plaintiff's domicile is incompatible with the special forum of the place of performance of the obligation. Moreover, they consider that the possibility that the place determined by reference to the *lex causae* may have no connection with the subject-matter in question is a risk inherent in all cases of special jurisdiction. The assumption that the connection exists justifies the creation of the special forum of the place of performance of the obligation. Nevertheless, when applying this special jurisdiction rule, a court may be guided only by the formal criteria adopted by the Convention.

81. The Court itself justifies its preference for recourse to the *lex causae* by invoking legal certainty and foreseeability.

82. In my opinion, recourse to the *lex causae* provides at most only a

certain degree of theoretical peace of mind. There is something attractive in the apparent mathematical logic of the *Tessili* method, in its theoretical formulation. In reality, the conflictualist solution offers no *advantage whatsoever* over autonomous interpretation, but it certainly has numerous disadvantages.

83. In default of agreement between the parties, the term 'place of performance' in Article 5, point (1), could be interpreted independently by treating it as the same as 'the place with which the contract is most closely connected'. This possibility is categorically rejected, in spite of its undeniable simplicity, because it would compel the court to examine the substance of the case in detail and, because of the uncertainty as to the result of the assessment of the facts which the court would have to make, would open the door to diverging judgments and, ultimately, to the multiplication of bases of jurisdiction. On the other hand, according to the conflictualists, supported on this point by the Court's settled case-law, recourse must be had to the *lex causae*. In other words, the court before which the matter is brought must first find the law applicable to the legal relationship in question. For this purpose it must, since it came into force, use the Rome Convention of 19 June 1980 on the Law Applicable to Contractual Obligations, Article 4(1) of which provides that 'to the extent that the law applicable has not been chosen ... the contract shall be governed by the law of the country with which it is most closely connected'. This is followed by a number of provisions which require the court to examine the substance of the case in more and more detail (raising of presumptions and exceptions to them, nature and subject-matter of the contract, determining the 'characteristic obligation'). The conflictualist method merely postpones to a later stage of the court's examination the inevitable assessment of the substance of the case. Moreover, I fail to see why the criterion of the closest connection provided for by the 1980 Rome Convention should permit solutions more uniform than those based on the criterion of the place of performance, which is itself also relatively indeterminate.

84. The difference between the two methods is that, whereas a court which would prefer autonomous interpretation already has a reply, with the potential errors and omissions inevitable in law, which is not an exact science, a court which chooses the conflictualist approach must still determine the place of performance of the obligation in question, in accordance with the law which it finds applicable. If the *lex fori*, which the court knows best, is applicable, the task will be easier. If, on the other hand, foreign law, perhaps of some distant country, is applicable, s the exercise will become appreciably more complicated. If it is a question of the characteristic obligation of the contract, as in the present case, whichever law is consulted will probably reply that the place of performance is the place chosen by the parties and, in default of agreement on the point, it must be designated in the light of the circumstances of the relationship creating the obligation in question, that is to say, by means of an assessment of the facts. Consequently we find ourselves back where we started.

To sum up, the method set out in the *Tessili* judgment guarantees no more legal certainty than an autonomous interpretation and it complicates unnecessarily the task of the court before which the matter is brought.

85. In addition, there is no guarantee that the *Tessili* method will designate a court closer to the facts or more closely connected with the obligation in question than the court which would be designated by recourse to an autonomous interpretation.

(c) Second provisional conclusion

86. Accordingly, I arrive at the second provisional conclusion of my analysis. The autonomous method has undoubted advantages by comparison with conflictualist interpretation, particularly with regard to the uniformity of criteria and the ease of designating the competent courts under Article 5, point (1). Regarding the aims of foreseeability, avoidance of a multiplicity of jurisdictions, and proximity or connection, the *Tessili* method merely succeeds in postponing recourse to a connecting element which necessitates examination of the facts of the case. However, because of its technical complexity, the conflictualist method encourages mistakes when it is applied and even when it is not applied, with the legal uncertainty which that entails.

XI - The criterion for interpretation proposed by Advocate General Lenz

87. Among the different criteria available for the purpose of autonomous interpretation, I think it would be helpful to study the proposal put forward by Mr Lenz in the *Custom Made* case.

Mr Lenz began his original analysis by observing that a forum designated as having jurisdiction on the basis of a concept of substantive law can be justified only on procedural grounds, namely a ground such as physical proximity to the relationship at issue. Therefore, according to Mr Lenz, it is necessary to distinguish clearly between the sharing of the economic risks, which is effected by substantive law, and the procedural grounds which are the subject of Article 5. It is dangerous to confuse the two concepts: under the Uniform Law on the International Sale of Goods (and particularly Article 59(1)), that is to say, the substantive law applicable by virtue of the *Tessili* judgment, the result would be to create, in the framework of Article 5, point (1), a true general jurisdiction of the defendant's domicile.

I share the concern expressed by Mr Lenz, although I still consider that the practical difficulties of applying it and the inevitable risk of divergence and legal uncertainty which it involves are the main defect of the conflictualist method.

88. Mr Lenz proposed that as, in disputes concerning the payment of the price - as opposed to those where the conclusion of the contract itself is disputed - the question in most cases is whether the seller duly fulfilled his obligations, the competent court under Article 5, point (1), is that which is best able to assess whether that is so.

89. As Mr Lenz himself admits, his proposal differs only very slightly from the *De Bloos* judgment, in so far as 'contractual obligation' must be taken to mean only the obligation 'which is far the more likely to result in the determination of a court physically proximate to the relationship than the

obligation at issue'. According to Mr Lenz, the *Tessili* case-law would continue to apply, albeit not for the purposes of determining the place of performance of the obligation at issue, but the place of performance of the counter-obligation of the other party (paragraph 78). However, the Advocate General then 'qualifies' that statement: 'As I used such elements when I examined the rules on the place of performance of the obligation to make payment as a reason for diverging from the substantive law of the contract, on the ground that those rules could not serve to determine a court which was physically proximate to the relationship at issue, it would seem illogical to use another method when considering the rules on the place of performance of the seller's obligation to deliver the goods'. And Mr Lenz concludes by proposing a completely independent interpretation of the place of performance in that case: '... in the case of disputes about the payment of the price arising on account of alleged defective performance of the counter-obligation ... the courts for the place at which the goods were intended to be supplied is, as a general rule, nearer to the facts than the court for the place from which they were sent. This is true irrespective as to which of those two places is the "place of performance" under the substantive law' (paragraph 80). And the Advocate General proposes that this same court be designated as the competent court for the purpose of Article 5, point (1), of the Convention.

90. To sum up, the conclusion reached by Advocate General Lenz implies a certain rectification of the *De Bloos* judgment (by introducing the concept of the characteristic obligation under a different name) and, in practice, the abandonment of the *Tessili* case-law in favour of an independent interpretation, according to which the *forum contractus* would be the place closest to the subject-matter.

91. Although I am in favour of the approach taken by my eminent colleague, I differ as to the *minimum theoretical criterion for the independent interpretation* preferred by Mr Lenz, that is to say, proximity to the subject-matter. Such proximity or, if you will, the connection with the contract, as objectives of the provision, are the foreseeable result of independent determination, and not the criterion for interpretation.

92. Mr Lenz ends by proposing that the Court's reply should be that the place of performance, within the meaning of Article 5, point (1), of the Convention, of the obligations arising from a contract for manufacture and supply is the place at which the goods are intended to be supplied.

93. This point leads me to what is perhaps the main criticism (or the main apprehension) of independent interpretation in this sense, which consists in saying that it would compel the Court to determine, case by case, the place of performance of each of the innumerable types of contract.

94. In my opinion, it is an illusion to think that it is possible to make an exhaustive list of every kind of contractual obligation, present and future, and to attribute theoretically a specific place of performance to each of them. Autonomy of intention does not lend itself to classification. Furthermore, without greater precision in the text of the Convention, this exercise would compel the national courts to request a preliminary ruling from the Court of Justice whenever they are confronted by a new type of obligation (the

possibilities are endless), thus defeating the Convention's aim of simplification. Any criterion for interpretation must be simple and unambiguous.

XII - The proposed solution: designation of the place of performance by reference to the particular circumstances of the case and the relationship creating the obligation in question

(a) Should the case-law be changed?

95. The difficulties created by the case-law laid down in the *Tessili* judgment suggest that the Court of Justice should take a new approach in its case-law. Although the interpretation proposed by the *Tessili* judgment has prevailed for 20 years and although it was solemnly followed in the *Custom Made* judgment, it has not gained acceptance by the national courts, which follow it very unequally and, above all, very imperfectly. The fact is that the correct application of the *Tessili* technique is a matter of fiendish difficulty.

96. The referring of a question by the French Cour de Cassation, which is familiar with the position adopted by Community case-law, must be understood as a desperate call for the aim of uniformity that the Court must pursue to be attained in the form of interpretive criteria, of more or less great scientific exactitude, but which meet the requirements of and the resources available to a lower court in the Community, without seriously affecting the other aims of the Convention.

97. I think the time has come for the wisdom and prudence of the Court of Justice to prevail once again. There must be a change of case-law to interpret Article 5, point (1), of the Brussels Convention in accordance with the requirements of social reality.

98. The temptation to wait for the necessary change to come from the negotiations concerning the amendment of the Brussels Convention now taking place within the Council should be resisted. Firstly, because such conduct would be incompatible with the characteristics of the judicial function: behind any particular case there are individual parties who, after years of litigation, are entitled to a reply in law, irrespective of the vicissitudes of some political negotiations. Secondly, because experience shows that the outcome of such negotiations is always uncertain, as is also the date by which a conclusion must be reached. Finally, since the question is one of procedural technique, no one is better placed than the national court to find a solution which most skillfully combines the interests of the proper administration of justice and sufficient protection for individuals.

(b) The new criterion of interpretation

99. The third method of interpretation which I mentioned above is, as I have said, a variant of the first or, rather, a concrete autonomous interpretation as opposed to what could be called a theoretical autonomous interpretation. Whereas in this last version there would be a theoretical definition of the place

of performance of each of the characteristic contractual obligations, in the version which I now put forward the theoretical aspect would be confined to setting out a very simple criterion for interpretation, leaving the national court to apply it to the particular case.

100. According to this proposal, thc court before which the matter is brought must determine 'the place of performance of the obligation' by reference to the particular circumstances of the case and taking account of the nature of the relationship creating the obligation in question.

101. I cannot deny that this approach obliges the court to assess the facts of the case, but any solution, as I explained above, requires some examination of the factual aspects of the action. What is more, I consider that a certain assessment of the factual aspects is not only inevitable, but legitimate. The concept of 'place of performance' of a contractual obligation has its *raison d'etre* in factual criteria, like the concept of 'the place where the harmful event occurred'. However, the Court has not had the slightest difficulty in giving an independent interpretation to the latter concept. Obviously, when assessing these circumstances in relation to the nature of the obligation in question, different courts may arrive at different conclusions, but is the location of the 'harmful event' always unequivocal?

102. It is a characteristic of administration of human justice that, when certain factual conditions are attached to a rule, it may happen that different courts reach different conclusions. That, however, is inevitable and the legal system must tolerate it. What is more difficult to accept, from the viewpoint of the proper administration of justice - which, after all, is the object of the whole Convention - is that, merely in order to ascertain whether the court before which the matter was brought has international jurisdiction, four sets of legal proceedings and more than seven years' litigation have been necessary.

103. Save with regard to obligations for the payment of a sum of money, reference to the circumstances of the case in relation to the nature of the obligation in question should enable the place or places of performance of an obligation to be determined with sufficient reliability in most cases.

I admit that this assertion does not apply to mere payment obligations. After all, it is easy to see that it is the existence of different rules in Europe regarding the place where such obligations must be fulfilled which has led to the use of the conflictualist method. It is all the fault of *De Bloos*! From the very beginning, the answer should have been to take account only of the characteristic obligation of the contract for the purpose of Article 5, point (1). Then it would have been possible, in the overwhelming majority of cases, to designate a place of performance for procedural purposes close to the essential elements of the contract. However, in order to avoid this reasonable construction of the text of the Convention, which would have been entirely appropriate to its aims, a method was introduced for obligations of all kinds which it is very difficult to apply.

Therefore I consider that, for the purpose of the *forum contractus*, the court must presume that the place of performance of an obligation is the place where the obligation which characterises the legal relationship in question was performed or was to be performed.

104. The solution proposed by Mr Lenz in the *Custom Made* case took an autonomous approach. However, in my opinion, proximity to the subject-matter (to which I prefer the 'connection with the dispute', as I explained) cannot in itself be the criterion for determining the *forum executionis*, but the main justification for creating that special jurisdiction. The draftsmen of the Convention considered it appropriate to provide for the possibility of bringing an action before the court of the place of performance of the contractual obligation in question *because*, among other things, that forum would in practice be close to the subject-matter. If the intention had been that, in matters relating to a contract, the court closest to the subject-matter should always have jurisdiction, why not have said so?

105. Although the connection with the dispute cannot be a criterion of interpretation in itself, for the national court it must offer correction or guidance if there is doubt, which could not otherwise be removed, as to the place of performance of the obligation. These situations arise more and more frequently in relation to certain obligations to deliver movable goods. However, I am sure that, in the overwhelming majority of disputes, an examination of the circumstances of the case in relation to the nature of the obligation in question is sufficient to designate a place of performance which corresponds, with reasonable reliability, to the aims of the Convention.

106. Consequently, I think that the criterion of 'proximity' should play only a secondary part in interpreting the Convention's criterion of 'place'. My choice is based not only on arguments supported by the authority of the text of the Convention, however important they may be, but it also has a deeper justification. Firstly, the concept of 'proximity to the subject-matter' seems to me relatively more imprecise than 'place of performance' (defined merely by reference to the circumstances of the case and the legal relationship in question), with the increased risk of multiplication of potential jurisdictions. Secondly, I consider that any provision, including procedural provisions, in contractual matters should be interpreted so as to take best into account the actual source of the relationship creating the obligation: the intention of the parties. When the court attempts to determine the place of performance of an obligation, clearly it must first and foremost establish what exactly was or could have been the will of the parties, without whose consensus the obligation would not exist. If the court can establish from the circumstances of the case the place of performance intended expressly or implicitly by the parties, taking into account the nature of the legal relationship in question, the *forum contractus* designated in this way will have the legitimacy of having been intended, albeit indirectly, by the parties, and will also be justified by its foreseeable proximity to the subject-matter. In other words, the defendant may be sued in the court for the place of performance of the contractual obligation because, in a certain way, he will have consented, by the expression of his will - which it will be the court's task to ascertain - to the creation of that special basis of jurisdiction. Clearly, the court which is competent by reason of the purely objective circumstance that it is close to the subject-matter will not have such legitimacy.

107. If the court of first instance had applied this criterion to the present

case, and on the basis of the information available to the Court of Justice, it seems that, taking account of the circumstances of the case and the fact that the obligation in question is to carry goods without damaging them, the court of first instance could easily have found that, in relation to parties actually bound by a contract of carriage, the place of performance of that obligation was the place designated as such by the parties. Without the need for long digressions concerning the law applicable to the legal transaction in question, it seems clear from the facts of the main proceedings that the port of destination is that specified by the bill of lading, which is Santos, in Brazil. On that ground, it must be deemed to be the place of performance. Where the courts of a State which is not a party to the Convention are designated, the special jurisdiction of Article 5 lapses. In the absence of other concurrent bases of jurisdiction, the French court must decline jurisdiction. I should point out, however, that this question must be examined by the national court and not by the Court of Justice.

108. To sum up, the forum designated by the place of performance of a contractual obligation by reference to the circumstances of the case, taking account of the relationship creating the obligation in question, combines the advantages of autonomous interpretation with those which follow from a simple, unequivocal criterion for all contracts. It does not in itself entail any greater dispersion of jurisdiction than that occasioned by the *Tessili* technique itself, and it observes scrupulously the letter and the spirit of the Convention. Any doubts which may arise in determining it must be resolved in conformity with the criterion of the connection which the dispute has with a specific place, as that is the specific purpose of the *forum contractus* created by the Convention.

XIII - Conclusion

109. For the reasons which I have given above, I propose that the Court reply as follows to the question from the national court: Article 5, point (1), of the Brussels Convention of 27 September 1968 on Jurisdiction and the Enforcement of Judgments in Civil and Commercial Matters must be interpreted as meaning that the *place of performance* of a contractual obligation means the place designated by reference to the circumstances of the case, taking account of the nature of the legal relationship in question, it being understood that it is presumed that that place is the same as the place where the obligation characterising the legal relationship in question was or is to be performed. If more than one place is designated, that having the closest connection with the dispute must be chosen.

Case C-420/97 - 5 October 1999

Leathertex Divisione Sintetici SpA
v
Bodetex BVBA

Interpretation of Articles 2 and 5(1) - Commercial agency agreement - Action founded on separate obligations arising from the same contract and regarded as equal in rank - Jurisdiction of the court seised to hear the whole action.

Summary

On a proper construction of Article 5(1) the same court does not have jurisdiction to hear the whole of an action founded on two obligations of equal rank arising from the same contract when, according to the conflict rules of the State where that court is situated, one of those obligations is to be performed in that State and the other in another Contracting State.

JUDGMENT OF THE COURT

Presiding, Lecourt, President, Rodriguez Iglesias, Presidents of Chambers, Kapteyn, Puissochet, Hirsch and Jann, Rapporteur, Mancini, Moitinho de Almeida, Gulmann, Murray, Edward Ragnemalm, Judges, Sevon, Wathelet and Schintgen, Advocate General, Léger.

1. By judgment of 4 December 1997, received at the Court on 11 December 1997, the Hof van Cassatie (Court of Cassation) referred to the Court for a preliminary ruling under the Protocol of 3 June 1971 on the interpretation by the Court of Justice of the Convention of 27 September 1968 on Jurisdiction and the Enforcement of Judgments in Civil and

Commercial Matters (hereinafter 'the Protocol') a question on the interpretation of Articles 2 and 5(1) of that Convention (OJ 1978 L 304, p. 36), as amended by the Convention of 9 October 1978 on the Accession of the Kingdom of Denmark, Ireland and the United Kingdom of Great Britain and Northern Ireland (OJ 1978 L 304, p. 1 and - amended text - p. 77, hereinafter 'the Convention').

2. That question was raised in proceedings between Leathertex Divisione Sintetici SpA (hereinafter 'Leathertex'), whose registered office is in Montemurlo, Italy, and Bodetex BVBA (hereinafter 'Bodetex'), whose registered office is in Rekkem-Menen, Belgium, concerning the payment of arrears of commission and of compensation in lieu of notice, which Bodetex, the commercial agent of Leathertex in the Belgian and Netherlands markets, is claiming from Leathertex.

The Convention

3. The first paragraph of Article 2 of the Convention states: 'Subject to the provisions of this Convention, persons domiciled in a Contracting State shall, whatever their nationality, be sued in the courts of that State.'

4. The first paragraph of Article 3 provides: 'Persons domiciled in a Contracting State may be sued in the courts of another Contracting State only by virtue of the rules set out in Sections 2 to 6 of this Title.'

5. Article 5 provides: 'A person domiciled in a Contracting State may, in another Contracting State, be sued: 1. in matters relating to a contract, in the courts for the place of performance of the obligation in question; ...'

6. Article 6(1) adds that where such a person is one of a number of defendants, he may be sued in the courts for the place where any one of them is domiciled.

7. Finally, the first paragraph of Article 22 provides: 'Where related actions are brought in the courts of different Contracting States, any court other than the court first seised may, while the actions are pending at first instance, stay its proceedings.'

The main proceedings

8. For a number of years Bodetex acted as commercial agent for

Leathertex in the Belgian and Netherlands markets under a long-term arrangement. It received 5% commission by way of remuneration.

9. After asking Leathertex to no avail during 1987 for payment of commission which it considered to be owing to it, Bodetex regarded its commercial agency agreement as terminated and, by letter of 9 March 1988, took formal note of the termination and demanded from Leathertex payment of arrears of commission and compensation in lieu of notice.

10. Since Leathertex did not reply to that letter, on 2 November 1988 Bodetex sued it for payment in the Rechtbank van Koophandel (Commercial Court), Courtrai.

11. By judgment of 1 October 1991, the Rechtbank van Koophandel found that two separate obligations formed the basis of the action. It held that the first, namely the obligation to give a reasonable period of notice on termination of a commercial agency agreement and, in the event of failure to give such notice, to pay compensation in lieu, was to be performed in Belgium, whereas the second, namely the obligation to pay commission, was to be performed in Italy under the principle that debts are payable where the debtor is resident. The Rechtbank van Koophandel accordingly found that it had jurisdiction in respect of the obligation to pay compensation in lieu of notice, by virtue of Article 5(1) of the Convention, and then declared that it had jurisdiction over the whole proceedings given the connection between that obligation and the obligation to pay commission. It ordered Leathertex to pay Bodetex arrears of commission and compensation in lieu of notice.

12. Leathertex appealed against that judgment to the Hof van Beroep (Court of Appeal), Ghent, which, by judgment of 29 October 1993, confirmed that the Rechtbank van Koophandel had jurisdiction to hear the action brought by Bodetex. The Hof van Beroep held that two separate obligations arising from the agency agreement formed the basis of the action, that the obligation to pay commission could not be regarded as the principal obligation and that the two obligations had to be regarded as equal in rank, so that there was nothing to prevent Bodetex from bringing its action before the courts for the place of performance of either of those two obligations. It therefore ruled that the Rechtbank van Koophandel had jurisdiction to hear the main proceedings as the court for the place where the obligation to give a reasonable period of notice was to be performed.

13. Leathertex appealed on a point of law to the Hof van Cassatie. It

submitted, first, that the Hof van Beroep had misconstrued Article 5(1) of the Convention in holding that it had jurisdiction to deal with the head of claim concerning payment of the arrears of commission when the obligation to pay that commission was to be performed in Italy. According to Leathertex, if a court is unable to identify the principal obligation and the ancillary obligations from among the various obligations forming the basis of an action, it is competent to rule only on the obligations for which the place of performance is located, in accordance with its own conflict rules, in its jurisdiction. Leathertex maintained, secondly, that the Hof van Beroep had misinterpreted Article 22 of the Convention in holding that it had jurisdiction to hear the whole of the dispute, since that provision can apply only where related actions have been brought in the courts of two or more Contracting States.

14. In its order for reference, the Hof van Cassatie states first of all that Article 22 of the Convention was not applied in the judgment under appeal and rejects on this ground Leathertex's plea based on the misinterpretation of that provision.

15. So far as concerns the alleged infringement of Article 5(1) of the Convention, the Hof van Cassatie notes that, in Case 266/85 *Shenavai* v *Kreischer* [1987] ECR 239, at paragraph 19, the Court held that, in the particular case of a dispute concerned with a number of obligations arising under the same contract and forming the basis of the proceedings brought by the plaintiff, the court before which the matter is brought should, when determining whether it has jurisdiction, be guided by the maxim *accessorium sequitur principale* so that, where a number of obligations are at issue, it will be the principal obligation which will determine its jurisdiction.

16. The Hof van Cassatie states that, in the present case, it is common ground that the obligation to pay commission cannot be regarded as the principal obligation in the context of the action brought by Bodetex, that the Belgian courts have jurisdiction to rule on the obligation to pay compensation in lieu of notice since that obligation is contractual in nature and is to be performed in Belgium, and that the two abovementioned obligations are of equal rank.

17. The Hof van Cassatie inquires whether it is possible to disapply the general rule set out in Article 2 of the Convention in the case of a dispute concerning various obligations arising under the same agency agreement where none of the obligations is subordinate to the others and only one,

having regard to its place of performance, supports the jurisdiction of the court before which the matter has been brought.

18. In those circumstances, the Hof van Cassatie decided to stay proceedings and to refer the following question to the Court for a preliminary ruling: 'Are Articles 5(1) and 2 of the Brussels Convention, in the version applicable to the present case, to be interpreted as meaning that a composite claim founded on different obligations arising from the same contract may be brought before the same court, even though, according to the jurisdictional rules of the State in which the proceedings are brought, one of the contractual obligations on which the claim is based is to be performed in that State and the other is to be performed in another EC Member State, having regard to the fact that the court before which the proceedings are brought decides, on the basis of the claim brought before it, that neither of the two obligations forming the subject-matter of the claim is subordinate to the other and that they are of equal rank?'

Consideration of the question submitted

19. By its question, the national court is essentially asking whether, on a proper construction of Articles 2 and 5(1) of the Convention, the same court has jurisdiction to hear the whole of an action founded on two obligations of equal rank arising from the same contract even though, according to the conflict rules of the State where that court is situated, one of those obligations is to be performed in that State and the other in another Contracting State.

20. The United Kingdom Government submits that, of the two obligations upon which the main action is founded, the obligation to pay commission forms its principal basis. According to the order for reference, the sole reason why Bodetex regarded the contract as having been terminated without notice was the failure to pay the disputed commission. So compensation in lieu of notice is to be paid only if it is established that the disputed commission is in fact due. The United Kingdom Government therefore proposes that the question referred for a preliminary ruling should be reformulated and the answer given that, in a situation such as that in the main proceedings, the contractual obligation which forms the principal basis of the legal proceedings and upon which jurisdiction may be founded under Article 5(1) of the Convention is the obligation to pay commission.

21. As to that, in view of the allocation of jurisdiction under the preliminary ruling procedure provided for by the Protocol, it is for the national court to assess the relative importance of the contractual obligations at issue in the main proceedings and for the Court of Justice to interpret the Convention in the light of the findings made by the national court.

22. Moreover, to alter the substance of the question referred for a preliminary ruling would be incompatible with the Court's function under the Protocol and with its duty to ensure that the Governments of the Member States and the parties concerned are given the opportunity to submit observations pursuant to Article 5 of the Protocol and Article 20 of the EC Statute of the Court, bearing in mind that, under Article 20, only the order of the referring court is notified to the interested parties (see, in relation to the procedure under Article 177 of the EC Treaty (now Article 234 EC), Case C-352/95 *Pytheron International* v *Bourdon* [1997] ECR I-1729, paragraph 14, and Case C-235/95 *AGS Assedic* v *Dumon and Froment* [1998] ECR I-4531, paragraph 26).

23. The question referred for a preliminary ruling must therefore be answered on the basis that, as stated in the order for reference, the two contractual obligations on which the action is founded are of equal rank.

24. Leathertex, the German Government and the United Kingdom Government, in an alternative submission, submit that a court of a Contracting State does not have jurisdiction under Article 5(1) of the Convention to hear the whole of an action founded on several obligations of equal rank arising from the same contract when the place of performance of one or a number of those obligations is in another Member State.

25. In their view, Article 5(1) of the Convention must be interpreted strictly. Where the two obligations which form the basis of an action are regarded as equal in rank by the court before which the action has been brought, jurisdiction to deal with each of them should lie with the court of the place where each is to be performed and any resultant fragmenting of jurisdiction should be accepted. Such an interpretation of Article 5(1) of the Convention is, they argue, consistent with the rationale for that provision, which is to guarantee to each party in matters relating to a contract that claims will be considered by the courts for the place where the obligation in dispute is to be performed.

26. Bodetex maintains, first, that the agreement giving rise to the two obligations at issue in the main proceedings is analogous to a commercial representative's contract of employment. Thus, when Article 5(1) of the Convention is applied in the case of an action founded on different obligations resulting from the same agency agreement, it is appropriate, as in the case of contracts of employment, to take account of the obligation which characterises that contract, namely, in the present case, the obligation to find new customers and to distribute Leathertex's products, in particular in Belgium. In a number of Contracting States, case-law and academic legal writing have extended that solution to concession agreements, with which commercial agency agreements likewise have similarities.

27. Bodetex argues, second, that the obligation to pay commission is linked to the obligation to pay compensation in lieu of notice. Both result from the agency agreement. In addition, failure to perform the obligation to pay commission was the reason why the agreement was terminated, thereby giving rise to the obligation to pay compensation in lieu of notice. That link provides the justification for the court with jurisdiction to rule on the obligation to pay compensation in lieu of notice to have jurisdiction to rule on the obligation to pay commission as well.

28. According to Bodetex, such an interpretation of Article 5(1) of the Convention allows proceedings to be conducted effectively while avoiding a fragmenting of jurisdiction.

29. Finally, the Commission submits that, where a plaintiff brings two claims based on two obligations of equal rank, a court which has jurisdiction to hear one of the claims under Article 5(1) of the Convention also has jurisdiction to hear the other claim if there is such a close relationship between the claims that it is advantageous to hear and decide them at the same time in order to avoid the possibility of irreconcilable decisions if the cases were decided separately.

30. According to the Commission, such a solution corresponds most closely to the scheme of the Convention. First, it is comparable, *mutatis mutandis*, with the solution for which Article 6(1) of the Convention provides where there are a number of defendants. Second, it is called for by Article 22 of the Convention. In a dispute such as that before the national court, if the plaintiff decided, in accordance with Article 5(1) of the Convention, to bring the action for payment of compensation in one Contracting State and that for payment of the arrears of commission in

another Contracting State, Article 22 of the Convention would apply because of the relation between the two actions. Article 5(1) of the Convention should therefore be interpreted in such a way as to avoid in advance situations to which Article 22 of the Convention would be applicable.

31. It should be noted first of all that, in paragraphs 8, 9 and 10 of the judgment in Case 14/76 *De Bloos v Bouyer* [1976] ECR 1497, after observing that the Convention was intended to determine the international jurisdiction of the courts of the Contracting States, to facilitate the recognition of judgments and to introduce an expeditious procedure for securing their enforcement, the Court held that those objectives implied the need to avoid, so far as possible, creating a situation in which a number of courts had jurisdiction in respect of one and the same contract and that Article 5(1) of the Convention could not therefore be interpreted as referring to any obligation whatsoever arising under the contract in question. The Court concluded, in paragraphs 11 and 13 of the same judgment, that, for the purposes of determining the place of performance within the meaning of Article 5(1), the obligation to be taken into account was that which corresponded to the contractual right on which the plaintiff's action was based. It stated in paragraph 14 that, in a case where the plaintiff asserted the right to be paid damages or sought dissolution of the contract on the ground of the wrongful conduct of the other party, that obligation was still that which arose under the contract and the non-performance of which was relied upon to support such claims.

32. This interpretation was corroborated by the Convention of 9 October 1978 on the Accession of the Kingdom of Denmark, Ireland and the United Kingdom of Great Britain and Northern Ireland, which amended certain language versions of Article 5(1) of the Convention in order to specify that the obligation whose place of performance determines which court has jurisdiction in matters relating to a contract is the obligation which forms the basis of the claim (in the English version 'the obligation in question').

33. Also, the Court has held on several occasions that the place of performance of the obligation in question is to be determined by the law governing that obligation according to the conflict rules of the court seised (Case 12/76 *Tessili* v *Dunlop* [1976] ECR 1473, paragraph 13, Case C-288/92 *Custom Made Commercial* v *Stawa Metallbau* [1994] ECR I-2913, paragraph 26, and Case C-440/97 *Groupe Concorde and*

Others v *The Master of the Vessel* Suhadiwarno Panjan *and Others* [1999] ECR I-0000, paragraph 32).

34. In the present case, the Belgian courts have held, in accordance with the case-law cited above, that the obligation to pay compensation in lieu of notice was to be performed in Belgium while the obligation to pay commission was to be performed in Italy.

35. Furthermore, it is apparent from the order for reference and the file forwarded by the national court that the contract at issue in the main proceedings, under which the claims for payment of commission and of compensation in lieu of notice have been brought, does not constitute a contract of employment.

36. When the specific features of a contract of employment do not exist, it is neither necessary nor appropriate to identify the obligation which characterises the contract and to centralise at its place of performance all jurisdiction, based on place of performance, over disputes concerning all the obligations under the contract (*Shenavai*, cited above, paragraph 17).

37. Therefore, the obligation which characterises the agency agreement is not to be taken into account in the main proceedings in order to determine jurisdiction based on place of performance.

38. Nor can the court which has jurisdiction to hear the claim for payment of compensation in lieu of notice found its jurisdiction in respect of the claim for payment of commission on any relation between those two claims. As the Court has made clear, Article 22 of the Convention is intended to establish how related actions which have been brought before courts of different Contracting States are to be dealt with. It does not confer jurisdiction. In particular, it does not accord jurisdiction to a court of a Contracting State to try an action which is related to another action of which that court is seised pursuant to the rules of the Convention (see Case 150/80 *Elefanten Schuh* v *Jacqmain* [1981] ECR 1671, paragraph 19, and Case C-51/97 *Réunion Européenne and Others* v *Spliethoff's Bevrachtingskantor and Another* [1998] ECR I-6511, paragraph 39).

39. Finally, when a dispute relates to a number of obligations of equal rank arising from the same contract, the court before which the matter is brought cannot, when determining whether it has jurisdiction, be guided by the maxim *accessorium sequitur principale* referred to by the Court in paragraph 19 of the judgment in *Shenavai*, cited above.

40. The same court does not therefore have jurisdiction to hear the whole of an action founded on two obligations of equal rank arising from the same contract when, according to the conflict rules of the State where that court is situated, one of those obligations is to be performed in that State and the other in another Contracting State.

41. It should be remembered that, while there are disadvantages in having different courts ruling on different aspects of the same dispute, the plaintiff always has the option, under Article 2 of the Convention, of bringing his entire claim before the courts for the place where the defendant is domiciled.

42. The answer to be given to the question referred for a preliminary ruling must therefore be that, on a proper construction of Article 5(1) of the Convention, the same court does not have jurisdiction to hear the whole of an action founded on two obligations of equal rank arising from the same contract when, according to the conflict rules of the State where that court is situated, one of those obligations is to be performed in that State and the other in another Contracting State.

On those grounds, the Court, in answer to the question referred to it by the Hof van Cassatie by judgment of 4 December 1997, hereby rules:

> **On a proper construction of Article 5(1) of the Convention of 27 September 1968 on Jurisdiction and the Enforcement of Judgments in Civil and Commercial Matters, as amended by the Convention of 9 October 1978 on the Accession of the Kingdom of Denmark, Ireland and the United Kingdom of Great Britain and Northern Ireland, the same court does not have jurisdiction to hear the whole of an action founded on two obligations of equal rank arising from the same contract when, according to the conflict rules of the State where that court is situated, one of those obligations is to be performed in that State and the other in another Contracting State.**

OPINION OF MR ADVOCATE GENERAL LÉGER

1. The Hof van Cassatie (Belgian Court of Cassation) has referred to the Court a request for interpretation of Articles 2 and 5(1) of the Brussels Convention, 1 in order to decide which court has territorial jurisdiction to hear and determine an application comprising several claims for payment of sums of money based on different obligations arising from the same contract.

2. The court making the reference seeks to ascertain whether in such circumstances the relevant provisions of the Convention allow multiple claims to be submitted to one court although the claims are based on contractual obligations of equal rank and, according to the Court's settled case-law, should be enforced in two different Contracting States.

I - The Brussels Convention

3. The first paragraph of Article 2 of the Convention lays down the principle whereby the court having jurisdiction is determined according to the place where the person being sued is domiciled. Thus it provides: 'Subject to the provisions of this Convention, persons domiciled in a Contracting State shall, whatever their nationality, be sued in the courts of that State'.

4. Article 5 of the Convention, however, provides the plaintiff with a choice of courts having jurisdiction. In particular, in matters relating to a contract, Article 5(1) states: 'A person domiciled in a Contracting State may, in another Contracting State, be sued ... in the courts for the place of performance of the obligation in question ...'.

5. Article 22, which lays down the rules applying in cases where related actions are brought in the courts of different Contracting States, reads:"Where related actions are brought in the courts of different Contracting States, any court other than the court first seised may, while the actions are pending at first instance, stay its proceedings.

A court other than the court first seised may also, on the application of one of the parties, decline jurisdiction if the law of that court permits the consolidation of related actions and the court first seised has jurisdiction over both actions.

For the purposes of this Article, actions are deemed to be related where they are so closely connected that it is expedient to hear and determine them together to avoid the risk of irreconcilable judgments resulting from separate proceedings.'

II - Facts and procedure

6. Bodetex BVBA (hereinafter 'Bodetex'), whose registered office is in Belgium, has operated for several years on the Belgian and Netherlands markets as a commercial agent for Leathertex Divisione Sintetici SpA (hereinafter 'Leathertex'), whose registered office is in Italy. Bodetex has acted as a commercial agent in return for a commission.

7. Since a number of commission payments for 1987 were outstanding despite its complaints, Bodetex, in a letter dated 9 March 1988, announced that the commercial agency agreement was terminated, and requested payment of the outstanding commission and compensation for termination of the agreement without notice. When it received no response from Leathertex, Bodetex sued the latter for payment before the Rechtbank van Koophandel te Kortrijk (hereinafter 'the Rechtbankz').

8. By judgment of 1 October 1991, the Rechtbank ruled that the two obligations forming the subject-matter of the application should be treated separately. It found that the first obligation, namely to give a reasonable period of notice in the event of terminating a commercial agency agreement and, if such notice is not given, to pay compensation for termination, should be performed in Belgium, whilst the second obligation, namely to pay commission, should be performed in Italy according to the principle whereby a debt must be collected at the place where the debtor is domiciled.

9. The Rechtbank thus declared it had jurisdiction under Article 5(1) of the Convention to hear and determine the claim relating to notice of termination, and also that it was competent to deal with the case as a whole since the two obligations were related. It proceeded to order Leathertex to pay Bodetex the outstanding commission and compensation for termination of the agreement.

10. Leathertex appealed against that judgment before the Hof van Beroop (Court of Appeal), Ghent. By judgment of 29 October 1993, that court confirmed that the Rechtbank was competent to hear and determine the claims made by Bodetex.

11. The Hof van Beroop, Ghent, noted that the application made by Bodetex was based on two separate obligations arising from the contested agreement. It ruled that since the obligation to pay commission could not be regarded as the principal obligation, the two obligations should be regarded as equal in rank.

12. In those circumstances, the Hof van Beroop, Ghent held that there was no reason why Bodetex should not bring its action before the court for the place of performance of either of the obligations. It was of the view that the Rechtbank was competent to hear and determine this particular case as it was the court for the place where the obligation to comply with a reasonable period of notice was to be performed.

13. Leathertex applied for review of that judgment.

III - The question submitted by the national court

14. The Hof van Cassatie held that the fact that the obligation to pay commission could not be regarded as the principal obligation was not disputed, that the Belgian court was competent to rule on the obligation to pay compensation for termination of the agreement, since that contractual obligation had to be performed in Belgium, and that the two obligations were equal in rank.

15. The question arose whether, in such circumstances, a plaintiff who is a commercial agent may derogate from the general rule laid down in Article 2 of the Convention and refer the matter to the court which is competent by reason of the place of performance, within the meaning of Article 5(1), of either of the obligations at issue.

16. The Hof van Cassatie stayed proceedings and referred the following question to the Court: 'Are Articles 5(1) and 2 of the Brussels Convention, in the version applicable to the present case, to be interpreted as meaning that a composite claim founded on different obligations arising from the same contract

may be brought before the same court, even though, according to the jurisdictional rules of the State in which the proceedings are brought, one of the contractual obligations on which the claim is based is to be performed in that State and the other is to be performed in another EC Member State, having regard to the fact that the court before which the proceedings are brought decides, on the basis of the claim brought before it, that neither of the two obligations forming the subject-matter of the claim is subordinate to the other and that they are of equal rank?'

IV - The answer to the question

17. By the question it has raised, the Hof van Cassatie is essentially asking the Court whether Article 5(1) of the Convention can be interpreted as meaning that the same court can hear and determine an application comprising several heads of claim based on obligations of equal rank arising from the same commercial agency agreement when, according to the respective places of performance of those obligations, within the meaning of Article 5(1) of the Convention, the courts of more than one Contracting State have jurisdiction.

18. The question expresses the concern of the referring court to comply with the provisions of the Convention, thereby avoiding fragmentation of the case, with the possibility of each of its parts being dealt with by courts located in different Contracting States, contrary to the objectives of the Convention.

19. May I point out that, as the Court has consistently held, the Convention 'is intended to determine the international jurisdiction of the courts of the Contracting States, to facilitate the recognition and to introduce an expeditious procedure for securing the enforcement of judgments'. Those objectives 'imply the need to avoid, so far as possible, creating a situation in which a number of courts have jurisdiction in respect of one and the same contract'. 2

20. The Court has also ruled that 'multiplication of the bases of jurisdiction in one and the same type of case is not likely to encourage legal certainty and effective legal protection throughout the territory of the Community' and involves litigants in the 'risk of irreconcilable decisions ...'.

21. I should like to make clear, before any other consideration, that the principle laid down in Article 2 of the Convention whereby the competent court is that of the place were the person being sued is domiciled, which is one of the options open to the plaintiff, would undoubtedly have meant it was possible to avoid the difficulties encountered by the Belgian court. As the Court of Justice has ruled, 'the plaintiff is always entitled to bring his action before [that] court ... in accordance with Article 2 of the Convention, which thereby provides a certain and reliable criterion'.

22. The forum of the person being sued may thus hear and determine all the heads of claim and does not need to concern itself with determining the place where they should be performed, as Article 5(1) requires, at the risk of having to decline jurisdiction in part where one of the claims has been or is to be performed elsewhere.

23. Is it necessary therefore to settle for Article 2 of the Convention, as the

Hof van Cassatie appears to be minded to do, where application of Article 5(1) would result in the case being split between several fora?

24. In the context of the case in the main proceedings and in view of the arguments contained in the order for reference, this question could be answered in three different ways.

25. Firstly, it is tempting, as the Government of the United Kingdom has done, to revert to the *respective rankings of the obligations concemed.* Establishing a hierarchy between the obligations on which the claim is founded where, as in the circumstances of the present case, their characteristics appear to lend themselves to so doing naturally leads to combining the claims within the jurisdiction of a single court - that for the place of performance of the principal obligation - without the need to resort to Article 2 (Part A below).

26. Secondly, if one assumes that the obligations at issue are, or should be, regarded as being of equal rank, and that their places of performance are located in different Contracting States, it seems appropriate to assess the *effect of that situation as regards determining jurisdiction* under Article 5(1) of the Convention and in the light of the objectives of the Convention (Part B below).

27. Lastly, it must not be forgotten that the multiplication of fora having jurisdiction as a result of applying Article 5(1) in the case in the main proceedings follows to a great extent from the interpretation which has traditionally been given of the concept of '*the place of performance*' since the *Tessili* judgment. It is therefore necessary to look at alternative solutions which would result in Article 5(1) being applied in a way which corresponded more closely to the objectives of the Convention, in order to make the choice of jurisdiction provided for in the Convention more relevant (Part C below).

28. Before reverting to each of these points, it should be noted that the version of the Convention applying to the case in the main proceedings, the relevant provisions of which the Hof van Cassatie is seeking interpretation, is the version contained in the Convention of 9 October 1978, cited above, which entered into force on 1 November 1986, since Bodetex instituted its proceedings by a writ dated 2 November 1988.

29. No-one disputes the fact that the case in question is a matter relating to a contract since, according to the file, the Court has already described as such the category to which the agreement at issue belongs.

A - *The contested obligations are of equal rank*

30. Referring to the above-mentioned *Shenavai* judgment in particular, which quotes the maxim *accessorium sequitur principale*, the United Kingdom Government states that it is important that the Court should emphasise the need, where there is more than one obligation, for a national court to identify the principal contractual obligation on which a claim is based for the purposes of Article 5(1) of the Convention.

31. It considers that in the present case it is the obligation to pay the commission sought which is the principal obligation, since the only ground on which Bodetex made the claim that Leathertex terminated the agreement without

notice, and therefore sought compensation, was Leathertex's failure to pay that commission. Thus, in the view of the United Kingdom Government, a single court should be designated, that of the place of performance of the obligation to pay commission, in pursuance of Article 5(1).

32. Observing that the order for reference regards the contested obligations as being of equal rank, the United Kingdom considers that, as it has consistently held it is entitled to do, the Court should reformulate the question referred to it, in order to provide the referring court with an answer which will be of use to it and, by establishing an order of precedence among the contested obligations, enable it to determine the case before it.

33. In the Shenavai judgment, cited above, the Court held that regard to be had 'solely to the contractual obligation whose performance is sought in the judicial proceedings' and stated that 'in the particular case of a dispute concerned with a number of obligations arising under the same contract and forming the basis of the proceedings commenced by the plaintiff ... it will be the principal obligation which will determine its jurisdiction.'

34. An action in contract should not therefore be brought before the court for the place of performance of any obligation of the contract at random, which is understandable if one wishes to avoid there being more than one court having jurisdiction.

35. The solution advocated by the United Kingdom Government, to put the points it makes in different terms, sets the case in the main proceedings in the context of that case-law and provides an answer which meets the objectives of the Convention by avoiding there being more than one court having jurisdiction.

36. The approach proposed by Bodetex is similar. In Bodetex's view, the situation in which it found itself in relation to Leathertex, to which it was bound by a commercial agency agreement, is similar to the business relationship between Mr Ivenel, a sales representative, and his employer in the *Ivenel* case: the duties of canvassing for new customers in order to negotiate and conclude contracts on behalf of the principal, the existence of a longstanding business relationship between the parties, the requirement to give notice or pay compensation in the event of termination of the agreement and the subordinate position of their contracting parties, which was of a legal nature in the case of Mr Ivenel and of an economic nature in the case of Bodetex, are the same in both cases.

37. Bodetex proposes, therefore, that the solution the Court adopted in the Ivenel case should be transposed to the present case, which means it is necessary to decide which work 'characterises the contract'. Bodetex suggests that the answer to this question should be that the work characterising the contract involves finding new customers and distributing the products named in the agreement. It considers that the place where the service should be provided is Belgium, in whose territory the claims should therefore be combined.

38. Like the Government of the United Kingdom, Bodetex seeks not merely to establish a hierarchy among the obligations at issue, but also to designate which of those obligations takes priority, in order to combine the heads of claim before the court for the place where that obligation should be performed.

39. I cannot agree with this reasoning, particularly in view of the procedural context of the case in the main proceedings.

40. Let me point out first of all that the question itself clearly describes the obligations at issue as being of equal rank. Moreover, the referring court expressly states that the fact that the two obligations are of equal rank is one of the given factors in the case on the basis of which the question was raised and that the reference for a preliminary ruling does not relate to that point.

41. Secondly, the Hof van Cassatie cites several of the grounds of the judgment delivered by the Hof van Beroep, Ghent, on 29 October 1993, which show that the Hof van Beroop clearly held that the 'two obligations ranked equally in importance ...'. The Hof van Cassatie, refers to the *Shenavai* judgment, cited above, and states that the equal importance of the obligations has not been challenged.

42. The wording of the question referred by the national court clearly reflects those elements of the national proceedings. As the parties to the main proceedings have not challenged the legal characterisation given by the appeal court, the referring court did not consider that it should of its own motion raise the issue that that characterisation might be wrong; it may have been that this was not a legal possibility. Unless the Hof van Cassatie subscribed to the characterisation put forward by the Hof van Beroop, Ghent.

43. At all events, whether it was a legal obligation incumbent upon the national court or that court's own choice, the answer the Court of Justice gives to the question raised cannot disregard uncontested elements of the order for reference in case by so doing it provides the national court with answers which are not directly relevant to the outcome of the case.

44. May I point out in this connection that, according to settled case-law, it is solely for the national court before which the dispute has been brought, and which must take responsibility for the subsequent judicial decision, to determine in the light of the particular circumstances of each case both the need for a preliminary ruling in order to enable it to deliver judgment and the relevance of the questions it submits to the Court.

45. I am therefore of the opinion that the finding made by the Hof van Cassatie that the obligations at issue are of equal rank should not be challenged.

B - *The effect of there being more than one "place of performance"*

46. In its question, the Hof van Cassatie states that, under the jurisdictional rules of the State in which the proceedings are brought, one of the contractual obligations on which the claim is based is to be performed in the State of the court before which the case has been brought and the other is to be performed in another Contracting State.

47. The national court is referring implicity to the Court's case-law resulting from the *Tessili* judgment, cited above, application of which in the present case would lead to more than one place of performance and therefore to more than one court having jurisdiction.

48. May I point out that according to that judgment it is for the court

before which the matter is brought to establish under the Convention whether the place of performance is situated within its territorial jurisdiction. For this purpose it must determine in accordance with its own rules of conflict of laws what is the law applicable to the legal relationship in question and define in accordance with that law the place of performance of the contractual obligation in question..."

49. The arguments put forward by the intervening parties provide an accurate summary of the substance of the problem, at least as it appears in the context of the *Tessili* judgment, cited above.

50. Either the plaintiff's choice of jurisdiction remains open and application of Article 5(1) of the Convention, under that case-law, results in the obligations at issue being performed in more than one place, which means that there can be more than one court having jurisdiction. This is the view held by the Italian Government and Leathertex.

51. Or, as the United Kingdom Government proposes in the alternative, the choice of jurisdiction should be abandoned in favour of the criterion of the domicile of the person being sued, in accordance with Article 2 of the Convention, which would avoid creating a situation in which a number of courts have jurisdiction in respect of one and the same case.

52. Or, lastly, the court having jurisdiction to hear and determine one of the claims based on obligations which are of equal rank, under Article 5(1) of the Convention, also has jurisdiction to hear and determine the other claim if there is a relationship between those two claims which is so close that it is in the interest of good justice to examine and rule on them together in order to avoid irreconcilable outcomes. This is the solution advocated by the Commission.

53. As regards the Commission's argument that jurisdictions should be combined since the claims are related, I consider this goes further than the wording of the Convention allows.

54. It should be stated that, although relatedness is taken into account in the Convention, it is not considered to confer jurisdiction. In other words, Article 22 of the Convention does not allow a court to decline jurisdiction in favour of another court on the ground that actions are related unless a related case has already been brought before that other court. The provision contained in Article 22 therefore applies only in such circumstances. It is only in that case that, as a result of a plea that the actions are related, the cases may both be brought before one court.

55. The Court of Justice clearly stated this in its judgment in *Elefanten Schuh*: 'Article 22 of the Convention is intended to establish how related actions *which have been brought before* courts of different Member States are to be dealt with. It does not confer jurisdiction'.

56. The Commission, however, accepts this view since it states that 'so long as only one court is seised there is no question of applying Article 22'.

57. It even adds that it is merely a matter of interpreting Article 5(1) in a way which will preclude situations likely to come within the scope of Article 22.

58. Although the objective sought by the Commission is clear and undoubtedly legitimate, I have difficulty understanding the reasoning which led

it to propose an interpretation of Article 5(1) which is so far removed from the text.

59. Direct combination of related actions before the same court, where the places of performance of the obligations on which they are based are situated in different Contracting States amounts to disregarding the criterion of the place of performance of one of those obligations, which is contrary to the provisions of Article 5(1).

60. In fact, the Commission's proposal amounts to altering the way the Convention deals with the question of related claims, going against the letter of its provisions and failing to take into account the intentions of the Contracting States, an outcome which was never actually envisaged, and this cannot be permitted.

61. The two other sets of arguments concern the choice to be made in the present case between Article 2 and Article 5(1), as interpreted in the light of the rule in *Tessili*, cited above. This choice is dictated by the objectives of the Convention themselves.

62. We should remember that the Convention seeks to strengthen in the Community the legal protection of persons therein established.

63. As can be seen from the case-law of the Court, as I have already mentioned, this requirement for legal protection is reflected in the need to avoid wherever possible a situation in which a number of courts have jurisdiction in respect of one and the same contract.

64. In order to ensure that the Convention is fully effective, it is essential to unify the jurisdiction rules of the courts of the Contracting States, so as to avoid as far as possible multiplication of the bases of jurisdiction, and allow the plaintiff to identify easily the court before which he may bring an action and the defendant reasonably to foresee the court before which he may be sued. It is thus a case of protecting legal certainty for persons within the territory of the Community by ensuring the predictability of the rules on jurisdiction that will apply.

65. Combining jurisdiction also precludes the risk of irreconcilable decisions and facilitates the recognition and enforcement of judgments in States other than those in which they were delivered.

66. This means that it is essential, if one wishes to comply with the spirit of the Convention, to promote solutions which favour the centralisation of proceedings and thus interpret the provision in this way.

67. The judgments delivered by the Court in cases involving multiple obligations confirm this course.

68. When it comes to identifying, among several obligations, the contractual obligation forming the basis of the legal proceedings, the principal obligation, or the obligation which characterises the contract, the Court has advocated establishing, wherever possible, a hierarchy within the obligations at issue in order to avoid related proceedings being split between different courts.

69. In this particular case we are presented with a situation which does not allow a hierarchy to be established within the obligations, since they are described as being of equal rank.

70. The question is therefore whether, in view of this fact, the text of the Convention allows jurisdiction to be combined on other grounds.

71. The Court has held on several occasions that the categories of 'special jurisdiction' enumerated in Article 5 of the Convention constitute derogations from the principle that jurisdiction is vested in the courts of the State where the defendant is domiciled, as laid down in the 'General provisions' of Articles 2 and 3, and as such must be interpreted restrictively.

72. One might gain from that case-law the idea that where recourse to a special jurisdiction produces results which clearly conflict with the objectives of the Convention it is necessary to reject the choice of jurisdiction and say, as in the *Humbert* judgment, cited above, that Article 5(1) of the Convention does not apply.

73. This solution seems to me to be of doubtful legal validity.

74. The Convention does not make the choice of jurisdiction subject to compliance with any prior condition. A plaintiff is always at liberty to choose any of its terms where a case comes within the scope of the Convention and provided, naturally, the legal nature of that case allows the plaintiff to have recourse to one of the categories of special jurisdiction, if he so chooses.

75. Moreover, the fact that in the Humbert judgment cited above the choice of jurisdiction was rejected in favour of the rule of jurisdiction contained in Article 2 of the Convention was due to the specific nature of the main proceedings in that case, which related to obligations performed outside the territorial scope of the Convention. Application of Article 5(1) would have resulted in jurisdiction being located outside the territory of the Contracting States, a situation which is contrary to both the letter and the spirit of Article 5, which provides that a person domiciled in a Contracting State may be sued elsewhere than in that State only in another Contracting State, and excludes third States.

76. The Court of Justice has, moreover, observed that, whilst it is true that disadvantages arise from different aspects of the same dispute being adjudicated upon by different courts, the plaintiff is always entitled to bring his action in its entirety before the courts for the domicile of the defendant, which thus provides a sure and reliable criterion.

77. In other words, the choice of jurisdiction provided in the interest of the parties, in particular of the plaintiff, still gives them the security of a predictable rule of jurisdiction, which the plaintiff may choose if, for his own particular reasons, the other rule of jurisdiction does not suit him.

78. The choice which is made may conflict with the objectives of the Convention: it is up to the plaintiff to assess to what extent the increased number of courts having jurisdiction as a result of applying Article 5(1) is the source of more inconvenience than would result from combining the heads of claim comprising his action before a single court situated in the place where the defendant is domiciled, if, under Article 5(1), one of the courts is situated in the Contracting State of his domicile.

79. I share the idea that Article 5(1) of the Convention cannot be prevented from applying on grounds other than those dictated by its own scope of

application, even where the use which the plaintiff seeks to make of it leads to determining jurisdiction in a way which is not in accordance with the principles of the Convention, if that is the choice of the plaintiff.

80. Using the rule for determining jurisdiction contained in Article 2 of the Convention only where application of Article 5(1) is likely to have undesirable effects would be adding to the text of the Convention a condition which is not there.

81. It follows, therefore, that claims relating to two obligations of equal rank arising from one and the same contract, whose respective places of performance according to the jurisdiction rules of the State of the court seised of the matter are in two different Contracting States, may, under Article 2 of the Convention, be submitted to the same court, namely that of the Contracting State of the person being sued.

82. However, in that same situation, Article 5(1) of the Convention precludes one and the same court having jurisdiction to entertain both those claims where their places of performance are located in the territory of two different Contracting States.

83. The Court may consider that it is for the plaintiff to choose the provision which he thinks provides greater protection of his interests, even if he sacrifices thereby the advantages stemming from the existence of a single forum. The proposed interpretation therefore constitutes one possible answer to the question referred by the national court.

84. However, the Court may also consider that observance of the principles of the Convention does not permit, in a case such as that now before it, that one of the terms of the choice of jurisdiction which is open to a party should result in a solution which is so far removed from those principles. This is the opinion which I support, which leads me to propose to the Court an alternative interpretation of the provisions.

C - *The effects of the content of the concept of 'places of performance'*

85. In referring to the conflict rules of the forum in order to determine the place of performance of the obligations at issue, the national court was naturally complying with the relevant Community case-law.

(1) The *Tessili* judgment

86. The method of determining the place of performance used by the Belgian courts is, as we have seen, in part the reason why there is more than one place of performance of the obligations at issue.

87. Since the Convention entered into force the question has constantly been raised as to whether the expressions and concepts it contains should be regarded as autonomous, and hence common to all the Contracting States, or as referring to the substantive rules of the law applying in each case according to the conflict rules of the court first seised of the matter.

88. In the *Tessili* judgment, cited above, the Court answered: 'Neither of

these two options rules out the other since the appropriate choice can only be made in respect of each of the provisions of the Convention to ensure that it is fully effective having regard to the objectives of Article 220 of the Treaty'.

89. The Court has on several occasions ruled in favour of an autonomous interpretation of some of the concepts of the Convention, stating that, 'according to settled case-law ... the Court will, in principle, interpret the terms of the Convention autonomously so as to ensure that it is fully effective having regard to the objectives of Article 220 of the EEC Treaty, for the implementation of which it was adopted'.

90. However, as regards the term Uplace of performance" of contractual obligations within the meaning of Article 5(1) of the Convention, the Court's initial choice of reference to the conflict rules of the forum was recently confirmed very clearly, thereby dismissing indirectly any autonomous definition.

91. The reference by the Court to the substantive law applicable was based on the differences obtaining between national laws of contract and in view of the absence, at the stage of legal development in 1976, of any unification of the substantive law applicable. It was stated that that position was justified also by the fact that determination of the place of performance of the obligations depends on the contractual context to which those obligations belong.

92. The position set out in the *Tessili* judgment cited above reflects a legitimate concern not to impose on all the Contracting States a definition which conflicted with their national laws and whose appropriateness as regard the objectives of the Convention was not clearly apparent.

93. Thus, the obligation to make payment, which obviously relates to a very large number of contracts and is directly at issue in the case in the main proceedings, clearly shows the unsatisfactory nature of an autonomous definition in this area, which derives its content from the way in which some of the Contracting States determine the place of performance of this type of obligation.

94. Depending on whether payment is to be collected at the place of the debtor's domicile or the creditor's domicile, the place of performance of the obligation to make payment will be the place where either the defendant or the plaintiff is domiciled. In addition to the difficulties relating to the choice between the national laws of the Contracting States, which are divided equally between the legal systems, there is no rational criterion enabling arbitration in accordance with the principles of the Convention.

95. Adopting an autonomous definition based on the payment being payable at the place where the creditor is domiciled amounts in fact to adopting a *forum actons* which was clearly not that intended by the Convention. This can be seen from the fact that Article 2 provides that the jurisdiction of the courts of the defendant's domicile is the fundamental jurisdiction. Moreover, as the Court itself pointed out: 'the hostility of the Convention towards the attribution of jurisdiction to the courts of the plaintiff's domicile was demonstrated by the fact that the second paragraph of Article 3 precluded the application of national provisions attributing jurisdiction to such courts for proceedings against defendants domiciled in the territory of a Contracting State'. The Court added

that: 'apart from the cases expressly provided for, the Convention appears clearly hostile towards the attribution of jurisdiction to the courts of the plaintiff's domicile'.

96. On the other hand, stating that the place of performance of an obligation to make payment is the place where the defendant is domiciled, which is the solution adopted by those Contracting States for whom the place where the obligation to make payment is to be performed is the place where the debtor is domiciled, removes the choice of jurisdiction provided for in the Convention, since this interpretation of Article 5(1), by adopting the place where the defendant is domiciled, means that Article 5(1) has the same tenor as Article 2.

97. In the *Custom Made Commercial*, cited above, the question submitted by the national court concerned application of the above-mentioned *Tessili* case-law to a claim for payment brought by a supplier against his customer under a contract for manufacture and supply, where the lex causue is constituted by a provision such as Article 59(1) of the Uniform Law on the International Sale of Goods annexed to the Hague Convention.

98. Application to the contractual relationship of a uniform law dispels the disadvantages attaching to the multiplicity of laws applicable. However, the meaning of the relevant provision of that law, under which the place of performance of the obligation on the buyer to pay the price to the seller is the seller's place of business or, if he does not have a place of business, his habitual residence, subject only to the proviso that the parties to the contract have not stipulated a different place for the performance of that obligation, determined that the court of the applicant was the court having jurisdiction.

99. The Court of Justice upheld its case-law, transposing it to the circumstances where a renvoi is made under conflict rules to a uniform law. It therefore declined to adopt an autonomous definition, establishing the place of business of the seller, and hence in this particular case, that of the applicant, as the place of performance of the obligation to make payment.

(2) Application to the present dispute

100. In the case in the main proceedings, the multiplicity of fora is the result of the differences between the national rules concerning the place of performance of obligations to make payment, as such differences appear following application of the conflict rules.

101. Although clearly contrary to the requirement to simplify the rules of jurisdiction, a multiplicity of courts having jurisdiction could be accepted if it was justified by other essential considerations resulting from the scheme of the Convention.

102. Besides the interest in having certainty regarding the rules of jurisdiction, it is also necessary to point out the importance of the connecting factor which must exist, so far as possible, between the dispute and the court having jurisdiction to resolve it. The special rules of jurisdiction, which apply to the *forum contractus* provided for in Article 5(1) of the Convention, are justified by the consideration that there is a close connecting factor between the dispute

and the court having jurisdiction to resolve it, in order to ensure the proper organisation of the case.

103. This principle stems from the idea that it will be easier for a court which is geographically proximate to the contractual relationship at issue, through the knowledge it has of the facts of the case, to rule on the matter before it.

104. Although the criterion of predictable certainly constitutes one criterion for interpreting Article 5(1), it should be remembered that it is the criterion of the connecting factor which lies at the origin of that provision. An acceptable interpretation of Article 5(1) must therefore ensure that the meaning ascribed to the concept of 'place of performance' reflects as far as possible a genuine connecting factor.

105. The Court's case-law moreover consistently refers to the fundamental nature of this principle, which justifies Article 5, and the freedom of choice which its existence gives alongside Article 2.

106. It is difficult in this particular case to find such a connection between the claim for payment of commission sought and the corresponding forum according to the substantive law applicable, which is that of Italy, when one realises that the commission is the consideration for the performance of the agreement by Bodetex, which is established in Belgium and responsible, under the terms of the agreement, for the Belgian and Netherlands markets.

107. May I add that, with regard this time to the criterion of the certainty or predictability of the rules of jurisdiction, identification of the competent forum by an indirect method is no more likely to promote comprehension of the rules of jurisdiction, since it means resorting to the private international law of the forum in order to determine the substantive law applicable, which localises the place of performance of the contested obligation.

108. It is clear therefore that, in the case in the main proceedings, application of Article 5(1) when interpreted for the purposes of the *Tessili* case-law cited above, comes up against several guiding principles of the Convention, to the extent that the situation clearly stimulated the Hof van Beroep, Ghent into seeking to bring the claims together by other means.

109. It seems to me that a solution which is closer to the requirements of the Convention could be applied in this case.

(3) To achieve a solution which is closer to the objectives of the Convention

(a) Place of performance: a term with a variety of meanings

110. It is necessary to start from the idea put forward by Advocate General Lenz that the place of performance of an obligation is not defined, for the purposes of substantive law, on the basis of requirements such as those laid down in the Convention.

111. The substantive provisions relating to the place of performance 'not only ... have, in the absence of agreement, to crystallise the parties' obligations, they must also demarcate the areas for which each of the parties are responsible, in case irregularities should arise in carrying out the contract...'.

112. Advocate General Lenz adds that 'the place of performance under substantive law generally determines merely the allocation of the risks and burdens connected with the transfer of money, the availability of which does not depend on the place of performance of the obligation in question'. so He considers that it is necessary to 'diverg[e] from the substantive law of the contract [if] ... those rules [cannot] serve to determine a court which [is] physically proximate to the relationship...'.

113. There is often therefore a discrepancy between the reasons which explain the definition of the place of performance of an obligation under substantive law, on the one hand, and the objectives sought by the Convention, on the other.

114. So, in addition to the drawback of the differences between the national laws, which conflict with the objective of harmonising rules of jurisdiction as sought by the Convention, it is also regrettable that application of the *lex causae* results in designating the forum on the basis of a place of performance which is legally determined for reasons other than those concerned with proper organisation of the proceedings.

115. May I say, lastly, that Mr Lenz's statement that 'in neither of [the] judgments [in *De Bloos* v *Bouyer* and *Tessili* v *Dunlop*] did the Court take physical proximity as a reason for examining whether it was necessary to deviate from the substantive law (of the contract) in interpreting Article 5(1) ..., could also be made with regard to the judgment in *Custom Made Commercial*, cited above.

116. This continuing tolerance of a version of a provision which is so far removed from what constitutes its main justification cannot be explained solely by the existence of a choice of jurisdiction, which enables a plaintiff facing procedural complications due, for example, to the multiplicity of fora or the existence of a negative conflict of jurisdiction, to base his claims on Article 2 of the Convention.

117. It reveals the proper quandary facing the Court when it has to provide an autonomous definition of the concept of the place of performance.

(b) The choice of an autonomous interpretation

118. There is no doubt that such an interpretation is difficult for a number of reasons.

119. Firstly, one wonders whether the very principle of an autonomous definition in the matter of contracts is not questionable from the point of view of legal certainty, since the Court has to define as many concepts of 'place of performance' as there are contracts, which includes contracts *sui generis* and this means that it is faced with a never-ending task.

120. Secondly, assuming this tricky undertaking is embarked upon, the Court is required to give substance to the concept of 'place of performance'. The existence of uniform laws, which are thought to remove the obstacle, referred to in the *Tessili* judgment cited above, of the absence of unification of the substantive law applicable, was not sufficient, as we have seen, to alter the direction of the Court's case-law in *Custom Made Commercial*, cited above.

121. The choice of consistency of case-law is the direct consequence of the

fact that a uniform law, for reasons already stated, is not always able to provide the Court with the information enabling it to devise an autonomous definition which complies with the objectives of the Convention.

122. I think, however, that, however tricky it may be, an autonomous definition of the place of performance is desirable.

123. The drawback to this process is that it depends on a case-by-case approach to each contract, which would lead to constant lack of legal certainty.

124. This factor, which is not entirely unfounded, does not, however, constitute a decisive criterion for dismissing the idea of an autonomous definition.

125. A case-by-case approach is in fact the way favoured by a *renvoi* to the rules of private international law. A definition of the place of performance of each contract forming the subject of a dispute which the Court would be called upon to give, according to the scheme of autonomous interpretation, has already been given by the national court according to a similar process.

126. In addition, it is quite justified to think that the drawbacks of this approach, in the circumstances of the *Tessili* judgment cited above, were exacerbated by the fact that in the absence of a uniform law the solutions thus devised still differ from one State to another. Even where the applicable conflict of laws rules are derived from international rules, the definition of the place of performance of an obligation stems from a national law. Lastly, where the rule is itself defined at international level, its content is determined on the basis of considerations other than those of procedure.

127. Thus, the concept of place of performance, applying to an indeterminate number of obligations, is all the more elusive because the way in which it is determined in each case only applies in respect of the court which defines it.

128. In those circumstances, an autonomous interpretation has some legitimacy, that conferred on it by the objective of harmonisation and simplification of the Convention.

129. However, the risk that this analytical process will affect legal certainty for litigants should not be exaggerated.

130. An autonomous definition of the place of performance of an obligation will often be transposable to other obligations, of which there may be many.

131. In its search for a solution which complies more closely with the objectives of the Convention, and more particularly Article 5(1) thereof, the Court will, so far as is possible, take care not to adopt an analytical approach which would lead to as many definitions as there are obligations.

132. Rather, I think that it would be more appropriate to determine a general criterion, whose application would serve to provide definitions applying, if not to every contractual obligation, at least to certain categories of contractual obligation.

133. I would add that the lack of legal certainty generated by the uncertainty affecting determination of the place of performance of the obligations seems to me to be greater in the case of application of the *lex causae* than of devising autonomous Community law.

134. The choice of an autonomous criterion is, in fact, likely to make it easier to devise pragmatic definitions applicable in a uniform and lasting manner to an increasing number of categories of obligation, according to one scheme, which meets the requirements of the Convention.

135. Recourse to rules derived from uniform laws is, however, desirable only to the extent that the concept of the place of performance which results from so doing complies with the requirements of the Convention.

136. I therefore conclude that it is necessary to follow the general direction of the Court's case-law on the Brussels Convention and provide an autonomous interpretation of the terms it uses.

(4) The place of performance of the contested obligations

137. In the case in the main proceedings, compliance with the criterion of the connecting factor between the dispute and the court having jurisdiction leads us to approach the process of determining the place of performance of the contested obligations in two stages:

(a) Obligations to make payment

138. It is appropriate to apply the Court's case-law in *De Bloos*, cited above.

139. The general principle in *De Bloos* would lead one to take into account the obligation corresponding to the contractual right on which the plaintiff's action is based. This therefore involves both the obligation to pay the commission sought in return for operating as an agent, as provided in the agreement, and the obligation to pay compensation for termination of the agreement in return for the obligation to comply with a term of notice at the end of the commercial agency agreement.

140. It should be remembered, however, that according to that judgment 'in a case where the plaintiff asserts the right to be paid damages or seeks a dissolution of the contract on the ground of the wrongful conduct of the other party, the obligation referred to in Article 5(1) is still that which arises under the contract and the non-performance of which is relied upon to support such claims'.

141. The *De Bloos* judgment cited above takes account of the fact that the claim is not seeking direct performance of a defaulting contractual obligation, but rather compensation for non-performance or draws the legal consequences therefrom, in order not to dissociate artificially the place of performance of the original contractual obligation from that of the 'obligation replacing the unperformed contractual obligation', which might also be termed a counter obligation.

142. Thus, in such a circumstance, the place of performance serving to determine jurisdiction is not, as the first principle set out in the above-mentioned judgment would have it, that of the obligation under the contractual law on which the plaintiff's action is based, but that of the unperformed obligation on which the claim for payment is based.

143. In this way, the multiplicity of heads of claim, which is sometimes the consequence of one and the same failure to perform a contractual obligation, does not result in a proliferation of jurisdictions.

144. The result is that, as regards the obligation to pay compensation for termination of the agreement, the obligation to which reference should be made for the purposes of Article 5(1) is the obligation to comply with a period of notice.

145. On the other hand, if one follows the sense of the *De Bloos* judgment, cited above, that reasoning cannot be transposed to a claim for payment of commission. The payment of commission does not in fact constitute an obligation replacing an unperformed contractual obligation, within the meaning of the judgment cited above, but, as the file shows, one of the main contractual obligations incumbent on the principal.

146. In these circumstances, the place of performance to be taken into account should be that of the actual obligation to make the payment.

147. I have already mentioned the difficulties involved in determining the place of performance of obligations to pay sums of money.

148. If one follows the *De Bloos* ruling, the place of performance of the original contractual obligations is still determined by the substantive law applicable, which inevitably means that the competent forum is chosen according to whether the payment is to be collected at the place where the debtor is domiciled or at the place where the creditor is domiciled, and involves a risk that no account will be taken of any connecting factor between the dispute and the court having jurisdiction.

149. There is no reason to draw a distinction between these obligations since they come under the same category of obligations to make payment.

150. As Mr Lenz pointed out in his Opinion in the *Custom Made Commercial* case, cited above, regarding the payment of the purchase price -'in the case of disputes about the payment of the price arising on account of the alleged defective performance of the counter-obligation ... the court for the place at which the goods were intended to be supplied is, as a general rule, nearer to the facts than the courts for the place from which they were sent ...'.

151. He therefore proposed that the Court should rule: 'Where a supplier makes *a claim* against a customer *for the payment of the price* due under a contract for manufacture and supply to which the Uniform Law is applicable and the first part of Article 59(1) of the Uniform Law is applicable to that payment under the substantive law, the place of performance within the meaning of Article 5(1) of the Brussels Convention is *the place* agreed in the contract *at which the goods are intended to be supplied ...*'.

152. The objective legal basis of a dispute, whether it be a claim for payment of a price or a claim for compensation, is often to be found at the place of performance of the obligation in kind, so that the corresponding forum is likely to be chosen according to the criterion of the close connecting factor between the dispute and the court having jurisdiction.

153. This is why I approve that view and I consider that it should be transposed to a case where a claim is for payment of commission allegedly due in respect of the proper performance of the service provided as part of a commercial agency.

154. The search for a close connecting factor between the court and the

dispute, which provides the logical basis for this reasoning, should not be regarded as a desire to establish this connecting factor as a direct criterion of jurisdiction.

155. I agree with the Court that 'Article 5 does not establish that connecting factor itself as the criterion for the choice of the competent forum' and 'It is not possible for an applicant to sue a defendant before any court having a connection with the dispute since Article 5 lists exhaustively the criteria for linking a dispute to a specific court'.

156. It seems to me, as it did to the Court, to be essential not to allow the use of criteria other than the place of performance where that place assigns jurisdiction to a forum which has no direct connection with the case.

157. Conferring jurisdiction on the court of the place of performance of the obligation forming the basis of the claim or, in the case of a claim for payment, of the place of performance of the relevant obligation in kind provides a way of improving the chances of ensuring there is a connecting factor. However, the rule is by no means automatic, since the subject-matter or legal basis of the dispute before the court may be located elsewhere than at the place of performance of the obligation at the time when proceedings are instituted.

158. To the extent that it was not possible to contemplate establishing a direct criterion of jurisdiction based on the connecting factor, which would have affected the predictability of the competent forum by forcing the parties to discuss in every instance the question of which forum was best placed to hear and determine the dispute in order to agree on jurisdiction, it was decided to select the place of performance as the criterion which was best suited to achieve this purpose. Its fixed nature, irrespective of whether a connecting factor with the dispute of the court it designates can be proved, guarantees a clear and precise determination of the rules of jurisdiction applicable.

159. This is the interpretation which the Court has given in this connection, ruling that 'under Article 5(1), in matters relating to a contract, a defendant may be sued in the courts for the place of performance of the obligation in question, even where the court thus designated is not that which has the closest connection with the dispute'.

160. Selection of the place of performance of the obligations to which payment of commission and compensation for termination of the agreement are the counter obligation must therefore take precedence, even where no close connection can be established between the dispute and the court.

161. To summarise, reference to the place of performance of contractual obligations in order to establish jurisdiction, where the claim is for payment of a price, seems to me to be likely to avoid, if not as a general rule at least to a significant extent, proliferation of jurisdictions. It also seems to me to promote the search for a forum close to the dispute' without thereby threatening litigant's legal certainty by resorting directly to that criterion.

(b) Obligations in kind

162. It is appropriate to examine the factors which make it possible to establish the place of performance, for the purposes of Article 5(1) of the Convention, of the obligations in respect of which commercial agency

commission and compensation for termination of the agreement are the counter obligations.

163. I think that, in order to remove from the definition of the concept of 'place of performance' considerations not related to the geographical location *stricto sensu* of the obligation at issue, which is only valid with regard to the requirement laid down in the Convention that there must be a close connecting factor between the dispute and the court having jurisdiction, it is appropriate to refer to the place where the contested obligation was or must be *actually* performed.

164. Situated on the spot, near to one of the strategic points in the contractual process, the court has the facilities which that proximity should normally afford it in order to rule more quickly, and in full knowledge of the facts, on the dispute before it.

165. It should be pointed out that this approach is not totally new since, in view of their specific nature, contracts of employment do not come within the scope of the Court's *Tessili* judgment cited above, since their place of performance is defined autonomously.

166. After observing that 'the obligation to be taken into consideration for the purposes of the application of Article 5(1) of the Convention to contracts of employment is always the obligation which characterises such contracts, namely *the employee's obligation to carry out the work stipulated*', the Court held that, in this area 'the place of performance of the relevant obligation must be interpreted as meaning, for the purposes of Article 5(1) of the Convention, *the place where the employee actually performs the work covered by the contract with his employer*'.

167. The interpretation is justified by two different considerations.

168. On the one hand, contracts of employment display certain particular features compared with other contracts in that they create a lasting bond which brings the worker to some extent within the organisational framework of the employer's business and they are linked to the place where the activities are pursued, which determines the application of mandatory rules and collective agreements protecting the employee.

The Court deduces from this that it is appropriate to determine the place of performance of the relevant obligation, for the purposes of applying Article 5(1) of the Convention, by reference not to the applicable national law in accordance with the conflict rules of the court seised but, rather, to uniform criteria which it is for the Court to lay down on the basis of the scheme and objectives of the Convention.

169. On the other hand, the interpretation is based on the concern to afford proper protection to the party to the contract who is the weaker from the social point of view, in this case the employee. The Court considers that protection of that kind is best assured if disputes relating to a contract of employment fall within the jurisdiction of the courts of the place where the employee discharges his obligation towards his employer. That is the place where it is least expensive for the employee to commence, or defend himself against, court proceedings.

170. I do not think that, as regards the balance of relations between

contracting parties, an agreement such as a commercial agency agreement is comparable to a contract of employment. The relationship of economic dependency in which an agent finds himself with regard to his principal is not such that the agent must necessarily, as a result of his position, be regarded as the weaker party. As a matter of law, being self-employed, a commercial agent has significant room for manoeuvre in the organisation of his activity. Save where he is prevented by an exclusive dealing contract, he may also be connected to more than one principal, which is likely to provide him with a minimum turnover sufficient to reduce any potential subjection.

171. Moreover, there are no regulations comparable to the law applying to contracts of employment, the mandatory provisions of which would apply at the place of performance of the contract. The law applicable can be that chosen by the parties.

172. The reasons why I am proposing an autonomous definition of the place of performance are not therefore the same as those on which the Court decided to do so in respect of contracts of employment and do not have the same specific nature.

173. On the contrary, this choice is dictated by the particular ability of the actual place of performance, in an agency agreement, to reconcile the two criteria of the connecting factor and the predictability of the rules of jurisdiction.

174. As Article 7(2) of Directive 86/653 provides, a commercial agency agreement produces its effects mainly within a territorial context determined by the agreement. At all events, whether or not the context is determined, examination of the agreement should make it possible to localise the actual place of performance of the obligations it contains, which is all the more justified because, in an agency agreement such as the one in the case in the main proceedings, the law applicable leaves it to the parties themselves to determine the place of performance of their obligations.

175. In the present case, it is apparent from the order for reference that Bodetex was acting as a commercial agent for Leathertex, without an exclusive dealing agreement, on the Belgian and Netherlands markets.

176. Agreements provide details of the geographical location where they are to be performed. However, reference to the obligation at issue means it is possible to avoid uncertainty in connection with agreements that can be performed simultaneously in the territories of more than one Contracting State, and at the same time designates the courts which are nearest to the case. It is thus the place of performance of the obligation itself which must take precedence, as Article 5(1) of the Convention provides. It will be for the national court, on the basis of the information at its disposal, to determine the place where, according to the agreement, the obligation at issue has been or should be performed.

177. This solution does not of course provide an automatic answer in cases where the proceedings are fragmented, since several obligations which arise from the same contract but are, or could be, performed in the territory of more than one Contracting State may, as in the present case, constitute the basis for the same proceedings.

178. However, the principle of determining the place of performance solely

of the obligations in kind, where the obligation at issue relates to the payment of a sum of money, reduces that risk.

179. In the case which concerns us, where the obligations at issue in the proceedings are of equal rank, the existence of a single forum having jurisdiction depends on the existence of a single place of performance of the obligations in kind, to which the claims for payment correspond.

180. With regard to the claim for payment of compensation for termination of the agreement, it is necessary to refer to the place of performance of the original claim, failure to perform which is being contended, that is to say, the period of notice. Since this period is constituted by the extension of the effects of the agreement as a whole, for a legally appointed time, its place of performance is the same as that of the agreement itself and not of any specific obligation.

181. As regards the claim for payment of commission, the place of performance to be taken into consideration is that of the agency mandate granted to the commercial agent, whose commission constitutes the consideration therefor, which again covers the localisation of the agreement itself.

182. Where, as in the present case, the place of performance of the obligations at issue is the same as that of the agreement itself, and the scope of the agreement covers the territories of several Contracting States, it is for the court making the reference to determine that place of performance on the basis of the factors which enable it to designate one of the States as the State in whose territory the commercial agent will engage in most of his activity.

183. From a more general viewpoint, this policy does not exempt the referring court from first checking whether a hierarchy can be established between the contested obligations arising from an agreement, in order, as the Court has consistently held, to determine the principal obligation so as to designate the court which has jurisdiction.

Conclusion

184. I therefore propose that the Court give the following answer to the question submitted by the Hof van Cassatie:

'Article 5(1) of the Brussels Convention of 27 September 1968 on Jurisdiction and the Enforcement of Judgments in Civil and Commercial Matters, as amended by the Convention of 9 October 1978 on the accession of the Kingdom of Denmark, Ireland and the United Kingdom of Great Britain and Northern Ireland, is to be interpreted as meaning that a composite claim for payment of commercial agency commission and a claim for payment of compensation for termination of an agreement, based on obligations presented as being of equal rank and arising from the same commercial agency agreement, may be brought before the same court if the place where the agency mandate to which the commission relates

has been or is due to be actually performed, and the place where the obligation to comply with the period of notice of termination has been or is due to be actually performed, to which the compensation for termination relates, are situated in the territory of the same Contracting State'.

TITLE II *[Chapter II]*

JURISDICTION *[Jurisdiction]*

Jurisdiction in matters relating to maintenance – Article 5(2) *[Article 5(2)]*

Case C-295/95 - 20 March 1997

Jackie Farrell
v
James Long

Jurisdiction in matters relating to maintenance - Protocol on the interpretation of the Convention - Jurisdiction of the Court - Limits - Jurisdiction in matters relating to maintenance.

Summary

1. In the light of the division of responsibilities in the preliminary ruling procedure laid down by the Protocol of 3 June 1971 on the interpretation by the Court of Justice of the Convention of 27 September 1968 on Jurisdiction and the Enforcement of Judgments in Civil and Commercial Matters, it is solely for the national court before which the dispute has been brought, and which must assume the responsibility for the subsequent judicial decision, to determine in the light of the particular circumstances of each case both the need for a preliminary ruling in order to enable it to deliver judgment and the relevance of the questions which it submits to the Court.

2. The terms of the Convention must, in principle, be interpreted autonomously. Such autonomous interpretation is alone capable of ensuring uniform application of the Convention, the objectives of which include unification of the rules on jurisdiction of the Contracting States, so as to avoid as far as possible multiplication of the bases of jurisdiction in relation to one and the same legal relationship, and reinforcement of the legal protection available to persons established in the Community by allowing both the plaintiff easily to identify the court before which he may bring an action and the defendant reasonably to foresee the court before which he may be sued.

Those considerations also apply to the term 'maintenance creditor' in the first limb of Article 5(2) of the Convention, which must be interpreted as covering any person applying for maintenance, including a person bringing a maintenance action for the first time, without any distinction being drawn between those already recognized and those not yet recognized as entitled to maintenance.

JUDGMENT OF THE COURT

Mancini, President of the Sixth Chamber, Kakouris, Hirsch, Ragnemalm and Schintgen, Judges

1. By order of 15 May 1995, received at the Court on 15 September 1995, the Circuit Court, County of Dublin, referred to the Court for a preliminary ruling under the Protocol of 3 June 1971 on the interpretation by the Court of Justice of the Convention of 27 September 1968 on jurisdiction and the enforcement of judgments in civil and commercial matters (OJ 1978 L 304, p.36, hereinafter 'the Convention'), as amended by the Convention of 9 October 1978 on the accession of the Kingdom of Denmark, Ireland and the United Kingdom of Great Britain and Northern Ireland (OJ 1978 L 304, p.1 and - in the amended version - at p. 77) and by the Convention of 25 October 1982 on the Accession of the Hellenic Republic (OJ 1982 L 388, p. 1), a question on the interpretation of Article 5(2) of the Convention.

2. That question was raised in proceedings between Ms Farrell, residing in Dalkey, Ireland, and Mr Long, who is habitually resident in Bruges, Belgium.

3. It appears from the documents in the main proceedings that Ms Farrell is the mother of a child born on 3 July 1988 whose father is, she claims, Mr Long. She brought an action against Mr Long before the District Court, applying for a maintenance order in favour of that child.

4. Mr Long denies that he is the father of the child and contests the jurisdiction of the Irish courts to entertain Ms Farrell's application.

5. Ms Farrell maintains that the Irish courts have jurisdiction under Article 5(2) of the Convention. That provision, which derogates from the rule in the first paragraph of Article 2 conferring jurisdiction on the

courts of the Contracting State in which the defendant is domiciled, is in the following terms: 'A person domiciled in a Contracting State may, in another Contracting State, be sued: (...) 2. in matters relating to maintenance, in the courts for the place where the maintenance creditor is domiciled or habitually resident or, if the matter is ancillary to proceedings concerning the status of a person, in the court which, according to its own law, has jurisdiction to entertain those proceedings, unless that jurisdiction is based solely on the nationality of one of the parties'.

6. Mr Long, on the other hand, maintains that that provision cannot apply. He contends that Ms Farrell is not a maintenance creditor within the meaning of Article 5(2) of the Convention because she has not obtained any maintenance order recognizing her as such.

7. At first instance, the District Court dismissed the application on the ground of lack of jurisdiction. Ms Farrell appealed against that judgment to the Circuit Court, which has referred the following question to the Court for a preliminary ruling: 'Do the provisions of Article 5(2) of the Convention on Jurisdiction and the Enforcement of Judgments in Civil and Commercial Matters, signed at Brussels on the 27th day of September 1968, require as a condition precedent to the institution of maintenance proceedings in the Irish courts by an applicant who is domiciled in Ireland against a respondent who is domiciled in Belgium that the applicant has previously obtained an order for maintenance against the respondent?'

8. By that question, the national court seeks in essence to ascertain whether the first limb of Article 5(2) of the Convention must be interpreted as meaning that the term 'maintenance creditor' covers any person applying for maintenance, including a person bringing a maintenance action for the first time, or only persons whose entitlement to maintenance has already been recognized by a previous judicial decision.

9. The national court's question is prompted by the fact that the Jurisdiction of Courts and Enforcement of Judgments (European Communities) Act, 1988, which introduced the Brussels Convention into Irish law, contains, in section 1, the following definition: 'maintenance creditor means, in relation to a maintenance order, the person entitled to the payments for which the order provides'.

Admissibility of the question referred

10. The respondent in the main proceedings denies that the question referred is pertinent, on the ground that the maintenance obligation at issue in the dispute before the national court is ancillary to the issue of paternity, which is a matter of status, and that the applicable provision is therefore not the first limb of Article 5(2), in which the term 'maintenance creditor' appears, but the second limb.

11. In the light of the division of responsibilities in the preliminary ruling procedure laid down by the Protocol of 3 June 1971 on the interpretation by the Court of Justice of the Convention, it is for the national court alone to define the questions which it proposes to refer to the Court. According to settled law, it is solely for the national court before which the dispute has been brought, and which must assume the responsibility of the subsequent judicial decision, to determine in the light of the particular circumstances of each case both the need for a preliminary ruling in order to enable it to deliver judgment and the relevance of the questions which it submits to the Court (Case C-127/92 *Enderby* [1993] ECR I-5535, paragraph 10).

The question referred

12. For the purpose of answering the question referred, it must be noted that, according to settled law (see, in particular, Case C-125/92 *Mulox IBC* v *Geels* [1993] ECR I-4075, paragraph 10, and Case C-383/95 *Rutten* v *Cross Medical* [1997] ECR I-57, paragraph 12), the Court will, in principle, interpret the terms of the Convention autonomously so as to ensure that it is fully effective having regard to the objectives of Article 220 of the EEC Treaty, for the implementation of which it was adopted.

13. Such autonomous interpretation is alone capable of ensuring uniform application of the Convention, the objectives of which include unification of the rules on jurisdiction of the Contracting States, so as to avoid as far as possible multiplication of the bases of jurisdiction in relation to one and the same legal relationship and to reinforce the legal protection available to persons established in the Community by, at the same time, allowing the plaintiff easily to identify the court before which he may bring an action and the defendant reasonably to foresee the court before which he may be sued (*Mulox IBC*, paragraph 11, and *Rutten*, paragraph 13).

14. Those considerations must also apply to the interpretation of the

term 'maintenance creditor' in the first limb of Article 5(2) of the Convention, since there is nothing to suggest that its meaning is intended under that provision to be determined in accordance with the *lex fori*.

15. As to the meaning of that term, two arguments in particular have been advanced before the Court. According to the first of those arguments, put forward by the respondent in the main proceedings, the term covers only persons whose entitlement to maintenance has already been recognized by a previous judicial decision. Consequently, an initial action brought by a maintenance applicant, seeking a finding that maintenance is payable in principle, does not fall within that provision.

16. According to the second argument, advanced by the appellant in the main proceedings, by the Irish, German and United Kingdom Governments and by the Commission, the term must be construed as referring to any person applying for maintenance, including a person bringing a maintenance action for the first time.

17. It is necessary in that regard to determine the objective of Article 5(2) of the Convention.

18. Article 5 introduces a series of derogations from the rule laid down in the first paragraph of Article 2, which confers jurisdiction on the courts of the Contracting State where the defendant is domiciled. Each of the derogations from that rule provided for by Article 5 pursues a specific objective.

19. In particular, the derogation provided for in Article 5(2) is intended to offer the maintenance applicant, who is regarded as the weaker party in such proceedings, an alternative basis of jurisdiction. In adopting that approach, the drafters of the Convention considered that that specific objective had to prevail over the objective of the rule contained in the first paragraph of Article 2, which is to protect the defendant as the party who, being the person sued, is generally in a weaker position.

20. It is common ground that that was the intention of the authors of the Convention in cases where the entitlement to maintenance of a plaintiff in an action brought on the basis of Article 5(2) has already been recognized by a previous judicial decision and the new action seeks an order fixing the amount of the maintenance, if it has not been fixed by the previous decision, varying the amount already fixed, or requiring the maintenance to be paid where the defendant is in arrears or refuses to pay.

21. It is necessary, therefore to examine whether that was also the intention of the authors of the Convention in cases where a person brings a maintenance action on the basis of Article 5(2) without having previously obtained a judicial decision recognizing his or her entitlement to maintenance.

22. That question must be answered in the affirmative.

23. Article 5(2) refers to 'the maintenance creditor' in general terms, without drawing any distinction between those already recognized and those not yet recognized as entitled to maintenance.

24. That finding is borne out by the report drawn up by the committee of experts who drafted the text of the Convention, known as the *Jenard Report* (OJ 1979 C 59, p. 1, in particular p. 25). As regards Article 5(2) of the Convention, that report states as follows: '... the court for the place of domicile of the maintenance creditor is in the best position to know whether the creditor is in need and to determine the extent of such need. However, in order to align the Convention with the Hague Convention, Article 5(2) also confers jurisdiction on the courts for the place of habitual residence of the maintenance creditor. This alternative is justified in relation to maintenance obligations since it enables in particular a wife deserted by her husband to sue him for payment of maintenance in the courts for the place where she herself is habitually resident, rather than the place of her legal domicile. ... As regards maintenance payments, the Committee did not overlook the problems which might be raised by preliminary issues (for example, the question of affiliation). However, it considered that these were not properly problems of jurisdiction, and that any difficulties should be considered in the chapter on recognition and enforcement of judgments'.

25. It follows that Article 5(2) of the Convention is framed in such a way as to apply to all actions brought in maintenance matters, including the initial action brought by a person applying for maintenance, and that consideration of the question of paternity as a preliminary issue in such proceedings did not prompt the authors of the Convention to adopt any different solution.

26. Moreover, no decisive argument has been advanced against such an interpretation.

27. Having regard to the foregoing considerations, the first limb of Article 5(2) of the Convention must be interpreted as meaning that the term 'maintenance creditor' covers any person applying for maintenance, including a person bringing a maintenance action for the first time.

On those grounds, the Court (Sixth Chamber), in answer to the question referred to it by the Circuit Court, County of Dublin, by order of 15 May 1995, hereby rules:

> **The first limb of Article 5(2) of the Convention of 27 September 1968 on Jurisdiction and the Enforcement of Judgments in Civil and Commercial Matters, as amended by the Convention of 9 October 1978 on the accession of the Kingdom of Denmark, Ireland and the United Kingdom of Great Britain and Northern Ireland and by the Convention of 25 October 1982 on the Accession of the Hellenic Republic, must be interpreted as meaning that the term 'maintenance creditor' covers any person applying for maintenance, including a person bringing a maintenance action for the first time.**

OPINION OF MR ADVOCATE GENERAL LÉGER

1. This reference for a preliminary ruling, made by the Circuit Court, County of Dublin, under Article 3 of the Protocol of 3 June 1971, presents a further opportunity for defining one of the terms used by the Convention of 27 September 1968 on jurisdiction and the enforcement of judgments in civil and commercial matters, as amended, in particular, by the 1978 Accession Convention ('the Convention').

2. The point in issue is the interpretation of the term 'maintenance creditor' in Article 5(2) of the Convention, which has not hitherto been defined by the Court. That term identifies those who may invoke the special jurisdiction provided for by Article 5(2), and thus serves to define the scope of the choice of jurisdiction open to them. The Court is requested, in essence, to rule whether 'maintenance creditor' is to be interpreted as covering any person claiming maintenance or only a person whose status as a maintenance creditor has been recognized by judicial decision.

I - The special jurisdiction provided for by the Brussels Convention of 27 September 1968

3. The provisions of the Convention giving rise to the question referred are contained in Title II, headed 'Jurisdiction'.

4. T he basic jurisdictional rule laid down by the Convention is set out in the first paragraph of Article 2, which provides: 'Subject to the provisions of this Convention, persons domiciled in a Contracting State shall, whatever their nationality, be sued in the courts of that State'.

5. Article 5 of the Convention lays down, in certain areas, jurisdictional rules providing alternatives to the principle that jurisdiction is conferred on the courts of the State in which the defendant is domiciled. It provides, *inter alia*: 'A person domiciled in a Contracting State may, in another Contracting State, be sued: ... 2. *in matters relating to maintenance*, in the courts for the place where the maintenance creditor is *domiciled or habitually resident* or, if the matter is ancillary to proceedings concerning the status of a person, in the court which, according to its own law, has jurisdiction to entertain those proceedings, unless that jurisdiction is based solely on the nationality of one of the parties'.

6. A maintenance creditor therefore enjoys a *choice of jurisdiction*, being entitled to bring proceedings either in the courts for the place where the defendant is domiciled or in those for his or her own place of domicile or residence.

II - Facts and procedure

7. According to the reference for a preliminary ruling in the present case, the applicant, Ms Jackie Farrell, an unmarried woman of 28 years of age, residing at Dalkey, Ireland, is the mother of a child born on 3 July 1988. Ms Farrell asserts that the father of her child is the respondent, Mr James Long, a married man who is habitually resident in Bruges, Belgium, where he also works.

8. The applicant applied to the District Court for an order requiring Mr Long to pay maintenance. The respondent contests the application on the ground that he denies being the father of the child.

9. On 11 February 1994 the District Court dismissed Ms Farrell's application on the ground that it lacked jurisdiction. On appeal to the Circuit Court, County of Dublin, Ms Farrell argued that the Irish courts had jurisdiction under Article 5(2) of the Convention. Mr Long maintained that the term 'maintenance creditor' referred only to a person already in possession of a maintenance order, and not to a person in the applicant's position, seeking such an order.

10. In the context of that appeal, the Circuit Court, County of Dublin, has referred the following question to the Court of Justice: 'Do the provisions of Article 5(2) of the Convention on jurisdiction and the enforcement of judgments in civil and commercial matters signed at Brussels on the 27th day of September 1968 require as a condition precedent to the institution of maintenance proceedings in the Irish courts by an applicant who is domiciled in Ireland

against a respondent who is domiciled in Belgium that the applicant has previously obtained an order for maintenance against the respondent?'

11. In his observations, the respondent argues that the maintenance proceedings are ancillary to the issue of paternity and that the applicant cannot therefore rely on the first part of Article 5(2). Consequently, only the second part of that provision is applicable.

12. Since the relevance of the question referred is thus contested, it is necessary first of all to examine that point before undertaking an assessment of the contested concept.

III - Applicability of Article 5(2)

13. As is apparent both from the question referred and the wording of the decision to seek a preliminary ruling, the national court's question concerns the firs part of Article 5(2), which applies to proceedings seeking payment of maintenance applications ancillary to proceedings concerning the status of a person.

14. The national court therefore considers that the question raised is decisive for the determination of the dispute.

15. The Court of Justice has consistently held that 'the considerations which may have led a national court or tribunal to its choice of questions as well as the relevance which it attributes to such questions in the context of a case before it are excluded from review by the Court of Justice'.

16. More particularly, it has ruled that 'when a national court or tribunal refers a provision of Community law for interpretation, it is to be supposed that the said court or tribunal considers this interpretation necessary to enable it to give judgment in the action' and that 'the Court cannot require the national court or tribunal to state expressly that the provision which appears to that court or tribunal to call for an interpretation is applicable'.

17. I am of the view, therefore, that the question referred by the national court must be answered, regardless of its relevance for the dispute before it, and that the answer to be given requires an interpretation of the term 'maintenance creditor'.

IV - The term 'maintenance creditor'

18. According to the referring court, the law governing jurisdiction in the present proceedings is set out in the Jurisdiction of Courts and Enforcement of Judgments (European Communities) Act, 1988 ('the 1988 Act'). That statute gives the force of law to the Convention in Ireland.

19. Whilst the term 'maintenance creditor', as used in Article 5(2) of the Convention, may call for interpretation, its meaning in the Irish statute cited by the national court appears less ambiguous.

20. First, Section 1 of the 1988 Act provides: '"maintenance creditor" means, in relation to a maintenance order, the person entitled to the payments for which the order provides'.

21. Second, Rule 20 of the District Court [Jurisdiction of Courts and Enforcement of Judgments (European Communities) Act, 1988] Rules, 1988, which deals with the procedure for bringing an application before the District Court, refers to an application brought by virtue of Article 5(2) of the Convention 'for the variation of a maintenance order'.

22. The national court, noting the divergence between the wording of the Convention and that of the Irish statute, states: '... it may be that the terms of the Irish statute do not fully reflect the intentions and purpose of the Convention'.

23. The question of the interpretation of the term 'maintenance creditor' appears, therefore, to be decisive.

24. The numerous terms used in the Convention may differ in meaning from one Contracting State to another. The Court of Justice has had occasions, in the exercise of its interpretative functions, to decide whether such legal concepts must be regarded as autonomous, and therefore given a uniform interpretation in all the Contracting States, or whether they may bear their ordinary meaning under national law.

25. As the Court has held: 'Neither of these two options rules out the other since the appropriate choice can only be made in respect of each of the provisions of the Convention to ensure that it is fully effective having regard to the objectives of Article 220 of the Treaty'.

26. In the light of that principle, I suggest, that the intended meaning of the term 'maintenance creditor' must be sought.

(1) An autonomous concept

27. Whilst the Court has not hitherto had occasion to interpret the term 'maintenance creditor', an autonomous definition has been given to other expressions used to define the scope of the types of special jurisdiction laid down by Article 5 of the Convention.

28. One instance is the term 'matters relating to a contract' in Article 5(1). The Court has stated: 'Having regard to the objectives and the general scheme of the Convention, it is important that, in order to ensure as far as possible the equality and uniformity of the rights and obligations arising out of the Convention for the Contracting States and the persons concerned, that concept should not be interpreted simply as referring to the national law of one or other of the States concerned'.

29. The concepts contained in the phrase 'dispute arising out of the operation of a branch, agency or other establishment', which determine the special jurisdiction provided for in Article 5(5), provide another example. In that connection, the Court has very clearly stated: 'Multiplication of the bases of jurisdiction in one and the same case is not likely to encourage legal certainty and the effectiveness of legal protection throughout the territory of the Community and therefore it is in accord with the objective of the Convention *to avoid a wide and multifarious interpretation of the exceptions to the general rule of jurisdiction* contained in Article 2'.

30. I propose that the Court should follow the line taken in those decisions,

and regard the term 'maintenance creditor' as referring to *an autonomous concept.*

31. To decide otherwise would be to allow a situation in which persons could exercise a choice of jurisdiction in one Contracting State and not in another, depending on whether the national authorities chose to group them together within the same category or, on the contrary, to distinguish between them in accordance with criteria which might themselves vary from State to State.

32. In the preamble to the Convention, the Contracting States express their concern to strengthen in the Community the legal protection of persons therein established and, for that purpose, to determine the international jurisdiction of their courts. By resorting to a common set of norms, they evince a desire to establish a unified corpus of rules of jurisdiction precluding, in my view, any possibility that terms may vary in meaning.

33. A variable definition would not only give rise to discrimination which, in the light of the objective of protection set forth in the preamble, cannot be justified. It would maintain a complex fabric of rules of jurisdiction, inherent in the plurality of national laws, which the Convention was intended to reduce.

(2) The meaning of the term 'maintenance creditor'

34. As the Court has consistently held, the autonomous concepts used in the Convention must, for the purpose of its application, be interpreted by reference, first, *to the system and objectives of the Convention and, second, to the general principles which stem from the corpus of the national legal systems.*

35. Among the *legal systems of the Member States*, several categories may be discerned.

36. Most of the laws in the Member States (in Austria, Belgium, Denmark, England and Wales, Finland, Greece, Italy, the Netherlands and Sweden) *do not use the term 'maintenance creditor'* to define a domestic rule of jurisdiction. The concept of 'maintenance creditor' is not found in German law either, although there is a rule of jurisdiction in respect of maintenance obligations. Under French law, the applicant may choose, in matters relating to maintenance, to bring proceedings before the courts of the place where the creditor resides. However, the French legislation does not define what is meant by 'creditor', and the meaning of that term has not been judicially defined. Spanish law uses the term 'maintenance creditor', but no conclusions as to its meaning can be drawn either from legal literature or from case-law. The position is the same under Scots law. In Luxembourg law, on the other hand, the statute concerning territorial jurisdiction in matters relating to maintenance uses the term 'creditor' and expressly refers to 'applications for the payment of maintenance or for variation of a maintenance order'. In Ireland, doubt remains as to whether the 1988 Act is restricted to the enforcement within Ireland of maintenance decisions given in other States, or whether its provisions constitute rules governing the domestic or international jurisdiction of the Irish courts in the determination of maintenance obligations or variation of maintenance orders.

37. It does not seem possible, therefore, to derive from the national legal

systems any general principle which may assist in the interpretation of the term 'maintenance creditor'. It is not used in most legal systems. Where it is, its meaning has not been determined with any certainty. Interpretation of the wording used in the Convention must therefore seek, primarily, to adhere as closely as possible to the objectives and system of the Convention.

38. What is meant by the term 'maintenance creditor' may be defined by examining, in turn, three possible meanings, ranging from the narrowest to the widest sense of the term.

39. First, as the respondent contends in part of his argument, 'maintenance creditor' may mean *a person in whose favour a maintenance order has been made*. On that basis, Article 5(2) offers a choice of jurisdiction to persons who, having obtained a maintenance order in another Member State, wish to obtain an additional order in the State where they are domiciled or habitually resident.

40. Second, 'maintenance creditor' may mean a person whose right to maintenance has not been established but who is legitimately entitled, by reason of his or her status, in particular a family link with the person against whom the application is made, to claim the payment of sums of money.

41. Lastly, in its widest sense, the term may apply to any person who seeks the payment of maintenance.

42. If the term is taken to mean a person in whose favour a maintenance order has been made, the scope of Article 5(2) appears remarkably restricted, especially if one attempts to identify the categories of cases in which a rule of special jurisdiction has been considered justified.

43. We may immediately discount those cases in which the maintenance creditor applies to the courts for the place where he or she is domiciled or habitually resident for recognition or enforcement of a judicial decision within the territorial jurisdiction of those courts. Article 5 forms part of Title II of the Convention, relating to jurisdiction. It does not fall within the scope of Title III, which lays down rules of jurisdiction specific to applications for recognition and enforcement of judgments and is thus designed to regulate such applications.

44. Two other categories of proceedings thus remain to be considered: those seeking determination of the amount of maintenance, where there has been an initial decision merely declaring that maintenance is in principle payable, and those seeking variation of the amount of maintenance originally ordered.

45. However, there is nothing in the Convention to justify dividing maintenance cases up into two categories: those seeking recognition of the claim and those seeking determination of the amounts due. Moreover, such a division does not appear compatible with the requirements as to simplified procedural rules and expeditious procedures by which the Treaty and the Convention seek to facilitate the reciprocal recognition and enforcement of judgments of courts or tribunals in the Member States. Nor, moreover, does either the Commission or any of the parties or intervening States propose such an interpretation.

46. We may therefore question why a choice of jurisdiction should be reserved to a category of cases as limited as those seeking variation of maintenance obligations in respect of which a judicial decision has already been

given. Nor is it clear why the initial maintenance proceedings should be excluded from such special jurisdiction.

47. It is true that the danger that putative maintenance debtors would have to bear the principal burden imposed by legal proceedings improperly brought against them abroad might justify providing for a choice of jurisdiction limited strictly to applications brought by creditors recognized as such.

48. But if that concern was the justification for such a demarcation within the rules of special jurisdiction, it is surprising that there is no indication of it in the wording of Article 5(2) of the Convention or in the reports of Mr P. Jenard and Professor Schlosser.

49. On the contrary, the Jenard Report states: '... the court for the place of domicile of the maintenance creditor is in the best position to know whether the creditor is in need and to determine the extent of such need.

However, in order to align the Convention with the Hague Convention, Article 5(2) also confers jurisdiction on the courts for the place of habitual residence of the maintenance creditor. This alternative is justified in relation to maintenance obligations since it enables in particular a wife deserted by her husband to sue him for payment of maintenance in the courts for the place where she herself is habitually resident, rather than the place of her legal domicile.'

50. Not only does Mr Jenard draw no distinction between the initial proceedings and the application for the determination or variation of the amount of maintenance payable, but the explanations given by him attest to the general character, applicable without distinction to all proceedings brought in maintenance matters, of the rule laid down.

51. The justification given for the rule contained in Article 5(2) of the Convention, namely the capacity of the court to know whether the creditor is in need and to determine the extent of such need, is not valid only for a single category of maintenance proceedings; it is perfectly applicable to the initial proceedings seeking the payment of maintenance. Moreover, the example of a wife deserted by her husband, which Mr Jenard gives to show why the maintenance creditor's habitual residence should serve as an alternative criterion of jurisdiction, quite clearly relates to an initial application for maintenance, as is shown by the terminology used (suing 'for payment' of maintenance, not for the 'determination', 'review' or 'variation' of maintenance).

52. Furthermore, counsel for the respondent referred at the hearing to a definition of the term 'debt' given in England in 1883, according to which 'a debt is a sum of money which is payable or which will become payable in the future by reason of a present obligation'. He inferred from this that, in the present case, entitlement to payment of this sum of money is not established whilst paternity remains in issue, which means that the question raised turns on the question of legal status.

53. I endorse the definition proposed, but, as stated above, I do not consider that it is for the Court to assess the relevance of the question or the extent to which the answer to be given to it may resolve the dispute pending before the referring court.

54. On the other hand, once it is agreed that a debt is an obligation arising

from some fact - which may be either a legal fact in the strict sense of the term or a legal act - by virtue of which the creditor *is entitled to payment* of a sum of money from his debtor, it becomes clear that a person does not need to have obtained a court judgment in order to qualify as a creditor. Such a judgment certainly constitutes undeniable proof of his status as a creditor. However, that status is not conditional on the existence of a judgment, since the fact giving rise to the obligation, and thus the debt, may well precede the judgment (as, for example, in the case of the loan of a sum of money giving rise to a repayment obligation or a blood relationship creating a maintenance obligation).

55. Consequently, the existence of a judgment does not in my view constitute a *sine qua non* for recognizing that a person is a maintenance creditor, which can be established by other criteria.

56. That is the position where it is possible to prove a *family relationship* between the person claiming maintenance and the person from whom it is claimed which is such as to render the maintenance claim legitimate.

0

58. In my view, however, any such distinction is again precluded by the broadness of the wording of Article 5(2) and the need for simplicity in the procedural rules laid down by the Convention pursuant to Article 220 of the Treaty.

59. Different approaches may be taken with regard to what constitutes a family relationship as a criterion for determining whether a person is a maintenance creditor.

60. In a narrow sense, a maintenance creditor might be a person who is able to rely on a legally recognized family relationship with the person from whom maintenance is claimed. That construction would afford a choice of jurisdiction to, for example, a spouse or former spouse, or a child whose affiliation is established by the fact of the marriage or an act of recognition.

61. The advantage of such a solution lies in the fact that it is based on an objective criterion. However, it is open to challenge in two respects: first, in order to be accepted, such a precise distinction would have to be evident from the wording of Article 5(2) of the Convention or from the reports cited above, which is not the case. Second, it deviates from the very definition of indebtedness, by denying the choice of jurisdiction to persons who are entitled to maintenance but who do not possess any legal status enabling them to establish such entitlement. A maintenance claim made, for example, on behalf of an unacknowledged child against his real parents would be excluded from the scope of Article 5(2) solely because of the denial of his parentage. It is not possible to define a creditor as a person entitled to the payment of a sum of money by reason of a fact giving rise to indebtedness and, at the same time, to deny a person the opportunity of proving the very fact - in this instance, parentage - giving rise to such status as a creditor.

62. In the broad sense, a maintenance creditor would then be a person who, in order to exercise a choice of jurisdiction, first proves the family relationship on which the indebtedness is based. In such circumstances, however, the criterion ceases to be objective, since the court seised is required,

in each individual case, to assess the likely veracity of the alleged relationship. There is therefore a risk that the outcome may vary from one State to another, or even from one court to another, contrary to the minimum objectives of legal certainty and simplicity of procedural rules. Moreover, and for the same reasons, it is unacceptable that the determination of a rule of jurisdiction should be thus dependent on the outcome of complex arguments on a substantive issue.

63. The use of family relationships, in that sense of the term, in order to establish that a person is a maintenance creditor, and thus to determine the right to exercise a choice of jurisdiction, may therefore be seen as awkward, arbitrary and open to challenge.

64. The remaining solution, advocated by all of the parties except for the respondent, is to apply the widest definition to the term 'maintenance creditor'. According to that construction, 'maintenance creditor' within the meaning of the Convention must mean *the person bringing a principal claim for maintenance*.

65. It is apparent from what has been stated above that that construction is most closely in accordance with the objectives pursued by the Convention, namely, simplicity, expeditiousness and legal protection of individuals.

66. The criterion for determining whether a person is eligible to effect a choice of jurisdiction is a very precise and objective one. Consequently, it reduces the risk of potential litigation arising from uncertainty as to its parameters, which may itself cause delay and unjustified differentiation between persons who may be entitled to make such a choice.

67. The claim relevant for that purpose may be one seeking either an initial maintenance order or the review of such an order. It does not require the bringing of separate proceedings, which would hardly accord with the efficacy which it is sought to achieve.

68. Lastly, the Court has held that 'although Article 5 makes provision in a number of cases for a special jurisdiction which the plaintiff may choose, this is because of the existence, in certain clearly-defined situations, of a particularly close connecting factor between a dispute and the court which may be called upon to hear it, with a view to the efficacious conduct of proceedings'.

69. Article 5(2) is designed to relieve the maintenance creditor from having to bring proceedings in a distant court. There are two main reasons for this.

70. First, the maintenance claimant is *ex hypothesi* and, in most cases, in practice the more impecunious of the parties to the proceedings, so that it seems fair that he or she should be spared the costs of an action abroad, including those incurred at the stage of the initial application.

71. Second, the court for the place where the applicant is domiciled or resident is best placed, by reason of its familiarity with the economic and social climate in which the applicant lives, to make findings as to the reality and extent of the needs expressed. It is in a position to determine the merits of the application and to appraise the amount to be awarded. Its suitability is no different whether it is seised of an initial application or a fresh stage in the litigation. This is confirmed by the Jenard Report, cited above, in which it is stated that the court for the place of domicile of the maintenance creditor is in

the best position to know whether the maintenance creditor is in need and to determine the extent of such need.

72. The term as thus defined appears to me, therefore, to accord with the systemand objectives of the Convention as previously interpreted by the Court with a view to clarifying the provisions concerning special jurisdiction.

73. On this view, there is no reason why the proximity intended by the legislature between an individual and the court which is called upon to determine his or her claim should not also benefit those making initial maintenance applications.

74. It thus appears that the objective of the Convention is not to differentiate according to the type of proceedings brought but to facilitate the institution of lawsuits by maintenance claimants, who are frequently at a disadvantage. Consequently, for the purposes of deciding upon a rule of jurisdiction, it must be accepted that 'maintenance creditor', within the meaning of the Convention, designates a person claiming to qualify as such.

Conclusion

75. In the light of the foregoing considerations, I propose that the Court give the following answer to the question referred: 'On a proper construction of Article 5(2) of the Convention on jurisdiction and the enforcement of judgments in civil and commercial matters, signed at Brussels on 27 September 1968, an applicant domiciled in Ireland, who wishes to bring maintenance proceedings under that provision before the Irish courts against a respondent domiciled in Belgium, does not need to have previously obtained an order requiring the respondent to pay maintenance. The term 'maintenance creditor' in the first part of Article 5(2) must be interpreted as meaning any person who brings a claim for maintenance by way of principal application.'

TITLE II *[Chapter II]*

JURISDICTION *[Jurisdiction]*

Jurisdiction in matters relating to tort, delict or quasi-delict – Article 5(3) *[Article 5(3)]*

See also

Case 21/76 - 30 November 1976

Handelskwekerij G. J. Bier B.V.
v
Mines de Potasse d'Alsace S.A.

Pollution of the atmosphere or of water - Dispute of an international character - Article 5(3) - Matters relating to tort, delict or quasi-delict - Courts having jurisdiction - Special jurisdiction - Place where the harmful event occurred - Place of the event giving rise to the damage and place where the damage occurred - Connecting factors of significance as regards jurisdiction - Right of plaintiff to elect.

Summary

Where the place of the happening of the event which may give rise to liability in tort, delict or quasi-delict and the place where that event results in damage are not identical, the expression 'place where the harmful event occurred', in Article 5(3) of the Convention of 27 September 1968 on jurisdiction and the enforcement of Judgments in Civil and Commercial Matters, must be understood as being intended to cover both the place where the damage occurred and the place of the event giving rise to it. The result is that the defendant may be sued, at the option of the plaintiff, either in the courts for the place where the damage occurred or in the courts for the place of the event which gives rise to and is at the origin of that damage.

JUDGMENT OF THE COURT

Kutscher, President, Donner and Pescatore, Presidents of Chambers, Mertens de Wilmars, Sorensen, Lord Mackenzie Stuart and O'Keeffe, Judges

1. By judgment of 27 February 1976, which reached the Court Registry on the following 2 March, the Gerechtshof (Appeal Court) of The Hague has referred a question, pursuant to the Protocol on 3 June 1971 on the interpretation of the Convention of 27 September 1968 on jurisdiction and the enforcement of Judgments in Civil and Commercial Matters (hereinafter called 'the Convention'), on the interpretation of Article 5(3) of the said Convention.

2. It appears from the judgment making the reference that at the present stage the main action, which has come before the Gerechtshof by way of appeal, concerns the jurisdiction of the court of first instance at Rotterdam, and in general, of the Netherlands courts, to entertain an action brought by an undertaking engaged in horticulture, established within the area for which the court before which the action was first brought has jurisdiction, and by the Reinwater Foundation, which exists to promote the improvement of the quality of the water in the Rhine basin, against Mines de Potasse d'Alsace, established at Mulhouse (France), concerning the pollution of the waters of the Rhine by the discharge of saline waste from the operations of the defendant into that inland waterway.

3. It appears from the file that as regards irrigation the horticultural business of the first-named appellant depends mainly on the waters of the Rhine, the high salt content of which, according to the said appellant, causes damage to its plantations and obliges it to take expensive measures in order to limit that damage.

4. The appellants consider that the excessive salinization of the Rhine is due principally to the massive discharges carried out by Mines de Potasse d'Alsace and they declare that it is for that reason that they have chosen to bring an action for the purposes of establishing the liability of that undertaking.

5. By judgment delivered on 12 May 1975, the court at Rotterdam held that it had no jurisdiction to entertain the action, taking the view that under Article 5(3) of the Convention the claim did not come within its jurisdiction but under that of the French court for the area in which the discharge at issue took place.

6. Bier and Reinwater brought an appeal against that judgment before the Gerechtshof, The Hague, which subsequently referred the following question to the Court: 'Are the words 'the place where the harmful event

occurred', appearing in the text of Article 5(3) of the Convention on jurisdiction and the enforcement of Judgments in Civil and Commercial Matters, concluded at Brussels on 27 September 1968, to be understood as meaning 'the place where the damage occurred (the place where the damage took place or became apparent)' or rather 'the place where the event having the damage as its sequel occurred (the place where the act was or was not performed)'?'

7. Article 5 of the Convention provides: 'A person domiciled in a Contracting State may, in another Contracting State, be sued: … (3) in matters relating to tort, delict or quasi-delict, in the courts for the place where the harmful event occurred'.

8. That provision must be interpreted in the context of the scheme of conferment of jurisdiction which forms the subject-matter of Title II of the Convention.

9. That scheme is based on a general rule, laid down by Article 2, that the courts of the State in which the defendant is domiciled shall have jurisdiction.

10. However, Article 5 makes provision in a number of cases for a special jurisdiction, which the plaintiff may opt to choose.

11. This freedom of choice was introduced having regard to the existence, in certain clearly defined situations, of a particularly close connecting factor between a dispute and the court which may be called upon to hear it, with a view to the efficacious conduct of the proceedings.

12. Thus in matters of tort, delict or quasi-delict Article 5(3) allows the plaintiff to bring his case before the courts for 'the place where the harmful event occurred'.

13. In the context of the Convention, the meaning of that expression is unclear when the place of the event which is at the origin of the damage is situated in a State other than the one in which the place where the damage occurred is situated, as is the case *inter alia* with atmospheric or water pollution beyond the frontiers of a State.

14. The form of words 'place where the harmful event occurred', used in all the language versions of the Convention, leaves open the question whether, in the situation described, it is necessary, in determining

jurisdiction, to choose as the connecting factor the place of the event giving rise to the damage, or the place where the damage occurred, or to accept that the plaintiff has an option between the one and the other of those two connecting factors.

15. As regards this, it is well to point out that the place of the event giving rise to the damage no less than the place where the damage occurred can, depending on the case, constitute a significant connecting factor from the point of view of jurisdiction.

16. Liability in tort, delict or quasi-delict can only arise provided that a causal connection can be established between the damage and the event in which that damage originates.

17. Taking into account the close connection between the component parts of every sort of liability, it does not appear appropriate to opt for one of the two connecting factors mentioned to the exclusion of the other, since each of them can, depending on the circumstances, be particularly helpful from the point of view of the evidence and of the conduct of the proceedings.

18. To exclude one option appears all the more undesirable in that, by its comprehensive form of words, Article 5(3) of the Convention covers a wide diversity of kinds of liability.

19. Thus, the meaning of the expression 'place where the harmful event occurred' in Article 5(3) must be established in such a way as to acknowledge that the plaintiff has an option to commence proceedings either at the place where the damage occurred or the place of the event giving rise to it.

20. This conclusion is supported by the consideration, first, that to decide in favour only of the place of the event giving rise to the damage would, in an appreciable number of cases, cause confusion between the heads of jurisdiction laid down by Articles 2 and 5(3) of the Convention, so that the latter provision would, to that extent, lose its effectiveness.

21. Secondly, a decision in favour only of the place where the damage occurred would, in cases where the place of the event giving rise to the damage does not coincide with the domicile of the person liable, have the effect of excluding a helpful connecting factor with the jurisdiction of a court particularly near to the cause of the damage.

22. Moreover, it appears from a comparison of the national legislative provisions and national case-law on the distribution of jurisdiction - both as regards internal relationships, as between courts for different areas, and in international relationships - that, albeit by differing legal techniques, a place is found for both of the two connecting factors here considered and that in several States they are accepted concurrently.

23. In these circumstances, the interpretation stated above has the advantage of avoiding any upheaval in the solutions worked out in the various national systems of law, since it looks to unification, in conformity with Article 5(3) of the Convention, by way of a systematisation of solutions which, as to their principle, have already been established in most of the States concerned.

24. Thus, it should be answered that where the place of the happening of the event which may give rise to liability in tort, delict or quasi-delict and the place where that event results in damage are not identical, the expression 'place where the harmful event occurred', in Article 5(3) of the Convention, must be understood as being intended to cover both the place where the damage occurred and the place of the event giving rise to it.

25. The result is that the defendant may be sued, at the option of the plaintiff, either in the courts for the place where the damage occurred or in the courts for the place of the event which gives rise to and is at the origin of that damage.

On those grounds the court in answer to the question referred to it by the Gerechtshof, The Hague, by judgment of 27 February 1976, hereby rules:

> **Where the place of the happening of the event which may give rise to liability in tort, delict or quasi-delict and the place where that event results in damage are not identical, the expression 'place where the harmful event occurred', in Article 5(3) of the Convention of 27 September 1968 on jurisdiction and the enforcement of Judgments in Civil and Commercial Matters, must be understood as being intended to cover both the place where the damage occurred and the place of the event giving rise to it.**
>
> **The result is that the defendant may be sued, at the option of the plaintiff, either in the courts for the place where the damage**

occurred or in the courts for the place of the event which gives rise to and is at the origin of that damage.

OPINION OF MR ADVOCATE GENERAL CAPOTORTI

1. The proceedings between Bier and Mines de Potasse d'Alsace falls into the category of cases raising problems of the interpretation of the Brussels Convention on Jurisdiction and the Enforcement of judgments in Civil and Commercial Matters. The provision to be interpreted is Article 5(3) of the Convention whereby: 'A person domiciled in a Contracting State may, in another Contracting State, be sued ... in matters relating to tort, delict or quasi-delict, in the courts for the place where the harmful event occurred'. In substance the Court is asked to decide what is meant by the words, 'place where the harmful event occurred' which in the said article have the status and function of a criterion of special jurisdiction.

The essential facts may be summarised as follows: the Netherlands undertaking, Bier, which has large nurseries near Rotterdam irrigated by water from the Rhine, and the Stichting Reinwater of Amsterdam instituted proceedings before the Arrondissementsrechtbank (District Court), Rotterdam, against the company Mines de Potasse d'Alsace, which has its registered office in Mulhouse, claiming compensation for damage caused by the pollution of the waters of the Rhine on the ground that the company has daily discharged approximately 11,000 tons of chloride into a canal which flows into the Rhine. It should be recalled that the Stichting Reinwater is required by law to promote all possible improvements in the quality of the water in the Rhine basin and to this end it may also institute civil proceedings to protect the individual rights of persons whose environment is affected by the quality of the water, in particular, of persons deriving their livelihood from the Rhine.

The defendant's acts, which are alleged to have occasioned the damage, occurred in France whereas the damage was recorded in the Netherlands. On the view that Rotterdam was, within the meaning of the said Article 5(3) of the Convention, 'the place where the harmful event occurred' the plaintiffs instituted proceedings before the Netherlands court. For its part the defendant objected that the Netherlands court did not have jurisdiction because, in its view, any unlawful act must be held to have taken place in France, within the jurisdiction of the courts of Mulhouse which are thus the only courts having jurisdiction, even under the said Article 5(3) of the Convention, to settle the claim for compensation.

In its judgment of 12 May 1975, the Arrondissementsrechtbank upheld the objection of lack of jurisdiction on the ground that the harmful event forming the subject - matter of the proceedings could only have been constituted by the discharge of waste into the Rhine in France. The Gerechtshof (Court of Appeal), The Hague, to which the plaintiffs appealed against this decision, has submitted to the Court of Justice, under Article 3 of the Protocol dated 3 June 1971 concerning the interpretation of the Convention of 27 September 1968, the following preliminary question: 'Must the phrase 'the place where the harmful event occurred' in Article 5(3) of the above-mentioned Treaty be interpreted in the sense that it means: 'the place where the damage occurred' or: 'the place where the action having the damage as its sequel was undertaken'?'

2. We must consider first of all whether the wording adopted in Article 5(3) of the Convention must be regarded as independent of the laws of the Member States or whether it entails a reference to the substantive provisions of law applicable in each particular case in accordance with the appropriate rules of the private international law of the national legal system of which the court seised of the case forms part. As you will recall this is the preliminary option, referred to in the judgment of the Court in Case 12/76 (*Società Industrie Tessili Italiana* v *Dunlop*) in which it was emphasised that the option may only be exercised in respect of each of the provisions of the Convention in such a way as to ensure that it is fully effective having regard to the aims of Article 220 of the Treaty.

In the present case neither the court submitting the question nor any of the parties has expressed reservations regarding the possibility that the wording in question might be given an independent meaning.

I am also of the view that this matter cannot be in doubt.

The difficulty which the Court in its said judgment in Case 12/76 discerned regarding an independent definition of the place where the obligation arising from the contract is performed does not appear to me to recur on the other hand in the definition of the place where the harmful event occurred. Specification of this latter place is not in fact linked with any contractual dispute or influenced in any way by differences between various types of contract: although the concept of a 'non-contractual harmful event' covers a number of cases it is much more homogeneous in its nature than the concept of a 'contractual obligation'. On the other hand, the differences existing between the national legal systems with regard to the substantive rules of non-contractual liability cannot be considered as ruling out an independent definition of the concept employed in Article 5(3): it must not be forgotten that in the above-mentioned judgment the Court indeed emphasised the independent nature of the interpretation of the concepts contained in the Convention with regard to the substantive rules applicable to the dispute. It may be further added that an independent definition, where it is possible, of the words employed by the Convention for the purposes of defining the jurisdiction of the courts undoubtedly helps to promote the recognition and the enforcement of judgments of courts in the Contracting States in accordance with the essential aims of the Convention itself and with the objectives of Article 220 of the EEC Treaty to which the Convention relates.

In conclusion the circumstance that the authors of the Convention intentionally employed wording for certain provisions, including the article in question, does not militate against an independent definition. When the meaning of provisions of this nature is to be determined the task must be performed with the help of all the systematic and rational means available.

3. The imprecision to which I have referred is not fortuitous. In fact it is clear from the preparatory documents that when the authors of the Brussels

Convention of 27 September 1968 employed the wording in Article 5(3), in order to allow persons claiming to be affected by an unlawful act not relating to a contract to avail themselves of another criterion of jurisdiction besides the general criterion laid down in Article 2, they intended to leave open the question concerning the meaning to be conferred upon these words, clearly preferring to charge the courts with their interpretation. In the 'Rapport Jenard' it was stated in this connexion: 'The Committee did not consider it appropriate to specify expressly whether account should be taken of the place in which the act causing the damage was effected or on the other hand of the place in which the damage had occurred; instead the Committee considered it preferable to employ wording adopted by various national legal systems (Germany and France).

The Commission and the two States which have submitted observations in the present proceedings have confirmed this statement.

The same wording 'fait dommageable' ('harmful event') employed in Article 5(3) of the Convention was subsequently repeated in Article 10 of the Preliminary Draft Convention on the Law applicable to Contractual and Non-Contractual Obligations drawn up in 1972 within the framework of the Community. In the accompanying report Professor Giuliano, considering cases in which the event causing the damage occurs to a State other than that in which the injurious effect is recorded, states that the draft leaves open the question whether by the place of the 'fait dommageable' one or other country must be understood and he maintains that the purpose of this was to leave untrammelled current developments in case-law.

We are thus confronted with a case in which the expletory nature of the judgments of the Court vis-à-vis the provisions of treaties is particularly clear.

4. The reference in the 'Rapport Jenard' to the fact that the wording employed in Article 5(3) of the Convention coincides with that adopted by certain national legal systems confers particular relevance upon an enquiry as to what meaning is attributed to the relevant wording within the legal systems of the said States. Nevertheless I should like to point out that, in my view, the fact that the wording of the Convention coincides with that of a specific provision in one of the Contracting States is insufficient to require the provisions of the Convention to be interpreted in the light of the tendencies in interpretation prevailing in that State. Interpretation is closely linked to the context of a measure and to the system within which it operates; thus it seems clear that once an expression taken from one or more national legal systems has been inserted in a multilateral international treaty it must be understood in accordance with the scope and objectives of such treaty and not those of any national system of law from which it may have originated.

This is of even greater significance in the present case in which the expression under consideration is amongst those employed within a State, either in the substantive law on non-contractual liability, in private international law or in the law of civil procedure; furthermore within the context of procedural law those words can relate both to the delimitation of territorial jurisdiction and the determination of the jurisdiction of the courts with regard to aliens. Even if we restrict ourselves to this latter application of the words it should not be forgotten that national courts display a certain tendency to understand jurisdictional criteria in such a way that they can declare themselves to have jurisdiction to settle the dispute submitted to them. This impulse in the direction of the national courts is capable of causing positive conflicts of jurisdiction on occasions and clearly cannot have any function in the interpretation of a convention, such as the Convention of Brussels, precisely because this Convention lays down uniform rules for all the Contracting States and has as its aim the prevention of conflicts of jurisdiction. When this point has been made however, it must be recognized that neither the interpretative tendencies which have developed in the French system nor those which have emerged in the Federal Republic of Germany provide an unambiguous solution to the problem. In France, it was laid down in the last paragraph of Article 59 of the Code of Civil Procedure (Code de Procedure Civile) in force until 31 December 1975 that the courts for the place 'où le fait dommageable s'est produit' ('where the harmful event occurred') should have jurisdiction. Case-law was divided on the interpretation of this provision: in some cases the phrase was considered as a reference to the place in which the act occasioning the damage occurred and in others it was seen as referring to the place in which the damage occurred (cf. the judgments of the Cour de Cassation of 8 March 1937, *Dalloz* 1938, 1, 76; of 6 December 1939, *Dalloz* 1940, 1, 40; of 28 March 1968, *Le Bulletin des Arrêts de la Cour de Cassation* (Chambre Civile) 1968, 11, No 100). In the new Article 46 of the Code of Civil Procedure which came into force on 1 January 1976 the legislature expressly provided plaintiffs with a choice of the court of the place where the act occurred or the court of the place where the damage occurred; this article thus distinguishes the place where the 'harmful event' occurred from the place where the damage occurred. The respondent in the national case has endeavoured to rely upon this distinction, maintaining that since Article 46 has added an express reference to damage this signifies that the concept of a 'harmful event' is restricted to the act causing the damage. This inference is indeed correct with regard to the new provision but, to clarify the intention of the authors of the Convention on the basis of French law, it would clearly be necessary to take account of the provision and of case-law at the time at which the Convention was drawn up.

Courts and academic lawyers in the Federal Republic of Germany have also dealt with the plaintiff's option between the place where the act was committed ('Tatort') and the place where the consequences of the act appeared ('Erfolgsort'), both with regard to domestic and international jurisdiction (concerning pollution of the environment, cf. judgment of the Oberlandesgericht Saarbrücken of 22 October 1957 in the *Neue Juristische Wochenscrift,* 1958, p. 752, and the judgment of the Oberlandesgericht Hamm of 3 July 1958 *op. cit.* 1958, p 1831). It should be further noted that where Article 32 of the German Code of Civil Procedure (Zivilprozessordnung) lays down the criteria for jurisdiction, which in accordance with the case-law of the Bundesgerichtshof (the Federal Court of Justice) are the same in domestic proceedings and with regard to foreigners, reference is made to the place where the act ('die unerlaubte Handlung') was committed. However, the wording does not coincide with that adopted in the Convention inasmuch as Article 5(3) of the German version provides that a person may be sued 'vor dem Gericht des Ortes, an dem das schädigende Ereignis eingetreten ist.'

Only within the framework of French law prior to 1976, then, is the wording of the phrase in Article 5(3) exactly the same as that adopted for the criterion of jurisdiction in the context of domestic law and it is difficult to draw definite conclusions from this, even if it were desired to disregard the considerations I have put forward on the propriety of accepting as one's premises the interpretative practice prevailing in a single State. Treated in isolation the wording actually lends itself to at least three interpretations: the place where the act was committed, the place where the damage occurred and a choice between one or other place, at the option of the plaintiff. For the sake of completeness, some reference should be added to the legal systems of certain other Contracting States and, in addition, to those of two Member States which are not yet parties to the Convention: those legal system confirm that there is no justification for making a choice on the basis of tendencies which have established themselves at the level of national law.

5. Before considering what evidence Italian case-law and Italian academic lawyers may supply regarding the point at issue we should recall that the Italian version of Article 5(3) of the Convention confers jurisdiction upon the court 'del luogo in cui *l'evento dannoso é avvenuto'*('for the place in which the harmful event occurred'). Interpreted literally the concept of 'harmful event' is to be, assimilated to the concept of damage and of 'injury', and indeed certain Italian academic lawyers treat the problem of determining the locality of the unlawful act in terms of a choice between the place where the act was committed and the place where the damage occurred. Nevertheless, I do not consider that the existence of such wording in one of the versions of the Convention is sufficient to resolve the ambiguity of the other versions: it merely confirms that it is impossible to understand 'fait dommageable' as simply equivalent to conduct resulting in damage. For the Italian legal system, the basic premise is provided by the words 'luogo in cui è sorta l'obbligazione' ('the place where the obligation arises') contained in Article 20 and in Article 4(2) of the Code of Civil Procedure (the Codice di Procedura Civile), relating respectively to territorial jurisdiction and international jurisdiction, and also to non-contractual obligations. The tendency in Italian case-law and amongst academic lawyers is to fix the point where a non-contractual obligation arises at the place where the damage has occurred: cf. in particular, amongst the decisions of the Italian Corte di Cassazione, the judgment delivered by the full court on 27 February 1962, No 390, (*British Petroleum Co.* v *Ente Petrolifero Italiano Medio Oriente*) in *Foro Italiano* 1962, 1, p. 1810 and the judgment of 25 June 1971, No 2011, in the *Rivista di Diritto Internazionale Privato e Processuale*, 1972, p. 292. Nevertheless, there are authoritative writers, such as Morelli, who suggest that the place where the act was committed and the place where the event occurred should be considered of equal relevance for the purposes of jurisdiction.

The legal position in Belgium is similar to that in Italy: in fact Article 624 of the Code Judiciaire (Judicial Code) lays down that the court of the place - in which the obligations in dispute have arisen or the court of the place where they are to be fulfilled shall have territorial jurisdiction. This provision, which is also applied to obligations arising from non-contractual unlawful acts, has also given rise to conflicting views amongst academic lawyers and in case-law, the former showing a certain preference for the place where the act was committed whilst the latter largely refer to the place where the damage occurred. In Article 635 the Code Judiciaire makes provision for the jurisdiction of the Belgian courts with regard to foreigners and likewise confers jurisdiction in cases in which the obligation forming the basis of the application has arisen, has been fulfilled or is to be fulfilled in Belgium.

Netherlands law is of no assistance in this matter. It excludes any special criterion in the sphere of unlawful acts, adopting instead the general criterion of domicile - the domicile of the defendant or, if the defendant has neither a known domicile nor a residence within the State, the address of the applicant (Article 126(2) and (3) of the Wetboek van Burgerlijke Rechtsvordering (Code of Civil Procedure)).

The criterion of the place in which negligence has occurred has sometimes been expressly preferred in English case-law (cf. *George Monro Ltd.* v *American Cyanamid and Chemical Corporation*, [1944] KB 432) whilst at other times judgments appear to favour the criterion of the place in which the damage has occurred (*Bata* v *Bata*, [1948] WN 366). It should be noted, however, that this concerned an action on the grounds of defamation and that jurisdiction was conferred upon the court in the place in which the defamatory words were published. Scottish case-law also affords examples of this latter tendency (cf. *Smith* v *Rosenbloom*, [1915] 2 Scots Law Times 18).

Finally, in Danish law, with regard to domestic territorial jurisdiction, it is possible, under Article 244 of the Retsplejelov (Law on the administration of justice), to choose between the place where the act was committed and the place where the damage occurred; with regard to international jurisdiction, the national courts have declared themselves to have jurisdiction even if the act giving rise to the injury was committed abroad, provided that the damage occurred in Denmark (cf. Ugeskrift for Retsvaesen 1940, p. 454, Hejesteret og Ugeskrift for Retsvaesen 1947, p. 187, Ostre Landsret).

6. It may be wondered whether other solutions, differing from those mooted above, should be taken into consideration. The question is all the more justified in that, unlike the court making the reference, which adopts the alternative put forward in the 'Rapport Jenard', the Government of the Netherlands and the Commission maintain that the wording of Article 5(3) also allows reference to be made to the criterion of the 'most significant relationship' which the situation arising from the harmful event has with a State - which might be a State other than that where the act was committed or where the harmful effect occurred. It is not clear whether the Commission considers that all or only one of these criteria must be applied.

To embark upon this train of thought would involve taking into consideration a flexible concept developed principally in terms of the choice of the substantive law, and in this context known as the theory of the 'proper law of the tort'.

This doctrine originates in countries whose legal traditions are based on the Common Law and was propounded, as is noted in a judgment of the House of Lords of 1951, in order to allow the courts to choose the substantive law which 'on policy grounds, seems to have the most significant connection with the chain of acts and circumstances in the particular situation' (quoted by Cheshire in *Private International Law*, 1974, p. 264). The purpose of this doctrine is not to replace the traditional criterion of the *locus delicti commissi* but merely to supplement it and to amend it in specific cases when it would lead to results at variance with common sense. Understood thus, the doctrine has also been expressed both in Article 3 of the Resolution on Delictual Obligations in Private International Law, approved by the Institute of International Law at its meeting in Edinburgh (1969), and in the second paragraph of Article 10 of the above-mentioned Preliminary Draft Convention on the Law applicable to Contractual and Non-contractual Obligations, drawn up in 1972 under the aegis of the EEC. This supplemental nature remains clear even if it is desired to extend that criterion to determining the court having jurisdiction so as to make it coincide with the court of the State whose substantive law is held to be applicable (cf. in this connexion the United States system, in Paragraphs 36 and 37 of the Restatement of the Law Second, Conflict of Laws adopted by the American Law Institute in Washington on 23 May 1969). However, if in the present case a criterion of this nature, which might lead to disregarding both the place where the act was committed and the place where the damage occurred, were extended, albeit as an alternative, to determining the Court having jurisdiction this would imply total disregard for the wording of Article 5(3) and would risk producing results at variance with it. It would also be difficult to reconcile adoption of a criterion of the 'most significant connection' with the intention of the Convention to make it easy to determine the Court having jurisdiction, on the basis of clear, precise and sufficiently objective criteria which could thus be applied uniformly in all the States adhering to the Convention. In this respect insufficient assurances are afforded by a criterion, such as that referred to above, which does not lend itself to abstract definition and which tends to rely upon the subjective appraisal of the court. Finally, to draw a close parallel between the question of the substantive law applicable and that of jurisdiction would not be in accordance with the objective of the Brussels Convention which is to simplify problems relating to determination of the national court having jurisdiction. Just as it was not intended that the Convention submitted to the Court for its interpretation should have any influence whatsoever on the application of the rules of the Contracting States' private international law, it was certainly not intended to render determination of jurisdiction dependent on determination of the substantive law.

7. Having thus discarded the theory of the 'most significant connection' we should accept that the cumulative solution, which would leave the plaintiff free to choose between the *court of the place* where the act was committed and the court of the place where the event occurred, may appear by its very liberality fairer and better able to accommodate the characteristics of the various types of unlawful act. Indeed we have seen that within the national legal systems this

solution has now been broadly adopted. Despite this it does not appear to me in accordance with the letter and the spirit of the Convention. It is at odds with the spirit of the Convention. It is at odds with the letter of the Convention because Article 5(3) refers to the court of the place where the harmful event occurred, that is, to a single court and a single place, and thus seems to rule out the possibility that more than one place could be taken into consideration or more than one court declare itself to have jurisdiction, under the provisions of the Convention, with regard to the same harmful event. What is certainly more important, it is at odds with its spirit, in that the objective pursued by the Convention, namely to divide international jurisdiction amongst the different States in accordance with a distributive criterion in such a way as to reduce instead of increasing the scope of the jurisdiction of each State precisely where there already exists an objective basis for conferring jurisdiction upon another. In its judgment in Case No 14/76, *De Bloos* v *Bouyer*, the Court rightly held that the objectives of the Convention 'imply the need to avoid, so far as possible, creating a situation in which a number of courts have jurisdiction in respect of one and the same contract'. I consider that this guide-line also holds good when an unlawful act and not a contract is involved.

The French Government and the respondent appear to rely on the idea that Article 5 must be considered an exceptional provision, derogating from the general principle, which must be strictly interpreted, that the court of the defendant's domicile has jurisdiction. I do not share this point of view: I regard this article as a provision which, with regard to the cases for which it provides, adds to the general criterion of jurisdiction in Article 2 other criteria of a special nature with regard to specific cases, and it seems to me that this can be inferred from the very position of Article 5 in a section of the Convention distinct from that in which the general rule in Article 2 appears. Notwithstanding this, it seems proper to refrain from a wide interpretation of a provision establishing an additional special jurisdiction unless positive grounds for this can be inferred from the Convention, which does not appear to me to be the case.

8. According to the French Government and the respondent company the wording adopted in Article 5(3) indicates exclusively the place in which the act giving rise to the damage was located.

The principal reason for this is that, if jurisdiction is accorded to the court of the place where the damage occurred, the aim of the Convention, of avoiding conflicting judgments, would be frustrated when damage is caused in several States by one and the same act. In such cases to allocate jurisdiction to each State where the damage has been caused would involve a multiplication of jurisdictions, which might lead to injustice, affecting both applicants, who might be treated differently according to the place in which they had suffered damage, and respondents, who for the same reason would be exposed to a plurality of procedures the results of which might conflict.

This consideration might be met with the rejoinder that the criterion of the place where the act was committed may also produce the same disadvantage of a division of jurisdiction and the risk of conflicting judgments where one harmful event is caused by a series of acts carried out by various persons in different States. This can happen precisely with regard to pollution of the environment and indeed in cases identical to the present one. Besides the respondent there are in fact German undertakings which also discharge similar pollutant material into the Rhine. In such cases justice requires that those responsible for the same damage should be judged in accordance with an identical criterion. This could be attained by recognizing the jurisdiction of the court of the place where the harmful event occurred. Such a court would also be more capable than the courts in other countries of determining the causal connection between the various acts and the damage complained of and of assessing the extent to which each of the undertakings contributing to the pollution was liable for the damage thereby caused to the plaintiff.

In the course of the oral procedure factors relating to the substance of the case were also raised, in particular the fact that the discharges of chloride into the Rhine were authorized by officers of the French prefecture, and reasons of convenience have been adduced, regarding the appellant's choice of court (it was stated that the court in Mulhouse would be better able than the Netherlands court to appraise the relevance of the administrative measure of authorization). Nevertheless, I am convinced that in interpreting a provision which relates purely to jurisdiction one must not be influenced by details pertaining to the substance of the case in question. The same conviction leads me to deny all relevance to the danger of the difficulties which it is feared might be encountered in the execution in France of a Netherlands judgment incorporating a finding against the respondent, without taking due account of the above-mentioned circumstance. In fact it is for the injured party to appraise the appropriateness of choosing one of the courts (the general court of the defendant's domicile or the special court of which I have spoken) before which he can summon the person responsible for the damage. On the other hand, we know that in the context of the implementation of a convention on the jurisdiction of courts, such as the present Convention, the difficulties which might arise in enforcing the judgment could never relate to questions of jurisdiction. It is indeed true that difficulties in execution might follow from the derogation regarding public policy laid down in Article 27(1) of the Brussels Convention, but that is another matter. I shall merely express the hope that the jurisdiction in matters of interpretation conferred upon the Court of Justice may also serve to clarify the meaning of this provision, avoiding distorted interpretations and risks of abuse.

Likewise, I do not think that great importance can be attached to the argument whereby the criterion of the place where the act was committed is more suited to the proper administration of justice in that it ensures legal certainty for the person responsible for the unlawful act who, in order to regulate his conduct, has merely to acquaint himself with the law in force in the place in which he acts. This argument risks confusing the aspect of jurisdiction, which alone is relevant here, with that of the substantive law applicable. Determination of the substantive law applicable is not necessarily prejudged by recognizing the jurisdiction of the court of the place in which the damage has occurred. Indeed, even if this place is situated in a State other than that in which the act was committed, this factor alone is not decisive without regard to the applicability of the substantive law of the place in which the act was committed for the purpose of determining liability. Likewise, it cannot be presumed that, even if the jurisdiction of the court of the place where the act was committed were recognized, this court might not, on the basis of the private international law of its own State, instead apply the substantive law of some other State in which the damage occurred or with which the dispute before the court was more closely connected, on the basis of the above-mentioned criterion of the 'proper law of the tort'.

9. It is clear from what has been said that the arguments advanced in favour of interpreting Article 5(3) so as to identity the 'fait dommageable' with the act of the person responsible for the damage are unconvincing. On the contrary I consider that there are good grounds for favouring the criterion of the place in which the damage has occurred and that they justify acceptance of that criterion alone.

I should like to observe first of all that the legal duty to make reparation arising from the civil wrong necessarily presupposes, for its very existence, that the damage should be established. Whereas in the case of a criminal act the liability of the offender to punishment arises from an act at variance with the criminal law, since the aims of the criminal law are retributive, with regard to a civil wrong liability arises only if and when injury occurs, since the aims of civil law, unlike criminal law, are essentially to provide compensation for damage. Even though negligence is socially and morally reprehensible, if it does not occasion damage it does not give rise to liability for compensation or therefore to any other legal proceedings.

It follows from this that a criterion of jurisdiction having as its basis the act leading to the legal obligation to provide compensation, that is, the criterion in Article 5(3), cannot disregard the consideration of damage otherwise that act will not present all the factors necessary for it to be invoked at law. A location for the criterion in question can thus only be established where the act is legally speaking complete, that is, where the injury to the legal rights of the person suffering it occurs. As soon as this occurs the claim for compensation, the basis of the legal action, comes into being.

This solution also has the advantage that it is in harmony with the solution adopted in other provisions of the same Convention, the necessity for which undoubtedly guided the authors of the Convention, as is clear from a number of its provisions, namely the protection of the weaker party in a legal relationship. I refer to Article 5(2) on the obligation to provide maintenance, in which jurisdiction is conferred upon the courts for the place where the maintenance creditor, who will thus normally be the applicant, is domiciled or habitually resident; to Article 7 et seq., in matters relating to insurance, which also confer jurisdiction upon the Courts of the place in which the insured has his domicile; to Article 14, relating to instalment sales and loans which provides that the courts of the State in which the buyer or borrower is domiciled shall have jurisdiction. The injured party, who must establish the unlawful act, is automatically deemed the weaker party and as such worthy of protection in the choice of the Court having jurisdiction.

Even apart from the present case, I consider that of the two criteria - the place where the act was committed and the place where the damage occurred - the latter is generally more satisfactory to the injured party since it tends to coincide with the State in which he will usually reside; on the other hand in most cases the place where the act was committed will tend to coincide with the place of domicile of the person responsible for the damage (motor accidents constitute an exception to this in that the place of the act and the place of the damage normally coincide). If, therefore, the criterion in Article 5(3) were to be understood as referring to the place where the act was committed, this special criterion would in most instances duplicate the function of the general criterion in Article 2 and ultimately would be of little use.

10. For all these reasons I conclude by suggesting that the Court should reply to the question submitted in the order of 27 February 1967 by the Gerechtshof, The Hague, to the effect that the interpretation of the provision in Article 5(3) of the Brussels Convention of 27 September 1968 is that the words 'place where the harmful event occurred' indicate the place in which the damage for which compensation is claimed occurred.

Case C-220/88 - 11 January 1990

Dumez France and Tracoba
v
Hessische Landesbank (Helaba) and Others

Special jurisdiction - Article 5(3) - Jurisdiction in tort, delict or quasi-delict - Place where the harmful event occurred - Place where the damage occurred- Concept - Place of occurrence of damage suffered by a third party through damage sustained by the immediate victim - Exclusion.

Summary

The expression 'place where the harmful event occurred' contained in Article 5(3) of the Convention of 27 September 1968 on jurisdiction and the enforcement of judgments in civil and commercial matters may refer to the place where the damage occurred, but the latter concept can be understood only as indicating the place where the event giving rise to the damage, and causing tortious, delictual or quasi-delictual liability to be incurred, directly produced its harmful effects upon the person who is the victim of that event.

Accordingly, the rule on jurisdiction laid down in that article cannot be interpreted as permitting a plaintiff pleading damage which he claims to be the consequence of the harm suffered by other persons who were direct victims of the harmful act to bring proceedings against the perpetrator of that act before the courts in the place in which he himself ascertained the damage to his assets.

JUDGMENT OF THE COURT

Kakouris and Schockweiler, Presidents of Chambers, Koopmans, Mancini and Díez de Velasco, Judges

1. By judgment of 21 June 1988, which was received at the Court on 4 August 1988, the French Cour de cassation referred to the Court for a preliminary ruling under the Protocol of 3 June 1971 on the interpretation by the Court of Justice of the Convention of 27 September 1968 on jurisdiction and the enforcement of judgments in civil and commercial matters (hereinafter referred to as 'the Convention') a question on the interpretation of Article 5(3) of the Convention.

2. That question was raised in proceedings to establish quasi-delictual liability brought before the French courts by the French companies Sceper and Tracoba, whose rights are now held by the companies Dumez France and Oth Infrastructure (hereinafter referred to as 'Dumez and Oth'), against Hessische Landesbank, Salvatorplatz-Grundstücksgesellschaft mbH & Co. oHG Saarland, and Lübecker Hypothekenbank, whose registered offices are in the Federal Republic of Germany (hereinafter referred to as 'the German banks').

3. Dumez and Oth seek compensation for the damage which they claim to have suffered owing to the insolvency of their subsidiaries established in the Federal Republic of Germany, which was brought about by the suspension of a property-development project in the Federal Republic of Germany for a German prime contractor, allegedly because of the cancellation by the German banks of the loans granted to the prime contractor.

4. By judgment of 14 May 1985 the tribunal de commerce (Commercial Court), Paris, upheld the objection of lack of jurisdiction raised by the German banks, on the ground that the initial damage was suffered by the subsidiaries of Dumez and Oth in the Federal Republic of Germany and that the French parent companies sustained a financial loss thereafter only indirectly.

5. By judgment of 13 December 1985, the cour d'appel, Paris, confirmed that judgment, taking the view that the financial repercussions which Dumez and Oth claimed to have experienced at their head offices in France were not of such a kind as to affect the location of the damage suffered initially by the subsidiaries in the Federal Republic of Germany.

6. In support of their appeal in cassation against that judgment, Dumez and Oth claimed that the decision of the Court in Case 21/76 *G. J. Bier BV* v *Mines de potasse d'Alsace SA* [1976] ECR 1735, according to which the expression 'place where the harmful event occurred' used in Article 5(3) of the Convention covered both the place where the damage occurred and the place of the event giving rise to the damage, with the result that the defendant may be sued, at the option of the plaintiff, in the courts for either of those places, was also applicable to cases of indirect damage. In those circumstances, the place where the harmful event occurred was, according to Dumez and Oth, for a victim who has sustained damage as a consequence of the loss suffered by the initial victim, the place where his interests were adversely affected; the plaintiffs in this case being French companies, the place of the financial loss which they suffered following the insolvency of their subsidiaries in the Federal Republic of Germany was therefore the registered offices of Dumez and Oth in France.

7. Considering that the dispute raised a problem of interpretation of Community law, the French Cour de cassation stayed the proceedings and referred the following question to the Court of Justice for a preliminary ruling: 'Is the rule on jurisdiction which allows the plaintiff, under Article 5(3) of the Convention, to choose between the court for the place of the event giving rise to damage and the court for the place where that damage occurs to be extended to cases in which the damage alleged is merely the consequence of the harm suffered by persons who were the immediate victims of damage occurring at a different place, which would enable the indirect victim to bring proceedings before the court of the State in which he is domiciled?'

8. Reference is made to the Report for the Hearing for a fuller account of the facts of the case, the course of the procedure and the written observations submitted to the Court, which are mentioned or discussed hereinafter only in so far as is necessary for the reasoning of the Court.

9. In order to answer the question submitted, it must first be borne in mind that, in the terms of Article 5 of the Convention, 'A person domiciled in a Contracting State may, in another Contracting State, be sued: ... (3) in matters relating to tort, delict or quasi-delict, in the courts for the place where the harmful event occurred'.

10. It must then be pointed out that, in its judgment in *Mines de potasse d'Alsace*, cited above, the Court ruled that where the place of the

happening of the event which may give rise to liability in tort, delict or quasi-delict and the place where that event results in damage are not identical, the expression 'place where the harmful event occurred' which appears in Article 5(3) of the Convention must be understood as being intended to cover both the place where the damage occurred and the place of the event giving rise to the damage, with the result that the defendant may be sued, at the option of the plaintiff, either in the courts for the place where the damage occurred or in the courts for the place of the event which gives rise to and is at the origin of that damage.

11. Dumez and Oth observe that in that judgment the Court interpreted Article 5(3) of the Convention without drawing any distinction between direct and indirect victims of damage. In their view, it follows that where an indirect victim claims to have suffered personal damage the court of competent jurisdiction is the court for the place where the victim sustained that damage.

12. It must first be stated in that connection that the judgment in *Mines de potasse d'Alsace* related to a situation in which the damage - to crops in the Netherlands - occurred at some distance from the event giving rise to the damage the discharge of saline waste into the Rhine by an undertaking established in France - but by the direct effect of the causal agent, namely the saline waste which had moved physically from one place to another.

13. By contrast, in the present case, the damage allegedly suffered by Dumez and Oth through cancellation, by the German banks, of the loans granted for financing the works originated and produced its direct consequences in the same Member State, namely the one in which the lending banks, the prime contractor and the subsidiaries of Dumez and Oth, which were responsible for the building work, were all established. The harm alleged by the parent companies, Dumez and Oth, is merely the indirect consequence of the financial losses initially suffered by their subsidiaries following cancellation of the loans and the subsequent suspension of the works.

14. It follows that, in a case such as this, the damage alleged is no more than the indirect consequence of the harm initially suffered by other legal persons who were the direct victims of damage which occurred at a place different from that where the indirect victim subsequently suffered harm.

15. It is therefore necessary to consider whether the expression 'place

where the damage occurred' as used in the judgment in *Mines de potasse d'Alsace* may be interpreted as referring to the place where the indirect victims of the damage ascertain the repercussions on their own assets.

16. In that connection the Convention, in establishing the system for the attribution of jurisdiction, adopted the general rule that the courts of the State of the defendant's domicile would have jurisdiction (Title II, Article 2). Moreover, the hostility of the Convention towards the attribution of jurisdiction to the courts of the plaintiff's domicile was demonstrated by the fact that the second paragraph of Article 3 precluded the application of national provisions attributing jurisdiction to such courts for proceedings against defendants domiciled in the territory of a Contracting State.

17. It is only by way of exception to the general rule whereby jurisdiction is attributed to the courts of the State of the defendant's domicile that Title II, Section 2, attributes special jurisdiction in certain cases, including the case envisaged by Article 5(3) of the Convention. As the Court has already held (*Mines de potasse d'Alsace*, paragraphs 10 and 11), those cases of special jurisdiction, the choice of which is a matter for the plaintiff, are based on the existence of a particularly close connecting factor between the dispute and courts other than those of the State of the defendant's domicile, which justifies the attribution of jurisdiction to those courts for reasons relating to the sound administration of justice and the efficacious conduct of proceedings.

18. In order to meet that objective, which is of fundamental importance in a convention which has essentially to promote the recognition and enforcement of judgments in States other than those in which they were delivered, it is necessary to avoid the multiplication of courts of competent jurisdiction which would heighten the risk of irreconcilable decisions, this being the reason for which recognition or an order for enforcement is withheld by virtue of Article 27(3) of the Convention.

19. Furthermore, that objective militates against any interpretation of the Convention which, otherwise than in the cases expressly provided for, might lead to recognition of the jurisdiction of the courts of the plaintiff's domicile and would enable a plaintiff to determine the competent court by his choice of domicile.

20. It follows from the foregoing considerations that although, by virtue of a previous judgment of the Court (in *Mines de potasse d'Alsace*, cited

above), the expression 'place where the harmful event occurred' contained in Article 5(3) of the Convention may refer to the place where the damage occurred, the latter concept can be understood only as indicating the place where the event giving rise to the damage, and entailing tortious, delictual or quasi-delictual liability, directly produced its harmful effects upon the person who is the immediate victim of that event.

21. Moreover, whilst the place where the initial damage manifested itself is usually closely related to the other components of the liability, in most cases the domicile of the indirect victim is not so related.

22. It must therefore be stated in reply to the question submitted by the national court that the rule on jurisdiction laid down in Article 5(3) of the Convention cannot be interpreted as permitting a plaintiff pleading damage which he claims to be the consequence of the harm suffered by other persons who were direct victims of the harmful act to bring proceedings against the perpetrator of that act in the courts of the place in which he himself ascertained the damage to his assets.

On those grounds, the Court (Sixth Chamber), in reply to the question submitted to it by judgment of the French Cour de cassation of 21 June 1988, hereby rules:

> **The rule on jurisdiction laid down in Article 5(3) of the Convention of 27 September 1968 on jurisdiction and the enforcement of judgments in civil and commercial matters cannot be interpreted as permitting a plaintiff pleading damage which he claims to be the consequence of the harm suffered by other persons who were direct victims of the harmful act to bring proceedings against the perpetrator of that act in the courts of the place in which he himself ascertained the damage to his assets.**

OPINION OF MR ADVOCATE GENERAL DARMON

1. The preliminary question submitted by the French Cour de cassation, which seeks a clearer definition of the purport of the Court's previous decisions concerning the jurisdiction of courts, will require the Court to determine the scope of its judgment in *Mines de potasse d'Alsace* with respect to the interpretation of Article 5(3) of the Brussels Convention (hereinafter referred to as 'the Convention'), a judgment which almost all the legal literature on the subject describes as definitive.

2. The facts of the main proceedings do not need to be set out in great detail. Two French companies, Sceper and Tracoba, whose rights are now held by the companies Dumez France and Oth Infrastructure, set up subsidiaries in the Federal Republic of Germany for the purposes of a property-development project. In June 1973 the German banks which had granted financing to the German promoter (Hessische Landesbank, Gebrüder Röchling Bank and Lübecker Hypothekenbank) decided to terminate the loan contracts. The promoter was put into receivership under the supervision of the court, as were the two German subsidiaries of Sceper and Tracoba. The two French companies brought an action before the French Commercial Court to establish the liability in delict of the German banks. The defendants alleged that that court lacked jurisdiction, taking the view that the damage suffered by Sceper and Tracoba had occurred in Germany and not in Paris, where their registered offices were located. The Paris Commercial Court upheld their objection by judgment of 14 May 1985, which was confirmed by judgment of the Paris Court of Appeal of 13 December 1985. Dumez and Tracoba lodged an appeal in cassation, claiming that the damage suffered by them had occurred in Paris, the place where they ascertained the financial losses suffered by them when their subsidiaries became insolvent.

3. The Cour de cassation then submitted a question for a preliminary ruling by this Court which essentially seeks to determine whether the solution adopted in its judgment in *Mines de potasse d'Alsace*, which allows a plaintiff seeking to establish liability in tort or delict, to choose between the courts for the place where the event giving rise to the damage occurred and those for the place where the damage took place, can be relied on by the indirect victims of the damage; if that is the case, those victims would, according to the national court, be entitled to commence proceedings before the courts for the place where they are domiciled.

4. In my view there are two aspects to the question. Application of the solution adopted in *Mines de potasse d'Alsace* to damage suffered indirectly does not in my view necessarily mean that the victims of that damage will be entitled to have recourse to the courts for the place where they are domiciled. In other words, must it be said that the place where 'ricochet' damage occurs is the same as the place of the victim's domicile? In order to answer that question, after considering whether or not the solution adopted in *Mines de potasse d'Alsace* should be applied to 'ricochet' damage, I must consider the separate question of determination of the place where the damage to an indirect victim actually occurs.

5. With regard to the first aspect of the problem, let me say straight away that in my view there is nothing in that judgment to support the view that the solution which it adopts is not to apply to 'ricochet' damage. On the contrary, the Court stated: 'To exclude one option seems all the more undesirable in that, by its comprehensive form of words, Article 5(3) of the Convention covers a wide diversity of kinds of liability'.

6. Academic legal writers have also taken that judgment to be of very general application.

7. In France, Mr Droz points in his commentary to the extent of the risk

that the option thus granted is liable to multiply the number of courts before which proceedings might be brought in regard to road accidents, in which there are not infrequently 'secondary' victims. Mr Bourel is of the same opinion but considers that the problem mentioned by Mr Droz could be solved by reference to the exceptions concerning related actions provided for in the Convention itself. Mr Huet associates himself with the latter view and deplores the absence, under the system of the Convention, of a general ground of jurisdiction based on related actions.

8. The United Kingdom commentators have also regarded the Court's decision as being of very general application. However, the fact has not escaped the attention of some commentators that the solution adopted by the Court did not exclude the eventual adoption of specific rules for particular torts, for instance defamation by the press. Attention has also been drawn to the difficulty of determining the place of injury in the case of purely financial losses.

9. The same generality has been attributed to the judgment in Portugal and in Spain. I should point out, however, that according to certain authors, such as Mr Desantes Real and Mrs Jallès, the solution adopted in the judgment is linked above all with the specific problem of determining which criteria should be used to define the 'harmful event' in relation to protection of the environment and more particularly to the prevention of pollution of international waterways. Those authors appear in fact to consider that the Court's judgment in *Mines de potasse d'Alsace* must be confined to the specific facts of that case.

10. Subject to the latter observation, there is no doubt as far as legal writers are concerned that the *Mines de potasse d'Alsace* judgment applies without any exception whatsoever to actions for compensation for indirect damage, even though they feel on occasion the need to point out the disadvantages of that solution.

11. For my part, I consider that such an exclusion would lead, in such a diverse and complex area as that of tortious liability, to unforeseeable consequences - one exception leading to another - which might undermine the simplicity and the consistency of the interpretation arrived at in the Court's judgment in *Mines de potasse d'Alsace.*

12. Let us remember that in that judgment It was stated that: 'the place of the event giving rise to the damage no less than the place where the damage occurred can, depending on the case, constitute a significant connecting factor from the point of view of jurisdiction'.

13. That statement, which is inspired by the close relationship between the constituent elements of any liability, seems to me to be just as relevant to indirect damage.

14. Accordingly, whilst it seems to me eminently desirable to continue to regard the solution arrived at in that judgment as being of general application, we must nevertheless consider whether the option available to the victim of 'ricochet' damage to bring proceedings before the courts for the place where the damage occurred must necessarily result in the victim's being allowed to commence proceedings before the courts having jurisdiction at the place where the victim is domiciled. This therefore means endeavouring to resolve the

difficulty, which I consider to be of essential importance, concerning identification of the place at which the damage must be deemed to have occurred.

15. Let us first consider the factors that militate against the view that the direct victim suffered the damage at the place of his domicile.

16. In his Opinion in *Rüffer*, Mr Advocate General Warner had occasion to express his views on the matter. After pointing out that, in the circumstances of *Mines de potasse d'Alsace*, the place of the harmful event and the place where the damage occurred were separate, he stated:

'It was never suggested ..., much less held by the Court, that the place where the harmful event occurred could be the place where the plaintiff company had its seat or the place where the amount of the damage to its business was quantified.' Mr Warner continued: 'to hold here that the place where the State has its seat could be regarded as being "the place where the harmful event occurred" would be tantamount to holding that, under the Convention, a plaintiff in tort had the option of suing in the courts of his own domicile, which would be quite inconsistent with the scheme of Article 2 *et seq.* of the Convention'.

17. For reasons which are not relevant here, the Court did not have to express a view on that point in *Rüffer*.

18. Messrs Bischoff and Huet, in a commentary on the judgment in that case, approved the solution proposed by the Advocate General, and stated that 'to distinguish between the immediate material damage which, being confined to the locality where the event giving rise to the damage occurred, constitutes therewith the "harmful event" referred to in Article 5(3), and the subsequent costs or loss of profit which, unless they occurred at the same place, would of themselves justify a further jurisdiction, would go precisely in the opposite direction to the policy followed in the cases decided to date'.

19. Although this Court has not yet had to make an express pronouncement on this point, numerous national courts have, since the *Mines de potasse d'Alsace* judgment, expressed their opinion on the matter.

20. Thus, the Gerechtshof, Hertogenbosch, in a judgment of 31 October 1978 took the view that the Netherlands courts had no jurisdiction to hear an action for compensation for damage suffered by a Netherlands company through a German company's refusal to conclude a contract, since the only factor arising in the Netherlands was the ascertainment of the financial losses caused by the refusal to enter into a contract. The national court distinguished between the causal event, the damage and the assets specifically affected by the adverse financial consequences thereof and held, first, that this Court, in its judgment in *Mines de potasse d'Alsace*, was referring only to the first two elements and, secondly, that the assets affected might be located anywhere in the world.

21. The Oberlandesgericht, Hamm, took the same approach in a judgment of 3 October 1978. The case concerned a German company which, having allegedly acted in breach of the competition rules in Belgium, was prohibited by a Belgian company from buying motor vehicles. The German company considered that the German courts had jurisdiction to hear its action in damages. The Oberlandesgericht found that any infringement of the competition rules had

occurred in Belgium and the refusal to supply the plaintiff, which gave rise to the damage suffered by it, also took place in Belgium. Consequently, it considered that it could not be inferred from *Mines de potasse d'Alsace* that a court which had no connection with the materialization of the tort and happened to be situated at a place where financial loss was suffered had jurisdiction.

22. The Italian courts have taken a similar line. Thus, it was held in a judgment of the tribunale di Roma of 15 March 1978 that the Italian courts had no jurisdiction to hear an action to establish liability in tort concerning a transfer of shares between two companies which was regarded as contrary to certain prior agreements and took place on British territory. In the tribunale's view, the place where the damage occurred was the place where the infringement of the protected right took place.

23. Similarly, the tribunale di Monza, in a judgment of 28 September 1979, having stated that the dilemma concerning the place of the harmful event and the place where the damage occurred had been resolved by this Court by a 'judgment of Solomon', refused to treat the place where the damage arose and the place where the damage was suffered as the same. The case concerned an action by an Italian company which considered itself the victim of conduct contrary to the competition rules on the part of German companies in the Federal Republic of Germany, the effect was of that conduct having been to reduce the number of sales which it achieved in that country. The Monza court stated that 'il danno insorge lì dove si è realizzato quel fatto che si assume avere la caratteristica di esserne la causa, rimanendo del tutto ininfluente il luogo, coincidente o diverso, ove tale danno ha causato la diminuzione patrimoniale subita dal soggetto'.

24. The distinction to which the Monza court drew attention between the place where the damage occurred and the place where it was suffered seems to me to be entirely pertinent. Indeed, it seems to me that the view that the court at the place where a body corporate's seat is situated has jurisdiction, as being the court of the place where the damage occurred, in so far as that is the place where the financial losses were ascertained, is indicative of a confusion between the place of occurrence of the damage and the place where the damage was suffered.

25. A similar distinction had already given rise to a controversy in France which throws light on the question before us today. The third indent of Article 46 of the new French Code of Civil Procedure referred originally to the court 'within whose judicial district the damage is suffered'. Certain courts, having regard to the element of continuity-inherent in the words '*is* suffered', inferred that the victim of physical injury suffered damage at his domicile and that the court within whose judicial district the victim resided therefore had jurisdiction. Other courts, however, took the opposite view.

26. A decree of 12 May 1981 removed the ambiguity entirely by amending the third indent of Article 46, which now refers to the court 'within whose judicial district the damage *was* suffered', which confers on the provision in question an undeniable character of instantaneity.

27. It will also be noted that certain types of damage which are particularly difficult to appraise, having regard to the rules of jurisdiction, have given rise to

solutions which have prompted the national courts to decline to treat the place of the damage as the same as the place of the victim's domicile. That has happened in actions for damages for defamatory publications.

28. Similarly, there are instances of refusal to take account of the place where the materiality of the damage was merely *ascertained*.

29. Legal writers in the United Kingdom appear to take the same view. Thus, Mr Collins, in his work entitled The Civil Jurisdiction and Judgments Act 1982, states: 'Even though in one sense a plaintiff may suffer economic loss at the place of its business, that is not sufficient to confer jurisdiction on that place, for otherwise the place of business of the plaintiff would almost automatically become another basis of jurisdiction'.

30. The position taken by German writers is similar. Mr Kropholler, in his work on European procedural law, stresses that concentration on the place where the damage occurs subsequently would lead to a move towards the *forum actoris*.

31. In other words, the solution which opts for the *forum actoris* finds little favour. Moreover, the very nature of the action by a 'ricochet' victim suggested that we should be even firmer in excluding, in this case, the jurisdiction of the courts of the victim's domicile.

32. I will not, however, conceal the fact that this touches upon one of the most delicate and polemical questions of the law of liability: the nature of 'ricochet' damage. Is it, to use the definition adopted by certain authors, merely 'the projection on to an indirect victim of damage suffered by an initial victim' or is it, on the contrary, entirely separate damage?

33. Furthermore, that question does not of course arise in the many Member States which do not give victims who suffer damage indirectly a right to compensation and thus are not familiar with the concept of 'ricochet' damage.

34. Thus in the Netherlands a remedy is available against a third party only to insurers and social security authorities, not to private persons.

35. Greece and Denmark also seem unaware of the concept of 'ricochet' damage in so far as their legal systems do not, in principle, grant the right to obtain compensation for indirect damage, except, in certain instances, against the State and employers.

36. Under German law, victims of 'ricochet' damage cannot as a general rule obtain compensation. On the other hand, Paragraphs 844 and 845 of the Civil Code make an exception to that rule by granting a right to compensation to those whom the direct victim had an obligation to maintain, unless that obligation was created by contract, and to those for whom the direct victim was under a statutory obligation to provide.

37. In the United Kingdom, although the victim of a severe psychological shock caused by the death of or injuries sustained by a member of his family, or even by a person unrelated by kinship, may obtain compensation from the author of the harmful event, the courts take a strict line concerning the need for an objectively identifiable physical or mental consequence and refuse to award any compensation for ordinary non-material damage ('grief or sorrow') which is not accompanied by any appreciable physical consequence. However, since the Fatal

Accidents Act 1976 and subsequent statutes, the members of a victim's family have been able to seek compensation for damage caused by his death, by way of exception to the common-law principle that 'in a civil court the death of a human being could not be complained of as an injury'. It must be added that, under section 5 of the Fatal Accidents Act 1976, where a person dies partly through his own fault and partly through that of a third party, the damages which can be awarded under the Fatal Accidents Act must be reduced proportionately.

38. Let us now consider the laws of the Member States which unreservedly subscribe to the concept of 'ricochet' damage.

39. Under Portuguese law, all those who could require to be maintained by the victim are entitled to compensation if, by reason of the bodily injury suffered, the latter is not in a position to provide for their needs. On the other hand, in the case of non-financial damage, only the direct victim and his heirs can seek compensation. It must be observed that Articles 494 and 496 of the Portuguese Civil Code provide that the fault of the initial victim can be set up against the secondary victims.

40. Under Italian law, Article 1227 of the Civil Code provides for reduction of the compensation if 'il fatto colposo del creditore ha concorso a cagionare il danno'. Legal writers are divided on the question whether a fault committed by the initial victim of the harmful event can be set up against secondary victims. Some consider that the wrongful act referred to in Article 1227 is only that of the initial victim and not that of a 'ricochet' victim who has committed no fault that contributed to the damage. Others take the opposite view. Italian case-law itself appears to be divided regarding the autonomy or otherwise of 'ricochet' damage.

41. In Spain, the very existence of 'ricochet' damage is the subject of divergences in the case-law. Whilst the Criminal Chamber of the Tribunal Supremo insists on passing on to the heirs of the victim any rights to compensation, the First Chamber of the same court grants the right to compensation to all those persons who, by virtue of being immediately related to the direct victim, suffer non-material or material damage, without its being necessary for them to prove their status as heirs of the deceased.

42. Legal writers are divided between the two differing trends in the case-law. The question of the extent to which 'ricochet' damage is separate and whether the fault of the initial victim can be set up against the indirect victims appears still be to open. Legal writers seem to favour the view that the degree of the liability attributed to the author of the harmful event should be reflected in the compensation awarded to the 'ricochet' victims.

43. The question of 'ricochet' damage raised numerous questions in Belgium both in legal literature and in the case-law, until the Cour de cassation delivered a series of definitive judgments which determined that the extent of the compensation due from the author of an infringement should vary pro-rata to the seriousness of the fault of a victim with whom the person seeking compensation had family and affective links. The Cour de cassation emphasized that the damage in question is damage 'by repercussion or by ricochet' deriving exclusively from the links between the initial victim and the person seeking

compensation. The theory that 'ricochet' damage is separate is thus not accepted in Belgian law.

44. In Luxembourg the Cour de cassation, by judgment of 22 December 1988, contested that a fault committed by the direct victim of damage could be relied on as against third-party 'ricochet' victims stating that 'although that third party's action is distinct - by virtue of its subject-matter, even where the third party is also the victim's heir - from any action which the said victim might have been able to bring, it nevertheless derives from the same originating event, having regard to all the circumstances'. That judgment brings an end to a degree of vacillation in the case-law, although a reading of the Luxembourg cases on that point shows that most courts were already ruling that 'ricochet' damage was not separate and consequently that any fault on the part of the direct victim of the damage could be set up as a defence.

45. In French law, after many differences of opinion in the case-law and amongst legal writers, a judgment of the Cour de cassation sitting in plenary session of 19 June 1981 held that whilst the action of a 'ricochet' victim is distinct as regards its subject-matter from any which the direct victim might have been able to bring, 'it nevertheless derives from the same originating event, having regard to all the circumstances'.

46. It will be observed therefore that in the Member States of the Community which accept the concept of indirect damage it has never been accepted that that damage is separate - so as to provide a ground for justifying separate bases of jurisdiction - from that suffered by the initial victim.

47. The general philosophy of the Convention prompts me to advocate rejection of a concept according to which jurisdiction attaches to the court of the place where the 'ricochet' victim suffers damage, that is to say the court of his domicile.

48. Even though a move in that direction appears attractive, in so far as it would be beneficial to the victim, it must be observed that, within the general scheme of the Convention, the concern to preclude the *forum actoris* and consequently - since it is so easy to change one's domicile - 'forum shopping' is much further to the fore than the idea of favouring the victim. Moreover, the judgment in *Mines de potasse d'Alsace* is based essentially on the requirements of the sound administration of justice.

49. In addition, the disadvantages of such a solution seem to me to be too great for it to be adopted. Where there are a number of indirect victims there would be as many competent courts as different domiciles. Admittedly, the claims would be connected but the fact is, as Mr Huet points out, the Brussels Convention 'does not use the fact that actions are related as the basis for a general head of secondary jurisdiction allowing related actions to be concentrated in a single court'. As Mr Droz also emphasizes, 'the court of the domicile, of the wrongful act or the materialization of the damage will be reluctant to stay the proceedings or decline jurisdiction in favour of the courts of another country where jurisdiction is justified only by the occurrence of damage suffered by a third party and confined to that country'. Moveover, the exception concerning related actions provided for in Article 22 of the Convention

presupposes that the courts seised have concurrent jurisdiction, which then raises the problem of determining whether the jurisdiction of the court before which an action is brought by reason of the place where the damage occurred will be limited to the matter of reparation for the damage occurring within its judicial district. Certain authors have analysed that question. That delicate problem is not before the Court today, but it may reasonably be concluded that the seeds of that difficulty were present in the solution adopted in the judgment in *Mines de potasse d'Alsace* and that sooner or later it will be submitted for consideration by the Court.

50. This multiplicity of courts of competent jurisdiction does not seem to me to be without consequences for the other aspect of the Convention, namely the recognition and enforcement of judgments. From that point of view, a solution whereby each 'secondary' victim could bring proceedings before the courts of his domicile encourages the dispersion of actions and thereby accentuates the risks of irreconcilable decisions, a ground for refusing recognition or an order for enforcement under Article 27(3) of the Convention.

51. In addition, many of the problems which certain commentators believe they perceive in the *Mines de potasse d'Alsace* judgment derive from those authors' - in my opinion incorrect - view that the solution adopted in that judgment leads to the possibility of jurisdiction being attributed to the court in whose judicial district the victim has his domicile. Here again, that view - which appears to reveal confusion between the place where the damage occurs (the very words used in the judgment) and the place where the damage is suffered - would have the disadvantage of conflicting with the line of authority usually followed on that point by the courts of the Member States.

52. Accordingly, the foregoing considerations lead me to consider that the place where the damage occurs is, for indirect victims, the place where the *initial* damage manifested itself, in other words, the place where the damage to the *direct* victim occurred. The need to avoid a large number of possible jurisdictions, with all the disadvantages to which I have referred, makes it necessary to use as a reference an element which can be common to all the indirect victims, that is to say either the place of the event giving rise to the damage or the place where the initial damage occurred. Such a solution also has the advantage of not over-turning the solutions usually adopted in the Member States which recognize the concept of 'ricochet' damage and which consider that such damage is not separate from the direct damage. In that regard, Messrs Geimer and Schutze, in their commentary on the Convention, state that the rights to compensation of indirect victims are *incidental* to those of the initial victim, a fact which must be taken into account as far as the rules concerning jurisdiction of the courts are concerned.

53. Furthermore, the place where the initial damage manifested itself is usually closely related to the other constituent elements of any liability, but the same cannot be said, in most cases, of the domicile of the 'ricochet' victim. It was the existence of that relationship which prompted this Court, in the *Mines de potasse d'Alsace* judgment, to opt for both the place of the event giving rise to the damage and the place where it occurred.

54. Finally - and most importantly - that solution seems to me to be in much greater harmony with the general objectives of the Convention since it does not contribute to the creation of a *forum actoris*, something which its authors, subject to specific exceptions, sought to exclude.

55. In conclusion, I propose that the Court should rule as follows:

'(1) The rule on jurisdiction which allows a plaintiff, under Article 5(3) of the Brussels Convention on jurisdiction and the enforcement of judgments in civil and commercial matters, to choose between the court for the place of the event giving rise to the damage and the court for the place where the damage occurs is applicable to indirect victims of damage.

(2) The place where the damage is suffered by such victims must be deemed to be the place where the damage suffered by the initial victim occurred.'

Case C-261/90 - 26 March 1992

Mario Reichert and Others
v
Dresdner Bank AG

Special jurisdiction - Article 5(3) - Jurisdiction 'in matters relating to tort, delict or quasi-delict' - Concept - 'Action paulienne' - Not included - Exclusive jurisdiction - Article 16(5) - 'Proceedings concerned with the enforcement of judgments' - Concept - Disputes regarding the action of authorities responsible for enforcement - 'Action paulienne' - Not included - Jurisdiction to adopt provisional or protective measures - Article 24 - Concept of provisional or protective measures - Measures seeking to maintain a factual or legal situation pending a decision on the substance of the matter - 'Action paulienne' - Not included.

Summary

1. An action provided for by national law, such as the so-called '*action paulienne*' in French law, the purpose of which is not to have the debtor ordered to make good the damage he has caused his creditor by fraudulent conduct, but to render ineffective, as against his creditor, the disposition which the debtor has made, cannot be regarded as a claim seeking to establish the liability of a defendant in the sense in which it is understood in Article 5(3) of the Convention on Jurisdiction and the Enforcement of Judgments in Civil and Commercial Matters. Such an action therefore does not come within the scope of that provision.

2. Article 16(5) of the Convention confers exclusive jurisdiction on the courts of the place in which the judgment has been or is to be enforced to deal with proceedings which may arise from recourse to force, constraint or distraint on movable or immovable property in order to ensure the effective implementation of judgments.

An action such as the 'action paulienne', by which the creditor seeks to obtain the revocation with regard to himself of the transaction whereby the debtor has effected a disposition in fraud of the creditor's rights and which therefore seeks to protect whatever security the creditor may have with a view to a subsequent enforcement of the obligation of his debtor, is not intended to obtain a decision in such proceedings and does not therefore come within the scope of that provision.

3. Provisional or protective measures within the meaning of Article 24 must be understood as being measures which, in matters within the scope of the Convention, are intended to preserve a factual or legal situation so as to safeguard rights the recognition of which is sought elsewhere from the court having jurisdiction as to the substance of the matter.

Whilst an action such as the 'action paulienne' enables the creditor's security to be protected by preventing the dissipation of his debtor's assets, its purpose is that the court may vary the legal situation of the assets of the debtor and that of the beneficiary of the disposition effected by the debtor, and it cannot be described as a provisional or protective measure.

JUDGMENT OF THE COURT

Joliet, President of the Chamber, Grévisse, Moitinho de Almeida, Rodríguez Iglesias and Zuleeg, Judges

1. By judgment of 7 May 1990, received at the Court Registry on 28 August 1990, the Cour d'Appel d'Aix-en-Provence referred to the Court for a preliminary ruling under the Protocol of 3 June 1971 on the interpretation by the Court of Justice of the Convention of 27 September 1968 on Jurisdiction and the Enforcement of Judgments in Civil and Commercial Matters (hereinafter referred to as 'the Convention') a question on the interpretation of Articles 5(3), 16(5) and 24 of the Convention.

2. The question was raised in proceedings between Mr and Mrs Reichert and their son Mario Reichert, on the one hand, and Dresdner Bank AG on the other,

3. Mr and Mrs Reichert, who reside in Germany, are the owners of immovable property in the Commune of Antibes, Alpes-Maritimes, France, the legal ownership of which they donated to their son, Mario

Reichert, by a notarial instrument executed at Creutzwald, Moselle, France, That donation was challenged by Dresdner Bank AG, a creditor of Mr and Mrs Reichert, in the Tribunal de Grande Instance (Regional Court), Grasse, in whose judicial district the property at issue lies, on the basis of Article 1167 of the French Civil Code, under which creditors may 'challenge in their own name transactions entered into by their debtors in fraud of their rights' by a procedure known as the 'action paulienne'.

4. By a judgment of 20 February 1987, the Tribunal de Grande Instance de Grasse held that it had jurisdiction (which the Reicherts denied) on the basis of Article 16(1) of the Convention, under which, 'in proceedings which have as their object rights *in rem* in immovable property, ... the courts of the Contracting State in which the property is situated' have exclusive jurisdiction, regardless of domicile.

5. The Reicherts appealed against the ruling on jurisdiction to the Cour d'Appel d'Aix-en-Provence which, by a judgment of 18 November 1987, decided to stay the proceedings and referred to the Court for a preliminary ruling a first question asking substantially whether a case in which a creditor challenges, by an action under national law, in this case the '*action paulienne*' under French law, a donation of immovable property which he regards as having been made by his debtor in fraud of his rights, comes within the scope of Article 16(1) of the Convention.

6. By judgment of 10 January 1990, in Case C-115/88 *Reichert and Others* v *Dresdner Bank* [1990] ECR I-27, the Court ruled as follows: 'An action whereby a creditor seeks to have a disposition of a right *in rem* in immovable property rendered ineffective as against him on the ground that it was made in fraud of his rights by his debtor does not come within the scope of Article 16(1) of the Convention.'

7. However, at the request of Dresdner Bank AG, which intended to rely, in its defence to the appeal on jurisdiction, on other articles of the Convention in addition to Article 16(1) mentioned in the first question, the Cour d'Appel d'Aix-en-Provence, by the aforesaid judgment of 7 May 1990, referred to the Court for a preliminary ruling the following further question: 'If Article 16(1) of the Brussels Convention of 27 September 1968 does not apply, is an action under Article 1167 of the French Civil Code, by which a creditor seeks to obtain the revocation in regard to him of a transfer of rights *in rem* in immovable property by his debtor in a way which he regards as in fraud of his rights, covered by the

rules on jurisdiction in Article 5(3), Article 24 or Article 16(5) of the said convention if regard is had to the tortious, delictual or quasi-delictual nature of the alleged fraud or to the existence of protective measures which the decision on the substance of the case is intended to make it possible to enforce against the property which is the subject of the rights *in rem* transferred by the debtor?'

8. Reference is made to the Report for the Hearing for a fuller account of the facts of the case, the procedure and the observations submitted to the Court, which are mentioned or discussed hereinafter only in so far as is necessary for the reasoning of the Court.

9. As the Court has replied in its judgment in Case C-115/88 *Reichert*, cited above, that an action such as the '*action paulienne*' under French law does not come within the scope of Article 16(1) of the Convention, it is appropriate to reply to the further question raised by the national court.

10. Under Article 2 of the Convention, subject to special provisions, persons domiciled in a Contracting State, whatever their nationality, are to be sued in the courts of that State. The Convention envisages exceptions to that general rule by making provision for the applicant, in certain cases, to sue the defendant in the courts of the State of the latter's domicile or in the courts of another State (as in Articles 5 and 24 of the Convention). The Convention also provides for certain cases of exclusive jurisdiction regardless of domicile (as in Article 16).

11. To reply to the question referred to the Court, it is thus appropriate to consider in turn whether an action such as the '*action paulienne*' in French law comes within the scope of one of the exceptions for which the Convention provides and which are referred to in the order for reference.

Interpretation of Article 5(3) of the Convention

12. Article 5 of the Convention provides that: 'A person domiciled in a Contracting State may, in another Contracting State, be sued: ... (3) in matters relating to tort, delict or quasi-delict, in the courts for the place where the harmful event occurred'.

13. The Dresdner Bank, the respondent in the main proceedings, maintains that the '*action paulienne*' comes within the scope of Article 5(3) of the Convention inasmuch as it is a revocatory action which, as such, aims at rendering ineffective a culpable or deliberate act or

omission which is contrary to the law or to unwritten rules of care and causes damage to a third party, that is, an act of a quasi-delictual nature.

14. The Commission, on the contrary, thinks that the '*action paulienne*', which may affect a third party acting in good faith, who has therefore not committed any wrongful act or omission, and which not only leads, in certain circumstances, to imposing on such a third party acquiring the property an obligation to make reparation but may also result in an indirect depletion of his assets, cannot be regarded as an action for liability in tort, delict or quasi-delict. It does not, therefore, come within the scope of Article 5(3) of the Convention.

15. As the Court held in the judgment in Case 189/87 *Kalfelis* v *Schroeder* [1988] ECR 5565, paragraphs 15 and 16, the concept of 'matters relating to tort, delict or quasi-delict' serves as a criterion for defining the scope of one of the rules concerning the special jurisdictions available to the plaintiff. Regard being had to the objectives and general scheme of the Convention, it is important that, in order to ensure as far as possible the equality and uniformity of the rights and obligations arising out of the Convention for the Contracting States and the persons concerned, that concept should not be interpreted as a simple reference to the national law of one or other of the States concerned. Accordingly, the concept of 'matters relating to tort, delict or quasi-delict' must be regarded as an independent concept which is to be interpreted, for the application of the Convention, principally by reference to the scheme and objectives of the Convention in order to ensure that the latter is given full effect.

16. The Court also held in its above-mentioned judgment in Case 189/87 *Kalfelis*, at paragraph 17, that in order to ensure uniformity in all the Member States, it must be recognized that the concept of 'matters relating to tort, delict and quasi-delict' covers all actions which seek to establish the liability of a defendant and which are not related to a 'contract' within the meaning of Article 5(1).

17. In the above-mentioned judgment in Case C-115/88 *Reichert*, at paragraph 12, the Court pointed out that the '*action paulienne*' in French law was based on the creditor's personal claim against the debtor and sought to protect whatever security he might have over the debtor's estate. If successful, its effect was to render the transaction whereby the debtor had effected a disposition in fraud of the creditor's rights ineffective as against the creditor alone.

18. It may be seen, moreover, from the Commission's observations, which are not challenged on this point, that in French law the '*action paulienne*' may be instituted both against dispositions made for consideration by the debtor when the beneficiary acts in bad faith and against transactions entered into without consideration by the debtor even if the beneficiary acts in good faith.

19. The purpose of such an action is not to have the debtor ordered to make good the damage he has caused his creditor by his fraudulent conduct, but to render ineffective, as against his creditor, the disposition which the debtor has made. It is directed not only against the debtor but also against the person who benefits from the act, who is not a party to the obligation binding the creditor to his debtor, even, in cases where there is no consideration for the transaction, where that third party has not committed any wrongful act.

20. In these circumstances an action such as the '*action paulienne*' in French law cannot be regarded as a claim seeking to establish the liability of a defendant in the sense in which it is understood in Article 5(3) of the Convention and therefore does not come within the scope of that provision.

Article 16(5) of the Convention

21. Article 16 of the Convention provides that: 'The following courts shall have exclusive jurisdiction, regardless of domicile: ... (5) in proceedings concerned with the enforcement of judgments, the courts of the Contracting State in which the judgment has been or is to be enforced.'

22. The Dresdner Bank claims that the '*action paulienne*', in so far as it is preparatory to the enforcement of a decision, does come within the exceptions set out in Article 16(5) of the Convention.

23. The Commission's view, on the contrary, is that the '*action paulienne*', as its purpose is not to obtain a decision of the court with regard to a difficulty in enforcing a judgment, but to obtain from the court a judgment varying the legal situation of the debtor's assets, does not come within the scope of that article.

24. It should be pointed out, in the first place, that, as the Court held in its judgment in Case 220/84 *AS-Autoteile Service* v *Malhé* [1985] ECR

2267, at paragraph 16, Article 16 of the Convention makes a number of exceptions to the general rule set out in Article 2 of the Convention by granting exclusive jurisdiction to the courts of a Contracting State other than that specified under Article 2 in proceedings which have a particular connection with that other State, on the basis of the location of immovable property, the seat of a company, an entry in a public register or, in the case of paragraph (5), the place where a judgment is to be enforced.

25. In the second place it should be pointed out that Article 16 must not be given a wider interpretation than is required by its objective, since it results in depriving the parties of the choice of forum which would otherwise be theirs and, in certain cases, in their being brought before a court which is not that of the domicile of any of them (judgments in Cases 73/77 *Sanders* v *Van der Putte* [1977] ECR 2383, at paragraphs 17 and 18, and C-115/88 Reichert, cited above, at paragraph 9).

26. From that point of view it is necessary to take account of the fact that the essential purpose of the exclusive jurisdiction of the courts of the place in which the judgment has been or is to be enforced is that it is only for the courts of the Member State on whose territory enforcement is sought to apply the rules concerning the action on that territory of the authorities responsible for enforcement.

27. Thirdly, it should be pointed out that the report drawn up by the committee of experts which prepared the text of the Convention (Official Journal 1979 C 59 p.1) states that the expression 'proceedings concerned with the enforcement of judgments' is to be understood as meaning proceedings which may arise from recourse to force, constraint or distraint on movable or immovable property in order to ensure the effective implementation of judgments and authentic instruments' and that 'problems arising out of such proceedings come within the exclusive jurisdiction of the courts for the place of enforcement.'

28. As has been stated in paragraph 17 above, an action such as the '*action paulienne*' under French law seeks to protect whatever security the creditor may have by requesting the court having jurisdiction to render the transaction whereby the debtor has effected a disposition in fraud of the creditor's rights ineffective as against the creditor. Although it thus preserves the interests of the creditor with a view in particular to a subsequent enforcement of the obligation, it is not intended to obtain a decision in proceedings relating to 'recourse to force, constraint or

distraint on movable or immovable property in order to ensure the effective implementation of judgments and authentic instruments' and does not therefore come within the scope of Article 16(5) of the Convention.

Article 24 of the Convention

29. Article 24 of the Convention provides that: 'Application may be made to the courts of a Contracting State for such provisional, including protective, measures as may be available under the law of that State, even if, under this Convention, the courts of another Contracting State have jurisdiction as to the substance of the matter.'

30. Dresdner Bank claims that the '*action paulienne*' seeks to give the creditor a provisional security and so constitutes a 'protective measure' within the meaning of Article 24 of the Convention.

31. The Commission's view, on the contrary, is that the '*action paulienne*' does not seek to preserve a factual or legal situation so as to safeguard rights the recognition of which is, moreover, sought from the court having jurisdiction as to the substance of the matter, but that it seeks to vary the legal situation of an asset. It therefore constitutes neither a provisional nor a protective measure within the meaning of Article 24 of the Convention.

32. The Court has already declared in the judgment in Case 143/78 *De Cavel* v *De Cavel* [1979] ECR 1055, at paragraph 8, that as provisional or protective measures may serve to safeguard a variety of rights, their inclusion in the scope of the Convention is determined not by their own nature but by the nature of the rights which they serve to protect. It added, in paragraph 9 of that judgment, that the provisions of Article 24 of the Convention cannot be relied upon to bring within the scope of the Convention provisional or protective measures relating to matters which are excluded therefrom.

33. The Court also pointed out in the judgment in Case 125/79 *Denilauler* v *Couchet Frères* [1980] ECR 1553, at paragraphs 15 and 16, that an analysis of the function attributed under the general scheme of the Convention to Article 24 leads to the conclusion that, where such types of measures are concerned, special rules were contemplated so as to take account of the particular care and detailed knowledge of the actual circumstances required by the granting of this type of measure as well as

the determination of procedures and conditions intended to guarantee the provisional and protective character of such measures.

34. The expression 'provisional, including protective, measures' within the meaning of Article 24 must therefore be understood as referring to measures which, in matters within the scope of the Convention, are intended to preserve a factual or legal situation so as to safeguard rights the recognition of which is sought elsewhere from the court having jurisdiction as to the substance of the matter.

35. Whilst an action such as the '*action paulienne*' under French law enables the creditor's security to be protected by preventing the dissipation of his debtor's assets, it does not seek to preserve a factual or legal situation pending a decision of the court having jurisdiction as to the substance of the matter. Its purpose is that the court may vary the legal situation of the assets of the debtor and that of the beneficiary by ordering the revocation as against the creditor of the disposition effected by the debtor in fraud of the creditor's rights. It cannot, therefore, be described as a provisional or protective measure within the meaning of Article 24 of the Convention.

36. It follows from the foregoing that the answer to the national court should be that an action provided for by national law, such as the '*action paulienne*' in French law, whereby a creditor seeks to obtain the revocation in regard to him of a transfer of rights *in rem* in immovable property by his debtor in a way which the creditor regards as being in fraud of his rights does not come within the scope of Articles 5(3), 16(5) or 24 of the Convention of 27 September 1968 on Jurisdiction and the Enforcement of Judgments in Civil and Commercial Matters.

On those grounds, the Court (Fifth Chamber), in answer to the question referred to it by the Cour d'Appel d'Aix-en-Provence, by judgment of 7 May 1990, hereby rules:

> **An action provided for by national law, such as the '*action paulienne*' in French law, whereby a creditor seeks to obtain the revocation in regard to him of a transfer of rights *in rem* in immovable property by his debtor in a way which the creditor regards as being in fraud of his rights does not come within the scope of Articles 5(3), 16(5) or 24 of the Convention of 27 September 1968 on Jurisdiction and the Enforcement of Judgments in Civil and Commercial Matters.**

OPINION OF MR ADVOCATE GENERAL GULMANN

The Cour d'Appel d'Aix-en-Provence (Court of Appeal, Aix-en-Provence) has again referred to the Court for a preliminary ruling a question on the interpretation of the Convention of 27 September 1968 on Jurisdiction and the Enforcement of Judgments in Civil and Commercial Matters (hereinafter referred to as 'the Brussels Convention') in the case pending before that court between Mario Reichert and others on the one hand and Dresdner Bank on the other. The first such reference was the subject of the judgment of the Court of Justice in Case C-115/88 *Mario Reichert and Others* v *Dresdner Bank.*

The Court will remember that the background to the case pending before the Court d'Appel is as follows: the German couple, Mr and Mrs Reichert, residing in Germany, donated to their son, also resident in Germany, at a time when they are stated to have had a considerable debt to the Dresdner Bank, the legal ownership of a flat in France. They reserved to themselves the right of use of the property.

The Dresdner Bank challenged the donation by bringing an action before the Tribunal de Grande Instance de Grasse (Regional Court, Grasse) within whose judicial district the property is situated. The bank relied on Article 1167 of the French Civil Code according to which creditors 'may challenge in their own name transactions entered into by their debtors in fraud of their rights'. In French law such an action is known as an '*action paulienne*'.

The Dresdner Bank claimed that the Tribunal de Grande Instance de Grasse had jurisdiction under Articles 16(1) and 5(3) of the Brussels Convention. The Grasse court held that Article 16(1) of the Brussels Convention on jurisdiction with regard to immovable property was applicable. it was therefore not called upon to give a ruling as to whether Article 5(3) of the Convention was applicable. An appeal against that judgment was entered before the Cour d'Appel d'Aix-en-Provence, which originally referred to the Court of Justice for a preliminary ruling a question on the interpretation of Article 16(1).

That question was answered by the Court in the judgment in Case C-115/88 (hereinafter referred to as 'the *Reichert I* judgment'), in which the Court ruled as follows: 'An action whereby a creditor seeks to have a disposition of a right *in rem* in immovable property rendered ineffective as against him on the ground that it was made in fraud of his rights by his debtor does not come within the scope of Article 16(1) of the Convention.'

Before the Court had delivered its judgment, the Dresdner Bank - no doubt in the light of the observations submitted in the *Reichert I* case - had requested the Cour d'Appel d'Aix-en-Provence to refer a further question to the Court of Justice for a preliminary ruling. The Cour d'Appel agreed to that request and has referred the following question to the Court: 'If Article 16(1) of the Brussels Convention of 27 September 1968 does not apply, is an action under Article 1167 of the French Civil Code, by which a creditor seeks to obtain the revocation in regard to him of a transfer of rights *in rem* in immovable property by his debtor in a way which he regards as in fraud of his rights, covered by the rules on jurisdiction in Article 5(3), Article 24 or Article 16(5) of the said convention if regard is had to the tortious, delictual or quasi-delictual nature of the alleged fraud or to the existence of protective measures which the decision on the substance of the case is intended to make it possible to enforce against the property which is the subject of the rights *in rem* transferred by the debtor?'

Whereas the interpretation of Article 16(1) of the Brussels Convention caused several Member States to submit observations in the *Reichert I* case, only the Dresdner Bank and the Commission have submitted observations on the question referred to the Court in this case.

Before I proceed to answer the question about the interpretation of the three relevant provisions of the Brussels Convention I shall make some brief remarks, partly about the problems facing the Dresdner Bank in pursuing its application to have the transaction set aside and partly about the specific rules for such an action, known in French law as an '*action paulienne*' *(actio pauliana).*

The grounds on which the Dresdner Bank bases its action

The Dresdner Bank's basic idea was that the most appropriate procedure for having the donation set aside and thus of improving its chances of collecting its debt from Mr and Mrs Reichert was to take proceedings in the judicial district in which the couple's French property was situated. In this connection the bank assumed that it would be French law, that is, the '*action paulienne*', which would form the basis of the decision on the substance of the case and that there would be no difficulty in obtaining enforcement of a judgment in the bank's favour in the judicial district in which the property was situated. The bank claims that there would be problems for it if it were compelled to bring the action before a court in the State of the defendants' domicile, that is, before a German court. It states, probably correctly, that there is some doubt about the content of the German rules on the choice of legislation applicable in this situation. According to the Dresdner Bank's information it is most likely that such rules would mean either that German law would be regarded as applicable or that a German court would require that the conditions of both German and French law for the revocation of the transaction must be met because it concerned a property situated in France. It is less likely that the German rules on the choice of legislation would result in French law being taken as the basis. It seems to emerge from this case that a German court's rules for setting a transaction aside are different from the French rules and that it may be more difficult to secure such an outcome under German than under French rules.

The Dresdner Bank also claims that there may be a risk that a French court will refuse on the basis of French public policy to recognize and enforce a German judgment of revocation relating to a property situated in France.

More generally, the Dresdner Bank also refers to the importance of the fact that the transaction to be set aside concerns immovable property, claiming inter alia that such property comes exclusively under the legislation of the State in which it is situated.

The bank's view is that in the necessary interpretation of the rules of the Brussels Convention the Court should take these considerations into account.

I cannot deny that I have a certain sympathy for the bank's wish for help in solving the problems it has had in obtaining a decision that Mr and Mrs Reichert's donation to their son may be revoked on the ground that it was made in order to restrict their creditors' opportunities of obtaining satisfaction. I also understand to a certain extent that at first sight there are arguments for regarding an application for revocation of the donation of a property situated in France as being most appropriately determined by a French court according to French law. But the arguments in favour of such an outcome are primarily relevant to an interpretation of Article 16(1) of the Brussels Convention. In the *Reichert I* case the Court ruled, correctly in my view, that the arguments were not sufficient to make it possible to interpret Article 16(1) in the sense desired by the Dresdner Bank. It is doubtful whether the fact that the action concerns immovable property is by itself significant as regards the rules on jurisdiction which are relevant in this case.

Although it is no doubt an important general consideration with regard to the interpretation of the rules of jurisdiction in the Convention that they should ascribe jurisdiction to the courts which will best be in a position to determine both legally and factually the issues involved, and though any views which may exist in the legal systems concerned on the rules relating to the choice of legislation may still be relevant, it should also be said that no significance can be attached, for the interpretation of the provisions of the Brussels Convention, to the fact that in this case there may be differences between German and French rules on revocation.

The '*action paulienne*' French law

As I have said, the Dresdner Bank bases its action on Article 1167 of the French Code Civil, according to which creditors 'may challenge in their own name transactions entered into by their debtors in fraud of their rights'. The question in this case is therefore whether one or more of the articles of the Brussels Convention mentioned in the question referred to the Court cover an action for revocation such as the '*action paulienne*' under French law. That action was discussed in detail in the *Reichert I* case. The doubt which apparently still exists in French law on this specific action is hardly of decisive importance for the Court's decision. In the *Reichert I* case the Court emphasized the following characteristics of the action: 'The '*action paulienne*' ... is based on the creditor's personal claim against the debtor and seeks to protect whatever security he may have over the debtor's estate. If successful, its effect is to render the transaction whereby the debtor has effected a disposition in fraud of the creditor's rights ineffective as against the creditor alone...'.

It is important that the revocation takes effect only on behalf of the creditor who has brought the action, that it is valid only for the satisfaction of the creditor's claim and that the transferee may bar the action by meeting the creditor's claim.

Moreover for the purposes of this case it is important to mention the following points:

- the action is based on allegedly deliberate illegal conduct on the part of the debtor, but by its nature must be directed against the third person who has acquired rights over the property concerned, or both against him and the debtor;

- in the case of a donation between the debtor and a third person, the creditor is not required to show that the transferee has acted in bad faith, but must do so if the transaction is not a donation;
- the creditor must show that he had a claim on the debtor before the transaction, but it is not necessary for the claim to have fallen due;
- the action is not dependent on the nature of the property which has been transferred.

Finally it should perhaps be mentioned that it will probably be neither right nor appropriate to take the view that the revocatory action is based on the law of contract. That is true even if the creditor's claim against the debtor has, as in this case, a contractual basis and even if the transaction at issue is a conveyance of property.

Interpretation of Article 16(5) of the Brussels Convention

Article 16(5) provides that: 'The following courts shall have exclusive jurisdiction, regardless of domicile: ... (5) in proceedings concerned with the enforcement of judgments, the courts of the Contracting State in which the judgment has been or is to be enforced.'

The Dresdner Bank claims that that provision must not be restrictively interpreted and that it may cover a revocatory action such as the '*action paulienne*' because the purpose of the action to set the transaction aside is to prepare for enforcement of the creditor's claim to the property in question.

That interpretation cannot be accepted. Neither the wording of the provision, the preparatory documents nor the points of view adopted by academic writers may be regarded as supporting such a wide interpretation. The Court has emphasized on several occasions, and most recently in the *Reichert I* judgment, that: '... Article 16 must not be given a wider interpretation than is required by its objective, since it results in depriving the parties of the choice of forum which would otherwise be theirs and, in certain cases, results in their being brought before a court which is not that of any of them...' (paragraph 9).

In the preparatory documents relating to this article, according to the Jenard Report, it is stated that 'proceedings concerned with the enforcement of judgments' is to be understood as meaning: '...those proceedings which can arise from recourse to force, constraint or distraint on movable or immovable property in order to ensure the effective implementation of judgments and authentic instruments'.

Clearly it should be accepted that courts in the State in which the judgment has been or is to be enforced have exclusive jurisdiction under Article 16(5) of the Convention only in cases directly connected with the enforcement of judicial decisions already taken or with other enforceable instruments. An action for the revocation of a transaction, such as the '*action paulienne*' does not concern the enforcement of a judgment already delivered or any other enforceable instrument, nor is it an action arising in connection therewith. The object of an '*action paulienne*' is, as the Commission states, to obtain a material alteration of the legal relationship between the creditor and the transferee.

Interpretation of Article 24 of the Brussels Convention

Article 24, the last of the provisions of the Brussels Convention with regard to jurisdiction, which is to be found in Section 9 of Title II on provisional and protective measures, provides as follows: 'For the purposes of this Convention, "judgment" means any judgment given by a court or tribunal of a Contracting State, whatever the judgment may be called, including a decree, order, decision or writ of execution, as well as the determination of costs or expenses by an officer of the court.'

It may be seen both from the position of the article and from its wording, as well as from the preparatory documents, that it has a limited purpose, namely to preserve the opportunity for each Member State to continue to apply its existing rules of jurisdiction as regards the adoption of provisional measures such as, for example, attachment or injunction. That may be the case irrespective of whether the court having jurisdiction as to the substance of the matter under the provisions of the Convention is that of another Member State.

The measures referred to in Article 24 are only such as will ensure provisional legal protection of certain claims and are dependent on the result of a subsequent judgment as to the substance of the matter.

It is clear, in my view, that Article 24 does not apply in an action, such as the '*action paulienne*' to set a transaction aside. The subject-matter of such an action is a claim that a transaction should be regarded as having no legal effect in relation to one of the transferor's creditors. It is not a question, as the Commission has stressed of a remedy ensuring the maintenance of a given factual or legal situation so as to protect the rights which it is claimed should be recognized by a subsequent judgment as to the substance of the matter.

This interpretation of Article 24 must be accepted even though it appears from the Jenard Report that 'as regards the measures which may be taken, reference should be made to the internal law of the country concerned', and even though, from certain points of view it may perhaps be reasonable to emphasize the protective nature of a revocatory action such as the '*action paulienne*'. Article 24, according to its wording and purpose, covers only such remedies as are provisional in the proper sense of the word because in all circumstances they pre-suppose a subsequent judgment as to the substance of the matter.

Interpretation of Article 5(3) of the Brussels Convention

Article 5(3) reads as follows: 'A person domiciled in a Contracting State may, in another Contracting State, be sued: ... (3) in matters relating to tort, delict or quasi-delict, in the courts for the place where the harmful event occurred.'

It is not an easy matter to determine whether an action such as the '*action paulienne*' for the setting aside of a transaction is covered by Article 5(3).

The Court's case-law makes a useful contribution to an interpretation, but in my view nothing which may clearly be regarded as providing a certain answer to the question. Nor can the wording of the provision be considered to provide a clear answer, in particular because there are considerable differences between the various linguistic versions, all of which are authentic. The preparatory documents contain certain aids to interpretation, but nothing decisive, and the question is dealt with only to a limited extent in academic writings which, moreover, express divergent views. In this case therefore there are, in my view, especially compelling grounds for interpreting the provision on the basis of its context and purpose.

To begin with it may be appropriate to mention that it appears in any event from the case-law of the Court that Article 5(3) should be interpreted autonomously and that, like the other provisions of the article, it should be restrictively interpreted.

The Court decided in the judgment in Case 189/87 *Kalfelis* v *Schroeder* that 'the concept of "matters relating to tort, delict or quasi-delict" must be regarded as an autonomous concept (paragraph 16) since '... having regard to the objectives and general scheme of the Convention, it is important that, in order to ensure as far as possible the equality and uniformity of the rights and obligations arising out of the Convention for the Contracting States and the persons concerned, that concept should not be interpreted simply as referring to the national law of one or other of the States concerned' (paragraph 15).

In the same judgment the Court stated that '...the "special jurisdictions" enumerated in Articles 5 and 6 of the Convention constitute derogations from the principle that jurisdiction is vested in the courts of the State where the defendant is domiciled and as such must be interpreted restrictively' (paragraph 19).

Article 5(3) raises two independent but related questions: first the legal description of the type of case covered by special jurisdiction, and secondly the determination of the 'place where the harmful event occurred'. That is the first of the questions to be answered in this case.

As I have already said, the preparatory documents relating to the provision contain little information on Article 5(3), which is dealt with in conjunction with Article 5(4) on the court having jurisdiction 'as regards a civil claim for damages or restitution which is based on an act giving rise to criminal proceedings...'. In the Jenard Report the two courts are referred to as '*forum delicti commissi*'. The report states that the jurisdiction of the court of the place where the harmful event occurred is recognized by the national laws of the majority of the Member States and that such jurisdiction is incorporated in a number of bilateral conventions. It states that: 'The fact that this jurisdiction is recognized under most of the legal systems, and incorporated in the majority of the bilateral conventions was a ground for including it in the Convention, especially in view of the high number of road accidents'.

The wording of the provision gives rise to problems of interpretation, *inter alia* because the various linguistic versions, each of which is authentic, differ to some extent from one another. I think it may be appropriate to quote the provision in the various versions. Article 5 begins as follows: 'A person domiciled in a Contracting State may, in another Contracting State, be sued...' and paragraph (3) then provides:

'wenn eine unerlaubte Handlung oder eine Handlung, die einer unerlaubten Handlung gleichgestellt ist, oder wenn Ansprüche aus einer solchen Handlung den Gegenstand des Verfahrens bilden, vor dem Gericht des Ortes, an dem das schadigende Ereignis eingetreten ist;'

'en matière délictuelle ou quasi délictuelle, devant le tribunal du lieu où le fait dommageable s'est produit;'

'in materia di delitti o quasi-delitti, davanti al giudice del luogo in cui l'evento dannoso è avvenuto;'

'ten aanzien van verbintenissen uit onrechtmatige daad: voor het gerecht van de plaats waar het schadebrengende feit zich heeft voorgedaan;

'in matters relating to tort, delict or quasi-delict, in the courts for the place where the harmful event occurred;'

'in ábhair a bhaineann le tort, míghníomh nó samhail mhíghnímh, sna cúirteanna don áit inar tharla an teagmhas diobhálach;'

'i sager om erstatning uden for kontrakt, ved retten på det sted, hvor skadetilffjelsen er foregået;'

'en materia delictual o cuasidelictual, ante el tribunal del lugar donde se hubiere producido el hecho dañoso;'

'em materia excontratual, perante o tribunal do lugar onde ocorreu o facto danoso;'.

The Court has consistently held that a provision is not to be interpreted in isolation on the basis of its wording in the language of the case but that in order to obtain a uniform interpretation it is necessary to interpret it in the light of its wording in all the language versions.

In his Opinions in Case 21/76 *Bier* v *Mines de Potasse d'Alsace* and Case 814/79 *Netherlands* v *Rüffer* Mr Advocate General Warner had occasion to scrutinize the various language versions of the provision. In the latter case he stated, *inter alia*: 'As, however, emerges from Professor André Tunc's Introduction to Volume XI of the International Encyclopedia of Comparative Law, the volume on "Torts", no-one has ever succeeded, even in the context of any national legal system, in formulating an accurate description of tort that did not beg one or more questions. Like the proverbial elephant, tort is easier to recognize than to define.'

Mr Advocate General Darmon quoted Mr Advocate General Warner in point 20 of his Opinion in the *Kalfelis* case, and moreover in point 21 he drew attention to the fact that academic writers considered that a very prudent approach should be adopted in defining the sphere of application of Article 5(3). He therefore drew the conclusion that 'in the present case ... no abstract standard should be formulated.'

I can only agree with that view. An attempt to give an abstract and general definition of the scope of Article 5(3) is risky.

There is an extensive field in which Article 5(3) may undoubtedly be used and where its application will give rise to no problems (apart from those which may be involved in the determination of the place where the harmful event occurred). That field is represented by the typical actions for damages in which a claimant has suffered economic loss by a tortfeasor's conduct giving rise to liability and in which it is clear that there is no contractual link between the parties in relation to the damage. But the provision gives rise in any event to difficulties of demarcation in two respects.

On the one hand there may be difficulties in distinguishing the actions covered by the jurisdiction in matters relating to a contract, falling under Article 5(1), from those falling under Article 5(3). Certainly there are difficulties in the legal systems of all Member States in the demarcation between matters of contract and matters of tort, delict or quasi-delict as regards liability for damages and such difficulties are undeniably accentuated in the application of the Brussels Convention, not least because there may be differences in the legal description of one and the same legal concept between the legal systems of the Member States before whose courts a case may in certain circumstances be brought.

On the other hand, there may be difficulties in distinguishing actions which may be regarded as actions for compensation covered by either Article 5(1) or 5(3) from those which cannot be regarded as actions for compensation in matters either of contract or of tort, delict or quasi-delict. In such cases the result of the demarcation may be that there is no special jurisdiction for the action in question, which can therefore be brought only before the court of the State in which the defendant is domiciled. This case concerns a problem of that kind.

The various language versions of Article 5(3) have in any case two features in common. One is that there must have been 'wrongful' conduct, and the other that that conduct must have caused a 'harmful event'.

If that is correct, it may also be seen that the scope of Article 5(3) is potentially very wide. The Court also stated in the judgment in *Mines de Potasse d'Alsace* that '... by its comprehensive form of words, Article 5(3) of the Convention covers a wide diversity of kinds of liability' (paragraph 18).

The position therefore presumably is, as was also mentioned by the Dresdner Bank and the Commission in the *Reichert I* case, that according to the wording of Article 5(3) there is hardly anything to prevent an '*action paulienne*' from being regarded as an action drawing the conclusions from a wrongful act which has led to a harmful event. That presumably was what the Cour d'Appel d'Aix-en-Provence was referring to in suggesting in the reference for a preliminary ruling that the answer to the question should have regard 'to the tortious, delictual or quasi-delictual nature of the alleged fraud...'.

If the case-law of the Court is examined for aids to interpretation in order to solve the demarcation problem at issue here, the judgment in the *Kalfelis* case is probably the only one which is directly relevant. The Court stated: 'In order to ensure uniformity in all the Member States, it must be recognized that the concept of "matters relating to tort, delict and quasi-delict" covers all actions which seek to establish the liability of a defendant and which are not related to a "contract" within the meaning of Article 5(1)' (paragraph 17).

The Court therefore attached importance to the concept of 'liability' which in the original German version of the judgment is referred to as 'Schadenshaftung'. It is presumably reasonable to state that an action such as the '*action paulienne*' to set aside a transaction cannot be directly regarded as an action which seeks to establish 'Schadenshaftung or 'liability' of a defendant.

However, it should be pointed out that in the *Kalfelis* judgment the Court dealt with a problem of interpretation other than that relevant in this case. In the *Kalfelis* judgment the Court considered whether 'in the case of an action based concurrently on tortious or delictual liability, breach of contract and unjust enrichment, ... the court having jurisdiction by virtue of Article 5(3) may adjudicate on the action in so far as it is not based on tort or delict' (paragraph 14).

Thus it was not contested that in the main action the claim for compensation related to matters both of contract and of tort, delict or quasi-delict and paragraph 17 of the Court's judgment, previously cited, therefore hardly had the purpose of laying down a 'definition' of the sphere of application of Article 5(3) involving a decisive position with regard to the question at issue in this case. I think, in any event, that it would not be right to take the view that the problem of demarcation at issue here can be solved exclusively on the basis of the *Kalfelis* judgment.

In my view the question should be examined in the light of the purpose and context of Article 5(3).

In any event the case-law of the Court contains two factors of essential importance in this respect.

In the first place the Court, as I have already said, has declared that the rules as to jurisdiction in Article 5, including paragraph (3), must be restrictively interpreted as being derogations from the general rule contained in Article 2 of the Brussels Convention regarding the court of the State of the defendant's domicile. On the other hand the Court declared in the judgment in *Mines de Potasse d'Alsace* that: 'That provision [Article 5(3)] must be interpreted in the context of the scheme of conferment of jurisdiction which forms the subject-matter of Title 13 of the Convention.

That scheme is based on a general rule, laid down by Article 2, that the courts of the State in which the defendant is domiciled shall have jurisdiction.

However Article 5 makes provision in a number of cases for a special jurisdiction, which the plaintiff may opt to choose.

This freedom of choice was introduced having regard to the existence, in certain clearly defined situations, of a particularly close connecting factor between a dispute and the court which may be called upon to hear it with a view to the efficacious conduct of the proceedings' (paragraphs 8 to 11).

The Court amplified these views in its judgment in Case C-220/88 *Dumez France and Tracoba*, in which it stated: '...those cases of special jurisdiction [including those of Article 5(3)], the choice of which is a matter for the plaintiff, are based on the existence of a particularly close connecting factor between the dispute and courts other than those of the State of the defendant's domicile, which justifies the attribution of jurisdiction to those courts for reasons relating to the sound administration of justice and the efficacious conduct of proceedings.

In order to meet that objective, which is of fundamental importance in a convention which has essentially to promote the recognition and enforcement of judgments in States other than those in which they were delivered, it is necessary to avoid the multiplication of courts of competent jurisdiction which would heighten the risk of irreconcilable decisions, this being the reason for which recognition or an order for enforcement is withheld by virtue of Article 27(3) of the Convention' (paragraphs 17 and 18).

When it is considered that:

- the wording of Article 5(3) does not preclude the possibility that an action such as the '*action paulienne*' for the setting aside of a transaction may be covered by that provision, whereas the judgment in the *Kalfelis* case may presumably be regarded as evidence of a contrary interpretation;
- the provision is to be interpreted restrictively; and
- in accordance with the case-law of the Court there must be a close connecting factor between the dispute at issue and the court having jurisdiction,

it is essential, for the interpretation of Article 5(3) in respect of an action such as the '*action paulienne*' for the setting aside of a transaction, that it should be possible to adduce reasons which in general will make it appropriate for the applicant to be given the opportunity to bring an action before a court other than that of the State of the defendant's domicile.

As the basis for the justification of the rule of jurisdiction laid down in Article 5(3) may be regarded as the fact that the court for the place where the harmful event occurred will typically be the court in which the 'claim for damages' may be best and most easily dealt with, it should be considered whether the court for the place where the harmful event occurred in an action such as the '*action paulienne*' to set a transaction aside has certain special advantages for handling and settling such an action in comparison with the court of the State of the defendant's domicile. In my view it does not. 'The place where the harmful event occurred' has hardly any special significance in determining the factual and legal circumstances relevant for settling such an action. In a case such as this the place where the harmful event occurred may well be either the place where the instrument of conveyance was drawn up or the place where the property conveyed is situated. But neither of these places seems to be of special significance in deciding whether the conditions for setting the transaction aside are met. The most essential such conditions are those concerning the existence of the debt owed to the creditor and the debtor's intention knowingly to restrict the creditor's opportunities for enforcement.

In my view there is no special ground for thinking that there is a general need for alternative jurisdictions in actions such as the '*action paulienne*' for setting transactions aside. Such cases may be dealt with by the court of the State of the defendant's domicile without any special procedural difficulties. In this case that would result in no difficulties since both the transferor and the transferee of the immovable property are domiciled within the same judicial district. Even if they were not, it would be possible for the applicant to bring proceedings against both the transferor and the transferee before the same court (cf. Article 6(1) of the Brussels Convention as interpreted in the *Kalfelis* judgment).

In my view the fact cannot be disregarded that the result which I propose has the advantage that the number of courts which may possibly be concerned is limited and that it avoids the need to decide where the harmful event took place in this case. As we know the Court declared in the judgment in *Mines de Potasse d'Alsace* that the expression 'the place where the harmful event occurred' must be understood as being intended 'to cover both the place where the damage occurred and the place of the event giving rise to it' (paragraph 24).

If Article 5(3) were applicable in a case such as this it would presumably follow from the judgment in *Mines de Potasse d'Alsace* that the applicant could in any case choose to bring proceedings - either before the court of the place where the instrument of conveyance was executed (the place where the tort, delict or quasi-delict was committed - in this case the Tribunal de Grande Instance de Sarreguemines, Department of the Moselle); or - the court for the place where the damage occurred (the place where it took effect - in this case the Tribunal de Grande Instance de Grasse in whose jurisdiction the property is situated).

However, there are no grounds for going further into these questions since for the reasons I have already mentioned I am able to suggest that the Court should answer the question referred to it to the effect that Article 5(3) does not apply to an action such as the '*action paulienne*' for setting a transaction aside. The Commission has come to the same conclusion, though it appears to restrict it to covering situations in which the revocation concerns transfers by donation. The Commission has stressed that the legal position in an action to set a transaction aside is more complicated than in a general action for damages since in the former case the legal position necessarily involves three interested parties - creditor, debtor and the transferee of the property transferred. The Commission particularly attaches importance to the fact that a donation may also be set aside as against a purchaser in good faith, so that in such cases there can be no question of a wrongful act as postulated in Article 5(3). From a narrow point of view the Commission's arguments may be regarded as correct, but their weak point is that they lead to the application of Article 5(3) being dependent on whether the contested transfer is or is not a donation. In my view it would be inappropriate to interpret Article 5(3) in such a way that its application depends on a distinction which does not appear relevant in relation to the considerations forming the background to the rule of jurisdiction under Article 5(3).

Conclusion

I shall accordingly propose that the Court should reply to the question referred to it by the Cour d'Appel d'Aix-en-Provence as follows: 'An action such as the '*action paulienne*' for the setting aside of a transaction does not fall within the scope of Article 5(3), Article 16(5) or Article 24 of the Convention of 27 September 1968 on jurisdiction and the Enforcement of Judgments in Civil and Commercial Matters'.

Case C-68/93 - 7 March 1995

Fiona Shevill and Others
v
Presse Alliance SA

Special jurisdiction - Jurisdiction 'in matters relating to tort, delict or quasi-delict' - Place where the harmful event occurred - Cross-border defamation by the press - Plaintiff's right to choose - Court of the place where the publisher is established - Jurisdiction in respect of all the harm - Courts of the places where the publication was distributed in each Contracting State where the reputation of the person harmed is injured - Jurisdiction limited to the harm caused in the State of the court seised - Defamation - Assessment of the harmful character of the event in question and the evidence required of the alleged harm - Application of the conflict of laws rules of the forum - Limits.

Summary

1. On a proper construction of the expression 'place where the harmful event occurred' in Article 5(3) of the Convention of 27 September 1968 on Jurisdiction and Enforcement of Judgments in Civil and Commercial Matters as amended by the Convention of 9 October 1978 on the accession of the Kingdom of Denmark, Ireland and the United Kingdom of Great Britain and Northern Ireland and by the Convention of 25 October 1982 on the accession of the Hellenic Republic, the victim of a libel by a newspaper article distributed in several Contracting States may bring an action for damages against the publisher either before the courts of the Contracting State of the place where the publisher of the defamatory publication is established, which have jurisdiction to award damages for all the harm caused by the defamation, or before the courts of each Contracting State in which the publication was distributed and where the victim claims to have suffered injury to his reputation, which

have jurisdiction to rule solely in respect of the harm caused in the State of the court seised.

2. The criteria for assessing whether the event in question is harmful and the evidence required of the existence and extent of the harm alleged by the plaintiff in an action in tort, delict or quasi-delict are not governed by the Convention but are determined in accordance with the substantive law designated by the national conflict of laws rules of the court seised on the basis of the Convention, provided that the effectiveness of the Convention is not thereby impaired. The fact that under the national law applicable to the main proceedings damage is presumed in libel actions, so that the plaintiff does not have to adduce evidence of the existence and extent of that damage, does not therefore preclude the application of Article 5(3) of the Convention.

JUDGMENT OF THE COURT

Rodríguez Iglesias, President, Schockweiler, Kapteyn, Gulmann, Presidents of Chambers, Mancini, Kakouris, Moitinho de Almeida, Murray, Edward, Puissochet and Hirsch, Judges.

1. By order of 1 March 1993, received at the Court on 15 March 1993, the House of Lords referred to the Court for a preliminary ruling under the Protocol of 3 June 1971 on the interpretation by the Court of Justice of the Convention of 27 September 1968 on Jurisdiction and the Enforcement of Judgments in Civil and Commercial Matters (*Journal Officiel* 1972, L 299, p. 32), as amended by the Convention of 9 October 1978 on the accession of the Kingdom of Denmark, Ireland and the United Kingdom of Great Britain and Northern Ireland (OJ 1978 L 304, p. 1 and - amended text - p. 77) and by the Convention of 25 October 1982 on the accession of the Hellenic Republic (OJ 1982 L 388, p. 1), hereinafter 'the Convention', seven questions on the interpretation of Article 5(3) of the Convention.

2. Those questions were raised in proceedings brought by Miss Fiona Shevill, a United Kingdom national residing in North Yorkshire, England, Chequepoint SARL, Ixora Trading Inc. and Chequepoint International Limited against Presse Alliance SA, a company incorporated under French law whose registered office is in Paris, and seek to establish which courts have jurisdiction to hear an action for damages for harm caused by the publication of a defamatory newspaper article.

3. According to the documents before the Court, on 23 September 1989 Presse Alliance SA, which publishes the newspaper *France-Soir*, published an article about an operation which drug squad officers of the French police had carried out at one of the *bureaux de change* operated in Paris by Chequepoint SARL. That article, based on information provided by the agency France Presse, mentioned the company 'Chequepoint' and 'a young woman by the name of Fiona Shevill-Avril'.

4. Chequepoint SARL, a company incorporated under French law whose registered office is in Paris, has operated *bureaux de change* in France since 1988. It is not alleged to carry on business in England or Wales.

5. Fiona Shevill was temporarily employed for three months in the summer of 1989 by Chequepoint SARL in Paris. She returned to England on 26 September 1989.

6. Ixora Trading Inc., which is not a company incorporated under the law of England and Wales, has since 1974 operated *bureaux de change* in England under the name 'Chequepoint'.

7. Chequepoint International Ltd, a holding company incorporated under Belgian law whose registered office is in Brussels, controls Chequepoint SARL and Ixora Trading Inc.

8. Miss Shevill, Chequepoint SARL, Ixora Trading Inc. and Chequepoint International Ltd considered that the above-mentioned article was defamatory in that it suggested that they were part of a drug-trafficking network for which they had laundered money. On 17 October 1989 they issued a writ in the High Court of England and Wales claiming damages for libel from Presse Alliance SA in respect of the copies of *France-Soir* distributed in France and the other European countries including those sold in England and Wales. The plaintiffs subsequently amended their pleadings, deleting all references to the copies sold outside England and Wales. Since under English law there is a presumption of damage in libel cases, the plaintiffs did not have to adduce evidence of damage arising from the publication of the article in question.

9. It is common ground that *France-Soir* is mainly distributed in France and that the newspaper has a very small circulation in the United Kingdom, effected through independent distributors. It is estimated that more than 237,000 copies of the issue of *France-Soir* in question were

sold in France and approximately 15,500 copies distributed in the other European countries, of which 230 were sold in England and Wales (5 in Yorkshire).

10. On 23 November 1989 *France-Soir* published an apology stating that it had not intended to allege that either the owners of Chequepoint *bureaux de change* or Miss Shevill had been involved in drug trafficking or money laundering.

11. On 7 December 1989 Presse Alliance SA issued a summons disputing the jurisdiction of the High Court of England and Wales on the ground that no harmful event within the meaning of Article 5(3) of the Convention had occurred in England.

12. That application to strike out was dismissed by order of 10 April 1990. The appeal brought against that decision was dismissed by order of 14 May 1990.

13. On 12 March 1991 the Court of Appeal dismissed the appeal brought by Presse Alliance SA against that decision and stayed the action brought by Chequepoint International Limited.

14. Presse Alliance SA appealed against that decision to the House of Lords pursuant to leave to appeal granted by the latter.

15. Presse Alliance SA argued essentially that under Article 2 of the Convention the French courts had jurisdiction in this dispute and that the English courts did not have jurisdiction under Article 5(3) of the Convention since the 'place where the harmful event occurred' within the meaning of that provision was in France and no harmful event had occurred in England.

16. Considering that the proceedings raised problems of interpretation of the Convention, the House of Lords by order of 1 March 1993 decided to stay the proceedings pending a preliminary ruling by the Court of Justice on the following questions:

'1. In a case of libel by a newspaper article, do the words "the place where the harmful event occurred" in Article 5(3) of the Convention mean: (a) the place where the newspaper was printed and put into circulation; or (b) the place or places where the newspaper was read by particular individuals; or (c) the place or places where the plaintiff has a significant reputation?

2. If and insofar as the answer to the first question is (b), is "the harmful event" dependent upon there being a reader or readers who knew (or knew of) the plaintiff and understood those words to refer to him?

3. If and insofar as harm is suffered in more than one country (because copies of the newspaper were distributed in at least one Member State other than the Member State where it was printed and put into circulation), does a separate harmful event or harmful events take place in each Member State where the newspaper was distributed, in respect of which such Member State has separate jurisdiction under Article 5(3), and if so, how harmful must the event be, or what proportion or the total harm must it represent?

4. Does the phrase "harmful event" include an event actionable under national law without proof of damage, where there is no evidence of actual damage or harm?

5. In deciding under Article 5(3) whether (or where) a "harmful event" has occurred is the local court expected to answer the question otherwise than by reference to its own rules and, if so, by reference to which other rules or substantive law, procedure or evidence?

6. If, in a defamation case, the local court concludes that there has been an actionable publication (or communication) of material, as a result of which at least some damage to reputation would be presumed, is it relevant to the acceptance of jurisdiction that other Member States might come to a different conclusion in respect of similar material published within their respective jurisdictions?

7. In deciding whether it has jurisdiction under Article 5(3) of the Convention, what standard of proof should a court require of the plaintiff that the conditions of Article 5(3) are satisfied: (a) generally; and (b) in relation to matters which (if the court takes jurisdiction) will not be re-examined at the trial of the action?'

The first, second, third and sixth questions

17. The national court's first, second, third and sixth questions, which should be considered together, essentially seek guidance from the Court as to the interpretation of the concept 'the place where the harmful event occurred' used in Article 5(3) of the Convention, with a view to establishing which courts have jurisdiction to hear an action for damages for harm caused to the victim following distribution of a defamatory newspaper article in several Contracting States.

18. In order to answer those questions, reference should first be made to Article 5(3) of the Convention, which, by way of derogation from the

general principle in the first paragraph of Article 2 of the Convention that the courts of the Contracting State of the defendant's domicile have jurisdiction, provides: 'A person domiciled in a Contracting State may, in another Contracting State, be sued: [...] (3) in matters relating to tort, delict or quasi-delict, in the courts for the place where the harmful event occurred; [...]'.

19. It is settled case-law (see Case 21/76 *Bier* v *Mines de Potasse d'Alsace* [1976] ECR 1735, paragraph 11, and Case C-220/88 *Dumez France and Tracoba* v *Hessische Landesbank* (Helaba) and Others [1990] ECR I-49, paragraph 17) that that rule of special jurisdiction, the choice of which is a matter for the plaintiff, is based on the existence of a particularly close connecting factor between the dispute and courts other than those of the State of the defendant's domicile which justifies the attribution of jurisdiction to those courts for reasons relating to the sound administration of justice and the efficacious conduct of proceedings.

20. It must also be emphasized that in *Mines de Potasse d'Alsace* the Court held (at paragraphs 24 and 25) that, where the place of the happening of the event which may give rise to liability in tort, delict or quasi-delict and the place where that event results in damage are not identical, the expression 'place where the harmful event occurred' in Article 5(3) of the Convention must be understood as being intended to cover both the place where the damage occurred and the place of the event giving rise to it, so that the defendant may be sued, at the option of the plaintiff, either in the courts for the place where the damage occurred or in the courts for the place of the event which gives rise to and is at the origin of that damage.

21. In that judgment, the Court stated (at paragraphs 15 and 17) that the place of the event giving rise to the damage no less than the place where the damage occurred could constitute a significant connecting factor from the point of view of jurisdiction, since each of them could, depending on the circumstances, be particularly helpful in relation to the evidence and the conduct of the proceedings.

22. The Court added (at paragraph 20) that to decide in favour only of the place of the event giving rise to the damage would, in an appreciable number of cases, cause confusion between the heads of jurisdiction laid down by Articles 2 and 5(3) of the Convention, so that the latter provision would, to that extent, lose its effectiveness.

23. Those observations, made in relation to physical or pecuniary loss or damage, must equally apply, for the same reasons, in the case of loss or damage other than physical or pecuniary, in particular injury to the reputation and good name of a natural or legal person due to a defamatory publication.

24. In the case of a libel by a newspaper article distributed in several Contracting States, the place of the event giving rise to the damage, within the meaning of those judgments, can only be the place where the publisher of the newspaper in question is established, since that is the place where the harmful event originated and from which the libel was issued and put into circulation.

25. The court of the place where the publisher of the defamatory publication is established must therefore have jurisdiction to hear the action for damages for all the harm caused by the unlawful act.

26. However, that forum will generally coincide with the head of jurisdiction set out in the first paragraph of Article 2 of the Convention.

27. As the Court held in *Mines de Potasse d'Alsace*, the plaintiff must consequently have the option to bring proceedings also in the place where the damage occurred, since otherwise Article 5(3) of the Convention would be rendered meaningless.

28. The place where the damage occurred is the place where the event giving rise to the damage, entailing tortious, delictual or quasi-delictual liability, produced its harmful effects upon the victim.

29. In the case of an international libel through the press, the injury caused by a defamatory publication to the honour, reputation and good name of a natural or legal person occurs in the places where the publication is distributed, when the victim is known in those places.

30. It follows that the courts of each Contracting State in which the defamatory publication was distributed and in which the victim claims to have suffered injury to his reputation have jurisdiction to rule on the injury caused in that State to the victim's reputation.

31. In accordance with the requirement of the sound administration of justice, the basis of the rule of special jurisdiction in Article 5(3), the courts of each Contracting State in which the defamatory publication was

distributed and in which the victim claims to have suffered injury to his reputation are territorially the best placed to assess the libel committed in that State and to determine the extent of the corresponding damage.

32. Although there are admittedly disadvantages to having different courts ruling on various aspects of the same dispute, the plaintiff always has the option of bringing his entire claim before the courts either of the defendant's domicile or of the place where the publisher of the defamatory publication is established.

33. In light of the foregoing, the answer to the first, second, third and sixth questions referred by the House of Lords must be that, on a proper construction of the expression 'place where the harmful event occurred' in Article 5(3) of the Convention, the victim of a libel by a newspaper article distributed in several Contracting States may bring an action for damages against the publisher either before the courts of the Contracting State of the place where the publisher of the defamatory publication is established, which have jurisdiction to award damages for all the harm caused by the defamation, or before the courts of each Contracting State in which the publication was distributed and where the victim claims to have suffered injury to his reputation, which have jurisdiction to rule solely in respect of the harm caused in the State of the court seised.

The fourth, fifth and seventh questions

34. The national court's fourth, fifth and seventh questions, which should be considered together, essentially ask whether, in determining whether it has jurisdiction *qua* court of the place where the damage occurred pursuant to Article 5(3) of the Convention as interpreted by the Court, it is required to follow specific rules different from those laid down by its national law in relation to the criteria for assessing whether the event in question is harmful and in relation to the evidence required of the existence and extent of the harm alleged by the victim of the defamation.

35. In order to reply to those questions, it must first be noted that the object of the Convention is not to unify the rules of substantive law and of procedure of the different Contracting States, but to determine which court has jurisdiction in disputes relating to civil and commercial matters in relations between the Contracting States and to facilitate the enforcement of judgments (see Case C-365/88 *Hagen* v *Zeehaghe* [1990] ECR I-1845, paragraph 17).

36. Moreover, the Court has consistently held that, as regards procedural rules, reference must be made to the national rules applicable by the national court, provided that the application of those rules does not impair the effectiveness of the Convention (paragraphs 19 and 20 of the same judgment).

37. In the area of non-contractual liability, the context in which the questions referred have arisen, the sole object of the Convention is to determine which court or courts have jurisdiction to hear the dispute by reference to the place or places where an event considered harmful occurred.

38. It does not, however, specify the circumstances in which the event giving rise to the harm may be considered to be harmful to the victim, or the evidence which the plaintiff must adduce before the court seised to enable it to rule on the merits of the case.

39. Those questions must therefore be settled solely by the national court seised, applying the substantive law determined by its national conflict of laws rules, provided that the effectiveness of the Convention is not thereby impaired.

40. The fact that under the national law applicable to the main proceedings damage is presumed in libel actions, so that the plaintiff does not have to adduce evidence of the existence and extent of that damage, does not therefore preclude the application of Article 5(3) of the Convention in determining which courts have territorial jurisdiction to hear the action for damages for harm caused by an international libel through the press.

41. The answer to the referring court must accordingly be that the criteria for assessing whether the event in question is harmful and the evidence required of the existence and extent of the harm alleged by the victim of the defamation are not governed by the Convention but by the substantive law determined by the national conflict of laws rules of the court seised, provided that the effectiveness of the Convention is not thereby impaired.

On those grounds, the Court, in answer to the questions referred to it by the House of Lords, by order of 1 March 1993, hereby rules:

1. On a proper construction of the expression 'place where the harmful event occurred' in Article 5(3) of the Convention of 27 September 1968 on Jurisdiction and the Enforcement of Judgments in Civil and Commercial Matters, as amended by the Convention of 9 October 1978 on the accession of the Kingdom of Denmark, Ireland and the United Kingdom of Great Britain and Northern Ireland and by the Convention of 25 October 1982 on the accession of the Hellenic Republic, the victim of a libel by a newspaper article distributed in several Contracting States may bring an action for damages against the publisher either before the courts of the Contracting State of the place where the publisher of the defamatory publication is established, which have jurisdiction to award damages for all the harm caused by the defamation, or before the courts of each Contracting State in which the publication was distributed and where the victim claims to have suffered injury to his reputation, which have jurisdiction to rule solely in respect of the harm caused in the State of the court seised.

2. The criteria for assessing whether the event in question is harmful and the evidence required of the existence and extent of the harm alleged by the victim of the defamation are not governed by the Convention but by the substantive law determined by the national conflict of laws rules of the court seised, provided that the effectiveness of the Convention is not thereby impaired.

OPINION OF MR ADVOCATE GENERAL DARMON

1. By order of 1 March 1993, the House of Lords seeks from the Court a preliminary ruling on the interpretation of Article 5(3) of the Brussels Convention of 27 September 1968 on jurisdiction and the enforcement of judgments in civil and commercial matters (hereinafter 'the Convention'), in the context of the delicate problem of ascertaining the place where the harmful event occurred in the case of defamation by a newspaper article.

2. The facts of the main action, which it is not necessary to go into at length, may be summarised as follows. Miss Shevill, who is domiciled in Great Britain, and three companies established in different Contracting States consider that they have been defamed by an article in the newspaper *France-Soir* suggesting that they were involved in a drug-trafficking network. On 17 October 1989 they brought proceedings before the High Court of England and Wales against Press Alliance SA, the publisher of *France-Soir*, for damages for the harm allegedly suffered by them both in France and in other States, as well as in

England and Wales. They pursued their claim despite the insertion in a later edition of a 'rectification' intended to make good the harm done to their reputation. Press Alliance contested the jurisdiction of the court applied to, alleging the absence of any harmful event. The plaintiffs in the main proceedings limited their claim in the course of the proceedings solely to damages for the harm occasioned in England and Wales.

3. Following the dismissal at first instance and on appeal of the application to strike out the action on the ground of lack of jurisdiction, the House of Lords, hearing the case on further appeal from the Court of Appeal, considered it necessary to seek a ruling from the Court of Justice.

4. Before the questions submitted for a preliminary ruling are discussed, it is necessary to establish whether an action for compensation for harm to a person's reputation and/or honour occurring as a result of a newspaper article falls within the scope of tort or delict within the meaning of Article 5(3).

5. It should be borne in mind that that provision establishes, by way of derogation from the principle laid down in Article 2 of the Convention whereby jurisdiction is conferred on the courts of the State in which the defendant is domiciled, and as an alternative thereto, that 'in matters relating to tort, delict or quasi-delict' special jurisdiction is to be conferred on the 'courts for the place where the harmful event occurred'.

6. With the notable exception of the judgment in *Tessili* v *Dunlop*, in which it was held that the 'place of performance of the obligation' within the meaning of Article 5(1) was to be determined in accordance with the national law governing the obligation in question, the Court has held that the concepts contained in the Convention should generally be given an independent interpretation.

7. In its judgment in *Kalfelis*, the Court further defined the concept of 'matters relating to tort, delict or quasi-delict' as covering '... all actions which seek to establish the liability of a defendant and which are not related to a "contract" within the meaning of Article 5(1)'.

8. Although very broad, the Court has limited its scope to actions for damages other than those, such as the *action paulienne* in French law, the purpose of which is not 'to have the debtor ordered to make good the damage he has caused his creditor by his fraudulent conduct, but to render ineffective, as against his creditor, the disposition which the debtor has made'.

9. Insofar as its purpose is to make good the damage resulting from an unlawful act, an action for defamation falls within the scope of Article 5(3). That is, at least, the prevailing view expressed by academic lawyers.

10. Furthermore, defamation is formally proscribed by the Universal Declaration of Human Rights, Article 12 of which provides:

'No one shall be subjected to arbitrary interference with his privacy, family, home or correspondence, nor to attacks upon his honour and reputation. Everyone has the right to the protection of the law against such interference or attacks'.

11. Although protection against 'such attacks' constitutes a recognised fundamental principle, there are striking differences between the laws of the Contracting States. Taking as an example the laws of France and England alone,

the former requires, as a condition of the tort, that there must be an intention to cause harm, so that there is no tort if good faith is established, whereas under English law the tort (known as 'libel') is committed where the writing is regarded as defamatory by the jury, without there being any requirement for the person harmed to show actual damage and without any consideration of the question of good faith. On the other hand, the reverse applies in relation to invasion of privacy, protection against which is particularly effective under French law. As Professor Badinter has written: '... by virtue of the recognition of a subjective right to privacy, any prejudice thereto is *ipso facto* wrongful, without there being any need for the person concerned to prove that he has suffered special harm'.

12. This difference of approach in relation to the protection of the victim, who is confronted with a diversity of laws applicable depending on the rules of conflict applied by the forum where the proceedings are brought (a diversity due to the calling in question and, on occasion, the abandonement of the traditional rule requiring the application of the law of the place where a tort has been committed) shows, if proof were needed, that the assertion of jurisdiction in favour of one forum as against another is not a neutral matter.

13. I now turn to an analysis of the seven questions submitted to the Court for a preliminary ruling, which may be reorganised under three headings relating respectively to the place where the harmful event occurred (Question 1), the possible limitation, where it is recognised that there is more than one competent forum, of the jurisdiction of each court within whose judicial district harm has occurred (Question 3) and the concept of damage, the standard of proof and the possible consequences of plurality of jurisdiction (Questions 2, 4, 5, 6 and 7).

I - The place where the harmful event occurred

14. As Mrs Gaudemet-Tallon has written:

'The wording of Article 5(3) creates difficulties of interpretation in three types of situation: where the place of the event giving rise to the damage and the place where the damage occurs are not the same, where the applicant suffers "ricochet" damage, and, lastly, where it is difficult to ascertain the place in which the damage occurred'.

15. The first of those situations was examined by the Court in its judgment in *Bier* v *Mines de Potasse d'Alsace*, the second was considered in the judgment in *Dumez France and Tracoba* and the third forms the subject-matter of the present case.

16. The *Mines de Potasse d'Alsace* case concerned cross-border pollution, responsibility for which was thought to lie with an undertaking established in France, causing harm to a horticultural undertaking domiciled in the Netherlands. The Netherlands court hearing the dispute, before whom the defendant raised the objection of lack of competence, asked the Court whether 'the place where the harmful event occurred' was to be understood as meaning the place where the damage occurred or the place where the event having the damage as its sequel occurred.

17. The Court, in its analysis of the basis of the special jurisdiction provided for in Article 5, held that 'this freedom of choice was introduced having regard to the existence, in certain clearly defined situations, of a particularly close connecting factor between a dispute and the court which may be called upon to hear it, with a view to the efficacious conduct of the proceedings'.

18. The Court held, therefore, without specifically taking into consideration the need to protect the victim, that the expression 'the place where the harmful event occurred' encompassed both '... the place where the damage occurred and the place of the event giving rise to it'.

19. The Court took the opportunity in the *Dumez* judgment to point out that the jurisdictional rule contained in Article 5(3) supports the need for a close connecting factor between the dispute and the court hearing the case, that is to say, the need for the sound administration of justice.

20. Consequently, the Court considered that 'the rule on jurisdiction laid down in Article 5(3) of the Convention of 27 September 1968 ... cannot be interpreted as permitting a plaintiff pleading damage which he claims to be the consequence of the harm suffered by other persons who were direct victims of the harmful act to bring proceedings against the perpetrator of that act in the courts of the place in which he himself ascertained the damage to his assets'.

21. The Court identified in those cases the independent concept of 'the place where the harmful event occurred', thereby departing from the position adopted by it in its judgment in *Tessili*, involving the notion of the place of performance of an obligation; it again adopted that position in its recent decision in *Custom Made Commercial*, in which it held, in the context of Article 5(1) that '... the place of performance of the obligation to pay the price is to be determined pursuant to the substantive law governing the obligation in dispute under the conflict rules of the court seised ...'.

22. In his Opinion in *Mines de Potasse d'Alsace*, Advocate General Capotorti stated, in terms still apposite today, that he favoured an independent definition of the concept of 'the place where the harmful event occurred'.

23. Furthermore, such a policy finds approval amongst the prevailing body of academic opinion, intended as it is to prevent position or - more worryingly - negative conflicts of jurisdiction.

24. However, in the view of the United Kingdom and the German Government, the question of uniqueness or plurality of harmful events falls within the scope of the national laws of each Contracting State. The Commission and the French and Spanish Governments, by contrast, suggest that there should be a Community definition both of the place where the damage occurred and of that of the event giving rise to it.

25. The latter solution would appear to reflect the purpose of the Convention, which is to allocate disputes consistently, and thus in accordance with an independent criterion, amongst the courts of the Contracting States, and which forms part of the logic underlying the Court's judgments in *Mines de Potasse d'Alsace* and *Dumez*.

26. The first of those judgments resulted, in certain Contracting States, in

the creation of a new class of jurisdiction. On the other hand, the second excluded any jurisdiction founded on damage suffered indirectly by a victim.

27. It would be paradoxical, at the very least, if the effectiveness of Article 5(3) were to be compromised in the event of variation, from one Contracting State to the next, in the location of the tortious act and thus of the competent forum.

28. Whilst it is certainly true that the diversity of the solutions offered by a comparative study of the laws of the Contracting States signally complicates the choice to be made, it must not bar the exercise altogether.

29. A brief comparative study is called for since, as the Court has pointed out, the interpretation of Article 5(3) in that context must also '... [avoid] any upheaval in the solutions worked out in the various national systems of law, since it looks to unification, in conformity with Article 5(3) of the Convention, by way of a systematization of solutions which, as to their principle, have already been established in most of the States concerned'.

30. In German law, jurisdiction is vested both in the courts of the place of publication and in those of the place of distribution, provided, in the latter case, that the distribution was effected by the publisher or was foreseeable by him. Under the national system, any court, whatever the basis of its jurisdiction, may order compensation for the whole of the damage. According to certain academic writers, that solution should also prevail in the international sphere, even though there has never, to my knowledge, been any decision to that effect.

31. Thus, according to Geimer and Schütze,

'*Die konkurrierende Zuständigkeit am Handlungs-wie am Erfolgsort eröffnet eine Klagemögluchkeit für den gesamten Schaden, wo immer er auch entstanden ist, nicht nur für den im Hoheitsgebiet des Gerichtsstaates entstandenen Schaden*'.

32. That is also Mr Kropholler's view:

'*So besteht bei der durch ein Druckerzeugnis verübten unerlaubten Handlung eine internationale Zuständigkeit nicht nur am Ort der Herstellung, sondern auch an den unter Umständen sehr zahlreichen Orten, an denen es bestimmungsgemäß verbreitet wird*'.

33. In Belgian law, the national courts appear to accept jurisdiction where a constituent element of the tort (distribution, publication) has been committed in Belgium, but without any recognition of the conferment of cumulative jurisdiction on the forums seised on the basis of those two elements. Academic writers generally consider that where any one of those forums is seised of the matter it must necessarily be competent, whatever the basis on which it is thus seised, to order compensation for the whole of the damage caused.

34. In French law, solutions to the problem of cross-border torts committed in the press have emerged in the context of invasion of privacy. The second indent in Article 46 of the New Code of Civil Procedure allows the plaintiff to sue either in the courts of the defendant's domicile or in those of the place of the causal event or, lastly, in those in whose judicial district the damage has been suffered. The choice between those two latter forums has been understood as relating, first, to the courts for the place in which publication

occurred and, second, to those for the places where distribution was effected. Whilst the former are competent to hear and determine claims in respect of the whole of the damage, wherever it may have occurred, the latter can only order compensation in respect of the harm suffered within their judicial district. As will be seen, certain academic writers have criticised the decisions given to that effect.

35. In Luxembourg law, Article 37 of the Code of Civil Procedure provides that 'in cases involving compensation for damage caused by tort, delict or quasi-delict, the plaintiff may sue, at his option, either before the courts for the place where the defendant is domiciled or before those for the place where the harmful event occurred'. The expression 'the place where the harmful event occurred' has not been clarified by the courts, but the prevailing view amongst academic writers, relying on the decisions of the French courts, is that '... in cases involving invasion of privacy by the press, it is acknowledged that the courts of the country in which distribution took place are competent to hear and determine claims for compensation for the damage resulting therefrom, as well as the courts of the country in which publication occurred...'.

36. The laws of Spain and Italy confer jurisdiction to award compensation for the whole of the damage solely on the courts for the place where the publication was printed and initially distributed, irrespective of where the damage occurred. Thus a central forum is designated in such matters.

37. The criterion applied in the United Kingdom and Ireland to determine the competent forum is the communication to a third party of material regarded by the victim as having harmed his reputation. However, although it has not proved possible to discover any decision by the English courts on the scope of jurisdiction where the damage has been suffered in more than one State, it appears from a judgment of the Supreme Court of Ireland that 'the extent of publication' constitutes a relevant factor in calculating the amount of the compensation sought.

38. In Portugal, the question of competence in cases of defamation in the press has been resolved principally in the context of the criminal law. Whilst in certain judgments it is the place of despatch of defamatory correspondence which has been held to be the decisive factor, in others it has been held to be the place of receipt.

39. Lastly, in the Netherlands, jurisdiction is conferred only on the courts for the place where the defendant is domiciled or, failing that, where he resides. If he is neither domiciled nor resident in the Netherlands, the *forum actoris* is adopted.

40. The diversity of the solutions adopted by the internal legal systems of the Contracting States reflects the difficulty in ascertaining the place where the damage arose in the event that such damage is non-material. Mrs Gaudemet-Tallon is accordingly quite correct in her observation that 'the *Mines de Potasse d'Alsace* decision is not easy to apply in the absence of agreement on the place where the event occurred and the place where the damage arose'.

41. Looking beyond those differences, however, it is possible to identify the twin criteria of publication or printing, on the one hand, and distribution or

communication, on the other, even though certain legal systems take only one of the two connecting factors into consideration, to the exclusion of the other, whereas other systems allow a choice to be made between the jurisdictions thus designated.

42. Some commentators have expressed doubt as to the relevance of those criteria, insisting, at least in the field of non-material damage, that the significant factor is the domicile of the victim, which is to be regarded as the place where the damage arose. Mrs Gaudemet-Tallon considers in that regard that the concept of distribution covers both the causal event and the harm itself, the result being that, even though publication may constitute the 'primary' cause, the 'secondary' cause is distribution. Consequently, for the purposes of the choice of jurisdiction, the place in which the victim is domiciled is to be regarded as that in which the damage arose.

43. According to Mr Bourel, '... that author's classification of the fact of distribution as a "generative act" stretches the bounds of reality somewhat'.

He continues:

'Furthermore, the expression "causal event", substituted for "generative act", is a good illustration of the difficulty in drawing a distinction here between the fact from which the damage originates and the damage itself. It shows, by means of the concept of causality thus introduced, the close link between the two elements making up civil liability and the difficulty in separating them from each other in terms of their spatial connection. If distribution is the final causal act, it must also be by such distribution that the damage is created and assumes concrete form'.

44. In the result, Mr Bourel states that he too is in favour of the attribution of jurisdiction to the courts of the victim's domicile, '... in the sense of ... the place where the tort taken as a whole, came into being'; in his view, neither publication nor distribution is of any relevance as regards jurisdiction, since they are 'neutral, unclassifiable and thus of no practical application'.

45. However, to sanction that forum would be tantamount to conferring jurisdiction on the *forum actoris*, an attribution to which, as the Court has pointed out on numerous occasions, the Convention is hostile. Thus it observed in its judgment in *Dumez* that '... the hostility of the Convention towards the attribution of jurisdiction to the courts of the plaintiff's domicile was demonstrated by the fact that the second paragraph of Article 3 precluded the application of national provisions attributing jurisdiction to such courts for proceedings against defendants domiciled in the territory of a Contracting State'.

46. Furthermore, that forum does not appear particularly to meet the requirements of the sound administration of justice, to which the Court has drawn attention in several of its judgments, even though it in fact allows the procedure to be centralised, as, after all, does the forum of the defendant's domicile. The example given by the United Kingdom is particularly apposite, concerning an Italian actor domiciled in England where he is totally unknown. An Italian newspaper not circulated in England damages his reputation. Even if the courts of the plaintiff's domicile were accepted as having jurisdiction, he

could bring proceedings before the English courts without there being any justification for such forum from the standpoint of the sound administration of justice.

47. Finally, it will be noted that none of the legal systems of any of the Contracting States has sanctioned the attribution of jurisdiction to that forum.

48. It is appropriate at this point to concentrate on the spatial separation of the two criteria for jurisdiction as regards the place of damage, namely the place where it arises and the place where the event giving rise to it occurred.

49. In *Mines de Potasse d'Alsace*, the separation of those two elements was, from the outset, not in doubt. Furthermore, as the Court pointed out in its judgment in *Dumez*: '... the judgment in *Mines de Potasse d'Alsace* related to a situation in which the damage - to crops in the Netherlands - occurred at some distance from the event giving rise to the damage - the discharge of saline waste into the Rhine by an undertaking established in France - but by the direct effect of the causal agent, namely the saline waste which had moved physically from one place to another'.

50. In the present case, the Commission and the Spanish and French Governments concur in their view that the event giving rise to the damage occurs in the place of publication of the periodical at issue, and that the damage arises in each of the Contracting States in which, as a result of the voluntary distribution of the text, a person's reputation is harmed. The United Kingdom considers for its part that the place of communication to third parties constitutes that of both the event giving rise to the damage and the damage itself.

51. It will be noted from a simple reference to the judgment in *Mines de Potasse d'Alsace* that the Court emphasized the significance, as criteria governing jurisdiction, of the 'place of the event giving rise to the damage' and the 'place where the damage occurred' in a case in which a causal event gave rise to a *single* instance of damage.

52. In the present case, the situation is more complex, involving as it does a causal event giving rise to *more than one* instance of damage. The harm occurs in the place of the final element making up the tort, that is to say, in the case of torts committed in a newspaper or in radio or television programmes, in each State where the newspaper is distributed or the broadcast programme is received. In objective terms, the place in which the causal event directly giving rise to such damage occurs is that in which the newspaper is published or the programme is broadcast.

53. Damage to a person's reputation and/or honour arises in the various places where a defamatory remark is revealed to third parties. Consequently, the damage becomes apparent when that 'information' is brought into public knowledge; the publication of the newspaper at issue constitutes the vehicle by which it is transmitted. Thus there is clearly a geographical separation between the causal event and the damage.

54. The scheme imposed by the decision in Mines de Potasse d'Alsace presents the problem, in relation to cross-border torts committed in the form of newspaper articles, that it gives rise to a multiplicity of competent jurisdictions, with the result that some commentators have proposed the adoption of specific criteria.

55. Thus, according to Lasok and Stone, '... it is thought that the *Bier* decision does not preclude the eventual adoption of specific rules for particular torts; e.g. a rule that for the purposes of defamation by a single publication, the relevant place is that of the publication to the third person'.

56. Kaye, for his part, states that '... it is considered that in the context of Article 5(3), when a defamatory statement is uttered, written, broadcast or posted in State A, published in State B and causes damage to reputation in State C (to which news of the publication spread by natural processes), it is the defendant's act in State A which should be held to be the event giving rise to the damage and consequently the harmful event for the purposes of Article 5(3)...'.

57. It is certainly true that such an approach avoids the multiplication of competent forums, which is one of the purposes of the Convention. However, quite apart from the fact that the principle of proximity cannot justify preference being given either to the courts for the place where the causal event occurred or to those for the place where the damage arose, it is my view, as I stated in my Opinion in *Dumez*, that the exclusion of one of those connecting factors in certain cases and of the other factor in other cases could undermine the consistency of the Court's case-law.

58. Thus, the plaintiff could bring the proceedings, at his option, either before the courts of the defendant's domicile, the courts of the place of the causal event or the courts of the place or places in which the damage arose.

59. The question immediately arises as to the scope of the jurisdiction of those courts, particularly those in whose judicial district an allegedly defamatory text has been distributed.

II - Scope of jurisdiction of the courts for the place in which the damage arose

60. Apart, therefore, from the courts of the place where the defendant is domiciled, those of the place of the causal event are competent in respect of the whole of the damage which has arisen, since all such damage originates from the unlawful act. On the other hand, do the courts within whose judicial district damage has arisen have jurisdiction to order compensation for the whole of the damage, including that which has arisen in other States?

61. I have referred above to the position of Geimer and Schütze, and also that of Mr Kropholler, all of whom consider that the courts of the place where the damage arose must necessarily be able to hear and determine claims in respect of the whole of the damage suffered, not only within their own judicial district but also in the territory of other Contracting States. However, Mr Kropholler is at pains to point out the danger of 'forum shopping' inherent in such an approach.

62. By contrast, Mr Lagarde, in an article much commented upon, has expressed the view that 'where an act gives rise to damage *in more than one country*, the courts of the place where that act was committed (in this case the courts of the place of publication) should hear and determine claims in respect of the whole of the damage caused by that act, wherever it may have arisen, since

each instance of such damage is connected in its entirety to that act. On the other hand, a court in one of the places where the damage arose can only be competent to hear and determine claims in respect of the harmful consequences of the act in the country in which it sits, since there exists no connection between the damage caused in another country and that court, by virtue of either the place where it arose or the place where the wrongful act was committed'.

63. Support for that view has been expressed by Mr Droz, as well as Gothot and Holleaux. Mr Huet has likewise taken the view, in a note on the judgment in *Mines de Potasse d'Alsace*, that where an unlawful act causes multiple damage in different places,

'the applicant is consequently able to sue in any of the courts in whose judicial district any damage has arisen...'.

64. That analysis is shared by most French courts, which do not regard themselves as competent to order compensation for any damage suffered in other Contracting States where the unlawful act has been committed in one of those other States.

65. Whilst the solution advocated by the German authors has the undeniable merit of avoiding a multiplicity of competent forums, it appears primarily to be prompted by a desire to protect the victim, who would thus not be obliged, in order to obtain compensation for the whole of the damage suffered, to sue in each of the courts of the Contracting States in whose judicial district damage had arisen.

66. However, I scarcely need to repeat that both the courts of the place of the causal event and those of the defendant's domicile already constitute two central forums having unlimited jurisdiction.

67. Besides, particularly in cases such as this, where the victim would be able, in practice, to sue in any of the courts in any of the Contracting States, such a solution would appear to conflict with the spirit of the Convention, which certainly does not favour 'forum shopping' but seeks instead to ensure the proper organisation of the attribution of special jurisdiction. It is obvious that the victim, confronted with such a system, would be bound to choose the forum in which he felt that he would be best compensated for the damage suffered by him.

68. First, it is clear from the Court's case-law that '... the "special jurisdictions" enumerated in Articles 5 and 6 of the Convention constitute derogations from the principle that jurisdiction is vested in the courts of the State where the defendant is domiciled and as such must be interpreted restrictively.

69. Second, such a solution would encourage the proliferation of concurrent forums. It should be borne in mind, as the Court pointed out in its judgment in *Effer* v *Kantner*, that '... the Convention provides a collection of rules which are designed *inter alia* to avoid the occurrence, in civil and commercial matters, of concurrent litigation in two or more Member States and which, in the interests of legal certainty and for the benefit of the parties, confer jurisdiction upon the national court territorially best qualified to determine a dispute'.

70. Above all, however, it does not appear to me to form any part of the principles established by the line of decisions commencing with the judgment in *Mines de Potasse d'Alsace*. The courts of the place of the causal event have

jurisdiction in respect of the whole of the damage arising from the unlawful act. They therefore constitute, along with the courts of the defendant's domicile, a firm basis of reference in respect of the whole of the damage. By contrast, in a situation such as that in the present case, the jurisdiction of the courts of the places where the damage arises is founded solely on the notion '... of a particularly close connecting factor between a dispute and the court which may be called upon to hear it, with a view to the efficacious conduct of the proceedings'.

71. Consequently, the courts of one of the places where damage arose cannot hear proceedings for compensation for damage arising in other Contracting States, inasmuch as there is no element of proximity connecting the forum with the dispute.

72. It cannot be denied that the main problem with such limitation of jurisdiction lies in the proliferation of competent forums and, consequently, in the danger of conflicting - abut not irreconcilable - decisions delivered by the courts seised. On the other hand, it is in conformity with many of the objectives of the Convention, as noted by the Court.

73. First, the courts of the place where the damage arises are best placed to assess the harm done to the victim's reputation within their judicial district, and to determine the extent of the damage.

74. Second, the adoption of such a criterion avoids the occurence of concurrent litigation in different forums. Its effect is that the competence of each of them is restricted to the damage arising within their respective judicial districts.

75. Third, the aim of providing legal protection can only be satisfied if the rules governing jurisdiction are foreseeable, a requirement to which the Court referred in its judgments in *Handte* and *Custom Made Commercial.* The defendant will be in a position to know precisely, on the basis of the place in which the newspapers are distributed, before which court or courts it risks being sued and the pleas on which it may be able to rely in its defence, having regard to the applicable law.

76. Lastly, in this area more than in any other, the restrictive interpretation of the rules of special jurisdiction calls for the solution which I am proposing. It should in that regard be borne in mind, as the Court held in *Kalfelis*, '... that a court which has jurisdiction under Article 5(3) over an action insofar as it is based on tort or delict does not have jurisdiction over that action insofar as it is not so based'.

77. It has previously been suggested by me that a claim founded simultaneously in tort, contract and unjust enrichment should be governed exclusively by the rules laid down for contractual matters by Article 5(1), having regard to the need to rationalise jurisdiction and to centralise the proceedings before a single forum.

78. That conclusion results both from the grounds of such a claim, based as they are for the most part on the non-performance of contractual obligations, and on the fact that the court dealing with the contract is best placed to understand its context and its implications as regards legal proceedings.

79. My view in this case does not in any way conflict with that to which I have just referred. In circumstances such as those in *Kalfelis*, the existence of a single court for the contract would allow an *objective* centralisation, without any risk of 'forum shopping'. In the present case, on the other hand, that risk would be considerable if, in order to avoid the problem of multiple forums, one such forum could be chosen by the plaintiff with a view to obtaining - for reasons of procedural and substantive legal strategy - compensation for the harm allegedly suffered in the territory of several Contracting States. As I have stated above, it is already possible for proceedings to be centralised in the courts of the defendant's domicile or in those of the causal event. Such centralisation should not be additionally obtainable by virtue of any special - and let me repeat, restrictive - jurisdiction.

80. Thus, to repeat the expression used by Mr Huet, there is certainly a 'fragmentation of international jurisdiction'. He has therefore suggested in a recent article that the Court's decision in *Shenavai* should be applied, by extension, to cross-border torts concerning invasion of privacy.

81. It will be recalled that the Court considered in that case that, where the dispute concerns a number of obligations arising under the same contract, '... the court before which the matter is brought will, when determining whether it has jurisdiction, be guided by the maxim *accessorium sequitur principale*; in other words, where various obligations are at issue, it will be the principal obligation which will determine its jurisdiction'.

82. According to Mr Huet, 'If transposed to matters of tort or delict, and particularly to invasions of privacy resulting from media exposure in several countries, the principle accessorium sequitur principale would enable the victim of multiple damage (occurring in the various places where distribution took place) to bring a single action before the courts of the place where the main harm suffered by him arose (such "main" damage not having necessarily arisen in the country where the magazine is published)'.

83. That author therefore seeks, without proposing the abandonment of the traditional criterion of the *locus delicti commissi*, to rectify its effects in situations where to apply it automatically might lead to a fragmentation of jurisdiction between several forums.

84. Attractive though that approach may be, and although the court must ascertain whether it has jurisdiction *ratione materiae*, I do not think that the intention of the Convention was to bind the court's jurisdiction to an assessment of the substance of the dispute; it is based upon an objective, impersonal view of the link of proximity, which cannot vary according to the specific nature of a given case. It may be very difficult, if not possible, to determine the 'main damage' in the case of international celebrities, particularly when they have no connection, in terms of nationality or residence, with the Community.

85. On the other hand, however, it is in the majority of cases a necessary, if sometimes delicate, task to determine objectively the place where the principal contractual obligation is to be performed.

86. Indeed, that approach was suggested by some of the interveners in *Mines de Potasse d'Alsace* and rejected by Advocate General Capotorti as follows:

'It would also be difficult to reconcile adoption of a criterion of the "most signficant connection" with the intention of the Convention to make it easy to determine the court having jurisdiction, on the basis of clear, precise and sufficiently objective criteria which could thus be applied uniformly in all the States adhering to the Convention. In this respect insufficient assurances are afforded by a criterion, such as that referred to above, which does not lend itself to abstract definition and which tends to rely upon the subjective appraisal of the court'.

87. Moreover, we appear here to be 'on the fringes' of civil matters, so that it seems preferable to adhere, within certain limits, to the concept of territoriality.

88. Furthermore, it was that concept which prompted those drafting the Community Patent Convention to insert in it Article 69(2), worded as follows: 'Actions for infringement of a Community patent may also be heard before the courts of the Contracting State in which an act of infringement was committed. The court hearing the action shall have jurisdiction only in respect of acts of infringement committed within the territory of that State'.

III - The concept of damage, the standard of proof and the consequences of allowing a plurality of forums

(A) 89. In asking the second, fourth and fifth questions, the national court seeks guidance as to the existence of damage where the law applicable to the tort or delict (English law in the present case) does not require the person claiming to be the victim of defamation to prove, first, that he or she was known to certain readers and, second, that he or she suffered actual harm, such harm being, as we have seen, presumed.

90. I have already drawn attention to the independent nature of the concept of 'matters relating to tort, delict or quasi-delict', as identified by the Court in its judgment in *Kalfelis*. Since an attack on the reputation of another person constitutes a 'harmful event' within the meaning of Article 5(3), and given the broad scope of that provision, any action which seeks compensation for damage resulting from the breach of a legal obligation other than one arising from the existence of contractual relations between the parties must be regarded as falling within its ambit.

91. It is necessary, however, to go beyond that somewhat general definition, and to specify the factors constituting the damage? That is the question to which the House of Lords seeks an answer.

92. Neither the Commission nor the interveners have sought to maintain that, for the purposes of the uniform application of the Convention, there was any need to unify the substantive law relating to tortious liability.

93. That is my view also, since the objective of the Convention is to allocate *jurisdiction* consistently amongst the courts of the Contracting States and not to unify the rules concerning the substantive law.

94. That is also the prevailing view amongst academic writers, particularly Mr Kaye, who states: '... no effort should be made, as part of the attempt to develop a uniform Convention concept, to define whether particular *facts* are to

be held to give rise to tortious liability or not, since it is not the function of the European Court, in drawing up such a definition, to stipulate whether tortious or any other form of liability *ought* to exist in a particular fact situation and reference must always be made to the applicable national law in order to determine the characteristics of the liability, if any, which is the subject of the national court proceedings...'.

95. It is for the national court alone, therefore, to determine, in accordance with the law applicable to the tort or delict, the circumstances in which damage arises.

96. The same applies in relation to the applicable procedural rules. I would merely draw attention in that regard to the Court's judgment in *Kongress Agentur Hagen*, in which it stated: '... the object of the Convention is not to unify procedural rules but to determine which court has jurisdiction in disputes relating to civil and commercial matters in intra-Community relations and to facilitate the enforcement of judgments. It is therefore necessary to draw a clear distinction between jurisdiction and the conditions governing the admissibility of an action'.

(B) 97. In asking the sixth question, the House of Lords seeks to know whether its decision to accept jurisdiction must be subject to the absence of any risk that the courts of another Contracting State, which also have jurisdiction, may arrive at a different solution.

98. As I have already stated, the jurisdiction of the courts of a Contracting State in which damage arises is limited to that part of the damage which occurred within their judicial district; consequently, where two courts are called upon, following the occurrence of the same causal event, to hear a claim for compensation for the damage, they do not have concurrent jurisdiction.

99. Article 22, relating to cases where jurisdiction is declined on the grounds of connexity, stipulates jurisdiction of that type as a condition of its application, and is consequently inapplicable. Mrs Gaudemet-Tallon states in that regard, moreover: 'If it is accepted that the courts of the place where damage occurs do not have jurisdiction in respect of any other damage arising from the same causal event but occurring in another Contracting State, Article 22 does not fall to be applied'.

100. Does there not exist, however, the risk that irreconcilable decisions may be given, within the meaning of Article 27(3) of the Convention, where certain courts are prepared to uphold the compensation claim whilst others, by contrast, find against the victim?

101. I do not think so, insofar as the condition of irreconcilability identified by the Court in its judgment in *Hoffmann* v *Krieg* is not met. In that judgment, the Court held that 'in order to ascertain whether the two judgments are irreconcilable within the meaning of Article 27(3), it should be examined whether they entail legal consequences that are mutually exclusive'.

102. The Court found in that judgment that a decision ordering a husband to pay maintenance to his wife was irreconcilable with a decision given in another Contracting State pronouncing the divorce. The present case does not fall within that hypothesis, and even though the decisions given might be regarded as contradictory, they would not be irreconcilable.

103. The recognition of its jurisdiction by the court of the place where the damage arises cannot be compromised on the ground of a risk of conflict between the decision to be given by it and that of a court in another Contracting State which has jurisdiction to order compensation for the damage occuring within its judicial district.

(C) 104. I now turn, lastly, to the seventh question, relating to the standard of proof required of the plaintiff in order to enable the national court to decide whether it has jurisdiction under Article 5(3).

105. The influence of the substance of a dispute on the determination of jurisdiction has previously been analysed by the Court in the case of *Effer*, which concerned Article 5(1) and in which the defendant contested the existence of contractual relations.

106. In his Opinion, Advocate General Reischl considered that 'If it were to be accepted that the presence of a dispute over the existence of a contractual relationship *ipso facto* excludes an action under Article 5(1) of the Convention, then it would be possible by a simple denial on the part of the defendant to render that provision largely ineffective, as well as that in Article 5(3) - jurisdiction in matters relating to tort - where indeed the defendant's defence as a rule consists of denying the existence of a tort'.

107. The Court held that '... the national court's jurisdiction to determine questions relating to a contract includes the power to consider the existence of the constituent parts of the contract itself, since that is indispensable in order to enable the national court in which proceedings are brought to examine whether it has jurisdiction under the Convention'.and that '... respect for the aims and spirit of the Convention demands that that provision should be construed as meaning that the court called upon to decide a dispute arising out of a contract may examine, of its own motion even, the essential preconditions for its jurisdiction, having regard to conclusive and relevant evidence adduced by the party concerned, establishing the existence or the inexistence of the contract'.

108. Thus, a dispute as to the existence of a contract does not preclude jurisdiction under Article 5(1), even if the court is prompted, for the purposes of determining its own jurisdiction, to examine substantive issues.

109. What is involved here is the application of the hallowed rule that it is for each court to determine its own jurisdiction.

110. The outcome is necessarily the same where a court before which proceedings are brought pursuant to Article 5(3) has to give a ruling on an objection to lack of competence raised by a defendant denying the existence of the tort. In order to be able to rule on that objection, the court has to verify, on the basis of the evidence adduced by the plaintiff, whether the defendant did or did not commit an act which might render him liable and giving rise to damage within the judicial district of the court.

111. I am according of the opinion that the questions referred to the Court should be answered as follows: 'In the case of defamation by a newspaper article circulated in more than one Contracting State, Article 5(3) of the Brussels Convention of 27 September 1968 on Jurisdiction and the Enforcement of Judgments in Civil and Commercial Matters must be interpreted as meaning that

the plaintiff may sue either in the courts of the place of publication, which have jurisdiction to order compensation for the whole of the damage arising from the unlawful act, or in the courts of the places where the newspaper is distributed, which have jurisdiction solely in respect of the damage arising, according to the law applicable to the tort or delict, within their judicial district.

The jurisdiction of any of the courts seised by reason of the damage suffered is not affected by the risk of conflicting decisions which may result from the multiplicity of courts having jurisdiction.

The fact that the defendant contests the existence of the factors constituting the tort or delict alleged by the plaintiff cannot in itself deprive the national court of its jurisdiction under Article 5(3).'

OPINION OF MR ADVOCATE GENERAL LÉGER

1. It very infrequently happens that, by reason of the reopening of the oral procedure and as a result of happenstance in the order of business of the Court, Opinions are successively delivered by two Advocates General in the same case.

2. Having been called upon to state my views following delivery of the Opinion of my predecessor, I have found that my task has been eased; I concur, in effect, with the position adopted by him on 14 July 1994, and will merely add a few observations in answer to certain arguments advanced after the delivery of his Opinion, particularly during the second oral procedure.

3. It will be recalled that the facts are as follows: Miss Shevill, domiciled in the United Kingdom, and three companies established in different Contracting States have brought an action for defamation in the High Court against the company which publishes the newspaper '*France-Soir*'. The High Court has dismissed an objection of want of jurisdiction, which has now come before the House of Lords on appeal. The latter court has sought a preliminary ruling from this Court on seven questions.

4. It cannot be seriously disputed that the defamation action falls within the class of actions concerning liability in tort and delict, and is covered by Article 5(3) of the Brussels Convention of 27 September 1968 on jurisdiction and the enforcement of judgments in civil and commercial matters (hereinafter 'the Convention').

5. Mr Darmon suggests that, apart from the courts of the State in which the defendant is domiciled, the courts having jurisdiction to hear and determine an action for defamation by a press article are either those of the place where the publication was printed, which are competent to award compensation in respect of the whole of the damage arising from the unlawful act, *or the courts of each Contracting State in whose territory the article has been distributed*, which have jurisdiction with regard to the specific damage caused in that State.

6. I am satisfied that that view is correct, for the following reasons.

7. As is well known, the jurisdictional options laid down by the rules of special jurisdiction contained in Article 5(3) of the Convention are justified by

reasons relating to '... the sound administration of justice and the efficacious conduct of proceedings'.

8. In circumstances as complex as those of the present case, the determination of the forum must necessarily result from a *compromise*. The point has been made that 'the objective of the sound administration of justice can be achieved only by maintaining a fine balance between, on the one hand, the requirement of *proximity* between the forum and the dispute and, on the other, the need for a degree of jurisdictional *concentration*'.

9. Given that the Convention embodies a *unified* system for the determination of judicial competence, the prime objective must be the designation of a *centralized forum*. The problem here lies in the special nature of non-material or non-pecuniary damage: it is difficult to identify, assess and compensate. Significantly, in certain areas of intellectual property law, such as that of trade marks, which also recognizes damage of that kind, international jurisdiction in cases of infringement is determined not according to the damage caused but on the basis of the *sole causal event*: the act of infringement itself.

10. That interpretation accords squarely with the case-law of the Court. Thus, according to Messrs Bischoff and Huet, commenting on the judgment in *Rüffer*, '... one of the major threads running through the Court's case-law on the interpretation of the Convention is its desire to avoid the "dismemberment" of the issues referred to it (and the jurisdictional fragmentation which that might cause), and to incline instead towards a degree of unification, by applying the maxim *accessorium sequitur principale* and thereby relating the consequential act or matter back to the causative *act or matter*'.

11. Consequently, Mr Darmon rightly concluded in his Opinion that the courts of the place where the publication was printed - that is to say, where the causal event occurred - must be defined as the central forum having jurisdiction to determine the whole of the damage caused throughout the Community.

12. Nevertheless, that forum cannot be the sole forum, for two reasons.

13. First, that forum coincides most frequently - if not invariably - with the courts of the State in which the defendant is domiciled. In its judgment in *Bier*, the Court held that '... to decide in favour only of the place of the event giving rise to the damage would, in an appreciable number of cases, cause confusion between the heads of jurisdiction laid down by Articles 2 and 5(3) of the Convention, so that the latter provision would, to that extent, lose its effectiveness'.

14. Second, the courts of the place where the damage arose (that is to say, the place of distribution) cannot be excluded as a potential forum. They must constitute a possible choice for the purposes of ensuring the '... particularly close connecting factor between the dispute and courts other than those of the State of the defendant's domicile' on which the special jurisdiction attributed by Article 5(3) of the Convention is founded.

15. For example, the victim of defamation arising from the publication in Contracting State A of a newspaper which is also distributed in Contracting State B, where that person is particularly well known, must be able, at his option, to sue in the courts of State A, if he considers that the damage suffered by him

extends to the whole of the Community, or in those of State B, if he considers that the damage is limited to the territory of that latter State.

16. For that reason, it is suggested that the plaintiff should be able, at his option, to sue not only in the courts of the defendant's domicile and those of the place in which the causal event occurred but also in the courts of the place in which the damage arose.

17. That solution obviates any risk of *forum-shopping*: each court before which proceedings are brought in places where distribution has occurred can award compensation for *separate damage*. Moreover, the courts of the place where the article was printed, having jurisdiction in respect of the whole of the damage, will generally apply, as regards damage arising in other Contracting States, the substantive laws of those States.

18. Such a solution accords with the principle that the rules of special jurisdiction must be interpreted restrictively.

19. It confers competence on the courts which are best qualified to assess the damage arising in their locality: the 'particularly close connecting factor' between the court seised and the dispute is undeniable.

20. It is true that one major objection may be raised against such a solution: it gives rise to a potential multiplicity of competent forums, whereas the concentration of proceedings is '... one of the primary objectives of the Convention'.

21. The tendency of the Convention is to avoid the proliferation of forums, because such proliferation increases the *risk of the irreconcilability of judgments*, which constitutes a ground for non-recognition (Article 27(3) and (5) of the Convention) or for refusing an application for enforcement in Contracting States other than that in which such judgments have been given.

22. *No such risk exists in the present case.*

23. It is true that the judgments of courts seised in different Contracting States may conflict with one another, since they are governed by different substantive laws. They will not be irreconcilable, because they will each relate to *compensation for a distinct head of damage* (that arising in the territory of the Contracting State concerned).

24. I would add that, in any event, the plaintiff will always have the option of suing in respect of the whole of his claim before the courts of the defendant's domicile and those of the place in which the causal event occurred.

25. I now turn to the four points which seem to me to be central to the matter following the re-opening of the oral procedure in this case.

26. First, the 'place where the harmful event occurred', within the meaning of Article 5(3), cannot amount to *the place of distribution* of the publication. In commenting on this point I will refer to the arguments submitted by the United Kingdom.

27. Second, the courts of the place in which the damage is suffered cannot constitute an appropriate forum.

28. Third, it appears to me that the solution arrived at in the judgment in *Shenavai* must also be rejected.

29. Fourth, the courts of each place in which distribution takes place cannot be competent to determine the whole of the damage.

I - Determination of the 'place where the harmful event occurred'

30. It is well known that, since delivering its judgment in *Bier*, cited above, the Court has regarded 'the place where the harmful event occurred' as an independent concept. It ruled that 'Where the place of the happening of the event which may give rise to liability in tort, delict or quasi-delict and the place where that event results in damage are not identical...', that expression covers both '... the place where the damage occurred and the place of the event giving rise to it'.

31. The United Kingdom's view as regards defamation is that the place of the causal event is the same as that in which the damage occurred. It is the place in which a defamatory document is communicated to a third party: '... the communication of defamatory material ..., rather than the editing or printing of the newspaper, is the causal event which, both as a matter of English law, and in fact, immediately damages the victim'.

'The communication of the material is the immediate and direct cause of the damage. This act, therefore, constitutes a harmful event, and jurisdiction ... may be taken at the place where it occurred'.

32. I do not agree.

33. In my view, the situation in this case is the same as that with which the judgment in *Bier* was concerned, namely the geographical separation between the causal event and the place where the damage occurred. The places where the newspaper was distributed do not coincide with the place where it was published.

34. Consequently, to maintain that the causal event occurred where the article was distributed is to forego a forum which the Convention, as interpreted in *Bier*, recognizes as being available to the victim.

35. The Court justified that duality of jurisdiction by pointing out, in its judgment in *Bier*, that: '... a decision in favour only of the place where the damage occurred would, in cases where the place of the event giving rise to the damage does not coincide with the domicile of the person liable, have the effect of excluding a *helpful connecting factor with the jurisdiction of a court particularly near to the cause of the damage*'.

36. The solution advocated by the United Kingdom effectively confuses the place where the causal event arose with the place in which the damage occurred, and does not take the Court's case-law into account.

37. Consequently, a distinction must be drawn between the place of the causal event, such as that in which the newspaper was printed, and the place in which the harmful event occurred, such as that in which it was distributed.

II - The courts of the place in which the damage is suffered cannot constitute an appropriate forum

38. In matters relating to tort, delict or quasi-delict, can the words 'place where the harmful event occurred' be construed as meaning the place where the damage is suffered, given that such an interpretation would effectively enshrine the concept of the *forum actoris* since the damage is generally suffered by the victim at his domicile?

39. The Convention is based on the general jurisdictional rule *actor sequitur forum rei,* laid down in Article 2. Only in the exceptional cases restrictively enumerated in Articles 5(2), 8 and 14 does the Convention confer jurisdiction on the *forum actoris*, a forum not contemplated by the ordinarily applicable rules of law: '... save in cases for which express provision is made, the Convention appears to be clearly hostile to the attribution of jurisdiction to the courts of the plaintiff's domicile ...'.

40. Furthermore, it seems to me particularly difficult to bring the *forum actoris* within the framework of the special jurisdiction established by Article 5(3), which makes no express provision for it. That jurisdiction constitutes a derogation from the principle that jurisdiction is vested in the courts of the State of the defendant's domicile, and as such must be interpreted *restrictively*.

41. In matters relating to liability in tort or delict, the Court has never attributed jurisdiction to the courts of the place where the damage is suffered. It has even formally excluded such jurisdiction in the case of an indirect victim. Advocate General Darmon has shown, in his Opinion in the *Marinari* case, currently at the stage of deliberation, that the rationale of Article 5(3) is based not on any compelling need to protect the victim but on '... the existence of a particularly close connecting factor between the dispute and courts other than those of the State of the defendant's domicile ...', and that the courts of the place where the damage was suffered do not meet that requirement.

42. Consequently, I am unable to see how jurisdiction to hear and determine an action for compensation for non-pecuniary damage resulting from defamation can vest in the courts of the place where the damage is suffered, when such special jurisdiction is excluded in actions for compensation for physical damage. Is it conceivable, for example, that a German tourist who has been seriously injured in an accident in Spain should have to sue in the courts of that State - Spain being the place where the damage occurred and where the causal event took place - whereas the victim of defamation perpetrated by a publication should enjoy the benefit of the *forum actoris*?

43. True, it could be maintained that the victim of a defamatory press article is the target of an act which he neither desired nor sought, and that there is no risk that, in conferring jurisdiction on the courts of his domicile, the Court is enabling the victim to choose his forum. Can it be said, however, that the victim of physical damage desired or sought to any greater extent the act from which he suffered? Why should the Court grant to the former a privilege which the Brussels Convention denies to the latter?

44. Lastly, it might be thought that damage as specific as an attack on a

person's reputation or honour is inseparable from that person and that it must necessarily occur in the place where he resides.

45. I am convinced that in such circumstances the place where the damage occurs coincides with the territory in which the publication is distributed. The damage is *severable* from the forum of the victim's domicile, which, as the United Kingdom has clearly shown, does not necessarily have any connection with the damage.

46. Finally, the adoption of the forum of the place where the damage is suffered - and thus of the *forum actoris* - would raise a particular problem in the dispute pending before the national court. Three of the four plaintiffs in the main proceedings are legal persons. How can their domicile be determined? Is it their *seat* or the place where they maintain their principal establishment?

47. The Convention does not define the domicile of legal persons any more than it defines that of natural persons. Article 53 provides that the seat of a company or other legal person is to be treated as its domicile and that, in order to determine that seat, '... the court shall apply its rules of private international law'. The solutions applied by the laws of the different Contracting States vary greatly. As has been pointed out, 'There is the risk that those differences may have unfortunate results', particularly as regards concurrent jurisdictions. Regrets have thus been expressed concerning 'the absence of any uniform conflicts rule which is capable of being applied with certainty to any given case'.

48. Even though this problem is specific to the dispute before the national court, I consider that it represents an additional argument for rejecting the idea that competence vests in the courts of the place where the damage is suffered.

III - It is inappropriate to apply the solution arrived at in *Shenavai*

49. In its judgment in *Shenavai*, cited above, the Court applied the maxim *accessorium sequitur principale*: '...in other words, where various obligations are at issue, it will be the principal obligation which will determine its jurisdiction'. The Court concluded from this that: 'For the purposes of determining the place of performance within the meaning of Article 5(1) of the Convention ..., the obligation to be taken into consideration in a dispute concerning proceedings for the recovery of fees commenced by an architect commissioned to draw up plans for the building of houses is the contractual obligation which forms the actual basis of legal proceedings'.

50. The defendant in the present case suggests that the Court should apply the same principle here.

51. That possibility has been convincingly dismissed in the earlier Opinion. I would add that the Court has previously declined to apply the principle *accessorium sequitur principale* in the context of Article 5(3). In its judgment in *Kalfelis*, it held that a court seised of an action by virtue of the special jurisdiction conferred by Article 5(3) does not also have jurisdiction 'over that action in so far as it is not so based'.

52. Lastly, how can the place where the main damage occurs be determined without appraising the reputation of the defamed person in the

various Contracting States concerned, without calculating the number of copies distributed in each of those States, *in short, without appraising the substance of the dispute?* The Court has expressed the view that an interpretation of Article 5 consistent with 'the purposes and spirit of the Convention' must enable '... the national court to rule on its own jurisdiction without being compelled to consider the substance of the case'.

53. Otherwise, a plaintiff could no longer be certain that the court in which he sues would accept jurisdiction. That would run counter to the requirement that jurisdictional rules must be predictable, as the Court ruled in *Rösler* and in *Handte*, cited above.

IV - The courts of each Contracting State in whose territory the article has been distributed are competent to determine the specific damage caused in that State

54. In matters relating to liability in tort and delict, '(the) jurisdiction (of the court of the place where the damage occurred) is ... by its nature functionally limited. According to the judgment in *Bier* v *Mines de potasse d'Alsace*, it is founded solely on the requirements of the sound administration of justice, and more precisely on the need for the existence of a connecting factor between the dispute and the court which is called upon to hear and determine it, particularly as regards matters of evidence and procedural organization'.

55. It follows that no sufficient link exists between the courts of a Contracting State and damage caused in another Contracting State, inasmuch as that damage is not connected with those courts by virtue either of the place where it occurred or of the place where the wrongful act was committed. The link of proximity between the forum and the dispute required by the Court's case-law exists only in respect of damage occurring in the territory of the State of the forum seised.

56. It is clear that any contrary solution would encourage forum shopping: the English courts could even find themselves in danger, by reason of their 'generosity' towards victims of defamation, of becoming the natural choice of forum in such matters.

57. The need to prevent any risk of forum shopping is particularly great when the subject-matter of the dispute is an area in which the substantive law applying in the Contracting States is not harmonized and gives rise to solutions which are markedly divergent from one Contracting State to another. That is particularly so in the case of the law of defamation.

58. For those reasons, I adopt the wording of the operative part of the Opinion delivered on 14 July 1994 by Mr Darmon.

Case C-364/93 - 19 September 1995

Antonio Marinari v Lloyds Bank Plc and Zubaidi Trading Company

Special Jurisdiction - Article 5(3) - Jurisdiction in 'matters relating to test, delict or quasi-delict' - Place where the harmful event occurred - Plaintiff's option - Place where the damage occurred and the place of the event giving rise to it - Scope - Place where financial damage was suffered in consequence of initial damage arising and suffered by a victim in another Contracting State - Excluded.

Summary

The term 'place where the harmful event occurred' in Article 5(3) of the Convention of 27 September 1968 on Jurisdiction and the Enforcement of Judgments in Civil and Commercial Matters does not, on a proper interpretation, cover the place where the victim claims to have suffered financial damage following upon initial damage arising and suffered by him in another Contracting State. Although that term may cover both the place where the damage occurred and the place of the event giving rise to it, it cannot be construed so extensively as to encompass any place where the adverse consequences can be felt of an event which has already caused damage actually arising elsewhere.

JUDGMENT OF THE COURT

Rodriguez Iglesias, President, Schockweiler, Kapteyn and Jann, Presidents of Chambers, Mancini, Kakouris, Moitinho de Almeida, Puissochet, Hirsch, Ragnemalm and Sevón, Judges

1. By order of 21 January 1993, received at the Court on 26 July 1993, the Corte Suprema di Cassazione (Supreme Court of Cassation) referred to the Court for a preliminary ruling under the Protocol of 3 June 1971 on the interpretation by the Court of Justice of the Convention of 27 September 1968 on Jurisdiction and the Enforcement of Judgments in Civil and Commercial Matters (OJ 1978 L 304, p.36), as amended by the Convention of 9 October 1978 on the accession of the Kingdom of Denmark, of Ireland, and of the United Kingdom of Great Britain and Northern Ireland (OJ 1978 L 304, p.1, and - amended text - p.77) and by the Convention of 25 October 1982 on the accession of the Hellenic Republic (OJ 1982 L 388, p.1, hereinafter 'the Convention') a question on the interpretation of Article 5(3) of the Convention.

2. That question was raised in the course of proceedings between Mr Marinari, who is domiciled in Italy, and Lloyds Bank, whose registered office is in London.

3. In April 1987, Mr Marinari lodged with a Manchester branch of Lloyds Bank a bundle of promissory notes with a face value of US $752 500 000, issued by the Negros Oriental province of the Republic of the Philippines in favour of Zubaidi Trading Company in Beirut. The bank staff, after opening the envelope, refused to return the promissory notes and advised the police of their existence, stating them of dubious origin, which led to Mr Marinari's arrest and sequestration of the promissory notes.

4. Having been released by the English authorities, Mr Marinari sued Lloyds Bank in the Tribunale di Pisa, seeking compensation for the damage caused by the conduct of its staff. The documents forwarded by the national court show that Mr Marinari is claiming not only payment of the face value of the promissory notes but also compensation for the damage he claims to have suffered as a result of his arrest, breach of several contracts and damage to his reputation. Lloyds Bank objected that the Italian court lacked jurisdiction on the ground that the damage constituting the basis of jurisdiction ratione loci had occurred in England. Mr Marinari, supported by Zubaidi Trading Company, applied to the Corte Suprema di Cassazione for a prior ruling on the question of jurisdiction.

5. In its order for reference, the Corte Suprema di Cassazione raises the issue of the jurisdiction of the Italian courts in relation to Article 5(3) of the Convention, as interpreted by the Court of Justice.

6. It observes that, in Case 21/76 *Bier* v *Mines de Potasse d'Alsace* [1976] ECR 1735, the Court considered that the term 'place where the harmful event occurred' was to be understood as intended to cover both the place where the damage occurred and the place of the event giving rise to it, and that Mr Marinari contends that the expression damage occurred relates not only to the physical result but also to damage in the legal sense, such as a decrease in a person's assets.

7. It also notes that in Case C-220/88 *Dumez France and Tracobo* v *Hessische Landesbank* [1990] ECR I-49, the Court held that account should not be taken, for the purpose of determining jurisdiction under Article 5(3) of the Convention, of indirect financial damage. The national court, in those circumstances, questions whether that also applies where the harmful effects alleged by the plaintiff are direct, not indirect.

8. In those circumstances, it decided to stay the proceedings pending a preliminary ruling on the following question: 'In applying the jurisdiction rule laid down in Article 5(3) of the Brussels Convention of 27 September 1968, as interpreted in the judgment of the Court of Justice of the European Communities of 30 November 1976 in Case 21/76 *Handelskwekerij G.J. Bier BV* v *Mines de Potasse d'Alsace SA* [1976] ECR 1735, is the expression 'place where the harmful event occurred' to be taken to mean only the place in which physical harm was caused to persons or things, or also the place in which the damage to the plaintiff's assets occurred?'

9. By way of derogation from the general principle laid down in the first paragraph of Article 2 of the Convention that the courts of the State where the defendant is domiciled are to have jurisdiction, Article 5 provides: 'A person domiciled in a Contracting State may, in another Contracting State, be sued: ... 3. in matters relating to tort, delict or quasi-delict, in the courts for the place where the harmful event occurred; ...'.

10. As the Court has held on several occasions (in *Mines de Potasse d'Alsace*, cited above, paragraph 11, *Dumez France and Tracoba*, cited above, paragraph 17, and Case C-68/93 *Shevill and Others* v *Presse Alliance* [1995] ECR I-415, paragraph 19), that rule of special jurisdiction, the choice of which is a matter for the plaintiff, is based on the existence of a particularly close connecting factor between the dispute and courts other than those of the State of the defendant's domicile which justifies the attribution of jurisdiction to those courts for reasons relating to the sound administration of justice and the efficacious conduct of proceedings.

11. In *Mines de Potasse d'Alsace* (paragraphs 24 and 25) and *Shevill* (paragraph 20), the Court held that where the place of the happening of the event which may give rise to liability in tort, delict or quasi-delict and the place where that event results in damage are not identical, the expression 'place where the harmful event occurred' in Article 5(3) of the Convention must be understood as being intended to cover both the place where the damage occurred and the place of the event giving rise to it, so that the defendant may be sued, at the option of the plaintiff, in the courts for either of those places.

12. In those two judgments, the Court considered that the place of the event giving rise to the damage no less than the place where the damage occurred could constitute a significant connecting factor from the point of view of jurisdiction. It added that to decide in favour only of the place of the event giving rise to the damage would, in an appreciable number of cases, cause confusion between the heads of jurisdiction laid down by Articles 2 and 5(3) of the Convention, so that the latter provision would, to that extent, lose its effectiveness.

13. The choice thus available to the plaintiff cannot however be extended beyond the particular circumstances which justify it. Such an extension would negate the general principle laid down in the first paragraph of Article 2 of the Convention that the courts of the Contracting State where the defendant is domiciled are to have jurisdiction and would lead to recognition, in cases other than those expressly indicated, of the jurisdiction of the courts for the plaintiff's domicile, a solution which the Convention does not favour since, in the second paragraph of Article 3, it excludes application of national provisions which make such jurisdiction available for proceedings against defendants domiciled in the territory of a Contracting State.

14. Whilst it has thus been recognized that the term 'place where the harmful event occurred' within the meaning of Article 5(3) of the Convention may cover both the place where the damage occurred and the place of the event giving rise to it, that term cannot be construed so extensively as to encompass any place where the adverse consequences of an event which has already caused damage actually arising elsewhere.

15. Consequently, that term cannot be construed as including the place where, as in the present case, the victim claims to have suffered financial damage following upon initial damage arising and suffered by him in another Contracting State.

16. The German Government submits, however, that, in interpreting Article 5(3) of the Convention, the Court should take account of the applicable national law on non-contractual civil liability. Thus, where, under that law, an actual adverse effect on goods or rights is a precondition for liability (inter alia, by virtue of Paragraph 823(1) of the Bürgerliches Gesetzbuch - the German Civil Code), the 'place where the harmful event occurred' means both the place of that adverse effect and the place of the event giving rise to it. On the other hand, it considers that where national law does not make redress conditional upon an actual adverse effect upon property or a right (as, for instance, under Article 1382 of the French Civil Code and Article 2043 of the Italian Civil Code), the victim may choose between the place of the event giving rise to the damage and the place where he suffered financial damage.

17. The German Government also considers that that interpretation would not be liable to lead to a multiplication of courts enjoying jurisdiction. Nor would it lead systematically to the result that the court for the place where the financial damage was suffered would be the same as the court for the plaintiff's domicile. Moreover, it would not enable the victim, by moving his assets, to determine the competent court, since account would be taken of the location of his assets when the obligation of reparation arose. Finally, that interpretation has the advantage of not according preference to the laws of certain States at the expense of others.

18. It must, however, be noted that the Convention did not intend to link the rules on territorial jurisdiction with national provisions concerning the conditions under which non-contractual civil liability is incurred. Those conditions do not necessarily have any bearing on the solutions adopted by the Member States regarding the territorial jurisdiction of their courts, such jurisdiction being founded on other considerations.

19. There is no basis for interpreting Article 5(3) of the Convention by reference to the applicable rules on non-contractual civil liability, as proposed by the German Government. That interpretation is also incompatible with the objective of the Convention, which is to provide for a clear and certain attribution of jurisdiction (see Case 241/83 *Rösler* v *Rottwinkel* [1985] ECR 99, paragraph 23, and Case C-26/91 *Handte* v *Traitments Mécano-Chimiques des Surfaces* [1992] ECR II-3967, paragraph 19). The delimitation of jurisdiction would then depend on uncertain factors such as the place where the victim's assets suffered subsequent damage and the applicable rules on civil liability.

20. Finally, as regards the argument as to the relevance of the location of the assets when the obligation to redress the damage arose, the proposed interpretation might confer jurisdiction on a court which had no connection at all with the subject-matter of the dispute, whereas it is that connection which justifies the special jurisdiction provided for in Article 5(3) of the Convention. Indeed, the expenses and losses of profit incurred as a result of the initial harmful event might be incurred elsewhere so that, as far as the efficiency of proof is concerned, that court would be entirely inappropriate.

21. The answer to the national court's question should therefore be that the term 'place where the harmful event occurred' in Article 5(3) of the Convention of 27 September 1968 on Jurisdiction and the Enforcement of Judgments in Civil and Commercial Matters does not, on a proper interpretation, cover the place where the victim claims to have suffered financial damage following upon initial damage arising and suffered by him in another Contracting State.

On those grounds, the Court, in answer to the question referred to it by the Italian Corte Suprema di Cassazione by order of 21 January 1993, hereby rules:

> **The term 'place where the harmful event occurred' in Article 5(3) of the Convention of 27 September 1968 on Jurisdiction and the Enforcement of Judgments in Civil and Commercial Matters does not, on a proper interpretation, cover the place where the victim claims to have suffered financial loss following upon initial damage arising and suffered by him in another Contracting State.**

OPINION OF MR ADVOCATE GENERAL DARMON

1. By an order of 21 January 1993, the Corte Suprema di Cassazione seeks clarification as to the interpretation of Article 5(3) of the Brussels Convention of 27 September 1968 on jurisdiction and enforcement of judgments in civil and commercial matters (hereinafter 'the Convention') in connection with a dispute, the facts of which may be summarized as follows.

2. In April 1987, Antonio Marinari, who was domiciled in Italy, lodged with a Manchester branch of Lloyds Bank, whose registered office is in London, promissory notes of an exchange value of US $752 500 000, issued by the Negros Oriental province of the Republic of the Philippines in favour of Zubaidi Trading Company of Beirut. According to the order from the national court, the

bank staff, after opening the envelope, refused to return the promissory notes and advised the police of the allegedly dubious origin of the notes, which led to the arrest of the plaintiff in the main proceedings and the sequestration of the promissory notes.

3. Having been released by the English authorities, Mr Marinari sued Lloyds Bank in the Tribunale di Pisa for compensation for the damage he claimed to have suffered as a result of the conduct of the bank's employees. As was made clear by his counsel at the hearing, he seeks not the return of the promissory notes but an order that the bank pay him US $795 500 000, representing the exchange value of the notes together with US $43 000 000 for interest, expenses and damages.

4. Lloyds Bank objected that the Italian court lacked jurisdiction on the ground that the damage constituting the basis of jurisdiction *ratione loci* had occurred in England. Mr Marinari, supported by Zubaidi, applied to the Corte Suprema di Cassazione for a prior ruling on that issue of jurisdiction.

5. It is for that reason that the latter court has submitted the following question for a preliminary ruling: 'In applying the jurisdiction rule laid down in Article 5(3) of the Brussels Convention of 27 September 1968, as interpreted in the judgment of the Court of Justice of the European Communities of 30 November 1976 in Case 21/76 *Bier* v *Mines de Potasse d'Alsace* [1976] ECR 1735, is the expression 'place where the harmful event occurred' to be taken to mean only the place in which physical harm was caused to persons or things, or also the place in which the damage to the plaintiff's assets occurred?'

6. Before the provision at issue is analysed, it is necessary to consider whether this Court has jurisdiction, having regard to the circumstances in which the case has been referred to it.

7. The Corte Suprema di Cassazione is not hearing an appeal against a decision of a lower court but is dealing with the matter on the basis of Article 41 of the Italian Code of Civil Procedure, under which any party may, by application, in any case where the jurisdiction of the court seised at first instance is in dispute, obtain an order that the latter stay the proceedings until the issue has been decided by the Corte Suprema di Cassazione.

8. Whilst it is undeniable that the latter court is a court within the meaning of Article 2(1) of the Protocol, it is not on the other hand called on directly to give judgment in so far as the case remains pending before the Tribunale di Pisa and it is not a court within the meaning of the Protocol since it is giving judgment neither on an appeal nor in the context of Article 37 of the Convention.

9. It will be recalled that Article 3(1) of the Protocol, on which the Corte Suprema di Cassazione seems to be relying, provides: 'Where a question of interpretation of the convention or of one of the other instruments referred to in Article 1 is raised in a case pending before one of the courts listed in Article 2(1), that court shall, if it considers that a decision on the question is necessary to enable it to give judgment, request the Court of Justice to give a ruling thereon.'

10. However, it must be noted that where that superior court makes a ruling on the basis of Article 41 of the Code of Civil Procedure, the decision

given constitutes a reply to a request for a preliminary ruling under domestic law for which it alone has jurisdiction and against which there is no appeal.

11. As Mr Mandrioli writes in his *Corso di Diritto Processuale Civile*: 'l'istanza di regolamento non apre affatto un nuovo grado di giudizio, ma apre solo una parentesi che si inserisce nell'ambito del giudizio di primo grado. Chiuso questa parentesi, il giudizio prosegue sui suoi normali binari; la pronuncia sulla giurisdizione appartiene alla sentenza di primo grado anche se, naturalmente, questa parte della sentenza non è più impugnabile'.

[Free translation: '... this procedure (before the Court of Cassation) does not take the matter to a higher level of jurisdiction but merely marks an interlude in the proceedings at first instance. Once that interlude comes to an end, the proceedings revert to their normal course; the decision on jurisdiction is a matter for the court of first instance even though, naturally, that aspect of the judgment is no longer appealable'.]

12. I therefore consider that the question has been properly submitted and should be answered.

13. The question relates essentially to the relevance, for the purpose of determining jurisdiction under Article 5(3), not only of the immediate effects of the causal event (physical damage caused to persons or things) but also of the harmful consequences of those effects for the plaintiff's assets (financial damage).

14. It should also be borne in mind that as well as being at issue in *Shevill*, which is now at the deliberation stage and in which I delivered my Opinion on 14 July of this year, that provision has already been the subject, as regards the term 'place where the harmful event occurred', of two of the Court's judgments, namely *Mines de Potasse d'Alsace* and *Dumez France and Tracoba*.

15. In the first of those judgments, the Court expounded its own view of the meaning of the expression 'place where the harmful event occurred' in a dispute concerning cross-frontier pollution affecting a market gardener established in the Netherlands, for which a French undertaking established in France was considered responsible.

16. The Court held that the special jurisdictions under Article 5 were based on 'the existence, in certain clearly defined situations, of a particularly close connecting factor between a dispute and the court which may be called upon to hear it, with a view to the efficacious conduct of the proceedings', although it did not refer to the need to protect the victim.

17. And the Court considered that 'the place where the harmful event occurred' should be taken to include 'both the place where the damage occurred and the place of the event giving rise to it'.

18. Legal writers have taken different views concerning the grounds of that judgment and the solution arrived at. Without going into the details of a debate that is now over, it will be remembered that Mr Droz criticized that decision on the ground that it enabled the 'secondary' victims to institute proceedings in the courts for the place where they lived and thus favoured the forum actoris. Mr Gothot and Mr Holleaux did not take the same view of that decision and expressed the opposite opinion, namely that it was confined 'to

cases in which the causative event and the first physical manifestation of the damage are separate from the outset'.

19. *Dumez* gave the Court an opportunity to settle the debate.

20. Let us recall the facts. Two French parent companies had brought proceedings in France against two German banks for compensation for damage resulting from the winding up of their two German subsidiaries which were carrying out a real-estate project in Germany, on the ground that they were wound up as a result of suspension of the works brought about by the banks' withdrawing credit facilities granted to the promoter.

21. I suggested that the Court should reject the approach whereby the courts of the place where the victim 'by ricochet' suffered damage were recognized as having jurisdiction. The Court agreed, stating: 'The rule on jurisdiction laid down in Article 5(3) of the Convention of 27 September 1968 ... cannot be interpreted as permitting a plaintiff pleading damage which he claims to be the consequence of the harm suffered by other persons who were direct victims of the harmful act to bring proceedings against the perpetrator of that act in the courts of the place in which he himself ascertained the damage to his assets.'

22. Let us be clear: the exclusion of the courts of the place where the damage is ascertained - that is to say, where the harm is suffered, not where it occurred - must apply both to the direct victim and to the indirect victim, otherwise the jurisdiction of the courts for the place where the plaintiff lived, which Article 3 of the Convention specifically takes care to remove, would be revived.

23. Advocate General Warner had already stated that view in his Opinion in *Rüffer*: 'It was never suggested ... much less held by the Court, that the place where the harmful event occurred could be the place where the plaintiff company had its seat or the place where the amount of damage to its business was quantified.'

24. That view was also shared by the national courts which had been called on to give their views concerning the jurisdiction of the courts for the place where the assets were situated, within whose territorial jurisdiction a financial loss had occurred in the wake of initial damage. I have already examined the decisions of certain courts in some of the contracting States and I shall merely refer in that connection to paragraphs 20 to 24 of my Opinion in *Dumez*.

25. And the *Mines de Potasse d'Alsace* judgment does not, contrary to the contention of the plaintiff in the main proceedings, provide any basis for a different interpretation merely because the Court held that 'where the place of the happening of the event which may give rise to liability in tort, delict or quasi-delict and the place where that event results in damage are not identical, the expression 'place where the harmful event occurred' ... must be understood as being intended to cover both the place where the damage occurred and the place of the event giving rise to it'.

26. That case concerned a complex situation in which the causal event and the harmful consequences occurred, from the outset, in two different contracting States. Here, by contrast, as rightly pointed out by the United Kingdom

Government, both the causal event (namely the conduct imputed to the employees of Lloyds Bank) and the initial damage (sequestration of the promissory notes and imprisonment) *occurred* in the United kingdom. Only the alleged consequential damage (financial losses) could have been *suffered* in Italy.

27. We are thus dealing with a particular situation in which the causal event and the direct harmful consequences are located in a single territory and that initial damage adversely affected the victim's assets in another contracting State.

28. Although the Court has not been called on to settle such a question directly, the basis for an answer is undeniably to be found in its judgments cited above since we are merely faced once more with the distinction - which is of essential importance for the purpose of determining jurisdiction - between the place where the damage arises and the place where it is suffered.

29. The Court regarded as relevant to the determination of the court of competent jurisdiction, in the first of its judgments on the issue, only the damage that had occurred. More clearly still, in *Dumez*, it displayed its hostility, it seems to me, to the taking into consideration of later financial consequences by referring to 'the place where the initial damage manifested itself', that is to say the place where that damage occurred.

30. Now, to confer jurisdiction on the court in the place where the financial losses were ascertained would be tantamount to disregarding the specificity of the *place of occurrence* as the criterion for the conferment of jurisdiction by placing it on the same footing as *the place* where the *damage is suffered.*

31. That broader approach would thus uphold the *forum actoris*, since a victim generally suffers harms at the place where he is domiciled. Such a result would be manifestly contrary to Article 5 of the Convention, which, as the Court has held, is intended to meet the requirements of the proper administration of justice.

32. The spirit of the Convention thus opposes that course. What is more, the solution that I propose is both logical and in conformity with the case-law of the Court.

33. Let us recall in the first place that '... the 'special jurisdictions' enumerated in Articles 5 and 6 of the Convention constitute derogations from the principle that jurisdiction is vested in the courts of the State where the defendant is domiciled and as such must be interpreted restrictively'.

34. To allow account to be taken, for the purpose of determining jurisdiction, of the financial damage resulting from initial damage would go in exactly the opposite direction to that objective.

35. But above all, that solution would favour the multiplication of competing courts, whereas the Court emphasized in *Effer* that 'the Convention provides a collection of rules which are designed *inter alia* to avoid the occurrence, in civil and commercial matters, of concurrent litigation in two or more Member States and which, in the interests of legal certainty and for the benefit of the parties, confer jurisdiction upon the national court territorially best qualified to determine a dispute'.

36. That concern to avoid such multiplication, with the danger on the horizon of 'fragmentation' of jurisdiction, was again expressed by the Court in *Dumez*. It stated 'it is necessary to avoid the multiplication of courts of competent jurisdiction which would heighten the risk of irreconcilable decisions, this being the reason for which recognition of an order for enforcement is withheld by virtue of Article 27(3) of the Convention'.

37. Thus, the solution which I advocate does not impinge upon the Court's judgment in *Dumez*. On the contrary, it constitutes a natural extension of it.

38. Commenting on that decision, Mme Gaudemet-Tallon considers that 'The *Dumez* judgment, by refusing to recognize the jurisdiction of the courts for the domicile of indirect victims, taking account only of the direct damage and using expressions such as 'place where the damage occurred', 'place where the initial damage manifested itself' (cf. paragraphs 10, 15, 20 and 21), gives the impression that it is only the courts for the place where the first damage became apparent that can have jurisdiction. Admittedly, here the Court of Justice is considering the case only of an indirect victim, but there is no reason for it to give a different answer regarding damage suffered by a direct victim, which later produces harmful consequences, located in most cases at the place where the victim is domiciled. It is not therefore a question of determining where the victim suffers the harm, since the aim pursued by the Convention is not essentially protection of the victim: if it had been, the forum actoris might have been favoured.'

39. I subscribe fully to that analysis: in fact, I expressed the same view in my Opinion in *Dumez*.

40. Furthermore, that position is fully supported by most legal writers on the subject.

41. Mr Huet also expresses the view, albeit in the form of a question, that the scope of the *Dumez* judgment goes beyond the hypothesis of the 'ricochet' victim: 'Does the Court not also mean to say that, where an immediate victim complains of subsequent damage, in particular of a financial nature, resulting from initial damage, only the place where the latter occurred is a basis for recognizing jurisdiction?'

42. Legal writers in the United Kingdom are also unwilling to accept any attribution of jurisdiction to the court for the place where subsequent financial losses occurred. Thus, according to Mr Collins, 'Even though in one sense a plaintiff may suffer economic loss at the place of its business, that is not sufficient to confer jurisdiction on that place, for otherwise the place of business of the plaintiff would almost automatically become another basis of jurisdiction.'

43. Mr O'Malley and Mr Leyton likewise consider that: 'It seems in such a case that the economic consequences of the damage should be distinguished from the damage itself (not necessarily an easy task in economic torts) and the location of the estate or person suffering damage by reason of the harmful event is not necessarily the location of the damage'.

44. There is agreement among German writers - although their view is not in conformity with that taken by the German Government in the present case - in particular Mr Kropholler, who draws attention to the danger of forum

shopping that would arise if precedence were given to the jurisdiction of the courts of the place where the subsequent damage occurs.

45. He says: 'Es spricht viel dafür, den Ort des (weiteren) Schadenseintritt nach erfolgter Rechtsgutverletzung für die Zuständigkeitsbegründung nicht ausreichen zu lassen. Denn sonst würde die Deliktszuständigkeit auf Kosten des in Art. 2 verankerten Grundsatzes des Beklagtenwohnsitzes stark ausgedehnt und einem Klägergerichsstand angenähert'. [Free translation: 'It would be preferable not to consider as relevant, for the purposes of jurisdiction, the place of subsequent damage, occurring after the infringement of the right. Otherwise jurisdiction for delictual matters would be considerably extended, contrary to the principle of the domicile of the defendant laid down in Article 2, and would come closer to the jurisdiction of the court of the plaintiff'.]

46. It is also interesting to note that even those writers who interpret Article 5(3) as being based on the idea of protection of the victim do not in any way suggest that that provision should be extended in the direction of conferring jurisdiction on the courts of the place where subsequent damage occurs. Mr Bourel writes: 'Thus, an analysis of both the legal literature and the case-law shows indisputably that the concept of 'place where the harmful event occurs' must be understood, for the purpose of determining the court with delictual jurisdiction, as being the location of the damage immediately suffered by the victim (directly or by ricochet) at the time when the causal event occurs, without account being taken of the repercussions or consequences of that damage, which might have manifested themselves somewhere else, in particular at the place where the plaintiff is domiciled.'

47. The victim could, in fact, at his option, institute proceedings not only in the courts for the defendant's domicile but also in those for the place where the causative event occurred or those for the place where the damage occurred or again those for the place where the damage was ascertained, which would inevitably encourage forum shopping.

48. I therefore consider that Article 5(3) of the Convention cannot be interpreted so as to enable the victim of financial loss consequent upon initial damage occurring in another contracting State to bring the alleged perpetrator before the courts of the place where that loss was suffered.

49. I therefore suggest that the Court rule as follows: 'Article 5(3) of the Brussels Convention of 27 September 1968 on jurisdiction and enforcement of judgments in civil and commercial matters must be interpreted as not allowing a plaintiff who claims to have suffered financial loss in consequence of initial damage suffered in another contracting State to institute proceedings against the defendant before the courts for the place where that loss was suffered'.

OPINION OF MR ADVOCATE GENERAL LÉGER

1. Since the oral procedure has been reopened I am once again as in Case C-68/93 *Shevill and Others* v *Presse Alliance*, called on to give an Opinion in the wake of one given by my predecessor.

2. As in that case, my observations will be very brief, endorsing the

position taken by Mr Darmon on 21 September 1994. Once again, the provision to be examined is Article 5(3) of the Brussels Convention.

3. The facts are these: Mr Marinari, living in Italy, brought an action for damages before the Tribunale di Pisa against Lloyds Bank, whose employees' conduct had led to his arrest in England and the seizure of promissory notes that he had presented there. Lloyds Bank disputed the jurisdiction of the Italian Court on the ground that the harm had arisen in England: an application was therefore made to the Suprema Corte di Cassazione for a prior ruling on the issue of jurisdiction.

4. The latter court has therefore asked the Court of Justice to interpret Article 5(3) of the Brussels Convention, in order to clarify whether the expression 'place where the harmful event occurred' is to be construed as referring only to the place where physical damage was suffered by persons or things or as also referring to the place where the financial loss suffered by the plaintiff occurred.

5. Mr Darmon suggests that the place where the financial loss was suffered (Italy, in this case), a loss which is merely *incidental* to the initial loss suffered in another contracting State (England in the present case), cannot be regarded as conferring jurisdiction within the meaning of Article 5(3).

6. I share that view: as the Court has held, only two bases of jurisdiction are available: the place where the harmful event occurred and the place where the causative event occurred, but not the place where a harmful event occurred which was incidental to the initial damage. And the judgment of 7 March 1995 in Case C-68/93 *Shevill and Other* v *Presse Alliance*, delivered after Mr Darmon gave his Opinion, certainly does not undermine that view, since it upholds that twofold possibility, whilst at the same time making it clear that, in cases of defamation by the press, the courts of each contracting State have jurisdiction to deal only with the initial damage caused in the State of the court seised.

7. I thus concur with the terms of the operative part of the Opinion delivered on 21 September 1994.

Case C-51/97 - 27 October 1998

Réunion Européenne SA and Others
v
Spliethoff's Bevrachtingskantoor BV and the Master of the Vessel Alblasgracht VOO2

Article 5(1) & (3) - Special jurisdiction in 'matters relating to a contract' and 'matters relating to tort, delict or quasi delict' - Goods damaged on completion of a voyage by sea then by land - Action for compensation by the consignee against the actual maritime carrier who did not issue the bill of landing - Action concerning a matter relating to tort, delict or quasi delict - Place where the harmful event occurred - Determination - Place where the damage arose - Place of delivery of the goods by the maritime carrier.

Special jurisdiction - More than one defendant - Jurisdiction of the courts for the place where any one of the co-defendants is domiciled - Condition - Co-defendant domiciled in a Contracting State.

Summary

1. An action by which the consignee of goods found to be damaged on completion of a transport operation by sea and then by land, or by which his insurer who has been subrogated to his rights after compensating him, seeks redress for the damage suffered, relying on the bill of landing covering the maritime transport, not against the person who issued that document on his headed paper but against the person whom the plaintiff considers to be the actual maritime carrier, does not fall within the scope of matters relating to a contract within the scope of matters relating to a contract within the meaning of Article 5, point 1, of the Convention of 27 September 1968 on Jurisdiction and the Enforcement of Judgements in Civil and Commercial Matters, as amended by the Convention of 9 October 1978 on the Accession of the Kingdom of Denmark, Ireland and the United Kingdom of Great Britain and Northern Ireland, by the Convention of 25 October 1982 on the Accession of the Hellenic republic

and by the Convention of 26 May 1989 on the Accession of the Kingdom of Spain and the Portuguese Republic, since the bill of lading in question does not disclose any contractual relationship freely entered into between the consignee and the defendant.

Such an action is, however, a matter relating to tort, delict or quasi-delect within the meaning of Article 5, point 3, of that Convention, since that concept covers all actions which seek to establish the liability of a defendant and are not related to matters of contract within the meaning of Article 5, point 1. As regards determining the 'place where the harmful event occurred' within the meaning of Article 5, point 3, the place where the consignee, on completion of a transport operation by sea and then by land, merely discovered the existence of the damage to the goods delivered to him cannot serve to determine that place. Whilst it is true that the above mentioned concept may cover both the place where the damage occurred and the place of the event giving rise to it, the place where the damage arose can, in the circumstances described, only be the place where the maritime carrier was to deliver the goods.

2. Article 6, point 1, of the Convention of 27 September 1968 must be interpreted as meaning that a defendant domiciled in a Contracting State cannot, on the basis of that provision, be sued in another Contracting State before a court seised of an action against a co-defendant not domiciled in a Contracting State on the ground that the dispute is indivisible rather than merely displaying a connection. The objective of legal certainty pursued by the Convention would not be attained if the fact that a court in a Contracting State had accepted jurisdiction as regards one of the defendants not domiciled in a Contracting State made it possible to bring another defendant, domiciled in a Contracting State, before that same court in cases other than those envisaged by the Convention, thereby depriving him of the benefit of the protective rules laid down by it.

JUDGMENT OF THE COURT

Puissochet, President of the Chamber, Moitinho de Almeida (Rapporteur) and Gulmenn, Judges

1. By judgment of 28 January 1997, received at the Court on 7 February 1997, the Cour de Cassation (Court of Cassation) referred to the Court for a preliminary ruling under the Protocol of 3 June 1971 on the interpretation by the Court of Justice of the Convention of 27 September

1968 on jurisdiction and the enforcement of judgments in civil and commercial matters four questions on the interpretation of Articles 5(1) and (3) and 6 of that convention (OJ 1975 L 204, p. 28), as amended by the Convention of 9 October 1978 on the Accession of the Kingdom of Denmark, Ireland and the United Kingdom of Great Britain and Northern Ireland (OJ 1978 L 304, p. 1 and - amended text - p. 77), by the Convention of 25 October 1982 on the Accession of the Hellenic Republic (OJ 1982 L 388, p. 1) and by the Convention of 26 May 1989 on the Accession of the Kingdom of Spain and the Portuguese Republic (OJ 1989 L 285, p. 1).

2. Those questions arose in proceedings brought by nine insurance companies and, as lead insurer, the company Réunion Européenne (hereinafter 'the insurers'), which have been subrogated to the rights of the company Brambi Fruits (hereinafter 'Brambi'), whose registered office is in Rungis (France), against Spliethoff's Bevrachtingskantoor BV, whose registered office is in Amsterdam (Netherlands), and the Master of the vessel Alblasgracht V002, residing in the Netherlands, following the discovery of damage to a cargo of 5,199 cartons of pears delivered to Brambi, in the carriage of which the defendants were involved.

The Convention

3. The first paragraph of Article 2 of the Convention provides: 'Subject to the provisions of this Convention, persons domiciled in a Contracting State shall, whatever their nationality, be sued in the courts of that State.'

4. The first paragraph of Article 3 provides: 'Persons domiciled in a Contracting State may be sued in the courts of another Contracting State only by virtue of the rules set out in Sections 2 to 6 of this Title.'

5. According to Article 5 of the Convention, '[A] person domiciled in a Contracting State may, in another Contracting State, be sued: 1. in matters relating to a contract, in the courts for the place of performance of the obligation in question ... 3. in matters relating to tort, delict or quasi-delict, in the courts for the place where the harmful event occurred; ...'

6. Article 6(1) of the Convention adds that where such a person is one of a number of defendants, he may also be sued in the courts for the place where any one of them is domiciled.

7. Finally, Article 22 provides: 'Where related actions are brought in the courts of different Contracting States, any court other than the court first seised may, while the actions are pending at first instance, stay its proceedings.'

The main proceedings

8. The goods at issue in the main proceedings were carried by sea, in eight refrigerated containers, from Melbourne (Australia) to Rotterdam (Netherlands) aboard the vessel Alblasgracht V002 under a bearer bill of lading issued on 8 May 1992 in Sydney, Australia, by Refrigerated Container Carriers PTY Ltd (hereinafter 'RCC'), whose registered office is in Sydney, then by road under an international consignment note, to Rungis in France, where Brambi discovered the damage. The fruit had ripened prematurely owing to a breakdown in the cooling system.

9. The insurers paid compensation for the damage suffered by Brambi. Having been subrogated to that company's rights as a result of that payment, they brought proceedings to recoup their loss against RCC on whose headed paper the bill of lading had been issued for the sea voyage, against Spliethoff's Bevrachtingskantoor BV, which actually carried the goods by sea despite not being mentioned on the bill of lading, and, finally, against the Master of the vessel Alblasgracht V002, as representative of the owners and charterers of that vessel, before the Tribunal de Commerce (Commercial Court), Créteil, in whose jurisdiction Rungis is situated.

10. By judgment of 17 May 1994 the Tribunal de Commerce, Créteil, declared that it had jurisdiction as regards RCC, on the basis that the goods were to be delivered to Brambi in Rungis. However, it declined jurisdiction under Article 5(1) of the Convention as regards Spliethoff's Bevrachtingskantoor BV and the Master of the vessel Alblasgracht V002, taking the view that the operation did not constitute a through transport operation from Melbourne to Rungis since an international consignment note had been drawn up for the carriage of the goods from Rotterdam to Rungis. The Tribunal de Commerce, Créteil, therefore considered that it should decline jurisdiction in the proceedings brought by the insurers against Spliethoff's Bevrachtingskantoor BV and the Master of the vessel Alblasgracht V002 in favour of the courts of Rotterdam, Rotterdam being the place of performance of the obligation within the meaning of Article 5(1) of the Convention, or those of Amsterdam or of Sydney pursuant to Article 6(1) of the Convention, according to which a person who is one

of a number of defendants may be sued before the courts for the place where any one of them is domiciled.

11. The Cour d'Appel (Court of Appeal), Paris, confirmed, by judgment of 16 November 1994, that the Tribunal de Commerce, Créteil, lacked international jurisdiction as regards Spliethoff's Bevrachtingskantoor BV and the Master of the vessel Alblasgracht V002, whereupon the insurers appealed to the Cour de Cassation, claiming that it had not been established that Brambi had concluded an agreement with those defendants and that the Cour d'Appel could not therefore apply Article 5(1) of the Convention to them. According to the insurers, the Cour d'Appel should have applied Article 5(3) of the Convention concerning jurisdiction in matters relating to tort, delict or quasi-delict.

12. In the alternative, the insurers claimed that the dispute was indivisible since RCC, as well as both Spliethoff's Bevrachtingskantoor BV and the Master of the vessel Alblasgracht V002, had been involved in the same transport operation. The Tribunal de Commerce, Créteil, having accepted jurisdiction for the proceedings against RCC, should have done so for the proceedings against the other two defendants.

13. Considering that the decision to be given depended on an interpretation of the Convention, the Cour de Cassation stayed proceedings pending a ruling from the Court of Justice on the following questions:

1. Is an action by which the consignee of goods found to be damaged on completion of a transport operation by sea and then by land, or by which his insurer who has been subrogated to his rights after compensating him, seeks redress for the damage suffered, relying on the bill of lading covering the maritime transport, not against the person who issued that document on his headed paper but against the person whom the plaintiff considered to be the actual maritime carrier, based on the contract of transport and does it, for that or any other reason, fall within the scope of matters relating to contract within the meaning of Article 5(1) of the Convention?

2. If the foregoing question is answered in the negative, is the matter one relating to tort, delict or quasi-delict within the meaning of Article 5(3) of the Convention or is it appropriate to have recourse to the principle laid down in Article 2 of the Convention that the courts of the State in whose territory the defendant is domiciled have jurisdiction?

3. In the event that the matter is to be regarded as one relating to tort, delict or quasi-delict, may the place where the consignee, after

completion of the maritime transport operation and then the final overland transport operation, merely discovered that the goods delivered to him were damaged, constitute - and if so under what conditions - the place of occurrence of the damage which, according to the judgment of the Court of Justice of 30 November 1976 in Case 21/76 *Bier* v *Mines de Potasse d'Alsace* [1976] ECR 1735, may be the place "where the harmful event occurred" within the meaning of Article 5(3) of the Convention?

4. May a defendant domiciled in the territory of a Contracting State be brought, in another Contracting State, before the court hearing an action against a co-defendant not domiciled in the territory of any Contracting State, on the ground that the dispute is indivisible, rather than merely displaying a connection?

The first and second questions

14. According to Spliethoff's Bevrachtingskantoor BV and the Master of the Alblasgracht V002, the dispute is a matter relating to a contract within the meaning of Article 5(1) of the Convention since the action against them is based on the bill of lading, the document containing the transport contract.

15. It must be pointed out that, according to settled case-law (Case 34/82 *Peters* v *ZNAV* [1983] ECR 987, paragraphs 9 and 10, Case 9/87 *Arcado* v *Haviland* [1988] ECR 1539, paragraphs 10 and 11, and Case C-26/91 *Handte* v *Traitements Mécano-Chimiques des Surfaces* [1992] ECR I-3967, paragraph 10), the phrase 'matter relating to a contract' in Article 5(1) of the Convention is to be interpreted independently, having regard primarily to the objectives and general scheme of the Convention, in order to ensure that it is applied uniformly in all the Contracting States; that phrase cannot therefore be taken to refer to how the legal relationship in question before the national court is classified by the relevant national law.

16. It is also settled case-law that, under the system of the Convention, the general principle is that the courts of the Contracting State in which the defendant is domiciled are to have jurisdiction and that it is only by way of derogation from that principle that the Convention provides for cases, which are exhaustively listed, in which the defendant may or must, depending on the case, be sued in the courts of another Contracting State. Consequently, the rules of jurisdiction which derogate from that general principle cannot give rise to an interpretation going beyond the cases envisaged by the Convention (see, in particular, Case C-269/95

Benincasa v *Dentalkit* [1997] ECR I-3767, paragraph 13).

17. It follows, as the Court held in paragraph 15 of *Handte*, cited above, that the phrase 'matters relating to contract', as used in Article 5(1) of the Convention, is not to be understood as covering a situation in which there is no obligation freely assumed by one party towards the other.

18. In this case, it is clear from the findings of the national courts at first instance and on appeal that the bearer bill of lading issued by RCC covers the carriage of the goods by sea to Rotterdam, the port of discharge and delivery, that it specifies Brambi as the person to whom the arrival of the goods must be notified and that it indicates that the goods are to be carried aboard the Alblasgracht V002.

19. It must therefore be held that that bill of lading discloses no contractual relationship freely entered into between Brambi on the one hand and, on the other, Spliethoff's Bevrachtingskantoor BV and the Master of the Alblasgracht V002, who, according to the insurers, were the actual maritime carriers of the goods.

20. In those circumstances, the action brought against the latter by the insurers cannot be a matter relating to a contract within the meaning of Article 5(1) of the Convention.

21. It is next necessary to determine whether such an action is concerned with a matter relating to tort, delict or quasi-delict within the meaning of Article 5(3) of the Convention.

22. In its judgment in Case 189/87 *Kalfelis* v *Schröder* [1988] ECR 5565, paragraph 18, the Court defined the concept of matters relating to tort, delict or quasi-delict within the meaning of Article 5(3) of the Convention as an independent concept covering all actions which seek to establish the liability of a defendant and which are not related to a 'contract' within the meaning of Article 5(1).

23. That is the position in the main proceedings. Where insurers who have been subrogated to the rights of the consignee of goods which, on completion of a sea voyage followed by overland transport, are found to be damaged claim compensation for the loss, relying on the bill of lading for the sea voyage, from the persons whom they regard as actually having carried the goods by sea, the purpose of their action is to establish the carriers' liability and does not, as is clear from paragraphs 18 to 20 of this

judgment, fall within the scope of 'matters relating to a contract' within the meaning of Article 5(1) of the Convention.

24. In those circumstances, it must be held that such an action is a matter relating to tort, delict or quasi-delict within the meaning of Article 5(3) of the Convention and that, therefore, the general principle that the courts of the State in which the defendant is domiciled are to have jurisdiction, laid down in the first paragraph of Article 2 of the Convention, is inapplicable.

25. The jurisdiction in matters relating to tort, delict or quasi-delict of the courts for the place where the harmful event occurred is one of the 'special jurisdictions' listed in Articles 5 and 6 of the Convention, which constitute exceptions to the general principle laid down in the first paragraph of Article 2.

26. The answer to the first two questions must therefore be that an action by which the consignee of goods found to be damaged on completion of a transport operation by sea and then by land, or by which his insurer who has been subrogated to his rights after compensating him, seeks redress for the damage suffered, relying on the bill of lading covering the maritime transport, not against the person who issued that document on his headed paper but against the person whom the plaintiff considered to be the actual maritime carrier, falls within the scope not of matters relating to a contract within the meaning of Article 5(1) of the Convention but of matters relating to tort, delict or quasi-delict within the meaning of Article 5 (3) of the Convention.

The third question

27. It must be borne in mind at the outset that, as the Court has held on several occasions (see the judgments in Case 21/76 *Bier* v *Mines de Potasse d'Alsace*, cited above, paragraph 11, Case C-220/88 Dumez France and Tracoba [1990] ECR I-49, paragraph 17, Case C-68/93 *Shevill and Others* v *Presse Alliance* [1995] ECR I-415, paragraph 19, and Case C-364/93 *Marinari* v *Lloyds Bank and Another* [1995] ECR I-2719, paragraph 10), the rule of special jurisdiction in Article 5(3) of the Convention, the choice of which is a matter for the plaintiff, is based on the existence of a particularly close connecting factor between the dispute and courts other than those of the State of the defendant's domicile which justifies the attribution of jurisdiction to those courts for reasons relating to the sound administration of justice and the efficacious conduct of proceedings.

28. It must next be observed that in the judgments cited above in *Mines de Potasse d'Alsace*, paragraphs 24 and 25, and *Shevill and Others*, paragraph 20, the Court held that, where the place of the happening of the event which may give rise to liability in tort, delict or quasi-delict and the place where that event results in damage are not identical, the expression 'place where the harmful event occurred' in Article 5(3) of the Convention must be understood as being intended to cover both the place where the damage occurred and the place of the event giving rise to it, so that the defendant may be sued, at the option of the plaintiff, in the courts for either of those places.

29. In *Marinari*, cited above, paragraph 13, the Court made it clear that the choice thus available to the plaintiff cannot however be extended beyond the particular circumstances which justify it, since otherwise the general principle laid down in the first paragraph of Article 2 of the Convention that the courts of the Contracting State where the defendant is domiciled are to have jurisdiction would be negated, with the result that, in cases other than those expressly provided for, jurisdiction would be attributed to the courts of the plaintiff's domicile, a solution which the Convention does not favour since, in the second paragraph of Article 3, it excludes application of national provisions which make such jurisdiction available for proceedings against defendants domiciled in the territory of a Contracting State.

30. The Court went on to infer, in paragraph 14 of that judgment, that whilst it has thus been recognised that the term 'place where the harmful event occurred' within the meaning of Article 5(3) of the Convention may cover both the place where the damage occurred and the place of the event giving rise to it, that term cannot be construed so extensively as to encompass any place where the adverse consequences can be felt of an event which has already caused damage actually arising elsewhere.

31. For the same reasons, in *Dumez France and Tracoba*, cited above, the Court held that the rule on jurisdiction laid down in Article 5(3) of the Convention cannot be interpreted as permitting a plaintiff pleading damage which he claims to be the consequence of the harm suffered by other persons who were direct victims of the harmful act to bring proceedings against the perpetrator of that act in the courts of the place in which he himself ascertained the damage to his assets.

32. It follows that a consignee of goods who, on completion of a transport operation by sea and then by land, finds that the goods delivered to him are

damaged may bring proceedings against the person whom he regards as the actual maritime carrier either before the courts for the place where the damage occurred or the courts for the place of the event giving rise to it.

33. As the Advocate General emphasises in points 54 to 56 of his Opinion, in an international transport operation of the kind at issue in the main proceedings the place where the event giving rise to the damage occurred may be difficult or indeed impossible to determine. In such circumstances, it will be for the consignee of the damaged goods to bring the actual maritime carrier before the courts for the place where the damage occurred. It must be pointed out in that regard that, in an international transport operation of the kind at issue in the main proceedings, the place where the damage occurred cannot be either the place of final delivery, which, as the Commission rightly pointed out, can be changed in mid-voyage, or the place where the damage was ascertained.

34. To allow the consignee to bring the actual maritime carrier before the courts for the place of final delivery or before those for the place where the damage was ascertained would in most cases mean attributing jurisdiction to the courts for the place of the plaintiff's domicile, whereas the authors of the Convention demonstrated their opposition to such attribution of jurisdiction otherwise than in the cases for which it expressly provides (see, to that effect, *Dumez France and Tracoba*, cited above, paragraphs 16 and 19, and Case C-89/91 *Shearson Lehman Hutton* v *TVB* [1993] ECR I-139, paragraph 17). Furthermore, such an interpretation of the Convention would make the determination of the competent court depend on uncertain factors, which would be incompatible with the objective of the Convention which is to provide for a clear and certain attribution of jurisdiction (see, to that effect, *Marinari*, paragraph 19, and *Handte*, paragraph 19, both cited above).

35. In those circumstances, the place where the damage arose in the case of an international transport operation of the kind at issue in the main proceedings can only be the place where the actual maritime carrier was to deliver the goods.

36. That place meets the requirements of foreseeability and certainty imposed by the Convention and displays a particularly close connecting factor with the dispute in the main proceedings, so that the attribution of jurisdiction to the courts for that place is justified by reasons relating to the sound administration of justice and the efficacious conduct of proceedings.

37. The answer to be given to the third question must therefore be that the place where the consignee of the goods, on completion of a transport operation by sea and then by land, merely discovered the existence of the damage to the goods delivered to him cannot serve to determine the 'place where the harmful event occurred' within the meaning of Article 5(3) of the Convention, as interpreted by the Court.

The fourth question

38. It must be noted at the outset that the Convention does not use the term 'indivisible' in relation to disputes but only the term 'related', in Article 22.

39. As the Court made clear in Case 150/80 *Elefanten Schuh* v *Jacqmain* [1981] ECR 1671, paragraph 19, Article 22 of the Convention is intended to establish how related actions which have been brought before courts of different Contracting States are to be dealt with. It does not confer jurisdiction; in particular, it does not accord jurisdiction to a court of a Contracting State to try an action which is related to another action of which that court is seised pursuant to the rules of the Convention.

40. In that judgment the Court held that Article 22 of the Convention applies only where related actions are brought before courts of two or more Contracting States.

41. It is clear from the documents before the Court in this case that separate actions have not been brought before the courts of different Contracting States, so that, in any event, the conditions for the application of Article 22 are not met.

42. It must next be borne in mind that, under Article 3 of the Convention, persons domiciled in a Contracting State may be sued in the courts of another Contracting State only by virtue of the rules set out in Sections 2 to 6 of Title II.

43. Those rules include, in Article 6(1) of the Convention, the rule that a person may also be sued, 'where he is one of a number of defendants, in the courts for the place where any one of them is domiciled'.

44. As is clear from the very wording of Article 6(1), it applies only if the proceedings in question are brought before the courts for the place where one of the defendants is domiciled.

45. That is not the case here.

46. It must be observed that the objective of legal certainty pursued by the Convention would not be attained if the fact that a court in a Contracting State had accepted jurisdiction as regards one of the defendants not domiciled in a Contracting State made it possible to bring another defendant, domiciled in a Contracting State, before that same court in cases other than those envisaged by the Convention, thereby depriving him of the benefit of the protective rules laid down by it.

47. In any event, the exception provided for in Article 6(1) of the Convention, derogating from the principle that the courts of the State in which the defendant is domiciled are to have jurisdiction, must be construed in such a way that there is no possibility of the very existence of that principle being called in question, in particular by allowing a plaintiff to make a claim against a number of defendants with the sole purpose of ousting the jurisdiction of the courts of the State where one of those defendants is domiciled (*Kalfelis*, cited above, paragraphs 8 and 9).

48. Accordingly, after pointing out that the purpose of Article 6(1) of the Convention, and of Article 22, is to ensure that judgments which are incompatible with each other are not given in the Contracting States, the Court held in *Kalfelis* that, for Article 6(1) of the Convention to apply there must exist between the various actions brought by the same plaintiff against different defendants a connection of such a kind that it is expedient to determine the actions together in order to avoid the risk of irreconcilable judgments resulting from separate proceedings.

49. In that connection, the Court also held in *Kalfelis* that a court which has jurisdiction under Article 5(3) of the Convention over an action in so far as it is based on tort or delict does not have jurisdiction over that action in so far as it is not so based.

50. It follows that two claims in one action for compensation, directed against different defendants and based in one instance on contractual liability and in the other on liability in tort or delict cannot be regarded as connected.

51. Finally, as the Court held in paragraph 20 of *Kalfelis*, whilst it is true that disadvantages arise from different aspects of the same dispute being adjudicated upon by different courts, it must be pointed out, on the one hand, that a plaintiff is always entitled to bring his action in its entirety

before the courts for the domicile of the defendant and, on the other, that Article 22 of the Convention allows the first court seised, in certain circumstances, to hear the case in its entirety provided that there is a connection between the actions brought before the different courts.

52. The answer to the fourth question must therefore be that Article 6(1) of the Convention must be interpreted as meaning that a defendant domiciled in a Contracting State cannot be sued in another Contracting State before a court seised of an action against a co-defendant not domiciled in a Contracting State on the ground that the dispute is indivisible rather than merely displaying a connection.

On those grounds, the Court (Third Chamber) in answer to the questions referred to it by the Cour de Cassation by judment of 28 January 1997, hereby rules:

1. **An action by which the consignee of goods found to be damaged on completion of a transport operation by sea and then by land, or by which his insurer who has been subrogated to his rights after compensating him, seeks redress for the damage suffered, relying on the bill of lading covering the maritime transport, not against the person who issued that document on his headed paper but against the person whom the plaintiff considered to be the actual maritime carrier, falls within the scope not of matters relating to a contract within the meaning of Article 5(1) of the Convention of 27 September 1968 on jurisdiction and the enforcement of judgments in civil and commercial matters, as amended by the Convention of 9 October 1978 on the Accession of the Kingdom of Denmark, Ireland and the United Kingdom of Great Britain and Northern Ireland, by the Convention of 25 October 1982 on the Accession of the Hellenic Republic and by the Convention of 26 May 1989 on the Accession of the Kingdom of Spain and the Portuguese Republic, but of matters relating to tort, delict or quasi-delict within the meaning of Article 5(3) of that Convention.**
2. **The place where the consignee of the goods, on completion of a transport operation by sea and then by land, merely discovered the existence of the damage to the goods delivered to him cannot serve to determine the 'place where the harmful event occurred' within the meaning of Article 5(3) of the Convention of 28 September 1968, as interpreted by the Court.**

3. Article 6(1) of the Convention of 27 September 1968 must be interpreted as meaning that a defendant domiciled in a Contracting State cannot be sued in another Contracting State before a court seised of an action against a co-defendant not domiciled in a Contracting State on the ground that the dispute is indivisible rather than merely displaying a connection.

OPINION OF MR ADVOCATE GENERAL COSMAS

I - Preliminary observations

1. By four preliminary questions the French Cour de Cassation (Court of Cassation) requests an interpretation from the Court of Article 5, paragraphs 1 and 3, and Article 6 of the Brussels Convention of 27 September 1968 on jurisdiction and the enforcement of judgments in civil and commercial matters, as amended most recently by the Convention of 26 May 1989 on the Accession of the Kingdom of Spain and the Portuguese Republic.

II - The facts

2. The facts of the present case do not emerge with all desirable clarity from the order for reference, from the observations of the parties or from the case-file in the main proceedings. According to the case-file, the French company Brambi Fruits, with its registered office in Rungis (hereinafter 'Brambi'), purchased, in May 1988, a large quantity of pears from the Australian company F.W. Year, with its registered office in Melbourne.

3. It was under cover of a bearer bill of lading issued, on 8 May 1992, in Sydney by the Australian company Refrigerated Container Carriers PTY Ltd, with its registered office in Sydney (hereinafter 'RCC') that the goods were loaded, in eight refrigerated containers containing 5 199 boxes of pears, in the port of Melbourne on board the vessel Alblasgracht V002, bound for the port of Rotterdam, which was designated as the place of delivery and unloading of the goods. This vessel was, it seems, operated by the Dutch company Spliethoff's, which is not referred to in the bill of lading and which has its registered office in Amsterdam. Brambi was merely to be notified of the bill of lading.

4. From Rotterdam, the containers were transported by road, under cover of international consignment notes, to Rungis in France, where the registered office of Brambi is situated. The consignment notes for this part of the journey indicate that they were issued by the company Transeco and refer to 'Conship' as the carrier.

5. When the consignment arrived at Rungis, Brambi noticed that it was damaged and entered reservations against delivery. The damage resulted from a premature ripening of the fruit, due to a breakdown in the cooling system.

Compensation for the damage was paid by the company Réunion Européenne and nine other insurance companies, all of whom were plaintiffs and are now appellants in the final appeal in the main proceedings.

6. After having paid out the compensation due, the insurers, subrogated to the rights of Brambi, brought an action before the Tribunal de Commerce (Commercial Court), Créteil, in the jurisdiction of which Rungis is situated. Their action was brought, on the one hand, against RCC, who had issued the bill of lading for the maritime part of the transport operation, and, on the other, against (a) Spliethoff's and (b) the master of the vessel Alblasgracht, in their capacity as the actual maritime transporters.

7. The Tribunal de Commerce held, having regard to the correspondence between Brambi and RCC, that the pears were intended to be delivered in Rungis and that, as a result, it had jurisdiction over the 'transaction' between these two companies. Thus, presumably under the first paragraph of Article 4 of the Convention, it applied French law and not the provisions of the said Convention, since the Commonwealth of Australia is not a party to the latter. In addition, the Tribunal de Commerce held that RCC had not respected its 'contract' and ordered it to pay compensation of some FRF 400 000 to the insurers, as well as the costs of the proceedings.

In contrast, the Tribunal de Commerce declared that it lacked jurisdiction in so far as the other two defendants were concerned, on the following grounds: there was nothing to show that there was combined joint transport from Melbourne to Rungis; the place where the defendants were to perform their obligation was Rotterdam; and, as a result, by virtue of the Convention, the competent courts were those of Rotterdam, where the goods were to be delivered, or those of Amsterdam, place of domicile of the defendants.

8. On appeal by the insurers, the Cour d'Appel (Court of Appeal), Paris, upheld the decision at first instance in holding that the liability of Spliethoff's and of the master of the vessel was necessarily based on contract and that, as a result, the abovementioned Netherlands courts had jurisdiction by virtue of Article 2 and Article 5(1) of the Brussels Convention.

9. The insurers brought a final appeal against this decision before the Cour de Cassation. They submitted that the dispute with the defendants was not contractual in character, as the Cour d'Appel had wrongly held, but was clearly a tortious dispute governed by Article 5(3) of the Convention, with the consequences which result therefrom as regards jurisdiction. In the alternative, the insurers submitted that, since all three of the defendants had taken part in the same maritime transport operation, the dispute was indivisible. As a result, the Cour d'Appel should also have declared that it had jurisdiction in regard to the other two defendants, since it had accepted that it had jurisdiction in regard to the first defendant.

10. Having decided that the resolution of the dispute required an interpretation of the Convention, in particular with regard to the autonomous nature of the concept of 'matters relating to a contract', the French Cour de Cassation referred the following four questions to the Court of Justice.

III - The questions for preliminary ruling

The French Cour de Cassation requests the Court of Justice to rule on the following questions:

'1. Is an action by which the consignee of goods found to be damaged on completion of a transport operation by sea and then by land, or by which his insurer who has been subrogated to his rights after compensating him, seeks redress for the damage suffered, relying on the bill of lading covering the maritime transport, not against the person who issued the document on his headed paper but against the person whom the plaintiff considered to be the actual maritime carrier, based on the contract of transport and does it, for that or any other reason, fall within the scope of matters relating to contract within the meaning of Article 5(1) of the Convention?

2. If the foregoing question is answered in the negative, is the matter one relating to tort, delict or quasi-delict within the meaning of Article 5(3) of the Convention or is it appropriate to have recourse to the principle laid down in Article 2 of the Convention that the courts of the State in whose territory the defendant is domiciled have jurisdiction?

3. In the event that the matter is to be regarded as one relating to tort, delict or quasi-delict, may the place where the consignee, after completion of the maritime transport operation and then the final overland transport operation, merely discovered that the goods delivered to him were damaged, constitute - and if so under what conditions - the place of occurrence of the damage which, according to the judgment of the Court of Justice of 30 November 1976 in Case 21/76 *Bier* v *Mines de Potasse d'Alsace* [1976] ECR 1735, may be the place "where the harmful event occurred" within the meaning of Article 5(3) of the Convention?

4. May a defendant domiciled in the territory of a Contracting State be brought, in another Contracting State, before the court hearing an action against a co-defendant not domiciled in the territory of any Contracting State, on the ground that the dispute is indivisible, rather than merely displaying a connection?'

IV - The legal framework

11. Article 2 of the Convention provides:

'Subject to the provisions of this Convention, persons domiciled in a Contracting State shall, whatever their nationality, be sued in the courts of that State ...'.

12. Article 3 provides: 'Persons domiciled in a Contracting State may be sued in the courts of another Contracting State only by virtue of the rules set out in Sections 2 to 6 of this Title'.

13. Article 4 provides: 'If the defendant is not domiciled in a Contracting State, the jurisdiction of the Courts of each Contracting State shall, subject to the provisions of Article 16, be determined by the law of that State.'

14. Article 5 of the Convention provides:

'A person domiciled in a Contracting State may, in another Contracting State, be sued:

(1) in matters relating to a contract, in the courts for the place of performance of the obligation in question ...

(3) in matters relating to tort, delict or quasi-delict, in the courts for the place where the harmful event occurred'.

15. Article 6 of the Convention provides: 'A person domiciled in a Contracting State may also be sued:

(1) where he is one of a number of defendants, in the courts for the place where any one of them is domiciled ...'.

16. Finally, Article 22 of the Convention provides: 'Where related actions are brought in the courts of different Contracting States, any court other than the court first seised may, while the actions are pending at first instance, stay its proceedings.

A court other than the court first seised may also, on the application of one of the parties, decline jurisdiction if the law of that country permits the consolidation of related actions and the court first seised has jurisdiction over both actions.

For the purposes of this Article, actions are deemed to be related where they are so closely connected that it is expedient to hear and determine them together to avoid the risk of irreconcilable judgments resulting from separate proceedings.'

V - The substance

The first question

17. The defendants submit that, to the extent that the action they are subject to has as its basis the bill of lading, i.e. the formal document of the contract of carriage, the dispute concerns matters relating to contract. In contrast, the German and French Governments, as well as the Commission, submit that, in the absence of a contractual link between the purchaser and the maritime carrier, the dispute is not contractual in nature.

18. The defendants' position cannot be accepted.

19. It should first be recalled that the Convention seeks to unify the rules of international jurisdiction of the Contracting States. Its objective is, in particular, to avoid, in so far as possible, multiplication of the bases of jurisdiction in relation to one and the same legal relationship and to reinforce the legal protection available to persons established in the Community by, at the same time, allowing the plaintiff easily to identify the court before which he may bring an action and the defendant reasonably to foresee the court before which he may be sued. The legal protection of persons established in the Community and legal certainty are thus reinforced.

20. Under the system of the Convention, the general principle is that the courts of the Contracting State in which the defendant is domiciled are to have jurisdiction (Article 2); it is only by way of derogation from this principle that

the Convention provides for cases, which are exhaustively listed, in which the defendant may (in the case of special jurisdiction) or must (in the case of exclusive jurisdiction or prorogation of jurisdiction), depending on the case, be sued in the courts of another Contracting State.

In fact, in general, the defendant is regarded, from a procedural point of view, to be the weaker party as a result of the fact that it is he who is being sued by the plaintiff, except in certain specified cases where it is the plaintiff who is considered to be the weaker party, and will thus be favoured by the Convention.

21. Thus, Article 5 provides for situations of special jurisdiction where the plaintiff may choose to sue the defendant other than in the place of his domicile.

This freedom of choice was introduced having regard to the existence, in certain clearly defined situations, of a particularly close connecting factor between a dispute and the court which may be called upon to hear it, with a view to the efficacious conduct of the proceedings.

22. One of these situations arises in disputes in matters relating to contract. The concept of 'matters relating to a contract' is not defined in the Convention. However, as the Court has repeatedly emphasised, in order to ensure the full effectiveness of the Convention, this concept has to be interpreted independently, by reference to the system and objectives of the Convention, and it cannot be understood as referring simply to the classification that national law gives to the legal relationship at issue before the national court.

23. The concept of matters relating to a contract was defined in particular in the Handte case. In that case, a French company having its registered office in Bonneville had purchased products from the subsidiary of a German company, which had its registered office in Strasbourg. As the products appeared to be defective, it brought an action before the Tribunal de Grande Instance (Regional Court), Bonneville, for compensation against both the seller and the German company which had manufactured the product. When asked to rule on the question of whether the relationship between the sub-buyer and the manufacturer was contractual in character (the only situation in which the manufacturing company could have been sued before the courts of the 'place of performance of the obligation'), the Court held, having recalled the objectives of the Convention, that the concept of 'matters relating to a contract' within the meaning of Article 5(1) could not to be understood as covering a situation in which there is no obligation freely assumed by one party towards another (paragraph 15), as in the case of the relationship between the sub-buyer of goods purchased from an intermediate seller and the manufacturer of those goods (paragraph 16).

The Court emphasised that 'where there is a chain of international contracts, the parties' contractual obligations may vary from contract to contract, so that the contractual rights which the sub-buyer can enforce against his immediate seller will not necessarily be the same as those which the manufacturer will have accepted in his relationship with the first buyer' (paragraph 17).

In those circumstances, the Court held that, in the absence of a contractual relationship between a manufacturer and a sub-buyer, where the identity and domicile of the latter may reasonably be unknown to the former, the manufacturer cannot foresee before which courts, other than those of his domicile, he may be sued, which would be incompatible with the principle of legal certainty which the Convention seeks to protect (paragraphs 18 and 20).

24. It follows from this case-law that, within the meaning of Article 5(1) of the Convention, which is to be strictly interpreted in so far as it derogates from Article 2, an action for compensation does not constitute a 'matter relating to a contract' except where there is an agreement freely entered into, not as between the plaintiff and a third party or between the defendant and a third party, but between the plaintiff and the defendant and on the condition that the plaintiff submits in his application that the defendant is in breach of the obligations imposed on him as a result of that agreement.

25. In the present case, the referring court asks whether, in the given circumstances, the dispute can be considered as having a contractual character because it has as its basis the 'contract of transport'. But which 'contract of transport' and between whom?

26. This point is not clear, and neither the plaintiffs nor the defendants, in their written submissions in the main proceedings and in their observations in the present proceedings, have really clarified things, not to say that they have studiously avoided clarifying them.

27. It follows in any event from the findings of the court of first instance and from those of the court of second instance that the delivery of the pears to Rungis was agreed between RCC and Brambi, probably in the context of a contract of transport between the two companies concerning the carriage of the goods from Melbourne to Rungis. The transport was in any event completed in two stages clearly separate and independent from each other, the first by sea and the second by land.

28. For the maritime stage, which is the only one of interest to us here, RCC issued a bill of lading to the bearer, on which the consigner is stated to be the Year company (i.e. the seller), while Brambi is mentioned as being the person to which the bill of lading should be notified and the transport is shown as having to be carried out on the vessel Alblasgracht. The courts of first and second instance decided that, although the form carried the pre-printed reference that it was combined transport (i.e. covering several types of transport), the bill of lading related in reality only to the maritime part of the transport, since the port of unloading and delivery was Rotterdam. From these factors, the courts at first instance and on appeal concluded that the actual maritime transporter was Spliethoff's, which was not referred to in the bill of lading, but which is the operator of the vessel on which the transport took place.

29. As regards the relationship between Brambi and Spliethoff's, we do not have any clear evidence. The allegations of the parties in the course of the main proceedings and their written observations before the Court do not in fact allow us to say whether there was a contractual link between the two companies. On the contrary, the plaintiffs submitted, without being contradicted on this point by any convincing argument on the part of the defendants, that RCC sub-contracted the performance of the maritime transport to Spliethoff's. This

implies, logically, that a contract must have been concluded between RCC and Spliethoff's. Whether or not such a contract existed, however, is irrelevant in the present case since, in any event, Brambi is a third party in relation to this contract. In fact, as indicated above (see point 20), in order for there to be a 'matter relating to a contract' within the meaning of Article 5(1) of the Convention, it is not sufficient that there is any kind of contract, even relating to the case, between the plaintiff or the defendant and a third party; there must be a contract between the plaintiff and the defendant.

30. Consequently, in the present case, irrespective of the legal nature of the bill of lading in question, and apart from the question of the link between RCC and Brambi, one can draw a reasonably clear conclusion from the documents on the case-file, namely that there was no contractual link freely entered into between Brambi, on the one hand, and Spliethoff's and the master, on the other hand.

31. As a result, to the extent that the national courts, who have sole jurisdiction to decide on the facts, concluded that there was no contractual link between Brambi and the defendants, or more precisely between the former and Spliethoff's, the dispute cannot in any sense be considered as having a contractual basis within the meaning of Article 5(1) of the Convention.

The second question

32. All of the parties agree that, to the extent that the liability of the maritime carrier transporter is engaged and the dispute does not have a contractual basis, it is a tortious matter.

33. This point of view should be accepted.

34. As I have stated previously, by way of derogation from the general principle of international jurisdiction of the place of domicile of the defendant, Article 5(3) of the Convention provides that the latter may be sued: 'in matters relating to tort, delict or quasi-delict, in the courts for the place where the harmful event occurred.'

35. According to the case-law of the Court, the concept of 'matters relating to tort, delict or quasi-delict' in Article 5(3), must, in a similar manner to the concept of 'matters relating to a contract' in Article 5(1), be regarded as an autonomous concept. In order to ensure uniformity in all the Member States, it must be recognised that the concept covers 'all actions which seek to establish the liability of a defendant and which are not related to a "contract" within the meaning of Article 5(1)'.

36. As, in the present case, the liability of the defendants is at issue because of the damage sustained to the goods during the maritime transport and since the dispute is not contractual, it necessarily concerns a dispute relating to tort, delict or quasi-delict within the meaning of Article 5(3) of the Convention. As a result, in so far as we are dealing with a case of special jurisdiction, it is not appropriate to apply Article 2 establishing general jurisdiction.

The third question

37. It should be noted that, by its third question, the referring court seeks to ascertain whether, in the circumstances of the main proceedings, the place where the damage was simply discovered is the 'place where the harmful event occurred', within the meaning of Article 5(3) of the Convention, as interpreted by the Court.

38. This questions raises two problems. The first is to determine the place where the harmful event occurred when the damage took place in the course of international transport, such as that in the main proceedings. The second problem is to determine whether this place corresponds with the place where the damage was simply discovered.

39. In principle, all of the parties are agreed that the place where the damage was simply discovered is irrelevant if it does not correspond with the place where the harmful event actually occurred or with the place where the damage arose. In addition, as can be inferred from their observations, the defendants and the French Government consider that, in circumstances such as those of the main proceedings, the place where the damage occurs is where the maritime voyage was concluded and where the defendants were required to deliver the goods.

40. These points of view call for consideration.

41. As the Court has consistently held, this rule of special jurisdiction contained in Article 5(3), which depends on the exercise of a choice by the plaintiff, is based on the existence of a particularly close connecting factor between the dispute and courts other than those of the domicile of the defendant, with a view to the sound administration of justice and the efficacious conduct of the proceedings.

42. The meaning of the expression 'place where the harmful event occurred' used in Article 5(3) as a criterion of special international jurisdiction is not particularly clear. The Jenard Report has already stated: 'The Committee did not think it should specify whether that place is the place where the event which resulted in damage or injury occurred, or whether it is the place where the damage or injury was sustained. The Committee preferred to keep to a formula which has already been adopted by a number of legal systems'.

43. In Mines de Potasse d'Alsace, the Court stated that the meaning of the above expression 'is unclear when the place of the event which is at the origin of the damage is situated in a State other than the one in which the place where the damage occurred is situated' (paragraph 13) and it asked whether, in such a case, it was necessary to choose as the connecting factor the place of the event giving rise to the damage, or the place where the damage occurred, or to accept that the plaintiff had an option between the one and the other of those two connecting factors (paragraph 14).

According to that judgment, the place of the event giving rise to the damage, no less than the place where the damage occurred, could, depending on the case, constitute a significant connecting factor from the point of view of jurisdiction. In fact, both could constitute significant factors connecting the dispute with the court seised, given that each of them could be particularly helpful from the point of view of the evidence and of the conduct of the proceedings (paragraphs 15 to 17).

Thus, the Court held that where the place of the occurrence of the event which might give rise to liability in tort, delict or quasi-delict and the place where that event resulted in damage were not identical, the expression 'place where the harmful event occurred' in Article 5(3) of the Convention had to be understood as being intended to cover both the place where the damage occurred and the place of the event giving rise to it, with the result that the defendant could be sued, at the option of the plaintiff, in the courts of either of them (paragraphs 24 and 25).

The Court also held that to opt only for the place of the event giving rise to the damage would, in an appreciable number of cases, cause confusion between the heads of jurisdiction laid down by Articles 2 and 5(3) of the Convention, so that the latter provision would, to that extent, lose its effectiveness (paragraph 20).

44. In Mines de Potasse d'Alsace, the place of the harmful event (that of the discharge of waste by the French company into the Rhine, leading to the pollution of its waters) was clearly different from the place where the damage was suffered (the place where the Dutch horticultural business irrigated its plantations with the polluted waters, causing considerable damage to them). However, this distinction is not always easy to make, all the more so where the exact determination of the place where the damage occurred presents certain difficulties in other respects. The Court has, in its case-law, ruled on a large number of similar questions in like circumstances.

45. In Shevill and Others, the Court had to answer the question of which court has jurisdiction in the case of defamation by the press, where the newspaper was published in one State, but the damage particularly resulted from its circulation in the State of domicile of the person defamed. The Court held that both the courts where the damage occurred and the courts where the harmful event originated, that is to say, the courts of the place of publication of the newspaper, had jurisdiction and that this was for all the harm caused by the unlawful act (paragraphs 24 and 25). This place where the damage occurred is 'the place where the event giving rise to the damage, entailing tortious, delictual or quasi-delictual liability, produced its harmful effects upon the victim' (paragraph 28). On the basis of these considerations, the Court concluded that the courts of each of the Member States in which the defamatory publication is circulated are only competent to rule on the question of compensation for injury caused to the reputation of the victim from the circulation of the newspaper in the corresponding State (paragraphs 29 to 33).

46. In Dumez France and Tracoba (C-220/88), French companies had brought an action before their national courts against German banks for compensation in respect of the damage they suffered following the insolvency of their subsidiaries established in Germany. According to the plaintiffs, the damage was brought about by the suspension of a property-development project in Germany for a German prime contractor: the damage was the direct result of

the cancellation by the German banks of the loans granted to the prime contractor.

In its judgment of 11 January 1990, the Court held in this case that the damage caused to the parent companies was merely an indirect consequence of the damage suffered by their subsidiaries in a different place (paragraphs 13 to 16) and, having rejected an interpretation of the Convention which would have allowed the plaintiff to determine, except in certain specified cases, the competent court by his choice of domicile (paragraph 19), the Court held that 'the rule on jurisdiction laid down in Article 5(3) of the Convention cannot be interpreted as permitting a plaintiff pleading damage which he claims to be the consequence of the harm suffered by other persons who were direct victims of the harmful act to bring proceedings against the perpetrator of that act in the courts of the place in which he himself ascertained the damage to his assets' (paragraph 22, emphasis added).

47. The decision in Marinari is of greater interest. In this case, Mr Marinari, domiciled in Italy, had lodged a bundle of promissory notes with an English bank. The employees of the bank, after opening the envelope, refused to return the promissory notes and advised the police of their existence, considering that they were of dubious origin, which led to Mr Marinari's arrest and sequestration of the promissory notes. Having been released by the English authorities, Mr Marinari brought an action against the bank in the Italian courts seeking, on the one hand, payment of the face value of the promissory notes, and on the other hand, compensation for damage suffered as a result of his detention, for breach of several contracts and for damage to his reputation.

When asked to rule on whether the Italian or English courts had jurisdiction over the matter, the Court, after recalling the principles set out in the case-law of Mines de Potasse d'Alsace, Dumez France and Tracoba and Shevill and Others, held that the option open to the plaintiff to choose between the place of the event giving rise to the damage and the place where the damage occurred cannot be extended beyond the particular circumstances which justify it, without negating the general principle that the courts of the Contracting State where the defendant is domiciled are to have jurisdiction; it would lead, in cases other than those expressly provided for, to recognition of the jurisdiction of the courts of the plaintiff's domicile, a solution which the Convention does not favour since, in the second paragraph of Article 3, it excludes application of national provisions which make such jurisdiction available for proceedings against defendants domiciled in the territory of a Contracting State (paragraph 13).

The Court thus held that the term 'place where the harmful event occurred' cannot be construed so extensively as to encompass any place where the adverse consequences can be felt of an event which has already caused damage actually arising elsewhere (paragraph 14).

More particularly, this concept cannot be construed as including the place where the victim claims to have suffered financial damage following upon initial damage arising and suffered by him in another Contracting State (paragraph 15).

48. In my opinion, the abovementioned case-law shows that, in order to determine the 'place where the damage occurred', it is essential to define the

relevant 'damage'. 'Damage' means any harm to the property or person of the plaintiff, where it relates to the event giving rise to the damage, that is to say to the illegal behaviour attributed to the defendant by a direct and causal link, to the exclusion of indirect, more remote damage or damage which is suffered by an indirect victim. Consequently, 'the place where the damage occurred' is that where the event giving rise to the damage caused injury, within the above meaning, to the plaintiff.

49. The above case-law provides sufficient elements to determine the 'place where the damage occurred' in the case where the damage occurs in the course of international carriage of goods, as in the present case.

50. First of all, it must be observed that the basic obligation imposed on every carrier is to load the goods at a given point and to deliver them intact at another point. As a result, carriers are, in principle, liable for any damage caused to the goods between the departure and the arrival points of the voyage, that is to say for the entire duration of that voyage.

51. When the consignee entered into a contract with one carrier only, the liability of the latter towards the former for damage caused to the goods during the voyage is contractual in nature. Consequently, where both are domiciled in the Community, Article 5(1) of the Convention allows the consignee to sue the carrier before the courts of the place where the goods were delivered or should have been delivered.

52. Let us suppose, however, that the carrier, without the consignee's knowledge, had entrusted part of the transport to another carrier (the sub-contractor), even domiciled in the Community, who caused the damage to the goods. In this case, the first carrier remains liable towards the consignee, by virtue of the contract which binds them. The sub-contractor is liable, on the one hand, towards the original carrier by virtue of the contract between them and, on the other hand, by reason of his tortious liability towards the consignee, to whom he is not bound by any contractual link.

53. In the latter case, the consignee may, according to Mines de Potasse d'Alsace, sue the sub-contractor either before the courts of the place where the harmful event occurred, or before the courts of the place where the damage occurred.

54. The place where the damage occurred may be known to the plaintiff and may be located in the Community, in which case the court having jurisdiction will be easily determined. It may also be impossible to locate this place, or the place may be outside the Community, so that it will not be possible to identify the court having jurisdiction. The harmful conduct may also have lasted for the entire voyage, and it would thus not be reasonable to require the plaintiff to seise the courts of all the places through which the vessel sailed. In such circumstances, the consignee must limit himself to the place where the damage occurred. We must now consider where this place is located.

55. First, the place where the damage occurred cannot be that of the 'final delivery' of the goods, that is to say the place where the initial carrier had to deliver the goods to the consignee, as the plaintiffs argue.

The reasons for this are obvious. In an international transport operation, such as that in the main proceedings, which is performed by several successive carriers, there is a succession of transport contracts under which the rights and obligations of the parties may vary significantly. The sub-contractor may not know the place where the initial carrier had agreed with the consignee to deliver the goods, and may be unaware of the existence and the address of the latter. As a result, this place does not have any organic link with the dispute between the consignee and the sub-contractor. In addition, as the Commission rightly points out, in international trade, goods may change destination in transit, with the result that their place of destination may not be determined easily, or it may even be determined arbitrarily by the plaintiff, which would encourage forum shopping. Moreover, as the place of final delivery of the goods is in general the place where the plaintiff's commercial establishment is located, choosing this place in the present case might amount to setting the place where the plaintiff is domiciled or where his professional establishment is located up as a new jurisdiction criterion, to which the Convention is expressly opposed. Such an outcome would be contrary to the rule set out in Article 2 of the Convention, as well as to the general scheme which the latter aimed at establishing.

56. In addition, the place where the damage occurred cannot be that where the damage was merely ascertained by the plaintiff.

Indeed, if an international transport operation is performed by several successive carriers, as in the present case, the damage allegedly caused to the goods by an intermediate carrier may be ascertained either in the course of one of the subsequent stages of the voyage, or at the place of delivery of the goods, or at the place to which the goods were sent subsequently, etc., all places which the defendant could not foresee in any way. If the place where the damage was ascertained was relevant, international jurisdiction would be subject to uncertain and fortuitous elements, which would be contrary to the fundamental objective of the Convention, which is 'to provide for a clear and certain attribution of jurisdiction'. In addition, such an interpretation could attribute jurisdiction to the court of a place having no connection with the subject-matter of the dispute, so that, as regards the quality of evidence, the court of that place would be irrelevant. Finally, the plaintiff could always assert that he ascertained the damage where his domicile or business is located, with the consequences which are explained in the above paragraph.

57. In my opinion, in a case such as that in the main proceedings, the place where the damage occurred may only be that up to which the sub-contractor against whom the plaintiff takes legal action was in charge of the goods, that is the place where he had to deliver the goods.

58. In the first place, there is indeed a causal link between the harmful event and the damage. The plaintiffs argue that, during the carriage, the defendants did not comply with the normal refrigeration temperature, and that this caused the pears to ripen prematurely. The defendants' conduct, if true, is likely to have caused the deterioration of such fragile goods.

This deterioration constitutes in itself direct damage to the property, in the broad sense of the term, of the consignee or the assignee of the goods. The fact that the deterioration of the goods was progressive (either because of its nature, or because of the negligence of the other carriers) is not relevant to what concerns us here and does not alter the fact that the damage occurred during the course of the transport and, at the latest, at the end of that transport.

59. In addition, this place is clear and foreseeable for the defendant and, as a result, it ensures legal certainty. Second, it is by nature closely linked to the dispute between the consignee and the defendant and it facilitates the gathering of evidence. As a result, it promotes the proper administration of justice. Moreover, it even favours the plaintiff to a certain extent, in so far as it entitles him to choose a place which may be closer to his domicile than the domicile of the defendant, when it is difficult or impossible to determine the place where the damage occurred, or where that place is very remote. In addition, if the initial carrier entrusted the transport to a single sub-contractor, the place of performance of the initial carrier's service and the place where the damage occurred will be the same, which limits the number of courts likely to have territorial jurisdiction, to the benefit of the proper administration of justice over the whole dispute. Consequently, this solution takes into account all the interests in question and does not lead to favouring one of the parties in particular.

60. In the present case, to the extent that, in the main proceedings, the defendants are alleged to be liable for the damage which occurred during the maritime transport from Melbourne to Rotterdam, it is in the latter port that the goods were, for the last time, under the defendants' responsibility and suffered the harmful consequences of the unlawful conduct attributed to the latter. As a result, that is where the damage occurred for the purposes of Article 5(3) of the Convention.

The fourth question

61. Considering the chronological background to the case set out above, the last question of the referring court must be construed as seeking to ascertain, essentially, whether the Convention allows persons domiciled in a Contracting State, against whom a claim has been brought under Article 5(3), to be sued before the court of another Contracting State, which is seised of another claim within the same action, brought against a defendant who is not domiciled in a Contracting State and which is, in addition, based on national law, on the ground that the dispute concerning the two cases is 'indivisible' rather than merely displaying a connection.

62. The question submitted does not refer to any concrete provisions for which it seeks the interpretation. Moreover, while the term 'related' is explained in Article 22, the term 'indivisible' applied to the dispute, as used in the question as a potential criterion of jurisdiction, is not referred to in the Convention.

63. In these circumstances, it should first be recalled that, under Article 3 of the Convention, a person domiciled in a Contracting State may not be sued before the courts of another Contracting State except in the cases expressly and exhaustively provided for in Sections 2 to 6 of Title II.

64. Article 22, which refers to related actions, forms part of Section 8 of Title II above. Thus, this Article does not apply in the present case.

As the Court held in Elefanten Schuh, 'Article 22 of the Convention is intended to establish how related actions which have been brought before courts of different Member States are to be dealt with. It does not confer jurisdiction; in particular, it does not accord jurisdiction to a court of a Contracting State to try an action which is related to another action of which that court is seised pursuant to the rules of the Convention' (paragraph 19).

'The answer ... should therefore be that Article 22 of the Convention applies only where related actions are brought before courts of two or more Contracting States' (paragraph 20).

In the circumstances, irrespective of whether the action brought against RCC and the action brought against the defendants are 'related actions' within the meaning of Article 22 of the Convention, the fact is that separate actions were not brought before the courts of different Member States. As a result, and in any event, the conditions for the application of Article 22 are not satisfied.

65. Let us return to Article 3 of the Convention. Of Sections 2 to 6 of Title II, sections 3 to 5 do not concern us in the present case. Since Article 5 does not offer the possibility of changing the court having jurisdiction, the only provision relating to the subject-matter of the preliminary question is Article 6(1). I will thus restrict myself to examining this provision.

66. It follows from the wording of this provision that an indispensable condition for its application is, in the first place, that the action is brought before the courts of the place of domicile of one of the defendants. This obviously means that the domicile of this defendant must be situated in a Contracting State and that, as a result, this defendant must be domiciled in a Contracting State. In addition, as the case-law shows, it is necessary in the second place that there is a connecting factor, within the meaning of Article 22, between the actions which concern the defendants.

67. As to the first condition, it should be recalled that RCC, to which the dispute with the defendants is allegedly linked, does not have a registered office in the jurisdiction of the Tribunal de Commerce of Créteil, before which it was sued, but rather in a non-Contracting State. As a result, and for this reason above all, the defendants cannot be sued before the Tribunal de Commerce of Créteil on the basis of Article 6(1) of the Convention.

68. As regards the second condition, it should be noted that the Court has already addressed, in the Kalfelis case, the question of whether a criterion of national law such as mere connection or indivisibility can be used for the definition of the concept of 'connection' for the purposes of Article 6(1) of the Convention, where several actions are brought against the same defendant.

69. The Court emphasised that the exception to the principle of Article 2 contained in Article 6(1) must be treated in such a manner that there is no possibility of the very existence of that principle being called into question (paragraph 8). That possibility might arise if a plaintiff were at liberty to make a claim against a number of defendants with the sole object of ousting the jurisdiction of the courts of the State where one of the defendants is domiciled; it is necessary for that purpose that there should be a connection

between the claims made against each of the defendants (paragraph 9), the nature of which must be determined independently (paragraph 10).

After having stated that Article 6(1), in the same manner as Article 22, seeks to avoid the risk in the Contracting States of judgments which are incompatible with each other (paragraph 11), the Court held that 'The rule laid down in Article 6(1) therefore applies where the actions brought against the various defendants are related when the proceedings are instituted, that is to say where it is expedient to hear and determine them together in order to avoid the risk of irreconcilable judgments resulting from separate proceedings. It is for the national court to verify in each individual case whether that condition is satisfied' (paragraph 12).

70. Such is the situation where several actions are brought against different defendants. In Kalfelis, however, the question arose as to whether, in the case of actions based concurrently on tortious liability, breach of contract or unjust enrichment, the court having jurisdiction under Article 5(3) for one of the heads of claim could adjudicate on the action in so far as it was not based on tort or delict.

On this point, the Court first observed that the special jurisdictions enumerated in Articles 5 and 6 of the Convention constitute derogations from the principle that jurisdiction is vested in the courts of the State where the defendant is domiciled and as such must be interpreted restrictively. Consequently, the Court ruled that 'a court which has jurisdiction under Article 5(3) over an action in so far as it is based on tort or delict does not have jurisdiction over that action in so far as it is not so based' (paragraph 19).

In fact, the Court went on, this solution presented a disadvantage arising from different aspects of the same dispute being adjudicated upon by different courts; however, this disadvantage was counterbalanced by the possibility for the plaintiff to bring his action in its entirety before the courts for the domicile of the defendant, as well as the possibility which Article 22 offers in certain conditions to the first court seised to hear the case (paragraph 20).

71. In view of the foregoing, it follows that two claims for compensation in the same action, brought against different defendants, with one based on contractual liability and the other on tortious liability, cannot be considered as having a connection.

72. This solution should also, for the same reason, be adopted in the present proceedings. As regards the action for compensation, if the court seised of the action based on tortious liability does not have jurisdiction to rule on the action which is founded on contractual liability, the court seised of this latter action (a fortiori, if this is under provisions other than those in the Convention) cannot rule on the former request either. Therefore, Article 6(1) cannot be applied in the present case.

VI - Conclusion

For those reasons, I propose that the questions submitted be answered as follows:

(1) In a situation such as that in the main proceedings, an action by which the consignee of goods seeks redress from the carrier for damage suffered at the hands of the carrier, who is assumed to have insured the maritime part of the transport, by reason of damage to the goods during this phase of the transport, is not a 'matter relating to a contract' within the meaning of Article 5(1) of the Brussels Convention of 27 September 1968 on jurisdiction and the enforcement of judgments in civil and commercial matters, as last amended by the Convention of 26 May 1989 on the Accession of the Kingdom of Spain and the Portuguese Republic, to the extent to which there is no contractual link freely entered into between the plaintiff and the defendant.

(2) The matter is tortious within the meaning of Article 5(3) of the Convention where this action brings into question the liability of the carrier for the damage and there is no contractual link between the plaintiff and the defendant.

(3) The place where the plaintiff only discovered the damage cannot be used to determine the 'place where the harmful event occurred' within the meaning of Article 5(3) of the Convention, as interpreted by the Court.

(4) Articles 3 and 6(1) of the Convention must be interpreted as meaning that a person domiciled in a Contracting State may not be sued before the courts of another Contracting State seised of an action brought against a co-defendant domiciled outside the territory of any Contracting State on the ground that the dispute is indivisible rather than merely displaying a connection.

TITLE II *[Chapter II]*

JURISDICTION *[Jurisdiction]*

Jurisdiction in matters arising out of the operations of a branch, agency or other establishment – Article 5(5) *[Article 5(5)]*

See also

Case 33/78 - 22 November 1978

Somafer SA
v
Saar-Ferngas AG

Interpretation - General rules - Special jurisdiction - Concepts in Article 5(5): 'operations of a branch, agency or other establishment' - Independent interpretation - Meaning - Jurisdiction of the national court.

Summary

1. The Convention of 27 September 1968 must be interpreted having regard both to its principles and objectives and to its relationship with the Treaty. The question whether the words and concepts used in the Convention must be regarded as having their own independent meaning and as being thus common to all the Contracting States or as referring to substantive rules of the law applicable in each case under the rules of conflict of laws of the court before which the matter is first brought must be so answered as to ensure that the Convention is fully effective in achieving the objects which it pursues.

2. The need to ensure legal certainty and equality of rights and obligations for the parties as regards the power to derogate from the general jurisdiction of Article 2 requires an independent interpretation, common to all the Contracting States, of the concepts in Article 5(5) of the Convention of 27 September 1968.

The concept of branch, agency or other establishment implies a place of business which has the appearance of permanency, such as the extension of a parent body, has a management and is materially equipped to negotiate business with third parties so that the latter, although knowing that there will if necessary be a legal link with the parent body, the head office of which is abroad, do not have to deal directly with such parent body but may transact business at the place of business constituting the extension.

The concept of 'operations' comprises:

- actions relating to rights and contractual or non-contractual obligations concerning the management properly so-called of the agency, branch or other establishment itself such as those concerning the situation of the building where such entity is established or the local engagement of staff to work there;
- actions relating to undertakings which have been entered into at the above-mentioned place of business in the name of the parent body and which must be performed in the Contracting State where the place of business is established and also actions concerning non-contractual obligations arising from the activities in which the branch, agency or other establishment within the above defined meaning, has engaged at the place in which it is established on behalf of the parent body.

It is in each case for the court before which the matter comes to find the facts whereon it may be established that an effective place of business exists and to determine the legal position by reference to the concept of 'operations' as above defined.

JUDGMENT OF THE COURT

Kutscher, President, Mertens de Wilmars and Lord Mackenzie Stuart, Presidents of Chambers, Donner, Pescatore, Sorensen, O'Keeffe, Bosco and Touffait, Judges

1. By order dated 21 February 1978, received at the Court on 13 March 1978, the Oberlandesgericht Saarbrücken referred to the Court under the Protocol of 3 June 1971 concerning the interpretation of the Convention of 27 September 1968 on Jurisdiction and the Enforcement of Judgments in Civil and Commercial Matters (Official Journal 1978, No L 304, p. 77) (hereinafter referred to as 'the Convention') three questions on the interpretation of Article 5(5) of the Convention. According to the provision, interpretation of which is sought, a person domiciled in a Contracting State may, in another Contracting State, be sued: '(5) as regards a dispute arising out of the operations of a branch, agency or other establishment, in the courts for the place in which the branch, agency or other establishment is situated'.

2. The questions put must enable the national court to decide whether it has jurisdiction under the said provision - without prejudice to its

jurisdiction on the basis of other provisions of the Convention - to try an action brought by a German undertaking against a French undertaking, the registered office of which is in French territory but which has an office or place of contact in the Federal Republic of Germany described on its note-paper as 'Vertretung für Deutschland' ['Representation for Germany'], for the recovery of the expenses incurred by the German undertaking to protect gas mains belonging to it from any damage which might be caused by demolition work which the French undertaking was carrying out in the vicinity on behalf of the Saarland.

The first question

3. The first question asks: 'Are the conditions regarding jurisdiction in the case of 'the operations of a branch, agency or other establishment' mentioned in Article 5(5) of the said Convention to be determined:

(a) under the law of the State before the courts of which the proceedings have been brought; or

(b) under the law of the States concerned (qualification according to the law to be applied in the main action); or

(c) independently, i.e. in accordance with the objectives and system of the said Convention and also with the general principles of law which stem from the corpus of the national legal system (Judgment of 14 October 1976 in Case 29/76 *LTU Lufttransportunternehmen GmbH & Go. KG* v *Eurocontrol* [1976] ECR 1541)?'

4. The Convention, concluded pursuant to Article 220 of the EEC Treaty, is intended according to the express terms of its preamble to implement the provisions of that article on the simplification of formalities governing the reciprocal recognition and enforcement of judgments of courts or tribunals and to strengthen in the Community the legal protection of persons therein established. In order to eliminate obstacles to legal relations and to settle disputes within the sphere of intra-Community relations in civil and commercial matters the Convention contains, *inter alia*, rules enabling the jurisdiction in these matters of the courts of Contracting States to be determined and facilitating the recognition and execution of courts' judgments. Accordingly, the Convention must be interpreted having regard both to its principles and objectives and to its relationship within the Treaty.

5. The Convention frequently uses words and legal concepts drawn from civil, commercial and procedural law and capable of a different meaning from one Contracting State to another. The question, therefore,

arises whether these words and concepts must be regarded as having their own independent meaning and as being thus common to all the Contracting States or as referring to substantive rules of the law applicable in each case under the rules of conflict of laws of the court before which the matter is first brought. The answer to this question must ensure that the Convention is fully effective in achieving the objectives which it pursues.

6. The meaning of the words 'dispute arising out of the operations of a branch, agency or other establishment', which are the basis of the jurisdiction given by Article 5(5), are different from one Contracting State to another, not only in the respective laws but also in the application given to bilateral conventions on the recognition and enforcement of foreign judgments.

7. Their function in the context of the Convention must be decided in relation to the general rule conferring jurisdiction contained in Article 2(1) of the Convention which states 'Subject to the provisions of this Convention, persons domiciled in a Contracting State shall, whatever their nationality, be sued in the courts of that State'. Although Article 5 makes provision in a number of cases for a special jurisdiction, which the plaintiff may choose, this is because of the existence, in certain clearly-defined situations, of a particularly close connecting factor between a dispute and the court which may be called upon to hear it, with a view to the efficacious conduct of the proceedings. Multiplication of the bases of jurisdiction in one and the same case is not likely to encourage legal certainty and the effectiveness of legal protection throughout the territory of the Community and therefore it is in accord with the objective of the Convention to avoid a wide and multifarious interpretation of the exceptions to the general rule of jurisdiction contained in Article 2. This is all the more so since in national laws or in bilateral conventions the similar exception is frequently due, as the United Kingdom rightly points out in its written observations, to the notion that a national State serves the interests of its nationals by offering them an opportunity to escape the jurisdiction of a foreign court and this consideration is out of place in the Community context, since the justification for the exceptions contained in Article 5 to the general rule of jurisdiction in Article 2 is solely in the interests of due administration of justice.

8. The scope and limits of the right given to the plaintiff by Article 5(5) must be determined by the particular facts which either in the relations between the parent body and its branches, agencies or other

establishments or in the relations between one of the latter entities and third parties show the special link justifying, in derogation from Article 2, the option granted to the plaintiff. It is by definition a question of factors concerning two entities established in different Contracting States but which in spite of this must be considered in the same way, whether from the point of view of the parent body or of an extension or extensions which the parent body has established in the other Member States or from that of the third parties with whom legal relations are created through such extensions. In these circumstances the need to ensure legal certainty and equality of rights and obligations for the parties as regards the power to derogate from the general jurisdiction of Article 2 requires an independent interpretation, common to all the Contracting States, of the concepts in Article 5(5) of the Convention which are the subject of the reference for a preliminary ruling.

The second and third questions

9. In the event of the words referred to being interpreted independently, the second question asks what criteria apply with reference to the capacity to take independent decisions (*inter alia* to enter into contracts) and also to the extent of the outward manifestation. The third question asks: 'Are the principles governing liability for holding oneself out in law to others, i.e. to third parties, to be applied to the questions whether there is, in fact, a branch or agency, with legal consequences that anyone who creates the appearance of such a situation is to be treated as having operated a branch or agency - as is, for example, the case under German law (cf. Article 21 of the Zivilprozessordnung[Code of Civil Procedure] Baumbach, 36th Edition Note 2 A, Stein-Jonas, 19th Edition, Note II 2; Oberlandesgericht Köln Neue Juristische Wochenschrift 1953, 1834, Oberlandesgericht Breslau Höchstrichterliche Rechtsprechung 1939 (Case No 111))?'

10. These two questions must be taken together.

11. Having regard to the fact that the concepts referred to give the right to derogate from the principle of jurisdiction of Article 2 of the Convention their interpretation must show without difficulty the special link justifying such derogation. Such special link comprises in the first place the material signs enabling the existence of the branch, agency or other establishment to be easily recognized and in the second place the connection that there is between the local entity and the claim directed against the parent body established in another Contracting State.

12. As regards the first issue, the concept of branch, agency or other establishment implies a place of business which has the appearance of permanency, such as the extension of a parent body, has a management and is materially equipped to negotiate business with third parties so that the latter, although knowing that there will, if necessary, be a legal link with the parent body, the head office of which is abroad, do not have to deal directly with such parent body but may transact business at the place of business constituting the extension.

13. As regards the second issue, the claim in the action must concern the operations of the branch, agency or other establishment. This concept of operations comprises on the one hand actions relating to rights and contractual or non-contractual obligations concerning the management properly so-called of the agency, branch or other establishment itself such as those concerning the situation of the building where such entity is established or the local engagement of staff to work there. Further, it also comprises those relating to undertakings which have been entered into at the above- mentioned place of business in the name of the parent body and which must be performed in the Contracting State where the place of business is established and also actions concerning non-contractual obligations arising from the activities in which the branch, agency or other establishment within the above defined meaning, has engaged at the place in which it is established on behalf of the parent body. It is in each case for the court before which the matter comes to find the facts whereon it may be established that an effective place of business exists and to determine the legal position by reference to the concept of 'operations' as above defined.

14. The above considerations make it unnecessary to answer the third question.

On those grounds, the court, in answer to the questions referred to it by the Oberlandesgericht Saarbrücken by order of 21 February 1978, hereby rules:

1. The need to ensure legal certainty and equality of rights and obligations for the parties as regards the power to derogate from the general jurisdiction of Article 2 requires an independent interpretation, common to all the Contracting States, of the concepts in Article 5(5) of the Convention.

2. The concept of branch, agency or other establishment

implies a place of business which has the appearance of permanency, such as the extension of a parent body, has a management and is materially equipped to negotiate business with third parties so that the latter, although knowing that there will, if necessary, be a legal link with the parent body, the head office of which is abroad, do not have to deal directly with such parent body but may transact business at the place of business constituting the extension.

3. The concept of 'operations' comprises:

- actions relating to rights and contractual or non-contractual obligations concerning the management properly so-called of the agency, branch or other establishment itself such as those concerning the situation of the building where such entity is established or the local engagement of staff to work there;

- actions relating to undertakings which have been entered into at the above-mentioned place of business in the name of the parent body and which must be performed in the Contracting State where the place of business is established and also actions concerning non-contractual obligations arising from the activities in which the branch, agency or other establishment within the above-defined meaning, has engaged at the place in which it is established on behalf of the parent body.

4. It is in each case for the court before which the matter comes to find the facts whereon it may be established that an effective place of business exists and to determine the legal position by reference to the concept of 'operations' as above-defined.

OPINION OF MR ADVOCATE GENERAL MAYRAS

I - Établissements Somafer, Uckange, Lorraine, submitted a tender pursuant to an invitation to tender by the Ministry of the Interior of the Saarland to carry out certain demolition work on the perimeter of the Röchling-Burbach factories. Since the security measures proposed by the French undertaking appeared inadequate the German company Saar-Ferngas, whose gas mains were in the immediate vicinity of the intended demolition work, considered it necessary itself to take additional protective measures of which it notified Établissements Somafer on 16 January 1974. After duly informing the Gewerbeaufsichtsamt of the Saarland, whose functions correspond to those of the Ponts et Chaussées and of the Service des Mines in France, Établissements Somafer on 29 January 1974 obtained a licence to carry out the work from the Mayor of Völklingen. On 29 October 1974 the German company with a view to obtaining compensation sent its bill to Établissements Somafer in respect of the costs incurred. The representative (Vertretung) for the Federal Republic at Beckingen in the Saar of the main establishment (Haupt-verwaltung) Uckange contended that the claim was barred. Saar-Ferngas therefore brought an action against Établissements Somafer before the local court of the 'representative' in the Federal Republic, the Landgericht Saarbrücken. Let me observe incidentally that in France actions relating to administrative contracts and damages for public works come within the jurisdiction of the administrative courts. The part played by the representative at Beckingen in the discussions conducted between the Ministry of the Interior on the one hand and Établissements Somafer on the other is disputed by the parties and it is to settle this question that the Oberlandesgericht Saarbrücken has referred the matter to you.

Before starting to consider the questions which have been referred to you it is appropriate to remember that Saar-Ferngas brought the case before the Landgericht Saarbrücken at first instance on the basis that Établissements Somafer had a branch at Beckingen within the meaning of German law (Article 21 of the German Code of Civil Procedure) and further on the basis that court was that of the 'place of performance of the obligation in question' within the meaning of Article 5(1) of the Brussels Convention of 1968.

The court of first instance accepted neither of these arguments but regarded itself as having jurisdiction under Article 5(5) of the Convention because in its view this goes further than German national law: it recognizes that a connection with the operation of the courts for the place in which the branch or agency is situated. The court considered that Somafar had at Beckingen, at least, an agency within the meaning of Article 5(5) of the Convention it used its office in that area to deal with third parties or in any event it gave Saar-Ferngas the impression that that office was such an agency. In doing this the court relied on criteria of German law but it considers that they could equally be relevant in the application of Article 5(5) of the Convention.

The Saarland undertaking adopted this argument on the appeal. It therefore dropped the claim that it put forward in the alternative at first instance based on Article 23 of the German Code of Civil Procedure. That article which constitutes an excessive rule of national law on jurisdiction provides that in the absence of any other court having jurisdiction in German territory actions *relating to property* brought against a person not resident within national territory come within the jurisdiction of the court of the place where the goods or objects in question are situate; this, however, can no longer be relied upon in view of Article 3 of the Convention of 1968.

II - The first question basically asks whether the concepts of 'branch, agency, or other establishment' must be interpreted by reference to national law or on the contrary independently.

1. In favour of reference to national law for determining place of the

court having jurisdiction it may be said that, in general, there is every advantage in applying the law of the State before whose courts the matter comes or the law applicable to the main action: it is important for questions of jurisdiction to be resolved speedily. It is always easier for a court to apply its own law; further almost all the criteria for jurisdiction referred to in the Convention are connected with concepts which are found used in the national law of the Member States for purposes other than the determination of jurisdiction.

As regards the concepts of domicile of natural persons or the seat of companies or legal persons, in respect of which after all the concepts of Article 5(5) represent only a breakdown or subclass, the Convention refers expressly to the application of the internal law of the court seised of the matter (first-paragraph of Article 52) or its rules of private international law (Article 53).

An independent interpretation of the concepts referred to in Article 5(5) would not, strictly, be in accord with 'the simplification of formalities governing the reciprocal recognition and enforcement of judgments of courts or tribunals' which is the objective assigned to the Convention by Article 220 of the EEC Treaty; on the contrary it would have been more expeditious for Saar-Ferngas to bring the action against Somafer before the court of the place where the head office of that undertaking is situated to obtain a judgment against it which would have been directly enforceable in France.

Moreover, it may be doubted whether the authors of the Convention intended to give a common and independent definition of the branch, agency or establishment. Such a definition would risk being overtaken by the development of the national laws and case-law. The very fact that they use the word 'other', which is a type of 'residuary' class to cover all other cases, would confirm that they have not sought to give a precise definition at least to the concept of establishment. Such an objective, which would come within the sphere of *uniform legislation*, would be alien to the Convention.

Finally, the Court decided in the judgment of 6 October 1976, *Tessili* ([1976] ECR 1473) in connection with the interpretation of the Convention *in general* that in certain circumstances the words and concepts used by the Convention (that case was concerned with the concept used in Article 5 of 'place of performance of the obligation in question') must be regarded as referring to the substantive rules of the law applicable under the rules of conflict of laws of the court before which the matter is first brought.

2. In favour of the independent nature of the words in Article 5(5) the following considerations, on the other hand, may be put.

Even if the national law of the court before which the matter is brought, or if the private international law applicable to the main action, make jurisdiction dependent on criteria more or less identical to those referred to in Article 5(5) of the Convention, it is not likely that the current interpretation of those criteria by the national court is appropriate to cases falling under the Convention.

In the judgment in *De Bloos* of 6 October 1976 ([1976] ECR 1497) the Court itself began to interpret the concepts referred to in Article 5(5) uniformly and independently in seeking to define the concept of 'branch'. This precedent does not appear to me completely decisive in itself for the definition not a full one - given in that judgment is purely negative and was arrived at in relation to the internal relationship between the grantee and grantor of an exclusive sales concession.

A little later on 14 October 1976 the Court in the case of the *Lufttranportunternehmen* ([1976] ECR 1541) ruled that the concept 'civil and commercial matters' used in Article 1 of the Convention cannot be interpreted solely in the light of the division of jurisdiction between the various types of courts existing in certain Member States and that the concept in question must, therefore, be regarded as independent and must be interpreted by reference, first, to the objectives and scheme of the Convention and, secondly, to the general principles which stem from the corpus of the national legal systems.

On 14 July 1977 in Joined Cases *Bavaria Fluggesellsehaft Schwabe and Germania Bedarfsluftfahrt* ([1977] ECR 1517) the Court ruled that this interpretation was based on the desire to ensure, in relation to Community law, that the Contracting States and parties concerned have equal and uniform rights and duties under the Brussels Convention and that the principle of legal certainty in the Community legal system and the objectives of the Convention in accordance with Article 220 of the EEC Treaty, which is at its origin, require in all Member States a uniform application of the legal concepts and legal classifications developed by the Court in the context of the Convention.

In the case of *Industrial Diamond Supplies* the Court ruled on 22 November 1977 ([1977] ECR 2175) that if the concept of 'ordinary appeal' were interpreted by reference to a national system, whether the legal system of the State in which the judgment was given or that of the State in which recognition or enforcement is sought, it would in certain cases be impossible to classify a specific appeal with the required degree of certainty for the purposes of Articles 30 and 38 of the Convention and that the interpretation of the concept of 'ordinary appeal' may usefully be sought only within the framework of the Convention itself.

The Court adopted the same attitude in the judgment of 21 June 1978 in Case 150/77 *Bertrand* v *Ott* [1978] ECR 1431 in relation to the 'sale of goods on instalment credit terms'.

On the basis of these precedents I think that the jurisdiction for disputes 'arising out of the operation of a branch, agency or other establishment' must be determined independently, that is to say, having regard to the objectives and the scheme of the Convention of 1968 and the general principles of the national legal systems. This 'independent' interpretation must be based on the laws and case-law of the Member States which are parties to the Convention as regards the consequences, from the point of view of the forum, of the concepts of branch, agency or other establishment and on the national case-law on the forum for subsidiary establishments of legal persons provided for in certain bilateral conventions entered into between Member States before the Brussels Convention.

These bilateral conventions recognise the criterion of attachment either on the basis of *direct* jurisdiction or on the basis of indirect jurisdiction by means of choice of domicile. It might be said that the Brussels Convention has 'codified' and multinationalized the bilateral provisions without in so doing unifying the case-law of the various States relating to their application.

The immediate predecessor of Article 5(5) of the Brussels Convention thus appears to be Article 4(1)(d) of the German-Netherlands Convention of 30 August 1962 which reads: 'The courts of the State where the decision has been given are recognized as having jurisdiction for the purposes of the present Convention:....if in the State where the decision has been given the defendant has been asserted at his place of business or at a branch in relation to disputes arising out of the operation of the said establishment or branch'.

It must be observed that Article 5(5) of the Brussels Convention provides a criterion of connection on the basis of direct jurisdiction for the purposes of recognition and enforcement and a presumption of choice of domicile.

Still following this line of reasoning, I shall invite you to answer Question 1(b) also in the negative for recourse in a case before a national court to the law applicable in the main action would finally lead to reference to national laws which are probably different.

III - In the event of jurisdiction relating to the operations of a branch, agency or other establishment having to be determined independently, the national court wishes to know by its second question what criteria of interpretation should be applied to the expressions 'branch' and 'agency' with reference to capacity to take independent decisions (*inter alia* to enter into contracts) and also to the extent of the outward manifestation. It must be observed that the question does not mention 'establishment', but it appears to me necessary to consider it.

Two observations will guide me in this endeavour. First of all, whatever the connection chosen, the concepts referred to in Section 2 of the Convention ('*special* jurisdiction') and in particular Article 5(5) must be interpreted strictly because the fact must not be lost sight of that there is another *general* criterion for jurisdiction, namely the defendant's domicile (Article 2). This rule is contained in the judgment in *Bier* of 30 November 1976 ([1976] ECR 1735).

In the second place, it is generally difficult to determine the characteristics of an establishment or agency to which the rule of jurisdiction in Article 5(5) applies. Although the definition of a branch may be relatively precise, the concepts of agency or establishment are very often tinged with questions of fact which in national case-law are generally left to the exclusive decision of the court trying the main action. Even if it is decided that the concepts of Article 5(5) are independent, it inevitably follows that in order to define them it is necessary to clarify questions of fact and this is a task for the national court.

1. The question concerns the concept of 'operations' as much, if not more than, that of a branch, agency or other establishment. It must therefore be a question of a dispute involving the operations of one of these entities and not of a dispute in relation to what comes simply under the activity of the parent company or is tied up with it. In other words, it is necessary for the foreign trading company to *operate* in the Federal Republic and it is necessary for the

entity in question to be able to develop its own activity there, distinct from that of the parent company without, nevertheless, being a legal person.

The Convention reveals a remarkable absence of precision: it refers not only to branch or agency, which never have legal personality, although they are governed by fairly precise legal regulations, at least the branch is, but also to '*other* establishment'. The common aspect of the concepts to which Article 5(5) refers is, therefore, of entities not having legal personality; it should be observed in particular that the *subsidiary* of an undertaking is not referred to for the good reason that such a subsidiary has legal personality and may, therefore, be brought before the courts where it is established.

Consequently, it is necessary for the company to have a *sufficient* industrial or commercial outward manifestation abroad for there to be operations. Certain criteria contained in the Convention on the Mutual Recognition of Companies and Bodies Corporate of 29 February 1968 could be applied by way of analogy, with the necessary adjustments, although this Convention has a different objective and has not yet entered into force: in order to obtain recognition it is necessary (Article 3) for the company or body corporate to have a *genuine connection* with the economy of one of the territories to which the Convention applies; the company or body corporate in question must show that it has *in fact exercised its activity for a reasonable period* in the Contracting State under whose law it was incorporated (Article 4).

2. Although the entity referred to in Article 5(5) must have a certain independence in taking decisions and although, in particular, it must have power to carry out operations on behalf of and binding the parent company, it must, nevertheless, be *subject to the latter's control and direction.*

The Court propounded this principle in the judgment in *De Bloos* which has already been cited: 'One of the essential characteristics of the concepts of branch or agency is the fact of being subject to the direction and control of the parent body' (paragraph 20). This criterion was extended to the establishment: 'it is clear from both the object and the wording of this provision that the spirit of the Convention requires that the concept of 'establishment' appearing in the same article shall be based on the same essential characteristics as a branch or agency' (paragraph 21).

However, it cannot automatically be inferred *a contrario* that in its relations with third parties every 'representation' which is bound by instructions emanating from the parent company can be described only as a branch or agency.

The delicate question of burden of proof arises here: on whom is the burden to show the existence of such control and direction by the parent company? Is it necessary to require that such control and direction should be based on the internal articles of the parent Company and of the subordinate entity so that the latter is *legally* able to bind the former or does it suffice that in the eyes of third parties the branch, agency or other establishment acts as though it had power even if in law it has exceeded its powers? The answer to this question thus merges with consideration of the third question raised by the national court.

IV - I think that having regard to the special nature of the jurisdiction under Article 5(5) appearances should be disregarded and the realities considered and is for third parties who wish to rely on this exception to adduce evidence that the entity which they wish to bring before the court was, in fact, subject to the control and direction of the parent company and that, in particular, the operation giving rise to the dispute was within the competence of the branch or agency and that there was sufficient connection with that operation.

In the present case it is for the Saarland company to show that the Saarland manager of the office of the Lorraine company was not a simple executive or technical agent but had the power and status to conclude the operation and that discussions were conducted by this representative and not by the head office.

In this respect it may be useful to refer to a provision of the Franco-German Treaty on the Saar of 26 October 1956, although that provision gave only indirect jurisdiction and is no longer in force. It is Article 46 of the Treaty which provided: 'Where a French national has in the Saar or a citizen of the Saar has in France an establishment or branch of an industrial, commercial or other nature they may, in respect of contracts concluded *directly* by such establishment or branch, be brought before the courts of the country where the establishment or branch is situate'.

In these circumstances, I think the argument based on appearances to which the Court refers in its last question should be rejected. I do not know how far such a doctrine is recognized in German law in respect of simple establishments and even if it is accepted that the question of the 'practical effects' of appearances is not something peculiar to such law, it appears to me doubtful whether it is part of the legal system of all the Member States which are parties to the Convention. Above all, if such a criterion was resorted to it would open the door to all interpretations and would renationalize, in a manner of speaking, a term which the premises require should be independent. I think there is support for this view too in the case-law of the Court according to which acts giving rise to *inferences* by one party to a contract cannot take the place of the express extension of jurisdiction required by Article 17 of the Convention (Case 24/76 *Estasis* [1976] ECR 1831 and Case 25/76 *Segoura* [1976] ECR 1851).

My opinion is that the Court should hold that in civil and commercial matters for the purposes of Article 5(5) of the Brussels Convention of 1968 it is sufficient that the entity which is referred to therein has entered directly into the contract out of which the claim arises.

Case 139/80 - 18 March 1981

Blanckaert & Willems PVBA
v
Luise Trost

Article 5(5) - Special jurisdiction - Disputes arising out of 'the operations of a branch, agency or other establishment' - Branch or other establishment - Concept - Commercial agent - Exclusion - Conditions.

Summary

An independent commercial agent who merely negotiates business [Handelsvertreter (Vermittlungsvertreter)], inasmuch as his legal status leaves him basically free to arrange his own work and decide what proportion of his time to devote to the interests of the undertaking which he agrees to represent and whom that undertaking may not prevent from representing at the same time several firms competing in the same manufacturing or marketing Sector, and who, moreover, merely transmits orders to the parent undertaking without being involved in either their terms or their execution, does not have the character of a branch, agency or other establishment within the meaning of Article 5(5) of the Convention of 27 September 1968 on Jurisdiction and the Enforcement of Judgments in Civil and Commercial Matters.

JUDGMENT OF THE COURT

Mertens de Wilmars, President, Lord Mackenzie Stuart and Everling, Judges

1. By an order of 21 March 1980 which was received at the Court on

11 June 1980 the Bundesgerichtshof [Federal Court of Justice] referred to the Court for a preliminary ruling under the Protocol of 3 June 1971 on the interpretation by the Court of Justice of the Convention of 27 September 1968 on Jurisdiction and the Enforcement of Judgments in Civil and Commercial Matters (hereinafter referred to as 'the Convention') two questions concerning the interpretation of Article 5(5) of that Convention.

2. According to that provision, which derogates from the general rule of *forum domicilii* set out in Article 2 of the Convention, a defendant domiciled in a Contracting State may be sued in another Contracting State 'as regards a dispute arising out of the operations of a branch, agency or other establishment, in the courts of the place in which the branch, agency or other establishment is situated'.

3. Blanckaert & Willems, a Belgian furniture manufacturer and the defendant in the main action (hereinafter referred to as 'Blanckaert') has according to its own statements had a business association since 1960 with the German undertaking Hermann Bey (hereinafter referred to as 'Bey'), a furniture agency (Möbelagentur), which it made responsible for the establishment in the Federal Republic of Germany of a sales network for the furniture which Blanckaert manufactured. In performance of that obligation Bey, acting on behalf of Blanckaert, entered into a commercial agency with Trost, the plaintiff in the main action, for the Rhine and Ruhr, Eifel and South Westphalia area. Under the terms of that contract Trost was to work as the direct representative of Blanckaert and receive from the latter a commission of 5%. The contract stipulated that Trost was to transmit the orders she obtained for Blanckaert through Bey at Aachen. On any such orders transmitted to it through Bey Blanckaert would pay the latter the extra commission customarily given to commercial agents who are responsible for supervising other commercial agents of an undertaking.

4. In December 1976 Blanckaert terminated its contract with Trost, leading to an action by the latter for payment of commission and agent's adjustment fees. Trost brought the action before the Landgericht [Regional Court] Aachen, on the ground that Bey was an agency or branch of Blanckaert and, therefore, the dispute could be brought before the court of the place in which that agency or branch was established.

5. The Landgericht Aachen did not accept that view and declined jurisdiction but the Oberlandesgericht Köln [Higher Regional Court,

Cologne], hearing the appeal, held that the conditions for the international jurisdiction of the Landgericht Aachen were fulfilled because Bey was an agency of Blanckaert's within the meaning of Article 5 of the Convention and because the amounts claimed were attributable to the operation of that agency.

6. Hearing the appeal on a point of law the Bundesgerichtshof held that the Oberlandesgericht Köln had rightly established that both Bey and Trost had worked for Blanckaert 'as a commercial agent [Handelsvertreter] and more specifically as a business negotiator [Vermittlungsvertreter], that is to say, both were charged on a permanent basis with negotiating business on behalf of an undertaking, namely the defendant, as independent businessmen within the meaning of the first paragraph in Article 84 of the German Commercial Code [Handelsgesetzbuch]', and ruled that the question whether the operations of an agency or other establishment within the meaning of Article 5(5) of the Convention include the activities of a commercial agent, and more particularly those of a business negotiator within the meaning of the above-quoted provision of German law, had yet to be decided by the Court of Justice.

7. Considering therefore that the dispute raised questions concerning the interpretation of the Convention the Bundesgerichtshof referred two questions to the Court of Justice for a preliminary ruling on the interpretation of Article 5(5) of that Convention.

First question

8. The first question asks in substance whether a commercial agent [Handelsvertreter] who is a business negotiator [Vermittlungsvertreter] within the meaning of Article 84 *et seq.* of the German Commercial Code is to be considered as an 'agency' or 'other establishment' within the meaning of Article 5(5) of the Convention.

9. As the national court correctly observes, the Court stated in its judgment of 6 October 1976 (Case 14/76 *De Bloos* v *Bouyer* [1976] ECR 1497) that one of the essential characteristics of the concept of a branch or agency is the fact of being subject of the direction and control of the parent body.

10. The Court did not have occasion in that decision to identify the factors enabling it to be determined whether or not an undertaking or

other business concern is subject to the direction and control of a parent body, because the main dispute concerned the relationship between the grantor and the grantee of an exclusive sales concession, and the national court had stated that the grantee was not subject to either the direction or the control of the grantor.

11. Furthermore, in its judgment of 22 November 1978 (Case 33/78 *Somafer* [1978] ECR 2183), the Court stated that 'the concept of a branch, agency or other establishment implies a place of business which has the appearance of permanency, such as the extension of a parent body, has a management and is materially equipped to negotiate business with third parties so that the latter, although knowing that there will if necessary be a legal link with the parent body, the head office of which is abroad, do not have to deal directly with such parent body but may transact business at the place of business constituting the extension'.

12. From the grounds given in those two judgments, and especially from the rule that a 'branch, agency or other establishment' within the meaning of Article 5(5) must appear to third parties as an easily discernible extension of the parent body, it is clear that the dependency on the direction and control of that parent body is not established when the representative of the parent body is 'basically free to organise his own work and hours of work' (Article 84(1), last sentence, of the German Commercial Code) without being subject to instructions from the parent body in that regard; when he is free to represent at the same time several rival firms producing or marketing identical or similar products and, lastly, when he does not effectively participate in the completion and execution of transactions but is restricted in principle to transmitting orders to the undertaking he represents. Those three factors preclude a concern having all those characteristics from being considered as the place of business having the appearance of permanency as extension of the parent body.

13. The reply to the first question must therefore be that an independent commercial agent who merely negotiates business [Handelsvertreter (Vermittlungsvertreter)], in as much as his legal status leaves him basically free to arrange his own work and decide what proportion of his time to devote to the interests of the undertaking which he agrees to represent and whom that undertaking may not prevent from representing at the same time several firms competing in the same manufacturing or marketing sector, and who, moreover, merely transmits orders to the parent undertaking without being involved in either their terms or their

execution, does not have the character of a branch, agency or other establishment within the meaning of Article 5(5) of the Convention.

Second question

14. The second question is asked only if the reply to the first question should be in the affirmative. A reply to it is therefore not required.

On those grounds, the court (Third Chamber), in answer to the questions referred to it by the Bundesgerichtshof by an order of 21 March 1980 hereby rules:

> **An independent commercial agent who merely negotiates business [Handelsvertreter (Vermittlungsvertreter)], in as much as his legal status leaves him basically free to arrange his own work and decide what proportion of his time to devote to the interests of the undertaking which he agrees to represent and whom that undertaking may not prevent from representing at the same time several firms competing in the same manufacturing or marketing sector, and who, moreover, merely transmits orders to the parent undertaking without being involved in either their terms or their execution, does not have the character of a branch, agency or other establishment within the meaning of Article 5(5) of the Convention of 27 September 1968 on Jurisdiction and the Enforcement of Judgments in Civil and Commercial Matters.**

OPINION OF MR ADVOCATE GENERAL REISCHL

Blanckaert & Willems, defendants and appellants in the appeal on a point of law in the main proceedings, run a furniture factory in Belgium. They, and apparently other Belgian furniture manufacturers, were represented under an oral agreement of 1960 by Hermann Bey [hereinafter referred to as 'Bey'], a furniture agency in Aachen which acted as an independent commercial agent [Handelsvertreter (Vermittlungsvertreter) - negotiating business on their behalf]. Bey received in return a commission of 5% on the value of each sale negotiated by it. Other activities on behalf of Blanckaert & Willems - organising customs clearance and transport for the goods, recruiting other representatives - were recompensed by the firm with a special commission of 2% of the net turnover in the Federal Republic of Germany.

By a letter dated 30 November 1975 Bey engaged as another commercial agent for Blanckaert & Willems Mrs Trost of Aachen, who is the plaintiff and the respondent in the appeal on a point of law in the main proceedings. The text of the letter was as follows: 'On behalf of Blanckaert & Willems of Eeklo,

Belgium, I hereby authorise you to represent the aforesaid undertaking in the Rhine and Ruhr, Eifel and South Westphalia area. You will be working as the direct representative of Blanckaert & Willems. You will also receive from them a commission of 5%. However, I would ask you kindly to send all orders exclusively to my address in Aachen. Please be understanding about this. The reason is that as I am answerable for you I must be kept informed of each order.

Naturally, your name will appear on all copies as representative. I look forward to a profitable association with you...'.

For the work brought in by Bey's collaboration with Mrs Trost, Blanckaert & Willems paid Bey what is known as a special commission.

From early in January 1977 Bey was apparently no longer working for Blanckaert & Willems. In a letter dated 14 December 1976 Blanckaert & Willems informed Mrs Trost that she, too, was to cease working for Blanckaert & Willems on 30 January 1977. The reason was evidently that Blanckaert & Willems were not satisfied with the amount of business brought by Mrs Trost and objected to the fact that she was also representing other furniture manufacturers.

Mrs Trost sued Blanckaert & Willems in the Landgericht [Regional Court] Aachen for payment of outstanding commission and for the agent's adjustment fees prescribed in Article 89(b) of the German Commercial Code [Handelsgesetzbuch] on termination of a commercial agency relationship by way of consideration for the new custom obtained. In the course of those proceedings Blanckaert & Willems contested the international jurisdiction of the court. The Landgericht Aachen dismissed the action as inadmissible on the ground that neither the requirements of Article 5(1) nor those of Article 5(5) of the Convention on Jurisdiction and the Enforcement of Judgments in Civil and Commercial Matters had been met. Those provisions state that: 'A person domiciled in a Contracting State may, in another Contracting State, be sued:
1. in matters relating to a contract, in the courts for the place of performance of the obligation in question; (...) 5. as regards a dispute arising out of the operations of a branch, agency or other establishment, in the courts for the place in which the branch, agency or other establishment is situated.'

The Oberlandesgericht Köln [Higher Regional Court, Cologne] quashed that decision and referred the case back to the Landgericht. In its view the Landgericht Aachen had jurisdiction because Bey constituted an agency within the meaning of Article 5(5) of the Convention and the dispute must be considered as arising out of the operations of that agency. The deciding factor for the decision lay in the fact that Bey described itself as an agency and had been a representative of Blanckaert & Willems for over 20 years. The court was of the opinion, moreover, that Bey had been instructed and authorised by Blanckaert & Willems to conclude a commercial agency agreement on a long-term basis with Mrs Trost, that Bey was subject to the direction and control of Blanckaert & Willems, that orders obtained by Mrs Trost were to be transmitted through Bey to Blanckaert & Willems and also that Bey had described itself as Blanckaert & Willems's sales manager.

In the appeal by Blanckaert & Willems on a point of law the Bundesgerichtshof [Federal Court of Justice] took the view that jurisdiction under Article 5(1) of the Convention was excluded because under the relevant German law the place of performance for claims concerning commission and compensation was the place where the debtor had his place of business. As regards Article 5(5) of the Convention, it must be assumed that Bey and Mrs Trost were commercial agents for Blanckaert & Willems and in that capacity they must be looked upon as independent businessmen within the meaning of Article 84(1) of the German Commercial Code. In any case, it had not been established that Bey's status was that of an employee within the meaning of Article 84(2) of the Commercial Code or that there was some other relationship of service or employment, even though in collecting and transmitting the orders negotiated by Mrs Trost it was subject to the direction and control of Blanckaert & Willems. The question therefore arose whether activities such as those of a commercial agent may be considered, despite the absence of full independence, as the operations of an agency within the meaning of Article 5(5) of the Convention. If the answer was in the affirmative it must be ascertained whether the claims for payment of Commission and agent's adjustment fees were based on a dispute arising out of the operations of Bey. If the answer to that was in the negative then it must be asked whether a dispute between Mrs Trost's agency and the undertaking she represented may be considered as a dispute arising out of the operations of an agency within the meaning of Article 5(5) of the Convention.

In view of those questions which concern the interpretation of the Convention on Jurisdiction and the Enforcement of Judgments the Bundesgerichtshof suspended the proceedings by an order of 21 March 1980 and referred the following questions to the Court for a preliminary ruling under Article 3 of the Protocol on the interpretation of that Convention:

1. Is a commercial agent [Handelsvertreter] who is a business negotiator [Vermittlungsvertreter] within the meaning of Article 84 *et seq.* of the Commercial Code [Handelsgesetzbuch] to be considered as an 'agency' or 'other establishment' within the meaning of Article 5(5) of the European Communities' Convention on Jurisdiction and the Enforcement of Judgments in Civil and Commercial Matters of 27 Sept- ember 1968 (hereinafter referred to as 'the Convention')?

2. If the answer to Question 1 is in the affirmative:

(a) Is there a dispute 'arising out of the operations' of an agency or other establishment within the meaning of Article 5(5) of the Convention if the agency or other establishment, acting under the authority of the undertaking in respect of which it operates as commercial agent, appoints a third person as an additional commercial agent for the undertaking, accepts against payment of a commission the documents relating to transactions negotiated by the third person and transmits them to the undertaking, and instructs and supervises the third person and if a dispute arises out of the activities of that third person in his capacity as a commercial agent between the undertaking and himself concerning his entitlement to commission and payment by way of adjustment on termination of the agency agreement?

(b) If the answer to Question 2 (a) is in the negative: Does a dispute between the undertaking and the agency or other establishment concerning the latter's entitlement to commission and payment by way of adjustment on termination of the agency agreement fall within the concept of 'a dispute arising out of the operations of ... [an] agency or other establishment' within the meaning of Article 5(5) of the Convention?

My views on these questions are as follows:

1. Question 1

In replying to this question Mrs Trost, the respondent in the appeal on a point of law in the main action, relies principally on the decision in Case 14/76 (*Ets A. de Bloos SPRL* v *Société en comandite par actions Bouyer*, judgment of 6 October 1976 [1976] ECR 1497) in which it was stated that the essential characteristic of a branch or an agency is 'the fact of being subject to the direction and control of the parent body' (paragraph 20). That requirement is certainly met in the case of Bey because it was bound in pursuing its business of selling the goods made by Blanckaert & Willems to follow the instructions of the latter in selecting contracting parties and determining the terms on which business was done, in soliciting, and serving the interests of, the clientele and in carrying out the business transactions. What was particularly significant here was that the agency agreement with Mrs Trost was made by Bey on behalf of, and in the name of, Blanckaert & Willems on the basis of instructions to that effect, as was shown, for instance, by the way in which the extent of the area of representation was determined, that the orders obtained by Mrs Trost were collected by Bey and transmitted by it to Blanckaert & Willems and that Bey, likewise in accordance with the instructions of the parent body, also took part in fixing the rate of the Commission. In the case of Bey which, as may be seen in a letter from Blanckaert & Willems, operated as the firm's intermediary, with a regular duty to furnish reports, it is therefore correct to say that there was a true relationship of dependency, a conclusion which is further borne out by the fact that Bey was forced to close its office when its contractual relationship with Blanckaert & Willems was terminated. A further argument in favour of the application of Article 5(5) of the Convention in the case of Bey is the underlying purpose of that provision which is to place jurisdiction wherever a thorough investigation into the facts can most easily be made, which in the present case is surely the place where the relevant agreements were made and where the decisive stages in the transactions occurred. Last but not least, regard should be had, in interpreting Article 5(5), to what might be termed 'social considerations'. These are based on the fact that as a rule only major business concerns have branches and agencies, whereas the other parties to agreements with them are for the most part small firms of limited means. It would not be fair to subject the latter to costly proceedings in another country.

Taking the opposite view the Commission, adopting the description of the legal relationships which was accepted by the court which has submitted the reference, believes that those concerned are commercial agents within the meaning of Article 84 of the German Commercial Code, that is to say, independent and legally autonomous persons, and that therefore the conditions which have been laid down in the case-law for the application of Article 5(5) of the Convention have not been met. Admittedly such persons have a duty to observe certain guidelines in negotiating business, but within those guidelines they are independent and therefore not subject to the 'direction' of those whom they represent. In those circumstances it is quite impossible for the conditions relating to Article 5(5) of the Convention, as laid down in recent case-law (judgment in Case 33/78, *Somafer SA* v *Saarferngas AG*, 22 November 1978 [1978] ECR 2183), to have been satisfied, according to which the essential requirement is that it must be easy to ascertain from its external features that the undertaking in question is a branch, agency or other establishment, and that a branch, agency or other establishment must be a place where the parent body conducts business. The first condition is rarely met in the case of commercial agents, who often neither maintain an office nor use a trade name. As to the second point it is not important that Bey described itself in a letter of 14 October 1975 as a 'sales manager' and that it collected the orders negotiated by Mrs Trost and passed them on, or in other words exercised a certain amount of supervision over Mrs Trost on behalf of Blanckaert & Willems. The significant factor is rather - and this prevents the conclusion that Bey was a place of business of Blanckaert & Willems - that business was *conducted* not by Bey but by Blanckaert & Willems.

In discussing this issue it should first be pointed out that, according to the case-law to date, not only are the concepts in Article 5(5) of the Convention to be interpreted independently, that is to say, so as to have the same content in all the Member States, but also, as I have already pointed out in my opinion in Case 14/76 ([1976] ECR 1512), the interpretation to be adopted is a *narrow* one, bearing in mind that derogations from the principle in Article 2 of the Convention are permissible only in the interests of the due administration of justice.

Similarly, it is clear from the case-law of the Court that for all three of the concepts employed in Article 5(5) of the Convention the same distinguishing criteria are to be retained which means that, for example, different standards cannot be applied with respect to agencies, as Wieczorek, for example, believed (Kommentar zur Zivilprozessordnung, 2nd edition, Note B I(a) 1 on Article 21 of the Zivilprozessordnung [Code of Civil Procedure]). The reference by Mrs Trost's representative in the course of the oral procedure to *insurance* agents is not relevant to the present question because special provisions relating to insurance agents are to be found in the second paragraph of Article 8 of the Convention.

If a solution is to be sought essentially in the earlier decisions, as was advocated in the course of the procedure, then, of course, the attempt must not be restricted to the decision in Case 14/76, as was done by the respondent in the main proceedings. All that was established in that case as far as the essential characteristics required by Article 5(5) of the Convention are concerned was that the principal feature of a branch, agency or other establishment is that it is subject to the direction and control of the parent body, no further explanation having been required in that case.

In my view the interpretation of that provision was given fairly conclusive clarification in the judgment in Case 33/78. There is stated that what is most significant as far as Article 5(5) is concerned is in the first place the material signs enabling the existence of the branch, agency or other establishment to be easily recognised (paragraph 11). It must be a place of business which has the appearance of permanency such as an extension of a parent body, has a management, and is materially equipped to negotiate business with third parties (paragraph 12). In addition third parties should be able to conclude their transactions at the place of business which constitutes the extension without having to deal directly with the parent body established in another country, even though they are aware that there may have to be *some* legal link with the latter.

That enables us to conclude that it is the objective activities of an agency or other establishment which are determinative and that therefore no significance can be attached to the description of itself adopted by Bey ('sales manager') and the various formulae used in individual letters ('profitable association') with Mrs Trost). The above-mentioned decision shows, furthermore, that in order to satisfy the requirements of Article 5(5) of the Convention the existence of *some* restrictions on the representative's independence and some opportunity for the principal undertaking to exercise its influence is not sufficient. The agency or other establishment must actually be a kind of decentralised office with essentially the same ability to conduct business as the principal undertaking, but restricted, of course, to the territory of the Member State in which it is situated. I think that is what is required by the words quoted above, in particular by the use of the words 'place of business'.

In a legal relationship of the kind in question in the main proceedings, therefore, it is not sufficient to consider the role of the agency or other establishment in attracting, and negotiating with, new customers. What is important is whether it also participates in *conducting* and executing transactions or whether that is exclusively the responsibility of the principal undertaking. A clear indication to that effect is to be found in the principle underlying the rule regarding jurisdiction in Article 5(5) which is that a departure from the general rule regarding jurisdiction is only allowed where it is expedient for the purpose of conducting the proceedings, that is to say, only where there exists an exceptionally close connection between the legal relationship in dispute and the place of jurisdiction of the court. It is important not to overlook the fact that proceedings involving, In connection with commercial representatives, consideration of Article 5(5) of the Convention usually occur in the course of conducting business. Consequently, where decisions concerning the conduct and execution of business are the responsibility of the principal undertaking the court having jurisdiction for the place where the undertaking has its principal place of business is naturally more appropriate than the court in the place in which the contractual relationship was solicited or entered into.

That is quite clearly the case in the main action. In the first place, it concerns payment of commission which, as we have been told, was always paid directly by Blanckaert & Willems and which pursuant to Article 87(a) of the Commercial Code may be payable on conclusion of the transaction and receipt of payment. The main action also concerns agents' adjustment fees, payment of which depends according to Article 89(b) of the Commercial Code on *inter alia*, whether the principal undertaking continues to benefit from the new customers brought in by the agent, that is to say, whether it maintains business relationships with those customers.

'Branch, agency or other establishment' therefore certainly does not mean a typical commercial agent such as the respondent in the main proceedings. A certain amount of independence is his hallmark; in any case the fact that the undertaking he represents can direct him to a certain extent in matters concerning the preparation and conclusion of agreements does not link him sufficiently strongly to the principal undertaking to satisfy Article 5(5) of the Convention.

The same must also apply in the case of Bey, however, whose responsibilities were even wider and who served in a certain sense as Blanckaert & Willems' 'contact' in the Federal Republic of Germany. The fact that Bey was plainly acting for *several* undertakings already raises doubt as to whether it constituted a branch of Blanckaert & Willems. In any case the fact remains that its duties in connection with the conclusion of representation agreements, supervision of the activities of other representatives, transmission of their orders and cooperation in calculating commission were not sufficient to enable it to have been considered as a place of business of Blanckaert & Willems, since decisions as to the nature and execution of transactions evidently lay exclusively within the province of the latter.

The answer to the first of the questions asked by the Bundesgerichtshof may therefore appropriately be, as the Commission has suggested, in the negative. Such an answer may be given without there being any need to consider the additional problem raised in the course of the oral procedure of whether, as far as Bey is concerned, jurisdiction under Article 5(5) of the Convention is precluded in any case because at the crucial time, that is to say, when the action was brought - I am referring to the observations in the Jenard report on the second paragraph of Article 8 of the Convention - Bey was no longer to be considered as an 'agency' of Blanckaert & Willems since the contractual relationship between them had already been terminated.

2. *Question 2(a)*

In the light of my observations as to the first question it is clear that consideration of the problem raised in the second question assumes subsidiary importance.

The respondent in the appeal in the main proceedings favours an answer in the affirmative for this question too. In her opinion it is significant that Bey concluded the representation agreement between Blanckaert & Willems and Mrs Trost and that the activities of Mrs Trost had a strong influence on Bey's business because, apart from the commission to which Bey thus became entitled, the orders obtained by Mrs Trost were given to Bey and transmitted by it to Blanckaert & Willems and because Bey had also to settle the commission due to Mrs Trost.

The Commission contends in particular that the claims by Mrs Trost which are the subject of the dispute are based on prior circumstances which must have arisen in the course of the operations of Blanckaert & Willems, that is to say, the conclusion and carrying-out of individual sales and the establishment of a clientele from which Blanckaert & Willems continues to benefit. Therefore, it may only be said that the dispute on the matter relates exclusively to the operations of Blanckaert & Willems.

Permit me to say immediately that, as far as this disagreement is concerned, the view taken by the Commission has the most convincing arguments in its favour.

According to the judgment in Case 33/78 to which reference has already been made, application of Article 5(5) of the Convention definitely requires the existence of a particularly close connecting factor between the dispute and the court which may be called upon to hear it (paragraph 7 of the decision). The subject-matter of the dispute relates to the operations of an agency if rights and duties concerning the actual management of the agency are at issue (for instance the renting of the property on which the agency stands, or the hiring of staff employed there). It does so likewise where the dispute involves undertakings entered into by the agency on behalf of the principal undertaking and which are to be performed in the Contracting State in which the agency is established, as well as in the case of non-contractual obligations arising from the activities pursued by an agency at its place of business on behalf of the principal undertaking.

The main proceedings in this case are not concerned with rights and duties relating to the actual management of the agency within the meaning of the examples cited from case-law. Nor do they concern obligations arising from the activities of Bey, for the dispute concerns claims arising out of the fact that Mrs Trost negotiated business for Blanckaert & Willems and won them a clientele; those claims, however, are attributable to circumstances brought about by the operations of Blanckaert & Willems. Lastly, the dispute is equally unconcerned with commitments entered into by Bey on behalf of Blanckaert & Willems. The claims to payment of commission derive directly from the orders taken by Mrs Trost for Blanckaert & Willems; however, insofar as the agents' adjustment fees are attributable to a contract which Bey concluded on behalf of Blanckaert & Willems, the essential point is still that such claims, as the Bundesgerichtshof itself pointed out, are not to be satisfied in the State in which Bey (the 'agency') was established.

Precisely because the close connection required by the law expressed in past decisions between the claims advanced and a German court is not evident, the answer to Question 2(a), should it still be required, must be in the negative.

3. Question 2(b)

This question, too, requires only subsidiary treatment from me.

In my opinion on Case 14/76 I have already explained the view, to which I still adhere, that it is not the intention and purpose of the provision in question to lay down rules governing jurisdiction in actions brought by subsidiaries against their parent companies, but that the essential purpose is to enable third parties involved in legal relationships with undertakings which have branches or other subsidiary establishments to bring actions in the court nearest to the place in which the cause of action arose. In fact it is difficult to imagine disputes between subsidiary establishments within the meaning of Article 5(5) of the

Convention and their parent undertaking because strictly speaking branches do not, as a general rule, have legal personality and because where they do the principal undertaking may be assumed to exercise its influence in commercial matters in a manner which amounts to *de facto* control.

In order to be able to speak of disputes arising out of the operations of an agency it is also important that the dispute involves obligations incurred on the responsibility of the agency, acting for the principal undertaking. There can surely be no question of that in the present circumstances. There is no doubt but that the claims in question are to be acted upon by the principal undertaking itself, and this concerns not only the agents' adjustment fees but also, even though the agency was involved in helping to settle the commission, the claims for commission themselves.

4. In conclusion I propose, therefore, that the reference submitted by the Bundesgerichtshof for a preliminary ruling be answered as follows:

A commercial agent within the meaning of Article 84 *et seq.* of the Commercial Code whose activities are concerned with negotiating transactions which are conducted and executed exclusively by the undertaking he represents is not to be considered as an agency or other establishment within the meaning of Article 5(5) of the Convention on Jurisdiction. That remains true even where, on the full authority of the undertaking for which he acts, he appoints third parties to be additional commercial agents, accepts orders negotiated by those third parties against payment of commission and transmits those orders to the undertaking, and instructs and supervises the third parties.

Case 218/86 - 9 December 1987

SAR Schotte GmbH
v
Parfums Rothschild SARL

Special jurisdiction - Article 5(5) - Dispute arising out of the 'operations of a branch, agency or other establishment' - Concept - Business conducted by a company through another company with the same name and identical management - Included.

Summary

Article 5(5) of the Convention of 27 September 1968 on Jurisdiction and Enforcement of Judgments in Civil and Commercial Matters must be interpreted as applying to a case in which a legal entity established in a Contracting State maintains no dependent branch, agency or other establishment in another Contracting State but, nevertheless, pursues its activities there through an independent company with the same name and identical management which negotiates and conducts business in its name and which it uses as an extension of itself.

JUDGMENT OF THE COURT

Due, President of the Chamber, Rodriguez Iglesias, Koopmans, Bahlmann and Kakouris, Judges

1. By an order of 10 July 1986, which was received at the Court on 7 August 1986, the Oberlandesgericht Düsseldorf referred to the Court for a preliminary ruling, under the Protocol of 3 June 1971 on the interpretation by the Court of Justice of the Convention of 27 September 1968 on Jurisdiction and the Enforcement of Judgments in Civil and

Commercial Matters (hereinafter referred to as 'the Convention'), a question on the interpretation of Article 5(5) of the Convention.

2. That question arose in the course of a dispute between a German undertaking, SAR Schotte GmbH, established at Hemer, and a French undertaking, Parfums Rothschild SARL, whose registered office is in Paris. The dispute concerns orders placed for the delivery by Schotte to the French undertaking of atomiser pumps and other accessories for perfumery articles. The purchaser complained that the atomisers did not work properly. When the matter was not settled by exchange of letters, Schotte brought an action before the Landgericht (Regional Court) Düsseldorf for payment of an amount representing six invoices which had not been paid.

3. It appears from the documents before the Court that the negotiations preceding the orders and deliveries were conducted by Schotte not with the French undertaking but with Rothschild GmbH, whose registered office is in Düsseldorf. Rothschild GmbH also exchanged extensive correspondence with Schotte concerning the complaints over the atomisers supplied. All the letters from Rothschild GmbH, both in the preliminary negotiations and in connection with the complaints, were signed by two persons, one of whom was a director of Rothschild GmbH and Parfums Rothschild SARL and the other a director of Parfums Rothschild SARL.

4. Initially Schotte brought proceedings before the Landgericht against Rothschild GmbH. However, in the course of the proceedings Rothschild GmbH contended that it was not liable for the debts in question since they concerned only Parfums Rothschild SARL. Schotte therefore, with the leave of the Landgericht, amended its claim by substituting the French undertaking as defendant.

5. Before the Landgericht, Parfums Rothschild SARL contended that the German courts had no jurisdiction to determine the dispute. Schotte, however, claimed that they had jurisdiction on the basis of Article 5(5) of the Convention, which provides that a defendant may be sued in a Contracting State other than that in which he is domiciled 'as regards a dispute arising out of the operations of a branch, agency or other establishment, in the courts for the place in which the branch, agency or other establishment is situated'. In its submission, Rothschild GmbH should be regarded as an 'establishment' of Parfums Rothschild SARL within the meaning of that provision.

6. The Landgericht held that it had no jurisdiction on the ground that the conditions laid down in Article 5(5) of the Convention were not satisfied. In particular, it considered that Rothschild GmbH could not be regarded as an agency or establishment of Parfums Rothschild SARL, since the latter was, on the contrary, a subsidiary of Rothschild GmbH.

7. On appeal, the Oberlandesgericht stayed the proceedings and asked the Court to give a preliminary ruling on the following question: 'Does the jurisdiction conferred by Article 5(5) of the Convention in regard to a branch, agency or other establishment extend to the case where a legal entity under French law (a "societe a responsabilite limitee"), whose registered office is in Paris, maintains no dependent establishment in another Contracting State (in this case, the Federal Republic of Germany) but where there is in that other Contracting State an independent legal entity under German law (a "Gesellschaft mit beschrankter Haftung") which has the same name and identical management, negotiates and conducts business in the name of the French legal entity and is used by the latter as an extension of itself?'

8. Reference is made to the Report for the Hearing for a fuller account of the facts, the course of the procedure and the written observations submitted to the Court by the German Government and the Commission, which are mentioned or discussed hereinafter only insofar as is necessary for the reasoning of the Court.

9. Article 5(5) of the Convention confers jurisdiction to hear disputes arising out of the operations of a branch, agency or other establishment. This jurisdiction forms part of the 'special jurisdiction' provided for by Articles 5 and 6 of the Convention, which is justified in particular by the existence of a close connection between the dispute and the court which is called upon to hear it.

10. In its judgment of 22 November 1978 in Case 33/78 *Somafer Saar-Ferngas* [1978] ECR 2183, the Court held that the concept of a branch, agency or other establishment implies a place of business which has the appearance of permanency, such as the extension of a parent body, has a management and is materially equipped to negotiate business with third parties so that the latter, although knowing that there will, if necessary, be a legal link with the parent body, the head office of which is abroad, do not have to deal directly with such parent body but may transact business at the place of business constituting the extension.

11. The national court considers that these conditions might also be satisfied in a case such as the present, where the undertaking which acted as an extension of a company established in another Contracting State is not a subsidiary of that company but is an independent company or even its parent company.

12. The German Government and the Commission share that view on the ground, first, that legal certainty requires the application of Article 5(5) of the Convention in any case in which an establishment which can negotiate business with third parties clearly appears to be the effective extension of an undertaking established in another Contracting State and, secondly, that undertakings which are in law independent companies may, nevertheless, display all the characteristics of an extension.

13. The question referred concerns a case in which two companies bear the same name and are under common management, and in which one of those undertakings; although not a dependent branch or agency of the other, nevertheless enters into transactions on behalf of the other and thus acts as its extension in business relations.

14. It should be added that in the present case Rothschild GmbH not only took part in the negotiations and in the conclusion of the contract but was also responsible, during the performance of the contract, for ensuring that the deliveries contracted for were made and that invoices were paid. Moreover, the correspondence addressed to Schotte seemed to indicate that it was acting as a place of business of Parfums Rothschild SARL.

15. In such a case, third parties doing business with the establishment acting as an extension of another company must be able to rely on the appearance thus created and regard that establishment as an establishment of the other company even if, from the point of view of company law, the two companies are independent of each other.

16. The close connection between the dispute and the court called upon to hear it must be assessed not only on the basis of the legal relations between legal entities established in different Contracting States but also by reference to the way in which these two undertakings behave in their business relations and present themselves vis-à-vis third parties in their commercial dealings.

17. Consequently, it should be concluded that Article 5(5) of the Convention must be interpreted as applying to a case in which a legal

entity established in a Contracting State maintains no dependent branch, agency or other establishment in another Contracting State but, nevertheless, pursues its activities there through an independent Company with the same name and identical management which negotiates and conducts business in its name and which it uses as an extension of itself.

On those grounds, the Court (Sixth Chamber), in answer to the question referred to it by the Oberlandesgericht Düsseldorf by order of 10 July 1986, hereby rules:

Article 5(5) of the Convention of 27 September 1968 on Jurisdiction and the Enforcement of Judgments in Civil and Commercial Matters must be interpreted as applying to a case in which a legal entity established in a Contracting State maintains no dependent branch, agency or other establishment in another Contracting State but, nevertheless, pursues its activities there through an independent company with the same name and identical management which negotiates and conducts business in its name and which it uses as an extension of itself.

OPINION OF ADVOCATE GENERAL SIR GORDON SLYNN

Firma SAR Schotte GmbH ('Schotte') whose registered office is in the Federal Republic of Germany claims in the German courts from Parfums Rothschild SARL ('French Rothschild') whose registered office is in France, DM 55 507.04 as the price of atomiser pumps and caps for perfume containers sold and delivered to French Rothschild. The latter disputes the jurisdiction of the German courts since it is domiciled in France. Schotte relies on Article 5(5) of the 1968 Convention on Jurisdiction and the Enforcement of Judgments in Civil and Commercial Matters which provides that: 'A person domiciled in a Contracting State may, in another Contracting State, be sued: ... as regards a dispute arising out of the operations of a branch, agency or other establishment, in the courts for the place where the branch, agency or other establishment is situated'.

The Landgericht (Regional Court) Düsseldorf held that it had no jurisdiction to hear the claim since Article 5(5) of the Convention was not applicable. On appeal the Oberlandesgericht, Düsseldorf (which appeared more sympathetic to the claim that the German courts had jurisdiction) referred to this Court the question: 'Does the jurisdiction conferred by Article 5(5) of the Convention in regard to a branch, agency or other establishment extend to the case where a legal entity recognised by French law (a 'société à responsabilité limitée'), whose registered office is in Paris, maintains no dependent establishment in another Contracting State (in this case, the Federal Republic of Germany) but where there is in that other Contracting State an independent legal entity recognized by German law (a 'Gesellschaft mit beschränkter Haftung') which has the same name and identical management, which negotiates and conducts business in the name of the French legal entity and which is used by the latter as an extension of itself?'

In the reference it is found that Rothschild GmbH, Düsseldorf, ('German Rothschild') conducted negotiations with Schotte in 1981 and 1982 for the manufacture and delivery of the atomisers. 'After the plaintiff's negotiations with Rothschild GmbH had come to a successful conclusion', French Rothschild placed orders with Schotte for the supply of different types of atomisers, delivery to be to Puteaux, France, where the containers were filled with perfume. Accounts were delivered by Schotte to French Rothschild in accordance with the agreement between them.

French Rothschild contended that it was a wholly-owned subsidiary of German Rothschild, both, it seems, formed in 1981. This is not found as a fact by the referring court but the claim has not been challenged. At any rate, at the material times the two Rothschild companies had one common director, a Mr Vehling; they also each had one other director, Mr Rothschild for the German company and Mrs Rodaks for the French company, though her domicile, like that of Mr Vehling, is said to be in the Federal Republic of Germany.

In 1983, German Rothschild complained to Schotte that it had received numerous complaints from customers that the atomisers were inefficient. Extensive correspondence followed between Schotte and German Rothschild on the latter's headed writing-paper though 'signed by one of the defendant's two directors'. Correspondence before the conclusion of each individual contract was apparently similarly conducted on German company headed paper, though similarly signed. Whether the common director signed and, if so, whether he signed on behalf of French or German Rothschild is not clear.

When sued, German Rothschild denied liability - it seems on the basis that it was not the contracting party ('disputed its capacity to be sued'). Hence the present proceedings were begun against French Rothschild.

It is clear that French Rothschild can only be sued in the Federal Republic under Article 5(5) firstly if German Rothschild is 'a branch, agency or other establishment' of French Rothschild and (if it is), secondly, if the dispute with Schotte arises 'out of the operations of' German Rothschild.

The Court has considered the meaning of 'a branch, agency or other establishment'. In Case 14/76 *De Bloos* v *Bouyer* [1976] ECR 1497, at p. 1510, it ruled that 'one of the essential characteristics of the concept of branch or agency is the fact of being subject to the direction and control of the parent body' and that the concept of 'establishment' must be based on the same essential characteristics. 'Establishment' must, it seems, be read *ejusdem generis* branch and agency. In Case 33/78 *Somafer* v *Saar-Ferngas* [1978] ECR 2183, at p. 2193, it stressed that, since Article 5(5) derogated from the principle of jurisdiction contained in Article 2 of the Convention, its interpretation must 'show without difficulty the special link justifying such derogation'. There must be material signs enabling the local entity to be easily recognised and a connection 'between the local entity and the claim directed against the parent body established in another Contracting State'. 'The concept of branch, agency or other establishment implies a place of business which has the appearance of permanency, such as the extension of a parent body, has a management and is materially equipped to negotiate business with third parties so that the latter, although knowing that there will, if necessary, be a legal link with the parent body, the head office of which is abroad, do not have to deal directly with such parent body may transact business at the place of business constituting the extension'.

In Case 139/80 *Blanckaert & Willems* v *Trost* [1951] ECR 819, at p. 829, it was ruled that an independent commercial agent, free to arrange his own time, and who 'merely transmits orders to the parent undertaking without being involved in either their terms or their execution' does not have the character of a branch, agency or other establishment.

Article 5(5) is beneficial to plaintiffs in that it enables them to sue in the State where a defendant has a branch with which the plaintiff has conducted business, rather than in the State of domicile of the defendant. It is beneficial to defendants in that it confers jurisdiction only where there is a branch, agency or other establishment; jurisdiction is not conferred where there is merely a temporary presence or some connection with the State in which it is desired to bring proceedings more tenuous than the existence of a branch.

A branch (as equally I understand to be a 'succursale' and a 'Zweigniederlassung') is as I see it an outpost of the main business (be it owned by a company or an individual) carrying out the affairs of the main business for the latter's benefit on a continuing basis and subject to the control of the main business. 'Agency' and 'establishment' I read in very much the same sense as indicating a place of business subsidiary to the business of the main business, though 'establishment' may be somewhat wider than 'branch'. I do not read 'agency' as covering simply the place where an agent acts for a principal. As a matter of ordinary usage, 'branch' normally connotes, it seems to me, a place belonging to the proprietor of a larger business. If these words in Article 5(5) are taken literally, it can be said that the branch, agency or establishment must be in law and in fact the property of the owner of the main business. *Per contra*, if the place of business in question belongs to another, it cannot be said that the place of business is the branch of the proprietor of the main business, even if that other may be his agent, representative or business partner.

Such a result would give the maximum protection to potential defendants and constitute the more restrictive interpretation of Article 5(5), thus making the least inroad into the principle enshrined in Article 2. It is an attractive result in that it is relatively simple to operate.

However, the position of plaintiffs must also be taken into account. If proprietors of a business set up in one State can avoid having what is technically their branch, agency or establishment in another Member State by creating a company there as, in fact if not in law, a complete *alter ego* it can be said with no less force that the object of Article 5(5) is frustrated. The person dealing through that other company with the main business is deprived of the right to sue, which he would have had if an office or other establishment had been opened by the main proprietor as his own property and in his own name. Yet the position of the two in reality is very similar.

Since it seems to me that Article 5(5) was drafted with the interests of both plaintiffs and defendants in mind, these divergent interests have, if possible, to be reconciled.

In *Somafer* the Court saw two elements as being necessary to create a branch, agency or other establishment - first, there must be a place of business with an appearance of permanency and a management which is equipped to conduct business (thus protecting defendants from suit as a result of transient or temporary presence) and, secondly, there must be awareness on the part of third parties that they do not have to deal directly with the parent body but may transact business at the place constituting the extension.

In the ordinary way it seems to me that this second test will normally be satisfied where the branch or other establishment is owned by (and perhaps bears the name of) the proprietor of the main business. On the other hand, if the proprietor causes another person or company to act in such a way that third parties are led to believe that they may deal with that other person or company as an extension or outpost of the proprietor, 'knowing that there will if necessary be a legal link with the parent body', then it seems to me that the place of business of that other person or company is capable of being a branch, agency or other establishment of the proprietor with whom the contract is made, who may be sued pursuant to Article 5(5) in the State where that place of business is to be found.

This kind of situation may well arise where a company sets up for whatever reason a wholly-owned subsidiary in another Contracting State. I do not, however, consider that the concept of 'branch' or 'establishment' is to be looked at in terms of formal company structure or shareholding. It depends on whether the owner of the main business has held out the place of business of the other company to be a place at which third parties can deal with the owner of the main business, and third parties have relied on that.

This could readily happen not only with a wholly-owned subsidiary but also with an associated company; it could happen, though no doubt more rarely, where the parent company dealt on behalf of the subsidiary (as, for example, where they were principally engaged in the production of different items, each dealing for the other to a small degree in respect of the other's major product). If the test is 'holding out' rather than 'shareholding' there is nothing unduly disturbing about such a consequence. The principle cannot, however, be limited to the situation where companies are involved. It must be capable of applying, if it applies at all, to individuals; the degree of factual control of one proprietor over an individual may indeed be no less than that exercised by a parent over a wholly-owned subsidiary.

This test is not lightly satisfied. There must be 'material signs enabling the existence of the branch...to be easily recognised' (*Somafer*, p. 2193). It must 'appear to third parties as an easily discernable extension of the parent body'

(*Blanckaert*, p. 829). It is obviously more difficult for a national court to resolve this question than mere legal ownership of the place of business, but it is not an impossible task. The national court has to decide on the facts whether there is such a holding out and whether it was relied on by the other contracting party. It will be relevant to take into account such matters as identity of name and management, the way in which the business is conducted, the degree of control exercised, whether one acts for the benefit and on behalf of the other, the way in which the alleged main business and branch recognise each other *vis-à-vis* third parties.

Despite the force and attraction of the contrary arguments (which unfortunately have not been developed before the Court) in favour of adopting the more limited view that the status of a 'branch, agency or other establishment' depends on ownership, I would accordingly take the view that if a place of business in one Member State is treated by the owner of a business who is domiciled in another Member State as if it were an integral part of his business under his direction and control, and is clearly seen to be so treated by third parties, then that place of business is capable of being a branch, agency or other establishment for the purposes of Article 5(5) even if it is owned and managed by another person or company. This seems to me not to be in conflict with, indeed to be closer in principle to, the statement in the Jenard Report that 'adoption of the "special" rules of jurisdiction is also justified by the fact that there must be a close connecting factor between the dispute and the court with jurisdiction to resolve it.

French Rothschild's second argument is that the dispute does not arise out of 'the operations' of German Rothschild since the contracts at issue were concluded exclusively with French Rothschild. The referring court does not seek a preliminary ruling on this question but quotes *Somafer* to the effect that 'operations' include actions 'relating to undertakings which have been entered into at the above-mentioned place of business in the name of the parent body and which must be performed in the Contracting State where the place of business is established'.

Since a ruling is not requested on it, it is perhaps better not to deal with the question. In case the Court takes the other view I comment briefly.

The concept of 'a dispute arising out of the operations of' a branch, etc. has not been investigated, save in *Somafer*. The words used in the judgment appear to indicate that the contractual undertaking must have been entered into at the branch in the name of the parent company. That would seem to exclude a case where the branch conducts all the negotiations but the final contract is signed by the parent company. But for that passage I would have read the preceding paragraph of the judgment, paragraph 12, as wide enough to cover the case where all negotiations were fully conducted by the branch on behalf of the parent body but the final contract ('if necessary a legal link') was signed by the latter. For my part, but for paragraph 13 of the judgment, I would have given 'dispute arising out of the operations of a branch' a wider meaning. Equally, but for that paragraph, I would find it difficult to spell out of Article 5(5) the limitation that undertakings entered into 'must be performed in the Contracting State where the place of business is established'. If here the contract had been signed by a German branch in the name of French Rothschild but stipulated delivery of the goods in Puteaux, France, it seems to me that the intention of Article 5(5) would be to enable Schotte to sue French Rothschild in Germany.

However, I do not deal with these matters in any further detail since they are not the object of a specific question. They may need to be considered by the national court if it is satisfied that there was here a branch, agency or other establishment of French Rothschild in the Federal Republic of Germany.

Accordingly, it seems to me that the question referred should be answered along the following lines: 'The jurisdiction conferred by Article 5(5) of the Convention in regard to a branch, agency or other establishment may extend to the case where a legal entity recognised by the law of one Contracting State and having its registered office in that State and an independent legal entity recognised by the law of another Contracting State and having its registered office there, have the same name and identical management, if in fact the latter carries out operations under the direction and control of the former and is held out to third parties as being an extension of, or as conducting a place of business of, the former and third parties have dealt with the latter on that basis.'

Case C-439/93 - 6 April 1995

Lloyd's Register of Shipping
v
Société Campenon Bernard

Article 5(5) - Dispute arising out of the operations of a branch, agency or other establishment - Definition.

Summary

The expression 'dispute arising out of the operations of a branch, agency or other establishment' in Article 5(5) of the Convention on Jurisdiction and the Enforcement of Judgments in Civil and Commercial Matters, as amended by the Convention of 9 October 1978 on the Accession of the Kingdom of Denmark, Ireland and the United Kingdom of Great Britain and Northern Ireland, does not presuppose that the undertakings giving rise to the dispute, entered into by a branch in the name of its parent body, are to be performed in the Contracting State in which the branch is established.

JUDGMENT OF THE COURT

Rodríguez Iglesias, President, Schockweiler, Kapteyn, Gulmann, Presidents of Chambers, Kakouris, Moitinho de Almeida, Murray, Edward and Puissochet, Judges

1. By judgment of 26 October 1993, received at the Court on 10 November 1993, the French Cour de Cassation (Court of Cassation) referred to the Court for a preliminary ruling pursuant to the Protocol of 3

June 1971 on the interpretation by the Court of Justice of the Convention of 27 September 1968 on Jurisdiction and the Enforcement of Judgments in Civil and Commercial Matters a question concerning the interpretation of Article 5(5) of that Convention, as amended by the Convention on 9 October 1978 on the Accession of the Kingdom of Denmark, Ireland and the United Kingdom of Great Britain and Northern Ireland (OJ 1978 L 304, p.1 and - the amended version - p. 77, hereinafter the 'Convention').

2. The question arose in proceedings which concerned the proper performance of a contract to test concrete reinforcing steel, between Campenon Bernard, a company governed by French law and established in Clichy (France), and Lloyd's Register of Shipping, an English registered charity, established in London.

3. At the end of November 1985, Campenon Bernard contacted the French branch of Lloyd's Register in order to arrange for the testing of concrete reinforcing steel which it was to use in the construction of a motorway in Kuwait. The object was to check that the concrete reinforcing steel complied with a United States technical standard which had been added to the tender specifications by the Kuwait Ministry of Public Works and, if so, to have a certificate of compliance issued.

4. Following negotiations, in a letter of 3 December 1985 Campenon Bernard placed the order with the French branch of Lloyd's Register. That letter specified that inspection would take place in Spain and would be carried out by the Spanish branch of Lloyd's Register. It also stated that payment would be effected in pesetas. On 9 December 1985 the French branch communicated its acceptance.

5. Although the Spanish branch of Lloyd's Register issued certificates of compliance, the Kuwait Ministry of Public Works refused to accept the concrete reinforcing steel on the ground that it did not comply with the United States technical standard.

6. On 2 February 1988 Campenon Bernard paid the invoice issued by the Spanish branch of Lloyd's Register, having been pressed to do so by the French branch, but without prejudice to its rights. Alleging that Lloyd's Register had wrongly stated that the steel complied with the United States technical standard, it then brought a claim for damages in the Tribunal de Commerce (Commercial Court), Paris, through the intermediary of the French branch.

7. Lloyd's Register pleaded that the French courts lacked jurisdiction.

8. The plea was rejected at first instance on the basis of domestic law. It was only on appeal that the plea was examined in the light of Article 5(1) and (5) of the Convention, pursuant to which: 'A person domiciled in a Contracting State may, in another Contracting State, be sued: 1. in matters relating to a contract, in the courts for the place of performance of the obligation in question; ... 5. as regards a dispute out of the operations of a branch, agency or other establishment, in the courts for the place in which the branch, agency or other establishment is situated.'

9. In its judgment of 5 June 1991 the Cour d'Appel (Court of Appeal), Paris, held that the case concerned the operations of the French branch of Lloyd's Register within the meaning of Article 5(5) of the Convention and that, consequently, it had jurisdiction. It pointed out that Campenon Bernard had had dealings solely with the French branch, since it had negotiated and concluded the contract and subsequently demanded payment. It was not significant that the undertakings entered into had been performed in Spain. According to the Cour d'Appel, Article 5(5) of the Convention did not require that the undertakings entered into were to be performed in the Contracting State where the place of business was established. To allow such a restriction would render Article 5(5) redundant in relation to Article 5(1), which already gave jurisdiction to the courts for the place of performance of the obligation in question.

10. Lloyd's Register applied for review *inter alia* on the ground that Article 5(5) had been infringed. In its view, a dispute arises out of the operations of a branch, agency or other establishment within the meaning of that provision insofar as the undertakings entered into by that place of business are to be performed in the Contracting State where it is established.

11. In the circumstances, by judgment of 26 October 1993, the Cour de Cassation asked the Court whether, 'in the light of the first paragraph of Article 5 of the Brussels Convention of 27 September 1968 on Jurisdiction and the Enforcement of Judgments in Civil and Commercial Matters, the expression "dispute arising out of the operations of a branch..." in Article 5(5) of the Convention necessarily presupposes that the undertakings in question entered into by the branch in the name of its parent body are to be performed in the Contracting State where the branch is established'.

12. Lloyd's Register contends that in its judgment in Case 33/78 *Somafer* v *Saar Ferngas* [1978] ECR 2183, at paragraph 13, the Court held that the rule set out in Article 5(5) applies to actions relating to undertakings which have been entered into by that establishment in the name of the parent body, provided that they are to be performed in the Contracting State of the ancillary establishment.

13. According to Lloyd's Register, such a requirement as to place is in accordance with the interests of the proper administration of justice which underlie the provision. It is aimed at enabling an action that has its origin in the actual activities of a branch to be heard by the courts for the place in which it is situated on practical and evidential grounds.

14. Moreover, it states, since an ancillary establishment may not confine itself to transmitting orders to its parent body but must also take part in their performance, and in that connection the range of activity of an ancillary establishment is naturally confined to the territory of the Contracting State in which it has been set up, jurisdiction under Article 5(5) is justified only where the undertakings in question entered into by the ancillary establishment in the name of its parent body are to be performed on the territory of the Contracting State in which it is situated.

15. That argument cannot be accepted.

16. Firstly, the actual wording of Article 5(5) of the Convention in no way requires that the undertakings negotiated by a branch should be performed in the Contracting State in which it is established in order for them to form part of its operations.

17. Secondly, the interpretation put forward by the appellant in the main proceedings would render Article 5(5) almost wholly redundant. Since Article 5(1) already allows the plaintiff to bring an action in contract in the courts for the place of performance of the obligation in question, Article 5(5) would duplicate that provision if it applied solely to undertakings entered into by a branch which were to be performed in the Contracting State in which the branch was established. At the very most it would create a second head of special jurisdiction where, within the Contracting State of the branch, the place of performance of the obligation in question was situated in a judicial area other than that of the branch.

18. Thirdly, it should be noted that an ancillary establishment is a place of business which has the appearance of permanency such as the

extension of a parent body, has a management and is equipped to negotiate business with third parties so that the latter, although knowing that there will, if necessary, be a legal link with the parent body, whose seat is in another Contracting State, do not have to deal directly with such parent body (see *Somafer*, cited above, at paragraph 12).

19. A branch, agency or other ancillary establishment within the meaning of Article 5(5) is therefore an entity capable of being the principal, or even exclusive, interlocutor for third parties in the negotiation of contracts.

20. There does not necessarily have to be a close link between the entity with which a customer conducts negotiations and places an order and the place where the order will be performed. Accordingly, undertakings may form part of the operations of an ancillary establishment within the meaning of Article 5(5) of the Convention even though they are to be performed outside the Contracting State where it is situated, possibly by another ancillary establishment.

21. That interpretation is, moreover, in conformity with the objective of the special rules of jurisdiction. As the Jenard Report (OJ 1979 C 59, p.22) makes clear, those rules allow the plaintiff to sue the defendant in courts other than those of his domicile because there is a specially close connecting factor between the dispute and the court with jurisdiction to resolve it.

22. In the light of the foregoing considerations, the answer to the question referred by the Cour de Cassation must be that the expression 'dispute arising out of the operations of a branch, agency or other establishment' in Article 5(5) of the Convention does not presuppose that the undertakings in question entered into by the branch in the name of its parent body are to be performed in the Contracting State in which the branch is established.

On those grounds, the Court in answer to the questions referred to it by the Cour de Cassation of the French Republic by judgment of 26 October 1993, hereby rules:

> **The expression 'dispute arising out of the operations of a branch, agency or other establishment' in Article 5(5) of the Convention of 27 September 1968 on Jurisdiction and Enforcement of Judgments in Civil and Commercial Matters**

does not presuppose that the undertakings in question entered into by the branch in the name of its parent body are to be performed in the Contracting State in which the branch is established.

OPINION OF MR ADVOCATE GENERAL ELMER

Introduction

1. According to Article 5(5) of the Brussels Convention of 27 September 1968 on Jurisdiction and the Enforcement of Judgments in Civil and Commercial Matters, a person domiciled in a Contracting State may, in another Contracting State, be sued as regards a dispute arising out of the operations of a branch, agency or other establishment, in the courts for the place in which the establishment is situated.

In this case the question referred to the Court for a preliminary ruling from the Cour de Cassation (Court of Cassation), Paris, is whether the plaintiff may avail himself of that special rule of jurisdiction only in cases in which the dispute concerns an obligation to be performed in the State in which the branch, agency or other establishment is situated.

Such a geographical limitation is not apparent from the wording of the provision. An observation in the Court's judgment in Case 33/78 *Somafer* v *Saarferngas* may however be understood as meaning that such a limitation applies in the sphere of application of that provision.

Facts

2. The French limited company Campenon Bernard was in 1985 awarded a contract by the Ministry of Public Works in Kuwait to construct a motorway from the port of Kuwait to the Iraqi border. The steel to be used for reinforcement of the concrete was, according to the contractor's specifications, to comply with a United States technical standard known as ASTM A 615.

Campenon Bernard ordered the steel from the French company Fercometal which sub-contracted the order to a Spanish company.

In order to ensure that the steel complied with the contractor's specifications, Campenon Bernard applied to the paris office of the British company, Lloyd's Register of Shipping, which, by a contract dated 3 December 1985, forwarded to Campenon Bernard by letter dated 9 December 1985, undertook to check that the steel complied with the prescribed standard. According to the contract the check was to be carried out by the Spanish sub-contractor of the Spanish branch of Lloyd's Register of Shipping and payment was to be made in pesetas.

On 17 and 24 January, 1986 the Spanish office of Lloyd's Register of Shipping issued certificates that the steel complied with the technical standards, whereupon Campenon Bernard paid Fercometal the purchase price and had the steel shipped to Kuwait.

In May 1986, however, the contractor in Kuwait refused the steel as not complying with the required standard.

Campenon Bernard thereupon brought an action before the Tribunal de Commerce (Commercial Court), paris, against Lloyd's Registet of Shipping, represented by its Paris office, claiming damages.

3. Lloyd's Register of Shipping claimed before the Tribunal de Commerce and later before the Cout d'Appel (Court of Appeal), paris, that the action was inadmissible, contending that Article 5(5) of the Brussels Convention did not confer on the French courts jurisdiction to deal with the matter. In the course of considering the appeal by Lloyd's Register of Shipping against the judgment of the Cout d'Appel dated 5 June 1991, the Cout de Cassation subsequently referred the following question to the Court of Justice for a preliminary ruling:

'In the light of the first paragraph of Article 5 of the Brussels Convention of 27 September 1968 on Jurisdiction and the Enforcement of Judgments in Civil and Commercial Matters, does the expression "dispute arising out of the operations of a branch (...)' in Article 5(5) of the Convention necessarily presuppose that the undertakings in question entered into by the branch in the name of *the parent body* are to be performed in the Contracting State in which the branch is established?'

Brussels Convention

4. The principal rule with regard to jurisdiction is to be found in the first paragraph of Article 2 of the Brussels Convention, which provides: 'Subject to the provisions of this Convention, persons domiciled in a Contracting State shall, whatever their nationality, be sued in the courts of that State.'

5. Article 5, which is to be found in Section 2 of Title 11 of the Convention, entitled 'Special jurisdiction' lists a number of cases of special jurisdiction of which the applicant may choose to avail himself instead.

'Article 5:

A person domiciled in a Contracting State may, in another Contracting State, be sued:

1. in matters relating to a contract, *in the courts for the place of performance of the obligation in question;*

2. ...

3. in matters relating to tort, delict or quasi-delict, in the courts for the place where the harmful event occurred;

4. ...

5. as regards a dispute arising out of the operations of a branch, agency or other establishment, in the courts for the place in which the branch, agency or other establishment is situated;

6. ...

7. ...

6. In the judgment of reference the Cour de Cassation refers to the

judgment in Case 33/78 *Somafer* v *Saar-Ferngas*, previously cited, where the Court declared: 'Although Article 5 makes provision in a number of cases for a special jurisdiction, which the plaintiff may choose, this is because of the existence, in certain clearly defined situations, of a particularly close connecting factor between a dispute and the court which may be called upon to hear it, with a view to efficacious conduct of the proceedings. Multiplication of the bases of jurisdiction in one and the same case is not likely to encourage legal certainty and the effectiveness of legal protection throughout the territory of the Community and therefore it is in accord with the objective of the Convention to avoid a wide and multifarious interpretation of the exceptions to the general rule of jurisdiction contained in Article 2 ...' (paragraph 7); and 'The scope and limits of the right given to the plaintiff by Article 5(5) must be determined by the particular facts which either in the relations between the parent body and its branches, agencies or other establishments or in the relations between one of the latter entities and third parties show the special link justifying, in derogation from Article 2, the option granted to the plaintiff ...' (paragraph 8).

The Court further declared: '... Such special link comprises in the first place the material signs enabling the existence of the branch, agency or other establishment to be easily recognized and in the second place the connection that there is between the local entity and the claim directed against the parent body established in another Contracting State' (paragraph 11).

In the case now pending it is the Court's definition of the expression '*operations' of* a branch, agency or other establishment which calls for consideration. In the *Somafer* judgment the Court stated: '...This concept of operations comprises on the one hand actions relating to rights and contractual or non-contractual obligations concerning the management properly so called of the agency, branch or other establishment itself such as those concerning the situation of the building where such entity is established or the local engagement of staff to work there. Further it also comprises those relating to undertakings which have been entered into at the above-mentioned place of business in the name of the parent body and *which must be performed in the Contracting State where the place of business is established* and also actions concerning non-contractual obligations arising from the activities in which the branch, agency or other establishment, within the above-defined meaning, has engaged at the place in which it is established on behalf *of the parent body'* (paragraph 13, my emphasis).

7. The Court's statement that the expression operations' also comprises the obligations which the branch, agency or other establishment has entered into on behalf of the parent body, in so far as it concerns the addition *and which must be performed in the Contracting State where the place of business is established',* has been criticized both in academic writings and in Advocate General Sir Gordon Slynn's Opinion in Case 218/86 *SAR Schotte* v *Palfums Rothschild.*

Procedure before the Court

8. In the written observations submitted to the Court, Campenon Bernard, the United Kingdom, the Greek Government and the Commission have all supported that criticism.

The observations emphasize that the wording of Article 5(5) contains no geographical limitation of the expression 'operations which is a purely economic concept.

If Article 5(5) were to apply only to disputes concerning obligations which were to be performed in the State in which the branch, agency or other establishment were situated, the independent practical significance of the provision would in addition be extremely slight. According to Article 5(1) the courts for the place of performance of the obligation already have jurisdiction in matters relating to a contract and under Article 5(3) the courts for the place where the harmful event occurred have jurisdiction in matters relating to tort, delict or quasi-delict. With such a limitation Article 5(5) would in reality be reduced to covering cases of choice between jurisdictions within the individual Contracting State, for which the provision cannot have been intended.

What is more, Article 5(5) is intended to apply to third persons contracting with a parent company's branch or agency and the same conditions apply to such third persons irrespective of where the contract is to be performed.

Finally, the United Kingdom mentions that in the second paragraph of Article 8 of the Convention (insurance matters) and the second paragraph of Article 13 thereof (certain consumer contracts) exactly the same wording is used as in the contested Article 5(5). The provisions must therefore, in the United Kingdom's view, be uniformly interpreted. The practical effect of the second paragraph of Article 8 and the second paragraph of Article 13 would, however, be very considerably reduced if those provisions were to be interpreted with the limitation ascribed to Article 5(5) in the *Somafer* judgment.

9. The French Government, in its observations, dissociates itself from a strictly literal interpretation of the requirements of the *Somafer* judgment. With particular reference to the Court's more recent decision in Case 218/86 *Schotte* it advocates a solution according to which there must be a real link between the dispute and the State in which it is to be heard, for instance that at least one part of the contract is to be performed in that State.

10. Lloyd's Register of Shipping in its observations has invited the Court to confirm in its entirety the geographical limitation of Article 5(5) referred to in the *Somafer* judgment and in doing so has mentioned *inter alia* that the reason for the provision is the practical procedural consideration of allowing disputes to be decided on the spot, as it were. Advocate General Reischl in his Opinion in Case 139/80 *Blanckaert and Willems* v *Trost* interprets the *Somafer* judgment as follows: '... The above-mentioned decision shows, furthermore, that in order to satisfy the requirements of Article 5(5) of the Convention the existence of *some* restrictions on the representative's independence and *some* opportunity for the principal undertaking to exercise its influence is not sufficient. The agency or other establishment must actually be a kind of decentralised office with

essentially the same ability to conduct business as the principal undertaking, but *restricted, of course, to the territory of the Member State in which it is situated.* I think that is what is required by the words quoted above, in particular by the use of the words "place of business".' (my emphasis).

In the view of Lloyd's Register of Shipping that requirement as to the place of performance does not create a textually unacceptable restriction of the provision.

Discussion

11. The Court has consistently held that the rules of the Convention on special jurisdiction - which are certainly derogations from the general rule of the first paragraph of Article 2 on the domicile of the defendant - are to be restrictively interpreted.

12. It may at first seem doubtful how much weight can be attached in cases such as this to the statements in the *Somafer* judgment on the concept of 'operations'.

In the first place the statement in paragraph 13 contains an indication of what *is* covered by the concept of 'operations', but there is no indication of what *is not* covered by the concept - see, for example, the expressions 'this concept of operations comprises on the one hand...' and 'Further it also comprises...'. The Court had no occasion to decide the question of whether to attribute a geographical limitation to Article 5(5). The dispute before the court of reference concerned a case which would also be covered by the provision even if such a limitation had applied and according to the report of the parties' observations the question of a geographical limitation was not even discussed.

Next, it must be stressed that the Court's statement that the concept of operations also comprises actions 'relating to undertakings which have been entered into at the above-mentioned place of business in the name of the parent body and which must be performed in the Contracting State where the place of business is established' is in the nature of an *obiter dictum.* The case before the court of reference concerned not this type of dispute but on the contrary a dispute 'concerning non-contractual obligations arising from the activities in which the branch, agency or other establishment within the above-defined meaning, has engaged at the place in which it is established on behalf of the parent body'.

I would refer to paragraph 2 of the grounds of judgment, according to which the action concerned the question whether the German court had jurisdiction: '... to try an action brought by a German undertaking against a French undertaking, the registered office of which is in French territory but which has an office or place of contract in the Federal Republic of Germany described on its note-paper as '*Vertretung für Deutschland'*, for the recovery of the expenses incurred by the German undertaking to protect gas mains belonging to it from any damage which might be caused by demolition work which the French undertaking was carrying out in the vicinity on behalf of the Saarland'.

The idea therefore suggests itself that in making its observations the

Court was not deciding the question of the application of Article 5(5) to a case such as this.

13. The same may be said of Case 139/80 *Blanckaert and Willems*, which concerned the jurisdiction of German courts to try a dispute regarding the plaintiff's agency in the Rhine and Ruhr, Eifel and South Westphalia area. Advocate General Reischl's observation to the effect that the undertaking must *of course* be restricted to the territory of the Member State in which it is situated was made therefore in a context in which it was not necessary to consider the consequences of the opposite point of view.

14. In its judgment in Case 218/86 *Schotte*, the Court did not discuss the question of whether a geographical limit applied to sub-paragraph 5 of Article 5, which, as I mentioned previously, was raised by Advocate General Sir Gordon Slynn. The question referred to the Court for a preliminary ruling did not concern that matter, but it was clear from the case that the perfume atomizer pumps to which the action related were *not* to be supplied in the Contracting State in which the branch, agency or other establishment was situated (Germany), but on the contrary in the Contracting State in which the defendant (parent) undertaking was situated (France).

In that judgment the Court declared that Article 5(5) could be applied in a situation 'in which two companies bear the same name and are under common management, and in which one of those undertakings, although not a dependent branch or agency of the other, nevertheless, enters into transactions on behalf of the other and thus acts as its extension in business relations' (paragraph 13).

It was also emphasized in the judgment that the German firm, not only 'took part in the negotiations and in the conclusion of the contract but was also responsible, during the performance of the contract, for ensuring that the deliveries contracted for were made and that invoices were paid' (paragraph 14).

The dispute concerned 'orders placed for the delivery ... to the French undertaking of atomizer pumps'.

The Court therefore mentioned expressly that the question concerned deliveries to a firm in France without raising the question of a geographical limitation in the application of Article 5(5) in a case in which such a limitation might possibly have led to the opposite result.

15. I certainly cannot concur with the United Kingdom's view that the same interpretation must be given to the identical provisions of Article 5(5) on the one hand and the second paragraphs of Article 8 and of Article 13 on the other. In my view that argument is significantly weakened by the very purpose of the two latter provisions: to protect the insured (second paragraph of Article 8) and the consumer (second paragraph of Article 13) respectively, who are by definition the weaker parties in the relevant contractual relationship. In addition, there is the important difference that Article 5(5) applies where the defendant is domiciled in a Contracting State, whereas the second paragraphs of Articles 8 and 13 deal expressly with situations in which the insurer or the party with whom the consumer has entered into a contract is not domiciled in the Contracting State. I naturally agree that it would be difficult for the provisions in question to be applied with a geographical limitation such as that at issue in this case. But

that does not mean that it may be immediately deduced that the limitation is untenable as far as Article 5(5) is concerned.

16. On the other hand, decisive importance must be attached to the fact that Article 5(5) would to all intents and purposes be devoid of independent content if it were applicable only to disputes regarding obligations which must be performed in the Contracting State in which the branch, agency or other establishment is situated. The courts for the place of performance of the obligation already have jurisdiction under Article 5(1) in matters relating to a contract and the courts for the place where the harmful event occurred already have jurisdiction under Article 5(3) in matters relating to tort, delict or quasi-delict. As emphasized by Campenon Bernard, the United Kingdom, the Greek Government and the Commission, with such a limitation of Article 5(5) would actually be reduced to cases of choice between several jurisdictions within the individual Contracting State.

17. If a geographical limitation were to be generally construed as being covered by the economic concept 'operations' in Article 5(5), that might also entail significant difficulties of interpretation, with the resultant legal uncertainty. Is it, for example, impossible to apply the provision if only a single part of the contract is to be performed outside the Contracting State? The French Government's suggestion that performance of at least one part of the contract must take place within the Contracting State raises the same difficulty, though in reverse. Can it be required, for example, that that part of the contract must be an essential one? Is the person with whom the contract is concluded to be able to avoid legal proceedings, for example, by having certain parts of the obligation he has assumed performed outside the Contracting State by engaging a sub-contractor, for instance, and will it be significant whether there has been agreement as to whether a (given) sub-contractor may be employed in the performance of the obligation? And what differences may the criterion possibly lead to as regards the delivery of foods or the performance of services?

Rather than creating clarity, a geographical limitation such as that at issue raises a series of problems and thus gives rise to legal uncertainty.

18. Furthermore, Article 5(5) serves two purposes:

- Partly to make it easier for the plaintiff to take proceedings in cases in which there is 'a place of business which has the appearance of permanency, such as the extension of a parent body, has a management and is materially equipped to negotiate business with third parties so that the latter, although knowing that there will, if necessary, be a legal link with the parent body, the head office of which is abroad, do not have to deal directly with such parent body but may transact business at the place of business constituting the extension' (*Somafer* judgment paragraph 12); and
- Partly, as mentioned in the United Kingdom's observations, to approximate the situation just described to the point of departure of the first paragraph of Article 2 of the Convention regarding general jurisdiction arising from the domicile of the defendant. For agencies such as those listed in Article 5(5) - non-legal persons - there is by definition no such jurisdiction arising from domicile.

Article 5(5) should therefore in my view be interpreted according to its clear wording, which entails no geographical limitation.

Opinion

19. On the foregoing grounds I shall suggest that the Court should answer the question referred to it as follows: The expression 'as regards a dispute arising out of the operations of a branch, agency or other establishment...' in Article 5(5) of the Brussels Convention of 27 September 1968 on Jurisdiction and the Enforcement of Judgments in Civil and Commercial Matters does not entail any requirement that the obligations undertaken by a branch (...) in the name of *the parent company* are to be performed in the Contracting State in which the branch ... is situated.

TITLE II *[Chapter II]*

JURISDICTION *[Jurisdiction]*

Plurality of defendants – Article 6 *[Article 6]*

See also

Case 189/87 - 27 September 1988

Athanasios Kalfelis
v
Bankhaus Schröder, Münchmeyer, Hengst and Co. and Others

Article 6(1) - Special jurisdictions - More than one defendant - Jurisdiction of the court for the place where one of the defendants is domiciled - Conditions - Connection between the actions within the meaning of the Convention - Special jurisdictions - Article 5(3) - Jurisdiction for 'matters relating to tort, delict or quasi-delict' - Concept - Independent interpretation - Action to establish liability unconnected with matter relating to a contract - Action based on several grounds - Exclusion of claims not based an grounds of tort or delict.

Summary

1. For Article 6(1) of the Convention of 27 September 1968 on Jurisdiction and the Enforcement of Judgments in Civil and Commercial Matters to apply, a connection must exist between the various actions brought by the same plaintiff against different defendants. That connection, whose nature must be determined independently, must be of such a kind that it is expedient to determine the actions together in order to avoid the risk of irreconcilable judgments resulting from separate proceedings.

2. The expression 'matters relating to tort, delict or quasi-delict' contained in Article 5(3) of the Convention must be regarded as an independent concept covering all actions which seek to establish the liability of a defendant and which are not related to a 'contract' within the meaning of Article 5(1).

A court which has jurisdiction under Article 5(3) over an action insofar as it is based on tort or delict does not have jurisdiction over that action insofar as it is not so based.

JUDGMENT OF THE COURT

Bosco, President of the Chamber, Everling, Galmot, Joliet and Schockweiler, Judges

1. By order of 27 April 1987, which was received at the Court Registry on 16 June 1987, the Bundesgerichtshof referred to the Court for a preliminary ruling under Article 3 of the Protocol of 3 June 1971 on the Interpretation by the Court of Justice of the Convention of 27 September 1968 on Jurisdiction and the Enforcement of Judgments in Civil and Commercial Matters (hereinafter referred to as 'the Convention') two questions on the interpretation of Articles 5(3) and 6(1) of the Convention.

2. The questions were raised in proceedings brought by Athanasios Kalfelis against Bankhaus Schröder, Münchmeyer, Hengst und Co., Frankfurt am Main, and Bankhaus Schröder, Münchmeyer, Hengst International SA, Luxembourg, and Ernst Markgraf, a procuration holder for the first-named bank.

3. Between March 1980 and July 1981 Mr Kalfelis concluded with the bank established in Luxembourg, through the intermediary of the bank established in Frankfurt am Main and with the participation of the latter's joint procuration-holder, a number of spot and futures stock exchange transactions in silver bullion and for that purpose paid DM 344 868.52 to the bank in Luxembourg. The futures transactions resulted in a total loss. The object of Mr Kalfelis's action is to obtain an order that the defendants, as jointly and severally liable for the debt, should pay him DM 463 019.08 together with interest. His claim is based on contractual liability for breach of the obligation to provide information, on tort, pursuant to Paragraph 823(2) of the Bürgerliches Gesetzbuch (Civil Code) in conjunction with Paragraph 263 of the Strafgesetzbuch (Criminal Code) and Paragraph 826 of the Bürgerliches Gesetzbuch, since the defendants caused him to suffer loss as a result of their conduct *contra bonos mores*. He also alleges unjust enrichment, on the ground that futures stock-exchange contracts, such as futures transactions in silver bullion, are not binding on the parties by virtue of mandatory provisions of German law and therefore reclaims the sums which he paid over.

4. Bankhaus Schröder, Münchmeyer Hengst International SA challenged the jurisdiction of the German courts at every stage of the

procedure and therefore the Bundesgerichtshof stayed the proceedings and referred the following questions to the Court for a preliminary ruling:

'(1) (a) Must Article 6(1) of the EEC Convention be interpreted as meaning that there must be a connection between the actions against the various defendants?

(b) If Question (a) must be answered in the affirmative, does the necessary connection between the actions against the various defendants exist if the actions are essentially the same in fact and law (einfache Streitgenossenschaft), or must a connection be assumed to exist only if it is expedient to hear and determine them together to avoid the risk of irreconcilable judgments resulting from separate proceedings (for example, in cases of "notwendige Streitgenossenschaft" (compulsory joinder))?

(2)(a) Must the term "tort" in Article 5(3) of the EEC Convention be construed independently of the Convention or must it be construed according to the law applicable in the individual case (*lex causae*), which is determined by the private international law of the court applied to?

(b) Does Article 5(3) of the EEC Convention confer, in respect of an action based on claims in tort and contract and for unjust enrichment, accessory jurisdiction on account of factual connection even in respect of the claims not based on tort?'

5. Reference is made to the Report for the Hearing for a fuller account of the facts of the case, the Community legislation and the observations submitted to the Court, which are mentioned or discussed hereinafter only insofar as is necessary for the reasoning of the Court.

The first question

6. The first question submitted by the Bundesgerichtshof is intended essentially to ascertain whether, for Article 6(1) of the Convention to apply, a connection must exist between the claims made by the same plaintiff against several defendants and, if so, what the nature of that connection is.

7. Pursuant to Article 2 of the Convention, persons domiciled in a Contracting State are, subject to the provisions of the Convention, 'whatever their nationality, to be sued in the courts of that State'. Section 2 of Title II of the Convention, however, provides for 'special jurisdictions', by virtue of which a defendant domiciled in a

Contracting State may be sued in another Contracting State. One of the special jurisdictions is that provided for in Article 6(1) according to which a defendant may be sued 'where he is one of a number of defendants, in the courts for the place where any one of them is domiciled'.

8. The principle laid down in the Convention is that jurisdiction is vested in the courts of the State of the defendant's domicile and that the jurisdiction provided for in Article 6(1) is an exception to that principle. It follows that an exception of that kind must be treated in such a manner that there is no possibility of the very existence of that principle being called in question.

9. That possibility might arise if a plaintiff were at liberty to make a claim against a number of defendants with the sole object of ousting the jurisdiction of the courts of the State where one of the defendants is domiciled. As is stated in the report prepared by the committee of experts which drafted the Convention (Official Journal C 59, 5.3.79, p. 1), such a possibility must be excluded. For that purpose, there must be a connection between the claims made against each of the defendants.

10. In order to ensure, as far as possible, the equality and uniformity of the rights and obligations under the Convention of the Contracting States and of the persons concerned, the nature of that connection must be determined independently.

11. In that regard, it must be noted that the above-mentioned report prepared by the committee of experts referred expressly, in its explanation of Article 6(1), to the concern to avoid the risk in the Contracting States of judgments which are incompatible with each other. Furthermore, account was taken of that preoccupation in the Convention itself, Article 22 of which governs cases of related actions brought before courts in different Contracting States.

12. The rule laid down in Article 6(1) therefore applies where the actions brought against the various defendants are related when the proceedings are instituted, that is to say where it is expedient to hear and determine them together in order to avoid the risk of irreconcilable judgments resulting from separate proceedings. It is for the national court to verify in each individual case whether that condition is satisfied.

13. It must therefore be stated in reply to the first question that for Article 6(1) of the Convention to apply there must exist between various actions brought by the same plaintiff against different defendants a connection of such a kind that it is expedient to determine those actions together in order to avoid the risk of irreconcilable judgments resulting from separate proceedings.

The second question

14. The second question submitted by the Bundesgerichtshof is intended essentially to ascertain, first, whether the phrase 'matters relating to tort, delict or quasi-delict' used in Article 5(3) of the Convention must be given an independent meaning or be defined in accordance with the applicable national law and, secondly, in the case of an action based concurrently on tortious or delictual liability, breach of contract and unjust enrichment, whether the court having jurisdiction by virtue of Article 5(3) may adjudicate on the action insofar as it is not based on tort or delict.

15. With respect to the first part of the question, it must be observed that the concept of 'matters relating to tort, delict or quasi-delict' serves as a criterion for defining the scope of one of the rules concerning the special jurisdictions available to the plaintiff. As the Court held with respect to the expression 'matters relating to a contract' used in Article 5(1) (see the judgments of 22 March 1983 in Case 34/82 *Peters* v *ZNAV* [1983] ECR 987, and of 8 March 1988 in Case 9/87 SPRL *Arcado and SA Haviland* [1988] ECR 1539), having regard to the objectives and general scheme of the Convention, it is important that, in order to ensure as far as possible the equality and uniformity of the rights and obligations arising out of the Convention for the Contracting States and the persons concerned, that concept should not be interpreted simply as referring to the national law of one or other of the States concerned.

16. Accordingly, the concept of matters relating to tort, delict or quasi-delict must be regarded as an autonomous concept which is to be interpreted, for the application of the Convention, principally by reference to the scheme and objectives of the Convention in order to ensure that the latter is given full effect.

17. In order to ensure uniformity in all the Member States, it must be recognized that the concept of 'matters relating to tort delict and quasi-

delict' covers all actions which seek to establish the liability of a defendant and which are not related to a 'contract' within the meaning of Article 5(1).

18. It must therefore be stated in reply to the first part of the second question that the term 'matters relating to tort, delict or quasi-delict' within the meaning of Article 5(3) of the Convention must be regarded as an independent concept covering all actions which seek to establish the liability of a defendant and which are not related to a 'contract' within the meaning of Article 5(1).

19. With respect to the second part of the question, it must be observed, as already indicated above, that the 'special jurisdictions' enumerated in Articles 5 and 6 of the Convention constitute derogations from the principle that jurisdiction is vested in the courts of the State where the defendant is domiciled and as such must be interpreted restrictively. It must therefore be recognized that a court which has jurisdiction under Article 5(3) over an action insofar as it is based on tort or delict does not have jurisdiction over that action insofar as it is not so based.

20. Whilst it is true that disadvantages arise from different aspects of the same dispute being adjudicated upon by different courts, it must be pointed out, on the one hand, that a plaintiff is always entitled to bring his action in its entirety before the courts for the domicile of the defendant and, on the other, that Article 22 of the Convention allows the first court seised, in certain circumstances, to hear the case in its entirety provided that there is a connection between the actions brought before the different courts.

21. In those circumstances, the reply to the second part of the second question must be that a court which has jurisdiction under Article 5(3) over an action insofar as it is based on tort or delict does not have jurisdiction over that action insofar as it is not so based.

On those grounds, the Court (Fifth Chamber), in reply to the questions submitted to it by the Bundesgerichtshof by order of 27 April 1987, hereby rules:

(1) For Article 6(1) of the Convention to apply there must exist between the various actions brought by the same plaintiff against different defendants a connection of such a

kind that it is expedient to determine the actions together in order to avoid the risk of irreconcilable judgments resulting from separate proceedings;

(2) (a) The term 'matters relating to tort, delict or quasi-delict' used in Article 5(3) of the Convention must be regarded as an independent concept covering all actions which seek to establish the liability of a defendant and which are not related to a 'contract' within the meaning of Article 5(1);

(b) A court which has jurisdiction under Article 5(3) over an action insofar as it is based on tort or delict does not have jurisdiction over that action insofar as it is not so based.

OPINION OF MR ADVOCATE GENERAL DARMON

1. The Bundesgerichtshof has referred to the Court two questions - each involving two difficulties - relating to the interpretation of the Convention of 27 September 1968 on Jurisdiction and the Enforcement of Judgments in Civil and Commercial Matters (which I shall refer to as 'the Convention'). The two provisions to be interpreted by the Court are Article 6(1) and Article 5(3) of the Convention.

I - Article 6(1)

2. It is necessary first to determine, in view of the lack of any guidance in that regard in Article 6(1), whether there must be a connection between the claims made against the various defendants. Both legal writers and the national case-law on the Convention are unanimous in answering that question in the affirmative. The *raison d'être* of such a requirement lies in the concern to ensure that the rule *actor sequitur forum rei* prevails as a principle, so as to 'prevent ... [Article 6(1)] from being used solely for the purpose of ousting the jurisdiction of the courts of the domicile of one of the parties'.

3. Notwithstanding an opinion put forward by some, definition of the connection cannot be left to the Contracting States. The terms used in the Convention must be interpreted uniformly 'having regard to the objectives and the general scheme of the Convention ... in order to ensure as far as possible the equality and uniformity of the rights and obligations arising out of the Convention for the Contracting States and the persons concerned'.

4. The national court offers an alternative: either jurisdiction is conferred by virtue of Article 6(1) whenever the claims are similar in fact and in law, or else it is conferred only where that course is necessary in order to avoid irreconcilable judgments in separate proceedings. This alternative appears in fact to relate to the distinction in German law between ordinary joinder of parties and compulsory joinder of parties.

5. The criterion to be chosen by the Court in this case must strike a balance between the following two imperatives: (i) ensuring the proper administration of justice by avoiding, in particular, the risk of incompatible decisions, and (ii) ensuring that the rule laid down in Article 2 of the Convention continues to prevail as a principle.

6. The terms 'un lien sérieux' and 'un lien qui ne serait pas artificiel' seem to me too vague in their definition.

7. A subjective criterion, which would involve trying to decide whether or not the plaintiff was trying to deny any of the defendants the right to be sued in the court which would normally have jurisdiction, would he difficult to apply in practice. Legal certainty would be poorly served by an analysis, as delicate as it would be uncertain, of the plaintiff's intentions.

8. A definition inspired by the concept of compulsory joinder as understood in German and Italian law seems to me excessively restrictive. The Commission rightly points out that if jurisdiction under Article 6(1) were restricted to cases of compulsory joinder of parties that provision would virtually cease to have any practical application in view of the infrequency of such cases.

9. The concept of 'litisconsorzio necessario' in Italian law provides interesting guidance as to the objective pursued. It presupposes that the *petitum* or the *causa petendi* is in part or in whole common to the claims. It is closely related to the 'einfache Streitgenossenschaft' of German law and also, albeit with subtle distinctions, to the 'connexité' of French law.

10. But it seems to me that an abstract formulation, based in particular on the concepts of identity of cause and of subject-matter is fraught with real difficulties. In particular the concept of cause is one so difficult to apply that I have very serious doubts as to whether it is appropriate to the requirements of an independent interpretation common to the Contracting States.

11. The approach which seems without doubt to be the most logical here consists in relying upon the third paragraph of Article 22 of the Convention. That provision describes as related those actions 'which are so closely connected that it is expedient to hear and determine them together to avoid the risk of irreconcilable judgments resulting from separate proceedings'.

12. The *prevention* of the irreconcilability of decisions is the *ratio legis* both of Article 6(1) and of the third paragraph of Article 22. In those circumstances I cannot see any good reason for not transposing the 'purpose-related' criterion of the latter provision to cases where there are several claims.

13. We should note however that the Bundesgerichtshof appears to place the need to preclude irreconcilable judgments and cases of compulsory joinder of parties on the same footing. Without doubt, in the case of irreconcilability, the national court has in mind 'the impossibility of enforcing two decisions simultaneously', a much more restrictive concept than a mere conflict of decisions which does not necessarily prevent each of them from being executed separately.

14. The following example will illustrate the distinction: two actions commenced separately against two persons allegedly responsible for an

accident may give rise to two judgments, one upholding the claim and the other dismissing it on the ground that the characteristics of the damage are such that it cannot be repaired. The decisions are certainly contradictory, if not irreconcilable. But that does not mean that there is any question of their simultaneous enforcement being impossible.

15. To emphasize this distinction, it will, without any doubt, be appropriate to refer expressly to 'contradictory decisions' in order to stress, unequivocally, that the choice made favours a solution of sufficient breadth.

II - Article 5(3)

16. Must the concept of 'matters relating to tort, delict or quasi-delict' mentioned in Article 5(3) be taken to have an independent meaning? This Court has not so far disposed of that question. But Mr Advocate General Warner, in his Opinion in the case of *Rüffer*, explained at length and, in my view, very accurately, the reasons for which an affirmative answer is called for. I shall confine myself to mentioning the two main reasons which he put forward in support of his view.

17. In the first place, with the exception of the case of *Tessili* v *Dunlop*, whenever the Court has been called upon to say whether a concept incorporated in the Convention must be interpreted by reference to the national legislation or must be given an independent meaning, it has opted for the second solution. It will be recalled that in *Peters* the Court attributed an independent meaning to the concept of 'matters relating to contract', and it may be considered that matters relating to tort, delict and quasi-delict' constitute the counterpart of that concept in Article 5(1).

18. Furthermore, insofar as the concepts used in the Convention do not correspond to legal concepts known in each Contracting State - and Mr Advocate General Warner clearly demonstrated that to be the case here - it cannot be considered that they are based on national law.

19. I would add that a lack of concordance between the meanings attributed to concepts, depending on whether the *lex causae* is being applied or jurisdiction is being determined under the Convention, will not militate against the adoption of an independent interpretation. A court may, drawing a very clear distinction, refer to different juridical categories for the purposes of determining that it has jurisdiction and, thereafter, adjudicating upon the case before it.

20. Is it in fact necessary, however, to work out a definition for the concept of 'matters relating to tort, delict and quasi-delict'? Closely examined, the wording of the question submitted by the national court does not call for such an analysis. In that regard, Mr Advocate General Warner made an amusing reference to the difficulties inevitably involved in arriving at such a definition: 'Like the proverbial elephant', he said, 'tort is easier to recognize than to define'.

21. Academic writers also consider that a very prudent approach should be adopted, which in the present case merely means that no abstract standard should be formulated, particularly when the Court has not been asked to

provide one. In any event, the interpretation which I propose that the Court should adopt in answering the last question should enable the difficulty facing the national court to be resolved.

22. The Bundesgerichtshof wishes to know to what extent Article 5(3) confers, as a result of connexity, accessory jurisdiction for matters not relating to tort, in an action based on 'claims in tort and contract and for unjustified enrichment'.

23. Needless to say, such an eventuality can arise only where national procedure allows the 'overlapping' of grounds for a single court action, as appears to be the case in the Federal Republic of Germany, the Netherlands and the United Kingdom.

24. The difficulty clearly arises only where the Court cannot *derive* from the Convention any *direct* jurisdiction regarding the accessory grounds.

25. Let me say at the outset that I agree with the Commission's analysis, which appears to take the most judicious points from the previous decisions of the Court and in particular from its judgment in Peters, in which it stated: '*multiplication of the bases of jurisdiction* in one and the same type of case is not likely to encourage legal certainty and effective legal protection throughout the territory of the Community. The provisions of the Convention should therefore be interpreted in such a way that the court seised is not required to declare that it has jurisdiction to adjudicate upon certain applications but *has no jurisdiction to hear certain other applications, even though they are closely related*'.

26. That need to rationalize jurisdiction provides justification for saying that 'because of the close links created by a contract between the parties thereto, it should be possible for all the difficulties which may arise on the occasion of the performance of a contractual obligation to be brought before the same court: that for the place of performance of the obligation'.

27. The Court thus formulated the reasons which militate in favour of an 'attraction' towards Article 5(1), an attraction which must extend to the *grounds* of the claims, whether they derive from a tort or unjust enrichment under the *lex causae*, provided that, as in the present case, they are based 'for the most part on the non-performance of contractual obligations'.

28. The manifest practical advantages must also be mentioned: the court dealing with the contract is best placed to understand its context and its implications as regards legal proceedings.

29. In other words, it is thus appropriate to conclude that where there are overlapping grounds of that kind, only Article 5(1) will determine the jurisdiction of the court, since the matters relating to contract will 'channel' all the aspects of the dispute.

30. The effect of such a solution thus, by implication but of necessity, is in such circumstances to *exclude* from the scope of Article 5(3) even those grounds relied on in a single action which are non-contractual under the national law in favour of the forum designated by Article 5(1), insofar as the action itself constitutes the expression of 'difficulties which may arise on the occasion of the performance of a contractual obligation'.

31. I therefore propose that the Court should rule as follows;

(i) The application of Article 6(1) of the Convention of 27 September 1968 requires that the claims should be related in such a way that it is expedient to hear and determine them at the same time in order to avoid the risk of irreconcilable judgments resulting from separate proceedings;

(ii) The term 'tort, delict and quasi-delict' in Article 5(3) of the Convention must be construed independently;

An action based on tort and contract and unjust enrichment is governed exclusively by the rules laid down for contractual matters in Article 5(1) of the Convention.

Case C-365/88 - 15 May 1990

Kongress Agentur Hagen GmbH
v
Zeehage BV

Articles 5(1) and 6(2) - Special jurisdiction - Action on a warranty or guarantee - Jurisdiction subject solely to the action on a warranty or guarantee being related to the main action - Action brought before the court seised of the original proceedings on the basis of Article 5(1) of the Convention - Included - Conditions of admissibility - Application of the procedural rules of the lex fori - Limits.

Summary

Where a defendant domiciled in a Contracting State is sued in a court of another Contracting State pursuant to Article 5(1) of the Brussels Convention of 27 September 1968 on jurisdiction and the enforcement of judgments in civil and commercial matters, that court also has jurisdiction by virtue of Article 6(2) of the Convention to entertain an action on a warranty or guarantee brought against a person domiciled in a Contracting State other than that of the court seised of the original proceedings. To enable the entire dispute to be heard by a single court, Article 6(2) simply requires there to be a connecting factor between the main action and the action on a warranty or guarantee, irrespective of the basis on which the court has jurisdiction in the original proceedings.

Article 6(2) must be interpreted as meaning that it does not require the national court to accede to the request for leave to bring an action on a warranty or guarantee and that the national court may apply the procedural rules of its national law in order to determine whether that action is admissible, provided that the effectiveness of the Convention in that regard is not impaired and, in particular, that leave to bring the action on the warranty or guarantee is not refused on the ground that the third party resides or is domiciled in a Contracting State other than that of the court seised of the original proceedings.

JUDGMENT OF THE COURT

Sir Gordon Slynn, President of the Chamber, Joliet and Rodríguez Iglesias, Judges

1. By judgment dated 9 December 1988 which was received at the Court on 15 December 1988, the Hoge Raad der Nederlanden referred to the Court pursuant to the protocol of 3 June 1971 on the interpretation by the Court of Justice of the Convention of 27 September 1968 on jurisdiction and the enforcement of judgments in civil and commercial matters (hereinafter referred to as 'the Convention') three questions for a preliminary ruling on the interpretation of Article 6(2) of that Convention.

2. Those questions were raised in proceedings between Kongress Agentur Hagen GmbH (hereinafter referred to as 'Hagen'), whose registered office is in Düsseldorf (Federal Republic of Germany), and Zeehaghe BV, whose registered office is in The Hague (The Netherlands).

3. It appears from the documents before the Court that Hagen cancelled a reservation made at the request and on behalf of Garant Schuhgilde e.G. (hereinafter referred to as 'Schuhgilde'), Düsseldorf, with Zeehaghe for a large number of hotel rooms, whereupon Zeehaghe summoned Hagen to appear before the Arrondissementsrechtbank (District Court), The Hague, claiming payment of a sum of money, together with interest and costs, for breach of contract. Hagen contended that the court should declare that it had no jurisdiction to entertain the action or, in the alternative, join Schuhgilde, as its principal, to answer a claim for indemnity.

4. The Arrondissementsrechtbank refused leave to bring an action on a warranty or guarantee on the ground that it would delay and complicate the main proceedings. Hagen appealed against that judgment to the Gerechtshof (Regional Court of Appeal), The Hague, arguing that Article 6(2) of the Convention required the court seised of the original proceedings to grant leave to bring an action on a warranty or guarantee 'unless these were instituted solely with the object of removing [the third

party] from the jurisdiction of the court which would be competent in his case', this exception being set out in Article 6(2) itself.

5. The Gerechtshof rejected that argument and upheld the decision of the Arrondissementsrechtbank on the ground that Article 6 did not impose an obligation but merely created a power to grant leave to bring an action on a warranty or guarantee.

6. Hagen appealed against that judgment on a point of law to the Hoge Raad der Nederlanden, which decided to refer the following questions to the Court for a preliminary ruling:

'A - If a defendant domiciled in a Contracting State is sued on the basis of Article 5(1) of the Brussels Convention in another Contracting State, may the court in the latter State derive from Article 6(2) of the Brussels Convention jurisdiction to entertain an action on a warranty or guarantee brought by the defendant against a person domiciled in a Contracting State other than that of the court?

B - Must Article 6(2) of the Brussels Convention be interpreted as meaning that the court is bound to grant leave for the action on a warranty or guarantee to be brought unless the exception provided for in that provision applies?

C - If question B is answered in the negative, may the court apply the procedural rules of its national law in assessing whether the request for leave to bring the action on a warranty or guarantee should be granted or do the provisions of the Brussels Convention mean that the court must consider the request in the light of criteria other than those laid down in its national procedural law and, if so, what are those criteria?'

7. Reference is made to the Report for the Hearing for a fuller account of the facts in the main proceedings, the course of the procedure and the written observations submitted to the Court, which are mentioned or discussed hereinafter only insofar as is necessary for the reasoning of the Court.

The first question

8. The first question is concerned with the case in which the court having jurisdiction under Article 5(1) of the Convention, which derogates from the general principle laid down in Article 2, is requested to grant the defendant leave to bring an action on a warranty or guarantee against a person domiciled in a Contracting State other than that of the court.

9. Hagen and the parties which have submitted observations to the Court infer from the general terms in which Article 6(2) is couched that the rule that a person may be sued as a third parry in an action on a warranty or guarantee 'in the court seised of the original proceedings' applies irrespective of the head of jurisdiction by virtue of which the court was seised of the original proceedings.

10. It is appropriate to point out *in limine* that Article 6(2), which occurs in Section 2 of the Convention entitled 'Special jurisdiction', constitutes, in the same way as Article 5(1), an exception to the rule of jurisdiction laid down in Article 2 under which the courts in the State in which the defendant is domiciled are to have jurisdiction.

11. Article 6(2) makes provision for a special jurisdiction, which the plaintiff may choose because of the existence, in clearly defined situations, of a particularly close connecting factor between a dispute and the court which may be called upon to hear it, with a view to the efficacious conduct of the proceedings (judgment of 22 November 1978 in Case 33/78 *Somafer SA* v *Saar-Ferngas AG* [1978] ECR 2183). The Convention thus enables the entire dispute to be heard by a single court. Consequently, the related nature of the main action and the action on a warranty or guarantee suffices to found jurisdiction on the part of the court in which the action on a warranty or guarantee has been brought, irrespective of the basis on which it has jurisdiction in the original proceedings; in this respect, the jurisdiction provided for in Article 2 and that provided for in Article 5 are equivalent.

12. The answer to the first question must therefore be that where a defendant domiciled in a Contracting State is sued in a court of another Contracting State pursuant to Article 5(1) of the Brussels Convention, that court also has jurisdiction by virtue of Article 6(2) of the Brussels Convention to entertain an action on a warranty or guarantee brought against a person domiciled in a Contracting State other than that of the court seised of the original proceedings.

The second and third questions

13. These two questions seek to establish whether Article 6(2) of the Convention requires the court to grant leave to bring an action on a warranty or guarantee, provided that proceedings were not brought with the object of removing the third party from the jurisdiction of the court which would be competent in his case, or whether, on the contrary, the

court may assess the admissibility of the application for leave in the light of the rules of the national procedural law.

14. Hagen, the French Government and the Government of the Federal Republic of Germany interpret Article 6(2) as an independent provision. In their view, this follows from considerations relating to the sound administration of justice: the full legal protection which the Contracting States are bound to guarantee the parties where one of their courts has jurisdiction cannot be restricted by the application of national procedural rules.

15. In its written observations, the Commission also supported this view, which, it stated, would have the advantage of simplicity and would ensure the uniform application of the Convention: on this view, the national court seised of the original proceedings would be bound to grant leave to bring an action on a warranty or guarantee.

16. At the hearing, the Commission argued that jurisdiction is only one of the conditions governing the admissibility of the application; the court seised must first decide whether it has jurisdiction under the provisions of the Convention and then determine whether the application satisfies such other conditions for an action on a warranty or guarantee as are laid down by the *lex fori.*

17. It should be stressed that the object of the Convention is not to unify procedural rules but to determine which court has jurisdiction in disputes relating to civil and commercial matters in intra-Community relations and to facilitate the enforcement of judgments. It is therefore necessary to draw a clear distinction between jurisdiction and the conditions governing the admissibility of an action.

18. With regard to an action on a warranty or guarantee, Article 6(2) therefore merely determines which court has jurisdiction and is not concerned with conditions for admissibility properly so called.

19. Moreover, the Court has consistently held that, as regards procedural rules, reference must be made to the national rules applicable by the national court (see in particular, as regards the concept of *lis alibi pendens*, the judgment of 7 June 1984 in Case 129/83 *Zelger* v *Salinitri* [1984] ECR 2397, and, as regards the conditions for the enforcement of a foreign judgment, the judgments of 2 July 1985 in Case 148/84 *Deutsche Genossenschaftsbank* v *Brasserie du pêcheur SA* [1985] ECR

1981, and of 4 February 1988 in Case 145/86 *Hoffmann* v *Krieg* [1988] ECR 645).

20. It should be noted, however, that the application of national procedural rules may not impair the effectiveness of the Convention. As the Court has held, in particular in its judgment of 15 November 1983 in Case 288/82 *Duijnstee* v *Goderbauer* [1983] ECR 3663, a court may not apply conditions of admissibility laid down by national law which would have the effect of restricting the application of the rules of jurisdiction laid down in the Convention.

21. Accordingly, an application for leave to bring an action on a warranty or guarantee may not be refused expressly or by implication on the ground that the third parties sought to be joined reside or are domiciled in a Contracting State other than that of the court seised of the original proceedings.

22. The answer to the second and third questions must therefore be that Article 6(2) must be interpreted as meaning that it does not require the national court to accede to the request for leave to bring an action on a warranty or guarantee and that the national court may apply the procedural rules of its national law in order to determine whether that action is admissible, provided that the effectiveness of the Convention in that regard is not impaired and, in particular, that leave to bring the action on the warranty or guarantee is not refused on the ground that the third party resides or is domiciled in a Contracting State other than that of the court seised of the original proceedings.

On those grounds, the Court (First Chamber), in answer to the questions referred to it by the Hoge Raad der Nederlanden, hereby rules:

> **(1) Where a defendant domiciled in a Contracting State is sued in a court of another Contracting State pursuant to Article 5(1) of the Brussels Convention, that court also has jurisdiction by virtue of Article 6(2) of the Brussels Convention to entertain an action on a warranty or guarantee brought against a person domiciled in a Contracting State other than that of the court seised of the original proceedings.**
>
> **(2) Article 6(2) must be interpreted as meaning that it does not require the national court to accede to the request for leave to bring an action on a warranty or guarantee and that the**

national court may apply the procedural rules of its national law in order to determine whether that action is admissible, provided that the effectiveness of the Convention in that regard is not inspired and, in particular, that leave to bring the action on the warranty or guarantee is not refused on the ground that the third party resides or is domiciled in a Contracting State other than that of the court seised of the original proceedings.

OPINION OF MR ADVOCATE GENERAL LENZ

A - The facts

1. The reference for a preliminary ruling submitted to the Court by the Hoge Raad der Nederlanden (Supreme Court of the Netherlands) concerns the interpretation of Article 6(2) of the Convention of 27 September 1968 on jurisdiction and the enforcement of judgments in civil and commercial matters (hereinafter referred to as 'the Convention' or 'the Brussels Convention').

2. In 1984 Kongress Agentur Hagen GmbH (hereinafter referred to as 'Hagen'), Düsseldorf, concluded an agreement with Zeehaghe BV for the reservation of hotel rooms in The Hague. Hagen acted in its own name but at the request and on behalf of Garant Schuhgilde e.G. (hereinafter referred to as 'Schuhgilde'), Düsseldorf. When the reservation was cancelled, Zeehaghe BV summoned Hagen to appear before the Arrondissementsrechtbank (District Court), The Hague, and claimed that Hagen should pay damages and interest for breach of contract.

3. In interlocutory proceedings, which concerned primarily the jurisdiction of the Arrondissementsrechtbank, Hagen claimed in the alternative that Schuhgilde, as its principal, should be joined in an action on a warranty or guarantee. The Arrondissements-rechtbank dismissed this application on the ground that it did not have to grant leave for such an action, since neither of the two companies concerned was domiciled in the Netherlands. As procedural difficulties might arise in the proceedings relating to the action on a warranty or guarantee, the main proceedings might be delayed. Zeehaghe did not have to be subjected to such a delay.

4. On appeal, the Gerechtshof (Regional Court of Appeal), The Hague, upheld the decision of the Arrondissementsrechtbank and added that Article 6 of the Convention only provided for the *possibility* of bringing an action on a warranty or guarantee but did not require the court to grant leave to bring such an action.

5. In the appeal on a point of law, the Hoge Raad referred to the Court of Justice three questions for a preliminary ruling in order to enable it to decide on the jurisdiction of the court seised and the admissibility of the action on a warranty or guarantee.

6. In this Opinion I shall discuss the observations submitted by the parties so far as is necessary. For the rest, I would refer to the Report for the Hearing.

B - Opinion

1. Question A

7. Question A reads as follows: 'If a defendant domiciled in a Contracting State is sued on the basis of Article 5(1) of the Brussels Convention in another Contracting State, may the court in the latter State derive from Article 6(2) of the Brussels Convention jurisdiction to entertain an action on a warranty or guarantee brought by the defendant against a person domiciled in a Contracting State other than that of the court?'

8. In other words, the Hoge Raad wishes to know whether the special jurisdiction provided for in Article 6(2) of the Convention applies even if the court's jurisdiction in the original proceedings is also based on a special rule of jurisdiction (in this case, Article 5(1) of the Convention), or whether it is limited to cases in which the jurisdiction of the court in the original proceedings is based on the general rule of jurisdiction set out in Article 2 of the Convention.

9. In the main proceedings, only Zeehaghe argued in favour of a strict interpretation of the rule of jurisdiction contained in Article 6(2) of the Convention. All the parties who have submitted written observations to the Court, however, support a broad interpretation, whereby the provision on which jurisdiction in the original proceedings is based is irrelevant.

10. No support is to be found in the terms of Article 6(2) of the Convention for a restrictive interpretation of this provision. Article 6(2) permits a person domiciled in a Contracting State to be joined as a third party in an action on a warranty or guarantee in the court seised of the original proceedings, regardless whether jurisdiction in the original proceedings is based on Article 2 or on Article 5 of the Convention. Article 6(2) refers simply to 'the court seised of the original proceedings' and not to 'the court having jurisdiction by virtue of Article 2'; such a formulation would have been necessary, however, to support a restrictive interpretation.

11. As the rule in Article 6 of the Convention is based on the idea of enabling related actions to be heard by a single court in order to avoid conflicting decisions, the existence of a substantive connection between the original proceedings and the action on a warranty or guarantee is of decisive importance for the interpretation of Article 6(2). Therefore the basis on which the court has jurisdiction in the original proceedings is irrelevant.

2. Question B

12. Question B reads as follows: 'Must Article 6(2) of the Brussels Convention be interpreted as meaning that the court is bound to grant leave for the action on a warranty or guarantee to be brought unless the exception provided for in that provision applies?'

13. This question seeks to establish whether the admissibility of an action on a warranty or guarantee must be assessed solely on the basis of Article 6(2) or whether any additional requirements laid down by national law must also be satisfied.

14. According to Hagen, the French Government and the Government of the Federal Republic of Germany, the admissibility of an action on a warranty or guarantee must be assessed solely in the light of Article 6(2) of the Convention. In their opinion, Article 6(2) must be interpreted independently and not by reference to provisions of national law. This view is supported by considerations of procedural economy and the sound administration of justice. If leave to bring an action on a warranty or guarantee could be refused on grounds other than the intention of disadvantaging the third party which is referred to in Article 6(2), a plaintiff might be forced to bring proceedings in two courts in two different Contracting States, which would give rise to additional expense, delays and visits. If one of its courts has jurisdiction, a Contracting State is bound to guarantee the parties full legal protection. This protection may not be restricted by the application of national procedural rules.

15. For its part, the Commission has put forward two alternative interpretations of Article 6(2) of the Convention. According to the *first interpretation,* the question of jurisdiction is only *one* of the conditions governing the admissibility of an action on a warranty or guarantee. The question of jurisdiction must first be determined in accordance with Article 6(2); subsequently, however, the national court must also establish whether the action satisfies the conditions laid down in the national procedural rules.

16. The Commission's *second*, alternative, interpretation, however, accords with that put forward by Hagen and the French and German Governments.

17. In its written observations, the Commission states that its preference is for the second interpretation. This solution was straightforward, as the national court's discretion was precisely defined by the Convention itself. Furthermore, the second interpretation was more likely to result in the uniform application of Article 6(2) of the Convention.

18. At the hearing, however, the Commission changed its mind and explained why it then preferred the first interpretation.

19. It is true that the Commission's second interpretation, which accords with the observations of the other interested parties, is attractive because of its simplicity. The national court would have to check only whether the express exception in Article 6(2) applied and then decide on the admissibility of the action on a warranty or guarantee solely on the basis of the Convention.

20. On closer inspection, however, this view is untenable. Admittedly, it must be held in the first place that the principle of legal certainty within the Community legal order and the objectives pursued by the Convention under Article 220 of the EEC Treaty, on which the Convention is based, require that the equality and uniformity of rights and obligations arising from the Convention for the Contracting States and the persons concerned must be ensured, regardless of the rules laid down in that regard in the laws of those States. Consequently, the Convention must override national provisions which are incompatible with it.

21. The Convention can in principle take priority, however, only within the limits of its scope *ratione materiae* or the scope of its individual provisions. In

the first place, therefore, it is necessary to determine the scope *ratione materiae* of Article 6(2) of the Convention.

22. Article 6(2) is contained in Title II of the Convention, which governs jurisdiction. Article 6(2) determines the court which has international and territorial jurisdiction to hear an action on a warranty or guarantee. The international and territorial jurisdiction of a court, however, constitutes only one of several factors which may be taken into account in order to determine whether an action is admissible but which are governed only in part by the Convention. In this regard I would refer to the Schlosser Report, which makes the following observations on 'other third-party proceedings' within the meaning of Article 6(2): 'In Article 6(2), the term "third-party proceedings" relates to a legal institution which is common to the legal systems of all the original Member States, with the exception of Germany. However, a jurisdictional basis which rests solely on the capacity of a third party to be joined as such in the proceedings cannot exist by itself. It must necessarily be supplemented by legal criteria which determine which parties may in which capacity and for what purpose be joined in legal proceedings. Thus the provisions already existing in, or which may in future be introduced into, the legal systems of the new Member States with reference to the joining of third parties in legal proceedings, remain unaffected by the 1968 Convention.'

Furthermore, the Court of Justice has acknowledged in its judgments that national procedural rules may be relied upon to supplement the provisions of the Convention.

23. Reference to national procedural rules is also to be found in the protocol to the Convention, which by virtue of Article 65 forms an integral part thereof. Thus Article V of the protocol provides that the jurisdiction specified in Article 6(2) in actions on a warranty or guarantee or in any other third-party proceedings may not be resorted to in the Federal Republic of Germany. In that State, any person domiciled in another Contracting State may be sued in the courts in pursuance of Articles 68, 72, 73 and 74 of the Code of Civil Procedure (Zivil-prozebordnung) concerning third-party notices (Streitverkündung).

24. Article 73 of the German Code of Civil Procedure does, however, contain provisions concerning the form of the Streitverkündung, since it provides that the party must serve a notice setting out the ground for the third-party proceedings and the place of the proceedings.

25. Admittedly, Article V is not directly concerned with actions on a warranty or guarantee but refers merely to the arrangement which takes the place of such actions in the Federal Republic of Germany. Regardless how the reference made in Article V of the protocol is to be categorized for legal purposes, Article V does at least provide an indication that in a type of action comparable to an action on a warranty or guarantee there may be procedural requirements in addition to the rules of jurisdiction laid down in the Convention. This confirms that Article 6(2) cannot be the last word on the admissibility of an action on a warranty or guarantee.

26. Accordingly, it is possible to draw an intermediate conclusion to the effect that it cannot be automatically assumed on the basis of the provisions of

Article 6(2) governing international and territorial jurisdiction that an action on a warranty or guarantee is admissible, as there may be in addition national rules which are outside the scope of Article 6(2). These may, for example, include provisions concerning the form of and the time-limit applicable to an action on a warranty or guarantee and substantive rules on the evidential burden to be discharged as regards the alleged relationship between the defendant and the third party.

27. In the section dealing with Question C I shall consider how far such national rules on admissibility must themselves be interpreted and applied in the light of the Convention.

3. *Question C*

28. Question C reads as follows: 'If question B is answered in the negative, may the court apply the procedural rules of its national law in assessing whether the request for leave to bring the action on a warranty or guarantee should be granted or do the provisions of the Brussels Convention mean that the court must consider the request in the light of criteria other than those laid down in its national procedural law and, if so, what are those criteria?'

29. If, as stated above, reference may be made to national procedural rules as regards those conditions governing the admissibility of an action on a warranty or guarantee which do not concern international or territorial jurisdiction, that does not necessarily mean that the possibility of such reference is unlimited. The application of the national procedural rules must not impair the practical effectiveness of the rules of the Convention. Consequently, national conditions governing admissibility may not be applied where they affect areas governed by the Convention, expressly or by implication.

30. As I cannot give an exhaustive list of examples here, I would refer to two factors which played a part in the main proceedings. The Arrondissements-rechtbank, The Hague, decided that the action on a guarantee or warranty was inadmissible because the third party to be joined was not domiciled in the State of the court seised and, if it were to be joined, the decision in the original proceedings would be delayed.

31. Even if national procedural rules permitted such circumstances to be taken into account, they would be incompatible with the meaning and purpose of Article 6(2) of the Convention. Since Article 6 refers merely to a person domiciled in a Contracting State, it precludes any difference in treatment between persons domiciled in different Contracting States. A refusal to grant leave to bring an action on a warranty or guarantee therefore may not be based on the fact that the third parties to be joined are established in a Contracting State other than that of the court seised of the original proceedings. Similarly, in order for third parties to be joined to the original proceedings in an action on a warranty or guarantee they need only have their registered office in one of the Contracting States.

32. It also follows that procedural delays which may occur precisely because the parties to the proceedings are established in different Contracting

States cannot be taken into consideration when balancing the conflicting interests of the parties to the original proceedings.

C - Conclusion

33. In conclusion, I propose that the Court should reply to the questions submitted to it by the Hoge Raad der Nederlanden as follows:

'(1) If a defendant domiciled in a Contracting State is sued on the basis of Article 5(1) of the Convention in a court of another Contracting State, that court also has jurisdiction under Article 6(2) of the Convention to entertain an action on a warranty or guarantee brought against a person domiciled in a Contracting State other than that of the court seised of the original proceedings.

(2) Article 6(2) of the Convention must be interpreted as meaning that, when assessing the admissibility of an action on a warranty or guarantee, reference may be made on a supplementary basis to national procedural rules, provided that those rules do not concern the international or territorial jurisdiction of the court seised of the original proceedings.

(3) Supplementary reference made to national procedural rules must not impair the practical effectiveness of the rules laid down in the Convention on the admissibility of an action on a warranty or guarantee; in particular, reliance may not be placed on the fact that the third party to be joined is domiciled in a Contracting State other than that of the court seised of the original proceedings.'

Case C-341/93 - 13 July 1995

Danvaern Production A/S
v
Schuhfabriken Otterbeck GmbH & Co.

Special Jurisdiction - Article 6(3) - Counterclaim - Definition - Defence seeking to set off a claim by the defendant against a claim by the plaintiff - Excluded.

Summary

Article 6(3) of the Convention of 27 September 1968 on Jurisdiction and the Enforcement of Judgments in Civil and Commercial Matters, as amended by the Convention of 9 October 1978 on the Accession of the Kingdom of Denmark, Ireland and the United Kingdom of Great Britain and Northern Ireland and by the Convention of 25 October 1982 on the Accession of the Hellenic Republic, is intended to establish the conditions under which a court has jurisdiction to hear a claim which could involve a separate judgment or decree. It therefore applies only to claims by defendants which seek the pronouncement of such a judgment or decree. It does not apply to the situation where a defendant raises, as a pure defence, a claim which he allegedly has against the plaintiff. The defences which may be raised and the conditions under which they may be raised are governed by national law.

JUDGMENT OF THE COURT

Rodríguez Iglesias, President, Schockweiler , Gulmann and Jann, Presidents of Chambers, Mancini, Moitinho de Almeida, Murray, Edward and Sevón, Judges

1. By decision of 30 June 1993, received at the Court Registry on 5 July 1993, the Vestre Landsret (Western Regional Court), Denmark, referred to the Court for a preliminary ruling under the Protocol of 3 June 1971 on the interpretation by the Court of Justice of the Convention of 27 September 1968 on Jurisdiction and the Enforcement of Judgments in Civil and Commercial Matters (OJ 1978 L 304, p. 36), as amended by the Convention of 9 October 1978 on the Accession of the Kingdom of Denmark, Ireland and the United Kingdom of Great Britain and Northern Ireland (OJ 1978 L 304, p. 1 and - as amended - p. 77) and the Convention of 25 October 1982 on the Accession of the Hellenic Republic (OJ 1982 L 388, p. 1 and - as amended - OJ 1983 C 97, p. 1) (hereinafter `the Convention'), two questions on the interpretation of Articles 6(3) and 22 of the Convention.

2. Those questions were raised in proceedings between Schuhfabriken Otterbeck GmbH & Co. ('Otterbeck'), the plaintiff in the main proceedings, established in Germany, and Danværn Production A/S ('Danværn'), the defendant in the main proceedings, established in Denmark.

3. Under an agency contract of 10 August 1979, Otterbeck appointed Danværn as its exclusive agent in Denmark for sales of its range of safety shoes.

4. By letter of 22 March 1990, Otterbeck terminated the agency contract with immediate effect, on the ground that Danværn had acted in gross bad faith by dismissing a certain employee.

5. On 11 September 1990 Otterbeck brought proceedings against Danværn in the Byret (District Court), Brønderslev, seeking payment of DKR 223 173.39 with interest, in respect of safety shoes delivered in January and February 1990.

6. Before the Byret, Danværn admitted that it owed the amount claimed, but, asserting that it had its own claims against Otterbeck, including a claim for loss and damage resulting from the wrongful termination of the agency contract, submitted that Otterbeck's claim should be dismissed and that a separate judgment should be entered against Otterbeck ordering it to pay DKR 737 018.34.

7. By judgment of 26 March 1991 the Byret dismissed Danværn's claim as inadmissible, both insofar as it sought a separate judgment and

insofar as it pleaded a set-off as a defence, on the basis that there was not the necessary degree of connection between Otterbeck's and Danværn's claims as required by Article 6(3) of the Convention, which provides: 'A person domiciled in a Contracting State may also be sued: ... (3). on a counterclaim arising from the same contract or facts on which the original claim was based, in the court in which the original claim is pending'.

8. Danværn appealed against that judgment to the Vestre Landsret, where it abandoned its application for a separate judgment and sought only to set-off the sum of DKR 233 173.39 with interest, which was equivalent to the amount of Otterbeck's original claim.

9. The Vestre Landsret considered that the proceedings raised a question of interpretation of the Convention.

10. It therefore stayed the proceedings and referred the following questions to the Court for a prelimary ruling: '1. Does Article 6(3) cover counterclaims for set-offs? 2. Is the expression in Article 6(3) "...arising from the same contract or facts on which the original claim was based..." to be treated as more restrictive than the expression "actions [which] are ... related" in the third paragraph of Article 22 of the Convention?'

Question 1

11. By its first question the national court asks whether Article 6(3) of the Convention applies to the situation where a defendant, who is being sued in a court which has jurisdiction over him, pleads in reply a claim which he allegedly has against the plaintiff.

12. The national laws of the Contracting States generally distinguish between two situations. One is where the defendant pleads, as a defence, the existence of a claim he allegedly has against the plaintiff, which would have the effect of wholly or partially extinguishing the plaintiff's claim. The other is where the defendant, by a separate claim made in the context of the same proceedings, seeks a judgment or decree ordering the plaintiff to pay him a debt. In the latter case, the separate claim can be made for an amount exceeding that claimed by the plaintiff, and it can be proceeded with even if the plaintiff's claim is dismissed.

13. Procedurally, a defence is an integral part of the action initiated by the plaintiff and therefore does not involve the plaintiff being 'sued' in

the court in which his action is pending, within the meaning of Article 6(3) of the Convention. The defences which may be raised and the conditions under which they may be raised are determined by national law.

14. Article 6(3) of the Convention is not intended to deal with that situation.

15. By contrast, a claim by the defendant for a separate judgment or decree against the plaintiff presupposes that the court in which the plaintiff has brought proceedings also has jurisdiction to hear such an application.

16. Article 6(3) is specifically intended to establish the conditions under which a court has jurisdiction to hear a claim which would involve a separate judgment or decree.

17. While the Danish version of Article 6(3) uses the word '*modfordringer*', a general term which can cover both situations referred to in paragraph 12 above, the legal terminology of other Contracting States expressly recognises the distinction between those two situations. French law distinguishes between '*demande reconventionnelle*' and '*moyens de défense au fond*', English law between 'counterclaim' and 'set-off as a defence', German law between '*Widerklage*' and '*Prozeßaufrechnung*', and Italian law between '*domanda riconvenzionale*' and '*eccezione di compensazione*'. The relevant language versions of Article 6(3) expressly adopt the terms '*demande reconventionnelle*', 'counterclaim', '*Widerklage*' and 'domanda riconvenzionale'.

18. The answer to the national court's first question must therefore be that Article 6(3) of the Convention applies only to claims by defendants which seek the pronouncement of a separate judgment or decree. It does not apply to the situation where a defendant raises, as a pure defence, a claim which he allegedly has against the plaintiff. The defences which may be raised and the conditions under which they may be raised are governed by national law.

Question 2

19. The order for reference indicates that Question 2 need only be answered if Article 6(3) of the Convention applies to the situation where

a defendant raises as a defence a claim which he allegedly has against the plaintiff. In the light of the answer to Question 1, there is therefore no need to answer Question 2.

On those grounds, the Court, in answer to the questions referred to it by the Vestre Landsret by decision of 30 June 1993, hereby rules:

> **Article 6(3) of the Convention of 27 September 1968 on Jurisdiction and the Enforcement of Judgments in Civil and Commercial Matters, as amended by the Convention of 9 October 1978 on the Accession of the Kingdom of Denmark, Ireland and the United Kingdom of Great Britain and Northern Ireland and by the Convention of 25 October 1982 on the Accession of the Hellenic Republic, applies only to claims by defendants which seek the pronouncement of a separate judgment or decree. It does not apply to the situation where a defendant raises, as a pure defence, a claim which he allegedly has against the plaintiff. The defences which may be raised and the conditions under which they may be raised are governed by national law.**

OPINION OF MR ADVOCATE GENERAL LÉGER

1. This case has been referred to the Court by the Vestre Landsret (Western Regional Court) pursuant to Article 3 of the Protocol of 3 June 1971 on the interpretation by the Court of Justice of the Convention on 27 September 1968 on Jurisdiction and the Enforcement of Judgments in Civil and Commercial Matters (hereinafter 'the Convention'). In the questions referred for a preliminary ruling, that court asks the Court of Justice to rule for the first time to my knowledge on the interpretation to be given to Article 6(3) of the Convention. The national court essentially asks whether a set-off must be regarded as a 'counterclaim' within the meaning of that provision and whether the requirement for there to be a sufficient connection set out therein is more restrictive than that appearing in the third paragraph of Article 22 of the Convention.

2. I shall briefly call to mind the context and content of those provisions before considering the facts which gave rise to the questions referred for a preliminary ruling.

Legal context

3. The Brussels Convention of 27 September 1968 on Jurisdiction and the Enforcement of Judgments in Civil and Commercial Matters, as amended by

the 1978 Accession Convention (Kingdom of Denmark, Ireland and the United Kingdom of Great Britain and Northern Ireland), the 1982 Accession Convention (Hellenic Republic) and the 1989 Accession Convention (Kingdom of Spain and Portuguese Republic), was drawn up pursuant to Article 220 of the Treaty of Rome to secure the 'simplification of formalities [as between Member States] governing the reciprocal recognition and enforcement of judgments of courts or tribunals...'. Its essential purpose is to secure the free movement of judgments between the Contracting States. The simplified mechanism for the recognition and enforcement of judgments of courts and tribunals in the Member States (Title III) falling within the scope of the Convention (Title I) is based on a standardised system for determining jurisdiction (Title II).

4. The jurisdiction rules set out in Title II enable it to be determined in which court proceedings may competently be brought. Various heads of jurisdiction are provided for in this way, but, under the 'general provisions' (Section 1: Articles 2, 3 and 4), general jurisdiction is conferred in principle on the courts of the defendant's domicile (Article 2). Supplementing that conferral of jurisdiction in principle, and by way of option, Section 2 (Articles 5, 6 and 6a) lists various concurrent jurisdictions, known as 'special jurisdictions', conferred on the courts of a Contracting State other than the courts of the defendant's domicile on account of the strong connection between a particular court and a dispute having regard to the specific character of the subject-matter in question or the specific nature of certain procedural situations.

5. Article 6 falls within the latter section. Consequently, it lists rules of special jurisdiction constituting an optional addition to the other ordinary jurisdiction rules in the following events: where there are a number of defendants (Article 6(1)), action on a warranty or a guarantee in pre-existing proceedings (Article 6(2)) and counterclaims (Article 6(3)).

6. Article 6(3), which is the subject of this request for an interpretative ruling, reads as follows: '(A person domiciled in a Contracting State may also be sued:) ... 3. on a counterclaim arising from the same contract or facts on which the original claim was based, in the court in which the original claim is pending'.

7. Consequently, that provision enables the defendant to enter a counterclaim against the plaintiff in the court seised of the original claim, irrespective as to the basis of that court's jurisdiction. In accordance with the aim of the Convention - that of determining a centralising forum - Article 6(3) enables a proliferation of courts having jurisdiction to be avoided. But this head of special jurisdiction is made expressly conditional on the existence of a contractual or factual connection with the original claim.

8. The difficulty here is that neither the concept of a 'counterclaim' nor that of the existence of a connection within the meaning of the provision is specified. Admittedly, the concept of a 'counterclaim' also appears in the body of the Convention in the specific context of insurance (second paragraph of Article 11) and in the context of consumer contracts (third paragraph of Article 14), but no more is it defined there. In contrast, the concept of relatedness or sufficient connection ('*connexité*') is defined in the third paragraph of Article 22 in the context of the provisions relating to jurisdiction based on '*Lis pendens* -

related actions' (Section 8 of Title II): 'For the purposes of this Article, actions are deemed to be related where they are so closely connected that it is expedient to hear and determine them together to avoid the risk of irreconcilable judgments resulting from separate proceedings'.

9. These were the difficulties that the national court was faced with in proceedings the facts of which are as follows.

Facts

10. On 10 August 1979, an exclusive sales agency contract was concluded between a German shoe manufacturer, *Schuhfabrik Otterbeck GmbH and Co.* (hereinafter 'the appellant in the main proceedings' or 'the appellant'), and a Danish company, *Danværn Production A/S* (hereinafter 'the respondent in the main proceedings' or 'the respondent'). The contract gave the respondent in the main proceedings the exclusive right to sell in Denmark a product range manufactured by the appellant in the main proceedings (safety shoes). Initially concluded for one year, the contract was renewable by tacit acquiescence every three years. It provided that it was governed by German law and that the courts at Duisburg would have jurisdiction.

11. On 22 March 1990, the appellant unilaterally terminated the contract with immediate effect.

12. Since the respondent had not paid for certain deliveries, the appellant brought an action for the recovery of its debts (DKR 223 173.39) in the Byret (District Court), Brønderslev, in spite of the jurisdiction clause in the contract. The respondent submitted that the claim should be dismissed and pleaded a number of counterclaims, one of which - amounting to DKR 909 684 - was for damage allegedly sustained on account of the wrongful termination of the contract.

13. By judgment of 26 March 1991, the Byret, Brønderslev, upheld the appellant's claim and dismissed as inadmissible the claim of the respondent in the main proceedings '...insofar as it sought a *separate decision* and insofar as it requested a set-off' on the ground that there was no 'connection between the claims (the one being for payment for goods supplied, the other for damages for the non-performance and wrongful termination of a contract) such as would enable the defendant, pursuant to Article 6(3) of the Brussels Convention, to have its counterclaim dealt with by the court in Brønderslev or have the amount requested set off...'.

14. In an appeal to the Vestre Landsret, the respondent withdrew its claim for a separate decision and simply asserted a claim to DKR 223 173.39, corresponding to the main claim, with a view to a set-off. It argued that the Vestre Landsret had jurisdiction under Article 6(3) of the Convention on the ground that that provision was applicable to set-offs. In order to establish that the requirement for sufficient connection laid down by that provision was fulfilled, it referred to the interpretation of that concept which is set out in the third paragraph of Article 22 of the Convention.

15. Since it questioned whether it had jurisdiction under the rules of the

Convention, the Vestre Landsret decided to stay the proceedings and refer the following questions to the Court of Justice: '1.Does Article 6(3) cover counterclaims for set-offs? 2. Is the expression in Article 6(3) " ... arising from the same contract or facts on which the original claim was based ..." in Article 6(3) to be treated as more restrictive than the expression "actions [which] are ... related ..." in the third paragraph of Article 22 of the Convention?'

Replies to the questions

16. Given that the Convention makes no stipulation regarding this matter, the national court's first question asks very precisely whether a claim for set-off is to be regarded as a 'counterclaim' within the meaning of Article 6(3). If that were so, under that provision the court seised of the original claim should also have heard and determined the set-off pleaded by the respondent, since it exhibited the requisite connection with the original claim. The second question is concerned with the meaning of the concept of sufficient connection.

First question

17. At first sight, this question may seem surprising. Article 6(3) refers only to a 'counterclaim' and not at all to a 'set-off'. At first water, the two terms seem completely different: the first seeks a separate decision, whilst, procedurally, the second is generally regarded as being simply a ground of defence. However, the order for reference explains the Danish court's questions. The national court mentions that in Danish different terms do not exist to designate a counterclaim with a view to a separate decision, on the one hand, and a counterclaim with a view to a set-off, on the other: the word '*modfordringer*' is used to cover both concepts and it is precisely that term which appears in the Danish version of the Convention.

18. The Danish procedural provisions governing counterclaims set out in Article 249(2) of the Retsplejelov (Law on the Administration of Justice) may seem unfamiliar and add to the confusion of lawyers of other nationalities. Article 249(2) of the Retsplejelov reads as follows: 'A defendant may, during proceedings in a case, submit a counterclaim ("*modkrav*") requesting that the court *find fully or partially in the defendant's favour in respect of the plaintiff's claim or that the court give judgment in favour of the counterclaim or a part thereof,* on condition that the counterclaim may be treated according to the same procedural rules as the plaintiff's claim. A separate decision in respect of the counterclaim, however, may be given only if there is a court with jurisdiction in respect of the claim in Denmark or if the claim arises from the same contract or facts as those on which the plaintiff's claim is based'. In French Law, for example, where the form of order sought is to the effect that the Court should 'find fully or partially in the defendant's favour in respect of the plaintiff's claim' this would be classed as '*conclusions en réponse*', the term 'counterclaim' being reserved for the second type of claim to the effect that 'the court [should] give judgment in favour of the counterclaim or a part thereof'.

19. Having regard to these difficulties, it falls to the Court to interpret Article 6(3) of the Convention in order to determine whether it also applies to set-offs.

20. The first question which should be answered relates to the choice of the method of interpretation: must the provision be interpreted in the light of national law ('national' interpretation; in this case, the Danish court would accept jurisdiction over the set-off) or must it be defined on the basis of the Convention itself ('independent' interpretation)? The Convention supplies no answer to this question and the Court has had recourse to both methods of interpretation. However, the Court has held that '...the appropriate choice can only be made in respect of each of the provisions of the Convention to ensure that it is fully effective having regard to the objectives of Article 220 of the Treaty', whilst to date giving much more prominence to 'independent' interpretation.

21. The Court has explained in general terms the basis for electing for an 'independent' interpretation in *Shearson Lehman Hutton*: '...the principle established by case-law (see in particular the judgments in Case 150/77 *Bertrand v. Ott* [1978] ECR 1431, paragraphs 14, 15, 16 and 19, and in Case C-26/91 *Handte* [1992] ECR I-3967, paragraph 10) must be borne in mind; according to that principle, the concepts used in the Convention, which may have a different content according to the national law of the Member States, must be interpreted independently, by reference principally to the system and objectives of the Convention, in order to ensure that the Convention is applied uniformly in all the Contracting States'.

22. More specifically, the Court has held that '...terminological differences... between the various language versions of the Convention', as exist in this case, justify opting for an 'independent' interpretation '...in order to ensure as far as possible that the rights and obligations of the Contracting States and of the persons concerned arising from the Convention are equal and uniform'. Hence it is that approach which I shall take.

23. Since the Convention does not provide, as I have mentioned, any definition of 'counterclaim' or *a fortiori* of set-off - since that term is not used in any provision whatsoever -, it will be necessary to agree on the meaning of those terms in order to determine whether there is any distinction between them. I shall therefore consider them in turn.

(a) The concept of counterclaim

24. The Jenard Report is also silent on this point. However, it does mention that the wording of Article 6(3) is based on the draft Belgian Judicial Code. Let us therefore refer to that code.

25. Article 15 of the draft Belgian Judicial Code defines a '*demande reconventionnelle*' (counterclaim) as '...an incidental claim made by the defendant which seeks a decision against the plaintiff'.

The draughtsman explains that provision more specifically as follows: 'This definition is aligned with the approach which the French Court of Cassation proposed to the government in its 1806 draft Code of Civil Procedure: that of a *contre-prétention* (counterclaim) which is admissible in every case where such a claim is not barred by law. In addition, it accords with academic writings and the case-law, which, in the absence of a definition of a *demande reconventionnelle* (counterclaim) in the Code itself, has identified its basic constituents in a manner which may be summarised as follows: (1) a counterclaim is *incidental*, that is to say, it is introduced into pending proceedings even though it could have given rise to separate main proceedings; (2) it goes beyond seeking to have the plaintiff's case dismissed and costs awarded against him: the defendant, acting as plaintiff in his turn, seeks a *ruling* against the defendant. Thus, in a judgment of 4 November 1949, the Court of Cassation recognised as being a counterclaim and not merely a ground of defence a head of claim seeking "compensation for damage independent of the performance on which the plaintiff's action was based". Such a claim must doubtless be made during the main proceedings, which makes sense and implies that the parties should be the same. But its course and its outcome are independent of the main claim; if the principal plaintiff withdraws, this does not terminate the counterclaim'.

26. It can therefore be held at this juncture that a counterclaim is characterised by the following essential aspects:

- it is a *new claim,* put forward during the proceedings by the defendant, who becomes in turn a plaintiff;
- it relates to a *right of any nature whatsoever;*
- it seeks a *separate decision against the opponent* and is not confined to seeking the dismissal of the original plaintiff's claims.

(b) The concept of set-off

27. As far as 'compensation' or 'set-off' is concerned, no reference is made to it either in the Jenard Report - as I have already mentioned - or in the draft Belgian Judicial Code on which it was based. The reason is simple: it is not a concept of procedural law but of civil law, more specifically of the law of obligations.

28. The mechanism is known to all the national legal systems of the States party to the Convention. A few examples may be mentioned:

- in Belgian law, the following articles of the Civil Code: *Article 1289*: 'Where two persons are indebted to one another, set-off shall be effected between them so as to extinguish the two debts in the manner and in the cases described hereinafter'.

Article 1290: 'Set-off shall be effected *ipso jure*, even unbeknown to the debtors; the two debts shall extinguish each other reciprocally, provided that they exist concurrently, up to their respective amounts'.

Article 1291: 'Set-off shall take place only between two debts which are both for a sum of money or for a certain amount of fungible things of the same kind which are also liquid and due'.

- In French law, Articles 1289, 1290 and 1291 of the Civil Code are drafted in exactly the same terms.

- In German law, set-off, which invariably requires a declaration of intention by one of the creditors to the other, is governed by Articles 387 to 396 of the Civil Code. Articles 387 makes set-off subject to the following conditions: reciprocity of claims; similar nature of the subject-matter of the claims (most often, money debts); the claim of the party taking the initiative of a declaration of set-off (*Gegenforderung* or *Aktivforderung*) must be due (*fällig*).

29. It can generally be held that set-off consists of a way of simultaneously extinguishing two separate obligations (generally pecuniary) which exist concurrently between two persons who are indebted to each other, to the extent of the smaller debt.

30. It can be seen from these few examples that, whilst the concept of 'set-off' does exist in the various national legal systems, it may mask different situations as regards the rules for implementing it, the procedural rules and its effects (Danish law affords a perfect example of this).

31. Taking a general perspective, a distinction can be drawn between three 'families' of national laws as regards the concept of set-off:

- laws adopting an approach based on *off-setting by operation of law* (Belgian, French, Italian and Portuguese law). In the case of those laws, off-setting is by operation of law once certain conditions are met: reciprocity and fungibility together with the fact that the debts must be due and liquid. If one of those conditions for off-setting by operation of law is not met, off-setting may nevertheless take place if the parties have agreed to it and provided for it (*contractual off-setting*) or if the court orders *judicial off-setting*;

- laws adopting an approach consisting of *off-setting by virtue of the declaration of one party* (German, Danish, Dutch, Finnish, Norwegian and Swedish law).

Under that approach debts are set-off by a declaration of intention made by one of the debts to the other, provided, leaving aside certain subtleties, that the following conditions are met: the debts must be reciprocal, fungible and due (the requirement that they must be liquid required for off-setting 'by operation of law' does not exist);

- laws providing for *off-setting allowed by the court* (English, Irish, Scots law). Those laws encompass both set-off properly so called (extinction of reciprocal debts up to their common amount) and the principle that the defendant may defer all or part of the satisfaction of his debt until there has been a judicial ruling on his own claim.

32. From the procedural point of view, the ambiguity depends on the fact that, depending on the 'family' of laws considered, or even within each of them, set-off may be regarded either as merely a substantive ground of defence or as a reconventional demand.

This point has already been considered by Advocate General Capotorti in *Meeth* v. *Glacetal*: 'With regard to procedure, ... two situations may arise: the case where the defendant relies on the plaintiff's debt exclusively *as a defence* and the case where the defendant submits a *counterclaim*. The difference is that the defence is concerned exclusively to obtain the dismissal of the plaintiff's claim, whilst the counterclaim is intended to establish a claim by the defendant and accordingly to obtain a ruling against the plaintiff. In the case of the set-off the defendant may rely on this defence to justify his non-payment of the debt claimed by the plaintiff; but he must introduce a counterclaim if he wishes his own debt to be recognised in its entirety and to obtain a ruling compelling the plaintiff to make payment (full payment if the court rules that the plaintiff's claim is unfounded; partial payment if it upholds the plaintiff's claim but the amount to which the defendant is entitled exceeds that owing to the plaintiff)'.

33. Consequently, it can be considered, in parallel to the above study of counterclaims, that set-offs are characterised by the following essential features:

- set-offs may, depending on the case, either be a *defence raised by way of objection by* the defence to justify its failure to fulfil the obligation as alleged by the plaintiff in the same proceedings brought by the plaintiff or a *counterclaim* brought by the defence and seeking a separate decision against the plaintiff;
- set-offs relate to an *obligation*, generally of a pecuniary nature;
- set-offs seek the *total or partial dismissal of a plaintiff's claims* (where they are a defence) or a separate decision (where they constitute counterclaims).

34. May it be inferred from this consideration of those two concepts central to this request for a preliminary ruling similarities such that they may be equated with each other in the intention of the draughtsmen of the Convention? As has just been shown, there are *two types* of set-off: that pleaded as part of a counterclaim and that pleaded as a ground of defence. As far as the first is concerned, it manifestly falls within the circumstances contemplated by Article 6(3), since it '[arises] from the same contract or facts on which the original claim was based'. In contrast, it is more doubtful whether the second type of set-off - and it would seem that it is to this type that the national court is referring - is caught by Article 6(3).

35. The aim sought by the head of jurisdiction provided for in Article 6(3) can clearly be understood. By enabling a counterclaim to be raised before the same court seised of the original claim, the draughtsmen of the Convention sought to obviate superfluous, multiple proceedings and to enable the parties to settle the whole of their reciprocal claims in the same proceedings and before the same court. Could not authorising the same head of jurisdiction to cover set-offs pursue the same aim? I think not, for the following reasons.

36. First, as has been seen, the national rules on set-off vary from one State to another and the connection which is to exist between the original claim and the claim to set-off may not be the same as the close connection which is required of counterclaims under Article 6(3) of the Convention (this connection will be considered in answering the second question). Thus, as the United Kingdom points out, the application of Article 6(3) to set-off could result in a significant narrowing of the circumstances in which set-off could competently be entertained in an action covered by the Convention and thereby lead to a multiplicity of separate actions in more than one country. This would miss one of the essential aims of the Convention.

37. I have already pointed out that Article 6(3) of the Convention is based on the Belgian Judicial Code, which covers only a counterclaim 'which seeks a *decision against* the plaintiff'. The opening words of Article 6 introducing paragraph 3, 'a person domiciled in a Contracting State may also be *sued*', should be given the same meaning: Article 6(3) of the Convention applies only to a claim seeking a separate decision. A set-off pleaded as a ground of defence, however, merely asks the court to dismiss the plaintiff's claims and does not seek a separate order.

38. In addition, I have pointed to the ambiguity of the Danish terminology used to designate a 'counterclaim' within the meaning of Article 6(3). It cannot be precisely inferred from the term used ('*modfordringer*') whether it designates a claim pleaded by way of defence or a claim seeking a separate decision or both (yet two different terms do exist in Danish, and one of them could have been used in Article 6(3): '*modrav til kompensation*' and 'modrav til selvstændig dom' which might be translated as 'claim set-off' and 'claim for a separate decision'). In the other legal systems, there also exist separate expressions to designate the two concepts: in French law, '*demande à titre d' exception*' and '*demande reconventionnelle*'; in English law, 'set-off as a defence' and 'counterclaim'; in German law, 'verteidigungsweise Geltendmachung einer Forderung' and '*Widerklage*'; and in Italian law, '*eccezione di compensazione*' and '*domanda riconvenzionale*'. However, unlike in the case of the Danish version, it is the expressions '*demande reconventionnelle*', 'counterclaim', '*Widerklage*' and '*domanda riconvenzionale*' which are set out in the relevant language versions of Article 6(3) of the Convention. Here again, the language versions clearly indicate that the concept of 'counterclaim' within the meaning of the Convention is intended to be that of a claim for a separate decision.

39. Lastly and more generally, I would point out that the head of jurisdiction provided for by Article 6(3) constitutes an exception to the general rule set out in Article 2. By introducing a counterclaim, the original defendant will become a plaintiff, and whereas in principle the plaintiff must bring his action in the courts of the defendant's domicile (the original plaintiff in these circumstances), Article 6(3) enables him, by way of exception, to assert his claim in the court originally seised, that is to say, generally in the court of his domicile, that is to say, the defendant's court. Consequently, Article 6(3) makes the *forum actoris* possible. Admittedly, as has been seen, that provision fulfils a quite specific aim of the Convention. However, to my mind, Article 6(3) must continue to be in the nature of an exception and must therefore not be too broadly interpreted. The opposite interpretation would ultimately end up by multiplying a head of jurisdiction based on the plaintiff's (even a person bringing a counterclaim's) domicile, thereby facilitating the *forum actoris*, whereas the whole system of jurisdiction introduced by the Convention gives preeminence to the defendant's domicile. Moreover, the Court has held that 'apart from the cases expressly provided for, the Convention appears clearly hostile towards the attribution of jurisdiction to the courts of the plaintiff's domicile (see judgment in Case C-220/88 *Dumez France and Tracoba* [1990] ECR I-49, paragraphs 16 and 19)'.

40. Moreover, the Court has held in a judgment concerned with Article 5, which deals, in common with Article 6, with 'special jurisdiction', that it is in accord with the objective of the Convention '... to avoid a wide and multifarious interpretation of the exceptions to the general rule of jurisdiction contained in Article 2'. More generally, the Court has held that provisions providing for heads of special jurisdiction or for exclusive jurisdiction must be strictly interpreted. This is why the Court has laid down the following principle: 'It is only by derogation from that general principle [set out in the first paragraph of Article 2] that the Convention provides for cases, exhaustively listed in Sections 2 to 6 of Title II, in which a defendant domiciled or established in a Contracting State may, where the situation comes under a rule of special jurisdiction, or must, where the situation comes under a rule of exclusive jurisdiction or of prorogation of jurisdiction, be sued in the courts of another Contracting State. Consequently, the rules of jurisdiction which derogate from that general principle cannot give rise to an interpretation going beyond the cases envisaged by the Convention (see the above-mentioned judgments in *Bertrand* v. *Ott*, at paragraph 17, and *Handte*, at paragraph 14)'.

41. By the same token, therefore, the Court should not give a broad interpretation to Article 6(3) so as to cover the term 'set-off', since it may encompass two separate concepts.

42. For all those reasons, I conclude that Article 6(3) should be interpreted as meaning that it covers only a claim pleaded with a view to obtaining a separate decision. If the claim is pleaded as a set-off seeking merely that the plaintiff's claims be dismissed, the Convention does not apply. There is no need to restrict its admissibility and reference should be made in such a case to the rules of national law in order to establish whether such a ground of defence may be pleaded. Moreover, this is the idea underlying the Court's case-law in which it has held that it is irrelevant '...that the defendant's claim for a set-off is not based on the same contract or subject-matter as the main application. The fact relates to the *admissibility of a claim for a set-off which depends on the law of the State in which the court seised of the proceedings is situated*'.

43. Let us now turn to the second question.

Second question

44. The national court raises the question of the interpretation of sufficient connection referred to in Article 6(3) only in the event '...Article 6(3) cover[s] counterclaims for set-offs'. Inasmuch as I take the view that Article 6(3) of the Convention is not applicable to a set-off pleaded as a defence, it is unnecessary to consider the second question where it is so pleaded. However, the question is still relevant where set-off is pleaded in a counterclaim. It is therefore in the light of that eventuality that I shall set out my observations on the second question.

45. The connection required according to Article 6(3) is expressed in the following terms: '...arising from the same contract or facts on which the original claim was based'.

The Jenard Report explains those words as follows: 'It has been made clear that in order to establish this jurisdiction the counterclaim must be related to the original claim. Since the concept of related actions is not recognised in all the legal systems, the provision in question, following the draft Belgian Judicial Code, states that the counterclaim must arise from the contract or the facts on which the original claim was based'.

46. I mentioned in the introductory part of this Opinion that more express reference is made to the concept of 'sufficient connection' in the third paragraph of Article 22. But that provision, albeit part of the provisions on 'Jurisdiction'(Title II), does not, unlike Article 6, come under the heading of 'Special jurisdiction' (Section 2), but under that of '*Lis pendens* - Related Actions' (Section 8).

47. Those two provisions therefore deal with different procedural situations.

48. The Jenard Report describes the objective of Article 22 of the Convention as follows: it serves 'to avoid the risk of conflicting judgments and thus to facilitate the proper administration of justice in the Community'. But the 'judgments' referred to are judgments liable to be given by two courts in *two different States* party to the Convention and not judgments handed down by a court in *one State*, the eventuality contemplated by Article 6(3).

49. Consequently, no general meaning to be attributed to the concept of 'sufficient connection' for the purposes of the Convention could be inferred from the wording of the third paragraph of Article 22, which is motivated by the very specific intention to avoid conflicting judgments *as between Contracting States*. The concept of sufficient connection is, moreover, stated in that provision to be 'for the purposes of this Article'.

50. In any event, this is the interpretation which the Court has adopted: 'Article 22 of the Convention is intended to establish how related actions which have been brought before courts of different Member States are to be dealt with. It does not confer jurisdiction; in particular, it does not accord jurisdiction to a court of a Contracting State to try an action which is related to another action of which that court is seised pursuant to the rules of the Convention'.

The Court concluded that '... Article 22 of the Convention applies only where related actions are brought before courts of two or more Contracting States'.

51. I therefore conclude that the requirements relating to sufficient connection referred to in Article 6(3) ('counterclaim arising from the same contract or facts on which the original claim was based') and in the third paragraph of Article 22 ('actions ... so closely connected that it is expedient to hear and determine them together to avoid the risk of irreconcilable judgments resulting from separate proceedings') ought not to be construed in the same way, since they relate to two completely distinct procedural situations.

52. In view of the foregoing considerations, I propose that the reply to be given to the national court's questions should be as follows:

- Article 6(3) of the Brussels Convention of 27 September 1968 on Jurisdiction and the Enforcement of Judgments in Civil and Commercial Matters must be interpreted as covering only counterclaims pleaded with a view to a separate decision and not set-offs pleaded simply as grounds of defence.

- The concept of sufficient connection within the meaning of the third paragraph of Article 22 of the Convention applies only where related actions are brought before courts of two or more Contracting States; it is distinct from the concept of sufficient connection within the meaning of Article 6(3), which covers only counterclaims pleaded before the same court in one Member State.

TITLE II *[Chapter II]*

JURISDICTION *[Jurisdiction]*

Jurisdiction in matters relating to insurance Articles 7 - 12a *[Articles 8 - 14]*

See

Gerling v Treasury Administration
[14 July 1983] p.930
Overseas Union Insurance v New Hampshire Insurance
[27 June 1991]. p.1152
Group Josi v UGIC
[15 September 1994] p.159

TITLE II *[Chapter II]*

JURISDICTION *[Jurisdiction]*

Jurisdiction over consumer contracts – (Articles 13 - 15) *[Articles 15 - 17]*

Case 150/77 - 21 June 1978

Société Bertrand
v
Paul Ott KG

Articles 13 and 14 - Jurisdiction in the case of sales and loans on instalments - Concept of 'sale of goods on instalment credit terms' - Independent classification within the context of the Convention - Description.

Summary

Since the concept of a contract of sale on instalment credit terms varies from one Member State to another, in accordance with the objectives pursued by their respective laws, it is necessary, in the context of the Convention, to consider that concept as being independent and, therefore, to give it a uniform substantive content allied to the Community order.

According to the principles common to the laws of the Member States, the sale of goods on instalment credit terms is to be understood as a transaction in which the price is discharged by way of several payments or which is linked to a financing contract. However, a restrictive interpretation of the second paragraph of Article 14 of the Convention, in conformity with the objectives pursued by Section 4, entails the restriction of the jurisdictional advantage for which provision is made by that article to buyers who are in need of protection, their economic position being one of weakness in comparison with sellers by reason of the fact that they are private final consumers and are not engaged, when buying the product acquired on instalment credit terms, in trade or professional activities.

JUDGMENT OF THE COURT

Kutscher, President, Sorensen and Bosco, Presidents of Chambers, Mertens de Wilmars, Pescatore, Lord Mackenzie Stuart and Touffain, Judges

1. By judgment of 8 November 1977, which was received at the Court Registry on 15 December 1977, the French Cour de Cassation referred to the Court of Justice a question, pursuant to Articles 1 to 3 of the Protocol of 3 June 1971 (Journal Officiel L 204, p. 28) on the Interpretation by the Court of Justice of the Convention of 27 September 1968 on Jurisdiction and the Enforcement of Judgments in Civil and Commercial Matters Journal Officiel L 299 of 31 December 1972, p. 32), hereinafter referred to as 'the Convention', for a preliminary ruling concerning the interpretation of Articles 13, 14 and 28 of the said Convention.

2. That question has been raised in the context of a dispute between two commercial undertakings, one having its registered office in Germany, the other in France, concerning a contract, dated 12 February 1972, for the sale of a machine tool, the price of which, fixed at DM 74 205, was to be paid by the French company by way of two equal bills of exchange payable at 60 and 90 days, which were only partially discharged.

3. By judgment of 10 May 1974 the Landgericht, Stuttgart ordered the French company, in its absence, to pay the sum of DM 7 139, plus interest.

4. That decision was declared to be enforceable in France, first by order of the Tribunal de Grande Instance, Le Mans, of 30 June 1975, and then by confirmatory judgment of the Cour d'Appel, Angers, of 20 May 1976.

5. An appeal was made against that judgment on a point of law.

6. The Cour de Cassation held that the judgment of the Cour d'Appel, Angers, 'would be valid under the third paragraph of Article 28 of the Brussels Convention, by virtue of which the jurisdiction of the courts of the State in which the judgment was given may not be reviewed by the court before which enforcement is sought unless the sale can be held to be a sale of goods on instalment credit terms within the meaning of Article 13 of the Convention, in which case, under the second paragraph of Article 14 and the first paragraph of Article 28, proceedings may be brought only in the courts of the State in which the respondent company

is domiciled, namely, the courts of France, and execution must be withheld from the decision of a German court'.

7. The Cour de Cassation deduced from this that the solution to the problem depended upon the status to be accorded to the contract and it, therefore, referred the case to the Court of Justice in order to ascertain by way of a preliminary ruling 'whether the sale of a machine which one company agrees to make to another company on the basis of a price to be paid by way of two equal bills of exchange payable at 60 and 90 days can be held to be a sale of goods on instalment credit terms within the meaning of Article 13 of the Brussels Convention'.

8. In relation to the sale of goods on instalment credit terms, the second paragraph of Article 14 of the Convention provides that 'proceedings may be brought by a seller against a buyer ...only in the courts of the State in which the defendant is domiciled'.

9. In consequence of that imperative rule of jurisdiction the Landgericht Stuttgart, the court in which the original judgment was given, the Tribunal de Grande Instance, Le Mans, and the Cour d'Appel, Angers, the courts in which enforcement was sought, refused, whether by implication or expressly, in defining their jurisdiction, to classify the contract of sale in question as a contract for the sale of goods on instalment credit terms.

10. The reservations of the Cour de Cassation regarding the precise status of the said contract persuaded it to refer the above-mentioned question to the Court of Justice.

11. By that question the Court is asked whether a contract of sale such as that described is entitled to the privileged position with regard to jurisdiction created by the second paragraph of Article 14 of the Convention.

12. The concept of a contract of sale on instalment credit terms varies from one Member State to another, in accordance with the objectives pursued by their respective laws.

13. Although all of those laws incorporate the idea of protection for the buyer 'on instalments' because, in general, he is the weaker party in economic terms in comparison with the seller, certain of them are also based on considerations of economic, monetary and savings policy,

which are intended to control the practice of sales on instalment credit terms, in particular in relation to consumer durable goods (cars, household electrical and audio-visual equipment, etc.), most often by the indirect expedient of provisions relating to minimum deposits or to the maximum duration of credit or by laying down minimum or maximum values for the total sale price.

14. Since these various objectives have led to the creation of different rules in the various Member States it is necessary, for the purpose of eliminating obstacles to legal relations and to the settlement of disputes in the context of intra-Community relations in matters of the sale of goods on instalment credit terms, to consider that concept as being independent and therefore common to all the Member States.

15. In fact, it would not be possible to guarantee the harmonious operation of Article 13 *et seq*. of the Convention if the expression in question were given different meanings in the various Member States according to the court first seised of a dispute concerning a contract for the sale of goods on instalment credit terms or the court having jurisdiction to order enforcement.

16. It is, therefore, indispensable, for the coherence of the provisions of Section 4 of the Convention, to give that expression a uniform substantive content allied to the Community order.

17. To this finding must be added the fact that the compulsory jurisdiction provided for in the second paragraph of Article 14 of the Convention must, because it derogates from the general principles of the system laid down by the Convention in matters of contract, such as may be derived in particular from Articles 2 and 5(1), be strictly limited to the objectives proper to Section 4 of the said Convention.

18. Those objectives, as enshrined in Articles 13 and 14 of the Convention, were inspired solely by a desire to protect certain categories of buyers who, having been parties to contracts for the 'sale of goods on instalment credit terms', may be sued by the seller only in the courts of the State on the territory of which the said buyers are domiciled, whereas sellers domiciled on the territory of a Contracting State may be sued either in the courts of that State or in the courts of the Contracting State in which the buyer is domiciled.

19. In order to reply to the question referred to the Court an attempt must

be made to elaborate an independent concept of the contract of sale on instalment credit terms in view of the general principles which are apparent in this field from the body of laws of the Member States and bearing in mind the objective of the protection of a certain category of buyers.

20. It is clear from the rules common to the laws of the Member States that the sale of goods on instalment credit terms is to be understood as a transaction in which the price is discharged by way of several payments or which is linked to a financing contract.

21. A restrictive interpretation of the second paragraph of Article 14, in conformity with the objectives pursued by Section 4, entails the restriction of the jurisdictional advantage described above to buyers who are in need of protection, their economic position being one of weakness in comparison with sellers by reason of the fact that they are private final consumers and are not engaged, when buying the product acquired on instalment credit terms, in trade or professional activities.

22. The answer to be given to the national court should therefore be that the concept of the sale of goods on instalment credit terms within the meaning of Article 13 of the Brussels Convention of 27 September 1968 is not to be understood to extend to the sale of a machine which one company agrees to make to another company on the basis of a price to be paid by way of bills of exchange spread over a period.

On those grounds, the court in answer to the question referred to it by the French Cour de Cassation by judgment of 8 November 1977, hereby rules:

The concept of the sale of goods on instalment credit terms within the meaning of Article 13 of the Brussels Convention of 27 September 1968 is not to be understood to extend to the sale of a machine which one company agrees to make to another company on the basis of a price to be paid by way of bills of exchange spread over a period.

OPINION OF MR ADVOCATE GENERAL CAPOTORTI

1. In the case which concerns us today the Court is required to interpret the provisions of the Brussels Convention of 27 September 1968 on jurisdiction and the enforcement of Judgments in Civil and Commercial Matters. The

question put by the French Cour de Cassation, Civil Chamber, is as follows: 'whether the sale of a machine which one company agrees to make to another company on the basis of a price to be paid by way of two equal bills of exchange payable at 60 and 90 days can be held to be a sale of goods on instalment credit terms within the meaning of Article 13 of the Brussels Convention'. I would emphasise the precise and circumscribed nature of that request: the answer thereto must determine the concept of 'sale of goods on instalment credit terms', to be found in the said Article 13, with reference to the stated case of the sale of machinery between two commercial undertakings. In accordance with my usual practice, I think it useful to give a brief summary of the facts. In February 1972 Bertrand, whose registered office is in France, purchased from the undertaking Paul Ott, whose registered office is in the Federal Republic of Germany, a machine tool which was duly sent to the purchaser and installed. In payment of the purchase price the purchaser issued two bills of exchange payable at 60 and 90 days, as stated above. However, Bertrand became partially insolvent; that prompted the vendor to bring proceedings against it before the Landgericht Stuttgart, which court gave judgment against the defendant on 10 May 1974. One year later the Tribunal de Grande Instance, Le Mans, issued an order for enforcement of that judgment within the meaning of Article 31 of the Brussels Convention. On 20 May 1976 the Cour d'Appel, Angers, dismissing the appeal by Bertrand, confirmed that *exequatur*. Thereafter, the dispute was brought before the Cour de Cassation; it is at that point that the question which I have restated to the Court has arisen.

2. In their written observations the parties to the judgment on the merits commented at considerable length on the problem of the criteria to be adopted for the interpretation of the Brussels Convention, and more particularly of Article 13 thereof. The decision of this Court of 6 October 1976 in Case 12/76 *Tessili* v *Dunlop* ([1976] ECR 1473) was cited, amongst others. Indeed, that decision, having stated that the Convention frequently uses words and legal concepts drawn from civil, commercial and procedural law, which are capable of a different meaning from one Member State to another, leaves open the choice between two methods of interpretation: such words and concepts may be considered either as independent and common to all the Member States or as implying a reference to the substantive law applicable in each case under the rules of conflict of laws of the court before which the matter is first brought. I would note, in this connexion, that the course followed in all successive case-law of the Court concerning the interpretation of the Brussels Convention has been clearly orientated towards attributing pre-eminence to the first of those choices, making every possible effort to give independent value to the concepts employed in the Convention, even when, at first sight, they display a marked relationship to the legal system of each Member State. The Court has constantly sought to identify a common nucleus of concepts incorporated into the Convention, even where the task appears rather arduous: this is demonstrated in particular by the judgment of 14 October 1976 in Case 29/76 *LTU* v *Eurocontrol* ([1976] ECR 1541) and of 22 October 1977 in Case 43/77 *Industrial Diamond Supplies* v *Riva* ([1977] ECR 2175). The reasons for this tendency are self-evident: uniformity of

interpretation of the rules contained in the Convention provides the fullest guarantee of that 'free movement of decisions' which has justly been seen as once of the primary objectives of the Convention itself. In short, therefore, the method consisting in reference to the national system applicable on the basis of the private international law of the forum could now be said to be a residual method, that is to say, a method which is called upon only when the search for the independent meaning of a given concept within the context of the Convention has given a decidedly negative result. It goes without saying that, in order to determine independently the meaning of an expression taken from the Brussels Convention, it is necessary to have recourse to certain fundamental points of reference. These have also been indicated by the case-law of the Court, where it has identified the objectives and general system of the Convention as well as the general principles which may be inferred from the national legal systems (cf. the above-mentioned judgment of 14 October 1976 in Case 29/76 *LTU* v *Eurocontrol*). It is therefore with the aid of those criteria that the case in point should be examined.

3. I shall begin by assessing the position and function of Articles 13 to 15 (that is to say, Section 4 of Title II, composed precisely of those three articles) in the general system of the Convention. It is clear, in the first place, that the rule as to jurisdiction contained in Article 14 is in the nature of a special rule; it is sufficient to consider its content in relation to other articles of the Convention which are of wider scope. The first paragraph of the provision in question allows a seller on instalment credit terms to be sued in the courts of the State in which the buyer is domiciled, as well as in the place where the seller is domiciled, by way of exception from the general rule contained in Article 2. However, where the seller is suing the buyer proceedings may be brought, pursuant to the second paragraph of Article 14, only in the courts of the State in which the defendant is domiciled; that provision is in accordance with the criterion contained in Article 2 but excludes the application of other provisions, such as Article 5(1) concerning jurisdiction in matters relating to contract and Article 6(1) on the eventuality of a number of defendants. The special nature of Article 14 is, furthermore, confirmed by the limitations which Article 15 places on the possibility of a change of jurisdiction by agreement between the parties. This first conclusion must incline the interpreter to caution in determining the meaning of Articles 13 to 15; it is accepted that provisions creating exceptions are to be interpreted strictly. That caution should consist in the choice of an interpretation which to the greatest extent takes account of the *ratio* of Section 4 of Title II, and gives the provisions therein contained a sphere of application exactly corresponding to that raison d'être. Concerning the *ratio* of Articles 13 to 15 there is no doubt; those provisions are designed to protect the weaker contracting party, that is, the purchaser in the case of the sale of goods on instalment credit terms and the borrower in the case of loans repayable by instalments expressly made to finance the sale of such goods. That appears clearly from the fact that the first paragraph of Article 14 permits such persons to choose between two jurisdictions, in order to bring proceedings against the seller or the lender, whereas in the second paragraph, which is concerned with

the case of proceedings brought by the seller against the buyer or by the lender against the borrower, the general rule contained in Article 2 is confirmed and rendered exclusive. It should, moreover, be borne in mind that the report on the Convention - the so-called Jenard Report - perceives in the desire to protect certain categories of persons - buyers and borrowers - the central motivation of the provisions of Section 4 (in the same vein, cf. Weser, *Convention Communautaire sur la Compétence Judiciaire et l'Exécution des Décisions*, Brussels, 1975, p. 291).

At this point, the interpretation of the concept 'sale on instalment credit terms' contained in Article 13 of the Convention cannot be undertaken without having regard to two criteria which emerge from the conclusions drawn so far: (a) a restrictive interpretation is to be preferred to a wider one; (b) the contract in question must have as its essential characteristic the fact that the parties are not on an equal footing in economic terms: the contract was entered into by a 'weak' party and a 'strong' party. In connexion with - criterion (a), the sale on instalment credit terms cannot be identified for the purposes of the Convention solely on the basis of the means of payment, in the sense that any contract of sale in which settlement of the price is undertaken by two or more payments may be said to be a 'sale on instalment credit terms', in disregard of any other subjective or objective factors. I therefore believe that the Court should dismiss the arguments of Bertrand, claiming that the Community definition must be sufficiently wide to include the definitions contained in all the national laws; this would lead to the result that the term 'sale on instalment credit terms' would have to be understood to refer to any credit sale in which the price is paid in successive amounts. On the other hand, in pursuance of criterion (b), we must move towards a concept of sale on instalment credit terms which is characterized *typically* by the economic inferiority of the buyer, such that it may be said that the latter was induced to purchase by the system of payment by instalments, insofar as payment in a lump sum would have been the cause of economic difficulties for him. In this connexion I would agree with the observation made in these proceedings by the Government of the United Kingdom, when it noted that it is illogical to regard all buyers who arrange for payment on deferred terms as being in need of protection, and that it is more sensible to speak of consumer protection. Indeed, the only method of identifying a category of buyers who may be said to be typically in a position of economic inferiority is to direct attention to the category of consumers, the protection of whom, as is well known, presents a general problem in Community law as well as in many national laws. Thus it is that the conclusions drawn with regard to the role of Articles 13 to 15 in the general system of the Brussels Convention lead to an interpretation of the concept of sale on instalment credit terms as a sale by a commercial undertaking (whether in production or marketing) to a consumer - and therefore as a sale of consumer goods in respect of which payment is spread over a certain number of successive amounts.

4. I referred above to the importance of having recourse to the general principles which may be derived from the various laws of the Member States in order to determine independently the meaning of the expressions adopted within

the Convention. It must therefore be asked whether such general principles exist in relation to the subject-matter with which we are concerned and, if so, what they provide.

It cannot be said that the phenomenon of sale on instalment credit terms is regulated in a uniform manner in the Member States. It is clear that the national legislatures have considered that phenomenon from three different points of view: sometimes in the context of the ordinary rules relating to contract (as has occurred in Italy and in the Netherlands), at others in special laws adopted for the purpose of protecting persons buying on instalment credit terms (such laws are at present in force in nearly all the Member States), and, finally, more rarely in the context of restrictive laws, with the objective of avoiding the inflationary consequences which the device of payment on instalment credit terms may entail (such is the case in France, in Belgium, in the United Kingdom and, during a certain period, in Italy). It is clear that, as the point of view changes, the description of the phenomenon may also change; this is one reason why a uniform concept of sale on instalment credit terms does not exist in the laws of the Member States.

By way of a first approximation we may say that at one extreme there is the very broad concept, according to which it is necessary and sufficient that the purchase price of a good, which passes immediately into the possession of the purchaser, is paid in two or more successive instalments; at the opposite extreme there are various restrictive concepts, the criteria for the definition of which are either subjective factors (status of the contracting parties) or objective factors (type, value and intended use of the article) or factors inherent in the price (minimum or maximum number of instalments, the total amount of the price, the maximum period for payment) or, finally, factors relating to the transfer of possession (clause relating to the retention of possession until the total price has been paid). Of course, beyond the field which may be traced by one or other of those factors there is, purely and simply, the sale by deferred payment in two or more instalments, which is not subject to any special rules: this type of commercial transaction is encountered very frequently, as was rightly noted by the undertaking Ott, in international trade, without it being identified without more ado - whether in practice or at law - with the sale on instalment credit terms.

In a situation which displays such wide divergencies, it may appear pointless to seek principles which are common to the Member States. However, a common tendency may be identified in the field of laws adopted for the protection of buyers on instalment credit terms; and I would emphasize that it is logical and appropriate to approach the matter from this angle, since Articles 13 to 15 of the Brussels Convention are themselves, as we saw above, provisions whose objective is to redress the balance in favour of the buyer on instalment credit terms. The common tendency of which I am speaking consists in the exclusion of certain categories of buyers from the protective system in relation to sales on instalment credit terms. This may occur either directly, where that system is stated to be inapplicable where the purchase is made by traders, entrepreneurs or legal persons, or indirectly, with reference to purchases of industrial plant and purchases which are connected with the buyer's professional activity. This course is common to the laws of nearly all the Member States, with the exception of Denmark and Italy.

I shall now turn to the problem which has to be resolved in this dispute. It seems to me that the above-mentioned tendency indicated by national laws, although it cannot be confused with the existence of common principles properly so-called, provides definite confirmation of the conclusions previously drawn by way of a systematic interpretation of the Convention. In short, as long as the buyer on instalment credit terms is a private consumer and the object of the purchase is a consumer good, special rules regarding sales on instalment credit terms are justified since in that situation on of the contracting parties is weaker and deserves special protection. Outside that context, there is no reason to extend the 'protective' rules relating to sales on instalment credit terms, and therefore the *nomen juris* itself of 'sale on instalment credit terms', within the meaning of Article 13 of the Convention, ceases to be applicable.

5. Mention should be made of two further circumstances which indicate how written Community law has been developing in the direction indicated. The first, and most important, is the following: the *ad hoc* Working Party on Adjustments to the Conventions under Article 220 of the EEC Treaty, in drafting the amendments to the Brussels Convention which were to accompany the accession of the United Kingdom, Ireland and Denmark, proposed modifications to Articles 13 to 15, and suggested, *inter alia* that the sphere of application of Article 13 should be restricted to contracts entered into by a person for a purpose which could be considered extraneous to his professional or trade activity, thereafter to be referred to as the consumer. In consequence, in Articles 14 and 15 reference would no longer be made to the buyer or the borrower, but to the 'consumer' (working document No 5, revised version; Article 9a of the Accession Convention). It is clear that draft cannot influence the interpretation of Article 13 which must now be provided; however, it seems to me interesting to be able to say that the solution suggested by myself coincides in this matter with the foreseeable course of development of the Brussels Convention. In the second place, I would recall that the draft proposal for a directive on consumer credit, drawn up by the Commission, places contracts for the sale of goods on deferred payment terms within the category of 'consumer credit agreements' and defines the consumer as a natural person who is not acting in pursuance of a commercial or professional activity. That means that Community action for the protection of the consumer impinges on the field of sales on instalment credit terms from an angle which coincides with the conception of that phenomenon accepted by the Brussels Convention.

6. In conclusion, it is my opinion that the question put by the French Cour de Cassation, Civil Chamber, in the case of *Bertrand* v *Ott* should be answered as follows by this Court: 'The sale of a machine agreed between two companies on the basis of a price to be paid by way of two deferred bills of exchange cannot be held to be a sale of goods on instalment credit terms within the meaning of Article 13 of the Brussels Convention'.

Case C-89/91 - 19 January 1993

Shearson Lehman Hutton
v
TVB Treuhandgesellschaft für Vermögensverwaltung und Beteiligungen mbH

Jurisdiction in proceedings concerning contracts concluded by consumers - Concept of 'consumer' - Plaintiff acting in pursuance of his trade or professional activity, as the assignee of the rights of a private individual - Excluded.

Summary

The special system established by Article 13 *et seq*. of the Convention of 27 September 1968 on Jurisdiction and Enforcement of Judgments in Civil and Commercial Matters is inspired by the concern to protect the consumer, as the party deemed to be economically weaker and less experienced in legal matters than the other party to the contract, so that the consumer must not be discouraged from suing by being compelled to bring his action before the courts in the Contracting State in which the other party to the contract is domiciled. Those provisions affect only a private final consumer not engaged in trade or professional activities, who is bound by one of the contracts listed in Article 13 and who is a party to the action, in accordance with Article 14. It follows that Article 13 of the Convention is to be interpreted as meaning that a plaintiff who is acting in pursuance of his trade or professional activity, and who is not, therefore, himself a consumer party to one of the contracts listed in the first paragraph of that provision, may not enjoy the benefit of the rules of special jurisdiction laid down by the Convention concerning consumer contracts.

JUDGMENT OF THE COURT

Kakouris, President of Chamber, acting for the President, Rodriguez Iglesias, Zuleeg and Murray, Presidents of Chambers, Mancini, Joliet, Schockweiler, Moitinho de Almeida, Grévisse, Diez de Velasco and Kapteyn, Judges

1. By order of 29 January 1991, received at the Court on 11 March 1991, the Bundesgerichtshof referred to the Court for a preliminary ruling under the Protocol of 3 June 1971 on the interpretation by the Court of Justice of the Convention of 27 September 1968 on Jurisdiction and the Enforcement of Judgments in Civil and Commercial Matters (OJ 1978 L 304, p. 36), as amended by the Convention of 9 October 1978 on the Accession of the Kingdom of Denmark, Ireland and the United Kingdom of Great Britain and Northern Ireland (OJ 1978 L 304, p. 1, hereinafter 'the Convention'), four questions on the interpretation of the first and second paragraphs of Article 13 of the Convention.

2. Those questions were raised in proceedings between TVB Treuhandgesellschaft für Vermögensverwaltung und Beteiligungen mbH, a company established in Munich (Federal Republic of Germany) (hereinafter 'TVB'), and E.F. Hutton & Co. Inc., a firm established in New York (United States of America), which has in the meantime been taken over by the company Shearson Lehman Hutton Inc., also established in New York (hereinafter 'Hutton Inc.').

3. It is apparent from the documents forwarded to the Court that TVB brought an action before the German courts against Hutton Inc., in reliance on a right assigned to it. The assignor, a German judge, had instructed the brokers Hutton Inc. to carry out currency, security and commodity futures transactions under an agency contract. To that end, the assignor paid over considerable sums in 1986 and 1987, but lost nearly all of his investments in those transactions.

4. Hutton Inc. had offered its services through press advertisements in the Federal Republic of Germany. The business relationship with the assignor was arranged through E.F. Hutton & Co. GmbH (hereinafter 'Hutton GmbH'), whose registered office is in Germany, which is dependent on Hutton Inc. and undertakes consultancy functions *vis-à-vis* its customers for the purposes of Hutton Inc.'s operations. Hutton GmbH had acted, at least in an intermediary capacity, in connection with all the orders to buy and sell given by the assignor. The shares in Hutton GmbH

belong to E.F. Hutton International Inc., a wholly-owned subsidiary of Hutton Inc. whose registered office is in New York. In addition, many persons having managerial responsibilities within Hutton Inc. also have like responsibilities within Hutton GmbH.

5. TVB claims from Hutton Inc. the return of the sums lost by the assignor. It bases its claims on unjust enrichment and on the right to damages for breach of contractual and pre-contractual obligations and for tortious conduct, on the ground that Hutton Inc. had not sufficiently informed the assignor of the risks involved in futures transactions.

6. The case was brought before the Landgericht München (Regional Court, Munich) which declined jurisdiction to hear TVB's claim. On appeal, the Oberlandesgericht München (Higher Regional Court, Munich) overturned that decision and held that the Landgericht did have jurisdiction. Hutton Inc. appealed on a point of law against that decision to the Bundesgerichtshof.

7. Taking the view that the dispute raised issues relating to interpretation of the Convention, the Bundesgerichtshof decided to stay the proceedings until the Court had given a preliminary ruling on the following questions:

'Question 1

Does subparagraph 3 of the first paragraph of Article 13 of the Convention cover agency contracts concerning currency, security and commodity futures dealings?

Question 2

Is it sufficient, for subparagraph 3(a) of the first paragraph of Article 13 of the Convention to apply, that before conclusion of the contract the other party to the contract with the consumer advertised in newspapers in the State of the consumer's domicile, or does the provision require a connection between the advertising and the conclusion of the contract?

Question 3

Does the other party to the contract with the consumer have a branch, agency or other establishment within the meaning of the second paragraph of Article 13 if, for the conclusion of and performance of the contract, it uses a company having its registered office in the State of the consumer's domicile, which is effectively owned by it and has staff links with it but has no authority to contract on its behalf, acting only as intermediary and advising the consumer, and are disputes which arise in connection with the relations so arranged between the consumer and the other party to the contract disputes arising out of the operation of the branch, agency or other establishment?

Question 4

(a) In addition to claims for damages for breach of contractual obligations, does the phrase 'proceedings concerning a contract' in the first paragraph of Article 13 of the Convention also cover claims arising out of the breach of pre-contractual obligations (*culpa in contrahendo*) and unjust enrichment in connection with the unwinding of contractual transactions?

(b) In an action in which claims for damages for breach of contractual and pre-contractual obligations, claims relating to unjust enrichment and claims for damages for tort or delict are put forward, does the first paragraph of Article 13 of the Convention give any ancillary jurisdiction to hear the non-contractual claims because of their relationship to the contractual claims?'

8. Reference is made to the Report for the Hearing for a fuller account of the facts of the case, the procedure and the pleas and arguments of the parties, which are mentioned or discussed hereinafter only insofar as is necessary for the reasoning of the Court.

9. As a preliminary point, it should be noted that the questions submitted by the national court all relate to the interpretation of the first and second paragraph of Article 13 of the Convention, which form part of Section 4, entitled 'Jurisdiction over consumer contracts', of Title II of the Convention, concerning the rules governing jurisdiction.

10. Consequently, it must first be ascertained whether the conditions for the application of that provision are satisfied in a situation such as that in point in the main proceedings, since the questions relating to the scope of application of the provisions of the Convention, which determine jurisdiction within the international legal order, must be regarded as being matters of public policy.

11. It is apparent from the order for reference that, in the case in the main proceedings, the action for the recovery of debts was brought against Hutton Inc., not by the private individual who was the other party to the contract with Hutton Inc., but by a company, the assignee of the rights of that individual.

12. It must therefore be considered whether a plaintiff, such as the plaintiff in the main proceedings, may be regarded as a consumer within the meaning of the Convention and must, therefore, benefit from the special rules governing jurisdiction laid down by the Convention with respect to consumer contracts.

13. For the purpose of answering that question, it is necessary to bear in mind the principle, established by case-law (see, in particular, the judgments in Case 150/77 *Bertrand* v *Ott* [1978] ECR 1431, paragraphs 14 to 16 and 19, and in Case C-26/91 *Handte* v *Traitements Mécano-chimiques des Surfaces* [1992] ECR I-3967, paragraph 10), according to which the concepts used in the Convention, which may have a different content depending on the national law of the Contracting States, must be interpreted independently, by reference principally to the system and objectives of the Convention, in order to ensure that the Convention is uniformly applied in all the Contracting States. This rule must apply, in particular, to the concept of 'consumer' within the meaning of Article 13 *et seq.* of the Convention, in so far as that concept is the principal factor in the determination of rules governing jurisdiction.

14. In that connection, it must first be noted that under the system of the Convention the general principle, stated in the first paragraph of Article 2, is that the national courts of the Contracting State in which the defendant is domiciled are to have jurisdiction.

15. It is only by way of derogation from that general principle that the Convention provides for the cases, exhaustively listed in Sections 2 to 6 of Title II, in which a defendant domiciled or established in a Contracting State may, where the situation comes under a rule of special jurisdiction, or must, where the situation comes under a rule of exclusive jurisdiction or of prorogation of jurisdiction, be sued in the courts of another Contracting State.

16. Consequently, the rules of jurisdiction which derogate from that general principle cannot give rise to an interpretation going beyond the cases envisaged by the Convention (see the judgments in *Bertrand*, paragraph 17, and *Handte*, paragraph 14, cited above).

17. Such an interpretation must apply *a fortiori* with respect to a rule of jurisdiction, such as that contained in Article 14 of the Convention, which allows a consumer, within the meaning of Article 13 of the Convention, to sue the defendant in the courts of the Contracting State in which the plaintiff is domiciled. Apart from the cases expressly provided for, the Convention appears clearly hostile towards the attribution of jurisdiction to the courts of the plaintiff's domicile (see judgment in Case C-220/88 *Dumez France and Tracoba* v *Hessische Landesbank* (Helaba) and Others [1990] ECR I-49, paragraphs 16 and 19).

18. Secondly, the special system established by Article 13 *et seq*. of the Convention is inspired by the concern to protect the consumer as the party deemed to be economically weaker and less experienced in legal matters than the other party to the contract, and the consumer must not therefore be discouraged from suing by being compelled to bring his action before the courts in the Contracting State in which the other party to the contract is domiciled.

19. The protective role fulfilled by those provisions implies that the application of the rules of special jurisdiction laid down to that end by the Convention should not be extended to persons for whom that protection is not justified.

20. In that regard, it is important to note, in the first place, that the first paragraph of Article 13 of the Convention defines the consumer as a person acting 'for a purpose which can be regarded as being outside his trade or profession' and provides that the various types of contracts listed in that article, and to which the provisions of Section 4 of Title II of the Convention apply, must have been concluded by the consumer.

21. Secondly, the first paragraph of Article 14 of the Convention provides for the courts of the Contracting State in which the consumer is domiciled to have jurisdiction to hear and determine the 'proceedings against the other party to a contract'.

22. It follows from the wording and the function of those provisions that they affect only a private final consumer, not engaged in trade or professional activities (see also, to that effect, the judgment in *Bertrand*, cited above, paragraph 21, and the Expert Report drawn up when the Kingdom of Denmark, Ireland and the United Kingdom of Great Britain and Northern Ireland acceded to the Convention, OJ 1979 C 59, p. 71, paragraph 153), who is bound by one of the contracts listed in Article 13 and who is a party to the action, in accordance with Article 14.

23. As the Advocate General pointed out in paragraph 26 of his Opinion, the Convention protects the consumer only in so far as he personally is the plaintiff or defendant in proceedings.

24. It follows that Article 13 of the Convention is to be interpreted as meaning that a plaintiff who is acting in pursuance of his trade or professional activity and who is not, therefore, himself a consumer party to one of the contracts listed in the first paragraph of that provision, may

not enjoy the benefit of the rules of special jurisdiction laid down by the Convention concerning consumer contracts.

25. It follows from the foregoing considerations that it is not necessary to give a ruling on the specific questions put to the Court by the Bundesgerichtshof.

On those grounds, the Court, in answer to the questions referred to it by the Bundesgerichtshof by order of 29 January 1991, hereby rules:

> **Article 13 of the Convention of 27 September 1968 on Jurisdiction and the Enforcement of Judgments in Civil and Commercial Matters is to be interpreted as meaning that a plaintiff who is acting in pursuance of his trade or professional activity and who is not, therefore, himself a consumer party to one of the contracts listed in the first paragraph of that provision, may not enjoy the benefit of the rules of special jurisdiction laid down by the Convention concerning consumer contracts.**

OPINION OF MR ADVOCATE GENERAL DARMON

1. Faced with the facts set out below, the Bundesgerichtshof has referred four questions to the Court, all relating to the interpretation of Article 13 of the Convention on Jurisdiction and the Enforcement of Judgments in Civil and Commercial Matters ('the Brussels Convention') in the version resulting from the Convention of 9 October 1978 on the accession of Denmark, Ireland and the United Kingdom.

2. Following the appearance of an advertisement in the German press, an individual, a judge by profession, instructed an American firm of brokers, Hutton Inc., to carry out currency and security futures transactions under an agency contract (Kommissions weise Durchführung von Devisen, Werpapier und Warentermingeschäften). In order to do so, he dealt with the American firm's German subsidiary, Hutton GmbH.

3. After investing considerable sums in 1986 and 1987, which were almost entirely consumed by losses, he assigned his claims to a German trust company, TVB Treuhandgesellschaft für Vermögensverwaltung und Beteiligungen mbH ('TVB').

4. TVB brought an action in the German courts for the recovery of the claims against the American firm of brokers (Brokenfirma), Hutton, which has in the meantime been taken over by another American company, Shearson Lehman Hutton Inc. ('Shearson Hutton').

5. The action is based on unjust enrichment and on claims for damages for breach of contractual and pre-contractual obligations and for tortious conduct inasmuch as, according to TVB, Shearson Lehman did not sufficiently explain to the other party to the contract the risks which he was running.

6. Whereas the Landgericht (Regional Court) held the action to be 'inadmissible', the appeal court held itself to have jurisdiction. Shearson Lehman appealed on a point of law against that decision.

7. The Bundesgerichtshof takes the view that the German courts can have international jurisdiction in this case only if Article 13 of the Brussels Convention is applicable and refers to the Court for a preliminary ruling four questions which are set out in the preliminary report.

8. Essentially those questions seek the Court's interpretation of the expressions set out below:

(a) 'any other contract for the supply of services' within the meaning of subparagraph 3 of the first paragraph of Article 13, in order to determine whether that expression also covers agreements of the type at issue in the main proceedings;

(b) prior 'advertising' within the meaning of subparagraph 3(a) of the first paragraph of Article 13, in order to establish whether it entails a link with the conclusion of the contract;

(c) 'branch, agency or other establishment' within the meaning of the second paragraph of Article 13, in order to determine whether that concept covers a company established in the State of the consumer's domicile which is effectively owned by the company which was the other party to the contract with the consumer, and acted only as intermediary, having no authority to conclude contracts;

(d) 'operations' of the branch, agency or establishment within the meaning of that same provision, in order to determine whether disputes arising in connection with the relations thus created are disputes arising out of such operations;

(e) 'concerning a contract' in the first paragraph of Article 13, in order to establish whether, above and beyond claims for damages for breach of contract, it also covers claims relating to the breach of pre-contractual obligations and unjust enrichment and whether that provision gives ancillary jurisdiction over non-contractual claims on account of connexity.

9. The Court has taken the view that, in order to answer those questions - or to establish whether it was necessary to answer them - it was appropriate to examine whether TVB, the assignee of the claims, might also claim to have the capacity of a consumer which attached to the assignor and whether the second paragraph of Article 13 of the Brussels Convention was applicable where the consumer was domiciled in the State in which the branch was established and where the parent company had its seat in a third State. The Court has put questions concerning those two points.

10. The jurisdiction rules of the Brussels Convention are set out in Title II (Articles 2 to 24), which is made up of nine sections. Section 1 (Articles 2 to 4) is headed 'General provisions', Section 4 (Articles 13 to 15) 'Jurisdiction over consumer contracts'.

11. The answers to all these questions - those of the national court and those of the Court of Justice - can be found only by comparing and contrasting the provisions set out in sections 1 and 4.

12. It has to be established whether a situation such as the one at issue falls within the scope of the Brussels Convention and, if so, what consequences have to be drawn with regard to the determination of the court having jurisdiction.

13. It should be borne in mind that the action for the recovery of assets has been brought by a company established in a Contracting State against another company having its seat in a third State.

14. The Brussels Convention, which was adopted pursuant to a mandate conferred on the Member States of the European Economic Community by the fourth indent of Article 220 of the Treaty of Rome, aims in particular at standardizing the international jurisdiction rules of courts in the Member States in order to secure, within the Community, the 'free movement of judgments' in civil and commercial matters. It is not intended to govern jurisdiction conflicts between signatory States and third countries. Its field of application is confined to the Contracting Parties.

15. That principle is expressly enshrined in the first paragraph of Article 4, which provides that 'if the defendant is not domiciled in a Contracting State, the jurisdiction of the courts of each Contracting State shall, subject to the provisions of Article 16, be determined by the law of that State'.

16. Since Article 16 is not in point here, the case falls prima facie under the law of the State of the court hearing the plaintiff's action, since the defendant is domiciled outside the territory of any Contracting State. On the face of it, therefore, the Convention seems to be inapplicable. '[W] here a defendant is not domiciled in a Contracting State the Convention does not contain any rules of its own but refers to the internal law of the State of the court hearing the action (Article 4, first paragraph). As against such a defendant, the Convention permits any person domiciled in a Contracting State, whatever his nationality, to avail himself of the law of that State (...).'

17. The specific provisions of Article 13 also prompted the Bundesgerichtshof to make the reference to the Court.

18. Admittedly the reference made to Article 4 in the first paragraph of Article 13 is a reminder that the scope of Articles 13, 14 and 15 is confined to cases where the defendant is domiciled in a Contracting State; if he is not, the court seised is to apply its own jurisdiction rules.

19. It is clear, however, that the second paragraph of Article 13 implicitly constitutes an exception to Article 4 and must be able to be applied where the other party to the contract with the consumer, the defendant to the proceedings, is domiciled in a State which is not a party to the Convention and has a branch, agency or other establishment in a Contracting State.

20. Consequently, the situation before the Court falls within the scope of the Brussels Convention only if the second paragraph of Article 13 is applicable to it. I would say straight out that this is not the case for three reasons: (1) where the person who initiated the judicial proceedings is not himself a party to one of the contracts listed in the first paragraph of Article 13, that person is not a

consumer within the meaning of Articles 13 and 14; (2) a secondary establishment which has no authority to conclude contracts is not a branch, agency or establishment within the meaning of the second paragraph of Article 13; and (3) even if it were, that provision would be inapplicable, in the absence of any extraneous element, where the branch had its seat in the State in which the consumer is domiciled. Let us consider those three points *seriatim*.

21. The alternative jurisdictions and the special jurisdiction for which a consumer qualifies under the first paragraph of Article 14 of the Brussels Convention apply only where 'a consumer (...) bring[s] proceedings against the other party to the contract'.

22. Yet the action for the recovery of claims was indeed not brought before the national court by the initial party to the contract with Shearson Lehman but by a commercial company, the assignor of that party's rights, which was acting within the terms of its corporate objects. May that company therefore claim that it is a consumer within the meaning of Articles 13 and 14 of the Brussels Convention in its action for the recovery of the claims?

23. To my mind, this is the key question. It seems clear to me that if TVB is not entitled validly to claim that it is a consumer, the dispute between it and Shearson Lehman does not fall within the scope of the Convention.

24. There is no doubt that, in order to preserve the coherence of the provisions of Article 4 of the Convention, the term 'consumer' must be given an independent interpretation in order to provide it with a uniform substantive content in the context of the Community order without reference to the law of the Contracting States. The Court has already given a ruling to that effect on the expression 'sale on instalment credit terms' which has been replaced by 'consumer contracts' in Section 4.

25. The question whether the assignee company can be regarded as a consumer does not depend, to my mind, on the nature of the assignment of rights made to it (was merely a claim assigned or also rights attached to the creditor in his personal capacity?). Consideration of the scope of that assignment, which presupposes an interpretation of domestic law, falls, moreover, exclusively within the jurisdiction of the court dealing with the substance.

26. Admittedly, to allow the assignee company to enjoy the benefit of Article 14 would also indirectly benefit the consumer himself (in particular by favouring the conditions for recovery and hence for the assignment of his claims). But the Brussels' Convention protects the consumer *expressis verbis* only inasmuch as he *personally is the plaintiff or defendant* in proceedings. That protection does not extend to proceedings to which he is not a party.

27. What is more, the concept of 'consumer' within the meaning of Article 14 necessarily refers to that contained in Article 13. It is inconceivable in the absence of any express provision that the term 'consumer' used in two consecutive articles should refer to two different things. According to Article 13, the status of consumer attaches only to a consumer who has concluded a certain type of contract. This must also be true for the purposes of the application of Article 14.

28. Consequently, only the party to the proceedings who himself satisfies

the requirements laid down by Article 13 and therefore took part in concluding the contract with the trader or professional person can benefit from the special jurisdiction rules applying to consumers. The action covered by Article 14 can therefore, in my view, be brought only by a consumer in relation to a contract which he himself concluded.

29. In other words, a consumer entitled to avail himself of the special jurisdiction rules set out in Section 4 must satisfy a two-fold requirement: (1) he must be a party to the proceedings (Article 14); and (2) he must be bound by one of the contracts listed in Article 13. Consequently, if the consumer, who was the other party to the original contract, assigns his claims to a third party who subsequently brings legal proceedings relating to those claims, the third party in question does not, in my view, satisfy the two-fold requirement laid down by those articles.

30. Not only textual analysis, but also the rationale of Articles 13 and 14 considered together, preclude a legal person in the situation of TVB from being regarded as a consumer. The moving spirit behind those provisions is to secure protection for the weaker or less experienced party. That does not apply to a company bringing legal proceedings within the ambit of its corporate objects.

31. In a case in which the Court was asked to interpret the second paragraph of Article 14 in its 1968 wording concerning the sale of goods on instalment credit terms, it was held that: 'A restrictive interpretation of the second paragraph of Article 14, in conformity with the objectives pursued by Section 4, entails the restriction of the jurisdictional advantage described above to buyers who are in need of protection, their economic position being one of weakness in comparison with sellers *by reason of the fact that they are private final consumers and are not engaged*, when buying the product acquired on instalment terms, *in trade or professional activities'*.

32. The Court concluded that: '(...) the concept of the sale of goods on instalment terms within the meaning of Article 13 of the Brussels Convention of 27 September 1968 is not to be understood to extend to the sale of a machine which one company agrees to make to another company on the basis of a price to be paid by way of bills of exchange spread over a period'.

33. As Professor Schlosser points out, the amendments made in 1978 to Section 4 are based on the same guiding spirit as the previous provisions. The field of application of Section 4 was enlarged to cover consumer contracts. Inspired by the judgment in *Bertrand* v *Ott*, the new Section 4 applies therefore only to the *final* consumer.

34. Furthermore, it seems to me to be impossible to vary the jurisdiction rules depending on the origin of the right on which the plaintiff relies: that is to say that, depending on whether he had his right from a consumer or whether he acted by virtue of a right of his own, he would, or would not, be entitled to claim the benefit of Article 14 although the action brought was of the same nature in each case.

35. It follows, in my view, that an initiator of legal proceedings who is not himself a party to one of the contracts listed in the first paragraph of Article 13 is not a consumer within the meaning of Articles 13 and 14.

36. The second paragraph of Article 13, which, I reiterate, is the only provision which might bring the situation described by the national court within the ambit of the Brussels Convention, is inapplicable for a second reason: the other party to the contract with the consumer does not have a branch, agency or other establishment within the meaning of that provision where he has recourse, for the purposes of his activities in a Contracting State, to a company which has its seat there and is effectively owned by it *but has no authority to conclude contracts.*

37. The concept of 'branch, agency or other establishment' which the national court has asked the Court to interpret in its third question is not unfamiliar to the Court. Although the second paragraph of Article 8 and the second paragraph of Article 13 have not yet had to be considered by the Court, Article 5(5), in which that expression also appears, has already been the subject of judgments of the Court.

38. Let us examine what distinguishes those three provisions: Article 5(5) is concerned only with undertakings whose registered office is in the territory of one of the Contracting States. If that undertaking has its seat in the territory of a third State, Article 4 applies. On the contrary, the second paragraph of Article 8 and the second paragraph of Article 13 may cause the strict application of that article to be defeated, since they are concerned with the case where the insurer or the other party to the contract with a consumer are not domiciled in the territory of a signatory State.

39. Since it constitutes an exception to the principle laid down by the first paragraph, in so far as it refers to Article 4, the second paragraph of Article 13, the provisions of which may be relied on against parties domiciled in a third State, must be interpreted strictly. Indeed, if it were given a broad interpretation, the concept of 'branch' would make it easy to defeat the fundamental principle set out in the first paragraph of Article 4.

40. What guidance can be obtained from the Court's caselaw on Article 5(5)?

41. The Court came down in favour of an independent interpretation of the concept of a 'dispute arising out of the operations of a branch, agency or establishment' and considered that, as a special jurisdiction constituting an exception to the general rule that the courts of the defendant's domicile should have jurisdiction, Article 5(5) had to be interpreted strictly.

42. In the judgment in *De Bloos* v *Bouyer*, the first to consider that provision, the Court observed that: 'One of the essential characteristics of the concepts of branch or agency is the fact of being subject to the direction and control of the parent body'.

The Court concluded that the holder of an exclusive concession who was not subject to the direction and control of a company could not be regarded as being a branch, agency or establishment.

43. In the judgment in *SAR Schotte* v *Parfums Rothschild* the Court held that Article 5(5) could apply to the two separate companies (one being the parent company, the other its wholly-owned subsidiary) bearing the same name and being under common management, one of which (the parent company) entered

into transactions on behalf of the other even though it was not a branch or an agency without any independence *vis-à-vis* that other company.

44. Consequently, a company should have acted in the State in which it has its seat as the extension in business relations of a company established in another Contracting State if the latter company is to be capable being sued in the courts of the place where the first company has its seat, even though, from the point of view of company law, the two companies are independent of each other.

45. The tie of dependency *vis-à-vis* the company established in another Member State is not the key criterion here. To my mind, the key criterion lies in the fact that the secondary establishment should have the authority to negotiate with third parties.

46. As long ago as the judgment of 18 March 1981 in *Blanckaert & Willems* v *Trost* the Court held that an independent commercial agent did not have the characteristics of a branch, agency or other establishment within the meaning of Article 5(5) *inter alia* because he merely transmitted orders to the parent undertaking *without being involved in either their terms or their execution.*

47. More specifically still, in *Somafer* v *Saar-Ferngas* the Court held as follows: 'the concept of branch, agency or other establishment implies a place of business which has the appearance of permanency, such as the extension of a parent body, has a management and is materially equipped *to negotiate business with third parties so that* the latter, although knowing that there will if necessary be a legal link with parent body, the head office of which is abroad, do not have to deal directly with such parent body but may transact business at the place of business constituting the extension.'

48. Lastly, in the aforementioned judgment in *SAR Schotte* v *Parfums Rothschild* the Court categorized as a branch a parent company which had the power to transact business on behalf of its subsidiary.

49. As has been seen, under the second paragraph of Article 13, the other party to a contract with a consumer may be sued in a court in a Contracting State where that party is not domiciled in a Contracting State. As has been pointed out, that constitutes an exception to Article 4. It cannot be given a broader interpretation than Article 5(5), which merely lays down, *within the territorial area to which the Convention applies,* an exception to Article 2.

50. Is it therefore possible to categorize as an establishment, branch or agency an entity which, although effectively owned by a company which has its seat in a non-Contracting State, does not have the authority to conclude contracts?

51. That authority seems to me to be the condition *sine qua non* for the existence of a secondary establishment within the meaning of the second paragraph of Article 13.

52. The rationale of that article is based on the existence of such a strong connecting link with the State in which the consumer is domiciled as to warrant an exception to Article 4 of the Convention, which is made capable of being relied on as against a person domiciled in a third State.

53. This is sufficient to establish that a company domiciled in a

Contracting State which serves merely as a forwarding body, a 'letter box', cannot 'fix' jurisdiction in the territory in which it is established when the contract for which it acted as the intermediary was not concluded by it and was performed in a third State. The contract's centre of gravity could not be located in the Contracting State in which it was perhaps prepared but not concluded. Only the conditions for the conclusion and performance of the contract in the third State may give rise to disputes between the parties. They are not capable of connecting the dispute to the branch's seat.

54. I consider that this point of view is confirmed by the last paragraph of Article 8 of the Convention. Mr Jenard observes that this exception 'applies only to branches and or agencies, i. e. when the foreign company is represented by a person *able to conclude contracts with third parties on behalf of the company'.*

55. I cannot see moreover how there could be a 'dispute arising out of the operations' of the branch if the latter has no authority to conclude contracts.

56. The Court held in paragraph 13 of the judgment in *Somafer* that there cannot be said to have been operations of the branch unless it entered into undertakings which are to be performed in the State in which it is established. That presupposes that the branch had the authority to enter into such undertakings. A dispute cannot be located at the branch's seat if the subject-matter of the dispute is not within the branch's 'range of activity'. As Shearson Lehman rightly observes 'if the agency acted merely as a forwarding body, the mere fact that it acted in that capacity precludes the possibility of there having been disputes arising out of its operations'. A mere intermediary could not 'shift' jurisdiction to the courts of its place of establishment.

57. My conclusion is that an operations centre which has no authority to conclude a contract cannot be regarded as being a branch, agency or establishment within the meaning of the second paragraph of Article 13 of the Brussels Convention. The requirements of consumer protection do not extend so far as to allow the consumer in such a case to sue the other party to the contract who is domiciled in a third State in the courts of the signatory State in which he is domiciled and in which the branch has its seat.

58. Lastly, even supposing that there was proof that the other party to the contract with the consumer had a branch within the meaning of the second paragraph of Article 13, we would still be outside the scope of the Convention, since the branch would have its seat in the State in which the consumer was domiciled. The dispute, which may be an international one *inter alia* as regards the applicable law, would not be international from the point of view of the Convention as it would lack the requisite extraneous element, which presupposes in principle the involvement of two States.

59. Where the other party to the contract with the consumer is not domiciled in the territory of a Contracting State but does have a branch, agency or any other establishment in a Contracting State other than that in which the consumer is domiciled, the second paragraph of Article 13 is definitely applicable.

60. As a result of that provision, the other party to the contract with the consumer is deemed to be domiciled by way of fiction in the Contracting State

where its branch has its seat. In such case, the Convention exercises a species of attraction on the dispute, which enables the application of the first paragraph of Article 4 to be avoided. The criterion for exclusion from the Convention's scope (the fact that the other party to the contract with the consumer is domiciled in a third State) is replaced by a connecting factor (the fact that the branch has its seat in a signatory State). As a result, an international situation arises within the meaning of the Convention, since the dispute concerns two Contracting States - the State in which the consumer is domiciled and the State in which the branch of the other party to the consumer contract has its seat.

61. But what is the position where the branch has its seat and the consumer is domiciled in the *same* Contracting State?

62. In his report on the Brussels Convention, Mr Jenard takes the view that 'Proceedings instituted in the courts of a Contracting State which involve only persons domiciled in that State will not normally be affected by the Convention'.

63. Admittedly, it could be argued that, through the operation of the Convention itself and the fiction provided for in the second paragraph of Article 13, the proceedings could be between two parties domiciled in the same Contracting State. But I can see one specific limit to the application of that provision: where the branch and the consumer are domiciled in the same Contracting State the dispute is no longer an 'international' one for the purposes of the Brussels Convention and the second paragraph of Article 13 cannot therefore apply.

64. As Mr Droz observes, 'each time that the Convention lays down a direct special jurisdiction, for example the courts of the place where the policyholder is domiciled, this will apply where the defendant is sued in the courts of a State *other* than the State in which he is domiciled'.

65. The purpose of the Convention is, I reiterate, to determine the international jurisdiction of the Contracting States' courts *within the intra-Community order.*

66. I further consider that a provision of the Convention, such as the second paragraph of Article 13, which *can be relied upon as against persons domiciled in a State which is not a party to the Convention*, has to be interpreted strictly, since that is a situation which the Convention is not intended in principle to govern.

67. Article 14 bears out that interpretation. Under its first paragraph the consumer may bring proceedings 'either in the courts of the Contracting State in which [the other party to the contract] is domiciled or in the courts of the Contracting State in which he is himself domiciled', which implies that there are in fact two States involved.

68. Further confirmation seems to be provided in my view by Article 15. That provision states that the provisions of Section 4 may be departed from only by an agreement: '(...) 3. which is entered into by the consumer and the other party to the contract, both of whom are *at the time of conclusion of the contract* domiciled or habitually resident in the same Contracting State, and which confers jurisdiction on the courts of that State, provided that such an agreement is not contrary to the law of that State.'

That provision - which is in the nature of a derogation and therefore has to be interpreted strictly - indeed seems to mean that the application of the Convention where only one Contracting State is involved at the time when the proceedings are initiated - contrary therefore to the wording of the preamble - is merely in the nature of an exception.

69. In such an event, jurisdiction must therefore be governed, not by the Convention but by the *lex fori* of the Contracting State in question, even if that law does not give the consumer the benefit of the *forum actoris*.

70. My conclusion is that the second paragraph of Article 13 of the Convention is not applicable where the branch of a company which has its seat in a third State is located in the territory of the same Contracting State in which the consumer has his domicile.

71. For all those reasons, a situation such as the one at issue does not, in my view, fall within the scope of the Brussels Convention.

72. I shall therefore tackle the Bundesgerichtshof's first, second and fourth questions in the alternative, since its third question, which is concerned with the concept of branch, has already been covered.

73. Let us turn to the first question. The only one of the contracts listed in the first paragraph of Article 13 in point here is the one mentioned in subparagraph 3, 'a contract for the supply of services', which has been taken over from the Convention on Contractual Obligations. Such a contract is not defined in the body of the conventions themselves or in the explanatory reports.

74. The amendment made to Section 4, and Article 13 in particular, of the Brussels Convention by the 1978 accession convention aimed at *extending* consumer protection without confirming it to the sphere of sales on instalment terms and loans repayable by instalments. Thus, the article sets out, using very comprehensive wording, a residual category of the contracts - 'any other contract for the supply of goods or a contract for the supply of services' - without making any distinction within that category as to the nature of the contract.

75. Admittedly, Article 5 of the Convention on the Law applicable to Contractual Obligations applies to a contract 'the object of which is the supply of goods and services to a person ("the consumer") for a purpose which can be regarded as being outside his trade or profession, or a contract for the provision of credit for that object' and, according to the Giuliano-Lagarde report, sales of securities are excluded.

76. For all that, it does not follow - as Shearson Lehman wrongly argues - that an agency contract concerning currency, security and commodity futures dealings is excluded from the category of contracts for the supply of services within the meaning of Article 13. The Rome Convention provides for exceptions to its scope which are unknown to the Brussels Convention. Moreover, such a contract is not a 'sale of securities' properly so called.

77. Neither can the protection of Article 13 be ruled out on the ground that the contract concerns security and commodity futures dealings 'which are speculative in nature and akin to games of chance, which are alien to the idea of social protection'.

78. As Professor Schlosser points out, even if stock-exchange speculators

are not 'paradigms for consumers deserving of protection', the field of Article 13 cannot conceivably be restricted by exclusions not provided for in that provision. Moreover, it seems to me to be dangerous to draw a distinction on the basis of the objective pursuant by the contracting party: how could it be argued that an agency contract concluded into order to manage one's assets prudently would fall within the scope of Article 13 whereas an agency contract concluded for purely speculative purposes would not?

79. It should therefore be considered that that provision also covers agency contracts concerning currency and security futures dealings.

80. Does such a contract satisfy the two concurrent conditions laid down by sub-paragraphs 3(a) and (b) of the first paragraph of Article 13? If the consumer has indisputably carried out in the State of his domicile the acts necessary to conclude the contract, was that *preceded* by advertising and does that advertising fulfil the conditions laid down in the Convention? In particular, does there have to be a connection between the advertising and the conclusion of the contract? This is the second question before the Court.

81. As the Schlosser report indicates, contracts for the supply of services can be caught by Article 13 only 'if there is a sufficiently strong connection with the place where the consumer is domiciled'.

82. Thus, the contract must have been preceded in the State of the consumer's domicile by *advertising*.

83. The Convention requires no other condition to be met in this regard: the consumer is not required to prove that he was actually affected by the advertising or that there was a causal link between the advertising and the conclusion of the contract.

84. Apart from the fact that it would generally be impossible to satisfy such a requirement, it seems to me that such requirement would be contrary to the aim pursued by Article 13: that of consumer protection. Consumer protection is to be fostered: any restrictions on the application of that provision must therefore ensue from the actual wording of the Convention. The only conceivable limitation is one of common sense: it seems to me that the advertising cannot have been too remote in time from the conclusion of the contract to which it is purported to have given rise. This assessment falls within the remit of the national court.

85. It follows that the conditions laid down in subparagraph 3(a) of the first paragraph of Article 13 of the Convention are met where the conclusion of the contract in the State of the consumer's domicile was preceded within a reasonable time by advertising, there being no requirement to prove a causal connection between the advertising and the conclusion of the contract. As a result, that article lays down a species of irrebuttable presumption that there is a link between the appearance of the advertising and the conclusion of the contract where the former preceded the latter.

86. Let us turn to question 4(a), which is concerned with the phrase 'concerning a contract'.

87. The phrase 'concerning a contract' in Article 13 of the Convention has never come before the Court. However, the Court has on many occasions

interpreted the phrase 'matters relating to a contract' contained in Article 5(1). Here again, there is in my view nothing to justify considering that those two provisions may cover two different things. It seems to me that the interpretations which the Court has given to the expression 'matters relating to a contract' in Article 5 have to be taken into account in interpreting the similar provisions of Article 13.

88. The Court held with regard to Article 5 in the judgment in *Peters* v *ZNAV* that: '(...) the concept of matters relating to a contract serves as a criterion to define the scope of one of the rules of special jurisdiction available to the plaintiff. Having regard to the objectives and the general scheme of the Convention, it is important that, in order to ensure as far as possible the equality and uniformity of the rights and obligations arising out of the Convention for the Contracting States and the persons concerned, that concept should not be interpreted simply as referring to the national law of one or other of the States concerned.

Therefore (...) the concept of matters relating to a contract should be regarded as an independent concept which, for the purpose of the application of the Convention, must be interpreted by reference chiefly to the system and objectives of the Convention, in. order to ensure that it is fully effective.'

89. In the case of *Arcado* v *Haviland*, following the termination of an independent commercial agency agreement by which the Haviland company appointed the Agecobel company as its agent for the sale of porcelain products in Belgium and Luxembourg, the latter company instituted proceedings against Haviland before the Tribunal de Commerce (Commercial Court), Brussels, seeking compensation for wrongful termination of the agreement and the balance of outstanding commission. In appeal proceedings Haviland relied on Article 5(3) of the Convention and contested the jurisdiction of the Belgian courts. The Cour d'Appel (Court of Appeal) took the view that the dispute concerning the payment of commission was contractual in nature but was uncertain as to the nature of the claim for indemnity for the sudden and premature repudiation of the contract, and referred to the Court for a preliminary ruling a question on that point.

90. The Court held that: 'There is no doubt that a claim for the payment of commission due under an independent commercial agency agreement finds its very basis in that agreement and consequently constitutes a matter relating to a contract within the meaning of Article 5(1) of the Convention.'

The same view must be taken of a claim for compensation for the wrongful repudiation of such an agreement as the basis for such compensation is the failure to comply with a contractual obligation.

91. The Court based itself in particular on Article 10 of the Rome Convention: '[That article] confirms the contractual nature of judicial proceedings such as those in point inasmuch as it provides that the law applicable to a contract governs the consequences of a total or partial failure to comply with obligations arising under it and consequently the contractual liability of the party responsible for such breach'.

92. In the earlier judgment in *De Bloos* v *Bouyer* the Court held that: 'In

disputes concerning the consequences of the infringement by the grantor of a contract conferring an exclusive concession, such as the payment of damages or the dissolution of the contract, the obligation to which reference must be made for the purposes of applying Article 5(1) of the Convention is that which the contract imposes on the grantor and the non-performance of which is relied upon by the grantee in support of the application for damages or for the dissolution of the contract.'

93. In my view, an action for damages for breach of contractual obligations by the grantee of a concession is not different in kind from an action for wrongful termination - and hence for failure to comply with contractual obligations - which is brought by a grantor or by the other party to a contract with a commercial agent: in both cases, the basis of the right to compensation is the contract.

94. Does the expression 'concerning a contract' in the first paragraph of Article 13 also cover claims based on infringement of the advisory duty in pre-contractual negotiations? Do such claims deserve the same treatment as claims based on the main contractual obligation?

95. During pre-contractual negotiations, the parties thereto are not bound by obligations based on the contract precisely because the contract does not yet exist and perhaps never will. It is generally considered that they are simply under a reciprocal obligation to act with care and diligence.

96. Of course, a claim for liability arising out of failure to fulfil that obligation cannot in itself be regarded as contractual. This is shown by the fact that it could be asserted even if, in the end, the contract has not been concluded.

97. However, once it is combined with a claim based on contractual liability under a contract to which the pre-contractual negotiations themselves succeeded in giving rise, it appears that the claim for pre-contractual liability becomes inseparable from the contract.

98. Lastly, the nature of the claim based on unjust enrichment with regard to the Brussels Convention raises a delicate issue.

99. In the judgment in *Kalfelis* the Court had to categorise such a claim.

100. In that case, the appellant in the main proceedings concluded with a bank established in Luxembourg, through the intermediary of the German affiliate of that bank, spot and futures stock-exchange transactions in silver bullion. The futures transactions resulted in a total loss and the appellant brought an action for payment of sums owed against Bankhaus Schröder in Luxembourg and its affiliate.

101. The action was based both on contractual liability (infringement of obligations to provide information) and on tortious liability (conduct *contra bonos mores*). The action was also based on unjust enrichment on the ground that futures stock-exchange transactions, such as futures transactions in silver bullion, were not binding on the parties.

102. Asked to interpret the expression 'matters relating to tort, delict or quasi delict' in Article 5(3) of the Convention, the Court held that: '[that expression] must be regarded as an independent concept covering *all* actions which seek to establish the liability of a defendant and which are not related to

a "contract" within the meaning of Article 5(1)', and therefore includes under matters relating to tort a claim based on unjust enrichment.

103. In my opinion on that case, I suggested, on the basis of the aforementioned judgment in *Martin Peters* v *ZNAV*, a solution which would enable the dispute to be brought before just one court where there was a multiplication of the bases of jurisdiction in one and the same case.

104. I should like to quote a brief passage. After setting out the wording of that judgment, to the effect that: '(...) the designation by Article 5(1) of the Convention of the courts for the place of performance of the obligation in question expresses the concern that, because of the close links created by a contract between the parties thereto, it should be possible for all the difficulties which may arise on the occasion of the performance of a contractual obligation to be brought before the same court: that for the place of performance of the obligation', I stated that: 'The Court thus formulated the reasons which militate in favour of an "attraction" towards Article 5(1), an attraction which must extend to the grounds of the claims, whether they derive from a tort or unjust enrichment under the *lex causae*, provided that, as in the present case, they are based "for the most part on the non-performance of contractual obligations". (...)

In other words, it is thus appropriate to conclude that where there are overlapping grounds of that kind, only Article 5(1) will determine the jurisdiction of the court, since the matters relating to contract will "channel" all the aspects of the dispute.'

105. This case prompts me to submit the same proposal for the determination of a single court having jurisdiction.

106.It is in fact impossible not to see that what 'federates' and 'unites' the various claims made before the national court is *the contract concluded by the parties.*

107. It follows that where a claim reflects difficulties which are liable to arise when contractual obligations are performed, it must fall within the scope of Article 5(1) of the Convention.

108. That 'centralisation' of jurisdiction which seemed to me to be necessary in connection with matters relating to a contract under Article 5 is even more necessary in my view where what is involved is contracts concluded by a consumer, on whom the multiplication of bases of jurisdiction could have a very particular adverse effect.

109. The desire to foster legal certainty and the effectiveness of legal protection throughout the territory of the Community can result only in the application of the first paragraph of Article 13, which was the solution which I advocated with regard to Article 5(1).

110. It follows in my view that the concept of matters relating to a contract within the meaning of the first paragraph of Article 13 covers a claim based on breach of contractual obligations, breach of pre-contractual obligations and unjust enrichment arising out of one and the same agency contract.

111. Since matters relating to a contract within the meaning of that article channel all the aspects of the dispute and the claims are interconnected in such a way that they can only be assessed together in accordance with the Court's

judgment in *Martin Peters* v *ZNAV*, jurisdiction must be determined by Article 14 alone.

112 As a result, the last question relating to connexity is otiose.

113. I propose therefore that the Court should rule as follows:

'(1) An initiator of legal proceedings who is not himself a party to one of the contracts listed in the first paragraph of Article 13 is not a consumer within the meaning of Articles 13 and 14 of the Brussels Convention.

(2) A company which is established in a signatory State of the Brussels Convention, is effectively owned by the other party to the contract with the consumer and has no authority to conclude contracts is not a branch, agency or other establishment within the meaning of the second paragraph of Article 13 of the Brussels Convention.

(3) The second paragraph of Article 13 of the Brussels Convention is not applicable, in the absence of any extraneous element, where the branch of the company based in a third State is situated in the territory of the same Contracting State in which the consumer has his domicile.'

In the alternative

(1) An agency contract concerning currency, security and commodity futures dealings is a contract for the supply of services within the meaning of subpara-graph 3 of the first paragraph of Article 13 of the Brussels Convention.

(2) The latter provision does not require there to be proof of a causal link between the advertising and the conclusion of the contract.

(3) The concept of matters relating to a contract within the meaning the first paragraph of Article 13 covers a claim based on breach of contractual obligations, breach of pre-contractual obligations and unjust enrichment arising out of the conclusion of one and the same contract.

Case C-318/93 - 15 September 1994

Wolfgang Brenner and Peter Noller
v
Dean Witter Reynolds Inc.

Articles 13 and 14 - Jurisdiction over consumer contracts - Contract with a party not domiciled in a Contracting State.

Summary

The courts of the State in which the consumer is domiciled have jurisdiction in proceedings under the second alternative in the first paragraph of Article 14 of the Convention of 27 September 1968 on Jurisdiction and Enforcement of Judgments in Civil and Commercial Matters, as amended by the Convention of 9 October 1978 on the Accession of the Kingdom of Denmark, Ireland and the United Kingdom of Great Britain and Northern Ireland, if the other party to the contract is domiciled in a Contracting State or is deemed under the second paragraph of Article 13 of that Convention to be so domiciled.

The latter provision, which applies where a consumer enters into a contract with a party who is not domiciled in a Contracting State but has a branch, agency or other establishment there and the dispute arises out of its operation, is, with respect to consumer contracts, the only exception to the rule in Article 4 that the jurisdiction of the courts in proceedings where the defendant is not domiciled in a Contracting State is governed not by the Convention but by the law of the Contracting State of the court in which the proceedings are brought.

JUDGMENT OF THE COURT

Moitinho de Almeida, President of the Chamber, Joliet, Rodríguez Iglesias, Grévisse and Zuleeg, Judges

1. By order of 25 May 1993, received at the Court on 16 June 1993, the Bundesgerichtshof (Federal Court of Justice) referred to the Court for a preliminary ruling under the Protocol of 3 June 1971 on the interpretation by the Court of Justice of the Convention of 27 September 1968 on Jurisdiction and the Enforcement of Judgments in Civil and Commercial Matters (OJ 1972 L 299, p. 32), as amended by the Convention of 9 October 1978 on the Accession of the Kingdom of Denmark, Ireland and the United Kingdom of Great Britain and Northern Ireland (OJ 1978 L 304, p. 1) (hereinafter 'the Brussels Convention'), on a number of questions on the interpretation of Articles 13 and 14 of that Convention.

2. Those questions were raised in separate proceedings between Mr Brenner, a self-employed master joiner, and Mr Noller, employed as a textile technician, both domiciled in the Federal Republic of Germany ('the plaintiffs'), and Dean Witter Reynolds Inc., a firm of brokers based in New York ('the defendant').

3. According to the order for reference, the plaintiffs, not acting within the scope of their profession or occupation, commissioned the defendant with the implementation of commodity futures transactions, on a commission basis.

4. The plaintiffs provided large sums of money, which apart from a small residual amount were entirely consumed by losses as a result of speculations.

5. The defendant advertises in Germany via Dean Witter Reynolds GmbH, a German company based in Frankfurt. However, it is common ground between the parties that contacts between them were mediated exclusively by Metzler Wirtschafts-und Börsenberatungsgesellschaft mbH ('MWB'), a company based in Frankfurt which advises on economic and stock market affairs, and is independent of the defendant.

6. The plaintiffs claimed damages on the grounds of breach by the defendant of its contractual and precontractual obligations, tortious conduct characterized by unjustified charges in connection with a large number of partly unreasonable transactions ('churning'), and unjust enrichment.

7. The Landgericht (Regional Court), in which the plaintiffs brought proceedings, held that it had no jurisdiction in respect of the defendant. Its decisions were upheld on appeal. Mr Brenner and Mr Noller thereupon each appealed on a point of law to the Bundesgerichtshof.

8. The Bundesgerichtshof considers that, on the basis of the findings made by the judges of fact, only Articles 13 and 14 of the Brussels Convention might establish the international jurisdiction of the German courts.

9. Under Article 13 of the Brussels Convention: 'In proceedings concerning a contract concluded by a person for a purpose which can be regarded as being outside his trade or profession, hereinafter called "the consumer", jurisdiction shall be determined by this Section without prejudice to the provisions of Articles 4 and 5(5), if it is:

1. a contract for the sale of goods on instalment credit terms; or
2. a contract for a loan repayable by instalments, or for any other form of credit, made to finance the sale of goods; or
3. any other contract for the supply of goods or a contract for the supply of services, and

(a) in the State of the consumer's domicile the conclusion of the contract was preceded by a specific invitation addressed to him or by advertising; and

(b) the consumer took in that State the steps necessary for the conclusion of the contract.

Where a consumer enters into a contract with a party who is not domiciled in a Contracting State but has a branch, agency or other establishment in one of the Contracting States, that party shall, in disputes arising out of the operations of the branch, agency or establishment, be deemed to be domiciled in that State.

This Section shall not apply to contracts of transport.'

10. The first paragraph of Article 14 then states that: 'A consumer may bring proceedings against the other party to a contract either in the courts of the Contracting State in which that party is domiciled or in the courts of the Contracting State in which he is himself domiciled.'

11. The Bundesgerichtshof observes that in the present case the other party to the contract is not domiciled in a Contracting State and no branch, agency or other establishment within the meaning of the second paragraph of Article 13 of the Brussels Convention acted as an intermediary in the conclusion or performance of the contract. It wonders

whether in those circumstances the consumer is precluded only from bringing proceedings against the other party to the contract in the courts of the State in which that party is domiciled, or whether the consumer is also precluded from bringing proceedings in the courts of the Contracting State in which he is himself domiciled. The Bundesgerichtshof considers that the first paragraph of Article 4 of the Brussels Convention might support the latter interpretation, since it makes the applicability of the Convention subject to the defendant being domiciled in a Contracting State.

12. In those circumstances the Bundesgerichtshof stayed the proceedings pending a preliminary ruling by the Court on the following questions:

'1. Is it a condition for the recognition of the international jurisdiction of the State in which the consumer is domiciled under the second alternative in the first paragraph of Article 14 of the Brussels Convention that the other party to the contract is domiciled in a Contracting State to the Brussels Convention or is deemed under the second paragraph of Article 13 of the Brussels Convention to be so domiciled?

2. Does subparagraph 3 of the first paragraph of Article 13 of the Brussels Convention cover contracts on a commission basis for the purpose of carrying out commodity futures transactions?

3. Is subparagraph 3(a) of the first paragraph of Article 13 of the Brussels Convention applicable whenever the party with whom the consumer enters into a contract has advertised in the State in which the consumer is domiciled prior to conclusion of the contract, or does that provision require there to be a connection between the advertisement and the conclusion of the contract?

4. (a) Does the term "proceedings concerning a contract" in the first paragraph of Article 13 of the Brussels Convention cover, in addition to the pursuit of claims for damages for breach of contractual obligations, also the pursuit of claims based on breach of precontractual obligations (*culpa in contrahendo*) and unjust enrichment in connection with reversal of contractual performance?

(b) In the case of proceedings in which damages are claimed for the breach of contractual and precontractual obligations, claims are put forward on the basis of unjust enrichment and damages are sought for tortious acts, does the first paragraph of Article 13 of the Brussels Convention create, by virtue of the factual connection, ancillary jurisdiction which extends also to the non-contractual claim?'

13. The Bundesgerichtshof notes that Questions 2, 3 and 4 are asked only in case the answer to Question 1 is that the first paragraph of Article 14 of the Convention is applicable in a case such as the present one.

14. It must be noted to begin with that Articles 13 and 14 form part of the section on 'jurisdiction over consumer contracts'.

15. In addition, the first subparagraph of Article 13 expressly states that that section, as a whole, applies 'without prejudice to the provisions of [Article] 4'.

16. According to the first paragraph of Article 4, 'if the defendant is not domiciled in a Contracting State, the jurisdiction of the courts of each Contracting State shall, subject to the provisions of Article 16, be determined by the law of that State'. Article 16 lays down rules for exclusive jurisdiction in proceedings which have as their object rights *in rem* in immovable property or tenancies of immovable property, the validity of the constitution, the nullity or the dissolution of companies or other legal persons, the validity of entries in public registers, the registration or validity of patents, trademarks, designs or other similar rights, and in proceedings concerned with the enforcement of judgments.

17. It follows that, subject to those cases of exclusive jurisdiction, the jurisdiction of courts in proceedings where the defendant is not domiciled in a Contracting State is governed not by the Brussels Convention but by the law of the Contracting State of the court in which proceedings are brought.

18. With respect to consumer contracts, the only exception to the rule in Article 4 is introduced by the second paragraph of Article 13, which applies where a consumer enters into a contract with a party who is not domiciled in a Contracting State but has a branch, agency or other establishment there and the dispute arises out of its operations.

19. It is sufficient to note that, according to the order for reference, no branch, agency or other establishment within the meaning of the second paragraph of Article 13 acted as an intermediary in the conclusion or performance of the contracts between Mr Brenner and Mr Noller and the defendant, and that that exception thus does not apply to the present case.

20. Accordingly, the answer to Question 1 must be that the courts of the State in which the consumer is domiciled have jurisdiction in proceedings

under the second alternative in the first paragraph of Article 14 of the Brussels Convention if the other party to the contract is domiciled in a Contracting State or is deemed under the second paragraph of Article 13 of that Convention to be so domiciled.

21. In view of the answer to Question 1, there is no need to answer the other questions.

On those grounds, the Court (Fifth Chamber), in answer to the questions referred to it by the Bundesgerichtshof, by order of 25 May 1993, hereby rules:

The courts of the State in which the consumer is domiciled have jurisdiction in proceedings under the second alternative in the first paragraph of Article 14 of the Convention of 27 September 1968 on Jurisdiction and the Enforcement of Judgments in Civil and Commercial Matters, as amended by the Convention of 9 October 1978 on the Accession of the Kingdom of Denmark, Ireland and the United Kingdom of Great Britain and Northern Ireland, if the other party to the contract is domiciled in a Contracting State or is deemed under the second paragraph of Article 13 of that Convention to be so domiciled.

OPINION OF MR ADVOCATE GENERAL DARMON

1. By order of 25 May 1993 the Bundesgerichtshof refers to the Court for a preliminary ruling four questions on the interpretation of Articles 13 and 14 of the Brussels Convention on Jurisdiction and the Enforcement of Judgments in Civil and Commercial Matters (hereinafter 'the Convention') as amended on 9 October 1978. Three of the questions are identical in content with those referred by the Bundesgerichtshof in the *Shearson Lehman* case.

2. The facts of the case may be summarised briefly. Two private individuals, Mr Brenner and Mr Noller, not acting in connection with their profession or occupation, commissioned the broking firm of Dean Witter Reynolds Inc., established in the United States of America, with the implementation of commodity futures transactions. That firm has an agency in Frankfurt am Main, Dean Witter Reynolds GmbH, which advertises for it, but the contract between the parties was mediated exclusively by Metzler Wirtschafts- und Börsenberatungs-gesellschaft mbH, a company which is independent of Dean Witter Reynolds Inc.

3. The result of the investments made by that firm on behalf of the plaintiffs in the main proceedings was that, following speculative transactions, they lost almost all the capital provided. Mr Brenner and Mr Noller therefore

brought proceedings for compensation against the broking firm, seeking repayment of the sums lost; they claimed on the basis of breach of contractual and precontractual obligations, tortious conduct in connection with inflating charges by carrying out a large number of sometimes unreasonable transactions ('churning'), and unjust enrichment.

4. The Landgericht, at first instance, held that it lacked jurisdiction, and its decision was upheld on appeal. The plaintiffs in the main proceedings thereupon appealed on a point of law to the Bundesgerichtshof, which now seeks a preliminary ruling from the Court on its jurisdiction with respect to the first paragraph *in fine* of Article 14 of the Convention where, as in the present case, the other party to the contract is domiciled in a non-Contracting State and no branch, agency or other establishment has acted as an intermediary in the conclusion or performance of the contract.

5. The other, subsidiary, questions essentially ask the Court for an interpretation of the following terms:

- 'contract for the supply of goods or a contract for the supply of services' in subparagraph 3 of the first paragraph of Article 13, in order to determine whether a contract on a commission basis for the purpose of carrying out commodity futures transactions comes within that category;
- 'advertising' within the meaning of that provision, in order to determine whether it means that there must be a link with the conclusion of a contract;
- 'proceedings concerning a contract' in the first paragraph of Article 13, so as to know whether it covers not only claims for damages for breach of contract but also claims on the basis of breach of precontractual obligations and unjust enrichment, and if so, whether it creates, by virtue of the factual connection, an ancillary jurisdiction for non-contractual claims.

6. I have already considered those questions in my Opinion in the *Shearson Lehman Hutton* case. The Court did not, however, answer them since it considered, as I had suggested, that '... Article 13 of the Convention is to be interpreted as meaning that where a plaintiff, party to one of the contracts mentioned in the first paragraph of that provision, is engaged in his trade or professional activity, and is not himself the consumer, he cannot enjoy the benefit of the special rules of jurisdiction laid down by the Convention concerning consumer contracts'.

7. The Court thus considered that the assignee of a claim acting in the course of his professional activity could not rely on the protective rules of Article 13 which the assigning consumer could have relied on.

8. The present case, on the other hand, according to the findings of the national court, in fact concerns two consumers who each concluded with a company established in a non-Contracting State a contract on a commission basis for the purpose of carrying out commodity futures transactions. The preliminary question to be answered in this case is that of the determination of the scope of the provisions on jurisdiction over consumer contracts in Section 4 of Title II of the Convention.

9. I may state straight away that in my opinion, where, as in the present

case, the defendant is not domiciled within the Community and no branch, agency or other establishment has acted in the conclusion and/or performance of the contract, the national court can apply only its own rules on jurisdiction, with the effect that it is not only one of the two alternatives in the first paragraph of Article 14 which is inapplicable, but the whole of Section 4.

10. The Brussels Convention is not intended to regulate jurisdictional disputes which may arise between courts in a Contracting State on the one hand and those in a non-Contracting State on the other hand. As the Jenard Report states, '... the territory of the Contracting States may be regarded as forming a single entity: it follows, for the purpose of laying down rules on jurisdiction, that a very clear distinction can be drawn between litigants who are domiciled within the Community and those who are not', with the result that 'if a person is not domiciled in a Contracting State, that is, if he is domiciled outside the Community, the rules of jurisdiction in force in each Contracting State, including those regarded as exorbitant, are applicable'.

11. The Evrigenis and Kerameus Report on the accession of the Hellenic Republic to the Convention on Jurisdiction and the Enforcement of Judgments in Civil and Commercial Matters similarly states that: 'where a defendant is not domiciled in a Contracting State the Convention does not contain any rules of its own but refers to the internal law of the State of the court hearing the action (Article 4, first paragraph). As against such a defendant, the Convention permits any person domiciled in a Contracting State, whatever his nationality, to avail himself of the law of that State ...'.

12. The first paragraph of Article 4 of the Convention indeed provides that: 'If the defendant is not domiciled in a Contracting State, the jurisdiction of the courts of each Contracting State shall, subject to the provisions of Article 16, be determined by the law of that State.'

13. Although Article 4 does not say so, other provisions in addition to Article 16 apply even where the defendant is domiciled in a non-Contracting State.

14. That is the case where jurisdiction is based on an agreement conferring jurisdiction within the meaning of the first paragraph of Article 17, since in such a case the parties have by joint agreement chosen to 'embed' the case in the Community legal order. It suffices here if one of them is domiciled in a Contracting State.

15. Similarly, Article 18 deals with the case of a defendant who enters an appearance before a court of a Contracting State, where he does not contest its jurisdiction and there is no conflict with the provisions of Article 16.

16. Article 21 also applies independently of any condition as to domicile. The Court held in the *Overseas Union Insurance and Others* judgment that '... Article 21 of the Convention must be interpreted as applying irrespective of the domicile of the parties to the two sets of proceedings'.

17. However, the plaintiff cannot be allowed to rely on the rules on jurisdiction in Section 4 if the defendant is not domiciled in a Contracting State and the conditions in the second paragraph of Article 13 are not fulfilled.

18. As Article 13 states, 'in proceedings concerning a contract concluded

by a person for a purpose which can be regarded as being outside his trade or profession, hereinafter called "the consumer", jurisdiction shall be determined by this Section, without prejudice to the provisions of Articles 4 and 5(5)'.

19. The express reference to Article 4 in the first paragraph of Article 13 is thus a reminder that the scope of Articles 13 to 15 is limited to cases where the defendant is domiciled in a Contracting State.

20. In the circumstances the rules on jurisdiction set out in the Convention do not apply to proceedings such as those pending before the national court, with the consequence that the rules of the *lex fori* on international jurisdiction remain applicable. In such a case the consumer must rely on those rules, including those which derogate from the ordinary law.

21. As Gothot and Holleaux write, '... if the defendant is not domiciled in the territory of a Contracting State, the first paragraph of Article 4 expressly refers to the law of each Contracting State for determination in such a case of the *international* jurisdiction of the courts of that State .... It is thus necessary - but also sufficient - that the defendant is domiciled outside the Community for all the rules of international jurisdiction of the court in which proceedings are brought to be applicable, including if appropriate so-called exorbitant rules of jurisdiction. Article 3 gives a list of them: ... the forum where the property is situated under Paragraph 23 of the German ZPO ... .

The mere fact that he is not domiciled in a Contracting State thus means that the defendant, even if he is a national of a Contracting State, loses the benefit of the European jurisdiction system in Articles 2 to 15 ...'.

22. In proceedings concerning consumer contracts, the only exception to the rule in Article 4 is introduced by the second paragraph of Article 13, which applies where the party with whom the consumer contracts is domiciled in a non-Contracting State but has a branch, agency or other establishment in a Contracting State which represents him and can bind him *vis-à-vis* third parties; that is not the case here.

23. As Professor Kaye writes, '... a non-Contracting State domiciled non-consumer, which possesses a branch, agency or other establishment within the Community from which *it transacts* with the consumer, is deemed to be domiciled in the Contracting State in which the branch, agency or other establishment is situated, so that instead of being subject to national jurisdiction rules by virtue of Article 4, it can be proceeded against by the consumer in the latter State, as its domicile, under Article 14, para. 1'.

24. I note, however, that even if that condition were fulfilled Articles 13 to 15 would still not apply, since the proceedings would not be international for the purposes of the Convention, as Dean Witter Reynolds GmbH and Mr Brenner and Mr Noller would be domiciled in the same Contracting State.

25. It was stated by Droz, in his work cited above, that '... wherever the Convention determines a special direct jurisdiction, for example, the court of the place where the holder of an insurance policy is domiciled, this is a case where the defendant is sued in the courts of a State which is not that where he is domiciled'.

26. Similarly, in her commentary on the Court's judgment in the *Shearson*

Lehman Hutton case, Gaudemet-Tallon also considers that '... the basic principle ... is that the Brussels Convention lays down rules for intra-Community proceedings, not for national proceedings ...'.

27. The main proceedings are therefore not covered by the rules on direct jurisdiction in the Convention, more particularly those in the first paragraph of Article 14.

28. There is therefore no need to answer the subsidiary questions.

29. That is, moreover, the approach adopted by the Court in the judgment in *Shearson Lehman Hutton*. I dealt with them in my Opinion on an alternative basis. I will therefore restrict myself to referring to my observations in that Opinion in case the Court, contrary to my conclusion, considers that Article 14 of the Convention does apply here.

30. Accordingly, I propose that the Court hold that Article 14 of the Brussels Convention of 27 September 1968 on Jurisdiction and the Enforcement of Judgments in Civil and Commercial Matters is not applicable where the proceedings are brought by a consumer in a Contracting State against the other party to the contract who is domiciled in a non-Contracting State, where the conditions in the second paragraph of Article 13 are not fulfilled. In any event, the latter provision is not applicable, for want of a foreign element, where the branch, agency or other establishment of a company based in a non-Contracting State is situated on the territory of the same Contracting State as that in which the consumer is domiciled.

Case C-269/95 - 3 July 1997

Francesco Benincasa
v
Dentalkit Srl

Jurisdiction in respect of contracts concluded by consumers - Concept of 'consumer' - Plaintiff who has concluded a contract with a view to pursuing a trade or profession in the future - Excluded - Article 17 - Prorogation of jurisdiction - Agreement conferring jurisdiction - Scope of the exclusive jurisdiction of the court designated - Action to have the main agreement declared void - Included.

Summary

1. In the context of the specific regime established by Article 13 et seq. of the Convention of 27 September 1968 on jurisdiction and the enforcement of judgments in civil and commercial matters, only contract concluded for the purpose of satisfying an individual's own needs in terms of private consumption come under the provisions designed to protect the consumer as the party deemed to be the weaker party economically. On the other hand, the specific protection sought to be afforded by those provisions in unwarranted in the case of contracts for the purpose of trade or professional activity, even if that activity is only planned for the future, since the fact that an activity is in the nature of a future activity does not divest it is any way of its trade or professional character. It follows that the regime in question applies solely to contracts concluded outside and independently of any trade or professional activity or purpose, whether present or future, so that a plaintiff who has concluded a contract with a view to pursuing a trade or profession, not at the present time, but in the future may not be regarded as a consumer within the meaning of the first paragraph of Article 13 and the first paragraph of Article 14 of the Convention.

2. Article 17 of the Convention of 217 September 1968 on jurisdiction and the enforcement of judgments and civil and commercial matters sets out to designate, clearly and precisely, a court in a Contracting State which is to have exclusive jurisdiction in accordance with the consensus formed between the parties, which is to be expressed in accordance with the strict requirements as to form laid down therein. The legal certainty which that provision seeks to secure could easily be jeopardised if one party to the contract could frustrate the rule simply by claiming that the whole of the contract which contained the clause was void on grounds derived from the applicable substantive law. It follows that the court of a Contracting State which is designated in a jurisdiction clause validly concluded under the first paragraph of Article 17 also has exclusive jurisdiction where the action seeks in particular a declaration that the contract containing that clause is void. Furthermore, it is for the national court to determine which disputes fall within the scope of the clause conferring jurisdiction invoked before it and, consequently, to determine whether that clause also covers any dispute relating to the validity of the contract containing it.

JUDGMENT OF THE COURT

Mancini, President of the Chamber, Murray, Kakouris, Kapteyn and Ragnemalm, Judges

1. By order of 5 May 1995, received at the Court on 9 August 1995, the Oberlandesgericht (Higher Regional Court), Munich referred to the Court for a preliminary ruling under the Protocol of 3 June 1971 on the interpretation by the Court of Justice of the Convention of 27 September 1968 on jurisdiction and the enforcement of judgments in civil and commercial matters (OJ 1978 L 304, p.36), as amended by the Convention of 9 October 1978 on the accession of the Kingdom of Denmark, Ireland and the United Kingdom of Great Britain and Northern Ireland (OJ 1978 L 304, p.1; amended version of the Convention at p. 77; hereinafter 'the Convention'), three questions on the interpretation of the first paragraph of Article 13, the first paragraph of Article 14 and the first paragraph of Article 17 of the Convention.

2. Those questions were raised in proceedings between the Dentalkit Srl ('Dentalkit') having its seat in Florence, and Mr Benincasa, an Italian national, relating to the validity of a franchising contract concluded between them.

3. According to the case-file relating to the main proceedings, in 1987 Dentalkit developed a chain of franchised shops in Italy specializing in the sale of dental hygiene products. In 1992 Mr Benincasa concluded a franchising contract with Dentalkit with a view to setting up and operating a shop in Munich. In that contract Dentalkit authorized Mr Benincasa to exploit the exclusive right to use Dentalkit trade mark within a particular geographical area. Dentalkit further undertook to supply goods bearing that trade mark, to support him in various spheres, to carry out the requisite training and promotion and advertising activities and not to open any shop within the geographical area covered by the exclusive right.

4. For his part, Mr Benincasa undertook to equip business premises at his own cost, to stock exclusively Dentalkit's products, not to disclose any information or documents concerning Dentalkit and to pay it a sum of LIT 8 million as payment for the cost and technical and commercial assistance provided when opening the shop and 3% of its annual turnover. By reference to Articles 1341 and 1342 of the Italian Civil Code, the parties specifically approved a clause of the contract reading 'The courts at Florence shall have jurisdiction to entertain any dispute relating to the interpretation, performance or other aspects of the present contract' by separately signing it.

5. Mr Benincasa set up his shop, paid the initial sum of LIT 8 million and made several purchases, for which, however, he never paid. In the meantime, he has ceased trading altogether.

6. Mr Benincasa brought proceedings in the Landgericht (Regional Court), Munich I, where he sought to have the franchising contract declared void on the ground that the contract as a whole was void under German law. He also claimed that the sales contracts concluded subsequently pursuant to the basic franchising contract were void.

7. Mr Benincasa argued that the Landgericht Munich I had jurisdiction as the court for the place of performance of the obligation in question within the meaning of Article 5(1) of the Convention. He argued that the clause of the franchising contract conferring jurisdiction on the courts at Florence did not have the effect of derogating from Article 5(1) as regards his action to avoid the contract because that action sought to have the whole franchising agreement declared void and, therefore, also the jurisdiction clause. Mr Benincasa further argued that, since he had not yet started trading, he should be regarded as a consumer within the meaning

of the first paragraph of Article 13 and the first paragraph of Article 14 of the Convention.

8. The relevant provisions of the Convention read as follows: Article 13 ‘In proceedings concerning a contract concluded by a person for a purpose which can be regarded as being outside his trade or profession, hereinafter called "the consumer", jurisdiction shall be determined by this Section, without prejudice to the provisions of point 5 of Articles 4 and 5, if it is: 1. a contract for the sale of goods on instalment credit terms, ...’. Article 14 ‘A consumer may bring proceedings against the other party to a contract either in the courts of the Contracting State in which that party is domiciled or in the courts of the Contracting State in which he is himself domiciled. ...’.

9. The Landgericht Munich I declined jurisdiction on the ground that the jurisdiction clause contained in the franchising contract was valid and that the contract was not a contract concluded by a consumer.

10. Mr Benincasa appealed against that decision to the Oberlandesgericht Munich, which stayed proceedings and referred the following questions to the Court for a preliminary ruling:

‘(1) Is a plaintiff to be regarded as a consumer within the meaning of the first paragraph of Article 13 and the first paragraph of Article 14 of the Convention even if his action relates to a contract which he concluded not for the purpose of a trade which he was already pursuing but a trade to be taken up only at a future date (here: a franchising agreement concluded for the purpose of setting up a business)?

(2) If Question 1 is answered in the affirmative: Does point 1 of the first paragraph of Article 13 of the Convention (contract for the sale of goods on instalment credit terms) cover a franchising agreement which obliges the plaintiff to buy from the other party to the agreement, over a period of several (three) years, the articles and goods required to equip and operate a business (without instalment credit terms having been agreed) and to pay an initial fee and, as from the second year of the business, a licence fee of 3% of turnover?

(3) Does the court of a Member State specified in an agreement conferring jurisdiction have exclusive jurisdiction pursuant to the first paragraph of Article 17 of the Convention even when the action is *inter alia* for a declaration of the invalidity of a franchising agreement containing the jurisdiction clause itself, which is worded ‘The courts at Florence shall have jurisdiction to entertain any dispute relating to the interpretation, performance or other aspects of the present contract’, that

clause having been specifically approved within the meaning of Articles 1341 and 1342 of the Italian Civil Code?'

The first question

11. The point sought to be clarified by the national court's first question is whether the first paragraph of Article 13 and the first paragraph of Article 14 of the Convention must be interpreted as meaning that a plaintiff who has concluded a contract with a view to pursuing a trade or profession, not at the present time but in the future, may be regarded as a consumer.

12. In this connection, regard should be had to the principle laid down by the case-law (see, in particular, Case 150/77 *Bertrand* [1978] ECR 1431, paragraphs 14, 15, 16 and 19, and Case C-89/91 *Shearson Lehman Hutton* [1993] ECR I-139, paragraph 13) according to which the concepts used in the Convention, which may have a different content depending on the national law of the Contracting States, must be interpreted independently, by reference principally to the system and objectives of the Convention, in order to ensure that the Convention is uniformly applied in all the Contracting States. This must apply in particular to the concept of 'consumer' within the meaning of Article 13 et seq. of the Convention, in so far as it determines the rules governing jurisdiction.

13. It must next be observed that, as the Court has consistently held, under the system of the Convention the general principle is that the courts of the Contracting State in which the defendant is domiciled are to have jurisdiction and that it is only by way of derogation from that principle that the Convention provides for cases, which are exhaustively listed, in which the defendant may or must, depending on the case, be sued in the courts of another Contracting State. Consequently, the rules of jurisdiction which derogate from that general principle cannot give rise to an interpretation going beyond the cases envisaged by the Convention (*Shearson Lehman Hutton*, paragraphs, 14, 15 and 16).

14. Such an interpretation must apply *a fortiori* with respect to a rule of jurisdiction, such as that contained in Article 14 of the Convention, which allows a consumer, within the meaning of Article 13 of the Convention, to sue the defendant in the courts of the Contracting State in which the plaintiff is domiciled. Apart from the cases expressly provided for, the Convention appears hostile towards the attribution of jurisdiction to the courts of the plaintiff's domicile (see Case C-220/88 *Dumez France and*

Tracoba [1990] ECR I-49, paragraphs 16 and 19, and *Shearson Lehman Hutton*, paragraph 17).

15. As far as the concept of 'consumer' is concerned, the first paragraph of Article 13 of the Convention defines a 'consumer' as a person acting 'for a purpose which can be regarded as being outside his trade or profession'. According to the settled case-law, it follows from the wording and the function of that provision that it affects only a private final consumer, not engaged in any trade or professional activities (*Shearson Lehamn Hutton*, paragraphs 20 and 22).

16. It follows from the foregoing that, in order to determine whether a person has the capacity of a consumer, a concept which must be strictly construed, reference must be made to the position of the person concerned in a particular contract, having regard to the nature and aim of that contract, and not to the subjective situation of the person concerned. As the Advocate General rightly observed at point 38 of his Opinion, the self-same person may be regarded as a consumer in relation to certain transactions and as an economic operator in relation to others.

17. Consequently, only contracts concluded for the purpose of satisfying an individual's own needs in terms of private consumption come under the provisions designed to protect the consumer as the party deemed to be the weaker party economically. The specific protection sought to be afforded by those provisions is unwarranted in the case of contracts for the purpose of trade or professional activity, even if that activity is only planned for the future, since the fact that an activity is in the nature of a future activity does not divest it in any way of its trade or professional character.

18. Accordingly, it is consistent with the wording, the spirit and the aim of the provisions concerned to consider that the specific protective rules enshrined in them apply only to contracts concluded outside and independently of any trade or professional activity or purpose, whether present or future.

19. The answer to the national court's first question must therefore be that the first paragraph of Article 13 and the first paragraph of Article 14 of the Convention must be interpreted as meaning that a plaintiff who has concluded a contract with a view to pursuing a trade or profession, not at the present time but in the future, may not be regarded as a consumer.

The second question

20. In view of the answer given to the first question, there is no need to answer the second.

The third question

21. The point sought to be clarified by the national court's third question is whether the courts of a Contracting State which have been designated in a jurisdiction clause validly concluded under the first paragraph of Article 17 of the Convention also have exclusive jurisdiction where the action seeks in particular a declaration that the contract containing that clause is void.

22. The national court also raises the question whether a jurisdiction clause validly concluded under the rules of the Convention and contained in the main contract must be considered on its own, independently of any allegations as to the validity of the remainder of the contract.

23. The first paragraph of Article 17 of the Convention provides as follows: 'If the parties, one or more of whom is domiciled in a Contracting State, have agreed that a court or the courts of a Contracting State are to have jurisdiction in connection with a particular legal relationship, that court or those courts shall have exclusive jurisdiction. Such an agreement conferring jurisdiction shall be either in writing ...'.

24. A distinction must first be drawn between a jurisdiction clause and the substantive provisions of the contract in which it is incorporated.

25. A jurisdiction clause, which serves a procedural purpose, is governed by the provisions of the Convention, whose aim is to establish uniform rules of international jurisdiction. In contrast, the substantive provisions of the main contract in which that clause is incorporated, and likewise any dispute as to the validity of that contract, are governed by the *lex causae* determined by the private international law of the State of the court having jurisdiction.

26. Next, as the Court has consistently held, the objectives of the Convention include unification of the rules on jurisdiction of the Contracting State's courts, so as to avoid as far as possible the multiplication of the bases of jurisdiction in relation to one and the same legal relationship and to reinforce the legal protection available to

persons established in the Community by, at the same time, allowing the plaintiff easily to identify the court before which he may bring an action and the defendant reasonably to foresee the court before which he may be sued (Case 38/81 *Effer* v *Kantner* [1982] ECR 825, paragraph 6, and Case C-125/92 *Mulox IBC* [1993] ECR I-4075, paragraph 11).

27. It is also consonant with that aim of legal certainty that the court seised should be able readily to decide whether it has jurisdiction on the basis of the rules of the Convention, without having to consider the substance of the case.

28. The aim of securing legal certainty by making it possible reliably to foresee which court will have jurisdiction has been interpreted in connection with Article 17 of the Convention, which accords with the intentions of the parties to the contract and provides for exclusive jurisdiction by dispensing with any objective connection between the relationship in dispute and the court designated, by fixing strict condition as to form (see, in this regard, Case C-106/95 *MSG* [1997] ECR I-0000, paragraph 34).

29. Article 17 of the Convention sets out to designate, clearly and precisely, a court in a Contracting State which is to have jurisdiction in accordance with the consensus formed between the parties, which is to be expressed in accordance with the strict requirements as to form laid down therein. The legal certainty which that provision seeks to secure could easily be jeopardised if one party to the contract could frustrate that rule of the Convention simply by claiming that the whole of the contract was void on grounds derived from the applicable substantive law.

30. That solution is consistent not only with the approach taken by the Court in *Effer* v *Kantner*, cited above, in which it ruled that the plaintiff may invoke jurisdiction of the courts of the place of performance in accordance with Article 5(1) of the Convention even when the existence of the contract on which the claim is based is in dispute between the parties, but also with the judgment in Case 73/77 *Sanders* v *Van der Putte* [1977] ECR 2383, paragraph 15, in which the Court held, in connection with Article 1691) of the Convention, that, in the matter of tenancies of immovable property, the courts of the State in which the immovable property is situated continue to have jurisdiction even where the dispute is concerned with the existence of the lease.

31. It must be added that, as the Court has held, it is for the national court

to interpret the clause conferring jurisdiction invoked before it in order to determine which disputes fall within its scope (Case C-214/89 *Powell Duffryn* [1992] ECR I-1745, paragraph 37). Consequently, in the instant case it is for the national court to determine whether the clause invoked before it, which refers to 'any dispute' relating to the interpretation, performance or 'other aspects' of the contract, also covers any dispute relating to the validity of the contract.

32. The answer to the national court's third question must therefore be that the courts of a Contracting State which have been designated in a jurisdiction clause validly concluded under the first paragraph of Article 17 of the Convention also have exclusive jurisdiction where the action seeks in particular a declaration that the contract containing that clause is void.

On those grounds, the Court (Sixth Chamber), in answer to the question referred to it by the Oberlandesgericht Munich by order of 5 May 1995, hereby rules:

> **1. The first paragraph of Article 13 and the first paragraph of Article 14 of the Convention of 27 September 1968 on jurisdiction and the enforcement of judgments in civil and commercial matters, as amended by the Convention of 9 October 1978 on the accession of the Kingdom of Denmark, Ireland and the United Kingdom of Great Britain and Northern Ireland, must be interpreted as meaning that a plaintiff who has concluded a contract with a view to pursuing a trade or profession, not at the present time but in the future, may not be regarded as a consumer.**
>
> **2. The courts of a Contracting State which have been designated in a jurisdiction clause validly concluded under the first paragraph of Article 17 of the Convention of 27 September 1968 also have exclusive jurisdiction where the action seeks in particular a declaration that the contract containing that clause is void.**

OPINION OF MR ADVOCATE GENERAL RUIZ-JARABO CLOMER

1. In this case the Oberlandesgericht (Higher Regional Court), Munich, requests a preliminary ruling on three questions concerning the interpretation of

Articles 13, 14 and 17 of the Convention of 27 September 1968 on jurisdiction and the enforcement of judgments in civil and commercial matters ('the Brussels Convention'), as amended by the Convention of 9 October 1978 on the accession of the Kingdom of Denmark, Ireland and the United Kingdom of Great Britain and Northern Ireland.

2. The questions, which have been referred to the Court pursuant to the Protocol of 3 June 1971 on the interpretation of the Brussels Convention by the Court of Justice relate to the concepts of consumer contract and sale of goods on instalment credit terms, both used in Article 13 of the Convention, and identification of the competent court to take cognizance of a dispute concerning an agreement conferring jurisdiction of the kind referred to in Article 17 of the Convention.

Facts and main proceedings according to the order for reference

3. Dentalkit Srl (hereinafter 'Dentalkit'), a company whose registered office is in Florence (Italy), is the promoter of a chain of franchise shops specializing in the sale of dental hygiene products.

4. On 28 September 1992 Dentalkit and Francesco Benincasa, an Italian national, concluded a franchise agreement in Florence for the opening and operation of a shop in Munich, where Mr Benincasa stated that he resided.

5. Under clause 2 of the agreement Dentalkit undertook, inter alia, (a) to allow use of the Dentalkit trade mark for naming the sales outlet; (b) to grant the exclusive right to use the mark within a specified area; (c) to give the necessary assistance in opening the establishment; (d) to supply a list of products; (e) to supply the goods; (f) to give assistance in the presentation of the products; (g) to pass on the technical and commercial expertise and know-how in its possession; (h) to give assistance in planning advertising and local sales promotion schemes; (i) to supply certain printed matter; (l) to provide theoretical and practical training; (m) to carry out an advertising and sales promotion campaign at national level; and (n) not to open any other sales outlet within the exclusive territory.

6. Under clause 3 of the agreement, Mr Benincasa for his part undertook (a) to arrange for registration in the commercial register and to obtain the requisite authorizations; (b) to keep the business premises available for the term of the agreement; (c) to fit out the premises in the same manner as existing Dentalkit shops; (d) to sell only products supplied by Dentalkit and to keep suitable stocks of them; (e) to suggest new products which could be introduced to fit in with the range; (f) to keep the premises in proper condition and to offer customers an efficient, skilled service; (g) to use the business name and logo in accordance with Dentalkit's instructions, without alteration; (h) to maintain secrecy with regard to information and documentation relating to the 'Dentalkit system'; and (i) to carry out advertising campaigns and local sales promotion at his own expense, by prior agreement with Dentalkit.

7. Finally, Mr Benincasa undertook to pay the defendant LIT 8 000 000 to cover the cost of technical and commercial assistance in opening the shop and, after the first 12 months of trading, 3% of the annual turnover in consideration of the use of the business names and marks granted exclusively for the specified territory.

8. When concluding the agreement, the original term of which was three years and could be extended tacitly, the two parties signed a document in Italian, which is generally used by Dentalkit for that purpose.

9. Mr Benincasa opened the shop, paid the initial sum of LIT 8 000 000 and made various purchases, for which he did not pay. In the meantime he ceased trading. Subsequently he brought an action against the defendant before the Landgericht (Regional Court) Munich I, seeking:

(a) repayment of LIT 8 000 000, together with 12% interest from the date of service of the writ (27 December 1993),

(b) a declaration that the franchise agreement of 28 September 1992 is void and that, consequently, the contracts of sale concluded thereunder are also void.

10. Mr Benincasa contends that the franchise agreement is void on the grounds, first, that it is contrary to Paragraph 138 of the Bürgerliches Gesetzbuch (German Civil Code, 'BGB') and, second, that the agreement lays down an obligation for more than two years without complying with Paragraph 11(12)(a), in conjunction with Paragraph 6, of the Gesetz über die Allgemeinen Geschäftsbedingungen (Law on standard business conditions). He also challenges the agreement on the grounds of mistake pursuant to Paragraph 119 of the BGB and fraudulent misrepresentation pursuant to Paragraph 123 of the BGB.

11. In its defence, Dentalkit asked the court to dismiss Mr Benincasa's claim, but first raised the objection that the German court before which the action had been brought had no international or local jurisdiction. In Dentalkit's opinion, the courts of Florence had exclusive jurisdiction by virtue of the jurisdiction clause included by the parties in the franchise agreement (clause 12).

12. Mr Benincasa's observations in reply to that procedural objection were in essence as follows:

(a) the Landgericht Munich was the court for the place of performance of the obligation in question, within the meaning of Article 5(1) of the Brussels Convention;

(b) the clause conferring jurisdiction on the courts of Florence did not have the effect of excluding jurisdiction to hear his action because he sought the annulment of the entire agreement, including that clause;

(c) application of the jurisdiction clause was also excluded by point 1 of the first paragraph of Article 13 and the first paragraph of Article 14 of the Brussels Convention so that, in accordance with the third paragraph of Article 17 and Article 15 of the Convention, that clause could not take effect.

13. In support of the last-mentioned submission, Mr Benincasa states that when he concluded the franchise agreement he was not carrying on a business and that therefore he should be regarded as a consumer within the meaning of the first paragraph of Article 13 of the Brussels Convention. He bases that view on a teleological interpretation of that provision in the light of an objective of the EC Treaty, namely to ensure a high level of protection for the final consumer.

14. By judgment of 19 July 1993 the Landgericht Munich I upheld Dentalkit's objection and therefore declared the action inadmissible for lack of international jurisdiction.

15. Consequently the national court took the view that the jurisdiction

clause in the franchise agreement was valid and, in accordance with Article 17 of the Brussels Convention, found that the courts of Florence had jurisdiction.

16. The judgment found that the agreement was not a consumer contract, which meant that in this case Article 13 of the Brussels Convention could not be relied on to defeat the jurisdiction clause. It was clear from the actual wording, as well as the purpose, of the first paragraph of Article 13 of the Convention that an agreement intended to establish a trade or profession must be deemed to have been concluded for the purpose of a trade or profession.

17. In the opinion of the Landgericht Munich I, the other conclusions reached by applying the German Verbraucherkreditgesetz (Law on consumer credit) are not relevant to the interpretation of Article 13 of the Brussels Convention, which must be construed independently. Finally, the agreement in question did not fulfil the other requirements for a consumer contract.

18. The plaintiff lodged an appeal against the judgment given at first instance, which Dentalkit considers should be dismissed. In the appeal proceedings both parties in essence repeat their opposing arguments concerning the international jurisdiction of the German courts.

19. In view of the doubts raised regarding interpretation of the Brussels Convention, the appeal court has referred the following questions to the Court of Justice:

'(1) Is a plaintiff to be regarded as a consumer within the meaning of the first paragraph of Article 13 and the first paragraph of Article 14 of the Brussels Convention even if his action relates to a contract which he concluded not for the purpose of a trade which he was already pursuing but a trade to be taken up only at a future date (here: a franchise agreement concluded for the purpose of setting up a business)?

(2) If Question 1 is to be answered in the affirmative: Does point 1 of the first paragraph of Article 13 of the Convention (contract for the sale of goods on instalment credit terms) cover a franchising agreement which obliges the plaintiff to buy from the other party to the agreement, over a period of several (three) years, the articles and goods required to equip and operate a business (without instalment credit terms having been agreed) and to pay an initial fee and, as from the second year of the business, a licence fee of 3% of turnover?

(3) Does the court of a Member State specified in an agreement conferring jurisdiction have exclusive jurisdiction pursuant to the first sentence of the first paragraph of Article 17 of the Convention even when an action is inter alia for a declaration of the invalidity of a franchising agreement containing the jurisdiction clause itself, which is worded: "The courts at Florence shall have jurisdiction to entertain any dispute relating to the interpretation, performance or other aspects of the present contract", that clause having been specifically approved within the meaning of Articles 1341 and 1342 of the Italian Codice Civile?'

The provisions of the Brussels Convention to be construed

20. Section 4 of the Brussels Convention is entitled 'Jurisdiction over consumer contracts'.

21. Article 13, which forms part of that Section, provides as follows:

'In proceedings concerning a contract concluded by a person for a purpose which can be regarded as being outside his trade or profession, hereinafter called "the consumer", jurisdiction shall be determined by this Section, without prejudice to the provisions of Articles 4 and 5(5), if it is:

(1) a contract for the sale of goods on instalment credit terms, or

(2) a contract for a loan repayable by instalments, or for any other form of credit, made to finance the sale of goods, or

(3) any other contract for the supply of goods or a contract for the supply of services, and

(a) in the State of the consumer's domicile the conclusion of the contract was preceded by a specific invitation addressed to him or by advertising, and

(b) the consumer took in that State the steps necessary for the conclusion of the contract.

Where a consumer enters into a contract with a party who is not domiciled in a Contracting State but has a branch, agency or other establishment in one of the Contracting States, that party shall, in disputes arising out of the operation of the branch, agency or establishment, be deemed to be domiciled in that State.

[...]'

22. Article 14 of the Brussels Convention provides as follows:

'A consumer may bring proceedings against the other party to a contract either in the courts of the Contracting State in which that party is domiciled or in the courts of the Contracting State in which he himself is domiciled.

Proceedings may be brought against a consumer by the other party to the contract only in the courts of the Contracting State in which the consumer is domiciled.

These provisions shall not affect the right to bring a counterclaim in the court in which, in accordance with this Section, the original claim is pending.'

23. Finally, Article 17 of the Brussels Convention, which forms part of Section 6 entitled 'Prorogation of jurisdiction', is worded as follows:

'If the parties, one or more of whom is domiciled in a Contracting State, have agreed that a court or the courts of a Contracting State are to have jurisdiction to settle any disputes which have arisen or which may arise in connection with a particular legal relationship, that court or those courts shall have exclusive jurisdiction. Such an agreement conferring jurisdiction shall be either:

(a) in writing or evidenced in writing, or

(b) in a form which accords with practices which the parties have established between themselves, or

(c) in international trade or commerce, in a form which accords with a usage of which the parties are or ought to have been aware and which in such trade or commerce is widely known to, and regularly observed by, parties to contracts of the type involved in the particular trade or commerce concerned.

Where such an agreement is concluded by parties, none of whom is domiciled in a Contracting State, the courts of other Contracting States shall have no jurisdiction over their disputes unless the court or courts chosen have declined jurisdiction.

[...]

Agreements ... conferring jurisdiction shall have no legal force if they are contrary to the provisions of Article 12 or 15, or if the courts whose jurisdiction they purport to exclude have exclusive jurisdiction by virtue of Article 16.

If an agreement conferring jurisdiction was concluded for the benefit of only one of the parties, that party shall retain the right to bring proceedings in any other court which has jurisdiction by virtue of this Convention.

[...]'

Question 1

24. To answer the first question from the national court, the Court of Justice must decide whether a franchise agreement signed by a person who has not previously carried on a business should be classified as a contract 'for a purpose which can be regarded as being outside his trade or profession', within the meaning of Article 13 of the Brussels Convention.

25. I shall begin by examining franchise agreements and go on to consider the Court's case-law relating to the term 'consumer contracts' in Article 13 of the Brussels Convention. This will lead to my conclusion that the term is not applicable to agreements of that kind.

(i) Franchise agreements

26. Franchise agreements are a widespread form of business arrangement whereby one undertaking, the franchiser, grants to another, the franchisee, the right to exploit its own system for marketing goods or services.

27. Natural or legal persons who act as franchisers normally establish a network of franchises in a particular field of commerce. They offer to include future franchisees in the network, by concluding a contract setting out the principal stipulations of the bilateral agreement. In most cases this a standard-form contract.

28. The franchisee is legally independent. He is a genuinely independent trader carrying on his own business and engaging in commercial transactions (he purchases goods from his supplier for resale to his customers).

29. The Court of Justice considered this form of business from the viewpoint of freedom of competition in its judgment of 28 January 1986 in Pronuptia, which relates to atypical distribution franchise agreements under which the franchisee merely sells certain products in a shop which bears the franchiser's business name.

30. In paragraph 15 of that judgment the Court outlined the main features of the relationship between franchisers and franchisees, stressing that the latter are independent traders:

'In a system of distribution franchises of that kind, an undertaking which has established itself as a distributor on a given market and thus developed certain business methods grants independent traders, for a fee, the right to establish themselves in other markets, using its business name and the business methods which have made it successful. Rather than a method of distribution, it is a way for an undertaking to derive financial benefit from its expertise without investing its own capital. Moreover, the system gives traders who do not have the necessary experience access to methods which they could not have learned without considerable effort and allows them to benefit from the reputation of the franchiser's business name.'

31. Article 1 of Commission Regulation (EEC) No 4087/88 of 30 November 1988 on the application of Article 85(3) of the Treaty to categories of franchise agreements also presumes that a franchise agreement is entered into by two 'undertakings', that is to say two economic entities operating on a commercial basis.

(ii) The Court's case-law relating to 'consumer contracts'

32. The Shearson Lehman Hutton judgment of 19 January 1993 clearly set out the requirements for contracts of this kind and the position to be taken by national courts when construing Article 13 of the Brussels Convention.

33. That judgment begins by referring to 'the principle, established by case-law [the judgments in Case 150/77 *Bertrand* [1978] ECR 1431, paragraphs 14 to 16 and 19; Case C-26/91 *Handte* [1992] ECR I-3967, paragraph 10], according to which the concepts used in the Convention, which may have a different content depending on the national law of the Contracting States, must be interpreted independently, by reference principally to the system and objectives of the Convention, in order to ensure that the Convention is uniformly applied in all the Contracting States. This rule must apply in particular to the concept of "consumer" within the meaning of Article 13 et seq. of the Convention, in so far as that concept is the principal factor in the determination of rules governing jurisdiction.'

34. The judgment goes on to describe the interaction between the general and the special rules concerning jurisdiction:

- under the system of the Convention, the general principle, stated in the first paragraph of Article 2, is that the national courts of the Contracting State in which the defendant is domiciled are to have jurisdiction.
- it is only by way of derogation from that general principle that the Convention provides for the cases, exhaustively listed in Sections 2 to 6 of Title II, in which a defendant domiciled or established in a Contracting State may, where the situation comes under a rule of exclusive jurisdiction or of prorogation of jurisdiction, be sued in the courts of another Contracting State.
- consequently, the rules of jurisdiction which derogate from that general principle cannot give rise to an interpretation going beyond the cases envisaged by the Convention.

35. In paragraph 17 of the judgment the Court observes that 'such an interpretation must apply a fortiori with respect to a rule of jurisdiction such as that contained in Article 14 of the Convention, which allows a consumer, within the meaning of Article 13 of the Convention, to sue the defendant in the courts of the Contracting State in which the plaintiff is domiciled. Apart from the cases expressly provided for, the Convention appears clearly hostile towards the attribution of jurisdiction to the courts of the plaintiff's domicile (see the judgment in Case C-220/88 *Dumez France* [1990] ECR I-49, paragraphs 16 and 19).'

36. After those detailed observations concerning the principles for construing the rules governing jurisdiction, the judgment clarifies the definition of 'consumer' for the purpose of Articles 13 and 14 of the Brussels Convention: 'It follows from the wording and the function of those provisions that they affect only a private final consumer, not engaged in trade or professional activities (see the

Bertrand judgment cited in paragraph 21 above, and the Expert Report drawn up when the Kingdom of Denmark, Ireland and the United Kingdom of Great Britain and Northern Ireland acceded to the Convention on jurisdiction and the enforcement of judgments in civil and commercial matters, OJ 1979 C 59, p. 71), who is bound by one of the contracts listed in Article 13 and who is a party to the action in accordance with Article 14.'

(iii) Application of those principles to franchise agreements

37. In view of those considerations, it cannot be said that the parties to a franchise agreement are 'consumers' for the purpose of Article 13 of the Brussels Convention.

38. The status of consumer referred to by Article 13 is not determined by a pre-existing subjective situation: thc same natural person may be a consumer for certain purposes and an entrepreneur for others. The decisive factor is, therefore, not thc personal circumstances of the individual but rather his position under a particular contract, having regard to its scope and purpose.

39. Where contracts such as franchise agreements are concerned, which are clearly of a commercial nature and necessarily relate to a trade or profession of the parties, the latter's personal circumstances before the formation of the contract are irrelevant for the purpose of Article 13.

40. Contrary to the appellant's view - which was expounded at greater length during the oral procedure - I certainly do not consider that the Court should disregard or water down the traditional principle of autonomous interpretation of the terms, including 'consumer', used in the Brussels Convention.

41. In my opinion, the autonomous interpretation of 'consumer' to which I referred in connection with the Shearson Lehman Hutton judgment is preferable to an interpretation which relies on national law, and there are two reasons for that view:

(a) national legislation need not coincide from one State to another and may differ slightly in certain respects, depending on the particular case. To rely on one body of legislation rather than another (and what would be the criterion for making the choice?) would prejudice the legal certainty which the Brussels Convention aims to ensure;

(b) the same national legislation may contain different definitions of 'consumer', depending on the field of law in which they occur.

42. In the opinion of counsel for the appellant, the Court should give primacy to the German definition of 'consumer' deriving from the German Law on consumer credit (Verbraucherkreditgesetz), which confers the status of consumers upon persons applying for credit in order to pursue an activity which they had not previously taken up.

43. I do not agree with that argument: it is also opposed by the German Government itself which, in its written observations, points out that that wider definition of 'consumer' was expressly and intentionally formulated by the national legislature to go beyond the minimum standard laid down by the Directive which the Law on consumer credit was intended to implement so as to offer consumers a higher level of protection than that provided for by the Community measure.

44. According to the German Government, the Community definition of 'consumer' in the Directive on consumer credit excludes not only persons who are parties to contracts relating to a trade or profession 'already taken up' (in the actual words of the Law on consumer credit), but also generally persons who are parties to contracts which are concluded for the purpose of a trade or profession.

45. In the same observations, the German Government adds that in its legal system a narrower definition of 'consumer' is used in other consumer protection measures: for example, the Law on the cancellation of doorstep sales (Haustürwiderrufsgesetz).

46. All this merely confirms the necessity to adhere to the autonomous interpretation of the definition of 'consumer' in Article 13 of the Brussels Convention, which need not be linked to the definitions used in individual cases in the respective national legal systems.

47. Finally, the view I have just put forward is not contradicted by the inclusion in the EC Treaty of a new Title XI on consumer protection, in which Article 129a lays down 'a high level of consumer protection' as an objective of the Community. First, the legal scope of that provision is limited and, secondly, Article 129a(3) expressly permits Member States to maintain or introduce more stringent protective measures. It follows logically that the Community level of protection need not be identified with the level obtaining in one or more of the Member States.

48. To sum up, it is in my view necessary to uphold the autonomous interpretation of the term 'consumer' used in the Brussels Convention, as the Court did in the Shearson Lehman Hutton judgment, which means that the term must be limited to private final consumers not acting in the capacity of parties to contracts concerning their trade or professional activities.

49. Sometimes, no doubt, franchisees do not have previous business experience, but this does not justify describing the activity covered by the franchise agreement as being outside a trade or profession. It is precisely the activity in question - and not, I emphasize, the existing personal circumstances of the party to the agreement - which was the factor taken into account when special rules of jurisdiction in relation to certain contracts were laid down in Article 13 of the Convention.

50. Therefore, the wording of Article 13 does not permit it to be extended to cover any contract, irrespective of its subject-matter and purpose, in which an economically weaker party is faced by a party in a position which is objectively superior or superior by reason of the circumstances.

51. Contracting parties are not normally in a position of equality in the area of business relationships, but that does not mean that contracts of that kind, including standard-form contracts, entered into by businessmen benefit from the special rule in Article 13. Although that provision aims to protect the weaker party in a contractual relationship, its scope is limited to contracts in which one party is acting for purposes unrelated to a business activity, that is to say as a 'private final consumer, not engaged in trade or professional activities'.

52. In other words, the mere fact that one of the parties to a contract concluded with a view to the pursuit of a trade or professional activity or in the

course of such activities is in an inferior position, as in the case of franchise agreements, is not regarded by the Brussels Convention as requiring special protection in relation to the attribution of jurisdiction.

53. Therefore I consider that the Court's reply to the first question should be that Article 13 of the Brussels Convention does not apply to a contract such as that in the present case.

Question 2

54. The national court's second question falls to be answered only if the Court's reply to the first is that Article 13 of the Brussels Convention does apply to a contract such as that in the present case. In view of my proposed reply to the first question, it is unnecessary, in my opinion, to answer the second.

55. Should the Court find that Article 13 is applicable, it will have to reply to the second question from the Oberlandesgericht Munich concerning the interpretation of point 1 of the first paragraph of Article 13, relating to the sale of goods on instalment credit terms.

56. Specifically, the national court asks whether or not the legal concept 'contract for the sale of goods on instalment credit terms' covers a franchise agreement under which one party undertakes to buy from the franchiser, over a period of three years, the articles and goods required to equip and operate a business, without instalment credit terms having been agreed. In that connection the franchisee's only obligations are to pay an initial fee and, as from the second year, a licence fee of 3% of his turnover.

57. The significance of the second question lies in the fact that Article 13 of the Brussels Convention not only requires the contract to have been concluded for a purpose which can be regarded as being outside any trade or profession, but also requires it to belong to one of the three categories described in points 1, 2 and 3 of the first paragraph, point 1 being 'contracts for the sale of goods on instalment credit terms'.

58. In my view, the reply to this question must also be in the negative. Contracts for the sale of goods on instalment credit terms cannot be confused with other contracts which, although entailing successive obligations, possess features quite different from those of a sale on instalment credit terms.

59. In the present case, the national court itself observes that the instalment credit rules do not apply to the purchases which the franchisee undertakes to make from the franchiser during the three-year term of the agreement, which makes no provision for the payment of instalments for the goods on successive, predetermined dates.

60. The fact that a contract provides for successive obligations to be performed by one or both parties does not in itself justify treating it as a 'sale of goods on instalment credit terms'.

61. The periodical purchases which the franchisee has to make under a franchise agreement are the consequence or effect of the initial contract which, as such, bears no resemblance at all to a sale on instalment credit terms for the purpose of Article 13 of the Brussels Convention.

62. Furthermore, those periodical purchases are not in this case even subject to provisions relating to the sale of goods on instalment credit terms.

63. Still less can it be concluded from the fact that the franchisee has to pay at regular intervals a sum equal to 3% of his annual turnover for the use of the franchiser's business names that there is a sale of goods on instalment credit terms. It is quite clear that in such circumstances no bilateral contract for the sale of goods exists, whether by instalments or for cash.

64. Consequently, if a reply is required to the second question, in my opinion the Court should answer in the negative.

Question 3

65. The third question is wider in scope. In essence, the national court asks whether, pursuant to the first paragraph of Article 17 of the Brussels Convention, the 'court with exclusive jurisdiction' designated by the parties in a jurisdiction clause is also competent to adjudicate in an action for the annulment of the contract containing the jurisdiction clause.

66. Let me begin with two points which seem to me important:

(a) it is not disputed that the jurisdiction clause in the agreement in question meets the formal requirements of Article 17 of the Brussels Convention;

(b) the jurisdiction clause is in the most general terms possible, as it relates to 'any dispute concerning the interpretation, performance or other aspect of this contract', and it is stipulated that any such dispute must be brought before the courts of Florence.

67. In my view, an agreement conferring jurisdiction such as that in the present case, which is formally valid under the Brussels Convention and has been stipulated by the parties in order to settle future differences of any kind concerning any aspect of the contract, is applicable to any legal disputes which may arise, including those relating to the requirements for the validity of the contract containing the jurisdiction clause.

68. In its judgment in Effer SpA the Court examined a similar problem relating to the ambit of Article 5 of the Brussels Convention. The question in that case was whether the courts for the place of performance of the contract had jurisdiction when the dispute between the parties concerned the very existence of the main contract or the conditions for its formation.

69. The Court found that the national court's jurisdiction to determine questions relating to a contract included the power to consider the existence of the constituent parts of the contract itself since that was indispensable in order to enable the national court to examine whether it had jurisdiction under Article 5 of the Convention.

70. That view was strengthened by consideration of the harmful effects on legal certainty if that were not the case. The provisions of the Brussels Convention would be liable to be deprived of their legal effect if it were accepted that, in order to defeat them, it would be sufficient for one of the parties merely to claim that the contract did not exist.

71. The Court added that, on the contrary, respect for the aims and spirit of the Convention demanded that its provisions should be construed as meaning that the court called upon to decide a dispute arising out of a contract may examine, even of its own motion, the essential preconditions for its jurisdiction, having regard to conclusive and relevant evidence adduced by

the party concerned, establishing the existence or the non-existence of the contract.

72. The same arguments are applicable by analogy to the present case, where the issue is the validity, not the existence, of the contract. The difference between this situation and that considered in the Effer judgment cited above is that territorial jurisdiction was determined in the latter case by a legal criterion (the place of performance of the obligation), and not by a jurisdiction clause in the contract. In my opinion, however, the legal reasoning used in the earlier case applies equally to both situations.

73. It is possible to reach the same conclusion by analysing the nature of the jurisdiction clauses provided for by Article 17 of the Brussels Convention. In my opinion, it must be recognized that they are to some extent independent of the contract of which they form part.

74. This question is the subject of a well-known academic controversy which has not been settled. However, I consider that, so far as Article 17 of the Brussels Convention is concerned, the Court should take the same approach as in the Effer judgment and incline towards the view which promotes legal certainty and which, specifically, means recognizing the court chosen in a jurisdiction clause (provided, of course, that the latter fulfils the requirements of Article 17) as the competent court, even when it is alleged that the contract containing the clause is void.

75. There are a number of reasons for taking this approach. First, jurisdiction clauses do not depend on the economic or legal factors forming the basis of the contract, nor is the causa of the contract the same as that of the jurisdiction clause, the purpose of which is merely procedural (to locate within a particular forum proceedings to deal with any future disputes). Consequently, any grounds of nullity which might affect the substantive elements of a contract should not have any impact on jurisdiction clauses.

76. Secondly, if one party alleges that there was no consensus ad idem - for example, that there was a mistake as to essential aspects of the subject-matter, rendering the mutual obligations void - the jurisdiction clause is not necessarily affected because the mistake does not extend to the express choice of the competent court. This applies a fortiori where the alleged grounds of nullity of the contract relate to its compatibility or otherwise with the substantive law of a particular national system.

77. Thirdly, if a court other than that designated by the parties in a jurisdiction clause were allowed to decide on the validity of the contract in general, the practical consequences would be rather disconcerting. If, for example, such proceedings led to a decision that the contract in general was valid, the court in question would immediately have to decline jurisdiction in favour of the court chosen by the parties, which has exclusive jurisdiction to settle their differences. It would be difficult to deny that the latter court in turn would not be competent to rule that the contract or any of its essential stipulations was invalid, even if by so doing it contradicted the judgment of the first court.

78. Finally, the approach that I advocate has the advantage of avoiding concurrent litigation and preventing circumvention of the very system whereby only

one forum should have jurisdiction, which forms the basis of the Brussels Convention. Merely by claiming that the contract containing the jurisdiction clause was void, either party would displace the jurisdiction rules and thereby render Article 17 ineffective. That would certainly detract from certainty and foreseeability in designating the competent court.

79. In that connection I should point out that neither party to this action has questioned the validity of the jurisdiction clause itself on substantive or on formal grounds. Mr Benincasa merely claims that the franchise agreement is void in general on grounds based on substantive German law (alleged infringement of the BGB and the German Law on standard business conditions).

80. The response to those allegations, that is to say the decision on the validity of the franchise agreement, will depend on the substantive law found to be applicable to it. However, I consider that the competent court to give a ruling on that point - since the parties have stipulated a jurisdiction clause in such general terms - must be precisely the court designated by them beforehand.

81. The parties' intention expressed in the jurisdiction clause is clear: 'any dispute' concerning any 'aspect' of the contract (which must include disputes on validity) falls within the jurisdiction of the courts of Florence.

82. On this point it is inevitable that the Court's reply cannot be limited to a hypothetical interpretation of Article 17 of the Brussels Convention, unconnected with the dispute with which the question from the national court is concerned. Without any intention to take the place of the competent national court in interpreting the agreement between the parties, a helpful reply from the Court of Justice, under the preliminary-ruling procedure, necessitates an analysis of the terms of the jurisdiction clause in order, by reference to its characteristics, to provide the national court with an interpretation of the Brussels Convention, as requested.

Conclusion

83. I therefore propose that the Court reply as follows to the questions from the Oberlandesgericht Munich:

(1) The parties to a franchise agreement for the forthcoming opening of a commercial establishment cannot be regarded as consumers within the meaning of the first paragraph of Article 13 and the first paragraph of Article 14 of the Brussels Convention.

(2) The court designated in a jurisdiction clause as having jurisdiction 'to entertain any dispute relating to the interpretation, performance or other aspect of this contract' has exclusive jurisdiction, in accordance with the first sentence of the first paragraph of Article 17 of the Brussels Convention, even where the action seeks, inter alia, annulment of the contract containing the jurisdiction clause.

Case C-99/96 - 27 April 1999

Hans-Hermann Mietz
v
Intership Yachting Sneek BV

Jurisdiction over consumer contracts - 'Sale of goods on instalment credit terms' - Contract for the manufacture of goods for a price payable in several instalments before the goods are transferred to the purchaser - Excluded - Contract for the supply of services or goods.
Article 24 - Enforcement - 'Provisional measure' ordering interim payment - Excluded - Conditions.
Articles 18 & 24 - Prorogation of jurisdiction - Interim proceedings designed to obtain provisional or protective measures - Appearance by the defendant - Effects.

Summary

1. In the area of consumer contracts, Article 13, first paragraph, point 1, of the Convention of 27 September 1968 on Jurisdiction and the Enforcement of Judgments in Civil and Commercial Matters must be construed as not applying to a contract between two parties having the following characteristics, that is to say, a contract:

- relating to the manufacture by the first contracting party of goods corresponding to a standard model, to which certain alterations have been made;
- by which the first contracting party has undertaken to transfer the property in those goods to the second contracting party, who has undertaken, by way of consideration, to pay the price in several instalments; and
- in which provision is made for the final instalment to be paid before possession of the goods is transferred definitively to the second contracting party.

That provision is intended to protect the purchaser only where the vendor has granted him credit, that is to say, where the vendor has transferred to the purchaser possession of the goods in question before the purchaser has paid the full price. A contract having the characteristics mentioned above, is however, to be classified as a contract for the supply of services or of goods within the meaning of Article 13, first paragraph, point 3, of the Convention.

2. A judgment cannot be the subject of an enforcement order under Title III of the Convention of 27 September 1968 in a case where

- it was delivered at the end of proceedings which were not, by their very nature, proceedings as to substance, but summary proceedings for the granting of interim measures;
- the defendant was not domiciled in the Contracting State of the court of origin and it does not appear from the judgement that, for other reasons, that court had jurisdiction under the Convention as to the substance of the matter;
- it does not contain any statement of reasons designed to establish the jurisdiction of the court of origin as to the substance of the matter and
- it is limited to ordering the payment of a contractual consideration, without, on the one hand, repayment to the defendant of the sum awarded being guaranteed if the plaintiff is unsuccessful as regards the substance of his claim or, on the other, the measure sought relating only to specific assets of the defendant located or to be located within the confines of the territorial jurisdiction of the court to which application is made.

In such a case, the court to which application for enforcement is made must conclude that the measure ordered is not a provisional measure within the meaning of Article 24 of the Convention.

3. The fact that the defendant appears before the court dealing with interim measures in the context of fast procedures intended to grant provisional or protective measures in case of urgency and which do not prejudice the examination of the substance cannot, by itself, suffice to confer on that court, by virtue of Article 18 of the Convention of 27 September 1968, unlimited jurisdiction to order any provisional or protective measure which the court might consider appropriate if it had jurisdiction under the Convention as to the substance of the matter.

JUDGMENT OF THE COURT

Presiding, Lecourt, President, Rodriguez Iglesias, Presidents of Chambers, Kapteyn, Puissochet, Hirsch and Jann, Rapporteur, Mancini, Moitinho de Almeida, Gulmann, Murray, Edward Judges, Ragnemalm, Sevon and Wathelet.

1. By order of 29 February 1996, received at the Court on 26 March 1996, the Bundesgerichtshof (Federal Court of Justice) referred to the Court for a preliminary ruling under the Protocol of 3 June 1971 on the Interpretation by the Court of Justice of the Convention of 27 September 1968 on Jurisdiction and the Enforcement of Judgments in Civil and Commercial Matters four questions on the interpretation of Article 13, first paragraph, points 1 and 3, Article 24, Article 28, second paragraph, and Article 34, second paragraph, of the above Convention of 27 September 1968 (OJ 1978 L 304, p. 36), as amended by the Convention of 9 October 1978 on the Accession of the Kingdom of Denmark, Ireland and the United Kingdom of Great Britain and Northern Ireland (OJ 1978 L 304, p. 1 and - amended text - p. 77) and by the Convention of 25 October 1982 on the Accession of the Hellenic Republic (OJ 1982 L 388, p. 1) ('the Convention').

2. Those questions have arisen in proceedings brought before a German court with a view to securing an order in Germany for the enforcement of a judgment delivered on 12 May 1993 ('the Netherlands judgment') by the President of the Arrondissementsrechtbank te Leeuwarden (Regional Court, Leeuwarden) (Netherlands) ('the court of origin') following adversarial interim proceedings ('*kort geding*') between Intership Yachting Sneek BV ('Intership Yachting'), a limited-liability company established in Sneek (Netherlands), and Mr Mietz, who is domiciled in Lüchow (Germany).

3. Under the system of the Convention, the general rule in regard to the jurisdiction of courts, set out in the first paragraph of Article 2, is that persons domiciled in a Contracting State must, whatever their nationality, be sued in the courts of that State.

4. The first paragraph of Article 3 of the Convention provides that persons domiciled in a Contracting State may be sued in the courts of another Contracting State only by virtue of the rules set out in Sections 2 to 6 of Title II, that is to say, the rules set out in Articles 5 to 18 of the Convention.

5. Articles 13 and 14 form part of Section 4, entitled 'Jurisdiction over consumer contracts', of Title II of the Convention. The first paragraph of Article 13 provides as follows:

'In proceedings concerning a contract concluded by a person for a purpose which can be regarded as being outside his trade or profession, hereinafter called "the consumer", jurisdiction shall be determined by this Section, without prejudice to the provisions of [Articles 4 and 5(5)], if it is:

1. a contract for the sale of goods on instalment credit terms; or
2. a contract for a loan repayable by instalments, or for any other form of credit, made to finance the sale of goods; or
3. any other contract for the supply of goods or a contract for the supply of services, and

(a) in the State of the consumer's domicile the conclusion of the contract was preceded by a specific invitation addressed to him or by advertising; and

(b) the consumer took in that State the steps necessary for the conclusion of the contract.'

6. The second paragraph of Article 14 of the Convention provides as follows: 'Proceedings may be brought against a consumer by the other party to the contract only in the courts of the Contracting State in which the consumer is domiciled.'

7. In addition, Article 24, which constitutes Section 9 of Title II of the Convention and specifically governs provisional and protective measures, provides as follows: 'Application may be made to the courts of a Contracting State for such provisional, including protective, measures as may be available under the law of that State, even if, under this Convention, the courts of another Contracting State have jurisdiction as to the substance of the matter.'

8. The rules governing recognition and enforcement of judgments are found in Title III of the Convention. Article 28, which appears in Section 1 of Title III, entitled 'Recognition', provides as follows: 'Moreover, a judgment shall not be recognised if it conflicts with the provisions of Sections 3, 4 or 5 of Title II, or in a case provided for in Article 59.

In its examination of the grounds of jurisdiction referred to in the foregoing paragraph, the court or authority applied to shall be bound by the findings of fact on which the court of the State of origin based its jurisdiction.

Subject to the provisions of the first paragraph, the jurisdiction of the court of the State of origin may not be reviewed; the test of public policy referred to in point 1 of Article 27 may not be applied to the rules relating to jurisdiction.'

9. Article 29, which also appears in Section 1 of Title III of the Convention, provides that:
'Under no circumstances may a foreign judgment be reviewed as to its substance.'

10. The second and third paragraphs of Article 34, which forms part of Section 2, entitled 'Enforcement', of Title III of the Convention, are worded as follows: 'The application may be refused only for one of the reasons specified in Articles 27 and 28.
Under no circumstances may the foreign judgment be reviewed as to its substance.'

11. Mr Mietz and Intership Yachting concluded in writing in Sneek a 'contract of sale' for the purchase of an Intership Type 1.150 G vessel, to which a number of alterations were to be made. As consideration, Mr Mietz was to pay DM 250 000 in five instalments.

12. Mr Mietz having failed to meet in full his obligation to pay the price, Intership Yachting obtained the Netherlands judgment, by which Mr Mietz was ordered, inter alia, to pay to Intership Yachting the sum of DM 143 750, plus interest. That judgment was declared to be provisionally enforceable.

13. On 29 October 1993 the Landgericht (Regional Court) Lüneburg (Germany), on the application of Intership Yachting, declared the Netherlands judgment to be enforceable and issued an order for its enforcement.

14. Mr Mietz appealed against that decision authorising enforcement to the competent Oberlandesgericht (Higher Regional Court). He argued that Intership Yachting and himself had agreed on all of the details of the order for the vessel in question, which was intended for his own personal use, at the Boat Show in Düsseldorf (Germany) and that, when they met again in Sneek one week later, they had merely signed the contract and he had made the agreed advance payment of DM 40 000. From this he concluded that, under the second paragraph of Article 14 of the Convention, the courts of the Contracting State in which the debtor was

domiciled, that is to say Germany, had exclusive jurisdiction in the matter.

15. The Oberlandesgericht dismissed that appeal and Mr Mietz appealed on a point of law ('Revision') against that decision to the Bundesgerichtshof.

16. The Bundesgerichtshof takes the view that recognition and enforcement of the Netherlands judgment could be refused, pursuant to the first paragraph of Article 28 of the Convention, only if Mr Mietz were able to rely on the rules governing jurisdiction over consumer contracts set out in Articles 13 and 14 of the Convention.

17. The Bundesgerichtshof notes in this regard the different definitions which the Member States have given to the concept of the sale of goods on instalment credit terms (Kauf beweglicher Sachen auf Teilzahlung) and to the concept of the supply of goods (Lieferung beweglicher Sachen), terms which are set out in points 1 and 3 respectively of the first paragraph of Article 13 of the Convention.

18. The Bundesgerichtshof also notes that the Netherlands judgment contains no information as to where the acts preparatory to the conclusion of the contract were performed, so that it finds it impossible on that basis to determine whether the court of origin did or did not infringe Article 13, first paragraph, point 3, of the Convention, which reserves to the courts of the Member State in which the consumer resides jurisdiction over disputes concerning contracts for the supply of services or goods in the case where certain preparatory acts have been performed in that State. During the appeal proceedings, Mr Mietz had argued that the creditor had advertised with a view to this sale during a specialist show organised in Germany and that the contract had been concluded orally during that show. The Bundesgerichtshof, however, is unsure whether it can take into account this new argument by Mr Mietz inasmuch as the second paragraph of Article 28 of the Convention prohibits review as to substance.

19. If the Court should take the view that Mr Mietz could indeed rely on the rules governing jurisdiction over consumer contracts, the Bundesgerichtshof questions whether the court of origin would not have been entitled to derogate from those rules by virtue of Article 24 of the Convention. Articles 13 and 14 would not then constitute an obstacle to recognition of the Netherlands judgment.

20. The Bundesgerichtshof accordingly decided to stay proceedings and refer the following questions to the Court for a preliminary ruling: '1. Is there a sale of goods on instalment credit terms within the meaning of point :

1. of the first paragraph of Article 13 of the Brussels Convention in the case where, in a document described by the parties as a "contract of sale", one of the parties undertakes to manufacture a specific type of motor yacht with nine specified alterations and to transfer it to the other party, and the latter is required to pay DM 250 000 for it in five instalments?

If the first question is answered in the negative:

2. Is the contract described in the first question a contract for the supply of goods within the meaning of point 3 of the first paragraph of Article 13 of thc Brussels Convention?

3. Under the second paragraph of Article 34 of the Brussels Convention, in conjunction with the second paragraph of Article 28 thereof, must account also be taken of new facts which, according to the debtor, establish that the court of the State of origin breached the provisions of Section 4 of Title II of that Convention?

If either the first or the second and third questions are answered in the affirmative:

4. Does the possibility provided for in Articles 289 to 297 of the Netherlands Wetboek van Burgerlijke Rechtsvordering (Code of Civil Procedure) for obtaining a judgment ordering payment of contractual consideration through application for an immediate interim order by way of an abbreviated procedure ("*kort geding*") constitute a provisional measure within the meaning of Article 24 of the Brussels Convention?'

21. It is appropriate first of all to reply to the first and second questions, which should be examined together, then to the fourth question, and finally to the third question.

The first and second questions

22. In order to determine the scope of the first and second questions, it should be borne in mind that the dispute in the main proceedings concerns a contract concluded between two parties which those parties described as a 'contract of sale' involving the construction of a yacht conforming to a standard model type but featuring a number of alterations. The first contracting party undertook to manufacture the yacht and to transfer the property in it to the second contracting party, who, by way of consideration, undertook to pay the price for it in five instalments. It appears from the order for reference that the final

instalment was to be paid at the time of the trial voyage, that is to say, before possession of the yacht passed definitively to the second contracting party.

23. In view of certain observations concerning the possible treatment of a registered vessel as immovable property, it follows from the order for reference that, without prejudice to the question whether the contract in issue is to be treated as a contract for the supply of services or for the supply of goods, the yacht in question must, in any event, be classified as goods within the meaning of the Convention.

24. In that context, the crux of the Bundesgerichtshof's first question is whether the concept of the sale of goods on instalment credit terms within the meaning of Article 13, first paragraph, point 1, of the Convention must be understood as extending to a contract:

- relating to the manufacture by the first contracting party of goods corresponding to a standard model, to which certain alterations have been made;
- by which the first contracting party has undertaken to transfer the property in those goods to the second contracting party, who has undertaken, by way of consideration, to pay the price in several instalments; and
- in which provision is made for the final instalment to be paid before possession of the goods is transferred definitively to the second contracting party.

If the answer is in the negative, the Bundesgerichtshof asks, by its second question, whether such a contract must be treated as a contract for the supply of goods within the meaning of Article 13, first paragraph, point 3, of the Convention.

25. It must be stressed that the Court has not been asked to address the question whether a person in the position of Mr Mietz satisfies the other conditions set out in Article 13 of the Convention in order to be treated as a consumer within the meaning of that provision.

26. According to settled case-law, the concepts used in Articles 13 and 14 of the Convention must be interpreted independently, by reference principally to the system and objectives of the Convention (see, in particular, Case 150/77 *Bertrand* v *Ott* [1978] ECR 1431, paragraphs 14, 15, 16 and 19, Case C-89/91 *Shearson Lehman Hutton* v *TVB* [1993] ECR I-139, paragraph 13, and Case C-269/95 *Benincasa* v *Dentalkit* [1997] ECR I-3767, paragraph 12).

27. Furthermore, the rules of jurisdiction which derogate from the general principle on jurisdiction, such as the rules featuring in Articles 13 and 14, cannot give rise to an interpretation going beyond the cases envisaged by the Convention (see *Bertrand*, paragraph 17, *Shearson Lehman Hutton*, paragraphs, 14, 15 and 16, and *Benincasa*, paragraphs 13 and 14, all cited above).

28. The Court held, in paragraph 20 of its judgment in *Bertrand*, that the sale of goods on instalment credit terms is to be understood as a transaction in which the price is discharged by way of several payments or which is linked to a financing contract.

29. A contract such as that described in paragraph 22 of the present judgment is indeed a transaction in which the agreed price is discharged by way of several payments, so that such a contract could be described as a contract of sale, since transfer of possession and property takes place only after the agreed price has been paid in full.

30. Such a contract cannot, however, be described as a 'sale ... on instalment credit terms' within the meaning of Article 13, first paragraph, point 1, of the Convention.

31. It follows from the wording of the Convention, and in particular from the expression 'instalment credit terms' in the English version, that Article 13, first paragraph, point 1, of the Convention is intended to protect the purchaser only where the vendor has granted him credit, that is to say, where the vendor has transferred to the purchaser possession of the goods in question before the purchaser has paid the full price. In such a case, on the one hand, the purchaser may, when the contract is concluded, be misled as to the real amount which he owes, and, on the other, he will bear the risk of loss of those goods while remaining obliged to pay any outstanding instalments. Such considerations do not, however, apply where the price must be paid in full before transfer of possession takes place. Where the full price must be paid before transfer of possession, the special protection referred to in the first paragraph of Article 13 of the Convention cannot be extended to the purchaser solely on the ground that he has been allowed to pay the price in several instalments.

32. As regards the second question, it must be stressed that the Bundesgerichtshof is asking the Court only whether a contract such as that in the main proceedings is to be treated as a contract for the supply

of goods within the meaning of Article 13, first paragraph, point 3, of the Convention. There can be no doubt that such a contract should be classified as a contract for the supply either of services or of goods. It is unnecessary, for the purposes of the present judgment, to decide whether, in this particular case, there was a supply of services or of goods.

33. The answer to the first and second questions must therefore be that Article 13, first paragraph, point 1, of the Convention must be construed as not applying to a contract between two parties having the following characteristics, that is to say, a contract:

- relating to the manufacture by the first contracting party of goods corresponding to a standard model, to which certain alterations have been made;
- by which the first contracting party has undertaken to transfer the property in those goods to the second contracting party, who has undertaken, by way of consideration, to pay the price in several instalments; and
- in which provision is made for the final instalment to be paid before possession of the goods is transferred definitively to the second contracting party.

It is in this regard irrelevant that the contracting parties have described their contract as a 'contract of sale'. A contract having the characteristics mentioned above is however to be classified as a contract for the supply of services or of goods within the meaning of Article 13, first paragraph, point 3, of the Convention. It is for the national court, should the need arise, to determine whether the particular case before it involves a supply of services or a supply of goods.

The fourth question

34. It should be noted at the outset that Articles 289 to 297 of the Netherlands Code of Civil Procedure ('the Netherlands Code') deal with a form of procedure known as '*kort geding*', which allows the President of the Arrondissementsrechtbank to grant enforceable measures 'in all cases which, having regard to the interests of the parties, require an immediate measure on grounds of urgency' (Article 289(1)).

35. Under Article 292 of the Netherlands Code, 'interim decisions are without prejudice to the main proceedings'. *Kort geding* may be instituted without the need to bring substantive proceedings before the court having jurisdiction. The President of the Arrondissementsrechtbank may, however, refer the parties back to the ordinary proceedings (Article 291).

36. In order to exercise his jurisdiction in respect of *kort geding*, the President of the Arrondissementsrechtbank is required to comply with the jurisdiction rules provided for under Netherlands law.

37. Under Article 289 of the Netherlands Code, *kort geding* may be instituted at very short notice and, in accordance with Article 295, an appeal must be lodged within two weeks, on pain of being declared inadmissible.

38. Under those circumstances, it must be held that *kort geding* is a procedure of the type envisaged in Article 24 of the Convention, under which a court is authorised, by the law of its State, to order provisional or protective measures even if, under the Convention, it does not have jurisdiction as to the substance of the matter.

39. The Bundesgerichtshof's fourth question must therefore be construed as seeking to ascertain whether a judgment ordering payment of contractual consideration, delivered at the end of a procedure such as *kort geding*, is a provisional measure which may be granted by virtue of the jurisdiction provided for under Article 24 of the Convention.

40. It is important to stress that it is not necessary for the court hearing an application for provisional or protective measures to have recourse to Article 24 of the Convention where it has, in any event, jurisdiction as to the substance of a case in accordance with Articles 2 and 5 to 18 of the Convention (see, to that effect, Case C-391/95 *Van Uden* v *Deco-Line* [1998] ECR I-7091, paragraph 19).

41. In this connection, the Court held at paragraph 22 of its judgment in *Van Uden* that the court having jurisdiction as to the substance of a case under one of the heads of jurisdiction laid down in the Convention also has jurisdiction to order provisional or protective measures, without that jurisdiction being subject to any further conditions.

42. In contrast, in the case of a judgment delivered solely by virtue of the jurisdiction provided for under Article 24 of the Convention and ordering interim payment of a contractual consideration, the Court ruled in *Van Uden* that such a judgment does not constitute a provisional measure within the meaning of Article 24 unless, first, repayment to the defendant of the sum awarded is guaranteed if the plaintiff is unsuccessful as regards the substance of his claim and, second, the measure ordered relates only to specific assets of the defendant located or to be located

within the confines of the territorial jurisdiction of the court to which application is made.

43. The answer to the fourth question must therefore be that a judgment ordering interim payment of contractual consideration, delivered at the conclusion of proceedings such as those provided for under Articles 289 to 297 of the Netherlands Code by a court not having jurisdiction under the Convention as to the substance of the matter is not a provisional measure capable of being granted under Article 24 of the Convention unless, first, repayment to the defendant of the sum awarded is guaranteed if the plaintiff is unsuccessful as regards the substance of his claim and, second, the measure ordered relates only to specific assets of the defendant located or to be located within the confines of the territorial jurisdiction of the court to which application is made.

The third question

44. By this question, the Bundesgerichtshof is asking in substance whether the court to which application for enforcement is made may, in the context of the procedure for ordering enforcement set out in Title III of the Convention, take account of new facts relied on by one party for the purpose of establishing that a contract such as that described in paragraph 22 of the present judgment satisfies the conditions listed in Article 13, first paragraph, point 3, heads (a) and (b), of the Convention.

45. It should, however, be noted that, even if Mr Mietz were allowed to prove that he ought to have been treated as a consumer within the meaning of Article 13 of the Convention, the court of origin could still have had jurisdiction to order provisional measures.

46. Article 24 of the Convention expressly provides that a court has jurisdiction under its national law to grant an application for such measures, even if it does not have jurisdiction as to the substance of the matter. That jurisdiction must be exercised within the limits set out in Article 24 of the Convention with regard, in particular, to the granting of measures ordering interim payment, limits which do not apply where the court has jurisdiction as to the substance of the matter (see, to that effect, *Van Uden*, paragraph 19).

47. However, it is important to ensure that enforcement, in the State where it is sought, of provisional or protective measures allegedly founded on the jurisdiction laid down in Article 24 of the Convention, but which go beyond the limits of that jurisdiction, does not result in

circumvention of the rules on jurisdiction as to the substance set out in Articles 2 and 5 to 18 of the Convention (see, to that effect, *Van Uden*, paragraph 46).

48. Next, it should be noted that although, in the main proceedings, the court of origin ordered only one measure - namely interim payment - it may happen, in other situations, that the court of origin orders several measures, some of which are to be classified as provisional or protective measures within the meaning of Article 24 of the Convention, while others go beyond the limits provided for in that provision.

49. The question which arises for the court to which application for enforcement is made therefore relates not to the jurisdiction, as such, of the court of origin, but rather to the extent to which it is possible to seek enforcement of a judgment delivered in the exercise of the jurisdiction recognised by Article 24. That jurisdiction constitutes, within the context of the Convention, a special regime (see, in that regard, Case 125/79 *Denilauler* v *Couchet Frères* [1980] ECR 1553, paragraph 15, and *Van Uden*, paragraph 42).

50. Finally, it must be stressed that this is not a case where the court of origin has expressly based its jurisdiction to order interim payment by reference to its jurisdiction under the Convention to deal with the substance of the matter, nor a case where such jurisdiction is evident from the actual terms of its judgment, as would in particular be the case if the judgment showed that the defendant was domiciled in the Contracting State of the court of origin and none of the types of exclusive jurisdiction set out in Article 16 of the Convention was applicable.

51. In such circumstances, only the provisions of Article 27 and, if appropriate, the first paragraph of Article 28 of the Convention would be capable of preventing recognition and enforcement of the judgment of the court of origin.

52. Contrary, however, to the submissions of the United Kingdom Government and the Commission, the fact that the defendant appears before the court dealing with interim measures in the context of fast procedures intended to grant provisional or protective measures in case of urgency and which do not prejudice the examination of the substance cannot, by itself, suffice to confer on that court, by virtue of Article 18 of the Convention, unlimited jurisdiction to order any provisional or protective measure which the court might consider

appropriate if it had jurisdiction under the Convention as to the substance of the matter.

53. Unlike the circumstances outlined above, the Netherlands judgment, for the enforcement of which an order is sought in the main proceedings, has the following characteristics:

- it was delivered at the end of proceedings which were not, by their very nature, proceedings as to substance, but summary proceedings for the granting of interim measures;
- the defendant was not domiciled in the Contracting State of the court of origin and it does not appear from the Netherlands judgment that, for other reasons, that court had jurisdiction under the Convention as to the substance of the matter;
- it does not contain any statement of reasons designed to establish the jurisdiction of the court of origin as to the substance of the matter and
- it is limited to ordering the payment of a contractual consideration, without, on the one hand, repayment to the defendant of the sum awarded being guaranteed if the plaintiff is unsuccessful as regards the substance of his claim or, on the other, the measure sought relating only to specific assets of the defendant located or to be located within the confines of the territorial jurisdiction of the court to which application is made.

54. It follows from the reply to the fourth question that, if the court of origin had expressly indicated in its judgment that it had based its jurisdiction on its national law in conjunction with Article 24 of the Convention, the court to which application for enforcement was made would have had to conclude that the measure ordered - namely unconditional interim payment - was not a provisional or protective measure within the meaning of that article and was therefore not capable of being the subject of an enforcement order under Title III of the Convention.

55. So, where the court of origin is silent as to the basis of its jurisdiction, the need to ensure that the Convention rules are not circumvented (see, in this respect, paragraph 47 of this judgment) requires that its judgment be construed as meaning that that court founded its jurisdiction to order provisional measures on its national law governing interim measures and not on any jurisdiction as to substance derived from the Convention.

56. It follows that, in a case having the characteristics set out in paragraph 53 of the present judgment, the court to which application for enforcement was made should conclude that the measure ordered is not a provisional measure within the meaning of Article 24 and for that reason cannot be the subject of an enforcement order under Title III of the Convention.

57. It is consequently unnecessary for that court to examine whether, and under what circumstances, it might take account of new facts for the purpose of possible application of the second paragraph of Article 28 of the Convention.

58. It follows that the Court need not reply to the third question.

On those grounds, the Court in answer to the questions referred to it by the Bundesgerichtshof by order of 29 February 1996, hereby rules:

1. Article 13, first paragraph, point 1, of the Convention of 27 September 1968 on Jurisdiction and the Enforcement of Judgments in Civil and Commercial Matters, as amended by the Convention of 9 October 1978 on the Accession of the Kingdom of Denmark, Ireland and the United Kingdom of Great Britain and Northern Ireland, and by the Convention of 25 October 1982 on the Accession of the Hellenic Republic, must be construed as not applying to a contract between two parties having the following characteristics, that is to say, a contract:

- relating to the manufacture by the first contracting party of goods corresponding to a standard model, to which certain alterations have been made;

- by which the first contracting party has undertaken to transfer the property in those goods to the second contracting party, who has undertaken, by way of consideration, to pay the price in several instalments; and

- in which provision is made for the final instalment to be paid before possession of the goods is transferred definitively to the second contracting party.

It is in this regard irrelevant that the contracting parties have described their contract as a 'contract of sale'. A contract having the characteristics mentioned above is however to be classified as a contract for the supply of services or of goods within the meaning of Article 13, first paragraph, point 3, of the Convention of 27 September 1968. It is for the national court,

should the need arise, to determine whether the particular case before it involves a supply of services or a supply of goods.

2. A judgment ordering interim payment of contractual consideration, delivered at the end of a procedure such as that provided for under Articles 289 to 297 of the Netherlands Code of Civil Procedure by a court not having jurisdiction under the Convention of 27 September 1968 as to the substance of the matter is not a provisional measure capable of being granted under Article 24 of that Convention unless, first, repayment to the defendant of the sum awarded is guaranteed if the plaintiff is unsuccessful as regards the substance of his claim and, second, the measure ordered relates only to specific assets of the defendant located or to be located within the confines of the territorial jurisdiction of the court to which application is made.

OPINION OF MR ADVOCATE GENERAL LÉGER

1. The Bundesgerichtshof (Federal Court of Justice), seeks a preliminary ruling, under Article 3 of the Protocol of 3 June 1971, on the interpretation of points 1 and 3 of the first paragraph of Article 13, Article 24, the second paragraph of Article 28, and the second paragraph of Article 34 of the Brussels Convention of 27 September 1968 on jurisdiction *and* the enforcement of judgments in civil and commercial matters, as amended by the accession agreements of 1978 and 1982 (hereinafter 'the Convention' or 'the Brussels Convention').

Legal framework: the relevant provisions of the Brussels Convention

2. It will be recalled that the Brussels Convention establishes a unified system for the determination of jurisdiction (Title II), accompanied by a simplified mechanism for the recognition and enforcement of judgments given by the courts of the Contracting States (Title III) within the scope of the matters covered by the Convention (Title I).

3. It is clear that, by way of derogation from the first paragraph of Article 2, which grants general jurisdiction to the courts of the State where the defendant is domiciled, in the situations restrictively set out by Sections 2 to 6 of Title II, the defendant may, in the case of special jurisdiction, by reason of the close ties linking a given court to a dispute (Section 2: Articles 5 to 6a), or shall, in the case of exclusive jurisdiction (Section 5: Article 16) or of voluntary prorogation of jurisdiction (Section 6: Articles 17 and 18), be sued, where appropriate, in the courts of another Contracting State.

4. The rules contained in Sections 3 and 4 of Title II operate as systems

of jurisdiction separate from that established by Article 2 and its exceptions. These are protective rules for parties considered to be weak, governing jurisdiction in matters relating to insurance and consumer contracts respectively.

5. The benefit of the protective rules provided for in Section 4 of Title II is subject to two cumulative conditions being satisfied. In the first place, the person who relies on them has to be a 'consumer' within the meaning of the first paragraph of Article 13, that is to say a person acting 'for a purpose which can be regarded as being outside his trade or profession'. Secondly, the contract concluded by the consumer has to be one of those set out in points 1 to 3 of this provision. The following types are envisaged:

'1. a contract for the sale of goods on instalment credit terms; or

2. a contract for a loan repayable by instalments, or for any other form of credit, made to finance the sale of goods; or

3. any other contract for the supply of goods or a contract for the supply of services, and

(a) in the State of the consumer's domicile the conclusion of the contract was preceded by a specific invitation addressed to him or by advertising; and

(b) the consumer took in that State the steps necessary for the conclusion of the contract.'

6. Where these conditions are satisfied, the consumer may only be sued, in accordance with the second paragraph of Article 14, in the courts of the Contracting State in which he is domiciled.

7. In setting out the relevant provisions of the Convention concerning jurisdiction Article 18 should also be mentioned, which permits the prorogation of jurisdiction as a consequence of the mere appearance of the defendant. This article provides as follows:

'Apart from jurisdiction derived from other provisions of this Convention, a court of a Contracting State before whom a defendant enters an appearance shall have jurisdiction. This rule shall not apply where appearance was entered solely to contest the jurisdiction, or whether another court has exclusive jurisdiction by virtue of Article 16.'

The principle is thus that the appearance of the defendant has an attributive effect on jurisdiction: a court which in principle lacks jurisdiction becomes competent when the defendant appears.

However, this provision does not apply in two situations. Where the dispute relates to a matter closely linked with the territory of a Contracting State, such as rights *in rem* in immovable property, the exclusive jurisdiction under Article 16 prevents the application of Article 18. Moreover, the appearance of the defendant does not confer jurisdiction if it seeks to challenge the jurisdiction of the court seised. That is the case where the defendant appears solely to contest the jurisdiction without challenging the substance. That is also the case where the defendant appears to contest both the jurisdiction *and* the substance. In the latter case, the defence on the substance must, however, be presented in the alternative to avoid the application of Article 18.

8. The final provision of Title II of interest to the present proceedings is Article 24, which allows a court not having jurisdiction over the substance of the

matter to take 'provisional, including protective, measures', within the scope of the matters covered by the Convention, where the plaintiff chooses to apply to it rather than to the courts of another Contracting State, having jurisdiction as to the substance of the matter. That article reads as follows:

'Application may be made to the courts of a Contracting State for such provisional, including protective, measures as may be available under the law of that State, even if, under this Convention, the courts of another Contracting State have jurisdiction as to the substance of the matter.'

9. Title III, which concerns the recognition and enforcement of judgments, seeks to ensure the 'free movement of judgments' in the common market. In keeping with this objective, Articles 31 and following put in place a summary enforcement procedure, more simplified than ordinary enforcement proceedings, which seeks to limit the requirements to which the enforcement of decisions given in one Contracting State may be subjected to in another Contracting State.

10. Thus, the first part of the procedure is not adversarial (Article 34, first paragraph).

11. Moreover, the principle is that enforcement is granted without the need for the court applied to to review the jurisdiction of the Court of the State of origin (Article 28, third paragraph).

12. It is only on an exceptional basis that such review is carried out, in particular where certain rules of jurisdiction are at issue. That is why, under the second paragraph of Article 34, 'The application may be refused only for one of the reasons specified in Articles 27 and 28.'

In particular, under the first paragraph of Article 28, enforcement may not be given to judgments given in disregard of the provisions on jurisdiction in matters relating to insurance (Section 3, Articles 7 to 12a), or of those concerning consumer contracts (Section 4: Articles 13 to 15), or of the rules relating to exclusive jurisdiction contained in Article 16 (Section 5).

Within this examination of the grounds of jurisdiction set out in the first paragraph of Article 28, 'the court or authority applied to shall be bound by the findings of fact on which the court of the State of origin based its jurisdiction' (Article 28, second paragraph).

13. Finally, according to the third paragraph of Article 34, 'Under no circumstances may the foreign judgment be reviewed as to its substance'.

Factual and procedural background

14. The dispute in the main proceedings concerns the enforcement of a contract between the creditor, Intership Yachting Sneek BV, a company incorporated under Dutch law and having its registered place of business in the Netherlands town of Sneek, and the debtor, Mr Mietz, who is domiciled in Lüchow, Germany, where he runs a construction business and trades in construction materials.

15. The parties agreed that the debtor would purchase an Intership boat of type 1.150 G. It was agreed that the boat would be subject to substantial

modifications before its final delivery. The total purchase price of DEM 250 000 was payable in five successive instalments, all due before final delivery. This agreement was set down in writing in a document called a 'contract of sale' signed at Sneek, Netherlands.

16. Following partial failure by the debtor to make certain payments, the creditor, through the procedure of '*kort geding*', in which both sides were heard, obtained on 12 May 1993 a provisionally enforceable judgment from the President of the Arrondissementsrechtbank (District Court) of Leenwarden, a Dutch court with interim jurisdiction, ordering the recovery of part of the debt (almost two thirds of the total amount payable).

17. Enforcement of this judgment having been granted in Germany by the Landgericht (Regional Court), Luneberg, the debtor lodged an appeal before the Oberlandesgericht (Higher Regional Court).

18. In support of this appeal, the debtor contested, for the first time, the jurisdiction of the Dutch court of origin, which he claimed had disregarded the consumer protection provisions of Articles 13 and 14 of the Convention granting jurisdiction to the courts of his place of domicile, Germany. Consequently, the court applied to, in examining the jurisdiction of the court of origin, could not, where it found an infringement of these provisions, grant the enforcement sought in Germany, in conformity with the second paragraph of Article 34, which refers back to the first paragraph of Article 28.

19. In order to claim the benefit of the provisions of Title II, Section 4, he put forward the following two arguments.

On the one hand, the boat ordered was only intended for strictly private use, so that his capacity as a 'consumer' under the first paragraph of Article 13 was established.

On the other hand, the transcription in Sneek (Netherlands) of the earlier agreement was purely formal, the contract having been orally concluded in Germany prior to signature in the Netherlands. It was at a visit to the creditor's exhibition stand at the Bootsmesse (Pleasure Boat Show) in Dusseldorf, Germany, that the debtor indicated his intention to buy the boat there on display; this not being possible, it was agreed between the parties that a boat of the same model would be built for him, incorporating the alterations specified by the debtor.

This second argument appears to seek to demonstrate that the disputed contract falls within the scope of point 3 of the first paragraph of Article 13 of the Convention.

20. The Oberlandesgericht dismissed the appeal and, as a result, refused not to grant enforcement of the Netherlands judgment for failure to observe the consumer protection rules in Section 4 of Title II.

21. Mr Mietz brought an appeal on a point of law before the Bundesgerichtshof.

The questions referred for a preliminary ruling

22. The court has set out in its order of referral the object and content of

its inquiries which form the basis of the questions submitted to this court. It asks whether there is any reason that would justify it in refusing to grant enforcement of the judgment obtained in the Dutch court of origin.

23. Its first two questions examine the arguments put forward by the debtor and seek to determine whether the case before it is of a kind which deserves special protection, either because the disputed agreement constitutes a 'sale of goods on instalment credit terms' (Article 13, first paragraph, point 1) or a 'contract for the supply of goods or a contract for the supply of services' concluded by a consumer (Article 13, first paragraph, point 3).

24. In the context of the examination of point 3 of the first paragraph of Article 13, the referring court wants to know whether it can take into account matters put forward by the debtor which were not considered in the judgment given in the court of origin. These concern matters of fact raised before the Oberlandesgericht seeking to establish that the conditions required under (a) and (b) of this provision are satisfied (in particular, in this case, the fact that the contract was orally concluded at the Bootsmesse in Dusseldorf). The Bundesgerichtshof observes that, by virtue of the second paragraph of Article 28, in carrying out a review of the jurisdiction of the court of the State of origin under the rules of Section 4 of Title II, the court of the State to which request is made is 'bound by the findings of fact on which the court of the State of origin based its jurisdiction'. In so far as the Dutch court did not base its jurisdiction on findings of fact, the referring court asks whether the wording of the second paragraph of Article 28 prevents it from taking account of these new matters. Those considerations form the basis of the third question.

25. The national court points out that, if the answers to these first three questions ruled out the application of the first paragraph of Article 28, it could not review the jurisdiction of the court of origin, and consequently could not oppose enforcement of the disputed decision. It would thus have to reject the appeal.

26. Hence its fourth question, for which an answer is only sought if the first paragraph of Article 28 applies. In this case, if enforcement in principle could not be granted by reason of the misapplication by the court of origin of the rules contained in Section 4 of Title II, the referring court proposes to examine the question of enforcement from a different perspective, that of Article 24 of the Convention. Thus it asks whether a measure granted by way of a procedure of '*kort geding*' is a 'provisional, including protective, measure' within the meaning of Article 24. In such a case, the Bundesgerichtshof thinks that 'Articles 13 and 14 of the Brussels Convention would, from the outset, not preclude recognition'.

27. The wording of the four questions which have been submitted is as follows:

'1. Is there a sale of goods on instalment credit terms within the meaning of point 1 of the first paragraph of Article 13 of the Brussels Convention in the case where, in a document described by the parties as a "contract of sale", one of the parties undertakes to manufacture a specific type of motor yacht with nine specified alterations and to transfer it to the other party, and the latter is required to pay DEM 250 000 for it in five instalments?

If the first question is answered in the negative:

2. Is the contract described in the first question a contract for the supply of goods within the meaning of point 3 of the first paragraph of Article 13 of the Brussels Convention?

3. Under the second paragraph of Article 34 of the Brussels Convention, in conjunction with the second paragraph of Article 28 thereof, must account also be taken of new facts which, according to the debtor, establish that the court of the State of origin has infringed the provisions of Section 4 of Title II of that Convention?

If either the first or the second and third questions are answered in the affirmative:

4. Does the possibility provided for in Articles 289 to 297 of the Netherlands Wetboek van Burgerlijke Rechtsvordering (Code of Civil Procedure) for obtaining a judgment ordering payment of contractual consideration through application for an immediate interim order by way of an abbreviated procedure ("*kort geding*") constitute a provisional measure within the meaning of Article 24 of the Brussels Convention?'

Answers to the questions

Position on the suggestion to deal first with Article 18 of the Convention

28. As stated above, within the system of the Convention, Article 18 provides for voluntary or implied submission to jurisdiction. The Commission relies on this provision and argues, first of all, that the questions referred would be without purpose if the debtor had entered an appearance before the court of origin without any reservation. The United Kingdom Government has, in essence, put forward the same argument.

29. However, it seems to me that a number of arguments prevent the adoption of such an approach.

30. First of all, in my opinion, there is insufficient information before us in the present case to allow us to form an opinion as to the applicability of Article 18.

That provision allows submission to jurisdiction only in so far as the defendant's appearance is entered solely to make submissions as to the substance of his defence. However, as the parties have not taken part in the proceedings before this Court, we cannot be certain in this regard. The order for reference only permits vague assumptions. The Bundesgerichtshof has stated that the debtor contested the jurisdiction of the court of origin only at the stage of the appeal against the decision of enforcement, from which one can deduce that the debtor did not contest the jurisdiction of the Dutch court during the proceedings before that court, and limited himself to submissions as to the substance of his defence. However, it is conceivable that the debtor's submissions as to the substance of the case before the president of the Arrondissementsrechtbank te Leeuwarden were merely ancillary to a challenge to jurisdiction. In that case, in accordance with the abovementioned case of *Elefanten Schuh*, his appearance could not be deemed to amount to submission to jurisdiction.

31. A further difficulty would arise if it were decided to apply Article 18 to the present matter: does this provision allow submission to jurisdiction irrespective of the rules of jurisdiction for the protection of consumers in Section 4 of Title II? If the contract at issue were to be regarded as within the types provided for in Article 13, this question would certainly have to be resolved as a preliminary point.

An argument based on the wording of Article 18 favours its applicability in such a case: the only limitation resulting from the wording of this provision is the existence of exclusive jurisdiction by virtue of Article 16. Conversely, Article 18 seems to allow the parties to submit to jurisdiction of the court of a State regardless of any other rules of jurisdiction. In particular, the wording of Article 18 appears to show that nothing prevents, by virtue of that implied consent, jurisdiction being conferred in consumer contract matters on a court other than that indicated by the second paragraph of Article 14.

The case-law of this Court may also be interpreted as being in favour of this argument. This Court has not been reluctant to bring into operation the effect of submission to jurisdiction when the jurisdiction which was departed from resulted from a clause conferring jurisdiction pursuant to Article 17: '... Article 18 of the Convention applies even where the parties have by agreement designated a court which is to have jurisdiction within the meaning of Article 17'. If it is considered that the defendant's wishes at the time of the proceedings can derogate from the previous wishes of the parties, his appearance should also permit derogations from the Convention rules which are favourable to him. The defendant is free, as it were, not to take advantage of the protection which is afforded to him.

However, another argument based on the wording of the Convention can be made against this proposition. By virtue of the fourth paragraph of Article 17, the rules of jurisdiction in matters of insurance and consumer contracts are expressly withdrawn from the intention of the parties. In such matters, the choice of forum cannot come into operation; the parties are, in a way, obliged to benefit from the protective rules provided for in their favour, without being able to depart from them by a demonstration of intent. It is true that such a limitation does not appear in the wording of Article 18. However, their observation alone could be considered insufficient to establish that, although the parties cannot depart from the protective rules by choosing a forum at the time of conclusion of the contract, their mere appearance results in de facto loss of the benefit of the protection provided for. Yet, it seems to me that, in admitting contractual prorogation of jurisdiction 'after the dispute has arisen', point 1 of Article 15 covers not only clauses conferring jurisdiction under Article 17 but also implied submission to jurisdiction under Article 18.

32. The purpose of the above exposition on this latter point is not to resolve the difficulty raised, but simply to highlight it. If the course suggested by the Commission and the United Kingdom Government were to be followed, it would first of all have to be decided whether the defendant's appearance in itself

can override the Convention's protective rules provided for in his favour. I now turn to the last aspect of this examination of the applicability of Article 18 to the present case.

33. We have already seen two of the difficulties which this question raises: on the one hand, the examination to be undertaken might become, for want of factual elements in our possession, hypothetical or academic, on the other hand, it needs to be demonstrated, first of all, that voluntary appearance allows derogation from the rules of jurisdiction provided for in the second paragraph of Article 14.

34. But, above all, we must remember that we find ourselves at the stage of enforcement proceedings. We saw the importance within the system of the Convention of the fact that the court of enforcement cannot, in principle, examine the jurisdiction of the court of origin. The only exceptions which are likely to be of interest in the present case deal with the grounds of jurisdiction provided for in Sections 3, 4 and 5 of Title II.

35. Therefore, the referring court can only examine the jurisdiction of the Dutch court of origin from the point of view of the rules provided for under those sections, to the exclusion of any other. Thus it can satisfy itself, as suggested by the debtor, that the rules of jurisdiction in the field of consumer protection have not been misapplied. On the other hand, the system of enforcement put in place does not entitle it to verify whether the court of origin has properly applied the rules of jurisdiction provided for in Article 18. Even if the Dutch court had, in applying this provision, assumed jurisdiction by virtue of the defendant's appearance, the court applied to would not be entitled to review the proper application of this provision. Yet, this would be the case if the court applied to was allowed to examine the question of the application of Article 18 by the court of origin. In so doing, the court applied to would carry out an analysis which could only be considered as a review, in a certain sense, of the jurisdiction of the court of origin in the light of Article 18. It would in fact have to resolve the two types of difficulties I mentioned above. Was the purpose of the defendant's appearance solely to challenge the substance of the case without contesting jurisdiction? If so, does Article 18 allow the wishes of the parties to prevail over the protective rules of the Convention? Even if the court applied to considered it had to answer these two questions in the affirmative, it would have to have carried out, beforehand, an analysis on the proper application of this provision by the court of origin, in order to reach that conclusion.

36. Given that the Convention does not entitle a review of the jurisdiction of the court of origin by the court applied to in the light of the Convention rules except in certain very specific instances, and that the jurisdiction provided for under Article 18 is not one of these instances, I think that the Court cannot ask the referring court to refrain from verifying that Articles 13 to 15 were complied with by suggesting that Article 18 should prevail.

37. As a result, I propose that the Court answer the national court's questions without examining beforehand the application of Article 18 in this instance.

The questions concerning the consumer protection rules

38. The first three questions seek to determine whether the consumer protection rules (Section 4 of Title II) were misapplied by the Dutch court of origin, in which case the referring court cannot grant the enforcement sought.

39. I have no doubt as to the personal application of these rules to the present case.

40. The first paragraph of Article 13 of the Convention defines a 'consumer' as someone acting 'for a purpose which can be regarded as outside his trade or profession'.

41. This Court has concluded that '...only contracts concluded for the purpose of satisfying an individual's own needs in terms of private consumption come under the provisions designed to protect the consumer as the party deemed to be the weaker party economically'.

42. This is very much the case here. The debtor acted not in a professional capacity, but as a private individual. The acquisition of the boat at issue was actually to satisfy his own private consumption needs. In particular, it was totally separate from the business activity of the debtor, who runs a construction business and trades in construction materials.

43. The hesitation of the referring judge to consider the debtor as a 'consumer' under the first paragraph of Article 13, by reason of the size of the transaction, seems to me to be without foundation. In fact, '... in order to determine whether a person has the capacity of consumer ... reference must be made to the position of the person concerned in a particular contract, having regard to the nature and aim of that contract, and not to the subjective situation of the person concerned.'

The status of consumer is thus not reserved only to those persons who are economically weak or disadvantaged.

44. Mr Mietz's capacity as a consumer in the disputed transaction thus not being in any doubt, it must be considered whether this transaction falls within the scope of Section 4 of Title II, since these provisions 'affect only ... a consumer ... who is bound by one of the contracts listed in Article 13'.

The first question: Article 13, first paragraph, point 1

45. Can the disputed transaction be considered as a 'sale of goods on instalment credit terms' within the meaning of point 1 of the first paragraph of Article 13? All the interveners in the present case have given a negative response to this first question. I propose that their analysis should be followed.

46. The disputed contract was treated as a 'works contract' by the President of the Arrondissementsrechtbank te Leeuwarden on the basis of Dutch law, whereas it might be a 'mixed commercial and sale contract' in German law. The parties, for their part, have called it a 'contract of sale'. The referring court also expresses an opinion that there is a sale of goods on instalment credit terms within the meaning of point 1 of the first paragraph of Article 13 only when a ready-made item or an item manufactured for stock for general use is handed over.

47. In this context, this Court has emphasised that the need for 'eliminating obstacles to legal relations and to the settlement of disputes in the context of intra-Community relations in matters of the sale of goods on instalment credit terms' leads to 'consider that concept as being *independent and therefore common* to all the Member States'.

48. As a result, neither the parties' own designation in the particular case nor the solutions adopted under differing national laws can prevail.

49. In the absence of a definition in the text of the Convention, the Court has considered '...that the sale of goods on instalment credit terms is to be understood as a transaction in which the price is discharged by way of several payments or which is linked to a financing contract.'

50. An operation by which the creditor agrees to transfer title in goods under construction to the debtor, in return for payment in a series of five instalments, could satisfy the above definition, were it not for a factor which seems to me to be decisive in the present case, but did not have to be examined in the *Bertrand* judgment.

51. This is because the series of instalments, in the case we are dealing with, all take place before the delivery of the goods contracted for.

52. However, as stated in the abovementioned *Bertrand* judgment, '...a restrictive interpretation of the second paragraph of Article 14, in conformity with the objectives pursued by Section 4, entails the restriction of the jurisdictional advantage...to buyers who are in need of protection, their economic position being one of weakness in comparison with sellers'. In this sense, a buyer who is granted credit by the seller is indeed in a position of weakness. However, this is certainly not the case where the buyer is billed for the total price *before* the delivery of the good, even if the obligation to pay is spread out over several instalments. Such a buyer cannot be regarded as having been '...induced to purchase by the system of payment by instalments, in so far as payment in a lump sum would have been the cause of economic difficulties for him'. In reality, in a situation such as the present, the buyer does not require any special protection.

53. Therefore, I am of the opinion that the disputed transaction cannot be considered as a sale of 'goods on instalment credit terms' within the meaning of point 1 of the first paragraph of Article 13 of the Convention in the absence of 'payments made *after* delivery'.

54. Thus, enforcement of the Dutch court's judgment cannot be refused on the ground of misapplication of the applicable rules on contracts of this kind.

The second and third questions: Article 28, second paragraph and Article 13, first paragraph, point 3

55. If it does not fall within the scope of point 1 of the first paragraph of Article 13 of the Convention, can the transaction at issue nevertheless be regarded as falling under point 3 of the first paragraph of Article 13? That is the purpose of the second question.

56. Before examining this point, it seems necessary to first consider the third question. In order to decide whether the disputed contract falls within the scope of point 3 of the first paragraph of Article 13, and in particular whether the

conditions provided for in (a) and (b) of this provision are satisfied in this instance, it must be shown that the court of the State applied to is entitled to base its assessment on matters put forward by the debtor which were not mentioned by the court of the State of origin in its decision. As a result, if the answer to the third question is in the negative, the second does not call to be answered.

57. According to the second paragraph of Article 28 of the Convention, 'In its examination of the grounds of jurisdiction referred to in the foregoing paragraph, the court or authority applied to shall be bound by the findings of fact on which the court of the State of origin based its jurisdiction'.

58. That provision, according to the Jenard Report, '...avoids recourse to time-wasting duplication in the exceptional cases where re-examination of the jurisdiction of the court of origin is permitted'.

59. It seems to me that if we do not allow the court applied to to disregard the findings of fact made by the court of origin, we cannot equally accept that it should receive new matters of fact which had not been put before the court of origin. The justification is the same in both cases: it is a question of avoiding all delaying tactics. Such an objective could be jeopardised if the court of the State applied to had to take into account new submissions of the debtor, capable of calling into question the jurisdiction of the court first seised, in order to prevent the enforcement sought, when the debtor could have submitted those arguments in the original proceedings. If the production of new arguments of fact before the court applied to were to be admitted, it would be open to any defendant seeking to disrupt the course of the fast procedure provided for in the Convention deliberately not to put forward certain essential arguments until the enforcement stage, in order to prevent enforcement of the judgment.

60. Although the Court has not yet had the opportunity to rule on such a situation under the second paragraph of Article 28, the case-law concerning the third paragraph of Article 34 gives useful indications which can be applied by analogy to the present case.

61. In the *Van Dalisen and Others* case, faced with '...the question whether the court with which the appeal is lodged may take into consideration, in a decision concerning an application for a stay of proceedings under the first paragraph of Article 38 of the Convention, arguments unknown to the foreign court at the time of its judgment because the appellant had failed to put them before it', the Court ruled that, by reason of the prohibition of review as to the substance set out in the third paragraph of Article 34, a court of appeal can take into account, in its decision concerning a request for a stay of proceedings under Article 38, '...only such submissions as the appellant was unable to put before the court of the State where the judgment was given'.

62. In my opinion, in the same way as the court applied to can take into consideration, in its decision concerning a request for a stay of proceedings under Article 38, 'only such submissions as the appellant was unable to put before the court of the State where the judgment was given', similarly, the court applied to can take into account, in its decision concerning enforcement, only the arguments which could not have been relied on before the court of origin.

This is clearly not the case here: Mr Mietz was perfectly able to put forward before the Dutch court of origin the matters of fact which he alleged in the course of the proceedings in the State applied to.

63. Consequently, I think that the matters put forward by the debtor before the courts of that State, seeking to establish that the disputed contract was one of those referred to in point 3 of the first paragraph of Article 13, in that it consisted of a contract for the supply of goods or a contract for the supply of services, concluded as a result of advertising taking place in the State of domicile of the consumer (the Bootsmesse in Dusseldorf) and with the consumer having taken in that State the steps necessary for the conclusion of the contract (contract concluded orally during the Bootsmesse), cannot be admitted by the court applied to, since they could have been put before the court of origin.

64. In view of the answer proposed to be given to the third question, the second does not need to be answered. Since the court applied to cannot take into account the matters of fact put forward in support of the application of point 3 of the first paragraph of Article 13, it cannot review the jurisdiction of the court of origin under that provision.

65. Thus it is only in the alternative that I offer the following observations on the second question submitted to the Court.

66. In this regard, were it not for the inability of the German court in the present case to take into account the factual elements put forward by the debtor, this question would have to be given a positive reply in my opinion.

67. Firstly, as noted above, the disputed contract at issue was concluded by a consumer within the meaning of Article 13.

68. Secondly, the subject of the contract, according to the information provided by the referring court, being the delivery of a boat to which a number of substantial modifications were to be made, the condition requiring, under point 3 of the first paragraph of Article 13, the contract to be 'for the supply of goods or ... for the supply of services' appears to be satisfied in the present case.

69. Finally, point 3 of the first paragraph of Article 13 requires that two cumulative conditions are satisfied, to ensure a sufficiently close connection between the contract and the country of domicile of the consumer.

70. The first of these conditions requires that the conclusion of the contract was preceded by a 'specific invitation addressed to him or by advertising' in that State. The Report by Professors M. Giuliano and P. Lagarde on the Rome Convention, to which the Schlosser Report refers, states that this includes all forms of advertising in the State where the consumer is domiciled, or a special offer addressed to him. In the present case, a display on a stand during a pleasure boat fair in Dusseldorf certainly amounts to a form of advertising in the State where the consumer is domiciled. It would in any event be for the court seised to satisfy itself as to the correctness of this factual element.

71. The second condition requires that the consumer has taken in his State of domicile 'the steps necessary for the conclusion of the contract'. The aforementioned Ginliano-Lagarde Report states that this expression avoids the problem of determining the *place* where the contract was concluded, and includes any written document (or any action) indicating the intention of the consumer to follow up the special offer or advertising. Likewise, if it were

established, as Mr Mietz claims, that he indicated his intention to purchase the boat contracted for at the Bootsmesse in Dusseldorf, this second condition would be satisfied. The court applied to would have to satisfy itself of this in any event.

The classification of a measure taken following a procedure of 'kort geding' as a 'provisional, including protective' measure underArticle 24 of the Convention.

72. The fourth question, by which the national court asks for the classification, from the point of view of Article 24 of the Convention, of a measure taken following a procedure of '*kort geding*', would not need to be answered if the Court follows my previous argument. This question is only submitted on the basis that the Court considers the disputed contract to be one of the types referred to in point 1 of paragraph 1 of Article 13 or point 3 of paragraph 1 of Article 13.

73. Furthermore, it is significant that, in asking this question, the referring court seems to be prepared to undertake a review of the jurisdiction of the court of origin, which it is prohibited from doing under the third paragraph of Article 28. In fact, the court applied to is permitted to verify that the court of origin has correctly applied the rules of the Convention only where the rules contained in Sections 3, 4 and 5 of Title II are at issue. Apart from these situations, any review is prohibited. Thus, if it were concluded, following the examination of the first two questions, that the consumer protection provisions were indeed wrongly applied by the court of origin, the court applied to could not in any event grant enforcement of the disputed decision. It could not engage in a lengthy search of the other grounds of jurisdiction on which the court applied to could have based jurisdiction, so as to 'make up for', as it were, its lack of jurisdiction under the consumer protection rules. Even should the fourth question have to be answered in the affirmative, this would not allow the court applied to to base the jurisdiction of the court of origin on Article 24 of the Convention rather than on Article 13, in order to avoid refusing enforcement on the ground of misapplication of the consumer protection provisions.

74. In addition, I should again point out the complexity of the question raised, which the present case invites the Court to examine for the third time.

75. While taking the opportunity to refer back to my Opinion in the afore-mentioned *Van Uden* case on this point, I emphasise, as I did there, that the wide range of measures which may be adopted under the '*kort geding*' procedure does not, in my opinion, allow an absolute and abstract answer to be given to the question of their classification under Article 24 of the Convention. Whereas, in the *Van Uden* case, it appeared to me that there were sufficient elements relating to the course of the Dutch proceedings and their subject-matter, to answer, in the alternative, the question posed, in the absence of any such elements in the present case, it seems dangerous for me to express an opinion, even in the alternative.

Conclusion

76. For the foregoing reasons, I propose to answer the questions submitted by the Bundesgerichtshof as follows:

(1) The concept of 'sale of goods on instalment credit terms', within the meaning of point 1 of the first paragraph of Article 13 of the Convention of 27 September 1968 on jurisdiction and the enforcement of judgments in civil and commercial matters, cannot be understood as including a transaction having as its object the supply of goods to a person acting for a purpose which can be regarded as being outside his trade or profession, when the price, payable in instalments, is fully due before the final delivery of the goods to the consumer who has purchased them.

(2) Within the system of the Convention, the second paragraph of Article 34 and the second paragraph of Article 28 must be interpreted as precluding the court of the State applied to from taking into account, in the exercise of its exceptional power of review of the jurisdiction of the court of origin under Section 4 of Title II, matters of fact other than those that the court of origin has taken into account or could have taken into account if the party putting them forward had not refrained from adducing them before it.

In the alternative,

(3) The concept of 'contract for the supply of goods or a contract for the supply of services', within the meaning of point 3 of the first paragraph of Article 13, must be interpreted as including the case of a contract for the supply of a motor boat, in so far as that contract fulfils the two cumulative conditions under (a) and (b) relating to its connection with the place of domicile of the consumer.

(4) The system put in place by the Convention and, in particular, the second paragraph of Article 34, in so far as it refers to the third paragraph of Article 28, does not permit the court of the State applied to to review the jurisdiction of the court of the State of origin under Article 24 of the Convention.

TITLE II *[Chapter II]*

JURISDICTION *[Jurisdiction]*

Exclusive Jurisdiction – Article 16 *[Article 22]*

See also

Case 73/77 - 14 December 1977

Theodorus Engelbertus Sanders
v
Ronald van der Putte

Exclusive jurisdiction - Matters relating to tenancies of immoveable property - Strict interpretation - Business carried on in immoveable property rented from a third party by the lessor - Agreement to run the business - Application of Article 16 excluded - Dispute as to the existence of such an agreement.

Summary

The assignment, in the interests of the proper administration of justice, of exclusive jurisdiction to the courts of one Contracting State in accordance with Article 16 of the Convention results in depriving the parties of the choice of the forum which would otherwise be theirs and, in certain cases, results in their being brought before a court which is not that of the domicile of any of them. Having regard to that consideration the provisions of Article 16 must not be given a wider interpretation than is required by their objective. Therefore, the concept of 'matters relating to ... tenancies of immovable property' within the context of Article 16 of the Convention must not be interpreted as including an agreement to rent under a usufructuary lease a retail business (verpachting van een winkelbedrijf) carried on in immovable property rented from a third person by the lessor. The fact that there is a dispute as to the existence of such an agreement does not affect the reply given as regards the applicability of Article 16 of the Convention.

JUDGMENT OF THE COURT

Kutscher, President, Sorensen and Bosco, Presidents of Chambers, Donner, Mertens de Wilmars, Pescatore and O'Keeffe, Judges

1. By judgment of 10 June 1977, received at the Court on 15 June 1977, the Hoge Raad der Nederlanden referred for a preliminary ruling under Articles 2 and 3 of the Protocol of 3 June 1971 (OJ L 204 of 2.8.75, p. 28) concerning the interpretation by the Court of Justice of the Convention of 27 September 1968 on Jurisdiction and the Enforcement of Judgments in Civil and Commercial Matters (OJ L 299 of 31.12.72, p. 32) certain questions concerning the interpretation of Article 16 down to the end of subparagraph (1) of the said Convention.

2. The questions were raised within the context of a dispute between two Netherlands citizens, at present domiciled in the Netherlands, in relation to an agreement made in 1973 by which they arranged that one would take over from the other the running of a florist's business in a shop which the latter had leased at Wuppertal-Elberfeld in the Federal Republic of Germany.

3. A dispute having arisen between the parties to the main action as regards the agreement which they had concluded and even as regards its existence the 'subtenant', Sanders, who had refused to start running the business, was ordered to do so by judgment delivered in summary proceedings by the President of the Arrondissementsrechtbank, Arnhem.

4. On appeal, the Gerechtshof, Arnhem, found that the agreement in dispute did exist and that Sanders owed to his lessor, Van der Putte, a sum representing the rent due under the head-lease of the shop and a further sum representing the usufructuary lease as such of the business, and also the 'goodwill' (the intangible elements of the business).

5. Sanders pleaded that the Gerechtshof had no jurisdiction on the basis, in particular, of Article 16 of the Convention of 27 September 1968, the first paragraph of which provides that the following courts shall have exclusive jurisdiction, regardless of domicile: '(1) in matters relating to rights *in rem* in, or tenancies of, immovable property, the courts of the Contracting State in which the property is situated;'.

6. Sanders was unsuccessful on the ground that in the agreement in question the emphasis fell less on the rent or lease of immovable property

than on the running of a business and that in that connexion the justification for the exclusive jurisdiction provided for in Article 16(1), namely that tenancies and rents of immovable property are generally governed by special legal provisions and it is preferable that such provisions should be applied by the courts of the State in which they are in force, does not apply.

7. Sanders appealed from that judgment on a point of law to the Hoge Raad, which asks the following questions:

1. Must 'tenancies of immovable property' within the meaning of Article 16 down to the end of subparagraph (1) of the Convention on Jurisdiction and the Enforcement of Judgments in Civil and Commercial Matters also include an agreement to rent under a usufructuary lease a retail business carried on in immovable property rented from a third person by the lessor?

2. If so, does the exclusive jurisdiction of the courts of the State where the immovable property is situated also apply to a claim on the basis of such an agreement for: (a) payment of the rent of the retail premises under the usufructuary lease; or (b) payment by the tenant under the usufructuary lease of the head-rent owed by the lessor to the owner of the immovable property; or (c) payment of consideration for the goodwill of the retail business?

3. Is the answer to the questions set out above affected by the fact that in the proceedings the defendant (the tenant under the usufructuary lease (pachter)) has contested the existence of the agreement?

The first two questions

8. Under the terms of Article 2 of the Convention and subject to any other provisions thereof, persons domiciled in a Contracting State shall, whatever their nationality, be sued in the courts of that State.

9. The Convention admits of exceptions to the general rule by allowing the plaintiff in certain cases to sue the defendant before the court of the State in which the latter is domiciled or before the court of another Contracting State, according to the special provisions in Articles 5, 6, 8, 9, 10, 13 and 14 of the Convention.

10. On the other hand, Article 16 of the Convention provides for exclusive jurisdiction, regardless of domicile.

11. As regards the matters listed under subparagraphs (2), (3), (4) and (5) of that article it is clear that the courts which are given exclusive jurisdiction are those which are the best placed to deal with the disputes in question.

12. The same applies to the assignment of exclusive jurisdiction to the courts of the Contracting State in which the property is situated in matters relating to rights *in rem* in, or tenancies of, immovable property.

13. In fact, actions concerning rights *in rem* in immovable property are to be judged according to the rules of the State in which the immovable property is situated since the disputes which arise result frequently in checks, inquiries and expert assessments which must be carried out on the spot, with the result that the assignment of exclusive jurisdiction satisfies the need for the proper administration of justice.

14. Tenancies of immovable property are generally governed by special rules and it is preferable, in the light of their complexity, that they be applied only by the courts of the States in which they are in force.

15. The foregoing considerations explain the assignment of exclusive jurisdiction to the courts of the State in which the immovable property is situated in the case of disputes relating to tenancies of immovable property properly so-called, that is to say, in particular, disputes between lessors and tenants as to the existence or interpretation of leases or to compensation for damage caused by the tenant and to giving up possession of the premises.

16. The same considerations do not apply where the principal aim of the agreement is of a different nature, in particular, where it concerns the operation of a business.

17. Furthermore, the assignment, in the interests of the proper administration of justice, of exclusive jurisdiction to the courts of one Contracting State in accordance with Article 16 of the Convention results in depriving the parties of the choice of the forum which would otherwise be theirs and, in certain cases, results in their being brought before a court which is not that of the domicile of any of them.

18. Having regard to that consideration the provisions of Article 16 must not be given a wider interpretation than is required by their objective.

19. Therefore, the concept of 'matters relating to ... tenancies of immovable property' within the context of Article 16 of the Convention must not be interpreted as including an agreement to rent under a usufructuary lease a retail business (verpachting van een winkelbedrijf) carried on in immovable property rented from a third person by the lessor.

20. In the light of the reply to the first question, the second question does not call for an answer.

The third question

21. The third question asks whether the reply to the questions set out above is affected by the fact that in the proceedings the defendant (the tenant under the usufructuary lease (pachter)) has contested the existence of the agreement.

22. It emerges from the clear terms of Article 16 of the Convention that the fact that there is a dispute as to the existence of the agreement which forms the subject of the action does not affect the reply given as regards the applicability of that article.

On those grounds, the court in answer to the questions referred to it by the Hoge Raad der Nederlanden by order of 10 June 1977, hereby rules:

1. The concept of 'matters relating to tenancies of immovable property within the context of Article 16 of the Convention must not be interpreted as including an agreement to rent under a usufructuary lease a retail business (verpachting van een winkelbedrijf) carried on in immovable property rented from a third person by the lessor;

2. The fact that there is a dispute as to the existence of the agreement which forms the subject of the action does not affect the reply given as regards the applicability of Article 16 of the Convention.

OPINION OF MR ADVOCATE GENERAL MAYRAS

I - The main action which has given rise to the present reference for a preliminary ruling arises out of settlement of accounts between Netherlands subjects who are florists in the Ruhr.

It emerges from the file that the action arose in the following way: according to the statement made by Mr Van der Putte, a Netherlands national, residing at that time at Wuppertal-Barmen and already the apparent owner of two flower shops, one of which was situated at Solingen and the other at Wuppertal-Barmen, Mr Sanders, another Netherlands national also residing at that time in the Federal Republic of Germany, took over from the said Van der Putte in February 1973 with effect from 5 March 1973 a florist's business situated at

Wuppertal-Elberfeld. The sum due under the usufructuary lease in respect of the occupation of the business premises was fixed at DM 750 per week. For 'reasons of simplicity' Sanders paid the rent due under the headlease, amounting to DM 1 900 per month, directly to the actual owner of the immovable property, a German insurance company. In addition, Sanders was to pay DM or Hfl 25 000 (that point remains obscure) in respect of the goodwill or key money. That agreement was, furthermore, to be governed by the provisions of an agreement concerning the taking over of another shop of the same type situated at Wuppertal-Barmen, which was executed before a notary on 21 August 1972 between Van der Putte, the lessor, and Sanders, the lessee, together with his wife.

Sanders was prepared to implement that agreement. However, he informed Van der Putte that the prior assent of his wife was necessary since she was also a party to the lease of the shop at Wuppertal-Barmen. She has not given her assent.

In fact, Sanders only implemented the agreement on 17 April 1973 and only began to run the business at Wuppertal-Elberfeld after the President of the Arrondissementsrechtbank (Regional Court), Arnhem, ordered him, by a judgment delivered in summary proceedings on 10 April 1973, to take possession of the said premises or to pay a fine of Hfl 300 for each day for which he was in default. However, the sums agreed by way of the rent due under the head-lease to the owner (DM 1 900 per month) and under the usufructuary lease of the business (DM 750 per week), as well as the consideration for the goodwill, were not paid.

By a writ of 3 July 1973 Van der Putte claimed, in addition to the payment in respect of the goodwill and the aforementioned arrears of rent, the payment of a sum of Hfl 21 794 agreed in writing in respect of the transfer of the stock and various goods. That sum was paid by Sanders up to the amount of Hfl 19 635.94.

By judgment of 10 January 1974 the Arrondissementsrechtbank, Arnhem, suspended the proceedings and ordered the parties to appear before an examining magistrate for the purposes of an inquiry. Van der Putte appealed against that judgment to the Gerechtshof (Regional Court of Appeal), Arnhem.

The owner of the premises situated at Solingen having subsequently terminated the lease to Van der Putte and having dealt directly with Sanders, it appears that Van der Putte requested the Landgericht Wuppertal to order Sanders to give up possession of the property. We have no further information concerning the outcome of those proceedings.

In an interim judgment of 3 December 1974 the Gerechtshof, Arnhem, awarded Van der Putte the balance owed to him by Sanders in respect of the transfer of the stock, that is, Hfl 2158.06. It considered that from the evidence put forward it was likely that an agreement existed but permitted Sanders to bring evidence to the contrary.

As no such evidence was brought by Sanders the Gerechtshof, Arnhem, gave a final ruling on 4 May 1976 on the heads of claim relating to the tenancy agreement and the goodwill. The claim for payment of the rents was held to be well founded up to 1 January 1976, the date on which Sanders gave notice to terminate the tenancy agreement in dispute and he was ordered to pay the sum of Hfl 25 000 to Van der Putte in respect of the goodwill.

During the proceedings before the Gerechtshof, Arnhem, Sanders had pleaded that court had no jurisdiction: even supposing that an agreement had been validly concluded between the parties - which Sanders disputed - such an agreement would have included a clause giving jurisdiction to the court at Wuppertal, the place where the shop was situated. In its final judgment the Gerechtshof, Arnhem, rejected that plea on the basis of the first paragraph of Article 17 of the Convention of 27 September 1968 on jurisdiction and the Enforcement of judgments in Civil and Commercial Matters, which entered into force on 1 February 1973: there was no agreement in writing or oral agreement confirmed in writing providing for such an extension of jurisdiction. In fact, Sanders did not appear solely in order to contest the jurisdiction of the Netherlands court and the question of jurisdiction was actually only raised at a subsequent stage of the proceedings. However, the Gerechtshof, Arnhem, added of its own motion, on the supposed basis of Article 19 of the Brussels Convention on Jurisdiction and the Enforcement of Judgments in Civil and Commercial Matters, a dictum relating to Article 16 of that Convention, which was worded as follows: 'Particular attention must be paid to the provisions of Article 16(1) of the Convention, to the effect that: 'The following courts shall have exclusive jurisdiction, regardless of domicile:

(1) in matters relating to rights *in rem* in, or tenancies of, immovable property, the courts of the Contracting State in which the property is situated.'

(a) In the opinion of the Gerechtshof, on the assumption that an agreement between the parties must be held to exist the emphasis falls less on the exploitation of certain immovable property against payment - which moreover Van der Putte himself merely rented - than on the exploitation of a complete business against payment which in the course of the proceedings was referred to as the usufructuary lease of the business;

(b) In that respect the reasons which, according to the commentary to the Convention by Paul Jenard, formed the grounds for bringing claims relating to rights *in rem* in, or tenancies of, immovable property under the exclusive jurisdiction of the courts of the State where the property is situated do not apply, namely that in general tenancies of immovable property are governed by special legal provisions and it is preferable that the application of such provisions should be judged solely by the courts of the State in which such provisions are in force;

(c) In those circumstances it is not a claim relating to tenancies within the meaning of Article 16 of the Convention which is at issue, with the result that there is no ground for holding that the Netherlands court lacks jurisdiction.'

It is those grounds which form the subject of an appeal brought by Sanders on a point of law and led the Supreme Netherlands court, with the concurrent opinion of its Procureur General, to refer certain questions to you for a preliminary ruling under Articles 2 and 3 of the Protocol of 3 June 1971. The Hoge Raad, in fact, considered that the exception laid down to the rule in Article 18 of the Convention found expression in Article 19 and that 'agreements conferring jurisdiction shall have no legal force if ... the courts whose jurisdiction they purport to exclude have exclusive jurisdiction by virtue of Article 16' (second paragraph of Article 17). The exclusive jurisdiction based on

Article 16 - which must be examined by the court even of its own motion when the recognition or the enforcement of a decision of a court is sought (first paragraph of Article 28 and second paragraph of Article 34) - does not depend on any particular conduct by the parties during or outside the proceedings.

It is in those circumstances that the Hoge Raad der Nederlanden requests you, by judgment of 10 June 1977, to give a preliminary ruling on the following questions:

1. 'Must 'tenancies of immovable property' within the meaning of Article 16 down to the end of subparagraph (1) of the Convention also include an agreement to rent under a usufructuary lease [verpachting] a retail business carried on in immovable property rented from a third person by the lessor?

2. If so, does the exclusive jurisdiction of the courts of the State where the immovable property is situated also apply to a claim on the basis of such an agreement for (a) payment of the rent of the retail premises under the usufructuary lease; or (b)payment by the tenant under the usufructuary lease of the head-rent owed by the lessor to the owner of the immovable property; or (c)payment of consideration for the goodwill of the retail business?

3. Is the answer to the questions set out above affected by the fact that in the proceedings the defendant (the tenant under the usufructuary lease) has contested the existence of the agreement?'

II - The terms used by the authors of the Convention to express in the different official languages the French expression 'en matière de droits réels immobilisers et de baux d'immeubles' ('in matters relating to rights *in rem* in, or tenancies of, immovable property') betray some uncertainty, which is perhaps at the origin of the questions raised by the supreme Netherlands court.

It must be noted, first of all, that the French version nowhere rules out disputes relating to tenancies of immovable property having to be brought before the court of the State in which the property is situated, whether or not they relate to a right *in rem* and whether the lease in question is for residential or business purposes. Mr Bellet (JDI, 1965, p. 857) has already pointed out that it is rather strange that the text refers not only to disputes concerning rights *in rem* but also those concerning tenancies of immovable property.

The corresponding terms in the Dutch text, which are extremely wide, also appear not to rule out *a priori* the bringing of all disputes relating to rights (whether or not *in rem*) arising out of a lease of immovable property before the *forum rei sitae*.

For my part, I consider that the authors of the Convention intended to provide for exclusive jurisdiction both in matters relating to rights *in rem* and to rights, even those *in personam*, arising out of tenancies of immovable property for residential or business purposes.

On that point, it is possible to put forward, first of all an argument based on the text. Translated literally into French the German text of Article 16(1) states: 'Pour les recours qui ont pour objet des droits réels sur les biens immobilisers ainsi que le loyer ou le bail de biens immobilisers ...' (in actions relating to rights *in rem* in immovable property, as well to the rent or to the lease of immovable property).

What the authors of the Convention were concerned to do appears to be generally recognized: as Monsier Droz writes (Compétence Judiciaire Internationale, p. 100), the exclusive nature of the jurisdiction in matters relating to rights *in rem* in immovable property 'is easily justified. Disputes in matters relating to rights *in rem* in immovable property often involve checks, inquiries and expert assessments which must necessarily be carried out in the place where the property is situated ... Furthermore, a judgment relating to immovable property will necessarily be enforced in the place where the property is situated.'

The importance attached by the authors of the Convention to the exclusive nature of the jurisdiction is shown by Article 19 (the Court shall declare of its own motion that it has no jurisdiction) and by Articles 28 and 34 (refusal of recognition and enforcement in the case of violation of the exclusive jurisdiction rule).

However, the magnetic attraction of the place where the immovable property is situated results in extending, on an international level, the rules of jurisdiction applied in internal law and, as Mr Droz says, 'overflows the area of pure rights *in rem* and extends to tenancies of immovable property'. Mr Bellet also notes that 'experts have considered that, whether it concerns a residence or the pursuit of an occupation, a tenancy in the six countries of the common market, has almost reached the point where it gives rise to rights *in rem*'. Tenancies of immovable property give rise not only to actions *in rem* concerning immovable property but also to mixed actions, that is to say, to actions which combine an action *in personam* arising out of an obligation with an action *in rem*. As regards that case, the internal law of four out of the six Contracting States allows the plaintiff to choose between the court of the domicile of the defendant and the court of the State in which the property is situated. For his part, Mr Battifol (Mèlanges Offerhaus-Kollewijn, p. 57) notes that English law also appears recently to have abandoned the maxim 'personality has no locality'. He points to a tendency in France and in Italy to interpret rights *in rem* in respect of immovable property more widely than rights *in rem* in respect of movable property because the locality of movable property is more transitory and therefore less significant and likely to raise difficulties from the point of view of proof.

Mr Droz writes: 'The position will not be the same in future by reason of the wording of Article 16. It has become clear that in the legislation of each of the Member States leases of dwellings or of premises used for the pursuit of an occupation, leases for business purposes and agricultural leases formed the subject of special rules ... It is therefore reasonable for those special and complex provisions to be applied only by the judges of the countries in which they are in force ...' it is also possible that national rules or special local customs may apply to a lease for business purposes which is connected with a lease for residential purposes. All things considered, the fact that the lessor of business is himself only the tenant of the immovable property in which the business leased is carried on is only of secondary importance.

With the support of Mme Weser (Convention Communautaire, p. 303), Mr Droz concludes that 'There is no doubt that disputes between lessors and tenants relating to the existence or interpretation of the lease, to giving up possession of the premises and to quitting them fall within the field of application of Article 16(1)'.

Thus, as regards actions which concern only payment of the rent Mr Droz considers, rightly in my opinion, although contrary to the view taken by Mr Jenard who drew up the Commentary on the Convention, that such an action cannot be separated from the immovable property rented. Among other relevant considerations Mr Droz refers to the fact that very often, if the tenant is ordered to pay, enforcement on an international level - which always raises difficult problems - will not even have to be considered. The judgment will also be directly enforceable against the movable property used to furnish the premises let. If it is accepted that the action for the payment of the rents may be brought in a country other than that in which the immovable property is situated, the tenant, assuming that he is domiciled in the first country, 'cannot bring a counterclaim before the court of that first country for compensation for costs incurred in the maintenance of the immovable property, imposed by local rules and paid by the user of the premises on behalf of the owner ... In the interests of the proper administration of justice one would therefore have to apply the provisions concerning related actions in order to allow the court other than the court first seised to stay its proceedings. It appears to be infinitely preferable to save time and money by concentrating all the problems in the country in which the immovable property is situated.'

That view was taken by the Landgericht Aachen, in its ruling of 24 October 1975 on the ground that an action for the payment of rent may call into question provisions of national law concerning the lease itself. The court considered that even as regards claims for the payment of rent, the provisions of the national law on leases which concern the subject-matter of the lease may be conclusive.

On the other hand, in a decision of 25 November 1975 the Arrondissementsrechtbank, (Regional Court) Amsterdam, dismissed a plea of lack of jurisdiction raised before it in an action relating to the payment of a sum of money claimed under a penalty clause provided in respect of the fulfilment of a condition precedent. The immovable property was situated in France, the defendant was domiciled in the Netherlands and the court considered that the action did not concern a right *in rem* in immovable property.

On that point, let me add a further consideration, for purely practical purposes: although it may seem going too far to compel two litigants domiciled in the same State to seise the Court of a third State or of another Member State in whose area the immovable property is situated, where the distance between the litigants and the seat of that court is considerable, that does not apply in this instance since Wuppertal is not much further from Arnhem than is the Hague.

III - Even if, on that first point, one was inclined to say that it is for the national court to decide whether the action with which it is seised is only vaguely connected with a lease of immovable property or, on the other hand, whether the question raised before it cannot be separated from the problem of the lease of the immovable property, consideration of the remainder of the questions referred to the Court by the Hoge Raad of the Netherlands leads one to take the contrary view.

In fact, the questions referred by that Court under No 2 help towards a better understanding of the problem before it. It is clear therefrom that the dispute concerns a series of obligations related to a lease of retail premises, that is, to the rent which, under the terms of an alleged agreement, was to be paid directly by the tenant of the retail premises to the owner of the premises in which the business was carried on, to the usufructuary lease of the business itself as well as to payment of consideration for the goodwill, or key money.

The action by which Van der Putte claims simultaneously payment of the sum for which he is himself liable to the owner, of the sum due under the usufructuary lease and of consideration for the goodwill is mixed: it is action *in personam* insofar as it seeks recognition of an obligation to take certain action but it is also an action *in rem* concerning immovable property insofar as it seeks to assert rights conferred upon him by his capacity as lessor or holder of the immovable property.

Furthermore, if the existence of such an agreement were to be acknowledged - and I shall say in reply to the third query that the existence of a question on that subject is a further reason for acknowledging the exclusive nature of jurisdiction within the meaning of Article 16(1) - such agreement would have to be interpreted in the same way as the usufructuary lease of the shop situated at Wuppertal-Barmen. Paragraph 2(2) of that written agreement states that 'a copy of the lease (entered into between the insurance company, owner of the premises, and Van der Putte) is annexed to the notarial act (usufructuary lease of the business between Sanders and Van der Putte) and forms an integral part thereof', Thus, the dispute *ipso facto* concerns that first lease of the immovable property.

Still on the same model, the parties declared German law to be applicable to the transaction (paragraph 14(1)) and they had agreed to an extension of jurisdiction in favour of the court at Wuppertal (paragraph 14(2)). Furthermore, the parties to the action were originally domiciled in the Federal Republic of Germany and only moved subsequently. All the factors seem therefore to point to the jurisdiction of the court at Wuppertal as being the most appropriate. Finally, it appears that by reason of the debts owed by Van der Putte by way of tax, the finance administration of Wuppertal-Barmen made several orders for sequestration and, knowing that Sanders had entered into the subtenancy agreement with Van der Putte, proceeded to sequester the debts owed by Sanders to Van der Putte both under the head-lease and under the usufructuary lease.

I am sorry to go into all those details but I wish to provide all the necessary criteria for the national court. Of course, it is for that court to consider whether, despite the terms used by Van der Putte in his initiating summons, it is properly seised of the principal question of the existence of a tenancy agreement, in which case it will have to apply Article 19.

As regards the consideration in respect of goodwill, it is a property right relating to intangible assets and, therefore, movable in nature but although the action of which it forms the subject may be regarded as an action *in personam*, it is mixed and concerns immovable property insofar as the right in question is claimed in relation to and in implementation of a lease of immovable property:

jurisdiction to deal with the action must, therefore, follow the rule set out above.

IV - The third question referred by the Hoge Raad of the Netherlands confirms the opinion which I have just expressed. The question itself acknowledges that at a given moment in the proceedings there was a dispute between the plaintiff, the lessor, and the defendant, the tenant, as to the existence of the lease and the interpretation of its clauses. When the summons to appear was issued by Van der Putte the action concerned chiefly payment of the rents and fulfilment of the other undertakings entered into when the lease was concluded. However, the very existence of a 'lease' is seriously contested by Sanders. It is, in fact, always possible to contest the title to payment when a claim payment is made. An action for the payment of arrears of rent becomes an action *in rem* when title to the arrears is contested; that is sufficient to make the action before the Netherlands court 'mixed' in nature and to justify the application of the rule in Article 16(1). Jurisdiction under that article is based on public policy even at the stage of recognition and enforcement, and cannot be dependent solely on the conduct of the parties during or outside the proceedings.

In the light of all of the foregoing I consider that you should rule that:

1. Tenancies of immovable property within the meaning of Article 16(1) of the Convention of 1968 must be understood to mean, in particular, an agreement relating to the lease of a business carried on in immovable property which is itself rented from a third party by the lessor;

2. The exclusive jurisdiction laid down by that provision applies, in particular, to a claim submitted on the basis of such an agreement, which seeks:

- payment of the amount due under the usufructuary lease of the retail premises;
- payment of the head-rent for which the lessor is himself liable to the owner of the immovable property;
- payment of consideration for the goodwill.

3. The fact that during the course of the proceedings the tenant under the usufructuary lease has contested the existence of such an agreement in no way affects the foregoing.

Case 288/82 - 15 November 1983

Ferdinand M. J. J. Duijnstee
v
Lodewijk Goderbauer

Object of the Convention - Primacy over domestic law - Articles 16 and 19 - Review of jurisdiction and of admissibility - Exclusive jurisdiction of the courts of a Contracting State - Obligation on a court in another Contracting State to declare of its own motion that it has no jurisdiction - Scope - Exclusive jurisdiction - Article 16(4) - Proceedings 'concerned with the registration or validity of patents' - Meaning - Independent interpretation - Limits.

Summary

1. The Convention of 27 September 1968, which seeks to determine the jurisdiction of the courts of the Contracting States in civil matters, must override national provisions which are incompatible with it.

2. Article 19 of the Convention of 27 September 1968 requires the national court to declare of its own motion that it has no jurisdiction whenever it finds that a court of another Contracting State has exclusive jurisdiction under Article 16 of the Convention, even in an appeal in cassation where the national rules of procedure limit the court's reviewal to the grounds raised by the parties.

3. The term 'proceedings concerned with the registration or validity of patents' contained in Article 16(4) of the Convention of 27 September 1968 must be regarded as an independent concept intended to have uniform application in all the Contracting States.

4. The term 'proceedings concerned with the registration or validity of patents' does not include a dispute between an employee for whose

invention a patent has been applied for or obtained and his employer, where the dispute relates to their respective rights in that patent arising out of the contract of employment.

JUDGMENT OF THE COURT

Mertens de Wilmars, President, Koopmans, Bahlmann, Presidents of Chambers, O'Keeffe and Bosco, Judges

1. By a judgment of 29 October 1982, which was received at the Court Registry on 3 November 1982, the Hoge Raad der Nederlanden [Supreme Court of the Netherlands] referred to the Court, for a preliminary ruling under the Protocol of 3 June 1971 on the Interpretation by the Court of Justice of the Convention of 27 September 1968 on Jurisdiction and the Enforcement of Judgments in Civil and Commercial Matters (hereinafter referred to as 'the Convention'), three questions on the interpretation of Articles 16(4) and 19 of the Convention.

2. Those questions arose in an appeal in cassation by Ferdinand M. J. J. Duijnstee against a judgment delivered on 20 May 1981 by the Gerechtshof [Regional Court of Appeal], 's-Hertogenbosch, confirming a judgment of the Arrondissementsrechtbank [District Court], Maastricht.

3. On 28 November 1979, Mr Duijnstee had, in his capacity as the liquidator in the winding-up of BV Schroefboutenfabriek, applied to the Arrondissementsrechtbank, Maastricht, for an interlocutory injunction requiring Lodewijk Goderbauer, the former manager of that company, to transfer to it the patents applied for or granted in 22 countries, including some which have acceded to the Convention, in respect of an invention which Mr Goderbauer had made while employed by that company. Mr Duijnstee's claim, which was based on the fact that the Netherlands Patent Office had decided that BV Schroefboutenfabriek was *entitled* to the Netherlands patent for Mr Goderbauer's invention, was dismissed on 19 December 1979.

4. On 21 December 1979, Mr Goderbauer in turn brought an action against the liquidator in the Arrondissementsrechtbank, Maastricht, claiming that, if and insofar as the patents and applications for patents referred to in the writ were the property of the insolvent company, Mr Goderbauer had a lien over them as against the liquidator. Mr Duijnstee then pleaded a counterclaim in the same terms as his application for an interlocutory injunction of 28 November 1979.

5. By judgment of 24 April 1980, the Arrondissementsrechtbank, Maastricht, dismissed both Mr Goderbauer's claim and Mr Duijnstee's counterclaim. That judgment was confirmed on appeal by the Gerechtshof, 's-Hertogenbosch, by judgment of 20 May 1981.

6. Mr Duijnstee appealed against that judgment to the Hoge Raad on the ground that it was contrary to the Octrooiwet [Netherlands Patents Law].

7. Although the only ground of appeal was the alleged infringement of the Netherlands Patents Law, the Hoge Raad nonetheless expressed doubt over its own jurisdiction on the ground that certain factors involving the law of other States might, by virtue of Article 16(4) of the Convention, mean that the courts of other Contracting States had exclusive jurisdiction.

8. In the first place, the Hoge Raad raised the question whether, on the assumption that the courts of another Contracting State had exclusive jurisdiction, that jurisdiction should be recognised even though the point had not been pleaded by any of the parties. Article 419(1) of the Netherlands Code of Civil Procedure provides that the Hoge Raad is to confine its consideration of the case 'to the grounds on which the appeal is based', whereas Article 19 of the Convention provides that 'where a court of a Contracting State is seised of a claim which is principally concerned with a matter over which the courts of another Contracting State have exclusive jurisdiction by virtue of Article 16, it shall declare of its own motion that it has no jurisdiction'.

9. In its first question, the Hoge Raad, therefore, asks the Court whether the obligation imposed by Article 19 on the court of a Contracting State to declare of its own motion that it has no jurisdiction implies that a provision such as Article 419(1) of the Netherlands Code of Civil Procedure has no effect, inasmuch as a court of cassation must include in its consideration of the case the question covered by Article 19 and, if that question is answered in the affirmative, must quash the judgment appealed against, even if the question has not been raised in the grounds of appeal.

10. In order to reply to that question, it is necessary to consider the aims of the Convention.

11. According to the preamble to the Convention, the Contracting States,

anxious to 'strengthen in the Community the legal protection of persons therein established', considered that it was necessary for that purpose 'to determine the international jurisdiction of their courts, to facilitate recognition and to introduce an expeditious procedure for securing the enforcement of judgments, authentic instruments and court settlements'.

12. Both the provisions on jurisdiction and those on the recognition and enforcement of judgments are, therefore, aimed at strengthening the legal protection of persons established in the Community.

13. The principle of legal certainty in the Community legal order and the aims pursued by the Convention in accordance with Article 220 of the Treaty, on which it is based, require that the equality and uniformity of rights and obligations arising from the Convention for the Contracting States and the persons concerned must be ensured, regardless of the rules laid down in that regard in the laws of those States.

14. It must be concluded that the Convention, which seeks to determine the jurisdiction of the courts of the Contracting States in civil matters, must override national provisions which are incompatible with it.

15. The reply to the first question must therefore be that Article 19 of the Convention requires the national court to declare of its own motion that it has no jurisdiction whenever it finds that a court of another Contracting State has exclusive jurisdiction under Article 16 of the Convention, even in an appeal in cassation where the national rules of procedure limit the court's reviewal to the grounds raised by the parties.

16. In its second question the Hoge Raad asks whether the concept of proceedings 'concerned with the registration or validity of patents' within the meaning of Article 16(4) of the Convention, which attributes exclusive jurisdiction to the courts of the Contracting State competent to grant the patent, must be defined on the basis of the law of the Contracting State whose courts are referred to in that provision, or according to the *lex fori*, or on the basis of an independent interpretation of the said provision.

17. The Court has several times had occasion to consider the criteria to be used for the definition of the concepts appearing in the Convention. Thus, in its judgment of 22 February 1979 in Case 133/78 (*Gourdain* v *Nadler* [1979] ECR 743), it stated that 'in order to ensure, as far as possible, that the rights and obligations which derive from [the

Convention] for the Contracting States and the persons to whom it applies are equal and uniform', it is necessary that the terms of Article 1 of the Convention should not be interpreted 'as a mere reference to the internal law of one or other of the States concerned', and 'the concepts used in Article 1 must be regarded as independent concepts which must be interpreted by reference, first, to the objectives and scheme of the Convention and, secondly, to the general principles which stem from the corpus of the national legal systems' The Court also stressed the need for an independent interpretation in its judgment of 21 June 1978 in Case 150/77 (*Bertrand* v *Ott* [1978] ECR 1432), in relation to the terms used in Article 13 and in the second paragraph of Article 14 of the Convention, and in its judgment of 22 March 1983 in Case 34/82 (*Martin Peters Bauuntemehmung* v *Zuid Nederlandse Aannemers Vereniging* [1983] ECR 987), in relation to the terms used in Article 5(1) of the Convention.

18. In the present case, both an interpretation according to the law of the Contracting State whose courts have jurisdiction under Article 16(4) and an interpretation according to the *lex fori* would be liable to produce divergent solutions, which would be prejudicial to the principle that the rights and obligations which the persons concerned derive from the Convention should be equal and uniform.

19. Thus the term 'proceedings concerned with the registration or validity of patents' contained in Article 16(4) must be regarded as an independent concept intended to have uniform application in all the Contracting States.

20. This reply to the second question compels the Court to define the term 'proceedings concerned with the registration or validity of patents', since the Hoge Raad has asked in its third question whether that concept may cover a dispute such as that concerned in the main action.

21. In order to reply to the third question, reference must again be made to the objectives and scheme of the Convention.

22. In that regard, it must be noted that the exclusive jurisdiction in proceedings concerned with the registration or validity of patents conferred upon the courts of the Contracting State in which the deposit or registration has been applied for is justified by the fact that those courts are best placed to adjudicate upon cases in which the dispute itself concerns the validity of the patent or the existence of the deposit or registration.

23. On the other hand, as is expressly stated in the report on the Convention (Official Journal 1979, C 59, p. 1 at p 36), 'other actions, including those for infringement of patents, are governed by the general rules of the Convention'. That statement confirms the restrictive nature of the provision contained in Article 16(4).

24. It follows that proceedings 'concerned with the registration or validity of patents' must be regarded as proceedings in which the conferring of exclusive jurisdiction on the courts of the place in which the patent was granted is justified in the light of the factors mentioned above, such as proceedings relating to the validity, existence or lapse of a patent or an alleged right of priority by reason of an earlier deposit.

25. If, on the other hand, the dispute does not itself concern the validity of the patent or the existence of the deposit or registration, there is no special reason to confer exclusive jurisdiction on the courts of the Contracting State in which the patent was applied for or granted and consequently such a dispute is not covered by Article 16(4).

26. In a case such as the present, neither the validity of the patents nor the legality of their registration in the various countries is disputed by the parties to the main action. The outcome of the case, in fact, depends exclusively on the question whether Mr Goderbauer or the insolvent company BV Schroefboutenfabriek is entitled to the patent which must be determined on the basis of the legal relationship which existed between the parties concerned. Therefore, the special jurisdiction rule contained in Article 16(4) should not be applied.

27. In that regard, it should be pointed out that a very clear distinction between jurisdiction in disputes concerning the right to the patent, especially where the patent concerns the invention of an employee, and jurisdiction in disputes concerning the registration or validity of a patent was made both in the European Patent Convention signed in Munich on 5 October 1973 and in the Community Patent Convention signed in Luxembourg on 15 December 1975 (Official Journal 1976, L 17), which has not yet entered into force. Although those two Conventions are not applicable in this case, the fact that they expressly accept such a distinction confirms the interpretation given by the Court to the corresponding provisions of the Brussels Convention.

28. The reply to the third question should therefore be that the term 'proceedings concerned with the registration or validity of patents' does

not include a dispute between an employee for whose invention a patent has been applied for or obtained and his employer, where the dispute relates to their respective rights in that patent arising out of the contract of employment.

On those grounds, the Court (Fourth Chamber), in answer to the questions submitted to it by the Hoge Raad der Nederlanden by judgment of 29 October 1982, hereby rules:

1. Article 19 of the Convention requires the national court to declare of its own motion that it has no jurisdiction whenever it finds that a court of another Contracting State has exclusive jurisdiction under Article 16 of the Convention, even in an appeal in cassation where the national rules of procedure limit the court's reviewal to the grounds raised by the parties.

2. The term 'proceedings concerned with the registration or validity of patents' contained in Article 16(4) must be regarded as an independent concept intended to have uniform application in all the Contracting States.

3. The term 'proceedings concerned with the registration or validity of patents' does not include a dispute between an employee for whose invention a patent has been applied for or obtained and his employer, where the dispute relates to their respective rights in that patent arising out of the contract of employment.

OPINION OF MRS ADVOCATE GENERAL ROZES

A request for a preliminary ruling has been submitted to the Court by the Hoge Raad der Nederlanden [Supreme Court of the Netherlands] in a dispute between F. M. J. J. Duijnstee, the liquidator in the winding-up of BV Schroefboutenfabriek, and Lodewijk Goderbauer, a former employee of that company who made a patented invention.

I - The facts are as follows: Lodewijk Goderbauer, of Schaesberg (Netherlands), the manager of a bolts factory owned by BV Schroefboutenfabriek [hereinafter referred to as 'the Company'], whose registered office is in Heerlen (Netherlands), had made an invention consisting in the mounting of a rail on a girder. He submitted to the Netherlands Patent Office an application for a patent in his own name for that invention (No 75.93593) and then made applications in 22 other countries, including five Contracting States.

Considering that the invention was made as a result of special knowledge which Mr Goderbauer had acquired in the ordinary performance of his duties with it, the Company on 26 August 1976 applied to the President of the Arrondissementsrechtbank [District Court], for an interlocutory injunction requiring Mr Goderbauer, subject to the payment of periodic penalties in the event of non-compliance, to transfer into its name the application for a Netherlands patent and the applications lodged and patents obtained abroad and, in the alternative, to refrain from disposing of those applications or patents or taking any measure necessary for the conservation of his own rights in those applications or patents.

By judgment of 7 December 1976 the President of that court dismissed the principal claim but granted the alternative claim.

Later, at an unspecified date, the Company submitted a claim to the Netherlands Patent Office, under the conditions laid down in Article 10 of the Netherlands Patents Law [Octroiwet], to the effect that it was entitled to the Netherlands patent which Mr Goderbauer had *applied for*.

The Claims Division of the Netherlands Patent Office granted the Company's claim on 28 December 1977, and that decision was confirmed by the Appeals Division of that office on 7 March 1979.

On 10 April 1979, the Company took action to transfer to its name the application for a patent in the Netherlands.

At a date also unspecified, but after that transfer and without any apparent causal link, the Company went into liquidation. Mr Duijnstee [hereinafter referred to as 'the Liquidator'], of Rekem (Belgium), was appointed liquidator.

On 28 November 1979 he applied to the President of the Arrondissements-rechtbank, Maastricht, for an interlocutory injunction requiring Mr Goderbauer to sign the forms needed for the purpose of the transfer of the applications lodged and patents granted in the 22 foreign countries.

On 19 December 1979 the President dismissed that application.

On 21 December 1979 Mr Goderbauer himself brought proceedings against the Liquidator before the Arrondissementsrechtbank, Maastricht, in order to obtain recognition, as against the Liquidator, of the '*right of lien*' over the application for a patent in the Netherlands and over the foreign applications and patents, which he claimed arose out of Article 60 of the Netherlands Insolvency Law.

For his part, the Liquidator pleaded a counterclaim identical to his previous claim of 28 November 1979. Mr Goderbauer's claim and the Liquidator's counterclaim were dismissed by the Arrondissementsrechtbank on 24 April 1980.

On 17 July 1980 the Liquidator appealed against that judgment to the Gerechtshof [Regional Court of Appeal], 's-Hertogenbosch, contending that Mr Goderbauer's claim should be declared unfounded and that his own counterclaim should be upheld, that is to say that Mr Goderbauer should be ordered to cooperate in the formalities requisite for the transfer of the applications or patents into the name of the Company or of the Liquidator, and that periodic penalty payments should be imposed upon failure to do so.

Mr Goderbauer himself lodged a cross-appeal, claiming that under the second paragraph of Article 10 of the Netherlands Patents Law, in the event of his being required to transfer the applications and patents to the Company, he should be accorded a *right of lien* as against the Liquidator until he had been compensated or the loss of the patent and the administrative expenses which he had incurred (fees for filing, designation and so forth).

On 28 May 1981 the Gerechtshof, s'-Hertogenbosch, upheld the contested decision.

The Liquidator lodged an appeal in cassation against that judgment to the Hoge Raad der Nederlanden. Mr Goderbauer, the respondent, contended that the appeal should be dismissed.

Neither of the parties raised the questions which have been submitted to this Court by the Hoge Raad der Nederlanden. The Advocate General at that court recommended that a reference should be made to the Court of Justice for a ruling on the interpretation of Articles 19, 16, 6 and 22 of the 1968 Convention on Jurisdiction and the Enforcement of Judgments in Civil and Commercial Matters.

II - By a judgment dated 29 October 1982 the Hoge Raad der Nederlanden referred the following questions to the Court:

'1. Does the obligation imposed on the Court of a Contracting State by Article 19 of the Convention of 27 September 1968 on Jurisdiction and the Enforcement of Judgments in Civil and Commercial Matters to declare of its own motion that it has no jurisdiction override a provision such as Article 419(1) of the Netherlands Code of Civil Procedure, with the result that the court of cassation must consider whether the judgment appealed against relates to a claim covered by Article 19 and, if that question is answered in the affirmative, quash the judgment appealed against, even if the question has not been raised in the grounds of appeal?

2. Must the question whether the proceedings are concerned with the registration or validity of patents within the meaning of Article 16(4) of the said Convention be determined: (a) according to the law of the Contracting State whose courts are referred to in that provision; (b) according to the *lex fori*; or (c) on the basis of an independent interpretation of the said provision?

3. If Question 2 is answered in the manner suggested under (c), must a claim such as that concerned here be considered to be a claim covered by Article 16(4)?'

III - I shall consider those questions in a different order, which has the advantage of following the numerical order of the provisions to be interpreted.

Second question submitted by the Hoge Raad

This question asks on what basis the term 'proceedings concerned with the registration or validity of patents' within the meaning of Article 16(4) of the Convention must be defined. In my view, that term must be interpreted on an *independent* basis.

The Commission rightly points out the inconveniences of recourse to a definition based either on the *lex fori* or on the law of the Contracting State within which the deposit or registration of the patent has been applied for, has taken place or is, under the terms of an international Convention, deemed to have taken place.

The adoption of an independent criterion for the definition of the scope of the Convention has already been recommended in the judgments of the Court. The Court has indeed stated that 'in order to ensure, as far as possible, that the rights and obligations which derive from [the Convention] for the Contracting State and the persons to whom it applies are equal and uniform' the terms of Article 1 should not be interpreted as a mere reference to the national law of one or other of the States concerned and that the concepts used in Article 1 should be regarded 'as independent concepts which must be interpreted by reference, first, to the objectives and scheme of the Convention and, secondly, to the general principles which stem from the corpus of the national legal systems'.

This approach should also be adopted in order to define the proceedings in which certain courts are to have exclusive jurisdiction under Article 16. Whilst Article 1 of the Convention in principle excludes certain proceedings from the scope of the Convention, for example bankruptcy (in paragraph (2)), it does not contain a similar exception in relation to disputes involving patents or other rights required to be deposited or registered: on the contrary, insofar as the dispute concerns the registration or validity of such rights, Article 16(4) *confers* exclusive jurisdiction upon the courts of the Contracting State in which registration takes place. For the rest, it does not affect the applicability in principle of the general and special provisions of the Convention.

The Court has adopted the same method in relation to sales by instalment (Article 13 and the second paragraph of Article 14) and in relation to special jurisdiction ('in matters relating to a contract', Article 5(1)). It follows that the concepts used in Article 16, and in particular paragraph (4) thereof, must also be interpreted independently.

Third question submitted by the Hoge Raad

(a) On the basis of an independent criterion, does the expression 'proceedings concerned with the registration or validity of patents' include a dispute such as that which is before the Hoge Raad?

In accordance with the previous judgments of the Court, I consider first that the exclusive jurisdictions created by the Convention in derogation from the general and special provisions must be interpreted narrowly.

The Court has indeed ruled that: '...the assignment, in the interests of the proper administration of justice, of exclusive jurisdiction to the courts of one Contracting State in accordance with Article 16 of the Convention results in depriving the parties of the choice of the forum which would otherwise be theirs and, in certain cases, results in their being brought before a court which is not that of the domicile of any of them'.

From that the Court inferred that 'the provisions of Article 16 must not be given a wider interpretation than is required by their objective'.

Like the exclusive jurisdiction provided for in Article 16(3) (validity of entries in public registers), the exclusive jurisdiction laid down in Article 16(4) is explained by the fact that patents and other similar rights involve - according to the systems in force in the Member States - either deposit or registration after prior examination, and obviously the courts of the State in which the deposit or registration has taken place or is deemed to have taken place are best placed to adjudicate upon cases in which the dispute (validity or existence of the patent, alleged right of priority by reason of earlier deposit, revocation, lapse, unity of the invention, etc.) itself centres on the validity or existence of the deposit or registration.

None of those questions seems to be *primarily* at issue in the dispute before the Hoge Raad. The legality of the grant of the patent was not disputed when the patent was applied for; nor is it the subject-matter of the proceedings before the Hoge Raad.

It appears from the papers before the Court that the outcome of the dispute depends, first, upon the classification of the relationship which existed between the Company and Mr Goderbauer and, secondly, upon the rights and obligations arising out of that relationship.

That question arises in advance of the formalities, properly so called, for the transfer of the applications lodged or patents registered by Mr Goderbauer in the Contracting States other than the Netherlands. It is not until a decision has been taken on any assistance which Mr Goderbauer might have to give to the Liquidator that the problem of the transfer, properly so called, of the rights of the applicant or the inventor will actually arise in the other Contracting States and in the countries which are not parties to the Convention.

In reality, what the Liquidator is seeking - and this is clearly demonstrated by the fact that at first instance he applied for an interlocutory injunction - is the adoption of an *interim* measure relating to an obligation *to act* on the part of Mr Goderbauer, since in order to wind up the insolvent company it is necessary that the formalities for transfer should be carried out.

The adoption of such a measure is dependent upon the civil or commercial relationship which existed between the Company and Mr Goderbauer. It is a question of whether the Liquidator, insofar as he is the assignee of the rights of the Company, may, on the basis of the links or the contract of employment between Mr Goderbauer and the Company, and notwithstanding the right to compensation which the latter continues to assert as against the insolvent Company, require his cooperation in order to carry out the preliminary formalities needed in order to realize the asset of the Company constituted by the applications lodged and the patents obtained abroad in the name of Lodewijk Goderbauer.

(b) Since the adoption of the 1968 Convention on Jurisdiction and the Enforcement and Judgments, two international Conventions have been drawn up concerning patents: the Convention on the Grant of European Patents, signed in Munich on 5 October 1973, and the Convention for the European Patent for the Common Market, signed in Luxembourg on 15 December 1975.

Only the Munich Convention is at present in force. It deals only with the

European patent. The applications made or patents held by Mr Goderbauer are national; therefore it appears that only the Paris Convention for the Protection of Industrial Property of 20 March 1883, most recently amended in Stockholm on 14 July 1967, should be applied to them.

That point was considered in the written observations submitted to the Court and it is not without interest to examine the problem of jurisdiction in the light of the solutions or approaches adopted by the two Conventions of Munich and Luxembourg. Those two Conventions, which are subsequent to the Brussels Convention, in fact contain special provisions on jurisdiction, in particular in relation to actions for the revocation of patents under the Luxembourg Convention. In addition, they deal with the special case of the inventor in the service of an employer.

Article 60(1) of the Munich Convention provides as follows: 'The right to a European patent shall belong to the inventor or his successor in title. If the inventor is an employee the right to the European patent shall be determined in accordance with the law of the State in which the employee is mainly employed; if the State in which the employee is mainly employed cannot be determined, the law to be applied shall be that of the State in which the employer has his place of business to which the employee is attached'. Article 4 of the Protocol on Jurisdiction and the Recognition of Decisions in respect of the Right to the Grant of a European Patent (known as 'the Protocol on Recognition'), annexed to that Convention, provides that: 'Subject to Article 5, if the subject-matter of a European patent application is the invention of an employee, the courts of the Contracting State, if any, whose law determines the right to the European patent pursuant to Article 60, paragraph 1, second sentence, of the Convention, shall have exclusive jurisdiction over proceedings between the employee and the employer. Article 68 of the Luxembourg Convention provides that: 'Unless otherwise specified in this Convention, the Convention on Jurisdiction and Enforcement of Judgments in Civil and Commercial Matters, signed at Brussels on 27 September 1968 ... shall apply to actions relating to Community patents and to decisions given in respect of such actions'.

Article 69(4) of that Convention provides that: 'The following courts shall have exclusive jurisdiction, regardless of residence: (a) ...; (b) in actions relating to the right to a patent in which an employer and an employee are in dispute, the courts of the Contracting State *under whose law the right to a European patent is determined* in accordance with the second sentence of Article 60(1) of the European Patent Convention. Any agreement conferring jurisdiction shall be valid only insofar as the national law governing the contract of employment allows the agreement in question'.

Finally, Article V(d) of the Protocol annexed to the Brussels Convention, after the adjustments made by the Convention on the Accession of Denmark, Ireland and the United Kingdom and by the Convention on the Accession of Greece, will, when it enters into force, provide that: 'Without prejudice to the jurisdiction of the European Patent Office under the Convention on the Grant of European Patents, signed at Munich on 5 October 1973, the courts of each Contracting State shall have exclusive jurisdiction, regardless of domicile, in proceedings concerned with the registration or validity of any European patent granted for that State which is not a Community patent by virtue of the provisions of Article 86 of the Convention for the European Patent for the Common Market, signed at Luxembourg on 15 December 1975'.

By stating that in disputes between employer and employee in relation to patents the courts of the State whose law determines the right to the patent (European or Community) are to have exclusive jurisdiction, all those texts by implication confirm the special nature of the concepts of registration and validity of patents.

Even if the patent were a European or Community patent, the courts of the State in which the employee is mainly employed, that is to say in this case the Netherlands courts, would have exclusive jurisdiction, provided that the dispute between Mr Goderbauer and the Liquidator could properly be described as an 'action in which an employer and an employee are in dispute'. It seems that Mr Goderbauer was employed mainly in the Netherlands; in addition, that part of the Company to which he was attached was also situated in the Netherlands.

Consequently, the jurisdiction of the Netherlands courts - subject to the national rules on jurisdiction contained in Article 5 of the Netherlands Patents Law - resulting in this case from the combined provisions of Articles 2 and 5 of the Brussels Convention would not be affected by the provisions of the two European Conventions on patents.

(c) The papers before the Court show that the dispute between Mr Goderbauer and the Liquidator arose before the Company went into liquidation.

Nevertheless, as the United Kingdom points out in its written observations, it is not impossible that, while not falling within the matters referred to in Article 16(4) and, therefore, being in principle within the scope of the general or special provisions of the Convention, the dispute exhibits a link with the rules on bankruptcy, which is specifically excluded by Article 1.

For example, there might be a problem in relation to the registration of a patent in the name of the Liquidator. It is in that case that Mr Goderbauer relies upon Article 60 of the Netherlands Insolvency Law.

However, it should be noted that, apart from the fact that the applications or patents in question are registered abroad and the Liquidator resides in Belgium, the dispute does not exhibit any foreign element.

As for the problem of the effect of the insolvency on the disposal of the intangible assets, which are subject to registration in the public registers of other Contracting States, it does not arise until a later stage: first, it must be determined whether those rights are part of the assets; the applications or patents in question can be involved in the insolvency proceedings relating to the Company only in the State in which such proceedings have been brought in the first place, that is to say in the Netherlands.

The question of what effects a reference, or failure to make reference, to the insolvency in the public registers of the other Contracting States in which the applications or patents in question have been registered will have on the disposal of those assets also does not arise until a later stage.

Consequently, if it is accepted that the Netherlands rules of private international law on bankruptcy are applicable, the same result is achieved as that reached by the interpretation which I have suggested of Article 16(4) of the Convention.

First question submitted by the Hoge Raad

Article 429(1) of the Netherlands Code of Civil Procedure provides that: 'The Hoge Raad shall confine its consideration of the case to the grounds on which the appeal is based.'

Since none of the parties has expressly pleaded the lack of jurisdiction of the Netherlands courts under international law, the Hoge Raad asks whether, notwithstanding that provision of national law, it is bound to examine of its own motion whether it has jurisdiction under Article 19 of the Convention, which provides as follows: 'Where a court of a Contracting State is seised of a claim which is *principally* concerned with a matter over which the courts of another Contracting State have exclusive jurisdiction by virtue of Article 16, it shall declare of its own motion that it has no jurisdiction.'

The Commission, the Federal Republic of Germany and the United Kingdom answer that question in the affirmative, which is fully in accordance with the tenor of the preamble to the Convention and with its general spirit. I for my part, however, consider that the explanations set out in relation to the second and third questions render consideration of this point superfluous.

In order that it should be necessary to consider whether or not the courts of a Contracting State are entitled to make the examination of their own jurisdiction dependent upon whether or not the lack of international jurisdiction has been pleaded during the proceedings, those courts must first have before them a claim which is principally concerned with a matter in which Article 16 confers exclusive jurisdiction upon the courts of another Contracting State.

As I have stated, it seems to me that the terms of Article 16(4) do not cover, at any rate principally, a dispute of the type brought before the Hoge Raad.

Another ground, based on practical considerations, may be added to that fundamental reason: I do not believe that it would be in the interests of the proper administration of justice to adjudicate upon a question of this importance when, apart from the Commission, only the governments of two Member States - amongst which not even the Netherlands Government was included - have submitted written observations and when no government of any Member State has presented oral argument.

The Commission itself laid no special emphasis on this point in its observations.

In reply to the questions submitted, I conclude that the Court should rule as follows:

1. The expression 'proceeding's concerned with the registration or validity of patents' used in Article 16(4) of the Brussels Convention must be given an independent interpretation.

2. That expression covers only disputes which are principally concerned with the registration or validity of a patent.

Case 241/83 - 15 January 1985

Erich Rösler
v
Horst Rottwinkel

Exclusive jurisdiction - Article 16(1) - Disputes concerning tenancies of immovable property - Concept - Short letting of a holiday home - Included - Obligations of the parties under the tenancy agreement - Obligations in respect of which courts have exclusive jurisdiction.

Summary

1. Article 16(1) of the Convention of 27 September 1968 applies to all lettings of immovable property, even for a short term, and even where they relate only to the use and occupation of a holiday home.

2. All disputes concerning the obligations of the landlord or of the tenant under a tenancy, in particular those concerning the existence of tenancies or the interpretation of the terms thereof, their duration, the giving up of possession to the landlord, the repairing of damage caused by the tenant or the recovery of rent and of incidental charges payable by the tenant, such as charges for the consumption of water, gas and electricity, fall within the exclusive jurisdiction conferred by Article 16(1) of the Convention on the courts of the State in which the property is situated. On the other hand, disputes which are only indirectly related to the use of the property let, such as those concerning the loss of holiday enjoyment and travel expenses, do not fall within that exclusive jurisdiction.

JUDGMENT OF THE COURT

Bosco, President of Chamber, Pescatore, O'Keeffe, Koopmans and Bahlmann, Judges

1. By order of 5 October 1983, which was received at the Court on 24 October 1983, the Bundesgerichtshof [Federal Court of Justice] referred to the Court for a preliminary ruling under the Protocol of 3 June 1971 to the Convention of 27 September 1968 on Jurisdiction and the Enforcement of Judgments in Civil and Commercial Matters (hereinafter referred to as 'the Convention') two questions on the interpretation of Article 16(1) of that Convention.

2. By a written agreement dated 19 January 1980, Horst Rottwinkel, the plaintiff in the main proceedings, let a flat in his holiday villa at Cannobio in Italy to Erich Rösler, the defendant in the main proceedings, for the period from 12 July to 2 August 1980. The rent agreed for four persons was DM 2 625. By the terms of the agreement visitors were not allowed to stay overnight. The incidental charges for gas, water and electricity had to be calculated according to the quantities consumed and there was also an extra charge for cleaning at the end of the letting. The parties further agreed that the agreement was to be governed by German law, that Bielefeld was to be the place of performance and that its courts were to have jurisdiction.

3. The plaintiff in the main proceedings spent his holiday in the holiday villa at the same time as the defendant.

4. On 7 January 1981 the plaintiff sued the defendant in the Landgericht [Regional Court] Berlin, for damages and for the payment of outstanding incidental charges. He claimed that throughout the holiday the defendant had accommodated more than four persons in the holiday home which caused the cesspool constantly to overflow, creating an intolerable smell, and was a considerable nuisance owing to the noise.

5. According to the plaintiff, his and his family's rest and quiet had been considerably disturbed. He claimed damages from the defendant for loss of holiday enjoyment, founding his claim on a breach of the lease, and sought reimbursement of the costs of travelling to the holiday resort. He also claimed, under the terms of the lease, payment of incidental charges in respect of gas, electricity and water and of cleaning at the end of the letting.

6. The Landgericht Berlin dismissed the action as inadmissible on the ground that, according to Article 16(1) of the Convention, the courts of the Contracting State in which the property was situated, namely Italy, had exclusive jurisdiction to entertain the plaintiff's claims. The Kammergericht [Higher Regional Court] in Berlin quashed the judgment of the Landgericht and referred the case back to that court for re-hearing and judgment.

7. The defendant appealed against the judgment of the Kammergericht to the Bundesgerichtshof on a point of law.

8. Considering that the dispute raised questions as to the interpretation of the Convention, the Bundesgerichtshof, by order of 5 October 1983, stayed the proceedings and submitted the following questions to the Court of Justice for a preliminary ruling: '(1) Is Article 16(1) of the Convention applicable if a lease concluded between persons resident in the Federal Republic of Germany is for the short letting only of a holiday home located in Italy and the parties to the lease have agreed that German law is to apply? (2) If Article 16(1) is applicable, does it apply to actions for damages for breach of the lease, particularly for compensation for loss of holiday enjoyment and for the recovery of incidental charges payable under the lease?'

9. The plaintiff submits that Article 16(1) of the Convention is not applicable to this case. In his view, the agreement in question is for the short letting of a holiday home which, on an economic view, is more akin to a lodging agreement than to a lease in the proper meaning of the word. The claims involved are primarily for compensation for the loss of holiday enjoyment and for damage to, or loss of, movable property. Furthermore, the place of performance is in the Federal Republic of Germany. The agreement provided that monies due, including the rent, had to be paid in the Federal Republic and the keys also had to be returned there. A court inspection of the premises is out of the question as a means of resolving the dispute.

10. The Government of the Federal Republic of Germany takes the view that it would be contrary to the spirit of Article 16(1) of the Convention to apply it to claims arising from short-term leases. It points out in this regard that in its judgment of 14 December 1977 in Case 73/77, *Sanders* v *van der Putte*, [1977] ECR 2383 the Court stated that Article 16(1) must not be given a wider interpretation than its objective requires. The *ratio legis* of Article 16(1) is that tenancies of immovable property, especially

of dwellings, are generally governed by complex legislation which is strongly influenced by social considerations and which is best applied by the courts of the country in which it is in force. However, that situation does not arise in the case of agreements which relate only to the short-term letting of holiday homes situated abroad. In such cases the interests involved do not require the application of social legislation in the matter of tenancies. In German legislation, for example, short-term lettings of housing accommodation, which cover lettings of holiday homes, are expressly excluded from the ambit of social legislation on tenancies.

11. The Government of the Federal Republic of Germany also considers that the inexpediency of applying Article 16(1) of the Convention to the letting of holiday homes becomes particularly clear if, as in this case, the parties have made their contract subject exclusively to German law and to the jurisdiction of the German courts. The primary purpose of entrusting the proceedings to the courts of the place where the property is situated, which is to enable the mandatory provisions of the law of that place to apply by making the forum and applicable law coincide and, generally, to simplify the proceedings, is irrelevant in this case.

12. A further aim of Article 16(1) is that the tenant of a dwelling, who as a general rule is socially in a comparatively weak position, should not be put at any further disadvantage by the fact that the trial takes place before a court far away from his place of residence. That aim is also irrelevant as far as leases of holiday homes are concerned because the lessee does not normally reside at the place where the holiday home is situated or require any special social consideration.

13. With regard to the second question, the Government of the Federal Republic of Germany points out that in its judgment in *Sanders* v *van der Putte*, cited above, the Court stated that the special considerations relating to tenancies of immovable property explained why exclusive jurisdiction was conferred on the courts of the State in which the immovable property was situated in the case of disputes relating to tenancies of immovable property properly so-called, that is to say, in particular, disputes between landlords and tenants as to the existence or interpretation of leases or to compensation for damage caused by the tenant and to the giving up of possession of the premises. According to the Rapporteur of the Committee of Experts on the Convention (*Official Journal*, 1979 C 59, p.1), the rule conferring exclusive jurisdiction does not apply to proceedings concerned only with the recovery of rent, since such proceedings can be considered to relate to a subject-matter which is

quite distinct from the rented property itself. That view must apply *a fortiori* to actions for compensation for indirect damage arising from a breach of the lease by one party and unrelated to the rented property itself. Therefore, the plaintiff's claims for compensation for loss of holiday enjoyment and unnecessarily incurred travel expenses do not fall under Article 16(1). Nor can there be any exclusive jurisdiction under that provision in respect of claims for the payment of incidental charges which form an integral part of the total rent.

14. The United Kingdom considers that the scope of Article 16(1) is to be determined by reference to the type of proceedings affecting the immovable property rather than to the nature of the lease or other interest in that property. In this case, the plaintiff is not making any claim for rent but is claiming damages for breaches of the lease and consequential loss flowing therefrom. The plaintiff's claims do not fall within the class of disputes mentioned by the Court in *Sanders* v *van der Putte*. The need for the proper administration of justice does not require claims, such as those in this case for breach of terms of a lease and for consequential loss, to be assigned to the exclusive jurisdiction of the courts of the State in which the property is situated. Similar arguments apply to the claim by the plaintiff for incidental charges, namely those relating to the consumption of gas, electricity and water and for cleaning. The claims concerning the loss of, or damage to, articles listed in the inventory do not affect the rented property and ought not to be regarded as disputes which have as their object tenancies of immovable property for the purposes of Article 16(1) of the Convention. For that provision to apply, the objective of the proceedings must be the determination, enforcement or giving effect to, or the termination of, rights of possession.

15. The Government of the Italian Republic takes the view that the reasons given by the national court for its decision, namely that considerations of expediency suggest that Article 16(1) should not be applied to cases in which the lease is only for the short-term letting of a holiday home, both parties habitually reside in a country other than the one in which the property is situated and have agreed to apply the substantive law of the State in which they habitually reside, are not of such a nature as to exclude the application of that provision. The rule laid down in Article 16(1) does not distinguish between short-term and long-term lettings or between the different uses to which the property is put: it may be used for professional, commercial or agricultural purposes, as a dwelling, for holidays and so forth. The fact that neither contracting party resides in Italy is immaterial. The argument based on the clause

concerning the application of the law of a Member State other than that in which the property is situated is unacceptable. In any event, in some circumstances at least the clause would not be valid, for example if it were meant to defeat the application of the 'fair rent' legislation in Italy. If it were accepted that an agreement of that kind incorporated into the contract by means of a jurisdiction clause, might even deprive the courts of the State in which the property is situated of jurisdiction, the way would be open to the possibility of evading mandatory rules of that State.

16. With regard to the incidental charges there can be no doubt, in the view of the Government of the Italian Republic that they are related to the lease itself since their payment is a contractual obligation undertaken by the tenant. A dispute over such charges must clearly fall within the exclusive jurisdiction conferred by Article 16(1). The possibility of depriving the courts of the State in which the property is situated of jurisdiction in such disputes might enable mandatory rules to be evaded by means of cleverly drafted agreements.

17. The Commission states that in some Contracting States furnished accommodation in general and furnished holiday accommodation in particular are expressly or impliedly excluded from the matters covered by special legislation for the protection of tenants. For those reasons it considers that the letting for consideration of furnished accommodation, particularly furnished holiday accommodation, does not come within the scope of application of Article 16(1).

18. Article 16 of the Convention provides as follows: 'The following courts shall have exclusive jurisdiction, regardless of domicile: (1) in proceedings which have as their object rights *in rem* in, or tenancies of, immovable property, the courts of the Contracting State in which the property is situated; ...'.

19. The *raison d'être* of the exclusive jurisdiction conferred by Article 16(1) on the courts of the Contracting State in which the property is situated is the fact that tenancies are closely bound up with the law of immovable property and with the provisions, generally of a mandatory character, governing its use, such as legislation controlling the level of rents and protecting the rights of tenants, including tenant farmers.

20. Article 16(1) seeks to ensure a rational allocation of jurisdiction by opting for a solution whereby the court having jurisdiction is determined on the basis of its proximity to the property since that court is in a better

position to obtain first-hand knowledge of the facts relating to the creation of tenancies and to the performance of the terms thereof.

21. The question submitted by the Bundesgerichtshof is designed to ascertain whether exceptions may be made to the general rule laid down in Article 16 owing to the special character of certain tenancies, such as short-term lettings of holiday homes, even though the wording of that article provides no indication in that respect.

22. It must be emphasised in this regard that, as the Italian Government has rightly pointed out, inherent in any exception to the general rule laid down in Article 16(1) is the risk of further extensions which might call in question the application of national legislation governing the use of immovable property.

23. Account must also be taken of the uncertainty which would be created if the courts allowed exceptions to be made to the general rule laid down in Article 16(1), which has the advantage of providing for a clear and certain attribution of jurisdiction covering all circumstances, thus fulfilling the purpose of the Convention, which is to assign jurisdiction in a certain and predictable way.

24. It follows that the provision in question applies to all tenancies of immovable property irrespective of their special characteristics.

25. The reply to the first question must therefore be that Article 16(1) of the Convention applies to all lettings of immovable property, even for a short term and even where they relate only to the use and occupation of a holiday home.

26. With regard to the second question, it must be noted that the Convention grants exclusive jurisdiction 'in proceedings which have as their object ... tenancies of immovable property'. In its judgment in *Sanders* v *van der Putte*, cited above, the Court considered that that expression covers disputes between landlords and tenants as to the existence or the interpretation of leases or to compensation for damage caused by the tenant. The Court must point out that that list is not exhaustive. The Government of the Italian Republic is right in arguing that disputes concerning payment of rent fall under that exclusive jurisdiction. It would, in fact, be contrary to one of the aims of the provision in question, namely the correct application of national legislation on tenancies, to excluded from that exclusive jurisdiction

disputes which are, in some Member States at least, governed by special legislation, such as the Italian 'fair rent' legislation.

27. Leases generally contain terms concerning entry into possession by the tenant, the use to which the property is to be put, the obligation of the landlord and tenant regarding the maintenance of the property, the duration of the lease and the giving up of possession to the landlord, the rent and the incidental charges to be paid by the tenant, such as water, gas and electricity charges.

28. Disputes concerning the obligations of the landlord or of the tenant under the lease come within the ambit of Article 16(1) of the Convention, being 'proceedings which have as their object ... tenancies of immovable property'. On the other hand, disputes which are only indirectly related to the use of the property let, such as those concerning the loss of holiday enjoyment and travel expenses, do not fall within the exclusive jurisdiction conferred by that article.

29. The reply to the second question must, therefore, be that any dispute concerning the existence of tenancies or the interpretation of the terms thereof, their duration, the giving up of possession to the landlord, the repairing of damage caused by the tenant or the recovery of rent and of incidental charges payable by the tenant, such as charges for the consumption of water, gas and electricity, falls within the exclusive jurisdiction conferred by Article 16(1) of the Convention on the courts of the State in which the property is situated. Disputes concerning the obligations of the landlord or of the tenant under the terms of the tenancy fall within that exclusive jurisdiction. On the other hand, disputes which are only indirectly related to the use of the property let, such as those concerning the loss of holiday enjoyment and travel expenses, do not fall within the exclusive jurisdiction conferred by that article.

On those grounds, the Court (Fourth Chamber), in answer to the questions referred to it by the Bundesgerichtshof, by order of 3 October 1983, hereby rules:

1. Article 16(1) of the Convention applies to all lettings of immovable property, even for a short term and even where they relate only to the use and occupation of a holiday home.

2. All disputes concerning the obligations of the landlord or of the tenant under a tenancy, in particular those concerning the

existence of tenancies or the interpretation of the terms thereof, their duration, the giving up of possession to the landlord, the repairing of damage caused by the tenant or the recovery of rent and of incidental charges payable by the tenant, such as charges for the consumption of water, gas and electricity, fall within the exclusive jurisdiction conferred by Article 16(1) of the Convention on the courts of the State in which the property is situated. On the other hand, disputes which are only indirectly related to the use of the property let, such as those concerning the loss of holiday enjoyment and travel expenses, do not fall within the exclusive jurisdiction conferred by that article.

OPINION OF ADVOCATE GENERAL SIR GORDON SLYNN

Article 16(1) of the Convention on jurisdiction and the Enforcement of Judgments in Civil and Commercial Matters provides that 'in proceedings which have as their object rights in, or tenancies of, immovable property' the Courts of the Contracting State in which the property is situated shall have exclusive jurisdiction regardless of domicile. Article 19 requires the Court of any other Contracting State which is seised of a claim which is principally concerned with such a matter to declare of its own motion that it has no jurisdiction.

Mr Rottwinkel and Mr Rösler both live in Germany.

By a contract dated 19 January 1980, Mr Rottwinkel let to Mr Rösler for three weeks from 12 July 1980 certain parts of a holiday villa in Italy which was furnished though not provided with linen. Mr Rösler undertook to pay a rent of DM 2625 for four persons to stay at the house, it being agreed that visitors were not permitted to stay overnight. In addition Mr Rösler undertook to pay charges of DM 295 and a final charge for cleaning at the end of the letting together with the costs of gas, water, electricity and heating. It was stipulated that Mr Rösler should comply with the agent's instructions, use the property and the furnishings carefully and pay the costs of any damage. German law was declared to be the law governing the contract, which was executed in Bielefeld whose courts were chosen as having jurisdiction.

Mr Rottwinkel stayed in the house for his holiday at the same time as Mr Rösler. As a result of what he alleges happened, Mr Rottwinkel brought an action in the Landgericht, Berlin, claiming that the terms of the lease had been broken in that more than four people stayed in the property, causing a great deal of noise. They also proved too much for the cesspool which overran causing a nuisance. In the result, Mr Rottwinkel's own holiday was spoiled and he claims that the cost of it is recoverable as damages for breach of the agreement. Secondly, Mr Rottwinkel alleges that some articles were damaged or missing at the end of the period of the letting and thirdly, he claims under the terms of the lease, monies due for gas, electricity, water and for the cleaning of the property.

The Landgericht considered that the action could only be brought in Italy because of the provisions of Article 16 of the Convention; the Kammergericht took the opposite view; on appeal by way of revision, the Bundesgerichtshof was inclined to think that proceedings could be brought in Germany, but asks two questions of this Court pursuant to the Protocol of 3 June 1971 on the interpretation of the Convention by the Court of Justice:

'(1) Is Article 16(1) of the Convention applicable if a lease concluded between persons resident in the Federal Republic of Germany is for the short letting only of a holiday home located in Italy and the parties to the lease have agreed that German law is to apply?

(2) If Article 16(1) is applicable, does it also apply to actions or damages for breach of the lease, particularly for compensation for lost holiday enjoyment and for the recovery of supplementary costs payable under the lease?'

At first sight it might seem astonishing that such a dispute as exists here could not be litigated in the Federal Republic; the varying reasons suggested by the parties why it is not caught by Article 16, however, only serve to show that on the present wording of the Article, the question is not so simple.

The German Government and the Commission support the plaintiff in the main action in saying that as a matter of interpretation Article 16(1) does not apply to short holiday lets at all. In the alternative, the German Government contends that, if Article 16 does cover such lettings, it only covers claims for damage to the property let and does not include claims for personal inconvenience suffered as the result of a breach of the contract, nor does it cover a claim for letting charges. The Commission argues, again in the alternative, that, if such lettings do fall within Article 16(1), the only litigation which must go before the court of the *situs* of the land is that which directly concerns the lettings, such as questions as to the existence or termination of the lease, or defects in or damage to the property let, but does not include claims for damages for loss of a holiday or for supplementary charges.

On the other hand, the United Kingdom Government and the Italian Government consider that it is not possible to distinguish tenancies by their length or purpose; they accept that, as a matter of interpretation, short-term holiday lettings do fall within Article 16. To avoid the result for which the defendant contends, the United Kingdom Government, however, says that the proper course is to consider not the type of lease but the type of proceedings. The only proceedings covered by Article 16 are those which concern the determination, enforcement, or giving effect to, or the termination of, rights of possession. In this case it is said that the claims are like other claims for damages for breach of contract or for a debt, and bear little direct relationship to the property let. The proper administration of justice does not require that they should be exclusively the province of the courts of the *situs*.

The Italian Government considers that once it is accepted that short holiday lettings do fall within the Article, claims for charges, even supplementary charges included in the terms of the lease, fall within Article 16, though it is recognised that a claim for damages for loss of a holiday may be outside the Article.

Although it is clear that Article 16 is a mandatory rule (Case 288/82

Duijnstee v *Goderbauer* 15 November 1983, paragraph 15) the Court has already held that, since it deprives the parties of the choice of forum which would otherwise be theirs, and may even require them to litigate in a court which is not that of the domicile of any of them, its provisions 'must not be given a wider interpretation than is required by their objective'. (See Case 73/77 *Sanders* v *van der Putte* [1977] ECR 2383, where the Court held that Article 16(1) must not be interpreted as including an agreement to rent under a usufructuary lease a retail business carried on in immovable property rented from a third person by the lessor.)

In the Jenard report on the Convention, the explanation given for adopting an exclusivity rule in relation to disputes regarding immovable property is, partly, that in Germany and Italy the exclusive jurisdiction of the courts of the *situs* is regarded as a matter of public policy, so that rulings by other courts would neither be recognised nor enforced there, and partly that the interests of the proper administration of justice were thought to be better served by adopting such a rule. The fact that checks and expert enquiries might have to be carried out on the spot, entries have to be made in land registries, and special customary rules be applicable, it was said, makes it much more convenient for the court of the *situs* to be seised of the case. Tenancies of immovable property in particular are 'usually governed by special legislation' which should preferably be administered only by the courts of the country where it is in force. Moreover, several States provide for exclusive jurisdiction in such proceedings. The Committee, therefore, intended Article 16 to 'cover disputes between landlord and tenant over the existence or interpretation of tenancy agreements, compensation for damage caused by the tenant, eviction etc.' but not claims for rent of the property leased.

That difficulties might arise in cases of short lettings or involving claims for damages arising from obligations included in tenancy agreements was recognised by the time that the accession of Denmark, Ireland and the United Kingdom to the Convention was being considered. However, a majority of Member States, it is said, opposed a proposal put forward by the United Kingdom that the Article should be altered so that jurisdiction was not exclusive where litigation involved personal obligations contained in tenancies of immovable property, or where agreements granted a right of possession for a limited period, as where holiday accommodation was the subject matter of a letting. Professor Schlosser's Report, on the questions arising on the accession of the three new Member States, shows that the Committee considering the question was not of the same view as the Jenard Report as to whether claims for rent were within Article 16(1). It does, however, state that 'the underlying principle of the provision quite clearly does not require its application to short-term agreements for use and occupation Such as, for example, holiday accommodation'.

It seems that in many Member States rules of social policy adopted in respect of lettings or accommodation (such as fair rents, periods of notice, supervision by special tribunals) do not apply to short lettings of holiday accommodation. Since special rules and registers may not exist in respect of such lettings and detailed site inspections may not be needed, it can be said, also, that the administration of justice does not necessarily require that such lettings be dealt with by the courts of the country where the property is situated.

Moreover, the convenience of the parties may not necessarily be best served by requiring that the courts of the *situs* should have exclusive jurisdiction in respect of short holiday lettings, if both parties live in another country. To this extent the principles which generally led the Committee to propose exclusive jurisdiction for disputes as to tenancies of immovable property and rights *in rem do not seem to apply to short holiday lettings.*

On the other hand, it is clear that the intention, when the Convention was made, was not to confer exclusive jurisdiction in respect of disputes as to rights *in rem*, or tenancies of immovable property, only for those countries which recognised exclusive jurisdiction as a matter of public order, nor for those countries which have special legislation dealing with the kind of tenancies in question. The rule adopted was to be uniformly applied; it was not to depend on whether the administration of justice in any particular case required that the courts of the *situs* should have exclusive jurisdiction. Nor does it seem to me that the question was to depend in each case on an assessment of the convenience of the parties, nor an assessment of the risk that injustice might arise in exceptional cases because of the distance of the parties from the courts of the *situs* and the consequent difficulty and cost of litigation.

The Commission, though in the end supporting the plaintiffs in the main action, clearly recognises the difficulties of creating exceptions to the general words used in the Article. The Commission considers, however, that, since the Member States were not able to agree which leases and claims were covered by Article 16(1), the uncertainty must be removed. It proposes as a guide that the purpose of Article 16 is to protect a specific group of persons, namely tenants of immovable property for whom such property forms an essential part of their livelihood and accordingly, that the letting of accommodation for consideration, particularly furnished holiday accommodation, does not fall within the scope of Article 16(1).

There seems to me very great force in the arguments that short holiday lettings of furnished property should not be the exclusive province of the courts of the *situs*, particularly if both parties reside in another country, though in some cases even if only one of them does so. The question, however, is not what the Member States could have agreed but what they did agree.

It is possible on a fair reading of the Article to say that some tenancies, in this case short holiday lettings, are excluded?

The Jenard Report says that the Article 'will include tenancies of dwellings and of premises for professional or commercial use, and agricultural holdings'.

It does not seem to me possible to adopt a clear-cut distinction between tenancies of furnished and tenancies of unfurnished accommodation. Both are of immovable property and usually primarily of immovable property. Nor do I think that the suggested test as to whether a letting is an essential part of a tenant's livelihood is an acceptable one for the purpose of introducing exceptions to the Article. I cannot see as a matter of interpretation of the Article any justification for saying that holiday lettings are excluded, but only holiday lettings. There is no real difference between a short letting to a man on holiday or to one attending a conference or undertaking a short course of study.

Nor does it seem to me that on the present Article there can be fairly read in a distinction between 'short lettings' and 'long lettings', whatever 'short' may mean in this context.

If it were possible to distinguish between a tenancy properly understood and an agreement which only grants a licence to use and occupy property, which is not itself a tenancy, then there would, of course, be no difficulty about categorising holiday accommodation agreements as being such licences.

However, if, as the Schlosser Report considered, rights *in rem* have to be defined by the law of the *situs*, then equally it would seem that what is a tenancy must be decided by the law of the *situs* (paragraph 168). In the present case it seems that no distinction is drawn in German law between a tenancy and such a licence. The agreement has to be treated as a tenancy and the question proceeds on the basis that there is a tenancy or lease of the accommodation.

Conversely, if 'tenancy' has to be defined as a matter of Community law, it seems difficult to introduce as a matter of interpretation and without clearly expressed words, such a distinction between a licence (which is outside Article 16) and a tenancy, when such a distinction may not exist in the law of several Member States.

Moreover, it is clearly not possible in my view to create an exception, for the purposes of Article 16, by reason of the fact that both parties to the contract were resident or domiciled in a Member State other than that of the *situs*, that they have specified the forum as being in their own country or specifically agreed that a particular system of law is to govern the contract. Those matters do not seem to me in any way to affect the question as to whether the courts of the *situs* have exclusive jurisdiction.

In my view, the wording of the Article requires clearly that the first question must be answered in the affirmative.

As to the second question, it is to be noted that exclusive jurisdiction is granted 'in proceedings which have as their object tenancies of immovable property' (in French 'de baux d'immeubles'; in Italian 'di contratti di affitto d'immobili'; in German 'die Miete oder Pacht von unbeweglichen Sachen'). The other language versions seem to indicate that what is covered is litigation the subject matter (rather than 'the object') of which is a tenancy agreement of immovable property rather than one which concerns simply the immovable property itself. In *Sanders* v *van der Putte*, the Court recognised this when adopting some of the examples of disputes given in the Jenard Report as falling within Article 16 - in particular, disputes between lessors and tenants as to the existence or interpretation of leases or to compensation for damage caused by the tenant and to giving up possession of the premises'. Accordingly it seems to me that the argument of the United Kingdom that Article 16(1) does not apply to actions for damages for breach of the lease, but only to proceedings whose objective is 'the determination, enforcement or giving effect to; or the termination of, rights of possession too narrow.

I consider that the answer to the first part of the second question is, therefore, that actions for damages for breach of a term of a tenancy agreement can fall within Article 16.

The second part of the second question, dealing with claims for lost holiday enjoyment and the recovery of supplementary costs payable under the lease, raises, however, the more difficult issue as to whether distinctions are to be drawn between different claims for breaches of a tenancy agreement or for monies due under a tenancy agreement.

I read the reference as making it quite clear that the complaints made about the overcrowding, the cesspool and the noise, which it is said spoiled the claimant's holiday, are claims for breach of the lease and not otherwise. If the claim had been put on a basis that the applicant was simply a neighbouring user, not relying on the terms of the lease, then clearly the matter would not fall within Article 16 but that is not the case.

If my reading is correct, it seems to me that the arguments have concentrated too much on the type of damage claimed. It is not in my view possible simply to dismiss the question in issue by saying that the loss of a good holiday and the waste of travel costs by the landlord are so far removed from immovable property that they cannot be within Article 16. What matters, as I see it, is the nature of the breach alleged rather than the damage caused, some of which in the present case may in any event be too remote.

Here two breaches are alleged. The first is a breach of a clause as to the nature of the user of the property (the number of people to be admitted), the second, breach of a clause as to the care to be exercised in the use of the property referred to in the lease.

In my opinion it is not possible to say that proceedings alleging a breach of a clause in a lease specifying the user of immovable property are always outside Article 16. If a house is let as a dwelling, but used as a shop or a factory, or land is let for grazing which is used for arable purposes, proceedings alleging breach of the user clause in the tenancy would in my view be within Article 16(1) and the courts of the *situs* would have exclusive jurisdiction. A distinction could be drawn between that kind of qualitative breach of user and the quantitative breach of user alleged here, namely using the premises for more people than agreed. For my part, I would not introduce that distinction, firstly, because I do not think that there is a real distinction of principle and, secondly, because it seems to me undesirable to encourage distinctions to be drawn, through litigation, between different breaches of different user clauses.

If, here, as I understand it, the damage claimed under this head results wholly or primarily from the breach of user clause, I consider the proceedings to be within Article 16 of the Convention to that extent.

The second head of damages relates to the loss of or damage to property. If the damage is said to have been done to the immovable property, in breach of a term of the lease, the proceedings to that extent fall within Article 16. If the items lost or damaged are chattels provided with the immovable property under the lease the position is more difficult.

It is tempting, in the modest circumstances of this case, to construe Article

16 as being limited to claims for damages to the immovable property, and to accept that claims for damages to the movable property can be litigated elsewhere. If one were drafting a convention *de novo* there might be arguments for so providing. Such a result would be more convenient where both parties live in the same Member State but one different from that where the land is situated. It has, however, to be borne in mind that such a combination of facts may be less usual than where the owner lives in the same country as the property let. It is also important to bear in mind that claims for damages to property may arise in all types of letting and the issues involved may be more complex than in the present case. A tenancy, not only for residential but also for business, professional and agricultural uses, may well include the provision of movable chattels in respect of which specific obligations are set out in the tenancy agreement. Damage to expensive movable equipment included in a business or agricultural lease may be more conveniently dealt with in the courts of the *situs* of the immovable property.

On balance, it is my view that if a tenancy of immovable property provides for the supply and use of movables as a part of the letting, then the tenancy should be treated as one legal transaction, and as falling within Article 16(1). It seems to me wrong to divide up the terms of the agreement between those concerned with immovables and those concerned with movables so long as the agreement provides for the letting of immovable property. It is artificial, for example, in a case like the present to say that a claim for damage to a door or a fixed bath falls within Article 16(1) but that a claim for damage to a chair provided for use in the property falls outside it.

That leaves the claim for the supplementary charges. The argument that they fall outside Article 16 is based partly on the views of the Jenard Committee (though not the Schlosser Committee) that a claim for rent falls outside Article 16(1). Whether that view is correct has not been fully argued, and since it may one day fall for decision, it is perhaps undesirable to express a concluded view about it. On what has been argued in this case, I find it very difficult to accept that the Jenard Committee view is right on the present wording of Article 16(1). Just as the primary obligation of the landlord is to make available the property, the primary obligation of the tenant is usually to pay the rent. Most disputes as to immovable property probably concern rent. To exclude rent disputes from Article 16(1) would seem to take away much of its content I find it difficult to accept that consequence when it is remembered that a primary reason for adopting Article 16(1) was that special legislation in several Member States deals with the letting of immovable property, and that one of the most important aspects of that legislation usually concerns rents. Proceedings involving a dispute as to the liability for rent or for unpaid rent due under an agreement seem to me, on the arguments advanced here, essentially to have as their subject matter a tenancy of immovable property. In this respect I find persuasive a number of the comments made by Dr Droz in 'Compétence Judiciaire et effets des jugements dans le Marché Commun' Vol. XIII *Bibliothèque de droit international privé* at p. 101-103 and, in particular, para. 153.

It is, of course, possible to distinguish rent from other charges for such matters as gas, electricity and heating and for cleaning the premises, on the basis that these are not part of the property let but are provided for, or in respect of, the property. If these goods and services are provided as an integral part of the letting, I would again not draw a distinction between them. To introduce refinements between what proceedings concerning the different terms of the lease are within, and what are without, Article 16(1) seems to me likely to increase and complicate rather than aid the solution of disputes. In such a case a dispute as to one overall rent for furnished accommodation, where the tenant holds back some rent because the furniture was not adequate, would lead to arguments as to which part of the rent fell within Article 16(1); a claim for cleaning charges could lead to a dispute as to whether the part withheld related to the cleaning of the walls and floor or the brushing of the carpets and furniture.

Although fully conscious of the inconvenience in a small case of the conclusion I have reached as to the interpretation of Article 16(1), it seems to me that such a result flows from a proper reading of the text, not least since the Member States were not able to reach agreement, at a later stage, that specific exceptions should be introduced in respect of what are called personal obligations or in respect of specific types of letting. The conclusion I have reached also, to my mind, produces a more consistent result overall.

I would accordingly read Article 16 as including all proceedings in respect of tenancies of immovable property albeit those proceedings include or involve claims in respect of movable property included in the letting of immovable property, or charges relating to the use of that property.

It is, of course, possible that some claims for damages arising out of the use of the property may well fall outside Article 16(1) as not arising under the tenancy agreement itself but under the general law, for example, of nuisance, negligence or malicious damage. In which case they are outside the Article because they are not part of the tenancy agreement. It does not, however, follow that, because claims under the lease are analogous to other claims under the general law of obligations, they cease to be within Article 16(1) automatically for that reason.

It is also to be borne in mind that by virtue of Article 19 of the Convention a court faced with a claim involving a tenancy agreement is not bound to reject jurisdiction if that claim is not the principal claim in the proceedings, or, as the Jenard report puts it at p. 39, 'If an issue which comes within the exclusive jurisdiction of another court is raised only as a preliminary or incidental matter'. It might, thus, be that in a situation where a package holiday was arranged through a travel agent which included air transport and the use of furnished accommodation that the dispute as to the accommodation might only be an incidental part of the dispute. In such a situation a court would be entitled to rely upon Article 19 of the Convention.

The difficulties revealed by this case may lead the Member States, parties to the Convention, to reconsider whether it would not be desirable to make specific exceptions, e.g. for holiday lettings or other defined categories, to the provisions of Article 16(1). That is not, however, a matter for the Court.

On the present Article, it seems to me that the questions put should be answered on the following lines:

(a) Article 16(1) of the Convention of Brussels 1968 is applicable to a tenancy agreement concluded between persons resident in one Member State for the short letting of a holiday home located in another Member State, even if those persons have agreed that the law of their State of residence is to govern the tenancy agreement.

(b) Article 16(1) applies to proceedings in which claims (i) for damages for breach of such a tenancy agreement and (ii) for the recovery of supplementary costs payable under the tenancy agreement are made.

Case 220/84 - 4 July 1985

AS-Autoteile Service GmbH
v
Pierre Malhé

Article 16(5) - Exclusive jurisdiction - Proceedings 'concerned with the enforcement of judgments' - Meaning - Applications to oppose enforcement under German law - Included - Claims which may be raised in such applications - Limits.

Summary

Applications to oppose enforcement, as provided for under Paragraph 767 of the German Code of Civil Procedure, fall, as such, within the jurisdiction provision contained in Article 16(5) of the Convention of 27 September 1968 on Jurisdiction and the Enforcement of Judgments in Civil and Commercial Matters; that provision does not, however, make it possible, in an application to oppose enforcement made to the courts of the Contracting State in which enforcement is to take place, to plead a set-off between the right whose enforcement is being sought and a claim over which the courts of that State would have no jurisdiction if it were raised independently.

JUDGMENT OF THE COURT

Due, President of Chamber, Pescatore and Bahlmann, Judges

1. By an order of 9 July 1984, which was received at the Court on 28 August 1984, the Bundesgerichtshof requested a preliminary ruling, under the Protocol of 3 June 1971 on the interpretation by the Court of Justice of the Convention of 27 September 1968 on Jurisdiction and the

Enforcement of Judgments in Civil and Commercial Matters (hereinafter referred to as 'the Convention'), on three questions concerning the interpretation of Article 16(5) of the Convention.

2. According to the documents before the Court, the plaintiff in the main proceedings, AS-Autoteile, whose registered office is in Bühl, is in the business of reconditioning used motor-vehicle parts; in the course of its business it had dealings with PAT GmbH, whose registered office was in Meckenheim, near Bonn, and one of whose shareholders was the defendant in the main proceedings, Pierre Malhé, who resides in Saleux (France) and is the owner of Société de Récupération de Pièces Automobiles. On 5 April 1978 AS-Autoteile obtained a default judgment in the Landgericht [Regional Court] Bonn against PAT in the amount of DM 1 001 476.95, plus interest, for the supply of defective goods.

3. When AS-Autoteile tried to enforce that judgment it discovered that PAT was insolvent. AS-Autoteile considers that the insolvency is due to the fact that PAT's assets were unlawfully transferred to Mr Malhé, in the form of fictitious profits. AS-Autoteile therefore obtained from the Amtsgericht [Local Court] Rheinbach, on 6 March 1980, an order for the attachment and transfer to it of the claim for unjust enrichment which, in its view, PAT could make against Mr Malhé.

4. On the basis of that order AS-Autoteile brought an action for payment against Mr Malhé before the Landgericht [Regional Court] Baden-Baden. The documents before the Court do not reveal on what basis the proceedings were brought before that court. In any event, the Landgericht Baden-Baden held that it had jurisdiction, and by a judgment dated 17 November 1981 it ordered Mr Malhé to pay to AS-Autoteile a sum representing his unjust enrichment at the expense of PAT, in an amount not exceeding the debt owed by PAT to AS-Autoteile.

5. Mr Malhé appealed against that judgment to the Oberlandesgericht [Higher Regional Court] Karlsruhe, which held on 15 October 1982 that under Article 2 of the Convention it had no jurisdiction, since the alleged debtor was domiciled in France. According to the Oberlandesgericht, the French courts have jurisdiction in such a case. AS-Autoteile's appeal to the Bundesgerichtshof against that judgment was dismissed by an order of 7 November 1983. The question of jurisdiction over the substance of the case has therefore been settled.

6. On 17 December 1982, while the proceedings were still pending, the Landgericht Baden-Baden made an order for costs against AS-Autoteile. Since that order was immediately enforceable, AS-Autoteile gave Mr Malhé a bank guarantee in the amount of DM 40 000, in order to avoid enforcement proceedings; Mr Malhé is still in possession of the instrument of guarantee.

7. AS-Autoteile thereupon lodged an application to oppose enforcement before the same court, under Paragraph 767 of the German Zivilprozessordnung [Code of Civil Procedure], which provides as follows:

(1) Objections against the judgment debt itself must be raised by the debtor before the court which heard the matter at first instance.

(2) Such objections are only admissible insofar as the grounds on which they are based arise after the close of the oral procedure in which, under this statute, objections should at the latest have been made and insofar as such matters may no longer be raised by way of appeal.

(3) In his application the debtor must make all the objections which he was in a position to make at the time of the application.

8. In its application AS-Autoteile seeks to set off against the order for costs the claim resulting from Mr Malhé's unjust enrichment at the expense of PAT, which had been transferred to it for the purpose of recovery. In the alternative, AS-Autoteile seeks the return of the instrument of guarantee.

9. By a judgment of 4 April 1983 the Landgericht Baden-Baden declared that it had no jurisdiction, since the action concerned a claim which had already been declared non-justiciable in Germany for want of jurisdiction.

10. AS-Autoteile brought a direct appeal to the Bundesgerichtshof against the Landgericht's decision that the German courts lacked jurisdiction. In the course of the proceedings on that appeal the Bundesgerichtshof referred the following three questions to the Court:

(1) Do applications to oppose enforcement within the meaning of Paragraph 767 of the German Code of Civil Procedure fall within the jurisdiction provision contained in Article 16(5) of the Convention?

(2) Pursuant to Article 16(5) of the Convention, in an application to oppose enforcement before the courts of the Contracting State in which enforcement is to take place, is it possible to resist enforcement

by pleading a set-off in respect of a claim over which the courts of that State would have no jurisdiction if it were raised independently?

(3) Does the jurisdiction recognised by Article 16(5) of the Convention cover proceedings in which the debtor, relying on a submission that the creditor's claim cannot be enforced, demands the return of the instrument of guarantee which he provided as security to avoid enforcement?

11. Article 16(5) of the Convention provides that 'in proceedings concerned with the enforcement of judgments, the courts of the Contracting State in which the judgment has been or is to be enforced' shall have exclusive jurisdiction, regardless of domicile.

12. In reply to the first question it must be held that proceedings such as those provided for under Paragraph 767 of the German Code of Civil Procedure fall, as such, within the jurisdiction provision contained in Article 16(5) by virtue of their close link with the enforcement procedure. However, that finding does not resolve the question of what objections a party may raise in such proceedings without going beyond the limits of Article 16(5). That is the problem addressed by the second question referred by the Bundesgerichtshof.

13. That question concerns the point whether, in enforcement proceedings a party may raise an objection based on a debt over which the courts of the Contracting State in which enforcement is to take place would have no jurisdiction if an independent action were brought on that debt.

14. In order to resolve that question it is necessary to have regard to the general scheme of the Convention, paying particular attention to the relationship between Article 2 and Article 16.

15. According to Article 2, persons domiciled in a Contracting State are to be sued in the courts of that State. That provision is intended to protect the rights of the defendant; it serves as a counterpoise to the facilities provided by the Convention with regard to the recognition and enforcement of foreign judgments. In this case the German courts have already held that since the defendant in the main proceedings is domiciled in France the debt raised by the plaintiff in the main proceedings is a matter for the French courts.

16. Article 16 of the Convention makes a number of exceptions to that general rule by granting exclusive jurisdiction to the courts of a

Contracting State other than that specified under Article 2 in proceedings which have a particular connection with that other State, on the basis of the location of immovable property, the seat of a company, an entry in a public register or, in the case of paragraph (5), the place where a judgment is to be enforced.

17. It follows from the specificity of the connection required by Article 16 that a party cannot make use of the jurisdiction conferred by Article 16(5) on the courts of the place of enforcement in order to bring before those courts a dispute which falls within the jurisdiction of the courts of another Contracting State under Article 2. The use for such a purpose of the application to oppose enforcement is contrary to the division of jurisdiction which the Convention intended to establish between the court of the defendant's domicile and the court of the place of enforcement.

18. In this case, since the German courts have already held that they have no jurisdiction over the claim relied on as a set-off, the use of that claim in order to oppose the enforcement of an order for the costs incurred in the same proceedings amounts to a clear abuse of the process on the part of the plaintiff for the purpose of obtaining indirectly from the German courts a decision regarding a claim over which those courts have no jurisdiction under the Convention.

19. The answer to the first two questions raised by the Bundesgerichtshof must therefore be that applications to oppose enforcement, as provided for under Paragraph 767 of the German Code of Civil Procedure, fall, as such, within the jurisdiction provision contained in Article 16(5) of the Convention, but that that provision does not make it possible, in an application to oppose enforcement made to the courts of the Contracting State in which enforcement is to take place, to plead a set-off between the right whose enforcement is being sought and a claim over which the courts of that State would have no jurisdiction if it were raised independently.

20. As a result of those replies, the third question has become otiose.

On those grounds, the Court (Second Chamber), in answer to the questions referred to it by the Bundesgerichtshof by order of 9 July 1984, hereby rules:

> **Applications to oppose enforcement, as provided for under Paragraph 767 of the German Code of Civil Procedure, fall, as**

such, within the jurisdiction provision contained in Article 16(5) of the Convention; that provision does not, however, make it possible, in an application to oppose enforcement made to the courts of the Contracting State in which enforcement is to take place, to plead a set-off between the right whose enforcement is being sought and a claim over which the courts of that State would have no jurisdiction if it were raised independently.

OPINION OF MR ADVOCATE GENERAL LENZ

A. The background of the proceedings with which this opinion deals goes back to 1977. The plaintiff, AS-Autoteile Service GmbH, buys used motor-vehicle parts, in particular, clutches and clutch parts, reconditions them and sells them as replacement parts. In connection with its business it had dealings in spring 1977 with PAT, a company whose head office was in Meckenheim, near Bonn. The defendant, who is normally resident in France, was a shareholder in PAT. The plaintiff paid PAT a total of DM 1 940 949,95 for a number of deliveries, the last of which was on 9 September 1977. After the last delivery made by PAT differences of opinion arose over the quality of the goods supplied. The plaintiff brought a claim against PAT for the repayment of DM 1 001 476.95 on the ground that PAT had for the most part delivered only unusable scrap, instead of used parts suitable for reconditioning, as had been agreed. The plaintiff obtained default judgment for that amount in the Landgericht [Regional Court], Bonn on 5 April 1978. That judgment could not, however, be enforced, since PAT had become insolvent and an application for a winding-up order had been dismissed by order of the Amtsgericht [Local Court] Euskirchen of 5 May 1978 on the ground that there were insufficient assets to cover the cost of the proceedings.

The plaintiff asserted that the defendant had received sums of money from PAT in a total amount in excess of its claim against PAT, and that he was obliged to repay them to that company under the law on unjust enrichment. On the application of the plaintiff PAT's alleged claims in unjust enrichment against the defendant were therefore attached and transferred to the plaintiff for recovery. The plaintiff thereupon brought an action against the defendant on those claims before the German courts in the amount of DM 1 008 741.25 plus interest. The action was dismissed as inadmissible, on the ground that the German courts lacked jurisdiction.

In the judgment dismissing the claim in that action, the antecedent of the present proceedings, costs were awarded against the plaintiff. The defendant obtained an order against the plaintiff for the payment of those costs. To avoid enforcement of that order the plaintiff put forward a bank guarantee as security. Against the defendant's claim for the costs of the previous proceedings (about DM 40 000) the plaintiff sought to set off the claims for unjust enrichment which had been attached and transferred to it for recovery and which it had unsuccessfully raised in those proceedings. In an application brought before the Landgericht [Regional Court] Baden-Baden, the plaintiff, relying on that right of set-off, claimed that the order to pay the costs of the previous proceedings should be declared unenforceable.

The Landgericht dismissed the application as inadmissible on the ground that the German courts had no jurisdiction. It left open the question whether the German courts could derive jurisdiction from Article 16(5) of the Brussels Convention. In its view there could be no jurisdiction over an application to oppose enforcement whereby the applicant, whose claim in previous proceedings was unsuccessful for lack of jurisdiction, sought to defeat the defendant's claim for costs arising out of those proceedings by setting off the claim in which he was unsuccessful.

As permitted by Paragraph 566 a of the Code of Civil Procedure the plaintiff brought a direct appeal against that judgment before the Bundesgerichtshof. In order to arrive at a decision on the appeal the Bundesgerichtshof considered it necessary to obtain replies to three questions regarding Article 16(5) of the Brussels Convention. It therefore referred the following three questions to the Court:

'(1) Do actions to oppose enforcement within the meaning of Paragraph 767 of the German Code of Civil Procedure fall within the jurisdiction provision contained in Article 16(5) of the Convention?

(2) Pursuant to Article 16(5) of the Convention, in an action to oppose enforcement before the courts of the Contracting State in which enforcement is to take place, is it possible to resist enforcement by pleading a set-off in respect of a claim over which the courts of that State would have no jurisdiction if it were raised independently?

(3) Does the jurisdiction recognized by Article 16(5) of the Convention cover proceedings in which the debtor, relying on a submission that the creditor's claim cannot be enforced, demands the return of the instrument of guarantee which he provided as security to avoid enforcement?'

The plaintiff in the main proceedings, the Government of the United Kingdom and the Commission of the European Communities submitted observations regarding the reference.

Those observations are in agreement with regard to the answers to be given to the first question and to the closely related third question. Both questions should, they say, be answered in the affirmative, since an action to oppose enforcement falls in principle within the scope of Article 16(5) of the Brussels Convention. In view of the factual circumstances described above the question regarding the return of the instrument of guarantee should also be answered in the affirmative.

There are differences of opinion, however, with regard to the second question, whether in an action to oppose enforcement claims may be pleaded over which the court hearing the matter, in the State in which enforcement is to take place, would have no jurisdiction under the general provisions of the Brussels Convention. The plaintiff in the main proceedings argues that the answer to that question should be in the affirmative, while the Government of the United Kingdom and the Commission are of the opposite view.

B. My views on the matter are as follows.

1. Since the main legal issue raised in this reference lies in question 2, I shall deal with that question first. In referring that question the Bundesgerichtshof wishes to know whether under Article 16(5) of the Brussels Convention, in an action to oppose enforcement before the courts of the Contracting State in which enforcement is to take place, it is possible to resist enforcement by pleading a set-off in respect of a claim over which the courts of that State would have no jurisdiction if it were raised independently.

The plaintiff in the main proceedings would like an affirmative reply to be given to that question. It takes the view that the wording of the Brussels Convention, which attributes exclusive jurisdiction over actions to oppose enforcement to the courts of the 'Contracting State in which the judgment has been or is to be enforced', implies that those courts have exclusive jurisdiction over the objections raised.

The Government of the United Kingdom and the Commission, on the other hand, take the opposite view. At first sight, they argue, there is something to be said for the idea that in the interest of the effective administration of justice the court of the place of enforcement should be able to determine all claims which may be associated with the enforcement of judgment. There are compelling reasons of principle, however, for opposing that result. Article 16 confers exclusive jurisdiction and must, the Court has held, be interpreted strictly. It does not create any additional jurisdiction over new claims or objections which would establish or, as in this case, extinguish liability. The departure from the general jurisdictional rules of the Brussels Convention laid down in Article 16 is only justified where there are objective reasons connected with the proper administration of justice: the basic provision of Article 2 (jurisdiction of the courts of the State where the debtor is domiciled) must not be overridden without compelling reason.

The intention and scheme of the Brussels Convention clearly favour the latter view.

The Brussels Convention makes it considerably easier for a plaintiff to obtain recognition and enforcement of a judgment. Conversely - as a counterbalance, in a way - Title II of the Convention includes provisions protecting defendants. In view of the fact that the recognition and enforcement of judgments is facilitated the defendant must be protected from being 'caught by surprise' by proceedings brought before courts which do not have jurisdiction, hampered in his defence and pursued on the basis of such judgments.

That would, however, be the case if under Article 16(5) he was obliged to defend an application to oppose enforcement based on a set-off with a claim over which the courts of the State of enforcement, according to their own final decision, had no jurisdiction. Although in the first proceedings the defendant was not obliged to reply to the claim made against him, since it was brought before a court which had no jurisdiction, he would still have to reply to it in connection with the proceedings on costs, merely in order to recover the costs incurred by him in his defence against the inadmissible claim. The defendant would, thus, be forced to defend himself against the claim even though in the proceedings in which it was raised he was not obliged to do so.

As the Landgericht Baden-Baden correctly stated in its judgment of 4 November 1983, 'having regard to the objectives and the protective nature of the jurisdictional provisions such a result cannot represent the law'.

The conclusion proposed by the United Kingdom and the Commission is also in accordance with Article 16(5) of the Brussels Convention. In the first place, the provisions regarding exclusive jurisdiction constitute exceptions which must, as I have already said, be interpreted strictly. Furthermore, the particular areas which fall under Article 16, certain disputes regarding tenancies, companies, registers, industrial property and the enforcement of judgments, are matters which, because of their particular difficulty or complexity, require that the court having jurisdiction should be particularly familiar with the relevant national law. As the Court held in its judgment of 14 December 1977 with regard to the exclusive jurisdiction provided for by Article 16(1), 'it is preferable, in the light of their complexity, that [rules regarding tenancies of immovable property] be applied only by the courts of the States in which they are in force'.

Such a 'proximity to the matter' can certainly be required of the competent court in matters involving the provisions on the 'recourse to force, constraint or distraint on movable or immovable property in order to ensure the effective implementation of judgments and authentic instruments', that is, in deciding on the lawfulness of measures of enforcement. It does not, however, constitute a sufficient ground for granting exclusive jurisdiction over a claim in ancillary proceedings where there was no jurisdiction over the same claim in the main proceedings and a final decision was given on that absence of jurisdiction.

2. Since in its order the Bundesgerichtshof itself stated that the appeal on the action to oppose enforcement would be dismissed if question 1 or question 2 received a negative answer, I do not think it necessary to go into question 1. The Court should not, I think, state a view on the general question of whether and to what extent actions to oppose enforcement within the meaning of Paragraph 767 of the German Code of Civil Procedure come under Article 16(5) of the Brussels Convention since, as the national court itself has stated, that question is no longer important to the decision. I do not think, moreover, that this general problem was sufficiently discussed in these proceedings to permit the Court to define exactly to what extent actions to oppose enforcement fall within the exclusive jurisdiction established by Article 16(5) (it seems to me certain, however, that in principle they may fall within the scope of that provision).

3. Although the Bundesgerichtshof's third question regarding the return of the instrument of guarantee is independent of questions 1 and 2, I do not think it is necessary for the Court to give an answer to that question either. I share the view expressed by the plaintiff in the main proceedings that the claim for the return of the instrument of guarantee is so closely connected with the enforcement procedure that jurisdiction over the one cannot be separated from jurisdiction over the other.

C. In view of the foregoing I propose that the Court give the following answer to the reference of the Bundesgerichtshof: 'Article 16(5) of the

Convention of 27 September 1968 on Jurisdiction and the Enforcement of Judgments in Civil and Commercial Matters must be interpreted as meaning that in an action to oppose enforcement before the courts of the Contracting State in which enforcement is to take place it is not possible to resist enforcement of an order for costs by pleading a set-off in respect of a claim over which it has been held in a final judgment of a court in that State that those courts would have no jurisdiction if it were raised independently'.

Case 158/87 - 6 July 1988

R. O. E. Scherrens
v
M. G. Maenhout and Others

Article 16(1) - Exclusive jurisdiction - Disputes regarding tenancies of immovable properties - Lease relating to a property consisting of parts situated in two contracting States - Exclusive jurisdiction of the courts of each State over the part situated in that State.

Summary

Article 16(1) of the Convention of 27 September 1968 on Jurisdiction and the Enforcement of Judgments in Civil and Commercial Matters must be interpreted as meaning that, in a dispute as to the existence of a lease relating to immovable property situated in two contracting States, exclusive jurisdiction over the immovable property situated in each contracting State is, in principle and subject to special cases in which the particular disposition of the property may necessitate a different solution, held by the courts of that State.

JUDGMENT OF THE COURT

Due, President of the Chamber, Koopmans, Bahlmann, Kakouris and O'Higgins, Judges

1. By judgment of 23 March 1987, which was received at the Court on 26 May 1987, the Gerechtshof, Arnhem, referred to the Court for a preliminary ruling under the Protocol of 3 June 1971 on the interpretation by the Court of Justice of the Convention of 27 September 1968 on Jurisdiction and the Enforcement of Judgments in Civil and Commercial

Matters (hereinafter referred to as 'the Convention') a question concerning the interpretation of Article 16(1) of the Convention.

2. The question was raised in the course of proceedings between Mr Scherrens and Maria Maenhout and others in a dispute as to whether a lease of a farm was concluded orally between Mr Schereens, as agricultural tenant, and Maria Maenhout and her (now deceased) husband, as landlords, in respect of a farm consisting of buildings and approximately five hectares of agricultural land situated at Maldegem (Belgium) and four plots of land, covering altogether twelve hectares, situated in the commune of Sluis (Netherlands).

3. It appears from the documents before the Court that the land in the Netherlands is not adjacent to the part of the holding in Belgium but is situated seven kilometres away.

4. The dispute over the lease was brought by Mr Scheerens not only before the Vrederechter (Cantonal Judge), Eeklo (Belgium) in respect of the land in Belgium but also before the Pachtkamer (chamber dealing with leasehold matters) of the Kantongerecht (Cantonal Court) Oostburg (Netherlands) in respect of the land situated in the Netherlands. The Kantongerecht was not satisfied that a lease had been concluded and accordingly it dismissed the action, whereupon Mr Scherrens appealed to the Pachtkamer of the Gerechtshof, Arnhem.

5. According to the judgment making the reference, the farmer, the appellant, claims that there is a single lease covering both the farm and the plots of land. Taking the view that it was therefore possible that the Belgian court and the Netherlands court might give contradictory rulings, the Gerechtshof considered that it was necessary to settle the question as to which court had jurisdiction under Article 16(1) of the Convention in cases such as this. It therefore stayed the proceedings and requested the Court to rule on 'how Article 16(1) of the Convention is to be interpreted with regard to the lease of a farm of which the buildings (with some of the land) are situated in one contracting State (Belgium) and (most of) the land in another (the Netherlands)'.

6. Reference is made to the Report for the Hearing for a fuller account of the facts of the case, the procedure and the observations submitted to the Court, which are mentioned or discussed hereinafter only insofar as is necessary for the reasoning of the Court.

7. Article 16 of the Convention provides as follows: '1. The following courts shall have exclusive jurisdiction, regardless of domicile: 1. In proceedings which have as their object rights *in rem* in, or tenancies of, immovable property, the courts of the contracting State in which the property is situated; ...'.

8. The question submitted by the Gerechtshof seeks to establish whether Article 16(1) of the Convention is to be interpreted as meaning that, in a dispute as to the existence of a lease relating to immovable property situated in two contracting States, exclusive jurisdiction over the property situated in each contracting State is held by the courts of that State.

9. It should be recalled that the Court, in its judgment of 15 January 1985 in Case 241/83 (*Rösler* v *Rottwinkel* [1985] ECR 99), ruled that the *raison d'être* of the exclusive jurisdiction conferred by Article 16(1) on the courts of the contracting State in which the property is situated is the fact that tenancies are closely bound up with the law of immovable property and with the provisions, generally of a mandatory character, governing its use, such as legislation controlling the level of rents and protecting the rights of tenants, including tenant farmers.

10. The Court further held that Article 16(1) seeks to ensure a rational allocation of jurisdiction by opting for a solution whereby the court having jurisdiction is determined on the basis of its proximity to the property since that court is in a better position to obtain first-hand knowledge of the facts relating to the creation of tenancies and to the performance of the terms thereof.

11. In the light of those considerations the Court concluded in that case, in respect of a letting of immovable property situated entirely within a single contracting State, that Article 16(1) applies to all tenancies of immovable property irrespective of their special characteristics.

12. The same considerations hold good in principle in the case of a tenancy of immovable property whose component parts are situated in two contracting States.

13. Article 16(1) of the Convention must therefore be interpreted as meaning that, in a dispute as to the existence of a lease relating to immovable property situated in two contracting States, exclusive jurisdiction over the immovable property situated in each contracting State is held by the courts of that State.

14. It is, however, possible that cases may arise in which immovable property whose component parts are situated in two contracting States but are the subject of a single lease has special characteristics such as will necessitate an exception to the general rule of exclusive jurisdiction described above. This might occur when, for example, the immovable property situated in one contracting State is adjacent to the property in another State and the property is situated almost entirely in one of those States. In those circumstances it might be appropriate to regard the property as a single unit and deem it to be entirely situated in one of those States for the purposes of conferring on the courts of that State exclusive jurisdiction over the tenancy of that property.

15. Consideration of the documents laid before the Court does not, however, disclose any such special characteristics in this case, since the component parts of the immovable property at issue situated in the two contracting States are neither adjacent to one another nor situated almost entirely in one of those States.

16. The reply to be given to the question referred to the Court is therefore that Article 16(1) of the Convention must be interpreted as meaning that, in a dispute as to the existence of a lease relating to immovable property situated in two contracting States, exclusive jurisdiction over the immovable property situated in each contracting State is held by the courts of that State.

On those grounds, the Court (Sixth Chamber), in answer to the question referred to it by the Gerechtshof, Arnhem, by judgment of 23 March 1987, hereby rules:

> **Article 16(1) of the Convention of 27 September 1968 on Jurisdiction and the Enforcement of Judgments in Civil and Commercial Matters must be interpreted as meaning that, in a dispute as to the existence of a lease relating to immovable property situated in two contracting States, exclusive jurisdiction over the unmovable property situated in each contracting State is held by the courts of that State.**

OPINION OF MR ADVOCATE GENERAL MANCINI

1. This reference for a preliminary ruling is concerned with the interpretation of Article 16(1) of the Convention of 27 September 1968 on Jurisdiction and the Enforcement of Judgments in Civil and Commercial Matters (Brussels Convention) which provides: 'The following courts shall have exclusive jurisdiction, regardless of domicile: (1) in proceedings which have as their object rights *in rem* in, or tenancies of, immoveable property, the courts of the contracting State in which the property is situated; ...'.

The facts are as follows. The court making the reference - the Pachtkamer (Chamber dealing with agricultural leases) of the Gerechtshof (Regional Court of Appeal), Arnhem - was called upon to settle as to the existence of a lease which Mr. Raphaël O.E. Scherrens claims to have concluded orally in the winter of 1972/73, tenant-farmer, with the landlords, who later became his parents-in-law, Mr B.P.J. van Poucke, who died on 8 November 1973, and Maria G. Maenhout. The particularity of the holding to which the alleged leasing agreement relates is that it consists of a building with about five hectares of land situated at Maldegem (Belgium) and four plots of land totalling 12 hectares, lying seven kilometres away in the Commune of Sluis (Netherlands). The dispute arose in 1982 from an event which soured relations between Mr Scherrens and his mother-in-law. She gave the land situated in the Netherlands to another daughter, Rita A. M. van Poucke, and the donee did not recognise Scherrens' right to lease them as he had done for the previous seven years.

In accordance with Article 11 of the Pachtwet (Agricultural Holdings Law) of 23 January 1958 (*Staatsblad* 1958, No 37), Schereens then brought proceedings against his mother-in-law, sister-in-law and wife, Lucie M. L. van Poucke, before the Pachtkamer of the Kantongerecht (Cantonal Court), Oostburg, asking that the lease agreement be set down in writing (9 December 1982); however, since he failed to prove that the transaction had ever taken place, his application was dismissed by a judgment of 2 May 1985.

The tenant, however, did not give up. In parallel with an action brought in Belgium for the refund of part of the rent paid in respect of the land there, he lodged an appeal with the Pachtkamer of the Gerechtshof, Arnhem. There then arose the question on which this Court is requested to rule. In Scherrens' view, the combined provisions of Article 16(1) of the Brussels Convention and the second sentence of Article 137(1) of the Pachtwet require that the ruling on the entire holding, the main part of which is on Netherlands territory, be given by the Netherlands court. However, in the opinion of Maria G. Maenhout and Rita A. M. van Poucke, the Gerechtshof, Arnhem, has jurisdiction only with regard to the land in the Netherlands, whereas that part of the holding which lies in Belgium is subject to the jurisdiction of the Belgian courts.

By a judgment of 23 March 1987 the Gerechtshof stayed the proceedings and asked the Court of Justice, under Article 2(2) of the Protocol of 3 June 1971, 'how Article 16(1) of the Convention should be interpreted with regard to the lease of a farm of which the buildings (with some of the land) are situated in one contracting State (Belgium) and (most of) the land in another (the Netherlands)'.

In the proceedings before this Court, written observations were submitted by Maria G. Maenhout, Rita A. M. van Poucke and the Commission of the European Communities. Only the Commission took part in the hearing.

2. As observed above, the judgment of the national court and the documents laid before it show that the question is whether there is a single lease concluded in respect of agricultural lands which are not adjacent, are of varying sizes and are situated in the territory of different States.

In a situation of this kind, jurisdiction is guided by the age-old principle of the *forum rei sitae* ('ne contra situs legem in immobilibus quidquam decerni possit privato consensu et par est sic judicari', as D'Argentré wrote in *De Statutis personalibus et realibus, Commentarii ad patrias Britonum leges, seu Consuetudines generales antiquissimi Ducatus Britanniae,* Article CCXVIII, GI. 6, Nos 2 and 3, Paris 1614, Col. 676). That rule was embodied in Article 16(1) of the Convention, and its adoption was rightly perceived by Batiffol and Lagarde as 'une manifestation nouvelle de la "puissance d'attraction" de la situation de l'immeuble qui, débordant les terrains des conflits de lois, où elle s'était conquise dèjá une situation privilegiée, s'annexe celui des conflits de compétence judiciaire' ['a further manifestation of the "power of attraction" of the situation of real property which, having expanded beyond the field of the conflict of laws, in which it had already secured a privileged position, is annexing the domain of conflicts of jurisdiction'] (*Droit international privé*, VII, Paris 1983, Vol. II, p. 492).

It follows that the jurisdiction to entertain a dispute concerning the lease of an agricultural holding divided between two contracting States vests exclusively, in respect of each part, in the courts of the State in whose territory that part lies; and even if the concomitant risk is that the same instrument (the lease) will be subject to the appraisal of different national courts, the terms and effects of the judgments cannot extend to those parts of the land which fall within another jurisdiction.

That solution accords fully with the purpose of the Convention and the rationale of Article 16(1). Indeed, this Court has recently held that to confer jurisdiction on the courts of the State in which the land is situated fulfils, better than any other rule, the requirement of 'providing for a clear and certain attribution of jurisdiction' and is due to at least three factors: 'the fact that tenancies are closely bound up with the law of immovable property', 'the provisions, generally of a mandatory character, governing [the] use of such property' and the 'first-hand knowledge [of the courts concerned] of the facts relating to the creation of tenancies and to the performance of the terms thereof' (judgment of 15 January 1985 in Case 241/83 *Rösler* v *Rottwinkel* [1985] ECR 109, at paragraphs 23, 19 and 20; see also the judgment of 14 December 1977 in Case 73/77 *Sanders* v *Van der Putte* [1977] ECR 2383, at paragraphs 12, 13 and 14).

As the defendants and the Commission point out, preference for the *forum rei sitae* is also in keeping with the principle of the sound administration of justice. Besides the reasons recited above, that preference is justified by (a) practical necessities, since it is clear that judgments concerning rights in rem in immovable property are enforced at the place where that property is situated; (b) the often special nature of the national laws on the letting of immovable property and of the courts applying them; and (c) the fact that agreements whereby ownership is transferred or a right over immovable property is granted are registered at the place where that property is situated (to this effect, see the Jenard Report, Official Journal 1979, C 59, p. 35, and in legal literature: Droz, *Compétence judiciaire et effets des jugements dans le Marché commun*, Paris, 1972, p. 101, and Bischoff's note on the judgment of the Court of 14 December 1977 in Case 73/77, published in the *Journal du droit international* 1978, p. 388 *et seq*., especially at p. 392).

3. Endorsing the opinion of certain authors (Droz, op. cit., p. 193; Gothot and Holleaux, L*a convention de Bruxelles du 27 Septembre 1968, compétence judiciaire et effets des jugements de la CEE*, Paris, 1985, p.126), the Commission maintains that, in special circumstances, the rule under Article 16 must be relinquished in favour of an exclusive jurisdiction which is undivided but concurrent and in practice governed, by virtue of Article 23, by the criterion of the court first seised. The hypothesis envisaged is one in which the land forms a single unit, either because it is regarded as such by the parties concerned in their contractual dealings or because its component parts cannot profitably be exploited as separate entities.

That view cannot be accepted. It must first be observed that Article 16(1) is to be interpreted strictly. That is shown by several arguments based on the text itself: first, by the imperative nature of exclusive jurisdiction, which cannot be overridden either by an agreement attributing jurisdiction to the courts of another contracting State or by way of tacit prorogation (Articles 17 and 18); secondly, by the obligation on the court of a contracting State other than that whose courts are recognised as having exclusive jurisdiction to declare that it has no jurisdiction (Article 19); lastly, by the fact that breach of those rules is authority for refusing to recognise or enforce the judgments concerned (Articles 28 and 34).

Furthermore, although in the case described by the Commission, the application of Article 16(1) may indeed, by involving duplication of the courts concerned and the laws applicable, give rise to certain disadvantages, the extent of those disadvantages does not appear to justify exceptions to the principle of exclusive jurisdiction. It may be added that the economic unity of land does not necessarily preclude its being divisible into separate parts for legal purposes and thus capable of falling under the jurisdiction of different national courts (see Niboyet, 'Les conflits de lois relatifs aux immeubles situés aux frontiéres des états', published in *Revue de droit international et de législation comparée*, 1933, p. 468 *et seq*.).

4. In the light of the foregoing considerations, I propose that the Court should give the following answer to the question referred to it by the Gerechtshof, Arnhem, by judgment of 23 March 1987 in the proceedings pending before it between Raphaël O. E. Scherrens on the one hand and Maria G. Maenhout and Rita A. M. van Poucke on the other: 'Article 16(1) of the Convention of 27 September 1968 on Jurisdiction and the Enforcement of

Judgments in Civil and Commercial Matters must be interpreted as meaning that jurisdiction over disputes concerning the lease of a farm situated partly in one contracting State and partly in another vests exclusively, with regard to each of the two parts and irrespective of their size, in the courts of the State in which that part lies.'

Case C-115/88 - 10 January 1990

Mario P. A. Reichert and Others
v
Dresdner Bank

Article 16(1) - Proceedings which have as their object rights in rem in immovable property - Concept - Independent interpretation - 'Action paulienne'- Not included.

Summary

The concept of 'proceedings which have as their object rights *in rem* in immovable property' mentioned in Article 16(1) of the Convention of 27 September 1968 on jurisdiction and the enforcement of judgments in civil and commercial matters must be given an independent interpretation. It encompasses only those actions concerning rights *in rem* in immovable property which both come within the scope of the Brussels Convention and are actions which seek to determine the extent, content, ownership or possession of immovable property or the existence of other rights *in rem* therein and to provide the holders of those rights with the protection of the powers which attach to their interest.

It does not apply to an action whereby a creditor seeks to have a disposition of a right *in rem* in immovable property rendered ineffective as against him on the ground that it was made in fraud of his rights by his debtor.

JUDGMENT OF THE COURT

Sir Gordon Slynn, President of the Chamber, Zuleeg, Joliet, Moitinho de Almeida and Grévisse, Judges

1. By judgment dated 18 November 1987 which was received at the Court on 11 April 1988, the cour d'appel, Aix-en-Provence, referred to the Court for a preliminary ruling pursuant to the Protocol of 3 June 1971 on the interpretation by the Court of Justice of the Convention of 27 September 1968 on jurisdiction and the enforcement of judgments in civil and commercial matters (hereinafter referred to as 'the Convention') a question on the interpretation of Article 16(1) of that Convention.

2. That question was raised during the course of proceedings between Mr and Mrs Reichert and their son, Mario Peter Antonio Reichert, on the one hand, and Dresdner Bank AG on the other hand.

3. Mr and Mrs Reichert, who reside in the Federal Republic of Germany, are the owners of immovable property in the commune of Antibes, Alpes-Maritimes, France, the legal ownership of which they donated to their son, Mario Reichert, by a notarial instrument executed at Creutzwald, Moselle, France. That donation was challenged by Dresdner Bank AG, a creditor of Mr and Mrs Reichert, in the tribunal de grande instance (Regional Court), Grasse, in whose judicial district the property in issue lies, on the basis of Article 1167 of the French civil code under which creditors may 'challenge in their own name transactions entered into by their debtors in fraud of their rights' by a procedure known as the '*action paulienne*'.

4. By a judgment of 20 February 1987 the tribunal de grande instance, Grasse, held that it had jurisdiction (which the Reicherts denied) on the basis of Article 16(1) of the Convention, under which 'in proceedings which have as their object rights *in rem* in immovable property ... the courts of the Contracting State in which the property is situated' have exclusive jurisdiction, regardless of domicile.

5. The Reicherts appealed against the ruling on jurisdiction to the cour d'appel, Aix-en-Provence, which decided to stay the proceedings and seek a preliminary ruling from the Court on whether 'by providing that the courts of the Contracting State in which the property is situated are to have exclusive jurisdiction in proceedings which have as their object rights *in rem* in immovable property or tenancies of immovable property, it was the intention of the Brussels Convention to lay down a rule of jurisdiction without any reference whatever to the classification of actions as personal, real or mixed actions, taking account only of the substantive legal issue, namely the nature of the rights concerned, and whether the rule of jurisdiction thus laid down entitles a creditor who

contests transactions entered into by his debtor in fraud of his rights - in this case a donation of rights *in rem* in immovable property - to bring his action before the courts of the Contracting State in which the property is situated'

6. Reference is made to the Report for the Hearing for a fuller account of the facts of the case in the main proceedings, the course of the procedure and the observations submitted to the Court, which are mentioned or discussed hereinafter only insofar as is necessary for the reasoning of the Court.

7. It is clear from the actual wording of the national court's question and from the grounds set out in its judgment that it seeks to determine whether Article 16(1) of the Convention covers a case in which a creditor applies, by means of an action available under national law, in the present case the *action paulienne* in French law, to have a donation of immovable property set aside on the ground that it was made by his debtor in fraud of his rights.

8. First of all, it is evident that in order to ensure that the rights and obligations arising out of the Convention for the Contracting States and for individuals concerned are as equal and as uniform as possible, an independent definition must be given in Community law to the phrase 'in proceedings which have as their object rights *in rem* in immovable property', as has been done by the Court, with regard to other grounds of exclusive jurisdiction laid down in Article 16, in its judgment of 14 December 1977 in Case 73/77 *Sanders* v *Van der Putte* [1977] ECR 2383 - concept of 'tenancies of immovable property' Article 16(1) - and in its judgment of 15 November 1983 in Case 288/82 *Duijnstee* v *Goderbauer* [1983] ECR 3663 - concept of 'proceedings concerned with the registration or validity of patents', Article 16(4).

9. Secondly, as the Court has already held, Article 16 must not be given a wider interpretation than is required by its objective, since it results in depriving the parties of the choice of forum which would otherwise be theirs and, in certain cases, results in their being brought before a court which is not that of any of them (judgment of 14 December 1977 in *Sanders* v *Van der Putte*, cited above).

10. In that regard, it is necessary to take into consideration the fact that the essential reason for conferring exclusive jurisdiction on the courts of the Contracting State in which the property is situated is that the courts of the *locus rei sitae* are the best placed, for reasons of proximity, to

ascertain the facts satisfactorily and to apply the rules and practices which are generally those of the State in which the property is situated (judgments of 14 December 1977 in *Sanders* v *Van der Putte*, cited above, and of 15 January 1985 in Case 241/83 *Rösler* v *Rottwinkel* [1985] ECR 99).

11. In those circumstances, Article 16(1) must be interpreted as meaning that the exclusive jurisdiction of the Contracting State in which the property is situated does not encompass all actions concerning rights *in rem* in immovable property but only those which both come within the scope of the Brussels Convention and are actions which seek to determine the extent, content, ownership or possession of immovable property or the existence of other rights *in rem* therein and to provide the holders of those rights with the protection of the powers which attach to their interest.

12. The *action paulienne*, however, is based on the creditor's personal claim against the debtor and seeks to protect whatever security he may have over the debtor's estate. If successful, its effect is to render the transaction whereby the debtor has effected a disposition in fraud of the creditor's rights ineffective as against the creditor alone. The hearing of such an action, moreover, does not involve the assessment of facts or the application of rules and practices of the *locus rei sitae* in such a way as to justify conferring jurisdiction on a court of the State in which the property is situated.

13. Finally, although in certain Member States the rules governing the public registration of rights in immovable property require public notice to be given of legal actions seeking to have transactions affecting such rights avoided or declared ineffective as against third parties and of judgments given in such actions, that fact alone is not enough to justify conferring exclusive jurisdiction on the courts of the Contracting State in which the property affected by those rights is situated. Such rules of national law are based on the need to afford legal protection to the interests of third parties, and such protection can be ensured, if need be, by public notice in the form and at the place prescribed by the law of the Contracting State in which the property is situated.

14. Consequently, such an action, brought by a creditor against a contract of sale of immovable property entered into, or a donation thereof made, by his debtor, does not come within the scope of Article 16(1).

15. The answer to the national court's question must therefore be that an action whereby a creditor seeks to have a disposition of a right *in rem* in immovable property rendered ineffective as against him on the ground that it was made in fraud of his rights by his debtor does not come within the scope of Article 16(1) of the Convention.

On those grounds, the Court (Fifth Chamber),in answer to the question referred to it by the cour d'appel, Aix-en-Provence, by judgment of 18 November 1987, hereby rules:

> **An action whereby a creditor seeks to have a disposition of a right *in rem* in immovable property rendered ineffective as against him on the ground that it was made in fraud of his rights by his debtor does not come within the scope of Article 16(1) of the Convention.**

OPINION OF MR ADVOCATE GENERAL MISCHO

1. Mr and Mrs Reichert, who are German nationals residing in Germany and the owners of immovable property at Antibes, in France, made a donation of the legal ownership of that property to their son Mario Reichert, also resident in Germany. The instrument was executed before a notary in the French *département* of Moselle.

2. The main proceedings concern a dispute between Dresdner Bank AG, a company governed by German law, whose registered office is at Frankfurt am Main, on the one hand, and Mr and Mrs Reichert and their son, on the other. On the basis of Article 1167 of the French civil code, Dresdner Bank brought proceedings before the tribunal de grande instance (Regional Court), Grasse, in the form of an *action paulienne*, seeking a declaration that the donation was ineffective as against the applicant, who was a creditor of Mr and Mrs Reichert. The tribunal de grande instance, Grasse, within whose judicial district the property is situated, held that it had jurisdiction to hear the proceedings pursuant to Article 16(1) of the Convention of 27 September 1968 on jurisdiction and the enforcement of judgments in civil and commercial matters, which provides: 'in proceedings which have as their object rights *in rem* in immovable property or tenancies of immovable property, the courts of the Contracting State in which the property is situated [shall have exclusive jurisdiction, regardless of domicile]'.

3. The Reicherts appealed to the cour d'appel (Court of Appeal), Aix-en-Provence, against the ruling on jurisdiction.

4. By a judgment of 16 November 1987, pursuant to Article 1 of the Protocol of 3 June 1971 on the interpretation by the Court of the Convention of 27 September 1968, the cour d'appel sought a preliminary ruling from the Court on whether 'by providing that the courts of the Contracting State in which the

property is situated are to have exclusive jurisdiction in proceedings which have as their object rights *in rem* in immovable property or tenancies of immovable property, it was the intention of the Brussels Convention to lay down a rule of jurisdiction without any reference whatever to the classification of actions as personal, real or mixed actions, taking account only of the substantive legal issue, namely the nature of the rights concerned, and whether the rule of jurisdiction thus laid down entitles a creditor who contests transactions entered into by his debtor in fraud of his rights - in this case a donation of rights *in rem* in immovable property - to bring his action before the courts of the Contracting State in which the property is situated'.

5. Let it be said at the outset that I agree with the French Government's view that the question should be restated in two parts, the first part being whether the concept of matters relating to rights *in rem* in immovable property should be interpreted in accordance with the laws of the Contracting States or in the light of the objectives and system of the Brussels Convention.

6. A - Without formulating a general principle in that regard, the Court has hitherto generally ruled in favour of an independent interpretation, although it accepts that neither of the two options rules out the other and that the choice must be made on a case-by-case basis, depending on the provision concerned. It has taken that approach, in particular, in two cases concerning the interpretation of the concept of 'tenancies of immovable property', which also appears in Article 16(1) of the Convention.

7. The cour d'appel considers that the wording of Article 16(1) should not be interpreted as merely a reference to French internal law' and its traditional classification of actions into personal, real and mixed actions.

8. The same view is held by most of the governments which have submitted observations in this case, which have pointed out that the concept of 'rights *in rem*' is not interpreted uniformly in all the Contracting States. It follows that only by giving that concept an independent interpretation can a uniform implementation of the Convention throughout the Community be achieved, and I propose that the Court should take that approach.

9. B - The second part of the question is, in effect, whether the concept of 'proceedings which have as their object rights *in rem* in immovable property', as interpreted within the framework of the Brussels Convention, covers proceedings such as the *action paulienne* in French law in cases where such an action - which may also concern movable property - is brought by a creditor to challenge the donation of the legal ownership of immovable property made by a debtor.

10. The national court observes that Article 16(1) refers not to the nature of the proceedings brought but to that of the rights in issue - in this case the right of legal ownership of immovable property, which is unquestionably a right *in rem* - and seeks confirmation from the Court that proceedings affecting such a right must be brought before the courts of the State in which the property is situated.

11. There is much to be said for such an approach. If the action is successful, will Mr and Mrs Reichert's son not cease to be able to rely, as against

the Dresdner Bank, on his right *in rem* - hitherto available *erga omnes* in the property? Is this not, therefore, a case of 'proceedings which have as their object rights *in rem* in immovable property?

12. Such an approach would also have the merit of answering the Court's concern, expressed in paragraph 23 of its judgment in Case 241/83 *Rösler* v *Rottwinkel* [1985] ECR 99, cited above, - in the context, it is true, of tenancies of immovable property that account must be taken 'of the uncertainty which would be created if the courts allowed exceptions to be made to the general rule laid down in Article 16(1), which has the advantage of providing for a clear and certain attribution of jurisdiction covering all circumstances, thus fulfilling the purpose of the Convention, which is to assign jurisdiction in a certain and predictable way'.

13. In addition, an *action paulienne* lies only if the debt is liquid and due for payment. It will therefore normally be followed by attachment, which can only be effected at the place where the property is situated. Moreover, Article 54 of the French code of civil procedure provides that any creditor may be authorized to enter a provisional registration of a judicial hypothec over immovable property if he can show that he has 'a prima-facie valid claim', that there are circumstances of urgency and that recovery of the debt is endangered. That step appears to have been taken in the present case. All those arguments, therefore, plead in favour of an interpretation allowing the courts of the place where the property is situated jurisdiction to hear an *action paulienne*, as 'the best placed' to deal with the dispute.

14. It is none the less certain, on the other hand, that the plaintiff in an *action paulienne* does not rely on any right *in rem* and, as the French Government has stated, if the action is successful, 'it does not give rise to a reverse transfer of a right *in rem* in immovable property. The avoidance of the donation of the property is purely relative. It means that the donation cannot be relied upon as against the creditor. It is an essential characteristic of rights *in rem*, however, that they have absolute effect *erga omnes*'.

15. It is striking to note that this conception of what constitutes the essence of a right *in rem* is shared by the United Kingdom - representing the common law tradition - which also proposes that the scope of Article 16(1) should be limited to proceedings brought directly to determine as against the whole world the lawful ownership or possession of the property. But, as the United Kingdom rightly pointed out, the principal object of the action in question is to establish that the defendant acted with the intention of defrauding his creditors rather than to determine the issue of lawful ownership or possession of immovable property.

16. Like the United Kingdom, the German and Italian Governments and the Commission consider that it is not enough that a right *in rem* in immovable property should be concerned by an action, or that the action should *relate* to or have a *connection with* immovable property for Article 16(1) to be applicable. On the contrary, the right *in rem* must be the actual cause of the action, which must have as it object to determine, *erga omnes*, the ownership of the property in question.

17. Even if the present instance is a borderline case, I too endorse the

solution put forward with pleasing unanimity by the German, United Kingdom, French and Italian Governments and by the Commission. I agree with them that Article 16(1) should be interpreted restrictively, since it forms an exception to the basic principle governing jurisdiction laid down in the first paragraph of Article 2 of the Convention: 'Subject to the provisions of this Convention, persons domiciled in a Contracting State shall, whatever their nationality, be sued in the courts of that State'.

18. The Court's case-law, cited above, which concerns the tenancies of immovable property to which Article 16(1) also refers, also takes a relatively restrictive approach. The Court held that Article 16 covers neither disputes concerning contracts whose principal object is not the tenancy (such as an agreement to rent under a usufructuary lease a retail business carried on in immovable property rented from a third person by the lessor *Sanders*) nor those which are only indirectly related to the use of the property let (such as those concerning the loss of holiday enjoyment and travel expenses - *Rösler*).

19. That interpretation of the Convention is also borne out by teleological considerations.

20. It is clear, first of all, that the aim of Article 2, which is to protect the defendant, would not be achieved if other provisions of the Convention were interpreted too broadly.

21. It is important, moreover, to bear in mind that the jurisdiction provided for in Article 16(1) is exclusive, a factor which would exacerbate yet further the consequences of too broad an interpretation.

22. Nor can Article 16(1) be applied without reference to its own *raison d'être*. In its judgment in *Sanders*, the Court considered that: 'the assignment, in the interests of the proper administration of justice, of exclusive jurisdiction to the courts of one Contracting State in accordance with Article 16 of the Convention results in depriving the parties of the choice of forum which would otherwise be theirs and, in certain cases, results in their being brought before a court which is not that of the domicile of any of them; having regard to that consideration, the provisions of Article 16 must not be given a wider interpretation than is required by their objective'.

23. Finally, there are very specific reasons for Article 16(1) providing that the courts of the State in which the property is situated are to have exclusive jurisdiction. Proceedings 'which have as their object rights *in rem* in immovable property' often entail a whole series of procedural steps which must be taken on the spot. There may be, for instance, checks, enquiries and expert examinations which, by definition, can only be carried out at the *locus rei sitae* and to which it is therefore logical to apply the *lex rei sitae*. Moreover, local practices which are not generally known except in the courts of the place are often important. Finally, account was also taken of the need to make entries in land registers located where the property is situated.

24. It may be assumed, by contrary inference, that the article should not be applied where the dispute is not such as to entail such procedural steps or when a knowledge of local practices is not relevant.

25. As regards the actual answer to be given to the cour d'appel, two

options are available: either an answer couched in negative terms, ruling that proceedings such as the *action paulienne* under Article 1167 of the French civil code do not come within the scope of the paragraph in question (which would undoubtedly be sufficient to enable the national court to settle the dispute before it) or one formulated in positive terms, stating which types of action are to be regarded as coming within the scope of Article 16(1). If the latter course were taken, it would be useful to take the first part of the answer proposed by the United Kingdom, thus ensuring that the ruling can also be properly understood in the countries whose legal systems are based on common law.

26. In the final analysis, I think it preferable to choose the first option, as the French and Italian Governments and the Commission have done. My consideration of the national court's question has necessarily been based on the aim and effects of the *action paulienne* in French law (disregarding, obviously, the classification of that action in the French legal system). It would, therefore, be prudent not to give an answer going beyond that framework.

27. I therefore propose that the Court should rule as follows:

'(1) The concept of "proceedings which have as their object rights *in rem* in immovable property" in Article 16(1) of the Brussels Convention of 27 September 1968 must be interpreted in the light of the objectives and system of that convention;

(2) An action such as the *action paulienne* under Article 1167 of the French civil code does not come within that concept'.

Case C-280/90 - 26 February 1992

Elisabeth Hacker
v
Euro-Relais GmbH

Exclusive jurisdiction - Article 16(1) - Proceedings relating to tenancies of immovable property - Concept - Letting of holiday accommodation by a business organising travel - Not applicable - Conditions.

Summary

Article 16(1) of the Convention of 27 September 1968 on Jurisdiction and the Enforcement of Judgments in Civil and Commercial Matters is to be interpreted as not applying to a contract concluded in a Contracting State whereby a business organizing travel with its seat in that State undertakes to procure for a client domiciled in the same State the use for several weeks of holiday accommodation not owned by it in another Contracting State, and to book the travel arrangements. A complex contract of that type, which concerns a range of services provided in return for a lump sum paid by the customer, is outside the scope within which the exclusive jurisdiction laid down in Article 16(1) finds its *raison d'être* and cannot constitute a 'tenancy agreement' within the meaning of that provision.

JUDGMENT OF THE COURT

Due, President, Grèvisse, Kapteyn, Presidents of Chambers, Mancini, Kakouris, Moitinho de Almeida, Diez de Velasco, Zuleeg and Murray, Judges

1. By order of 28 June 1990, which was received at the Court on 14

September 1990, the Landgericht Köln (District Court, Cologne) referred to the Court, pursuant to the Protocol of 3 June 1971 on the interpretation by the Court of Justice of the Convention of 27 September 1968 on Jurisdiction and the Enforcement of Judgments in Civil and Commercial Matters (hereinafter referred to as 'the Convention'), two questions on the interpretation of Article 16(1) of the Convention.

2. Those questions were raised in the course of proceedings between Mrs Hacker, who is domiciled in the Federal Republic of Germany, and Euro-Relais GmbH ('Euro-Relais'), carrying on a business as a travel organiser with a head office in the Federal Republic of Germany and which advertises by way of brochures. The proceedings concern a contract described as a 'tenancy agreement' concluded by the parties on 5 April 1989 also in the Federal Republic of Germany.

3. Under that contract Euro-Relais undertook, in return for payment, to procure a holiday home situated in Ameland, in the Netherlands, not owned by Euro-Relais, for the use of Mrs Hacker and six other persons accompanying her, for the period from 29 July to 12 August 1989. The contract also provided that, in return for an additional payment, Euro-Relais undertook to arrange the booking of the ferry crossing to Ameland for Mrs Hacker; the cost of the crossing itself was to be paid separately by Mrs Hacker to the ferry company.

4. Mrs Hacker considered that the size of the holiday home was less than that indicated in the Euro-Relais brochure, so that she had been compelled first to rent an additional room and then to cut short her holiday. She commenced proceedings in the Amtsgericht Köln (Local Court, Cologne) against Euro-Relais, claiming a reduction in the price paid, damages for the cost of renting an additional room and damages for loss of holiday enjoyment.

5. The Amtsgericht rejected Mrs Hacker's claim and she then appealed to the Landgericht Köln, which considered that the outcome of the proceedings depended on the interpretation of Article 16(1) of the Convention; it therefore stayed the proceedings and referred the following questions to the Court for a preliminary ruling:

'(1) Is there a tenancy agreement within the meaning of Article 16(1) of the Convention when a travel organiser and a customer who are both domiciled in the Federal Republic of Germany conclude a contract in the Federal Republic of Germany under which the travel organiser undertakes to provide for the use of the customer for a number of weeks a holiday home in the Netherlands not owned by the travel organiser and to arrange the booking of the ferry crossing?

(2) If so, does Article 16(1) of the Convention also apply to actions in which the travel organiser's customer claims: (a) a reduction owing to an alleged shortcoming in the holiday home; (b) damages on the ground that, because of an alleged shortcoming in the holiday home, it was necessary to rent an additional room; (c) damages for loss of holiday enjoyment?'

6. Reference is made to the Report for the Hearing for a fuller account of the facts of the case, the procedure and the written observations submitted to the Court, which are mentioned or discussed hereinafter only in so far as is necessary for the reasoning of the Court.

Question 1

7. Article 16 of the Convention, in the version applicable at the time the dispute arose, provides: 'The following courts shall have exclusive jurisdiction, regardless of domicile: 1. In proceedings which have as their object rights *in rem* in, or tenancies of, immovable property, the courts of the Contracting State in which the property is situated; ...'.

8. As the Court pointed out in its judgment in Case 241/83 *Rösler* v *Rottwinkel* [1985] ECR 99, at paragraph 19, the *raison d'être* of the exclusive jurisdiction conferred by Article 16(1) on the courts of the Contracting State in which the property is situated is the fact that tenancies are closely bound up with the law of immovable property and with the provisions, generally of a mandatory character governing its use, such as legislation controlling the level of rents and protecting the rights of tenants, including tenant farmers.

9. In the above judgment, the Court also pointed out that Article 16(1) seeks to ensure a rational allocation of jurisdiction by opting for a solution whereby the court having jurisdiction is determined on the basis of its proximity to the property since that court is in a better position to obtain first-hand knowledge of the facts relating to the creation of tenancies and to the performance of the terms thereof (paragraph 20).

10. On those considerations the Court held (at paragraph 24 of the judgment) that the provision in question applied to all tenancies of immovable property irrespective of their special characteristics.

11. However, it must be borne in mind that the Court had previously stated, in its judgment in Case 73/77 *Sanders* v *Van der Putte* [(1977] ECR 2383, at paragraphs 15 and 16), that although those considerations explained the assignment of exclusive jurisdiction to the courts of the State in which the immovable property was situated in the case of tenancies of immovable property properly so-called they did not apply where the principal aim of the agreement was of a different nature.

12. It is also apparent from the same judgment that the assignment, in the interests of the proper administration of justice, of exclusive jurisdiction to the courts of one Contracting State in accordance with Article 16 of the Convention deprives the parties of the choice of the forum which would otherwise be theirs and, in certain cases, results in their being brought before a court which is not that of the domicile of any of them (paragraph 17). Having regard to that consideration the provisions of Article 16 must not be given a wider interpretation than is required by their objective (paragraph 18).

13. On those grounds the Court held that Article 16(1) did not apply to a contract which concerned the operation of a business.

14. The situation is similar with regard to an agreement of the type in dispute in the main proceedings, which is concluded between a travel organizer and a customer in the place where they are both domiciled. Irrespective of its title, and although providing a service concerning the use of short-term holiday accommodation, such an agreement also includes other services, such as information and advice, where the travel organiser proposes a range of holiday offers, the reservation of accommodation during the period chosen by the customer, the reservation of seats in connection with travel arrangements, the reception at the destination and, possibly, travel cancellation insurance.

15. A complex contract of that type, which concerns a range of services provided in return for a lump sum paid by the customer, is outside the scope within which the exclusive jurisdiction laid down by Article 16(1) finds its *raison d'être* and cannot constitute a 'tenancy agreement' within the meaning of that article as interpreted in the judgment in *Sanders* v *Van der Putte*, cited above.

16. Consequently, the reply to the first question put by the national court must be that Article 16(1) of the Brussels Convention is to be interpreted as not applying to a contract concluded in a Contracting State whereby a

business organizing travel with its seat in that State undertakes to procure for a client domiciled in the same State the use for several weeks of holiday accommodation not owned by it in another Contracting State and to book the travel arrangements.

The second question

17. Having regard to the answer given to the first question, it is not necessary to reply to the second question.

On those grounds, the Court, in answer to the questions referred to it by the Landgericht Köln by order of 28 June 1990, hereby rules:

> **Article 16(1) of the Brussels Convention is to be interpreted as not applying to a contract concluded in a Contracting State whereby a business organizing travel with its seat in that State undertakes to procure for a client domiciled in the same State the use for several weeks of holiday accommodation not owned by it in another Contracting State, and to book the travel arrangements.**

OPINION OF MR ADVOCATE GENERAL DARMON

1. Article 16(1) of the Brussels Convention gives exclusive jurisdiction in proceedings which have as their object tenancies of immovable property to the courts of the Contracting State in which the property is situated.

2. That provision has once again been submitted to the Court for interpretation by the Landgericht Köln in connection with a contract for the letting of a holiday home.

3. By a contract dated 5 April 1989, formally described as a 'tenancy agreement', Euro-Relais of Cologne, a travel organizer, undertook to make available for the use of Mrs Hacker, who is domiciled in Cologne, a holiday home in the Netherlands which was not owned by the agency. The holiday home, which was chosen from a catalogue, was to be let for a fortnight, at a price of DM 1 520. The agency also undertook to make bookings for the ferry crossing to the island of Ameland.

4. Although the catalogue specified that the size of the holiday home was 100 square metres, according to Mrs Hacker it was only 55 square metres in area, which meant that she was obliged to rent additional accommodation locally at a cost of DM 288. Mrs Hacker was not satisfied with the arrangements and finally cut short her holiday.

5. In the Amtsgericht and then the Landgericht Köln Mrs Hacker claimed DM 760 as a reduction in the cost of the holiday, damages representing the cost of renting the extra room, and DM 3046.35 damages as compensation for lost holiday enjoyment on behalf of herself and her husband.

6. The Landgericht Köln asks the Court essentially: (1) if there is a tenancy agreement within the meaning of Article 16(1) of the Convention in circumstances such as those arising in this case; (2) if so, does Article 16(1) also apply for the purpose of establishing which court has jurisdiction over claims such as those made by the plaintiff in the main proceedings as described above.

7. The Court has already been called upon to interpret the concept of 'tenancies of immovable property' within the meaning of Article 16(1) of the Convention three times. The Court established the principle that the concept should be *interpreted independently* on the basis of the Convention itself, without reference to the law applicable under the conflict rules of the national court hearing the main proceedings.

8. Only if there is *uniformity of interpretation will uniform application* of the Convention in all the Contracting States be ensured in this area and the 'free movement of decisions' which constitutes the primary objective of the Convention guaranteed.

9. As regards the method of interpretation the Court will recall the particularly instructive formula it offered in its judgment in *LTU* v *Eurocontrol*: 'In the interpretation of the concept "civil and commercial matters" for the purposes of the application of the Convention reference must not be made to the law of one of the States concerned but, *first to the objectives and scheme of the Convention and, secondly, to the general principles which stem from the corpus of the national legal systems*'.

10. Article 16 appears in Title II, Section 5 'Exclusive jurisdiction'. It lists a series of exceptions to the basic principle set out in the first paragraph of Article 2 of the Convention, according to which persons domiciled in a Contracting State shall, whatever their nationality, be sued in the courts of that State.

11. As the Jenard Report points out, Article 16 provides for exclusive jurisdiction which may not be departed from either by an agreement purporting to confer jurisdiction on the courts of another Contracting State (Article 17) or by an implied submission to the jurisdiction (Article 18). Under Article 19 of the Convention any court of a State other than the State whose courts have exclusive jurisdiction pursuant to Article 16 must declare of its own motion that it has no jurisdiction. Finally, a foreign decision given in disregard of exclusive jurisdiction will not be recognized (Article 28) or enforced (Article 34).

12. In its judgment in *Sanders* the Court emphasized that: 'the assignment, in the interests of the proper administration of justice, of exclusive jurisdiction to the courts of one Contracting State in accordance with Article 16 of the Convention results in depriving the parties of the choice of the forum which would otherwise be theirs and, in certain cases, results in their being brought before a court which is not that of the domicile of any of them'; and that '*Having regard to that consideration the provisions of Article 16 must not be given a wider interpretation than is required by their objective.*' The Court concluded that the concept of a tenancy did not cover a contract relating to a business carried on in immovable property rented from a third person by the lessor.

13. However, precisely in a case where there was a contract for the letting

of a holiday home, the Court held in *Rösler* that Article 16(1) of the Convention 'applies to all lettings of immovable property, even for a short term and even where they relate only to the use and occupation of a holiday home', and that disputes concerning the obligations of the landlord or of the tenant under the lease fell within the exclusive jurisdiction of the courts of the State in which the property was situated except disputes 'which are only indirectly related to the use of the property let, such as those concerning the loss of holiday enjoyment and travel expenses'.

14. In that case *two private individuals*, both domiciled in Germany, concluded a letting agreement, which they expressly stated was to be governed by German law, for a holiday villa in Italy. It was agreed that the letting would be for four persons for a period of three weeks and that the tenant was not permitted to accommodate visitors. The owner, who spent his holiday in the same villa at the same time as the tenant, brought proceedings against the tenant in the courts of his domicile on the ground that the clauses in the contract had not been complied with, in particular in respect of the number of persons to be accommodated.

15. The Court stated: 'The *raison d'être* of the exclusive jurisdiction conferred by Article 16(1) on the courts of the Contracting State in which the property is situated is the fact that tenancies are closely bound up with the law of immovable property and with the provisions, generally of a mandatory character, governing its use, such as legislation controlling the level of rents and protecting the rights of tenants, including tenant farmers. Article 16(1) seeks to ensure a rational allocation of jurisdiction by opting for a solution whereby the court having jurisdiction is determined on the basis of its proximity to the property since that court is in a better position to obtain first-hand knowledge of the facts relating to the creation of tenancies and to the performance of the terms thereon.

The question submitted by the Bundesgerichtshof is designed to ascertain whether exceptions may be made to the general rule laid down in Article 16 owing to the special character of certain tenancies, such as short-term lettings of holiday homes, even though the wording of that article provides no indication in that respect.

It must be emphasized in this regard that (...) inherent in any exception to the general rule laid down in Article 16(1) is the risk of further extensions which might call in question the application of national legislation governing the use of immovable property.'

16. It follows that when two nationals of a single Member State, both domiciled in that State, make a tenancy agreement for a holiday home in another Member State, actions arising from that tenancy fall within the exclusive jurisdiction of the courts of the latter State.

17. The Court's judgment failed, however, to dispel the unease caused in the national legal systems and academic writing by the provision contained in Article 16 which is general and does not make distinctions.

18. In their commentary on the Brussels Convention, Gothot and Holleaux had already stated: 'It may well be thought excessive to give exclusive

jurisdiction over any dispute whatsoever arising from a tenancy of immovable property to the courts of the country where the immovable property is situated when the dispute will sometimes be purely a matter for the ordinary law governing contracts or rentals'.

19. Speaking at a seminar on the Brussels Convention held in Luxembourg on 11 and 12 March 1991, Mr M. Carpenter concluded on the subject of Article 16 'it may be that parties to such lettings (of holiday accommodation) will increasingly resort to arbitration in future to avoid the inconveniences caused by Article 16'.

20. Noting the solution arrived at in the *Rösler* judgment, the States who were parties to the San Sebastian Convention 'on the accession of Spain and Portugal' of 26 May 1989 decided to insert a new subparagraph (b) in Article 16(1) concerning short-term tenancies, in particular tenancies for holiday purposes.

21. That Convention, which has not yet entered into force, provides in the new Article 16(1)(b) for the concurrent jurisdiction of the courts of the defendant's domicile 'in proceedings which have as their object tenancies of immovable property concluded for temporary private use for a maximum period of six consecutive months (...) provided that the landlord and the tenant are natural persons and are domiciled in the same Contracting State'.

22. The exclusive jurisdiction rule contained in Article 16(1) of the Brussels Convention is applicable 'regardless of domicile' and links jurisdiction to a territory: the territory where the property is situated.

23. It follows that if there was a departure from that rule the Convention might not be applied where, for instance, all the parties to the dispute were domiciled in the same contracting State.

24. As the law stands at present, should the contract whereby a travel firm makes holiday accommodation available to an individual for a limited period and undertakes at the same time to make connected arrangements be characterized as a tenancy within the meaning of Article 16 of the Brussels Convention?

25. It should first be noted that, as a business organizing holiday accommodation, the agency undertakes in that type of contract more than just to make a holiday home available. It seems clear to me that the travel agency's obligations are not at an end once it has made the holiday home available.

26. All the other services provided by the agency must be taken into account when characterizing the contract: advising the client, booking the chosen villa, making ferry bookings, providing cancellation insurance, paying the rental to the owner (avoiding the need for the holidaymaker to do so), etc. That multitude of services is reflected in the fact that the price paid by the holidaymaker represents not merely the rent but also the cost of insurance, 'booking fees' and the agency's remuneration.

27. There is thus a complex contract that includes certain services which do not fall under the heading of a tenancy and are not bound up with that concept.

28. It does not therefore appear that the specific feature of such a contract

necessarily lies in the nature of what is rented. In particular it does not confer on the holidaymaker the benefit of legislation protecting lessees.

29. If the holidaymaker were to benefit from protective legislation it would be in order to put him back on equal terms with the business rather than to safeguard his right to accommodation or to stay in the property, for instance. The adoption by the Council of a directive on package travel, package holidays and package tours is significant in this connection.

30. With regard to the jurisdiction *ratione loci* it might well be considered that disputes concerning whether the accommodation was in conformity with that offered in the catalogue, cancellation insurance, the validity of clauses limiting liability or the duty to give professional advice fall within the jurisdiction of the courts where the contract was negotiated and concluded rather than the courts for the place in which the property is situated. The same is true of the price: as the Landgericht Frankfurt judiciously observed, the price of accommodation is often a catalogue price determined by the state of supply and demand in travel agencies rather than by the state of the rental market in the place where the property is situated.

31. In circumstances such as those that arose in this case, there is not, therefore, a *tenancy* within the meaning of Article 16 of the Brussels Convention which makes a strong link between the rules on tenancies and those on rights *in rem*. It is striking to note that in this case the claims of the plaintiff in the main proceedings are *personal* claims in contractual liability which, moreover, in no sense put at issue the status of the property.

32. Finally, it should be remembered that because Article 16 provides for exclusive jurisdiction, the Court interprets the article narrowly, stating in the *Sanders* judgment that it applies only to tenancies of immovable property *properly so-called*, that is to say, in particular, disputes between lessors and tenants as to the existence or interpretation of leases or to compensation for damage caused by the tenant and to giving up possession of the premises'. The Court held that Article 16 does not apply 'where the *principal aim* of the agreement is of a different nature'.

33. I do not therefore think it possible to describe as a tenancy, within the meaning of Article 16 of the Convention, a contract in which the principal aim is the provision of a bundle of services and to make subject to the exclusive jurisdiction of the courts where the property is situated a contract whose 'centre of gravity' is the place where it was concluded.

34. The Landgericht Köln asks solely in the event that the Court should find that there was a tenancy within the meaning of Article 16(1) of the Convention whether a distinction should be drawn between the different claims put forward by the plaintiff in the main proceedings. I shall therefore examine the question only in the alternative. The Court will recall that the plaintiff is seeking a reduction in the price because of a shortcoming in the holiday home (which was smaller in area than had been specified), claiming damages for having had to rent an extra room and compensation for a disturbed holiday.

35. In the *Rösler* case the Court held: 'All disputes concerning the obligations of the landlord or of the tenant under a tenancy, in particular those

concerning the existence of tenancies or the interpretation of the terms thereof, their duration, the giving up of possession to the landlord, the repairing of damage caused by the tenant or the recovery of rent and of incidental charges payable by the tenant, such as charges for the consumption of water, gas and electricity, fall within the exclusive jurisdiction conferred by Article 16(1) of the Convention on the courts of the State in which the property is situated. *On the other hand, disputes which are only indirectly related to the use of the property let such as those concerning the loss of holiday enjoyment and travel expenses, do not fall within the exclusive jurisdiction conferred by that article.*'

36. The action which the Court considered in that case to be inseparable from the tenancy agreement was brought by the owner who, having spent his holiday at the same time as the tenant in the villa that he had let, complained about the noise and excessive number of people in the villa. He was seeking compensation for 'lost holiday enjoyment' as a *holiday-maker* staying in the same villa as the tenant, not as its owner.

37. Conversely, in this case all the claims before the Landgericht Köln are made by the tenant against the travel organizer that let the property on the ground that it failed to perform its contractual obligations. The claims for a reduction in the rent and for damages, in so far as they relate to renting an additional room, must be regarded as claims directly connected with the use of the property let. Similarly, the claim for damages for a disturbed holiday is here also linked to the failure by the travel organizer to perform its obligation to make available to the tenant property that conformed to what had been agreed. There is thus a close link between that claim and the letting agreement.

38. All the claims put forward by the plaintiff in the main proceedings therefore relate directly to the use of the property let within the meaning of the Court's judgment in *Rösler*.

39. Finally we should not underestimate the major practical difficulties which could result from a 'Zuständigkeitssplitting', referred to by the Landgericht Köln in its decision: the risk of conflicting decisions, the risk of both courts declining jurisdiction with no possibility of any court resolving the issue, and in addition the excessive costs and burden on the parties.

40. The Court will recall that in the *Peters* judgment it stated: 'multiplication of the bases of jurisdiction in one and the same type of case is not likely to encourage legal certainty and effective legal protection throughout the territory of the Community. The provisions of the Convention should therefore be interpreted in such a way that the court seised is not required to declare that it has jurisdiction to adjudicate upon certain applications but has no jurisdiction to hear certain other applications, even though they are closely related.'

41. The Court concluded that obligations in regard to the payment of a sum of money which have their basis in the relationship existing between an association and its members by virtue of membership are 'matters relating to a contract' within the meaning of Article 5(1) of the Convention, whether or not the obligations in question arise simply from the act of becoming a member or from that act in conjunction with one or more decisions made by organs of the association.

42. Consequently, I consider that in the event that the Court should not share my opinion but takes the view that a contract such as that concluded by the parties to the main proceedings should be regarded as a tenancy within the meaning of Article 16(1) of the Convention, all the plaintiff's claims are sufficiently connected with that tenancy and therefore fall within the ambit of that article.

43. I therefore conclude that the Court should hold that:

(1) Article 16(1) of the Brussels Convention should he interpreted as not applicable to a contract concluded in a Contracting State between a travel organiser and a client, both of whom are domiciled in that State, which obliges the travel organiser, amongst other services provided, to procure for the use of the client for a few weeks holiday accommodation - whether or not the travel organizer owns the accommodation - situated in another Contracting State;

(2) in the alternative, if Article 16 of the Convention does apply to such a contract, it must also apply to the claim for a reduction in the cost linked to a shortcoming in the holiday home, to the claim for damages for having had to rent an additional room and to the claim for compensation for a disturbed holiday.

Case C-294/92 - 17 May 1994

George Lawrence Webb
v
Lawrence Desmond Webb

Exclusive jurisdiction - Article 16(1) - Proceedings which have as their object rights in rem in immovable property - Concept - Proceedings relating to the existence of a trust attaching to immovable property - Excluded.

Summary

In order for Article 16(1) of the Convention on Jurisdiction and the Enforcement of Judgments in Civil matters to apply, it is not sufficient that a right *in rem* in immovable property be involved in the action or that the action have a link with immovable property: the action must be based on a right *in rem* and not on a right *in personam*, save in the case of the exception concerning tenancies of immovable property.

It follows that an action for a declaration that a person holds immovable property as trustee and for an order requiring that person to execute such documents as should be required to vest the legal ownership in the plaintiff does not constitute an action *in rem* within the meaning of Article 16(1) of the Convention.

JUDGMENT OF THE COURT

Due, President, Moitinho de Almeida, Diez de Velasco, Edward, Presidents of Chambers, Kakouris, Joliet, Rodriguez Iglesias, Zuleeg and Kapteyn, Judges

1. By order of 27 February 1992, received at the Court on 3 July 1992, the Court of Appeal, London, referred to the Court for a preliminary ruling under Article 3 of the Protocol of 3 June 1971 on the interpretation by the Court of Justice of the Convention of 27 September 1968 on Jurisdiction and the Enforcement of Judgments in Civil and Commercial Matters (OJ 1972 L 299, p. 32, hereinafter 'the Convention') a question on the interpretation of Article 16(1) of the Convention.

2. The question arose in proceedings between George Lawrence Webb ('the father') and his son, Lawrence Desmond Webb ('the son') relating to immovable property situated in France.

3. In 1971 the father concluded an agreement for the purchase of a flat in Antibes. He raised the necessary funds in England.

4. The Bank of England authorizations required by United Kingdom exchange control legislation were obtained on the footing that the property would be purchased in the name of the son. The necessary funds were then transferred from the father's bank account in England to an account opened in Antibes by the son. In October 1971 the vendor conveyed legal ownership of the flat to the son.

5. Since then, both the father, with his wife, and the son have used the flat as a holiday home, with the father bearing the bulk of the outgoings.

6. On 26 March 1990 the father brought an action against the son before the High Court of Justice for a declaration that the son held the property as trustee and for an order that the son should execute such documents as should be required to vest legal ownership of the property in the father.

7. The son challenged the jurisdiction of the English courts. He contended that, since the action related to a right *in rem* in immovable property, the French courts had exclusive jurisdiction. On this point, he relied on Article 16(1) of the Convention, which provides that:

'The following courts shall have exclusive jurisdiction, regardless of domicile: (1)(a) in proceedings which have as their object rights *in rem* in immovable property or tenancies of immovable property, the courts of the Contracting State in which the property is situated.'

8. In its judgment of 23 May 1991 the High Court found that the father's claim was based on a fiduciary relationship between himself and

the son and, further, that the father was not seeking a declaration that he was the owner, an order for possession, or rectification of the land register but an order requiring the son to execute such documents as should be necessary to convey ownership in the flat. The High Court accordingly concluded that the claim did not relate to rights *in rem* in immovable property within the meaning of Article 16(1) of the Convention and dismissed the objection of lack of jurisdiction.

9. On the merits, the High Court found that the son held the flat under a resulting trust. In English law, where a person finances the purchase of property in the name of another, that person is presumed, in the absence of clear intention to bestow a gift, to have retained the beneficial interest in the property and the nominal owner is presumed to be a trustee. In order to rebut that presumption, the son, relying on the presumption of advancement, contended that the flat had been a gift to him. However, that argument did not convince the High Court which deduced from the fact that the flat was used by the father that he intended to keep the property for himself.

10. The son appealed on the ground that the High Court was wrong to hold Article 16(1) of the Convention inapplicable. The Court of Appeal, which was in doubt as to the interpretation to be given to that provision, requested the Court of Justice to give a preliminary ruling on the following question: 'Whether on the true interpretation of Article 16(1) of the Brussels Convention the proceedings in the Chancery Division of the High Court of Justice, the short title and reference to the record of which is *Webb* v *Webb* 1990 W. No 2827, are proceedings in respect of which the courts of France have exclusive jurisdiction'.

11. By its question the national court asks whether an action for a declaration that a person holds immovable property as trustee and for an order requiring that person to execute such documents as should be required to vest the legal ownership in the plaintiff constitutes an action *in rem* within the meaning of Article 16(1) of the Convention.

12. The son and the Commission, who consider that the test for applying Article 16(1) is the plaintiff's ultimate purpose and that by his action the father is ultimately seeking to secure ownership of the flat, contend that the main proceedings are covered by Article 16(1).

13. That argument cannot be accepted.

14. Article 16 confers exclusive jurisdiction in the matter of rights *in rem* in immovable property on the courts of the Contracting State in which the property is situated. In the light of the Court's judgment in Case C-115/88 *Reichert and Kockler* [1990] ECR 1-27, where the Court had to rule on the question whether the exclusive jurisdiction prescribed by that article applied in respect of an action by a creditor to have a disposition of immovable property declared ineffective as against him on the ground that it was made in fraud of his rights by his debtor, it follows that it is not sufficient, for Article 16(1) to apply, that a right *in rem* in immovable property be involved in the action or that the action have a link with immovable property: the action must be based on a right *in rem* and not on a right *in personam*, save in the case of the exception concerning tenancies of immovable property.

15. The aim of the proceedings before the national court is to obtain a declaration that the son holds the flat for the exclusive benefit of the father and that in that capacity he is under a duty to execute the documents necessary to convey ownership of the flat to the father. The father does not claim that he already enjoys rights directly relating to the property which are enforceable against the whole world, but seeks only to assert rights as against the son. Consequently, his action is not an action *in rem* within the meaning of Article 16(1) of the Convention but an action *in personam*.

16. Nor are considerations relating to the proper administration of justice underlying Article 16(1) of the Convention applicable in this case.

17. As the Court has held, the conferring of exclusive jurisdiction in the matter of rights *in rem* in immovable property on the courts of the State in which the property is situated is justified because actions concerning rights *in rem* in immovable property often involve disputes frequently necessitating checks, inquiries and expert assessments which must be carried out on the spot (see the judgment in Case 73/77 *Sanders* v *Van der Putte* [1977] ECR 2383, at paragraph 13).

18. As the father and the United Kingdom rightly point out, the immovable nature of the property held in trust and its location are irrelevant to the issues to be determined in the main proceedings which would have been the same if the dispute had concerned a flat situated in the United Kingdom or a yacht.

19. The answer to be given to the question submitted to the Court must

therefore be that an action for a declaration that a person holds immovable property as trustee and for an order requiring that person to execute such documents as should be required to vest the legal ownership in the plaintiff does not constitute an action *in rem* within the meaning of Article 16(1) of the Convention.

On those grounds, the Court, in answer to the question referred to it by the Court of Appeal, London, by order of 27 February 1992, hereby rules:

> **An action for a declaration that a person holds immovable property as trustee and for an order requiring that person to execute such documents as should be required to vest the legal ownership in the plaintiff does not constitute an action *in rem* within the meaning of Article 16(1) of the Convention of 27 September 1968 on Jurisdiction and the Enforcement of Judgments in Civil and Commercial Matters.**

OPINION OF MR ADVOCATE GENERAL DARMON

1. In this reference from the Court of Appeal this Court is asked to rule upon the interpretation of Article 16(1) of the Brussels Convention of 27 September 1968 on Jurisdiction and the Enforcement of Judgments in Civil and Commercial Matters (hereinafter referred to as 'the Convention'). The main facts of the dispute are as follows.

2. During 1971 George Lawrence Webb concluded an agreement for the purchase of a flat in Antibes (France). The authorizations required by the Bank of England under exchange control legislation were granted in the name of his son, Lawrence Desmond Webb.

3. The funds necessary for the purchase were transferred from the bank account of the plaintiff in the main proceedings to one opened in Antibes by his son in whose name the property was registered.

4. In March 1990, the father, George Webb, brought an action against his son in the High Court primarily for a declaration that the son held the property upon trust and for an order that his son should execute such documents as should be required to vest the legal ownership of the property in himself.

5. The son, Lawrence Webb, besides contending that the property was a gift to him, challenges the jurisdiction of the English courts on the ground that, since the action concerns a right *in rem* in immovable property, only the French court of the place where the property is located has jurisdiction. He relies in this regard on Article 16(1) of the Convention, which provides that: 'The following courts shall have exclusive jurisdiction, regardless of domicile: ... in proceedings which have as their object rights *in rem*, or tenancies of, immovable property, the courts of the Contracting State in which the property is situated'.

6. By judgment of 23 May 1991 the High Court dismissed that objection on the ground that the father's claim is based on a fiduciary relationship, the father not seeking an order for possession, rectification of the land register or a declaration that he is the owner.

7. An appeal was lodged and the Court of Appeal has referred the following question: 'Whether on the true interpretation of Article 16(1) of the Brussels Convention the proceedings in the action in the Chancery Division of the High Court of Justice the short title and reference to the record of which is *Webb* v *Webb* [1090] W.No287 are proceedings in respect of which the courts of France have exclusive jurisdiction'.

8. A preliminary observation is called for. Although the referring court has made its reference on the basis of Article 177 of the EEC Treaty, the relevant provision in this case is Article 3 of the Protocol of 3 June 1971. Even under that provision, the Court may not rule directly on the case before the Court of Appeal but must provide it with the necessary criteria for interpretation so that it may give judgment. The question must therefore be reframed and could be put in these terms: does an action brought by a person against another person for a declaration that the other person holds immovable property as trustee and for an order requiring the latter to execute such documents as should be required to vest the legal ownership in the plaintiff constitute an action *in rem* within the meaning of Article 16(1) of the Convention?

9. The Convention does take account of trusts and their specific nature since it lays down jurisdiction in matters concerning trusts in Article 5(6). However, that provision is inapplicable in the present case owing to the very particular nature of the trust in question. Whereas the aforesaid provision can only govern 'a trust created by the operation of a statute, or by a written instrument, or created orally and evidenced in writing', the resulting trust involved here is to be deduced '... from the presumed intention of the person who furnishes the property, or the purchase price of the property'.

10. As regards a resulting trust, Mr Béraudo gives the example '... of a person who buys property in another's name. In the absence of a clear intention to make a gift, the person who financed the purchase is presumed to have retained equitable title, the beneficial interest in the property. The nominal owner has only the legal title. He is presumed trustee of the property'.

11. Where Article 16 is concerned, it should be borne in mind that this provision appears in Section 5 of Title II of the Convention and determines which courts are to have jurisdiction where the *principal subject-matter* of the claim relates to a matter mentioned therein. Article 16, which confers exclusive jurisdiction, has the effect of ousting the jurisdiction of the courts of the place where the defendant is domiciled and applies irrespective of any contrary agreement between the parties.

12. As Droz wrote '... the heads of jurisdiction enumerated in Article 16 will normally be the subject of exclusive jurisdiction only if they relate to the *principal subject-matter* of the proceedings of which the court is to be seised. This follows a *contrario*, but quite clearly, from Article 19 of the Convention which requires the court to decline jurisdiction, where a court of another

Member State has exclusive jurisdiction under Article 16, only if it is seised of the principal subject-matter of the issue reserved for the courts of another Member State'.

13. Finally, a judgment given in another Contracting State in disregard of that jurisdiction rule cannot be recognized (Article 28) nor enforced (Article 34).

14. Article 16 may therefore have the effect of bringing parties before a court which is not that of any of them.

15. That provision, in the part conferring exclusive jurisdiction 'in proceedings which have as their object rights *in rem* in immovable property' on the courts of the Contracting State in which the property is situated, has given rise to only one judgment of the Court, in *Reichert I*, on which the observations of the parties concentrated, though it was not mentioned during the proceedings before the English courts.

16. In the case in which that ruling was given, a man and wife domiciled in the Federal Republic of Germany had donated to their son, who was also domiciled in that State, the legal ownership of immovable property located in France, taking a life interest for themselves. The German bank, which was a creditor of the couple, had brought in France an '*action paulienne*' which had the effect of making the transfer of property ineffective against itself. After the defendants had challenged the jurisdiction of the French court in favour of the German court of their domicile, the Cour d'Appel, Aix-en-Provence, referred a question asking in substance whether the '*action paulienne*' constituted an action *in rem* within the meaning of Article 16(1) of the Convention.

17. In its ruling the Court referred to its judgment in Sanders, relating to the concept of 'tenancies of immovable property' and its judgment in *Duijnstee*, on proceedings concerned with the registration or validity of patents', and repeated its concern to ensure that concepts used in the Convention should be applied uniformly, this requiring '... an independent definition [to] be given in Community law to the phrase "proceedings which have as their object rights *in rem* in immovable property"'.

18. After then observing that Article 16 provided for a forum different from that ordinarily having jurisdiction, the Court came to the conclusion that it '... must not be given a wider interpretation than is required by its objective ... ' the *ratio legis* of that provision resting on the principle of proximity which justified conferring jurisdiction on the courts of the *locus rei sitae*, which '... are the best placed, for reasons of proximity, to ascertain the facts satisfactorily and to apply the rules and practices which are generally those of the State in which the property is situated...'

19. Those considerations led the Court to interpret that provision as meaning that '... the exclusive jurisdiction of the Contracting State in which the property is situated does not encompass all actions concerning rights *in rem* in immovable property but only those which both come within the scope of the Brussels Convention and are actions which seek to determine the extent, content, ownership or possession of immovable property or the existence of other rights *in rem* therein and to provide the holders of these rights with the protection of the powers which attach to their interest'.

20. The Court found it necessary to consider the basis and purpose of the action brought and refused to apply Article 16(1) on the ground that: 'The '*action paulienne*' ... is based on the creditor's personal claim against the debtor and seeks to protect whatever security he may have over the debtor's estate'.

21 As Bischoff states: 'It would not therefore be rash to venture the view that the implications of the judgment certainly extend beyond the *action paulienne* alone and embrace all actions for annulment, rescission or avoidance which, although they might have a bearing on title to property, are based on a right *in personam* of the plaintiff'.

22. Thus, being based on an enforceable claim, the *action paulienne* has as its purpose to preserve the creditor's general security over the debtor's estate but without giving him a *ius in rem*, so that, as Ancel States: 'Claims seeking to strike down a right *in rem* in immovable property by challenging the transaction by which the property was transferred do not concern that category of rights as directly as those striking at their structure and protection. Unlike the latter,the former arise away from the core of the "substance" - the legal nature of the property - and are therefore liable to be barred by the rule of strict interpretation'.

23. The positions taken before the Court are as follows.

24. On the one hand, we have the United Kingdom, which takes the view that the object of the father's action is 'the determination of the question whether land is held under a trust' and that the action concerns only the relations internal to the trust so that it cannot be regarded as concerning a right *in rem*.

25. That view is shared by the plaintiff in the main proceedings who considers that 'where the dispute concerns the existence or otherwise of a right arising out of a contract between the parties, or out of their conduct towards each other, the courts of the *situs* will be no better qualified to determine the dispute than the courts of any other Contracting State'.

26. On the other hand, we have both the Commission and the defendant - the Commission expressly and the defendant more implicitly - laying stress on the purpose of the claim and submitting that the action is one *in rem*, with the father claiming to be the owner, which at the hearing led Counsel for the defendant to sum up the plaintiff's claim, not without humour, in these words: 'What is the plaintiff's claim? My Lords, the plaintiff's claim is to own the flat!'

27. The question is not an easy one and I have pondered on the correct approach to take, for the claim of ownership undeniably underlies the claim for the recognition of such a trust.

28. However, the approach which looks at the actual *aim* pursued by the plaintiff in the main proceedings is not supported by the relevant provision, by prevailing academic opinion or by the case-law of the Court. The jurisdiction *ratione materiae* of a court must necessarily be assessed in the light of the *subject-matter* of the claim, as defined in the originating application, without looking at purpose.

29. Exclusive jurisdiction is conferred provided that the principal subject-matter of the claim relates to rights *in rem* in immovable property. Reading the French, Spanish and Italian texts ('en matière de droits réels immobiliers', 'en materia de derechos reales imobiliarios', in materia di diritti reali immobiliari'),

one notices the slight difference in the English text ('in proceedings which have as their object rights *in rem*').

30. As Advocate General Sir Gordon Slynn stated in his Opinion in the *Rösler* case: 'The other language versions seem to indicate that what is covered is litigation the subject-matter (rather than "the object") of which is a tenancy agreement of immovable property rather than one which concerns simply the immovable property itself'.

31. Jenard also explained in this report that '... the matters referred to in this article will normally be the subject of exclusive jurisdiction only if they constitute the principal subject-matter of the proceedings of which the court is to be seised 'and [t]hese rules (on exclusive jurisdiction), which take as their criterion the subject-matter of the action, are applicable regardless of the domicile or nationality of the parties'.

32. As far as the case-law of the Court is concerned, the requirement or a restrictive interpretation of Article 16, laid down for the first time in the *Sanders* judgment, cited above, reflects the Court's refusal to extend the scope of that provision to cover claims which only indirectly or incidentally concern rights *in rem*.

33. The question to be determined, therefore, is whether or not an action for a declaration that a person holds property in trust for another person and for an order that the defendant execute such documents as are necessary to vest the legal ownership in the plaintiff constitutes an action *in rem* for the purposes of Article 16(1).

34. The distinction between rights *in personam* and rights *in rem*, which is well known in continental legal systems, was defined in this way in the Schlosser Report: 'A right *in personam* can only be claimed against a particular person .... A right *in rem*, on the other hand, is available against the whole world. The most important legal consequence flowing from the nature of a right *in rem* is that its owner is entitled to demand that the thing in which it exists be given up by anyone not enjoying a prior right'.

35. Where property is transferred to a trustee to be held in trust, dual ownership' arises since title stands in the name of the trustee or in the name of another person on behalf of the trustee, and the beneficiary holds the beneficial interest which is an equitable interest.

36. According to the Schlosser Report, equitable interests '... are not, however, merely the equivalent of personal rights on the Continent. Some can be registered and then, like legal rights, have universal effect, even against purchasers in good faith. Even if not registered they operate in principle against all the world; only purchasers in good faith who had no knowledge of them are protected in such a case'.

37. Lasok and Stone also suggest that equitable interests in land should be included to the concept of rights *in rem*. According to them: '... there can be no doubt that an equitable interest in land, as known to English law, qualifies as a "right *in rem*" for the purpose of Article 16(1); such an interest is binding on all persons, with the limited exceptions of certain purchasers, viz. those who purchase without notice, or benefit of non-registration, or purchase from a vendor exercising powers of overreaching'.

38. However, in the case in point, can the action brought by the plaintiff in the main proceedings be regarded as an action laying claim to the immovable property situated in France on the basis of an equitable interest if the subject-matter of the dispute relates to the possible existence of a trust between himself and his son, or, alternatively, to the question of the parties' intention when the property was purchased? Is this not rather a *preliminary question*, which, whilst indeed having decisive consequences as regards ownership, is intrinsically based at this stage on a purely personal relationship?

39. Although the circumstances of the *Duijnstee* case, cited above, were quite different since it concerned Article 16(4), that case presents certain similarities. The relevant facts were as follows.

40. Mr Goderbauer, the employee of a company had been granted patents in his name in various Contracting States. The liquidator in the winding-up of the company, Mr Duijnstee, claimed that those patents belonged to the person in whose name he sought their transfer. Article 16(4) confers jurisdiction 'in proceedings concerned with the registration or validity of patents' on 'the Courts of the Contracting State in which the deposit or registration ... has taken place'.

41. After pointing out that none of the claims primarily concerned validity or registration, Advocate General Rozès continued: 'That question (of the relationship between the company and the employee) arises in advance of the formalities, properly so-called, for the transfer of the applications lodged or patents registered .... It is not until a decision has been taken on any assistance which Mr Goderbauer might have to give to the Liquidator that the problem of the transfer, properly so-called, of the rights of the applicant or the inventor will actually arise in the other Contracting States ...'

42. In its judgment the Court held that Article 16(4) was not applicable on the ground that '... neither the validity of the patents nor the legality of their registration in the various countries is disputed by the parties to the main action. The outcome of the case in fact depends exclusively on the question whether Mr Goderbauer or the insolvent company ... is entitled to the patent, which must be determined on the basis of the legal relationship which existed between the parties concerned.

43. Although the legality of the registration was not the principal subject-matter of the dispute, nevertheless it was closely linked to the intention of, and relations between, the parties at the time of deposit so that this question had to be examined prior to the completion of the transfer formalities.

44. It is for that reason that I find the Commission's arguments in this case, based on the authority of Professor Kaye, unconvincing. According to Professor Kaye,'[a]n action for a declaration that land purchased by one person in the name of another is subject to a resulting trust in favour of the former' is covered by Article 16(1) in so far as the dispute concerns an equitable interest in land and'[t]here seems no good reason why Article 16(1) should not also be held to apply when the immovable property, rights *in rem* in which form the object of the proceedings, is or is alleged to be property subject to a trust, since the sound policy reasons for subjecting such proceedings to the exclusive

jurisdiction of courts of the Contracting State *situs* are no less applicable than would be the case if the property were not held on trust'.

45. However, besides expressing doubt about actions which might be considered as being *in rem*, Kaye, after giving the example of an action for the recognition of a resulting trust as an action *in rem*, goes on to mention likewise as an action *in rem* proceedings brought under section 172 of the Law of Property Act 1925, which penalizes the conveyance of property by a settlor to trustees with intent to defraud creditors, these being proceedings which may be equated with the *action paulienne*, which, in its judgment in *Reichert I*, however, the Court held to be *in personam*.

46. I myself take the view that only actions bearing *directly*, upon 'the extent, content or ownership of immoveable property' fall within the scope of Article 16(1).

47. In this regard, Schlosser draws such a distinction: 'One could ... envisage a dispute arising between two people as to which of them was trustee of certain property. If one of them instituted proceedings against the other in a German court claiming the cancellation of the entry in the land register showing the defendant as the owner of the property and the substitution of an entry showing the plaintiff as the true owner, there can be no doubt that, under Article 16(1) or (3), the German court would have exclusive jurisdiction. However, if a declaration is sought that a particular person is a trustee of a particular trust which includes certain property, Article 16(1) does not become applicable merely because that property includes immovable property'.

48. The dividing line therefore appears to lie between actions whose principal subject-matter is a dispute over ownership between persons who do not claim *inter se* any fiduciary relationship and actions concerning a breach of fiduciary duty which, if found to have been committed, will have effects *in rem*. In such a case, the personal nature of the relations is, in my view, the overriding factor.

49. There can be no ground here for applying Article 16 since that provision, interpreted in the light of Article 19, is designed to govern only situations in which the *in rem* nature is predominant.

50. This is precisely the logic adopted in the Schlosser Report with regard to actions in connection with obligations to transfer immovable property. According to Schlosser, in French, Belgian and Luxembourg law, which is largely followed by Italian law, ownership is transferred as soon as the contract is concluded, which is the time from which the purchaser may proceed to effect transcription which has the effect of making his title effective against third parties. In the United Kingdom, the purchaser has an equitable interest in the property which is effective against third parties even though he must obtain the vendor's cooperation in order to make his legal title fully effective.

51. Although he considers that the purchaser may claim transfer of ownership on the basis of his right *in rem*, such an action must, according to Schlosser, be regarded as one *in personam* falling outside the scope of Article 16(1). Schlosser concludes: 'Actions based on contracts for the transfer of ownership or other rights *in rem* affecting immovable property do not therefore have as their object rights *in rem*.

52. According to Gothot and Holleaux: 'Mixed actions by which a person relies on both a right *in rem* and a right *in personam* arising from the same legal transaction also appear to lie outside the scope of Article 16 (1) ...'.

They also consider that an action for dividing immovable property should not be subject to special jurisdiction.

53. However, as the High Court points out, the plaintiff in the main action relies solely on the *existence of a fiduciary relationship*, a situation which indeed appears to correspond to that described in the Schlosser Report.

54. In my view, the provision does not cover an action by which a person seeks a declaration that property is held by another on trust since the person is not the holder of rights *erga omnes*, that is to say rights effective against the whole world. Nor are the rights of third parties acting in good faith affected by any recognition of a trust since *ex hypothesi* they were not previously informed of its existence.

55. The fact that the plaintiff in the main proceedings seeks an order requiring the defendant to execute such documents as should be required to vest the legal ownership of the property in the plaintiff cannot alter the nature of the action, since the order sought is a mandatory injunction directed at the defendant alone whose non-performance would lead the plaintiff to bring proceedings for the rectification of the land register.

56. It is true that the *ratio legis* of Article 16(1) is partly based on procedural economy which is mentioned by Jenard; '... the system adopted also takes into account the need to make entries in land registers located where the property is situated'.

57. This idea of procedural economy which forms the basis for exclusive jurisdiction has been supported in particular by Huet, who, in his Commentary on the *Rösler* case, stated that '... the only consideration which would account for the *exclusive* jurisdiction provided for in Article 16(1) is the necessity for the judgment which is to be delivered in the proceedings to be enforced at the place where the property is situated'.

58. However, the Court has never expressly adopted that principle. Thus, in the *Sanders* case, it stated that '... actions concerning rights *in rem* in immovable property are to be judged according to the rules of the State in which the immovable property is situated since the disputes which arise result frequently in checks, inquiries and expert assessments which must be carried out on the spot, with the result that the assignment of exclusive jurisdiction satisfies the need for the proper administration of justice'.

59. Similarly, in *Reichert I*, it held: '... although in certain Member States the rules governing the public registration of rights in immovable property require public notice to be given of legal actions seeking to have transactions affecting such rights avoided or declared ineffective as against third parties and of judgments given in such actions, that fact alone is not enough to justify conferring exclusive jurisdiction on the courts of the Contracting State in which the property affected by those rights is situated'.

60. However, no-one doubts that the need to have a judgment enforced at the place where the property is situated is part if the *ratio legis* of Article 16(1)

so that in the present case the conferral of jurisdiction on the French courts could meet that need.

61. If the Court should hold, however, that an action for a declaration that a person is a trustee of a trust attaching to immovable property is an action *in rem*, that analysis would necessarily be the same in the case of a trust which attached to various properties situated in different Contracting States. The plaintiff would in that case be compelled to bring proceedings in the courts of each place where property is situated, which would have sole jurisdiction. Who cannot fail to see that such a situation would entail a serious risk of conflicting decisions, with the courts of each State having a monopoly on the recognition of the existence of any trust relating to the property situated in their area of jurisdiction? Article 22 of the Convention, which deals with related actions, could not counteract that risk in every case since it does not constitute a head of jurisdiction. In such a situation, the proper administration of justice requires that the plaintiff should apply to one court only, which would assess the question of the possible existence of a trust by a judgment followed either by enforcement proceedings if the defendant complies with the order or by a direct action for claiming right of ownership.

62. Finally, I would observe that the essential reason for conferring sole jurisdiction under Article 16(1), as recognized by the Court in *Reichert I* namely that the courts of the *locus rei sitae* are better placed to ascertain the facts satisfactorily and to apply the rules and practices of that *locus*, is irrelevant where, as in this case, the principal subject-matter of the dispute is the possible existence of a fiduciary relationship between the parties.

63. I accordingly propose that the Court should rule that an action brought by a person against another person for a declaration that the latter holds immovable property as trustee and for an order requiring the latter to execute such documents as should be required to vest the legal ownership in the plaintiff does not constitute an action *in rem* within the meaning of Article 16(1) of the Brussels Convention of 27 September 1968 on Jurisdiction and the Enforcement of Judgments in Civil and Commercial Matters.

Case C-292/93 - 9 June 1994

Norbert Lieber
v
Willi S. Göbel and Siegrid Göbel

Exclusive jurisdiction - Article 16(1) - Proceedings 'which have as their object rights in rem in immovable property or tenancies of immovable property' - Definition - Claim for compensation for the use of real property following the annulment of a transfer of ownership - Excluded - Calculation of compensation according to the principles of the law on tenancies - No effect.

Summary

A claim for compensation for use of a dwelling after the annulment of a transfer of ownership is not included in the matters governed by Article 16(1) of the Convention on Jurisdiction and the Enforcement of Judgments in Civil and Commercial Matters, as amended by the Convention on the Accession of the Kingdom of Denmark, Ireland and the United Kingdom of Great Britain and Northern Ireland.

Article 16 must not be given a wider interpretation than is required by its objective, since it results in depriving the parties of the choice of forum which would otherwise be theirs and, in certain cases, in their being brought before a court which is not that of any of them. The fact that the compensation payable is to be calculated according to the principles governing tenancies does not justify the application of Article 16(1) to a situation where no tenancy is involved, since where there is no relationship of landlord and tenant, which is governed by special legislative provisions, some of a mandatory nature, of the State where the immovable property which is the subject of the lease is situated, the reasons, relating to the complex nature of that relationship and the interest of the State in which the property is situated in ensuring that those provisions are complied with, which justify the exclusive jurisdiction conferred by that provision on the courts of that State in cases concerning tenancies do not apply.

JUDGMENT OF THE COURT

Moitinho de Almeida, President of the Chamber, Edward, Joliet, Rodriguez Iglesias, and Grévisse, Judges

1. By order of 10 June 1992, received at the Court on 19 May 1993, the Oberlandesgericht (Higher Regional Court), Frankfurt am Main, referred to the Court for a preliminary ruling under the Protocol of 3 June 1971 on the Interpretation by the Court of Justice of the Convention of 27 September 1968 on Jurisdiction and the Enforcement of Judgments in Civil and Commercial Matters a question on the interpretation of Article 16(1) of that Convention (OJ 1972 L 299, p. 32), as amended by the Convention of 9 October 1978 on the Accession of the Kingdom of Denmark, Ireland and the United Kingdom of Great Britain and Northern Ireland (OJ 1978 L 304, p. 1) (hereinafter 'the Brussels Convention').

2. That question was raised in proceedings between Mr Lieber and Mr and Mrs Göbel.

3. It can be seen from the case file that Mr and Mrs Göbel, who are domiciled in Germany, are the owners of an apartment in Cannes (France).

4. In 1978 Mr Lieber, who is also domiciled in Germany, brought proceedings against Mr and Mrs Göbel in the Landgericht (Regional Court), Frankfurt am Main. Following those proceedings, the parties reached a friendly settlement under which ownership of the apartment was to be transferred to Mr Lieber. In execution of that settlement, Mr and Mrs Göbel allowed Mr Lieber into possession of the apartment. He used it until 1987.

5. In that year the 1978 settlement on the transfer of ownership of the apartment was declared void *ex tunc* for reasons of German law. Mr Lieber then brought proceedings in the Landgericht Frankfurt am Main. Mr and Mrs Göbel counterclaimed for an order that Mr Lieber should pay them compensation for the nine years during which he had used the apartment in Cannes.

6. After obtaining a report from a French expert on the value of the use of the apartment, the Landgericht Frankfurt am Main upheld the counterclaim to the amount of DM 200 791.78.

7. Mr Lieber appealed to the Oberlandesgericht Frankfurt am Main against that decision, arguing that under Article 16(1) of the Brussels Convention a court of the Contracting State where the immovable property was situated, in other words a French court, not a German court, had jurisdiction on the counterclaim.

8. The Oberlandesgericht Frankfurt am Main considered that the case raised a question of interpretation of the Brussels Convention. It therefore stayed the proceedings and referred thc following question to the Court for a preliminary ruling: 'Do the matters governed by Article 16(1) of the Brussels Convention also cover questions of compensation for use of a dwelling after a failed property transfer?'

9. Article 16(1) of the Brussels Convention provides that: 'The following courts shall have exclusive jurisdiction, regardless of domicile: 1. in proceedings which have as their object rights *in rem* in immovable property or tenancies of immovable property, the courts of the Contracting State in which the property is situated ...'.

10. It must be noted to begin with that, as the German Government correctly pointed out, a settlement such as that in issue here, the object of which was to transfer ownership of immovable property, does not constitute a tenancy of immovable property within the meaning of Article 16(1) of the Brussels Convention. That term applies to agreements for the letting of immovable property (see the judgment in Case 241/83 *Rösler* v *Rottwinkel* [1985] ECR 99, paragraphs 24 and 25). It follows that compensation for the use of property following the annulment of a transfer of ownership of that property cannot be regarded as a right relating to a tenancy of immovable property and fall within Article 16(1) of the Brussels Convention on that basis.

11. The Court must therefore consider whether the compensation in question is a right *in rem* in immovable property within the meaning of that provision.

12. The Court has consistently held (see *inter alia* the judgment in Case C-115/88 *Reichert and Kockler* [1990] ECR I-27, paragraph 9) that Article 16 must not be given a wider interpretation than is required by its

objective, since it results in depriving the parties of the choice of forum which would otherwise be theirs and, in certain cases, results in their being brought before a court which is not that of any of them.

13. It follows from that judgment and from the judgment in Case C-294/92 *Webb*, 17 May 1994 [1994] ECR I-1717, paragraph 14, that in order for Article 16(1) to apply, it is not sufficient that the action concerns a right *in rem* in immovable property or that the action is connected with immovable property. The action must be based on a right *in rem* and not, apart from the exception for tenancies of immovable property, on a right *in personam*.

14. The difference between a right *in rem* and a right *in personam* is that the former, existing in an item of property, has effect against the whole world, whereas the latter can only be claimed against the debtor (see the *Schlosser Report*, OJ 1979 C 59, p. 71, paragraph 166).

15. It is evident that a claim for compensation for the use of immovable property can be raised only against the debtor and thus constitutes a right *in personam*, at any rate where the debtor does not dispute that the person bringing the claim is the owner of the immovable property in question.

16. Mr Lieber points out, however, that in the *Rösler* judgment, cited above, the Court held that the *raison d'être* of the exclusive jurisdiction conferred by Article 16(1) of the Brussels Convention was the fact that tenancies are closely bound up with the law of immovable property and with the provisions, generally of a mandatory character, governing its use, such as legislation controlling the level of rents and protecting the rights of tenants, including tenant-farmers. In Mr Lieber's opinion that is why the Court held that the recovery of rent payable by the tenant pursuant to a lease fell within Article 16(1).

17. Mr Lieber considers that those considerations also apply to a claim for compensation for use of property, such as that in issue in the main proceedings, in particular because the compensation sought must be calculated according to principles analogous to those governing tenancies. The calculation cannot be done without recourse to an expert based in France, given that local knowledge is a precondition for drawing up an expert report.

18. That argument cannot be accepted.

19. Firstly, unlike the present case, the judgment in *Rösler*, cited above, concerned a letting agreement, which was therefore covered by the term 'tenancies of immovable property'.

20. Secondly, the mere fact that in a case such as the present one the compensation payable is to be calculated according to the principles governing tenancies does not justify the application of Article 16(1) to a situation where no tenancy is involved. The relationship of landlord and tenant comprises a series of rights and obligations in addition to that relating to rent. That relationship is governed by special legislative provisions, some of a mandatory nature, of the State where the immovable property which is the subject of the lease is situated, for example, provisions determining who is responsible for maintaining the property and paying land taxes, provisions governing the duties of the occupier of the property as against the neighbours, and provisions controlling or restricting the landlord's right to retake possession of the property on expiry of the lease. It is the complex nature of that relationship and the interest of the State in which the property is situated in ensuring that those provisions are complied with which justify the exclusive jurisdiction conferred on that State in cases concerning tenancies. Those reasons do not apply where there is no relationship of landlord and tenant.

21. Thirdly, while it may be easier for the court of the Contracting State in which the immovable property is situated to ascertain the level of rents within its area with a view to determining the amount of compensation payable, it is equally possible for a court in another Member State to consult a local expert in order to obtain the necessary information, as indeed the Landgericht Frankfurt am Main did at first instance in the main proceedings.

22. The answer to the question referred by the national court must therefore be that a claim for compensation for use of a dwelling after the annulment of a transfer of ownership is not included in the matters governed by Article 16(1) of the Brussels Convention.

On those grounds, the Court (Fifth Chamber), in answer to the question referred to it by the Oberlandesgericht Frankfurt am Main by order of 10 June 1992, hereby rules:

> **A claim for compensation for use of a dwelling after the annulment of a transfer of ownership is not included in the matters governed by Article 16(1) of the Convention of 27**

September 1968 on Jurisdiction and the Enforcement of Judgments in Civil and Commercial Matters, as amended by the Convention of 9 October 1978 on the Accession of the Kingdom of Denmark, Ireland and the United Kingdom of Great Britain and Northern Ireland.

OPINION OF MR ADVOCATE GENERAL DARMON

1. By order of 10 June 1992, received at the Court on 19 May 1993, the Oberlandesgericht (Higher Regional Court) Frankfurt am Main asks the Court for an interpretation of Article 16(1) of the Brussels Convention of 27 September 1968 on jurisdiction and the enforcement of judgments in civil and commercial matters ('the Convention'), in the context of proceedings between Norbert Lieber; the appellant in the main proceedings, and Mr and Mrs Göbel, the owners of an apartment in Cannes (France), all three being domiciled in the Federal Republic of Germany.

2. Following earlier proceedings, the parties reached a settlement on 27 April 1978 in which Mr and Mrs Göbel agreed to transfer the ownership of the said apartment to Mr Lieber. The appellant in the main proceedings was thus put in possession of the apartment and used it from 1 June 1978 to 30 April 1987. The settlement was declared void under Paragraphs 313 and 125 of the Bürgerliches Gesetzbuch (German Civil Code), and the respondents in the main proceedings brought before the Landgericht (Regional Court) Frankfurt am Main a claim for compensation for use for the period in question.

3. The Landgericht, in order to assess the value of the use of the property, appointed a French expert, and on the basis of his report that court determined the amount of compensation payable to Mr and Mrs Göbel.

4. Mr Lieber appealed against that decision. He considered that in view of the location of the property, the French courts had exclusive jurisdiction under Article 16(1) of the Convention, which provides that: 'The following courts shall have exclusive jurisdiction, regardless of domicile: ... in proceedings which have as their object rights *in rem* in immovable property or tenancies of immovable property, the courts of the Contracting State in which the property is situated ...'.

5. In those circumstances the Oberlandesgericht Frankfurt am Main puts the following question to the Court: 'Do the matters governed by Article 16(1) of the Brussels Convention also cover questions of compensation for use made of a dwelling after a failed property transfer?'

6. To answer that question, the Court will have to determine the scope of Article 16(1) with respect not only to 'tenancies of immovable property' but also to 'rights *in rem* in immovable property'. I shall therefore examine those two aspects in turn.

7. I. The appellant in the main proceedings argues that although 'the counterclaim does not put forward any claims relating to the law on tenancies', it must be regarded as relating to the law on tenancies with respect in particular to

the determination of the amount of rent and the rules on protection for tenants, with the result that the French courts must be allowed exclusive jurisdiction.

8. Let me say straight away that neither the underlying objective of the rule nor the case-law of the Court supports such an argument.

9. The intention of the authors of the Convention was to limit the scope of Article 16(1) to tenancies in the strict sense. Thus the Jenard Report states that tenancies of immovable property 'will include tenancies of dwellings and of premises for professional or commercial use, and agricultural holdings. In providing for the courts of the State in which the property is situated to have jurisdiction as regards tenancies in immovable property, the Committee intended to cover disputes between landlord and tenant over the existence or interpretation of tenancy agreements, compensation for damage caused by the tenant, eviction, etc.'.

10. The reasons for conferring exclusive jurisdiction in this respect are that: 'This type of dispute often entails checks, enquiries and expert examinations which have to be made on the spot. Moreover, the matter is often governed in part by customary practices which are not generally known except in the courts of the place ... where the immovable property is situated.'

11. Moreover, that exclusive jurisdiction cannot be derogated from by an agreement conferring jurisdiction (Article 17) or by an implied extension of jurisdiction (Article 18). Under Article 19 of the Convention, a court from a State other than the State whose courts have exclusive jurisdiction by virtue of Article 16 must declare of its own motion that it has no jurisdiction. Finally, a judgment given in another Contracting State which conflicts with a rule conferring exclusive jurisdiction cannot be recognized (Article 28) or enforced (Article 34).

12. The exclusive jurisdiction conferred in this respect on the courts of the place where the property is situated has incidentally been regarded as 'curious' by an authority on the subject.

13. The Court for its part stated in the *Sanders* judgment that 'the assignment, in the interests of the proper administration of justice, of exclusive jurisdiction to the courts of one Contracting State in accordance with Article 16 of the Convention results in depriving the parties of the choice of the forum which would otherwise be theirs and, in certain cases, results in their being brought before a court which is not that of the domicile of any of them', and concluded that 'having regard to that consideration the provisions of Article 16 must not be given a wider interpretation than is required by their objective'.

14. In that judgment, and also in three other judgments, the Court had to rule on the interpretation of 'tenancies of immovable property' within the meaning of Article 16(1) of the Convention and in each case upheld the principle of an independent interpretation without reference to the rules of national law.

15. Thus in the *Sanders* judgment the Court refused to apply that provision to an agreement whose principal aim concerned the operation of a business. In the *Hacker* judgment the Court likewise declined to regard as a tenancy an agreement which 'irrespective of its title, and although providing a service concerning the use of short-term holiday accommodation, ... also includes other services ...'.

16. In the *Rösler* judgment, on the other hand, the Court held that Article

16(1) applied 'to all lettings of immovable property, even for a short term and even where they relate only to the use and occupation of a holiday home'.

17. The conclusion reached by the Court in that judgment cannot be regarded as having extended the scope of that provision. As Huet writes in his observations on the decision, although '... the conclusion may appear inappropriate, or even absurd, in that it makes the procedure considerably more complicated', it was nevertheless dictated by the provision itself.

18. However, in that case the parties had indeed concluded an agreement for a tenancy within the meaning of Article 16(1), certain characteristics of which were defined by the Court as follows: 'Leases generally contain terms concerning entry into possession by the tenant, the use to which the property is to be put, the obligations of the landlord and tenant regarding the maintenance of the property, the duration of the lease and the giving up of possession to the landlord, the rent and the incidental charges to be paid by the tenant, such as water, gas and electricity charges.'

19. An agreement relating to immovable property does not necessarily relate to a *transfer* of use and occupation as defined by the Court, and in that case Article 16(1) cannot be applied. A *fortiori*, there cannot be a transfer of occupation if, as a result of its being declared void, there is no contractual relationship. That is the case in particular with respect to compensation for use for the period during which a person has occupied immovable property following a void contract for sale, in other words with no legal right or title.

20. Moreover, I believe that that conclusion is in harmony with the 'rule of reason' relating to this head of jurisdiction in cases concerning residential tenancies of immovable property, expressed as follows in the Court's judgment in *Sanders*: 'Tenancies of immovable property are generally governed by special rules and it is preferable, in the light of their complexity, that they be applied only by the courts of the States in which they are in force.'

21. Assessment of the compensation for use will indeed depend on the letting value of the dwelling (already determined at first instance in the main proceedings after consulting a French expert), but it should be noted that national rules restricting or indexing rents are intended to protect persons holding under a lease, not mere occupiers.

22. I note, however, that the fact that some Member States have mandatory rules relating to commercial tenancies was not considered by the Court to justify the application of Article 16(1) in the aforesaid *Sanders* judgment, contrary incidentally to the opinion of the Advocate General.

23. Moreover, according to *Gothot and Holleaux*, '... the scope of Article 16(1) cannot be extended on the pretext that reasons of the proper administration of justice and the concordance of the judicial and legislative functions, which are the basis of that provision, are also met with in cases other than those expressly provided for'.

24. II. If the compensation in question cannot be based on the concept of a tenancy of immovable property, can it be regarded as relating to a right *in rem* in immovable property, in so far as it follows from a void contract of sale?

25. With respect to the scope of that part of Article 16(1) which refers to

'rights *in rem* in immovable property' the Court has handed down only one judgment to date, the judgment in *Reichert I*, since judgment has not yet been given in the *Webb* case, which concerns the same provision and in which I delivered my Opinion on 8 February 1994.

26. In the *Reichert I* case a married couple domiciled in the Federal Republic of Germany had donated to their son, who was also domiciled in that State, the legal ownership of immovable property situated in France, reserving to themselves the right to use it. The German bank which was their creditor brought proceedings in France, namely the '*action paulienne*' provided for in Article 1167 of the French Civil Code, the effect of which is to render a transfer of property made in fraud of the creditor's rights ineffective as against him.

27. On a question being referred by the Cour d'Appel, Aix-en-Provence, on the nature of such an action with respect to Article 16(1), the Court, referring expressly to its judgments in *Sanders*, cited above, and *Duijnstee*, noted that 'an independent definition must be given in Community law to the phrase "in proceedings which have as their object rights *in rem* in immovable property" ...'.

28. The Court then held that that provision had to be given a restrictive interpretation, and stated that 'the exclusive jurisdiction of the Contracting State in which the property is situated does not encompass all actions concerning rights *in rem* in immovable property but only those which both come within the scope of the Brussels Convention and are actions which seek to determine the extent, content, ownership or possession of immovable property or the existence of other rights *in rem* therein and to provide the holders of those rights with the protection of the powers which attach to their interest'.

29. On the distinction between rights *in personam* and rights *in rem*, the Schlosser Report states: 'A right *in personam* can only be claimed against a particular person ... A right *in rem*, on the other hand, is available against the whole world. The most important legal consequence flowing from the nature of a right *in rem* is that its owner is entitled to demand that the thing in which it exists be given up by anyone not enjoying a prior right.'

30. Schlosser then states with reference to the particular field of actions concerning the obligation to transfer the ownership of immovable property, 'Where a purchaser of German immovable property brings proceedings on the basis of a contract for sale of immovable property which is governed by German law, the subject-matter of such proceedings is never a right *in rem* in the property. The only matter in issue is the defendant's personal obligation to carry out all acts necessary to transfer and hand over the property.'

31. Although such an action may have an effect on a right *in rem*, its basis is thus a relationship of a personal nature, so that in Professor Schlosser's opinion it should not come within the scope of Article 16(l). That situation is different from the one before the national court, which is characterized by a legal relationship corresponding to a mere claim for protection of a right *in personam* by virtue of which a creditor's estate includes an asset, while conversely as a result of the same relationship there is a liability - in other words, a debt - in the debtor's estate.

32. An action claiming compensation for use as a result of the annulment

of a contract of sale is a consequence of the annulment of a contractual relationship which furthermore has no bearing on the existence, content or structure of the property right. It thus does not come within the category of rights *in rem*.

33. Moreover, as L. Collins writes 'The expression (rights *in rem* in ... immovable property) is clearly aimed at actions involving title or possession. Thus, it does not include an action for damages caused to an immovable. Nor is it concerned, it seems, with an action concerning the purely contractual aspects of a property transaction ...'.

34. It would moreover be paradoxical, as the French Government has incidentally rightly pointed out, if such an action came under the rule on jurisdiction in Article 16, even though the action for annulment did not.

35. Although the latter action altered the structure of a right *in rem*, that does not mean that it can be regarded as being strictly of an *in rem* nature, since it is based on a legal relationship of a personal nature.

36. That opinion is shared by Professor Schlosser in his report, and is also supported by the most authoritative writers, in particular by *Gothot and Holleaux* who write that: 'Mixed actions in which a person at one and the same time asserts a right *in rem* and a right *in personam* deriving from the same legal operation also appear to be outside the scope of Article 16(1), since that provision is probably not intended to reserve to the courts of the country where the immovable property is situated actions such as those for the annulment, cancellation or rescission of a sale, or even actions for delivery of the immovable property which has been sold.'

37. Bischoff, commenting on the Court's judgment in *Reichert I*, also considers that: 'the fact that immovable property is concerned is not enough to impose exclusive jurisdiction under Article 16. It is necessary, much more narrowly, that the action constitutes the exercise of a right *in rem* in immovable property ...'.

38. I therefore propose that the Court should rule as follows: 'A claim for compensation for the use of immovable property after the annulment of a contract of sale does not fall within the scope of Article 16(1) of the Brussels Convention of 27 September 1968 on jurisdiction and the enforcement of judgments in civil and commercial matters'.

Case C-8/98 - 27 January 2000

Dansommer A/S
v
Andreas Götz

Article 16(1) - Exclusive jurisdiction in proceedings having as their object tenancies of immovable property - Scope.

Summary

The rule laid down in Article 16(1)(a) of the Convention conferring exclusive jurisdiction in proceedings having as their object tenancies of immovable property is applicable to an action for damages for taking poor care of premises and causing damage to accommodation which a private individual had rented for a few weeks' holiday, even where the action is not brought directly by the owner of the property but by a professional tour operator from whom the person in question had rented the accommodation and who has brought legal proceedings after being subrogated to the rights of the owner of the property.

The ancillary clauses relating to insurance in the event of cancellation and to guarantee of repayment of the price paid by the client, which are contained in the general terms and conditions of the contract concluded between that organiser and the enant, and which do not form the subject of the dispute in the main proceedings, do not affect the nature of the tenancy as a tenancy of immovable property within the meaning of that provision of the Convention.

JUDGMENT OF THE COURT

Schintgen (Rapporteur), President of the Second Chamber, acting as President of the Sixth Chamber, Kapteyn and Hirsch, Judges

1. By order of 16 June 1997, received at the Court on 14 January 1998, the Landgericht (Regional Court) Heilbronn (Germany) referred to the Court for a preliminary ruling under the Protocol of 3 June 1971 on the Interpretation by the Court of Justice of the Convention of 27 September 1968 on Jurisdiction and the Enforcement of Judgments in Civil and Commercial Matters a question on the interpretation of Article 16(1)(a) of that Convention (OJ 1978 L 304, p. 36), as amended by the Convention of 9 October 1978 on the Accession of the Kingdom of Denmark, Ireland and the United Kingdom of Great Britain and Northern Ireland (OJ 1978 L 304, p. 1 and - amended text - p. 77), by the Convention of 25 October 1982 on the Accession of the Hellenic Republic (OJ 1982 L 388, p. 1) and by the Convention of 26 May 1989 on the Accession of the Kingdom of Spain and the Portuguese Republic (OJ 1989 L 285, p. 1) (hereinafter 'the Convention').

2. That question has arisen in a dispute between Dansommer A/S, a company incorporated under Danish law and having its registered office in Denmark ('Dansommer'), and Andreas Götz, a German national who is resident in Germany.

The Convention

3. Article 16(1) of the Brussels Convention, in the version prior to the amendment made by the Convention of 26 May 1989, provided as follows:

'The following courts shall have exclusive jurisdiction, regardless of domicile: 1. in proceedings which have as their object rights *in rem* in, or tenancies of, immovable property, the courts of the Contracting State in which the property is situated'.

4. As amended by the Convention of 26 May 1989 ('the San Sebastián Convention'), that provision is now worded as follows:
'The following courts shall have exclusive jurisdiction, regardless of domicile:

1. (a) in proceedings which have as their object rights *in rem* in immovable property or tenancies of immovable property, the courts of the Contracting State in which the property is situated;

(b) however, in proceedings which have as their object tenancies of immovable property concluded for temporary private use for a maximum period of six consecutive months, the courts of the Contracting State in which the defendant is domiciled shall also have jurisdiction, provided that the landlord and the tenant are natural persons and are domiciled in the same Contracting State'.

5. Article 29(1) of the San Sebastián Convention provides:

'The 1968 Convention and the 1971 Protocol, as amended by the 1978 Convention, the 1982 Convention and this Convention, shall apply only to legal proceedings instituted ... after the entry into force of this Convention in the State of origin ...'.

6. The San Sebastián Convention entered into force in Germany on 1 December 1994.

The dispute in the main proceedings

7. On 27 February 1995, Mr Götz rented from Dansommer a house in Denmark owned by a private individual resident in Denmark, with a view to spending his holidays there from 29 July 1995 to 12 August 1995.

8. In its capacity as a professional tour operator, Dansommer merely acted as intermediary.

9. Under the general terms and conditions of the contract concluded between Dansommer and Mr Götz, the price payable by the latter as consideration for the provision of the accommodation during the contractual period included a premium for insurance to cover the costs in the event of cancellation of the contract.

10. Those general terms and conditions also provided that, in accordance with Article 651k(3) of the Bürgerliches Gesetzbuch (German Civil Code), Dansommer guaranteed reimbursement of the price paid by Mr Götz in the event of the organiser's insolvency.

11. It is common ground that Dansommer was not under an obligation to provide any other services.

12. After Mr Götz had stayed in the house in question, Dansommer brought proceedings against him as lessee before the Amtsgericht (Local Court) Heilbronn. In those proceedings, Dansommer, which had

previously been subrogated to the rights of the owner of the house rented by Mr Götz, claimed damages from him on the ground that he had failed to clean the house properly before his departure and had damaged the carpeting and the oven safety mechanism.

13. Following the dismissal of its action, Dansommer appealed to the referring court.

14. Since it was unsure whether it had jurisdiction to hear the dispute, the Landgericht Heilbronn decided to stay the proceedings and to refer the following question to the Court for a preliminary ruling: 'Is Article 16(1)(a) of the Brussels Convention applicable if the tour operator's performance obligation is limited to making available a holiday home and automatic provision of travel cost and cancellation insurance, but the owner and lessee of the holiday home are not domiciled in the same Contracting State?'

The question referred for preliminary ruling

15. By way of derogation from the general principle set out in the first paragraph of Article 2 of the Convention, according to which persons domiciled in a Contracting State must be sued in the courts of that State, Article 16(1) of the Convention provides that, in proceedings which have as their object rights *in rem* in immovable property or tenancies of immovable property, exclusive jurisdiction lies with the courts of the Contracting State in which the property is situated.

16. The dispute in the main proceedings is, however, manifestly unconnected with any right *in rem* in immovable property, within the meaning of Article 16(1).

17. Although the case of which the national court is seised results from the short-term letting of a holiday home, it must be stressed, as the Landgericht Heilbronn points out in its order for reference, that Article 16(1)(b), which contains a specific provision relating to short-term tenancies which was added to Article 16(1) of the Brussels Convention by the San Sebastián Convention, is not relevant to this case since not all the conditions laid down in that provision are satisfied. Thus, in the case before the national court, the owner and tenant of the property are not domiciled in the same Contracting State.

18. The national court is thus asking the Court whether Article 16(1)(a),

resulting from the San Sebastián Convention, which is applicable to the dispute in the main proceedings, but the wording of which has remained unchanged in relation to Article 16(1) of the Brussels Convention in its earlier versions, covers judicial proceedings such as those of which it is seised.

19. Finally, it must be pointed out that the fact, mentioned in the question submitted, that the owner of the property and the lessee are not domiciled in the same Contracting State is immaterial, since, as is clear from the actual wording of Article 16 and subject to the proviso in subparagraph 1(b) thereof, which, as has just been held in paragraph 17 above, is not applicable to this case, the domicile of the parties is irrelevant for the purposes of Article 16 of the Convention (see, to this effect, Casc 73/77 *Sanders* v *Van der Putte* [1977] ECR 2383, paragraph 10).

20. In those circumstances, the question submitted must be construed as essentially seeking to ascertain whether the rule laid down in Article 16(1)(a) of the Convention conferring exclusive jurisdiction in proceedings having as their object tenancies of immovable property is applicable to an action for damages for taking poor care of premises and causing damage to accommodation which a private individual had rented for a few weeks' holiday, even where the action is not brought directly by the owner of the property but by a professional tour operator from whom the person in question had rented the accommodation and who has brought legal proceedings after being subrogated to the rights of the owner of the property.

21. It should be noted in this regard that Article 16, being an exception to the general rule of jurisdiction set out in the first paragraph of Article 2 of the Convention, must not be given an interpretation broader than is required by its objective, since the article deprives the parties of the choice of forum which would otherwise be theirs and, in certain cases, results in their being brought before a court which is not that of the domicile of any of them (see *Sanders*, cited above, paragraphs 17 and 18; Case C-115/88 *Reichert and Kockler* [1990] ECR I-27, paragraph 9; and Case C-292/93 *Lieber* [1994] ECR I-2535, paragraph 12).

22. So, it is established in case-law that, in order for Article 16(1) of the Brussels Convention to apply, it is not sufficient for the action to be connected with immovable property (Case C-294/92 *Webb* [1994] ECR I-1717, paragraph 14, and *Lieber*, cited above, paragraph 13).

23. Nevertheless, it follows from that same case-law that, in a case such as that before the national court, which concerns not a right *in rem* in immovable property but a tenancy of immovable property, Article 16(1) applies to any proceedings concerning rights and obligations arising under an agreement for the letting of immovable property, irrespective of whether the action is based on a right *in rem* or on a right *in personam* (*Lieber*, paragraphs 10, 13 and 20).

24. That is precisely the position in the instant case, since the proceedings brought by Dansommer, after partial failure to perform a tenancy agreement, is based on the tenant's obligation to maintain the property let in a proper condition and to repair any damage which he has caused to it.

25. The subject-matter of the proceedings before the referring court is thus directly linked to a leasing contract concerning immovable property and consequently to a tenancy of immovable property within the meaning of Article 16(1)(a) of the Convention, with the result that those proceedings fall within the exclusive jurisdiction rule laid down in that provision.

26. This interpretation, which is, moreover, the only interpretation which does not render ineffective the rule of exclusive jurisdiction in regard to tenancies of immovable property, is borne out by the underlying purpose of the provision in question.

27. It is clear from both the Jenard Report on the Brussels Convention (OJ 1979 C 59, p. 1, at p. 35) and case-law that the essential reason for conferring exclusive jurisdiction on the courts of the Contracting State in which the property is situated is that the courts of the *locus rei sitae* are the best placed, for reasons of proximity, to ascertain the facts satisfactorily, by carrying out checks, inquiries and expert assessments on the spot, and to apply the rules and practices which are generally those of the State in which the property is situated (see, in particular, *Sanders*, paragraph 13, and *Reichert and Kockler*, paragraph 10).

28. This interpretation is also borne out by the fact that the Jenard Report (cited above, pp. 34 and 35) states that the jurisdiction rules set out in Article 16 of the Brussels Convention take as their criterion the subject-matter of the action and, with specific regard to the rule of exclusive jurisdiction in the matter of tenancies of immovable property in Article 16(1), the Convention draftsmen intended it to cover, *inter alia*, disputes over compensation for damage caused by tenants.

29. The reasoning set out above cannot be called in question by the judgment in Case C-280/90 *Hacker* [1992] ECR I-1111.

30. In that judgment, the Court held, in paragraph 15, that a complex contract concerning a range of services provided in return for a lump sum paid by the customer did not constitute a tenancy of immovable property within the meaning of Article 16(1) of the Brussels Convention.

31. The contract at issue in *Hacker* had been concluded between a professional travel organiser and its customer at the place where both were domiciled, and even though that contract provided for a service concerning the use of short-term holiday accommodation, it also included other services, such as information and advice, where the travel organiser proposed a range of holiday offers, the reservation of accommodation during the period chosen by the customer, the reservation of seats in connection with travel arrangements, reception at the destination and the possibility of travel cancellation insurance (*Hacker*, cited above, paragraph 14).

32. However, the unavoidable conclusion is that the circumstances of the case now under consideration are different from those of *Hacker*.

33. The contract now at issue concerns exclusively the letting of immovable property.

34. The clause in the general terms and conditions of the contract relating to insurance to cover the costs in the event of cancellation is only an ancillary provision which cannot alter the status of the tenancy agreement to which it relates, especially since this clause is not in issue before the referring court.

35. The same applies in regard to the guarantee - which is, moreover, required by German legislation - of repayment of the price paid in advance by the customer in the event of the organiser's insolvency.

36. Finally, Article 16(1)(a) of the Convention is not rendered inapplicable merely because the dispute in this case is not directly between the owner and the tenant of the immovable property, given that Dansommer brought legal proceedings against the tenant after being subrogated to the rights of the owner of the property which was the subject of the lease concluded between Dansommer and Mr Götz.

37. Suffice it to note in this regard that, through subrogation, one person steps into the shoes of another in order to enable the former to exercise rights belonging to the latter, so that, in the main proceedings in this case, Dansommer is not acting in its capacity as a professional tour operator but as if it were the owner of the property in question.

38. In view of the foregoing, the answer to be given to the question referred must be that the rule laid down in Article 16(1)(a) of the Convention conferring exclusive jurisdiction in proceedings having as their object tenancies of immovable property is applicable to an action for damages for taking poor care of premises and causing damage to accommodation which a private individual had rented for a few weeks' holiday, even where the action is not brought directly by the owner of the property but by a professional tour operator from whom the person in question had rented the accommodation and who has brought legal proceedings after being subrogated to the rights of the owner of the property.

The ancillary clauses relating to insurance in the event of cancellation and to guarantee of repayment of the price paid by the client, which are contained in the general terms and conditions of the contract concluded between that organiser and the tenant, and which do not form the subject of the dispute in the main proceedings, do not affect the nature of the tenancy as a tenancy of immovable property within the meaning of that provision of the Convention.

On those grounds, the Court (Sixth Chamber), in answer to the question referred to it by the Landgericht Heilbronn by order of 16 June 1997, hereby rules:

The rule laid down in Article 16(1)(a) of the Convention of 27 September 1968 on Jurisdiction and the Enforcement of Judgments in Civil and Commercial Matters, as amended by the Convention of 9 October 1978 on the Accession of the Kingdom of Denmark, Ireland and the United Kingdom of Great Britain and Northern Ireland, by the Convention of 25 October 1982 on the Accession of the Hellenic Republic, and by the Convention of 26 May 1989 on the Accession of the Kingdom of Spain and the Portuguese Republic, conferring exclusive jurisdiction in proceedings having as their object tenancies of immovable property is applicable to an action for damages for taking poor care of premises and causing damage to

accommodation which a private individual had rented for a few weeks' holiday, even where the action is not brought directly by the owner of the property but by a professional tour operator from whom the person in question had rented the accommodation and who has brought legal proceedings after being subrogated to the rights of the owner of the property.

The ancillary clauses relating to insurance in the event of cancellation and to guarantee of repayment of the price paid by the client, which are contained in the general terms and conditions of the contract concluded between that organiser and the tenant, and which do not form the subject of the dispute in the main proceedings, do not affect the nature of the tenancy as a tenancy of immovable property within the meaning of that provision of the Convention.*

* Opinion of AG not yet available in English.